RACISM IN
CONTEMPORARY
AMERICA

Recent Titles in
Bibliographies and Indexes in Ethnic Studies

Annotated Bibliography of Puerto Rican Bibliographies
Fay Fowlie-Flores, compiler

Racism in the United States:
A Comprehensive Classified Bibliography
Meyer Weinberg, compiler

Ethnic Periodicals in Contemporary America:
An Annotated Guide
Sandra L. Jones Ireland, compiler

Latin American Jewish Studies:
An Annotated Guide to the Literature
Judith Laikin Elkin and Ana Lya Sater, compilers

Jewish Alcoholism and Drug Addiction:
An Annotated Bibliography
Steven L. Berg, compiler

Guide to Information Resources in Ethnic Museum, Library, and
Archival Collections in the United States
Lois J. Buttlar and Lubomyr R. Wynar, compilers

RACISM IN CONTEMPORARY AMERICA

Compiled by
MEYER WEINBERG

Bibliographies and Indexes in Ethnic Studies,
Number 6

GREENWOOD PRESS
Westport, Connecticut • London

Library of Congress Cataloging-in-Publication Data

Weinberg, Meyer.
    Racism in contemporary America / compiled by Meyer Weinberg.
      p. cm.—(Bibliographies and indexes in ethnic studies, ISSN
1046–7882 ; no. 6)
    Includes bibliographical references and index.
    ISBN 0–313–29659–6 (alk. paper)
    1. Racism—United States—Bibliography. 2. United States—Race
relations—Bibliography. I. Title. II. Series.
Z1361.N39W45   1996
[185.61]
016.3058′00973—dc20   95–38637

British Library Cataloguing in Publication Data is available.

Library of Congress Catalog Card Number: 95–38637
ISBN: 0–313–29659–6
ISSN: 1046–7882

First published in 1996

Greenwood Press, 88 Post Road West, Westport, CT 06881
An imprint of Greenwood Publishing Group, Inc.
Printed in the United States of America

The paper used in this book complies with the
Permanent Paper Standard issued by the National
Information Standards Organization (Z39.48–1984).

10 9 8 7 6 5 4 3 2

To the memory of Faith Rich

CONTENTS

Introduction	xi
Affirmative Action	1
Africa	18
Anti-Racism	21
Antisemitism	24
Autobiography and Biography	30
Black Towns	43
Blacks and Jews	44
Business	53
Children	59
Citizenship	65
Civil Rights	69
Class Structure	81
Collective Self-Defense	90
Colonialism	93
Community Development	99
Concentration Camps	104
Crime	107
Desegregation	120
Discrimination	135
Du Bois	149
Economic Standards	150
Economics of Racism	164
Education -- Elementary and Secondary	166
Education -- Higher	203
Employment	252
Environment	255
Family	261
Forced Labor	270
Free Blacks	271
Ghetto	273
Government and Minorities	275
Health	284
History	314
Housing	330
Humor	345
Immigration	350
Industry	359
IQ and Race	360
Ku Klux Klan	365
Labor	369
Land	384

Language	391
Law	405
Libraries	426
Literature	428
Locality	
Alabama	437
Alaska	438
Arizona	439
Arkansas	440
California	441
Colorado	445
District of Columbia	446
Delaware	447
Florida	448
Georgia	449
Hawaii	450
Illinois	452
Indiana	453
Iowa	454
Kansas	455
Kentucky	456
Louisiana	457
Maryland	458
Massachusetts	459
Michigan	460
Mississippi	461
Missouri	463
Montana	464
Nebraska	465
Nevada	466
New Hampshire	467
New Jersey	468
New Mexico	469
New York	470
North Carolina	473
North Dakota	474
Ohio	475
Oklahoma	476
Oregon	477
Pennsylvania	478
South Carolina	479
South Dakota	480
Tennessee	481
Texas	482
Vermont	484
Virginia	485
Washington	487
West Virginia	488
Wisconsin	489
Wyoming	490
Mass Media	491
Migration	515
Military	519
Minorities in Conflict	528
Multiculturalism	533
Nationalism	552
Occupations	556
Oppression	560
Philosophy	561

Planning	563
Pluralism	564
Politics and Racism	566
Puplic Opinion	596
Racism -- Defining	600
Racism -- Exporting	605
Racism -- Institutional	607
Racism -- Psychology	608
Racism -- Scholarly	611
Racism -- Testing	614
Racism -- Theory	615
Racist Groups	621
Racist Thoughtways	626
Recreation	627
Religion	629
Science and Technology	640
Sexism	643
Slavery	650
Socialism and Racism	656
Sports	657
Stereotypes	665
Surveillance	674
Tests	683
Undoing Personal Racism	688
Unemployment	691
Violence vs. Minorities	694
Wealth and Income	702
Whites	706
Women of Color	710
General	719
Bibliographies	725
Author Index	729
Subject Index	827

INTRODUCTION

The present volume is the third in a series of book-length bibliographies of racism. Its predecessors were *Racism in the United States* (1990) and *World Racism and Related Inhumanities* (1992). All have been published by Greenwood Press. Together, they contain over 36,650 entries. None of the volumes was produced with the aid of a foundation or other granting agency. To my knowledge there is no foundation or agency in the United States which promotes the scholarly study of racism by helping create research bibliographies. Few if any universities in the country undertake research into the subject except in a minor and unsystematic way.

Racism in Contemporary America provides to readers and researchers a comprehensive array of books, dissertations, legislative hearings, monographs, journal articles, investigative accounts, and other materials bearing on racism. The contents are grouped under 87 subject-headings and are thoroughly indexed. Empirical studies and commentaries make up a principal part of the contents. Definitional and theoretical aspects are also covered, with a broad range of viewpoints represented. This is not, however, a debate handbook. The compiler's basic interest is to end racism, not merely study it.

Racism has entered every major institution of American society, and marked virtually every era of American history. A bibliography of the subject must reflect these facts. Historical studies are noted throughout the volume under many subject-headings in addition to "History." Wherever possible, historical actors' articles or books are cited as in the case of Frederick Douglass writing on the vagaries of citizenship in the United States. Many works by W.E.B. Du Bois are listed.

There is very little evidence in the literature of the subject that racism is disappearing in the United States. Autobiographies and biographies of Americans of many ethnicities demonstrate the across-the-board nature of racist discrimination. Even in the stories of socially successful persons, discrimination has left many tracks. The same is true of the entries under "Localities." Whatever conclusions one might arrive at in general, the literature of localities indicates clearly that racial discrimination endures. This can be seen also in the section on "Black Towns."

The subject index illustrates another important aspect of racism in America: entries by ethnic and racial group permit us to compare and contrast the experience of racism for each group. At the heart of racism lies a refusal to acknowledge the equal human worth of distinctive groups of people in customary spheres of social life. That failure is especially injurious when backed by governmental force or private economic power, or both. Many entries in this volume document this fact. A Chicana leader put it this way: "Texas is our Mississippi." Sharing a common oppression does not, of course, obliterate the characteristics of time and place that distinguish the groups. Nor are all deprivations equal in intensity and consequence.

A common misunderstanding of racism is to equate it with racial prejudice exercised by some individuals against other individuals and actuated by sentiments of hate. Racism, however, is far more than the sum of individual hates or dislikes. It may, in fact, have little or nothing to do with such sentiments. Racism is an ideology or system of ideas that allocates superiority and inferiority to separate sections of people so as to award privileges to the former and deprivations to the latter. Thus, racism rests on a base of differential worth of human beings and the legitimacy of unequal treatment according to presumed superiority and inferiority.

Racism operates most effectively when it seems not to emanate from individual hate. Instead of discrimination resulting from an individual act, it may seem to be accidental. Thus, certain schools have enrolled only students of certain racial backgrounds; others were simply not enrolled. The decision not to enroll them was not made by the head administrator, though he might have agreed with it. In some distant past, persons in authority- a legislature, court, or school board- had decided on the exclusion policy. This racism thereupon became institutional. Thereafter, the racist policy did not depend for its existence on this or that prejudiced official. Instead, the rule was enforced impersonally, regardless of the individual opinions of administrators. The vitality of the exclusion depended on the degree to which administrators stuck to the rule. At times, when the rule was challenged, legal authorities reminded administrators of their institutional duty to maintain racial separation.

Institutional racism complements, but it does not replace, individual prejudice and discrimination. A study of the 87 subject headings in *Racism in Contemporary America* indicates that institutional racism is much more widespread than individual racism. Yet, most educational programs against racism are aimed almost exclusively against individual racism. This is most unfortunate. Individual racism can exist to some degree regardless of what else is going on in society. Institutional racism, however, cannot thrive without constant replenishment of new personnel who are able to accept the human cost of racist policies without challenging their legitimacy. Not only that. People who are victimized by institutional racism may combat it most readily by organizing and changing public policies. Altering public policies solely by changing personal opinions of racists is a hopeless, endless endeavor. As part of a general strategy of anti-racism, however, changing personal opinions has a place.

The literature of racism has little to say about the relative effectiveness of various anti-racist approaches. Some entries relevant to this concern can be found under "Anti-racism" and "Undoing personal racism."

The present work chooses to be inclusive rather than exclusive. In the view of the compiler, there is no satisfactory definition of racism that will embrace all the aspects of the subject. To a significant extent, racism bears a relationship to sexism, antisemitism, and extreme nationalism. Some writers have subsumed all these subjects under a classification of "racisms." As indicated above, this bibliography bases its choice of references on violations of equal human worth which are involved in racism as well as in sexism, antisemitism, and extreme nationalism.

Following are indications of the contents of nearly a fifth of the subject-headings.

In "Affirmative Action" can be found references to evaluations of specific plans, legal and political analyses, as well as occasional historical studies. "Crime" contains items referring to capital punishment, racial differentials in sentencing, imprisonment, economic and social causes and consequences, and trend analysis. In "Desegregation" are listed materials describing the course of court-ordered desegregation in many specific cities, legal problems and concepts, opposition, public opinion, and unresolved problems. "Discrimination" has entries covering a very broad range of subjects, stressing definitional issues, and touching on legal problems. Readers interested in discrimination should also examine sections dealing with specific areas of action such as education, health, housing, and others.

"Elementary and Secondary Education" guides the reader to references related to discrimination on those levels of schooling. Among the topics covered are tracking, testing, and teacher bias, as well as the role of supervision and policy management. A few entries deal with intra-district, or school-by-school, material inequalities. Another number analyze political factors affecting school systems. "Higher Education" highlights racism at work in specific colleges and universities, and examines racist potentials in admissions, curricular changes, graduation trends, and other subjects. A number of articles are listed which relate to the issue of control over racist speech.

Racial-ethnic differentials in a range of diseases and health conditions are discussed in many articles listed in "Health," as are interrelated issues of health and society. Racism in the health professions and severe inequalities in hospital and other facilities are examined. "Housing" includes references on discrimination in purchase and sale as well as in rentals, bias in mortgage credit, governmental programs, role of real estate industry, public housing, analysis of specific housing markets, jurisprudence of fair and unfair housing, and effects of housing segregation on other spheres such as schooling. Historical material makes up a significant part of "Immigration" which is complemented by extensive references on the immigration experience of specific groups from widely-separated areas of the world, the politics of immigration regulation, legal studies of cases and trends, class differences among immigrants, and discrimination in economic and educational life.

"Localities" contains references primarily to city-wide and less so, state-wide studies and reports on racist structures and policies. Strikingly, much agreement exists among the historians and others about the past and present salience of racism in those places. This is true even in cases (such as California and New York) where a number of writers have viewed the subject. The role of politics and the local economy is prominent in these writings. A special effort has been made to take note of materials written by minorities. The variation between places is great; three or four cities or states may greatly outnumber the articles and studies on ten other places. By cross-reference, however, many more citations can be found; this is especially true of entries in other subject-headings which deal with specific places and are so described in a bracketed annotation.

The extensive use of litigation and legislation in American racial affairs determines the salience of the "Law" section. Here can be found entries on leading personalities, landmark court rulings and laws, the heritage of legalized segregation and discrimination, bias in the administration of justice and contemporary conflicts over unresolved issues of the law. "Mass Media," one of the longest sections, contains many references to racism in television, movies, the print press, radio, including talk-radio, and the stage. Specific personalities and productions are amply represented. A stream of progress reports is available in most of the media. Problems of affirmative action, stereotyping of roles, and minor changes in access to mass audiences, persist into the present.

Ten years ago, "Multiculturalism" was of interest to barely more than a small circle of academicians. Since then, a neo-conservative critique has made it a principal political issue, involving even the U.S. Senate and election campaigns. In this section can be found many references to the debate. Concrete problems of multiculturalism are discussed such as the teaching of history, concepts of citizenship and collective and individual identity. "Politics and Racism," the longest section in the book, deals with every level of government in historical and contemporary perspective. Many of the references analyze deliberate manipulation of racial issues for political advantage. The consequences for those victimized are dwelt on. Political ideologies with a major racist component are described.

"Slavery," a topic which has faded from many schoolbooks over recent years, directs readers' attention especially to concrete, empirical portrayal of operating slave systems. Entries in the "Free Negroes" section are significant because they show how restrictively non-slave blacks were treated under slavery. In fact, the status of the emancipated African American after the Civil War closely resembled that of the free Negro under enslavement. Many, if not most, of the items listed under "Stereotypes" demonstrate behavior patterns that did not exist under slavery. Nor did they after slavery, but they were used nevertheless as racist weapons against the former slaves.

Anita Weigel helped immensely in producing this book. Her mastery of the computer was indispensable. Aiding her in various ways were: Rob Schweitzer, Elise Young, Nancy Perman, and Martha Braun.

AFFIRMATIVE ACTION

1. Adrogue, Sofia. "When Injustice is the Game, What is Fair Play?" *Houston Law Review* 28 (March 1991): 363-411.

2. "Affirmative Action and Social Justice." *Social Justice Research* 5 (1992): Entire Issue.

3. "Affirmative Action Reaffirmed." *Minerva* 26 (1988): 598-99, 600-10. [Duke University]

4. "Affirmative Action Revisited." *Annals of the American Academy of Political and Social Science* 523 (September 1992): entire issue.

5. Akemann, Charles. "Affirmative Action Misplaces Unprepared Students in UC." *Daily Nexus (UC Santa Barbara)*, 1 February 1990.

6. Anderson, George Edward. *The Effect of Affirmative Action Programs on Female Employment and Earnings.* Ph.D. diss., University of California, 1988. UMO # 8826004.

7. Anderson, Talmadge. "Black Affirmative Action : A Discussion of Economic Strategies Towards Self-Help and Self-Determination." *Humboldt Journal of Social Relations* 14 (1987): 185-194.

8. Bacchi, C. "Affirmative Action - Is It Really Un-American?" *International Journal of Moral & Social Studies* 7 (Spring 1992): 19-31.

9. Badgett, M.V. Lee. *Racial Differences in Umemployment Rates and Employment Opportunities.* Ph.D. diss., University of California, 1990. UMO # 9126472.

10. Barbezat, D. A. "Affirmative Action in Higher Education - Have Two Decades Altered Salary Differentials by Sex and Race?" in *Research in Labor Economics*, Vol. 10. ed. Ronald G. Ehrenberg. Greenwich, CT: JAI Press, 1989.

11. Barnes, Robin. "Politics and Passion : Theoretically a Dangerous Liaison." *Yale Law Journal* 101 (1992).

12. Bartlett, Robin and others. "We Still Need Affirmative Action." *New York Times*, 3 September 1990. [On the American stage]

13. Baylor, D. E. "The Three R's of Faculty Affirmative Action Programs in Public Schools: Race, Reverse Discrimination, and the Rehnquist Court." *University of Chicago Legal Forum* (1991): 231- 252.

14. Beer, William R. "Resolute Ignorance: Social Science and Affirmitive Action." *Society* 24 (May-June 1987): 63-69.

15. Bell, Derrick. "The Final Report: Harvard's Affirmative Action Allegory." *Michigan Law Review* 87 (August 1989): 2382- 2410.

16. _____. "Preferential Affirmative Action." *Harvard Civil Rights - Civil Liberties Law Review* 16 (1982): 855-873.

17. _____. "Xerces and the Affirmative Action Mystique." *George Washington Law Review* 15 (August 1989): 1595-1613.

18. Belz, Herman. "Equal Protection and Affirmative Action." in *The Bill of Rights in Modern America*, eds. David J. Bodenhamer, and Ely, James W. Jr. Indiana University Press, 1993.

19. _____. *Equality Transformed; A Quarter Century of Affirmative Action*. New Brunswick, NJ: Transaction, 1991.

20. Bennett-Alexander, Dawn D. "The State of Affirmative Action in Employment; A Post-Stotts Retrospective." *American Business Law Journal* 27 (Winter 1990).

21. Benokraitis, Nina, and Joe R. Feagin. *Affirmative Action and Equal Opportunity*. Boulder, Co: Westview, 1978.

22. Berger, Joseph. "The Bakke Case 10 Years Later; Mixed Realities." *New York Times*, 13 July 1988.

23. Bernstein, Richard. "Law School Calls Bias Ruling a Victory." *New York Times* (21 August 1994). [U. of Texas affirmative-action policy]

24. Betsey, Charles L. "The Role of Race-Conscious Policies in Addressing Past and Present Discrimination." *Review of Black Political Economy* 21 (Fall 1992): 5-35.

25. Bigelow, Donovan R. "Equal But Separate: Can the Army's Affirmative Action Program Withstand Judicial Scrutiny after Croson?" *Military Law Review* 131 (Winter 1991): 147-167.

26. Black, Albert Jr. "Affirmative Action and the Black Academic Situation." *Western Journal of Black Studies* 5 (1981): 87-94.

27. Blanchard, F., and Faye J. Crosby, eds. *Affirmative Action in Perspective*. New York: Springer-Verlag, 1989.

28. Block, W. E., and M. A. Walker, eds. "Discrimination, Affirmative Action and Equal Opportunity." Vancouver, British Columbia: The Fraser Institute, 1982.

29. Blumrosen, Alfred W. *Modern Law: The Law Transmissions System and Equal Opportunity*. University of Wisconsin Press, 1993.

30. Bobo, Lawrence, and Kluegel, James R. "Opposition to Race- Targeting: Self-interest, Stratification Ideology, or Racial Attitudes." *American Sociological Review* 58 (August 1993): 443- 464.

31. Bonacich, Edna. "The Limited Social Philosophy of Affirmative Action." *Insurgent Sociologist* 14 (Winter 1987): 99- 118.

32. _____. "Racism in the Deep Structure of U.S. Higher Education: When Affirmative Action Is Not Enough." in *International Perspectives on Education and Society*, vol.1. pp. 3-15. eds. Sally Tomlinson, and Abraham Yogev. Greenwich, CT: JAI Press, 1989.

33. Bowen, E. J. *Affirmative Action Employment Programs in Mississippi Public Universities; 1972-1979*. Ph.D. diss., University of Mississippi, 1981.

34. Boyes-Watson, Carolyn F. *The Institutionalization of Judgment: Dynamics of the Formal Hiring Process*. Ph.D. diss., Harvard University, 1991. UMO # 9131915.

35. Brenner, Aaron. "The Politics of Affirmative Action." *Against the Current* 7 (May 1992): 48-52. [Review essay of Gertrude E. Ezorsky, *Racism and Justice; The case for Affirmative Action*, 1991]

36. Brett, Armand George. *Stages of Affirmative Action and Diversity Policy in the California State University System*. Ph.D. diss., University of the Pacific, 1992. UMO # 9315959.

37. Brooks, Roy L. "The Affirmative Action Issue: Law, Policy, and Morality." *Connecticut Law Reviw* 22 (Winter 1990): 323-372.

38. Bryden, David P. "On Race and Diversity." *Constitutional Commentary* 6 (Summer 1989): 383-430.

39. Bunzel, John H. "Affirmative-Action Admissions: How It Works at UC Berkeley." *Public Interest* (Fall 1988): 111-129.

40. _____. "Minority Faculty Hiring: Problems and Prospects." *American Scholar* 59 (Winter 1990): 39-52.

41. Burns, Michael M. "Lessons from the Third World: Spirituality as the Source of Commitment to Affirmative Action." *Vermont Law Review* 14 (Winter 1990): 401-456.

42. Burstein, Paul. "Affirmative Action & the Rhetoric of Reaction." *The American Prospect* 14 (Summer 1993): 138-147.

43. _____. "'Reverse Discrimonation Cases in the Federal Courts: Legal Mobilization by a Countermovement." *Sociological Quarterly* 32 (Winter 1991): 511-528.

44. Butterfield, Bruce D. "Affirmative Action Under Fire." *Boston Globe*, 20 October 1991. series of articles.

45. "Can Equal Opportunity Be Made More Equal?" *Harvard Business Review* 70 (March 1992): 138-158 (debate).

46. Carnegie Council on Policy Studies in Higher Education. *Making Affirmative Action Work in Higher Education*. San Francisco, CA: Jossey-Bass, 1975.

47. Carter, George E. *Affirmative Action in Higher Education: Another Political Myth for Ethnic Americans*. April 1981. ERIC ED 217 114.

48. Carter, Stephen L. "The Best Black, and Other Tales." *Reconstruction* 1 (Winter 1990).

49. _____. *Reflections of an Affirmative Action Baby*. New York: Basic Books, 1991.

50. Cazanave, Noel. "From a Committed Achiever to a Radical Social Scientist: The Life Course Dialectics of a 'Marginal' Black American Sociologist." *American Sociologist* (Winter 1988): 347-354.

51. Chamberlain, Marian K., ed. "Affirmative Action." in *Women in Academe: Progress and Prospects*, chapter 8. Russell Sage Foundation, 1988.

52. Chang, David. "Discriminatory Impact, Affirmative Action, and Innocent Victims: Judicial Conservatism or Conservative Justices?" *Columbia Law Review* 91 (May 1991): 790-844.

53. Chavez, Linda. *Out of the Barrio: Toward a New Politics of Hispanic Assimilation*. New York: Basic Books, 1991.

54. Cherry, David L. *Affirmative Action A Kuhnian Anomaly for the Liberal Democratic Paradigm?* Ph.D. diss., Northern Arizona University, 1991. UMO # 9136508.

55. Clayton, Susan D., and Faye J. Crosby. *Justice, Gender, and Affirmative Action*. University of Michigan Press, 1993.

56. Coate, S., and G. C. Lowry. "Will Affirmative Action Policies Eliminate Negative Stereotypes?" *American Economic Review* 83 (December 1993).

57. Cohn, Bob, and Tom Morgenthau. "The Q-Word Charade." *Newsweek* (3 June 1991). [Racial-ethnic quotas in employment]

58. Collins, Sharon M. "Failure in Affirmative Action: The Marginality of Black Executives." *Sociological Abstracts* Accession No. 89S 21316.

59. Committee on the University of California SCR 43 Task Force. *The Challenge: A Plan for Universitywide Diversity*. Riverside, CA: University of California Consortium on Mexico and the United States, 1989.

60. Corfman, Tom. "State Takes No Action on Asian Hiring goals." *Chicago Reporter* 20 (June 1991): 2,13.

61. Cortese, Anthony J.P. "Affirmative Action: Are White Women Gaining at the Expense of Black Men?" *Equity & Excellence* 25 (December 1992): 77-89.

62. Cose, Ellis. "Are Quotas Really the Problem?" *Time*, 24 June 1991.

63. _____. "To the Victors, Few Spoils." *Newsweek* (29 March 1993): 54.

64. Crosby, Faye J. "Affirmative Action is Worth It." *Chronicle of Higher Education*, 15 December 1993.

65. Crosby, Faye J., and Susan Clayton. "Affirmative Action and the Issue of Expectancies." *Journal of Social Issues* 46 (1990): 61-79.

66. Curran, Jeanne and others. "In the Trenches: A Response to Discrimination and Affirmative Action in the 1990s." *Wisconsin Sociologist* 28 (Spring-Summer 1991): 24-36.

67. Curry, Barbara K. *The Institutionalization of Affirmative Action of the University of Massachusetts at Boston.* Ph.D. diss., Harvard University, 1988. UMO # 8823313.

68. Danforth, John C. "Stop the Brawling About Quotas." *New York Times*, 20 June 1991.

69. Daniel, Cletus E. *Chicano Workers and the Politics of Fairness. The FEPC in the Southwest, 1941-1945.* Austin: University of Texas Press, 1991. [Fair Employment Practices Committee]

70. Dansicker, A. M. "A Sheep in Wolf's Clothing: Affirmative Action, Disparate Impact, Quotas and the Civil Rights Act." *Columbia Journal of Law and Social Problems* 25 (1991): 1-50.

71. Davila, A., and A. K. Bohara. "Equal Employment Opportunity Across States: The EEOC 1979-1989." *Public Choice* 80 (September 1994): 223-244.

72. Davis, Christopher H., and Darrell D. Jacobsen. "The Sunset of Affirmative Action." *National Black Law Journal* 12 (Spring 1990): 73-87. [Richmond v. Croson]

73. Deale, Frank. "Affirmative Action: Unsolved Questions Amidst a Changing Judiciary." *New York University Review of Law & Social Change* 18 (March 1990): 81-92.

74. Delgado, Richard. "Affirmative Action as a Majoritarian Device: Or, Do You Really Want To Be a Role Model." *Michigan Law Review* 89 (March 1991): 1222-1232.

75. Dembner, Alice. "UMass Poll Shows Gap on Equality Policy." *Boston Globe* (7 July 1994). [White students...overwhelmingly voice strong support for racial integration, but...are much less supportive of affirmative action or other policies that they believe could affect their own chances of success.]

76. Dershowitz, Alan M., and Laura Hanft. "Affirmative Action and the Harvard College Diversity-Discretion Model: Pradigm or Pretext?" *Cardozo Law Review* no. 1 (September 1979).

77. Devins, Neal. "Affirmative Action after Reagan." *Texas Law Review* 68 (December 1989): 353-379.

78. Dingerson, Michael R. and others. "The Hiring of Underrepresented Individuals in Academic Administrative Positions: 1972-1979." *Research in Higher Education* 23 (1985): 115-134.

79. Edmond, Beverly C. *The Impact of Federal Equal Employment Opportunity and Affirmative Action Policies on the Employment of Black Women in the Higher Grades (1982-1986).* Ph.D. diss., Georgia State University, 1990. UMO # 9032152.

80. Edwards, John. "Group Rights v. Individual Rights: The Case of Race-conscious Policies." *Journal of Social Policy* 23, part 1 (January 1994): 55-70.

81. _____. *Positive Discrimination, Social Justice and Social Policy: Moral Scrutiny of a Policy Practice.* London: Tavistock, 1987. [Anti-Affirmative action]

82. Eisenstein, Z. "Privatizing the State: Reproductive Rights, Affirmative Action, and the Problem of Democracy." *Frontiers* 12 (1991): 98-140.

83. Engels, Chris. "Voluntary Affirmative Action in Employment for Women and Minorities under Title VII of the Civil Rights Act: Extending Possibilities for Employers to Engage in Preferential Treatment to Achieve Equal Employment Opportunity." *John Marshall Law Review* 24 (Summer 1991): 731-813.

84. Espinosa, D. J. "Affirmative Action: A Case Study of an Organized Effort." *Sociological Perspectives* 35 (Spring 1992): 119-136.

85. Espinoza, Leslie G. "Empowerment and Achievment in Minority Law Student Support Programs: Constructing Affirmative Action." *University of Michigan Journal of Law Reform* 22 (Winter 1989): 281-302.

86. Exum, William H. "Climbing the Crystal Stair: Values, Affirmative Action and Minority Faculty." *Social Problems* 30 (1983): 383-399.

87. Ezorsky, Gertrude. "Affirmative Action and Layoffs." *Academe* 78 (July-August 1992): 50-51.

88. _____. *Racism and Justice: The Case for Affirmative Action*. Ithaca, NY: Cornell University Press, 1991.

89. Farber, David, and P.P. Frickey. "Is Carolene Products Dead? Reflections on Affirmative Action and the Dynamics of Civil Rights Legislation." *California Law Review* 79 (May 1991): 685- 728.

90. Feagins, Ken. "Affirmative Action or the Sanction." *Denver University Law Review* 67 (Spring 1990): 421-451.

91. *Federal Affirmative Action Efforts in Mid-America*. Washington, DC: U.S Commision on Civil Rights, 1983.

92. Feinberg, W. E. "The Inertia of Social Structure: Affirmative Action or Seniority in Layoffs." *Journal of Mathemetical Sociology* 15 (1990).

93. Feraca, Stephen E. "Inside the Bureau of Indian Affairs." *Society* 27 (May-June 1990): 29-39.

94. Fife, M. D. "A Critical Assessment of Equal Employment Opportunity Policy in Telecommunication Industries." *Mass Comm Review* 15 (1988): 3-9.

95. Finder, Alan. "Errors Inflated New York Success At Affirmative-Action Contracts." *New York Times* (27 June 1994).

96. Finder, Alan, and Thomas J. Lueck. "Flaws Are Found in Contract Plan to Aid Minorities." *New York Times* (26 June 1994). [New York City]

97. Finn, Chester E., Jr. "Quotas and the Bush Administration." *Commentary* 9217-23 (November 1991): 17-23.

98. Fiscus, Ronald J. "The Constitutional Logic of Affirmative Action." in ed. Stephen L. Wasby. : Duke University Press, 1992.

99. "Fla., N.Y. Bars Act To Forbid Hiring Bias by Lawyers." *Bar Leader* 14 (January 1989): 10.

100. Fletcher, Arthur A. "For Civil Rights, It's Back to the Future." *New York Times* (19 August 1990).

101. Follett, R. S. and others. "Problems in Assessing Employment Discrimination." *American Economic Review* 83 (May 1993).

102. Forman, James, Jr. "Saving Affirmative Action." *Nation* (9 December 1991).

103. Fosu, Augustin K. "Occupational Mobility of Black Women, 1958-1981: The Impact of Post-1964 Anti-discrimination Measures." *Industrial and Labor Relations Review* 45 (January 1992): 281-294.

104. French, S., and A. Wells. "Affirmative Action in the 1980s: A Study of Compliance in Higher Education." *Sociological Focus* 24 (October 1991).

105. Fried, Charles. "Affirmative Action After City of Richmond v. J. A. Croson Co.: A Response to the Scholars Statement." *Harvard Law Review* 99 (October 1989) [See also,"Scholars' Reply to Professor Fried, same issue]

106. _____. "Rehnquist Court Ruled for Affirmative Action." *New York Times*, 23 September 1994. (letter)

107. Funk, Nanette. "Affirmative Action and Universality." *Socialism & Democracy* 8 (Summer-Fall 1992): 207-222.

108. Galster, George C. "Neighborhood Racial Change, Segregationist, and Affirmative Marketing Policies." *Journal of Urban Economics* 27 (May 1990).

109. Gamson, William A., and Andre Modigliani. "The Changing Culture of Affirmative Action." in *Research in Political Sociology*, Vol.3. pp. 137-177. ed. Richard S. Braungart. Greenwich, CT: JAI Press, 1987.

110. Garcia, Luis T. and others. "The Effect of Affirmative Action on Attributions About Minority Group Members." *Journal of Personality* 49 (December 1981).

111. Garibaldi, Antoine. "The Paradoxical Impact of Affirmative Action on the Supply of Black Teachers." *Educational Policy* 2 (1988): 177-188.

112. Garrett, Robert. "Action Becomes Affirmative." *Boston Globe*, 29 July 1990. [Some improvement in use of Black and Hispanic actions in films]

113. Glaberson, William. "Panel Faults Racial Pattern of Court Staffs." *New York Times*, 12 July 1989. [Report by New York State Judicial Commission on Minorities]

114. Glackman, Howard and others. "Race in the Workplace: Is Affirmative Action Working?" *Business Week* (8 July 1991): 50-53.

115. Glaviano, Cliff, and R. Errol Lam. "Academic Libraries and Affirmative Action. Approaching Cultural Diversity in the 1990s." *College & Research Libraries* 51 (November 1990).

116. Goldstein, Morris, and Smith Robert S. "The Estimated Impact of the Antidiscrimination Program Aimed at Federal Contractors." *Industrial and Labor Relations Review* 29 (July 1976): 523-543.

117. Gorin, Stephen. "The [Reagan] Administration and Original Intent: The Curious Case of Affirmative Action." *Journal of Intergroup Relations* 15 (1987): 3-9.

118. Greenburgh, Deborah M. "Public Policy in the Quota Controversy." *Education and Urban Soociety* 8 (November 1975): 73- 85.

119. Greene, Kathanne W. *Affirmative Action and Principles of Justice*. Westport, CT: Greenwood Press, 1989.

120. Griffin, Peter B. *The Impact of Affirmative Action on Labor Demand: A Test of Some Implications of the Le Chatelier Principle*. Ph.D. diss., University of California, 1990. UMO # 9104498.

121. Groarke, Leo. "Affirmative Action as a Form of Restitution." *Journal of Business Ethics* 9 (March 1990).

122. Grossman, Deidre A. "Voluntary Affirmative Action Plans in Italy and the United States: Differing Notions of Gender Equality." *Comparative Labor Law Journal* 14 (Winter 1993): 185- 225.

123. Guidry, William B. "Affirmative Action." *American Opinion* (March 1979): 19-34. [Public opinion polls]

124. Hacker, Andrew. "Affirmative Action: The New Look." *New York Review of Books*, 12 October 1989.

125. _____. "Affirmative Action: A Negative opinion." *New York Times Book Review*, 1 July 1990. [Review of Thomas Sowell's *Preferential Policies*]

126. Hadreas, Peter. "Foucault & Affirmative Action." *Praxis International* 11 (July 1991): 214-226.

127. Haley, R. B. "Back to the Future: An Economic Approach to Affirmative Action." *Labor Law Journal* 41 (December 1990).

128. Hamilton, Charles V. "Affirmative Action and the Clash of Experiential Realities." *Annals of the American Academy of Political and Social Science* 523 (September 1992).

129. Hampden, Brenda S. "Preparing Undergraduate Minority Students for the Law School Experience." *Seton Hall Legislative Journal* 12 (Winter 1989): 207-231.

130. Haney-Lopez, Ian. "Community Ties, Race and Faculty Hiring: The Case for Professors Who Don't Think White." *Reconstruction* 1 (1991): 46-62.

131. Hankin, Joseph N. *Affirmative Action and Inaction: The Status of Minorities and Women at Public Two-Year Colleges in New York State and the Nation*. November 1986. ERIC ED 279 380.

132. Harvey, E. B., and J. H. Blakely. "Employment Equity Goal Setting and External Availability Data." *Social Indicators Research* 28 (March 1993): 245-266.

133. Haygood, Wil. "Shelby Steele, New Darling of the Right." *Boston Globe*, 6 June 1991.

134. Heckman, James J., and Brook S. Payner. "Determining the Impact of Federal Anti-discrimination Policy on the Economic Status of Blacks: A Study of South Carolina." *American Economic Review* 79 (March 1989): 138-177.

135. Heilman, M. E. "Affirmative Action: Some Unintended Consequences for Working Women." in *Research in Organizational Behavior*, Vol.16. pp. 125-170. eds. B. M. Staw, and L. L. Cummings. Greenwich, CT: JAI Press, 1994.

136. Henry, William A. III. "What Price Preference?" *Time* September 30, 1991.

137. Hentoff, Nat. "Affirmative Action. What of Those Left Behind?" *Village Voice*, 8 October 1991.

138. Hicks, Jonathan P. "Guiliani Is Halting or Scaling back Affirmative-Action Efforts." *New York Times*, 23 August 1994. [NYC Mayor Rudolph W. Giuliani]

139. Hill, Herbert. "Affirmative Action and the Quest for Job Equality." *Review of Black Political Economy* 6 (Spring 1976): 263-278.

140. Hill, T. E. "The Message of Affirmative Action." *Social Philosophy & Policy* 8 (Spring 1991): 108-129.

141. Holdeman, Linda L. "Civil Rights in Employment: The New Generation." *Denver University Law Review* 67 (1990).

142. Holmes, Peter. "The Ineffective Mechanism of Affirmative Action Plans in an Academic Setting." in *Chicanos in Higher Education*, pp. 76-83. eds. H. G. Casso, and G. D. Rowan. Albuquerque: University of New Mexico Press, 1975.

143. Holmes, Steven A. "Mulling the Idea of Affirmative Action for Poor Whites." *New York Times*, 18 August 1991.

144. _____. "Workers Find It Tough Going Filing Lawsuits Over Job Bias." *New York Times*, 24 July 1991.

145. Hoogland, K. A. "Metro Broadcasting, Inc. v. FCC: Nonremedial Affirmative Action Becomes an Exclusive Prerogative of Congress." *Employee Relations Law Journal* 16 (Winter 1991).

146. Horne, Gerald. *Reversing Discrimination. The Case for Affirmative Action*. International Publishers, 1992.

147. House, Ernest R., and William Madura. "Race Gender, and Jobs: Losing Ground on Employment." *Policy Science* 21 (1988).

148. Howard, Curtis D. *Career Paths of African-American Who Were Promoted to Upper Echelon Positions in the School District of Philadelphia: 1964-1974*. Ph.D. diss., University of Pennsylvania, 1989. UMO # 8922520.

149. Hsia, Jayjia. "Limits of Affirmative Action: Asian American Access to Higher Education." *Educational Policy* 2 (1988): 117- 136.

150. Hubler, Shaun. "Heeding Concerns of White Backlash." *Los Angeles Times*, 17 May 1993. ["Workplace diversity" Supplement]

151. Hudson, Richard. "Nonsense Clouds Affirmative Action Debate." *New York Times*, 30 September 1991. (letter). [Argues against stigma in affirmative action]

152. Hugo, Pierre. "Sins of the Fathers: Affirmative Action and the Redressing of Racial Inequality in the United States. Towards the South African Debate." *Politikon* 13 (June 1986): 54-74.

153. Hux, S. "Affirmative Action, Anti-Semitism and the Politics of Brave Triviality." *Moment* 9 (June 1984): 59-62.

154. Hyclak, Thomas and others. "Some New Historical Evidence on the Impact of Affirmative Action: Detroit, 1972." *Review of Black Political Economy* 21 (Fall 1992): 81-98.

155. Hyer, Patricia. "Affirmative Action for Women Faculty: Case Study of Three Successful Institutions." *Journal of Higher Education* 56 (1985): 282-299.

156. Isaac, Daniel. "Abuse Seen of Antibias Contracts Law." *Boston Globe*, 3 July 1989. [Laws to help minorities and women obtain public contracts.]

157. Ivers, G., and M. O'Connor. "Minority Set-aside Programs after City of Richmond v. J.A. Croson." *Publius* 20 (Summer 1990).

158. Jacobson, Cardell. "Resistance to Affirmative Action: Self- interest or Racism?" *Journal of Conflict Resolution* 29 (June 1985): 306-329.

159. Jacobson, Derrick Z. "Self-Help for Whom?" *Boston Globe*, 22 September 1991.

160. Jaschick, Scott. "Affirmative-Action Ruling on Connecticut. Called a 'Big Step' for Asian Americans." *Chronicle of Higher Education*, 19 May 1993. [U.S. Dept. of Education rules against Conn. Board of Governors for Higher Education]

161. _____. "Asian Americans and American Indians Added to Connecticut's Affirmative Action Program." *Chronicle of Higher Education*, 5 October 1994. [Colleges]

162. _____. "Court Backs Use of Race in Admission." *Chronicle of Higher Education*, 7 September 1994. [Affirmative Action at the University of Texas Law School]

163. _____. "Suit Against U. of Texas Challenges Law Schools' Affirmative-Action Effort." *Chronicle of Higher Education*, 9 February 1994. [Complaint of white students]

164. Johnson, Robert C., Jr. "Affirmative Action and the Academic Profession." *Annals of the American Academy of Political and Social Science* 448 (March 1980): 102-114.

165. Johnson, Roberta Ann. "Affirmative Action as a Woman's Issue." *Journal of Political Science* 17 (1989): 114-126.

166. _____. "Affirmative Action Policy in the United States: Its Impact on Women." *Policy and Politics* 18 (April 1990).

167. Jones, Augustus J., Jr. *Affirmative Talk, Affirmative Action: A Comparative Study of the Politics of Affirmative Action*. Westport, CT: Praeger, 1991. [Alucha County and Gainesville, FL]

168. Jones, Augustus J., Jr., and Clyde Brown. "State Responses to Richmond v. Croson: A Survey of Equal Employment Opportunity Officers." *National Political Science Review* 2 (1990): 40-61.

169. Jones, James E., Jr. "The Rise and Fall of Affirmative Action." in *Race in America*, eds. Herbert Hill, and James E. Jones, Jr. University of Wisconsin Press, 1993.

170. Jones, Stephen. "Affirmative Action, Promise and Passion, MSU finds Fairness Is a Balancing Act." *Detroit Free Press*, 31 January 1990. [Michigan State University]

171. Joseph, Antoine. "The Resurgence of Racial Conflict in Post Industrial America." *International Journal of Politics, Culture & Society* 5 (Fall 1991): 81-93. [Affirmative Action]

172. Judges, Donald P. "Light Beams and Particle Dreams: Rethinking the Individual vs. Group Rights Paradigm in Affirmative Action." *Arkansas Law Review* 44 (Fall 1991): 1007- 1061.

173. Justus, Joyce B., Sandra Freitag, and Leann Parker. *The University of California in the Twenty-First Century: Successful Approaches to Faculty Diversity*. Berkeley: University of California Press, 1987.

174. Kahn, Lawrence M. "Customer Discrimination and Affirmative Action." *Economic Inquiry* 29 (July 1991): 555-571.

175. Kauffman, Albert H., and Carmen Rumbaut. "Let's Look at Reverse Discrimination Suit." *New York Times*, 31 July 1994.

176. Keith, S. N. and others. "Effects of Affirmative Action in Medical Schools: A Study of the Class of 1975." *New England Journal of Medicine* 313 (December 1985): 1519-1525.

177. Kellough, J. Edward. "Federal Agencies and Affirmative Action for Blacks and Women." *Social Science Quarterly* 71 (March 1990): 83-92.

178. Kemp, Evan J.,Jr. "Rights and Quotas, Theory and Practice." *Washington Post*, 8 December 1992.

179. Kennedy, Duncan. "A Cultural Pluralist Case for Affirmative Action in Legal Academia." *Duke Law Journal* (September 1990): 705-757.

180. Kennedy, Randall L. "Persuasion and Distrust: A Comment on the Affirmative Action Debate." *Harvard Law Review* 99 (1986).

181. Kilborn, Peter T. "A Company Recasts Itself to Erase Decades of Bias." *New York Times*, 4 October 1990. [Corning, Inc., Corning, NY]

182. Kilson, Martin L., Jr. "Thoughts on Black Conservatism: A Review Essay." *Trotter Institute Review* (Winter/Spring 1992): 8-14. [Review of Stephen L. Carter, *Reflection of an Affirmative Action Baby* (1991)]

183. Kinder, Donald R., and Lynn M. Sanders. "Mimicking Political Debate with Survey Questions: The Case of White Opinion on Affirmative Action for Blacks." *Social Cognition* 8 (Spring 1990): 73-103. [1985 data]

184. King, N. J. "Racial Jurymandering: Cancer or Cure? A Contemporary Review of Affirmative Action in Jury selection." *New York University Law Review* 68 (October 1993): 707-776.

185. Kinsley, Michael. "Class, Not Race." *New Republic*, 19 August 1991. [Analysis of proposal to base affirmative action on class, not race]

186. Kleiman, H. "Content Diversity and the FCCs Minority and Gender Licensing Policies." *Journal of Broadcasting & Electronic Media* 35 (Autumn 1991): 411-430.

187. Konrad, A. M., and J. Pfeffer. "Understanding the Hiring of Women and Minorities in Educational Institutions." *Sociology of Education* 64 (July 1991): 141-157.

188. Krauthammer, Charles. "Reparations for Black Americans." *Time*, 31 December 1990. [As a substitute for affirmative action on behalf of blacks and other groups]

189. Landes, W. M. "The Economics of Fair Employment Laws." *Journal of Political Economy* 76 (1968): 507-552.

190. Laney, Garrine. *The Evolution of Equal Employment Programs, 1940-1985*, Paper Prepared for the Committee on the Status of Black Americans, National Research Council, Washington, DC., 1986.

191. Lanoue, G. R. ,. "Social Science and Minority Set-Asides." *Public Interest* 110 (Winter 1993): 49-62.

192. Lear, E. N. "Affirmative Action: An International Perspective." *American Zionist* 66 (May-June 1976): 16-18.

193. Leonard, Jonathan S. "The Impact of Affirmative Action Regulation and Equal Employment Law on Black Employment." *Journal of Economic Perspectives* 4 (Autumn 1990).

194. _____. *Splitting Blacks? Affirmative Action and Earnings Inequality Within and Across Races*. National Bureau of Economic Research, 1985.

195. _____. "Women and Affirmative Action." *Journal of Economic Perspectives* 3 (Winter 1989).

196. Lesher, Richard L. and others. "The Quota Question." *Business and Society Review* (Spring 1991): 4-8.

197. Levin, Michael. "Implications of Race and Sex Differences for Compensatory Affirmative Action and the Concept of Discrimination." *Journal of Social, Political & Economic Studies* 15 (1990): 175-212.

198. Lipset, Seymour M. "Equal Chances versus Equal Results." *Annals of the American Academy of Political and Social Science* 523 (September 1992).

199. Lively, Donald E. "The Supreme Court and Affirmative Action: Whose Classification is Suspect?" *Hastings Constitutional Law Quarterly* 17 (Spring 1990): 483-502.

200. Lokos, Lionel. *The New Racism: Reverse Discrimination in America*. Arlington House, 1971.

201. Lowe, Rosemary H., and Michele A. Wittig (eds.). "Approaching Pay Equity Through Comparable Worth." *Journal of Social Issues* 45 (Winter 1989): entire issue.

202. Lowry, L. D., and D. Garman. "Affirmative Action in Higher Education." *American Economic Review* 83 (May 1993).

203. Lundberg, S. J. "The Enforcement of Equal Opportunity Laws under Imperfect Information: Affirmative Action and Alternatives." *Quarterly Journal of Economics* 106 (February 1991).

204. Lunn, J. and H.L. Perry. "Justifying Affirmative Action: Highway Construction in Louisiana." *Industrial and Labor Relations Review* 46 (April 1993).

205. Lynch, Frederick R. *Invisible Victims: White Males and the Crisis of Affirmative Action*. NY: Greenwood Press, 1989.

206. Lynch, Frederick R., and William R. Beer. "'You Ain't the Right Color, Pal'." *Policy Review* (Winter 1990): 64-67.

207. Martin, Susan E. "White Male, black Male, Female: Affirmative Action and the Status of Women in Policing." *Sociological Abstracts* (1989). Accession No. 89 S 21563.

208. Marx, J. "Affirmative Action and Impact theory." *Sociological Focus* 25 (February 1992): 15-26.

209. Mathews, Thomas. "Quotas." *Newsweek* (31 December 1990).

210. Matsuda, Mari J. "Affirmative Action and Legal Knowledge." *Harvard Women's Law Journal* 11 (Spring 1988).

211. Matteson, Kevin. "The Dialectic of Powerlesness: Black Identity Culture and Affirmative Action." *Telos* 84 (Summer 1990): 177-184.

212. McArthur, Harvey. "Affirmative Action, Challenged by Rail Union Officialdom, Is Debated by Workers." *Militant* (19 March 1993) [United Transportation Union]

213. McDowell, Douglas S. *Affirmative Action after the Johnson Decision: Practical Guidance for Planning and Compliance*. Washington, DC: National Foundation for the Study of Employment Policy, 1989.

214. Mercer, Joyce. "Assault on Affirmative Action." *Chronicle of Higher Education*, 16 March 1994. [California]

215. *Minorities in Management: the Program to Increase Minorities in Business*. American Assembly of Collegiate Schools of Business, August 1988.

216. Mixon, J. W., Jr., and K. W. Pool. "Federal Funding of Public Schools: De Facto Affirmative Action?" *Atlantic Economic Journal* 18 (March 1990).

217. Monroe, Sylvester. "Does Affirmative Action Help or Hurt?" *Time*, 27 May 1991. [Contains some public opinion poll results]

218. _____. "Up from Obscurity." *Time*, 13 August 1990. [Shelby Steele]

219. Morton, F. A. "Class-Based Affirmative Action: Another Illustration of America Denying the Impact of Race." *Rutgers Law Review* 45 (Summer 1993).

220. Moss, Philip I. *Changing Public Sector Employment and the Occupational Advancement of Blacks, Women, and Hispanics*. Paper prepared for the Committee on the Status of Black Americans, National Research Council, Washington, DC, 1986.

221. _____. "Employment Gains by Minorities, Women in Large City Government, 1976-83." *Monthly Labor Review* 111 (November 1988).

222. Murray, Hugh. "The Case Against Affirmative Action." *Telos* 93 (Fall 1992): 145-158.

223. Myers, Steven L. "Racial Barriers Hard to Break in Fire Department." *New York Times*, 17 April 1992. [NYC]

224. Nacoste, R. W., and B. Hummels. "Affirmative Action and the Behavior of Decision Makers." *Journal of Applied Social Psychology* 24 (1 April 1994): 595-613.

225. Nay, Leslie A., and James E. Jones, Jr. "Equal Employment and Affirmative Action in Local Governments: A Profile." *Law & Inequality* 8 (November 1989): 103-149.

226. Nemeth, Charles P. "Judicially Imposed Quotas and Local 28, A Sheetmetal Worker's Union: A Search for Equal Opportunity or a 'Scorched Earth' Policy of Affirmative Action." *Labor Law Journal* 41 (May 1990).

227. Neuborne, Burt. "Notes for the Restatement (First) of the Law of Affirmative Action." *Tulane Law Review* 64 (June 1990): 1543-1556.

228. Newton, Jim. "White Male Applicants Struggle for LAPD Jobs." *Los Angeles Times*, 25 August 1993.

229. Nieli, Russell, ed. *Racial Preference and Racial Justice: The New Affirmative Action Controversy*. Ethics and Public Policy Center, 1991.

230. Niemi, A. W., Jr. "Impact of Recent Civil Rights Laws." *American Journal of Economics and Sociology* 33 (1974): 137-144.

231. Oliensis, Sheldon. "Minority Lawyer Recruitment and Hiring." *The Record of the Association of the Bar of the City of New York* 43 (December 1988): 922-932.

232. Orlans, Harold, and June O'Neill,eds. "Affirmative Action Revisited." *Annals of the American Academy of Political and Social Science* 523 (September 1992): entire issue.

233. Parikh, Sunita. "The Supreme Court, Civil Rights, and Preference Policies: Judicial Decision Making Process in the United States and India." *Teachers College Record* 92 (Winter 1990): 192-211.

234. Parker, Johnny C., and Parker Linda C. "Affirmative Action: Protecting the Untenured Minority Professor during Extreme Finacial Exigency." *North Carolina Central Law Journal* 17 (Fall 1988): 119-134.

235. Pear, Robert. "Courts Are Undoing Efforts to Aid Minority Contractors." *New York Times*, 16 July 1990.

236. Pearlsten, Mitchell B. *Selected Jewish Responses to Affirmative Action Admission. Toward a Conceptual Understanding*. Ph.D. diss., University of Minnesota, 1980.

237. Pendleton, Clarence M., Jr. "Time Is Running Out: Revise Executive Order 11246." *Ohio Northern University Law Review* 13 (Summer 1986): 403-409.

238. Peterson, Iver. "U.S. Appeals Case It Won For Teacher." *New York Times*, 14 August 1994. [Involves issue of teacher layoffs based on race]

239. Phelan, Pamela E. "An Affirmance of Equal Employment Opportunities for Women." *Creighton Law Review* 25 (December 1991): 185-211. [UAW v. Johnson Controls, Inc.]

240. Phillips, Tasha. "Whites & Asians Get Affirmative Action Too." *Daily Nexus*, 8 February 1990.

241. Pinzler, Isabelle K., and Deborah Ellis. "Wage Discrimination and Comparable Worth: A Legal Perspective." *Journal of Social Issues* 45 (Winter 1989).

242. "Politics, Intellectuals and the University." *Telos* 86 (December 1990): 103-140. [Symposium on affirmative action in higher education]

243. Posner, Richard A. "Duncan Kennedy on Affirmative Action." *Duke Law Journal* 5 (November 1990): 1157-1162. [See D. Kennedy, above]

244. Prager, Jeffrey. "Equal Opportunity and Affirmative Action- The Rise of New Social Understanding." *Research in Law, Deviance and Social Control* 4 (1982).

245. Prestage, Jewel L. "Duelling the Mythical Revolution in Higher Education: Retreat from the Affirmative Action Concept." *Journal of Politics* 1 (1979): 763-783.

246. "Race in the Workplace: Does Affirmative Action Work?" *Business Week*, 8 July 1991.

247. Rai, Kul B., and John W. Critzer. "Affirmative Action in Connecticut: A Comparison of Connecticut State University and the University of Connecticut." *Connecticut Review* 13 (Spring 1991): 55-68.

248. Ransom, Michael R., and S. B. Megdal. "Sex Differences in the Academic Labor Market in the Affirmative Action Era." *Economics of Education Review* 12 (March 1993).

249. Raspberry, William. "When Affirmative Action Ends." *Washington Post*, 2 August 1993.

250. Rebell, Michael A., and Arthur R. Block. "Chance v. Board of Examiners." in their *Educational Policymaking and the Courts*, Chicago, IL: University of Chicago Press, 1982. [Affirmative action to remedy discrimination in educational employment]

251. Reed, Merl E. *Seedtime for the Modern Civil Rights Movement. The President's Committee on Fair Employment Practice, 1941-1946*. Baton Rouge, LA: Louisiana State University Press, 1991.

252. Reid-Bookhart, Patricia A. *Blacks in Higher Education: A Study of Some of the Perceived Side Effects of Affirmative Action Policy Implementation on Designated Beneficiaries*. Ph.D. diss., University of Pennsylvania, 1984. UMO # 8416974.

253. *Report of the Task Force to Review Affirmative Action within the Division of Agriculture and Natural Resources*. Berkeley: Office of the President of the University of California, 1988.

254. Rhoads, Steven E. *In Comparable Worth, Pay Equity Meets the Market*. Cambridge University Press, 1993.

255. Riccucci, Norma M. *Women, Minorities, and Unions in the Public Sector*. New York: Greenwood Press, 1989.

256. Rice, Mitchell F. "State and Local Government Set-Aside Programs, Disparity Studies, and Minority Business Development in the Post- Croson Era." *Journal of Urban Affairs* 15 (1993): 529-554.

257. Robbs, Lloyd F.,Sr. *The Aura of Equal Opportunity: A Study- profile Concerning Affirmative Action*. Ph.D. diss., Claremont Graduate School, 1990. [County government of Los Angeles] UMO # 9016776.

258. Roberts, Sam. "Racial Quota That Was Upset Was a Means to an End." *New York Times*, 8 February 1993.

259. Rockwell, Paul. "Fighting the Fires of Racism." *Nation*, 11 December 1989. [The campaign against affirmative action by the International Association of Fire Fighters]

260. Rodin, M. J. "Affirmative Action Rhetoric." *Social Philosophy & Policy* 8 (Spring 1991): 130-149.

261. Rodriguez, Adriene and others. "UCLA Law School's Faltering Commitment to the Latino Community: The New Admissions Process." *Chicago Law Review* 9 (1988): 73-96.

262. Rodriguez, Santiago. "Affirmative Action and the Hispanic Community." *Civil Service Journal* 18 (October-December 1977): 18- 22.

263. Rodriguez, Ray. "Prejudice at the L.A. Fire Dept." *Long- Beach Press-Telegram*, 2 March 1994. [Affirmative action]

264. Rogers, Edward D. "When Logic and Reality Collide: The Supreme Court and Minority Business Set-asides." *Columbia Journal of Law and Social Problems* 24 (Winter 1990): 117-168.

265. Romero, Mary. "Twice Protected? Assessing the Impact of Affirmative Action on Mexican-American Women." in *Ethnicity and Women*, ed. Winston A. Van Horne. Milwaukee: University of Wisconsin Press, 1986.

266. Rose, David L. "Twenty-Five Years Later: Where Do We Stand on Equal Employment Opportunity Law Enforcement?" *Vanderbilt Law Review* 42 (May 1989): 1121-1182.

267. Rose, Patricia S. "Going Too Far or Just Doing their Job: The Double Bind Facing EEO and AA Officers." *The Labor Lawyer* 6 (Spring 1990): 439-478.

268. Rosenbloom, David H. "What Have Policy Studies Told Us About Affirmative Action and Where Can We Go From Here?" *Policy Studies Review* 4 (1984): 43-48.

269. Rosenfeld, Michel. *Affirmative Action and Justice: A Philosophical and Constitutional Inquiry*. Yale University Press, 1991.

270. _____. "Decoding Richmond: Affirmative Action and the Elusive Meaning of Constitutional Equality." *Michigan Law Review* 87 (June 1989): 1729-1794.

271. Ross, Thomas. "Innocence and Affirmative Action." *Vanderbilt Law Review* 43 (March 1990).

272. _____. "A Matter of Character." *Reconstruction* 1 (1991): 109-114. [Critique of Shelby Steele, *The Content of Our Character*]

273. Rucker, Robert E., and Jerry D. Bailey. "The Fall and Demise of Affirmative Action." in *Policy Controversies in Higher Education*, eds. Samuel K. Gove, and Thomas W. Stauffer. Westport, CT: Greenwood Press, 1986.

274. Scanlon, Anthony J. "The History and Culture of Affirmative Action." *Brigham Young University Law Review* (Spring 1988): 343- 361.

275. Scanlon, J. P. "The Curious Case of Affirmative Action for Women." *Society* 29 (January-February 1992): 36-41.

276. Schnapper, Eric. "Affirmative Action and the Legislative History of the Fourteenth Amendment." *Virginia Law Review* 71 (1985).

277. Schwartz, Bernard. *Behind Bakke: Affirmative Action and the Supreme Court.* New York: New York University Press, 1988.

278. Schwartz, Herman. "Affirmative Action." in *Minority Report*, ed. Leslie W. Dunbar. New York: Pantheon, 1984.

279. Scott, Marvin B. "Playing at Affirmative Action." *Integrated Education* 77 (September 1975): 37-38.

280. Sedler, Robert A. "The Constitution, Racial Preference, and the Supreme Court's Institutional Ambivalence; Reflections on Metro Broadcasting." *Wayne Law Review* 36 (Spring 1990): 1187-1236.

281. Selig, Joel L. "Affirmative Action in Employment after Croson and Martin: The Legacy Remains Intact." *Temple Law Review* 63 (Spring 1990).

282. Selinker, Michael. "Blacks Lose to Women in Construction Game." *Chicago Reporter* 18 (September 1989): 6-7,9.

283. Semple, Jesse B. [pseud.] "Invisible Man: Black and Male under Title VII." *Harvard Law Review* 104 (January 1991): 749-768.

284. Shanker, Albert. "Flip-flop at Justice." *New York Times*, 4 September 1994.

285. "A Sheep in Wolf's Clothing: Affirmative Action, Disparate Impact, Quotas, and the Civil Rights Act." *Columbia Journal of Law and Social Problems* 25 (1991): 1-50.

286. Simmons, Ross. *Affirmative Action.* Cambridge, MA: Schenkman, 1982.

287. Sims, Calvin. "The Unbreakable Glass Ceiling." *New York Times*, 7 June 1993. [Military contractor industries]

288. Sloan, Allan. "Minority Buyer Means Big Tax Benefit for Times Mirror in Sale of TV Stations." *Los Angeles Times*, 6 June 1993.

289. Smien, Eulius. "The Law School Admission Test as a Barrier to Almost Twenty Years of Affirmative Action." *Thurgood Marshall Law Review* 12 (Summer 1987): 359-393.

290. Smith, Earl, and Stephanie L. Witt. "Black Faculty and Affirmative Action at Predominantly White Institutions." *Western Journal of Black Studies* 14 (Spring 1990): 9-16.

291. Smith, J. P. "Affirmative Action and the Racial Wage Gap." *American Economic Review* 83 (May 1993).

292. Smolla, Rodney A. "Affirmative Action in the Marketplace of Ideas." *Arkansas Law Review* 44 (Fall 1991): 935-969.

293. "Social Psychological Perspectives On Affirmative Action." *Basic and Applied Social Psychology* 15 (April 1994): nine articles.

294. Son, In Soo and others. "Polarization and Progress in the Black Community: Earnings and Status Gains for Young Black Males in the Era of Affirmative Action." *Sociological Forum* 4 (1989): 309-327.

295. Sowell, Thomas. "'Affirmative Action': A Worldwide Disaster." *Commentary* 88 (December 1989).

296. Starr, Paul. "Civil Reconstruction: What To Do Without Affirmative Action." *American Prospect* 8 (Winter 1992).

297. *State Government Affirmative Action in Mid-America: An Update.* Washington, D.C.: Commission on Civil Rights, 1982.

298. Stavitsky, Jerome J. *A Theoretical Analysis of the Labor Market Wage and Employment Effects of Title VII of the Civil Rights Act of 1964*. Ph.D. diss., Virginia Polytechnic Institute and State University, 1989. UMO # 9000642.

299. Steele, Claude M., and Green, Stephen G. "Affirmative Action and Academic Hiring: A Case of a Value Conflict." *Journal of Higher Education* 47 (1976): 413-535.

300. Steele, Shelby. "A Negative Vote on Affirmative Action." *New York Times Magazine*, 13 May 1990.

301. _____. "The New Sovereignty: Grievance Groups Have Become Nations unto Themselves." *Harper's* (July 1992): 47-54.

302. Steinberg, Ronnie. "The Debate on Comparable Worth." *New Politics* 1 (Summer 1986): 108-126.

303. Steinberg, Stephen and others. "Critique of Stephen Carter's *Reflections of an Affirmative Action Baby*." *Reconstruction* 1 (1992): 114-127.

304. Steinberg, Stephen. "Occupational Apartheid." *Nation*, 9 December 1991.

305. Stetson, Jeffrey. "The Illusion of Inclusion: Affirmative Inaction in the Eighties- A Practitioner Speaks." *Journal of the College and University Personnel Association* 35 (1984): 9-15.

306. Stewart, Joseph, Jr. and others. "In Quest of Role Models: Change in Black Teacher Representation in Urban School Districts, 1968-1986." *Journal of Negro Education* 58 (Spring 1989): 141-152.

307. Stickler, K. Bruce. "For Job-Bias Suits, Ballooning Costs." *New York Times*, 17 July 1994.

308. Stimpson, Catharine R. "Has Affirmative Action Gone Astray?" *Thought & Action* 8 (Winter 1993): 5-26.

309. Stokes, Larry D. *Policy Intervention in Social Problems Development: A Case for Affirmative Action*. Ph.D. diss., Harvard University, 1990. UMO # 9134078.

310. Sue, Newton. *Review of Equal Employment Opportunity and Affirmative Action at the University of Hawaii*. Honolulu: Legislative Auditor, 1991.

311. Suggs, Robert E. "Rethinking Minority Business Development Strategies." *Harvard Civil Rights-Civil Liberties Law Review* 25 (Winter 1990): 101-145.

312. Summers, R. J. "The Influence of Affirmative Action on Perceptions of a Beneficiary's Qualifications." *Journal of Applied Social Psychology* 21 (1 August 1991): 1265-1276.

313. Takagi, Dana Y. "From Discrimination to Affirmative Action: Facts in the Asian American Admissions Controversy." *Social Problems* 37 (November 1990): 578-592.

314. Taylor, Bron R. *Affirmative Action and Moral Meaning: A Descriptive and Normative Ethical Analysis of Attitudes of Affected Groups*. Ph.D. diss., University of Southern California, 1988.

315. _____. *Affirmative Action at Work. Law, Politics, and Ethics*. Pittsburgh, PA: University of Pittsburgh Press, 1991.

316. Thomas, Clarence W. "Affirmative Action: Cure or Contradiction?" *Center Magazine* (November-December 1987).

317. _____. "The Equal Employment Opportunity Commission: Reflections on a New Philosophy." *Stetson Law Review* 15 (1985).

318. Thomas, R. Roosevelt, Jr. "From Affirmative Action to Affirming Diversity." *Harvard Business Review* 68 (March-April 1990).

319. Thornberry, Mary C. "Affirmative Action: History of an Attempt to Realize Greater Equality." in *Elusive Equality: Liberalism, Affirmative Action, And Social Change in America*, eds. James C. Foster, and Mary C. Segers. Port Washington, NY: Associated Faculty Press, 1983.

320. Tollett, Kenneth S., Sr. "Racism and Race-conscious Remedies." *American Prospect* 5 (Spring 1991): 91-93.

321. Torres, Frank. "Battling the System: Prejudicial Barriers Must Be Attacked." *Bar Leader* 14 (March-April 1989): 19-21. [Minority Lawyers]

322. Tougas, F. and others. "Why Women Approve Affirmative Action: The Study of a Predictable Model." *International Journal of Psychology* 26 (1991): 761-777.

323. Townsend-Smith, Richard. "The Role of Affirmative Action Officers in North American Universities." *Anglo-American Law Review* 19 (October-December 1990): 325-344.

324. Turner, Marlene E., and Anthony R. Pratkanis, eds. *Social Psychological Perspectives on Affirmative Action*. Lawrence Erlbaum Associates, 1994.

325. Turner, Ronald. *The Past and Future of Affirmative Action. A Guide and Analysis for Human Resource Professionals and Corporate Counsel*. Westport, CT: Quorum, 1990.

326. Turque, Bill, and Bob Cohn. "Black Conservatives Quarrel Over Quotas." *Newsweek*, 24 December 1990.

327. Tushnet, Mark V. "Change and Continuity in the Concept of Civil Rights: Thurgood Marshall and Affirmative Action." *Social Philosophy & Policy* (Spring 1991): 150-171.

328. Twale, D. J. and others. "Affirmative Action Strategies and Professiona; Schools: Case Illustrations of Exemplary Programs." *Higher Education* 24 (September 1992): 177-192.

329. UCLA Pilipino Affirmative Action Student Task Force. "Redefining Affirmative Action: A Case Study on Filipinos." *Philippine-American Journal* 1 (Winter 1989): 1-5.

330. Uri, N. D., and J. W. Mixon, Jr. "Effects of U.S. Affirmative Action Programs on Women's Employment." *Journal of Policy Modeling* 13 (Fall 1991).

331. _____. "Effects of United States Equal Employment Opportunity and Affirmative Action Programs on Women's Employment Stability." *Quality & Quantity* 26 (May 1992): 113-126.

332. _____. "Impact of the Equal Employment Opportunity and Affirmative Action Programs on the Employment of Women in the U.S." *Labour* 5 (Autumn 1991): 89-104.

333. Urofsky, Melvin J. *A Conflict of Rights. The Supreme Court and Affirmative Action*. New York: Scribner, 1991.

334. U.S. Commission on Civil Rights. *Consultations on the Affirmative Action Statement of the U.S. Commission on Civil Rights*. Washington, D.C.: The Commision, 1982.

335. U.S. Congress, 102nd, 1st session, House of Representatives, Committee on Education and Labor. *Hearings on H.R.1, the Civil Rights Act of 1991*. Washington, D.C.: GPO, 1991.

336. U.S. Equal Employment Opportunity Commission. *Indicators of Equal Employment Opportunity Status and Trends*. Washington, D.C.: The Commission,

337. Verkerke, J. Hoult. "Compensating Victims of Preferential Employment Discrimination Remedies." *Yale Law Journal* 98 (May 1989).

338. Virtanen, Simo V. *Group Conflict and Racial Prejudice as Sources of White Opposition to Policies Assisting Black Americans*. Ph.D. diss., SUNY Stony Brook, 1992. UMO # 9318961.

339. Vonnegut, Kurt. "Harrison Bergeron." *Arkansas Law Review* 44 (Fall 1991): 927-933.

340. Wagner, J. "Groups, Individuals and Constitutive Rules: The Conceptual Dilemma in Justifying Affirmative Action." *Polity* 23 (Autumn 1990).

341. Waldinger, Roger. "Changing Ladders amd Musical Chairs: Ethnicity and Opportunity in Post-Industrial New York." *Politics and Society* 15 (1987).

342. Ward, Nicole. "Cheering for Ability, Not Quotas." *Cleveland Plain Dealer*, 10 July 1994. [A black former cheerleader at Ellet High School in Akron, Ohio]

343. Ware, Leland. "A Remedy for the Extreme Case: The Status of Affirmative Action after Croson." *Missouri Law Review* 55 (Summer 1990): 631-702.

344. Washington, Valora, and William B. Harvey. *Affirmative Rhetoric, Negative Action: African-American and Hispanic Faculty at Predominantly White Institutions*. Washington, D.C.: School of Education and Human Development, George Washington University, 1990.

345. Watts, Jerry G. "The Race Problem and 'Moral Innocence." *Dissent* 38 (Winter 1991): 78-81. [Review of Shelby Steele, *The Content of Our Character*]

346. Weeden, L. Darnell. "Black Law School and the Affirmative Action Rationale." *Thurgood Marshall Law Review* 12 (Summer 1987): 395-413.

347. _____. "City of Richmond v. J. A. Croson and the Aborted Affirmative Action Plan." *Southern University Law Review* 16 (Spring 1989): 73-100.

348. Weiner, Tim. "The Men in the Gray Federal Bureaucracy." *New York Times*, 10 April 1994. ["White faces at the top"]

349. Weiss, Robert G. "Affirmative Action: A Brief History." *Journal of Intergroup Relations* 15 (1987): 40-53.

350. Welch, Finis K. "Affirmative Action and Discrimination." in *The Question of Discrimination. Racial Inequity in the U.S. Labor Market*, pp. 153-189. eds. Steven Shulman, and William A. Darity, Jr. Middletown, CT: Wesleyan University Press, 1989.

351. Westerhaus, C. F. "Resurrecting State and Local Race- conscious Set-aside Programs." *Indiana Law Journal* 67 (Winter 1991): 169-186.

352. Wicker, Tom. "Justice or Hypocrisy?" *New York Times*, 15 August 1991.

353. Wilgoren, Debbi. "'Downsizing' Plan Raises Ire." *Washington Post* [Race and order of layoffs in Washington, D.C. fire department]

354. Wilkerson, Isabel. "A Remedy for Old Racism Has New Kind of Shackles." *New York Times*, 15 September 1991.

355. Wilkins, Roger W. "Bush's Quota Con." *Mother Jones* (March- April 1991): 22-23.

356. Williams, Adolphus L., Jr. "A Critical Analysis of the Bakke Case." *Southern University Law Review* 16 (Spring 1989): 129-230.

357. Williams, J. B. "Affirmative Action at Harvard." *Annals of the American Academy of Political and Social Science* 523 (September 1992): 207-223.

358. Williams, Loretta J. "Ramifications of Affirmative Action." in *Dilemmas of the New Black Middle Class*, ed. Joseph R. Washington, Jr. , 1980.

359. Williams, P. J. "Metro Broadcasting, Inc. v. FCC: Regrouping in Singualr Times." *Harvard Law Review* 104 (December 1990).

360. Williams, Walter E. "Race, Scholarship, and Affirmative Action." *National Review* (5 May 1989): 36-38.

361. Willis, Dana L. "Best Schools Have White Affirmative Action." *New York Times*, 23 June 1991. [Children of alumni]

362. Wilson, Reginald. "An Elitist Attack on Affirmative Action." *New Politics* 3 (Winter 1992): 183-189. [Critique of Stephen L. Carter, *Reflections of an Affirmative Action Baby*, 1991]

363. Wilson, William J. "Race Neutral Policies and the Democratic Coalition." *American Prospect* 1 (Spring 1990): 74-81.

364. Wingfield, Harold L. *Affirmative Action: The Shootout Over Racism and Sexism at the Academy. The Case of Minority (Black) Faculty Recruitment and Hiring at the University of Oregon, 1973-1975*. Ph.D. diss., University of Oregon, 1982.

365. Witt, Stephanie L. *The Pursuit of Race and Gender Equity in American Academe*. New York: Praeger, 1990.

366. _____. *Self-Interest, Community Welfare and the Pursuit of Gender and Race Equity in American Academia: The Dynamics of Black/White and Male/Female Perspectives on Affirmative Action*. Ph.D. diss., Washington State University, 1989. UMO # 9007818.

367. Wonnell, Christopher T. "Circumventing Racism: Confronting the Problem of the Affirmative Action Ideology." *Brigham Young University Law Review* (Winter 1989): 95-144.

368. Wood, B. Dan. "Does Politics Make a Difference at the EEOC?" *American Journal of Political Science* 34 (1990): 503-530. [Equal Employment Opportunity Commission]

369. Woodard, Maurice C. "An Evaluation of Equal Employment Policies in Virginia." *Review of Black Political Economy* 5 (Summer 1975): 423-437.

370. Woods, Geraldine. *Affirmative Action*. New York: Watts, 1989. [Written for young People]

371. Work, John W. "After Affirmative Action, What?" *New York Times*, 27 August 1989.

372. _____. *Toward Affirmative Action and Racial/Ethnic Pluralism: How to Train in Organizations: A Handbook for Trainers*. Arlington, VA: Belvedere Press, 1990.

373. Wycliff, Don. "Blacks Debate the Costs of Affirmative Action." *New York Times*, 10 June 1990.

374. Wyzan, Michael L. ed. *The Political Economy of Ethnic Discrimination and Affirmative Action. A Comparative Perspective*. Westport, CT: Praeger, 1990.

375. Yogev, A., and S. Tomlinson, eds. *Affirmative Action and Positive Policies in the Education of Ethnic Minorities*. Greenwich, CT: JAI Press, 1989.

AFRICA

376. *African-American Baseline Essays*. Multicultural/MultiethnicEducation Office, 501 N. Dixon street, Portland, Oregon 97227.

377. "The Afrocentric Idea." *Social Studies' Review* 7 (Winter 1991): 3-6. [Critique of concept]

378. Alleyne, Mervyn. *Comparative Afro-American: A Historical- Comparative Study of English-Based Afro-American Dialects in the New World*. Ann Arbor, MI: Karoma Publishers, 1980.

379. Apter, Andrew. "Herskovits's Heritage: Rethinking Syncretism in the African Diaspora." *Diaspora* 1 (Winter 1991): 231-260.

380. Asante, Molefi. *Afrocentricity*. Trenton, NJ: Africa World Press, 1990.

381. Asgill, E. O. *The Endangered Species: The African Character in American Fiction*. Ph.D. diss., University of South Florida, 1988. UMO # 8907638.

382. "The Atlanta Conference [on Afrocentric Education]" *Social Studies Review* 7 (December 1991): 7-10. [Reprinted from *New Republic*]

383. Bell, Muriel, and Malcolm Bell, Jr. *Drums and Shadows. Survival Studies Among the Georgia Coastal Negroes*. Athens, GA: University of Georgia Press, 1986.

384. Bruce, Dickson C., Jr. "Ancient Africa and the Early Black American Historian, 1883-1915." *American Quarterly* 36 (Winter 1984): 684-699.

385. Busby, Margaret, ed. *Daughters of Africa: An International Anthology of Words & Writings by Women of African Descent: From the Ancient Egyptian to the Present*. Pantheon, 1992.

386. Chocolate, Deborah N. *Kwanzaa*. Chicago, IL: Children's Press, 1990. [Written for young people]

387. Cromwell, Adelaide M., ed. *Dynamics of the African/Afro- American Connection, from Dependency to Self-reliance*. Washington, D.C.: Howard University Press, 1987.

388. Erhogbe, Edward O. *African Americans' Ideas and Contributions to Africa, 1900-1985: From "Idealistic Rhetoric" to "Realistic Pragmatism"?* Ph.D. diss., Boston University, 1992. UMO # 9202866.

389. Feierman, Steven. "Struggles for Control: The Social Roots of Health and Healing in Modern Africa." *African Studies Review* 28 (1985): 73-145.

390. Garrett, Romeo B. "African Survivals in American Culture." *Journal of Negro History* 51 (1966): 239-245.

391. Gonzalez, Fernando. "Roots, Recognition and Radio." *Boston Globe*. [Why Afropop Hasn't Found an African-American]

392. Holloway, Joseph E., ed. *Africanisms in American Culture*. Bloomington, IN: Indiana University Press, 1990.

393. Holloway, Joseph E., and Winifred K. Vass. *The African Heritage of American English*. Bloomington, IN: Indiana University Press, 1993.

394. Jean, Clinton M. *Behind the Eurocentric Veils: The Search for African Mysteries*. Ph.D. diss., Brandeis University, 1988.

395. Jenkins, David. *Black Zion: Africa Imagined and Real as Seen by Today's Blacks*. New York: Harcourt Brace Jovanovich, 1975.

396. Jones, Lisa. "Africa." *Village Voice*, 24 August 1993. [Using word "Africa" in naming a commercial hair grease]

397. Littlefield, Daniel C. "'Abundance of Negroes of That Nation': The Significance of African Ethnicity in Colonial South Carolina." in *The Meaning of South Carolina History*, eds. David R. Chesnutt, and Clyde N. Wilson. University of South Carolina Press, 1991.

398. Magubane, Bernard. *The Ties that Bind*. Trenton, NJ: 1987.

399. Moore, Richard B. "Africa-conscious Harlem." *Freedomways* (Summer 1963).

400. Mullin, Michael. *Africa in America: Slave Acculturation and Resistance in the American South and the British Caribbean, 1736- 1831*. University of Illinois Press, 1992.

401. Murphy, Joseph M. *Working the Spirit. Ceremonies of the African Diaspora*. Beacon Press, 1994.

402. Okafor, V. O. "Diop and the African Origin of Civilization: An Afrocentric Analysis." *Journal of Black Studies* 22 (December 1991): 252-268.

403. Raver, Anne. "In Georgia's Swept Yards, a Dying Tradition." *New York Times*, 8 August 1993. [Persecution of West African traditions]

404. Roediger, David. "The Meaning of Africa for the American Slave." *Journal of Ethnic Studies* 4,1 (1977): 1-16.

405. Schroeder, Walter A. and others. "Sickle Cell Anaemia Genetic Variations, and the Slave Trade to the United States." *Journal of African History* 31 (1990): 163-180.

406. Scuttles, William C., Jr. "African Religious Survivals as Factors in American Slave Revolts." *Journal of Negro History* 56 (1971): 97-104.

407. Skinner, Elliot P. *African American and U.S. Policy toward Africa, 1850-1924: In Defense of Black Nationality*. Washington, D.C.: Howard University Press, 1992.

408. Staniland, Martin. *American Intellectuals and African Nationalists, 1955-1970*. Yale University Press, 1991.

409. Terrell, Robert L. "Problematic Aspects of U.S. Press Coverage of Africa." *Gazette: International Journal for Mass Communication Studies* 43 (1989): 131-153.

410. Thompson, Vincent Bakpetu. *The Making of the African Diaspora in the Americas: 1441-1900*. London: Longmans, 1987.

411. Thornton, John K. "African Dimensions of the Stono Rebellion [of 1739]." *American Historical Review* 96 (October 1991): 1101- 1113.

412. Thornton, Michael C., and Robert J. Taylor. "Black American Perception of Black Africans." *Ethnic and Racial Studies* 11 (1988): 139-150.

413. Turner, Lorenzo D. *Africanism in the Gullah Dialect*. Chicago, IL: University of Chicago Press, 1949.

414. _____. "Linguistic Research and African Survivals." *American Council of Learned Societies Bulletin* 32 (1941): 68-89.

415. _____. "Our African Heritage." *Say: Alumni Magazine of Roosevelt University* (1957): 15-19.

416. Twining, Mary A., and Keith E. Baird, eds. *Sea Island Roots: African Presence in the Carolinas and Georgia*. Africa World, 1991.

417. Vass, Winifred K. *The Bantu Speaking Heritage of the United States*. Los Angeles: Center for Afro-American Studies, University of California, Los Angeles, 1979.

418. Walters, Ronald W. *Pan Africanism and the African Diaspora: An Analysis of Modern Afrocentric Political Movements*. Wayne State University Press, 1993.

419. Warlaw, Alvia J. and others. *Black Art, Ancestral Legacy: The African Impulse in African-American Art*. New York: Abrams, 1990.

420. Westbury, Susan. "Slaves of Colonial Virginia: Where They Came From." *William and Mary Quarterly* 42 (April 1985): 228-237.

ANTI-RACISM

421. Albert, Michael. "At the Breaking Point." *Z Magazine* 3 (May 1990): 16-18.

422. Aptheker, Herbert. *Anti-Racism in U.S. History: The First Two Hundred Years*. Westport, CT: Greenwood, 1992.

423. _____. "Bibliographic Essay: Anti-Racism in the U.S.: An Introduction." *Sage Race Relations Abstracts* 12 (November 1987): 3-32.

424. _____. "Resistance and Afro-American History: Some Notes on Contemporary Historiography and Suggestions for Further Research." in *Resistance: Studies in African, Caribbean and Afro-American History*, ed. Gary Y. Okihiro. Amherst, MA: University of Massachusetts Press, 1986.

425. Baird, Susan. "The Face of Bigotry. Oregon Students Examine White Supremacy." *Teaching Tolerance* 1 (March 1992): 58-59. Ashland Middle School, Ashland, OR.

426. Baker, Lee D. "The Location of Franz Boas Within the African-American Struggle." *Critique of Anthropology* 14 (June 1994): 199-218.

427. _____. "The Location of Franz Boas Within the African- American Struggle." *Critique of Anthropology* 14 (June 1994): 199- 218.

428. Bejin, A., and J. Freund, eds. *Racismes, antiracismes*. Paris: Meridiens-Klincksieck, 1986.

429. Braham, Peter and others, eds. *Racism and Antiracism: Inequalities, Opportunities and Policies*. London: Sage, 1992.

430. Brandt, Godfrey L. *The Realization of Anti-Racist Teaching*. London: Falmer Press, 1986.

431. Byrnes, Deborah A., and Gary Kiger, eds. *Common Bonds: Anti- Bias Teaching in a Diverse Society*. Association for Childhood Education International, 1992.

432. Caldwell, Janet. "The Need for 'Anti-Racism' Education." *Education Week* (20 September 1989).

433. Cambridge, Alrick X., and Stephen Feuchtwang. *Antiracist Strategies*. Aldershot: Avebury, 1990.

434. Davis, Ray. "Anti-racist Organizing, Then and Now." *Socialist Review* 20 (October 1990): 29-35.

435. Derman-Sparks, Louise. *Anti-Bias Curriculum: Tools for Empowering Young Children*. National Association for the Education of Young Children, 1989.

436. Foster, Peter. *Policy and Practice in Multicultural and Anti-Racist Education*. Routledge, 1990.

437. Garnett, Cynthia M. "Look at the Lies- See the Truth. Confronting the Divide and Rule Strategy of White Supremacy." *African Commentary* (August 1990): 9-11.

438. Goldberg, David T. "Racism and Rationality: The Need for a New Critique." *Philosophy of the Social Sciences* 20 (September 1990).

439. Greer, Colin. "We Must Take a Stand." *Parade* (28 April 1991). [Local organizing against hate groups]

440. Harber, C. "Anti-Racism and Political Education for Democracy." in *Education for Democratic Citizenship. A Challenge for Multi-Ethnic Societies*, eds. Roberta S. Sigel, and Marilyn Hoskin. Hillsdale, New Jersey: Lawrence Erlbaum Associate, 1990.

441. Heller, Celia, and J. A. Hawkins. "Teaching Tolerance: Notes from the Front Line." *Teachers College Record* 95 (March 1994): 337-68.

442. Hennessy, M. "Undoing Racism: What Are the 'Next Steps?'." *Peace and Freedom* 49 (1989).

443. Horne, Gerald. "Race Matters: The Trajectory of Anti- Racism." *Science and Society* 57 (December 1993): 441-45.

444. Hulteen, Bob, and Jim Wallis, eds. *America's Original Sin: A Study Guide on White Racism*. Revised edition. Washington, D.C.: Sojourners, 1992.

445. ILEA Centre for Anti-Racist Education. "Is Anti-Racist Education Really Necessary?" *Contemporary Issues in Geography and Education* 1 (March 1984): 26-29.

446. Jenkins, Adelbert H. "The Liberating Value of Constructionism for Minorities." *Humanistic Psychologist* 17 (June 1989): 161-68.

447. Jenkins, Olga C. "A Lifetime Fighting Racism: Was It Worth It?" *New York Times*, 17 May 1992. Letter.

448. John, Rupert. *Racism and Its Elimination*. New York: UN Institute for Training and Research, 1981.

449. Jones, James. "Piercing the Veil: Bi-Cultural Strategies for Coping with Prejudice and Racism." in *Opening Doors*, eds. Harry J. Knopke and others. : University of Alabama Press, 1991.

450. Katz, Phyllis A., and Dalmas A. Katz, eds. *Eliminating Racism: Profiles in Controversy*. New York: Plenum, 1989.

451. Ketabgian, Tamara. "You Can't Stop Racism With a Class." *Pasadena Star-News*, 4 August 1989.

452. Landerman, Donna. "Breaking the Racism Barrier: White Anti- Racism Work." in *Reweaving the Web of Life: Feminism and Life*, ed. Pam McAllister. Philadelphia: New Society, 1982.

453. Linzie, Roderick K. *Analysis of the Anti-Racist Student at the University of Michigan- Ann Arbor*. Ph.D. diss., University of Michigan, 1994. UMO # 9332123.

454. McKissack, Patricia, and Frederick McKissack. *Taking a Stand against Racism and Racial Discrimination*. New York: F. Watts, 1990. [Written for young people]

455. Mitchell, H. L. "Socialism, Anti-Racism and the Southern Tenant Farmers Union." in *Within the Shell of the Old*, eds. Don Fits, and David Roediger. : Kerr, 1990.

456. Moore, Basil S. "The Prejudice Thesis and the De- politization of Racism." *Discourse* 14 (October 1993): 52-64.

457. Parry, G. "Anti-racist Anthropology." *Rain. Royal Anthropological Institute Newsletter* 60 (1984): 3-4.

458. Parsons, Dana. "Group Fails to Figure Out Racism, but at Least It's Trying." *Los Angeles Times*, December 1992. [Community efforts in Orange Country. CA]

459. Peterson, Iver, Country-by-Country Fight Against Bias. *New York Times*, 5 January 1993. [New Jersey]

460. Silk, Catherine and John Silk. *Racism and Anti-racism in American Popular Culture: Portrayals of African-Americans in Fiction and Film*. Manchester: Manchester University Press, 1990.

461. Simon, Roger I. and others. *Decoding Discrimination: A Student-based Approach to Anti-racist Education Using Film*. London: University of Western Ontario-Althouse Press, 1988.

462. Steinerkhamsi, G. "Community Languages and Anti-Racist Education." *Educational Studies* 16 (1990).

463. Walcott, Rinaldo. "Theorizing Anti-Racist Education: Decentering White Supremacy in Education." *Western Canadian Anthropologist* 1 (1990): 109-120.

464. Whitaker, Ben ed. *Teaching about Prejudice*. London: Minority Rights Group, 1983.

ANTISEMITISM

465. "ADL-Harris Poll: Anti-Semitism in the Farm Belt." *ADL Bulletin* 43 (April 1986): 8-9.

466. Agassi, J. "Anti-Semitism (according to M. Mushkat & E. Delisle)." *International Problems. Society & Politics* 32 (November 1993).

467. Alexander, Jeffrey C., and Chaim Seidler-Feller. "False Distinctions and Double Standards: The Anatomy of Antisemitism at UCLA." *Tikkun* 7 (January-February 1992): 12-14.

468. Alter, Jonathan and others. "Is It Bad For the Jews?" *Newsweek*, 7 October 1991. [Antisemitism in the U.S.]

469. Alter, Jonathan. "Is Pat Buchanan Anti-Semitic?" *Newsweek*, 23 December 1991.

470. Alterman, Eric. "The Pat and Abe Show." *Nation*, 5 November 1990. [The danger in calling people anti-semites]

471. "Anti-Semitism." *Commentary* 92 (October 1991): 8-9 (four letters).

472. "Anti-Semitism." *Commentary* 93 (June 1992): 4-11. [Letters on the subject]

473. "Anti-Semitism in the United States." *American Jewish History* 71 (1981): entire issue.

474. Athans, Mary C. *The Coughlin-Fahey Connection: Father Charles E. Coughlin, Father Denis Fahey, C.S. Sp., and Religious Anti-Semitism in the United States, 1938-1954*. New York: Peter Lang, 1992.

475. Banton, Michael. "The Relationship between Racism and Antisemitism." *Patterns of Prejudice* 26 (1992): 17-27.

476. Bellant, Russ. *Old Nazis, the New Right and the Reagan Administration: The Role of Domestic Fascist Networks in the Republican Party and Their Effect on U.S. Cold War Policies*. Boston, MA: Political Research Associates, 1988.

477. Bergmann, Werner, ed. *Current Research on Antisemitism. Vol.2: Error Without Trial: Psychological Research on Antisemitism*. Berlin/New York: W. de Gruyter, 1988.

478. Bergmann, Werner. "Psychological & Sociological Theories of Antisemitism." *Patterns of Prejudice* 26 (1992): 34-47.

479. Bishop, Katherine. "Hoping to Change Minds of Young on Holocaust." *New York Times*, 23 December 1991. [Bradley R. Smith, organizer of "The Committee for the Open Debate of the Holocaust", denying the reality of the Holocaust.]

480. Braham, Randolph L. "Boring From Within: The Case of Laszlo Pasztor." *Midstream* 35 (June-July 1989): 25-28. [Activity of former Hungarian Nazi in U.S. Republican Party.]

481. Braverman, William A. *The Ascent of Boston's Jews, 1630- 1918*. Ph.D. diss., Harvard University, 1990. UMO # 9021785.

482. Brown, Cherie. "The Dynamics of Anti-Semitism." *Tikkun* 6 (March-April 1991): 26-28.

483. Buckley, William F. "In Search of Anti-Semitism." *National Review*, 30 December 1991.

484. "A Bum Rap: [Henry} Ford's International Jew Gets New Life." *Moment* 15 (February 1990): 23. [Professor Griff of Public Enemy rap music group]

485. Carmichael, Joel. *The Satanizing of the Jews: Origin & Development of Mystical Anti-Semitism.* Fromm, 1992.

486. Carroll, James. "Boston's Jews and Boston's Irish - Conflict and Common Ground." *Boston Globe*, 12 January 1992.

487. Carvajal, Doreen. "Extremist Institute Mired in Power Struggle." *Los Angeles Times*, 15 May 1994. [Institute for Historical Review, Holocaust-denier group in Costa Mesa, CA]

488. Cellini, Joseph, ed. *Anti-Semitism in America, 1878-1939.* New York: Arno Press, 1977.

489. Chavez, Jerome A. "Anti-Semitism in the United States: On the Rise or On the Decline?" *Midstream* (January 1990): 26-30.

490. Chavez, Stephanie, and Jill Gottesman. "Anti-Semitism Harassment Alleged." *Los Angeles Times*, 24 September 1992. [Jewish detective in Huntington Park, CA]

491. Clymer, K. J. "Anti-Semitism in the Late Nineteenth Century: The Case of John Hay." *American Jewish Historical Quarterly* 60 (June 1971): 344-354.

492. Cohen, Naomi W. "Antisemitism in the Gilded Age: The Jewish View." *Jewish Social Studies* 41 (Summer-Fall 1979): 187-210.

493. _____. *Jews in Christian America: The Pursuit of Religious Equality.* Oxford University Press, 1992.

494. _____. "Shaare Tefila Congregation v. Cobb: A New Departure in American Jewish Defense?" *Jewish History (Haifa)* (Spring 1988): 95-108.

495. Cohen, Richard. "The Gotcha Game." *Washington Post Magazine*, 27 December 1992. [Public-opinion poll on antisemitism in the U.S.]

496. Cohen, Steven M. "Undue Stress on American Anti-Semitism?" *Sh'ma* (1 September 1989): 113-115.

497. Cohler, Larry. "Bush Campaign Committee Contains Figures Linked to Anti-Semitic and Fascist Backgrounds." *Washington Jewish Week*, 8 September 1988.

498. Corevan, James. *Bitter Harvest: Gordon Kahl and the Posse Comitatus: Murder in the Heartland.* New York: Viking Press, 1990. [Antisemitism in the farm belt]

499. Curtis, Michael. "Anti-Semitism in the United States." *Midstream* (January 1990): 20-26.

500. Dajani, Souad. "Anti-Semitism." *Z Magazine* 5 (November 1992): 7. [See Bell Hooks, below]

501. D'Alessio, Stewart J., and Lisa Stolzenberg. "Anti-Semitism in America: The Dynamics of Prejudice." *Sociological Inquiry* 61 (Summer 1991): 359-366.

502. Dawidowicz, L. S. "How They Teach the Holocaust." *Commentary* 90 (December 1990).

503. Dershowitz, Alan M. *Chutzpah.* Boston, MA: Little, Brown, 1991.

504. _____. "Sleeper's Ad Hominem Attack: Alan Dershowitz responds." *Reconstruction* 1 (1992): 89-90. [See Sleeper, below]

505. Dinnerstein, Leonard. *Antisemitism in America.* Oxford University Press, 1994.

506. Dobkowski, Michael N. "American Antisemitism: A Reinterpretation." *American Quarterly* 29 (1977): 166-181.

507. Duffy, Bernard K. "The Rhetoric of Ezra Pound's World War II Radio Broadcast." *Rendezvous* 22 (1986): 48-58. [Antisemitism]

508. Eber, Linda and others, eds. *Awareness and Action. A Resource Book on Anti-Semitism.* New Jewish Agenda, 1991.

509. Eber, Linda, and Irena Klepfisz eds. *The Proceedings of CARRYING IT ON. A National Conference Organizing Against Anti- Semitism and Racism for Jewish Activists and College Students*. New Jewish Agenda, 1992.

510. Farrell, John A. "[Patrick] Buchanan's Views of Jews in Question." *Boston Globe*, 7 February 1992.

511. Fein, Helen, ed. *Current Research on Antisemitism: Vol. 1: the Persisting Question: Sociological Perspectives and Social Contexts of Modern Antisemitism*. Berlin/New York: W. de Gruyter, 1987.

512. Feingold, Henry L. "Finding a Conceptual Framework for the Study of American Antisemitism." *Jewish Social Studies* 47 (Summer-Fall 1985): 313-326.

513. Feldman, Egal. *Dual Destinies. The Jewish Encounter with Protestant America*. Urbana, IL: University of Illinois Press, 1990.

514. Flynt, J. Wayne. "Religion in the Urban South: The Divided Religious Mind of Birmingham, 1900-1930." *Alabama Review* 30 (1977): 108-134.

515. Freiling, Harald. "Der Holocaust als Thema amerikanischer Schulcurricula." *Int. Schulbuchforschung* 11 (1989): 255-282.

516. Freudmann, Lillian C. *Antisemitism in the New Testament*. University Press of America: 1994.

517. Ginsberg, Benjamin. *The Fatal Embrace: Jews and the State*. University of Chicago Press, 1993.

518. Glazer, Nathan. "The Enmity Within." *New York Time Book Review*, 27 September 1992. [Review of William F. Buckley, *In Search of Anti-Semitism*]

519. Glock, Charles Y., and Rodney Stark. "Do Christian Beliefs Cause Anti-Semitism? - A Comment." *American Sociological Review* 38 (February 1975): 53-59.

520. Goodstein, Laurie. "Holocaust of Mirrors." *Washington Post* [Deniers of the Holocaust]

521. Hagedorn, Leah E. *The Southern Jewish Ethos: Jews, Gentiles, and Interfaith Relations in the American South, 1877-1917*. Master's thesis: University of North Carolina, 1989.

522. Hall, Sidney G. III. *Christian Anti-Semitism and Paul's Theology*. Fortress Press, 1993.

523. Haupt, Peter I. "A Universe of Lies: Holocaust Revisionism and the Myth of a Jewish World-Conspiracy." *Patterns of Prejudice* 25 (Summer 1991): 75-85.

524. Hentoff, Nat. "God Must Have Loved Anti-Semites, He Made So Many of Them." *Village Voice*, 7 May 1991.

525. _____. "How To Find Out If You're Anti-Semitic." *Village Voice*, 19 January 1993.

526. _____. "Why Do They Hate Us?" *Village Voice*, 28 May 1991. [Antisemitism at UCLA]

527. Hertzberg, Arthur. "Is Anti-Semitism Dying Out?" *New York Review of Books*, 24 June 1993.

528. *Highlights from an Anti-Defamation League Survey on Anti- Semitism and Prejudice in America*. Anti-Defamation League, November 1992.

529. Hirsch, Herbert, and Jack D. Spiro, eds. *Persistent Prejudice: Perspectives on Anti-Semitism*. Fairfax, VA: George Mason University Press, 1988.

530. Houseman, Gerald L. "Antisemitism in City Politics: The Separation Clause and the Indianapolis Nativity Scene Controversy, 1976-1977." *Jewish Social Studies* 42 (1980): 21-36.

531. Husock, Howard. "Red, White, and Jew: Holocaust Museum on the Mall." *Tikkun* 5 (July-August 1990): 32-34, 92-93.

532. Jaher, Frederic C. *The Origins and the Rise of Anti-Semitism in America*. Harvard University Press, 1994.

533. Jenifer, Franklin G. "Decrying Antisemitism." *Washington Post*, 7 March 1994. [President of Howard University]

534. Judis, John B. "Slurs Fly in Right's Uncivil War." *In These Times*, 18 October 1989. [Antisemitism as weapon of paleoconservatives against neoconservatives]

535. Kakutani, Michiko. "Examining T.S. Eliot and Anti-Semitism: How Bad Was It?" *New York Times*, 22 August 1989.

536. Katz, J. "Accounting for Anti-Semitism." *Commentary* 91 (June 1991): 52-54.

537. Kessler, Sidney H. "Fascism under the Cross: The Case of Father Coughlin." *Wiener Library Bulletin* 33 (1980): 8-12.

538. King, Dennis, and Chip Berlet. "ADLgate." *Tikkun* 8 (July- August 1993): 31-36, 100-102. [Charges that the Anti Defamation League's commitment against antisemitism has been compromised by increasing identification with neoconservatism]

539. King, Kathleen P., and Dennis E. Clayson. "Perceptions of Jews, Jehovah's Witnesses, and Homosexuals." *California Sociologist* 7 (winter 1984): 49-67.

540. Klausner, Samuel Z. "Jews in the Executive Suite: The Ambiance of Jewish and Gentile Firms," in *Social Class and Democratic Leadership*, pp. 147-179. ed. Harold J. Bershady. Philadelphia, PA: University of Pennsylvania Press, 1989.

541. Knee, Stuart. "Tensions in Nineteenth Century Russo-American Diplomacy: The 'Jewish Question'." *East European Jewish Affairs* 23 (1993): 79-90.

542. Kolodny, R. L. "Father Coughlin and the Jews: A Reminiscence for Younger Colleagues." *Journal of Jewish Communal Service* 53 (Summer 1977): 309-319.

543. Korman, Abraham K. "Anti-Semitism and the Behavioral Sciences Towards a Theory of Discrimination in Work Settings." *Contemporary Jewry* 9 (Fall 1988): 63-85.

544. Kosinski, Jerry. "The Second Holocaust." *Boston Globe*, 4 November 1990. [American Jews' "obsession" with Nazi Holocaust]

545. Lagnado, Lucette. "The Jewish Non-Defense League." *Village Voice*, 10 August 1993. [Failure of Jewish defense organizations to intervene in anti-Jewish events in Crown Heights, NYC in August 1991]

546. Lerner, Michael. *Anti-Semitism on the Left*. Oakland, CA: Tikkun, 1992.

547. Liberman, Arthur. "Anti-Semitism in the Left?" in *Anti- Semitism in American History*, pp. 321-347. ed. David A. Gerber. Urbana, IL: University of Illinois Press, 1986.

548. Lipstadt, Deborah E. *Denying the Holocaust: The Growing Assault on Truth & Memory*. Free Press, 1993.

549. _____. "Holocaust-Denial and the Compelling Force of Reason." *Patterns of Prejudice* 26 (1992): 64-76.

550. Littell, Marcia S. *The Anne Frank Institute of Philadelphia, the First Interfaith Holocaust Education Center: A Critique of the Educational Philosophy and History, 1975-1988*. Ph.D. diss., Temple University, 1990. UMO # 9100307.

551. Lotz, Roy. "Another Look at the Orthodoxy-Anti-Semitism Nexus." *Review of Religious Research* 18 (Winter 1977): 126-133.

552. Maclean, N. "The Leo Frank Case Reconsidered: Gender and Sexual Politics in the Making of Reactionary Populism." *Journal Of American History* 78 (December 1991): 917-948.

553. Marcus, Jacob R. *United States Jewry, 1776-1985. Vol. IV: The East European Period, the Emergence of the American Jew*. Wayne State University Press, 1993.

554. Margolick, David. "To a New York Lawyer, Greener Pastures Turn Out To Be a Home for Anti-Semitism." *New York Times*, 4 June 1993.

555. Masters, Brooke A. "Georgetown U. Criticized After Antisemitism Probe." *Washington Post*, 19 May 1994.

556. Mayo, Louise A. *The Ambivalent Image: Nineteenth-century America's Perception of the Jew*. Fairleigh Dickinson University Press, 1988.

557. Medding, Peter Y. *A New Jewry? America Since the Second World War*. Oxford University Press, 1992.

558. Medoff, Rafael. "How Alaska Could Have Saved Jewish Refugees." *Jewish Frontier* 58 (July-August 1991): 28-29. [1941 measure buried in congressional committee.]

559. Michael, Robert. "Christian Theological Antisemitism: Jewish Values Turned Upside Down." *Menorah Review* (Spring 1992).

560. Middleton, Russell. "Do Christian Beliefs Cause Anti- Semitism?" *American Sociological Review* 38 (February 1973): 33- 52, 59-61.

561. _____. "Regional Differences in Prejudice." *American Sociological Review* 41 (February 1976): 94-117.

562. Miller, Marvin D. *Wunderlich's Salute: The Interrelationship of the German-American Bund, Camp Siegfried, Yaphank, Long Island and their Relationship with American and Nazi Institutions.* Smithstown, NY: Malamud-Rose Publishers, 1983.

563. Modras, Ronald. "Father Coughlin and Anti-Semitism: Fifty Years Later." *Journal of Church and State* 31 (Spring 1989): 231- 247.

564. Muravchik, Joshua. "Challenging the Taboo on Antisemitism: Patrick Buchanan's Continued Quest for the U.S. Presidency." *Analysis (Institute of Jewish Affairs)* No.3 (July 1992).

565. _____. "Patrick J. Buchanan and the Jews." *Commentary* 91 (January 1991).

566. Nelson, Jack. *Terror in the Night: The Klan's Campaign Against the Jews.* Simon & Schuster, 1993.

567. _____. "White Knights, Dark Hearts." *Los Angeles Times Magazine,* 10 January 1993. [Ku Klux Klan terror campaign against Mississippi's Jews in 1960's]

568. Newport, Frank. *Nationwide Attitudes Survey: A Confidential Report Presented to the Anti-Defamation League of B'nai B'rith.* Houston, TX: Tarrairee, Hill, Newport & Ryan, 1986.

569. Obenzinger, Hilton. "False Anti-Semitism Charges Stifle Debate." *Palestine Focus* (January-February 1991).

570. "An Open Letter from Alan Dershowitz Concerning a Conflict of Interest Hidden From the Readers of the New York Times Book Review." *New York Times,* 17 October 1991. D7.

571. Ostow, Mortimer. "A Contribution to the Study of Anti- Semitism." *Conservative Judaism* 38 (Summer 1986): 51-73.

572. Peretz, Don. "The Semantics of Zionism, Anti-Zionism and Anti-Semitism." in *Judaism or Zionism? What Difference for the Middle East?*, pp. 76-87. eds. Earford, and Ajaz. London: Zed Books, 1986.

573. Podhoretz, Norman. "What Is Anti-Semitism - An Open Letter to William F. Buckley." *Commentary* 93 (February 1992): 15-20.

574. Rabinowitz, Howard N. "Nativism, Bigotry and Anti-Semitism in the South." *American Jewish History* 77 (1988): 437-451.

575. Rausch, David. "American Evangelicals and the Jews." *Midstream* 23 (1977): 38-41.

576. Rosenbaum, Alan S. *Prosecuting Nazi War Criminals.* Westview Press, 1993.

577. Russ, Shlomo M. *The "Zionist Hooligans": The Jewish Defense League.* Ph.D. diss., CUNY, 1981.

578. Sachar, Howard M. *A History of the Jews in America.* Knopf, 1992.

579. Sarna, Jonathan D. "American Anti-Semitism." in *History and Hate,* pp. 115-128.

580. Sato, Tadayuki. "The Expansion of the Jewish Community and the Formation of the Anti-Semitism Movement in Atlanta, 1845- 1913." *Seiyo Shigaku* No.140 (1986): 2-37. [In Japanese]

581. Schneider, William. *Anti-Semitism and Israel: A Report on American Public Opinion.* New York: American Jewish Committee, 1978.

582. Selznick, Gertrude J., and Stephen Steinberg. *The Ferocity of Prejudice: Anti-Semitism in Contemporary America.* New York: Harper & Row, 1969.

583. Shafir, S. "American Jewish Leaders and the Emerging Nazi Threat (1928-January 1933)." *American Jewish Archive* 31 (November 1979): 150-183.

584. Shalom, Stephen R. "Anti-Semitism and the Left." *New Politics* 4 (Summer 1993): 51-61.

585. Shapiro, Edward S. "The Approach of War: Congressional Isolationism and Anti-Semitism, 1931-1941." *American Jewish History* 74 (September 1984): 45-65.

586. _____. "John Higham and American Anti-Semitism." *American Jewish History* 76 (1986): 201-213.

587. Short, Geoffrey. "Combatting Anti-Semitism: A Dilemma for Anti-Racist Education." *British Journal of Educational Studies* 39 (February 1991): 33-44.

588. Sifry, Micah L. "Anti-Semitism In the Mind of America." *Nation*, 25 January 1993. pp. 92-99.

589. Silberstein, Fred B., and Norman Fogel. "The Roots of Christian Anti-Semitism." *Free Inquiry in Creative Sociology* 14 (November 1986): 123-128.

590. Silverberg, David. "'Heavenly Deception': Rev. Moon's Hard Sell." *Present Tense* 4 (1976): 49-56.

591. Simpson, Christopher. *Blowback, America's Recruitment of Nazis and Its Effects on the Cold War*. New York: Weidenfeld & Nicolson, 1988.

592. Singerman, Robert. "The American Career of the Protocols of the Elders of Zion." *American Jewish History* 71 (September 1981): 48-78.

593. Sleeper, Jim. "Alan Dershowitz's Chutzpah: The Making of a 'Race Man'." *Reconstruction* 1 (1992): 84-88. [See Dershowitz, above]

594. Smiga, George M. *Pain and Polemic. Anti-Judaism in The Gospels*. Paulist Press, 1993.

595. Smith, Tom W. "Actual Trends or Measurement Artifacts? A Review of the Three Studies of Anti-Semitism." *Public Opinion Quarterly* 57 (Fall 1993): 380-393.

596. _____. *What Do Americans Think About Jews?* New York: American Jewish Committee, December 1991.

597. Smothers, Ronald. "Hate Fliers Inflame Mayoral Race in New Orleans." *New York Times*, 27 February 1994. [Charges that Jewish candidate issued antisemitic fliers to create sympathy for himself.]

598. Soifer, S. "Infusing Content About Jews and Anti-Semitism into the Curricula." *Journal of Social Work Education* 27 (Spring- Summer 1991): 156-167.

599. Steinfels, Peter. "Jews Assail Bible Videos for Children." *New York Times*, 5 September 1991.

600. Stern, Norton B., and William M. Kramer. "Anti-Semitism and the Jewish Image in the Early West." *WSJHQ* (January 1974): 129- 140.

601. Stewart, James B. "Wild Card." *New Yorker*, 25 January 1993. pp. 38-45. [Charges of antisemitism in high corporate affairs]

602. Tobin, Gary A. *Jewish Perceptions of Anti-Semitism*. New York: Plenum Press, 1988.

603. Tucker, Gordon. "A Half-Century of Jewish-Christian Relations." in *Altered Landscapes: Christianity in America: 1935- 1985*, ed. David W. Lotz. Grand Rapids, MI: William B. Eerdmans, 1989.

604. Weinstein, Henry. "Attorney Sanctioned for Criticizing Judge." *Los Angeles Times*, 20 May 1994. [Among other things, civil rights attorney called federal judge an antisemite]

605. Westreich, Budd. *The Stow Affair: Anti-Semitism in the California Legislature*. Sacramento, Ca: Press of Arden Park, 1981.

606. Windsor, Pat. "Anti-Semitism Charges Resurface in Church." *National Catholic Reporter*, 22 September 1989.

607. Wistrich, Robert S. *Anti-Semitism: The Longest Hatred*. Pantheon, 1992.

608. Wolfson, Adam. "The Boston Jewish Community and the Rise of Nazism, 1933-1939." *Jewish Social Studies* 48 (1986): 305-313.

AUTOBIOGRAPHY AND BIOGRAPHY

609. Aaron, Hank. *I Had a Hammer. The Hank Aaron Story.* New York: Harper Collins, 1991.

610. Abernathy, Ralph D. *And the Walls Came Tumbling Down. An Autobiography.* New York: Harper and Row, 1989.

611. Adamo, Mark. "Watts's Incidental Achievement." *Washington Post,* 16 April 1993. [Andre Watts]

612. Adams, Frank. *James A. Dombrowski: An American Heretic, 1897-1983.* Knoxville: University of Tennesse Press, 1992.

613. Aldred, Lisa. *Thurgood Marshall.* New York: Chelsea House, 1990. [Written for young people]

614. Andrews, William L. *To Tell a Free Story: The First Century of Afro-American Autobiography, 1760-1865.* Urbana: University of Illinois Press, 1986.

615. Apess, William. *On Our Own Ground: The Complete Writings of William Apess, a Pequot.* University of Massachusetts Press, 1992.

616. Ashe, Arthur, and Arnold Rampersad. *Days of Grace. A Memoir.* Knopf, 1993.

617. Athill, Diana. *Make Believe. A True Story.* Box 70, South, Royalton, Vermont 05068: Steerforth Press, 1994. [About Hakim Jamal]

618. Augenbraun, Harold and Stavans, Ilan, eds. *Growing Up Latino. Memoirs and Stories.* Houghton Mifflin, 1993.

619. Avery, Sheldon. *Up from Washington. William Pickens and the Negro Struggle for Equality, 1900-1954.* Newark: University of Deleware Press, 1989.

620. Barlow, William. "Bessie Smith." *Black Women in America, II* 1074-1078.

621. Beals, Melba Patillo. *Warriors Don't Cry. A Searing Memoir of the Battle to Integrate Little Rock's Central High.* Pocket Books, 1994.

622. Bell, Derrick. *Confronting Authority: Reflections of an Ardent Protester.* Beacon Press, 1994.

623. Berger, Elmer. "Memoirs of an Anti-Zionist Jew." *Journal of Palestine Studies* 5 (1975-1976): 3-55.

624. Berlin, Ira. "In Praise of John Hope Franklin." *Reconstruction* 1 (1991): 93-95.

625. Beth, Loren. *John Marshall Harlan. The Last Whig Justice.* University Press of Kentucky, 1992.

626. "Bethune, Mary McLeod." *Black Women in America, I* 113-126.

627. Blackett, R. J. M. *Beating Against the Barriers: The Lives of Six Nineteenth Century Afro-Americans.* Ithaca, New York: Cornell University Press, 1989.

628. Blackman, Margaret B. *Sadie Brown Neakok, An Inpiaq Woman.* Seattle: University of Washington Press, 1989.

629. Boelhower, William. "The Brave New World of Immigrant Autobiography." in *The Impressions of a Gilded Age: The American Fin de Siecle*, eds. Marc Chenetier, and Rob Krols. Amsterdam: Amerika Institut, Universiteit von Amsterdam, 1983.

630. Bogle, Kathryn H. "Kathryn Hall Bogle on the Writing of 'An American Negro Speaks of Color'." *Oregon Historical Quarterly* 89 (1988): 82-91. [Growing up Black in Portland, Oregon]

631. Booth, William. "The Woman From Liberty City." *Washington Post*, 16 December 1992. [Carrie Meek, first Black elected from Florida since Reconstruction]

632. Bracey, Derek. "Do Pathfinder, SWP Seek to Monopolize Malcolm X?" *Militant* (29 November 1991). [Pathfinder Press, Socialist Workers Party, and the published works of Malcolm X]

633. Bracey, John H., Jr., ed. "The Horace Mann Bond Papers." Frederick, MD: University Publications of America, 1989.

634. Bradford, Sarah. *Harriet Tubman: The Moses of Her People*. Secaucus, NJ: Citadel Press, 1987.

635. Bramlett-Solomon, S. "Civil Rights Vanguard in the Deep South: Newspaper Portrayal of Fannie Lou Hamer, 1964-1977." *Journalism Quarterly* 68 (1991): 515-521.

636. Braxton, Joanne M. *Black Women Writing Autobiography: A Tradition within a Tradition*. Philadelphia, PA: Temple University Press, 1990.

637. Bray, Rosemary L. "A Black Panther's Long Journey." *New York Times Magazine*, 31 January 1993. [Elaine Brown]

638. Broussard, Albert S. "McCants Stewart: The Struggle of a Black Attorney in the Urban West." *Oregon Historical Quarterly* 89 (1988): 157-179.

639. Brown, A. W. "A Social Work Leader in the Struggle for Racial Equality: Lester Blackwell Granger." *Social Service Review* 65 (June 1991): 266-280.

640. Brown, Elaine. *A Taste of Power. A Black Woman's Story*. Pantheon, 1993. [Rise and fall of the Black Panther Party]

641. Brown, Oscar, Sr. *By a Thread*. New York: Vantage Press, 1983.

642. Brown, Richard D. "'Not Only Extreme Poverty, But the Worst Kind of Orphanage': Samuel Haynes and the Boundaries of Racial Tolerance on the Yankee Frontier, 1770-1833." *New England Quarterly* 61 (1988): 502-518.

643. Bruce, Dickson C., Jr. *Archibald Grimke*. LSU Press, 1993.

644. Brumble, H. David III. *American Indian Autobiography*. Berkeley: University of California Press, 1988.

645. Bryant, Flora R. *An Examination of the Social Activism of Pauli Murray*. Ph.D. diss., University of South Carolina, 1991. UMO # 9214921.

646. Burner, Eric R. *And Gently He Shall Lead Them: Robert Parris Moses and Civil Rights in Mississippi*. New York University Press, 1994.

647. Butterfield, Fox. "Old Rights Campaigner Leads a Harvard Battle." *New York Times*, 21 May 1990. [Derrick Bell]

648. Campbell, James. *Talking At the Gates. A Life of James Baldwin*. New York: Penguin, 1991.

649. Carroll, John M. *Fritz Pollard; Pioneer in Racial Advancement*. University of Illinois Press, 1992. [Frederick Douglass Pollard, football player, coach, and film producer]

650. Carson, Clayborne and others, eds. *The Papers of Martin Luther King, Jr. Vol. I: Called to Serve, January 1929-June 1951*. Berkeley: University of California Press, 1992.

651. Celis, Willliam 3rd. "An Impatient Advocate Stirs Up the Education Department's Rights Office." *New York Times*, 3 August 1994. [Norma V. Cantu, Assistant Education Secretary for Civil Rights]

652. Cheek, William, and Aimee Lee Cheek. *John Mercer Langston and the Fight for Black Freedom, 1829-1865*. Urbana: University of Illinois Press, 1989.

653. Chestnut, J. L., Jr., and Julia Cass. *The Uncommon Life of J.L. Chestnut*. New York: Farrar, Straus & Giroux, 1990. [Black lawyer in Selma, AL.]

654. Christy, Marian, Dr. Margaret Lawrence: Overcoming All Odds. *Boston Globe*, 23 October 1991.

655. Clark, Kenneth B. "Racial Progress and Retreat: A Personal Memoir." in *Race in America*, eds. Herbert Hill, and James E. Jones, Jr. : University of Wisconsin Press, 1993.

656. Clarke, Donald. *Wishing On the Moon. The Life and Times of Billie Holiday*. Viking, 1994.

657. Clifton, James A., ed. *Being and Becoming Indian: Biographical Studies of North American Frontiers*. Chicago, IL: Dorsey Press, 1989.

658. Codije, Corinn. *Vilma Martinez*. Milwaukee, WI: Raintree Publishers, 1989. [Mexican American lawyer; written for young people]

659. Conroy, Sarah B. "A Century of Being Sisters." *Washington Post*, 25 November 1993. [Elizabeth 'Bessie' Delany, 102, and Sarah 'Sadie' Delaney, 104]

660. Cooper, Arnold. *Between Struggle and Hope: Four Black Educators in the South, 1893-1915*. Ames: Iowa State University Press, 1989.

661. Cooper, Wayne F. *Claude McKay: Rebel Sojourner in the Harlem Renaissance*. New York: Random House, 1990.

662. Courlander, Harold, ed. *Hopi Voices: Recollections, Traditions, and Narratives of the Hopi Indians*. Albuquerque: University of New Mexico Press, 1982.

663. Crow Dog, Mary, and Richard Erdoes. *Lakota Woman*. New York: Grove Weidenfeld, 1990.

664. Cunningham, Bill, and Daniel Golden. "Malcolm. The Boston Years." *Boston Globe Magazine*, 16 February 1992. [Malcolm X]

665. Darity, William A. Jr., and J. Ellison. "Abram Harris, Jr.: The Economics of Race and Social Reform." *History of Political Economy* 22 (December 1990).

666. Davies, Mark. *Malcolm X: Another Side of the Movement*. Englewood Cliffs, NJ: Silver Burdett Press, 1990. [Written for young people]

667. Davis, Benjamin O., Jr. *Benjamin O. Davis, Jr., American. An Autobiography*. Washington, D.C.: Smithsonian Institution Press, 1991.

668. Davis, Charles T., and Henry Louis Gates, Jr., eds. *The Slave's Narrative*. New York: Oxford University Press, 1985.

669. Davis, Frank Marshall. *Living the Blues. Memoirs of a Black Journalist and Poet*, ed. John Edgar Tidwell. : University of Wisconsin Press, 1992.

670. Davis, Gwenn, and Beverly A. Joyce, comps. *Personal Writings by Women to 1900. A Bibliography of American and British Writers*. Norman: University of Oklahoma Press, 1989.

671. Davis, Leroy Jr. *John Hope of Atlanta: Race Leader and Black Educator*. Ph.D. diss., Kent State University, 1989. UMO # 9014825.

672. Davis, Michael D., and Hunter R. Clark. *Thurgood Marshall. Warrior at the Bar, Rebel on the Bench*. Birch Lane Press/Carol Publishing, 1993.

673. Delaney, Sarah and Delaney, Elizabeth A. *Having Our Say. The Delaney Sisters' First 100 years*. Kodansha, 1993.

674. Denard, Carolyn. "Toni Morrison." *Black Women in America* II 815-819.

675. DeVries, Hilary. "Drama Lesson." *Boston Globe Magazine*, 24 June 1990. [Lloyd Richards, artistic director of the Yale Repertory Theatre]

676. _____. "He's Hot." *Boston Globe Magazine*, 5 August 1990. [Denzel Washington]

677. Drake, St. Clair. "Bibliographic Essay: Studies of the African Diaspora: The Work and Reflections of St. Clair Drake." *Sage Race Relations Abstracts* (14 August 1989): 3-29.

678. Duberman, Martin B. *Paul Robeson*. New York: Knopf, 1988.

679. Dudley, David Lewis. *The Trouble I've Seen: Visions and Revisions of Bondage, Flight, and Freedom in Black American Autobiography.* Ph.D. diss., Louisiana State University, 1988. UMO # 19934.

680. Dunham, Katherine. *A Touch of Innocence. Memoirs of Childhood.* University of Chicago Press, 1994.

681. Dyson, Michael E. "Who Speaks for Malcolm X? The Writings of Just About Everybody." *New York Times Book Review*, 29 November 1992.

682. Eakin, Paul J. ed. *American Autobiography: Retrospect and Prospect.* University of Wisconsin Press, 1991.

683. Eakin, Paul J. *Fictions in Autobiography.* Princeton University Press, 1985.

684. Edwards, William J. *Twenty-Five Years in the Black Belt.* Boston, MA: Cornhill Co., 1918.

685. Elliot, Jeffrey, ed. *Conversations with Maya Angelou.* London: Virago, 1989.

686. "Ethnic Autobiography." *Melus* 14 (Spring 1987): entire issue.

687. Evanzz, Karl. *The Judas Factor. The Plot to Kill Malcolm X.* Thunder's Mouth Press, 1992.

688. Fendrich, James M. *Ideal Citizens: The Legacy of the Civil Rights Movement.* SUNY Press, 1993.

689. Fox- Genovese, Elizabeth. "My Statue, My Self: Autobiographical Writings of Afro-American Women." in *The Private Self: Theory and Practice of Women's Autobiographical Writings*, pp. 63-89. ed. Shari Benstock. Chapel Hill: University of North Carolina Press, 1988.

690. Frady, Marshall. "The Children of Malcolm." *New Yorker* (12 October 1992).

691. French, Mary Ann. "The Radical Departure of Bobby Rush." *Washington Post*, 3 May 1993. [Congressman from Illinois, former Black Panther leader]

692. Friedly, Michael. *Malcolm X, The Assassination.* Carroll and Graf, 1992.

693. Galanis, Diane E. "Climbing the Mountain: Pioneer Black Lawyers Look Back." *ABA Journal* 77 (April 1991): 60.

694. Gallen, David. *Malcolm X: As They Knew Him.* Carroll and Graf, 1992.

695. Gambino, Ferruccio. "The Transgression of a Laborer: Malcolm X in the Wilderness of America." *Radical History Review* 55 (Winter 1993): 7-31.

696. Garcia, Mario T. *Memoirs of Chicano History. The Life and Narrative of Bert Corona.* University of California Press, 1993.

697. Garrow, David J. "Does Anyone Care Who Killed Malcolm X?" *New York Times*, 21 February 1993.

698. Garrow, David J., ed. *Martin Luther King, Jr.: Civil Rights Leader, Theologican, Orator.* Brooklyn, New York: Carlson Publishing Inc., 1990. [3 volumes of scholarly articles]

699. Gates, Henry Louis, Jr., ed. *Bearing Witness. Selections from African-American Biography in the Twentieth Century.* New York: Pantheon, 1991.

700. Gates, Henry Louis, Jr. *Colored People. A Memoir.* Knopf, 1994.

701. _____. "A Fragmented Man: George Schuyler and the Claims of Race." *New York Times Book Review*, 20 September 1992.

702. Getlin, Josh. "I'm a Troublemaker, Too." *Washington Post*, 5 November 1992. [Derrick Bell]

703. _____. "Raising Hell for a Cause." *Washington Post*, 5 November 1992. [Derrick Bell]

704. Ginger, Ann Fagan. *Carol Weiss King: Human Rights Lawyer, 1895-1952.* University Press of Colorado, 1993.

705. Goggin, Jacqueline. *Carter G. Woodson and the Black History Movement.* Louisiana State University Press, 1993.

706. _____. "Countering White Racist Scholarship: Carter G. Woodson and the Journal of Negro History." *Journal of Negro History* (Fall 1983).

707. Goldman, Peter. *The Death and Life of Malcolm X*. University of Illinois Press, 1979.

708. Goldman, Roger M. with David Gallen. *Thurgood Marshall. Justice For All*. Carroll and Graf, 1992.

709. Gomez, Jewelle. "Retta's House." *Village Voice*, 15 February 1994. [Sketch of Henrietta Walker, African-American woman, in Boston]

710. Gomillion, Charles G. "An Interview with Charles G. Gomillion." *Callaloo* 12 (1989): 575-599.

711. Gonzalez, David and Martin Gottlieb. "Power Built on Poverty: A New Yorker's Odyssey." *New York Times*, 14 May 1993. [Ramon S. Velez, South Bronx]

712. Goodheart, Lawrence B. "The Odyssey of Malcolm X: An Eriksonian Interpretation." *Historian* 53 (Autumn 1990): 47-62.

713. Goodson, Martia G., ed. *Chronicles of Faith. The Autobiography of Frederick D. Patterson*. Tuscaloosa: University of Alabama Press, 1991.

714. Gottlieb, Martin with Baquet Dean. "Street-Wise Impressario." *New York Times*, 19 December 1991. [Reverend Al Sharpton, New York City]

715. Gourse, Leslie. *Sassy. The Life of Sarah Vaughn*. Scribners, 1993.

716. Greene, Lorenzo J. *Working with Carter G. Woodson, the Father of Black History. A Diary, 1928-1930*. Baton Rouge: Louisiana State University Press, 1989.

717. Greider, Katherine. "Frances Sandoval: Against the Gangs." *In These Times* (20 June 1990). [Founder of Mothers Against Gangs in Marquette Square neighborhood, Chicago]

718. Grove, Lloyd. "The Man in Transition." *Washington Post*, 19 November 1992. [Vernon Jordan]

719. Guinier, Lani. "Who's Afraid of Lani Guinier?" *New York Times*, 27 February 1994.

720. Haizlip, Shirlee Taylor. *The Sweeter the Juice: A Family Memoir in Black and White*. Simon and Schuster, 1994.

721. Hamilton, Charles V. *Adam Clayton Powell, Jr. The Political Biography of an American Dilemma*. New York: Atheneum, 1991.

722. Harrington, Oliver W. *Why I Left America and Other Essays*. University Press of Mississippi, 1993.

723. Haygood, Wil. *King of the Cats: The Life and Times of Adam Clayton Powell Jr*. Houghton Mifflin, 1993.

724. Hemenway, Robert. *Zora Neale Hurston: A Literary Biography*. Urbana, IL: 1980.

725. Hendricks, Wanda A. "Ida Bell Wells-Barnett." *Black Women in America* II 1242-1246.

726. Henig, Robin M. "For Many, Pediatric Neurosurgeon Is a Folk Hero." *New York Times*, 8 June 1993. [Benjamin S. Carson, African- American chief of pediatric neurosurgery, Johns Hopkins University]

727. Hentoff, Nat. "A Hero of Our Time." *Village Voice*, 19 October 1993. [Michael Meyers]

728. Hess, Debra. *Thurgood Marshall: Changing the Legal System*. Englewood Cliffs, New Jersey: Silver Burdett Press, 1990. [written for young readers]

729. Hillard, David, and Lewis Cole. *This Side of Glory. The Autobiography of David Hillard and the Story of the Black Panther Party*. Little, Brown and Co., 1993.

730. Hine, Darlene Clark. "Harriet Ross Tubman." *Black Women in America* II 1176-1180.

731. Hinkle, Don. *Fannie Lou Hamer: From Sharecropping to Politics*. Englewood Cliffs, New Jersey: Silver Burdett Press, 1990. [written for young people]

732. Hobbs, Richard S. *The Cayton Legacy: Two Generations of a Black Family, 1859-1976*. Ph.D. diss., University of Washington, 1989. UMO # 8911626.

733. Horne, Gerald. *Black Liberation/Red Scare: Ben Davis and the Communist Party*. University of Delaware Press, 1994.

734. Horowitz, Irving Louis. *Daydreams and Nightmares: Reflections of a Harlem Childhood*. Jackson: University Press of Mississippi, 1990.

735. Hunter, Carol Margaret. *To Set the Captives Free: Reverend Germain Wesley Loguen and the Struggle for Freedom in Central New York, 1835-1872*. Ph.D. diss., State University of New York at Binghamton, 1985. UMO # 8926260.

736. Hunton, Dorothy. *Alphaeus Hunton: The Unsung Valiant*. Privately printed, 1986.

737. Hurmence, Belinda, ed. *Before Freedom: 48 Oral Histories of Former North and South Carolina Slaves*. New York: Mentor, 1990.

738. Jackson, Carlton. *Hattie. The Life of Hattie McDaniel*. Lanham, MD: Madison Books, 1989.

739. Jackson, Walter A. "Between Socialism and Nationalism: The Young E. Franklin Frazier." *Reconstruction* 1 (1991): 124-134.

740. Jacoby, Tamar. "Malcolm X's Bitter Legacies." *Commentary* (February 1993).

741. Janken, Kenneth R. *The Life of Rayford W. Logan*. Ph.D. diss., Rutgers University, 1991. UMO # 9213976.

742. _____. *Rayford W. Logan and the Dilemma of the African- American Intellectual*. University of Massachusetts Press, 1993.

743. Jeffries, John C., Jr. *Justice Lewis F. Powell, Jr.: A Biography*. Scribner's, 1994.

744. Jenkins, Kent, Jr., The Many Lives of Kweisi Mfume. *Washington Post*, 8 December 1992. [Congressman from West Baltimore, MD]

745. Johnson, Charles, The Singular Vision of Ralph Ellison. *Washington Post*, 18 April 1994.

746. Johnson, Jacqueline. *Stokely Carmichael: The Story of Black Power*. Englewood Cliffs, New Jersey: Silver Burdett Press, 1990. [Written for young people.]

747. Johnson, Joni L. "Ella Baker: An Unknown Soldier." *Sage* (1988): 48-50. [student supplement]

748. Jone, Carole. *Pride of Family. Four Generations of American Women of Color*. New York: Summit Books, 1991.

749. Jones, Bessie, and John Stewart. *For the Ancestors: Autobiographical Memoirs*. Urbana: University of Illinois Press, 1983.

750. Jones, Beverly W. *Quest for Equality: The Life and Writings of Mary Eliza Church Terrell, 1863-1954*. Brooklyn, New York: Carlson, 1990.

751. Jones, Charisse. "Memories of the Revolution." *Los Angeles Times*, 24 February 1993. [About Elaine Brown, Head of the Black Panther Party, 1974-1977]

752. Jones, Hettie. *How I Became Hettie Jones*. New York: Dutton, 1990. [First wife of Leroi Jones]

753. Jones, James E., Jr., and Penelope Niven. *James Earl Jones. Voices and Silences*. Scribner's, 1993.

754. Jones, Kirkland C. *Renaissance Man from Louisiana: A Biography of Arna Wendell Bontemps*. Greenwood, 1992.

755. Jones, Lewis W. "Fred L. Shuttlesworth, Indigenous Leader." in *Birmingham, Alabama, 1956-1963: The Black Struggle for Civil Rights*, David J. Garrow, ed. Brooklyn, New York: Carlson Publishing, Inc., 1990.

756. Karcher, Carolyn L. "Lydia Maria Child and the Example of John Brown." *Race Traitor* 2 (Winter 1993): 21-44.

757. Karim, Benjamin and others. *Remembering Malcolm*. Carroll and Graf, 1993.

758. Katzman, David M., and William M. Tuttle, Jr., eds. *Plain Folk, The Life Stories of Undistinguished Americans*. Urbana: University of Illinois Press, 1982. [Material first published between 1902 and 1906]

759. Kent, George E. *A Life of Gwendolyn Brooks*. Lexington: University Press of Kentucky, 1990.

760. Kerman, Cynthia E. and Richard Eldridge. *The Lives of Jean Toomer. A Hunger for Wholeness*. Baton Rouge: Louisiana State University Press, 1989.

761. Ketner, Joseph D. *The Emergence of the African-American Artist: Robert S. Duncanson, 1821-1872*. University of Missouri Press, 1993.

762. Klein, Michael. *Sharpton*. New York: Castillo International, 1991. [Rev. Al Sharpton]

763. Klepp, Susan E., and Billy G. Smith, eds. *The Unfortunate. The Voyage and Adventures of William Moraley, an Indentured Servant*. Pennsylvania State Press, 1992.

764. Kondon, Zak. *Conspiracy: Unravelling the Assassination of Malcolm X*. Nubia Press, 1994.

765. Kornweibel, Theodore, Jr. "Race, Radicalism, and Rage: The Life of Joseph J. Jones." *Afro-Americans in New York Life and History* 13 (1989): 19-38.

766. Kremer, Gary R. *James Milton Turner and the Promise of America. The Public Life of a Post-Civil War Black Leader*. Columbia: University of Missouri Press, 1991. [Missouri]

767. Krupat, Arnold. *For Those Who Come After. A Study of Native American Autobiography*. Berkeley: University of California Press, 1990.

768. Kunstler, William M., and Sheila Isenberg. *My Life As a Radical Lawyer*. Birch Lane Press, 1994.

769. Kurnick, David. "Malcolm X Beyond Labels." *Race Traitor* No.1 (Winter 1993): 108-113.

770. Ladd, Jerrold. *Out of the Madness. From the Projects to a Life of Hope*. Warner Books, 1994. [Growing up Black in Dallas]

771. Ladner, Joyce A. "Fannie Lou Hamer. In Memoriam." *Black Enterprise* (May 1977).

772. Lamar, Jake. *Bourgeois Blues: An American Memoir*. New York: Summit, 1991. [Upper middle-class Black person who became a journalist at Time Magazine]

773. Larson, Louise Leung. *Sweet Bamboo. A Saga of a Chinese American Family*. Los Angeles, California: Chinese Historical Society of Southern California, 1990.

774. Lee, Chana Kai. *A Passionate Portrait of Justice: The Life and Leadership of Fannie Lou Hamer, 1917-1967*. Ph.D. diss., University of California at Los Angeles, 1993. UMO # 9332619.

775. Lee, Mary Paik. *Quiet Odyssey: A Pioneer Korean Woman in America*. Seattle: University of Washington Press, 1990.

776. Leeming, David. *James Baldwin*. Knopf, 1994.

777. Leff, Gladys. *George G. Sanchez*. Ph.D. diss., North Texas State University, 1976.

778. Leroux, Charles. "Man Spared by 1930 Lynch Mob Spurns Bitterness." *Long Beach Press-Telegram*, 21 February 1993. [James Cameron]

779. Lesher, Stephen. *George Wallace: American Populist*. Addison-Wesley, 1994.

780. Levine, Lawrence W. "The Historical Odyssey of Nathan Irvin Huggins." *Radical History Review* No. 55 (Winter 1993): 113-132.

781. Levy, Jacques E. *Cesar Chavez: Autobiography of La Causa*. New York: Norton, 1975.

782. Logan, Jonnie Lee. *Motherwit. An Alabama Midwife's Story*. New York: Dutton, 1989. [As told to Katherine Clark]

783. Lubasch, Arnold. "Finding His Voice and Learning How to Use It." *New York Times*, 21 October 1993. [Paul Robeson, Jr.]

784. Lucas, Maria Elena. *Forged Under the Sun. Forjado Bajo el Sol: The Life of Maria Elena Lucas*. University of Michigan Press, 1993. [Edited by Fran Leeper Buss]

785. Mabee, Carleton. *Sojourner Truth: Slave, Prophet, Legend*. New York University Press, 1993.

786. Manegold, Catherine S. "The Reformation of a Street Preacher." *New York Times Magazine*, 24 January 1993. [Al Sharpton]

787. Mankiller, Wilma. *Mankiller: A Chief and Her People*. St. Martin's Press, 1993. [Principal chief of the Cherokee Nation]

788. Mann, Eric. *Comrade George*. New York: Harper and Row, 1972. [George Jackson]

789. Martin Luther King, Jr. Papers Project. *A Guide to Research on Martin Luther King, Jr., and the Modern Black Freedom Struggle*. Stanford, California: Stanford University Libraries, 1989.

790. Massengill, Reed. *Portrait of a Racist. The Man Who Kkilled Medgar Evers?* St. Martin's Press, 1994. [Byron De La Beckwith]

791. Mathabane, Mark. *Kaffir Boy in America: An Encounter with Apartheid*. New York: Collier Books, 1990.

792. McCall, Nathan. *Makes Me Wanna Holler: A Young Black Man in America*. Random House, 1994.

793. McCunn, Ruthanne Lum. *Chinese American Portraits: Personal Histories 1828-1988*. San Francisco, CA: Chronicle Books, 1988.

794. McKenna, Kristine. "Louie Perez of Los Lobos." *Los Angeles Times*, 5 July 1992.

795. McLaurin, Melton A. *Celia, A Slave*. Athens: University of Georgia Press, 1991.

796. Means, Howard. *Colin Powell- Statesman /Soldier*. Donald G. Fine, 1993.

797. Mehren, Elizabeth. "And Justice for All." *Los Angeles Times*, 10 April 1994. [Deval L. Patrick, assistant U.S. attorney general for civil rights]

798. Meier, August. *A White Scholar and the Black Community, 1945-1965*. University of Massachusetts Press, 1992.

799. Meier, Matt S. *Mexican-American Biographies: A Historical Dictionary, 1836-1987*. Westport, CT: Greenwood, 1988.

800. Miller, Edward. *Gullah Statesman: Robert Smalls from Slavery to Congress, 1839-1915*. University of South Carolina Press, 1994.

801. Miller, Jay, ed. *Mourning Dove. A Salishan Autobiography*. Lincoln: University of Nebraska Press, 1990.

802. Mills, David. "The West Alternative." *Washington Post Magazine*, 8 August 1993. [Cornel West]

803. Mills, Kay. *This Little Light of Mine. The Life of Fannie Lou Hamer*. Dutton, 1993.

804. _____. "Unita Blackwell." *Los Angeles Times*, 2 August 1992. [Black mayor of Mayersville, MI.]

805. Muccigrosso, Robert and Suzanne Niemeyer, eds. *Research Guide to American Historical Biography*. Washington, D.C.: Beacham, 1988.

806. Mura, David. *Turning Japanese. Memoirs of a Sansei*. New York: Atlanta Monthly Press, 1991.

807. Muro, Mark. "Derrick Bell- In Protest." *Boston Globe*, 25 March 1992.

808. Murray, David. "Authenticity and Text in American Indian Hispanic and Asian Autobiography." in *First Person Singular: Studies in American Autobiography*, ed. Robert A. Lee. New York: St. Martin's Press, 1988.

809. _____. "From Speech to Text: The Making of American Indian Autobiographies." in *American Literary Landscapes: The Fiction and the Fact*, eds. F. A. Bell and others. New York: St. Martin's Press, 1988.

810. Mydans, Seth. "Giving Voice to the Hurt and Betrayal of Korean-Americans." *New York Times*, 2 May 1993. [Angela Oh, Los Angeles]

811. Myers, Walter D. *Malcolm X: By Any Means Necessary*. Scholastic, 1993.

812. New York Panther Twenty-One. *Look for Me in the Whirlwind: The Collective Autobiography of the New York Twenty-One*. New York: Random House, 1971.

813. Newby, Robert G. "The Making of a Class-Conscious 'Race Man'." *Critical Sociology* (Summer 1988).

814. Noel, Peter. "The Player. Al Sharpton Comes Out Running- From His Past." *Village Voice*, 4 August 1992.

815. Norcini, Marilyn J. *The Education of a Native American Anthropologist: Edward P. Dozier (1916-1971)*. Master's thesis, University of Arizona, 1988.

816. North, Oliver L., I Don't Have a Racist Bone in My Body. *Washington Post*, 24 March 1993.

817. Oishi, Gene. *In Search of Hiroshi*. Rutland, VT: Tuttle, 1988. [Autobiography]

818. Olney, James, ed. *Autobiography: Essays Theoretical and Critical*. Princeton University Press, 1980.

819. O'Rourke, Lawrence M. *Geno: The Life and Mission of Geno Baroni*. Paulist Press, 1991.

820. Owens, Don B. and Walter Ellis. *I Am a Black Panther*. New York: Vantage Commonsense Press, 1970.

821. Parks, Rosa with Hoskins, Jim. *Rosa Parks, My Story*. New York: Dial, 1992. [Written for young people]

822. Patterson, Tiffany R. L. "Zora Neale Hurston." *Black Women in America* I 598-603.

823. Payne, James R., ed. *Essays in Multicultural American Autobiography*. Knoxville: University of Tennessee Press, 1988.

824. Payne, James R. *Multicultural Autobiography*. *American Lives*. Knoxville: University of Tennessee Press, 1992.

825. Pear, Robert. "A Champion of Civil Liberties Lays Down His Lance." *New York Times*, 3 April 1994. [Rep. Don Edwards]

826. Pearson, Hugh. *The Shadow of the Panther. Huey Newton and the Price of Black Power in America*. Addison-Wesley, 1994.

827. Peery, Nelson. *Black Fire: The Making of an American Revolutionary*. New Press, 1994.

828. Peretti, Burton W. *Music, Race, and Culture in Urban America: The Creators of Jazz*. Ph.D. diss., University of California, Berkeley, 1989. UMO # 9006472.

829. Perl, Peter. "The Mayor's Mystique." *Washington Post Magazine*, 31 January 1993. [Mayor Sharon Pratt Kelly of Washington, D.C.]

830. Perry, Bruce. *Malcolm. The Life of a Man Who Changed Black America*. Barrytown, New York: Station Hill Press, 1991.

831. Pfeffer, Paula F. *A. Philip Randolph, Pioneer of the Civil Rights Movement*. Baton Rouge: Louisiana State University, 1990.

832. Platt, Tony. "E. Franklin Frazier Reconsidered." *Social Justice* 16 (Winter 1989): 186-195.

833. Podilla, Genaro M. *My History, Not Yours. The Formation of Mexican American Autobiography*. University of Wisconsin Press, 1993.

834. _____. "The Recovery of Chicano Nineteenth-Century Autobiography." *American Quarterly* 40 (September 1988): 286-306.

835. Prather, Patricia S., and Jane C. Monday. *From Slave to Statesman. The Legacy of Joshua Houston, Servant To Sam Houston*. University of North Texas Press, 1993.

836. Rainerie, Vivian M. *The Red Angel. The Life and Times of Elaine Black Yoneda, 1906-1988*. New York: International Publishers, 1991.

837. Raines, Howell. "Grady's Gift." *New York Times Magazine*, 1 December 1993. [Gradystein Williams Hutchinson, Birmingham, Alabama]

838. Rampersad, Arnold. "Psychology and Afro-American Biography." *Yale Review* 78 (1989): 1-18.

839. Rankin-Hill, L. M., and Blakey M. L. "Montague W. Cobb (1904-1990): Physical Anthropologist, Anatomist, and Activist." *American Anthropologist* 96 (March 1994): 74-96.

840. Ransby, Barbara. "A Life of Defiance: Dhoruba on Struggle Past and Present." *Guardian (NYC)* (6 June 1990). [Interview with Dhoruba bin Wahad (formerly Richard Moore), a former Black Panther leader]

841. Rasmussen, Cecilia. "L.A. Scene. The City Then and Now." *Los Angeles Times*, 22 February 1993. [Charlotta Bass, publisher of the California Eagle, an African American newspaper published in Los Angeles]

842. Rayson, Ann. "Beneath the Mask: Autobiographies of Japanese- American Women." *MELUS* 14 (Spring 1987): 43-57.

843. Revesz, R. L. "Thurgood Marshall's Struggle." *New York Univerity Law Review* 68 (May 1993): 237-264.

844. Ribes Tovar, Federico. *Albizu Campos*. New York: Plus Ultra Press, 1971.

845. Ribowsky, Mark. *Don't Look Back: Satchel Paige in the Shadows of Baseball*. Simon and Schuster, 1994.

846. Rice, Sarah. *He Included Me. The Autobiography of Sarah Rice*. Athens: University of Georgia Press, 1989. [Edited by Louise Westling]

847. Riley, Michael. "Confessions of a Former Segregationist." *Time* (2 March 1992). [George Wallace of Alabama]

848. Ringle, Ken. "Against the Drift of History." *Washington Post*, 27 August 1993. [Lerone Bennett]

849. _____. "A Southern Road to Freedom." *Washington Post*, 20 July 1993. [Ernest Gaines, author]

850. Rivlin, Benjamin, ed. *Ralph Bunche. The Man and His Times*. New York: Holmes and Meier, 1989.

851. Roberts, Randy. "Galveston's Jack Johnson: Flourishing in the Dark." *Southern Historical Quarterly* 87 (1983): 37-56.

852. Romano-V., Octavio L. *Geriatric Fu: My First Sixty-Five Years in the United States, 1990*. TQS Publications, P.O. Box 9275, Berkeley, CA 94709,

853. Ronda, Bruce A. *Intellect and Spirit: The Life and Work of Robert Coles*. New York: Continuum, 1989.

854. Rosenfeld, Megan. "Before the Dream." *Washington Post*, 26 August 1993. [Pauline Myers, pioneer African-American civil rights activist in Washington, D.C.]

855. Rouse, Jacqueline A. *Lugenia Burns Hope, Black Southern Reformer*. Athens: University of Georgia Press, 1990.

856. Rout, Kathleen. *Eldridge Cleaver*. Twayne, 1991.

857. Rowan, Carl T. *Breaking Barriers. A Memoir*. Boston, MA: Little, Brown, 1991.

858. _____. *Dream Makers, Dream Breakers. The World of Justice Thurgood Marshall*. Little, Brown, 1993.

859. Rubin, Steven J. "American-Jewish Autobiography, 1912 to the Present." in *Handbook of American-Jewish Literature*, ed. Lewis Fried. Westport, CT: Greenwood, 1988.

860. Santino, Jack. *Miles of Smiles, Years of Struggle. Stories of Black Pullman Porters*. Urbana: University of Illinois Press, 1989.

861. Shakur, Sanjika a. k. a. Monster Kody Scott. *Monster. The Autobiography of an L.A. Gang Member*. Atlantic Monthly Press, 1993.

862. Simone, Nina. *I Put a Spell on You. The Autobiography of Nina Simone*. New York: Pantheon, 1992.

863. Simons, Marlene. "To Heal a Nation." *Los Angeles Times*, 1 March 1994. [Dr. David Satcher]

864. Sipchen, Bob. "Face to Face, Race to Race." *Los Angeles Times*, 11 March 1994. [Controversy over Nathan McCall's autobiography, Makes Me Wanna Holler- A Young Black Man in America]

865. Skorapa, Olga L. *Feminist Theory and the Educational Endeavor of Mary McLeod Bethune*. Ph.D. diss., Georgia State University, 1989. UMO # 8922919.

866. Sleeper, Jim. "A Man of Too Many Parts." *New Yorker*, 25 January 1993. 55-67. [Al Sharpton]

867. Sloss Vento, Adela. *Alonso S. Perales: His Struggle for the Rights of Mexican-Americans*. San Antonio Texas: Artes Graficas, 1977.

868. Smith, Eric C. *Bert Williams. A Biography of the Pioneer Black Comedian*. Jefferson, NC: McFarland, 1992.

869. Smith, Gerald L. *A Black Education in the Segregated South: Kentucky's Rufus B. Atwood*. University of Kentucky Press, 1994. [President of Kentucky State College, 1929-1962]

870. Smith, Joyce O. *Channing H. Tobias: An Educational Change Agent in Race Relations, 1940-1960*. Ph.D. diss., Loyola University of Chicago, 1993. [Worker for YMCA, NAACP, and other organizations] UMO # 9311907.

871. Spaid, Elizabeth L. "Rebuilding a Nation." *Los Angeles Times*, 4 October 1992. [Cherokee Chief Wilma Mankiller]

872. Span, Paula. "Marvel Cooke's Tour of the Century." *Washington Post*, 11 August 1993.

873. Staples, Brent. *Parallel Time: Growing Up in Black and White*. Pantheon, 1994.

874. Stetson, Erlene and Linda David. *Glorying in Tribulation: The Lifework of Sojourner Truth*. Michigan State University Press, 1994.

875. Streit-Matter, R. "No Taste for Fluff: Ethel L. Payne, African-American Journalist." *Journalism Quarterly* 68 (Autumn 1991): 528-540.

876. Sundquist, Eric J., ed. *Frederick Douglass: New Literary and Historical Essays*. Cambridge University Press, 1990.

877. Swan, Robert J. *Thomas McCants Stewart and the Failure of the Mission of the Talented Tenth in Black America, 1880-1923*. Ph.D. diss., New York University, 1990. UMO # 9025148.

878. Sweeney, Edwin R. *Cochise: Chirichua Apache Chief*. University of Oklahoma Press, 1991.

879. Takara, Kathryn W. *The Fire and the Phoenix: Frank Marshall Davis (an American Biography)*. Ph.D. diss., University of Hawaii, 1993. UMO # 9334944.

880. Taulbert, Clifton L. *Once Upon a Time When We Were Colored*. Tulsa, OK: Council Oak Books, 1989. [Growing up in Glen Allen, Mississippi]

881. Taylor, Ula Y. *The Veiled Garvey: The Life and Times of Amy Jacques Garvey*. Ph.D. diss., University of California, Santa Barbara, 1992. UMO # 9226580.

882. Teamoh, George. *God Made Man, Man Made the Slave: The Autobiography of George Teamoh*. Macon, GA: Mercer University Press, 1992. [Edited by F. N. Boney and others]

883. Terry, Gayle Pollard. "Spike Lee. Espousing the Multiple Messages of His Malcolm X." *Los Angeles Times*, 29 November 1992. [Interview]

884. Terry, Wallace. "It's Such a Pleasure to Learn." *Parade*, 8 March 1990. [John Morton-Finney]

885. _____. "Make Things Better For Somebody." *Parade*, 14 February 1993. [Marion Wright Edelman]

886. Thomas, Lamont D. *Paul Cuffe: Black Entreprenuer and Pan- Africanist*. Urbana: University of Illinois Press, 1988.

887. Thorp, Daniel B. "Chattel with a Soul: The Autobiography of a Moravian Slave." *Pennsylvania Magazine of History and Biography* 112 (1988): 433-435. [Bethlehem, PA]

888. Thurman, Howard. *The Luminous Darkness: A Personal Interpretation of the Anatomy of Segregation and the Ground of Hope*. Richmond, Indiana: Friends United Press, 1989.

889. Tillery, Tyrone. *Claude McKay: A Black Poet's Struggle for Identity*. Amherst: University of Massachusetts Press, 1992.

890. Tobar, Hector. "The Politics of Anger." *Los Angeles Times Magazine*, 3 January 1993. [Gloria Molina]

891. Travis, Dempsey T. *An Autobiography of Black Chicago*. Chicago, Illinois: Urban Research Institute, 1981.

892. Trescott, Jacqueline. "Betty Shabazz, Recalling the Life Behind the Image [of Malcolm X]" *Washington Post*, 18 November 1992. [Widow of Malcolm X]

893. Urban, Wayne J. *Black Scholar. Horace Mann Bond, 1904-1972*. University of Georgia Press, 1992.

894. _____. "Philanthropy and the Black Scholar: The Case of Horace Mann Bond." *Journal of Negro Education* 58 (Fall 1989): 478-493.

895. Viadero, Debra. "Separate and Unequal." *Education Week*, 28 September 1994. [About the work of Gary Orfield]

896. Villasenor, Victor. *Rain of Gold*. Houston, Texas: Arte Publico Press, 1991.

897. Vizenor, Gerald. *Interior Landscapes. Autobiographical Myths and Metaphors*. Minneapolis: University of Minnesota Press, [Chippewa]

898. Wade-Gayles, Gloria. *Pushed Black to Strength. A Black Woman's Journey Home*. Beacon Press, 1993.

899. Wade-Lewis, Margaret. *Lorenzo Dow Turner: First African American Linguist: A Monograph*. Philadelphia, PA: Institute of African and African American Affairs, Temple University, 1988.

900. _____. "Lorenzo Dow Turner: Pioneer African American Linguist." *Black Scholar* 21 (Fall 1991): 10-24.

901. Walsh, Mark. "Counsel for the Cause." *Education Week* (11 May 1994). [David S. Tatel]

902. Washington, Mary H. "Anna Julia Cooper: The Black Feminist Voice of the 1890's." *Legacy* 4 (1987): 3-14.

903. Watts, Jerry G. *Heroism and the Black Intellectual. Ralph Ellison, Politics, and Afro-American Intellectual Life*. University of North Carolina Press, 1994.

904. Welch, Marvis O. *Prudence Crandall. A Biography*. Hartford, CT: Jason Publishers, 1987.

905. Westling, Louise, ed. *He Included Me: The Autobiography of Sarah Rice*. Athens: University of Georgia Press, 1989.

906. Wideman, John Edgar. *Fatheralong. A Meditation on Fathers and Sons, Race and Society*. Pantheon, 1994.

907. Wilson, Raymond. *Ohiyesa: Charles Eastman, Santee Sioux*. Urbana: University of Illinois Press, 1983.

908. Wong, Hertha D. *Sending My Heart Back Across the Years: Tradition and Innovation in Native American Autobiography*. Oxford University Press, 1992.

909. Wood, Joe. "Looking for Malcolm. The Man and the Meaning Behind the Icon." *Village Voice*, 29 May 1990. [Malcolm X]

910. Wood, Joe, ed. *Malcolm X. In Our Own Image*. St. Martin's Press, 1992.

911. Wooden-Byrant, Sharon. "Remembering a Kansas Childhood." *Los Angeles Times*, 17 May 1994. [Growing up Black in mid- 1950s Kansas]

912. Woods, Richard D., comp. *Mexican Autobiography/La Autobiographia Mexicana*. Westport, CT: Greenwood, 1988. [Translated by Josefina Cruz-Melendez]

913. Wynes, Charles E. *Charles Richard Drew: The Man and the Myth*. Urbana: University of Illinois Press, 1988.

914. Yancy, Dorothy C. "Dorothy Bolden, Organizer of Domestic Workers: She Was Born Poor But She Would Not Bow Down." *Sage* 3 (1986): 53-55. [Organizer of National Domestic Workers Union, 1968]

915. Yates, James. *Mississippi to Madrid: Memoir of a Black American in the Abraham Lincoln Brigade*. Seattle, WA: Open Hand Publishers, 1989.

916. Young, Andrew J. *A Way Out of The Way: The Spiritual Memoirs of Andrew Young*. Thomas Nelson, 1994.

917. Young, Coleman. *Hard Stuff. The Autobiography of Coleman Young*. Viking, 1994.

918. Zepp, Ira G., Jr. *The Social Vision of Martin Luther King, Jr.* Brooklyn, New York: Carlson Publishing Inc., 1990.

BLACK TOWNS

919. Crockett, Norman L. "Witness to History: Booker T. Washington Visits Boley." *Chronicle of Oklahoma* 67 (1989): 382- 391.

920. Gasper, Michele C. "Robbins' New Mayor Faces Uphill Struggle." *Chicago Reporter*, July-August 1989. 18. [Robbins, IL, a virtually all-Black suburb of Chicago]

921. Gray, Linda C. "Taft: Town on the Black Frontier." *Chronicles of Oklahoma*, 1988. 66, 430-447.

922. Hamilton, Kenneth M. *Black Towns and Profit. Promotion and Development in the Trans-Appalachian West, 1877-1915.* Baltimore, MD: University of Illinois Press, 1991.

923. Landers, Jane L. "Gracia Real de Santa Teresa de Mose: A Free Black Town in Spanish Colonial Florida." *American Historical Review* 95 (February 1990): 9-30.

924. Lewis, Earl, and David Organ. "Housing, Race and Class: The Government's Creation of Truxton, Virginia, a Model Black War Workers' Town." *Research in Urban Sociology* 1 (1989): 53-78.

925. Mobley, Joe. "In the Shadows of White Society: Princeville, a Black Town in North Carolina, 1886-1915." *North Carolina Historical Review* 63 (July 1986): 340-384.

926. Nichols, Elaine. *No Easy Run to Freedom: Maroons in the Great Dismal Swamp of North Carolina and Virginia, 1677-1850.* Ph.D. diss., University of South Carolina, 1989.

927. Orser, Edward W. "Secondhand Suburbs: Black Pioneers in Baltimore's Edmondson Village, 1955-1980." *Journal of Urban History* 16 (1990): 227-262.

928. Pittman, Ruth. "Allen Allensworth: Man of Ambition." *Crisis* 98 (February 1990): 34-35. [Founder of Allensworth, CA]

929. Ramsay, E. *Allensworth: A Study of Social Change.* Ph.D. diss., University of California, Berkeley, 1977. [California]

930. Thomas, Chleyon D. *Boley [Oklahoma]: An All-Black Pioneer Town and the Education of Its Children.* Ph.D. diss., University of Akron, 1989. UMO # 8922328.

931. Watson, Wilbur H. *The Village: An Historical and Ethnographic Study of a Black Community.* Atlanta, GA: Village Vanguard, 1989. [Cleveland, Ohio region]

932. Wiese, Andrew. "Places of Our Own: Suburban Black Towns before 1960." *Journal of Urban History* 19 (May 1993): 30-54.

BLACKS AND JEWS

933. Adler, Jerry and others. "The Rap Attitude." *Newsweek*, 19 March 1990.

934. American Jewish Committee. *Jewish Attitudes Toward Blacks and Race Relations*. New York: AJC, 1990.

935. *The Anti-Semitism of Black Demagogues and Extremists*. Anti- Defamation League, June 1992.

936. Aptheker, Herbert. "African-Americans and Jewish-Americans: Common Aspirants for the Good Life." *Jewish Affairs* 21 (Sept.- Oct., Nov.-Dec., 1991): 5-6, 14.

937. Austen, Ralph. "The Uncomfortable Relationship. African Enslavement in the Common History of Blacks and Jews." *Tikkun* (March 1994): 65-68,86. [Analysis of the Secret Relationship between Blacks and Jews,1991]

938. Baldwin, James. "Blacks and Jews." *Black Scholar* no. 19 (November 1988): 3-15.

939. Bauman, Mark K. *Harry R. Epstein and the Rabbinate as Conduit for Change*. Fairleigh Dickinson University Press, 1994.

940. Bender, Eugene I. "Reflections on Negro-Jewish Relationships." *Phylon* 30 (1969).

941. Benjamin, Playthell. "What the Minister Said." *Village Voice*, 15 August 1989. [Analysis of Louis Farrakhan's allegedly antisemitic remarks]

942. Ben-Jochannan, Yosef. *We the Black Jews: Witness to the 'White Jewish Race' Myth*. New York: Alkebu-lan Books and Education Materials Associates, 1982.

943. Berman, Paul, ed. *Blacks and Jews. Thirty Years of Alliance and Argument*. Delacorte Press, 1994.

944. Berman, Paul. "The Other and the Almost the Same." *New Yorker* (28 February 1994). [African Americans and Jews in the U.S.]

945. "Beyond Crown Heights- Strategies for Overcoming Anti- Semitism and Racism in New York." *Tikkun* 8 (January 1993): 59-62, 78-80. [Roundtable discussion]

946. Bick, Abraham. *Veker un kemper: Amerikaner Yidn in kamf kegn shlaferay (1848-1865)*. New York: Aroysgegebn fun a komitet, 1955. [Awakers and Fighters: American Jews in the Struggle Against Slavery]

947. Bikales, William G. "Where Jewish and Black Victimizations Differ." *New York Times*, 5 February 1993. [letter]

948. "Black Anti-Semitism." *Commentary* 98 (July 1994). [ten letters]

949. "Blacks and Anti-Semitism." *Militant* (13 September 1992). [editorial]

950. *Blacks and Jews. National Conference on African American/ Jewish American Relations*. Savannah, GA: 1983. [Savannah State College, 1983]

951. Blakeney, Ronnie A. F. *Prejudice or Discordance? The Cross- racial Moral Reasoning of Jews and Blacks*. Ph.D. diss., Howard University, 1984.

952. Blanchard, Tsvi. "Jews and Latinos." *Tikkun* 7 (November 1992): 47-48, 76-77.

953. Blauner, Robert. "That Black-Jewish Thing: What's going On?" *Tikkun* 9 (September 1994): 27-32, 103.

954. Boyd, Herb. "Blacks and Jews. Conflict on the Cultural Front." *Crisis* 96 (November 1989): 34-36.

955. Brackman, Harold D. *The Ebb and Flow of Conflict: A History of Black-Jewish Relations through 1900.* Ph.D. diss., University of California, Los Angeles, 1977.

956. Branch, Taylor. "The Uncivil War." *Esquire* (May 1989): 89- 90,92,94. [Blacks and Jews in Chicago]

957. Brent, Jonathan. "Parting of the Ways." *Midstream* 35 (May 1989): 59-61. [Negative review of Jonathan Kaufman's Broken Alliance: The Turbulent Times Between Blacks and Jews (1988)]

958. Breslin, Jimmy. "Trials Without End." *Village Voice*, 4 October 1994. letter, [On the second trial of Lemrick Nelson for the murder of Yankel Rosenbaum]

959. Brooklyn Chapter of New Jewish Agenda. "Statement on Crown Heights." *Jewish Affairs* 21 (Sept.-Oct., Nov.-Dec. 1991): 13,15.

960. Cage, Mary C. "A Life spent Interpreting the History of Slavery." *Chronicle of Higher Education* (4 May 1994). [David Brion Davis]

961. Cherry, Robert. "Middleman Minority Theories: Their Implications for Black-Jewish Relations." *Journal of Ethnic Studies* (Winter,1990): 117-138.

962. Christgau, Robert. "Jesus, Jews, and the Jackass Theory." , 16 January 1990. [Discusses charges of antisemitism against Black rap group]

963. Cohen, Debra Nussbaum. "Caught in the Cross Fire of the Crown Heights Crisis." *Moment* no. 16 (December 1991): 48-49.

964. Cohen, Kitty O. *Black-Jewish Relations: The View from the State Capitol.* New York: Cornwell Books, 1988.

965. Cohen, Richard. "Tolerating Race Hatred." *Washington Post*, 11 January 1994. [Louis Farrakhan]

966. _____. Farrakhan's False Choice. *Washington Post*, 27 January 1994.

967. Cox, Oliver C. "Jewish Self-Interest in 'Black Pluralism'." *Sociological Quarterly* 15 (March 1974): 183-198.

968. Cruse, Harold W. "My Jewish Problem and Theirs." in *Black AntiSemitism and Jewish Reaction*, James Baldwin, ed. New York: Baron, 1969.

969. Cudjoe, Selwyn R. "Time for Serious Scholars to Repudiate Nation of Islam's Diatribe Against Jews." *Chronicle of Higher Education* (11 May 1994). [Critique of 'The Secret Relationship Between Blacks and Jews,' 1991]

970. Davis, D. S. "Ironic Encounter: African-Americans, American Jews, and the Church-State Relationship." *Catholic University Law Review* 43 (Autumn 1993): 109-142.

971. "Diary Shows Nixon Wary of Blacks and Jews." *New York Times*, 18 May 1994.

972. Dinnerstein, Leonard. "The Origins of Black Anti-Semitism in America." *American Jewish Archives* 38 (1986): 113-122. [See critique by Stephen J. Whitfield, 39 (1987) 193-198]

973. "Dr. King and Anti-Semitism." *ADL Bulleting* 43 (January 1986).

974. Duke, Lynn. "New York, Jewish Tension Not Seen As indicative of Groups' Relations." *Washington Post*, 27 December 1992.

975. Dunbar, Leslie W. "Blacks and Jews on the Margins of Captivity." *Social Policy* 11 (1980): 54-58.

976. Eickhoff, Harold W. "When Khallid Abdul Muhammad Came to Call at Trenton State." *Education Week* (22 June 1994). [Representative of Nation of Islam]

977. Ellis, Joseph V., and James M. Cargal. "Khallid Abdul Muhammad at Trenton State." *Chronicle of Higher Education* (13 July 1994). [Two letters]

978. "The Farrakhan Furor." *Washington Post*, 7 February 1994. [editorial]

979. Farrakhan, Louis. "I Will Not Grovel: An Exclusive Interview with Louis Farrakhan." *Baltimore Jewish Times*, 27 August 1993.

980. _____. *A Torchlight for America*. Chicago: FCN Publishing Co., June 1993. [See Schapper, below]

981. Feuer, M. J. "Affirmative Action and Black-Jewish Relations." *Jewish Frontier* 52 (June-July 1985): 7-8.

982. Friedman, Murray. "Rewriting the History of Blacks and Jews." *Washington Post*, 4 December 1993.

983. Friedman, Robert J. "Conventional Wisdom. How 'Newsweek' Flubbed the 'Shwartzer Story'." *Village Voice*, 17 October 1989. [About Jackie Mason's racist remarks about Blacks]

984. _____. "The Origins of Black/Jewish Hatred in New York." *Village Voice*, 10 April 1990. [Role of FBI in fomenting Black- Jewish conflict in New York City during 1960s]

985. Gabler, Neal. "Jews, Blacks and Trouble in Hollywood." *New York Times*, 3 September 1990.

986. Gans, Herbert J. "Negro-Jewish Conflict in New York City." *Midstream* 15 (1969): 3-15.

987. Gates, Henry Louis, Jr. "Black Demagogues and Pseudo- Scholars." *New York Times*, 20 July 1992. [Antisemitism among some Black leaders]

988. _____. "Memoirs of an Anti-Anti-Semite." *Village Voice*, 20 October 1992.

989. Gelb, Joyce. *Beyond Conflict: Black-Jewish Relations- Accent on the Positive*. New York: Institute on Pluralism and Group Identity of the American Jewish Committee, 1980.

990. Gershman, Carl. "Blacks and Jews." *Midstream* 22 (1976): 8- 17.

991. Glazer, Nathan. "Negroes and Jews: The New Challenge to Pluralism." in *Ethnic Dilemmas, 1964-1982*, Cambridge, MA: Harvard University Press, 1983.

992. Glazer, Nathan, and Michel Giraud. "Juifs et noirs." *Traces* 11 (1984): 108-177.

993. Goldberg, J. J. "Justice and the Hasidim." *New York Times*, 1 September 1993. [The Crown Heights issue]

994. Goldstein, Richard. "Enough Already! The Jackson-Detente." *Village Voice*, 21 July 1992.

995. _____. "The New Anti-Semitism. A Geshrei." *Village Voice*, 1 October 1991. 33-38. [A "cry" against antisemitism by Blacks in Crown Heights, Brooklyn riot]

996. Golub, Jennifer L. *What Do We Know About Black Anti- Semitism?* New York: American Jewish Committee, 1990.

997. Greenberg, Cheryl L., and Barton Kunstler. "The History of Relations Between Blacks and Jews." *Chronicle of Higher Education* (16 February 1994). [Two letters]

998. Hacker, Andrew. "Jewish Racism, Black Anti-Semitism." *Reconstruction* 1 (1991): 14-17.

999. Haggard-Gibson, Nancy J. *Wounded in the House of Friends: Black and Jewish Ethnic Identity in the 1930s and 1940s*. Ph.D. diss., University of California, 1988. UMO # 8916685.

1000. Halpern, Stanley. "[Letter on Black-Jewish relations]." *Jewish Affairs* 21 (Sept.-Oct., Nov.-Dec. 1991): 4.15.

1001. Halpern, Stanley and others. "Still More on [Henry] Foner on [Leonard] Jeffries." *Jewish Currents* 48 (February 1994): 37-39. [Three letters]

1002. Heller, Celia, and Alphonso Pinkney. "The Attitudes of the Negro Toward Jews." *Social Forces* 43 (1965): 364-369.

1003. Hellwig, David J. "Black Images of Jews; from Reconstruction to Depression." *Societies* 8 (1978): 205-223.

1004. Henry, William A. III. "Pride and Prejudice." *Time* (28 February 1994). [Louis Farrakhan]

1005. Hentoff, Nat. "A Black Student Stands Up to Black Racism." *Village Voice*, 22 February 1994. [Khalid Abdul Muhammad at Kean College, Union, New Jersey]

1006. _____. "Blacks and Jews: Those Were the Days." , 13 August 1991.

1007. _____. "Let All Hate Speech Be Heard." *Village Voice*, 1 March 1994. [Controlling Louis Farrakhan's speech]

1008. _____. "My Introduction to Black Anti-Semitism." *Village Voice*, 29 September 1992.

1009. _____. "The Politics of Hate." *Village Voice*, 22 March 1994. [Al Sharpton and Louis Farrakhan]

1010. _____. "Skip Gates: Speaking Truth to Bigotry." *Village Voice*, 6 October 1992. [Antisemitism in the African-American community]

1011. _____. "Why Do They Hate Us?" *Village Voice*, 28 May 1991. [Black-Jewish strident conflict at UCLA]

1012. Herbert, Bob. "The Hate Game." *New York Times*, 9 February 1994. [Charges that Louis Farrakhan and Khalid Abdul Muhammad are "teaching young black Americans that they can hate without struggling."]

1013. Hill, Herbert and others. "Bridges and Boundaries: Black- Jewish Relations." *Race Traitor* (Winter 1993): 50-72. [Racial policies of the International Ladies Garment Workers Union]

1014. _____. "Bridges and Boundaries: Black-Jewish Relations." *Race Traitor* (Winter 1993): 50-72. [Racial policies of the International Ladies Garment Workers Union]

1015. Hirschorn, Michael W. "At Cross-Purposes: Blacks and Jews in Political Conflict." *Mosaic* 2 (1987): 7-20.

1016. Historical Research Department, The Nation of Islam. *The Secret Relationship Between Blacks and Jews*. Boston, MA: Nation of Islam, 1991.

1017. Holmes, Steven A. "Islamic Figure's Speech Plunges Howard University Into Debate on Racism." *New York Times*, 4 March 1994. [Khallid Abdul Muhammad]

1018. Hooks, Bell. "Keeping a Legacy of Shared Struggle." *Z Magazine* 5 (September 1992): 23-25. [Blacks, Jews, and antisemitism] [See Souad Dajani, above]

1019. Horne, Gerald. "Black-Jewish Relations and the 'New World Order'." *Jewish Affairs* 21 (Sept.-Oct., Nov.-Dec. 1991): 7-8,15.

1020. Hurvitz, Nathan. "Blacks and Jews in American Folklore." *Western Folklore* 33 (1974): 301-325.

1021. Jackson, Jesse L. "My Brother's Keeper" (Part 1). *Jewish Currents* 47 (February 1993): 20-24,40.

1022. _____. "My Brother's Keeper" (Part II). *Jewish Currents* 47 (March 1993): 14-17,37-38.

1023. _____. "No Group has Won Its Rights Without Help." *Los Angeles Times*, 6 March 1994. [African Americans and Jews]

1024. James, Caryn. "Spike Lee's Jews and the Passage from Benign Cliche Into Bigotry." *New York Times*, 16 August 1990. [See Spike Lee, below]

1025. Jenifer, Franklyn G. "Hate Speech Is Still Free Speech." *New York Times*, 13 May 1994. [Howard University]

1026. Jordan, Vernon E., Jr. "Racists, Antisemites And the 'Rights of Humanity'." *Washington Post*, 8 May 1994.

1027. Kadetsky, Elizabeth. "Racial Politics in New York." *Nation* (30 November 1992).

1028. Kamin, Leon J., and Dan B. Landt. "Scholars' Responsibility to Combat Racism." *Chronicle of Higher Education* (15 June 1994). [Nation of Islam, The Secret Relationship Between Blacks and Jews]

1029. Karp, Walter, and H. R. Shapiro. "Exploding the Myth of Black Anti-Semitism." in *Black Anti-Semitism and Jewish Racism*, Nat Hentoff, ed. New York: Baron, 1969.

1030. Kaufman, Jonathan. *Broken Alliance: The Turbulent Times between Blacks and Jews in America*. New York: Scribner, 1988.

1031. King, Dennis. "The Farrakhan Phenomenon: Ideology, Support, Potential." *Patterns of Prejudice* 20 (January 1986): 11-22.

1032. Klein, Joe. "The Threat of Tribalism." *Newsweek*, 14 March 1994.

1033. Krakoff, Sarah. "White Lies." *Village Voice*, 15 June 1993. [Are Jews whites?]

1034. Krause, Allen P. "Rabbis and Negro Rights in the South, 1954-1967." *American Jewish Archives* 21 (1969): 20-47.

1035. Laness, Thomas, and Richard Quinn. *Jesse Jackson and the Politics of Race*. Ottawa, IL: Jameson Books, 1985.

1036. Lecomte, Monique. "Noirs et Juifs: des frères ennemis?" *Le Monde Juif* 33 (1977): 23-34.

1037. Lee, Spike. "I Am Not an Anti-Semite." *New York Times*, 22 August 1990. [See Caryn James, above]

1038. Lerner, Michael. *Facing Anti-Semitism (on the Left and Among African-Americans and Other Oppressed Groups)*. Oakland, CA: Fighting Anti-Semitism Project, CJSJ, 1991.

1039. Lester, Julius. "The Simple Truth About Blacks and Jews." *Reform Judaism* (Summer 1989): 8-9.

1040. Levine, Burton. "Jews and Blacks." *Jewish Spectator* (Winter 1988): 49-57.

1041. Locke, Herbert G. *The Black Anti-Semitism Controversy: Protestant Views and Perspectives*. Susquehanna University Press: 1994.

1042. Logan, Andy. "Syzygy." *New Yorker* (23 September 1991): 102- 107. [Jews and Blacks in New York City]

1043. Logan, Paul E. "The Voice of Howard [University]." *Washington Post*, 13 May 1994. [The issue of antisemitism]

1044. Lopez, Manuel, and Jim Matthews. "Alan Dershowitz: Blacks, Jews, and Selective Morality." *Harvard Salient* (April 1985).

1045. Magner, Denise K. "A Charge of Anti-Semitism." *Chronicle of Higher Education* (12 January 1994). [Tony Martin's The Jewish Onslaught]

1046. Malev, William S. "The Jews of the South in the Conflict on Segregation." *Conservative Judaism* 13 (1958): 35-46.

1047. Mazrui, Ali A. "Negritude, the Talmudic Tradition and the Intellectual Performance of Blacks and Jews." *Ethnic and Racial Studies* 1 (January 1978): 19-30.

1048. McMillan, Lewis K. "An American Negro Looks at the German Jew." *Christian Century* 55 (August 31, 1938): 1034-36.

1049. McPherson, James A. "To Blacks and Jews: Haim Rachmones." *Tikkun* 4 (September-October 1989): 15-18.

1050. Miller, David. "Half-Truths and History: The Debate Over Jews and Slavery." *Washington Post*, 17 October 1993. [Critical discussions of The Secret Relationship Between Blacks and Jews]

1051. Miller, E. Ethelbert and others. "Blacks and Jews Must Reunite Against Injustice." *New York Times*, 3 August 1992. [five letters]

1052. Mohammed, Khalid Abdul. "Excerpts, Out of Sequence, from a Transcript of Remarks..., Nation of Islam National Spokesman, at Kean College, NJ, 11/29/93." *New York Times*, 16 January 1994.

1053. *Moment* 19 (October 1994): 4-11. [Series of letters discussing Blacks and Jews]

1054. "Mr. Bellow's Planet." *New Yorker* (25 May 1994). [Among other things, Saul Bellow's views on antisemitism]

1055. Muhammed, Askia. "Face the Nation." *Washington Post*, 8 May 1994. [Defense of Nation of Islam]

1056. Muwakkil, Salim. "Disharmony." *In These Times* (14 June 1993). [Blacks and Jews]

1057. _____. "Farrakhan's Dilemma." *In These Times* (21 February 1994).

1058. _____. "Muhammad Speaks." *In These Times* (16 May 1994). [Khalid Abdul Muhammad]

1059. _____. "Visible Man." *In These Times* (2 September 1992). [Commentary on Henry Louis Gates'critique of Black antisemitism]

1060. NAACP and Union of American Hebrew Congregations. *Common Road to Justice.* 2027 Massachusetts Avenue, N.W., Washington, D.C. 20036: Marjorie Kovler Institute for Black-Jewish Relations, 1991.

1061. Newsome, Yvonne D. *A House Divided: Conflict and Cooperation in African-American-Jewish Relations, 2 volumes.* Ph.D. diss., Northwestern, 1991. UMO # 9213520.

1062. _____. "International Issues and Domestic Ethnic Relations: African Americans, American Jews, and the Israel-South African Debate." *International Journal of Politics, Culture, and Society* 5 (Fall, 1991): 19-48.

1063. Niebuhr, Gustav. "Anti-Jewish Feelings By African Americans Have a Long History." *Washington Post*, 4 February 1994.

1064. Noel, Peter. "Kill the Jew! Kill the Nigger!" *Village Voice*, 27 October 1992.

1065. _____. "Word to My Brother." *Village Voice*, 6 July 1993. [An African-American reflects on having saved two Jews from mob death at Crown Heights.]

1066. Nordheimer, Jon. "College Speech leaves Angry Echoes." *New York Times*, 26 January 1994. [Nov. 29, 1993 speech by Khalid Abdul Muhammad at Kean College, N.J.][See Mohammed, above]

1067. Okami, P. "Intolerable Grievances Patiently Endured: Referent Cognitions and Group Conflict as Mediators of Anti- Jewish Sentiment." *Political Psychology* 13 (December 1992): 727- 754.

1068. "An Open Letter to the Nation. The Truth About Howard University." *New York Times*, 15 May 1984. [advertisement]

1069. Owens, Major R. "A Statement on Farrakhan." *Jewish Currents* 48 (April 1994): 14-17.

1070. Page, Clarence. "The Fault Line Is Words vs. Deeds." *Los Angeles Times*, 4 August 1992. [Jesse Jackson and the Jews]

1071. Pearlman, Jill. "Repentant Professor." *Spin* 6 (April 1990): 94-96. [Professor Griff takes a second look at the Jews.]

1072. Petigny, Alan. "Black-Jewish Tensions Analyzed. An African- American Journalist's View." *Jewish Currents* 48 (February 1994): 7-11,29.

1073. Phillips, William M., Jr. *An Unillustrious Alliance. The African American and Jewish American Communities.* Westport, CT: Greenwood, 1991.

1074. Pinkney, Alphonso. "Recent Unrest Between Blacks and Jews: The Claims of Anti-Semitism and Reverse Discrimination." *Black Sociologist* 8 (Fall-Summer 1978-79): 38-57.

1075. Pogrebin, Letty Cottin. "Different Kinds of Survival." *Nation* (23 September 1991). [Blacks and Jews]

1076. Porter, Jack N. "John Henry and Mr. Goldberg: The Relationship Between Blacks and Jews." *Journal of Ethnic Studies* 7 (Fall 1979): 73-86.

1077. Puddington, Arch. "Black Anti-semitism and How It Grows." *Commentary* 97 (April 1994): 19-24.

1078. Raab, Earl. "Interracial Conflict and American Jews." *Patterns of Prejudice* 25 (Summer 1991): 46-61.

1079. _____. "The Riddle of Jewish/Black Relations." *Reform Judaism* (Summer 1989): 10-11.

1080. Raspberry, William. "Facing the Farrakhan Question." *Washington Post*, 26 January 1994.

1081. _____. "The NAACP's Burden." *Boston Globe*, 20 June 1994. [Blacks and Jews]

1082. Rich, Frank. "Bad for the Jews." *New York Times*, 3 March 1994. [Louis Farrakhan as a guest on the Arsenio Hall television program]

1083. Ringle, Ken. "The Real Life and Death of Nat Turner." *Washington Post*, 24 April 1994.

1084. Roberts, Sam. "To Owens, Most Blacks Don't Seem Anti- Semitic." *New York Times*, 5 July 1993. [Rep. Major R. Owens, Brooklyn]

1085. Robeson, Paul Jr. "Blacks and Jews: Allies Still." *Jewish Currents* (September 1993).

1086. Roiphe, Anne. "He's Not the Enemy." *Present Tense* 17 (January-February 1990): 57-59. [Jews and Jesse Jackson]

1087. Rose, Peter. "Blacks and Jews- The Strained Alliance." *Annals of the American Academy of Political and Social Science* 454 (1980): 55-69.

1088. Rosenberg, Henry. "Arsenio Hall vs. Louis Farrakhan: It's a Rout." *Los Angeles Times*, 28 February 1994.

1089. Rosenthal, A. M. "On Black Anti-Semitism." *New York Times*, 11 January 1994.

1090. Rubin, Gary E. *Jews and Race in America*. Los Angeles: Wilstein Institute, University of Judaism, 1992.

1091. Sacks, Karen B. "On Michael Levin's 'Why Black Antisemitism?'." *Jewish Currents* (June 1992).

1092. Salzman, Jack and others. *Bridges and Boundaries. African Americans and American Jews*. Braziller, 1992.

1093. Santamaria, Ulysses. "Black Jews: The Religious Challenge or Politics versus Religion." *European Journal of Sociology* 28 (1987): 217-240.

1094. Schappes, Morris U. "Farrakhan Khalid Muhammad, Jews and Slavery." *Jewish Currents* 48 (April 1994): 11.

1095. _____. "Farrakhan's 'A Torchlight for America'." *Jewish Currents* 48 (January 1994): 18-20. [See Farrakhan, above]

1096. _____. "Schappes' Challenge to Farrakhan." *Jewish Currents* 48 (March 1994): 15.

1097. Schindler, Alexander M. "Look Beyond the Grievance of the Past." *Los Angeles Times*, 4 August 1992. [Jesse Jackson and the Jews]

1098. Schoen, David, and Marshall Field Stevenson, Jr. "Teaching Ethnic Identity and Intergroup Relations: The Case of Black-Jewish Dialogue." *Teachers College Record* 91 (Summer 1990).

1099. Seiden, Melvin. "An Open Letter to Derrick Bell." *Jewish Currents* (September 1993).

1100. Shankman, Arnold. "Brothers across the Sea: Afro-Americans on the Persecution of Russian Jews, 1881-1917." *Jewish Social Studies* 37 (1975): 114-121.

1101. _____. "Friend or Foe? Southern Blacks View the Jew, 1880-1935." in *Turn to the South: Essays on Southern Jewry*, Melvin J. Urofsky, ed. Waltham, MA, 1979.

1102. Silver, Nina. "Growing Up with Jewish Racism." *Jewish Currents* 45 (February 1991): 8-9.

1103. Sinden, Peter G. "Anti-Semitism and the Black Power Movement." *Ethnicity* 7 (March 1980): 34-46. [School strike in New York City, 1968-1969]

1104. Singer, David G. "An Uneasy Alliance: Jews and Blacks in the United States, 1945-1953." *Conservative Judaism* 4 (1978): 35- 50.

1105. Sipchen, Bob. "L.A. Jews Look Past the Riots." *Los Angeles Times*, 16 October 1992.

1106. Smothers, Ronald. "[Jesse] Jackson and the Jews." *New York Times*, 7 November 1983.

1107. Solomon, Alisa. "Lost in America. Solomon Mengstie: A Case of Mistaken Identity." *Village Voice*, 3 May 1994. [An Ethiopian Jew in New York City]

1108. Sowell, Thomas. "Scapegoating." *Forbes Magazine* (11 April 1994). [Jews in the slave trade] [Reprinted on Op-Ed page of New York Times, May 24, 1994]

1109. Steinberg, Stephen. "Blacks and Jews: The Politics of Memory." *New Politics* 3 (Winter 1991): 64-70.

1110. Stern, Marc D. "The Problem of Crown Heights." *Congress Monthly* (January 1993).

1111. Stevenson, Marshall Field, Jr. *Points of Departure, Acts of Resolve: Black-Jewish Relations in Detroit, 1937-1962.* 2 vols. Ph.D. diss., University of Michigan, 1988. UMO # 8907150.

1112. Stith, Barbara J. "A Black-Jewish Student Bond." *Jewish Currents* 48 (February 1994): 4-5. [Thomas Jefferson High School, Brooklyn, 1966-1970]

1113. _____. "The Holocaust Memorial Museum: An African American Perspective." *Jewish Currents* 48 (February 1994): 5-7.

1114. Strasser, Steven and others. "Jesse Jackson and the Jews." *Newsweek* (5 March 1984).

1115. Thomas, Laurence M. "Jews, Blacks and Group Autonomy." *Social Theory and Practice* 14 (Spring 1988): 55-70.

1116. _____. "Liberalism and the Holocaust: An Essay on Trust and the Black-Jewish Relationship." in *Echoes from the Holocaust: Philosophical Reflections on a Dark Time*, Alan Rosenberg, and Gerald E. Myers, eds. Philadelphia, PA: Temple University Press, 1988.

1117. *Tikkun* 4 (July-August 1989): 88-101. [Five articles on Black-Jewish relations]

1118. Toll, William. "Pluralism and Moral Force in the Black- Jewish Dialogue." *American Jewish History* 77 (September 1987): 87-105.

1119. Tollett, Kenneth S., Sr. "Fiery Words Are More Likely Smothered With Neglect." *Washington Post*, 13 April 1994. [On Blacks and Jews]

1120. Trescott, Jacqueline. "The Student Warrior. Malik Shabazz and His Fighting Words." *Washington Post*, 6 April 1994. [Malik Zulu Shabazz, Howard University law student, and his antagonism toward Jews]

1121. Tsukashima, Ronald T. *The Social and Psychological Correlates of Black Anti-Semitism.* San Francisco, CA: R & E Research Associate, 1978.

1122. _____. "A Test of Competing Contact Hypotheses in the Study of Black Anti-Semitic Beliefs." *Contemporary Jewry* 7 (1986): 1-17.

1123. *Village Voice*, 15 February 1994. [Series of articles critical of Louis Farrakhan]

1124. Wagner, Stephen T. *Reconstruction* 1 (1992): 157-160. [Letters commenting on Andrew Hacker's Jewish Racism, Black Anti- Semitism]

1125. Weisbord, R. G. "Farrakhan, Blacks and Jews." *Jewish Frontier* 53 (February-March 1986): 8-11.

1126. Weisbord, R. G., and A. Stein. "Negro Perceptions of Jews between the World Wars." *Judaism* 18 (Fall 1969): 428-447.

1127. Weisman, Seymour S. "Black-Jewish Relations in the USA..." *Patterns of Prejudice* 14 (1980): 15(1981), 45-52.

1128. Weiss, Avi, and Martin Hochbaum. "What About Antisemitism at Howard University." *Washington Post*, 8 May 1994. [Two letters]

1129. West, Cornel. "Black Anti-Semitism and the Rhetoric of Resentment." *Tikkun* 7 (January-February 1992): 15-16.

1130. _____. "How to End the Impasse." *New York Times*, 14 April 1993. [Blacks and Jews]

1131. _____. "On Black-Jewish Relations." in *Race Matters*, pp. 69-79 : Beacon Press, 1993.

1132. _____. "Why I Write for Tikkun." *Tikkun* 5 (September- October 1990): 59.

1133. Whitfield, Stephen J. "A Critique of Leonard Dinnerstein's 'The Origins of Black Antisemitism in America'." *American Jewish Archives* 39 (November 1987): 193-198. [See rejoinder by Dinnerstein, 199-202]

1134. Wilkins, Roger W. "The Farrakhan Paradox. A Search for Moral Authority." *Los Angeles Times*, 6 February 1994.

1135. Williams, Juan. "The Farrakhan Paralysis." *Washington Post*, 13 February 1994.

1136. Williams, Lena. "Blacks, Jews and 'This Thing That Is Suffocating Us'." *New York Times*, 29 July 1990.

1137. Winkler, Karen J. "Debating the History of Blacks and Jews." *Chronicle of Higher Education* (19 January 1994).

1138. Zakim, Leonard. "A Partnership Forged in Blood." *Boston Globe*, 30 June 1994. [Blacks and Jews]

1139. Zucker, Ben-Ami. "Black Americans' Reaction to the Persecution of European Jews." *Simon Wiesenthal Center Annual* 3 (1986): 177-197.

BUSINESS

1140. Adams, Robert H. *A Little Black Book of Business Inspirations*. Hempstead, New York: 1987.

1141. Allen, Joyce E. "The Growth and Diversification of Black Business." *Focus* 18 (October 1990): 5-6.

1142. "Asians, Native Americans Top Minority Entrepreneurs." *USA Today* (5 December 1986): 11A.

1143. Baris, Jay G. "Inner-City Banking's Catch-22." *New York Times*, 1 August 1992.

1144. Bates, Timothy. *Banking on Black Enterprise: The Potential of Emerging Firms for Revitalizing Urban Economics*. Joint Center for Political and Economic Studies, 1993.

1145. _____. "The Changing Nature of Minority Business: A Comparative Analysis of Asian, Nonminority, and Black-Owned Businesses." *Review of Black Political Economy* 18 (Fall 1989): 25-42.

1146. _____. "Commercial Bank Financing of White- and Black- owned Small Business Start-ups." *Quarterly Review of Economics and Business* 31 (Spring 1991): 64-80. [1982-1986]

1147. _____. "Do Black-owned Businesses Employ Minority Workers? New Evidence." *Review of Black Political Economy* 16 (Spring 1988)

1148. _____. *Paper on Black Entrepreneurship*. Prepared for the Committee on the Status of Black Americans, National Research Council, Washington, D.C., 1986.

1149. _____. "The Potential of Black Capitalism." *Public Policy* 21 (1973): 135-148.

1150. _____. "Small Business Viability in the Urban Ghetto." *Journal of Regional Science* (November 1989)

1151. Betsey, Charles L. *Birmingham's Changing Economy: Opportunitites for Disadvantaged Business*. City of Birmingham: Office of Economic Development, December 1991.

1152. Biddle, Frederic M. "The Collapse of Harlem's Freedom National [Bank]." *Boston Globe*, 18 November 1990.

1153. Big Record Labels Making Big Investments in Rap Music. *New York Times*, 10 August 1990.

1154. Boneparth, E. "Black Businessmen and Community." *Phylon* 37 (1976): 26-43.

1155. Boyd, Robert L. "Black Business Transformation, Black Well- Being, and Public Policy." *Population Research and Policy Review* 9 (May 1990).

1156. _____. *Ethnic Entrepreneurs in the New Economy: Business Enterprise among Asian-Americans and Blacks in a Changing Urban Enironment*. Ph.D. diss., University of North Carolina, UMO # 9007267.

1157. Brimmer, Andrew F. "The Dilemma of Black Banking: Lending Risks vs. Community Service." *Review of Black Political Economy* 20 (Winter 1992): 5-29.

1158. Brooks, Nancy Rivera. "Crenshaw S & L Viewed as Model for Inner-City Banks." *Los Angeles Times*, 16 April 1993. [Family Savings Bank, largest Black-owned financial institution in California]

1159. Brown, Ken. "Korean Groceries Failing in New York as Recession Drags On." *New York Times*, 29 November 1993.

1160. Bryant, John. "Let's Look at the Inner City As an Opportunity." *Los Angeles Times*, 23 August 1993.

1161. Byrd, Veronica. "Black Bankers Seek Broader Market." *New York Times*, 6 September 1993.

1162. Carroll, James R. "Avalanche of Paperwork Foils Move to Aid Latino Business." *Long Beach Press-Telegram*, 29 November 1992. [Minority business programs in government]

1163. Carter, Bill. "Fox Praise of NAACP Raises Eyebrows." *New York Times*, 10 October 1994. [Fox Broadcasting Company]

1164. Caskey, J. P. "Bank Representation in Low-Income and Minority Urban Communities." *Urban Affairs Quarterly* 29 (June 1994): 617-138.

1165. Chapelle, Tony. "A Pioneer Who's Skeptical of 'Minority' Brokerages." *September 18, 1994*[The First Black to buy a Big Board seat sees many of today's dealers as fronts]

1166. Clair, R. T. "The Performance of Black-owned Banks in Their Primary Market Areas." *Federal Reserve Bank of Dallas Economic Review* (November 1988).

1167. Cochran, Thomas. *The Puerto Rican Businessman: A Study in Cultural Change*. Philadelphia: University of Pennsylvania Press, 1959.

1168. Coleman, L., and S. Cook. "The Failures of Minority Capitalism: The Edapco Case." *Phylon* 37 (1976): 44-58.

1169. Coopers and Lybrand. *Minority Business Utilization Study: Report to the State of Maryland, Department of Transportation (DOT)*. Coopers and Lybrand, 1990. [Contract DOT-OTS-90-001]

1170. Cruz, Laura. "Chicano Capitalism." *La Luz* 5 (March 1976).

1171. Daniels, George M. "The Rise and Fall of Freedom National Bank." *Crisis* 99 (April-May 1992): 40-42. [One of original stockholders in the Freedom National Bank of Harlem]

1172. Eastman, Dale. "The Price of Pawning." *Chicago Reporter*, October 1991. 20, 3-5, 10-11.

1173. Edmond, Alfred Jr. "Drexel's Fall: The Price of Backing Blacks?" *Black Enterprise* 20 (May 1990): 14.

1174. Edwards, Ellen. "A Battle for Public TV Dollars." *Washington Post*, 20 May 1994. [Minority Groups, Stations, Fight for Control of $5 Million]

1175. Elliott, Stuart. "Retailers Reach Out to Minorities." *New York Times*, 31 December 1991. [Employment of minority advertising agencies]

1176. Farhi, Paul. "Hair Care Battle Lines Drawn in Black, White." *Washington Post*, 27 December 1993. [The Black hair care market]

1177. Fitzgerald, Michael W. "Railroad Subsidies and Black Aspirations: The Politics of Economic Development in Reconstruction Mobile, 1865-1879." *Civil War History* no. 39 (September 1993): 240-256.

1178. Flynn, Michael S. "The Big Three [AutoMakers] and Black America." *New York Times*, 8 November 1992.

1179. Fratoe, Frank A., and Ronald L. Meeks. *Business Participation Rates and Self-employed Incomes: Analysis of the Fifty Largest U.S. Ancestry Groups*. Los Angeles: UCLA Center for Afro-American Studies,

1180. Garreau, Joel. "Ethics of 'Ethnicated' Mailing Lists." *Washington Post*, 14 November 1992. [Marketers, Fund-raisers Target names by race or background]

1181. George, Nelson. "Forty-Acres and An Empire." *Village Voice*, 7 August 1990. [Spike Lee's investments and expenditures in Black areas]

1182. Glover, Glenda. "Enterprise Zones: Incentives Are Not Attracting Minority Firms." *Review of Black Political Economy* 22 (Summer 1993): 73-99.

1183. Gonzalez, Henry S. "Banks in Poor Neighborhoods." *Los Angeles Times*, 17 August 1993.

1184. Green, Shelley, and Paul Pryde. *Black Entrepreneurship in America*. New Brunswick, New Jersey: Transaction, 1989.

1185. Handy, John W. *An Analysis of Black Business Enterprise*. New York: Garland, 1989.

1186. Harris, Abram L. *The Negro as Capitalist*. College Park, MD: McGrath Publishing Co., 1968.

1187. Harrison, Bennett. *Lean and Mean. The Changing Landscape of Corporate Power in the Age of Flexibility*. Basic Books, 1994.

1188. Hatchett, David. "The Future of Black Financial Institutions." *Crisis* 99 (April-May 1992): 44-46.

1189. Hemp, Paul. "Chicago's Grand Experiment." *Boston Globe*, 25 August 1991. [Grand Boulevard Plaza]

1190. _____. "Why Retailers Shun Boston's Minority Neighborhoods." *Boston Globe*, 25 August 1991.

1191. Henderson, Alexa B. *Atlanta Life Insurance Company: Guardian of Black Economic Dignity*. Tuscaloosa: University of Alabama Press, 1990.

1192. Henriques, Diana B. "Piercing Wall Street's 'Lucite Ceiling'." *New York Times*, 11 August 1991. [Minority-owned investment banking]

1193. Hinds, Michael de Courcy. "Minority Business Set Back Sharply by Courts' Rulings." *New York Times*, 23 December 1991.

1194. Holmes, Steven A. "Most Securities Arbiters Found to Be White Men Over 60." *New York Times*, 5 April 1994. [Securities firms eroding civil rights laws]

1195. Horovitz, Bruce. "Asian Americans Appear To Be Hot Market for the 90's." *Los Angeles Times*, 8 September 1992.

1196. _____. "Blacks Flex Buying Power." *Los Angeles Times*, 18 May 1993.

1197. _____. "Harmonic Convergence. Racial Tolerance Is Suddenly a Hot Topic in Advertising." *Los Angeles Times*, 19 January 1993.

1198. _____. "Penny's Stores to Feature Items for Minorities." *Los Angeles Times*, 9 September 1993.

1199. Hylton, Richard D. "Minority Firms Feel the Pinch. Times are Tougher in Municipal Bonds, But Racism is Blamed Too." *New York Times*, 16 April 1989.

1200. Jackson, L. Duane. "Minority [Real Estate] Developers." *Boston Globe*, 12 April 1992. [Interview]

1201. Judge, Paul C. "Minority Auto Dealers Face More Than Just the Recession." *New York Times*, 17 February 1991.

1202. Kenzer, Robert C. "The Black Businessman in the Postwar South: North Carolina, 1865-1880." *Business History Review* 63 (Spring 1989).

1203. Kimbro, Dennis. "Dreamers. Black Sales Heroes and Their Secrets." *Success Everybody Sells* 37 (May 1990): 40-41.

1204. Kinsey, Bernard W. "Nothing Else has Worked. Buy Black." *New York Times*, 1 August 1993.

1205. Kraul, Chris. "Lock of South-Central Banks 'Appalling'." *Los Angeles Times*, 8 September 1993. [South-Central Los Angeles]

1206. Krikorian, Greg. "The Minority Community's Shopping-Mall Hard Sell." *New York Times*, 20 May 1990.

1207. Kwon, S. C. "Korean Small Businesses in the Bronx, New York: An Aternative Perspective of Occupational Adaptation of New Immigrants." *Urban Geography* 11 (September-October 1990).

1208. Lang, Curtis J., and Timothy L. O'Brien. "Who Killed Harlem's Bank?" *Village Voice*, 30 April 1991. [Freedom National Bank; first of two articles]

1209. Lee, Dong Ok. *The Socio-spatial Incorporation of New Immigrants in the Post-industrial City: Korean Immigrant Entrepreneurs in Los Angeles.* Ph.D. diss., University of Kentucky, 1989. UMO # 9014285.

1210. Lee, Gary. "Black PR Firms Charge Business Bias." *Washington Post*, 15 February 1993. [Washington, D.C. area]

1211. Lee, Patrick. "Blacks Seek to Nurture an Entrepreneurial Class." *Los Angeles Times*, 8 June 1992.

1212. Lesly, Elizabeth. "Inside the Black Business Network: A Farflung Web of Entrepreneurs and Executives is Driving African American Economics Growth." *Business Week* (29 November 1993).

1213. Lewis, Diane E. "Going Shopping- the Hard Way." *Boston Globe*, 25 August 1991. [Difficulties of retail shopping in Roxbury, Dorchester, and Mattapan]

1214. Lueck, Thomas J. "Into the World of Banking Comes a Hip-Hop Credit Union." *New York Times*, 25 April 1993. [Central Brooklyn Federal Credit Union, Bedford Stuyvesant, N.Y.C.]

1215. Mabry, Marcus and others. "An Endangered Dream." *Newsweek* (3 December 1990). [Black business in the U.S.]

1216. MacDonald, J. M., and P. E. Nelson. "Do the Poor Still Pay More? Food Price Variations in Large Metropolitan Areas." *Journal of Urban Economics* 30 (November 1991): 344-359.

1217. Maier, Andrea. "Who Owns Businesses?" *Los Angeles Times*, 29 July 1992.

1218. Meier, Barry. "A Friend of the Consumer Says She Will Keep Fighting." *New York Times*, 26 October 1991. [Ms. Florence Rice, of Harlem Consumer Education Council]

1219. Meyer, Bruce D. D. *Why Are There So Few Black Entrepreneurs?* Cambridge, MA: National Bureau of Economic Research, 1990.

1220. Min, F. G. "Problems of Korean Immigrant Entrepeneurs." *International Migration Review* 24 (Autumn 1990).

1221. Min, Pyond Gap. "A Structural Analysis of Korean Business in the United States." *Ethnic Groups* 6 (1984): 1-25.

1222. "Minority Auto Dealers Call for U.S. Assistance." *Los Angeles Times*, 6 June 1992.

1223. Monroe, Sylvester. "The Gospel of Equity." *Time* (10 May 1993).

1224. Myerson, Allen R. "Twin Spotlights on Parsons of the Dime." *New York Times*, 26 August 1990. [Richard D. Parsons, Black pesident of the Dime Savings Bank of New York]

1225. O'Barr, William M. *Culture and the Ad: Explaining Otherness in the World of Advertising.* Westview Press, 1994.

1226. O'Hare, William P. "Black Business Ownership in the Rural South." *Review of Black Political Economy* 18 (Winter 1990): 93-104.

1227. Osborne, A., and M. Granfield. "The Potential of Black Capitalism in Perspective." *Public Policy* 24 (1976): 529-544.

1228. O'Toole, Patrician. "Battle of the Beauty Counter." *New York Times Business World* (3 December 1989). [Black cosmetics]

1229. Owsley, Beatrice R. *Hispanic American Entrepreneurs: An Oral History of the American Dream.* Twayne Publishers, 1992.

1230. Pearlstein, Steven. "Wealth of Impressions." *Washington Post*, 15 March 1993. [Industrial Bank of Washington, the only African-American owned bank in D.C.]

1231. Penley, L. E. and others. "The Comparative Salary Position of Mexican American College Grduates in Business." *Social Science Quarterly* 65 (June 1984).

1232. Pennington, Jody. "Don't Knock the Rock: Race, Business and Society in the Rise of Rock 'n' Roll." in *Cracking the Ike Age*, Dale Carter, ed. : Aarhus University Press, 1992.

1233. Raspberry, William. "Where Are the Black Entrepreneurs?" *Washington Post*, 9 August 1993.

1234. Reich, Kenneth. "Private Investment Pools Dealt Blow." *Los Angeles Times*, 25 September 1993. [Legality of Korean-American Kyes]

1235. Reinhold, Robert. "The Koreans' Big Entry Into Business." *New York Times*, 24 September 1989.

1236. Rice, F. "The Rise of Black Auto Dealers." *Fortune* 120 (14 August 1989).

1237. Schweninger, Loren. "Black-owned Businesses in the South, 1790-1880." *Business History Review* 63 (Spring 1989): 22-59.

1238. Shin, Eui-Hang, and Shin-Kap Han. "Korean Immigrant Small Businesses in Chicago: An Analysis of the Resource Mobilization Processes." *Amerasia Journal* 16 (1990): 39-60.

1239. Sims, Calvin. "Black Enterprises Grow and Get Noticed." *New York Times*, 11 July 1993.

1240. _____. "'Buying Black' Approach Paying Off in Los Angeles." *New York Times*, 23 May 1993.

1241. Skotnes, A. "Buy Where You Can Work: Boycotting for Jobs in African-American Baltimore, 1933-1934." *Journal of Social History* 27 (Summer 1994): 735-762.

1242. Sloan, Leslie J. "American Indian Banking-Beyond the Gordon Report." *ILSA Journal of International Law* 12 (Winter 1988): 155- 170.

1243. Spraggins, Tinsley L. *The History of the Negro in Business Prior to 1860*. Ph.D. diss., Howard University, 1935.

1244. Suggs, Robert E. *Recent Changes in Black-Owned Businesses*. Washington, D.C.: Joint Center for Political Studies, 1986.

1245. _____. "Rethinking Minority Business Strategies." *Harvard Civil Rights Civil Liberties Law Review* 25 (Winter 1990).

1246. Tassy, Elaine. "Hard Times. Black-Owned Cosmetics Firms Finding the Going Tough." *Los Angeles Times*, 27 December 1993.

1247. Thompson, Marilyn W. *Feeding the Beast. How Wedtech Became the Most Corrupt Little Company in America*. New York: Scribner's, 1990.

1248. Traub, James. *Too Good To Be True. The Outlandish Story of Wedtech*. New York: Doubleday, 1990.

1249. Treadwell, David. "Hard Rock for Black Businesses." *Los Angeles Times*, 20 September 1991.

1250. U.S. Department of Commerce. *Survey of Minority-owned Business Enterprises*. U.S. Department of Commerce, various years.

1251. U.S.Congress, 102nd session ,. House of Representatives, Committee on Government Operations, Employment and Housing Subcommittee. *Racial Discrimination in Awarding Toyota Dealerships; Hearing...* Washington, D.C.: GPO, 1993.

1252. Waldinger, Roger, and Howard E. Aldrich. "Trends in Ethnic Business in the United States." in *Ethnic Entrepreneurs: Immigrant Business in Industrial Societies*, (eds. Waldinger and others.) : Sage, 1990.

1253. Walker, Juliet E. K. "Prejudices, Profits, Privileges: Commentaries on 'Captive Capitalists', Antebellum Black Entrepreneurs." *Essays in Economic and Business History* 8 (1990): 399-422.

1254. _____. "Racism, Slavery, and Free Enterprise: Black Entrepreneurships in the United States before the Civil War." *Business History Review* 60 (Autumn 1986): 343-382.

1255. Watrous, Peter. "Laying Claim To the Mantle of Motown." *New York Times*, 4 July 1993.

1256. Watson, Milton H. "Black Star Line." *Steamboat Bill* 46 (1989): 264-272.

1257. Wayne, Leslie. "Big Firms Take Business Slated for Minorities." *New York Times*, 11 August 1994. [See letter of response by Paul W. Critchlow in issue of August 24, 1994]

1258. _____. "Politics and Municipal Bonds: A Bubbling Stew in Louisiana." *New York Times*, 6 July 1994. [Cutting in a Black owned bond house]

1259. Weems, Robert E., Jr. "The Revolution Will Be Marketed: American Corporations and Black Consumers During the 1960s." *Radical History Review* No. 59 (Spring 1994): 94-107.

1260. Weinraub, Judith. "The Group That Means Business." *Washington Post*, 4 March 1994. [African-American Business Association]

1261. Whatley, Warren C. "Getting a Foot in the Door: 'Learning,' State Dependence, and the Racial Integration of Firms." *Journal of Economic History* 50 (March 1990): 43-66.

1262. White, George. "Drive to Bolster Black Banks is a Hit." *Los Angeles Times*, 28 July 1992. [Three Black-owned banks in Los Angeles]

1263. _____. "'Rising Star' Threads 4 Life Forced to Sell the Operations." *Los Angeles Times*, 2 March 1994. [Black-owned clothing company]

1264. Woolf, A. G. "Market Structure and Minority Presence: Black-Owned Firms in Manufacturing." *Review of Black Political Economy* 14 (Spring 1986).

1265. Working Group on Section 936. "A Corporate License to Steal." *Against the Current* No. 48 (January-February 1994): 24- 29. [Tax incentives for business in Puerto Rico]

1266. Yarrow, Andrew L. "In Harlem, Freedom Bank's Collapse Is Like a Family Death." *New York Times*, 12 November 1990. [Freedom National Bank of New York]

1267. Young, Philip K. Y. "Family Labor, Sacrifice, and Competition: Korean Greengrocers in New York City." *Amerasia Journal* 10 (1983): 53-71.

CHILDREN

1268. Atwood, Barbara Ann. "Fighting Over Indian Children: The Uses and Abuses of Jurisdictional Ambiguity." *UCLA Law Review* 36 (August 1989): 1051-1108.

1269. Augenbraun, Harold, and Ilan Stavans, eds. *Growing Up Latino. Memoirs and Stories*. Houghton Mifflin, 1993.

1270. Bane, Mary Jo, and Ellwood David T. "One Fifth of the Nation's Children: Why Are They Poor?" *Science* 245 (8 September 1989): 1045-1053.

1271. Barsh, Russell Lawrence. "Indian Child Welfare Act of 1978: A Critical Analysis." *Hastings Law Journal* 31 (1980).

1272. Batten, Laura. "Teaching the Very Young to Battle Prejudice." *Boston Globe*, 28 April 1991.

1273. Bernal, Martha E. and others. "The Development of Ethnic Identity in Mexican-American Children." *Hispanic Journal of Behavioral Sciences* 12 (February 1990).

1274. Besharov, Douglas J. "Fresh Start." *New Republic* (14 June 1993). [Headstart program]

1275. Bianchi, Suzanne M. "America's Children: Mixed Prospects." *Population Bulletin* 45 (June 1990).

1276. Black Community Crusade for Children. *Progress and Peril: Black Children in America*. 1993. [Available from Children's Defense Fund]

1277. Braden, William and others. "The Critical Years: City Kids Left Behind at the Start." *Chicago Sun-Times*, June 26-30, 1988.

1278. Brown, Sara A. and others. *Children Working in the Sugar- Beet Fields of Certain Districts of the South Platte Valley, Colo*. New York: National Child Labor Committee, 1925.

1279. Carrasquillo, Angela L. *Hispanic Children and Youth in the United States. A Resource Guide*. Garland, 1991.

1280. Cater, Sandy. "Children of Crisis." *Z magazine* 4 (January 1991): 33-36.

1281. Cavenaugh, David N. and others. *Migrant Child Welfare: Final Report*. Washington, D.C.: Inter America Research Associates, 1977.

1282. Cazenave, N. A. "Philadelphia's Children in Need: Black, White, Brown, Yellow and Poor." in *The State of Black Philadelphia: 1988*, pp. 47-62. Philadelphia, PA: Urban League of Philadelphia.

1283. Chambers, T. "Black Child in a White Place." *Journal of Counseling and Development* 70 (March-April 1992).

1284. Chew, Kenneth S. Y. and others. "American Children in Multiracial Households." *Sociological Perspectives* 32 (Spring 1989): 65-85.

1285. *Child Poverty in America*. Washington, D.C.: Children's Defense Fund, 1991.

1286. Children's Defense Fund. *A Briefing Book on the Status of American Children in 1988*. Washington, D.C.: The Fund, 1988.

1287. _____. *Children 1990: A Report Card, Briefing Book, and Action Power*. Washington, D.C.: Children's Defense Fund, 1990.

1288. _____. *S.O.S. America! A Children's Defense Budget*. Washington, D.C.: Children's Defense Fund, 1990.

1289. Chira, Susan. "Worry and Distrust of Adults Beset Teenagers, Poll Says." *New York Times*, 10 July 1994.

1290. Christensen, John W. "Steeped in Prejudice." *New York Times*, 17 May 1992.

1291. Cohen, Cynthia P. and others. "Deaf Children from Ethnic, Linguistic and Racial Minority Backgrounds: An Overview." *American Annals of the Deaf* 135 (April 1990).

1292. Cohen, Cynthia P., and Howard A. Davidson. *Children's Rights in America. UN Convention on the Rights of the Child Compared with United States Law*. Defense for Children International-USA, 210 Forsyth Street, New York, N.Y. 10002, 1990.

1293. Cohen, Deborah. "Perry Preschool Graduates Show Dramatic New Social Gains at 27." *Education Week* (21 April 1993).

1294. Comer, James P. "What Makes the New Generation Tick?" *Ebony* 45 (August 1990).

1295. *Conditions of Children in California*. Berkeley: Policy Analysis for California Education, School of Education, University of California, 1989.

1296. Congressional Research Service. *Hispanic Children in Poverty*. Washington, D.C.: CRS, 13 September 1985.

1297. Cooper, Peter. "The Development of the Concept of War." *Journal of Peace Research* 1 (1965): 1-18. [A sense of "We" and "They" at nine years of age]

1298. Cronin, Mary E. "Deterring Racist Messages." *Long Beach Press-Telegram* (10 August 1992).

1299. Day, Dawn. *The Adoption of Black Children: Counteracting Institutional Discrimination*. Lexington, MA: Lexington Books, 1978.

1300. Edelman, Peter B., and Joyce Ladner, eds. *Adolescence and Poverty: Challenge for the 1990s*. Washington, D.C.: Center for National Policy Press, 1991.

1301. *Facing the Facts: A Progress Report on Ohio's Black Children*. Cleveland: Ohio Children's Defense Fund, 1993.

1302. *First National Conference on Latino Children in Poverty*. Washington, D.C.: The National Association of Latino Elected and Appointed Officials, NALEO Education Fund, 1987.

1303. *Five Million Children, a Statistical Profile of Our Poorest Young Citizens*. New York: National Center for Children in Poverty, School of Public Health, Columbia University, April 1990.

1304. Foderaro, Lisa W. "In Harlem, Children Reflect the Ravages U.N. Seeks to Relieve." *New York Times*, 30 September 1990.

1305. Ford, Royal and others. "Children of Poverty. Living in the Shadows." *Boston Globe*, 14 May 1989, supplement.

1306. French, Mary Ann. "The Noose of Racism." *Washington Post*, 23 February 1994. [The hazards of growing up Black in Indiana]

1307. George, Nelson. "Marilyn." *Village Voice*, 1 August 1989. [Black children and white dolls]

1308. Gittens, Joan. *Poor Relations: The Children of the State in Illinois, 1818-1990*. University of Illinois Press, 1994.

1309. Goldberg, David T. "The Poison of Racism and the Self-poisoning of Adolescents." *Journal of Family Therapy* 14 (February 1992): 51-68.

1310. Goldsmith, Donna J. "Individual vs. Collective Rights: The Indian Child Welfare Act." *Harvard Women's Law Journal* 13 (Spring 1990): 1-12.

1311. Goldstein, Naomi. *Why Poverty Is Bad for Children*. Ph.D. diss., Harvard University, 1991. UMO # 9123057.

1312. Goleman, Daniel, Black Scientists Study the 'Rose' of the Inner City. *New York Times*, 21 April 1992. [The "aloof swagger and studied unflappability projected by young black men" from inner cities]

1313. Hansberry, Lorraine. "The Scars of the Ghetto." *Monthly Review* (February 1965). [Reprinted in issue of July-August 1989, pp.52-55]

1314. Hare, B. R. "Black Youth at Risk." in *The State of Black America:1988*, New York: National Urban League, 1988.

1315. Harris, Frederick W. *The Racial Attitudes of Black Preschoolers: An Exploratory Study*. Ph.D. diss., University of Pitttsburgh, 1990. UMO # 9028405.

1316. Haveman, Robert H. and others. "The Well-being of Children and Disparities among Them Over Two Decades: 1962-1983." in *The Vulnerable*, eds. J. L. Palmer and others. Washington, D.C.: Urban Institute Press, 1988.

1317. Haveman, Robert H., and Barbara Wolfe. *Succeeding Generations. On the Effects of Investments in Children*. Russell Sage Foundation, 1994.

1318. Hayes, Cheryl D. and others. *Who Cares for America's Children*. Washington, D.C.: National Academy Press, 1990.

1319. Heinz, Martha C. *Racial and Ethnic Identification, Preference, and Acceptance in Hispanic and Caucasian Preschool Children*. Ph.D. diss., University of South Carolina, 1984. UMO # 8427735.

1320. Hill, R. P. "Homeless Children: Coping with Material Losses." *Journal of Consumer Affairs* 26 (Winter 1992).

1321. Hollinger, Joan H. "Beyond the Best Interests of the Tribe: The Indian Child Welfare Act and the Adoption of Indian Children." *University of Detroit Law Review* 66 (Spring 1989): 451-501.

1322. Holloran, Peter C. *Boston's Wayward Children: Social Services for Homeless Children, 1830-1930*. Rutherford, NJ: Fairleigh Dickinson University, 1989.

1323. Howlett, Scott W. *"My Child, Him Is Mine": Plantation Slave Children in the Old South*. Ph.D. diss., University of California, 1993. UMO # 9316412.

1324. Husemoller, Carl. *On the Edge: A History of Poor Black Children and Their American Dreams*. Basic Books, 1994.

1325. Jackson, Derrick Z. "US Falls Behind on Treatment of Children." *Boston Globe*, 29 June 1994.

1326. Jones, Reginald L. *Black Adolescents*. Berkeley, CA: Cobb & Henry, 1989.

1327. Jordan, Mary. "Head Start's Big Test. Can '60's Success Story Fill 90's Role?" *Washington Post*, 29 March 1993.

1328. Jordan, Robert A. "Poll Shows Hope- If Society Listens." *Boston Globe*, 12 June 1994. [Black Children and adults discuss the future of Black children; Peter D. Hart public-opinion poll.]

1329. Juhasz, Anne M. "Black Adolescents' Significant Others." *Social Behavior and Personality* 17 (1989).

1330. Karp, Robert J., ed. *Malnourished Children in the United States: Caught in the Cycle of Poverty*. Springer, 1993.

1331. Kerwin, Christine. *Racial identity Development in Biracial Children of Blck/White Racial Heritage*. Ph.D. diss., Fordham University, 1991. UMO # 9136328.

1332. Kotlowitz, Alex. *There Are No Children Here. The Story of Two Boys Growing Up*. New York: Doubleday, 1991. [Chicago public housing project]

1333. Kraly, Ellen P., and Charles Hirschman. "Racial and Ethnic Inequality among Children in the United States: 1940 and 1950." *Social Forces* 69 (1990): 33-51.

1334. Lambert, Wallace E., and O. Klineberg. *Children's Views of Foreign Peoples*. New York: Appleton-Century-Crafts, 1967.

1335. Lash, Trude W. and others. *State of the Child: New York City II*. New York: Foundation for Child Development, 1980.

1336. Lawson, Carol. "Nurturing Black Children In a Hostile World." *New York Times*, 10 June 1993.

1337. Lerner, M. J. *The Belief in a Just World: A Fundamental Delusion*. Plenum, 1980.

1338. Lew, Bill. "A Letter to My Children." *Amerasia Journal* 15 (1989): 91-94.

1339. Low, Ronald. "No Child Should Be Without Love and Protection: The Legal Problems of Amerasians." *Howard Law Journal* 26 (Fall 1983): 1527-1546.

1340. Lubeck, S., and P. Garrett. "The Social Construction of the At-risk Child." *British Journal of Sociology of Education* 11 (1990).

1341. Majors, Richard, and Janet M. Billson. *Cool Rose: The Dilemmas of Black Manhood in America*. Lexington, MA: Lexington Books, 1992.

1342. *Massachusetts Childwatch '90: A Report on the Status of Children in Boston*. Boston, MA: Massachusetts Office for Children, October 1990.

1343. McKenny, Patrick C. and others. "Research on Black Adolescents: A Legacy of Cultural Bias." *Journal of Adolescent Research* 4 (April 1989): 254-264.

1344. Miller, G., ed. *Giving Children a Chance: The Case for More Effective Natural Policies*. Washington, D.C.: Center for National Policy Press, 1989.

1345. Miller-Jones, D. "Informal Reasoning in Inner-City Children." in *Informal Reasoning and Education*, James F. Voss and others, eds. Hillsdale, NJ: Lawrence Erlbaum Associates, 1990.

1346. Miranda, Leticia C. *Latino Child Poverty in the United States*. Children's Defense Fund, 1991.

1347. Miringoff, Marc L. *The Index of the Social Health of the Children of New York City*. Tarrytown, NY: Institute for Innovation in Social Policy, Fordham University, July 1990.

1348. Morganthau, Tom and others. "Children of the Underclass." *Newsweek* (11 September 1989).

1349. Mori, Aisha Kiko. "I Wish People Would Ask My Name, Not Mix." *Los Angeles Times*, 13 December 1993. [Young women of Japanese-American and Afro-American parentage]

1350. Murry, Velma M. *Black Adolescence: Current Issues and Annotated Bibliography*. Boston, MA: Hall, 1990.

1351. National Commission on Children. *Beyond Rhetoric. A New American Agenda for Children and Families*. Washington, D.C.: GPO, 1991.

1352. Nightingale, Carl H. *On the Edge. A History of Poor Black Children and Their American Dreams*. Basic Books, 1993.

1353. O'Donnell, S. M. "The Care of Dependent African-American Children in Chicago: The Struggle between Black Self-help and Professionalism." *Journal of Social History* 27 (Summer 1994): 763-776.

1354. Parker, S. and others. "Double Jeopardy: The Impact of Poverty on Early Childhood Development." *Pediatric Clinics of North America* 35 (December 1988).

1355. Perkins, Darlene. "Meeting the Issue of Color. Kids Must Learn When Very Young." *Long Beach Press-Telegram*, 27 September 1992.

1356. Phinney, Jean S., and Mary J. Rotheram, eds. *Children's Ethnic Socialization. Pluralism and Development*. Newbury Park, CA: Sage, 1987.

1357. Piaget, Jean, and A. M. Weil. "The Development in Children of the Idea of the Homeland and of Relations with Other Countries." *International Social Science Bulletin* (1955).

1358. Pittman, Karen, and Luis Duany. *Latino Youths at a Crossroads*. Washington, D.C.: Children's Defense Fund, 1990.

1359. Porter, C. P. "Social Reasons for Skin Tone Preferences of Black School-age Children." *American Journal of Orthopsychiatry* 61 (January 1991): 149-154.

1360. Poussaint, Alvin, and James P. Comer. *Raising Black Children*. Plume, 1993.

1361. Ramsey, P. G. "The Salience of Race in Young Children Growing Up in an All-White Community." *Journal of Educational Psychology* 83 (March 1991): 28-34.

1362. Rector, Robert. "Food Fight. How Hungry Are America's Children?" *Policy Review* No. 58 (Fall 1991): 38-43.

1363. Reed, Sally, and Craig R. Sautter. "Children of Poverty. The Status of 12 Million Young Americans." *Phi Delta Kappa Special Report* (June 1990).

1364. Rosenberg, M. L. and others. "The Emergence of Youth Suicide: An Epidemiologic Analysis and Public Health Perspective." *Annual Review of Public Health* 8 (1987): 417-440.

1365. Rowe, D. C. and others. "No More Than Skin Deep: Ethnic and Racial Similarity in Developmental Process." *Psychological Review* 101 (July 1994): 369-413.

1366. Schultz, Valerie. "Racism Rears Its Hateful Head in Kindergarten." *Los Angeles Times*, 8 February 1993. [A mother of a five-year old writes about her child's education in racism]

1367. Smith, Charlene L. "Children on Kansas Poor Farms: 1860- 1900." *Legal Studies Forum* 13 (Summer 1989): 239-266.

1368. Smith, Paul. *The Relation of Black and Jewish Students Living in the Residence Halls of a Multi-racial Midwestern University*. Ph.D. diss., Eden Theological Seminary, 1977.

1369. *Speaking of Kids: A National Survey of Children and Parents*. 1111 18th Street, NW, Suite 810, Washington, D.C. 20036: National Commission on Children, 1991.

1370. "Special Issue on Minority Children." *Child Development* 61 (April 1990).

1371. Spencer, Margaret B., and Carol Markstrom-Adams. "Identity Processes among Racial and Ethnic Minority Children in America." *Child Development* 61 (1990): 290-310.

1372. Terris, Daniel. "What Place Can There Be for me?" *Boston Globe Magazine*, 14 June 1987. [Amerasian children from Southeast Asia]

1373. Turner, Bobbie G. *An Analysis of Title IV of the Social Security Act of 1935- Aid to Dependent Children and Its Relationship to the Social-Economic Well-being of Black, Needy Children in America, 1935-1985*. Ph.D. diss., University of Pittsburgh, 1986. UMO # 8926479.

1374. Tuthill, Nancy M. "State Implementtion of the Indian Child Welfare Act. 1982 Report." *American Indian Law Newsletter* 16 (March-April 1983): 10-26.

1375. *Two Americas: Comparisons of U.S. Child Poverty in Rural, Inner City, and Suburban Areas*. 11 Curtis Ave., Medford, MA 02155: Center on Hunger, Poverty, and Nutrition Policy, 1994.

1376. Ugwu-Oju, Dympna. "Black and No Place to Hide." *New York Times*, 17 May 1992. [Effect on children]

1377. U.S. Congress, House of Representatives, Select Committee on Children, Youth and Families. *No Place to Call Home: Discarded Children in America*. Washington, D.C.: GPO, 1989.

1378. Washington, Valora. "Afro-American Children: A Bibliography." *Interchange* (December 1977).

1379. Werner, Emmy S., and Ruth S. Smith. *Overcoming the Odds. High Risk Children from Birth to Adulthood*. Ithaca, New York: Cornell University Press, 1992.

1380. White, Jack E. "Growing Up in Black and White." *Time* (17 May 1993). [Effect on children]

1381. Williams, Leon F. "The Challenge of Education to Social Work." *Social Work* 35 (May 1990): 236-242.

1382. Williams, Portia. "Beyond the Pale. Why My 'Too-Black' Friends Want Light-Skinned Babies." *Washington Post*, 25 April 1993.

1383. Wilson, James. "Reconstructing Section Five of the Fourteenth Amendment to Assist Impoverished Children." *Cleveland State Law Review* 38 (Summer 1990): 391-453.

1384. Wollons, Roberta, ed. *Children at Risk in America: History, Concepts, and Public Policy*. SUNY Press, 1993.

1385. Wrigley, Julia. "Different Care for Different Kids: Social Class and Child Care Policy." *Educational Policy* 3 (December 1989).

1386. Zigler, Edward. "Head Start Falls Behind." *New York Times*, 27 June 1992.

1387. _____. "Head Start, the Whole Story." *New York Times*, 24 July 1993.

1388. Zill, N., and C. C. Roberts. "Recent Trends in the Well- being of Children in the United Sttes and Their Implications for Public Policy." in *The Changing American Family and Public Policy*, ed. A. J. Cherlin. Washington, D.C.: Urban Institute Press, 1988.

CITIZENSHIP

1389. Alvarez Gonzalez, Jose J. "The Empire Strikes Out: Congressional Ruminations on the Citizenship Status of Puerto Ricans." *Harvard Journal on Legislation* 27 (Summer 1990): 309- 365.

1390. Anderson, Kristi. "Women and Citizenship in the 1920's." in *Women, Politics, and Change*, eds. Louise A. Tilly, and Patricia Gurin. : Russell Sage Foundation, 1990.

1391. Barbalet, J. M. *Citizenship*. Minneapolis: University of Minnesota Press, 1989.

1392. Bartholomew, Amy. "Democratic Citizenship, Social Rights and the 'Reflexive Continuation' of the Welfare State." *Studies in Political Economy* No. 42 (Autumn 1993): 141-156.

1393. Bernasconi, Robert. "The Constitution of the People: Frederick Douglass and the Dred Scott Decision." *Cardozo Law Review* 13 (December 1991): 1281-1296.

1394. Bodayla, Stephen D. "'Can An Indian Vote?'Elk v. Wilkins, A Setback for Indian Citizenship." *Nebraska History* 67 (1986): 372- 380.

1395. Bosch, Norma. "Reconstructing Female Citizenship: Minor v. Happersett." in *The Constitution, Law, and American Life*, Donald G. Nieman, ed. : University of Georgetown Press, 1992.

1396. Bredbenner, Candice D. *Toward Independent Citizenship: Married Women's Nationality Rights in the United States: 1855- 1937*. Ph.D. diss., University of Virginia, 1990. UMO # 9100825.

1397. Brock, Jacobus and others. "Citizenship." in *Prejudice, War and the Constitution*, : University of California Press, 1968.

1398. Brubaker, William R., ed. *Immigration and the Politics of Citizenship in Europe and North America*. Lanham, MD: University Press of America, 1989.

1399. Cabranes, Jose A. *Citizenship and Empire: A Legislative History of American Citizenship for Puerto Ricans*. New Haven, Conn.: Yale University Press, 1979.

1400. Calvert, Robert E., ed. *"The Constitution of the People": Reflections on Citizens and Civil Society*. University of Kansas Press, 1991.

1401. Calvo, Janet M. "Alien Status Restrictions on Eligibility for Federally Funded Assistance Programs." *New York University Review of Law and Social Change* 16 (June 1988): 395-432.

1402. Carter, Edward C. II. "Naturalization in Philadelphia, 1789-1806." *Proceedings of the American Philosophical Society* 133 (1989): 175-189.

1403. Collins, Donald E. *Native Aliens: Disloyalty and the Renunciation of Citizenship by Japanese Americans during World War II*. Westport,CT: Greenwood, 1985.

1404. Conover, P. J. and others. "The Nature of Citizenship in the United States and Great Britain: Empirical Comments on Theoretical Themes." *Journal of Politics* 53 (August 1991): 800- 834.

1405. Du Bois, W. E. B. "The Negro Citizen." in *The Negro in American Civilization*, Charles S. Johnson, ed. New York: Holt, 1930.

1406. Fendrich, James M. *Ideal Citizens: The Legacy of the Civil Rights Movement*. SUNY Press, 1993.

1407. Finger, John R. "Conscription, Citizenship, and 'Civilization': World War I and the Eastern Board of Cherokee." *North Carolina Historical Review* 63 (1986): 283-308.

1408. Flacks, D. "The Revolution of Citizenship." *Social Policy* 21 (Autumn 1990).

1409. Fraser, Nancy, and Linda Gordon. "Contract versus Charity. Why Is there No Social Citizenship in the United States." *Socialist Review* 22 (July-September 1992): 45-67.

1410. Garcia, Mario T. "Mexican Americans and the Politics of Citizenship: The Case of El Paso, 1936." *New Mexico Historical Review* 59 (1984): 187-204.

1411. _____. "Mexican Americans and the Politics of Citizenship: The Case of El Paso, 1936." *New Mexico Historical Review* 59 (April 1984): 187-204.

1412. Glasser, T. L. "Communication and the Cultivation of Citizenship." *Communication* 12 (1991): 235-248.

1413. Gordon, Charles. "The Racial Barrier to American Citizenship." *University of Pennsylvania Law Review* 93 (1945).

1414. Heisler, Barbara S. "A Comparative Perspective on the Underclass: Questions of Urban Poverty, Race and Citizenship." *Theory and Society* 20 (August 1991): 455-483.

1415. Heuterman, T. H. "'We Have the Same Rights as Other Citizens': Coverage of Yakima Valley Japanese Americans in the 'Missing Decades' of the 1920s and 1930s." *Journalism History* 14 (Winter 1987): 94-103.

1416. Hraba, Joseph. "Citizenship and Ethnicity: The American Case." *Politics and the Individual* 2 (1992): 99-112.

1417. Janoski, Thomas. "Conflicting Approaches to Citizenship Rights: The Passage of Active Labor Market Policy Legislation in West Germany and the United States from 1946-1985." *Comparative Social Research* 12 (1990): 209-238.

1418. Karst, Kenneth I. "Citizenship, Race, and Marginality." *William and Mary Law Review* 1-49 (Fall 1988).

1419. _____. "Equal Citizenship Under the Fourteenth Amendment." *Harvard Law Review* 91 (1977).

1420. Kerber, Linda K. "The Paradox of Women's Citizenship in the Early Republic." *American Historical Review* 97 (April 1992): 349- 378.

1421. King, Richard H. "Citizenship and Self-respect: The Experience of Politics in the Civil Rights Movement." *Journal of American Studies* 22 (April 988): 7-24.

1422. Leonardo, Micaela di. "White Lies Black Myths. Rape, Race, and the Black Underclass." *Village Voice*, 22 September 1992.

1423. Logsdon, Joseph. "Americans and Creoles in New Orleans: The Origins of Black Citizenship in the United States." *Amerikastudien/American Studies* 34 (1989): 187-202.

1424. Lothyan, Phillip E. "A Question of Citizenship." *Prologue* 21 (1989): 267-273. [Pacific northwest region]

1425. Mann, Michael. "Ruling Class Strategies and Citizenship." *Sociology* 21 (1987): 339-354.

1426. Manville, Philip B. *The Origins of Citizenship in Ancient Athens*. Princeton, NJ: Princeton University Press, 1990.

1427. Marston, Sallie A. "Who Are the People? Gender, Citizenship, and the Making of the American Nation." *Environment and Planning, D, Society and Space* 8 (December 1990): 449-458.

1428. Martin, Jill E. "Neither Fish, Flesh, Fowl, Nor Good Red Herring: The Citizenship Status of American Indians, 1830-1924." *Journal of the West* 29 (1990): 75-87.

1429. McGovney, D. O. "Race Discrimination in Naturalization." *Iowa Law Bulletin* 8 (1923): 129-211.

1430. Parsons, Talcott. "Full Citzenship for the Negro American? A Sociological Problem." *Daedalus* 94 (1965).

1431. Passalacqua, John L. A. de. "The Involuntary Loss of United States Citizenship of Puerto Ricans upon Accession to Independence by Puerto Rico." *Denver Journal of Internatinal Law and Policy* 19 (Fall 1990): 139-161.

1432. Pinceti, S. "Challenge to Citizenship: Latino Immigrants and Political Organizing in the Los Angeles Area." *Environment and Planning A* 26 (June 1994): 895-914.

1433. Player, Mack A. "Citizenship, Alienage, and Ethnic Origin: Discriminatioin in Employment under the Law of the United States." *Georgia Journal of International and Comparative Law* 20 (Spring 1990): 29-55.

1434. Przybyszewski, Linda C. A. *The Republic According to John Marshall Harlan: Race, Republicanism, and Citizenship.* Ph.D. diss., Stanford University, 1989. UMO # 9011562.

1435. Reisler, Mark. "Always the Laborer, Never the Citizen: Anglo Perceptions of the Mexican Immigrant During the 1920s." *Pacific Historical Review* 45 (May 1976): 231-254.

1436. Riesenberg, Peter. *Citizenship in the Western Tradition: Plato to Rousseau.* University of North Carolina Press, 1993.

1437. Rouse, Joy. *Rhetorics of Citizenship in Nineteenth Century America.* Ph.D. diss., Miami University, 1991. UMO # 9200976.

1438. Salvatore, Nick. "Some Thoughts on Class and Citizenship in America." in *In the Shadow of Liberty: Immigrants, Workers, and Citizens in the American Republic, 1880-1920*, Marianne Debouzy, ed. Saint Denis: Presses Universitaires de Vicennes, 1988.

1439. Sapiro, Virginia. "Women, Citizenship and Nationality: Immigration and Naturalization Policies in the United States." *Politics and Society* 13 (1984): 1-26.

1440. Schmid, Carol. "Social Class, Race, and the Extension of Citizenship: The English Working Class and the Southern Civil Rights Movements." *Comparative Social Research* 9 (1986): 27-46.

1441. Schuck, Peter H. "Membership in the Liberal Polity: The Devaluation of American Citizenship." *Georgetown Immigration Law Journal* 3 (Spring 1989): 1-18.

1442. Schuck, Peter H., and Rogers M. Smith. *Citizenship Without Consent: Illegal Aliens in the American Polity.* Yale University Press, 1985.

1443. Shklar, Judith N. *American Citizenship. The Quest for Inclusion.* Cambridge, MA: Harvard University Press, 1991.

1444. Slattery, Jim, and Howard Bauleke. "The Right to Govern Is Reserved to Citizens: Counting Undocumented Aliens in the Federal Census for Reapportionment Purposes." *Washburn Law Journal* 28 (Winter 1988): 227-237.

1445. Smith, Rogers M. "The Meaning of American Citizenship." *This Constitution* No.8 (1985): 12-18.

1446. _____. "One United People: Second-Class Female Citizenship and the American Quest for Community." *Yale Journal of Law and the Humanities* 1 (May 1989): 229-293.

1447. Spinner, Jeff. *The Boundaries of Citizenship: Race, Ethnicity, and Nationality in the Liberal State.* John Hopkins University Press, 1994.

1448. Stellings, Brande. "The Public Harm of Private Violence: Rape, Sex Discrimination and Citizenship." *Harvard Civil Rights- Civil Liberties Law Review* 28 (Winter 1993): 185-216.

1449. Stoskopf, Alan L., and Margot Stern Strom. *Choosing to Participate: A Critical Examination of Citizenship in American History.* Brookline, MA: Facing History and Ourselves National Foundation, 1990.

1450. Taylor, David. "Citizenship and Social Power." *CSP, Critical Social Policy* 9 (Autumn 1989): 19-31.

1451. Thorin, Elizabeth and others. "Measuring Knowledge of Citizenship Rights and Responsibilities." *Research in Developmental Disabilities* 9 (1988): 85-92. [On the part of mentally retarded persons]

1452. U.S. Congress, 79th, 1st session, House of Representatives, Committee on Immigration and Naturalization. *To Grant a Quota to Eastern Hemisphere Indians and To Make Them Racially Eligible for Naturalization.* G.P.O., 1945.

1453. Viadero, Debra. "School-Funding Cuts Close Off One Path to Citizenship." *Education Week* (31 March 1993).

1454. Winicki, Norine M. "The Denaturalization and Deportation of Nazi Criminals: Is it Constitutional?" *Loyola of Los Angeles International and Comparative Law Journal* (Winter 1989): 117-143.

1455. Woodruff, Nan E. "African-American Struggles for Citizenship in the Arkansas and Mississippi Deltas in the Age of Jim Crow." *Radical History Review* No. 55 (Winter 1993): 33-51.

1456. Yamashita, Robert C., and Peter Park. "The Politics of Race: The Open Door, Ozawa and the Case of the Japanese in America." *Review of Radical Political Economics* 17 (Fall 1985): 135-156.

1457. Yeatman, Anna. "Beyond Natural Right: The Conditions for Universal Citizenship." *Social Concept* 4 (June 1988).

CIVIL RIGHTS

1458. "25 Years After the Civil Rights Act of 1964: Special Section." *Ebony* (August 1989): 29-78.

1459. Abernathy, Ralph D. "The Natural History of a Social Movement: The Montgomery Improvement Association." Atlanta University, 1958. Masters's Thesis. Reprinted in David J. Garrow (ed.), *The Walking City: The Montgomery Bus Boycott, 1955-1956*, Brooklyn, NY: Carlson Publ. Inc.: 1990.

1460. Adelman, David C. "Strangers: Civil Rights of Jews in the Colony of Rhode Island." *Rhode Island History* (July 1954).

1461. Albert, Peter J., and Ronald Hoffman. *We Shall Overcome: Martin Luther King, Jr. and the Black Freedom Struggle*. New York: Pantheon, 1991.

1462. Alvarez-Gonzalez, Jose J. "The Protection of Civil Rights in Puerto Rico." *Arizona Journal of International and Comparative Law* 6 (Spring 1989): 88-134.

1463. Amaker, Norman C. "De Facto Leadership and the Civil Rights Movement: Perspective on the Problems and Role of Activists and Lawyers in Legal and Social Change." *Southern University Law Review* 16 (Spring 1989): 1-54.

1464. Ansley, Frances L. "Stirring the Ashes: Race, Class, and the Future of Civil Rights Scholarships." *Cornell Law Review* 74 (September 1989): 993-1077.

1465. Ashmore, Harry S. *Civil Rights and Wrongs: A Memoir of Race and Politics, 1944-1994*. Pantheon: 1994.

1466. Bains, Lee E. "Birmingham 1963: Confrontation Over Civil Rights." B.A. Honors Thesis, Harvard University, 1977. [Reprinted in David J. Garrow (ed.), *Birmingham, Alabama, 1956-1963: the Black Struggle for Civil Rights*. Brooklyn, NY: Carlson]

1467. Baithorpe, Robin B. "The Civil Rights Act of 1866: A Courageous Beginning." Master's Thesis, John Carroll University, 1988.

1468. Baker, Peter. "Voters Rebel in Richmond." *Washington Post*, 19 May 1994.

1469. Baldwin, Lewis V. "Malcolm X and Martin Luther King, Jr. and What They Thought about Each Other." *Islamic Studies* 25 (1986): 395-416.

1470. Barkan, Steven. "Legal Control of the Southern Civil Rights Movements." *American Sociological Review* 49 (August 1984): 525- 565.

1471. Barksdale, Marcellus C. "Robert F. Williams and the Indigenous Civil Rights Movement in Monroe, North Carolina, 1961." *Journal of Negro History* 69 (1984): 73-89.

1472. Barlow, Andrew. "Building Movements for Racial Equality after the Civil Rights Era: Rethinking Advocacy in the 1990's." *Sociological Abstracts* Supplement 167 (August 1991): 91 S24923/ ASA/1991/6282

1473. Beifuss, Joan T. *At the River I Stand: Memphis, the 1968 Strike, and Martin Luther King*. Brooklyn NY: Carlson Publishing, Inc., 1989. (orig. 1985).

1474. Belknap, Michal R., ed. *Civil Rights, the White House, and the Justice Department 1945-1968*. Hamden CT: Garland Publishing, 1991. 18 Volumes

1475. Bell, Derrick. "Foreword: The Final Civil Rights Act." *California Law Review* 79 (May 1991): 597-611.

1476. _____. "Remembrances of Racism Past: Getting Beyond the Civil Rights Decline." in *Race in America*, eds. Herbert Hill, and James E. Jones, Jr. University of Wisconsin Press, 1993.

1477. Benjamin, Lois. *The Color Line in the Twilight of the 20th Century: The Talented 100*. Chicago, IL: Nelson-Hall, 1990.

1478. Bernstein, David. "The Supreme Court and Civil Rights, 1886-1908." *Yale Law Journal* 100 (December 1990): 725-744.

1479. Bettis, P. J. and others. "It's Not Steps Anymore, But More Like Shuffling: Student Perceptions of the Civil Rights Movement and Ethnic Identity." *Journal of Negro Education* 63 (Spring 1994): 197-211.

1480. Bloch, Farrell. *Antidiscrimination Law and Minority Employment: Recruitment Practices and Regulatory Constraints*. University of Chicago Press, 1994.

1481. Blumberg, Rhonda L. "Women in the Civil Rights Movement: Reform or Revolution?" *Dialectical Anthropology* 15 (1990): 133- 139.

1482. Bok, Marcia. *Civil Rights and the Social Programs of the 1960's: The Social Justice Functions of Social Policy*. Praeger, 1992.

1483. Bolick, Clint. *Changing Course: Civil Rights at the Crossroads*. New Brunswick, NJ: Transaction, 1988.

1484. Bond, Julian. "Reconstruction and the Southern Movement for Civil Rights-Then and Now." *Teachers College Record* 93 (Winter 1991): 221-235.

1485. Boxill, Bernard R. "Is Civil Rights Legislation Irrelevant to Black Progress?" in *Race: Twentieth-Century Dilemmas-Twenty- First-Century Prognoses*, eds. Winston A. VanHorne, and Thomas V. Tonneson. Milwaukee, WI: Institute on Race and Ethnicity, University of Wisconsin, 1989.

1486. Bracey, John H., Jr. "The Black Community and Civil Rights." in *The Study of American History*, pp. 482-509. ed. J. T. Chase. : Dushkin Publishing Group, 1974.

1487. Braeman, John. *Before the Civil Rights Revolution: The Old Court and Individual Rights*. Westport, CT: Greenwood Press, 1988.

1488. Bridges, Roger. "Equality Deferred: Civil Rights for Illinois Blacks, 1865-1885." *Journal of the Illinois State Historical Society* 74 (Spring 1981).

1489. Brownstein, Ronald. "Key Civil Rights Post Left Empty as Search Falters." *Los Angeles Times*, 22 May 1994. [Chairman of the Equal Employment Opportunity Commission]

1490. Bryan, Dianetta G. "Her-Story Unsilenced: Black Female Activists in the Civil Rights Movement." *Sage* 5 (Fall 1988): 60- 64.

1491. Burk, Robert F. "Dwight D. Eisenhower and Civil Rights: Reflections On a Portrait in Caution." *Kansas History* 13 (1990): 178-89.

1492. Burner, Eric R. *And Gently He Shall Lead Them: Robert Parris Moses and Civil Rights in Mississippi*. New York, NY: New York University Press, 1994.

1493. Burns, Haywood. "A Late Spring." *Rights* (April-June 1993). [A celebration of Thomas Paine and Civil Rights]

1494. Burns, James MacGregor, and Stewart Burns. *The Pursuit of Rights in America*. NY: Knopf, 1992.

1495. Burns, Stewart. "Martin Luther King, Jr.'s Empowering Legacy." *Tikkun* 8 (March-April 1993): 49-53, 67-68.

1496. Butler, Richard J. and others. "The Impact of the Economy and State on the Economic Status of Blacks." in *Markets in History*, ed. David W. Galenson. NY: Cambridge University Press, 1989.

1497. Button, James W. *Blacks and Social Change: Impact of the Civil Rights Movement in Southern Communities*. Princeton, NJ: Princeton University Press, 1989.

1498. Button, James W., and Richard K. Scher. "Impact of the Civil Rights Movement: Perceptions of Black Municipal Service Changes." *Social Science Quarterly* 60 (December 1979): 497-510.

1499. Carson, Clayborne. "Civil Rights Reform and the Black Freedom Struggle." in *The Civil Rights Movement in America*, ed. Charles W. Eagles. Jackson, MI, 1986.

1500. Carson, Clayborne and others, eds. *The Eyes on the Prize Civil Rights Reader: Documents, Speeches, and Firsthand Accounts from the Black Freedom Struggle, 1954-1990*. Penguin, USA, 1991.

1501. Carson, Clayborne. *A Guide to Research on Martin Luther King, Jr. and the Modern Black Freedom Struggle*. Stanford, CA: 1989.

1502. Carson, Clayborne, ed. *The Movement 1964-1970*. Greenwood: 1993.

1503. _____. *The Student Voice, 1960-1965: Periodical of the Student Nonviolent Coordinating Committee*. Westport, CT: Meckler, 1990.

1504. Carter, G. L. "Hispanic Rioting During the Civil Rights Era." *Sociological Forum* 7 (June 1992): 301-322.

1505. Carter, Robert Lee. "The Federal Rules of Civil Procedure as a Vindicator of Civil Rights." *University of Pennsylvania Law Review* 137 (June 1989): 2179-2196.

1506. Cashman, Sean D. *African-Americans and the Quest for Civil Rights*. New York: U.P., 1992.

1507. Chambers, Julius L. "Brown v. Board of Education." in *Race in America*, eds. Herbert Hill, and James E. Jones, Jr. University of Wisconsin Press, 1993.

1508. _____. "Twenty-five Years of the Civil Rights Act: History and Promise." *Wake Forest Law Review* 25 (Summer 1990): 159-195.

1509. Chandler, Robert J. "Friends in Time of Need: Republicans and Black Civil Rights in California during the Civil War Era." *Arizona and the West* 24 (Winter 1982): 319-340.

1510. Chappell, David L. *Inside Agitators: White Southerners in the Civil Rights Movement*. Johns Hopkins University Press: 1994. [Montgomery, AL and Albany GA]

1511. Chong, Dennis. "All-or-Nothing Games in the Civil Rights Movement." *Social Science Information* 30 (December 1991): 677- 698.

1512. _____. *Collective Action and the Civil Rights Movement*. Chicago, IL: University of Chicago Press, 1991.

1513. Citizens' Commission on Civil Rights. *Lost Opportunities: The Civil Rights Record of the Bush Administration Mid-Term, 1991*. The Commission, 2000 M St., NW, Suite 400, Washington DC, 20036:

1514. *Civil Right Issues in Arkansas*. Washington DC: U.S. Commission on Civil Rights, 1989.

1515. "The Civil Rights Act of 1990." *Record of the Association of the Bar of the City of New York* 45 (May 1990): 430-477.

1516. "The Civil Rights Act of 1991." *Employee Relations Law Journal* 17 (Spring 1992): six articles.

1517. "The Civil Rights Act of 1991: Unraveling the Controversy." *Rutgers Law Review* 45 (Summer 1993): six articles.

1518. *Civil Rights Enforcement in Vermont*. Washington DC: U.S. Commission on Civil Rights, 1987.

1519. *Civil Rights Issues in Birmingham*. Washington DC: U.S. Commission on Civil Rights, 1988.

1520. *Civil Rights Issues in Wyoming*. Washington DC: U.S. Commission on Civil Rights, 1988.

1521. *Civil Rights Issues in Kentucky*. Washington DC: U.S. Commission on Civil Rights, 1989.

1522. "Civil Rights Legislation in the 1990's." *California Law Review* 79 (May 1991): 597-805. (six articles)

1523. Clark, Benjamin F., Sr. *The Editorial Reaction of Selected Black Newspapers to the Civil Rights Movement, 1954-1968.* 1989. UMO #9006612.

1524. Clark, Leroy D. "The Future Civil Rights Agenda: Speculation on Litigation, Legislation, and Organization." *Catholic University Law Review* 38 (Summer 1989): 795-846.

1525. Cobb, James C. "Somebody Done Nailed Us on the Cross: Federal Farm and Welfare Policy and the Civil Rights Movement in the Mississippi Delta." *Journal of American History* 77 (1990): 912-936.

1526. Colburn, David R. *Racial Change and Community Crisis: St. Augustine, Florida, 1877-1980.* New York: Columbia University Press.

1527. Cornelius, Janet D. "Civil Rights in Illinois." *Illinois History* 42 (March 1989): 101-120.

1528. Couto, Richard A. *Ain't Gonna Let Nobody Turn Me Around: The Pursuit of Racial Justice in the Rural South.* Temple University Press, 1991.

1529. Crawford, Vicki L. "Grassroots Activists in the Mississippi Civil Rights Movements." *Sage* 5 (Fall 1988): 24-29.

1530. Davidson, Chandler, and Bernard Grofman, eds. *Quiet Revolution in the South: The Impact of the Voting Rights Act, 1965-1990.* Princeton University Press: 1994.

1531. Dees, Morris, and Steve Fiffer. *A Season for Justice: The Life and Times of Civil Rights Lawyer Morris Dees.* New York: Scribner's, 1991.

1532. Delgado, Richard. "On Taking Back Our Civil Rights Promises: When Equality Doesn't Compute." *Wisconsin Law Review* (May-June 1989): 579-587.

1533. Detlefsen, Robert R. *Civil Rights Under Reagan.* San Francisco, CA: Institute for Contemporary Studies, 1991.

1534. _____. *Triumph of the Race-Conscious State: The Politics of Civil Rights, 1980-86.* 1988. UMO #8902074.

1535. Dittmer, John. *Local People: The Struggle for Civil Rights in Mississippi.* University of Illinois Press: 1994.

1536. Donohue, John, Jr. III. "The Impact of Federal Civil Rights Policy on the Economic Status of Blacks." *Harvard Journal of Law and Public Policy* 14 (Winter 1991): 41-52.

1537. Donohue, John, Jr. III, and James J. Heckman. "Continuous versus Episodic Change: The Impact of Civil Rights Policy on the Economic Status of Blacks." *Journal of Economic Literature* 29 (December 1991): 1603-1643.

1538. Draper, Alan. *Conflict of Interests: Organized Labor and the Civil Rights Movement in the South 1954-1968.* ILR Press: 1994.

1539. Dudziak, Mary L. *Cold War Civil Rights: The Relationship between Civil Rights and Foreign Affairs in the Truman Administration.* Ph.D. diss., Yale University, 1992. UMO #9314801.

1540. Duke, Lynne. "A New Challenge Faces an Evolving Black Leadership." *Washington Post*, 28 August 1993.

1541. Dulaney, W. Marvin, and Kathleen Underwood, eds. *Essays on the American Civil Rights Movement.* Texas A + M University Press: 1993.

1542. Epstein, Richard A. "Two Conceptions of Civil Rights." *Social Philosophy and Policy* 8 (Spring 1991): 38-59.

1543. Eskew, Glenn T. *But for Birmingham: The Local and National Movement in the Civil Rights Struggle.* 1993. UMO #9320687.

1544. Farmer, James, [Interview] *Boston Globe Magazine*, 19 January 1991.

1545. Filippatos, Parisis. "The Doctrine of Stare Decisis and the Protection of Civil Rights and Liberties in the Rehnquist Court." *Boston College Third World Law Journal* 11 (Summer 1991): 335-377.

1546. Finkelman, Paul R. "The Protection of Black Rights in Seward's New York." *Civil War History* 34 (September 1988): 211- 234. [Pre-Civil War]

1547. Fiss, Owen. "Groups and the Equal Protection Clause." *Philosophy and Public Affairs* 5 (1976).

1548. Flanders, Todd R. *A Civil Rights Crucible: Martin Luther King, Jr.'s Enigmatic Albany, Georgia Campaign*. Kirksville: Master's Thesis, Northeast Missouri State University, 1988.

1549. Fleming, Cynthia G. "Black Women Activists and the Student Non-violent Coordinating Committee: The Case of Ruby Doris Smith Robinson." *Journal of Women's History* 4 (Winter 1993): 64-83.

1550. _____. "White Lunch Counters and Black Consciousness: The Story of the Knoxville Sit-ins." *Tennessee Historical Quarterly* 49 (Spring 1990): 40-52.

1551. Flug, Michael. "Organized Labor and the Civil Rights Movement of the 1960's: The Case of the Maryland Freedom Union." *Labor History* 31 (Summer 1990).

1552. Fort, Vincent D. *The Atlanta Sit-in Movement, 1960-61: An Oral Study*. Master's Thesis, Atlanta University, 1980, [Reprinted in David J. Garrow (ed.), *Atlanta, Georgia, 1960-1961: Sit-ins and Student Activism*. Brooklyn NY: Carlson Publ. Inc. 1990]

1553. Freilich, Robert H. and others. "Reagan's Legacy: A Conservative Majority Rules on Civil Rights, Civil Liberties, and State and Local Government Issues." *Urban Lawyer* 21 (Fall 1989): 633-731.

1554. Galst, Liz. "Voting With the Enemy. Why Some Blacks Oppose Gay Rights." *Village Voice* (14 December 1993).

1555. Garrow, David J., ed. *Atlanta, Georgia, 1960-1961. Sit-Ins and Student Activism*. Brooklyn, NY: Carlson Publishing, Inc., 1990.

1556. _____. *Birmingham, Alabama, 1956-1963. The Black Struggle for Civil Rights*. Brooklyn, NY: Carlson Publishing, Inc., 1990.

1557. _____. *Chicago 1966. Open Housing Marches, Summit Negotiations, and Operation Breadbasket*. Brooklyn, NY: Carlson Publishing, Inc., 1990.

1558. _____. *St. Augustine, Florida, 1963-1964. Mass Protest and Racial Violence*. Brooklyn, NY: Carlson Publishing, Inc., 1990.

1559. _____. *The Walking City. The Montgomery Bus Boycott, 1955-1956*. Brooklyn, NY: Carlson Publishing, Inc., 1990.

1560. _____. *We Shall Overcome. The Civil Rights Movement in the United States in the 1950's and 1960's*. Brooklyn, NY: Carlson Publishing, Inc., 1990. 3 vols.

1561. George, R. P. "Natural Law and Civil Rights: From Jefferson's 'Letter to Henry Lee' to Martin Luther King's 'Letter from Birmingham Jail'." *Catholic University Law Review* 43 (Autumn 1993): 143-158.

1562. Glennon, Robert J. "The Role of Law in the Civil Rights Movement: The Montgomery Bus Boycott." *Law and History Review* 9 (Spring 1991): 59-112.

1563. Goering, John, and Steven J. Sachs. "Civil Rights Enforcement in a Federalist System: An Analysis of Policy Formation and Implementation." in *Public Policy Across States and Communities*, ed. Dennis R. Judd. Greenwich, CT: JAI Press, 1985.

1564. Goldfield, David R. *Black, White, and Southern: Race Relations and Southern Culture, 1940 to the Present*. Baton Rouge: Louisiana State University Press, 1990.

1565. Govan, Reginald C. "Honorable Compromises and the Moral High Ground: The Conflict Between the Rhetoric and the Content of the Civil Rights Act of 1991." *Rutgers Law Review* 46 (Autumn 1993): 1-242.

1566. Govan, Reginald C., and William L. Taylor. *One Nation Indivisible: The Civil Rights Challenge for the 1990's*. Washington, DC: Citizens' Commission on Civil Rights, 1990.

1567. Graham, Hugh D. *The Civil Rights Era. Origins and Development of National Policy*. New York: Oxford University Press, 1990.

1568. Grossman, Joel P., and Charles R. Epp. "The Reality of Rights in an 'Atolerant' Society." *This Constitution* no. 19 (Fall 1991): 20-28.

1569. Gyant, LaVerne. *Contributions of African-American Women to Nonformal Education during the Civil Rights Movement, 1955-1965*. Ph.D. diss., Pennsylvania State University, 1990, UMO #9111336.

1570. Hagen, Susan M. "Fannie Lou Hamer and SNCC's Mississippi Campaign for Civil Rights, 1962-1964." Master's Thesis, University of Calgary, 1989.

1571. Haines, Herbert H. *Black Radicals and the Civil Rights Mainstream, 1954-1970*. Knoxville: University of Tennessee Press, 1988.

1572. Hall, Kermit L., ed. *Civil Rights in American History: Major Historical Interpretations*. New York: Garland, 1987.

1573. Hampton, Henry, Steve Fayer, and Sarah Flynn. *Voices of Freedom: An Oral History of the Civil Rights Movement From the 1950's through the 1980's*. New York: Bantam Books, 1990.

1574. Harding, Vincent. *Hope and History: Why We Must Share the Story of the Movement*. Maryknoll, NY: Orbis Books, 1991.

1575. Harris, Clarissa M. *Miror of the Movement: The History of the Free Southern Theatre as a Microcosm of the Civil Rights and Black Power Movements, 1963-1978*. Ph.D. diss., Emory University, 1988. UMO #8827899.

1576. Hemeryck, Sondra and others. "Reconstruction, Deconstruction and Legislative Response: The 1988 Supreme Court Term and the Civil Rights Act of 1990." *Harvard Civil Rights- Civil Liberties Law Review* 25 (Summer 1990): 475-590.

1577. Henderson, Jacquie. "Mass Movement Dismantled Jim Crow Segregation." *Militant* (12 March 1993).

1578. Herring, Cedric. "Do Blacks Still Support Civil Rights Leaders?" *Sociology and Social Research* 72 (January 1988): 87-90.

1579. Holmes, Steven A. "In Fighting Racism, Is Sexism Ignored?" *New York Times*, 11 September 1994. [Absence of women in leadership of NAACP and other civil-rights groups]

1580. Honey, Michael. "Labour Leadership and Civil Rights in the South: A Case Study of the CIO in Memphis, 1935-1955." *Studies in History and Politics* 5 (1986): 97-120.

1581. Horton, Aimee L. *The Highlander Folk School: A History of Its Major Programs, 1932-1961*. Brooklyn, NY: Carlson Publishing, Inc., 1990.

1582. Irons, Peter. "New Deal Symposium: Politics and Principle: An Assessment of the Roosevelt Record on Civil Rights and Liberties." *Washington Law Review* 59 (1984).

1583. Jaschick, Scott. "New Focus on Civil Rights. An Aggressive Education Dept. Goes After Colleges for Violating Anti-Bias Laws." *Chronicle of Higher Education* (22 June 1994).

1584. _____. "A New Philosophy and New Style at the Office for Civil Rights." *Chronicle of Higher Education* (14 July 1993): Norma V. Cantu, head of OCR

1585. Jones, Nathaniel R. "Civil Rights after Brown: 'The Stormy Road We Trod'." in *Race in America*, Herbert Hill, and James E. Jones, Jr., eds. University of Wisconsin Press, 1993.

1586. Kaczorowski, Robert J. "The Enforcement Provisions of the Civil Rights Act of 1866: A Legislative History in Light of Runyon v. McCrary." *Yale Law Journal* 98 (January 1989): 565-595.

1587. _____. *The Nationalization of Civil Rights: Constitutional Theory and Practice in a Racist Society, 1866- 1883*. New York: Garland, 1989.

1588. Kelleher, Richard V. "The Black Struggle for Political and Civil Rights in Broward County, 1943-1989." Master's Thesis, Florida Atlantic University, 1989.

1589. Kilbaner, Irwin. *Conscience of a Troubled South. The Southern Conference Educational Fund, 1946-1966.* Brooklyn, NY: Carlson Publishing, Inc., 1990.

1590. King, A. G., and R. Marshall. "Black-White Economic Convergence and the Civil Rights Act of 1964." *Labor Law Review* 25 (1974): 462-471.

1591. King, Martin Luther, Jr. "The Role of the Behavioral Scientist in the Civil Rights Movement." *American Psychologist* (March 1968): 180-186.

1592. King, Richard H. *Civil Rights and the Idea of Freedom.* Oxford University Press: 1992.

1593. Kornbluh, Felicia. "Taken for a Ride by '60's Nostalgia." *In These Times* (2 August 1989). [June 1989 caravan from NYC to Philadelphia, MS and back to NYC, commemorating 1964 murders of three civil rights activists.]

1594. Kornbluh, Jesse. "The Struggle Continues." *New York Times Magazine* (23 July 1989). [Civil Rights in Mississippi since the 1964 murders of three civil rights workers]

1595. Kosof, Anna. *The Civil Rights Movement and Its Legacy.* New York: Watts, 1989.

1596. Lacy, Michael G. *Toward a Rhetorical Conception of Civil Racism.* Ph.D. diss., University of Texas, 1992. UMO #9239293.

1597. Lave, James H. *Direct Action and Desegregation, 1960-1962. Toward a Theory of the Rationalization of Protest.* Brooklyn, NY: Carlson Publishing, Inc., 1990.

1598. Lawson, Steven F. "Freedom Then, Freedom Now: The Historiography of the Civil Rights Movement." *American Historical Review* 96 (April 1991): 456-471. [Review of literature on subject]

1599. Leahy, E. Molly. "The National Symbol of Contempt for Civil Rights. United States v. Yonkers Board of Education, 837 F.2d 1181." *Hamline Journal of Public Law and Policy* 10 (Fall 1989): 441-456.

1600. Levine, Ellen. *Freedom's Children. Young Civil Rights Activists Tell Their Own Stories.* S.P. Putnam: 1993. [Written for children 12 years and up]

1601. Levy, Leonard W. and others, eds. *Civil Rights and Equality: Selections from the Encyclopedia of the American Constitution.* New York: MacMillan, 1989.

1602. Levy, Peter B., ed. *Documentary History of the Modern Civil Rights Movement.* Westport, CT: Greenwood, 1992.

1603. Levy, Peter B. "Teaching the History of the Modern Civil Rights Movement." *Perspectives (American Historical Association)* (October 1991): 20-22.

1604. Lewis, David Levering. *The Civil Rights Movement in America.* Jackson, MS: 1986.

1605. Liffmann, Karla L. "Civil Rights-Discrimination in Private Clubs." *Illinois Bar Journal* 77 (November 1989): 830.

1606. Limas, Vicki J. "Employment Suits Against Indian Tribes: Balancing Sovereign Rights and Civil Rights." *Denver University Law Review* 70 (1993): 359-392.

1607. Ling, Peter. "Dusk and Dawn: Black Protest in the Fifties and Forties." in *Cracking the Age,* ed. Dale Carter. Aarhus University Press, 1992.

1608. Liss, Susan M., and William L. Taylor, eds. *New Opportunities: Civil Rights at a Crossroads.* Citizens Commission on Civil Rights, 2000 M Street, NW, Suite 400, Wash., D.C. 20036: 1993.

1609. Loevy, Robert D. *To End All Segregation: The Politics of the Passage of the Civil Rights Act of 1964.* Lanham, MD: University Press of America, 1990.

1610. Lowery, Charles D., and John F. Marszalek, eds. *Encyclopedia of African-American Civil Rights From Emancipation to the Present.* Greenwood: 1992.

1611. Lyman, Stanford M. "Race Relations as Social Process: Sociology's Resistance to a Civil Rights Orientation." in *Race in America*, eds. Herbert Hill, and James E. Jones, Jr. University of Wisconsin Press, 1993.

1612. Lyon, Danny. *Memories of the Southern Civil Rights Movement*. University of North Carolina Press: 1992.

1613. Mainwaring, Wm. T., Jr. *Community in Danville, Virginia, 1880-1963*. Ph.D. diss., University of North Carolina at Chapel Hill, 1988. UMO #8905667.

1614. Maltz, Earl M. *Civil Rights, the Constitution, and Congress, 1863-1869*. Lawrence: University Press of Kansas, 1990.

1615. Marable, Manning. *Race, Reform and Rebellion: The Second Reconstruction in Black America, 1945-1990*. 2nd ed. Jackson: University Press of Mississippi, 1991.

1616. Marable, Manning, and Leith Mullings. "The Divided Mind of Black America: Race, Ideology and Politics in the Post Civil Rights Era." *Race and Class* 36 (July-September 1994): 61-72.

1617. Marshall, Thurgood. "The View from Inside." *Bill of Rights Journal* 22 (December 1989): 1.

1618. Marwell, Gerald and others. "The Persistence of Political Attitudes among 1960's Civil Rights Activists." *Public Opinion Quarterly* 51 (Fall 1987): 359-375.

1619. Mayer, Michael S. "The Eisenhower Administration and the Civil Rights Act of 1957." *Congress and the Presidency* 16 (1989): 137-154.

1620. McAdam, Douglas. "The Decline of the Civil Rights Movement." in *The Social Movements of the 1960's and 1970's*, pp. 279-319. ed. Jo Freeman. New York: Longman, 1983.

1621. _____. "Gender as a Mediator of the Activist Experience: The Case of Freedom Summer." *American Journal of Sociology* 97 (March 1992): 1211-1240.

1622. McAlpine, Robert and others. "Civil Rights and Social Justice: From Progress to Regress." in *Black Americans and Public Policy: Perspectives of the National Urban League*, New York: National Urban League, 1988.

1623. McCoy, Donald. *Quest and Response: Minority Rights and the Truman Administration*. Lawrence: University of Kansas Press, 1973.

1624. McDevitt, Jack. *The Study of the Implementation of the Massachusetts Civil Rights Act*. Boston, MA: Center for Applied Social Research, Northeastern University, 1989.

1625. McDougall, Harold A. "Jesse Jackson and the New Civil Rights Movement." *Mississippi College Law Review* 9 (Fall 1988): 155-165.

1626. McGrane, Donald J., and Richard J. Hardy. "Civil Rights Policies and the Achievement of Racial Economic Equality." *American Journal of Political Science* 22 (February 1978): 1-17.

1627. Meier, August. "Toward a Synthesis of Civil Rights History." in *New Directions in Civil Rights Studies*, eds. Armstead L. Robinson, and Patricia Sullivan. University Press of Virginia, 1991.

1628. Miller, C. M., and Walton Hanes, Jr. "Congressional Support of Civil Rights Public Policy: From Bipartisan to Partisan Convergence." *Congress and the Presidency* 21 (Spring 1994): 11- 28.

1629. Mills, Nicolaus. *Like a Holy Crusade-Mississippi 1964-The Turning of the Civil Rights Movement in America*. Ivan R. Dee: 1992.

1630. Milner, Neal. "The Denigration of Rights and the Persistence of Rights Talk: A Cultural Portrait." *Law and Social Inquiry* 14 (Fall 1989): 631-675.

1631. *Minds Stayed on Freedom. The Civil Rights Struggle in the Rural South*. Boulder, CO: Westview, 1991.

1632. Moore, Charles. *Powerful Days. The Civil Rights Photography of Charles Moore*. Stewart, Tabori, and Chang: 1991.

1633. Motley, Constance Baker. "The Supreme Court, Civil Rights Litigation, and Deja Vu." *Cornell Law Review* 76 (March 1991): 643-655.

1634. Munk, Erika. "Mississippi Yearning. You Can't Go Home Again." *Village Voice* (18 July 1989). [25th anniversary of killing of James Cheney, Michael Schwerner, and Andrew Goodman]

1635. Nelson, William E., Jr., and Michael S. Bailey. "The Weakening of State Participation in Civil Rights Enforcement." in *Public Policy Across States and Communities*, ed. Dennis R. Judd. Greenwich, CT: JAI Press, 1985.

1636. Norman, Mary Ann. "Civil Rights in Colorado: An Examination of Five Cases." *Journal of the West* 25 (1986): 38-43.

1637. Nossiter, Adam. *Of Long Memory. Mississippi and the Murder of Medgar Evans*. Addison-Wesley: 1994.

1638. Nye, M. A. "Changing Support for Civil Rights: House and Senate Voting 1963-1988." *Political Research Quarterly* 46 (December 1993): 799-822.

1639. _____. "The United States Senate and Civil Rights Roll- call Votes." *Western Political Quarterly* 44 (December 1991): 971- 986.

1640. O'Connor, Karen. "The Impact of the Civil Rights Movement on the Women's Movement." *Update on Law-Related Education* 12 (Fall 1988).

1641. O'Hanlon, Ann. "Grass Roots and Glass Ceilings." *Washington Post*, 18 April 1993. [Lack of women at head of national civil rights organizations]

1642. Oppenheimer, Martin. *The Sit-In Movement of 1960*. Brooklyn, NY: Carlson Publishing, Inc., 1990.

1643. Orozco, Cynthia E. *The Origins of the League of United Latin American Citizens (LULAC) and the Mexican-American Civil Rights Movement in Texas With an Analysis of Women's Political Participation in a Gendered Context, 1910-1929*. Ph.D. diss., UCLA, 1992. UMO #9302444.

1644. Pachon, Harry. "Crossing the Border of Discrimination: Has the Civil Rights Movement Ignored Generations of Hispanics?" *Human Rights* 15 (Fall 1988).

1645. Payne, Charles. "Ella Baker and Models of Social Change." *Signs* 14 (Summer 1989): 885-899.

1646. Pear, Robert. "With [Civil] Rights Act Comes Fight to Clarify Congress's Intent." *New York Times*, 18 November 1991. [Civil Rights Act of 1991]

1647. Pfeffer, Paula F. *A. Philip Randolph, Pioneer of the Civil Rights Movement*. Baton Rouge: Louisiana State University Press, 1990.

1648. Pinderhughes, Dianne M. "Civil Rights Movement." *Black Women in America* I 239-241.

1649. Powledge, Fred. "Civil Rights: A Backward March." *Boston Globe*, 4 August 1991.

1650. _____. *Free At Last? The Civil Rights Movement and the People Who Made It*. Boston, MA: Little, Brown, 1991.

1651. Ralph, James R., Jr. *Northern Protest. Martin Luther King Jr., Chicago, and the Civil Rights Movement*. Harvard University Press, 1993.

1652. _____. *Northern Protest: Martin Luther King, Jr., Chicago, and the Civil Rights Movement*. Ph.D. diss., Harvard University, 1990. UMO #9035541.

1653. Reed-Mundell, C. A. "Days of Defiance." *Free Times (Cleveland, Ohio)* 2 (April 6-12, 1994). [The death on April 7, 1964 of Rev. Bruce W. Klunder, a civil rights demonstrator against school segregation in Cleveland]

1654. Riker, William H. "Civil Rights and Property Rights." in *Liberty, Property, and the Future of Constitutional Development*, eds. Ellen F. Paul, and Howard Dickman. SUNY Press, 1990.

1655. Robinson, Armstead L., and Patricia Sullivan, eds. *New Directions in Civil Rights Studies*. Charlottesville: University Press of Virginia, 1991.

1656. Robnett, Belinda. *African-American Women in Southern-based Civil Rights Movement Organizations, 1954-1965: Gender, Grass Roots Leadership, and Resource Mobilization Theory*. Ph.D. diss., University of Michigan, 1991. UMO #9208635.

1657. _____. "African-American Women in Southern-based Civil Rights Movement Organizations, 1954-1965: Gender and 'Behind-the- Scenes Leadership'." *Sociological Abstracts* supplement 167 (August 1991) 91S25388/ASA/1991/6747.

1658. "The Rodney King Trials: Civil Rights Prosecutions and Double Jeopardy." *UCLA Law Review* 41 (February 1994): 4 articles.

1659. Rogers, Kim Lacy. *Righteous Lives: Narratives of the New Orleans Civil Rights Movement.* New York University Press: 1993. [1950's and 1960's]

1660. Romo, Ricardo. "Southern California and the Origins of Latino Civil-rights Activism." *Western Legal History* 3 (Summer- Fall 1990): 379-406.

1661. Ryce, Drew M. "Enforcement of Indian Civil Rights." *Rutgers Law Review* 37 (Summer 1985): 1019-1033.

1662. Salmond, John A. *The Conscience of a Lawyer: Clifford J. Durr and American Civil Liberties, 1899-1975.* Tuscaloosa: University of Alabama Press, 1990.

1663. Salter, John R., Jr. *Jackson, Mississippi: An American Chronicle of Struggle and Schism.* Malabar, FL: R.E. Krieger, 1987. (orig. pub. 1979).

1664. Sanger, Kerran L. *The Rhetoric of the Freedom Songs in the American Civil Rights Movement.* Ph.D. diss., Pennslyvania State University, 1991. UMO #9204283.

1665. Schultz, Jon S. *Legislative History and Analysis of the Civil Rights Restoration Act [of 1987].* Littleton, CO: F.B. Rothman, 1989.

1666. Setser, Gregorio. *La violacion de los derechos humanos en los Estados Unidos.* Mexico City, Mexico: Editorial Mestiza, 1989.

1667. Shapiro, Walter. "The Glory and the Glitz." *Time* (5 August 1991). [National Civil Rights Museum, Memphis, TN]

1668. Shull, Steven A. *A Kinder, Gentler Racism? The Reagan-Bush Civil Rights Legacy.* Sharpe: 1993.

1669. Sigelman, Lee, and J.S. Todd. "Clarence Thomas, Black Pluralism, and Civil Rights Policy." *Political Science Quarterly* 107 (Summer 1992): 231-248.

1670. Sims, Calvin. "N.A.A.C.P. Revises the Prize." *New York Times*, 31 August 1993. [Economic rights as civil rights]

1671. Skotnes, Andor D. *The Black Freedom Movement and the Workers' Movement in Baltimore, 1930-1939.* Ph.D. diss., Rutgers University, 1991. UMO #9200274.

1672. Smith, Charles U., and Lewis M. Killian. "Sociological Foundations of the Civil Rights Movement." in *Sociology in America*, ed. Herbert J. Gans. Newbury Park, CA: Sage, 1990.

1673. Sowell, Thomas. *Civil Rights: Rhetoric or Reality?* New York: Morrow, 1984.

1674. "Special Report: Civil Rights Act of 1991." *Human Rights* 19 (Summer 1992): 4 articles.

1675. Spivack, John M. *Race, Civil Rights, and the United States Court of Appeals for the Fifth Judicial Court.* New York: Garland, 1990.

1676. Squires, Gregory D. "Economic Restoration, Urban Development and Race: The Political Economy of Civil Rights in 'Post Industrial' America: A Review Essay." *Western Political Quarterly* 43 (1990): 201-217.

1677. Staples, Brent. "The End of 'the Movement'." *New York Times*, 4 September 1994.

1678. *The Status of Civil Rights in Louisiana.* Washington D.C.: U.S. Commission on Civil Rights, 1988.

1679. Stefan, S. "Leaving Civil Rights to the 'Experts': From Deference to Abdication under the Professional Judgment Standard." *Yale Law Journal* 102 (December 1992).

1680. Steinberg, Stephen. "Et Tu Brute: The Liberal Betrayal of the Black Liberation Struggle." *Reconstruction* 2 (1992).

1681. Steinkraus, Warren E. "The Dangerous Ideas of Martin Luther King." *Scottish Journal of Religious Studies* 6 (1985): 16-25.

1682. Stern, Mark. *Calculating Visions: Kennedy, Johnson, and Civil Rights*. New Brunswick, NJ: Rutgers University Press, 1992.

1683. _____. "Lyndon Johnson and the Democrats' Civil Rights Strategy." *Humboldt Journal of Social Relations* 16 (1990): 1-29.

1684. _____. "Presidential Strategies and Civil Rights: Eisenhower, the Early Years, 1952-54." *Presidential Studies Quarterly* 19 (1989): 769-795.

1685. Stone, Robert B. *The Legislative Struggle for Civil Rights in Iowa: 1947-1965*. Ames: Master's Thesis, Iowa State University, 1990.

1686. Stoper, Emily. *The Student Nonviolent Coordinating Committee. The Growth of Radicalism in a Civil Rights Organization*. Brooklyn, NY: Carlson Publishing, Inc., 1990.

1687. Sunstein, Cass R. "Three Civil Rights Fallacies." *California Law Review* 79 (May 1991): 751-774.

1688. *Texas: The State of Civil Rights: Ten Years Later, 1968- 1978*. Washington, DC: U.S. Commission on Civil Rights, 1980.

1689. Thomas, Clarence W. *The Journalistic Civil Rights Advocacy of Harry Golden and the "Carolina Israelite"*. Ph.D. diss., University of Florida, 1990. UMO #9116054.

1690. Thompson, John H. L. *The Little Caesar of Civil Rights: Roscoe Dunjee in Oklahoma City, 1915 to 1955*. Ph.D. diss., Purdue University, 1990. UMO #9104715.

1691. Tokayi, D. P. "The Persistence of Prejudice: Process-based Theory and the Retroactivity of the Civil Rights Act of 1991." *Yale Law Journal* 103 (November 1993).

1692. Tushnet, Mark V. *Making Civil Rights Law. Thurgood Marshall and the Supreme Court, 1936-1961*. Oxford University Press: 1993. [The NAACP Legal Defense Fund at work]

1693. U.S. General Accounting Office. *Within-School Discrimination-Inadequate Title VI Enforcement by the Office for Civil Rights*. G.A.O.: 1991.

1694. Varma, Premdatta. *The Asian Indian Community's Struggle for Legal Equality in the United States, 1900-1946*. Ph.D. diss., University of Cincinnati, 1989. UMO #9019869.

1695. Verhovek, Sam H. "Case Backlog Is Swamping Rights Agency." *New York Times*, 17 July 1989. [New York State Division of Human Rights]

1696. Walker, Jack L. *Sit-Ins in Atlanta*. New York: McGraw-Hill, 1964.

1697. Walker, Melissa. *Down from the Mountaintop. Black Women's Novels in the Wake of the Civil Rights Movement, 1966-1989*. New Haven, CT: Yale University Press, 1991.

1698. Walters, Ronald W. "Federalism, Civil Rights, and Black Progress." *Black Law Journal* 8 (Fall 1983): 220-234.

1699. Weinberg, Jack. "Students and Civil Rights in the 1960's." *History of Education Quarterly* 30 (Summer 1990): 213-224.

1700. Weinreb, L. L. "What Are Civil Rights?" *Social Philosophy and Policy* 8 (Spring 1991): 1-21.

1701. Weisbrot, Robert. *Freedom Bound. A History of America's Civil Rights Movement*. New York: Norton, 1990.

1702. Weiss, Nancy J. *Whitney M. Young, Jr. and the Struggle for Civil Rights*. Princeton, NJ: Princeton University Press, 1989.

1703. West, Louis Jolyon. "Pioneer of Sit-In Movement Remembered." *New York Times*, 15 March 1990. Letters. [Mrs. Clara Luper, Oklahoma City, Oklahoma, August 19, 1958]

1704. West, W. Richard, Jr., and Kevin Gover. "Indians in United States Civil Rights History." *Update on Law-Related Education* 27 (Fall 1988).

1705. _____. "The Struggle for Indian Civil Rights." in *Indians in American History*, pp. 275-293. ed. Fredrick E. Hoxie. Arlington Heights, IL: Harlan Davidson, Inc., 1988.

1706. Williams, Juan. "Reaganite on Civil Rights?" *Washington Post*, 26 December 1993. [Is Clinton a Reaganite in the area of civil rights?]

1707. Williams, Lena. "Blacks Reject Gay Rights Fight as Equal to Theirs." *New York Times*, 28 June 1993.

1708. Williams, Patricia J. "The Obliging Shell: An Informal Essay on Formal Equal Opportunity." *Michigan Law Review* 87 (August 1989): 2128-2151.

1709. Willie, Charles V., and Sanford J.S. "Martin Luther King, the Civil Rights Movement, and Educational Reform." *Educational Policy* 5 (March 1991): 29-43.

1710. Wilson, Paula. *Hubert Humphrey's Civil Rights Rhetoric: 1948-1964.* Ph.D. diss., Pennsylvania State University, 1990. UMO #9117759.

1711. Wolfinger, Raymond E., ed. "Roundtable of Participants in the Passage of the Civil Rights Act of 1964." *this Constitution* no. 19 (Fall 1991): 29-43. [John G. Stewart, Andrew J. Young, David B. Filvaroff, Stephen Horn, and Raymond Wolfinger]

1712. Wolfson, Evan. "Civil Rights, Human Rights, Gay Rights: Minorities and the Humanity of the Different." *Harvard Journal of Law and Public Policy* 14 (Winter 1991): 21-39.

1713. Woliver, Laura R. "A Measure of Justice-Police Conduct and Black Civil Rights, the Coalition for Justice for Ernest Lacy." *Western Political Quarterly* 43 (1990): 415-436.

1714. Wright, Mary E. "Natural Rights versus Civil Rights in the African-Americans' Elusive Quest for Parity." *Thurgood Marshall Law Review* 16 (Fall 1990): 1-34.

1715. Youth of the Rural Organizing and Cultural Center. *Minds Stayed on Freedom: The Civil Rights Struggle in the Rural South, An Oral History.* Boulder, CO: Westview, 1991.

1716. Zasloff, Jonathan. "The Varied Dominion of Thurgood Marshall." *Boston Globe*, 19 June 1994. [Dwells on limitations of civil rights through court action]

CLASS STRUCTURE

1717. Acuna, Rodolfo F. "The Struggle of Class and Gender: Current Research in Chicano Studies." *Journal of American Ethnic History* 8 (1989): 134-38. [Review essay]

1718. Althauser, Robert, and Michael Wallore, eds. *Research in Social Stratification and Mobility, 1993.* JAI Press: 1993.

1719. Anctil, Pierre. *Aspects of Class Ideology in a New England Ethnic Minority: The Franco-Americans of Woonsocket, Rhode Island (1865-1929).* Ph.D. diss., New School for Social Research, 1980.

1720. Andrews, M. "Schools, Jails, and the Dynamics of an Educational Underclass: Some Dreadful Social Arithmetic." *Journal of Economic Behavior and Organization* 22 (October 1993).

1721. Anthias, Floya. "Race and Class Revisited-Conceptualizing Race and Racisms." *Sociological Review* 38 (1990): 19-42.

1722. Aronowitz, Stanley, and Henry A. Giroux. "Class, Race, and Gender in Educational Politics." in their *Postmodern Education. Politics, Culture, and Social Criticism*, Minneapolis: University of Minnesota Press, 1990.

1723. Austin, Roy L., and Steven Stack. "Race, Class, and Opportunity: Changing Realities and Perceptions." *Sociological Quarterly* 29 (1988): 357-369.

1724. Bailey, David T. *Stratification and Ethnic Differentiation in Santa Fe, 1860-1870.* Ph.D. diss., University of Texas, 1975.

1725. Banner-Haley, Charles P. *The Fruits of Integration: Black Middle-Class Ideology and Culture, 1960-1990.* University Press of Mississippi: 1993.

1726. Barrera, Mario. "Class Segmentation and the Political Economy of the Chicano, 1900-1930." *New Scholar* 6 (1977): 167- 181.

1727. _____. *Race and Class in the Southwest: A Theory of Racial Inequality.* Notre Dame, IN: University of Notre Dame Press, 1979.

1728. Benjamin, Lois. *The Black Elite: Facing the Color Line in the Twilight of the Twentieth Century.* Nelson-Hall: 1991. [Upper middle class U.S. Blacks]

1729. Berberoglu, Berch. *The Legacy of Empire: Economic Decline and Class Polarization in the United States.* New York: Praeger, 1992.

1730. Bird, Van S. "Race or Class: A New Chapter in an Old Story." in *Symposium on Race and Class*, Philadelphia, PA: Black Scholars Foundation, 1984.

1731. Blalock, Hubert M., Jr. "Race versus Class: Distinguishing Reality from Artifacts." *National Journal of Sociology* 3 (1989): 127-142.

1732. Bonacich, Edna. "Class Approaches to Ethnicity and Race." *Insurgent Sociologist* 10 (Fall 1980): 9-23.

1733. _____. "Inequality in America: The Failure of the American System for People of Color." *Sociological Spectrum* 9 (1989): 77-101.

1734. Boston, Thomas D. "Racial Inequality and Class Stratification: Contributions to a Critique of Black Conservatism." *Review of Black Political Economics* 17 (1985): 47- 71.

1735. Bottomore, Tom. "Classes in Modern Society." 2nd ed. New York: Harper Collins, 1991.

1736. Boyle, Susan C. *Social Mobility in the United States: Historiography and Methods.* New York: Garland, 1990.

1737. Bradbury, Katharina L. "The Shrinking Middle Class." *New England Economic Review* (September-October 1986): 41-55.

1738. Brueggemann, John F. "Class, Race, and Symbolic Community." *Sociological Abstracts* (August 1991): supplement 167. 91S24970/ASA/1991/6329.

1739. Calderon, Garcia, and Homer Dennis. *Chicano Social Class, Assimilation, and Nationalism.* 2 vols Ph.D. diss., Yale University, 1980. UMO #8024801.

1740. Camacho, Eduardo, and Ben Joravsky. *Against the Tide: The Middle Class in Chicago.* Chicago, IL: Community Renewal Society, 1989.

1741. Campbell, Bruce A. "The Interaction of Race and Socioeconomic Status in the Development of Political Attitudes." *Social Science Quarterly* 60 (March 1980): 651-58.

1742. Cannon, Lynn W. "Trends in Class Identification Among Black Americans from 1952 to 1978." *Social Science Quarterly* 65 (March 1984): 112-126.

1743. Carrion, Juan M. *The Petty Bourgeoisie in Puerto Rico.* Ph.D. diss., Rutgers University, 1978. UMO #7910371.

1744. Carson, Emmett D. "The Black Underclass Concept: Self-Help vs. Government Intervention." *American Economic Review* 76 (1986): 347-350.

1745. Carter, Robert T., and Janet E. Helms. "The Relationship between Racial Identity Attitudes and Social Class." *Journal of Negro Education* 57 (Winter 1988): 22-30.

1746. Collins, Sharon M. "The Making of the Black Middle Class." *Social Problems* 30 (April 1983): 369-382.

1747. "A Continuation of the Underclass Debate." *Urban Geography* 12 (November-December 1991): 491-569 (five articles).

1748. Cordasco, Francesco. "Charles Loring Brace and the Dangerous Classes: Historical Analogues of the Urban Black Poor." *Kansas Journal of Sociology* 7 (Winter 1971).

1749. Cromwell, Adelaide M. *The Other Brahmins. Boston's Black Upper Class, 1750-1950.* University of Arkansas Press: 1994.

1750. The Damned. *Lessons from the Damned: Class Struggle in the Black Community,* 2nd ed. Ojai, CA: Times Change Press, 1990.

1751. Dardanoni, V. "Measuring Social Mobility." *Journal of Economic Theory* 61 (December 1993).

1752. "Debate: Are Social Classes Dying?" *International Sociology* 8 (September 1993): 259-316.

1753. Delgado, Richard. "Zero-based Racial Politics: An Evaluation of the Three Best-case Arguments on Behalf of the Nonwhite Underclass." *Georgetown Law Journal* 78 (August 1990): 1929-1948.

1754. DeMott, Benjamin. "In Hollywood, Class Doesn't Put Up Much of a Struggle." *New York Times,* 20 January 1991.

1755. DeParle, Jason. "Responding to Urban Alarm Bells At Scholarship's Glacial Pace." *New York Times,* 19 July 1992. [William J. Wilson's theory of the underclass]

1756. Emerson, Michael O. *The Rise of the Underclass: A Theory of Separate Spheres.* Ph.D. diss., University of North Carolina, 1991. UMO #9207944.

1757. Fainstein, Norman Q. "Race, Class and Segregation: Discourses about African Americans."
International Journal of Urban and Regional Research 17 (September 1993): 384-403.
[Underclass]

1758. _____. "The Underclass / Mismatch Hypothesis As an Explanation for Black Economic
Deprivation." *Politics and Society* 15 (1986): 403-451.

1759. Farley, Reynolds, and Suzanne M. Bianchi. "Social Class Polarization: Is It Occurring among
Blacks?" *Research in Race and Ethnic Relations* 4 (1985): 1-31.

1760. Feagin, Joe R., and Leslie B. Inniss. "Conceptualization of the Black Underclass: Its Political Uses
and Abuses." *Sociological Abstracts* (1989) 9S21380.

1761. Fixico, Donald L. "Modernization and the Native American Middle Class, 1945-1970." in *Sharing
a Heritage*, pp. 75-87. eds. Charlotte Heth, and Michael Swarm. American Indian Studies
Center, UCLA, 1984.

1762. Forbath, Jean. "The Poor Are the Underpinnings of Our Lifestyle." *Los Angeles Times*, 7 June
1993. [Orange County, CA]

1763. Foster, Edward M. *Childhood Poverty and the Underclass: Unraveling the Effects of Constraints
and Preferences*. Ph.D. diss., University of North Carolina, Chapel Hill, 1990. UMO
#9115623.

1764. Franklin, Raymond. *Shadows of Race and Class*. Minneapolis: University of Minnesota Press,
1991.

1765. Fredrickson, George M. "Race, Class, and Consciousness." introduction to his *The Arrogance of
Race: Historical Perspectives on Slavery, Racism, and Social Inequality*, Wesleyan U. P.,
1989.

1766. Gaines, Kevin K. *Uplifting the Race: Black Middle-class Ideology in the Era of the 'New Negro',
1890-1935*. Ph.D. diss., Brown University, 1991. UMO #9204864.

1767. Gaiter, Leonce. "The Revolt of the Black Bourgeoisie." *New York Times Magazine* (26 June 1994).
["The bad boys in the 'hood are the image of black America. Some black Americans are
getting sick of it."]

1768. Gallman, Vanessa. "Black and Blue. Our Besieged Middle Class." *Washington Post*, 21 February
1993.

1769. Gans, Herbert J. "Deconstructing the Underclass: The Term's Dangers as a Planning Concept."
Journal of the American Planning Association 56 (Summer 1990): 271-277.

1770. _____. "From 'Underclass' to 'Undercaste': Some Observations about the Future of the
Postindustrial Economy and Its Major Victims." *International Journal of Urban and Regional
Research* 17 (September 1993): 327-335.

1771. _____. "Positive Functions of the Undeserving Poor: Uses of the Underclass in America."
Politics and Society 22 (September 1994): 269-283.

1772. Garcia, Richard A. "Class, Consciousness, and Ideology-The Mexican Community of San Antonio,
Texas: 1930-1940." *Aztlan* 9 (1978): 23-69.

1773. _____. *Rise of the Mexican American Middle Class. San Antonio, 1929-1941*. College Station:
Texas A and M University Press, 1990.

1774. Gatewood, Willard B., Jr. *Aristocrats of Color. The Black Elite, 1880-1920*. Bloomington: Indiana
University Press, 1990.

1775. George, Lynell. "Unearthing an Unspoken Rage." *Los Angeles Times*, 3 March 1994. [Interview
with Ellis Cose, author of *The Rage of a Privileged Class*, i.e., middle-class Blacks]

1776. Gephart, Martha A., and Robert W. Pearson. "Contemporary Research on the Urban Underclass."
Items (Social Science Research Council) (June 1988).

1777. Gilliam, Frank. "Black America: Divided By Class?" *Public Opinion* (February-March 1986):
53-57.

1778. Glasco, Lawrence. "Internally Divided: Class and Neighborhood in Black Pittsburgh." *Amerikastudien/American Studies* 34 (1989): 223-230.

1779. Glasgow, Douglas S. "The Black Underclass in Perspective." *State of Black America* (1987): 129-144.

1780. Gonzales, Manuel G. *The Hispanic Elite of the Southwest*. El Paso: University of Texas, 1989.

1781. Greene, R. "Poverty Concentration Measures and the Urban Underclass." *Economic Geography* 67 (July 1991): 240-252.

1782. Greenwood, Janette T. *Bittersweet Legacy: The Black and White "Better Classes" in Charlotte, 1850-1910*. University of North Carolina Press: 1994.

1783. Gregory, S. "The Changing Significance of Race and Class in an African-American Community." *American Ethnologist* 19 (May 1992): 255-274.

1784. Griswold del Castillo, Richard. "Myth and Reality: Chicano Economic Mobility in Los Angeles, 1850-1880." *Aztlan* 6 (Summer 1976): 151-171.

1785. Grusky, D. B., and DiPrete, T.A. "Recent Trends in the Process of Stratification." *Demography* 27 (November 1990).

1786. Harley, Sharon. "The Middle Class." *Black Women in America*, II, 786-789.

1787. Harrison, Bennett, and Lucy Gorham. "Growing Inequality in Black Wages in the 1980's and the Emergence of an African- American Middle Class." *Journal of Policy Analysis and Management* 11 (Spring 1992): 235-253.

1788. Haywood, Harry. "Is the Black Bourgeoisie the Leader of the Black Liberation Movement?" *Soulbook* 5 (Summer 1966): 70-75.

1789. Heisler, Barbara S. "A Comparative Perspective on the Underclass Questions of Urban Poverty, Race, and Citizenship." *Theory and Society* 20 (August 1991): 455-484.

1790. Hill, Robert B. "The Black Middle Class: Past, Present, and Future." in *The State of Black America 1986*, pp. 43-64. Washington, DC: National Urban League, 1987.

1791. _____. "The Black Middle Class Defined." *Ebony* 42 (August 1987).

1792. Hochschild, Jennifer L., B. R. Boxhill, and W. J. Wilson. "Symposium on William Julius Wilson, The Truly Disadvantaged." *Ethics* 101 (April 1991): 560-609.

1793. Holden, Matthew, Jr., ed. *The Challenge to Racial Stratification*. Transaction: 1993.

1794. Holloway, S. R. "Urban Economic Structure and the Urban Underclass: An Examination of Two Problematic Social Phenomena." *Urban Geography* 11 (July-August 1990).

1795. Horne, Gerald. "Re-educating the U.S. Working Class on Race and Class." in *The Re-education of the American Working Class*, eds. Joseph Wilson and others. Greenwood, 1990.

1796. Horton, James O., and L. Horton. "Race and Class." *American Quarterly* 35 (Spring/Summer 1983): 155-168.

1797. Huckfeldt, Robert, and Carol W. Kohfeld. *Race and the Decline of Class in American Politics*. Urbana: University of Illinois Press, 1989.

1798. Hughes, Mark A. "Misspeaking Truth to Power: A Geographical Perspective on the 'Underclass' Fallacy." *Economic Geography* 65 (July 1989).

1799. Ignatiev, Noel. "The American Intifada." *Race Traitor* no. 1 (Winter 1993): 45-49. [Class revolution]

1800. Inniss, Leslie B., and Joe R. Feagin. "The Black 'Underclass' Ideology in Race Relations Analysis." *Social Justice* 16 (Winter 1989): 13-34.

1801. Irizarry, Annabelle. *Economic Relations for Class Reproductions: The Class of Puerto Ricans*. Ph.D. diss., City University of New York, 1983. UMO #8401903.

1802. Jacoby, Susan. "The Underclass." *Present Tense* 17 (January- February 1990): 10-11.

1803. Jean, Clinton M. "Inside the American Stratification System: Imageries from Black Writers." *Trotter Institute Review* (Winter/Spring 1992): 18-21.

1804. Jencks, Christopher. *Rethinking Social Policy. Race, Poverty, and the Underclass*. Cambridge, MA: Harvard University Press, 1991.

1805. Jencks, Christopher, and Paul E. Peterson, eds. *The Urban Underclass*. Washington, DC: Brookings Institution, 1991.

1806. Jones, Jacqueline. *The Dispossessed. America's Underclass from the Civil War to the Present*. New York: Basic Books, 1992.

1807. Kalleberg, Arne L., ed. *Research in Social Stratification and Mobility, 1990: A Research Annual*. Greenwich, CT: JAI Press, 1990.

1808. Kantrowitz, Nathan. "Social Mobility of Puerto Ricans: Education, Occupation, and Income Changes among Children of Immigrants, New York, 1950-1960." *International Immigration Review* 2 (Spring 1968): 53-72.

1809. Katz, Michael B. *The "Underclass" Debate. Views From History*. Princeton University Press: 1992.

1810. Keith, Verna M., and Cedric Herring. "Skin Tone and Stratification in the Black Community." *American Journal of Sociology* 97 (November 1991): 760-768.

1811. Kilson, Martin L., Jr. "Black Social Classes and Intergenerational Poverty." *Public Interest* 64 (Summer 1981): 58-78.

1812. Kloby, Gerald S. *Class Polarization in the United States, 1973-1985*. Ph.D. diss., Rutgers University, 1988. UMO #8914237.

1813. Kornblum, William. "Who Is the Underclass?" *Dissent* 38 (Spring 1991): 202-211.

1814. Kotkin, Joel. "A Multiethnic Middle Class Is Growing in California." *Los Angeles Times*, 14 November 1993.

1815. Krieger, Nancy. "Women and Social Class: A Methodological Study Comparing Individual Household and Census Measures as Predictors of Black/White Differences in Reproductive History." *Journal of Epidemiology and Community Health* 45 (1991): 35-42.

1816. Kuttner, Robert. "The Declining Middle Class." *Atlantic* (July 1983): 60-72.

1817. _____. "Notes from Underground: Clashing Theories About the 'Underclass'." *Dissent* 38 (Spring 1991): 212-217.

1818. "La classe mayenne ecartelee." *Revue Francaise d' Etudes Americaines* (February 1991): 7-89 (10 articles). [French and English]

1819. Landry, Bart. "Growth of the Black Middle Class in the 1960's." *Urban League Review* 3 (Winter 1978): 68-82.

1820. _____. *The New Black Middle Class*. Berkeley: University of California Press, 1987.

1821. Lawrence-Lightfoot, Sara. *I've Known Rivers: Lives of Loss and Liberation*. Addison Wesley: 1994. [Life in the African- American middle class]

1822. Lemann, Nicholas. "The Origins of the Underclass." *Atlantic Monthly* (July 1986): 54-68. [Chicago]

1823. _____. "The Other Underclass." *Atlantic* (December 1991). [Puerto Ricans]

1824. Lichtenstein, Nelson. "The Making of the Postwar Working Class: Cultural Pluralism and Social Structure in World War II." *The Historian* 51 (November 1988): 42-63.

1825. Littman, Mark S. "Poverty Areas and the 'Underclass': Untangling the Web." *Monthly Labor Review* 114 (March 1991): 19- 32.

1826. Loren, C. *Classes in the United States*. Davis, CA: Cardinal Publishers, 1977.

1827. Lucal, B. "Class Stratification in Introductory Textbooks: Relational or Distributional Models." *Teaching Sociology* 22 (April 1994): 139-150.

1828. Macnicol, John. "The Pursuit of the Underclass." *Journal of Social Policy* 16 (1988): 293-318.

1829. "Making It in America. On the Move But Going Nowhere." *Dollars and Sense* no. 108 (July-August 1985): 3-5.

1830. Marable, Manning. "Race, Class and Conflict: Intellectual Debates on Race Relations Research in the United States since 1960, a Social Science Bibliographical Essay." *Sage Race Relations Abstracts* 6 (November 1981): 1-38.

1831. Marks, Carole. "The Urban Underclass." *Annual Review of Sociology* (1991): 445-466.

1832. Mason, Carol. "Natchez Class Structure." *Ethnohistory* 11 (1964): 120-133.

1833. Massey, Douglas S. "American Apartheid: Segregation and the Making of the Underclass." *American Journal of Sociology* 96 (September 1990).

1834. _____. "Latinos, Poverty, and the Underclass: A New Agenda for Research." *Hispanic Journal of Behavioral Sciences* 15 (November 1993): 449-475.

1835. Massey, Douglas S. and others. "Segregation, the Concentration of Poverty, and the Life Chances of Individuals." *Social Science Research* 20 (December 1991): 397-420.

1836. Massey, Douglas S., and Nancy A. Denton. *American Apartheid: Segregation and the Making of the Underclass*. Harvard University Press: 1993.

1837. Menchaca, Martha. "Chicano-Mexican Cultural Assimilation and Anglo-Saxon Cultural Dominance." *Hispanic Journal of Behavioral Sciences* 11 (August 1989): 203-231.

1838. Mincy, Ronald. *Is There a White Underclass?* Washington, DC: Urban Institute, 1988.

1839. Miranda, Gloria E. "Racial and Cultural Dimensions in Gente de Razon Status in Spanish and Mexican California." *Southern California Quarterly* 70 (Fall 1988): 265-278.

1840. Monroy, Douglas G. *Mexicans in Los Angeles, 1930-1941: On Ethnic Group Relations to Class Forces*. Ph.D. diss., University of California, Los Angeles, 1978.

1841. Moore, Joan. "Is There a Hispanic Underclass?" *Social Science Quarterly* 70 (1989): 265-284.

1842. Moore, Joan, and Raquel Pinderhughes, eds. *In the Barrios: Latinos and the Underclass Debate*. Russell Sage Foundation: 1993.

1843. Morrissey, Marietta. "Ethnic Stratification and the Study of Chicanos." *Journal of Ethnic Studies* 10 (Winter 1983): 71-99.

1844. Moss, E. Yvonne, and Wornie L. Reed. "Stratification and Subordination: Change and Continuity." in *Social, Political, and Economic Issues in Black America*, vol. 4. pp. 1-28. ed. Wornie L. Reed. Boston: William Monroe Trotter Institute, University of Massachusetts at Boston, 1990.

1845. Mucha, Janusz. "Ethnicity or Class. Economic Interpretations of Ethnic Relations in American Society. Review Article." *Europa Ethnica* 44 (1987): 9-16.

1846. Mullings, Leith. "Ethnicity and Stratification in the Urban United States." in *Racism and the Denial of Human Rights: Beyond Ethnicity*, pp. 121-138. eds. M. Berlowitz, and Ronald S. Edari. Minneapolis, MN: MEP Press, 1984.

1847. Mullins, Elizabeth, and Paul Sites. "The Contribution of Black Women to Black Upper Class Maintenance and Achievement." *Sociological Spectrum* 10 (1990).

1848. Murray, Charles. "Here's the Bad News on the Underclass." *Wall Street Journal*, 8 March 1990.

1849. Muwakkil, Salim. "Increased Polarization: Aesthetics or Economics?" *In These Times* (1 November 1989).

1850. Navarro, Vicente. "Class and Race: Life and Death Situations." *Monthly Review* 43 (September 1991): 1-13.

1851. _____. "The Middle Class-A Useful Myth." *Nation* (23 March 1992).

1852. _____. "Race or Class, or Race and Class." *International Journal of Health Services* 19 (1989): 311-314.

1853. Nee, Victor, and J. Sanders. "The Road to Parity: Determinants of the Socioeconomic Achievements of Asian Americans." *Ethnic and Racial Studies* 9 (January 1985): 75-93.

1854. O'Connor, Alice Mary. *From Lower Class to Underclass: The Poor in American Social Science, 1930-1970.* Ph.D. diss., Johns Hopkins University, 1991. UMO #9132699.

1855. Ogbu, John U. "The Consequences of the American Caste System." in *The School Achievement of Minority Children; New Perspectives*, ed. Ulric Neisser. Hillsdale, NJ: Erlbaum, 1986.

1856. Oliver, Melvin L., and Mark A. Glick. "An Analysis of the New Orthodoxy on Black Mobility." *Social Problems* 29 (1984): 511- 523.

1857. O'Sullivan, Katherine, ed. "Special Issue on the Underclass in the United States." *Social Problems* 38 (November 1991): 427- 561 (eight articles).

1858. Parenti, Michael. "The Stampede from Class." *NST. Nature, Society, and Thought* 2 (1989).

1859. Passell, Peter. "Chronic Poverty, Black and White." *New York Times*, 6 March 1991. [Underclass, black and white]

1860. Pearson, R. W. "Social Statistics and an American Urban Underclass: Improving the Knowledge Base for Social Policy in the 1990's." *Journal of the American Statistical Association* 86 (June 1991).

1861. Pemberton, Gayle. *The Hottest Water in Chicago. On Family, Race, Time, and American Culture.* Faber and Faber: 1992.

1862. Pena, Devon G. "Las maquiladoras: Mexican Women and Class Struggle in the Border Industries." *Aztlan* 11 (Fall 1980): 159- 229.

1863. Perdue, Theda. "The Conflict Within: The Cherokee Power Structure and Removal." *Georgia Historical Society* 73 (Fall 1989): 467-491.

1864. Pessen, Edward. "Status and Social Class in America." in *Making America*, ed. Luther S. Luedtke. University of North Carolina Press, 1992.

1865. Peterson, Paul E. "The Urban Underclass and the Poverty Paradox." *Political Science Quarterly* 106 (Winter 1992): 617-638.

1866. Pilling, Arnold R. "Yurok Aristocracy and 'Great Houses'." *American Indian Quarterly* 13 (1989): 421-436.

1867. Popov, O. "Towards a Theory of Underclass Review." *Stanford Law Review* 43 (May 1991): 1095-1132.

1868. Quintero Rivera, Angel G. *Conflictos de clase y politica en Puerto Rico.* Rio Piedras: Huracan, 1976.

1869. Ramirez, Rafael L. and others. *Problems of Social Inequality in Puerto Rico.* Rio Piedras, PR: Ediciones Liberia Internacional, 1972.

1870. Reed, Adolph, Jr. "The Underclass as Myth and Symbol: The Poverty of Discourse About Poverty." *Radical America* 24 (January- March 1990).

1871. Reich, Robert B. "The Fracturing of the Middle Class." *New York Times*, 31 August 1994.

1872. Resnick, S., and R. Wolff. "Power, Property, and Class." in *Research in Political Economy*, vol. 9. ed. Paul Zarembka. Greenwich, CT: JAI Press, 1986.

1873. Riches, W. T. M. "Industrialization and Class Conflict in a Slave Society." *Amerikastudien* 30 (1985): 353-361.

1874. Ricketts, Erol R., and Ronald Mincy. "Growth of the Underclass: 1970-1980." *Journal of Human Resources* 25 (Winter 1990).

1875. Ricketts, Erol R., and Isabel V. Sawhill. "Defining and Measuring the Underclass." *Journal of Policy Analysis and Management* 7 (1988).

1876. Riley, Norman. "Attitudes of the New Black Middle Class." *Crisis* 93 (1986): 14-18, 31-32.

1877. Rios-Bustamante, Antonio. "The Barrioization of Nineteenth- Century Mexican Californians: From Landowners to Laborers." *Masterkey* 60 (1986): 26-35.

1878. Rodriquez, Clara E. "Prisms of Race and Class." *Journal of Ethnic Studies* 12 (Summer 1984): 99-120. [Review essay of Thomas Sowell's *Ethnic America*, as applied to Puerto Ricans]

1879. Roediger, David. "Notes on [White] Working Class Racism." *New Politics* 2 (Summer 1989): 61-66.

1880. Rolison, Garry L. "An Exploration of the Term Underclass As It Relates to African-Americans." *Journal of Black Studies* 21 (March 1991): 287-301.

1881. Rose, Stephen. *Social Stratification in the United States*, Revised and expanded ed. The New Press, 1992.

1882. Rousseau, M. O. "Distinguishing Ethnic Competition and Class Conflict." in *Perspectives on Social Problems*, vol. 3. eds. J. A. Holstein, and G. Miller. JAI Press, 1992.

1883. Sacks, Karen b. "Toward a Unified Theory of Class, Race, and Gender." *American Ethnologist* 16 (August 1989).

1884. Sandis, E. E. "The Socio-Economic Integration of Puerto Ricans in the Continental United States." *Annales du Centre de Recherches sur L'Amerique Anglophone* 9 (1984): 155-176.

1885. Schmalz, Jeffrey. "Roots of the Looting on St. Croix Lie in Racial and Class Tensions." *New York Times*, 26 September 1989. [Aftermath of Hurricane Hugo, September 1989]

1886. Schweninger, Loren. "Prosperous Blacks in the South, 1790- 1880." *American Historical Review* 95 (February 1990): 31-56. [References to many other studies and sources of information]

1887. Segura, Denise A. "Labor Market Stratification and Chicanas." *Berkeley Journal of Sociology* 29 (1984).

1888. Shanks, Ronald D. *Race and Ethnic Relations: A Modernization and Stratification Perspective 1876-1896.* Ph.D. diss., University of California, 1973.

1889. Sheppard, E. "Ecological Analysis of the Urban Underclass." *Urban Geography* 11 (May-June 1990).

1890. Singh, V. P. "The Underclass in the United States: Some Correlates of Economic Change." *Sociological Inquiry* 61 (Autumn 1991): 505-521.

1891. The Staff of the Chicago Tribune. *The American Millstone: An Examination of the Nation's Permanent Underclass.* Chicago, IL: Contemporary Books, 1986.

1892. Stafford, Walter W., and Joyce A. Ladner. "Political Dimensions of the Underclass Concept." in *Sociology in America*, ed. Herbert J. Gans. Newbury Park, CA: Sage, 1990.

1893. Steinberg, Stephen. "Stephen Steinberg Comments." *New Politics* 2 (Winter 1990): 48-58. [On debate around issue of underclass]

1894. _____. "The Underclass: A Case of Color Blindness." *New Politics* 2 (Summer 1989): 42-60.

1895. Steinmetz, George, and Erik O. Wright. "The Fall and Rise of the Petty Bourgeoisie: Changing Patterns of Self-Employment in the Postwar United States." *American Journal of Sociology* 94 (1989): 973-1018.

1896. Strobel, Fredrick R. *Upward Dreams, Downward Mobility: The Economic Decline of the American Middle Class.* Rowman and Littlefield: 1993.

1897. Swain, Johnnie Dee, Jr. "Black Mayors: Urban Decline and the Underclass." *Journal of Black Studies* 24 (September 1993): 16-28.

1898. Thurow, Lester. "The Disappearance of the Middle Class." *New York Times*, 5 February 1984. sec. 5, p.2.

1899. Tienda, Marta. "Puerto Ricans and the Underclass Debate." *Annals of the American Academy of Political and Social Science* no. 501 (January 1989): 105-119.

1900. _____. "Race, Ethnicity and the Portrait of Inequality: Approaching the 1990's." *Sociological Specturm* 9 (1989): 23-52.

1901. Torres, David L. "Dynamics Behind the Formation of a Business Class: Tuscon's Hispanic Business Elite." *Hispanic Journal of Behavioral Sciences* 12 (February 1990): 25-49.

1902. Torres, R. D., and A. Delatorre. "Latinos, Class and the United States Political Economy: Income Inequality and Policy Alternatives." in *Hispanics in the Labor Force*, pp. 265-288. eds. E. Melendez and others. New York: Plenum, 1991.

1903. Trevino, Roberto R. "Prensa y patria: The Spanish-Language Press and the Biculturation of the Tejano Middle Class, 1920- 1940." *Western Historical Quarterly* 22 (November 1991): 451-472.

1904. Turner, James. "Implications of Class Conflict and Racial Cleavage for the U.S. Black Community." *Review of Black Political Economy* 6 (Winter 1976): 133-144.

1905. "The Underclass in the United States." *Social Problems* 38 (November 1991): entire issue.

1906. Vaillancourt, Meg. "Middle-Class Blacks Emerge in Hyde Park." *Boston Globe*, 29 July 1994.

1907. Van Haitsma, Martha. "A Contextual Definition of the Underclass." *Focus* 12 (Summer 1989): 27-31.

1908. Vannerman, Reeve, and Lynn W. Cannon. *The American Perception of Class*. Philadelphia, PA: Temple University Press, 1987.

1909. Wacquant, Loic J. D., and William J. Wilson. "The Cost of Racial and Class Exclusion in the Inner City." *Annals of the American Academy of Political and Social Science* no. 501 (January 1989): 8-25.

1910. Waddoups, Jeffrey. "Racial Differences in Intersegment Mobility." *Review of Black Political Economy* 20 (Fall 1991): 23- 43.

1911. Wagenaar, Hendrick, and Dan A. Lewis. "Ironies of Inclusion: Social Class and Deinstitutionalization." *Journal of Health Politics, Policy and Law* 14 (Fall 1989): 503-522.

1912. Welch, Susan, and Lorn Foster. "Class and Conservatism in the Black Community." *American Politics Quarterly* 15 (1987): 445- 470.

1913. Wilkerson, Isabel. "Middle-Class but Not Feeling Equal, Blacks Reflect on Los Angeles Strife." *New York Times*, 4 May 1993.

1914. Williams, Vernon J., Jr. *From a Caste to a Minority. Changing Attitudes of American Sociologists Toward Afro- Americans, 1896-1945*. Westport, CT: Greenwood, 1989.

1915. Willie, Charles V., ed. *Caste and Class Controversy on Race and Poverty*, 2nd ed. Dix Hills, NJ: General Hall, Inc., 1989.

1916. Wilson, D., and J. Browning. "Politics and Community: Chicago's Near West Side Black Underclass." *Tydschrift voor economische en sociale geographie* 85 (1994): 53-66.

1917. Wilson, William J. "Another Look at the Truly Disadvantaged." *Political Science Quarterly* 106 (Winter 1992): 639-656.

1918. Wilson, William Julius and others. "The Ghetto Underclass and the Changing Structure of American Poverty." in *Quiet Riots: Race and Poverty in the United States*, eds. Fred R. Harris, and Roger W. Wilkins. New York: Pantheon, 1988.

1919. Wilson, William Julius, ed. "The Ghetto Underclass. Social Science Perspectives." *Annals of the American Academy of Political and Social Science* 501 (January 1989): entire issue.

1920. Winch, Julie. *Philadelphia's Black Elite: Activism, Accommodation, and the Struggle for Autonomy, 1787-1848*. Philadelphia, PA: Temple University Press, 1988.

1921. Wright, Erik Olin. "Class Analysis, History and Emancipation." *New Left Review* no. 202 (November-December 1993): 15-35. [Esp. 31-34, "The Underclass"]

1922. Wright, Erik Olin and others. *The Debate on Classes*. New York: Verso, 1989.

1923. Wright, Erik Olin, and Joachim Singlemann. "Proletarianization in American Class Structure." *American Journal of Sociology* 88 (1982): supplement.

COLLECTIVE SELF-DEFENSE

1924. Allsup, Carl. *The American G.I. Forum: Origin and Evolution*. Austin: University of Texas Press, 1982.

1925. Barrera, Mario. "The Historical Evolution of Chicano Ethnic Goals: A Bibliographic Essay." *Sage Race Relations Abstracts* 10 (February 1985): 1-48.

1926. Basu, T. K. "Beyond the National Question: Shifting Agendas of African-American Resistance." *Economic and Political Weekly* 29 (12 February 1994): 377-385.

1927. Baylor, Timothy J. "Social Control of an Insurgent Social Movement: A Case Study of the American Indian Movement." Master's Thesis, University of North Carolina, Chapel Hill, 1990.

1928. Beardsley, Richard K. "Ethnic Solidarity Turned to New Activism in a California Enclave: The Japanese Americans of 'Delta'." *California History* 68 (Fall 1989): 100-115.

1929. Borrego, John G. *Capitalist Accumulation and Revolutionary Accumulation: The Context for Chicano Struggle*. Ph.D. diss., University of California, 1978. 2 vols. UMO #7904383.

1930. Bowers, Cynthia. "Building from the Grassroots." *Against the Current* 5 (July-August 1990): 6-8. [New African Voices Alliance, Philadelphia]

1931. Brew, Sarah L. ""Making Amends for History": Legislative Reparations for Japanese Americans and Other Minority Groups." *Law and Inequality* 8 (November 1989): 179-201.

1932. Brisbane, Robert H. "Black Protest in America." in *The Black American Reference Book*, ed. Mabel M. Smythe. Englewood Cliffs, NJ: Prentice-Hall, 1976.

1933. Calvo Buezas, Tomas. "Analisis de un movimiento social: la lucha de los chicanos en los Estados Unidos." *Debates en Antropologia* no. 8 (1982): 107-127. [Departamento de Ciencias Sociales, Pontificia Universidad, Lima, Peru]

1934. Campos Tapia, Javier. *Cultural Reproduction: Funds of Knowledge as Survival Strategies in the Mexican-American Community*. Ph.D. diss., University of Arizona, 1991. UMO #9202090.

1935. Cose, Ellis. "The Fall of Benjamin Chavis." *Newsweek* (29 August 1994). [Executive director of NAACP]

1936. Cristobal, Hope Alvarez. "The Organization of People for Indigenous Rights: A Commitment towards Self-determination." *UCLA Pacific Ties* (March 1990): 10-11.

1937. Dewart, Janet, ed. *The State of Black America: 1987*, vol. 11. New Brunswick, NJ: Transaction, 1987.

1938. _____, ed. *The State of Black America: 1988*, vol. 12. New Brunswick, NJ: Transaction, 1988.

1939. _____, ed. *The State of Black America: 1989*, vol. 13. New Brunswick, NJ: Transaction, 1989.

1940. Dowd, Gregory E. *A Spirited Resistance. The North American Indian Struggle for Unity, 1745-1815*. Baltimore, MD: Johns Hopkins University Press, 1991.

1941. Dyson, Michael E. "Ben Chavis Wasn't the Problem." *New York Times*, 1 September 1994. [Critique of NAACP]

1942. Fullwood, Sam, III. "Chavis a Riddle for NAACP." *Los Angeles Times*, 10 July 1993. [Benjamin F. Chavis Jr., national executive director of NAACP]

1943. Fullwood, Sam, III. "NAACP at the Crossroads." *Emerge* (October 1991).

1944. Garcia, John A. and others. *The Chicano Struggle: Analyses of Past and Present Efforts*. Binghamton, NY: Bilingual Press, Office of the Graduate School, State University of New York, 1984.

1945. Gates, Henry Louis, Jr. "The Black Leadership Myth." *New Yorker* (24 October 1994).

1946. Greenberg, Jack. "Identity Crisis." *New York Times*, 23 May 1994. [NAACP]

1947. Herbert, Bob. "Chavis's Noisy 15 Minutes." *New York Times*, 24 August 1994. [Ben Chavis, ousted executive director of NAACP]

1948. Holmes, Steven A. "Uncharted Change at the NAACP." *New York Times*, 16 April 1994. [Ben Chavis]

1949. Hughes, C. Alvin. "The Negro Sanhedrin Movement." *Journal of Negro History* 69 (1984): 1-13.

1950. Johnson, Dirk. "Census Finds Many Claiming New Identity: Indian." *New York Times*, 5 March 1991.

1951. Johnson, Terry. "Land, a Jackass, or Cold Cash." *Village Voice* (20 June 1989). [Demands for African-American reparations]

1952. Keith, Damon J., Jr. "The Myth and Reality of Racial Progress: Why We Must 'Keep on Keeping on'." *Journal of Intergroup Relations* 15 (1987): 15-21.

1953. Kolsky, Thomas A. *Jews Against Zionism. The American Council for Judaism, 1942-1948*. Philadelphia, PA: Temple University Press, 1990.

1954. Marin, Marguerite V. *Social Protest in an Urban Barrio: A Study of the Chicano Movement, 1966-1974*. Lanham, MD: University Press of America, 1991.

1955. Marquez, Benjamin. "The Politics of Race and Class: The League of United Latin American Citizens in the Post-World War II Period." *Social Science Quarterly* 68 (1987): 84-101.

1956. _____. "The Problems of Organizational Maintenance and the League of United Latin American Citizens." *Social Science Journal (Fort Worth)* 28 (1991): 203-225.

1957. Martin, Marguerite V. *Social Protest in an Urban Barrio: A Study in an Urban Barrio: A Study of the Chicano Movement, 1966- 1974, Vol. I*. University Press of America: 1990,

1958. Marx, Andrew. "The United League of Mississippi." *Dollars and Sense* no. 60 (October 1980): 12-14.

1959. McClellan, E. Fletcher. *The Politics of American Self- Determination, 1958-75: The Indian Self-Determination and Education Assistance Act of 1975*. Ph.D. diss., University of Tennessee, 1988. UMO #8911737.

1960. Meyers, Michael. "The Right to Save the NAACP." *New York Times*, 3 August 1994.

1961. Milloy, Courtland. "We Have Met the Enemy..." *Washington Post*, 19 September 1993.

1962. Munoz, Carlos, Jr. *Youth, Identity, Power: The Chicano Movement*. New York: Verso, 1990.

1963. Nightingale, Carl H. *"It Makes Me Wonder How I Keep From Going Under": Young People in Poor Black Philadelphia and the Formation of a Collective Experience, 1940-1990*. Ph.D. diss., Princeton University, 1992. UMO #9216812.

1964. Orozco, Cynthia E. *The Origins of the League of United Latin American Citizens (LULAC) and the Mexican-American Civil Rights Movement in Texas with an Analysis of Women's Political Participation in a Gendered Context, 1910-1929*. Ph.D. diss., UCLA, 1992. UMO #9302444.

1965. Ortiz, Isidro D., and Marguerite V. Marin. "Reaganomics and Latino Organizations." in *Social and Gender Boundaries in the United States*, ed. Sucheng Chan. Lewiston, NY: Edwin Mellen Press, 1989.

1966. Patterson, Orlando. "The Black Community: Is There a Future?" in *The Third Century: America as a Post-Industrial Society*, ed. Seymour M. Lipset. Stanford, CA: Hoover Institution Press, 1979.

1967. Reed, Ishmael. "The Black Pathology Biz." *Nation* (20 November 1989).

1968. Roberto, Rita Jean. *In Quest of Autonomy: Northern Black Activism between the Revolution and Civil War*. Ph.D. diss., University of California, Berkeley, 1988. UMO #8916863.

1969. Rodriguez, Clara E. and others, eds. *The Puerto Rican Struggle: Essays on Survival in the U.S.* Maplewood, NJ: Waterfront Press, 1980.

1970. Rosenbaum, Robert J. *Mexicano Resistance in the Southwest: The Sacred Right of Self-Preservation*. Austin: University of Texas Press, 1981.

1971. Shepard, Paul. "Chavis Emerges Victor at NAACP Convention." *Cleveland Plain Dealer*, 17 July 1994.

1972. Sheridan, Earl. "the Diminishing Soul of Black America." *Social Theory and Practice* 14 (Summer 1988): 131-140.

1973. Sides, W. Hampton. "A Crisis of Leadership." *Los Angeles Times*, 8 April 1993. [The national NAACP]

1974. Smith, Preston H. *The Limitations of Racial Democracy: The Politics of the Chicago Urban League, 1916-1940*. Ph.D. diss., University of Massachusetts, 1990. UMO #9035403.

1975. Smith-Irvin, Jeannette. *Footsoldiers of the Universal Negro Improvement Association: Their Own Words*. Trenton, NJ: Africa World Press, 1990.

1976. Sommers, Laurie Kay. "Inventing Latinismo: The Creation of 'Hispanic' Panethnicity in the United States." *Journal of American Folklore* 104 (1991): 32-53.

1977. Spero, Robert. "Speaking for the Jews." *Present Tense* 17 (January-February 1990): 15-27. ["Who does the Conference of Presidents of Major American Jewish Organizations really represent?"]

1978. Tenayuca, Emma, and Homer Brooks. "The Mexican Question in the Southwest." *The Communist* 18 (March 1939): 261. [1st author was leader in San Antonio Pecan Shellers strike of 1938]

1979. Terry, Don. "NAACP Shows Split As Leaders Hold Meeting." *New York Times*, 13 June 1994.

1980. Torres, Richard S. *Virtues and Vices, Hearts and Histories: A Theory of Emotional Injustice, Stratification, Solidarity Rituals, and Habitus Production*. Ph.D. diss., Harvard University, 1989. UMO #8926187.

1981. Vigil, Maurillio E. "The Ethnic Organization As An Instrument of Political and Social Change: MALDEF, A Case Study." *Journal of Ethnic Studies* 18 (Spring 1990). [Mexican American Legal Defense and Educational Fund]

1982. Wald, Alan. "Roots of Chicano Power." *Against the Current* 6 (July-August 1991): 41-43. [Essay-review of Carlos Munoz, Jr., *Youth, Identity, Power: The Chicano Movement*]

1983. White, Vilbert L. "Charles Houston and Black Leadership of the 1930's and 1940's." *National Black Law Journal* 11 (Fall 1990): 331-347.

1984. Wilkins, Roger W. "Now or Never for the NAACP." *New York Times*, 12 October 1994.

1985. Woo, Merle. "What Have We Accomplished? From the Third World Strike Through the Conservative Eighties." *Amerasia Journal* 15 (1989): 81-89. [Asian-American movement]

COLONIALISM

1986. Albizu Campos, Pedro. *Obras Escogodes*. 3 vols. San Juan, PR: Editorial Jelope, 1975.

1987. Balandier, G. "The Colonial Situation: A Theoretical Approach." in *Social Change: The Colonial Situation*, ed. Immanuel Wallenstein. New York: Wiley 1966.

1988. Barrera, Mario and others. "The Barrio as Internal Colony." *Urban Affairs Annual Review* 6 (1972): 465-498.

1989. Bee, Robert, and Ronald Gingerich. "Colonialism, Classes, and Ethnic Identity: Native Americans and the National Political Economy." *Comparative International Development* 12 (1977): 70-93.

1990. Benitez-Nazario, Jorge A. *Teachers and Politics: A Case Study on Compliance and Resistance*. Ph.D. diss., University of Wisconsin, 1989. [Puerto Rico]. UMO #8923777.

1991. Binder, Wolfgang. "The Tropical Garden and the Mahanesque Resting-Place in the Caribbean: Remarks on the Early Incorporation of Puerto Rico by the United States of America." in *An American Empire: Expansionist Cultures and Policies, 1881- 1917*, ed. Serge Ricard. Six-en-Provence. Universite de Provence, 1990.

1992. Bonilla, Frank. "Puerto Rico: Exchanging People for Capital." *Crossrouds* no. 36 (November 1993): 14-16.

1993. Bonilla, Frank, and Ricardo Campos. "Imperialist Initiatives and the Puerto Rican Workers: From Foraker to Reagan." *Contemporary Marxism* no. 5 (1982).

1994. Boyer, W. W. "The Navy and Labour in St. Croix, 1917-1931." *Journal of Caribbean History* 20 (1985): 78-104.

1995. Caban, Pedro A. "The Colonial State and Capitalist Expansion in Puerto Rico." *Centro 2* no. 6 (1989).

1996. _____. "Industrialization, the Colonial State, and Working Class Organizations in Puerto Rico." *Latin American Perspectives* 11 (Summer 1984): 149-172.

1997. Campos, Ricardo, and Frank Bonilla. *La economia politica de la relacion colonial: la experiencia puertorriquena*. New York: Centro de Estudios Puertorriquena, City University of New York, 1977.

1998. Canny, Nicholas, and Anthony Pagden, eds. *Colonial Identity in the Atlantic World, 1500-1800*. Princeton, NJ: Princeton University Press, 1987.

1999. Carr, Raymond. *Puerto Rico, A Colonial Experiment*. New York: Vintage Books, 1984.

2000. Cesaire, Aime. *Discourse on Colonialism*. New York: Monthly Review Press, 1972.

2001. Cheyfitz, Eric. *The Poetics of Imperialism: Translation and Colonialization from The Tempest to Tarzan*. New York: Oxford University Press, 1990.

2002. Churchill, Ward. *Fantasies of the Master Race. Literature, Cinema and the Colonization of American Indians*, ed. M. Annette Jaimes. Monroe, ME: Common Courage Press, 1992.

2003. _____. "Indigenous Peoples of the United States: A Struggle Against Internal Colonialism." *Black Scholar* 16 (January-February 1985): 29-35.

2004. _____. "Literature and the Colonization of the American Indian." *Journal of Ethnic Studies* 10 (Fall 1982): 37-56.

2005. _____. "Sam Gill's Mother Earth: Colonialism, Genocide, and the Expropriation of Indigenous Spiritual Tradition in Contemporary Academia." *American Indian Culture and Research Journal* 12 (1988): 49-67. [See also Gill's reply, pp. 69-84]

2006. Churchill, Ward, and Winona La Duke. "Radioactive Colonization and the Native American." *Socialist Review* 15 (May- June 1985): 95-119.

2007. Clark, Truman R. "'Educating the Natives in Self- Government': Puerto Rico and the United States, 1900-1933." *Pacific H. Rev.* 42 (1973): 220-233.

2008. Collo, Martin J. "Development of Food-import Dependence: the Puerto Rican Experience." *Journal of Developing Societies* 5 (1989): 141-156.

2009. Colon Morera, Jose J. "Puerto Rico: A Nation in Search of Self Determination." *National Lawyers Guild Practitioner* 46 (Fall 1989): 98-103.

2010. Comptroller General of the United States. *Welfare and Taxes: Extending Benefits and Taxes to Puerto Rico, Virgin Islands, Guam, and American Samoa*. Washington, DC: General Accounting Office, September 1987.

2011. Congressional Budget Office. *Potential Economic Impacts of Changes in Puerto Rico's Status under SB 712*. Washington, DC: CBO, April 1990.

2012. de Albuquerque, Klaus, and Jerome L. McElroy. "Race and Ethnicity in the United States Virgin Islands." *Ethnic Groups* 6 (1985): 125-153.

2013. del Valle, Manuel. "Puerto Rico Before the United States Supreme Court." *Revista Juridicia de la Universidad Interamericana de Puerto Rico* 19 (1984).

2014. Dexter, L. A. "A Dialogue on the Social Psychology of Colonialism and Certain Puerto Rican Professional Personality Patterns." *Human Relations* 11 (1949).

2015. Dietz, James L. "Imperialism and Underdevelopment: A Theoretical Perspective and a Case Study of Puerto Rico." *Review of Radical Political Economics* 11 (Winter 1979).

2016. Diffie, Bailey W., and Justine W. F. Diffie. *Puerto Rico: A Broken Pledge*. New York: Vanguard Press, 1931.

2017. Eliza Colon, Sylvia M. *Colonialism and Education in Puerto Rico: Appraisal of the Public Schools during the Commonwealth Period-1952 to 1986*. Ph.D. diss., Washington University, 1989. UMO #9017364.

2018. Epica Task Force. *Puerto Rico: A People Challenging Colonialism*. Washington, DC: EPICA, 1976.

2019. Fitzpatrick, Joseph P. "Puerto Ricans as a Social Minority on the Mainland." *International Journal of Group Tensions* 19 (Fall 1989): 195-208.

2020. Forbes, E. "African-American Resistance to Colonization." *Journal of Black Studies* 21 (December 1990).

2021. Forbes, Jack D. "Envelopment, Proletarianization and Inferiorization: Aspects of Colonialism's Impact upon Native Americans and Other People of Color in Eastern North America." *Journal of Ethnic Studies* 18 (Winter 1991): 95-122.

2022. Frickey, P. P. "Marshalling Past and Present: Colonialism, Constitutionalism, and Interpretation in Federal Indian Law." *Harvard Law Review* 107 (December 1993): 381-441.

2023. Garcia, Mario T. "Internal Colonialism: A Critical Essay." *Revista Chicano-Riquena* 6 (Summer 1978): 38-41.

2024. Gautier-Mayoral, Carmen. *One Aspect of the Political Dependence of Puerto Rico: The Politics of Federally Financed Poor Relief 1927-1980.* Ph.D. diss., University of London, 1986.

2025. Golden, Daniel. "The Legacy of Wounded Knee." *Boston Globe Magazine*, 26 November 1989. [Oglala Sioux, Pine Ridge Reservation, South Dakota]

2026. Gonzalez Casanova, Pablo. "Internal Colonialism and National Development." *Studies in Comparative International Development* 1 (1965): 27-37.

2027. Grimshaw, Patricia. *Paths of Duty: American Missonary Wives in Ninteenth-Century Hawaii.* Honolulu: University of Hawaii Press, 1989.

2028. Grupo de Investigadores Puertottiquenos. *Breakthrough from Colonialism.* Rio Piedras: Editorial de la Universidad de Puerto Rico, 1984.

2029. Henrikson, Markku. *The Indian on Capitol Hill: Indian Legislation and the United States Congress, 1862-1907.* Helsinki: SHS, 1988.

2030. Hickerson, Harold. "Fur Trade Colonialism and the North American Indians." *Journal of Ethnic Studies* 1 (1973): 15-44.

2031. Hornblower, Margot. "Puerto Rico. The Underside of Paradise." *Washington Post*, 21 June 1981. (Three articles).

2032. Houghton, Richard H., III. "An Argument for Indian Status for Native Hawaiians-The Discovery of a Lost Tribe." *American Indian Law Review* 14 (Spring 1988): 1-55.

2033. Howard, J. "How to End Colonial Domination of Black America: A Challenge to Black Psychologists." *Negro Digest* 19 (1970): 4-10.

2034. Huang, Hsiao-ping. *Chinese Merchant Background and Experience in Hawaii under the Monarchy.* Ph.D. diss., University of Hawaii, 1989.

2035. Hurwitz, Emanuel and others. *Educational Imperialism: American School Policy and the U.S. Virgin Islands.* Landham, MD: University Press of America, 1987.

2036. Jaimes, M. Annette, ed. *The State of Native America. Genocide, Colonization, and Resistance.* Bsoton, MA: South End Press, 1991.

2037 Jones, Dorothy V. *License for Empire: Colonialism by Treaty in Early America.* Chicago, IL: University of Chicago Press, 1982.

2038. Katz, Stephen. "The Problems of Europocentrism and Evolutionism in Marx's Writings on Colonialism." *Political Studies* 38 (December 1990): 672-687.

2039. König, Rene. *Navajo Report: von der Kolonie zur Nation*, 2nd ed. W. Berlin: Dietrich Riemer Verlag, 1983.

2040. La Motta, Gregory R. *The Americanization of the Virgin Islands, 1917-1946: Politics and Class Struggle during the First Thirty Years of American Rule.* Ph.D. diss., University of Maryland, 1992. UMO #9315673.

2041. Larsen, Lauren C. *Chaos or Continuity? The Problems of Americanization in the United States Virgin Islands to 1936.* Ph.D. diss., Howard University, 1989. UMO #9006615.

2042. Leibowitz, Arnold H. *Defining Status: A Comprehensive Analysis of United States Territorial Relations.* Boston, MA: Nyhoff, 1989.

2043. Lewis, Gordon K. *Notes on the Puerto Rican Revolution. An Essay on American Dominance and Caribbean Resistance.* New York: Monthly Review Press, 1975.

2044. Lewis, Rupert. *Marcus Garvey: Anti-Colonial Champion.* Trenton, NJ: African World Press, 1988.

2045. Linnekin, Jocelyn. *Sacred Queens and Women of Consequence: Rank, Gender, and Colonialism in the Hawaiian Islands.* Ann Arbor: University of Michigan Press, 1990.

2046. Liu, J. "Toward an Understanding of the Internal Colonial Model." in *Counterpoint*, pp. 160-168. ed. Emma Gee. Los Angeles: UCLA Asian American Studies Center, 1976.

2047. Lopez, Alfredo. *Dona Lieha's Island: Modern Colonialism in Puerto Rico.* Boston, MA: South End Press, 1988.

2048. Lopez, Alfredo, ed. *The Puerto Ricans: Their History, Culture, and Society*. Cambridge, MA: Schenkman, 1980.

2049. Lopez-Rivera, Oscar, and Bernard D. Headly. "Who Is the Terrorist? The Making of a Puerto Rican Freedom Fighter." *Social Justice* 16 (Winter 1989).

2050. Maldonado-Denis, Manuel. "'El destino de todos los pueblos es la independcia'." *QueHacer* no. 18 (August 1982): 94-103. [Interview]

2051. _____. *Puerto Rico: A Socio-Historic Interpretation*. New York: Random House, 1972. Translated by Elena Vialo

2052. _____. "Puerto Rico: sociedad colonial en el Caribe." in *Problemas dominico haitianos y del Caribe*, Gerard Piere-Charles and others. Mexico City: Universidad Nacional Autonomos de Mexico, 1973.

2053. _____. *Puerto Rico y Estados Unidos: Emmigracion y Colonialismo*. Mexico City: Siglo XXI, 1976.

2054. _____. "Toward a Marxist Interpretation of the History of Puerto Rico." *Rican* 2 (October 1974): 32-53.

2055. Maldonado, Rita M. "Why Puerto Ricans Migrated to the United States [sic] in 1947-73." *Monthly Labor Review* 99 (September 1976): 7-15.

2056. Martinez, Jose V., Jr. *Internal Colonialism and Decolonization in El Centro: A Socio-historical Analysis of Chicanos in a Texas City*. Ph.D. diss., University of Texas, 1981. UMO #8119331.

2057. Mattei, A. R. "The Plantations of the Southern Coast of Puerto Rico: 1880-1910." *Social and Economic Studies* 37 (March- June 1988).

2058. Mattos Cintron, Wilfredo. "La formacion de la hegemoina de Estados Unidos en Puerto Rico y el independentismo." *Homines* 2 (1987-1988).

2059. _____. "La formacion de la hegemoina de Estados Unidos en Puerto Rico y el independentismo, los derechos civiles y la cuestion nacional." *Caribe Contemporaneo* (January-June 1988): 21- 57.

2060. Melendez, Edgardo. *Puerto Rico: Statehood Movement*. Westport, CT: Greenwood, 1988.

2061. Melendez, Edwin, and Edgardo Melendez, eds. *Colonial Dilemma. Critical Perspectives on Contemporary Puerto Rico*. Boston, MA: South End Press, 1992.

2062. Melendez, Edwin, and Edgardo Melendez. "Puerto Rico: A Colonial Dilemma." *Racial America* 23 (January-February 1989): entire issue.

2063. Mendez, J. L., ed. *La Agresion Cultural Norteamericana en Puerto Rico*. Mexico City: Editorial Gryalbo, 1980.

2064. Miranda, Luis A. *La Justicia Social en Puerto Rico*. San Juan, PR: Talleres de la Correspondencia, 1943.

2065. Monet, Don, and Ardythe Wilson. *Colonialism on Trial: Indigenous Land Rights and the Citksan and Wet'suwet'en Sovereignty Case*. New Society Publishers, 1992.

2066. Moore, Joan W. "Colonialism: The Case of the Mexican Americans." *Social Problems* 17 (Spring 1970): 463-472.

2067. Morris, Nancy E. *National Identity Under Challenge: Puerto Rico in the Twentieth Century*. Ph.D. diss., University of Pennsylvania, 1992. UMO #9235178.

2068. Morse, Bradford W., and Kazi A. Hamid. "American Annexation of Hawaii: An Example of the Unequal Treatment Doctrine." *Connecticut Journal of International Law* 5 (Spring 1990): 407-456.

2069. Murguia, Edward. *Assimilation, Colonialism, and the Mexican American People*. Austin: Center for Mexican American Studies, University of Texas, 1975.

2070. Nelson, Anne. *Murder under Two Flags: The U.S., Puerto Rico and the Cerro Maravilla Cover-Up*. Boston, MA: Ticknor and Fields, 1986.

2071. Nistal-Moret, Benjamin. *El Pueblo de Neuestra Senora de la Candelaria y del Apostol San Matias 1800-1880, Its Ruling Classes and the Institution of Black Slavery [in Puerto Rico]*. Ph.D. diss., State University of New York at Stony Brook, 1977. UMO #7803168.

2072. Ojeda Rios, Filiberto. "History Will Judge All of Us." *National Lawyers Guild Practitioner* 46 (Fall 1989): 114-117. [Puerto Rico]

2073. Ortiz, Roxanne Dunbar. "Wounded Knee 1890 to Wounded Knee 1973: A Study in United States Colonialism." *Journal of Ethnic Studies* 8 (1980): 1-15.

2074. Passell, Peter. "Debate on Puerto Rico's Future Has a Bottom Line." *New York Times*, 15 May 1990.

2075. Peterson, Patti M. "Colonialism and Education: The Case of the Afro-American." *Comparative Education Review* 15 (June 1971): 146-157.

2076. Pomeroy, Earl S. *The Territories and the United States 1861-1890: Studies in Colonial Administration*. Philadelphia: University of Pennsylvania Press, 1947.

2077. Quintero Rivera, Angel G. "Background to the Emergence of Imperialist Capitalism in Puerto Rico." *Caribbean Studies* 13, no. 3 (1973): 31-63.

2078. _____. *Conflicts de clase y politica en Puerto Rico*. Rio Piedras: Editorial Huracan, 1976.

2079. Ramos Mattei, Andres A. "The Growth of the Puerto Rican Sugar Industry under North American Domination, 1899-1910." in *Crisis and Change in the International Sugar Economy, 1860-1914*, eds. Bill Albert, and A. Graves. Norwich, England: ISC, 1984.

2080. _____. *La sociedad del azucar en Puerto Rico*. Rio Piedras: University of Puerto Rico, 1988.

2081. Rivera, Angel G. "A Hesitant Unveiling of America's Colonial Problem in Puerto Rico." *Journal of Latin American Studies* 18 (November 1986): 425-433.

2082. Rivera Lugo, Carlos. "La politica del derecho internacional de descolonizacion en el caso de Puerto Rico." *Revista de Derecho Puertorriqueno* 25 (July-October 1985): 55-78.

2083. Rodriguez, Clara E. *Puerto Ricans. Born in the U.S.A.* Boston, MA: Unwin Hyman, 1990.

2084. _____. "Race, Class, and Gender: Puerto Ricans in New York." *Sociological Abstracts* (1989) 89S2/674.

2085. Said, Edward W. "Representing the Colonized: Anthropology's Interlocutors." *Critical Inquiry* 15 (Winter 1989): 205-225.

2086. Santiago-Valles, Kelvin A. *"Subject People" and Colonial Discourses: Economic Transformation and Social Disorder in Puerto Rico, 1898-1947*. SUNY Press, 1994.

2087. Smith, Jane M. "Republicanism, Imperialism, and Sovereignty: A History of the Doctrine of Tribal Sovereignty." *Buffalo Law Review* 37 (Spring 1989): 527-582.

2088. Snipp, C. Matthew. "The Changing Political and Economic Status of American Indians: From Captive Nations to Internal Colonies." *American Journal of Economics and Sociology* 45 (1986): 145-157.

2089. Solomon, Mark I. "Black Critics of Colonialism and the Cold War." in *Cold War Critics*, pp. 205-211. ed. T. G. Paterson. Chicago, IL: Quadrangle, 1971.

2090. Staples, Robert. *The Urban Plantation: Racism and Colonialism in the Post Civil Rights Era*. Oakland, CA: Black Scholar Press, 1987.

2091. Stavenhagen, Rodolfo. "Classes, Colonialism, and Acculturation." *Studies in Comparative International Development* 1 (1965): 53-77.

2092. Taller de Formacion Politica. "The Meaning of the Plebiscite." *Against the Current* 5 (July-August 1990): 29-34. [Puerto Rico]

2093. Tolan, Sandy. "Showdown At Window Rock." *New York Times Magazine*, 26 November 1989. [Peter MacDonald and the Navajo Nation.]

2094. Vandermeer, John, and Ivette Perfecto. "The Politics of Neo-Colonialism: The Case of the Puerto Rican 15." *Against the Current* 4 (July-August 1989): 5-8. [Puerto Rican nationalist movement]

2095. Villamil, Jose J. "Puerto Rico 1948-1976: The Limits of Dependent Growth." in *Transnational Capitalism and National Development*, ed. Villamil. Atlantic Highlands, NJ: Humanities Press, 1979.

2096. Wagenheim, Karl. *Puerto Ricans in the U.S.* New York: Minority Rights Group, 1983. Report no. 58

2097. Wald, Alan. "The Literature of Internal Colonialism: A Marxist Perspective." *MELUS* 8 (Fall 1981): 18-27.

2098. Wendt, Bruce H. *An Administrative History of the Warm Springs, Oregon, Indian Reservation, 1855-1955.* Ph.D. diss., Washington University, 1989. UMO #9025432.

2099. Williams, Walter L. "American Imperialism and the Indians." in *Indians in American History*, pp. 231-249. ed. Fredrick E. Hoxie. Arlington Heights, IL: Harlan Davidson, Inc, 1988.

2100. _____. "From Independence to Wardship: The Legal Process of Erosion of American Indian Sovereignity, 1810-1903." *American Indian Culture and Research Journal* 7 (1984): 5-32.

2101. _____. "United States Indian Policy and the Debate over Philippine Annexation: Implications for the Origins of American Imperialism." *Journal of American History* 66 (1980): 810-831.

2102. Zavala, Iris M., and Rafael Rodriguez. *The Intellectual Roots of Independence: An Anthology of Puerto Rican Political Essays*. New York: Monthly Review Press, 1980.

COMMUNITY DEVELOPMENT

2103. Ambler, Marjane. *Breaking the Iron Bonds: Indian Control of Energy Development*. Lawrence: University Press of Kansas, 1990.

2104. Ambrecht, Biliana C. S. *Politicizing the Poor: The Legacy of the War on Poverty in a Mexican American Community*. New York: Praeger, 1976. [Los Angeles]

2105. Anders, Gary C. "Theories of Underdevelopment and the American Indian." *Journal of Economic Issues* 14 (September 1980): 681-701.

2106. Anderson, T. L., and D. Lueck. "Land Tenure and Agricultural Productivity on Indian Reservations." *Journal of Law and Economics* 35 (October 1992).

2107. Bates, Timothy. *The Role of Black Enterprise in Urban Development*. Washington, DC: Joint Center for Political Studies, 1989.

2108. Billy, Bahe. *The Missing Link in Navajo Indian Economic Development*. ERIC ED 204 048: 24 April 1980. [On-reservation development]

2109. Brazier, Arthur M. *Black Self-Determination: The Story of the Woodlawn Organization*. Grand Rapids, MI: Erdmans, 1969. [Chicago]

2110. Brenner, Robert. "The Social Basis of Economic Development." in *Analytical Marxism*, ed. John Roemer. Cambridge, 1986.

2111. Burt, Larry W. "Factories on Reservations: The Industrial Development Programs of Commissioner Glenn Emmons, 1953-1960." *Arizona and the West* 19 (1977): 317-332.

2112. Ciaramitaro, Bridget and others. "The Development of Underdevelopment in the Mid-South: Big Farmers and the Persistence of Rival Poverty." *Humanity and Society* 12 (November 1988): 347-365.

2113. Cornell, Stephen, and Joseph P. Kalt. "Pathways from Poverty: Economic Development and Institution-building on American Indian Reservations." *American Indian Culture and Research Journal* 14 (1990): 89-125.

2114. Cruz, Wilfredo. *The Nature of Alinsky-Style Community Organizing in the Mexican American Community of Chicago*. Ph.D. diss., University of Chicago, 1987.

2115. _____. "UNO: Organizing at the Grass Roots." in *After Alinsky: Community Organizing in Illinois*, ed. Peg Knoeple. Springfield, IL: Illinois Issues, Sangamon State University, 1990. [Hispanic organization in Chicago]

2116. De Maille, Raymond J. "Pine Ridge Economy: Cultural and Historical Perspectives." *American Indian Economic Development*, pp. 237-312. The Hague: Mouton, 1978.

2117. Dreier, P. "Redlining Cities: How Banks Color Community Development." *Challenge* 34 (November-December 1991).

2118. *Economic Development in American Indian Reservations*. Albuquerque: Native American Studies, University of New Mexico, 1979.

2119. Edwards, Jeffrey B. *The Resolution of an "Urban Crisis": Racial Formation in Detroit, 1961-1981*. Ph.D. diss., University of Minnesota, 1992. UMO #9215977.

2120. Ellison, Christopher G., and B. London. "The Social and Political Participation of Black Americans: Compensatory and Ethnic Community Perspectives Revisited." *Social Forces* 70 (March 1992): 681-702.

2121. Fish, John. *Black Power/White Control: The Struggle of the Woodlawn Organization of Chicago*. Princeton, NJ: Princeton University Press, 1973.

2122. Fisher, Robert. *Let the People Decide*. Boston, MA: Twayne, 1984. [Critique of Alinsky]

2123. Fisher, Robert, and Peter Romanofsky, eds. *Community Organizing for Urban Social Change: A Historical Perspective*. Westport, CT: Greenwood, 1981.

2124. Fite, Gilbert C. "Development of the Cotton Industry by the Five Civilized Tribes in Indian Territory." *Journal of Southern History* 15 (1949): 342-353.

2125. Flores, Henry. "The Selectivity of the Capitialist State: Chicanos and Economic Development." *Western Political Quarterly* 42 (1989): 377-395.

2126. Franklin, Vincent P. "'They Rose and Fell Together': African American Educators and Community Leadership, 1795-1954." *Journal of Education* 172 (1990): 39-64.

2127. Frye, Hardy, and Charles F. Underwood. "Schooling as a Focus for African American Community Development." *Sociological Abstracts* 91S24805/SSSP/1991/2999.

2128. Gite, Lloyd. "The New Agenda of the Black Church: Economic Development for Black America." *Black Enterprise* (December 1993).

2129. Goodman-Draper, Jacqueline. "The Development of Underdevelopment of Akwesasne: Cultural and Economic Subversion." *American Journal of Economics and Sociology* 53 (January 1994): 41-56.

2130. Gore, Al, and Daniel P. Moynihan. "The Myth of Community Development." *New York Times Magazine*, 30 January 1994. [Two letters commenting on Lemann, below]

2131. Gray, P. A. "Economic Development and African Americans in the Mississippi Delta." *Rural Sociology* 56 (Summer 1991): 238- 246.

2132. Grim, Valerie. *Black Farm Families in the Yazoo-Mississippi Delta: A Study of the Brooks Farm Community, 1920-1970*. Ph.D. diss., Iowa State University, UMO #9101352.

2133. Hall, Thomas D. "Patterns of Native American Incorporation into State Societies." in *Public Policy Impacts on American Indian Economic Development*, pp. 23-38. ed. C. Matthew Snipp. Albuquerque: University of New Mexico Press, 1988.

2134. Handy, John W. "Community Economic Development: Some Critical Issues." *Review of Black Political Economy* 21 (Winter 1993): 41-64.

2135. Henderson, Al. *The Navajo Nation Energy Policy: A Means to Economic Prosperity for the Navajo Nation*. Master's thesis, University of New Mexico, 1981.

2136. "Heroes and Heroines." *Mother Jones* (January 1989): 27-35.

2137. Hickey, Jo Ann S. "Economic Well-being in North Carolina Counties 1980-85: Some Gray Areas, but Mostly a Case of Black and White." *Sociological Abstracts* (1989): 89S21034.

2138. _____. *Uneven Development in the South, 1959-1984: An Analysis of Economic Well-being for Rural Black and Rural White Counties*. Ph.D. diss., Cornell University, 1992. UMO #9300745.

2139. Hucles, Harold D. *Postbellum Urban Black Economic Development: The Case of Norfolk, Virginia, 1860-1890*. Ph.D. diss., Purdue University, 1990. UMO #9031341.

2140. Jaynes, Gerald D., and Robin M. Williams, Jr., eds. "Identity and Institutions in the Black Community." in *A Common Destiny. Blacks and American Society*, pp. 161-204. Washington, DC: National Academy Press, 1989.

2141. Jennings, James, ed. *Race, Politics, and Economic Development. Community Perspectives*. Verso: 1992.

2142. Johnson, Dirk. "Economics Come to Life on Indian Reservations." *New York Times*, 3 July 1994.

2143. Johnson, Louise A. and others, eds. *The People of East Harlem: The Needs of the Community and the Resources for Meeting Them*. New York: Mount Sinai School of Medicine, 1974.

2144. Kling, Joseph M., and Prudence S. Posner, eds. *Dilemmas of Activism: Class, Community, and the Politics of Local Mobilization*. Philadelphia, PA: Temple University Press, 1990.

2145. Knoepfle, Peg, ed. *After Alinsky: Community Organizing in Illinois*. Springfield, IL: Illinois Issues, Sangamon State University, 1990.

2146. Kusmer, Kenneth L., ed. *Black Communities and Race Relations in American Cities 1712-1990*. Garland: 1992. [9-volume collection of reprinted articles]

2147. La Duke, Winona. "The Mortality of Wealth: Native America and the Frontier Mentality." *Radical America* 17 (March-June 1983): 69-79.

2148. Lamb, David. "A Tribe That Means Business." *Los Angeles Times*, 2 December 1992. [Passamaquoddy Indians in Maine]

2149. Lasch, Elisabeth D. *Black Neighbors: Race and the Limits of Reform in the American Settlement House Movement, 1890-1945*. Ph.D. diss., University of Massachusetts, 1990. UMO #9110172.

2150. Legters, Lyman H., and Fremont J. Lyden, eds. *American Indian Policy: Self-governance and Economic Development*. Greenwood: 1994.

2151. Leibhart, Barbara G. *Law, Environment, and Social Change in the Columbia River Basin: The Yakima Indian Nation as a Case Study, 1840-1933*. Ph.D. diss., University of California, Berkeley, 1990. UMO #9126657.

2152. Lemann, Nicholas. "The Myth of Community Development." *New York Times Magazine*, 9 January 1994.

2153. Lewter, Merri G. *Inner-city Reinvestment and Public Policy: A Study of Minority and Non-minority Historic Districts*. Ph.D. diss., University of Lousiville, 1992. UMO #9313801.

2154. Loury, Glenn. "Internally Directed Action for Black Community Development: The Next Frontier for 'The Movement'." *Review of Black Political Economy* 13 (Summer-Fall 1984): 31-46.

2155. Malan, Vernon. *The Dakota Indian Economy. Factors Associated with Success in Ranching*. Brookings: South Dakota State College Agricultural Experiment Station, 1963.

2156. Manta, Ben. "Toward Economic Development of the Chicano Barrio: Alternative Strategies and Their Implications." *Southwest Economy and Society* 1 (Spring 1976): 35-41.

2157. Marcuse, Peter. "Neighborhood Policy and the Distribution of Power: New York City's Community Boards." *Policy Studies Journal* 16 (Winter 1987-1988): 277-289.

2158. Miner, H. Craig. "The Cherokee Oil and Gas Co., 1889-1902: Indian Sovereignty and Economic Change." *Business History Review* 46 (1972): 45-66.

2159. _____. *The Corporation and the Indian: Tribal Sovereignty and Industrial Civilization in Indian Territory, 1865-1907*. Columbia: University of Missouri Press, 1976.

2160. Mohawk, John C. "Indian Economic Development: An Evolving Concept of Sovereignty." *Buffalo Law Review* 39 (Spring 1991): 495-506.

2161. Monti, Daniel J. *Race, Redevelopment, and the New Company Town*. Albany: State University of New York Press, 1990. [St. Louis, MO]

2162. Morrison, James D. "Problems in the Industrial Progress and Development of the Choctaw Nation, 1865-1907." *Chronicles of Oklahoma* 32 (1954): 71-91.

2163. Naples, N. A. "Contradictions in the Gender Subtext of the War on Poverty. the Community Work and Resistance of Women from Low Income Communities." *Social Problems* 38 (August 1991): 316- 332.

2164. Obama, Barack. "Why Organize? Problems and Promise in the Inner City." in *After Alinsky: Community Organizing in Illinois*, ed. Peg Knoeple. Springfield, IL: Illinois Issues, Sangamon State University, 1990.

2165. Ortiz, Roxanne Dunbar, ed. *Economic Development in American Indian Reservations*. 1979: ERIC ED 182 078.

2166. Pasternak, Judy. "Chicago's Shorebank Earns Interest as Model for Rebirth." *Los Angeles Times*, 22 February 1993. [South Shore Bank]

2167. Patterson, Orlando. "The Black Community: Is There a Future?" in *The Third Century*, ed. Seymour M. Lipset. Hoover Institution Press, 1979.

2168. Pierce, Neal R., and Carol F. Steinbach. *Corrective Capitalism: The Rise of America's Community Development Corporation*. New York: Ford Foundation,

2169. Reardon, Kenneth M. *Local Economic Development in Chicago, 1983-1987: The Reform Efforts of Mayor Harold Washington*. Ph.D. diss., Cornell University, 1990. UMO #9027058.

2170. Richardson, Bill. "More Power to the Tribes." *New York Times*, 7 July 1993. [Chairman of the House Subcommittee on Native American Affairs on tribal autonomy]

2171. Robinson, Carla J. "Minority Political Representation and Local Economic Development Policy." *Journal of Urban Affairs* 12 (1990): 49-57.

2172. Rogers, Mary Beth. *Cold Anger. A Story of Faith and Power Politics*. College Station: Texas A + M University.

2173. Rury, John L. "Education and Black Community Development in Ante-bellum New York City." Master's Thesis, City University of New York, 1975.

2174. Sanchez Korrol, Virginia E. *From Colonia to Community: The History of Puerto Ricans in New York City, 1917-1948*. Westport, CT: Greenwood, 1983.

2175. _____. *Settlement Patterns and Community Development Among Puerto Ricans in New York City, 1917- 1948*. Ph.D. diss., University of New York at Stony Brook, 1981. UMO #8119239.

2176. Sandoval, Raymond E. *Intrusion and Domination: A Study of the Relationship of Chicano Development to the Exercise and Distribution of Power in a Southern City*. Ph.D. diss., University of Washington, 1980. [Las Cruces, NM] UMO #8026300.

2177. Shamon, Janet H. *Community Formation: Blacks in Northern Liberties, 1790-1850*. Ph.D. diss., Temple University, 1991. [Philadelphia] UMO #9135006.

2178. Snipp, C. Matthew. "Old and New Views of Economic Development in Indian Country." *Overcoming Economic Dependency: Papers and Comments from the First Newberry Library Conference on Themes in American Indian History*, Chicago, IL: Newberry Library, 1988.

2179. Stea, D. "Energy Resource Development, Energy Use, and Indigenous Peoples: A Case Study of Native North Americans." *Geography Research Forum* 7 (1984).

2180. Stull, Donald D. "Reservation Economic Development in the Era of Self-Determination." *American Anthropologist* 92 (March 1990): 206-210.

2181. Tabb, W. "What Happened to Black Economic Development?" *Review of Black Political Economy* 17 (Fall 1988): 65-88.

2182. Taibi, A. D. "Banking, Finance, and Community Economic Empowerment: Structural Economic Theory, Procedural Civil Rights, and Substantive Racial Justice." *Harvard Law Review* 107 (May 1994): 1463-1546.

2183. Task Force on Indian Economic Development. *Report...* Washington, DC: GPO, 1986.

2184. Thomas, Richard W. *Life for Us Is What We Make It. Building Black Community in Detroit, 1915-1945*. Indiana University Press: 1992.

2185. Till, T. E. "The Share of Southeastern Black Counties in the Southern Rural Renaissance: Were They Bypassed by Factory Job Gains, 1959-1977?" *Growth and Change* 17 (April 1986).

2186. Valle, Victor, and Rudy D. Torres. "Fighting With Blacks for Jobs is Self-Defeating." *Los Angeles Times*, 2 August 1992.

2187. Vidal de Haynes, Maria R. "'Successful Minorities': A Re- examination of the Cuban American Case." *Sociological Abstracts* (August 1991): supplement 166. 91S24866/SSSP/1991/3060.

2188. Vinje, David L. "Economic Development on Reservations in the Twentieth Century." in *Overcoming Economic Dependency*, Chicago, IL: Newberry Library, 1988.

CONCENTRATION CAMPS

2189. Amsden, Charles. "The Navaho Exile at Bosque Redondo." *New Mexico Historical Review* 8 (January 1933): 31-50.

2190. Bailey, Lynn R. *Bosque Redondo: An American Concentration Camp*. Pasadena, CA: Socio-Technical Books, 1970.

2191. Baker, Lillian. *American and Japanese Relocation in World War II: Fact, Fiction, and Fallacy*. Medford, OR: Webb Research Group, 1989. [Rejects characterization of concentration camps]

2192. Bearden, Russell. "Life Inside Arkansas's Japanese-American Relocation Centers." *Arkansas H. Quarterly* 48 (Summer 1989): 169- 196.

2193. Chiasson, L. "Japanese-American Relocation During World War II: A Study of California Editorial Reactions." *Journalism Quarterly* 68 (Spring-Summer 1991): 263-269.

2194. Daniels, Roger. *Concentration Camps: North American Japanese in the United States and Canada During World War II*. Krieger: 1989.

2195. Emi, Frank. "Resistance: The Heart Mountain Fair Play Committee's Fight for Justice." *Amerasia Journal* 17 (1991): 47- 51.

2196. Fox, Stephen R. *The Unknown Resistance: An Oral History of the Relocation of Italian-Americans during World War II*. Boston, MA: Twayne, 1990.

2197. Fukuda, Yoshiaki. *My Six Years of Internment: An Issei's Struggle for Justice*. San Francisco, CA: Konko Church of San Francicso, 1990.

2198. Gentile, Nancy J. "Survival Behind Barbed Wire: The Impact of Imprisonment on Japanese-American Culture during World War II." *Maryland Historian* 19 (Fall-Winter 1988): 15-32.

2199. Hansen, Arthur A., ed. *Japanese American World War II Evacuation Oral History Project. Vol. 1, Internees*. Westport, CT: Meckler, 1991.

2200. Hansen, Arthur A., and Betty E. Mitson, eds. *Voices Long Silent: An Oral Inquiry into the Japanese American Evacuation*. Fullerton, CA: 1974.

2201. Harth, Erica. "Concentration and Memory." *In These Times* (24 June 1992). [Written by a white person who, as a child, had lived at Manzanar concentration camp.]

2202. Hayashi, Haruo, and P. R. Abramson. "Self-identity of Japanese Americans Interned during World War 2: An Archival Study." *Psychologia* 30 (September 1987): 127-136.

2203. Hohri, William. *Repairing America: An Account of the Movement for Japanese-American Redress*. Washington, DC, 1988.

2204. Ichioka, Yuji, ed. *Views from Within: The Japanese American Evacuation and Resettlement Study*. Los Angeles: UCLA Asian American Studies Center, 1989.

2205. Iiyama, Patty. "American Concentration Camps: Racism and Japanese-Americans During World War II." *International Socialist Review* 34 (1973): 24-33.

2206. Irons, Peter, ed. *Justice Delayed: The Record of the Japanese American Internment Cases.* Middletown, CT: Wesleyan University Press, 1989.

2207. Irons, Peter. "Race and the Constitution: The Case of the Japanese American Internment." *This Consitution* no. 13 (1986): 18-26.

2208. Johnson, Melyn. "At Home in Amache: A Japanese-American Relocation Camp in Colorado." *Colorado Heritage* no. 1 (1989): 2- 11. [Granada Relocation Center]

2209. Kessler, Lauren. "Fettered Freedoms: The Journalism of World War II Japanese Internment Camps." *Journalism History* (Summer/August 1988).

2210. Matsuda, Kazue. *Poetic Reflections of the Tule Lake Internment Camp 1944.* California: 1987.

2211. Nagata, D. K. "The Japanese-American Internment-Perceptions of Moral Community, Fairness, and Redress." *Journal of Social Issues* 46 (Spring 1990).

2212. Nagata, D. K., and Faye J. Crosby. "Comparisons, Justice, and Internment of Japanese Americans." in *Social Comparison: Contemporary Theory and Research*, eds. J. Suls, and T. A. Wills. Hillsdale, NJ: Lawrence Erlbaum Associates, 1990.

2213. Nakagawa, Gordon. "'No Japs Allowed': Negation and Naming as Subject-Constituting Strategies Reflected in Contemporary Stories of Japanese-American Internment." *Communication Reports* 3 (Winter 1990): 22-27.

2214. Nakanishi, Don T. "Seeking Convergence in Race Relations Research: Japanese-Americans and the Resurrection of the Internment." in *Eliminating Racism*, pp. 159-180. eds. Phyllis A. Katz, and Dalmas A. Taylor. New York: Plenum, 1988.

2215. Nash, Philip Tajitsu. "A More Perfect Union: Japanese Americans and the Constitution." *Radical History Review* no. 45 (Fall 1989): 139-142.

2216. Okamura, Raymond Y. "The American Concentration Camps: A Cover-Up through Euphemistic Terminology." *Journal of Ethnic Studies* 10 (Fall 1982): 95-108.

2217. Osburn, Katherine M. B. "The Navajo at Bosque Redondo: Cooperation, Resistance, and Initative, 1864-1868." *New Mexico Hist. Review* 60 (October 1985): 399-413.

2218. Petonito, Gina. "Loyal Americans, Disloyal Enemies: An Interactionist Analysis of One Justification of Japanese Internment during World War II." *Sociological Abstracts* 90S24365/ASA/1990/6063.

2219. Rabinovitz, Jonathan. "Revisiting Japanese Internment." *New York Times Education Life* (7 April 1991). [Public-school curriculum about Japanese-Americans in camps, 1942-1945; call 415-431-5007]

2220. Romanowski, Michael H. *The Ethical Treatment of the Japanese-American Internment Camps: A Content Analysis of Secondary American History Textbooks.* Ph.D. diss., Miami University, 1993. UMO #9320240.

2221. Scheiber, Harry N., and Jane L. Scheiber. "Constitutional Liberty in World War II: Army Rule and Martial Law in Hawaii, 1941-1946." *Western Legal History* 3 (Summer-Fall 1990): 340-378.

2222. Schonberger, Howard. "Dilemmas of Loyalty: Japanese Americans and the Psychological Warfare Campaigns of the Office of Strategic Services, 1943-1945." *Amerasia Journal* 16 (1990): 20-38.

2223. Schweik, Susan. "The 'Pre-Poetics' of Internment: The Example of Toyo Suyemoto." *American Literary History* 1 (Spring 1989): 89-109.

2224. Strum, Harvey. "Jewish Internees in the American South, 1942-1945." *American Jewish Archives* 42 (1990): 27-48.

2225. Suzuki, Peter T. "For the Sake of Inter-University Comity: The Attempted Suppression by the University of California of Morton Grodzins' Americans Betrayed." in *Views from Within. The Japanese American Evacuation and Resettlement Study*, ed. Yuji Ichioka. Los Angeles: Asian American Studies Center, University of California, Los Angeles, 1989.

2226. Takaki, Janie Hitomi. "The Later Generations: How Has the Internment of Japanese in America Impacted Them?" Master's Thesis, California State University, Long Beach, 1988.

2227. Takezawa, Yasuko I. *"Breaking the Silence": Ethnicity and the Quest for Redress among Japanese-Americans.* Ph.D. diss., University of Washington, 1989. UMO #9020972.

2228. Taylor, Sandra C. "Japanese Americans and Keetley Farms: Utah's Relocation Colony." *Utah Historical Quarterly* 54 (1986): 328-344.

2229. Turner, Stanton B. "Japanese-American Internment at Tule Lake, 1942-1946." *Journal of the Shaw Historical Library* 2 (1987): 1-34.

2230. Weglyn, Michi N. *Years of Infamy. The Untold Story of America's Concentration Camps.* Morrow Quill Paperbacks: 1976.

CRIME

2231. Abney, D. "Capital Punishment in Arizona, 1863-1963." Master's Thesis, Arizona State University, 1989.

2232. Abramson, Jeffrey. "When Lawyers Play the Race Card." *New York Times*, 9 September 1994. [O.J. Simpson Case]

2233. Abu-Jamal, Mumia. "B-Block Days and Nightmares." *Nation* (25 April 1990). [Letter from Death Row]

2234. Acker, James R. "Social Science in Supreme Court Criminal Cases and Briefs." *Law and Human Behavior* 14 (February 1990): 25- 42.

2235. _____. "Thirty Years of Social Science in Supreme Court Criminal Cases." *Law and Policy* 12 (January 1990): 1-23.

2236. Albonetti, Celesta A. and others. "Criminal Justice Decision Making as a Stratification Process: The Role of Race and Stratification Resources in Pretrial Release." *Journal of Quantitative Criminology* 5 (March 1989): 57-82.

2237. Albonetti, Celesta A. "Race and the Probability of Pleading Guilty." *Journal of Quantitative Criminology* 6 (September 1990): 315-334.

2238. Allen, Derek B. *From the Ghetto to the Joint: A Study of Black Urban Survival Crime in Detroit.* Ph.D. diss., Michigan State University, 1989. UMO #8923826 2 Vols.

2239. Altschuler, D. M., and P. J. Brownstein. "Patterns of Drug Use, Drug Trafficking, and Other Delinquency among Inner-City Adolescent Males in Washington D.C." *Criminology* 29 (November 1991): 589-622.

2240. *Americans Behind Bars*. Edna McConnell Clark Foundation: 1993.

2241. Amsterdam, Anthony. "Race and the Death Penalty." *Criminal Justice Ethics* 7 (1988): 2, 84-86.

2242. Applebome, Peter. "2 Years, 10 Murders and 1 Question." *New York Times*, 24 March 1994. [Racism and official investigation of murders in Charlotte, NC]

2243. _____. "Alabama Releases Man Held On Death Row for Six Years." *New York Times*, 3 March 1993. [Walter McWilliams, African-American]

2244. _____. "Atlanta Watches Nervously As Corruption Trial Begins." *New York Times*, 5 January 1994.

2245. _____. "Conditions in 18 Mississippi Jails Found Unsanitary and Dangerous." *New York Times*, 11 December 1993.

2246. _____. "Death in a Jailhouse: The Ruling, A Suicide: The Fear, a Lynching." *New York Times*, 21 February 1993. [Mendenhall, Mississippi]

2247. _____. "Rise Is Found in Hate Crimes Committed by Blacks." *New York Times*, 13 December 1993.

2248. Aquirre, Adalberto, Jr., and David Baker. "The Execution of Mexican American Prisoners in the Southwest." *Social Justice* 16 (Winter 1989).

2249. Arneklev, Bruce J. "Racial Disparity and Incarceration in the Juvenile Justice System: A Test of Differential Involvement and Discrimination Theory." Master's Thesis, Western Washington University, 1988.

2250. Arnold, R. A. "Processes of Victimization and Criminalization of Black Women." *Social Justice* 17 (Autumn 1990).

2251. Arthur, John A. "Criminal Victimization, Fear of Crime and Handgun Ownership among Blacks: Evidence from National Survey Data." *American Journal of Criminal Justice* 16 (1992): 121-141.

2252. Arvanites, Thomas M. "The Differential Impact of Deinstitutionalization on White and Nonwhite Defendants Found Incompetent to Stand Trial." *Bulletin of the American Academy of Psychiatry and the Law* 17 (1989): 311-320.

2253. Bachman, Ronet. "An Analysis of American Indian Homicide: A Test of Social Disorganization and Economic Deprivation at the Reservation County Level." *Journal of Research in Crime and Delinquency* 28 (November 1991): 456-471.

2254. Baker, Karin. "Geronimo Pratt, Political Prisoner." *Against the Current* no. 51 (July-August 1994). [Former Black Panther Leader]

2255. Baldus, David C. and others. *Equal Justice and the Death Penalty: A Legal and Empirical Analysis.* Boston, MA: Northeastern University Press, 1990.

2256. Balkwell, J. W. "Ethnic Inequality and the Rate of Homicide." *Social Forces* 69 (September 1990).

2257. Barak, Gregg, ed. *Media, Process, and the Social Construction of Crime.* Garland: 1994.

2258. Barker, Rodney. *The Broken Circle. A True Story of Murder and Magic in Indian Country.* Simon and Schuster: 1992. [Navajo reservation]

2259. Baxter, Brent I.. *The Contextual Influences of County Racial Characteristics on Racial Disparities in Criminal Sanctions.* Ph.D. diss., University of Washington, 1991. UMO #9216103.

2260. Beaty, Jonathan and others. "Race and the Death Penalty." *Time* (29 April 1991).

2261. Bell, Derrick. "Stuart's Lie: An American Tradition." *New York Times*, 14 January 1990. [Exploiting fears of black people among whites]

2262. Benjamin, Stacy E. "Color Blind? The Influence of Race on Perception of Crime Severity." *Journal of Negro Education* 58 (1989): 442-448.

2263. Berk, Richard A. "Thinking About Hate-Motivated Crimes." *Journal of Interpersonal Violence* 5 (September 1990): 334-349.

2264. "Bias Crimes. Truth and Hysteria [in NYC]." *Village Voice* (28 January 1992). [Four articles and an editorial]

2265. Birnbaum, Jesse. "When Hate Makes a Fist." *Time* (26 April 1993). [hate crimes]

2266. Black Horse, Francis D. "Prison and Native People." *Indian Historian* 8 (1975): 54-56.

2267. Blecker, Robert. "Haven or Hell? Inside Lorton Central Prison: Experiences of Punishment Justified." *Stanford Law Review* 42 (May 1990): 1149-1249.

2268. Bodenhamer, David J. "The Efficiency of Criminal Justice in the Antebellum South." *Criminal Justice History* (1983).

2269. Bodinger-De Uriarte, Christina, and Anthony R. Sancho. *Hate Crime: Sourcebook for Schools.* Research for Better Schools, Philadelphia, 1992.

2270. Boritch, H. "Gender and Criminal Court Outcomes: An Historical Analysis." *Criminology* 30 (August 1992): 293-326.

2271. Bouza, Anthony V. *How to Stop Crime.* Plenum: 1993.

2272. Boyer, Peter J. "Looking for Justice in L.A." *New Yorker* (15 March 1993).

2273. Braithwaite, J. "Poverty, Power, White-collar Crime and the Paradoxes of Criminological Theory." *Austrialian and New Zealand Journal of Criminology* 24 (March 1991): 40-58.

2274. Bridge, George S., and Robert D. Crutchfield. "Law, Social Standing, and Racial Disparities in Imprisonment." *Social Forces* 66 (1988): 699-724.

2275. Bright, S. B. "Counsel for the Poor: The Death Sentence Not for the Worst Crime But for the Worst Lawyer." *Yale Law Journal* 103 (May 1994): 1835-1854.

2276. Brownstein, Ronald. "Clinton's 'New Democrat' Agenda Reopens Racial Divisions." *Los Angeles Times*, 9 February 1994. [On welfare and crime policy]

2277. Bruck, David I. "Does the Death Penalty Matter? Reflections of a Death Row Lawyer." *Reconstruction* 1 (1991): 35-39.

2278. Butler, Anne M. "Still in Chains: Black Women in Western Prisons, 1865-1910." *Western Historical Quarterly* 20 (1989): 18- 35.

2279. Byrne, J. M., and F. S. Taxman. "Crime Control Policy and Community Corrections Practice: Assessing the Impact of Gender, Race, and Class." *Evaluation and Program Planning* 17 (April-June 1994).

2280. Cameron, Samuel. "Race and Prosecution Expenditures." *Review of Black Political Economy* 19 (Summer 1990): 79-90.

2281. Carrico, Richard L. "Spanish Crime and Punishment: The Native American Experience in Colonial San Diego, 1769-1830." *Western Legal History* 3 (Winter-Spring 1990): 21-33.

2282. "Challenging the Dealth Penalty: A Colloquium." *New York University Review of Law and Social Change* 18 (1990-1991): entire issue.

2283. Charen, Mona. "Racial Justice Fallacies." *Boston Globe*, 25 July 1994. [Race and death penalty]

2284. Chin, Do-lin. *Chinese Subculture and Criminality. Non- Traditional Crime Groups in America*. Westport, CT: Greenwood, 1990. [Asian crime groups in the U.S.]

2285. Churchill, Ward, and Jim Vander Wall, eds. *Cages of Steel: The Politics of Imprisonment in the United States*. Maisonneuve Press, PO Box 2980. Washington, DC 20013-2980: 1992. [Political prisoners]

2286. Clary, Mike. "Rising Toll of Hate Crimes Cited in Student's Slaying." *Los Angeles Times*, 10 October 1992. [Death of Luyen Phan Nguyen, in Coral Springs, FL]

2287. Clines, Francis X. "Ex-Inmates Urge Return to Areas of Crime to Help." *New York Times*, 23 December 1992.

2288. Cohen, Laurie P. "White Collar Offender Discovers Little Mercy in the Toils of the Law." *Wall Street Journal*, 18 December 1990.

2289. Cohen, Richard. "Common Ground On Crime." *Washington Post*, 21 December 1993.

2290. _____. "Justice-or Mandatory Revenge?" *Washington Post*, 13 July 1993. [The politics of crime statistics]

2291. Cohen, Steven F. and others. "Punitive Attitudes Toward Criminals: Racial Consensus or Racial Conflict?" *Social Problems* 38 (1991): 287-296.

2292. Colbert, Douglas L. and others. "For Simpson, a Multiracial Jury Insures Justice." *New York Times*, 16 September 1994. [Three separate letters on O.J. Simpson]

2293. Combs, M., and J. Comer. "Race and Capital Punishment: A Longitudinal Analysis." *Phylon* 43 (1982): 350-359.

2294. Conrad, John P. "From Barbarian Toward Decency: Alabama's Long Road to Prison Reform." *Journal of Research in Crime and Delinquency* 26 (November 1989).

2295. Conyers, John, Jr., and Craig A. Washington. "Senate Crime- Custer's Got It Wrong." *Washington Post*, 23 November 1993.

2296. Corfman, Tom, and Muriel L. Whetstone. "Hate Crimes [in Chicago] Headed for Record Year." *Chicago Reporter* (July 1992).

2297. Covington, Jeanette. "Crime and Heroin: The Effects of Race and Gender." *Journal of Black Studies* 18 (June 1988): 486-506.

2298. Crabb, Beth. "May 1930: White Man's Justice for a Black Man's Crime." *Journal of Negro History* 75 (Winter, Spring 1990): 29-40. [Lynching]

2299. Culver, J. H. "Capital Punishment, 1977-1990: Characteristics of the 143 Executed." *Sociology and Social Research* 76 (January 1992): 59-62.

2300. Cummings, Eric. *The Rise and Fall of California's Radical Prison Movement*. Stanford University Press: 1994. [Deals with George Jackson, among others]

2301. Curry, G. David, and J. A. Spergel. "Gang Involvement and Delinquency Among Hispanic and African-American Adolescent Males." *Journal of Research in Crime and Delinquency* 29 (August 1992): 273-291.

2302. Daly, Kathleen. "Neither Conflict nor Labeling nor Paternalism Will Suffice: Intersections of Race, Ethnicity, Gender, and Family in Criminal Court Decisions." *Crime and Delinquency* 35 (January 1989): 136-168.

2303. Darity, William A., Jr., and Samuel L. Myers, Jr. "Impacts of Violent Crime on Black Family Structure." *Contemporary Policy Issues* 8 (1990): 15-29.

2304. Davis, John A. "Blacks, Crime, and American Culture." *Annals of the American Academy of Political and Social Science* no. 423 (1976): 89-98.

2305. De Parle, Jason. "Young Black Men in Capital: Study Finds 42% in Courts." *New York Times*, 18 April 1992. [District of Columbia]

2306. Defeis, Elizabeth F. "Freedom of Speech and International Norms: A Response to Hate Speech." *Stanford Journal of International Law* 29 (Fall 1992): 57-130.

2307. Deutsch, J. and others. "Crime and Income Inequality: An Economic Approach." *Atlantic Economic Journal* 20 (December 1992).

2308. Deutsch, M. E., and J. Susler. "Political Prisoners in the United States: The Hidden Reality." *Social Justice* 18 (Autumn 1991): 92-106.

2309. Didion, Joan. "New York: Sentimental Journeys." *New York Review of Books* (17 January 1991): 45-56.

2310. Dolan, Maura, and Tracy Shryer. "2 Murdered for Helping People Look 'Aryan'." *Los Angeles Times*, 11 August 1993. [Neo- Nazi supporter was murderer]

2311. Donnelly, Samuel J. M. "The Goals of Criminal Punishment: A Rawlsian Theory." *Syracuse Law Review* 41 (Summer 1990): 741-800.

2312. Dunne, Bill. "The U.S. Penitentiary at Marion, Illinois: An Instrument of Oppression." *New Studies on the Left* 14 (Spring- Summer 1989).

2313. Edmundson, William A. "The 'Race-of-the-Victim' Effect in Capital Sentencing: McClesky v. Kemp and Underadjustment Bias." *Jurimetrics. Journal of Law, Science, and Technology* 31 (Fall 1990): 125-141.

2314. Ekland-Olson, Sheldon. "Structured Discretion, Racial Bias, and the Death Penalty: The First Decade after Furman in Texas." *Social Science Quarterly* 69 (December 1988): 853-873.

2315. Elias, Robert. *Victims Still: The Political Manipulation of Crime Victims*. Sage: 1993.

2316. Fadaei-Tehrani, R. "The Costs of Crime: Unemployment and Poverty." *International Journal of Social Economics* 16 (1989).

2317. Fagan, J. and others. "Delinquency and Substance Use Among Inner-City Students." *Journal of Drug Issues* 20 (Summer 1990).

2318. Feeley, M. M., and D. L. Little. "The Vanishing Female: The Decline of Women in the Criminal Process, 1687-1912." *Law and Society Review* 25 (1991): 719-758.

2319. Filbert, M. Shanara. "Racism and Retrenchment in Capital Sentencing: Judicial and Congressional Haste toward the Ultimate Injustice." *New York University Review of Law and Social Change* 18 (1990-91): 51-80.

2320. Fingerhut, L. A., and J. C. Kleinman. "International and Interstate Comparison of Homicide Among Young Males." *Journal of the American Medical Association* (June 1990).

2321. Finn, Peter, and Taylor McNeil. *The Response of the Criminal Justice System to Bias Crime: An Exploratory Review*. Cambridge, MA: Abt Associates, October 1987.

2322. Flanigan, Daniel J. "Criminal Procedure in Slave Trials in the Antebellum South." *Journal of Southern History* 40 (November 1974).

2323. _____. *The Criminal Law of Slavery and Freedom*. New York: Garland, 1989.

2324. Flowers, Ronald B. *Demographics and Criminality. The Characteristics of Crime in America*. Westport, CT: Greenwood, 1989.

2325. _____. *Minorities and Criminality*. Westport, CT: Greenwood, 1988.

2326. Forst, Brian, ed. *The Socio-Economics of Crime and Justice*. Sharpe, 1994.

2327. Fox, James G. *Organizational and Racial Conflict in Maximum-Security Prisons*. Lexington, MA: Lexington Books, 1982.

2328. Frazier, C. E. and others. "The Social Context of Race Differentials in Juvenile Justice Dispositions." *Sociological Quarterly* 33 (Autumn 1992): 447-458.

2329. Freeman, Richard B. "The Relation of Criminal Activity to Black Youth Employment." *Review of Black Political Economy* 16 (1987): 99-107.

2330. Friedman, Lawrence. *Crime and Punishment in American History*. Basic Books, 1993.

2331. Garcia, Velia. *My Momma the State: A Sociological Study of the Criminialization of Chicanos*. Ph.D. diss., University of California, Berkeley, 1990. UMO # 9126569.

2332. George, Nelson, ed. *Stop the Violence: Overcoming Self- Destruction*. New York: Pantheon, 1990.

2333. Georges-Abeyle, Daniel E. "Race, Ethnicity and the Spatial Dynamic: Toward a Realistic Study of Black Crime, Crime Victimization, and Criminal Justice Processing of Blacks." *Social Justice* 16 (1989): 35-54.

2334. Glover, Danny. "A Fervor to Kill in a Doubtful Case." *Los Angeles Times*, 8 August 1993. [Criticism of impending execution of Gary Graham at Huntsville prison, Texas]

2335. Goldberg, M. Z. "Hate Crimes Alleged in Florida Suit." *Trial* 27 (October 1991): 86-87.

2336. Goldstein, Paul J. and others. "Crack and Homicide in New York City, 1988: A Conceptually Based Event Analysis." *Contemporary Drug Problems* 16 (Winter 1989): 651-687.

2337. Goldstock, Ronald, and Thomas Thatcher, II. *Corruption and Racketeering in the New York City Construction Industry*. New York: New York University Press, 1991.

2338. Gotfredson, Michael R., and Travis Hirschi. *A General Theory of Crime*. Stanford, CA: Stanford University Press, 1990.

2339. Greenberg, Jack. "Death Row, U.S.A." *New York Times*, 2 June 1993. [Racism and capital punishment in the U.S.]

2340. Greene, Dwight L. "Abusive Prosecutors: Gender, Race, and Class Discretion and the Prosecution of Drug-addicted Mothers." *Buffalo Law Review* 39 (Fall 1991): 737-802.

2341. Guilfoyle, Michael H. "Indians and Criminal Justice Administration: The Failure of the Criminal Justice System for the American Indian." Master's Thesis, University of Arizona, 1988.

2342. Hagan, J. "The Poverty of a Classless Criminology: The American Society of Criminology, 1991." *Criminology* 30 (February 1992): 1-20.

2343. Harlow, Caroline Wolf. *Female Victims of Violent Crime*. Washington, DC: U.S. Department of Justice, Bureau of Justice Statistics, January 1991. [Contains racial breakdowns]

2344. Harris, D. A. "Factors for Reasonable Suspicion: When Black and Poor Means Stopped and Frisked." *Indiana Law Journal* 69 (Summer 1984): 659-688.

2345. Harris, Ron. "Hand of Punishment Falls Heavily on Black Youths." *Los Angeles Times*, 24 August 1993.

2346. Harrison, Eric. "Jail Cell Hangings Revive Old Ghosts in Mississippi." *Los Angeles Times*, 30 May 1993.

2347. "Hate Is Not Speech: A Constitutional Defense of Penalty Enhancement for Hate Crimes." *Harvard Law Review* 106 (April 1993): 1314-1331.

2348. Hawkins, Darnell F. "Explaining the Black Homicide Rate." *Journal of Interpersonal Violence* 5 (1991): 157-163.

2349. Hawkins, Darnell F., ed. *Homicide among Black Americans*. Lanham, MD: University Press of America, 1986.

2350. Hawkins, Darnell F., and Kenneth A. Hardy. "Black-White Imprisonment Rates: A State-by-state Analysis." *Social Justice* 16 (1989): 75-94.

2351. Hawkins, Steve. "Utah Shows Death Penalty's Racism." *New York Times*, 19 August 1992. Letter.

2352. Headley, Bernard D. "Black on Black Crime: The Myth and the Reality." *Crime and Social Justice* no. 20 (1983): 50-62.

2353. _____. "Crime, Justice, and Powerless Racial Groups." *Social Justice* 16 (Winter 1989).

2354. Heilbrun, Alfred B., Jr. and others. "The Death Sentence in Georgia, 1974-1987: Criminal Justice or Racial Injustice?" *Criminal Justice and Behavior* 16 (June 1989): 139-154.

2355. Henderson, William C. *The Slave Court System in Spartanburg County*. Publications of the South Carolina Historical Association, 1976.

2356. Hentoff, Nat. "The Executioner Who Would Be a Judge." *Village Voice* (7 July 1992) [The politics of the death penalty in Alabama]

2357. Hill, Gary D., and Elizabeth M. Crawford. "Women, Race, and Crime." *Criminology* 28 (November 1990): 601-626.

2358. Hoffman, Charles, and Tess Hoffman. *Brotherly Love: Murder and the Politics of Prejudice in Nineteenth-Century Rhode Island*. University of Massachusetts Press: 1994.

2359. Holmes, Steven A. "Blacks Convene to Seek Ways to Fight Crime." *New York Times*, 8 January 1994.

2360. Hooker, Mark. "Racism Isn't Issue In Crack Sentencing." *Boston Globe*, 1 August 1994. letter.

2361. Horn, Joseph. "Robbed By a Young Black." *New York Times*, 15 May 1990.

2362. Hudson, Barbara. "Discrimination and Disparity: The Influence of Race on Sentencing." *New Community* 16 (1989): 23-34.

2363. _____. *Penal Policy and Social Justice*. University of Toronto Press, 1993.

2364. Hutchinson, Earl Ofari. *The Mugging of Black America*. African American Images: 1990.

2365. *The Impact of Crime of Race Relations in New York City*. New York: Catholic Interracial Council, 1985.

2366. "It's Not Easy Being Green: Feds Blind to Reactionary Hate Crimes." *In These Times* (15 August 1990).

2367. Jackson, Derrick Z. "Equal Justice Takes a Loss." *Boston Globe*, 3 August 1994. [President Clinton and failure to support passage of the Racial Justice Act.]

2368. _____. "How the Crime News Gets Colorized." *Boston Globe*, 17 August 1994.

2369. _____. "So Who Really Gets the Juice?" *Boston Globe*, 29 July 1994. [The O.J. Simpson case in the perpective of African-American men in prison]

2370. _____. "The Wrong Face on Crime." *Boston Globe*, 19 August 1994. [Race and crime]

2371. Jackson, Pamela I. *Minority Group Threat, Crime, and Policing: Social Context and Social Control*. New York: Praeger, 1989.

2372. Jeffers, Sidonie C. "The Confrontation Clause and the Establishment of Bias in Criminal Prosecutions." *Harvard Law Review* 32 (Summer 1989): 149-161.

2373. Johnson, Dirk. "2 Out of 3 Young Black Men in Denver Are on Gang Suspect List." *New York Times*, 11 December 1993.

2374. Johnson, Robert C., Jr., "The Political Economy of Criminal Oppression." *Black Scholar* (April 1977): 14-22.

2375. Joselit, Jenna W. *Our Gang: Jewish Crime and the New York Jewish Community, 1900-1940*. Bloomington: Indiana University Press, 1983.

2376. Kazyaka, Ann-Marie. *Guarding the Gateway to Discrimination: Developing a Constitutional Model of Capital Sentencing*. Ph.D. diss., University of Maryland, 1990. UMO #9012842.

2377. Keil, Thomas J., and G. F. Vito. "Race, Homicide Severity, and Application of the Death Penalty: A Consideration of the Barnett Scale." *Criminology* 27 (August 1989): 511-535.

2378. Kennedy, Lisa. "Crime and Feminism." *Village Voice* (2 July 1991). [Crime, feminism, and racism]

2379. Kennedy, Randall L. "McCleskey v. Kemp: Race, Capital Punishment, and the Supreme Court." *Harvard Law Review* 101 (May 1988): 1388-1443.

2380. Klein, Stephen P. and others. "Race and Imprisonment Decisions in California." *Science* 247 (1990): 812-816.

2381. Klein, Stephen P. *Racial Disparities in Sentencing Decisions*. Santa Monica, CA: Rand Corp., 1991.

2382. Knepper, Paul E. *Imprisonment and Society in Arizona*. Ph.D. diss., Arizona State University, 1990. [1876-1909]. UMO #9025769.

2383. _____. "Southern-Style Penal Repression: Ethnic Stratification, Economic Inequality, and Imprisonment in Territorial Arizona." *Social Justice* 16 (Winter 1989).

2384. Kroll, Michael A. "How Much Is a Victim Worth?" *New York Times*, 24 April 1991. [Race and the death penalty]

2385. Kruttschnitt, Candace, and Maude Dornfeld. "Childhood Victimization, Race, and Violent Crime." *Criminal Justice and Behavior* 18 (December 1991): 448-463.

2386. Labaton, Stephen. "Poor Cooperation Deflates F.B.I. Report on Hate Crime." *New York Times*, 6 January 1993.

2387. Lafree, G. and others. "Race and Crime in Postwar America: Determinants of African-American and White Rates, 1957-1988." *Criminology* 30 (May 1992): 157-188.

2388. Lakshmann, India A. R. "Hate-crime Reports Rise in Boston." *Boston Globe*, 20 June 1994.

2389. Laurie, Pantell. "A Pathfinder on Bias Crimes and the Fight against Hate Groups." *Legal Reference Services Quarterly* 11 (1991): 39-75.

2390. Lawson, Bill E. "Crime, Minorities, and the Social Contract." *Criminal Justice Ethics* 9 (Summer-Fall 1990): 16-24.

2391. Le Flore, Larry. "Minority Youth in the Juvenile Justice System: A Judicial Response." *Juvenile and Family Courts Journal* 41 (Summer 1990): 1-71.

2392. Lessan, G. T. "Macro-economic Determinants of Penal Policy: Estimating the Unemployment and Inflation Influences on Imprisonment Rate Changes in the United States, 1948-1985." *Crime, Law, and Social Change* 16 (September 1991): 177-198.

2393. Levesque, George A. "Black Crime and Crime Statistics in Ante-Bellum Boston." *Australian Journal of Politics and History* 2 (1979).

2394. Levin, Jack, and Jack McDevitt. *Hate Crimes. The Rising Tide of Bigotry and Bloodshed*. Plenum: 1993.

2395. Lieberman, Paul. "51% of Riot Arrests Were Latino, Study Says." *Los Angeles Times*, 18 June 1992. [April 30, 1992 riot in Los Angeles]

2396. _____. "Criminals, Unlikely Targets Were Snared in Curfew Nets." *Los Angeles Times*, 2 August 1992. [Arrests in Los Angeles riots of April 30-May 5, 1992]

2397. Love, Sherri, and Rich Stuart. "Indian Rights Activist Gets 18-Year Sentence for Antiracist Action." *Militant* (9 March 1990). [Robeson County, NC]

2398. Lynch, Rene. "Grand Jury Still Fails to Reflect Racial Makeup of L.A. County." *Long Beach Press Telegram* (22 June 1992).

2399. Manly, Howard. "Harsh Line Drawn on Crack Cocaine. Tough Penalties Found to Affect Blacks Most." *Boston Globe*, 24 July 1994.

2400. Manly, Howard, and Adam Pertman. "Races See Simpson Differently." *Boston Globe*, 10 July 1994. [Views on O.J. Simpson's possible treatment in legal process trying charge of double-murder.]

2401. Mann, Coramae Richey. "Minority and Female: A Criminal Justice Double Bind." *Social Justice* 16 (Winter 1989).

2402. Margolick, David. "As Venues Are Changed, Many Ask How Important a Role Race Should Play." *New York Times*, 23 May 1992.

2403. _____. "In Land of Death Penalty, Accusations of Racial Bias." *New York Times*, 10 July 1991. [Columbus, GA]

2404. _____. "White Dies for Killing Black, for the First Time in Decades." *New York Times*, 7 September 1991. [Donald Gaskins, Columbia, SC]

2405. Marquart, James W. and others. *The Rope, the Chair, and the Needle: Capital Punishment in Texas, 1923-1990*. University of Texas Press, 1994.

2406. Martens, F. T. "African-American Organized Crime, an Ignored Phenomenon." *Federal Probation* 54 (December 1990): 43-50.

2407. Masur, Louis P. *Rites of Execution: Capital Punishment and the Transformation of American Culture, 1776-1865*. New York: Oxford University Press, 1989.

2408. Mauer, Marc, and Cathy Shine. *Does the Punishment Fit the Crime? Drug Users and Drunk Drivers, Questions of Race and Class*. The Sentencing Project, March 1993.

2409. McFadden, Robert D. "A Long Slide From Privilege Ends With Chaos on a Train." *New York Times*, 12 December 1993. [Colin Ferguson]

2410. McKenna, Clare V., Jr. "Ethnics and San Quentin Prison Registers: A Comment on Methodology." *Journal of Social History* 18 (March 1985).

2411. _____. "The Treatment of Indian Murderers in San Diego, 1850-1900." *Journal of San Diego History* 36 (1990): 65-77.

2412. McMillan, Theodore, and Christopher J. Petrini. "Batson V. Kentucky: A Promise Unfulfilled." *UMKC Law Review* 58 (Spring 1990): 361-374.

2413. Mercer, Le Ann W. "Constitutional Law-Racial Discrimination Within a Death Penalty System-The Petitioner's Heavy Burden." *Mississippi College Law Review* 9 (Fall 1988): 203-221.

2414. Messner, S. F., and R. M. Golden. "Racial Inequality and Racially Disaggregated Homicide Rates: An Assessment of Alternative Theoretical Explanations." *Criminology* 30 (August 1992).

2415. Messner, S. F., and South, S.J. "Interracial Homicide: A Macrostructural Opportunity Perspective." *Sociological Forum* 7 (September 1992): 517-540.

2416. Meyers, Christopher. "Racial Bias, the Death Penalty, and Desert." *Philosophical Forum* 22 (Winter 1990-91): 139-148.

2417. Miller, Arthur S., and Jeffrey H. Bowman. *Death by Installments. The Ordeal of Willie Francis*. Westport, CT: Greenwood, 1988. [Fate of Blacks who kill Whites]

2418. Miller, Jerome G. *Search and Destroy: The Plight of African American Males in the Criminal Justice System*. Alexandria, VA: National Center on Institutions and Alternatives, August 1992.

2419. Mitchell, John L. "Gangs in Affluent Black Turf." *Los Angeles Times*, 13 November 1992. [Upper-middle class Black gangs in Los Angeles suburbs]

2420. Monteiro, Tony. "Criminalization of African Americans: The New Face of Racism." *Political Affairs* 70 (April 1991): 4-12.

2421. *Murder in Families*. U.S. Department of Justice, July 1994.

2422. Muwakkil, Salim. "The Criminal Just-Us System." *In These Times* (19 April 1993).

2423. Myers, Martha A. "Black Threat and Incarceration in Postbellum Georgia." *Social Forces* 69 (December 1990): 373-393.

2424. _____. "Economic Threat and Racial Disparities in Incarceration: The Case of Postbellum Georgia." *Criminology* 28 (November 1990): 627-656.

2425. Myers, Martha A., and James L. Massey. "Race, Labor, and Punishment in Postbellum Georgia." *Social Problems* 38 (1991): 267-286. [1868-1936]

2426. Myers, Samuel L., Jr., and William J. Sabol. *Crime and the Black Community: Issues in the Understanding of Race and Crime in America*. Paper prepared for the Committee on the Status of Black Americans, National Research Council, Washington DC: 1987.

2427. Myers, Samuel L., Jr., and Margaret C. Simms, eds. *The Economics of Race and Crime*. New Brunswick, NJ: Transaction, 1988.

2428. Naison, Mark. "Outlaw Culture and Black Neighborhoods." *Reconstruction* 1 (1992): 128-131.

2429. New Jersey Committee of Investigation. *Afro-lineal Organized Crime*. 28 W. State St., CN 045, Trenton, NJ 08625: March 1991.

2430. Newton, Jim. "Harsher Crack Sentences Criticized as Racial Inequality." *Los Angeles Times*, 23 November 1992.

2431. Nieman, Donald G. "Black Political Power and Criminal Justice: Washington County, Texas, 1868-1884." *Journal of Southern History* 55 (August 1989): 391-420.

2432. O'Brien, Robert M. "The Interracial Nature of Violent Crimes: A Reexamination." *American Journal of Sociology* 92 (1987): 817-835.

2433. O'Kane, James M. *The Crooked Ladder. Gangsters, Ethnicity, and the American Dream*. New Brunswick, NJ: Transaction Publishers, 1992.

2434. Olivero, J. Michael, and James B. Roberts. "The United States Federal Penitentiary at Marion, Illinois: Alcatraz Revisited." *New England Journal on Criminal and Civil Confinement* 16 (Winter 1990): 21-51.

2435. Owens, Charles E. *The Impact of Black Criminal Justice Practitioners on the Criminal Justice System*. Paper prepared for the Committee on the Status of Black Americans, National Research Council, Washington, D.C.: 1987.

2436. Pain, R. "Space, Sexual Violence, and Social Control: Integrating Geographical and Feminist Analyses of Women's Fear of Crime." *Progress in Human Geography* 15 (December 1991): 415-432.

2437. Palley, Howard A., and Dana A. Robinson. "Black on Black Crime." *Society* 25 (1988): 59-62.

2438. Parkes, Keith D. "Criminal Victimization among Black Americans." *Journal of Black Studies* 22 (December 1991): 186-195.

2439. Patrick-Stamp, Leslie Cheryl. *Ideology and Punishment: The Crime of Being Black (Pennsylvania, 1639-1804)*. Ph.D. diss., University of California, Santa Cruz, 1989. UMO #8926508.

2440. Patterson, E. Britt. "Poverty, Income Inequality, and Community Crime Rates." *Criminology* 29 (November 1991): 755-776.

2441. Peak, Ken. "Criminal Justice, Law, and Policy in Indian County: A Historical Perspective." *Journal of Criminal Justice* 17 (September 1989): 393-407.

2442. Phillips, Charles D. "Social Structure and Social Control: Modeling the Discriminatory Execution of Blacks in Georgia and North Carolina, 1925-1935." *Social Forces* 65 (1986): 458-475.

2443. Pinkerton, James P. "Crime Succeeds in Keeping Us Segregated." *Los Angeles Times*, 12 May 1994.

2444. Pitts, Bruce. "Eliminating Hate: A Proposal for a Comprehensive Bias Crime Law." *Law and Psychology Review* 14 (Spring 1990): 139-157.

2445. "Race and the Criminal Process." *Harvard Law Review* 101 (May 1988): 1473-1641.

2446. Radelet, Michael L. "Executions of Whites for Crimes against Blacks: Exceptions to the Rule?" *Sociological Quarterly* 30 (1989): 529-544.

2447. Radosh, Polly F. "Women and Crime in the United States: A Marxian Explanation." *Sociological Spectrum* 10 (1990).

2448. Rakowsky, Judy. "US Charges Four With Hate Crimes." *Boston Globe*, 21 July 1994. [New Dawn Hammerskins]

2449. Ramirez, David E. "The Overincarceration Rate of Minority Youth: A Judicial Response." *Colorado Lawyer* 19 (September 1990).

2450. Ray, John. "The Issue is Crime, Not Race, Mr. President." *Washington Post*, 20 November 1993.

2451. Reed, Little Rock. "The American Indian in the White Man's Prisons: A Story of Genocide." *Humanity and Society* 13 (1989): 403-420.

2452. Reed, Wornie L. and others. "Trends in Homicide Among African-Americans." in *The Health and Medical Care of African Americans*, William Monroe Trotter Institute, University of Massachusetts at Boston, 1992.

2453. Reich, Kenneth. "Changes Seen as Inmates' Racial Brawls Escalate." *Los Angeles Times*, 12 October 1992. [Jails in Los Angeles County]

2454. Reidel, M. and others. *The Nature and Patterns of American Homicide*. Washington, DC: GPO, 1985.

2455. Reiman, Jeffry H. *The Rich Get Richer and the Poor Get Prison: Ideology, Class, and Criminal Justice*, 3rd ed. New York: Macmillan, 1990.

2456. Reitman, Judith. "Jungle Fever. Is Violence in the Genes?" *Village Voice* (17 August 1993).

2457. Reuter, Peter and others. *Money from Crime: A Study of the Economics of Drug Dealing in Washington, D.C.* The Rand Corporation: 1990.

2458. Rise, Eric W. *The Martinsville Seven and Southern Justice: Race, Crime, and Capital Punishment in Virginia, 1949-1951*. Ph.D. diss., University of Florida, 1993. UMO #9331205.

2459. Rithman S., and S. Powers. "Execution by Quota." *Public Interest* no. 116 (Summer 1994): 3-17.

2460. Roberts, Julian V., and Thomas Gabor. "Lombrosian Wine in a New Bottle: Research on Crime and Race." *Canadian Journal of Criminology* 32 (April 1990): 291-313. [For reply by J. Philippe Rushton, see pp. 315-334]

2461. Rodriguez, Luis J. *Always Running. La Vida Loca: Gang Days in L.A.* Curbstone Press: 1993. [1960's]

2462. Rodriguez, O., and Weisburd D. "The Integrated Social Control Model and Ethnicity: The Case of Puerto Rican American Delinquency." *Criminal Justice and Behavior* 18 (December 1991): 464-479.

2463. Rodriguez, Salvador F. *Patterns of Homicide in Texas: A Descriptive Analysis of Racial/Ethnic Involvement by Crime- specific Categories*. Ph.D. diss., University of Texas, 1990. UMO #9031701.

2464. Roehrenbeck, Carol A. *People vs. Goetz: the Summations and the Charges to the Jury*. Buffalo, NY: W.S. Hein Co., 1989.

2465. Rose, Harold M., and Paula D. McClain. *Race, Place, and Risk: Black Homicide in Urban America*. Albany: State University of New York Press, 1990.

2466. Rothman, David J. "The Crime of Punishment." *New York Review of Books* (17 February 1994). [Review essay]

2467. Rowe, G. S. "Black Offenders, Criminal Courts, and Philadelphia Society in the Late Eighteenth Century." *Journal of Social History* 22 (Summer 1989): 685-712.

2468. Rushton, J. Philippe. "Race and Crime: A Reply to Roberts and Gabor." *Canadian Journal of Criminology* 32 (April 1990). [See rejoinder by Roberts and Gabor in same issue.]

2469. Sabol, William J. "Racially Disproportionate Prison Populations in the United States: An Overview of Historical Patterns and Review of Contemporary Issues." *Contemporary Crises* 13 (December 1989): 405-432.

2470. Sagatun, Inger J. "Gender Discrimination in Criminal Justice: Relevant Law and Future Trends." *Women and Criminal Justice* 2 (1990): 63-81.

2471. Savage, David G. "Shaky Future for Statutes on Hate Crimes." *Los Angeles Times*, 10 December 1992.

2472. Schatzberg, Rufus. *Black Organized Crime in Harlem: 1920- 1930*. Ph.D. diss., City University of New York, 1990. UMO #9108171.

2473. Schauer, Frederick. "The Sociology of the Hate Speech Debate." *Villanova Law Review* 37 (1992): 805-819.

2474. Schulhofer, Stephen J. "Rethinking Mandatory Minimums." *Wake Forest Law Review* 28 (Summer 1993): 199-222. [Racial discrimination in pleading guilty to lesser crimes]

2475. Schwarz, Philip J. *Twice Condemned: Slaves and the Criminal Laws of Virginia, 1705-1865*. Baton Rouge: Louisiana State University Press, 1988.

2476. Scott, Robin F. "The Sleepy Lagoon Case and the Grand Jury Investigation." in *An Awakened Minority: The Mexican Americans*, ed. Manuel P. Servin. 2nd ed. Beverly Hills, 1974.

2477. Secret, Philip E., and James B. Johnson. "Racial Differences in Attitudes Toward Crime Control." *Journal of Criminal Justice* 17 (September-October 1989): 361-375.

2478. Seeley, David S. "The Debate Over Free Speech and Hate Speech." *Chronicle of Higher Education* (16 March 1994).

2479. Sege, Irene. "Race, Violence Make Complex Picture." *Boston Globe*, 31 January 1990.

2480. Sheldon, Randall F. "From Slave to Caste Society: Penal Change in Tennessee, 1830-1915." *Tennessee Historical Society* 38 (1979): 462-478.

2481. Sidanius, Jim. "Race and Sentence Severity: The Case of American Justice." *Journal of Black Studies* 18 (March 1988): 273- 281.

2482. Silverman, R. A. and others. "Murdered Children: A Comparison of Racial Differences Across Two Jurisdictions." *Journal of Criminal Justice* 18 (1990).

2483. Silvestrini de Pacheco, Blanca. *Violencia y criminalidad en Puerto Rico (1898-1973): apuntes para un estudio de historia social*. Rio Piedras: Editorial Universitaria, 1980.

2484. Simms, Margaret C., and Samuel L. Myers, Jr., eds. *Economics of Race and Crime*. New Brunswick, NJ: Transaction Publishers, 1988.

2485. Simon, Jonathan. *Poor Discipline: Parole and the Social Control of the Underclass, 1890-1990*. University of Chicago Press, 1993.

2486. Sisk, Glenn N. "Crime and Justice in the Alabama Black Belt, 1875-1917." *Mid-America* 40 (1958).

2487. Smith, Christopher E. "Black Muslims and the Development of Prisoners' Rights." *Journal of Black Studies* 24 (December 1993).

2488. Smith, M. D., and E. S. Kuchta. "Trends in Violent Crime against Women, 1973-1989." *Social Science Quarterly* 74 (March 1993).

2489. Snifen, Michael J. "Fear of Crime Rising Faster among Blacks than among Whites." *Boston Globe*, 20 June 1994. [National, 1985-1991]

2490. Sorensen, Jonathan R. *The Effects of Legal and Extralegal Factors on Prosecutorial and Jury Decision-making in Post-Furman Texas Capital Cases.* Ph.D. diss., Sam Houston State University, 1990. UMO #9024569.

2491. South, S. J., and R. B. Felson. "The Racial Patterning of Rape." *Social Forces* 69 (September 1990).

2492. Spindel, Donna J. *Crime and Society in North Carolina 1663- 1776.* Baton Rouge: Louisiana State University Press, 1989.

2493. Staples, Robert. "White Racism. Black Crime, and American Justice: An Application of the Colonial Model to Explain Crime and Race." *Phylon* 36 (1975): 14-22.

2494. Stark, Evan. "Rethinking Homicide: Violence, Race, and the Politics of Gender." *International Journal of Health Services* 20 (1990).

2495. Stern, Kenneth S. *Loud Hawk: The United States versus the American Indian Movement.* University of Oklahoma Press: 1994. [The 13 year trial of Dennis Banks]

2496. Stewart, Jocelyn Y. "A Black Cycle." *Los Angeles Times*, 11 February 1993. [Social consequences of incarceration of large number of African American men]

2497. Stolberg, Sheryl. "Fears Cloud Search for Genetic Roots of Violence." *Los Angeles Times*, 30 December 1993.

2498. _____. "Nipping Violence in the Bud." *Los Angeles Times*, 31 December 1993. [Role of genetic and other factors in violence]

2499. Sullivan, Kevin. "Former MD Man Claims He Killed Two To Defend 'Aryan Beauty', Police Say." *Washington Post*, 10 August 1993.

2500. Sullivan, Mercer. *"Getting Paid": Youth Crime and Work in the Inner City.* Ithaca, NY: Cornell University Press, 1990.

2501. Tabor, Mary B. W. "Judge Finds Bias Against Minority Inmates." *New York Times*, 3 October 1991. [Black and Hispanic inmates at Elmira Correctional Facility, NY]

2502. Takayi, Paul, and Tony Platt. "Behind the Guilded Ghetto: An Analysis of Race, Class, and Crime in Chinatown." *Crime and Social Justice* 9 (Spring and Summer 1978).

2503. Taylor, William Banks. *Brokered Justice: Race, Politics, and Mississippi Prisons, 1798-1992.* Ohio State University Press: 1994.

2504. Tesner, Michael A. "Racial Paranoia as a Defence to Crimes of Violence: An Emerging Theory of Self-defense or Insanity?" *Boston College Third World Law Journal* 11 (Summer 1991): 307-333.

2505. Tolnay, Stewart E. and others. "Black Competition and White Vengeance: Legal Execution of Blacks as Social Control in the Cotton South, 1890 to 1929." *Social Science Quarterly* 73 (September 1992): 627-644.

2506. Towry, M. "Racial Disproportion in United States Prisons." *British Journal of Criminology* 34 (1994): 97-115.

2507. "A Twenty year Retrospective on the Attica Rebellion." *Social Justice* 18 (Fall 1991): entire issue.

2508. U.S. Congress, 101st, 2nd session, Senate, Committee on Governmental Affairs, Subcommittee on Investigations. *Asian Organized Crime: The New International Criminal: Hearings...* Washington, DC: GPO, 1992.

2509. U.S. Congress, 100th, 1st session, Senate, Committee on the Judiciary. "Fighting Crime in America: An Agenda for the 1990's." *Congressional Record* (12 March 1991): (daily edition) S3067-3073. [Contains international and historical comparisons of US crime and violence]

2510. U.S. Congress, 101st, 2nd session, House of Representatives, Committee on the Judiciary, Subcommittee on Crime and Criminal Justice. *Bias Crimes: Hearing...* Washington, DC: GPO, 1992.

2511. U.S. Congress, 101st, 2nd session, House of Representatives, Committee on the Judiciary, Subcommittee on Civil and Constitutional Rights. *Death Penalty Legislation and the Racial Justice Act: Hearings...Serial No. 125.* Washington, DC: GPO, 1991.

2512. U.S. Department of Justice, Office of Juvenile Justice and Delinquency Prevention. "Growth in Minority Detentions Attributed to Drug Law Violators." *OJJDP Update on Statistics* (March 1990): 1-2.

2513. _____. "Juvenile Gangs: Crime and Drug Trafficking." *Juvenile Justice Bulletin* (September 1988): 1-2.

2514. U.S. Dept. of Health and Human Services, National Center for Health Statistics. "Firearm Mortality among Children, Youth, and Young Adults 1-34 Years of Age. Trends and Current Status 1979-1988." *Monthly Vital Statistics Report* 39, no.11, supp. (14 March 1991): 1-5.

2515. "U.S. Had More Than 7,000 Hate Crimes in '93, FBI Head Says." *New York Times*, 29 June 1994.

2516. Walsh, A. "Race and Discretionary Sentencing: An Analysis of Obvious and Nonobvious Cases." *International Journal of Offender Therapy and Comparative Criminology* 35 (Spring 1991): 7-20.

2517. Wasserman, David. "In Defense of a Conference on Genetics and Crime: Assessing the Social Impact of a Public Debate." *Chronicle of Higher Education* (23 September 1992).

2518. Waters, Robert C. "Gender Bias in Florida's Justice System." *Florida Bar Journal* 64 (May 1990): 10-16.

2519. Weinstein, Henry. "Probation Dept. Biased, Suit Charges." *Los Angeles Times*, 26 May 1994. [Los Angeles County Probation Department]

2520. Welte, J. W., and E. L. Abel. "Homicide and Race in Erie County, New York." *American Journal of Epidemiology* 124 (1986): 666-670.

2521. Whitaker, Catherine J., and Lisa D. Bastrain. *Teenage Victims: A National Crime Survey Report.* Bureau of Justice Statistics, Box 6000, Rockville, MD 20850: May 1991.

2522. White, Welsh S. *The Death Penalty in the Eighties.* Ann Arbor, MI, 1987.

2523. Wicker Tom. *A Time to Die.* New York: Quadrangle, 1975. [Attica prison riot]

2524. Will, George F. "A Law to End Capital Punishment." *Los Angeles Times*, 19 May 1994. [Racial Justice Act portion of pending crime bill]

2525. Williams, Stanley Tookie. "[Interview with Barbara Cottman Becnel]." *Los Angeles Times*, 22 August 1993. [Co-founder of the Crips, presently in San Quentin Prison's Death Row]

2526. Williams, Terry. *The Cocaine Kids: The Inside Story of a Teenage Drug Ring.* Cambridge, MA: Adison-Wesley, 1991.

2527. Wong, Doreena, and Karen K. Narasaki. "Hate Crimes Do More Harm." *Washington Post*, 22 June 1993. Letter.

2528. Wyatt, G. E. "The Sociocultural Context of African American and White American Women's Rape." *Journal of Social Issues* 48 (Spring 1992): 77-92.

2529. Young, Robert L. "Race, Conceptions of Crime and Justice, and Support for the Death Penalty." *Social Psychology Quarterly* 54 (March 1991): 67-75.

2530. Young, T. J. "Poverty, Suicide, and Homicide among Native Americans." *Psychological Reports* 67 (December 1990): 1153-1154.

2531. Young, V., and A. T. Sulton. "Excluded: The Current Status of African-American Scholars in the Field of Criminology and Criminal Justice." *Journal of Research in Crime and Delinquency* 28 (February 1991).

2532. Zatz, Majorie S., and Kathleen A. Cameron. *Racial Disparities in Prosecutorial Decisions and Plea Bargaining.* Paper prepared for the Committee on the Status of Black Americans, National Research Council, Washington, DC: 1987.

DESEGREGATION

2533. "1954 Topeka Desegregation Case Continues Odyssey in the Courts." *New York Times*, April 1992.

2534. Ailes, Roger. "A Bittersweet Victory: Public School Desegregation in Memphis." *Journal of Negro Education* 55 (1986): 470-483.

2535. "Allocating the Burden of Proof after a Finding of Unitariness in School Desegregation Litigation." *Harvard Law Review* 100 (January 1987): 653-671.

2536. "Appendix to Brief for Respondents-School Segregation and Residential Segregation: A Social Science Statement." *Columbus Board of Education, et al. v. Gary Pennick et al.*, 443 U.S. 449 (1979).

2537. Applebome, Peter. "Busing Is Abandoned Even in Charlotte." *New York Times*, 15 April 1992.

2538. _____. "Legacy of a Southern Town: Schools Still Split on Racial Lines." *New York Times*, 21 April 1991. [Summerton, SC]

2539. Archbold, Douglas A. *Magnet Schools, Voluntary Desegregation and Public Choice Theory: Limits and Possibilities in a Big City School System.* Ph.D. diss., University of Wisconsin, 1988. UMO #8810443.

2540. Arias, M. Beatriz. "Hispanics, School Desegregation and Educational Opportunity." in *Readings in Equal Education*, Vol. 8. pp. 207-218. eds. Marguerite Ross Barnett, and Charles C. Harrington. New York: AMS Press, 1985.

2541. Arkin, Daniel J. *Regime Politics Surrounding Desegregation Decision-Making During Massive Resistance in Richmond, Virginia.* Ph.D. diss., Virginia Commonwealth University, 1991. UMO #9135919.

2542. Armor, David J. "After Busing: Education and Choice." *Public Interest* (Spring 1989): 24-37.

2543. Armstrong, Liz S. "Court Reinstates Desegregation Plan for Little Rock." *Education Week* (9 January 1991).

2544. Baier, Paul R. "Framing and Reviewing a Desegregation Decree: Of the Chancellor's Foot and Fifth Circuit Control." *Louisiana Law Review* 47 (September 1986): 123-151.

2545. Baker, R. Scott. *Ambiguous Legacies: The NAACP's Legal Campaign against Segregation in Charleston, South Carolina, 1935- 1975.* Ph.D. diss., Columbia University, 1993. UMO #9333721.

2546. Barnett, Marilyn F. *Superintendents, Desegregation and the Politics of Compliance: Wilkinsburg, Pennsylvania: 1968-1986.* Ph.D. diss., University of Pittsburgh, 1990. UMO #9120102.

2547. Barrett, Paul M. "[U.S. Supreme] Court to Ponder Issue of School Integration as Some Blacks Shift." *Wall Street Journal*, 4 October 1991. [DeKalb County, GA]

2548. Bartel, Virginia B. *The Shattered Dream: An Ethnographic Social History of An Integrated "Model" School.* Ph.D. diss., University of Michigan, 1988. UMO #8906994.

2549. Batchelor, John E. *Rule of Law: North Carolina School Desegregation from Brown to Swann, 1954-1974.* Ph.D. diss., N.C. State University, 1992. [Swann, 1971]. UMO #9300014.

2550. Bates, Joseph H. "Out of Focus: The Misapplication of Traditional Equitable Principles in the Nontraditional Arena of School Desegregation." *Vanderbilt Law Review* 44 (November 1991): 1315-1354. [Little Rock School District v. Pulaski County Special School District No. 1]

2551. Batson, Ruth M., and Robert C. Hayden. *A History of METCO.* Boston, MA: Select Publications, 1987.

2552. Beady, C., and S. Hansell. "Teacher Race and Expectations for Student Achievement." *American Educational Research Journal* 18 (1983): 191-206.

2553. Bell, Derrick A., Jr. "Integration Can Be Unequal, Too." *Nation* (7 July 1979).

2554. Bennett, Rob. "Missouri v. Jenkins: A Case of Legislative Underreaching." *Tax Notes* 48 (2 July 1990): 115-116. [Kansas City school segregation case]

2555. Black, Chris. "South Carolina Schools Draw Whites Back." *Boston Globe*, 28 September 1989. [Orangeburg]

2556. Blank, R. and others. *Survey of Magnet Schools.* Washington, DC: U.S. Department of Education, Office of Planning, Budget, and Evaluation, 1984.

2557. Blume, Howard, and John D. Wagner. "Virtual Integration." *Los Angeles Times*, 26 May 1994. [Use of interactive television to "desegregate" classes in schools of varying racial-ethnic composition]

2558. Bobo, Lawrence. "'Whites' Opposition to Busing: Symbolic Racism or Realistic Group Conflict?" *Journal of Personality and Social Psychology* 45 (December 1983): 1196-1210.

2559. Bojar, Karen. "Cross-District Integration Needed." *Education Week* (14 October 1987).

2560. Bosma, Boyd. *Planning for and Implementing Effective School Desegregation: The Role of Teacher Associations.* Washington, DC: GPO, 1980.

2561. Braddock, Jomills Henry II, and James M. McPartland. "Social-Psychological Processes that Perpetuate Racial Segregation: The Relationship between School and Employment Desegregation." *Journal of Black Studies* 19 (March 1989): 267- 289.

2562. Braun, Stephen. "A Surprise Roadblock for Busing." *Los Angeles Times*, 16 November 1993. [Blacks in St. Louis, MO]

2563. Brenner, Scott C. "Judicial Taxation as a Means of Remedying Public School Segregation under Missouri v. Jenkins: Boldly Going Where No Federal Court Has Gone Before." *Whittier Law Review* 12 (Winter 1991): 551-589.

2564. Broder, David S. "Desegregation by Moving Van." *Boston Globe*, 8 June 1994. [The Gautreaux program]

2565. Brooks, Roy L. "The Painful Realities of Integrated Schools." *Hartford Courant*, 28 February 1993.

2566. Brown, Kevin. "Termination of Public School Desegregation: Determination of United States Based on the Elimination of Invidious Value Inculcation." *George Washington Law Review* 58 (August 1990): 1105-1164.

2567. Brown, Tony. "Integration: A Tragedy of Exaggerated Expectations." *Cleveland Call and Post*, 12 December 1991.

2568. Brownstein, Ronald. "4 Decades Later, Legacy of Brown vs. Topeka Is Cloudy." *Los Angeles Times*, 15 May 1994.

2569. Bullock, Charles S. III. "The Office of Civil Rights and Implementation of Desegregation Programs in the Public Schools." *Policy Studies Journal* 8 (1980): 597-615.

2570. Camp, William E. and others. "Within-district Equity: Desegregation and Microeconomic Analysis." in *The Impacts of Litigation and Legislation on Public School Finance*, eds. Julie K. Underwood, and Deborah A. Verstegen. Harper and Row, 1990.

2571. Canady, John E., Jr. "Overcoming Original Sin: The Redemption of the Desegregated School System." *Houston Law Review* 27 (May 1990): 557-597.

2572. Carr, Leslie G. "Resegregation: The Norfolk Case." *Urban Education* 24 (January 1990).

2573. Carr, Leslie G., and Donald J. Zeigler. "White Flight and White Return in Norfolk: A Test of Predictions." *Sociology of Education* 63 (October 1990): 272-282.

2574. Casebeer, Linda S. *Magnet Schools and Desegregation: A Study in Educational and Social Change.* Ph.D. diss., Indiana University, 1991. UMO #9205938.

2575. Casserly, Michael. "Urban Segregation: Who's To Blame?" *Education Week* (2 March 1994). [Critique of 1994 Orfield study on desgregation]

2576. Celis, William 3rd. "40 Years After Brown, Segregation Persists." *New York Times*, 18 May 1994. [The present national scene in school desegregation]

2577. _____. "District Finds Way to End Segregation and Restore Neighborhood Schools." *New York Times*, 4 September 1991. [A plan to integrate housing in Palm Beach County, Florida]

2578. _____. "In Effort to Improve Schools, Pupils To Be Assigned on Basis of Income." *New York Times*, 22 January 1992. [Hmong in LaCrosse, WI]

2579. _____. "Kansas City [Mo.] Praises Desegregation, But State Officials Say It Isn't Enough." *New York Times*, 25 September 1991.

2580. Chabotar, K. J. "Measuring the Costs of Magnet Schools." *Economics of Education Review* 8 (1989).

2581. Chafetz, Gary. "The Cambridge Schools, Choice Pays Off." *Boston Globe*, 15 September 1991. [Controlled-choice desegregation in Cambridge, Mass.]

2582. Chandler, Mittie O. "Obstacles to Integration Efforts." *The City in Black and White*, eds. Ned Hill, and George C. Galster. Center for Urban Policy Research, Rutgers University, 1992.

2583. Cheekoway, Marjorie B. *Toward Equity in the Schools: From Policy to Practice in Three Michigan Communities.* Ph.D. diss., University of Michigan, 1988. UMO #8821557.

2584. Chira, Susan. "Busing the Smallest Pupils: How Much Is Enough?" *New York Times*, 3 April 1990. [Oklahoma City desegregation]

2585. _____. "Housing and Fear Upend Integration." *New York Times*, 14 February 1993.

2586. Clark, E. Culpepper. "The Schoolhouse Door: An Institutional Response to Desegregation." in *Opening Doors*, eds. Harry J. Knopke and others. University of Alabama Press, 1991.

2587. Clark, Kenneth B. "The Brown Decision: Racism, Education, and Human Rights." *Journal of Negro Education* 57 (1988): 125-132.

2588. Clark, W. A. V. "School Desegregation and White Flight: A Reexamination and Case Study." *Social Science Research* 16 (1987): 211-228.

2589. Clark, W. A. V. and others. "School Segregation: Managed Integration or Free Choice." *Environment and Planning* 10 (February 1992): 91-104.

2590. Cohen, Muriel. "After 25 Years, Lincoln Takes a Hard Look at Metco." *Boston Globe*, 9 June 1990. [Lincoln, MA public schools and voluntary busing of black students from Boston]

2591. _____. "Officials Say Metco Students Suffer an Achievement Gap." *Boston Globe*, 27 June 1989. [Voluntary minority student transfers from Boston and Springfield to suburbs]

2592. _____. "Wisconsin City Will Mix Students By Family Income." *Boston Globe*, 26 December 1991. [Hmong in LaCrosse]

2593. Colburn, David R. "Florida's Governors Confront the Brown Decision: A Case Study of the Constitutional Politics of School Desegregation, 1954-1970." in *An Uncertain Tradition:*

Constitutionalism and the History of the South, eds. Kermit L. Hall, and James W. Ely, Jr. Athens: University of Georgia Press, 1989.

2594. Combs, Ron. "Schoolbooks in the Missouri River? A Possible Response to Missouri v. Jenkins." *Missouri Law Review* 56 (Spring 1991): 389-410.

2595. Cooper, Donald G. *The Controversy over Desegregation in the Los Angeles Unified School District, 1962-1981*. Ph.D. diss., University of Southern California, 1991.

2596. Crain, Robert L., and others. *Finding Niches: The Long-Term Effects of a Voluntary Interdistrict School Desegreation Plan*. New York: Department of Philosophy and Social Sciences, Teachers College, Columbia University, 1986.

2597. _____. *A Longitudinal Study of a Metropolitan Voluntary School Desegregation Plan*. New York: Institute for Urban and Minority Education, Teachers College, 1991. [Project Concern, Connecticut]

2598. Crain, Robert L., and Rita E. Mahard. "The Effect of Research Methodology on Desegregation-Achievement Studies: A Meta- analysis." *American Journal of Sociology* 88 (1983): 839-854.

2599. Dash, Steven. *A Case Study in Microcosm of the Voluntary Desegregation Efforts of a large Urban City School System: An Analysis of the L.C. Springwood Elementary School from 1954 to 1984*. Ph.D. diss., University of Pennslyvania, 1988. UMO #8816895.

2600. De Bona, Joseph. "The Resegregation of Schools in Small Towns and Rural Areas of North Carolina." *Journal of Negro Education* 57 (Winter 1988): 43-50.

2601. De Witt, Karen. "'Clustering' of White Pupils Stirs Richmond Furor." *New York Times*, 9 December 1992.

2602. Deeb, Norma Jean. *An Analysis of the Implemented Desegregation Plan of the Elementary Schools of Omaha, Nebraska*. Ph.D. diss., University of Nebraska, 1988. UMO #8910693.

2603. Dickens, Nicole P. "Life Is Black and White and In Between." *Hartford Courant*, 28 February 1993. [African-American student on school integration]

2604. "Does Brown Still Belong?" *Nation* (23 May 1994). [19 short statements]

2605. Donato, R. *Pajaro Valley Unified Schools: Bilingual Education and Desegregation*. Ph.D. diss., Stanford University, 1987.

2606. Dudziak, Mary L. "Desegregation as a Cold War Imperative." *Stanford Law Review* 41 (November 1988): 61-120.

2607. _____. "The Limits of a Good Faith: Desegregation in Topeka, Kansas, 1950-1956." *Law and History Review* 5 (Fall 1987): 351-391.

2608. Dugas, Carroll J. *The Dismantling of De Jure Segregation in Louisiana, 1954-1974*. 2 vols. Ph.D. diss., Louisiana State University, 1989. UMO #9002138.

2609. Dunne, John R. "Desegregation Guidelines." *Cleveland Plain Dealer*, 9 March 1991. [Reference to implications of Supreme Court's January 15, 1991 ruling in Oklahoma City desegregation case.]

2610. Eckford, Elizabeth. "The First Day: Little Rock, 1957." in *Growing Up Southern*, pp. 257-261. ed. Chris Mayfield. New York: Pantheon, 1981. [Central High School]

2611. Edwards, Audrey, and Craig K. Polite. *Children of the Dream: The Psychology of Black Success*. New York: Doubleday, 1992. [Nine Blacks who desegregated Central High School, Little Rock, Arkansas, in 1957]

2612. _____. "Don't Let Them See You Cry." *Parade* (16 February 1992). [Reunion of nine Blacks who desegregated Central High School, Little Rock, Arkansas in 1957.]

2613. Epstein, Joyce. *After the Bus Arrives: Resegregation in Desegregated Schools*. Baltimore, MD: Johns Hopkins University, Center for the Social Organization of Schools, 1983.

2614. _____. "After the Bus Arrives." *Journal of Social Issues* 41 (1985): 23-43.

2615. Fava, Eileen M. "Desegregation and Parental Choice in Public Schooling: A Legal Analysis of Controlled Choice Student Assignment Plans." *Boston College Third World Law Journal* 11 (Winter 1991): 83-105.

2616. Ficocelli-Lepore, Sandra. "Desegregation in Los Angeles: A Critical Assessment for Metropolitan Planning." Master's thesis, California State University, Dominguez Hills, 1980.

2617. Fife, Brian L. *Comparative Intervention Strategies: Desegregation of American Schools*. Ph.D. diss., State University of New York at Binghamton, 1991. UMO #9100622.

2618. Finley, Stephanie A. "Eradicating Dual Educational Systems through Desegregation: Missouri v. Jenkins." *Southern University Law Review* 17 (Spring 1990): 119-132.

2619. Formisano, Ronald P. *Race, Class, and Ethnicity in the 1960's and 1970's*. Chapel Hill: University of North Carolina Press, 1991. [Boston desegregation and busing]

2620. Fuerst, J. S. "School Desegregation in the Hartford Connecticut Area." *Urban Education* 22 (1987): 73-84.

2621. Galvan, Armando. "Diaz v. San Jose Unified School District." *La Raza Law Journal* 4 (Spring 1991): 98-123.

2622. Genova, W., and Herbert Walberg. *A Practitioner's Guide for Achieving Student Integration in City High Schools*. Washington, DC: GPO, 1981.

2623. Giles, Robert W. *Government, Race and Elementary Education in Oak Park, Illinois: A Case History of Decision Making*. Ph.D. diss., University of Illinois, 1988. UMO #8823134.

2624. Gilliam, Dorothy. "Turning the Tide on School Desegregation." *Washington Post*, 21 May 1994.

2625. Glenn, Charles L., Jr. "Controlled Choice in Massachusetts Public Schools." *Public Interest* no. 103 (Spring 1991): 88-105.

2626. Goetz, Judith P., and E. R. Breneman. "Desegregation and Black Students' Experiences in Two Rural Southern Elementary Schools." *Elementary School Journal* 88 (May 1988): 489-502.

2627. Goldsmith, Kory. "The Civil Rights Act of 1964 and School Desegregation." *School Law Bulletin* 22 (Fall 1991): 17-24.

2628. Gordon, William M. "School Desegregation: A Look at the 70's and 80's." *Journal of Law and Education* 18 (Spring 1988): 189-214.

2629. Graham, Renee. "To Worcester Minorities, Jury Still Out." *Boston Globe*, 26 March 1990. [Segregation and desegregation in Worcester, MA]

2630. Grant, Carl A. "Desegregation, Racial Attitudes, and Intergroup Contact: A Discussion of Change." *Phi Delta Kappan* 72 (September 1990): 25-32.

2631. Grant, Linda M. "Black Females' Place in Desegregated Classrooms." *Sociology of Education* 57 (April 1984): 58-76.

2632. Green, Charles W. and others. "Development and Validation of the School Interracial Climate Scale." *American Journal of Community Psychology* 16 (April 1988): 241-259.

2633. Green, Donald P., and Jonathan A. Cowden. "Who Protests? Self-Interest and White Opposition to Busing." *Journal of Politics* 54 (May 1992): 471-496.

2634. Green, K. C. *Integration and Educational Attainment: A Longitudinal Study of the Effects of Integration on Black Educational Attainment and Occupational Outcomes*. Ph.D. diss., University of California, Los Angeles, 1982.

2635. Greenfeld, Helaine. "Some Constitutional Problems with the Resegregation of Public Schools." *Georgetown Law Review* 80 (December 1991): 363-386. [Special schools for Black males]

2636. Gurwitt, Rob. "Getting Off the Bus." *Governing* 5 (May 1992): 30-36. [The courts and busing in Cleveland]

2637. Gutierrez, Henry J. *The Chicano Education Rights Movement and School Desegregation: Los Angeles, 1962-1970*. Ph.D. diss., University of California, Irvine, 1990. UMO #9103389.

2638. Hallinan, Maureen T., and Ruy A. Teixeira. "Students' Interracial Friendships: Individual Characteristics, Structural Effects, and Racial Differences." *American Journal of Education* 95 (August 1987): 563-583.

2639. Hanley, Robert. "A High School Braces for Segregation's End." *New York Times*, 10 September 1991. [Dwight Morrow High School, Englewood, NJ]

2640. Hanna, Judith L. *Descriptive School Behavior: Class, Race, and Culture.* New York: Holmes and Meier, 1988. [Magnet school in Dallas]

2641. Hansen, Chris. "School Desegregation Has, in Fact, Succeeded." *New York Times*, 11 August 1994. Letter.

2642. Harrison, Eric. "Desegregation Called Peril to Black Colleges." *Los Angeles Times*, 1 May 1994. [Mississippi]

2643. Hawley, Willis D., and Mark A. Smylie. "The Contribution of School Desegregation to Academic Achievement and Racial Integration." in *Eliminating Racism: Profiles in Controversy*, eds. Phyllis A. Katz, and D. Taylor. New York: Plenum, 1988.

2644. Heise, Michael R. *A Quantitative and Legal Analysis of Racial Ceilings and Equal Educational Opportunity.* Ph.D. diss., Northwestern University, 1990. [Conflict between school-choice in Chicago and desegregation]. UMO #9114556.

2645. Henderson, Ronald and others. "Remedies for Segregation: Some Lessons from Research." *Educational Evaluation and Policy Analysis* (1981).

2646. Henig, Jeffrey R. "Choice, Race, and Public Schools: The Adoption and Implementation of a Magnet Program." *Journal of Urban Affairs* 11 (1989): 243-259. [Montgomery County, MD]

2647. Herbert, Bob. "After Brown, What?" *New York Times*, 18 May 1994.

2648. Hess, G. Alfred, Jr., and Christina A. Warden. "Who Benefits from Desegregation Now?" *Journal of Negro Education* 57 (Fall 1988): 536-551.

2649. Hillson, Jon. "School Desegregation Had Wide Support." *New York Times*, 31 May 1994. Letter.

2650. Hinds, Michael de Courcy. "Busing Debated in Philadelphia." *New York Times*, 1 March 1993.

2651. Hornsby, Alton, Jr. "Black Public Education in Atlanta, Georgia, 1954-1973: From Segregation to Segregation." *Journal of Negro History* 76 (1991): 21-47.

2652. Huie, H. Mark. *Factors Influencing the Desegregation Process in the Atlanta School System.* Ph.D. diss., University of Georgia, 1967.

2653. Hunt, Frankie L. C. *A History of the Desegregation of the Fayette County School System: Fayette County, Tennessee, 1954- 1980.* Ph.D. diss., University of Mississippi, 1981.

2654. Husock, Howard. *Integration Incentives in Suburban Cleveland.* Kennedy School of Government Case Program, Harvard University, 1989.

2655. Hutchinson, Dennis. "Unanimity and Desegregation: Decision- making in the Supreme Court 1948-1958." *Georgetown Law Journal* 68 (October 1979): 1-96.

2656. Ingersoll, Gary M. and others. "Inter-racial Attitudes among Elementary and Secondary Students." *International Journal of Group Tensions* 20 (Fall 1990): 267-277.

2657. Jackson, Charles C. *The Struggle for Quality Desegregated Education Beyond the Alternative School Program: Cincinnati, Ohio, 1974-1988.* Ph.D. diss., University of Cincinnati, 1988. UMO #8908454.

2658. Jackson, Stephanie M. "School Desegregation: The Myth and the Reality: an Essay Based on Common Ground." *National Black Law Journal* 11 (Fall 1990): 361-368.

2659. Jacobs, Barbara D. *The Los Angeles Unified School District's Desegregation Case: A Legal History.* Ph.D. diss., Pepperdine University, 1989. UMO #9014170.

2660. James, David R. "City Limits on Racial Equality: The Effects of City-Suburb Boundaries on Public-School Desegregation, 1968-1976." *American Sociological Review* 54 (1989): 963-985.

2661. Jason, Carl E. *Integrating a Major Public High School.* Ph.D. diss., Saint Louis University, 1989. [McCluer North High School, Ferguson-Florissant School District, MO]. UMO #9014795.

2662. Johnson, Bill. "School District Merger, Busing and the Courts: Implications for School Administrators." *Urban Review* 19 (1987): 49-64.

2663. Johnson, Clarence B., Sr. *Integration versus Segregation in Mississippi Schools.* Vantage Press: 1993.

2664. Jones, Charisse. "Years on Integration Road: New Views of an Old Goal." *New York Times,* 10 April 1994.

2665. Joondeph, B. W. "Killing Brown Softly: The Subtle Undermining of Effective Desegregation in Freeman v. Pitts." *Stanford Law Review* 46 (November 1993): 147-174.

2666. Joravsky, Ben. "Integration and Education: What Can We Learn from Evanston's Public Schools?" *The Reader* (3 November 1989). [Evanston, Illinois]

2667. Judson, George. "Integration By Choice: Connecticut Struggles." *New York Times,* 7 October 1994.

2668. _____. "Parents Wary of Change As Integration Looms." *New York Times,* 26 February 1993. [West Hartford, CT]

2669. _____. "Planning Desegregation: Guides to Lead Forums." *New York Times,* 16 December 1993. [Connecticut]

2670. _____. "Poverty, Not Race, Is Linked to Hartford School Failure." *New York Times,* 20 February 1993.

2671. _____. "Regional School Planning On Integration Is Praised." *New York Times,* 20 October 1994. [Hartford, CT area]

2672. Karlan, Pamela S. "End of the Second Reconstruction?" *Nation* (23 May 1994). [Desegregation]

2673. Kaufman, Julie E. *Low-income Black Youth in White Suburbs: Education and Employment Outcomes.* Ph.D. diss., Northwestern University, 1991. UMO #99213483.

2674. Kaufman, Polly Welts. "Building a Constituency for School Desegregation: African-American Women in Boston, 1962-1972." *Teachers College Record* 92 (Summer 1991): 619-631.

2675. Kazal-Threshen, D. M. "Desegregation Goals and Educational Finance Reform: An Agenda for the Next Decade." *Educational Policy* 8 (March 1994): 57-67.

2676. Kelly, P., and W. Miller. "Assessing Desegregation Efforts- No Best Measure." *Public Administration Review* 49 (September- October 1989).

2677. Kemper, Donald J. "Catholic Integration in St. Louis, 1935- 1947." *Missouri Historical Review* 73 (1978): 1-22.

2678. Kingsley, David E. *Racial Attitudes in Liberty, Missouri: Implications for School Desegregation.* Ph.D. diss., Kansas State University, 1989. [Predominantly white suburb of Kansas City, MO]. UMO #9005064.

2679. Lacey, W. and others. "Fostering Constructive Intergroup Contact in Desegregated Schools." *Journal of Negro Education* 52 (1983).

2680. Lane, Daniel M., Jr. "Durable School Desegregation in the Tenth Circuit: A Focus on Effectiveness in the Remedial Stage." *Denver University Law Review* 67 (Summer 1990): 489-513.

2681. Larkin, Joseph M. *School Desegregation, Race, and Discipline: A Case Study Aggregation Analysis.* Ph.D. diss., University of Wisconsin, Milwaukee, 1982. UMO #8313240.

2682. Lassman, Barbara. *The Morris School District, 1988: Sixteen Years After Integration.* Ph.D. diss., Seton Hall University, 1989. [Morristown, NJ]. UMO #8911558.

2683. Lawson, Raneta J. "The Child Seated Next To Me: The Continuing Quest for Equal Educational Opportunity." *Thurgood Marshall Law Review* 16 (Fall 1990): 35-55.

2684. Leff, Lisa. "Blacks and Busing. Prince George's Ongoing Dilemma." *Washington Post* September 13-15, 1993. [Three articles on desegregation in Maryland county schools]

2685. "The Legacy of Desegregation." *Boston Globe*, 19 June 1994. [A review of 20 years of desegregation in Boston]

2686. Lemann, Nicholas. "Brown, Now." *New York Times*, 18 May 1994. [The continuing need for school integration]

2687. "Let the Students Be." *Cleveland Plain Dealer*, 8 September 1994. Editorial. [Busing to meet court-ordered desegregation plan]

2688. Liebman, James S. "Desegregating Politics: All-out School Desegregation Explained." *Columbia Law Review* 90 (October 1990): 1463-1664.

2689. _____. "Implementing Brown in the Nineties: Political Reconstruction, Liberal Recollection, and Litigatively Enforced Legislative Reform." *Virginia Law Review* 76 (April 1990): 349-435.

2690. Lowe, Denis S. *Social Climate in Integrated Schools: A Comparative Study of Social Interaction in Alternative and Neighborhood Elementary Schools.* Ph.D. diss., University of Cincinnati, 1989. [Role of gender and race]. UMO #8917962.

2691. Macdonald, Mary Lou P. *Teacher Learning in a Desegregated School District.* Ph.D. diss., Fordham University, 1990. UMO #9109262.

2692. Marriott, Michel. "For Old Foe of Racism, A New Test." *New York Times*, 11 December 1991. [School desegregation in Louisville, KY]

2693. _____. "Lousiville Debates Plan to End Forced Busing in Grade School." *New York Times*, 11 December 1991.

2694. Maslow-Armand, Laura. "Desegregation, Social Mobility, and Political Participation, Los Angeles, 1978-1982." *Revue Francaise d'Etudes Americaines* 12 (1987): 419-436.

2695. _____. "Ecoles noires, bulletins blancs: la desegregation scolaire et la participation politique des Noirs aux Etats-Unis." *Revue Francaise de Science Politique* 32 (1982): 1000-1022.

2696. Matney, Brian K. *Two Decades After Swann: A Qualitative Study of School Desegregation Efforts in Charlotte and Mecklenburg County, North Carolina.* Ph.D. diss., University of North Carolina at Chapel Hill, 1992. UMO #9234993.

2697. McCendon, McKee J., and Fred P. Pestello. "White Opposition: To Busing or Desegregation?" *Social Science Quarterly* 63 (1982): 70-81.

2698. McConahay, John B. "Reducing Racial Prejudice in Desegregated Schools." in *Effective School Desegregation: Equity, Quality, and Feasibility*, ed. W. Hawley. Beverly Hills, CA: Sage, 1981.

2699. McKenzie-Wharton, Lou B. V. *New Rochelle Board of Education's Policy Toward Racial Imbalance at the Lincoln Elementary School (1947-1962).* Ph.D. diss., Columbia University, 1973. UMO #7331659.

2700. McLarin, Kimberly J. "The Specter of Segregation." *New York Times*, 11 August 1994. [Montclair, NJ]

2701. Michaelides, Sandra. *PTA Members' Attitudes toward Integration and Quality Education in Connecticut's Public Schools.* Ph.D. diss., Columbia University Teachers College, 1990. UMO #9033920.

2702. Michelotti, Cecelia. "Arlington School Desegregation: A History." *Arlington Historical Magazine* 8 (1988): 5-20. [Virginia]

2703. Middleton, Jeanne M. *The History of Singleton v. Jackson Municipal Separate School District: Southern School Desegregation from the Perspective of the Black Community.* Ph.D. diss., Howard University, 1978.

2704. Miller, John Daniel. *Oral Histories of Elementary Principals in Relation to the Implementation of a Court-ordered School Desegregation Plan*. Ph.D. diss., University of Pittsburgh, 1991. UMO #9129205.

2705. Miller, Norman, and M. B. Brewer, eds. *Groups in Contact: The Psychology of Desegregation*. Orlando, FL: Academic Press, 1984.

2706. Miller, Norman, and G. Davidson-Podgorny. "Theoretical Models of Intergroup Relations and the Use of Cooperative Teams as an Intervention for Desegregated Settings." in *Group Processes and Intergroup Relations*, ed. Clyde Hendrick. Newbury Park, CA: Sage, 1987.

2707. Miller, Randi L. "Beyond Contact Theory: The Impact of Community Affluence on Integration Efforts in Five Suburban High Schools." *Youth and Society* 22 (September 1990): 12-34.

2708. _____. "Desegregation Experiences of Minority Students: Adolescent Coping Strategies in Five Connecticut High Schools." *Journal of Adolescent Research* 4 (April 1989): 173-189.

2709. *Milwaukee's City-Suburban Interdistrict Integration Programs: A Review of the Student Application and Assignment Process*. Milwaukee, WI: Compact for Educational Opportunity, January 1990.

2710. Mitchell, George. *An Evaluation of State-financed School Integration in Metropolitan Milwaukee*. Milwaukee: Wisconsin Policy Research Institute, June 1989.

2711. Moore, Thelma R. *Desegregation Revisited: Seeking Common Ground in Designing a New Student Assignment Plan for Boston Public Schools*. Ph.D. diss., University of Southern California, 1990.

2712. Moran, Rachel F. "Foreword-the Lessons of Keyes: How Do You Translate the American Dream?" *La Raza Law Journal* 1 (Fall 1986): 195-212.

2713. Moreno, Patricia A. *Desegregation of Mexican-American Students in Southwest School District*. Ph.D. diss., University of Arizona, 1991. UMO #9136856.

2714. Morrill, Richard L. "School Busing and Demographic Change." *Urban Geography* 10 (July-August 1989): 336-354.

2715. Moses, James C. *Desegregation in Catholic Schools in the Archdiocese of Chicago, 1964-1974, including a Case Study of a Catholic High School*. Ph.D. diss., Loyola University of Chicago, 1977.

2716. Muir, Donal E., and Leslie W. Muir. "Social Distance between Deep-South Middle-School 'Whites' and 'Blacks'." *Sociology and Social Research* 72 (April 1988): 177-180.

2717. Nee, Judy Silva. "Too Bad No One Listened to Antibusing Forces." *Boston Globe*, 30 June 1994. [Boston]

2718. Noboa, Abdin. "Hispanics and Desegregation: Summary of Aspira's Study on Hispanic Segregation Trends in U.S. School Districts." *Metas* 1 (Fall 1980): 1-24.

2719. Note. "Race-biased Faculty Hiring and Layoff Remedies in School Desegregation Cases." *Harvard Law Review* 104 (June 1991): 1917-1936.

2720. *Office on School Monitoring and Community Relations' July 1989 Quarterly Compliance Report*. Submitted July 21, 1989 to the United States District Court, Northern District of Ohio, Eastern Division: [Cleveland]

2721. Ollie, Bert W., Jr. "School Desegregation Efforts in the City of Brotherly Love." *Equity and Excellence* 24 (Winter 1989): 48-52. [Philadelphia, PA]

2722. Olson, Lynn. "Black Community Is Frustrated Over Lack of Results From Desegregation." *Education Week* (17 October 1990).

2723. Orfield, Gary. "America Lacks Equal Opportunity...And It Shows Acutely in Los Angeles." *Los Angeles Times*, 26 December 1993. [Desegregation]

2724. _____. *Desegregation of Black and Hispanic Students for 1968-1980*. Washington, DC: Joint Center for Political Studies, 1982.

2725. _____. "Lessons of the Los Angeles Desegregation Case." *Education and Urban Society* 16 (May 1984): 338-353.

2726. Orfield, Gary and others. *School Desegregation: A Social Science Statement*. Chicago, IL: University of Chicago, Department of Political Science, 14 June 1991.

2727. Orfield, Gary. "School Desegregation after Two Generations: Race, Schools, and Opportunity in Urban Society." in *Race in America*, eds. Herbert Hill, and James E. Jones, Jr. University of Wisconsin Press, 1993.

2728. _____. "Why it Worked in Dixie: Southern School Desegregation and Its Implications for the North." in *Race and Schooling in the City*, eds. Adam Yarmolinsky and others. Cambridge, MA: Harvard University Press, 1981.

2729. Orfield, Gary, and Franklin Monfort. *Racial Change and Desegregation in Large School Districts*. National School Boards Association, 1988.

2730. _____. *Status of School Desegregation: The Next Generation*. National School Boards Association, 1992.

2731. Orfield, Gary, and Peskin, L. "Metropolitan High Schools: Income, Race and Inequality." in *Education Politics for the New Century*, pp. 27-53. eds. Douglas E. Mitchell, and Margaret E. Goertz. London: Falmer Press, 1990.

2732. Pasternak, Judy. "Integration, Rockford Style: Schools Divided by Race." *Los Angeles Times*, 9 November 1993. [Rockford, IL]

2733. Perkins, Drew A. "Constitutional Law-When the Prohibition on Judicial Taxation Interferes with an Equitable Remedy in a School Desegregation Case (Missouri v. Jenkins, 110 S.Ct. 1651 [1990])." *Land and Water Law Review* 26 (Winter 1991): 373-384.

2734. Perry, Michael J. *The Constitution in the Courts: Law or Politics?* Oxford University Press: 1994. [Includes desegregation]

2735. Pertusati, L. "Beyond Segregation or Integration: A Case Study from Effective Native American Education." *Journal of American Indian Education* 27 (1988): 10-20.

2736. Praeger, J. and others. *School Desegregation Research*. New York: Plenum, 1986.

2737. Pratt, Robert A. *School Desegregation in Richmond, Virginia, 1954-1984: A Study of Race and Class in a Southern City*. Ph.D. diss., University of Virginia, 1987. UMO #8906783.

2738. Presser, Arlynn L. "Broken Dreams: A Federal Judge in Kansas City Had a Utopian Vision for Desegregating the City's Schools." *ABA Journal* 77 (May 1991): 60-64.

2739. Price, Janet R., and Jane R. Stern. "Magnet Schools as a Strategy for Integration and School Reform." *Yale Law and Policy Review* 5 (1987).

2740. Ptasiewicz, Seth. "The Unitariness Dilemma: The First Circuit's Attempt to Develop a Text for Determining When a System is Unitary." *Washington University Law Quarterly* 66 (Summer 1988): 615-642.

2741. Radelet, Joseph. "Stillness at Detroit's Racial Divide: A Perspective on Detroit's School Desegregation Court Order: 1970- 1989." *Urban Review* 23 (September 1991): 173-190.

2742. Rawls, Alfred. "The Attitudes of Black and White Community Leaders Toward Integration and Consolidation of Schools in West Carroll Parish, Louisiana." Master's thesis, Northeast Louisiana University, 1989.

2743. Reid, Evelyn M. *Desegregation Planning: A Case Study of Community Groups*. Ph.D. diss., University of Wisconsin, Madison, 1989. UMO #8915556.

2744. Ribadeneira, Diego, and Larry Tye. "Racial Gap Widens in Boston Schools." *Boston Globe*, 8 January 1992.

2745. Robbins, William. "Kansas City Tries to Revive School, but the Cost is Criticized." *New York Times*, 10 October 1989. [Central High School, Kansas City, MO]

2746. Roberts, Sam. "White Tilt to Balance A Project." *New York Times*, 3 August 1992. [Efforts to increase number of white students in school adjacent to Starrett City housing project in Canarsie, Brooklyn]

2747. Rodgers, Harrell R., Jr., and Charles S. Bullock III. *Coercion to Compliance*. Lexington, MA: D.C. Heath, 1976. [Implementation of desegregation in 31 Georgia school districts between 1965-6 and 1973-4]

2748. Rosenbaum, James E. and others. "White Suburban Schools' Responses to Low-Income Black Children: Sources of Successes and Problems." *Urban Review* 20 (Spring 1988): 28-41.

2749. Rossell, Christine H. *The Carrot or the Stick for School Desegregation Policy: Magnet Schools or Forced Busing*. Philadelphia, PA: Temple University Press, 1990.

2750. _____. "The Carrot or the Stick for School Desegregation Policy?" *Urban Affairs Quarterly* 25 (March 1990).

2751. _____. "Using Multiple Criteria to Evaluate Public Policies: The Case of School Desegregation." *American Politics Quarterly* 21 (April 1993): 155-184.

2752. Rossell, Christine H., and R. Clarke. *The Carrot or the Stick in School Desegregation Policy?* Washington, DC: National Institute of Education, 1987.

2753. Rossell, Christine H., and Charles L. Glenn, Jr. "The Cambridge Controlled Choice Plan." *Urban Review* 20 (Summer 1988): 75-94.

2754. Rossell, Christine H., and Willis D. Hawley, eds. *The Consequences of School Desegregation*. Philadelphia, PA: Temple University Press, 1983.

2755. Rutti, Ronald and others. "Cleveland in the Balance." *Cleveland Plain Dealer*, 21 April 1991. [First of series of articles on quality of education and the progress of desegregation in Cleveland]

2756. Samuels, Benjamin. "Resisting Equality: The Boston School Desegregation Conflict." Senior Essay, Amherst College, 1989.

2757. San Miguel, Guadalupe, Jr. "The Struggle Against Separate and Unequal Schools: Middle Class Mexican-Americans and the Desegregation Campaign in Texas, 1929-1957." *History of Education Quarterly* 23 (Fall 1983): 343-360.

2758. Scales-Trent, Judy. "A Judge Shapes and Manages Institutional Reform: School Desegregation in Buffalo." *New York University Review of Law and Social Change* 17 (March 1989): 119-169. [U.S. District Judge John Curtin]

2759. Schmidt, Peter. "Language Minorities Seek Place in Desegregation Case]." *Education Week* (17 February 1993).

2760. _____. "Magnets' Efficacy As Desegregation Tool Questioned." *Education Week* (2 February 1994).

2761. _____. "Palm Beach Shifts Integration Focus to Housing." *Education Week* (26 February 1992).

2762. _____. "Pursuing a Vision of Equality in Conn. Court." *Education Week* (6 May 1992). [Hartford and suburbs]

2763. Schmitt, Eric. "L.I. School District Strives to Integrate." *New York Times*, 27 November 1987. [Sewanhaka Central High School District, Long Island]

2764. Schofield, Janet Ward. *Review of School Desegregation's Impact on Elementary and Secondary School Students*. Hartford, CT: State Department of Education, 1989.

2765. _____. *School Desegregation and Black Americans*. Paper prepared for the Committee on the Status of Black Americans, National Research Council, Washington, D.C., 1986.

2766. *School Desegregation in Metro Atlanta, 1954-1973*. Research Atlanta: 1973.

2767. "School Desegregation Policy: Federal Role in the 1990's." *Education and Urban Society* 23 (November 1990): entire issue.

2768. "Seeking Private Schooling at Public Expense." *New York Times*, 3 August 1989. [Some black students in Kansas City, MO desegregation litigation]

2769. Shanker, Albert. "A Dream Deferred." *New York Times*, 4 April 1993. Advertisement. [Criticism of desegregation lawsuit in Hartford, Connecticut]

2770. Sheehan, J. B. *The Boston School Integration Dispute: Social Change and Legal Maneuvers*. New York: Columbia University Press, 1984.

2771. Sides, W. Hampton. "Southern Discomfort." *Los Angeles Times*, 15 September 1992. [Former Arkansas governor Orval E. Fabus, who tried to stop school desegregation in 1957]

2772. Simmons, Cassandra A. *Racial Bias of Teachers and Counselors in the Assignment of Incoming Seventh Graders to Ability of Groups Within a Desegregated School District*. Ph.D. diss., Michigan State University, 1979. UMO #8013797.

2773. Sivitz, T. E. "Eliminating the Continuing Effects of the Violation: Compensatory Education as a Remedy for Unlawful School Segregation." *Yale Law Journal* 97 (May 1988).

2774. Slavin, Robert E. "Cooperative Learning: Applying Contact Theory in Desegregated Schools." *Journal of Social Issues* 41 (1985): 45-62.

2775. Smith, Douglas. "'When Reason Collides with Prejudice': Armistead Lloyd Boothe and the Politics of Desegregation in Virginia, 1948-1963." *Virginia Magazine of History and Biography* 102 (January 1994): 5-46.

2776. Smith, Gladys E. *Defining Organizational Mission: The St. Louis Desegregation Monitoring Committee*. Ph.D. diss., Saint Louis University, 1993. UMO #9314500.

2777. Smith, P. J. "Is Brown Dead? Is There an Affirmative Duty to Eliminate Prior De Jure Segregation and Its Vestiges in Higher Education." *Tulane Law Review* 66 (November 1991): 231-245. [Ayers V. Allain]

2778. Smock, Pamela J., and Franklin D. Wilson. "Desegregation and the Stability of White Enrollments: A School-Level Analysis 1968-1984." *Sociology of Education* 64 (October 1991): 278-292.

2779. Smollar, David. "Schools Size Up the Effectiveness of Integration." *Los Angeles Times*, 3 December 1990. [San Diego, CA schools]

2780. Smothers, Ronald. "At Little Rock, 30 Years Later: Starting Over." *New York Times*, 27 September 1987. [Central High School]

2781. Snavely, Barbara J. "New Jersey's Sending-receiving Statute: Burden of Proof Tug-of-War." *Rutgers Law Journal* 22 (Fall 1990): 199-229.

2782. Sproat, John. "'Firm Flexibility': Perspectives on Desegregation in South Carolina." in *New Perspectives on Race and Slavery in America*, eds. Robert H. Abzug, and Steven Maizlish. Lexington, KY: University of Kentucky Press, 1986.

2783. Stein, Eric S. "Attacking School Segregation Root and Branch." *Yale Law Journal* 99 (June 1990): 2003-2022.

2784. Stein, Robert C. *A Qualitative and Quantitative Analysis of Factors Related to Resegregation in Desegregated Schools*. Ph.D. diss., Claremont Graduate School, 1987. UMO #8709300.

2785. Stephan, Walter G. "School Desegregation: Short-Term and Long-Term Effects." in *Opening Doors*, Harry J. Knopke and others. University of Alabama Press, 1991.

2786. Stringfellow, Christina H. *Desegregation Policies and Practices in Chicago during the Superintendencies of James Redmond and Joseph Hannon*. Ph.D. diss., Loyola University of Chicago, 1991. UMO #9125923.

2787. Synnott, Marcia G. "Desegregation in South Carolina, 1950- 1963: Sometime Between "Now" and "Never"." in *Looking South: Chapters in the Story of an American Region*, eds. Winfred B. Moore, Jr., and Joseph F. Tripp. Westport, CT: Greenwood, 1989.

2788. Tabariet, Joseph O. "Ross Barnett and Desegregation in Mississippi: A Situational Analysis of Selected Speeches." Master's thesis, Louisiana State University, 1987.

2789. Taeuber, Alma. *Memorandum on Issues of Resegregation in Public Schools...* Paper prepared for the Committee on the Status of Black Americans, National Research Council, Washington, D.C. 1987.

2790. Taeuber, Karl E. "Desegregation of Public School Districts: Persistence and Change." *Phi Delta Kappan* 72 (September 1990): 18-24.

2791. Taylor, Mary J. *Leadership Responses to Desegregation in the Denver Public Schools, a Historical Study: 1959-1977.* Ph.D. diss., University of Denver, 1990. UMO #9030097.

2792. Terez, Dennis G. "Protecting the Remedy of Unitary Schools." *Case Western Reserve Law Review* 37 (Fall 1986): 41-71.

2793. Thomas, J. C., and D. H. Hoxworth. "The Limits of Judicial Desegregation Remedies after Missouri v. Jenkins." *Publius* 21 (Summer 1991): 93-108.

2794. Thomas, Karen M. "Report Card on School Integration." *Chicago Tribune*, 23 August 1987. [Suburban Cook County]

2795. Thomas, Pamela D. *The Oklahoma City School Board's 1984 Decision to Curtail Busing and Return to Neighborhood Elementary Schools.* Ph.D. diss., University of Oklahoma, 1990. UMO #9110004.

2796. Thornton, Alvin, and Eva Wells Chuun. "Desegregating with Magnet and One-Race Elementary and Secondary Schools." *Urban League Review* 11 (Summer 1987/Winter 1987-88): 146-157.

2797. Thornton, Clarence H., and William T. Trent. "School Desegregation and Suspension in East Baton Rouge Parish: A Preliminary Report." *Journal of Negro Education* 57 (Fall 1988): 482-501.

2798. Todd, Gillien. "School Desegregation and the Decline of Liberalism: New Haven, Connecticut in 1964." *Connecticut History* 30 (1989): 1-40.

2799. Tompkins, Gay M. *An Historical Study of Voluntary Interdistrict School Desegregation in St. Louis County, Missouri: 1980-1986.* Ph.D. diss., Saint Louis University, 1991. UMO #9131030.

2800. Traub, James. "Oklahoma City: Separate and Equal." *Atlantic* 268 (September 1991): 24-37.

2801. Treadwell, David. "Seeking a New Road to Equality." *Los Angeles Times*, 7 July 1992. [School integration and separate schools in Oklahoma City]

2802. Tye, Larry. "Diversity, Separation Coexist in L.A." *Boston Globe*, 6 January 1992.

2803. _____. "In Louisville, a Model of Success is Threatened." *Boston Globe*, 7 January 1992.

2804. _____. "A Pair of Success Stories in Lousiville." *Boston Globe*, 5 January 1992.

2805. _____. "Poll Shows Wide Support Across U.S. for Integration." *Boston Globe*, 5 January 1992.

2806. _____. "U.S. Senate Retreat in School Integration." *Boston Globe*, 5 January 1992.

2807. _____. "Vision, Hard Choices Needed to Make Integration Work." *Boston Globe*, 8 January 1992.

2808. _____. "Walls of Separation Return to Norfolk, VA." *Boston Globe*, 7 January 1992.

2809. U.S. Commission on Civil Rights, North Carolina Advisory Committee. *In-School Segregation in North Carolina Public Schools.* Washington, DC: The Commission, 1991.

2810. U.S. District Court, Northern District of Ohio, Eastern Division. *Office on School Monitoring and Community Relations Report Pursuant to the Order of July 10, 1990.* Cleveland, Ohio: The Office on School Monitoring and Community Relations, 29 July 1991. [A 15-year review of the progress of desegregation in Cleveland, Ohio, 1976-1991]

2811. Vervack, Jerry J. "The Hoxie Imbroglio." *Arkansas Historical Quarterly* 48 (1989): 17-33. [School desegregation, 1955]

2812. Wachter, Kenneth W. "Disturbed by Meta-analysis." *Science* 241 (16 September 1988): 1407-1408. [Educational effects of desegregation]

2813. Walsh, Amy. "The Yonkers Case: Separation of Powers as a Yardstick for Determining Official Immunity." *Fordham Urban Law Review* 17 (July-August 1989): 217-255. [School and housing segregation]

2814. Walsh, Edward. "Des Moines Cites 'White Flight' in Curbing School Choice." *Washington Post*, 12 December 1992.

2815. Watson, Frederick D. *Removing the Barricades from the Northern Schoolhouse Door: School Desegregation in Denver.* Ph.D. diss., University of Colorado, 1993. UMO #9310488.

2816. Welch, Finis R., and Audrey Light. *New Evidence on School Desegregation.* Los Angeles, CA: Unican Research Corp., 1987. [Study for the U.S. Commission on Civil Rights]

2817. Wells, Amy S. "Once a Desegregation Tool, Magnet School Becoming School of Choice." *New York Times*, 9 January 1991.

2818. _____. *The Sociology of School Choice: A Study of Black Students' Participation in a Voluntary Transfer Plan.* Ph.D. diss., Columbia University, 1991. [St. Louis, MO]. UMO #9209903.

2819. West, K. C. "A Desegregation Tool That Backfired: Magnet Schools and Classroom Segregation." *Yale Law Journal* 103 (June 1994): 2567-2592.

2820. White, Forrest R. *School Desegregation and Urban Renewal in Norfolk, 1950-1959.* Ph.D. diss., Old Dominion University, 1991. UMO #9130688.

2821. White, James C., and John C. Larson. "Interracial Contact and Desegregation in Magnet Schools." *Sociological Abstracts* (August 1991, supplement 167) 91S25529/ASA/1991/6888.

2822. Wildman, Stephanie M. "Integration in the 1980's: The Dream of Diversity and the Cycle of Exclusion." *Tulane Law Review* 64 (June 1990): 1625-1676.

2823. Wilkerson, Isabel. "Des Moines Acts to Halt White Flight After State Allows Choice of Schools." *New York Times*, 16 December 1992.

2824. _____. "One City's 30-Year Crusade for Integration." *New York Times*, 30 December 1991. [Shaker Heights, Ohio}

2825. Wilkins, Roger W. "Dream Deferred But Not Defeated." *Nation* (23 May 1994). [Desegregation]

2826. Williams, Patricia J. "Among Moses' Bridge-Builders." *Nation* (23 May 1994). [Desegregation]

2827. Williams, Terry, and The Harlem Writers Crew. "The World of Brown's Children." *Nation* (23 May 1994). [Desegregation]

2828. Williard, Eric. "Federal Practice: Clarifying the Desegregation Process." *Oklahoma Law Review* 39 519-539.

2829. Willie, C. V. "A 10-year Perspective on the Role of Blacks in Achieving Desegregation and Quality Education in Boston." in *Research in Inequality and Social Conflict*, Vol. 1. eds. I. Wallimann, and Michael N. Dobkowski. Greenwich, CT: JAI Press, 1989.

2830. Willie, Charles V. "The Intended and Unintended Benefits of School Desegregation." *Urban League Review* 11 (Summer 1987/Winter 1987-88): 127-135.

2831. Wilson, Paul. "Speech on Brown v. Board of Education, May 1, 1981." *Kansas Law Review* 30 (1981).

2832. Wolohojian, G. R. "Judicial Taxation in Desegregation Cases." *Columbia Law Review* 89 (March 1989): 332-346.

2833. Wood, Robert, ed. *Remedial Law. When Courts Become Administrators.* Amherst: University of Massachusetts Press, 1990. [Discusses Keyes et al. v. School District No. 1, school desegregation case in Denver]

2834. Woods, Henry, and Beth Deere. "Reflections on the Little Rock School Case." *Arkansas Law Review* 44 (Fall 1991): 971-1006.

2835. Yanofsky, Saul M., and Laurette Young. "A Successful Parents' Choice Program." *Phi Delta Kappan* (February 1992): 476- 479. [White Plains, NY]

2836. Yazurlo, Michael V., Sr. *Desegregation: Yesterday, Today, and Tomorrow, a Case Study of the Yonkers Public Schools.* Ph.D. diss., Fordham University, 1990. UMO #9109275.

2837. Yee, Laura. "Most Parents Support Integration, Poll Finds." *Cleveland Plain Dealer*, 29 July 1991. [793 Cuyahoga County residents on the Cleveland public schools]

2838. Zisman, P., and V. Wilson. "Table Hopping in the Cafeteria: An Exploration of Racial Integration in Early Adolescent School Groups." *Anthropology and Education Quarterly* 23 (September 1992): 199-220.

DISCRIMINATION

2839. Aguirre, B. E. and others. "Discrimination and the Assimilation and Ethnic Competition Perspectives." *Social Science Quarterly* 70 (1989): 594-606. [Mexican-Americans]

2840. Alexander, L. "What Makes Wrongful Discrimination Wrong? Biases, Preferences, Stereotypes, and Profiles." *University of Pennsylvania Law Review* 141 (November 1992): 149-220.

2841. Alexis, M., and Marshall Medoff. "Becker's Utility Approach to Discrimination: A Review of the Issues." *Review of Black Political Economy* 12 (1984): 41-58.

2842. Ambrose, David M. "Retail Grocery Pricing: Inner City, Suburban, and Rural Comparisions." *Journal of Business* 52 (January 1979).

2843. "America's Asians: The Glass Ceiling." *Economist* (3 June 1989): 23-26.

2844. "The Antidiscrimination Principle in the Common Law." *Harvard Law Review* 102 (June 1989): 1993-2013.

2845. Armendariz, Albert. "Discrimination Against Mexican- Americans in Private Employment." in *Pain and Promise: The Chicano Today*, ed. Edward Simmen. New York: New American Library, 1972.

2846. Arrow, Kenneth. *Some Models of Racial Discrimination in the Labor Market*. Santa Monica, CA: RAND, 1971.

2847. _____. "The Theory of Discrimination." in *Discrimination in Labor Markets*, pp. 3-33. eds. Orley Ashenfelter, and A. Rees. Princeton, NJ: Princeton University Press, 1974.

2848. Austin, B. W. "White Attitudes Toward Black Discrimination." *Urban League Review* 2 (1976): 37-42.

2849. Ayres, Ian. "Fair Driving: Gender and Race Discrimination in Retail Car Negotiations." *Harvard Law Review* 104 (February 1991): 817-872.

2850. Badgett, M. V. Lee, and Rhonda M. Williams. "The Changing Contours of Discrimination: Race, Gender, and Structural Economic Change." in *Understanding American Economic Decline*, eds. David Adler, and Michael Bernstein. Cambridge University Press, 1994.

2851. Bailey, Thomas, and Roger Waldinger. "The Continuing Significance of Discrimination: Racial Discrimination and Racial Conflict in Construction." *Sociological Abstracts* 90S23995/ASA/1990/5693.

2852. Barringer, Felicity. "Mixed-Race Generation Emerges but Is Not Sure Where It Fits." *New York Times*, 24 September 1989.

2853. Bays, Martha D. *Drawing the Color Line: The Uses of Race in Manipulating Labor Markets*. Ph.D. diss., Northwestern University, 1988. UMO #8902613.

2854. Bell, Derrick, and Claire Conway. "The Legacy of Racial Discrimination: Who Pays the Cost?" *Update on Law-Related Education* 12 (Fall 1988).

2855. Bellman, Richard F., and Richard Cohn. "Housing Discrimination." *Touro Law Review* 6 (Fall 1989): 137-158. [Local government]

2856. Bender, Leslie. "Sex Discrimination or Gender Inequality?" *Fordham Law Review* 57 (May 1989): 941-953.

2857. Bender, Mike. "Civil Rights: Race and Sex Discrimination in Refusal to Train Correctional Officer Is Not Excused by Contract under North Dakota Human Rights Act." *North Dakota Law Review* 66 (Summer 1990): 537-551.

2858. Berry, Bertice B. *Black-on-Black Discrimination: The Phenomenon of Colorism among African Americans.* Ph.D. diss., Kent State University, 1988. UMO #8827158.

2859. Betten, Neil, and Raymond A. Mohl. "From Discrimination to Repatriation: Mexican Life in Gary, Indiana, During the Great Depression." *Pacific Historical Review* 42 (August 1973): 370-388.

2860. Biskupic, Joan. "After 19 Years, Racial Job-Bias Case Isn't Over Yet." *Washington Post*, 23 November 1992. [E.I. du Pont de Nemours and Co. plant in Louisville, KY]

2861. Black, Donald. *Sociological Justice.* Oxford University Press: 1989.

2862. Blair, Philip M. "Job Discrimination and Education: Rates of Return to Education of Mexican-Americans and Euro-Americans in Santa Clara County, California." in *Schooling in a Corporate Society*, pp. 80-99. ed. Martin Carnoy. New York: McKay, 1972.

2863. Block, W. "Discrimination: An Interdisciplinary Analysis." *Journal of Business Ethics* 11 (April 1992): 241-254.

2864. Blumrosen, Alfred W. "Society in Transition. 2. Price- Waterhouse and the Individual Employment Discrimination Case." *Rutgers Law Review* 42 (Summer 1990): 1023-1066.

2865. Bogas, K. L. "Discrimination Cases: What to Expect." *Trial* 27 (June 1991): 41-45. [Safeguarding the workplace]

2866. Bohara, A. K., and A. Davila. "A Reassessment of the Phenotypic Discrimination and Income Differences among Mexican Americans." *Social Science Quarterly* 73 (March 1992): 114-119.

2867. Bohing, Edward A. "A Coherent Method for Weighing the Discriminatory Effect of Exclusionary Zoning." *Washington University Journal of Urban and Contemporary Law* 37 (Spring 1990): 257-271.

2868. Boswell, Terry, and David Jorjani. "Uneven Development and the Origins of Split Labor Market Discrimination: A Comparison of Black, Chinese, and Mexican Immigrant Minorities in the United States." in *Racism, Sexism, and the World System*, eds. Joan Smith and others. Westport, CT: Greenwood, 1988.

2869. Bowen, James S. "Peremptory Challenge Discrimination Revisited: Do Batson and McClesky Relieve or Intensify the Swain Paradox?" *National Black Law Journal* 11 (Fall 1990): 291-330.

2870. Bracey, John H., Jr., and August Meier, eds. "Discrimination in the U.S. Armed Forces, 1918-1955." *Papers of the NAACP*, Bethesda, MD: University Publications of America.

2871. _____. "Discrimination in the Criminal Justice System, 1910-1955." *Papers of the NAACP*, Bethesda, MD: University Publications of America.

2872. Briggs, V. M. "Employer Sanctions and the Question of Discrimination: The GAO Study in Perspective." *International Migration Review* 24 (Winter 1990).

2873. Brodin, Mark S. "Reflections on the Supreme Court's 1988 Term: The Employment Discrimination Decisions and the Abandonment of the Second Reconstruction." *Boston College Law Review* 31 (December 1989): 1-30.

2874. Brooks, D. H. M. "Why Discrimination Is Especially Wrong." *Journal of Value Inquiry* 17 (1983). [Reprinted in T.A. Mappes and J.S. Zeinbaty (eds.) *Social Ethics*. 3rd Edition. NY: McGraw Hill, 1987]

2875. Brown, Walt K. and others. "The Negative Effect of Racial Discrimination on Minority Youth in the Juvenile Justice System." *International Journal of Offender Therapy and Comparative Criminology* 34 (September 1990): 87-93.

2876. Bullard, Robert D. "Ecological Inequities and the New South: Black Communities Under Siege." *Journal of Ethnic Studies* 17 (Winter 1990): 101-115.

2877. Burman, George. *The Economics of Discrimination: The Impact of Public Policy.* Ph.D. diss., University of Chicago, 1973.

2878. Burstein, Paul. *Discrimination, Jobs, and Politics.* Chicago, IL: University of Chicago Press, 1985.

2879. _____. "Intergroup Conflict, Law, and the Concept of Labor Market Discrimination." *Sociological Forum* 5 (September 1990).

2880. Buss, William. "Discrimination by Private Clubs." *Washington University Law Quarterly* 67 (Summer 1989): 815-853.

2881. Calhoun, Emily. "Workplace Discrimination: Truthfulness and the Moral Imagination." *Vermont Law Review* 16 (Summer 1991): 137- 182.

2882. Campbell, Patricia B. *The Hidden Discrimination: Sex and Race Bias in Educational Research.* Groton, MA: Educational Equity Act Program, U.S. Department of Education, 1989.

2883. Carter, Stephen L. "Racial Harassment as Discrimination: A Cautious Endorsement of the Anti-oppression Principle." *University of Chicago Legal Forum* (1991): 13-42.

2884. Castaneda, Ruben. "A Bad Excuse for Bias." *Washington Post*, 5 March 1994. [The inexcusability of racism against any group]

2885. Celis, William, 3rd. "Bias Found in Exclusion of Bright Minority People." *New York Times*, 5 November 1993. [Rockford, IL]

2886. Chavez, Margaret M. "Relationships between Levels of Acculturation and Perceptions of Discrimination of Mexican Americans in East Los Angeles." Master's thesis, California State University, Long Beach, 1985. UMO #1327183.

2887. Cherry, Robert. *Discrimination: Its Economic Impact on Blacks, Women, and Jews.* Lexington, MA: Lexington Books, 1989.

2888. Cherry, Robert, and Susan Fenier. "The Treatment of Racial and Sexual Discrimination in Economics Journals and Economics Textbooks: 1972 to 1987." *Review of Black Political Economy* 21 (Fall 1992): 99-118.

2889. Claussen, Cheryl, ed. *Women in Archaelogy.* University of Pennslyvania Press, 1994. [Discrimination]

2890. Cloud, Cathy, and George C. Galster. "What Do We Know About Racial Discrimination in Mortgage Markets." *Review of Black Political Economy* 22 (Summer 1993): 101-120.

2891. Connolly, Catherine R. *Hidden Gender Discrimination in the Work Status Distinction in Federal Labor Policy.* Ph.D. diss., SUNY Buffalo, 1992. UMO #9301834.

2892. Cooney, Mark. "Racial Discrimination in Arrest." *Virginia Review of Sociology* (1992): 99-119.

2893. Cooper, Christine G. "Employment Discrimination Law and the Need for Reform." *Vermont Law Review* 16 (Summer 1991): 183-221.

2894. Cornwall, Richard R., and P. V. Wunnawa, eds. *New Approaches to Economic and Social Analyses of Discrimination.* Praeger, 1991.

2895. Cotton, Jeremiah. "Discrimination and Favoritism in the U.S. Labor Market: A Cost/Benefit Analysis of Sex and Race." *American Journal of Economics and Sociology* 47 (January 1988).

2896. Cranor, Carl, and Kurt Nutting. "Scientific and Legal Standards of Statistical Evidence in Toxic Tort and Discrimination Suits." *Law and Philosophy* 9 (May 1990): 115-156.

2897. Crenshaw, Kimberle. "Demarginalizing the Intersection of Race and Sex: A Black Feminist Critique of Antidiscrimination Doctrine, Feminist Theory, and Antiracist Politics." *University of Chicago Law Forum* (1989).

2898. _____. "Race, Reform, and Retrenchment: Transformation and Legitimation in Anti-Discrimination Law." *Harvard Law Review* 101 (May 1988).

2899. Crosby, Faye J. and others. "Judgment and Prejudgment: Recognizing and Dealing with Discrimination: Anti-semitism, Racism, and Sexism." *Women's Rights Law Reporter* 12 (Winter 1991): 275-291.

2900. Cross, Harry and others. *Employer Hiring Practices, Differential Treatment of Hispanic and Anglo Job Seekers.* Washington, DC: Urban Institute Press, 1990.

2901. Culp, Jerome M., and Bruce H. Dunson. "Brothers of a Different Color: A Preliminary Look at Employer Treatment of White and Black Youth." in *The Black Youth Employment Crisis*, pp. 233-260. eds. Richard B. Freeman, and Harry J. Holzer. Chicago, IL: University of Chicago Press, 1986.

2902. Curry-Swann, Lynne. *Managing Equally and Legally: A Practical Business Guide to Preventing Discrimination Complaints and Termination Lawsuits.* Jefferson, NC: McFarland, 1990.

2903. Dahlback, Olof. "Analyzing Judicial Discrimination." *Quality and Quantity* 27 (November 1993): 315-334.

2904. Davis, Martha F. and others. "Report of the Committee on Immigration and Nationality Law of the Association of the Bar of the City of New York: An Analysis of the Discrimination Resulting from Employer Sanctions and a Call for Repeal." *San Diego Law Review* 26 (September-October 1989): 711-738.

2905. Dearden, I. F. M. "Sexual Harassment and Racial Discrimination: A Practitioner's Guide to the Legislation." *Queensland Law Society Journal* 20 (June 1990): 189-199.

2906. "Deciphering a Racist Business Code." *Time* (19 October 1992). [Employment agency's racially discriminatory practices.]

2907. del Valle, Manuel. *The National Origin Paradigm. The Processes and Consequences of Labor Market Discrimination Sanctioned by Law Against Hispanics.* New York: Social Science Research Council-Inter-University Program for Latino Research, 1987.

2908. Dex, Shirley. *The Costs of Discriminating.* London: Home Office Research and Planning Unit, 1986.

2909. Diamond, Stanley. "Battleground of Bilingual Education: The Challenge to Local Control in the Berkeley Unified School District." *Journal of Law and Politics* 6 (Spring 1990): 579-587.

2910. *Discrimination Against Chippewa Indians in Northern Wisconsin.* Washington, DC: U.S. Commission on Civil Rights, 1989.

2911. *Discrimination and Low Incomes: Social and Economic Discrimination against Minority Groups in Relation to Low Incomes in New York State.* New York: Studies of New York State Commission against Discrimination, New School for Social Research, 1959.

2912. *Discrimination and the Audit: State of the Art.* Washington, DC: U.S. Department of Housing and Urban Development, 1984. [Housing audits of discrimination by "testers" of differing races]

2913. Donohue, J. J., and P. Siegelman. "The Changing Nature of Employment Discrimination Litigation." *Stanford Law Review* 43 (May 1991): 983-1034.

2914. Duran, Joseph D. "The 1984 Riots in Lawrence, Massachusetts: Intergovernmental and Community Level: Interpretations and Responses." Master's thesis, Massachusetts Institute of Technology, 1986.

2915. Ellison, Mary. *Lyrical Protest: Black Music's Struggle Against Discrimination.* New York: Praeger, 1989.

2916. England, Paula, and Peter Lewin. "Economic and Sociological Views of Discrimination in Labor Markets: Persistence or Demise?" *Sociological Spectrum* 9 (Fall 1989): 239-257.

2917. Etaugh, C., and T. Duits. "Development of Gender Discrimination: Role of Stereotypic and Counter-stereotypic Gender Cues." *Sex Roles* 23 (September 1990).

2918. Feagin, Joe R. "The Continuing Significance of Race: Antiblack Discrimination in Public Places." *American Sociological Review* 56 (February 1991): 101-116.

2919. Feiner, Susan, and Bruce B. Roberts. "Hidden by the Invisible Hand: Neo-Classical Theory and the Textbook Treatment of Race and Gender." *Gender and Society* (June 1990): 159-181.

2920. Fernandez, Ferdinand F. "Except a California Indian: A Study in Legal Discrimination." *Southern California Quarterly* 50 (1968): 161-175.

2921. Field, Hubert S. and others. "Personal Selection in Police and Fire Departments: A Study of Employment Discrimination Case Characteristics and Outcomes." *Labor Law Journal* 41 (September 1990): 622-632.

2922. Flicker, Barbara ed. *Justice and School Systems: The Role of the Courts in Education Litigation.* Philadelphia, PA: Temple University Press, 1990.

2923. Floerchinger, Teresa D. *Earnings Differentials among Asian Indian, Black and White Workers Residing in Pennsylvania, New Jersey, New York, and Connecticut.* Ph.D. diss., University of Delaware, 1989. UMO #9010380.

2924. Foderaro, Lisa W. "Japanese in the New York Region Begin to Feel the Sting of Prejudice." *New York Times*, 22 July 1990.

2925. Fowler, G. A., and S. Moore. "When Discrimination Supersedes Confidentiality." *Nursing Outlook* 39 (March-April 1991): 77-81.

2926. Franck, Michael. "Invidious Discrimination [in Justice Administration]." *Michigan Bar Journal* 68 (January 1989).

2927. Frederick, Kenneth L. "State's Use of Peremptory Strikes Made More Difficult to Challenge on Grounds of Racial Discrimination." *South Carolina Law Review* 41 (Autumn 1989): 39- 46.

2928. Freshman, C. "Beyond Atomized Discrimination: Use of Acts of Discrimination Against Other Minorities to Prove Discriminatory Motivation under Federal Employment Law." *Stanford Law Review* 43 (November 1990).

2929. Frias, Albert. "Hispanics Remember Signs." *Indio News* (15 May 1980). [Older Hispanics recall anti-Hispanic discrimination in Indio]

2930. Fuchs, Stephan A. "Discriminatory Lending Practices: Recent Developments, Causes and Solutions." *Annual Review of Banking Law* 10 (1991): 461-490.

2931. Galster, C. George. "Assessing the Causes of Racial Segregation: A Methodological Critique." *Journal of Urban Affairs* 10 (1988): 395-407.

2932. Gardner, John. "Liberals and Unlawful Discrimination." *Oxford Journal of Legal Studies* 9 (Spring 1989): 1-22.

2933. Gewertz, Catherine. "Bias: It's Still a Fact of Business Life." *Los Angeles Times*, 16 May 1994. Supplement: "Work Force Diversity".

2934. Gill, Andrew M. "The Role of Discrimination in Determining Occupational Structure." *Industrial and Labor Relations Review* 42 (1989): 610-623. [1976 and 1981 data]

2935. Ginger, Ann Fagan. "Enforcing the Hidden U.S. Equal Rights Law." *Golden Gate University Law Review* 20 (Fall 1990): 385-478. [Sex discrimination]

2936. *Glass Ceiling Initiative Report.* U.S. Department of Labor, 1991.

2937. Goggin, Jacqueline. "Challenging Sexual Discrimination in the Historical Profession: Women Historians and the American Historical Association, 1890-1940." *American Historical Review* 97 (June 1992): 769-802.

2938. Goodman, Denise. "Black Workers at Maine Plant Win in Bias Suit." *Boston Globe*, 14 April 1991. [International Paper Co., Jay, Maine]

2939. Gouke, Cecil G. *Blacks and the American Economy.* Lexington, MA: Ginn Press, 1987.

2940. Gould, William B., IV. "The Supreme Court and Employment Discrimination Law in 1989: Judicial Retreat and Congressional Response." *Tulane Law Review* 64 (June 1990): 1485-1514.

2941. Graglia, Lino A. "The Remedy Rationale for Requiring or Permitting Otherwise Prohibited Discrimination: How the Court Overcame the Constitution and the 1964 Civil Rights Act." *Suffolk University Law Review* 22 (Fall 1986): 569-621.

2942. _____. "Title VII of the Civil Rights Act of 1964: From Prohibiting to Requiring Racial Discrimination in Employment." *Harvard Journal of Law and Public Policy* 14 (Winter 1991): 68- 77. [See Randall L. Kennedy, below]

2943. Grown, Caren, and Timothy Bates. "Commercial Bank Lending Practices and the Development of Black owned Construction Companies." *Journal of Urban Affairs* 14 (1992): 25-41.

2944. Grunig, L. A. "Court-ordered Relief from Sex Discrimination in the Foriegn Service: Implications for Women Working in Development Communication." in *Public Relations Research Annual*, vol. 3. eds. L. A. Grunig, and J. E. Grunig. Hillsdale, NJ: Erlbaum, 1991.

2945. *The Guidelines for Recognizing Race and Gender Bias in Economics*. Committee for Race and Gender Balance in the Economics Curriculum, [Write: Prof. Susan Feiner, Committee Chair, Hampton U., Hampton, VA 23668]

2946. Haberfeld, Yitchak. "Employment Discrimination: An Organizational Model." *Academy of Management Journal* 35 (March 1992): 161-180.

2947. Hacker, Andrew. "The Delusion of Equality." *Nation* (4 April 1994). [Review of Ellis Cose, The Rage of a Privileged Class: Why Are Middle-class Blacks Angry? Why Should America Care?]

2948. Hakken, Jon. *Discrimination Against Chicanos in the Dallas Rental Housing Market: An Experimental Extension of the Housing Market Practices Survey*. Washington, DC: Office of Policy Development and Research, U.S. Dept. of Housing and Urban Development, August 1979.

2949. Hartman, C. A. and others. "Disentangling Discrimination: Victim Characteristics as Determinants of the Perception Behavior as Racist or Sexist." *Journal of Applied Social Psychology* 24 (1 April 1994): 567-579.

2950. Hartmann, D., and L. A. Woolbright. "The New Segregation: Asians and Hispanics." *Urban Affairs Annual Reviews* 32 (1987).

2951. Haskell, Thomas L., Linda B. Hall, and Blanche Wiesen Cook. "[An exchange on possible gender discrimination in programs at the annual meetings of the American Historical Association]." *Perspectives* 30 (April 1992): 13-16.

2952. Heckman, James J., and J. Hoult Verkerke. "Racial Disparity and Employment Discrimination Law: An Economic Perspective." *Yale Law and Policy Review* 8 (Fall 1990): 276-298.

2953. Heevitt, William L. "Mexican Workers in Wyoming during World War II: Necessity, Discrimination and Protest." *Annals of Wyoming* 54 (Fall 1982): 20-33.

2954. Heywood, J. S. "Wage Discrimination by Race and Gender in the Public and Private Sectors." *Economic Letters* 29 (1989).

2955. Hicks, Jonathan P. "Blacks See Bias Trend in Job Cuts." *New York Times*, 23 September 1991. [Black professionals in industry]

2956. Hill, Robert B. "Structural Discrimination: The Unintended Consequences of Institutional Processes." in *Surveying Social Life: Papers in Honor of Herbert Hyman*, pp. 353-375. ed. H. J. O. Gorman. Middletown, CT: Wesleyan University Press, 1988.

2957. Hirsch, B. T., and Schumacher E.J. "Labor Earnings, Discrimination, and the Racial Composition of Jobs." *Journal of Human Resources* 27 (Fall 1992).

2958. Hoadley, Diane L. "Fetal Protection Policies: Effective Tools for Gender Discrimination." *Journal of Legal Medicine* 12 (March 1991): 85-104.

2959. Hoffman, Emily P., ed. *Essays on the Economics of Discrimination*. Kalamazoo, MI: W.E. Upjohn Institute, 1992.

2960. Holmes, Eleanor H. "Discrimination Actions in Federal Court." *New Hampshire Bar Journal* 30 (Summer 1989): 219-226.

2961. Janofsky, Michael. "Race and the American Workplace." *New York Times*, 20 June 1993. [Miller Brewing Co. plant in Fulton, NY]

2962. Johnson, Glen. "Job Bias Cases on the Rise." *Boston Globe*, 4 July 1994. [Dramatic increase nationally]

2963. Jordan, Robert A. "Getting Past the Racial Bar." *Boston Globe*, 3 March 1990. [Failure of Boston law firms to employ black law graduates.]

2964. Kadetsky, Elizabeth. "Muscling In on Construction Jobs." *Nation* (13 July 1992). [Racial discrimination in New York City construction industry]

2965. Kamalich, Richard F., and Solomon Polachek. "Discrimination: Fact or Fiction?" *Southern Economic Journal* 49 (October 1982).

2966. Katz, Martin J. "The Economics of Discrimination: The Three Fallacies of Croson." *Yale Law Journal* 100 (January 1991). [Richmond, VA set-aside case]

2967. _____. "Insurance and the Limits of Rational Discrimination." *Yale Law and Policy Review* 8 (Fall 1990): 436- 458.

2968. Kazyaka, Ann-Marie. *Guarding the Gateway to Discrimination: Developing a Constitutional Model of Capital Sentencing*. Ph.D. diss., University of Maryland, 1989. UMO #9012482.

2969. Kelman, M. "Concepts of Discrimination in General Ability Job Testing." *Harvard Law Review* 104 (April 1991): 1157-1248.

2970. Kennedy, Joseph P., II. "A Lending-Bias Battle." *Boston Globe*, 3 October 1989. [Racial discrimination in bank lending]

2971. Kennedy, Randall L. "The State, Criminal Law, and Racial Discrimination: A Comment." *Harvard Law Review* 107 (April 1994): 1225-1278.

2972. Kennedy, Randall L. "Competing Conceptions of Racial Discrimination: A Response to Cooper and Graglia." *Harvard Journal of Law and Public Policy* 14 (Winter 1991): 93-101. [See Lino A. Graglia, above]

2973. Kenny, William R. "Mexican-American Conflict on the Mining Frontier, 1848-1852." *Journal of the West* 6 (October 1967): 582- 592.

2974. Kerr, Peter. "Insurance Industry Bias Seen in National Study." *New York Times*, 5 February 1993. [Study of 13 cities]

2975. Kilborn, Peter T. "Labor Dept. Wants to Take On Job Bias in the Executive Suite." *New York Times*, 30 July 1990.

2976. Kilson, Martin L. Jr., and George C. Bond. "Marginalized Blacks." *New York Times*, 17 May 1992. Letter.

2977. Kim, Marlene. *Compensation and Discrimination in the California State Civil Service*. Ph.D. diss., University of California, Berkeley, 1990. UMO #9103757.

2978. _____. "Gender Bias in Compensation Structures: A Case Study of Its Historical Basis and Persistence." *Journal of Social Issues* 45 (1989): 39-50.

2979. King, N. J. "Postconviction Review of Jury Discrimination: Measuring the Effects of Juror Race on Jury Decisions." *Michigan Law Review* 92 (October 1993).

2980. Kingrea, Nellie. *Texas Good Neighbor Commission*. Texas Christian University Press, 1954.

2981. Kirchheimer, Anne. "The Woman Leading Fight Against Dual Discrimination." *Boston Globe*, 5 August 1981. [Ms. Maria Jimenez Van Hoy, president, National Conference of Puerto Rican Women]

2982. Kirschenman, Joleen, and Kathryn M. Neckerman. "'We'd Love to Hire Them, But...': The Meaning of Race for Employers." in *The Urban Underclass*, eds. Christopher Jencks, and Paul E. Peterson. Washington, DC: Brookings Institution, 1991.

2983. Kohn, E. and others. *Are Mortgage Lending Policies Discriminatory? A Study of 10 Savings Banks*. New York State Banking Department, Consumer Studies Division, 1992.

2984. Kousser, J. Morgan. "The Supremacy of Equal Rights: The Struggle against Racial Discrimination in Antebellum Massachusetts and the Foundations of the Fourteenth Amendment." *Northwestern University Law Review* 82 (Summer 1982): 941-1010.

2985. Kovacic-Fleischer, Candace S. "Proving Discrimination after Price Waterhouse and Wards Cove: Semantics as Substance." *American University Law Review* 39 (Spring 1990): 615-666.

2986. La Van, H.N. "Litigated Employment Discrimination Cases Based on National Origin: Comparison of Hispanic National Origin to All National Origin Cases." in *Hispanics in the Workplace*, eds. Stephen B. Knouse and others. Newbury Park, CA: Sage, 1992.

2987. Lagnado, Lucette. "Educating Rita." *Village Voice* (20 October 1992). [Non-implementation of order to stop discrimination against white worker]

2988. _____. "Old and Out of Work." *Village Voice* (25 June 1991). [Charges that Jewish civil servants in New York City are being discriminatorily discharged]

2989. Larson, David A. "Title VII Compensation Isues Affecting Bilingual Hispanic Employees." *Arizona State Law Journal* 23 (Fall 1991): 821-830. [Discrimination in employment]

2990. "The Law and Economics of Racial Discrimination in Employment." *Georgetown Law Journal* 79 (August 1991): 1619-1782 (seven articles).

2991. Lawrie, J. "Subtle Discrimination Pervades Corporate America." *Personnel Journal* 69 (January 1990).

2992. Lee, Barbara A. "Sex Discrimination and the Supreme Court Implications for Women Faculty." *Women's Studies Quarterly* 18 (Spring-Summer 1990): 155-173.

2993. "Legislative Attempts to Eliminate Racial and Religious Discrimination." *Columbia Law Review* 39 (1939).

2994. Lewin, Tamara. "Working Women Say Bias Persists." *New York Times*, 15 October 1994.

2995. Lieberson, Stanley, and Mary C. Waters. *From Many Strands: Ethnic and Racial Groups in Contemporary America*. New York: Russell Sage Foundation, 1988.

2996. Lippi-Green, Rosina. "Accent, Standard Language Ideology, and Discriminatory Pretext in the Courts." *Language in Society* 23 (June 1994): 163-198.

2997. Lively, Donald E. "Colorblindness and Context." *New York University Review of Law and Social Change* 18 (April 1990): 291- 301. [Discrimination in the workplace]

2998. Locust, Carol. "Wounding the Spirit: Discrimination and Traditional American Indian Belief Systems." *Harvard Educational Review* 58 (1988): 315-330.

2999. Long, James E. "Employment Discrimination in the Federal Sector." *Journal of Human Resources* 11 (Winter 1976): 86-97.

3000. Luebben, Ralph A. "Prejudice and Discrimination Against Navahos in a Mining Community." *Kiva* 30 (October 1964): 1-18.

3001. Luna, Gaye. "Understanding Gender-based Wage Discrimination: Legal Interpretation and Trends of Pay Equity in Higher Education." *Journal of Law and Education* 19 (Summer 1990): 371-384.

3002. Lykes, M. Brinton. "Discrimination and Coping in the Lives of Black Women." *Journal of Social Issues* 39 (1983): 79-100.

3003. Mabury, Marcus and others. "Past Tokenism." *Newsweek* (14 May 1990). [Corporate failure to promote women and minority employees.]

3004. Maitzen, Stephen. "The Ethics of Statistical Discrimination." *Social Theory and Practice* 17 (Spring 1991): 23- 45.

3005. Maltz, Earl M. "Legislative Inputs and Gender-based Discrimination in the Burger Court." *Michigan Law Review* 90 (March 1992): 1023-1027.

3006. Mark, Gregory Y. "The 1935 Oakland Laundry Ordinance: The Genesis of Discriminatory Justice." *Quarterly Journal of Ideology* 11 (1987): 41-57.

3007. Marshall, Ray. "The Economics of Racial Discrimination: A Survey." *Journal of Economic Literature* 12 (1974): 849-871.

3008. Martinez, Elizabeth. "That Old White (male) Magic." *Zeta Magazine* 2 (July-August 1989): 48-52. [The invisibility of Latinos in Left political analysis.]

3009. Mason, Philip L. "Accumulation, Segmentation and the Discrimination Process in the Market for Labor Review." *Review of Radical Political Economics* 25 (June 1993).

3010. Mathews, Jay. "Denny's Tackles a Stained Image." *Washington Post*, 1 August 1993. [Discrimination at Denny's restaurant chain]

3011. _____. "Use of Testers to Fight Bias Stirs Backlash." *Washington Post*, 14 December 1992. [District of Columbia and environs]

3012. Mayfield, Bonnie L. "Batson and Groups Other than Blacks: A Strict Scrutiny Analysis." *American Journal of Trial Advocacy* 11 (Spring 1988): 377-416. [Discriminatory jury selection].

3013. McAllister, Bill. "Postal Workers Cite Bias, Lack of Job Safety." *Washington Post*, 22 November 1993.

3014. McQuiston, John T. "Accord Gives Black Firefighters Benefits." *New York Times*, 10 March 1994. [Roosevelt, NY]

3015. McShane, S. L. "Two Tests of Direct Gender Bias in Job Evaluation Ratings." *Journal of Occupational Psychology* 63 (June 1990).

3016. McWilliams, Carey. "Race Discrimination and the Law." *Science and Society* 9 (1945): 1-22.

3017. Meier, Kenneth J. and others. *Race, Class, and Education: The Politics of Second-Generation Discrimination*. Madison: University of Wisconsin Press, 1989.

3018. Meier, Kenneth J. "Teachers, Students, and Discrimination: The Policy Impact of Black Representation." *Journal of Politics* 46 (1984): 252-263.

3019. Mindiola, Tatcho, Jr. *The Cost of Being Mexican American and Black in Texas, 1960-1970*. Ph.D. diss., Brown University, 1978. UMO #7906587.

3020. _____. "The Cost of Being a Mexican Female Worker in the 1970 Houston Labor Market." *Aztlan* 11 (Fall 1980): 231-247.

3021. Minow, Martha. "Making All the Difference: Three Lessons in Equality, Neutrality, and Tolerance." *De Paul Law Review* 39 (Fall 1989): 1-13.

3022. Mitchell, Alison. "White Jewish Woman's Bias Charge Is Upheld by U.S. Civil Rights Office." *New York Times*, 19 June 1992. [Ms. Rita Arno, NYC] [See nos. 2987 and 2988]

3023. Modjeska, Lee. "Employment Discrimination and the Reconsideration of Runyon." *Kentucky Law Journal* 78 (January 1990): 377-391.

3024. Moore, Helen J. "Patterson v. McLean Credit Union: Racial Discrimination by Private Actors and Racial Harassment under Section 1981." *Golden Gate University Law Review* 20 (Fall 1990): 617-645.

3025. Murphy, Clyde E. "Racial Discrimination in the Criminal Justice System." *North Carolina Central Law Journal* 17 (Fall 1988): 171-190.

3026. National Senior Citizens Law Center. "Race Discrimination in Nursing Homes." *Nursing Home Law Letter* Nos. 39 and 40 (1980).

3027. Naughton, Jim. "Black and Catholic in Washington: The Movie." *Washington Post*, 31 July 1993. [Discrimination against Black Catholics within the Catholic Church]

3028. Newburger, Harriet B. "Discrimination by a Profit-Maximizing Real Estate Broker in Response to White Prejudice." *Journal of Urban Economics* 26 (1989): 1-19.

3029. Newman, Robert. "Remedies for Discrimination in Supervisorial and Managerial Jobs." *Harvard Civil Rights-Civil Liberties Law Review* 13 (Summer 1978): 633-679.

3030. Niemi, A. W., Jr. "How Discrimination against Female Workers Is Hidden in U.S. Industry Statistics: Sex Differences in Wages in the Cotton, Textile, and Boot and Shoe Industries between the World Wars." *American Journal of Economics and Sociology* 48 (October 1989).

3031. Note. "State Power and Discrimination by Private Clubs: First Amendment protection for Nonexpressive Associations." *Harvard Law Review* 104 (June 1991): 1835-1856.

3032. O'Brien, Raymond C. "Discrimination: The Difference with AIDS." *Journal of Contemporary Health Law and Policy* 6 (Spring 1990): 93-125.

3033. Olson, Paulette. "The Persistence of Occupational Segregation: A Critique of Its Theoretical Underpinnings." *Journal of Economic Issues* 24 (March 1990).

3034. Pasternak, Judy. "Service Still Skin-Deep for Blacks." *Los Angeles Times*, 1 April 1993. [Anti-black discrimination in restaurants and public places in Milwaukee, WI]

3035. Perry, P. L. "Two Faces of Disparate Impact Discrimination." *Fordham Law Review* 59 (March 1991): 523-596.

3036. Peterson, Susan C. "Discrimination and Jurisdiction: Seven Civil Rights Cases in South Dakota, 1976-1982." *Journal of the West* 25 (1986): 44-48.

3037. Pinzler, Isabelle K., and Deborah Ellis. "Wage Discrimination and Comparable Worth: A Legal Perspective." *Journal of Social Issues* 45 (1989): 51-65.

3038. *Pipelines of Progress: A Status Report on the Glass Ceiling.* U.S. Department of Labor, 1992.

3039. Polionard, J. L. and others. "Education and Governance: Representational Links to Second Generation Discrimination." *Western Political Quarterly* 43 (September 1990).

3040. Poston, D. L., Jr. and others. "Earnings Differences Between Anglo and Mexican American Male Workers in 1960 and 1970: Changes in the 'Cost' of Being Mexican American." *Social Science Quarterly* 57 (1976): 618-631.

3041. Poston, D. L., Jr., and D. Alvirez. "On the Cost of Being a Mexican American Worker." *Social Science Quarterly* 53 (March 1973): 695-709.

3042. Quint, Michael. "Tracking Bias in Banks." *New York Times*, 16 February 1992.

3043. Ralston, Charlie S. and others. "Employment Discrimination." *Touro Law Review* 6 (Fall 1989): 55-112. [Symposium]

3044. Reich, Michael. "Segmented Labour, Time Series Hypothesis and Evidence." *Cambridge Journal of Economics* 8 (March 1984): 63- 81.

3045. Reid, Clifford E. "The Reliability of Fair Housing Audits to Detect Racial Discrimination in Rental Housing Markets." *Journal of the American Real Estate and Urban Economics Association* 12 (1984): 86-96.

3046. Reynolds, Vernon. "Sociology and the Idea of Primordial Discrimination." *Ethnic and Racial Studies* 3 (1980): 303-315.

3047. Riach, P. A., and J. Rich. "Testing for Racial Discrimination in the Labour Market." *Cambridge Journal of Economics* 15 (September 1991): 239-256.

3048. Robinson, James K. "Discrimination and the Legal System." *Michigan Bar Journal* 69 (December 1990): 12-52.

3049. Rockwell, Llewellyn H., Jr. "Call for Quotas Ignores Facts on Mortgages." *Los Angeles Times*, 10 December 1992. [Denies racial discrimination in mortgage lending by branches]

3050. Rodriguez, Clara E. "Puerto Ricans: Between Black and White." *Journal of New York Affairs* 1 (1974): 492-501.

3051. Rohlik, Josef. "Employment Discrimination in the United States in 1989: Revisions or a Pause." *Georgia Journal of International and Comparative Law* 20 (Spring 1990): 57-70.

3052. Roise, Anne. "A Big Oversight in the Study of Bias in Mass. Courts." *Boston Globe*, 9 October 1994. [Charges of bias inside the Supreme Judicial Court]

3053. Rubin, Laurie, and Susan Forward. *Systemic Discrimination in the Private Rental Market*. Boston: Massachusetts Commission Against Discrimination, 1984.

3054. Rubin, Margot S. "Advertising and Title VIII: The Discriminatory Use of Models in Real Estate Advertisements." *Yale Law Journal* 98 (November 1988): 165-185.

3055. Rust, Ben. "Racial Discrimination and the Teachers Shortage in California." *Frontier* 8 (May 1956): 16.

3056. Sagatun, Inger J. "Gender Discrimination in Criminal Justice: Relevant Law and Future Trends." *Women and Criminal Justice* 2 (1990): 63-81.

3057. Salamon, Lester, and S. Van Evera. "Fear, Apathy, and Discrimination." *American Political Science Review* 67 (1973): 1290-1299.

3058. Scaperlanda, Michael A. "The Paradox of a Title: Discrimination Within the Anti-discrimination Provisions of the Immigration Reform and Control Act of 1986." *Wisconsin Law Review* (November-December 1988): 1043-1091.

3059. Sexton, Donald E. *Groceries in the Ghetto*. Lexington, MA: D.C. Heath, 1973.

3060. Sexton, Edwin A. *Residential Location, Journey to Work, and Black Earnings*. Ph.D. diss., University of Illinois, 1988. UMO #8823246.

3061. Shanley, Jean M. "The Discriminatory Use of Peremptory Challenges after Holland." *Seton Hall Law Review* 22 (Winter 1991): 58-90.

3062. Shelton, Beth Ann. "Racial Discrimination at Initial Labor Market Access." *National Journal of Sociology* 1 (Spring 1987): 101-117.

3063. Shenon, Philip. "F.B.I. Settles Suit By Black Workers on Discrimination." *New York Times*, 12 January 1990.

3064. Shogren, Elizabeth. "Black Flood Victims Charge Bias in Allocating Relief Aid." *Los Angeles Times*, 19 August 1993. [Crystal City, MO]

3065. Shoop, Julie G. "Senate Panel Urges Judicial Nominees to Quit Discriminatory Clubs." *Trial* 26 (October 1990): 85-86.

3066. Short, G., and B. Carrington. "Unfair Discrimination: Teaching the Principles to Children of Primary School Age." *Journal of Moral Education* 20 (1991): 157-176.

3067. Shulman, Steven, and William A. Darity, Jr., eds. *The Question of Discrimination: Racial Inequality in the U.S. Labor Market*. Middletown, CT: Wesleyan University Press, 1989.

3068. Siegelman, P., and J. J. Dononhue. "Studying the Iceberg from Its Tip: A Comparison of Published and Unpublished Employment Discrimination Cases." *Law and Society Review* 24 (1990): 1133-1170.

3069. Slonaker, W. M., and A. C. Wendt. "Pregnancy Discrimination: An Empirical Analysis of a Continuing Problem." *Labor Law Journal* 42 (June 1991): 343-350.

3070. Soo, In Soo. *Problems in Black Economic Attainment: Racial Discrimination or Class Subordination?* Ph.D. diss., University of Massachusetts, 1990. UMO #9035405.

3071. Souza, Steven J. *A Decade of Institutional Discrimination in a School District: A Participatory Study*. Ph.D. diss., University of San Francisco, 1992. UMO #9307506.

3072. Spector, B. "Women Astronomers Say Discrimination in Field Persists." *Scientist* 5 (1 April 1991): 20-21.

3073. Spurr, Stephen J. "Sex Discrimination in the Legal Profession: A Study of Promotion." *Industrial and Labor Relations Review* 43 (April 1990): 406-417.

3074. Squires, Gregory D. and others. "Insurance Redlining, Agency Location, and the Process of Urban Disinvestment." *Urban Affairs Quarterly* 26 (June 1991): 567-588.

3075. Steele, R. W. "'No Racials': Discrimination Against Ethnics in American Defense Industry, 1940-1942." *Labor History* 32 (Winter 1991): 66-90.

3076. Steen, J. E. and others. "A Reexamination of Gender Bias in Arbitration Decisions." *Labor Law Journal* 45 (May 1994): 298-305.

3077. Stegman, L. M. "An Administrative Battle of the Forms: The EEOC's Intake Questionnaire and Charge of Discrimination." *Michigan Law Review* 91 (October 1992).

3078. Stewart, Gail. *Discrimination*. New York: Crestwood House, 1989. [Written for young people]

3079. Strauss, David A. "The Law and Economics of Racial Discrimination in Employment: The Case for Numerical Standards." *Georgetown Law Journal* 79 (August 1991): 1619-1658.

3080. Sunstein, Cass R. "Why Markets Don't Stop Discrimination." *Social Philosophy and Policy* 8 (Spring 1991): 22-37.

3081. Swoboda, Frank. "Labor Report Calls Secretary's Office 'Burial Ground' for Bias Cases." *Washington Post*, 26 May 1993.

3082. "Systematic Discrimination in the Indian Claims Commission: The Burden of Proof in Redressing Historical Wrongs." *Iowa Law Review* 57 (June 1972): 1300-1319.

3083. Szymanski, Albert. "Racial Discrimination and White Gain." *American Sociological Review* 41 (1970): 403-419.

3084. Tauer, C. A. "The Concept of Discrimination and the Treatment of People with AIDS." in *Meaning of AIDS*, eds. E. T. Juengst, and B. A. Koenig. New York: Praeger, 1989.

3085. Taylor, P. A., and S. W. Shields. "Mexican Americans and Employment Inequality in the Federal Civil Service." *Social Science Quarterly* 65 (June 1984).

3086. Telles, E. E., and Edward Murguia. "Phenotypic Discrimination and Income Differences among Mexican Americans." *Social Science Quarterly* 71 (December 1990): 682-696.

3087. Teltsch, Kathleen. "Aid Groups Rated on Puerto Ricans." *New York Times*, 3 January 1988. [Negligible philanthropic support by foundations for Puerto Rican groups]

3088. Terborg-Penn, Rosalyn. "Discrimination Against Afro-American Women in the Women's Movement, 1830-1920." in *The Afro-American Woman*, eds. Sharon Harley, and Rosalyn Terborg-Penn. Port Washington, NY, 1978.

3089. Thomas, J. Alan. "Resource Allocation in School Districts and Classrooms." *Journal of Education Finance* 5 (Winter 1980): 246-261.

3090. Thomas, Lawrence. "Next Life, I'll Be White." *New York Times*, 13 August 1990.

3091. Torres, Andrea. "Nativity, Gender, and Earnings Discrimination." *Hispanic Journal of Behavioral Sciences* 14 (February 1992).

3092. Turner, Margery A. and others. *The Housing Discrimination Study*. Urban Institute, 1991.

3093. _____. *Housing Discrimination Study: Synthesis*. Washington, DC: U.S. Dept. of Housing and Urban Development, Office of Policy Development and Research, August 1991. [1989 data]

3094. _____. *Opportunities Denied, Opportunities Diminished: Discrimination in Hiring*. Washington, DC: Urban Institute, 1991.

3095. Uchitelle, Louis. "Unequal Pay Widespread in U.S." *New York Times*, 14 August 1990.

3096. U.S. Congress, 100th, 2nd session, Senate, Committee on Banking, Housing, and Urban Affairs, Subcommittee on Consumer and Regulatory Affairs. *Mortgage Discrimination: Hearing*. Washington, DC: GPO, 1990.

3097. U.S. Congress, 99th, 1st session, House of Representatives, Committee on Banking, Finance, and Urban Affairs, Subcommittee on Housing and Community Development. *Discrimination in Federally Assisted Housing Programs*. Serial No. 99-83. Washington, DC: GPO, 1985.

3098. U.S. Department of Housing and Urban Development. *Measuring Racial Discrimination*. Washington, DC: GPO, 1979.

3099. U.S. General Accounting Office. *Within-School Discrimination: Inadequate Title VI Enforcement by the Office for Civil Rights*. Washington, DC: GPO, 1991.

3100. Vasu, Michael I., and Ellen Storey Vasu. "Gender Stereotypes and Discriminatory Behaviors toward Female Attorneys: The North Carolina Case." *Campbell Law Review* 13 (Spring 1991): 183-207.

3101. Vedder, Richard K. and others. "Discrimination and Exploitation in Antebellum American Cotton Textile Manufacturing III." in *Research in Economic History*, ed. Roger L. Ransom. JAI Press, 1978.

3102. Wainscott, Stephen H., and J. David Woodard. "Second Thoughts on Second-Generation Discrimination: School Resegregation in Southern States." *American Politics Quarterly* 16 (1988): 171-192.

3103. Waldinger, Roger, and T. Bailey. "The Continuing Significance of Race: Racial Conflict and Racial Discrimination in Construction." *Politics and Society* 19 (September 1991): 291-324.

3104. Walker, Adrian. "Boston Shows Bias in Awarding Contracts, Study Says." *Boston Globe*, 26 June 1994.

3105. Watkins, Steve. "Racism Du Jour At Shoney's." *Nation* (18 October 1993).

3106. Weddle, Kevin J. "Ethnic Discrimination in Minnesota Volunteer Regiments during the Civil War." *Civil War History* 35 (September 1989): 239-259.

3107. Weiss, Marley S. "Risky Business: Age and Race Discrimination in Capital Redevelopment Decision." *Maryland Law Review* 48 (Fall 1989): 910-1017.

3108. Welch, Finis R. "Education and Racial Discrimination." in *Discrimination in Labor Markets*, eds. Orley Ashenfelter, and Albert Rees. Princeton University Press, 1973.

3109. Wells, Julian W. "Housing Discrimination: The Fair Housing Act and Discriminatory Advertising." *Annual Survey of American Law* (October 1989): 811-827.

3110. Westman, J. C. "Juvenile Ageism: Unrecognized Prejudice and Discrimination against the Young." *Child Psychiatry and Human Development* 21 (Summer 1991): 237-256.

3111. Wharton, Amy S. "Gender Segregation in Private-sector, Public-sector, and Self-employed Occupations." *Social Science Quarterly* 70 (December 1989).

3112. Wienk, R. "Discrimination in Urban Credit Markets: What We Don't Know and Why We Don't Know It." *Housing Policy Debate* 3 (1992): 217-240.

3113. Wilbanks, William. "Statistical Libel: The Times Herald Racial Bias in Justice Study." *Prosecutor, Journal of the National District Attorneys Association* 23 (Spring 1990).

3114. Williams, Bruce B. *Black Workers in an Industrial Suburb: The Stuggle Against Discrimination*. New Bruswick, NJ: Rutgers University Press, 1987.

3115. Williams, Walter E. "A Coup for White Racists and Black Criminals." *Los Angeles Times*, 20 October 1993. [Denies discrimination has little to do with plight of blacks in Los Angeles]

3116. Wilson, S. B. "Eliminating Sex Discrimination in the Legal Profession: The Key to Widespread Social Reform." *Indiana Law Journal* 67 (Summer 1992): 817-852.

3117. Winston, Judith A. "Mirror, Mirror on the Wall: Title VII, section 1981, and the Intersection of Race and Gender in the Civil Rights Act of 1990." *California Law Review* 79 (May 1991): 775-805.

3118. Withey, Ellen. "Discrimination in Private Employment in Puerto Rico." *Revista Puertorriquena/sobre los Derechos Humanos/ Puerto Rican Journal of Human Rights* 1 (August 1977): 43-47.

3119. Wolkinson, B. W., and Nicol V. "The Arbitration of Discrimination Claims in Employment Cases." *Arbitration Journal* 47 (September 1992): 20-30.

3120. Woodhead, Mary J. "Ethnic Origin Discrimination as Race Discrimination under Section 1981 and Section 1982." *Utah Law Review* (Summer 1989): 741-758.

3121. Ydstie, John. "Dollars and Sense." *Modern Maturity* 36 (August-September 1993): 64-68, 81, 84, 88. [Interview with economist Gary Becker on racial discrimination and other subjects]

3122. Yinger, John. "Acts of Discrimination: Evidence from the 1989 Housing Discrimination Study." *Journal of Housing Economics* 1 (December 1991).

3123. _____. "Measuring Racial Discrimination with Fair Housing Audits." *American Economic Review* 76 (1986): 881-893.

3124. Yoder, J. D. "Rethinking Tokenism: Looking Beyond Numbers." *Gender and Society* 5 (June 1991): 178-192.

3125. York, Michael. "Wheels of Justice Turn Bias Suit Into 18- Year Ordeal." *Washington Post*, 2 June 1993. [Employment discrimination lawsuit filed in 1975]

3126. Young-Bruehl, Elizabeth. "Discriminations: Kinds and Types of Prejudice." *Transition* 60 (1993): 53-69.

DU BOIS

3127. Cain, William E. "From Liberalism to Communism. The Political Thought of W.E.B. Du Bois." in *Cultures of United States Imperialism*, eds. Amy Kaplan, and Donald E. Pease. Duke University Press, 1993.

3128. _____. "Violence, Revolution, and the Cost of Freedom: John Brown and W.E.B. Du Bois." *Boundary 2* 17 (Spring 1990): 305- 330.

3129. Du Bois, W. E. B. "Negroes and the Crisis of Capitalism in the United States." *Monthly Review* 41 (1989): 27-35. [Reprinted from issue of April 1953]

3130. Hufford, Donald E. *Polarity Thinking in the Educational Philosophy of W.E.B. Du Bois.* Ph.D. diss., University of Kansas, 1992. UMO #9323078.

3131. Hwang, H-S. *Booker T. Washington and W.E.B. Du Bois: A Study in Race Leadership, 1895-1915.* Ph.D. diss., University of Hawaii, 1988.

3132. Weinberg, Meyer, ed. *The World of W.E.B. Du Bois. A Quotation Sourcebook*. Greenwood, 1992.

ECONOMIC STANDARDS

3133. "The 1990 Federal Poverty Income Guidelines." *Social Security Bulletin* 53 (March 1990): 15-16.

3134. Aaron, Henry J. "Symposium on the Economic Status of African-Americans." *Journal of Economic Perspectives* 4 (Fall 1990): 3-7.

3135. Abramowitz, Mimi. *Regulating the Lives of Women. Social Welfare Policy from Colonial Times to the Present*. Boston, MA: South End Press, 1988.

3136. Adams, Terry K. and Others. "The Persistence of Urban Poverty." in *Quiet Riots*, eds. Fred R. Harris, and Roger W. Wilkins. New York, N.Y.: Pantheon, 1988.

3137. Agee, M. L., and R. W. Walker. "Is There Any Truth to the Buzz Words 'Feminization of Poverty'?" *International Journal of Social Economics* 17 (1990).

3138. Allen, J. E., and A. Thompson. "Rural Poverty among Racial and Ethnic Minorities." *American Journal of Agricultural Economics* 72 (December 1990): 1161-1168.

3139. Allen, Walter R., and Reynolds Farley. "The Shifting Social and Economic Tides of Black America, 1950-1980." *American Sociological Review* 12 (1986): 277-306.

3140. Amenia, Richard F. *Developing the Afro-American Economy*. Washington D.C.: Heath, 1977.

3141. Amott, Teresa. *Caught in the Crisis. Women and the U.S. Economy Today*. Monthly Review Press, 1993.

3142. Anders, Gary C. "The Reduction of a Self-Sufficient People to Poverty and Welfare Dependence: An Analysis of the Causes of Cherokee Indian Underdevelopment." *American Journal of Economics and Sociology* 40 (1981): 225-238.

3143. Angle, J. "The Inequality Process and the Distribution of Income to Blacks and Whites." *Journal of Mathematical Sociology* 17 (1992).

3144. Aponte, R. "Urban Hispanic Poverty: Disaggregations and Explanations." *Social Problems* 38 (November 1991): 516-528.

3145. Baldwin, M., and J. A. Bishop. "An Analysis of Racial Differences in Wage Distributions." *Economics Letters* 37 (September 1991).

3146. Barcelo, Cosme J., and Toni Breiter. "Hispanics on Welfare- The Facts and Figures." *Agenda* 7 (March-April 1977): 4-10.

3147. Barringer, Herbert R. and Others. "Education, Occupational Prestige, and Income of Asian Americans." *Sociology of Education* 63 (1990): 27-43.

3148. Beauford, E. Yvonne, and Mack C. Nelson. "Social and Economic Conditions of Black Farm Households: Status and Prospects." in *The Rural South in Crisis: Challenges of the Future*, ed. Lionel J. Beaulieu. Boulder, CO: Westview, 1988.

3149. Bennett, Gerald G. "Racial Inequality and the Poor: A Critique of W. J. Wilson's The Truly Disadvantaged." *Social Justice* 16 (Winter 1989).

3150. Billingsley, Andrew. "The Sociology of Knowledge of William J. Wilson: Placing The Truly Disadvantaged in Its Socio- historical Context." *Journal of Sociology and Social Welfare* 16 (December 1989): 7-39.

3151. Blackburn, McKinley L. and Others. "The Declining Economic Position of Less Skilled American Men." in *A Future of Lousy Jobs? The Changing Structure of U.S. Wages*, ed. Gary Burtless. Washington, D.C.: Brookings Institution, 1990.

3152. Blackburn, McKinley L. "Trends in Poverty in the United States, 1967-1984." *Review of Income and Wealth* 36 (March 1990): 53-66.

3153. Blackwelder, Julia K. *Women of the Depression: Caste and Culture in San Antonio, 1929-1939.* College Station, TX: Texas A & M University Press, 1984.

3154. Bluestone, Barry. "The Impact of Schooling and Industrial Restructuring on Recent Trends in Wage Inequality in the United States." *Papers and Proceedings of the American Economic Association* 80 (May 1990): 303-307.

3155. Bonacich, Edna. "Inequality in America: The Failure of the American System for People of Color." *Sociological Spectrum* 9 (1989): 77-101.

3156. Bonilla, Frank, and Ricardo Campos. "A Wealth of Poor: Puerto Ricans in the New International Order." *Daedalus* 110 (Spring 1981): 133-176.

3157. Boston Foundation. *In the Midst of Plenty: A Profile of Boston and Its Poor.* Boston, MA: The Foundation, 1990.

3158. Bound, John, and Richard B. Freeman. "Black Economic Progress: Erosion of the Post-1965 Gains in the 1980s?" in *The Question of Discrimination: Racial Inequality in the U.S. Labor Market*, eds., Darity, William A. and Steven Shulman. Middletown, CT: Wesleyan University Press, 1989.

3159. _____. "What Went Wrong? The Erosion of Relative Earnings and Employment Among Young Black Men in the 1980s." *Quarterly Journal of Economics* 107 (February 1992): 201-232.

3160. Boxill, Bernard R. "Wilson on the Truly Disadvantaged." *Ethics* 101 (April 1991): 579-592.

3161. Breiter, Toni. "The Welfare System: A Dangerous and Divisive Dilemma." *Agenda* 7 (March-April 1977).

3162. Bridges, Larry D. *Historical Sources of Daniel P. Moynihan's Theory of Cultural Deprivation as a Cause of Poverty.* Ph.D. diss., University of Oregon, 1989. UMO # 9003298.

3163. Briggs, Vernon M., Jr. *Chicanos and Rural Poverty.* Baltimore, MD: Johns Hopkins University Press, 1973.

3164. Brimmer, Andrew F. *The Economic Position of Black Americans, 1976.* Washington, D.C.: National Commision for Manpower Policy, 1976.

3165. Brown, Charles. "Black/White Earnings Ratios Since the Civil Rights Act of 1964: The Importance of Labor Market Dropouts." *Quarterly Journal of Economics* 99 (February 1984): 31- 44.

3166. Brown, Irene A. *Into and Out of Poverty: Changes in the Demographic Composition of the U.S. Poor, 1967-1987.* Ph.D. diss., University of Arizona, 1991. UMO # 9210310.

3167. Browne, Robert S. "The Economic Basis for Reparations to Black America." *Review of Black Political Economy* 21 (Winter 1993): 99-110. [Written in 1971]

3168. Business-Higher Education Forum. *Three Realities: Minority Life in the United States.* Washington, D.C.: Business-Higher Education Forum, 1990.

3169. Buss, Fran L. *Dignity: Lower Income Women Tell of Their Lives and Struggles: Oral Histories.* Ann Arbor, MI: University of Michigan Press, 1985.

3170. Butler, Richard J. and others. "The Impact of the Economy and the State on the Economic Status of Blacks: A Study of South Carolina." in *Markets in History: Economic Studies of the Past*, ed. David W. Galenson. New York, N.Y.: Cambridge University Press, 1989.

3171. Campano, F. "Recent Trends in U.S. Family Income Distribution: A Comparison of All, White, and Black Families." *Journal of Post Keynesian Economics* 13 (Spring 1991).

3172. Carson, Emmett D. *The Charitable Appeals Fact Book: How Blacks and Whites Respond to Different Types of Fundraising Efforts*. Lanham, MD: Joint Center for Political Studies Press, 1989.

3173. Castro, Raymond. "Chicanos and Poverty: Four Ideological Perspectives." *Aztlan* 3 (Spring 1972): 133-154.

3174. Center on Budget and Policy Priorities. "Falling Behind: A Report on How Blacks Have Fared Under Reagan." *Journal of Black Studies* 17 (1986): 148-171.

3175. Chang, Grace. "Undocumented Latinos. Welfare Burdens or Beasts of Burden?" *Socialist Review* 23 (1994): 151-185.

3176. Christensen, Kimberly. "Political Determinants of Income Changes for African-American Women and Men." *Review of Radical Political Economics* 24 (Spring 1992).

3177. Coil, Suzanne M. *The Poor in America*. Englewood Cliffs, N.J.: J. Messner, 1989. [Written for young people]

3178. Collo, Martin J. "The Development of Food-Import Dependence: The Puerto Rican Experience." *Journal of Developing Societies* 5 (1989): 141-156.

3179. Community Service Society. *Poverty in New York, 1980-1985*. New York, N.Y.: Community Service Society, 1987.

3180. Comptroller General of the U.S. *Problems Persist in the Puerto Rican Food Stamp Program, the Nation's Largest*. Washington, D.C.: General Accounting Office, 1974.

3181. Conrad, Cecilia A. "A Different Approach to the Measurement of Income Inequality." *Review of Black Political Economy* 22 (Summer 1993): 19-31. [1954-1989]

3182. Copp, D. "The Right to an Adequate Standard of Living: Justice, Autonomy, and the Basic Needs." *Social Philosophy and Policy* 9 (Winter 1992): 231-261.

3183. Corrado Guerrero, Rafael. "Los desigualdades del ingresso familiar en Puerto Rico." *Revista de Ciencias Sociales* 26 (1987): 73-102.

3184. Cotton, Jeremiah. "The Gap at the Top: Relative Occupational Earnings Disadvantage of the Black Middle Class." *Review of Black Political Economy* 18 (Winter 1990): 21-38.

3185. _____. "Opening the Gap: The Decline in Black Economic Indicators in the 1980s." *Social Science Quarterly* 70 (December 1989).

3186. _____. "A Regional Analysis of Black-White Male Wage Differences." *Review of Black Political Economy* 22 (Summer 1993): 55-71.

3187. Coulton, Claudia J. and others. *An Analysis of Poverty and Related Conditions in Cleveland Area Neighborhoods*. Ph.D. diss., Case Western University, Center for Urban Poverty and Social Change, 1990.

3188. Cray, Robert E. , Jr. "White Welfare and Black Stategies: The Dynamics of Race and Poor Relief in Early New York, 1700- 1825." *Slavery and Abolition* 7 (1986): 273-289.

3189. Cuciti, Peggy, and Franklin James. "A Comparison of Black and Hispanic Poverty in Large Cities of the Southwest." *Hispanic Journal of Behavioral Sciences* 12 (February 1990): 50-75.

3190. Dagum, Camilo. "Medida de la diferencial de ingreso entre familias blancas, negras y de origen hispanico en los Estados Unidos." *El Trimestre Economico* 50 (April-June 1983): 963-990.

3191. Daniel, Leon. "Indians Battle Poverty, Discouragement in City that is Number 1 for Quality of Life." *Los Angeles Times*, 9 December 1981. [Minneapolis- St. Paul]

3192. Danziger, Sheldon H. "Antipoverty Policies and Child Poverty." *Social Work Research and Abstracts* 26 (December 1990).

3193. Danziger, Sheldon H. and Others. *Confronting Poverty, Prescriptions for Change*. Boston, MA: Harvard University Press, 1994.

3194. Danziger, Sheldon H., and Peter Gottschalk, eds. *Uneven Tides: Rising Inequality in America*. Russell Sage Foundation, 1993.

3195. Darden, Joe T. "Afro-American Inequality within the Urban Structure of the United States, 1967-1987." *Journal of Developing Societies* 5 (January-April 1989): 1-14.

3196. _____. "The Status of Urban Blacks 25 Years Old after the Civil Rights Act of 1964." *Sociology and Social Research* 73 (July 1989): 160-173.

3197. Darity, William A. "Racial Inequality in the Managerial Age: An Alternative Vision to the NRC Report." *American Economic Review* 80 (May 1990).

3198. Davila, A. and Others. "Accent Penalties and the Earnings of Mexican Americans." *Social Science Quarterly* 74 (December 1993): 902-916.

3199. Dawes, Robyn M., and Lloyd G. Humphreys. "Racial Norming: A Debate." *Academe* 79 (May-June 1993): 31-37.

3200. *The Declining Economic Status of Black Children: Examining the Change*. Washington, D.C.: Joint Center for Political and Economic Studies, 1990.

3201. Dehavenson, Anna Lou. "Charles Dickens Meets Franz Kafka: The Maladministration of New York City's Public Assistance Program." *New York University Review of Law and Social Change* 18 (April 1990): 231-254.

3202. DeLeon, Arnoldo. "Wresting a Competence in Nineteenth Century Texas: The Case of the Chicanos." *Red River Valley Historical Review* 4 (1979): 52-64.

3203. DeParle, Jason. "What to Call the Poorest Poor?" *New York Times*, 26 August 1990.

3204. DeParle, Jason, and Peter Applebome. "The Missing Agenda. Poverty and Policy." *New York Times*, 27 January 1991. [three articles]

3205. Dodoo, F. N. A. "Earnings Differences Among Blacks in America." *Social Science Research* 20 (June 1991): 93-108.

3206. Doherty, Julian C. "Poverty in America- The Historic Problem of the 'Deserving' and 'Undeserving' Poor." in *Wege in die Zeitgeschichte*, eds. Jürgen Heidkind and others. New York, N.Y.: Walter de Gruyter, 1989.

3207. Duin, Virginia. "The Problem of Indian Poverty. The Shrinking Land Base and Ineffective Education." *Albany Law Review* 36 (1971): 143-181.

3208. Duncan, Greg J., and W. Rodgers. "Has Children's Poverty Become More Persistent?" *American Sociological Review* 56 (August 1991): 538-550.

3209. Duncan, Kevin C. "The Vintage Schooling Hypothsis and Racial Differences in Earnings and On-the-Job Training: A Longitudinal Analysis." *Review of Black Political Economy* 20 (Winter 1992): 99-117.

3210. Dusenberry, Verne. "Waiting for a Day that Never Comes: The Tragic Story of the Dispossessed Metis of Montana." *Montana* 8 (1958): 26-39.

3211. *The Economic Progress of Black Men in America*. Washington, D.C.: U.S. Commission on Civil Rights, 1986.

3212. *The Economic Status of Black Women: An Exploratory Investigation*. Washington, D.C.: U.S. Commission on Civil Rights, 1990.

3213. Edelman, Peter B., and Joyce Ladner eds. *Adolescence and Poverty: Challenge for the 1990s*. Washington, D.C.: Center for National Policy Press, 1991.

3214. Eggers, M. L., and Douglas S. Massey. "The Structural Determinants of Urban Poverty: A Comparison of Whites, Blacks and Hispanics." *Social Science Research* 20 (September 1991): 217-255.

3215. Ellison, J., and R. S. Browne. "Impact of the 1975 Tax Cut on Income and Employment in the Black Community." *Review of Black Political Economy* 17 (Fall 1988).

3216. Engerman, Stanley L. "The Economic Response to Emancipation and Some Economic Aspects of the Meaning of Freedom." in *The Meaning of Freedom*, eds. Frank McGlynn, and Seymour Drescher. Pittsburgh, PA: University of Pittsburgh Press, 1991.

3217. Fainstein, Susan S., and Norman Q. Fainstein. "The Racial Dimension in Urban Political Economy." *Urban Affairs Quarterly* 24 (December 1989).

3218. Falk, W. W., and Bruce H. Rankin. "The Cost of Being Black in the Black Belt." *Social Problems* 39 (August 1992).

3219. *Falling by the Wayside: Children in Rural America*. Washington, D.C.: Children's Defense Fund, 1992.

3220. Farley, Reynolds, and Lisa J. Neidert. *A Comparison of Racial Differences in Labor Force Participation, Unemployment, Earnings, and Income : 1940 to 1985*. Paper prepared for the Committee on the Status of Black Americans, National Research Council, Washington, D.C., 1986.

3221. Fatemi, Khosrow, ed. *The Maquiladora Industry. Economic Solution or Problem?* Westport, CT: Praeger, 1990.

3222. Feinberg, Renee, and Kathleen E. Knox. *The Feminization of Poverty in the United States: A Selected, Annotated Bibliography of the Issues, 1978-1989*. New York, N.Y.: Garland, 1990.

3223. Ferleger, Lou, and Jay R. Mandle. "Whose Common Destiny? African Americans and the U.S. Economy." *Socialist Review* 20 (January-March 1990): 151-157.

3224. Ferleger, Lou, and Jay R. Mandle. "African Americans and the Future of the U.S. Economy." *Trotter Institute Review* 5 (Winter/Spring 1991): 3-7.

3225. Fessehatzion, Tekie, and Bichaka Fayissa. "Public Assistance and Job Search Behavior of the Rural Poor- Evidence from the Mississippi Delta." *Review of Black Political Economy* 18 (Winter 1990): 79-91.

3226. Fisher, G. M. "The Development and History of the Poverty Thresholds." *Social Security Bulletin* 55 (Winter 1992).

3227. *Five Million Children: 1991 Update*. 154 Haven Ave., New York, N.Y.: National Center for Children in Poverty, 1992.

3228. Forbath, Jean. "The Poor Are the Underpinnings of our Lifestyle." *Los Angeles Times*, 7 June 1993. [Orange County, CA]

3229. Gabe, T. *Progress Against Poverty in the United States (1959 to 1987)*. Washington, D.C.: Library of Congress, 1989.

3230. Gallman, Robert E., and John J. Wallis, eds. *American Economic Growth and Standards of Living Before the Civil War*. Chicago, IL: University of Chicago Press, 1992.

3231. Gautier Mayoral, Carmen. "Interrelation of the United States Poor Relief, Massive Unemployment and Weakening of Legitimacy in Twentieth Century Puerto Rico." *Carribean Stud.* 19 (October 1979 - January 1980): 5-46.

3232. Geschwender, James A., and Rita Carroll-Seguin. "Exploding the Myth of African-American Progress." *Signs* 15 (Winter 1990): 285-299.

3233. Gimenez, Martha E. "The Feminization of Poverty : Myth or Reality?" *International Journal of Health Service* 19 (1989): 45- 61.

3234. Goldsmith, William W., and Edward J. Blakely. *Separate Societies. Poverty and Inequality in U.S. Cities*. Temple University Press, 1992.

3235. Gottschalk, Peter. "AFDC Participation Across Generations." *American Economic Review* 80 (May 1990): 367-371.

3236. Governor's Commission on Socially Disadvantaged African- American Males. *Ohio's African-American Males : A Call to Action*. Columbus, OH: The Governor's Office, June 1990.

3237. Gree, Gordon and others. *Factors Affecting Black-White Income Differentials : A Decomposition.* Presented at the 66th Annual Conference of the Western Economic Association International, Seattle, WA, 30 June 1991.

3238. Greenberg, Cheryl L. *Community and Crisis : Black Harlem in the Great Depression.* Ph.D. diss., Columbia University, 1988. UMO # 9102420.

3239. Griffith, David. *Jones's Minimal : Low Wage Labor in the United States.* State University of New York Press, 1993.

3240. Gugliotta, Guy. "Drawing the Poverty Line : A Calculation of Necessity and Self-Image." *Washington Post*, 10 May 1993. [How the annual poverty-line income is calculated]

3241. _____. "War on Poverty : Three Decades And No Victory." *Washington Post*, 26 December 1993. [Kentucky-Appalachia]

3242. Haber, Carole, and Brian Gratton. "Old Age, Public Welfare and Race : The Case of Charleston, South Carolina 1800-1949." *Journal of Social History* 21 (1987): 263-279.

3243. Haberfeld, Yitzhak, and Y. Shenhav. "Are Women and Blacks Closing the Gap? Salary Discrimination in American Science during the 1970s and 1980s." *Industrial and Labor Relations Review* 44 (October 1990).

3244. Hagan, William T. "Private Property : The Indian's Door to Civilization." *Ethnohistory* 3 (Spring 1956): 126-137.

3245. Hamilton, David. "Poverty Is Still With Us - and Worse." in *Quiet Riots : Race and Poverty in the United States*, eds. Fred R. Harris, and Roger Wilkins. New York, N.Y.: Pantheon, 1988.

3246. Handler, J., and Y. Hasenfeld. *The Moral Construction of Poverty : Welfare Reform in America.* Sage, 1991.

3247. "Hard Times for Black America." *Dollars and Sense* 115 (April 1986): 5-7.

3248. Harriman, Helga H. "Economic Conditions in the Creek Nation, 1865-1871." *Chronicles of Oklahoma* 51 (1973): 325-334.

3249. Harris, Donald J. "Economic Growth, Structural Change, and the Relative Income Status of Blacks in the U.S. Economy, 1947- 1978." *Review of Black Political Economy* 12 (Spring 1983): 75-92.

3250. Harvey, J. T. "Institutions and the Economic Welfare of Black Americans in the 1980s." *Journal of Economic Issues* 25 (March 1991): 115-136.

3251. Hathorn, Clay. "Down and Out in the Delta." *Nation* (9 July 1990). [Mississippi Delta]

3252. Haveman, Robert, and L. Buron. "Escaping Poverty through Work : The Problem of Low Earnings Capacity in the United States, 1973- 1988." *Review of Income and Wealth* 39 (June 1993).

3253. Hayes-Bautista, David E. and others. *The Burden of Support : Young Latinos in an Aging Society.* Stanford, CA: 1988.

3254. Heckman, James J. "The Central Role of the South in Accounting for the Economic Progress of Black Americans." *American Economic Review* 80 (May 1990).

3255. Hertzberg, Hazel W. "Reaganomics on the Reservation." *New Republic* (11 November 1982).

3256. Hoffman, Emily P. "Aid to Families with Dependent Children and Female Poverty." *Growth and Change* 22 (Spring 1991): 36-47. (1959-1988).

3257. _____. "Racial Differences in the Feminization of Poverty." *Review of Black Political Economy* 21 (Summer 1992): 19- 31.

3258. Holmes, Steven A. "The Rights Leader Minimizes Racism as a Poverty Factor." *New York Times*, 24 July 1994. [Hugh P. Price, President, National Urban League]

3259. Holt, Sharon Ann. *A Time to Plant : The Economic Lives of Freedpeople in Granville County, North Carolina, 1865-1900.* Ph.D. diss., University of Pennsylvania, 1991. UMO # 9200345.

3260. Hubler, Shaun, and Stuart Silverstein. "Schooling Doesn't Close Minority Earning Gap." *Los Angeles Times*, 10 January 1993.

3261. Hurt, R. Douglas. *Indian Agriculture in America : Prehistory to the Present*. Lawrence, KS: University Press of Kansas, 1987.

3262. "The Impact of Poverty on Children." *American Behavioral Scientist* 35 (January-February 1992): Eight Articles

3263. *In the Midst of Plenty : A Profile of Boston : An In-Depth Study on the Working Age Population of Boston*. Boston, MA: Boston Foundation, 1989.

3264. James, Bernard. "Continuity and Emergence in Indian Poverty Culture." *Current Anthropology* 11 (October-December 1970): 435- 452.

3265. Jargowsky, Paul A., and David T. Ellwood. *Ghetto Poverty : A Theoretical and Empirical Framework*. Malcolm Weiner Center for Social Policy, 1990.

3266. Jaynes, Gerald D. "The Labor Market Status of Black Americans : 1939-1985." *Journal of Economic Perspectives* 4 (Fall 1990): 9-24.

3267. Jaynes, Gerald D., James Tobin, and Reynolds Farley, eds. *Manuscript Prepared for the Panel on Income, Employment, and Occupation*. Committee on the Status of Black Americans, National Research Council, Washington, D.C., 1986.

3268. Jaynes, Gerald D., and Robin M. Williams, Jr., eds. "Blacks in the Economy." in *A Common Destiny. Blacks in American Society*, pp. 269-328. Washington, D.C.: National Academy Press, 1989.

3269. Jencks, Christopher, and Kathryn Edin. "The Real Welfare Problem." *The American Prospect* (1990).

3270. Jones, John Paul III, and Janet E. Kodras. "Restructured Regions and Families : The Feminization of Poverty in the U.S." *Annals of the Association of American Geographere* 80 (1990): 163-183.

3271. Katz, Michael B. "The History of an Impudent Poor Woman in New York City from 1918 to 1923." in *The Uses of Charity*, ed. Peter Mandler. : University of Pennsylvania Press, 1990.

3272. _____. *The Undeserving Poor. From the War on Poverty to the War on Welfare*. New York, N.Y.: Pantheon, 1990.

3273. Kaus, Mickey. *The End of Equality*. Basic Books, 1992. [Critical view of the welfare system]

3274. Kelly, William H. "The Economic Basis of Indian Life." *Annals of the American Academy of Political and Social Science* 311 (May 1957): 71-79.

3275. Kessler-Harris, Alice. *A Woman's Wage. Historical Meanings and Social Consequences*. University Press of Kentucky, 1992.

3276. Kilborn, Peter T. "Sad Distinction for the Sioux : Homeland Is Number 1 in Poverty." *New York Times*, 20 September 1992.

3277. Klein, B. W., and P. L. Rones. "A Profile of the Working Poor." *Monthly Labor Review* 112 (October 1989).

3278. Klotter, James C. "The Black South and White Appalachia." *Journal of American History* 66 (March 1980): 832-849.

3279. Kohlert, Nance. "Welfare Reform : A Historical Consensus." *Social Work* 34 (July 1989): 303-306.

3280. Korbin, Jill E., ed. "The Impact of Poverty on Children." *American Behavioral Scientist* 35 (January-February 1992): 213- 339. [seven articles]

3281. Labaton, Stephen. "Benefits Are Refused More Often to Disabled Blacks, Study Finds." *New York Times*, 11 May 1992. [Social Security disability programs]

3282. *Latino Child Poverty in the United States*. Washington, D.C.: Children's Defense Fund, 1991.

3283. Lav, Iris and others. *The States and the Poor : How Budget Decisions Affected Low Income People in 1992*. Center on Budget and Policy Priorities and Center for the Study of the States, February 1993.

3284. Lazear, Edward. "The Narrowing of the Black-White Wage Differentials is Illusory." *American Economic Review* 69 (September 1979): 553-564.

3285. Lewis, Gordon H., and Richard J. Morrison. "Interactions among Social Welfare Programs." *Evaluation Review* 14 (December 1990): 632-663.

3286. Lewis, W. Arthur. *Racial Conflict and Economic Development*. Cambridge, MA: Harvard University Press, 1985.

3287. Littman, Mark S. "Poverty in the 1980s : Are the Poor Getting Poorer." *Monthly Labor Review* 112 (1989): 13-18.

3288. Love, Roger, and Susan Poulin. "Family Income Inequality in the 1980s." *Perspectives on Labor and Income* 3 (Autumn 1991): 51- 57.

3289. Lydon, Mary T. *Movements in the Earnings-Schooling Relationship : 1940-1988*. Ph.D. diss., Stanford University, 1990. [Racial distinction]. UMO # 9108866.

3290. Magee, Rhonda V. "The Master's Tools, from the Bottom Up : Responses to African-American Reparations Theory in Mainstream and Outsider Remedies Discourse." *Virginia Law Review* 79 (May 1993): 863-916.

3291. Malveaux, Julianne. *The Economic Status of Black Women : An Overview and Note on Interpretation*. Paper prepared for the Committee on the Status of Black Americans, National Research Council, Washington, D.C., 1986.

3292. _____. "The Political Economy of Black Women." in *The Year Left : An American Socialist Yearbook : Race, Ethnicity, Class, and Gender*, eds. M. Davis and Others. New York, N.Y.: Verso, 1987.

3293. Manchester, J. M., and D. C. Stapleton. "On Measuring the Progress of Women's Quest for Economic Equality." *Journal of Human Resources* 26 (Summer 1991).

3294. Mancy, Ardith L. *Still Hungry After All These Years : Food Assistance Policy from Kennedy to Reagan*. Westport, CT: Greenwood, 1989.

3295. Mandle, Jay R. *Not Slave, Not Free : The African American Economic Experience Since the Civil War*. Durham, N.C.: Duke University Press, 1992.

3296. Mandler, Peter ed. *The Uses of Charity. The Poor on Relief in the Nineteenth Century Metropolis*. Philadelphia, PA: University of Pennsylvania Press, 1990.

3297. Maril, Robert Lee. *Poorest of Americans. The Mexican- Americans of the Lower Rio Grande Valley of Texas*. Notre Dame, IN: University of Notre Dame Press, 1989.

3298. Massachusetts, State of. *Income and Employment Problems in Boston's Low Income Neighborhoods: The Persistence of Poverty Amidst Increasing Affluence in Boston and Massachusetts*. Boston, MA: Executive Office of Economic Affairs, 1989.

3299. Massey, Douglas S. and others. *Disentangling the Causes of Concentrated Poverty*. Chicago, IL: Population Research Center, University of Chicago, 1989.

3300. _____. "Segregation, the Concentration of Poverty, and the Life Changes of Individuals." *Social Science Research* 20 (December 1991): 397-420.

3301. Massey, Douglas S., and Mitchell L. Eggers. "The Ecology of Inequality : Minorities and the Concentration of Poverty, 1970- 1980." *American Journal of Sociology* 95 (March 1990): 1153-1188.

3302. Mayer, Susan E., and Christopher Jencks. "Poverty and the Distribution of Material Hardship." *Journal of Human Resources* 24 (Winter 1989): 88-113.

3303. McFate, Katherine. *Poverty, Inequality and the Crisis of Social Policy*. Joint Center for Political and Economic Studies, 1991.

3304. McKee, Nancy P. *Living in La Fabrica : Environment, Opinion, and Stategies for Survival Among Low-Income Mexican- Americans in Laredo, Texas*. Ph.D. diss., Washington State University, 1985. UMO # 8527146.

3305. McLanahan, Sara J. and Others. "Sex Differences in Poverty, 1950-1980." *Signs* 15 (Fall 1989): 102-122.

3306. Michel, Richard C., and Frank S. Levy. "Family Income : Slower Growth and Less Equity." *Forum for Applied Research and Public Policy* 6 (Summer 1991): 40-49. [Since 1950]

3307. Miller, Michael V. *Poverty in the Lower Rio Grande Valley of Texas : Historical and Contemporary Dimensions*. College Station, TX: Texas Agricultural Experiment Station, Texas A & M University System, 1979.

3308. _____. *Poverty, Development, and the Quality of Life in a Texas Border City*. Ph.D. diss., Texas A & M University, 1981. [Brownsville]. UMO # 8206650.

3309. Mincy, Ronald B. "Paradoxes in Black Economic Progress : Incomes, Families, and the Underclass." *Journal of Negro Education* 58 (1989): 255-269.

3310. Miranda, Leticia C. *Latino Child Poverty in the United States*. Washington, D.C.: Children's Defense Fund, 1991.

3311. Mishel, Lawrence R., and David M. Frankel. *The State of Working America. 1990-1991 Edition*. Armonk, N.Y.: Sharpe, 1991. [U.S. standard of living during the 1980s]

3312. Moen, J. R. "Poverty in the South." *Federal Reserve Bank of Atlanta Economic Review* 74 (January - February 1989).

3313. Moffitt, Robert. "Incentive Effects of the U.S. Welfare System : A Review." *Journal of Economic Literature* 30 (March 1992): 1-61.

3314. Mohl, Raymond A. *Poverty in New York, 1785 - 1825*. New York, N.Y., 1927.

3315. Monaco, Anthony. "Blacks, Immigrants, and the Roots of Poverty in America." *Notre Dame Journal of Law, Ethics and Public Policy* (September 1985): 297-327.

3316. Moore, John. "The Myth of the Lazy Indian : Native American Contributions to the U.S. Economy." *NST. Nature, Society, and Thought* 2 (1989).

3317. Morganthau, Tom and Others. "Losing Ground." *Newsweek* (6 April 1992). [Black life problems in the U.S.]

3318. Myers, Patricia. "Minority Households : A Comparison of Selected Characteristics and Expenditures Contributing to Future Economic Well-being." *Family Economic Review* 4 (June 1991): 2-8.

3319. Nagel, Gerald S. "Economics of the Reservation." *Current History* 67 (1974): 245-249, 278-279.

3320. National Urban League. *Stalling Out : The Relative Progress of African Americans*. New York, N.Y.: National Urban League, August 1989.

3321. National Center for Children in Poverty. *A Statistical Profile of Our Poorest Young Citizens*. New York, N.Y.: NCCP, Columbia University School of Public Health, April 1990. [Children under six years of age]

3322. Nechyba, T. J. "The Southern Wage Gap, Human Capital and the Quality of Education." *Southern Economic Journal* 57 (October 1990).

3323. Nelson, Emily. "Black American Buying Power Up, But Family Income Lower, Study Says." *Boston Globe*, 6 August 1994.

3324. *The Next Step Toward Equality. A Comprehensive Study of Puerto Ricans in the United States Mainland*. New York, N.Y.: National Puerto Rican Forum, Inc., September 1980.

3325. Ng, Kenneth, and Nancy Virts. "The Value of Freedom." *Journal of Economic History* 49 (December 1989): 958-965. [Value to freedmen after Civil War]

3326. Norton, Eleanor Holmes. "America's Welfare Wake-Up Call." *Washington Post*, 3 April 1994.

3327. O'Hare, William P. and others. *Real Life Poverty in America*. Washington, D.C.: Families U.S.A. Foundation, 1990.

3328. O'Neill, June. "The Role of Human Capital in Earnings Differences between Black and White Men." *Journal of Economic Perspectives* 4 (Fall 1990): 25-45.

3329. Ong, Paul M. *The Widening Divide : Income Inequality and Poverty in Los Angeles*. Los Angeles, CA: Graduate School of Architecture and Urban Planning, University of California, Los Angeles, June 1990.

3330. Osterman, Paul. *In the Midst of Plenty : A Profile of Boston and Its Poor*. Boston, MA: The Boston Foundation, December 1989.

3331. Patterson, Orlando. "Inequality, Freedom, and the Equal Opportunity Doctrine." in *Equality and Social Policy*, pp. 15-41. ed. Walter Feinberg. Urbana, IL: University of Illinois Press, 1978.

3332. Pear, Robert. "Auditors Want to Change Federal Poverty Definition." *New York Times*, 5 August 1994.

3333. _____. "Many States Cut Food Allotments for Poor Families." *New York Times*, 29 May 1990.

3334. Perez, Sonia M. *Moving from the Margins : Puerto Rican Young Men and Family Poverty*. National Council for La Raza, 1993.

3335. Perez, Sonia M. and Deirdre Martinez. *State of Hispanic America 1993 : Toward a Latino Anti-Poverty Agenda*. National Council of La Raza, July 1993.

3336. Perez, Sonia M., and Denise De La Rosa Salazar. "Economic Labor Force, and Social Implications of Latino Education and Population Trends." *Hispanic Journal of Behavioral Sciences* 15 (May 1993).

3337. Perlo, Victor. "Deterioration of Black Economic Conditions in the 1980s." *Review of Radical Political Economics* 20 (Summer and Fall 1988): 55-60.

3338. Peterson, Jonathan. "Life in the U.S., Graded on the Curve." *Los Angeles Times*, 11 April 1993. ["First in Billionaires, Poverty"]

3339. Phillips, George H. "Indians in Los Angeles, 1781-1875 : Economic Integration, Social Disintegration." *Pacific Historical Review* 49 (August 1980): 427-451.

3340. Plotnick, Robert D. "Directions for Reducing Child Poverty." *Social Work* 34 (November 1989): 523-530.

3341. Porter, Kathryn H. *Poverty in Rural America : A National Overview*. Washington, D.C.: Center on Budget and Policy Priorities, April 1989.

3342. *Poverty In New York City, 1985 - 1988 : The Crisis Continues*. New York, N.Y.: Community Service Society, 1989.

3343. Rankin, Bruce H., and W. W. Falk. "Race, Region, and Earnings : Blacks and Whites in the South." *Rural Sociology* 56 (Summer 1991): 224-237.

3344. Redburn, Tom. "Study Finds Women Closer to Men in Pay in New York." *New York Times*, 2 February 1994. [Includes some data on Hispanics and African Americans]

3345. Reich, Michael. "Postwar Racial Income Differentials." in *The Three Worlds of Labor Economics*, eds. Garth Mangrum, and Peter Phillips. : Sharpe, 1989.

3346. Research Group on the Los Angeles Economy. *The Widening Divide : Income Inequality and Poverty in Los Angeles*. Los Angeles, CA: U.C.L.A. School of Urban Planning, 1989.

3347. Rexroat, Cynthia. *The Declining Economic Status of Black Children Examining the Change. Summary of Findings*. Washington, D.C.: Joint Center for Political and Economic Studies, 1990.

3348. Riemer, David R. *The Prisoners of Welfare : Liberating America's Poor from Unemployment and Low Wages*. Westport, CT: Praeger, 1988.

3349. Roberts, Shirley J. "Minority Group Poverty in Phoenix : A Socio-Economic Survey." *Journal of Arizona History* 14 (Winter 1973): 347-362.

3350. Rochin, Refugio Q. "Economic Deprivation of Chicanos - Continuing Neglect in the Seventies." *Aztlan* 4 (Spring 1973): 85- 102.

3351. Rodgers, Harrell R., Jr. *Poor Women, Poor Families : The Economic Plight of America's Female-headed Households.* 2nd Edition, Armonk, N.Y.: Sharpe, 1990.

3352. Rodgers, Harrell R., Jr., and G. Weiher. *Rural Poverty and Policy Reforms.* New York, N.Y.: Greenwood, 1989.

3353. Rodgers, J. R., and J. L. Rodgers. "Chronic Poverty in the United States." *Journal of Human Resources* 28 (Winter 1993).

3354. Rodgers, J. L., and J. R. Rodgers. "Measuring the Intensity of Poverty among Subpopulations : Applications to the United States." *Journal of Human Resources* 16 (Spring 1991).

3355. Rodriguez, Clara E. "Economic Survival in New York City." in *The Puerto Rican Struggle*, pp. 31-46. eds. Clara E. Rodriguez and Others. New York, N.Y.: Puerto Rican Migration Research Consortium, 1980.

3356. Rodriguez, Havidan. *Household Composition, Employment Patterns and Economic Well-being : Puerto Ricans in the United States and Puerto Rico, 1970 - 1980.* Ph.D. diss., University of Wisconsin, 1991. UMO # 9120063.

3357. Rohrlich, Ted. "Cuts May Double Homelessness, Experts Say." *Los Angeles Times*, 16 August 1993. [Reductions in welfare payments for single adults]

3358. Rosenberg, Terry J. *Poverty in New York City, 1985-1988 : The Crisis Continues.* New York, N.Y.: Community Service Society, 1989.

3359. Ruggles, Patricia. *Drawing the Line : Alternative Poverty Measures and Their Implications for Public Policy.* Urban Institute, 1992.

3360. Saenz, R., and J. K. Thomas. "Minority Poverty in Nonmetropolitan Texas." *Rural Sociology* 56 (June 1991): 204-223.

3361. Safa, Helen I. *The Urban Poor of Puerto Rico : A Study in Development and Inequality.* New York, N.Y.: Holt, Rinehart and Winston, 1974.

3362. Sanchez, Armand J. "Affluence and Poverty." *El Grito* 3 (Summer 1970): 64-84.

3363. Scanlan, J. P. "Sex Differences in Poverty, 1950 - 1980. Comment." *Signs* 16 (December 1991). [See, also, reply by Watson and others, following]

3364. Schlossman, Steven L. "The 'Culture of Poverty' in Ante- bellum Social Thought." *Science and Society* 38 (June 1974).

3365. Schram, Sanford F. and Others. "Child Poverty and Welfare Benefits : A Reassessment with State Data of the Claim that American Welfare Breeds Dependency." *American Journal of Economics and Sociology* 47 (October 1988).

3366. Schram, Sanford F., and Paul Wilken. "It's No 'Laffer' Matter : Claim that Increasing Welfare Aids Breeds Poverty and Dependence Fails Statistical Test." *American Journal of Economics and Sociology* 48 (April 1989): 203-218.

3367. Schwarz, John E., and Thomas J. Volgy. *The Forgotten Americans.* Norton, 1992. [Full-time workers earning poverty wages]

3368. Segal, Elizabeth A. "The Juvenilization of Poverty in the 1980s." *Social Work* 36 (September 1991): 454-457.

3369. Sege, Irene. "Data Show '80s 'Miracle' Did Little for Poverty Rate." *Boston Globe*, 9 April 1992. ["Massachusetts Miracle" of the 1980s]

3370. Shapiro, Isaac. *Laboring for Less : Working but Poor in Rural America.* Washington, D.C.: Center on Budget and Policy Priorities, October 1989.

3371. Sherraden, Michael A., and Isaac Shapiro. *The Working Poor : America's Contradiction.* St. Louis, MO: School of Social Work, Washington University, 1990.

3372. Shogren, Elizabeth. "Food Stamps : America's Rising Gauge of Lean Times." *Los Angeles Times*, 8 August 1993.

3373. _____. "Welfare Reform Rhetoric Rings Hollow in the Delta." *Los Angeles Times*, 9 May 1994. [Racial-economic differentials in Shelby, MS]

3374. Shulman, S. "The Causes of Black Poverty : Evidence and Interpretation." *Journal of Economic Issues* 24 (December 1990).

3375. Simms, Margaret C., ed. "Black Economic Progress : An Agenda for the 1990s." Washington, D.C.: Joint Center for Political and Economic Studies, 1988.

3376. Simpson, Patricia. "Trends in Illinois Poverty : 1979 to 1988." *Illinois Issues* 17 (April 1991): 16-18.

3377. Sjoquist, David L. *The Economic Status of Black Atlantans*. Atlanta, GA: Atlanta Urban League, 1988.

3378. Skora, C. L., and D. A. Johnson. "Establishing an Updated Standard of Need for AFDC Recipients." *Social Work Research and Abstracts* 27 (September 1991): 22-27.

3379. Slesnick, D. T. "The Standard of Living in the United States." *Review of Income and Wealth* 4 (December 1991): 363-386.

3380. Smith, James P., and Finis R. Welch. "Black Economic Progress After Myrdal." *Journal of Economic Literature* 27 (June 1989): 519-564. [since around 1940]

3381. Smith, James P., and Finis R. Welch. "Race and Poverty : A Forty-Year Record." *American Economic Review* 77 (May 1987): 152- 158.

3382. Speck, Frank. "Notes on Social and Economic Conditions among the Creek Indians of Alabama in 1941." *America Indigena* 7 (1947): 195-198.

3383. *State Lotteries : Seducing the Less Fortunate?* Chicago, IL: Heartland Institute, 1991.

3384. Stillwaggon, Eileen M., comp. "Native American Economic Studies : A Bibliographic Essay." *Sage Race Relations Abstracts* 9 (February 1984): 1-14.

3385. Stoddard, Ellwyn R. *Patterns of Poverty Along the U.S.- Mexico Border*. El Paso, TX: Center for Inter-American Studies, University of Texas, 1978.

3386. Sum, Andrew, and Neal Fogg. "The Changing Economic Fortunes of Young Black Men in America." *Black Scholar* 21 (January 1990): 47-55.

3387. Sung Lee, B. "A Different Index of Black/White Income Inequality, 1965-1974." *Review of Black Political Economy* 9 (September 1978): 90-94.

3388. Super, David, and Carrie M. Lewis. "Introduction to the Foodstamp Program." *Clearinghouse Review* 25 (November 1991): 905- 915.

3389. Swinton, David H. "The Economic Status of African Americans : 'Permanent Poverty' and Inequality." in *The State of Black America*, pp. 25-75. ed. Janet Dewart. New York, N.Y.: National Urban League, 1991.

3390. Thanawala, Kishor, and Robert H. De Fina. "The Misery Index, Only Half the Story." *New York Times*, 20 December 1992. [Considers Poverty and Inequality on pain index]

3391. Thomas, Melvin, and M. Hughes. "The Continuing Significance of Race : A Study of Race, Class and Quality of Life in America, 1972 - 1985." *American Sociological Review* 51 (December 1986): 830-841.

3392. Thomas, Susan L. *American Women in Poverty : A Gender Class Analysis*. Ph.D. diss., University of California, Riverside, CA, 1990. UMO # 9023970.

3393. *Three Realities : Minority Life in the United States*. Washington, D.C.: Business-Higher Education Forum, American Council on Education, June 1990.

3394. Tienda, Marta, and Leif Jensen. "Poverty and Minorities : A Quarter-Century Profile of Color and Socioeconomic Disadvantage." in *Divided Opportunities : Minorities, Poverty, and Social Problems*, eds. Gary D. Sandefur, and Marta Tienda. New York, N.Y.: Plenum Press, 1988.

3395. Tienda, Marta, and Gary Sandefur. *Divided Opportunity : Minorities, Poverty and Social Policy*. New York, N.Y.: Plenum Press, 1988.

3396. Torres, Andrea. "Explaining Puerto Rican Poverty." *Boletin del Centro de Estudios Puertorriquenos* 11 (Winter 1987 - 1988).

3397. "Tribal Assets $279 Million." *Navajo Times* (27 August 1981).

3398. U. S. Bureau of the Census. *Income, Poverty, and Wealth in the United States : A Chartbook*. Washington, D.C.: GPO, 1992.

3399. _____. *Measuring the Effect of Benefits and Taxes on Income and Poverty : 1990*. Washington, D.C.: GPO, August 1991.

3400. _____. *Money Income and Poverty Status in the United States, 1989*. Washington, D.C.: GPO, 1990.

3401. _____. *Money Income of Households, Families, and Persons in the United States : 1990*. Washington, D.C.: GPO, August 1991.

3402. _____. *Poverty in the United States : 1990*. Washington, D.C.: GPO, August 1991.

3403. _____. *Poverty in the United States*. Washington, D.C.: The Bureau, August 1992.

3404. U. S., Congress, 101st, 2nd session, Joint Economic Committee, Subcommittee on Investment, jobs, and Prices. *The Economic Status of African-Americans : Hearing*. Washington, D.C.: GPO, 1991.

3405. Valenzuela, Abel. "Hispanic Poverty, Is It An Immigrant Problem?" *Journal of Hispanic Policy* 5 (1991).

3406. Verdugo, R. R. "Earnings Differentials Between Black, Mexican American and Non-Hispanic White Male Workers : On the Cost of Being a Minority Worker, 1972 - 1987." *Social Security Quarterly* 73 (September 1992): 663-673.

3407. Vogt, Daniel C. "Poor Relief in Frontier Mississippi, 1798 - 1832." *Journal of Mississippi History* 51 (August 1989): 181- 199.

3408. Vroman, Wayne. "Black Men's Relative Earnings: Are the Gains Illusory?" *Industrial and Labor Relations Review* 44 (October 1990): 83-98.

3409. Weill, James D. "Child Poverty in America." *Clearinghouse Review* 25 (1991): 336-348.

3410. Weisskopf, Richard. *Factories and Food Stamps : The Puerto Rico Model of Development*. Baltimore, MD: Johns Hopkins University Press, 1985.

3411. "Welfare as We've Known It." *New York Times*, 19 June 1994. [Graphs illustrating central aspects of U.S. welfare system]

3412. Wilber, George L., and W. B. Bock. "Rural Poverty in Puerto Rico." in President's National Advisory Commission on Rural Poverty, Rural Poverty in the United States. Washington, D.C.: GPO, May 1968.

3413. Wilkerson, Margaret B., and Jewell H. Gresham. "The Racialization of Poverty." *Nation* (24 July 1989).

3414. Wilkie, Curtis. "Poor of Mississippi Delta See No Way Out." *Boston Globe*, 26 June 1994. [Issaquena County]

3415. Wilkins, Roger W., Sheila B. Kamerman, and Alfred J. Kahn. "Discussion of Poverty Can't Leave Out Race." *New York Times*, 12 November 1991. [Poverty rates in Europe and U.S.]

3416. Will, Jeffry A. *The Deserving Poor*. Garland, 1993. [1986 data]

3417. Willhelm, Sidney M. "The Economic Demise of Blacks in America : A Prelude to Genocide?" *Journal of Black Studies* 17 (1986): 201-254.

3418. Williams, B. "Poverty Among African Americans in the Urban United States." *Human Organization* 51 (Summer 1992): 164-173.

3419. Wilson, G. "The Juvenilization of Poverty." *Public Administration Review* 45 (1985): 880-884.

3420. Wilson, William J. "A Response to Cities of The Truly Disadvantaged." *Journal of Sociology and Social Welfare* 16 (December 1989): 133-148.

3421. _____. "The Truly Disadvantaged Revisited : A Response to Hochschild and Boxill." *Ethics* 101 (April 1991): 593-609.

3422. Woodson, Robert L. "Race and Economic Opportunity." *Vanderbilt Law Review* 42 (May 1989): 1017-1047.

3423. Zelman, Donald L. "Mexican Migrants and Relief in Depression California." *Journal of Mexican American History* 5 (1975): 1-23.

ECONOMICS OF RACISM

3424. Adu-Febiri. "The State, Racism, and Domination in Contemporary Capitalist Societies." *Berkeley Journal of Sociology* 38 (1993).

3425. Almaguer, Tomas. *Class, Race, and Capitalist Development : The Social Transformation of a Southern California County, 1848 - 1903.* Ph.D. diss., University of California, Berkeley, 1979.

3426. _____. "Racial Domination and Class Conflict in Capitalistic Agriculture : The Oxnard Sugar Beet Workers' Strike of 1903." *Labor History* 25 (Summer 1984).

3427. Baron, Harold M. "The Demand for Black Labor : Historical Notes on the Political Economy of Racism." *Radical America* (March - April 1971): 1-46.

3428. Bell, Derrick. "Does Discrimination Make Economic Sense? For Some, It Did - and Still Does." *Human Rights* 15 (Fall 1988).

3429. Bonacich, Edna, and John Modell. *The Economic Basis of Ethnic Solidarity.* Berkeley, CA: University of California Press, 1980.

3430. Cloutier, Norman R. "Who Gains from Racism? The Impact of Racial Inequality on White Income Distribution." *Review of Social Economy* 45 (October 1987): 152-162.

3431. Cobas, Jose A. "Six Problems in the Sociology of the Ethnic Economy." *Sociological Perspectives* 32 (Summer 1989): 201-214.

3432. Darity, William A. ,. Jr. "Race and Inequality in the Managerial Age." in *Social, Political, and Economic Issues in Black America, vol. 4*, pp. 29-81. ed. Wornie L. Reed. Boston, MA: William Monroe Trotter Institute, University of Massachusetts at Boston, 1990.

3433. Darity, William A. Jr, and J. Ellison. "Abram Harris : The Economy of Race and Social Reform." *History of Political Economy* 22 (Winter 1990).

3434. Evans, Arthur S. "The Relationship between Industrialization and White Hostility toward Blacks in Southern Cities : 1865 - 1910." *Urban Affairs Quarterly* 25 (1989): 322- 341.

3435. Feiner, Susan, and Bruce B. Roberts. "Hidden by the Invisible Hand : Neoclassical Economic Theory and the Textbook Treatment of Race and Gender." *Gender and Society* 4 (June 1990): 159-181.

3436. Franklin, Raymond, and Solomon Resnick. *The Political Economy of Racism.* New York, N.Y.: Holt, 1973.

3437. Gerstacker, Friedrich. *Scenes of Life in California.* San Francisco, CA: J. Howell, 1942. [Racism in gold mines]

3438. Handlin, Oscar. "Prejudice and Capitalist Exploitation : Does Economics Explain Racism?" *Commentary* 6 (July 1948): 79-85.

3439. Hardin, Bristow. *The Militarized Social Democracy and Racism : The Relationships between Militarism, Racism, and Social Welfare Policy in the United States.* Ph.D. diss., University of California, 1991. UMO # 9132416.

3440. Kaiwar, Vasant. "Some Reflections on Capitalism, Race and Class." *South Asian Bulletin* 2 (Spring 1982).

3441. Kushnick, Louis. "Racism and Class Consciousness in Modern Capitalism." in *Impacts of Racism on White America*, pp. 191-216. eds. Benjamin P. Bowser, and R. G. Hunt. Beverly Hills, CA: Sage, 1981.

3442. Mac Leod, William C. "Big Business and the North American Indian." *American Journal of Sociology* 34 (November 1928): 480- 491.

3443. Miles, Robert, and Annie C. Phizacklea. "Racism and Capitalist Decline." in *New Perspectives in Urban Change and Conflict*, pp. 80-100. ed. Michael Harloe. London: Heinemann Educational Books, 1981.

3444. Montejano, David. "Frustrated Apartheid : Race." in *The World System of Capitalism : Past and Present*, ed. W. L. Goldfrank. Beverly Hills, CA: Sage, 1979. [Depression, and Capitalist Agriculture in South Texas, 1920 - 1930.]

3445. _____. *Race, Labor Repression, and Capitalist Agriculture : Notes from South Texas, 1920 - 1930.* Berkeley, CA: Institute for the Study of Social Change, 2420 Bowditch St., Berkeley, CA 94720, 1977.

3446. Nee, Victor, and Jimmy Sanders. "The Road to Parity : Determinants of the Socioeconomic Achievements of Asian Americans." *Ethnic and Racial Studies* 8 (January 1985): 75-93.

3447. Peterson, Richard H. *Manifest Destiny in the Mines : A Cultural Interpretation of Anti-Mexican Nativism in California, 1848 - 1853.* San Francisco, CA: R & E Research Associates, 1975.

3448. Roback, J. "Racism as Rent Seeking." *Economic Inquiry* 27 (October 1989).

3449. Samuelson, Robert J. "Racism and Poverty." *Newsweek* (7 August 1989).

3450. Stillwaggon, Eileen M. "Anti - Indian Agitation and Economic Interests." *Monthly Review* 33 (November 1981).

3451. Swinton, David H. "Racial Parity under Laissez Faire : An Impossible Dream." in *Race : Twentieth-Century Dilemmas - Twenty- first-Century Prognoses*, eds. Winston A. Van Horne, and Thomas V. Tonneson. Milwaukee, WI: Institute on Race and Ethnicity, University of Wisconsin System, 1989.

3452. _____. "What's Wrong With the Theory of Racial Inequality : Toward a More Effective Theory of Racial Inequality in Economic Life." *Review of Black Political Economy* 21 (December 1993): 27-40.

3453. Valocchi, S. "The Racial Basis of Capitalism and the State, and the Impact of the New Deal on African Americans." *Social Problems* 41 (August 1994): 347-362.

3454. Wallis, J. "Violence, Poverty, and Separation : No One Really Expects the Children of the Inner Cities to Enter the Economic Mainstream." *Public Welfare* 50 (1992): 14-15.

3455. Wilkins, Roger W. "The Black Poor Are Different." *New York Times*, 22 August 1989. [Op-Ed Page]

EDUCATION -- ELEMENTARY AND SECONDARY

3456. Adams, David W. "Schooling the Hopi: Federal Indian Policy Writ Small." *Pacific H. Rev.* 48 (1979): 335-356.

3457. "Alabama Student Settles Lawsuit Over Principal's Racial Remark." *New York Times*, 22 June 1994. [Randolph County High School]

3458. Alberts, John B. "Black Catholic Schools: The Josephite Parishes during the Jim Crow Era." *U. S. Catholic Historian* 12 (Winter 1994): 77-98.

3459. Alexander, James S. *Post-Rodriquez School Finance Reform in Texas.* Ph.D. diss., University of Texas, 1989. UMO # 9016837.

3460. Allen, Charlotte. "Blackboard Jumble." *Washington Post*, 15 August 1993. [Alleges long record of non-productive teaching fads in Washington, D.C. public schools]

3461. Allen-Meares, Paula. "Educating Black Youths: The Unfulfilled Promise of Equality." *Social Work* 35 (May 1990): 283- 286.

3462. American Indian Science and Engineering Society. *Our Voices, Our Vision: American Indians Speak Out for Educational Excellence.* Boulder, CA, 1989.

3463. Ammar, Marie B. and others. "Single-Race, Single-Sex Schools." *Los Angeles Times*, 25 January 1994. [four letters]

3464. Anderson, James D. "The Schooling and Achievement of Black Children: Before and After Brown v. Topeka, 1900 - 1980." *Advances in Motivation and Achievement* 1 (1984): 103-122.

3465. _____. "Secondary School History Textbooks and the Treatment of Black History." in *The State of Afro-American History : Past, Present, and Future*, ed. Darlene Clark Hine. Baton Rouge, LA: Louisiana State University Press, 1989.

3466. Andrews, Donald R. and others. "An Estimation of the Aggregate Educational Production Function for Public Schools in Louisiana." *Review of Black Political Economy* 20 (Summer 1991): 25-47.

3467. Anyon. "Ideology and U.S. History Textbooks." *Harvard Educational Review* 49 (1979).

3468. Apple, Michael W. *Teachers and Texts: A Political Economy of Class and Gender Relations in Education.* Boston, MA: Routledge and Kegan Paul, 1986.

3469. Applebome, Peter. "Boarding Schools for Blacks: Need Born of Segregation Is on the Rise." *New York Times*, 21 September 1994. [Southern Normal School, Brewton, Alabama]

3470. _____. "Its Schools Ruled Inadequate, Alabama Looks for Answers." *New York Times*, 4 June 1993.

3471. Arias, B. "The Context of Education for Hispanic Students: An Overview." *American Journal of Education* 95 (1986): 26-57.

3472. Armor, David J. "Response to Carr and Zeigler's White Flight and White Return in Norfolk." *Sociology of Education* 64 (1991): 134-139.

3473. Armour-Thomas, E. and others. "Toward an Understanding of Higher-Order Thinking among Minority Students." *Psychology in the Schools* 29 (July 1992): 273-280.

3474. Arnez, Nancy L. "Equity and Access in the Instructional Materials Area." *Journal of Black Studies* 23 (January 1993): 500- 514.

3475. Arries, Jonathan F. *Ideology and Social Studies Textbooks Used in the Education of Hispanic Americans.* Ph.D. diss., University of Wisconsin, 1988. UMO # 8813115.

3476. Ascher, Carol. "Black Students and Private Schooling." *Urban Review* 18 (1986): 137-145.

3477. Aspira, Inc. *Trends in Segregation of Hispanic Students in Major School Districts Having Large Hispanic Enrollment.* 5 vols. 1979 - 1980. ERIC ED 190270-190275.

3478. Associated Press. "Adults Seeking Diploma Equivalent." *Boston Globe*, 20 June 1994. [Recent data on GED tests]

3479. Bahr, M. W. and others. "Are Teachers' Perceptions of Difficult-to-Teach Students Racially Biased?" *School Psychology Review* 20 (1991): 599-608.

3480. Baker, Donald P. "G.O.P. Helps All-White Virginia School." *Washington Post*, 22 July 1993. [Segregation academy created in 1964 to avoid school desegregation in Amelia, VA]

3481. _____. "A School Left Behind By the Times." *Washington Post*, 9 August 1993. [Amelia Academy, Virginia, all-white school created in 1969 to avoid desegregated public schools]

3482. Baker, Russ W. "Robbin' the 'Hood." *Village Voice*, 25 May 1993. [Kenneth W. Drummond in School District 12, New York City]

3483. "Baltimore Refuses Free Tuition [to Puerto Rican Children]." *New York Times*, 12 January 1902.

3484. Banks, Sandy. "Dissatisfaction Fuels Drive to Dismantle L. A. Unified." *Los Angeles Times*, 17 May 1993. [proposal to break up Los Angeles Unified School District]

3485. Banks, Sandy, and Stephanie Chavez. "L. A. Unified Breakup Drive Stirs Minorities' Suspicions." *Los Angeles Times*, 18 May 1993. [Los Angeles Unified School District]

3486. Barnett, Marguerite Ross. "Educational Policy Trends in a Neoconservative Era." *Urban League Review* 11 (Summer 1987/Winter 1987-1988): 36-46.

3487. Baron, Harold M. "Racism Transformed: The Implications of the 1960s." *Review of Radical Political Economics* 17 (1985): 10- 33.

3488. Bates, Steve. "Academic Mixing Stirs Pot in Alexandria." *Washington Post*, 31 January 1993. [Heterogenous classrooms]

3489. _____. "More Parents Are Challenging School Quality. Gifted Students Said to Suffer In a Push to Help the Needy." *Washington Post*, 20 April 1993.

3490. Beck, Nicholas. "The Vanishing Californians: The Education of Indians in the Nineteenth Century." *Southern California Quarterly* 69 (1987): 33-50.

3491. *Before It's Too Late: Dropout Prevention in the Middle Grades.* Boston, MA: Massachusetts Advocacy Center, 1988.

3492. Bell, Derrick. "The Case for a Separate Black School System." *Urban League Review* 11 (Summer 1987/Winter 1987-1988): 136-145.

3493. Benjamin, Gerald, and Charles Brecher, eds. "The Two New Yorks: State-City Relations in the Changing Fdereal System." : Russell Sage Foundation, 1988.

3494. Benmayor, Rina. "Testimony, Action Research, and Empowerment: Puerto Rican Women and Popular Education." in *Women's Worlds: The Feminist Practice of Oral History*, eds. Sherna Berger Gluck, and Daphne Patai. : Routledge, 1991.

3495. Berg, S. Carol. "Memories of an Indian Boarding School: White Earth, Minnesota, 1909-1945." *Midwest Review* 11 (Spring 1989): 27-36.

3496. Berger, Joseph. "New York Panel Backs School for Minority Men." *New York Times*, 10 January 1991. [NYC]

3497. _____. "Proposal Presents Features of a School for Black Boys." *New York Times*, 22 January 1991. [NYC]

3498. Bernal, M. E. and others. "Ethnic Identity and Adaptation of Mexican American Youths in School Settings." *Hispanic Journal of Behavioral Sciences* 13 (May 1991): 135-154.

3499. Berne, Robert. "Equity Issues in School Finance." *Journal of Educational Finance* 14 (Fall 1988).

3500. Berne, Robert, and Leanna Stiefel. *The Measurement of Equity in School Finance*. Johns Hopkins University Press, 1984.

3501. Bernstein, Sharon, and Josh Meyer. "4 Arrested in Racial Melee in High School." *Los Angeles Times*, 27 October 1992. [North Hollywood High School, CA]

3502. Berry, Gordon L., and Joy K. Asamen, eds. *Black Students : Psychosocial Issues and Academic Achievement*. Newbury Park, CA: Sage, 1989.

3503. Bickel, Robert N. *Achievement and Equity in Public and Private Secondary Schools: An Analytical and Empirical Response to the Continuing Debate*. Ph.D. diss., Florida State University, 1987. [Contra : Coleman]. UMO # 8713304.

3504. Bilbao, Elena, and Maria A. Gallart. *Los chicanos: segregacion y educacion*. Mexico City: Editorial Nueva Imagen, 1981.

3505. Bivins, Karin C. *The Formation, Activities, Agenda, Decline or Persistence of Three Black Educational Special Interest Groups in the School District of Philadelphia, 1965 - 1985*. Ph.D. diss., Temple University, 1992. UMO # 9301128.

3506. Black, Chris. "New New Jersey Superintendent Takes Reins of Troubled System." *Boston Globe*, 23 November 1989. [Jersey City whose school district was taken over by the state]

3507. Blume, Howard. "The Anatomy of a School's Disaster." *Los Angeles Times*, 21 March 1993. [Whaley Middle School, Compton, CA]

3508. _____. "Ethnic Standoffs Continue to Plague City's High Schools." *Los Angeles Times*, 18 November 1993. [Black - Latino conflict in Compton, CA]

3509. _____. "Failing in Math." *Los Angeles Times*, 12 December 1993. [Questionable business practices in school district affairs]

3510. _____. "A School Success Story." *Long Beach Press- Telegram*, 27 September 1992. [Whittier Elementary School, Long Beach, CA]

3511. Boggs, Stephen T. and others. *Speaking, Relating, and Learning: A Study of Hawaiian Children at Home and at School*. Norwood, N.J.: Ablex, 1985.

3512. Bond, Horace Mann. *Negro Education in Alabama: A Study in Cotton and Steel*. New York, N.Y.: Octagon Books, 1969.

3513. Boozer, M. A. and others. "Race and School Quality since Brown v. Board of Education." *Brookings Papers on Economic Activity, Microeconomics* (1992). [See, in same issue, comments and reply]

3514. Boundy, Kathleen. "Changing Educational Outcomes for Young Children from Low-Income Families." *Clearinghouse Review* 25 (1991): 375-390.

3515. Bowditch, Christine. "Getting Rid of Troublemakers: High School Disciplinary Procedures and the Production of Dropouts." *Social Problems* 40 (November 1993): 493-509.

3516. Boyd, William L. "What Makes Ghetto Schools Succeed or Fail?" *Teachers College Record* 92 (Spring 1991): 331-362.

3517. Bracey, Gerald W. "Why Can't They Be Like We Were?" *Phi Delta Kappa* 73 (October 1991): 105-117.

3518. Braddock, Jomills Henry III, and Marvin P. Dawkins. "Ability Grouping, Aspirations and Attainments: Evidence from the National Educational Longitudinal Study of 1988." *Journal of Negro Education* 62 (Summer 1993): 324-336.

3519. Bradley, Ann. "Equation for Equality." *Education Week* (14 September 1994). [Lawsuit decided against Los Angeles city schools to increase flow of funds to Chicano schools]

3520. _____. "Racial Incidents, 'End the Innocence' in Cleveland Suburb, Schools." *Education Week* (15 May 1991). [Cleveland Heights, OH]

3521. Brady, Patricia. "Trials and Tribulations: American Missionary Association Teachers and Black Education in Occupied New Orleans, 1863 - 1864." *Louisiana History* 31 (Winter 1990): 5-20.

3522. Brez Stein, Colman, Jr. "Hispanic Students in the Sink or Swim Era, 1900 - 1960." *Urban Education* 20 (July 1985): 189-198.

3523. Briggs, Carl M. and others. "Changes in Race and Class Inequalities in Central Public and Private School Enrollments : 1970 - 1980." *Sociological Abstracts* (August 1991). 91S24963/ASA/1991/6322.

3524. Broden, F. Clinton. "Litigating State Constitutional Rights to an Adequate Education and the Remedy of State-operated School Districts." *Rutgers Law Review* 42 (Spring 1990): 779-815.

3525. Brooks-Gunn, J. and others. "Who Drops Out of and Who Continues Beyond High School? A 20-year Follow-Up of Black Urban Youth." *Journal of Research on Adolescence* 3 (1993).

3526. Brown, De Neen L. "Homecoming's Slow Dance With Change." *Washington Post*, 2 November 1992. [Annandale High School, Fairfax County, VA]

3527. Brown, George H. and others. *The Condition of Education for Hispanic Americans*. National Center for Education Statistics, U.S. Department of Education, 1980.

3528. Brown, K. "Do African-Americans Need Immersion Schools? The Paradoxes Created by Legal Conceptualization of Race and Public Education." *Iowa Law Review* 78 (May 1993): 813-882.

3529. Brown, Linda B. *Schooling for Blacks in Henrico County, Virginia, 1870 - 1933, with an Emphasis on the Contributions of Miss Virginia Estelle Randolph*. Ph.D. diss., Virginia Polytechnic Institute and State University, 1990. UMO # 9028019.

3530. Browne, Joseph L. "The Expenses Are Borne by Parents: Freedman's Schools in Southern Maryland, 1865 - 1870." *Maryland Historical Magazine* 86 (Winter 1991): 407-422.

3531. Brumberg, Stephan F. *Going to America, Going to School: The Jewish Immigrant Public School Encounter in Turn-of-the-Century New York City*. New York, N.Y.: Praeger, 1986.

3532. Burke, Fred G. *Public Education. Who's in Charge?* Westport, CT: Praeger, 1990.

3533. Butchart, Ronald E. "Recruits to the 'Army of Civilization': Gender, Race, Class and the Freedmen's Teachers, 1862 - 1875." *Journal of Education* 172 (1990): 76-87.

3534. _____. "'We Best Can Instruct Our Own People': New York African Americans in the Freedman's Schools, 1861 - 1875." *Afro- Americans in New York Life and History* 12 (January 1988): 27-49.

3535. Butler, Amy C. *The Effect of AFDC Guarantees on Poor Children's Educational Attainment*. Ph.D. diss., University of Michigan, 1987. UMO # 8720251.

3536. Byars, Lauretta F. "Lexington's Colored Orphan Industrial Home, 1892 -1913." *Register of the Kentucky Historical Society* 89 (Spring 1991): 147-178.

3537. Cahan, E. D. *Past Caring: A History of the U. S. Preschool Care and Education of the Poor, 1820 - 1965*. New York, N.Y.: National Center for Children in Poverty, 1989.

3538. Calabrese, Raymond L. "The Public School: A Source of Alienation for Minority Parents." *Journal of Negro Education* 59 (Spring 1990): 148-154.

3539. "California District Is Accused of Betraying a Trust." *New York Times*, 9 March 1994. [Mendota Unified School District and low quality of education given migrant workers' children]

3540. Calitri, Ronald. *Racial and Ethnic High School Dropout Rates in New York City: A Summary Report/ 1983*. New York, N.Y.: Aspira of New York, 1983.

3541. Camacho, Annie M. *Family, Community, and Social Capital: The Missing Pieces in Chicago's School Reform*. Ph.D. diss., Northern Illinois University, 1993. UMO # 9324962.

3542. Camayd-Freixas, Yohel. "Public Education in Boston: A Social Policy Challenge." *Boston Bar Journal* 32 (November - December 1988).

3543. Cameron, J. W. *The History of Mexican Public Education in Los Angeles, 1910 - 1930*. Ph.D. diss., University of Southern California, 1976.

3544. Cameron, Stephen, and James J. Heckman. "High School Equivalency Guarantees Second-class Status." *New York Times*, 31 January 1994. (Letter)

3545. Capitanini, Lisa. "Sex Education Marked Absent at Black Neighborhood Schools." *Chicago Reporter* 20 (November 1991).

3546. Card, David, and Alan B. Krueger. "Does School Quality Matter? Returns to Education and the Characteristics of Public Schools in the United States." *Journal of Political Economy* 100 (February 1992): 1-40.

3547. _____. *School Quality and Black/White Relative Earnings : A Direct Assessment*. National Bureau of Economic Research, May 1991.

3548. Cardenas, Jose. *The Undereducation of American Youth*. San Antonio, TX: Intercultural Development Research Association, 1988.

3549. Carnegie Foundation for the Advancement of Teaching. *School Choice: A Special Report*. Princeton, N.J.: Princeton University Press, 1992.

3550. Carpenter-Stevenson, Sandy. *A Descriptive Study of Administrators of Afro-American Descent in the Oakland Unified School District, 1970 - 1985*. Ph.D. diss., University of San Francisco, 1988. UMO # 8900610.

3551. Carter, Hodding. "In Public Schools, Class Will Tell." *New York Times*, 13 June 1990.

3552. Carter, R. T., and A. L. Goodwin. "Racial Identity and Education." in *Review of Research in Education*, pp. 291 - 336. ed. Linda Darling-Hammond. : American Educational Research Society, 1994.

3553. Cary, Jean M. "Title IX: Sex Discrimination in Public Elementary and Secondary Schools." *School Law Bulletin (University of North Carolina)* 22 (Spring 1991): 8-18.

3554. Cary, Lorene. *Black Ice*. New York, N.Y.: Knopf, 1991. [Black student at St. Paul's boarding school in New Hampshire]

3555. Cataldo, Everett F. *Analysis of High School Dropout Rates and Patterns in Cleveland Public Schools*. Cleveland, OH: Office on School Monitoring and Community Relations, July 1989.

3556. Cecelski, David S. *Along Freedom Road: Hyde County, North Carolina, and the Fate of Black Schools in the South*. University of North Carolina Press, 1994.

3557. _____. *The Hyde County School Boycott: School Desegregation and the Fate of Black Schools in the Rural South, 1954 - 1969*. Ph.D. diss., Harvard University, 1991. [N.C.]. UMO # 9118818.

3558. Celis, William 3rd. "Cities Innovate in a Search for Minority Men to Teach." *New York Times*, 3 November 1993.

3559. _____. "Hispanic Youths Quitting at a Higher Rate." *New York Times*, 14 October 1992. [Nationwide]

3560. _____. "International Report Card Shows U.S. Schools Work." *New York Times*, 9 December 1993. [Report by Organization for Economic Cooperation and Development]

3561. Center for Demographical Cultural Research. *Education in Alabama: A Demographic Perspective*. Montgomery, AL: Auburn University, November 1990.

3562. Chalfant, John. "Celina Schools Buck Proficiency Test Law." *Cleveland Plain Dealer*, 7 September 1993. [Celina, OH school district chooses to graduate students with a diploma in the absence of passing grades on state proficiency tests]

3563. Chall, Jeanne S. and others. *The Reading Crisis. Why Poor Children Fall Behind.* Cambridge, MA: Harvard University Press, 1990.

3564. Chapa, Jorge. "The Myth of Hispanic Progress: Trends in the Educational and Economic Attainment of Mexican Americans." *Journal of Hispanic Policy* 4, 3-18.

3565. Chapman, Bernadine S. *Northern Philanthropy and African- American Adult Education in the Rural South: Hegemony and Resistance in the Jeanes Movement.* Ph.D. diss., Northern Illinois University, 1990. UMO # 9110735.

3566. Chateauvert, Melinda. "The Third Step: Anna Julia Cooper and Black Education in the District of Columbia, 1910 - 1960." *Sage (Student Supplement 1988)* (1988): 7-13.

3567. Chavez, F. R. *The Impact of a Chicano Gang in an Alternative School in Orange County, California.* Irvine, CA: Master's thesis, University of California, Irvine.

3568. Chavez, Stephanie. "An E for Excellence or Elitism?" *Los Angeles Times*, 23 March 1994. [Gretchen Whitney High School, Cerritos, CA]

3569. _____. "Hard Times at Fairfax High." *Los Angeles Times*, 23 January 1993. [Los Angeles]

3570. _____. "An L.A. Teachers Strike Is Justified, Many Say." *Los Angeles Times*, 7 February 1993. [Public opinion poll on Los Angeles schools]

3571. _____. "Little Progress Made With Classroom Racial Tensions." *Los Angeles Times*, 21 September 1992. [Los Angeles]

3572. _____. "Parents Say Vote on School Calender Doesn't Add Up." *Los Angeles Times*, 21 April 1994. [In local referendum at Euclid Avenue Elementary School, teachers' votes counted 6.32 times more than parents' votes]

3573. Chavira, Ricardo. "Blackboard Jungle." *Time* (30 April 1990). [San Fernando High School, Los Angeles]

3574. Chepyator-Thomson, Jepkorir R. *Stratification in an American Secondary School: Issues of Race, Class, Gender, and Physical Ability in Physical Education.* Ph.D. diss., University of Wisconsin, 1990. UMO # 9024757.

3575. Chiara, Susan. "Lamar Alexander's Self-Help Course." *New York Times Magazine*, 24 November 1991. [Secretary of Education]

3576. Chicago Panel on Public School Policy and Finance. *Illegal Use of Chapter I Funds By the Chicago Public Schools.* Chicago, IL: The Panel, 8 November 1988.

3577. Chimezie, Amuzie. "Black Children's Characteristics and the School: A Selective Adaptation Approach." *Western Journal of Black Studies* 12 (Summer 1988): 77-85.

3578. Chira, Susan. "Black Churches Turn to Teaching the Young." *New York Times*, 7 August 1991.

3579. _____. "Money's Value Questioned at Schools Debate." *New York Times*, 4 May 1991.

3580. _____. "Push for Better Schools in Memphis Takes on Importance for Nation." *New York Times*, 15 January 1992.

3581. _____. "Rethinking Deliberately Segregated Schools." *New York Times*, 11 July 1993.

3582. _____. "Where Children Learn How to Learn: Inner-City Pupils in Catholic Schools." *New York Times*, 20 November 1991.

3583. Chriss, B. and others. "The Rise and Fall of Choice in Richmond, California." *Economics of Education Review* 11 (December 1992).

3584. Chu, Henry, and Sandy Banks. "School Power-Sharing Plan Fall Far Short of Goals." *Los Angeles Times*, 5 January 1993. [Los Angeles public school system]

3585. Chubb, John E., and Terry M. Moe. *Politics, Markets and America's Schools.* Washington, D.C.: Brookings Institution, 1990.

3586. Chujo, Ken. *The Black Struggle for Education in North Carolina, 1877 - 1900*. Ph.D. diss., Duke University, 1988. UMO # 8827409.

3587. Chunn, Eva Wells. "Sorting Black Students for Success and Failure: The Inequity of Ability Grouping and Tracking." *Urban League Review* 11 (Summer 1987 / Winter 1987-1988): 93-106.

3588. Cintron Ortiz, Rafael. "A Colonial Experience: Schools in Puerto Rico as Agents of Domination." *Critical Anthropology* 2 (Spring 1972): 104-112.

3589. *Civil Rights Implications of Minority Student Dropouts*. Washington, D.C.: U.S. Commission on Civil Rights, 1990. [Massachusetts]

3590. *Civil Rights Implications of Minority Student Dropouts*. Washington, D.C.: U.S. Commission on Civil Rights, 1990. [Michigan]

3591. Clark, Joe, and Joe Picard. *Laying Down the Law. Joe Clark's Strategy for Saving Our Schools*. Washington, D.C.: Regnery Gateway, 1989. [Principal of Eastside High School, Paterson, N.J.]

3592. Claudio, Rafael R. *The Experience of Puerto Rican Urban Youth on the Mainland As It Affects Academic Success within the American School System*. Ph.D. diss., Union for Experimenting Colleges and Universities, 1987. UMO # 8720614.

3593. Clayton, Constance. "We Can Educate All Our Children." *Nation*, 24 July 1989.

3594. Coakley, Tom. "Norwood High Reviews, Repudiates Racism Charges." *Boston Globe*, 18 May 1991. [Norwood, MA]

3595. Coakley, Tom, and Ray Richard. "Racial Tensions Disrupt Randolph High School." *Boston Globe*, 26 September 1991. [Massachusetts]

3596. Cobbs, Lewis. "A Selma Reunion." *Education Week*, 6 November 1991. [20th anniversary of "the first class to graduate from a fully integrated public school in Selma, Alabama"]

3597. Cohen, Deborah, and Benjamin T. Smith. "Streets of Despair." *Education Week*, 1 December 1993. [Ida B. Wells Preparatory School, Chicago]

3598. Cohen, Muriel. "Whites Main Users of School Choice." *Boston Globe*, 29 October 1991. [In Massachusetts]

3599. Cohen, Muriel, and Diego Ribodeneira. "Schooling by Selection." *Boston Globe*, 11 August 1991. [Interdistrict school- choice plan in Massachusetts]

3600. Cohen, Ronald. *Children of the Mill. Schooling and Society in Gary, Indiana, 1906 - 1960*. Bloomington, IN: Indiana University Press, 1989.

3601. Cole, Beverly P. "The School Reform of the Eighties and Its Implications for the Restructuring of the Nineties." *Crisis* 98 (October 1991): 23-26.

3602. Cole, Charles E. *Reports of High School Freshmen on their Perceptions of Racial Prejudice During Junior High School*. Ph.D. diss., National College of Education, 1990. UMO # 9033922.

3603. Cole, Mike, ed. *Bowles and Gintis Revisited : Correspondence and Contradiction in Educational Theory*, Philadelphia, PA: Falmer Press, 1988.

3604. Coleman, James S. "Equality and Excellence in Education" in *Surveying Social Life: Papers in Honor of Herbert H. Hyman*, ed. Hubert J. O'Gorman. Middletown, CT: Wesleyan University Press, 1988.

3605. _____. *Equality and Achievement in Education*. Boulder, CO: Westview, 1990.

3606. Coleman, Michael C. *American Indian Children at School, 1850 - 1930*. University Press of Mississippi, 1993.

3607. _____. "The Mission Education of Francis La Flesche: An American Indian Response to the Presbyterian Boarding School in the 1860s." *American Stud. Scand.* 18 (1986): 67-82.

3608. _____. "Motivations of Indian Children at Missionary and U.S. Government Schools, 1860 - 1918: A Study through Published Reminiscences." *Montana* 40 (1990): 30-45.

3609. Collins, Timothy. "Reform and Reaction: The Political Economy of Education in Kentucky." *Sociological Abstracts* supplement 164 (June 1991) 91S24712/RSS/1991/2350.

3610. Colon-Tarrats, Nelson L. *Cimarrones: A Life History Analysis of Puerto Rican Dropouts in Boston.* Ph.D. diss., Harvard University, 1988. UMO # 8823311.

3611. Comer, James P. *A Conversation between James Comer and Ronald Edmonds: Fundamentals of Effective School Improvement.* Dubuque, IA: Kendall/Hunt, 1989.

3612. _____. "Educating Poor Minority Children." *Scientific American* 259 (November 1988): 42-48.

3613. _____. "Racism and the Education of Young Children." *Teachers College Record* 90 (Spring 1989): 352-361.

3614. Commission of Chapter I. "Making Schools Work for Children in Poverty." *Education Week*, 13 January 1993, 46-51.

3615. Committee on Policy for Racial Justice. *Visions of a Better Way: A Black Appraisal of Public Schooling.* Washington, D.C.: Joint Center for Political and Economic Studies, 1989.

3616. "Comparison Links Poverty, Test Scores." *Cleveland Plain Dealer*, 15 March 1993. [608 school districts in Ohio]

3617. Connell, R. W. "Poverty and Education." *Harvard Educational Review* 64 (Summer 1994): 125-149.

3618. Cookson, P. W., and C. H. Persell. "Race and Class in America's Elite Preparatory Boarding Schools: African Americans as the Outsiders Within." *Journal of Negro Education* 60 (Spring 1991): 219-228.

3619. Cooper, Eric, and John Sherk. "Addressing Urban School Reform: Issues and Alliances." *Journal of Negro Education* 58 (1989): 315-331.

3620. Cornelison, Alice and others. *History of Blacks in Howard County, Maryland: Oral History, Schooling, and Contemporary Issues.* Columbia, MD: Howard County, Maryland, NAACP, 1986.

3621. Cornelius, Janet D. *When I Can Read My Title Clear: Literacy, Slavery, and Religion in the Antebellum South.* University of South Carolina Press, 1991.

3622. Coulon, John R., and Mwangi S. Kimenyi. "Attitudes Towards Race and Poverty in the Demand for Private Education: The Case of Mississippi." *Review of Black Political Economy* 20 (Fall 1991): 5-22.

3623. Council of Chief State School Officers. *School Success for Limited - English - Proficient Students: The Challenge and State Response.* Resource Center on Educational Equity, 1990.

3624. Crowther, Edward R. "Alabama's Fight to Maintain Segregated Schools, 1953 - 1956." *Alabama Review* 43 (July 1990): 206-225.

3625. Cuban, Larry. "Desperate Remedies for Desperate Times." *Education Week*, 20 November 1991. [Black, all male academies] [see below, Jawanza Kunjufu]

3626. Daly, Charles U., ed. *The Quality of Inequality: Urban and Suburban Public Schools*, Chicago, IL: University of Chicago Center for Policy Study, 1968.

3627. Darling, Juanita. "Caught Between Two Educational Systems." *Los Angeles Times*, 29 November 1993. [Migrants' children who attend school in Mexico and the United States]

3628. Darling-Hammond, Linda. *Equality and Excellence: The Educational Status of Black Americans.* New York, N.Y.: College Entrance Examination Board, 1985.

3629. _____. "The Implications of Testing Policy for Quality and Equality." *Phi Delta Kappan* 73 (November 1991): 220-225.

3630. _____. "Instructional Policy Into Practice: 'The Power of the Bottom Over the Top'." *Educational Evaluation and Policy Analysis* 12 (1990): 339-348.

3631. _____. "Teacher Quality and Equality." in *Access to Knowledge: An Agenda for Our Nation's Schools*, eds. John Goodlad, and Pamela Keating. New York, N.Y.: College Board, 1990.

3632. Darnell, Frank. "Education Among the Native Peoples of Alaska." *Polar Record* 19 (1979): 431-446.

3633. Datcher-Loury, Linda. "Family Background and School Achievement among Low-income Blacks." *Journal of Human Resources* 24 (1988): 528-543.

3634. De Jong, David H. *Friend or Foe? Education and the American Indian.* Master's thesis, University of Arizona, 1990. UMO # MA1339909.

3635. De La Rosa, Denise, and Carlyle E. Maw. *Hispanic Education: A Statistical Portrait 1990.* Washington, D.C.: The National Council of La Raza, October 1990.

3636. De Leon, Arnoldo. "Blowout 1910: A Chicano School Boycott in West Texas." *Texana* 12 (November 1974).

3637. De Palma, Anthony. "Free Speech and a Flag, but This Time It's the Stars and Bars." *New York Times*, 12 March 1991. [The Confederate flag at James F. Byrnes High School, Duncan, S.C.]

3638. De Parle, Jason. "Without Fanfare, Blacks March to Greater High School Success." *New York Times*, 9 June 1991.

3639. De Santis, J. P. and others. "Black Adolescents' Concerns that They Are Academically Able." *Merrill - Palmer Quarterly* 36 (April 1990): 287-299.

3640. De Vore, Donald E. *Race Relations and Community Development: The Education of Blacks in New Orleans, 1862 - 1960.* Ph.D. diss., Louisiana State University Press, 1989. UMO # 9025300.

3641. De Young, A. J. "Economic Underdevelopment and Its Effects on Formal Schooling in Southern Appalachia." *American Educational Research Journal* 28 (Summer 1991): 297-315.

3642. Delany, B. "Allocation, Choice, and Stratification within High Schools: How the Sorting Machine Copes." *American Journal of Education* 99 (February 1991): 181-207.

3643. Deloria, Vine, Jr. *Indian Education in America: 8 Essays by Vine Deloria, Jr.* Boulder, CO: American Indian Science and Engineering Society, 1991.

3644. Dent, David J. "A Mixed Message in Black Schools." *New York Times*, 4 April 1993. [Black Christian and fundamentalist private schools]

3645. Dentler, Robert A. *Decentralization in the Cleveland Public Schools: An Evaluation.* Cleveland, OH: Office on School Monitoring and Community Relations, 1 July 1985.

3646. Denton, Virginia L. *Booker T. Washington and the Adult Education Movement, 1856 - 1915.* Ph.D. diss., University of Southern Mississippi, 1988. UMO # 8902483.

3647. _____. *Booker T. Washington and the Adult Education Movement.* University Press of Florida, 1993.

3648. Designs for Change. *Barriers to Excellence: Our Children at Risk in Illinois.* Chicago, IL: Designs for Change, 1985.

3649. Deutsch, Claudia H. "Corporate Takeovers?" *New York Times Education Life*, 6 August 1989. [Participation of business in the public schools]

3650. "The Development of Human Potential : Education of Latinos in California." in *The Challenge : Latinos in a Changing California*, pp. 49-63. University of California SCR 43 Task Force. Riverside, CA: The University of California Consortium on Mexico and the United States (UCMEXUS), 1989.

3651. Dhand, Harry. "Bias in Social Studies Textbooks: New Research Findings." *History and Social Science Teacher* 24 (1988): 23-27.

3652. Diamond, Raymond T. "Confrontation as Rejoinder to Compromise: Reflections on the Little Rock Desegregation Crisis." *National Black Law Journal* 11 (Spring 1989): 151-176.

3653. Dickinson, S. L. J. "Just How Effective Are the Science and Math Magnet Schools?" *The Scientist* 6 (11 May 1992): 4-6.

3654. Diegmueller, Karen. "Conservative - Learning Think Tanks Putting Imprint on Education Policy." *Education Week*, 24 March 1993.

3655. Dillon, Sam. "Change in Focus for P.T.A.'s: From Status Quo to Advocacy." *New York Times*, 13 October 1993.

3656. Donelan, Richard W. *Equity in Michigan's School Finance System for Students Participating in the State Compensatory Education Program*. Ph.D. diss., University of Michigan, 1991. UMO # 9123961.

3657. Dove, Dorothy E. N. *Racism and Resistance in the Schooling of Africans*. Ph.D. diss., State University of New York at Buffalo, 1993. UMO # 9330056.

3658. Doyle, Anne M. "Winning Numbers." *Village Voice*, 28 January 1992. [School aid funding and state of New York lottery revenue]

3659. Drago, Edmund L. *Initiative, Paternalism, and Race Relations. Charleston's Avery Normal Institute*. Athens, GA: University of Georgia Press, 1990.

3660. Drazen, Shelley M. *Relationship between Chapter 1 Program Characteristics and Local School District Poverty and Student Achievement*. Ph.D. diss., Cornell University, 1991. UMO # 9131443.

3661. *Early Childhood Education Issues in Texas: Implications for Civil Rights*. Washington, DC: U.S. Commission on Civil Rights, 1990.

3662. Eberhard, D. R. "American Indian Education: A Study of Dropouts, 1980 - 1987." *Journal of American Indian Education* 28 (1989): 32-40.

3663. Echewa, Willie W. *A Documentary Investigation of Non-elite Black Attitudes toward Public Education in Nineteenth Century Philadelphia : 1823 - 1860*. 2 vols. Ph.D. diss., Temple University, 1993. UMO # 9316542.

3664. Edwards, Ralph. *How Boston Selected Its First Black Superintendent of Schools*. Ph.D. diss., Harvard University, 1989. UMO # 9014291.

3665. Egerton, John. "A Gentlemen's Fight in Prince Edward County, Virginia." in *Shades of Gray. Dispatches from the Modern South*, John Egerton. Baton Rouge, LA: Louisiana State University Press, 1992. [Closing of public schools, 1959 - 1964]

3666. Eleazer, R. B. "School Books and Racial Antagonism: A Study of Omissions and Inclusions That Make for Misunderstanding." *High School Journal* 18 (October 1935): 197-199.

3667. Elliot, Roger. "Larry P., PASE, and Social Science in the Courtroom: The Science and Politics of Identifying and Educating Very Slow Learners." in *Interactive Assessment*, pp. 470 - 503. eds. H. C. Haywood, and D. Tzuriel. : Springer-Verlag, 1991.

3668. Entwisle, Doris R., and Karl L. Alexander. "Factors Affecting Achievement Test Scores and Marks of Black and White First Graders." *Elementary School Journal* 88 (May 1988): 449-471.

3669. Epps, P. "Who Shall Write Unbiased Textbooks?" *School and Society* 74 (1951).

3670. *Equal Educational Opportunity for Minority Students in the Morris School District*. Washington, DC: U.S. Commission on Civil Rights, 1990. [N.J.]

3671. Espinosa, Ruben. *Report on the Los Angeles Ufied School District: A Comparison of School Finance and Facilities between Hispanic and Non-Hispanic Schools during Fiscal Year 1980 - 1981*. Los Angeles, CA: Mexican American Legal Defense and Education Fund, 1982.

3672. Evans, Christopher. "The School Board Jungle. Is Al Tutela the Hunter or the Hunted in Cleveland's Most Savage Political Zoo?" *Cleveland Plain Dealer Magazine*, 10 September 1989.

3673. Evans, M. O. "An Estimate of Race and Gender Role-Model Effects in Teaching High School." *Journal of Economic Education* 23 (Summer 1992).

3674. Fairchild, H. H. "School Size, Per-pupil Expenditure, and Academic Achievement." *Review of Public Data Use* 12 (1984): 121- 129.

3675. Farber, M. A. "'Africa Centered' School Plan Is Rooter in 60's Struggles." *New York Times*, 5 February 1991. [Projected Ujaama Institute, New York City]

3676. Farkas, George and others. "Coursework Mastery and School Success: Gender, Ethnicity, and Poverty Groups within and Urban School District." *American Educational Research Journal* 27 (Winter 1990).

3677. Farkas, George and others. "Cultural Resources and School Success: Gender, Ethnicity, and Poverty Groups Within An Urban District." *American Sociological Review* 55 (February 1990).

3678. Fass, Paula S. *Outside In: Minorities and the Transformation of American Education*. New York, NY: Oxford University Press, 1989.

3679. Felice, Lawrence G. "Black Student Dropout Behavior: Disengagement from School Rejection and Racial Discrimination." *Journal of Negro Education* 50 (1981): 415-424.

3680. Fenyo, Mario D. "Columbus and All That: 'Discovery' and 'Expansion' in American Textbooks." *Perspectives* 24 (1986): 14- 16.

3681. Ferguson, Ronald F. "Paying for Public Education: New Evidence on How and Why Money Matters." *Harvard Journal on Legislation* (Summer 1991).

3682. Finkenbine, Roy E. "'Our Little Circle': Benevolent Reformers, the Slater Fund, and the Argument for Black Industrial Education, 1882 - 1908." *Hayes Historical Journal* 6 (1986): 6-22.

3683. "Fire Damages School Split By Race Issue." *New York Times*, 7 August 1994. [Wedowee, AL]

3684. Firestone, W. A. and others. "State Educational Reform since 1983: Appraisal and the Future." *Educational Policy* 5 (September 1991): 233-250.

3685. First, Joan M., and John W. Carrera. *New Voices: Immigrant Students in U.S. Public Schools*. Boston, MA: National Coalition of Advocates for Students, 1988.

3686. Fishback, Price V. "Can Competition among Employers Reduce Governmental Discrimination? Coal Companies and Segregated Schools in West Virginia in the Early 1900s." *Journal of Law and Economics* 32 (October 1989): 311-328.

3687. Fitzpatrick, Joseph P. "Problems of Race and Ethnic Relations among High School Youth: A Sociological Perspective." *International Journal of Group Tensions* 18 (1988): 33-43. [Puerto Rican students in New York City]

3688. Flicker, Barbara, ed. *Justice and the Schools Systems: The Role of the Courts in Education Litigation*, Philadelphia, PA: Temple University Press, 1990.

3689. Flores, Estevan T. "Research on Undocumented Immigrants and Public Policy: A Study of the Texas School Case." *International Migration Review* 18 (Fall 1984): 505-523.

3690. Foehrenbach, Josie. "Preparing for Learnfare: Setting the Conditions for a Questionable Experiment." *Clearinghouse Review* 22 (February 1989): 1060-1073. [Poor children]

3691. Foley, D. E. "Reconsidering Anthropological Explanations of Ethnic School Failure." *Anthropology and Education Quarterly* 22 (March 1991): 60-86.

3692. Ford, Michael D. "Defending the Common School." *Nation*, 9 December 1991.

3693. Fordham, Signithia M. *Black Students' School Success as Related to Fictive Kinship : A Study in the Washington, D.C. Public School System*. Ph.D. diss., American University, 1987. UMO # 8720997.

3694. _____. "On Research Interpretations and Black Students' Success." *Education Week*, 4 August 1993.

3695. _____. "Racelessness as a Factor in Black Students' School Success : Pragmatic Strategy or Pyrrhic Victory?" *Harvard Educational Review* 58 (February 1988): 54-84.

3696. _____. "Racelessness in Private Schools : Should We Deconstruct the Racial and Cultural Identity of African-American Adolescents." *Teachers College Record* 92 (Spring 1991): 470-484.

3697. _____. "Those Loud Black Girls." *Anthropology and Education Quarterly* 24 (March 1993): 3-32.

3698. Fordham, Signithia, and John U. Ogbu. "Black Students' School Success: Coping with the Burden of 'Acting White'." *Urban Review* 18 (1986): 176-206.

3699. Fouquette, Danielle A. "Largely Latino High School Fights Ethnic Stereotyping." *Los Angeles Times*, 13 April 1993. [Valencia High School, California]

3700. Franco, Jere. "Howard Billman and the Tucson Indian School: 1888 - 1894." *Social Science Journal* 26 (Spring 1989).

3701. Frank, Nyle C. *An Analysis of the March 1968 East Los Angeles High School Walkouts*. Master's thesis, Chapel Hill, NC: University of North Carolina, 1968.

3702. Frantz, Douglas, and Elizabeth Shogren. "Conservative Fire Spreads With School Board Sparks." *Los Angeles Times*, 11 December 1993. [Meridian, Idaho]

3703. Freedman, Samuel G. *Small Victories. The Real World of a Teacher, Her Students, and Their High School*. New York, NY: Harper and Row, 1990. [Seward Park High School, New York City]

3704. Frolik, Joe. "East Harlem Schools Offer Oasis Amid Strife." *Cleveland Plain Dealer*, 27 April 1991.

3705. Gabe, J. "'Race'-education Policy or Social Control?" *Sociological Review* 42 (February 1994): 26-61.

3706. Gallegos, Bernardo P. *Literacy, Schooling, and Society in Colonial New Mexico: 1692 - 1821*. Ph.D. diss., University of New Mexico, 1988. UMO # 8916129.

3707. _____. *Literacy, Education, and Society in New Mexico, 1693 - 1821*. University of New Mexico Press, 1992.

3708. Gamoran, Adam. "Microeconomics of Learning : Students, Teachers, and Classrooms." in *Microlevel School Finance : Issues and Implications for Policy*, eds. David Monk, and K. Julie Underwood. 1988.

3709. _____. "Rank, Performance, and Mobility in Elementary School Grouping." *Sociological Quarterly* 30 (Spring 1989).

3710. _____. "The Variable Effects of High School Tracking." *American Sociological Review* 57 (December 1992): 812-828.

3711. Gamoran, Adam, and Mark Berends. *The Effects of Stratification in Secondary Schools: Synthesis of Survey and Ethnographic Research*. Madison, WI: National Center on Effective Secondary Schools, University of Wisconsin, 1987.

3712. Gamoran, Adam, and R. D. Mare. "Secondary School Tracking and Education Inequality : Compensation, Reinforcement, or Neutrality." *American Journal of Sociology* 94 (1989): 1146-1183.

3713. Gandara, Patricia. "Language and Ethnicity as Factors in School Failure: The Case of Mexican-Americans." in *Children at Risk in America: History, Concepts and Public Policy*, ed. Roberta Wollons. : State University of New York Press, 1993.

3714. Garcia, Eugene E. "'Hispanic' Children: Effective Schooling Practices and Related Policy Issues." in *Literacy. A Redefinition*, eds. Nancy J. Ellsworth and others. : Lawrence Erlbaum Associates, 1994.

3715. Garvey, John. "Reading, 'riting, and Race." *Race Traitor* 1 (Winter 1993): 73-87.

3716. "Gender and Educational Achievement." *Educational Psychologist* 28 (Autumn 1993). [five articles]

3717. "Georgia School Denies Segregating Students on Bus." *Cleveland Plain Dealer*, 17 May 1993. (Associated Press story) [Lincoln County, GA]

3718. Gerber, J. "Public School Expenditures in the Plantation States, 1910." *Explorations in Economic History* 28 (July 1991): 309-322.

3719. Geske, T. G., and B. Y. LaCost. "The Student Equity Effects of the Public School Finance System in Louisiana." *Economics of Education Review* 9 (1990).

3720. Getz, Lynne M. "Extending the Helping Hand to Hispanics: The Role of the General Education Board in New Mexico in the 1930s." *Teachers College Record* 93 (Spring 1992): 500-515.

3721. _____. *Progressive Ideas for New Mexico: Educating the Spanish-speaking Child in the 1920s and 30s.* Ph.D. diss., University of Washington, 1989. UMO # 9000237.

3722. Gewertz, Catherine. "Big Racial Gap Persists in O. C. GATE Programs." *Los Angeles Times*, 22 March 1993. [Orange County, CA, Gifted and Talented Education program]

3723. _____. "GATE Is Opening for More Gifted O. C. Minority Pupils." *Los Angeles Times*, 23 March 1993. [Orange County, CA, Gifted and Talented Education program]

3724. Gholar, Cheryl R. *The Evolution of Equality in Educational Thought: An Historical Biography of the Ethnological Ideology that Supported a System of Dual Education in America from 1865 to 1954.* Ph.D. diss., Loyola University of Chicago, 1990. UMO # 9030282.

3725. Gibson, Margaret A. *Accommodation Without Assimilation: Sikh Immigrants In An American High School.* Ithaca, NY: Cornell University Press, 1988.

3726. _____. "The School Performance of Immigrant Minorities : A Comparative View." *Anthropology and Education Quarterly* 18 (1987): 262-275.

3727. Gibson, Margaret A., and John U. Ogbu eds. *Minority Status and Schooling: A Comparative Study of Immigrant and Involuntary Minorities.* New York, NY: Garland, 1991.

3728. Gilhousen, M. R. and others. "Veracity and Vicissitude: A Critical Look at the Milwaukee Project." *Journal of School Psychology* 28 (Winter 1990).

3729. Gill, Dawn and others, eds. *Racism and Education: Structures and Strategies*, : Sage, 1992.

3730. Gill, W. "Jewish Day Schools and Afrocentric Programs as Models for Educating African American Youth." *Journal of Negro Education* 60 (Autumn 1991): 566-580.

3731. Gillispie, Mark. "Garfield Hts. Board Didn't Discriminate." *Cleveland Plain Dealer*, 7 September 1994. [Heavily white school system refuses to absorb heavily-black neighborhood into its attendance area]

3732. Glenn, Charles L., Jr. "How to Integrate Bilingual Education Without Tracking." *School Administrator*, May 1990.

3733. _____. *The Myth of the Common School.* Amherst, MA: University of Massachusetts Press, 1988.

3734. Gonzalez, David. "Poverty Raises Stakes for Catholic School." *New York Times*, 17 April 1994. [St. Francis de Sales and St. Lucy Academy, East Harlem, New York City]

3735. Gonzalez, Gilbert G. *Chicano Education in the Era of Segregation.* Philadelphia, PA: Balch Institute Press, 1989.

3736. Goode, Victor. "Cultural Racism in Public Education: A Legal Tactic for Black Texans." *Harvard Law Review* 33 (Summer 1990): 321-338.

3737. Goodrich, Linda S. *A Historical Survey of Cultural Racism and Its Subsequent Impact on the Education of Black Americans.* Ph.D. diss., Ohio State University, 1976. UMO # 7624651.

3738. Gopaul-McNicol, Sharon-Ann. "Racial Identification and Racial Preference of Black Preschool Children in New York and Trinidad." *Journal of Black Psychology* 14 (February 1988): 65-68.

3739. Gottfredson, Denise C. "Black-White Differences in the Educational Process: What Have We Learned?" *American Sociological Review* 46 (October 1981): 542-557.

3740. Gottlieb, Stephen E. "In the Name of Patriotism: The Constitutionality of 'Bending' History in Public Secondary Schools." *New York University Law Review* 62 (June 1987): 497-578. [Reprinted in *History Teacher*, 22 (1989) 411-495]

3741. Gouldner, Helen. *Teachers' Pets, Troublemakers and Nobodies: Black Children in Elementary School.* Greenwood Press, 1978.

3742. "Grading the Schools." *Cleveland Plain Dealer*, 2 October 1991. [Arrangement of achievement scores in all school districts in Ohio by family income and type of residence, tax effort, tax base of community, and percent AFDC]

3743. Grady, Michael K. *Confronting the Presumption of Unconstitutionality: An Assessment of the Implementation of Milliken II Relief for the All-Black Schools of St. Louis, Missouri*. Ph.D. diss., Harvard University, 1988. UMO # 8907628.

3744. Grant, Carl A., and Christine E. Sleeter. "Race, Class and Gender and Abandoned Dreams." *Teachers College Record* 90 (Fall 1988): 19-40.

3745. Grant, Twala M. "The Legal and Psychological Implications of Tracking in Education." *Law and Psychology Review* 15 (Spring 1991): 299-312.

3746. Gray, C. Boyden, and Evan J. Kemp, Jr. "Flunking Testing: Is Too Much Fairness Unfair to School Kids?" *Washington Post*, 19 September 1993. [See below, Stanley G. Greenspan and Jacqueline L. Salmon]

3747. Gray, Jerry. "Gap Narrowing for Poor School Districts, Study Finds." *New York Times*, 12 October 1993. [N.J.]

3748. Greenspan, Stanley G., and Jacqueline L. Salmon. "The Tracking Trap." *Washington Post*, 19 September 1993. [See above, C. Boyden Gray and Evan J. Kemp, Jr.]

3749. Grey, M. A. "Immigrant Students in the Heartland: Ethnic Relations in Garden City, Kansas, High School." *Urban Anthropology* 19 (1990): 409-427.

3750. Griffith, Stephanie. "As Belts Tighten, PTAs Reach Into Parents' Pockets." *Washington Post*, 5 February 1993. [Washington, D.C. area]

3751. Gross, Jane. "A City's Determination to Rewrite History Puts Its Classroom in Chaos." *New York Times*, 18 September 1991.

3752. _____. "Coach Suspended Over Ethnic Slurs." *New York Times*, 30 July 1991. [Susanville, CA school district]

3753. Gross, Jane, and Ronald Smothers. "In Prom Dispute, a Town's Race Divisions Emerge." *New York Times*, 15 August 1994. [Wedowee, Alabama]

3754. Guerrero, Andre L. *The Presence of Undocumented Mexican Children in Texas Public Schools*. Ph.D. diss., Harvard University, 1990. UMO # 9032435.

3755. Gugliotta, Guy. "Operation Exodus's Path is Education." *Washington Post*, 16 March 1993. [Operation Exodus in Walker, Iowa]

3756. Guiney, Ellen. "A School That Works." *Boston Globe Magazine*, 27 September 1987. [Trinity Middle School, Roxbury]

3757. Gup, Ted. "What Makes This School Work?" *Time*, 21 December 1992. [Malcolm X Elementary School, Washington, D.C.]

3758. Haertel, Edward H. and others. *Comparing Public and Private Schools Vol. II: School Acheivment*. Philadelphia, PA: Taylor and Francis, 1987.

3759. Hallinan, Maureen T., and J. Oakes. "[An Exchange on Tracking]." *Sociology of Education* 67 (April 1994): 79-91.

3760. Halvorsen, Kate. "Notes on the Realization of the Human Right to Education." *Human Rights Quarterly* 12 (August 1990): 341-364.

3761. Hamm, Roger. "School's Free If You Can Pay." *Cleveland Plain Dealer*, 10 April 1991. [Charging of fees in public schools in the state of Ohio]

3762. Hanchett, Thomas W. "The Rosenwald Schools and Black Education in North Carolina." *North Carolina Historical Review* 65 (October 1988): 387-444.

3763. Hancock, Lynell. "The Chancellor Express." *Village Voice*, 3 July 1990. [Joseph Fernandez, chancellor of New York City public schools]

3764. _____. "The Chiseler of School District 27." *Village Voice*, 31 October 1989. [James Conroy Sullivan, leader of local school board in Queens, N.Y.]

3765. Hancock, Lynell. "Death to the Reading Score." *Village Voice*, 25 July 1989. [Reading tests taken in New York City public schools, Spring 1989]

3766. _____. "Joltin' Joe Fernandez." *Village Voice*, 24 October 1989. [Superindentent of Miami, Florida public schools]

3767. _____. "Ujamaa Means Controversy." *Village Voice*, 6 November 1990. [A proposed all black school for young men in New york City]

3768. _____. "Whose America Is This, Anyway?" *Village Voice*, 24 April 1990. [Ethnic unrepresentativeness of public school textbooks in New York state]

3769. _____. "Young, Gifted and (Mostly) White." *Village Voice*, 6 October 1987. [P.S. 9, Upper West Side]

3770. Hanley, Robert. "Tortuous Course to Equal Schools." *New York Times*, 17 September 1994. [New Jersey and elsewhere]

3771. Hanushek, Eric A. and others. *Making Schools Work: Improving Performance and Controlling Costs*. Brookings Institution, 1994.

3772. Harp, Lonnie. "Texas Governor Preaches the Gospel of Finance Equity." *Education Week*, 28 April 1993. [School finance in Texas]

3773. Harris, Carl V. "Stability and Change in Discrimination Against Black Public Schools: Birmingham, Alabama, 1871 - 1931." *Journal of Southern History* 51 (1985): 375-416.

3774. Harris, Hamil R. "Will Magnets Have Pull Here?" *Washington Post*, 1 April 1993. [Magnet schools in Washington, D.C.]

3775. Hart, Jordana. "Math Skills Don't Add Up in City." *Boston Globe*, 12 June 1994. [Few black and Hispanic students taking calculus in Boston high schools]

3776. _____. "Most Expelled Students Get No Schooling." *Boston Globe*, 14 June 1994. [Massachusetts]

3777. Hart, Thomas, and Linda Lumsden. "Confronting Racism in the Schools." *Oregon School Study Council Bulletin* 32 (1989).

3778. Harter, Kevin, and Patricia A. Jones. "School Discards Flags Some Viewed as Racist." *Cleveland Plain Dealer*, 27 March 1993. {Willoughby South High School, Willoughby, Ohio]

3779. Harvey, William B. and others. "Between a Rock and a Hard Place: Drugs and Schools in African American Communities." *Urban League Review* 13 (Summer 1989 - Winter 1989 - 1990): 113-128.

3780. Hauser, Robert M., and D. K. Anderson. "Post-High-School Plans and Aspirations of Black and White High School Seniors, 1976 - 1986." *Sociology of Education* 64 (October 1991): 263-277.

3781. Haw, K. F. "Interactions of Gender and Race: A Problem for Teachers: A Review of the Emerging Literature." *Educational Research* 33 (March 1991): 12-21.

3782. Hax, Elizabeth R. and others. "We're All Racist Now." *New York Times Magazine*, 19 June 1994. [Seven letters on Proviso West High School, Illinois, suburb of Chicago]

3783. Hayes, Constance L. "A Neighborhood School Is Out of Bounds for Some." *New York Times*, 16 June 1990. [P.S. 234, Greenwich and Chamber Streets, TriBeCa, Manhattan]

3784. Hayes, Floyd W. III. "Race, Urban Politics, and Educational Policy-making in Washington, D.C.: A Community's Struggle for Quality Education." *Urban Education* 25 (October 1990): 237-257.

3785. Hays, Kristen L. "Topeka Comes Full Circle." *Modern Maturity* 37 (April - May 1994): 34.

3786. Heller, Kirley A. and others, eds. *Placing Children in Special Education*. Washington, DC: National Academy Press, 1982.

3787. Hemmings, Annette B. *Making Model Students: How High- Acheiving Black Students Were Prepared for College in Two Urban High Schools.* Ph.D. diss., University of Wisconsin, 1992. UMO # 9223879.

3788. Hendrick, Irving G. "Early Schooling for Children of Migrant Farmworkers in California: The 1920's." *Aztlan* 8 (1977): 11-26.

3789. Hening, Jeffrey R. *Rethinking School Choice. Limits of the Market Metaphor.* Princeton, NJ: Princeton University Press, 1993.

3790. Henry, Annie B. *Philanthropic Foundations and Their Impact on Public Education for Blacks in Florida, 1920 - 1947.* Ph.D. diss., Florida State University, 1988. UMO # 8825739.

3791. Hentoff, Nat. "Black Self-Segregation in the Schools." *Village Voice*, October 1993.

3792. _____. "Can Apartheid Ever Be Desirable?" *Village Voice*, 14 June 1994. [Racism and segregation in the schools]

3793. Herbert, Bob. "The Prom And the Principal." *New York Times*, 16 March 1994. [Outlawing of a prom in Randolph County High School, Wedowee, Alabama for fear of interracial dancing]

3794. Herbert, Gayle. "Does Racism Still Exist?" *Philadelphia New Observer*, 18 October 1989. [Girard College]

3795. Hernandez, Peggy. "Beating the odds." *Boston Globe*, 11 June 1990. [Hispanic family support for school success]

3796. Hess, G. Alfred Jr. *The Reallocation of Funds Under the Chicago School Reform Act.* Chicago, IL: Chicago Panel on Public School Policy and Finance, 4 April 1991.

3797. _____. "Taking the Pulse of School Reform [in Chicago]." *Chicago Tribune*, 27 April 1992.

3798. Hess, G. Alfred Jr., and James L. Greer. *Bending the Twig: The Elementary Years and Dropout Rates in the Chicago Public Schools.* Chicago, IL: Chicago Panel on Public School Policy and Finance, 1987.

3799. Hess, G. Alfred Jr., and Diana Lauber. *Dropouts from the Chicago Public Schools.* Chicago, IL: Chicago Panel on Public School Policy and Finance, 1985.

3800. Hevies, Gregory N. "Redefining Segregation in a Connecticut Court." *In These Times*, 3 October 1990.

3801. Hicks, Desiree F. "Ability 'Tracks' in Schools Spur Controversy." *Cleveland Plain Dealer*, 29 May 1994. [Cleveland Heights, Ohio]

3802. Hill, Retha. "Pitching P. G. to Minority Teachers." *Washington Post*, 4 May 1994. [Prince George's County, MD, "a national leader in recruiting black males" as teachers]

3803. Hispanic Policy Development Project. *Make Something Happen.* Washington, DC: National Commission of Secondary Schooling for Hispanics, 1984.

3804. *Hispanic Student Dropout Problem in Colorado.* Washington, DC: U.S. Commission on Civil Rights, 1987.

3805. "History and Voice in African-American Pedagogy." *Journal of Education* 172 (1990): entire issue.

3806. Holison, Larry. "Ranchers Take 'Last Stand' in Chicano School Strike." *Guardian (NYC)*, 12 February 1992. [Dinuba, CA]

3807. Holyan, Regina. *Indian Education vs. Indian Schooling: An Educational Critique.* Ph.D. diss., Stanford University, 1993. UMO # 9317776.

3808. Horst, Samuel L. *Education for Manhood: The Education of Blacks in Virginia during the Civil War.* Lanham, MD: University Press of America, 1987.

3809. Houppert, Karen. "Separatist But Equal?" *Village Voice*, 19 May 1992. [Girls and boys, black schools in Detroit]

3810. Hubler, Shaun. "School Scores Can Make or Break a Neighborhood." *Los Angeles Times*, 14 March 1994. [Academic- achievement scores and house prices in California]

3811. Hull, Jon D. "Do Teachers Punish According to Race?" *Time*, 4 April 1994. [Cincinnati, Ohio]

3812. Hyde, Arthur, and Donald R. Moore. *Education Equity and Parent and Citizen Involvement in School District Decisions*. Washington, DC: National Institute of Education, 1984. Grant No. 79-0173.

3813. "In a Minority District in Maryland, A Magnet School that Really Draws." *New York Times*, 3 March 1993. [Enriched mathematics, science, and computer program at Montgomery Blair High School, Silver Spring, MD]

3814. *In-School Segregation in North Carolina Public Schools*. Washington, D.C.: U.S. Commission on Civil Rights, 1991.

3815. "Investing in Our Children's Future: School Finance Reform in the '90s." *Harvard Journal of Legislation* 28 (Summer 1991): 293-568. [14 articles]

3816. Irvine, Jacqueline J. *Black Students and School Failure. Policies, Practices, and Prescriptions*. Westport, CT: Greenwood Press, 1990.

3817. Iverson, Katherine. "Civilization and Assimilation in the Colonized Schooling in Native America." in *Education and Colonialism*, pp. 149-180. eds. Philip G. Altbach, and Gail P. Kelly. New York, NY: Longman, 1978.

3818. Jackson, G., and C. Cosca. "The Inequality of Educational Opportunity in the Southwest: An Observational Study of Ethnically Mixed Classrooms." *American Educational Research Journal* 11 (1974): 219-229.

3819. Jackson, Jimmie. "Teachers' Union Chief Looks at Herself and the System." *Washington Post*, 11 March 1993. [Dorothy Gilliam interviews the President of Washington, D.C. teachers union]

3820. Jaffe, Mark, and Kenneth Kersch. "Guaranteeing a State Right to a Quality Education: The Judicial-Political Dialogue in New Jersey." *Journal of Law and Education* 20 (Summer 1991): 271- 300.

3821. Jaynes, Gerald D., and Robin M. Williams Jr., eds. "The Schooling of Black Americans." in *A Common Destiny. Blacks and American Society*, pp. 329-389. Washington, DC: National Academy Press, 1989.

3822. Jetter, Alexis. "Mississippi Learning." *New York Times Magazine*, 21 February 1993. [Bob Moses]

3823. John, Gus. "Anti-racist Education in White Areas: A Movement in Search of a Focus." *Sage Race Relations Abstracts* 13 (February 1988): 17-24.

3824. Johnson, Dirk. "Milwaukee Creating 2 Schools Just for Black Boys." *New York Times*, 30 September 1990.

3825. Johnson, Sylvia T. *Extra-School Factors in Achievement, Attainment, and Aspirations Among Junior and Senior High School- Aged Black Youth*. Paper prepared for the Committee on the Status of Black Americans, National Research Council, 1987.

3826. Jones, Charisse. "Amid Doubts, Schools Tackle Upgrade of Math and Science." *New York Times*, 30 August 1994. [Includes ethnic curriculum data on New York City public schools]

3827. _____. "Test Scores Show Gaps By Ethnicity." *New York Times*, 8 July 1994. [New York City public schools]

3828. Jones, Lyle. *Trends in School Achievement of Black Children*. Chapel Hill, NC: Department of Psychology, University of North Carolina, 1987.

3829. Jones, M. "Education and Racism." *Journal of Philosophy of Education* 22 (1988).

3830. Jones, Patricia A. "Educating Black Males - Several Solutions, But No Solution." *Crisis* 98 (October 1991): 12-18.

3831. Jones, Rachel L. "Audubon Fights to Save Indian Studies Program." *Chicago Reporter* 20 (July - August 1991): 1-12. [American Indian Resource Center, John J. Audubon Elementary School, Chicago, IL]

3832. Jones-Wilson, Faustine C. "Equity in Education:Low Priority in the School Reform Movement." *Urban Review* 18 (1986): 31-39.

3833. _____. "Race, Realities, and American Education: Two Sides of the Coin." *Journal of Negro Education* 59 (Spring 1990).

3834. Jordan, Mary. "For-Profit Schools Plan Math Is Faulty, Critics Say." *Washington Post*, 8 February 1993. [Christopher Whittle's Edison project]

3835. _____. "In Cities Like Atlanta, Whites Are Passing on Public Schools." *Washington Post*, 24 May 1993.

3836. Jordan, Mary, and Tracy Thompson. "Across U.S. Schools Are Falling Apart." *Washington Post*, 22 November 1993.

3837. Jordan, William Chester. "Segregation Won't Work." *New York Times*, 21 October 1990. [Critique of Milwaukee proposal for two schools to be attended only by black male students]

3838. Joyner, Edward T. *The Comer Model: School Improvement for Students at Risk.* Ph.D. diss., University of Bridgeport, 1990. UMO # 9119318.

3839. Judson, George. "19th Century School Raises 20th Century Question About Burden of Racial Balance." *New York Times*, 21 November 1991. [Maloney School, Waterbury, CT]

3840. _____. "School Segregation Case Too Knotty, Lawyers Say." *New York Times*, 22 November 1991. [Sheff v. O'Neill, concerning Hartford, CT and its suburbs]

3841. Kallen, Horace M. "Black Power, White Power, and Education." in *Toward a Humanistic Science of Politics*, pp. 213- 226. eds. Dalmas H. Nelson, and Richard L. Sklar. Ranham, MD: University Press of America, 1983.

3842. Kantrowitz, Barbara, and Susan Miller. "Still Separate After 20 Years. Segregated Reunions for an Integrated Class." *Newsweek*, 7 September 1992. [Class of 1972, Captain Shreve High School, Shreveport, LA]

3843. Karp, Stan. "Money, Schools, and Justice." *Z Magazine* 5 (October 1992): 31-35.

3844. Karweit, Nancy. *Elementary Education and Black Americans: Raising the Odds.* Washington, DC: Paper prepared for the Committee on the Status of Black Americans, National Research Council, 1986.

3845. Katz, Michael B. "Chicago School Reform as History." *Teachers College Record* 94 (Autumn 1992): 56-72.

3846. Kaufman, P., and M. J. Frase. *Dropout Rates in the United States: 1989.* Washington, DC: U.S. Department of Education, 1990.

3847. Kaye, Stan. "Is All Black and All Male All Right?" *Z Magazine* 4 (June 1991): 87-91. [Schools for Black males]

3848. Kearney, C. Philip, and Li-Ju Chen. "Race and Equality of Opportunity: A School Finance Perspective." *Journal of Education Finance* 15 (Winter 1990).

3849. Kelmendi, John P. *The Community, Change and the Office of Civil Rights: A Case Study of the Process for Equality of Access for Limited English Proficient School Children and Youth in Detroit Public Schools.* 2 vols. Ph.D. diss., Wayne State University, 1990. UMO # 9115212.

3850. Kershaw, T. "The Effects of Educational Tracking on the Social Mobility of African Americans." *Journal of Black Studies* 23 (September 1992): 152-169.

3851. Kessen, Thomas P. *Segregation in Cincinnati Public Education: The Nineteenth - Century Black Experience.* Ph.D. diss., University of Cincinnati, 1973. UMO # 7329456.

3852. Kindleberger, Richard. "Schools, Labor in Dispute over Jobs." *Boston Globe*, 23 September 1989. [Boston public schools bar union-sponsored apprentice training program because of failure to enroll more minority and women apprentices]

3853. King, J. E. "Dysconscious Racism: Ideology, Identity, and the Miseducation of Teachers." *Journal of Negro Education* 60 (Spring 1991): 133-146.

3854. Kingston, Paul W., and L. S. Lewis eds. *The High Status Track: Studies of Elite Schools and Stratification.* Albany, NY: State University of New York Press, 1989.

3855. Kirp, David L. "Textbooks and Tribalism in California." *Public Interest* 104 (Summer 1991): 20-36.

3856. _____. "What School Choice Really Means." *Atlantic* 270 (November 1992): 119-132. [District Four, East Harlem]

3857. Kirsch, Irwin S., and Ann Jungeblut. *Literacy: Profiles of America's Young Adults*. Princeton, NJ: National Assessment of Educational Progress, Educational Testing Service, September 1986.

3858. Kitchen, Daniel J. *Ability Grouping and Dropping Out*. Ph.D. diss., Claremont Graduate School, 1990. UMO # 9032583.

3859. Kleg, Milton and others. "Elementary Student Attitudes and Perceptions of Select Racial, Religious, and Ethnic Groups." *Journal of Social Studies Research* 16-17 (1993): 31-36.

3860. Kleg, Milton, and Robert Karabinus. "Middle School Teachers' Ethnic and Racial Attitudes." *CSERV Bulletin* 3 (1994): 44-53. [Center for the Study of Ethnic and Racial Violence]

3861. Klompmaker, John. *The American Indian and American History Textbooks: In Pursuit of a Just and Fair Presentation*. Master's thesis, Calvin College, 1988.

3862. Knapp, Michael S., and Patrick M. Shields eds. *Better Schooling for the Children of Poverty: Alternatives to Conventional Wisdom - Volume II : Commissional Papers and Literature Review*. Washington, DC: Office of Planning, Budget, and Evaluation, U.S. Department of Education, January 1990.

3863. Koretz, Daniel. "Differences in Achievement Trends Among Black, Hispanic, and Nonminority Students." in *Trends in Educational Achievement*, pp. 149-165. Washington, DC: Congressional Budget, 1986.

3864. Koski, William S. "Equity in Public Education : School - finance Reform in Michigan." *University of Michigan Journal of Law Reform* 26 (Fall 1992): 195-243.

3865. Kousser, J. Morgan. "Making Separate Equal: Integration of Black and White School Funds in Kentucky." *Journal of Interdisciplinary History* 11 (Winter 1980): 399-428.

3866. Kozol, Jonathan. "Romance of the Ghetto School." *Nation*, 23 May 1994.

3867. _____. *Savage Inequalities: Children in American Schools*. New York, NY: Crown, 1991.

3868. _____. "Widening the Gap." *Boston Globe*, 3 November 1991. [Per- student expenditures in Massachusetts between poor and rich]

3869. Kramer, Betty Jo. "Education and American Indians: The Experience of the Ute Indian Tribe." in *Minority Status and Schooling*, pp. 287-307. eds. Margaret A. Gibson, and John U. Ogbu.*: Garland, 1991.

3870. KRS-One. "A Survival Curriculum for Inner-City Kids." *New York Times*, 9 September 1989.

3871. Krug, Mark. "'Safe' Textbooks and Citizenship Education." *School Review* 68 (1960).

3872. Kunjufu, Jawanza. "Detroit's Male Academics: What the Real Issue Is." *Education Week*, 20 November 1991. [See above, Larry Cuban]

3873. Kyle, Charles L., and Edward R. Kantowicz. *Kids First/ Primero Los Ninos: Chicago School Reform in the 1980's*. Institute for Public Affairs, Sangamon State University, 1992.

3874. La France, Joan L. *Redefining American Indian Education: Evaluation Issues in Tribally Controlled Schools*. Ph.D. diss., Harvard University, 1990. UMO # 9111441.

3875. Lachman, Seymour P., and Barry A. Kosmin. "Black Catholics Get Ahead." *New York Times*, 14 September 1991. [Blacks in parochial schools]

3876. Ladson-Billings G. "Like Lightning in a Bottle: Attempting to Capture the Pedagogical Excellence of Successful Teachers of Black Students." *Qualitative Studies in Education* 3 (1990): 335-344.

3877. Lait, Matt. "Few Minority Teachers in O.C., Educators Say." *Los Angeles Times*, 18 September 1993. [Orange County, CA]

3878. Lamon, Lester C. "Black Public Education in the South 1861- 1920: By Whom, For Whom and Under Whose Control." *Journal of Thought* 18 (Fall 1983): 76-90.

3879. Lamotey, Kofi, ed. *Going to School: The African-American Experience*. Albany, NY: State University Press of New York, 1990.

3880. Lane, Mary Beth. "Too Rich and Too Poor - Ohio School Dilemma." *Cleveland Plain Dealer*, 3 July 1994. [Differences in per-pupil spending]

3881. Lawton, Millicent. "Two Schools Aimed for Black Males Set in Milwaukee." *Education Week*, 10 October 1990.

3882. Leake, D. O., and B. L. Leake. "Islands of Hope: Milwaukee's African American Immersion Schools." *Journal of Nego Education* 61 (Winter 1992): 24-29.

3883. Lee, Boon T. *Education for Assimilation, Integration or Liberation? A Critical Analysis of Black Educational Thought in the Late Sixties and Early Seventies*. Ph.D. diss., University of North Carolina at Greensboro, 1991. UMO # 9204448.

3884. Lee, John H. "Scuffle Draws Attention to School's Racial Tensions." *Los Angeles Times*, 21 June 1992. [Poway Unified School District, near San Diego]

3885. Lee, Mathelle K. *A History of Luther P. Jackson High School: A Report of a Case Study on the Development of a Black High School*. Ph.D. diss., Virginia Polytechnic and State University, 1993. UMO # 9323776.

3886. Lee, Valerie E., and Anthony Bryk. "Curriculum Tracking as Mediating the Social Distribution of High School Achievement." *Sociology of Education* 61 (1988): 78-94.

3887. Lee, Valerie E., and Ruth B. Ekstrom. "Student Access to Guidance Counseling in High School." *American Educational Research Journal* 24 (1987): 287-310.

3888. Leff, Lisa. "Black, Hispanic Students Show Gains in Maryland Testing." *Washington Post*, 3 June 1993.

3889. Leicester, U. "Racism, Responsibility and Education." *Journal of Philosophy of Education* 22 (1988).

3890. Lester, Suzanne S. *Indian Education: Evolution of Policy Determination*. Ph.D. diss., University of Oklahoma, 1989. UMO # 9003671.

3891. Levin, Henry M. "Market Approaches to Education: Vouchers and Social Choice." *Economics of Education Review* 11 (December 1992).

3892. Lewis, Dan A. "School Decentralization in Large American Cities: Myrdal Resolved." *Sociological Abstracts* Supplement 166 (August 1991) 91S24827/SSSp/1991/3021.

3893. Lewis, Diane E. "The School With a UN Flavor." *Boston Globe*, 21 January 1990. [Cambridge Rindge and Latin High School, Cambridge, MA]

3894. Lewis, James H., and D. Garth Taylor. *Racial Equity and Local School Council Elections*. Chicago, IL: Chicago Urban League, 1990. [Chicago public schools]

3895. _____. "Racial, Ethnic Groups Fairly Represented." *Catalyst* 1 (May 1990): 18-19. [Local school councils in Chicago public schools]

3896. Lewis, Neil A. "Students Poor in Math Pose Job Problem." *New York Times*, 25 July 1989. [New York City public schools, grades 2 to 8]

3897. Lichtenstein. "Children, the Schools, and the Right to Know: Some Thoughts at the Schoolhouse Gate." *University of South Florida Law Review* 19 (1985).

3898. Lieberman, Myron. *Privatization and Educational Choice*. New York, NY: St. Martin's Press, 1989.

3899. Lightfoot, Sara Lawrence, and Michael Fultz. *Visions of a Better Way. A Black Appraisal of Public Schooling*. Washington, DC: Joint Center for Political Studies Press, 1989.

3900. Lindsay, Drew. "No Racial Bias Found in Ohio's School Exit Test." *Education Week*, 12 October 1994.

3901. Link, C. R., and J. G. Mulligan. "'Classmates' Effects on Black Student Achievement in Public School Classrooms." *Economics of Education* 10 (1991).

3902. Linn, Robert L., and Stephen B. Dunbar. "The Nation's Report Card Goes Home: Good News and Bad About Trends in Achievement." *Phi Delta Kappan* 72 (October 1990): 127-133.

3903. Littlefield, Alice. "The B.I.A. Boarding School: Theories of Resistance and Social Reproduction." *Humanity and Society* 13 (1989): 428-441. [Mount Pleasant Indian Boarding School, Michigan, 1893-1933]

3904. Lobbia, J. A. "Scratch Off." *Village Voice*, 3 December 1991. [Discriminatory school financing through the N.Y. State lottery]

3905. *Locked In / Locked Out: Tracking and Placement Practices in Boston Public Schools.* Boston, MA: Massachusetts Advocacy Center, 1990.

3906. Lomawaima, K. Tsianina. *The Called It Prairie Light: The Story of Chilocco Indian School.* University of Nebraska Press, 1994.

3907. Lookadoo, Linda K. *Analysis of the Existing Legal Basis for Educating Undocumented Alien Children.* Ph.D. diss., Texas Tech University, 1988. [Texas]. UMO # 8900950.

3908. Los Angeles County Human Relations Commission. *Intergroup Conflict in Los Angeles County Schools. Report on a Survey of Hate Crime.* October 1989.

3909. *Lost in the Labyrinth: New York City High School Admissions.* New York, NY: Educational Priorities Panel, 1985.

3910. Lowe, Robert E. "Choosing Inequality in the Schools." *Monthly Review* 44 (May 1992): 21-34.

3911. _____. *Ravenwood High School and the Struggle for Racial Justice in the Sequoia Union High School District.* Ph.D. diss., Stanford University, 1989. UMO # 9011537.

3912. Loya, Anamaria C. "Chicanos, Law, and Educational Reform." *La Raza Law Journal* 3 (Spring 1990): 28-50.

3913. Lucas, Tamara and others. "Promoting the Success of Latino Language- Minority Students: An Exploratory Study of Six High Schools." *Harvard Educational Review* 60 (August 1990): 315-340.

3914. Maat, Anasa. *An Analysis of Dropout Behavior in High Schools in the United States.* Ph.D. diss., Rutgers University, 1990. UMO # 9124968.

3915. Mabee, Carleton. "Control by Blacks Over Schools in New York State, 1830 - 1930." *Phylon* 40 (1979): 29-40.

3916. Mabry, Marcus. "The Ghetto Preppies." *Newsweek*, 4 November 1991.

3917. Macenczak, Kimberly P. *Educators to the Cherokees at New Echota, Georgia: A Study in Assimilation.* Ph.D. diss., Georgia State University, 1991. UMO # 9131872.

3918. Macias, Reynaldo F. *Parto de palabra: Biliteracy and Illiteracy Amongst Chicanos in the U.S.* Los Angeles, CA: Center for Multicultural Research, University of Southern California, October 1988.

3919. Madenwald, Abbie M. *Artic Schoolteacher: Kubulak, Alaska, 1931 - 1933.* University of Oklahoma Press, 1993. [Bristol Bay region]

3920. Mahoney, Brenna B. "Children at Risk: The Inequality of Urban Education." *New York Law School Journal of Human Rights* 9 (Fall 1991): 161-215.

3921. Marcus, Grania, and others. "Black and White Students' Perceptions of Teacher Treatment." *Journal of Educational Research* 84 (July - August 1991): 363-367.

3922. Margis-Noguera, Taylor. "The Swastika Effect." *Long Beach Press Telegram*, 16 December 1992. [Los Alamitos High School, CA]

3923. Margo, Robert A. "Accounting for Racial Differences in School Attendance in the American South, 1900: The Role of Separate- But- Equal." *Review of Economics and Statistics* 69 (November 1987).

3924. _____. *Race and Schooling in the South, 1880 - 1950. An Economic History*. Chicago, IL: University of Chicago Press, 1991.

3925. _____. "Segregated Schools and the Mobility Hypothesis: A Model of Local Government Discrimination." *Quarterly Journal of Economics* 106 (February 1991): 61-74.

3926. Margolis, Edwin, and Stanley Moses. *The Elusive Quest: The Struggle for Equality of Educational Opportunity*. Apex Press, 1992. [Rich and poor school districts in N.Y. state]

3927. Marisnerus, Laura. "Should Teaching Be Derailed?" *New York Times Education Life*, 1 November 1992. [see graph, "Ability Grouping by Race and Ethnicity... and by Socioeconomics"]

3928. Markowitz, Ruth J. *My Daughter, the Teacher: Second- generation Jewish Teachers in the New York City Public School System, 1920 - 1940*. Ph.D. diss., State University of New York at Stony Brook, 1990. UMO # 9106820.

3929. _____. *My Daughter, the Teacher: Jewish Teachers in the New York City Schools*. New York, NY: Rutgers University Press, 1993.

3930. Marriott, Michel. "The Home- Nigger Revolution." *Village Voice*, 20 August 1991. [the black prep-schooler]

3931. _____. "A New Road to Learning: Teaching the Whole Child." *New York Times*, 13 June 1990. [James P. Comer and the New Haven, CT schools]

3932. _____. "Value of G.E.D. Diplomas to High School Dropouts Questioned." *New York Times*, 15 June 1993.

3933. Marsh, Frances K. "The Case for Imposing a Legal Duty on Educators in Educational Malpractice Actions: Improving Minority Education." *Thurgood Marshall Law Review* 16 (Spring 1991): 295- 309.

3934. Martinez, Carlos. "Agitators Blocking Agricultural School's Expansion Draws Fire from Parents As City Hall Steps In." *Substance* (April - May 1993): 6-7. [Anti-black and Hispanic students in Chicago school]

3935. Marura, William A. *Black Educational Achievement and the Educational Underclass*. Ph.D. diss., University of Colorado, 1990. UMO # 9122626.

3936. Mascia, Patrick E. "Open Enrollment: Social Darwinism at Work." *Creighton Law Review* 23 (Winter 1990): 441-465.

3937. Massachusetts Advocacy Center. *Locked In/ Locked Out: Tracking and Placement Practices in Boston Public Schools*. Boston, MA: Massachusetts Advocacy Center, 1990.

3938. _____. *The Way Out: Student Exclusion Practices in Boston Middle School*. Boston, MA: Massachusetts Advocacy Center, 1986.

3939. Mateer, G. Dirk. *A Logit Analysis of the High School Dropout Problem in Florida*. Ph.D. diss., Florida State University, 1991. UMO # 9130955.

3940. Mathis, William J. *Political Socialization in a Mexican American High School*. Ph.D. diss., University of Texas, 1973.

3941. Matute-Bianchi, Maria E. "Situational Ethnicity and Patterns of School Performance among Immigrant and Nonimmigrant Mexican - Descent Students." in *Minority Status and Schooling*, pp. 205-247. eds. Margaret A. Gibson, and John U. Ogbu : Garland, 1991.

3942. Maxwell, N. L. "The Effect on Black - White Wage Differences of Differences in the Quantity and Quality of Education." *Industrial and Labor Relations Review* 47 (January 1994).

3943. McBeth, Sally J. *Ethnic Identity and the Boarding School Experience of West Central Oklahoma American Indians*. Washington, D.C.: University Press of America, 1983.

3944. McBride, Judith Ann. *Public School Performances of Disadvantaged Children with Extensive Preschool Experience: A Study of the Milwaukee Project Children Through High School*. Ph.D. diss., University of Wisconsin, 1989. UMO # 9003103.

3945. McCarthy, Cameron R. *Race and Curriculum*. Ph.D. diss., University of Wisconsin, 1988. UMO # 8822259.

3946. _____. *Race and Curriculum: Social Inequality and the Theories and Politics of Difference in Contemporary Research on Schooling*. Philadelphia, PA: Falmer, 1990.

3947. McCarthy, Peggy. "Connecticut City Vetoes Breakfast at Schools." *Boston Globe*, 9 February 1992. [Meriden]

3948. McCaul, E. J. and others. "Consequences of Dropping Out of School: Findings from High School and Beyond." *Journal of Educational Research* 85 (March - April 1992): 198-207.

3949. McCaul, Robert L. *The Black Struggle for Public Schooling in Nineteenth-Century Illinois*. Carbondale, IL: Southern Illinois University, 1987.

3950. McClure, Phyllis. "The School Choice Issue." *Trotter Institute Review* 5 (Winter/Spring 1991): 11-12.

3951. McCluskey, Audrey T. "The Historical Context of the Single- Sex Schooling Debate among African Americans." *Western Journal of Black Studies* 17 (Winter 1993): 193-201.

3952. _____. *Mary McLeod Bethune and the Education of Black Girls in the South, 1904 - 1923*. Ph.D. diss., Indiana University, 1991. UMO # 9205952.

3953. McCombs, Regina C., and Judith Gay. "Effects of Race, Class and IQ Information on Judgments of Grade School Teachers." *Journal of Social Psychology* 128 (1988): 647-652.

3954. McCormick, R. L. *Evolution of Indian Education*. Hayward, WI: 1901.

3955. McDonald, Dennis. "A Special Report on the Education of Native Americans. 'Stuck in the Horizon'." *Education Week*, 2 August 1989. (16 page supplement)

3956. McGowan, Sharon S. "Chicago Public Schools Flunk Black Students at Higher Rate." *Chicago Reporter* 20 (October 1991): 1, 6-9.

3957. McGrory, Mary. "From Dunbar to Despair." *Washington Post*, 30 January 1994. [Dunbar High School, Washington, D.C.]

3958. McKay, R. H. and others. *The Impact of Head Start on Children, Families, and Communities*. Washington, D.C.: Department of Health and Human Services, 1985.

3959. McKee, Nancy P. "Learning and Earning: Education and Well- being in a Texas Border Barrio." *Urban Education* 24 (1989): 308- 322. [Laredo]

3960. McLarin, Kimberly J. "A 1960s Throwback Leads the Challenge to the Financing of Public Schools in New Jersey." *New York Times*, 22 July 1994. [Marilyn Morheuser]

3961. _____. "Jersey City Schools Audit Complicates State Control." *New York Times*, 10 July 1994.

3962. _____. "New Jersey Prepares a Takeover of Newark's Desperate Schools." *New York Times*, 23 July 1994.

3963. McNeil, Teresa B. "St. Anthony's Indian School in San Diego, 1886 - 1907." *Journal of San Diego History* 34 (Summer 1988): 187-200.

3964. Means, Harrison J. *Analysis of the District's "Reading Parity" Study 1987 - 1988, Dated February 1989*. Cleveland, OH: Office on School Monitoring and Community Relations, July 1989.

3965. Medina, M. "Hispanic Apartheid in American Public Education." *Educational Administration Quarterly* 24 (August 1988): 336-349.

3966. Mehan, H. "Understanding Inequality in Schools: The Contribution of Interpretive Studies." *Sociology of Education* 65 (January 1992): 1-20.

3967. Meier, August, ed. *Papers of the NAACP. Part 3: The Campaign for Educational Equality, 1913 - 1950*. Frederick, MD: University Publications of America, 1989. 41 microfilm reels

3968. Meier, Deborah W. "The Little Schools That Could." *Nation*, 23 September 1991. [School reform through small, innovative schools]

3969. _____. "Obsession With Test Scores Distorts Education." *New York Times*, 22 August 1989. [Letter]

3970. Meier, Kenneth J. and others. "The Politics of Bureaucratic Discretion: Educational Access as an Urban Service." *American Journal of Political Science* 35 (1991): 155-177.

3971. _____. *Race, Class, and Education: The Politics of Second-Generation Discrimination.* Madison, WI: University of Wisconsin Press, 1990.

3972. Meier, Kenneth J., and Joseph Stewart, Jr. "Cooperation and Conflict in Multiracial School Districts." *Journal of Politics* 53 (November 1991): 1123-1133.

3973. Meier, Kenneth J., and Joseph Stewart Jr. *The Politics of Hispanic Education. Un paso pa'lante y dos patras.* Albany, NY: State University of New York Press, 1991. [The politics of "second generation discrimination" against Hispanic minorities]

3974. Menacker, Julius. "Equal Educational Opportunity: Is It an Issue of Race or Socioeconomic Status?" *Urban Education* 25 (October 1990): 317-325. [Chicago]

3975. Menchaea, Martha, and Richard R. Valencia. "Anglo-Saxon ideologies in the 1920s - 1930s: Their Impact on the Segregation of Mexican Students in California." *Anthropology and Education Quarterly* 21 (September 1990): 222-249. [Santa Paula, CA]

3976. Merl, Jean. "One Giant Leap for Education?" *Los Angeles Times*, 8 March 1993. [The Edison Project, a for-profit plan of schools organized by Christopher Whittle]

3977. _____. "Troubled Schools Able to Help Pupils Realize Dreams." *Los Angeles Times*, 15 January 1992. [Ten elementary schools in Black and Mexican American areas of Los Angeles]

3978. Merl, Joan. "Students' Scores on Placement Exams Soar." *Los Angeles Times*, 15 October 1992. [Advanced placement exams in Los Angeles County school districts]

3979. "Mexican Children in County Have No School Facilities." *Greenville Delta Democratic Times*, 6 September 1945. [Mississippi]

3980. Meyer, Josh. "Suit Changes Race Bias at Prep School." *Los Angeles Times*, 7 July 1992. [Stratford Preparatory School and the California Preparatory School in Van Nuys, CA]

3981. Michel, G. J. "School Politics and Conflict in Racially Isolated Schools." *Journal of Negro Education* 60 (Autumn 1991): 502-511.

3982. Mikell, Edna F. *The Influence of Community Interest Groups on School Board Decision-making in a Predominantly Minority Southern California Urban Community.* Ph.D. diss., University of Southern California, 1989.

3983. Miller, Julie A. "Threat To Halt Funds Latest Chapter in Racially Charged Drama in California." *Education Week*, 17 February 1993. [Centinela Valley (California) Union High School District]

3984. Miller, S. M. and others. *Too Late to Patch: Reconsidering Second-Chance Opportunities for Hispanic and Other Dropouts.* Washington, DC: Hispanic Policy Development Project, 1988.

3985. Milloy, Courtland. "No Respect, No Discipline, No Learning." *Washington Post*, 20 April 1994. [Career day at Evans Junior High School in Washington, D.C.]

3986. Mincberg, Elliot M. and others. "The Problems of Segregation and Inequality of Educational Opportunity." in *One Nation Indivisible: The Civil Rights Challenge of the 1990s*, Chapter 7. Washington, DC: Citizens' Commission on Civil Rights, 1988.

3987. Minkowitz, Donna. "Wrong Side of the Rainbow." *Nation*, 28 June 1993. [Religious right in New York City school board elections]

3988. Minorini, Paul, and Jonathan Stein. "Placing School Lunch and Breakfast Programs Back On the Advocacy Menu." *Clearinghouse Review* 24 (April 1991): 1358-1361.

3989. Miranda, Leticia C., and Julie Teresa Quiroz. *The Decade of the Hispanic: An Economic Retrospective.* Washington, DC: National Council of La Raza, March 1990.

3990. Mirel, Jeffrey. *The Rise and Fall of an Urban School System. Detroit, 1907 - 1981.* University of Michigan Press, 1992.

3991. Mirel, Jeffrey, and David Angus. "High Standards for All." *American Educator* (Summer 1994).

3992. Mitchell, Emily. "Do the Poor Deserve Bad Schools?" *Time*, 14 October 1991.

3993. Mitgang, Lee. "School Choice, Carnegie, and Alum Rock." *Education Week*, 24 February 1993.

3994. Molnar, Alex. "Public Schools and the Ties that Bind." *In These Times*, 16 September 1992. [School choice]

3995. Moore, Donald R., and Suzanne Davenport. *School Choice: The New Improved Sorting Machine*. Chicago, IL: Designs for Change, May 1989. [Secondary schools in New York City, Philadelphia, Boston and Chicago]

3996. Moore, Donald R., and Sharon W. Soltman. *The Bottom Line. Chicago's Failing Schools and How to Save Them*. Chicago, IL: Designs for Change, January 1985. [High schools, 1980 - 1984]

3997. Morley, Jefferson. "Taking Public Schools Private." *Washington Post*, 13 March 1994. [District of Columbia schools]

3998. Morris, Robert C. "Educational Reconstruction." in *The Facts of Reconstruction: Essays in Honor of John Hope Franklin*, eds. Eric Anderson, and Alfred A. Moss Jr. : Louisiana State University Press, 1991.

3999. _____. "Freedmen's Education." *Black Women in America* I 462-469.

4000. Morris, William V. *Los Angeles Proprietary Business Schools and the Training of Disadvantaged and Underrepresented Students*. Ph.D. diss., University of California at Los Angeles, 1991. UMO # 9128822.

4001. Moses, Maryann I. I. *Universal Education for African- Americans in North Carolina: A Historical Survey of the Beginning Years Through 1927*. Ph.D. diss., North Carolina State University, 1989. UMO # 8918980.

4002. Mufson, Steven. "A Dream Deferred. Ocean Hill - Brownsville Remembers." *Village Voice*, 6 June 1989. [United Federation of Teachers vs. Black community, Fall 1968]

4003. Mullis, Ina V. S., and Lynn B. Jenkins. *The Reading Report Card, 1971 - 1988: Trends from the Nation's Report Card*. Princeton, NJ: National Assessment of Educational Progress and Educational Testing Service, 1990.

4004. Myers, Steven L. "Schools Find That Diversity Can Place Values in Conflict." *New York Times*, 6 October 1992. [P.S. 87, Queens]

4005. National Advisory Council on Indian Education. *Indian Education: Focus on Past, Present and Future, 13th Annual Report*. Washington, DC: National Advisory Council on Indian Education, 1987.

4006. National Commission on Migrant Education. *Invisible Children: A Portrait of Migrant Education in the United States*. Washington, DC: National Commission on Migrant Education, 1992.

4007. National Commission on Secondary Education for Hispanics. *Make Something Happen: Hispanics and Urban School Reform*. Washington, DC: Hispanic Policy Development Project, 1984.

4008. National Council of La Raza. *The Education of Hispanics: Status and Implications*. Washington, DC: 1987.

4009. Neely, Charlotte. "The Forced Acculturation of the Eastern Cherokees: Bureau of Indian Affairs Schools, 1892 - 1933." in *Political Organization of Native North Americans*, pp. 85-106. Washington, DC: University Press of America, 1981.

4010. Nelson, Sheila. *Catholic Elementary Schools in Chicago's Black Inner City: Mission and Organizational Effectiveness, 2 vols*. Ph.D. diss., Loyola University of Chicago, 1992. [1960 - 1985]. UMO # 9215273.

4011. Nielsen, Francois, and Roberto M. Fernandez. *Hispanic Students in American High Schools: Background Characteristics and Achievement*. Washington, DC: National Opinion Research Center, National Center for Education Statistics, 1981.

4012. Oakes, Jeannie. "Limiting Opportunity: Student Race and Curricular Differences in Secondary Vocational Education." *American Journal of Education* 91 (1983): 328-355.

4013. Oakes, Jeannie and others. *Multiplying Inequalities: The Effects of Race, Social Class, and Tracking in Opportunities to Learn Mathematics and Science*. Santa Monica, CA: Rand Publications Department, September 1990.

4014. O'Connell, Mary. *School Reform, Chicago Style*. Chicago, IL: Center for Neighborhood Technology, 1991.

4015. Odum, Howard W. "Negro Children in the Public Schools of Philadelphia." *Annals* 49 (1913): 186-208.

4016. "Off Track in Alexandria." *Washington Post*, 10 March 1993. [Racial politics in the form of classroom tracking in Alexandria, Virginia schools]

4017. Ogbu, John U. "Cultural Boundaries and Minority Youth Orientation Toward Work Preparation." in *Adolescence and Work: Influences of Social Structure, Labor Markets, and Culture*, eds. D. Stern, and D. Eichorn. Hillsdale, NJ: Lawrence Elbaum Institute, 1989.

4018. _____. "Cultural Diversity and School Experience." in *Literacy as Praxis: Culture, Language, and Pedagogy*, ed. Catherine E. Walsh. Norwood, NJ: Ablex, 1990.

4019. _____. "Diversity and Equality in Public Education: Community Forces and Minority School Adjustment and Performance." in *Policies for America's Public Schools: Teachers, Equity, and Indicators*, pp. 127-170. eds. R. Haskins, and D. MacRae. Norwood, NJ: Ablex, 1988.

4020. _____. "The Individual in Collective Adaptation: A Framework for Focusing on Academic Underperformance and Dropping Out Among Involuntary Minorities." in *Dropouts from School. Issues, Dilemma, and Solutions*, pp. 181-204. eds. Lois Weis and others. Albany, NY: State University of New York Press, 1989.

4021. _____. "Low School Performance as an Adaptation: The Case of Blacks in Stockton, California." in *Minority Status and Schooling*, pp. 249-285. eds. Margaret A. Gibson, and John U. Ogbu. : Garland, 1991.

4022. _____. "Minority Education in Comparative Perspective." *Journal of Negro Education* 59 (Winter 1990): 45-57.

4023. _____. "Minority Coping Responses and School Experience." *Journal of Psychohistory* 18 (1991): 433-456.

4024. _____. "Variability in Minority School Performanance: A Problem in Search of an Explanation." *Anthropology and Education Quarterly* 18 (1987): 312-334.

4025. Oguntoyinbo, Lekan. "Parents Vote Down Requiring Uniforms at Akron School." *Cleveland Plain Dealer*, 2 July 1994. [Racial and economic factors]

4026. Ola, Akinshiju C. "Why Create Single-race, Single-sex Schools?" *Guardian*, 20 February 1991.

4027. *On the Road to Success: Students at Independent Neighborhood Schools*. Washington, DC: Institute for Independent Education, October 1991.

4028. Ortiz, Flora Ida. "Hispanic-American Children's Experiences in Classrooms: A Comparison Between Hispanic and Non-Hispanic Children." in *Class, Race and Gender in American Education*, ed. Lois Weis. : State University of New York Press, 1988. [Unequal resources]

4029. Orum, Lori S. *The Education of Hispanics: Status and Implications*. Washington, DC: National Council of La Raza, August 1986.

4030. _____. *Hispanic Dropouts: Community Responses*. Washington, DC: National Council of La Raza, 1984.

4031. Pallas, Aaron M. *Extra - School Factors in the Achievement of Black Adolescents*. Washington, DC: 1986, [Paper prepared for the Committee on the Status of Black Americans, National Research Council]

4032. _____. *Black - White Differences in Adolescent Educational Outcomes*. Washington, DC: 1987. [Paper prepared for the Committee on the Status of Black Americans, National Research Council]

4033. Palmer, Leola. *The Evolution of Education for African- Americans in Pointe Coupee Parish (New Roads, Louisiana): 1889 - 1969.* Ph.D. diss., Fordham University, 1992. UMO # 9228107.

4034. Paquette, Jerry and others. "Minority Education Policy: Assumptions and Propositions." *Curriculum Inquiry* 19 (Winter 1989). [Dialogue]

4035. Paris, Phillip L. *The Mexican American Informal Policy and the Political Socialization of Brown Students: A Case Study in Ventura County.* Ph.D. diss., University of Southern California, 1973.

4036. Parker, Tony V. *A Comparison of the Chickasaw Cession School Districts and Those Districts Holding Sixteenth Section Lands.* Ph.D. diss., Mississippi State University, 1991. UMO # 9131221.

4037. Patthey-Chavez, G. Genevieve. "High School As an Arena for Cultural Conflict and Acculturation for Latino Angelenos." *Anthropology and Education Quarterly* 24 (March 1993): 33-60.

4038. Patton, J. M. "Assessment and Identification of African- American Learners with Gifts and Talents." *Exceptional Children* 59 (October - November 1992): 150-159.

4039. Pay, Elaine. "All-male Black Schools Put On Hold in Detroit." *Boston Globe*, 1 September 1991.
4040. Payne, Charles. "Urban Teachers and Dropout-Prone Students: The Uneasy Partners." in *Dropouts from School, Issues, Dilemmas, and Solutions*, pp. 113-128. eds. Lois Weis and others. Albany, NY: State University of New York Press, 1989.

4041. Payne, Les. "Measuring Segregated Schooling." *Cleveland Plain Dealer*, 4 August 1987. [A black journalist recalls personal educational costs of attending segregated schools]

4042. Peltzman, S. "The Political Economy of the Decline of American Public Education." *Journal of Law and Economics* 36, part 2 (April 1993). [see comment, same issue, by D. D. Friedman]

4043. Perkins, Linda M. "The History of Blacks in Teaching: Growth and Decline Within the Profession." in *American Teachers: Histories of a Profession at Work*, ed. Donald Warren. New York, NY: Macmillan, 1989.

4044. Perlmutter, Philip. "Ethnicity, Education, and Prejudice: The Teaching of Contempt." *Ethnicity* 8 (1981): 50-66.

4045. Perry, Tony. "Teacher Is Ousted Over Movie Plan." *Los Angeles Times*, 4 May 1994. [Japanese-American teacher in San Diego suburb prevented from showing film, *Zoot Suit*, to classes]

4046. Persell, Caroline H. "Social Clan and Educational Quality." in *Multicultural Education: Issues and Perspectives*, eds. James A. Banks, and Cherry A. McGee Banks. Boston, MA: Allyn and Bacon, 1989.

4047. Peshkin, Alan, and Carolyne J. White. "Four Black American Students: Coming of Age in a Multiethnic High School." *Teachers College Record* 92 (Fall 1990): 21-38. [Northern California]

4048. Peterkin, Robert, and Dorothy Jones. "Schools of Choice in Cambridge, Massachusetts." in *Public Schools by Choice: Expanding Opportunities for Parents, Students, and Teachers*, ed. Joe Nathan. Minneapolis, MN: Institute for Learning and Teachers, University of Minnesota, 1989.

4049. Peterson, Iver. "Insurgent Parents Group in Princeton [N.J.] Pressing Goals for Minority Students." *New York Times*, 10 February 1992. [Robeson Group]

4050. _____. "More Get Delinquency Diploma Amid Questions About Its Value." *New York Times*, 21 October 1992. [G.E.D.]

4051. Pettit, Kenneth J. *The Status of Private Fund Raising in the Virginia Public Schools.* Ph.D. diss., George Washington University, 1987. UMO # 8707549.

4052. Pflaum, Susanna W., and Theodore Abramson. "Teacher Assignment, Hiring and Preparation: Minority Teachers in New York City." *Urban Review* 22 (March 1990): 17-31.

4053. Phillips, Donna C. *Educational Attainment in a Chicano Population: The Effects of Field Dependence.* Ph.D. diss., University of California, Riverside, 1989. UMO # 8915939.

4054. Pilgrim, David. "The Anatomy of a Racist Incident." *Journal of Ethnic Studies* 17 (Summer 1989): 121-126. [Indiana]

4055. Piller, Charles, and Liza Weiman. "America's Computer Ghetto." *New York Times*, 7 August 1992.

4056. Pitsch, Mark. "School Boycott Threatens 'Lifeblood' of Louisiana Town." *Education Week*, 16 December 1992. [Bonita, Morehouse Parish, LA]

4057. _____. "Suit Seeks To Halt Border Town's Education of Mexicans." *Education Week*, 17 March 1993. [Columbus, NM]

4058. Plank, David N., and Rick Ginsberg, eds. *Southern Cities, Southern Schools. Public Education in the Urban South*. Westport, CT: Greenwood, 1990.

4059. Plank, David N., and Margery E. Turner. "Contrasting Patterns in Black School Politics: Atlanta and Memphis, 1865 - 1985." *Journal of Negro Education* 60 (Spring 1991): 203-218.

4060. Podair, Jerald E. "'White' Values, 'Black' Values: The Ocean Hill - Brownsville Controversy and New York City Culture, 1965 - 1975." *Radical History Review* 59 (Spring 1994): 36-59.

4061. Poinsett, Alex. "School Reform, Black Leaders: Their Impact on Each Other." *Catalyst* 1 (May 1990): 7-11, 43. [Chicago public schools]

4062. Polite, Vernon C. *All Dressed Up with No Place to Go: A Critical Ethnography of African-American Male Students in an Urban High School*. Ph.D. diss., Michican State University, 1991. UMO # 9129487.

4063. Pratt, Robert A. *The Color of their Skin: Education and Race in Richmond, Virginia, 1954 - 1989*. Charlottesville, VA: University Press of Virginia, 1992.

4064. "Prep Schools and Minorities: A Place at the Table." *New York Times*, 7 July 1993.

4065. Pressley, Sue Anne. "Matter of Principal Shatters Small- Town Illusion of Racial Harmony." *Washington Post*, 11 April 1994. [Wedowee, Alabama]

4066. Price, Daniel O. "Educational Differentials Between Negroes and Whites in the South." *Demography* 5 (1968): 23-33.

4067. Price, Janet R., and Jane R. Stern. "Magnet Schools as a Strategy for Integration and School Reform." *Yale Law and Policy Review* 5 (Spring/ Summer 1987): 291 - 321.

4068. Priest, Diana H. *A Historical Study of the Royal Elementary School*. Ph.D. diss., University of Akron, 1993. [Segregated black school, Midvale Schools, Tuscarawas County, Ohio]. UMO # 9319697.

4069. Pritchett, Jonathan B. "The Burden of Negro Schooling: Tax Incidence and Racial Redistribution in Postbellum North Carolina." *Journal of Economic History* 49 (December 1989): 966- 973.

4070. _____. "North Carolina'a Public Schools: Growth and Local Taxation." *Social Science History* 9 (Summer 1985): 277-291.

4071. _____. *The Racial Division of Education Expenditures in the South, 1910*. Ph.D. diss., University of Chicago, 1986.

4072. Punter, David ed. *Introduction to Contemporary Cultural Studies*. Longman, 1986. [touches on racism in textbooks]

4073. Putka, Gary. "Course Work Stressing Blacks' Role Has Critics But Appears Effective." *Wall Street Journal*, 1 July 1991. [Atlanta public schools' Afrocentric curriculum]

4074. Quality Education for Minorities Project. *Education that Works: An Action Plan for the Education of Minorities*. Cambridge, MA: Massachusetts Institute of Technology, 1990.

4075. Quintero Rivera, Angel G. *Educacion y cambio social en Puerto Rico: una epoca critica*. Rio Piedras, PR: Editorial Edil, 1972.

4076. Rabb, Harriet and others. *Promoting Integration in the New York City High Schools*. New York, NY: Education Law Project, Columbia Law School, July 1987.

4077. "[Racial] Slur Accusation Imperils California School District." *New York Times*, 28 April 1991. [Teacher in Susanville Elementary School District]

4078. Radwin, Eugene and others. *A Case Study of New York City's Citywide Reading Testing Program*. Cambridge, MA: Huron Institute, May 1981.

4079. Raichle, Donald R. "The Great Newark School Strike of 1912." *New Jersey History* 106 (1988): 1-17. [In part, protest against alleged anti-semitism by teachers]

4080. Ramey, C. T., and S. L. Ramey. "Intensive Educational Intervention for Children of Poverty." *Intelligence* 14 (January - March 1990).

4081. Ramirez, Francisco O. "Institutions and Interests: A Critical Comment on Walters, McCammon, and James." *Sociology of Education* 63 (April 1990). [See also Walters, McCammon, and James reply, same issue] [Education in the South, 1910]

4082. Raspberry, William. "Good Students, Good Schools." *Washington Post*, 21 February 1994. [Argues cultural factors as explanation of Asian American school superiority]

4083. Raudenbush, S. W. "Neighborhood Effects on Educational Attainment: A Multicultural Analysis." *Sociology of Education* 64 (October 1991): 251-262.

4084. *Ready to Learn: A Mandate for the Nation*. New York, NY: Carnegie Foundation for the Advancement of Teaching, December 1991.

4085. "Report Cards of D. C. Elementary Schools." *Washington Post*, 22 October 1992. [Also, junior high and senior high schools]

4086. *Resolving a Crisis in Education: Latino Teachers for Tomorrow's Classrooms*. 710 N. College Avenue, Claremont, CA 91711: Tomas Rivera Center, 1993.

4087. Reyhner, J. "Native Americans in Basal Reading Textbooks: Are There Enough?" *Journal of American Indian Education* (October 1986): 14-21.

4088. Ribadeneira, Diego. "Boston Pupils Repeat Grades Too Often, Advocacy Group Says." *Boston Globe*, 19 April 1991. [Racial differentials]

4089. _____. "Can Anyone Save the Boston Public Schools?" *Boston Globe Magazine*, 23 September 1990.

4090. _____. "City Group Was Parents' First Choice." *Boston Globe*, 9 October 1989. [Citywide Parents Council, Boston]

4091. _____. "In Lawrence, [Mass,] Fears for Schools' Fate." *Boston Globe*, 14 October 1991. [Largely Hispanic public schools system shortchanging poor and other students]

4092. _____. "Poll: Most Parents Want School Panel Abolished." *Boston Globe*, 23 December 1990. [School Committee in Boston]

4093. _____. "Roxbury School Breaks the Mold." *Boston Globe*, 12 June 1990. [Rafael Hernandez Elementary School, Boston]

4094. Ribadeneira, Diego, and Peggy Hernandez. "Boston Schools Steer Hispanics Down a Path to Failure." *Boston Globe*, 10 June 1990. [First of three articles]

4095. Rice, Bobbylyne. *High School Teachers' Perceptions of African-American Male High School Students in San Francisco*. Ph.D. diss., University of San Francisco, 1988. UMO # 8926015.

4096. "Rich Are Wary of Michigan's Revolt." *New York Times*, 23 March 1994. [Financing of public schools]

4097. Richardson, Barbara B. *Negotiating Your Child's Experience in the Public Schools, a Handbook for Black Parents*. Washington, DC: National Black Child Development Institute, 1988.

4098. Richardson, Lynda. "Minority Students Languish In Special Education System." *New York Times*, 6 April 1994. [New York City public schools]

4099. _____. "New York Schools Falling Behind Homeless." *New York Times*, 2 January 1992.

4100. *The Road to College, Educational Progress by Race and Ethnicity*. Boulder, CO: Western Interstate Commission for Higher Education, July 1991.

4101. Roberts, Sam. "Separate Schools for Male Blacks Igniting Debate." *New York Times*, 12 November 1990. [Interview with Kenneth B. Clark]

4102. Roemwe, J. E. "Providing Equal Educational Opportunity: Public vs. Voucher Schools." *Social Philosophy and Policy* 9 (Winter 1992).

4103. Romo, Harriet. "The Mexican Origin Population's Differing Perceptions of their Children's Schooling." *Social Science Quarterly* 65 (1984): 635-649.

4104. Ross, William G. *Forging New Freedoms: Nativism, Education, and the Constitution, 1917 - 1927.* University of Nebraska Press, 1994.

4105. Rotberg, Iris C. "Separate And Unequal." *Education Week*, 9 March 1994. [For a more equitable and effective system of Chapter I services]

4106. Rotberg, Iris C., and James J. Harvey. *Federal Policy Options for Improving the Education of Low-income Students, 2 vols.* Rand, 1993.

4107. Rothman, Robert. "Wide Racial Gap Found on Open-Ended Math Stems." *Education Week*, 23 June 1993.

4108. Rothstein, Stanley W. *Schooling the Poor: A Social Inquiry into the American Educational Experience.* Bergin and Garvey, 1994.

4109. Rumberger, R. W. "Dropping Out of High School: The Influence of Race, Sex, and Family Background." *American Educational Research Journal* 20 (1983): 199-220.

4110. Rury, John L., and Frank A. Cassell eds. *Seeds of Crisis. Public Schooling in Milwaukee Since 1920.* University of Wisconsin Press, 1993.

4111. Sadker, Myra, and David Sadker. *Failing at Fairness: How America's Schools Cheat Girls.* Scribner's, 1994.

4112. San Miguel, Guadalupe, Jr. *Endless Pursuits: Chicano Educational Experience in Corpus Christi, Texas, 1880 - 1960.* Ph.D. diss., Stanford University, 1979.

4113. _____. *"Let All of Them Take Heed": Mexican Americans and the Campaign for Educational Equality in Texas, 1910 - 1981.* Austin, TX: University of Texas Press, 1987.

4114. _____. "Status of Historiography of Chicano Education: A Preliminary Analysis." *History of Education Quarterly* 26 (Winter 1986): 523-536.

4115. Sanchez, Carmen M. T. *An Historical Inquiry into the Role of Community Activist Organizations in Dealing with the Problem of Overcrowded Elementary Schools in the Hispanic Community of Chicago, 1970 - 1990.* Ph.D. diss., Northern Illinois University, 1993. UMO # 9324995.

4116. Sandler, Andrew B., and David E. Kapel. "Educational Vouchers: A Viable Option for Urban Settings?" *Urban Review* (Winter·1988): 267-282.

4117. Santiago Santiago, Isaura. "The Education of Hispanics in the United States." in *Education and the Integration of Ethnic Minorities*, pp. 150-184. eds. Dietwar Rothermund, and John Simon. New York, NY: St. Martin's Press, 1986.

4118. Santos, Joseph M. *Poverty and Problems of the Mexican Immigrant.* Master's thesis, University of the Pacific, 1931. [Deals with segregated schools]

4119. Santow, Dan. "Is Oak Park and River Forest High Set to Explode?" *Chicago* (October 1990). [Illinois]

4120. Sarrel, Robert. *Resource Allocation and Productivity: A Financial Analysis of New York City High Schools.* Ph.D. diss., Fordham University, 1991. UMO # 9123124.

4121. Schmidt, Peter. "District Proposes Assigning Pupils Based on Income." *Education Week*, 30 October 1991. [Hmong students in La Crosse, WI]

4122. _____. "Idea of 'Gender Gap' in Schools Under Attack." *Education Week*, 28 September 1994.

4123. Schnaiberg, Lynn. "Frustrated Hispanics Call for School Boycott in Denver." *Education Week*, 21 September 1994.

4124. _____. "O.M.B. Study Puts Price Tag on Educating Illegal Immigrants." *Education Week*, 21 September 1994. [Office of Management and Budget]

4125. Schneider, Keith. "School Renovation Plan Divides Carolina Village." *New York Times*, 2 January 1991. [McClellanville, SC]

4126. Schofield, Janet Ward. *Black and White in School: Trust, Tension, or Tolerance?* New York, NY: Teachers College Press, 1989.

4127. Scott, Janny. "Boys Only: Separate But Equal?" *Los Angeles Times*, 15 January 1994. [Black males attending separate classes or schools]

4128. Scott, Ralph. *Education and Ethnicity: The U. S. Experiment in School Education*. Washington, DC: Journal of Social, Political and Economic Studies, 1988.

4129. Scott-Jones, Diane. *Black Families and the Education of Black Children: Current Issues*. Washington, DC: 1987. Paper prepared for the Committee on the Status of Black Americans, National Research Council

4130. Secada, W. G. "Needed: An Agenda for Equity in Mathematics Education." *Journal for Research in Mathematics Education* 21 (November 1990).

4131. *Selected Civil Rights Issues in Iowa's Public Education*. Washington, DC: U. S. Commission on Civil Rights, 1990.

4132. Serwatka, Thomas S. and others. "Correlates of the Underrepresentation of Black Students in Classes for Gifted Students." *Journal of Negro Education* 58 (1989): 520-530.

4133. Shanker, Albert. "Afrocentric Education." *New York Times*, 31 March 1991.

4134. _____. "All 'A's' Are Not Equal." *New York Times*, 11 September 1994.

4135. _____. "Congress Remakes a Law." *New York Times*, 10 July 1994. [Chapter I program and performance-level requirements]

4136. _____. "Noah Webster Academy." *New York Times*, 3 July 1994. [Charter school in Michigan]

4137. Shea, Christine M. and others, eds. *The New Servants of Power. A Critique of the 1980s School Reform Movement*. Westport, CT: Praeger, 1990.

4138. Shepardson, D. P., and E. L. Pizzini. "Gender Bias in Female Elementary Teachers' Perceptions of the Scientific Ability of Students." *Science Education* 76 (April 1992): 147-154.

4139. Sherman, J. D., and P. S. Tomlinson. "Impact of School Finance on Minorities: A Study of Seven Southern States." *Journal of Law and Education* 9 (July 1980): 353-367.

4140. Shin, Barbara J. S. *A Study to Describe Culture Fair Schooling in Relation to Student Achievement for a Culturally Diverse Population*. Ph.D. diss., University of Minnesota, 1989. UMO # 9019095.

4141. Shiver, Jube, Jr. "Survey Finds 1 in 3 Homes Has a Computer." *Los Angeles Times*, 24 May 1994. [Maldistribution by education and income]

4142. *Shortchanging the Language Minority Student*. Washington, DC: U. S. Commission on Civil Rights, 1982. [N. H.]

4143. Shuster, Beth. "Blacks-Only Campus Event Draws Fire." *Los Angeles Times*, 13 January 1994. [Cleveland High School in Los Angeles, CA]

4144. Simmons, Doug. "A Liberal Education." *Village Voice*, 17 April 1990. [Neighbors' protests close down a mainly black school in Cambridge, MA]

4145. Simms, Margaret C. "Transformation in the Educational System: Catalysts for Black Change." *Review of Black Political Economy* 17 (Summer 1988): 57-65.

4146. Sizemore, Barbara A. "The Politics of Curriculum, Race, and Class." *Journal of Negro Education* 59 (Winter 1990).

4147. Slaughter, Diana T. *Ethnicity, Poverty, and Children's Educability; A Developmental Perspective*. Washington, DC: Science and Public Policy Seminars, Federation of Behavioral, Psychological, and Cognitive Sciences, 30 September 1988.

4148. Slavin, Robert E. "Synthesis of Research on Cooperative Learning." *Educational Leadership* 48 (February 1991): 71-82.

4149. Sleeter, Christine E., and Carl A. Grant. "Race, Class, Gender, and Disability in Current Textbooks." in *The Politics of the Textbook*, eds. Michael W. Apple, and Linda K. Christian-Smith. New York, NY: Routledge, 1991.

4150. Smith, Frank and others. *High School Admission and the Improvement of Schooling: A Report of the University Consultants*. New York, NY: The Author, 1986.

4151. Smith, J. and others. "Underrepresentation of Minority Students in Gifted Programs: Yet, A Matters." *Gifted Child Quarterly* 35 (Spring 1991): 81-83.

4152. Smith, Vern E. "What Did You Do in the Struggle?" *Newsweek* Feb. 21, 1994. [Lack of instruction about civil rights period in Mississippi public schools]

4153. Smith, Walter E., Jr. *Mexicano Resistance to Schooled Ethnicity: Ethnic Student Power in South Texas, 1930 - 1970*. Ph.D. diss., University of Texas, 1978. UMO # 7900637.

4154. Smith, Willy D., and Eva Wells Chumm, eds. *Black Education. A Quest for Equity and Excellence*. New Brunswick, NJ: Transaction, 1989.

4155. Smothers, Ronald. "Mississippi Schools Facing Move to Stem Resegregation Tide." *New York Times*, 7 September 1989.

4156. _____. "Principal Causes Furor On Mixed-Race Couples." *New York Times*, 16 March 1994. [Hulond Humphries, Randolph County, Alabama]

4157. _____. "School Fire Fuels Passions in a Racially Torn Town." *New York Times*, 8 August 1994. [Wedowee, AL]

4158. _____. "U. S. Motion to Oust Principal On Racial Remarks Stirs Talk." *New York Times*, 19 May 1994. [Randolph County School District, eastern Alabama]

4159. Snider, William. "In Milwaukee, Dissatisfied Black Leaders Draw Ire with 'Mostly Black' District Plan." *Education Week*, 4 November 1987.

4160. _____. "Local Fights Over Superintendents Are Seen Rekindling Racial Tensions." *Education Week*, 28 March 1990. [five school districts]

4161. Snyder-Joy, Zoann Kay. *American Indian Education in the Southwest: Issues of Self-determination and Local Control*. Ph.D. diss., Arizona State University, 1992. UMO # 9237288.

4162. Solis, Jose. *Public School Reform in Puerto Rico: Sustaining Colonial Models of Development*. Greenwood, 1994.

4163. Sontag, Deborah. "Caribbean Pupils' English Seems Barrier, Not Bridge." *New York Times*, 28 November 1992. [New York City schools]

4164. Sopapavon, Ricardo. "Spelling the 'R' Word." *Los Angeles Times*, 24 February 1993. [Racism in the Los Angeles Unified School District]

4165. Soto, L. D. "The Home Environment of Higher and Lower Achieving Puerto Rican Children." *Hispanic Journal of Behavioral Sciences* 10 (1988): 161-167.

4166. "Special Report: New Classroom Consciousness Minority Needs Become Majority Concerns." *New York Times Education Life*, 4 November 1990. five articles

4167. Spindler, George D. "Why Have Minority Groups in North America Been Disadvantaged by Their Schools?" in *Education and Cultural Process: Anthropological Approaches*, George D. Spindler. 2nd Edition ed. Prospect Heights, IL: Waveland Press, 1987.

4168. Sreedhar, M. V. "Educational Issues of the Socially Disadvantaged Children." *International Journal of Dravidian Linguistics* 17 (June 1988): 64-84.

4169. Stancik, Edward F. *Power, Politics and Patronage- Education in Community School District 12*. Office of the Special Commissioner of Investigation for the New York City School District, April 1993.

4170. *State Enforcement of Nondiscrimination Requirements in Education Programs*. Washington, DC: U. S. Commission on Civil Rights, 1986.

4171. Steele, Claude M. "Race and the Schooling of Black Americans." *Atlantic*, April 1992.

4172. Stefon, Frederick J. "Richard Henry Pratt and His Indians." *Journal of Ethnic Studies* 15 (Summer 1987): 86-112. [Carlisle Indian School]

4173. Stevens, Floraline Q., ed. "The Opportunity to Learn: Implications to Learn." *Journal of Negro Education* 62 (Summer 1993): 232-393. (ten articles)

4174. Stevens, Floraline Q. *Opportunity to Learn: Issues of Equity for Poor and Minority Students*. National Center for Education Statistics, 1993.

4175. Stevens, Leonard B. "'Separate But Equal' Has No Place." *Education Week*, 31 October 1990. [Special schools for black male students in Milwaukee]

4176. Stewart, Joseph, Jr. and others. "In Quest of Role Models: Change in Black Teacher Representation in Urban School Districts, 1968 - 1986." *Journal of Negro Education* 58 (Spring 1989): 140- 152.

4177. Stewart, Joseph, Jr. "Policy Models and Equal Educational Opportunity." *PS-Political Science and Politics* 24 (June 1991): 167-173.

4178. Stewart, Kenneth L., and Arnoldo De Leon. "Education is the Gateway: Comparative Patterns of School Attendance and Literacy Between Anglos and Tejanos in Three Texas Regions, 1850 - 1900." *Aztlan* 16 (Spring 1985): 177-195.

4179. Stewart, Sharon. "Area Schools Confront Campus Bigotry." *Long Beach Press - Telegram*, 21 February 1993. [Long Beach, CA]

4180. Stock, Carolyn H. *The Impact of California Policies on the Education of Indochinese Children: The Implementation of AB 507 Effective 1980*. Ph.D. diss., Fielding Institute, 1993. UMO # 9403379.

4181. Stone, Donald P. *Fallen Prince: William James Edwards, Black Education, and the Quest for Afro-American Nationality*. Snow Hill, AL: Snow Hill, 1990.

4182. Strane, Susan. *A Whole-Souled Woman. Prudence Crandall and the Education of Black Women*. New York, NY: Norton, 1990.

4183. Strefling, Donna and others. "High School for Gifted Students." *Los Angeles Times*, 30 March 1994. [five letters on Whitney High School, Cerritos, CA]

4184. Strum, Charles. "Trenton To Study Newark Schools." *New York Times*, 14 May 1993.

4185. Suarez-Orozco, Marcelo M. *Central American Refugees and U.S. High Schools: A Psychosocial Study of Motivation and Achievement*. Stanford University Press, 1989.

4186. _____. "Immigrant Adaptation to Schooling: A Hispanic Case." in *Minority Status and Schooling*, pp. 37-61. eds. Margaret A. Gibson, and John U. Ogbu : Garland, 1991.

4187. Suro, Roberto. "Equality Plan on School Financing Is Upsetting Rich and Poor in Texas." *New York Times*, 9 October 1991.

4188. Sutton, R. E. "Equity and Computers in the Schools: A Decade of Research." *Review of Educational Research* 61 (Winter 1991): 475-504.

4189. Szasz, Margaret C. *Indian Education in the American Colonies, 1607 - 1783*. Albuquerque, NM: University of New Mexico Press, 1988.

4190. _____. "Listening to the Native Voice: American Indian Schooling in the Twentieth Century." *Montana* 39 (Summer 1989): 42-53.

4191. Taeuber, Karl E., and David R. James. "Racial Segregation Among Public and Private Schools." *Sociology of Education* 55 (April - July 1982): 133-143.

4192. Tashman, Billy. "Reading and Hyping." *Village Voice*, 7 April 1992. [reading scores in New York City public schools]

4193. Taylor, R. D. and others. "Explaining the Performances of African-American Adolescents." *Journal of Research on Adolescence* 4 (1994): 21-44.

4194. "Teaching Inequality: The Problem of Public School Tracking." *Harvard Law Review* 102 (April 1989): 1318-1341.

4195. Thapa, Megh P. *Gender and Ethnic Inequality in Alaska: Changes in Educational and Occupational Attainment, 1970 - 1980.* Ph.D. diss., Stanford University, 1989. UMO # 8912943.

4196. Theiss, Evelyn. "Educator Says Pupils Still Suffer." *Cleveland Plain Dealer*, 25 July 1993. [Joseph A. Fernandez, former chancellor of New York City schools, says "the Cleveland school system seems to hurt, rather than help, African-American students"]

4197. _____. "Low Standards Faulted in Kids' Failures." *Cleveland Plain Dealer*, 6 March 1994. [Cleveland Public schools]

4198. Thompson, Victoria E. "A Parent's Dilemma: How Can We Take a Chance?" *Los Angeles Times*, 11 January 1993. [sending one's child to public or private school]

4199. Thornton, Mona W. *Racial Attitudes in White Preschoolers: An Exploratory Investigation.* Ph.D. diss., University of Massachusetts, 1978. UMO # 7903853.

4200. Timar, T. B. "Politics, Policy, and Categorical Aid: New Inequities in California School Finance." *Educational Evaluation and Policy Analysis* 16 (Summer 1994): 143-160.

4201. Torres Gonzales, Roame. *Democracy and Personal Autonomy in the Puerto Rican School System: A Socio-Historical Survey and Critique of Educational Development.* Ph.D. diss., University of Massachusetts, 1983.

4202. Torruellas, Rosa M. "The Failure of the New York Public Educational System to Retain Hispanic and Other Minority Students." *Centro de Estudios Puertorriquenos Newsletter* (June 1986).

4203. "Transforming Schools for African Americans: How Well Are We Doing?" *Journal of Negro Education* 63 (Winter 1994): entire issue.

4204. Trebilcock, Bob. "Reading, 'Riting, 'Rithmetic...Racism." *Redbook*, October 1993.

4205. Trennert, Robert A. "From Carlisle to Phoenix: The Rise and Fall of the Indian Outing System, 1878 - 1930." *Pacific Historical Review* 52 (August 1983): 267-291.

4206. Trent, S. C. "School Choice for African-American Children Who Live in Poverty: A Commitment to Equity or More of the Same?" *Urban Education* 27 (October 1992): 291-307.

4207. Trombley, William. "School Project at Heart of Whittle's Empire." *Los Angeles Times*, 9 March 1993. [Christopher Whittle, organizer of for-profit private schools]

4208. Trueba, Henry T. "Culturally Based Explanations of Minority Students' Academic Achievement." *Anthropology and Education Quarterly* 19 (September 1988): 270-287.

4209. Tyack, David, and Robert E. Lowe. "The Constitutional Movement: Reconstruction and Black Education in the South." *American Journal of Education* 94 (1986): 236-256.

4210. Tye, Larry. "Tracking Can Undo What Integration Builds." *Boston Globe*, 6 January 1992.

4211. "Untracking for Equity." *Educational Leadership* 50 (October 1992): 7 articles.

4212. U.S. Commission on Civil Rights, North Carolina Advisory Committee. *In-School Segregation in North Carolina Public Schools.* U.S. Commission on Civil Rights, March 1991.

4213. U.S. Congress, 101st, 2nd Session, Senate Committee on Finance, Subcommittee on Social Security and Family Policy. *Wisconsin Learnfare Program: Hearing.* Washington, DC: Government Printing Office, 1990.

4214. U.S. Education Department. *Dropout Rates in the United States: 1991.* Washington, DC: Government Printing Office, 1992.

4215. _____. *Dropout Rates in the United States: 1993.* Washington, DC: Government Printing Office, 1994.

4216. U.S., National Center for Education Statistics. *National Education Longitudinal Study of 1988: A Profile of Schools Attended by Eighth Graders in 1988*. Washington, DC: NCES, September 1991.

4217. U.S. Office for Civil Rights. *Racial and Ethnic Conflict in Elementary Schools*. U.S. Office for Civil Rights, 1993.

4218. Valencia, Richard R. ed. *Chicano School Failure and Success: Research and Policy Agendas for the 1990s*. Falmer, 1991.

4219. Valverde, Leonard A., and Albert Cortez. *The Impact of Mandated Enrollment of Undocumented Students in Selected Texas Public Schools*. Austin, TX: Office of Advanced Research in Hispanic Education, College of Education, University of Texas, 1983.

4220. van Geel, Tyll. "The Search for Constitutional Limits on Governmental Authority to Inculcate youth." *Texas Law Review* 62 (1983): 262-289.

4221. Vander Weele, Maribeth. *Reclaiming Our Schools: The Struggle for Chicago School Reform*. Loyola University Press, 1994.

4222. Vann, K. R., and Jawanza Kunjufu. "The Importance of an Afrocentric Multicultural Curriculum." *Phi Delta Kappan* 74 (February 1993): 490-491.

4223. Verhovek, Sam H. "District Cracking Down on Non-Resident Students." *New York Times*, 14 December 1993. [La Joya, Texas, Independent School District]

4224. _____. "Poorer New York School Districts Challenging State Aids as Unequal." *New York Times*, 6 May 1991.

4225. _____. "To These Children, Border's No Barrier." *New York Times*, 30 June 1993. [Children from Las Palomas, Mexico, who attend public school in Columbus, New Mexico]

4226. Viadero, Debra. "Schools Witness a Troubling Revival of Bigotry." *Education Week*

4227. Vickers, Robert J. "Heights' School Chief Aims to End Disparities." *Cleveland Plain Dealer*, 4 September 1994. [Superintendent of Cleveland Heights-University Heights public schools and black-white differences in academic achievement]

4228. Vinovskis, M. A. "Schooling and Poor Children in 19th Century America." *American Behavioral Scientist* 35 (January - February 1992): 313-331.

4229. *Voices from the Inside, 1992*. Claremont, CA: Institute for Education in Transformation, Claremont Graduate School, 121 E. 10th Street, Claremont, CA 91711-6160.

4230. Vold, David J., and Joseph L. De Vitis eds. *School Reform in the Deep South. A Critical Appraisal*. Tuscaloosa, AL: University of Alabama Press, 1990.

4231. Waldman, Peter. "On the Playing Fields of a Private Academy, Racism Makes a Stand." *Wall Street Journal*, 13 December 1989. [East Holmes Academy, Mississippi]

4232. Walsh, Catherine E. *Pedagogy and the Struggle for Voice. Issues of Language, Power, and Schooling for Puerto Ricans*. New York, NY: Bergin and Garvey, 1991.

4233. _____. "Schooling and the Civic Exclusion of Latinos: Toward a Discourse of Dissonance." *Journal of Education* 169 (1987): 115-131.

4234. Walsh, Edward. "At Chicago's Agricultural High School, Life Is Less Than Pastoral." *Washington Post*, 20 February 1994.

4235. Walsh, Mark. "War Hits Close to Home for Arab-Americans in Detroit-Area Schools." *Education Week*, 30 January 1991. [Persian Gulf War]

4236. Walters, Pamela B. and others. "Schooling or Working? Public Education, Racial Politics, and the Organization of Production in 1910." *Sociology of Education* 63 (1990): 1-26.

4237. Walters, Pamela B., and David R. James. "Schooling for Some: Child Labor and School Enrollment of Black and White Children in the Early 20th Century South." *American Sociological Review* 57 (October 1992): 635-650.

4238. Wang, M. C. and others. "Synthesis of Research: What Helps Students Learn." *Educational Leadership* 51 (1993): 74-79. [based on 11,000 statistical findings]

4239. Wang, M. C., and Edmund W. Gordon, eds. *Educational Resilence in Inner-City America*. Lawrence Erlbaum Associates, 1994.

4240. Watkins, John M. "Grouping Defenders Need Instruction." *Amherst Bulletin*, 3 January 1992. [Equity and classroom grouping]

4241. Weber, Michael J. "Immersed in an Educational Crisis: Alternative Programs for African-American Males." *Stanford Law Review* 45 (April 1993): 1099-1113.

4242. Weidner, Catherine S. *Debating the Future of Chicago's Black Youth: Black Professionals, Black Labor and Educational Politics during the Civil Rights Era, 1950 - 1965*. Ph.D. diss., Northwestern University, 1989. UMO # 9001885.

4243. Weiler, Kathleen. "The School at Allensworth." *Journal of Education* 172 (1990): 9-38. [Black town in California]

4244. _____. "Schooling Migrant Children: California, 1920 - 1940." *History Workshop* 37 (Spring 1994): 117-142.

4245. Weiss, Michael J. "America's Best Schools." *Redbook*, April 1992. 61-76.

4246. Weissbourd, Richard. "Schools That Work." *Boston Globe Magazine*, 17 November 1991.

4247. Wells, Amy S. "Choice in Education: Examining the Evidence on Equity." *Teachers College Record* 93 (Autumn 1991): 137-155.

4248. _____. "Quest for Improving Schools Finds Role for Free Market." *New York Times*, 14 March 1990.

4249. Welsh, Patrick. "Board Silly. How Politics Are Wrecking Alexandria's Schools." *Washington Post*, 20 June 1993.

4250. _____. "Staying on Tracks. Can We Teach Honors Kids and Hard Cases Together?" *Washington Post*, 7 March 1993.

4251. Wenglisky, Harold. "In Michigan School-Tax Shift, the Poor Lose." *New York Times*, 1 April 1994. [Four letters]

4252. Werum, Regina E. "Industrial and Vocational Education: Differences in the Education of Black Men and Women, 1900 - 1920." *Sociological Abstracts* Supplement 167 (August 1991). 91S25518/ASA/1991/6877.

4253. *What Americans Study*. Princeton, NJ: Educational Testing Service, August 1989. [Racial-ethnic data, 1982 and 1987]

4254. Wheelock, Anne. *Crossing the Tracks: How 'Untracking' Can Save America's Schools*. The New Press, 1992.

4255. White, Sammis B. and others. "Socioeconomic Status and Achievement Revisited." *Urban Education* 28 (October 1993): 328- 343.

4256. "Whites in Detroit Teach Students at Black School a 4th R: Racism." *New York Times*, 2 December 1992. [Malcolm X Academy]

4257. Whitman, Mark ed. *Removing the Badge of Slavery: The Record of Brown v. Board of Education*. Princeton, NJ: Markus Wiener, 1992.

4258. Wiese, M. R. R. "Racial/ Ethnic Minority Research in School Psychology." *Psychology in the Schools* 29 (July 1992): 267-272.

4259. Wilkerson, Isabel. "36 Years Later, an Integrated Georgia Prom." *New York Times*, 14 May 1990. [Peach County High School, Fort Valley, GA]

4260. _____. "Decentralized, Chicago Finds Change to Be Slow." *New York Times*, 20 October 1993. [Chicago Public Schools under "experiment" in school governance]

4261. _____. "Graduation: Where 500 Began, 150 Remain." *New York Times*, 13 June 1994. [Paul Robeson High School, Chicago]

4262. _____. "Separate Senior Proms Reveal An Unspanned Racial Divide." *New York Times*, 5 May 1991. [Brother Rice High School, Chicago]

4263. _____. "To Save Its Men, Detroit Plans Black Boys-Only School." *New York Times*, 14 August 1991.

4264. Wilkie, Curtis. "Alabama Town's Troubles Leave Races Split, Anguished." *Boston Globe*, 11 August 1994. [Wedowee]

4265. Will, George F. "Lofty Language, Goofy Goals." *Washington Post*, 17 February 1994. ["Goals 2000" education bill]

4266. Williams, Juan. "The New Segregation." *Modern Maturity* 37 (April - May 1994): 24-26, 28.

4267. Willie, Charles V. and others, eds. *The Education of African-Americans*. New York, NY: Auburn House, 1991.

4268. Wilson, Kenneth L. "The Effects of Integration and Class on Black Educational Attainment." *Sociology of Education* 52 (1979): 84-98.

4269. Wilson, Margaret A. *Culture Change and Academic Achievement: The Transition from Indian Reserve Elementary School to Public High School*. Ph.D. diss., University of California, 1989. [Dakota Indian Students]. UMO # 9029585.

4270. Winerip, Michael. "America Can Save Its City Schools." *New York Times Education Life*, 7 November 1993. [the work of Robert Slavin]

4271. Winfield, Linda F. ed. "Resilience, Schooling, and Development in African-American Youth." *Education and Urban Society* 24 (November 1991): 5-161. (11 articles)

4272. Winfield, Linda F., and Michael D. Woodard. "Where Are Equity and Diversity in America 2000?" *Education Week*, 29 January 1992.

4273. Winters, Wendy G. *African American Mothers and Urban Schools: The Power of Participation*. Lexington Books, 1993.

4274. Witte, John. "Public Subsidies for Private Schools." *Educational Policy* (June 1992).

4275. Wright, C. T. "The Development of Public Schools for Blacks in Atlanta, 1879 - 1900." *Atlanta Historical Bulletin* 21 (Spring 1977): 115-128.

4276. Wyckoff, J. H. "The Intrastate Equality of Public Primary and Secondary Education Resources in the U. S., 1980 - 1987." *Economics of Education Review* 11 (March 1992).

4277. Yeakey, Carol C. "The Social Consequences of Public [Education] Policy." *Journal of Negro Education* 62 (Spring 1993): 125-143.

4278. Yeakey, Carol C., and Clifford T. Bennett. "Race, Schooling, and Class in American Society." *Journal of Negro Education* 59 (1990): 3-18.

4279. Yoon, Yong-Sik. *Equity Trends in Wisconsin School Finance from 1980-81 to 1988-89*. Ph.D. diss., University of Wisconsin, 1991. [Milwaukee]. UMO # 9124700.

4280. Zigler, Edward, and Susan Muenchow. *Head Start: The Inside Story of America's Most Successful Educational Experiment*. Basic Books, 1992.

EDUCATION -- HIGHER

4281. Abbott, Devon I. *History of the Cherokee Female Seminary: 1851-1910.* 1989. UMO # 8919932.

4282. Abel, Emily. "Collective Protest and the Meritocracy: Faculty Women and Sex Discrimination Lawsuits." *Feminist Studies* 7 (1981).

4283. Abrams, Sheila. "Goddard and Racism." *Barre Times Argus*, 14 June 1989. (letter) [Goddard College, Vermont]

4284. Achenbach, James. "Some Call ASU Probe Whitewash." *Tempe Daily News Tribune*, 31 January 1990. [Arizona State University]

4285. Acuna, Rodolfo F. "A Professor's Refusal to Take Psychiatric Tests." *Chronicle of Higher Education*, 23 March 1994.

4286. Adelman, Clifford. *Women at Thirtysomething: Paradoxes of Attainment.* Washington, DC: Division of Higher Education, U.S. Department of Education, 1991.

4287. Adler, Jerry and others. "Taking Offense. Is This the New Enlightenment or the New McCarthyism?" *Newsweek*, 24 December 1990. [The newest stereotype- "political correctness" on college campuses]

4288. "Afro-American Studies in the Twenty-First Century." *Black Scholar* 22 (Summer 1992): entire issue.

4289. "After Complaint, Aid is Cut Off to Hispanic Paper." *New York Times*, 17 June 1990. [University of Texas, Austin]

4290. Aguirre, Adalberto, Jr. and others. "Majority and Minority Faculty Perceptions in Academe." *Research in Higher Education* 34 (June 1993): 371-385. [University of Colorado system, 1987-1988]

4291. Aguirre, Adalberto, Jr., and Ruben O. Martinez. *Chicanos in Higher Education: Issues and Dilemmas for the 21st Century.* ASHE- ERIC Higher Education Reports, George Washington University, 1994.

4292. Alexander, Karl L. and others. "Consistency and Change in Educational Stratification: Recent Trends Regarding Social Background and College Access." in *Research in Social Stratification*, ed. Robert V. Robinson. Greenwich, CT: JAI, 1987.

4293. Alexander, William S. "Regulating Speech on Campus: A Plea for Tolerance." *Wake Forest Law Review* 26 (Winter 1991): 1349- 1387.

4294. Alkalimat, Abdul. "Summing Up Black Studies after Two Decades." *Sage Race Relations Abstracts* 12 (August 1987): 23-31.

4295. "Alleging Bias, Seniors Leave Honor Society." *New York Times* [Cornell University]

4296. Allen, Anita L. "The Role Model Argument and Faculty Diversity." *Philosophical Forum* 24 (Fall-Spring 1992-1993): 167- 281.

4297. Allen, Robert L. "Politics of the Attack on Black Studies." *Black Scholar* 6 (September 1974): 2-7.

4298. Allen, Walter R. "Black Colleges vs. White Colleges. The Fork in the Road for Black Students." *Change* 28-34 (May-June 1987).

4299. _____. "Black Students in U.S. Higher Education: Toward Improved Access, Adjustment, and Achievement." *Urban Review* 20 (1988): 165-188.

4300. Allen, Walter R. and others, eds. *College in Black and White.* State University of New York Press, 1991.

4301. Allen, Walter R. "The Color of Success: African-American College Student Outcomes at Predominantly White and Historically Black Public Colleges and Universities." *Harvard Educational Review* 62 (Spring 1992): 26-44.

4302. Allen, Walter R. and others. *Preliminary Report: 1982 Survey of Black Undergraduate Students Attending Predominantly White, State Supported Universities.* Ann Arbor, MI: Center for Afro-American and African Studies, 1984.

4303. Almeida, Deirdre A. "Introduction to Campus Tensions in Massachusetts." *Equity and Excellence in Education* 26 (April 1993): 6-18.

4304. Alston, Denise. *Recruiting Minority Classroom Teachers: A National Challenge.* Washington, DC: National Governors' Association, 1988.

4305. Altbach, Philip G., and Kofi Lomotey, eds. *The Racial Crisis in American Higher Education.* Albany, NY: State University of New York Press, 1991.

4306. Alterman, Eric. "Black Universities: In Demand and In Trouble." *New York Times Magazine,* 5 November 1989.

4307. "American Indian Voices in Higher Education." *Change* (March-April 1991): entire issue.

4308. Anderson, Elijah. "Can We All Get Along? Not Yet." *Los Angeles Times,* 26 May 1993. [University of Pennsylvania]

4309. Anderson, Elizabeth. "Racism Versus Academic Freedom." *Against the Current* 32 (May-June 1991): 24-28.

4310. Anderson, Martin and others. "Why the Shortage of Black Professors?" *Journal of Blacks in Higher Education* 1 (Autumn 1993): 25-34.

4311. Anderson, Talmadge. "Black Encounter of Racism and Elitism in White Academe: A Critique of the System." *Journal of Black Studies* 18 (March 1988): 259-272.

4312. Andrew, Loyd D., and Rocco Russo. "Who Gets What? Impact of Financial Aids Policies." *Research in Higher Education* 30 (October 1989).

4313. Ansley, Frances L. "Race and the Core Curriculum in Legal Education." *California Law Review* 79 (December 1991): 1511-1597.

4314. Applebome, Peter. "At Two Universities, Homecoming Weekend Become An Event That Divides Students." *New York Times,* 19 October 1994. [University of Georgia and University of North Carolina]

4315. _____. "Bold Leap Into a Minority: White at Black Colleges." *New York Times,* 5 May 1993.

4316. _____. "A College Becomes a Mirror of Black Campuses' Troubles." *New York Times,* 2 January 1993. [Morris Brown College, Atlanta]

4317. _____. "Duke Learns of Pitfalls in Promise of Hiring More Black Professors." *New York Times,* 19 September 1993.

4318. _____. "Epilogue to Integration Fight at South's Public Universities." *New York Times,* 29 May 1991.

4319. _____. "Pain and Generosity at Ole Miss." *New York Times,* 12 November 1989.

4320. Archambault, David L., and Michael P. Gross. "Tribal Colleges Helping Renew Indians' Spirit." *New York Times,* 5 October 1992. [Two letters]

4321. Arcinega, Tomas. *Hispanic Underrepresentation: A Call for Reinvestment and Innovation*. Long Beach, CA: Office of the Chancellor, California State University, 1988.

4322. Arcinega, Tomas, and Ann I. Morey. *Hispanics and Higher Education: A CSU Imperative*. Long Beach, CA: Office of the Chancellor, California State University, 1985.

4323. Aruri, Naseer H. "Israel's Strategy for the American Campus: A Threat to Academic Freedom?" *Search* 6 (1985): 102-141.

4324. Asante, Molefi. "A Note on Nathan Huggins' Report on the Ford Foundation on African-American Studies." *Journal of Black Studies* 17 (1986): 255-262.

4325. Ashley, Mary Ellen. *A Model for Combatting Racism on Your Campus*. Cincinnati, OH: Office of the Vice Provost, Division of Student Affairs, University of Cincinnati, 1989.

4326. Ashraf, J. "Differences in Returns to Education: An Analysis by Race." *American Journal of Economics and Sociology* 53 (July 1994): 281-190.

4327. "Asian American Studies... Can the Asian American Movement Ever Become a Reality in Arizona?" *Brushstrokes, Journal of Asian American Experiences in Arizona, University of Arizona* (Fall 1992). [University of Arizona]

4328. "ASV Chooses Committee to Study Racism." *Scottsdale Progress*, 24 June 1989. [Investigation of Arizona State University police in arresting two black students who were attacked by large group of white students.]

4329. Avalos, M. "The Status of Latinos in the Profession: Problems in Recruitment and Retention." *PS-Political Science and Politics* 244 (June 1991): 241-251.

4330. Avorn, Jerry and others. *Up Against the Ivy Walls: A History of the Columbia Crisis*. New York, NY: Atheneum, 1969.

4331. Ayers, David John. "My Days and Nights in the Academic Wilderness." *Heterodoxy* 1 (January 1993): 1, 12-13. [Dallas Baptist University]

4332. Ayres, B. Drummond, Jr. "Students at Virginia Resort Erupt in Violence; Four Hurt." *New York Times*, 4 September 1989. [Greekfest in Virginia Beach, VA]

4333. Azares, Tania. "Educational Attainment and Upward Mobility: Prospects for Filipino Americans." *American Journal* 13 (1986- 1987): 39-52.

4334. Badwound, Elgin. *Leadership and American Indian Values: The Tribal College Dilemma*. Ph.D. diss., Pennsylvania State University, 1990. UMO # 9104847.

4335. Baida, A. H. "Not All Minority Scholarships Are Created Equal: Why Some May Be More Constitutional Than Others." *Journal of College and Univversity Law* 18 (Winter 1992): 333-366.

4336. Bair, J. H., and M. Boor. "The Academic Elite in Law: Linkages Among Top-Ranked Law Schools." *Psychological Reports* 68 (June 1991): Part 1, 891-894.

4337. Baratz, Joan C., and Myra Finklen. *Participation of Recent Black College Graduates in the Labor Market and in Graduate Education*. Princeton, NJ: Educational Testing Service, 1983.

4338. Barber, William J. *Breaking the Academic Mould*. Middletown, CT: Wesleyan University Press, 1988.

4339. Barlow, Andrew. "The Student Movement of the 1960s and the Politics of Race." *Journal of Ethnic Studies* 19 (Fall 1991): 1- 22.

4340. Barnett, Stephen R. "Who Gets In? A Troubling Policy." *Los Angeles Times*, 11 June 1992. [University of California, Berkeley]

4341. Barrow, Clyde W. "Corporate Liberalism, Finance Hegemony and Central State Intervention in the Reconstruction." in *Studies in American Political Development*, Vol. 6, #2. eds. Karen Orren, and Stephen Skowrovek. : Cambridge University Press, 1992.

4342. Bartlett, Katharine T., and Jean O'Barr. "The Chilly Climate on College Campuses: An Expansion of the Hate Speech Debate." *Duke Law Journal* (June 1990): 574-586.

4343. Baruch, Chad. "Dangerous Liaisons: Campus Racial Harassment Policies, the First Amendment, and the Efficacy of Suppression." *Whittier Law Review* 11 (Winter 1990): 697-721.

4344. Baxter, Tom. "With Award, Lewis's Life Comes Full Circle." *Atlanta Journal*, 3 June 1989. [Rep. John Lewis, honorary degree at Troy State University; had been excluded from institution in 1958 on racial grounds]

4345. Beale, Lewis. "The Right to Speak Up But Not to Talk Down." *Detroit Free Press* (13 July 1989). [regulation at the University of Michigan forbidding racial and other harassment speech]

4346. Beckham, Edgar F. "Campus Snapshots- A Misleading Picture." *Los Angeles Times*, 20 December 1993.

4347. Bell, Derrick A. "Desegregation and the Meaning of Equal Educational Opportunity in Higher Education." *Harvard Civil Rights- Civil Liberties Law Review* 17 (1982).

4348. _____. "Why We Need More Black Professors in Law School." *Boston Globe*, 29 April 1990.

4349. Bell-Scott, Patricia and others. "The Promise and Challenge of Black Women's Studies." *National Women's Studies Association Journal* 3 (Spring 1991): 281-288.

4350. Bender, Eric D. "The Viability of Racist Speech from High Schools to Universities: A Welcome Matriculation?" *University of Cincinnati Law Review* 59 (Winter 1991): 871-903.

4351. Benezet, Louis T. "Schools of the Rich." *New York Times*, 7 August 1994. ["Colleges of top prestige"]

4352. Bereman, M. A., and J. A. Scott. "Using the Compa-Ratio to Detect Gender Bias in Faculty Salaries." *Journal of Higher Education* 62 (September-October 1991): 556-569.

4353. Berger, Joseph. "Are Blacks Excluded?" *New York Times Education Life*, 1 August 1993. [Campus life in higher education]

4354. _____. "Campus Racial Strains Show Two Perspectives on Inequality." *New York Times*, 22 May 1989.

4355. _____. "College Paper Article Called Blatant Anti- Semitism." *New York Times*, 25 September 1990. [City College, C.U.N.Y.]

4356. Berman, Paul, ed. *Debating P.C.: The Controversy Over Political Correctness on College Campuses*. New York, NY: Laurel/ Dell, 1992.

4357. Berman, Paul. "The Fog of Political Correctness." *Tikkun* 7 (January - February 1992): 53-58, 94-96.

4358. Bernstein, Alison R. and Jacklyn Cock. "A Troubling Picture of Gender Equality." *Chronicle of Higher Education*, 15 June 1994. [Higher education]

4359. Berry, Gordon L., and Joy K. Asamen, eds. *Black Students: Psychosocial Issues and Academic Achievement*. Newbury Park, CA: Sage, 1989.

4360. Berube, Michael, and Cary Nelson. *Higher Education Under Fire*. Routledge, 1994.

4361. Beyer, Eric and others. "How Cornell Student Housing Really Works." *New York Times*, 4 May 1994. [Three letters on race and housing on Ivy League campuses]

4362. *Bigotry and Violence on Missouri's College Campuses*. Washington, DC: U.S. Commission on Civil Rights, 1990.

4363. *Bigotry and Violence on Nebraska's College Campuses*. Washington, DC: U.S. Commission on Civil Rights, 1990.

4364. Bishop, David. "The Consent Decree between the University of North Carolina System and the U.S. Department of Education, 1981-1982." *Journal of Negro Education* 52 (1983): 350-361.

4365. Bjork, Lars G., and T. E. Thompson. "The Next Generation of Faculty: Minority Issues." *Education and Urban Society* 21 (May 1989): 341-351.

4366. Black, Elias. "Is Higher Education Desegregation a Remedy for Segregation But Not Educational Inequality? A Study of the Ayers v. Mabus Desegregation Case." *Journal of Higher Education* 60 (Autumn 1991): 538-565.

4367. "A Black and White Issue." *Columbus [Ohio] Dispatch*, 4 March 1990. [Racism on college campuses in Central Ohio]

4368. "[Black Intellectualism and the Controversy at U Mass]." *Black Scholar* 19 (1988): 3-43. [James Baldwin, Julius Lester, and the W. E. B. DuBois Department of Afro-American Studies]

4369. "Black Professors." *Commentary* 90 (December 1990): 4-8. [Series of letters]

4370. "Black Students Get a Yearbook Of Their Own." *New York Times*, 23 July 1989. [Black Students League, University of Pennsylvania]

4371. "Black Students March in Protest of Race Incident." *New York Times*, 27 October 1991. [University of Alabama, Tuscaloosa]

4372. "Blacks-Only Group May Soon Forfeit Status and Money." *New York Times*, 9 December 1990. [Student African-American Society, Syracuse University]

4373. Blum, Debra E. "10 Years Later, Questions Abound Over Minnesota Sex-Bias Settlement." *Chronicle of Higher Education*, 13 June 1990. [Detailed account of aftermath of Rajender case, at University of Minnesota]

4374. _____. "Are Athletes Graduating?" *Chronicle of Higher Education*, 6 July 1994. [Accompanied by tables covering institutions in each state]

4375. _____. "Athletes' Graduation Rates Lag at Some Division I Colleges." *Chronicle of Higher Education*, 13 July 1994.

4376. _____. "'Eyes on the Prize'." *Chronicle of Higher Education*, 13 July 1994. [Black coaches]

4377. Boas, Phil. "Officers' Conduct Supported." *Mesa Tribune*, 23 June 1989. [Arrest of two black Arizona State University students under attack by white students]

4378. Bogen, David S. "The First Integration of the University of Maryland School of Law." *Maryland Historical Magazine* 84 (Spring 1989): 39-49.

4379. Bonacich, Edna. "Racism in the Deep Structure of United States Higher Education- When Affirmative Action is Not Enough." in *Affirmative Action and Positive Policies in the Education of Ethnic Minorities*, eds. A. Yogev, and S. Tomlinson. Greenwich, CT: JAI Press, 1989.

4380. Bonilla, Frank and others. "Puerto Rican Studies: Prompting for the Academy and the Left." in *The Left Academy*, vol. 3. pp. 67-102. eds. B. Ollman, and E. Vernoff. New York, NY: Praeger, 1986.

4381. Bonner, Thomas N. *To the Ends of the Earth, Women's Search for Education in Medicine*. Boston, MA: Harvard University Press, 1992.

4382. Boone, Young and Associates. *Minority Enrollment in Graduate and Professional Schools*. Washington, DC: Government Printing Office, 1984.

4383. Borunda, Mario R. *Emerging Hispanic Colleges and Universities*. Ph.D. diss., Harvard University, 1990. UMO # 9032410.

4384. Boulard, Garry. "Deep-South Campus Chips Away at Entrenched Biases." *Los Angeles Times*, 9 June 1992. [Tulane University]

4385. _____. "Learning to Get by at Cash-strapped Black Colleges." *Los Angeles Times*, 2 September 1993. [Southern University, New Orleans]

4386. Boyer, Ernest L. "Is College a Privilege or a Right?" *Cleveland Plain Dealer*, 14 August 1991.

4387. Boyer, Paul. *Tribal Colleges. Shaping the Future of Native America*. Princeton, NJ: Carnegie Foundation for the Advancement of Teaching, 1989.

4388. Boynton, Robert S. "Princeton's Public Intellectual." *New York Times Magazine*, 15 September 1991. [Cornel West]

4389. Braiman, Eva. "Students Against Racism." *Militant*, 10 November 1989. [State University of New York at New Paltz]

4390. Brazzell, Johnetta C. *Education as a Tool of Socialization: Agnes Scott Institute and Spelman Seminary, 1881-1910*. Ph.D. diss., University of Michigan, 1991. UMO # 9135559.

4391. _____. "Bricks Without Straw: Missionary- sponsored Black Higher Education in the Post-emancipation Era." *Journal of Higher Education* 63 (January - February 1992): 26-49.

4392. Brigham, J. C. "College Students' Racial Attitudes." *Journal of Applied Social Psychology* 23 (1 December 1993): 1933- 1967.

4393. Brighouse, Harry and others. "N.S.C. Out of South Africa!" *Against the Current* 5 (July - August 1990): 9-10.

4394. Brint, Steven, and Jerome Karabel. "American Education, Meritocratic Ideology, and the Legitimation of Inequality- The Community College and the Problem of American Exceptionalism." *Higher Education* 18 (1989).

4395. Brisbay, Erin. "College Women in the 1930s: The Possibilities and the Realities." *Filson Club History Quarterly* 64 (1990): 32-59.

4396. Bromwich, David. *Politics By Other Means. Higher Education and Group Thinking*. New Haven, CT: Yale University Press, 1992.

4397. Brough, C. H. "Work of the Commission of Southern Universities on the Race Question." *Annals* 49 (1913): 47-57.

4398. Brown, Darryl. "Racism and Race Relations in the University." *Virginia Law Review* 76 (March 1990): 295-335.

4399. Brown, De Neen L. "Members of Fraternities Drink More on Virginia College Campuses, Survey Says." *Washington Post*, 10 March 1993. [Racial differentials]

4400. _____. "Violence Muscles Its Way Onto Campus." *Washington Post*, 15 February 1994. [Nationwide]

4401. Brown, Shirley V. *Increasing Minority Faculty: An Elusive Goal*. Princeton, NJ: Educational Testing Service, 1988.

4402. _____. *Minorities in the Graduate Education Pipeline*. Princeton, NJ: Educational Testing Service, 1987.

4403. Brownstein, Alan E. "Regulating Hate Speech at Public Universities: Are First Amendment Values Functionally Incompatible with Equal Protection Principles?" *Buffalo Law Review* 39 (Winter 1991): 1-52.

4404. Bryden, David P. "On Race and Diversity." *Constitutional Commentary* 6 (Summer 1989): 383-430. [Law schools]

4405. Buchsbaum, Tamar. "A Note on Antisemitism in Admissions at Dartmouth." *Jewish Social Studies* 49 (Winter 1987): 79-84.

4406. *Building a Multiracial, Multicultural University Community: Final Report of the University Committee on Minority Issues*. Stanford, CA: Stanford University, 1989.

4407. Bunch, Kenyon D. "Patrick E. Higginbotham's Third Road to Desegregating Higher Education: Something Old or Something New?" *Ohio Northern Law Review* 18 (Winter 1991): 11-34.

4408. Bunzel, John H. "Black and White at Stanford." *Public Interest* 105 (Autumn 1991): 61-77.

4409. _____. "Choosing Freshmen: Who Deserves an Edge?" *Wall Street Journal*, 1 February 1988.

4410. _____. *Race Relations on Campus: Stanford Students Speak*. Stanford Alumni Association, 1992.

4411. Burke, William T. III, and Frank J. Cavaliere. "Equal Employment Opportunity on Campus: Strengthening the Commitment." *Labor Law Review* 42 (January 1991): 19-27.

4412. Burnside, Jacqueline G. *Philanthropists and Politicians: A Sociological Profile of Berea College, 1855-1908*. Ph.D. diss., Yale University, 1988. UMO # 8917149.

4413. Butterfield, Fox. "Colleges Luring Black Students With Incentives." *New York Times*, 18 February 1993.

4414. _____. "Worker on Dartmouth Paper Added Hitler Quote, Investigators Say." *New York Times*, 10 January 1991.

4415. Byrne, J. Peter. "Racial Insults and Free Speech within the University." *Georgetown Law Journal* 79 (February 1991): 399-443.

4416. Cadet, Marc V. *An Exploratory Analysis of a Profile of Black and White Doctoral Holders and their Perceived Labor Market Demands: 1976-1986*. Ph.D. diss., Kansas State University, 1991. UMO # 9122741.

4417. Cage, Mary C. "Graduation Rates of American Indians and Blacks Improve, Lag Behind Others." *Chronicle of Higher Education* (26 May 1993).

4418. _____. "Rancor at York College." *Chronicle of Higher Education* (22 June 1994). [CUNY]

4419. _____. "Report on Minority Hiring Angers University of Michigan Officials." *Chronicle of Higher Education* (13 July 1994).

4420. _____. "Students, Parents, and Alumni Seek Sweeping Changes at Tuskegee University." *Chronicle of Higher Education* (21 April 1993).

4421. Calabresi, Massimo. "Bakke as Pseudo Tragedy." *Catholic University Law Review* 28 (1979).

4422. _____. "Skin Deep 101." *Time*[Racial theory of CUNY Professor Leonard Jeffries]

4423. California Postsecondary Education Commission. *Toward an Understanding of Campus Climate. A Report to the Legislature in Response to Assembly Bill 4071 (Chapter 690, Statutes of 1980)*. Sacramento, CA: June 1990.

4424. Camburn, E. "College Completion among Students from High Schools Located in Large Metropolitan Areas." *American Journal of Education* 98 (1990): 551-569.

4425. Cammack, Mark, and Susan Davies. "Should Hate Speech Be Prohibited in Law Schools?" *Southwestern University Law Review* 20 (Spring 1991): 145-173.

4426. *Campus Ethnoviolence Kit*. Baltimore, MD: National Institute Against Prejudice and Violence, n.d.

4427. *Campus Ethnoviolence and the Policy Options*. Baltimore, MD: National Institute Against Prejudice and Violence, March 1990.

4428. "Campus Hate Speech and the Constitution in the Aftermath of Doe v. University of Michigan." *Wayne Law Review* 37 (Spring 1991): entire issue.

4429. "Campus Is Split Over Statements by a Professor." *New York Times*, 23 December 1990. [U.C. Berkeley and statements by anthropology professor on gender and racial issues]

4430. "Campus Police Attend Racial Sensitivity Class." *New York Times*, 16 February 1992. [University of Arizona]

4431. Caranese, A. V. "Faculty Role Models and Diversifying the Gender and Racial Mix of Undergraduate Economics Majors." *Journal of Economic Education* 22 (Summer 1991): 276-284.

4432. Card, David, and Alan B. Krueger. "School Quality and Black- White Relative Earnings: A Direct Assessment." *Quarterly Journal of Economics* 107 (February 1992): 151-200.

4433. Carnegie Foundation for the Advancement of Teaching. *Campus Life: In Search of Community*. Lawrenceville, NJ: Princeton University Press, 1990.

4434. Carter, Deborah J. and others. "Double Jeopardy: Women of Color in Higher Education." *Educational Record* 68 (Fall-Winter 1988): 98-103.

4435. Carter, Stephen L. "Academic Tenure and White Male Standards: Some Lessons from the Patent Law." *Yale Law Journal* 100 (May 1991): 2065-2086.

4436. Celis, William, 3rd. "Colleges Battle Culture and Poverty to Swell Hispanic Enrollments." *New York Times*, 24 February 1993.

4437. _____. "Kansas Campus Debates Ouster of Black Leader." *New York Times*, 16 September 1991. [University of Kansas]

4438. _____. "Tenure Dispute at S. M. U. Raises Suspicions of Racism." *New York Times*, 11 November 1992. [Southern Methodist University]

4439. Center for the Study and Prevention of Campus Violence. *National Campus Violence Survey*. Towson State University, CSPCV, 1988.

4440. Chacon, Maria. *Chicanas in Post Secondary Education*. Intercambios Femeniles, 1982.

4441. Chaikind, Stephen. *College Enrollment Patterns of Black and White Students*. Washington, DC: Decision Resources Corporation, 1987.

4442. Chait, Richard P. *The Desegregation of Higher Education: A Legal History*. University of Wisconsin, 1972.

4443. Chamberlain, Marian K., ed. "Women's Colleges." *Women in Academe: Program and Prospects*, : Chapter 6. Russell Sage Foundation, 1988.

4444. Chambers, Raymond M. *Black Students' Perceptions of the Environment at a Predominantly White Public University*. Ph.D. diss., University of Massachusetts, 1991. UMO # 9132827.

4445. Chan, Sucheng. "On the Ethnic Studies Requirement. Part I: Pedogogical Implications." *Amerasia Journal* 15 (1989): 267-280.

4446. Chandras, Kan V. "Race Discrimination on Black Campuses." *Chronicle of Higher Education* (17 November 1993). [Discrimination against "non-white" faculty]

4447. Chang, Edward C., and Edward H. Ritter. "Ethnocentrism in Black College Students." *Journal of Social Psychology* 100 (1976): 89-98.

4448. "The Changing Culture of the University." *Partisan Review* 58 (Spring 1991): entire issue.

4449. "Changing Patterns of Opportunity in Higher Education." *American Journal of Education* 98 (August 1990): entire issue.

4450. Chao, Suzie, and William Fitzsimmons. "Statement on Asian American Admissions." *Harvard Gazette*, 22 January 1988.

4451. Chasan, Alice. "Walk Like an Egyptian. Reflections on Leonard Jeffries." *Tikkun* 8 (July - August 1993): 5-6. [City College, CUNY]

4452. Chestam, H. E. and others. "Institutional Effects on the Psychosocial Development of African American College Students." *Journal of Counseling Psychology* 37 (October 1990).

4453. Chideya, Faroi, and Mark Starr. "Dashed Hopes at Harvard." *Newsweek*, 14 May 1990. [Afro-American Studies Department]

4454. Chira, Susan. "Minority Students Tell of Bias In Quest for Higher Education." *New York Times*, 4 August 1992. [High school guidance counselors]

4455. Christy, Ralph D., and Lionel Williamson, eds. *A Century of Service. Land-Grant Colleges and Universities*. New Brunswick, NJ: Transaction Publishers, 1991. [Black land-grant institutions]

4456. Churaman, Charlotte V. "Financing of College Education by Minority and White Families." *Journal of Consumer Affairs* 26 (Winter 1992): 324-350.

4457. Churchill, Ward. "White Studies: The Intellectual Imperialism of Contemporary U.S. Education." *Integrateducation* 19 (January 1982): 51-57.

4458. Churchill, Ward, and Norbert S. Hill, Jr. "Indian Education at the University Level: An Historical Study." *Journal of Ethnic Studies* 7 (Fall 1979): 43-58.

4459. Chused, Richard H. "The Hiring and Retention of Minorities and Women on American Law School Faculties." *University of Pennsylvania Law Review* 137 (December 1988): 537-569.

4460. Clague, Monique W. "Legal Aspects of Minority Participation in Higher Education." *Education and Urban Society* 21 (May 1989): 260-282.

4461. Clark, E. Culpepper. "The Schoolhouse Door. An Institutional Response to Desegregation." in *Opening Doors*, pp. 40-63. eds. Harry J. Knopke and others. : University of Alabama Press, 1991. [Desegregation of the University of Alabama]

4462. Clarke, David A. "The Chairman and the Law School." *Washington Post*, 13 April 1994. (letter), [Financial aid by the D.C. government to the District of Columbia School of Law]

4463. "A Class Sends Message to Harvard Law School." *New York Times*, 21 November 1990. [Non-credit class taught by Derrick A. Bell, Jr., protesting the absence of minority women from the faculty]

4464. Clay, Camille A. "Campus Racial Tensions: Trend Or Aberration?" *Thought and Action* 5 (Fall 1989): 21-30.

4465. Clayton, Cornell W. "Politics and Liberal Education. An Apolitical Curriculum Is a Dangerous Mirage." *Chronicle of Higher Education*, 8 April 1992. pp. B1-B2.

4466. Coakley, Jay, and Lynda Dickson. *The Perceptions and Experiences of Minority Students at the University of Colorado, Colrado Springs*. Colrado Springs, CO: The University, 1988.

4467. Cohen, Adam. "White Supremacists Find Recruits on Campus." *Klanwatch Intelligence Report*, February 1989.

4468. Cohen, Dov. "Equity Program Can Equal Success at EMU." *Ann Arbor News*, 10 June 1989. [Minority students at Eastern Michigan University]

4469. Cohen, Robert. *When the Old Left Was Young. Student Radicals and America's First Mass Student Movement, 1929-1941*. Oxford University Press, 1993.

4470. Cole, Johnnetta B. "Another Day Will Find Us Brave." *Sage* 6 (Summer 1989). [First black woman president of Spelman College]

4471. _____. *Conversations. Straight Talk with America's Sister President*. Doubleday, 1993. [President of Spelman College]

4472. Cole, Stephen. "Sex Discrimination and Admission to Medical School, 1929-1984." *American Journal of Sociology* 92 (1986): 549- 567.

4473. Coliver, Sandra, ed. *Striking a Balance: Hate Speech, Freedom of Expression and Non-Discrimination*. Article 19. London: 1992.

4474. Collison, Michele N-K. "Black Students Complain of Abuse by Campus Police." *Chronicle of Higher Education*, 14 April 1993.

4475. _____. "In Chapel Hill, Geography Is an Issue as Students Demand a Central Location for Black Cultural Center." *Chronicle of Higher Education*, 28 April 1993.

4476. _____. "Network of Black Students Hopes to Create a New Generation of Civil Rights Leaders." *Chronicle of Higher Education*, 30 September 1992.

4477. _____. "A Twist on Affirmative Action." *Chronicle of Higher Education*, 24 November 1993. [Italian American Legal Defense and Higher Education Fund and CUNY]

4478. Colon, Alan K. *A Critical Review of Black Studies Programs*. Ph.D. diss., Stanford University, 1980.

4479. Committee on Admissions and Enrollment. *Freshman Admissions at Berkeley: A Policy for the 1990s and Beyond*. Berkeley, CA: Berkeley Division, Academic Senate, University of California, 1989.

4480. Conable, Charlotte W. *Women at Cornell: The Myth of Equal Education*. Ithaca, NY: 1977.

4481. Conarroe, Joel. "How I'm PC." *New York Times*, 12 July 1991. ["Politically correct"]

4482. "Conflict Escalates Over Organization Devoted to Racism." *New York Times*, 20 October 1991. [White Student union, University of Minnesota]

4483. Conklin, Paul. "Bleak Outlook for Academic History Jobs." *Perspectives (American Historical Association)* (April 1993).

4484. Conley, Darlene J. *Philanthropic Foundations and Organizational Change: The Case of Southern Educational Foundation (SEF) During the Civil Rights Era*. Ph.D. diss., Northwestern University, 1990. [Desegregation of higher education]. UMO # 9114537.

4485. Conrad, Clifton F. *Mississippi Curriculum Study: A Report for the U.S. Department of Justice.* Washington, DC: U.S. Department of Justice, 1987. [Comparison of black and white public colleges in state]

4486. Conrad, Clifton F., and Paul E. Shrode. "The Long Road: Desegregating Higher Education." *Thought and Action* 6 (Spring 1990): 35-45.

4487. Constantine, J. M. "The Added Value of Historically Black Colleges." *Academe* 80 (May-June 1994): 12-18.

4488. Conti, Gina. "Minority Organizations Perceived as Being Separatist." *Daily Orange*, 29 January 1990. [Syracuse University]

4489. _____. "Racial Polarization Increasing on Syracuse University Campus." *Daily Orange*, 22 January 1990. [Syracuse University]

4490. Cook, Blanche Wiesen, and Sandra E. Cooper. "The Trashing of C.U.N.Y." *New York Times*, 8 September 1994.

4491. "The Court's Decision Against the U." *Daily Pennsylvanian*, 11 January 1990. [Excerpts from U.S. Supreme Court ruling in the tenure case of Professor Rosalie Tung, University of Pennsylvania]

4492. Crist, Alan N. *The Role of the Undergraduate Minority Student Recruiter in Selected Major Public Midwestern Universities.* Ph.D. diss., University of Wisconsin, 1987.

4493. Cross, Dorothy. *Aid and Access.* Albany, NY: New York State Higher Education Services Corporation, 1984.

4494. Cross, Robert D. "The Historical Development of Anti- intellectualism in American Society: Implications for the Schooling of African Americans." *Journal of Negro Education* 59 (Winter 1990).

4495. Cross, Theodore. "Black Faculty At Harvard: Does the Pipeline Defense Hold Water?" *Journal of Blacks in Higher Education* 4 (Summer 1994): 42-46.

4496. _____. "Suppose There Was No Affirmative Action At the Most Prestigious Colleges and Graduate Schools." *Journal of Blacks in Higher Education* 3 (Spring 1994): 44-51.

4497. Crum, Steven J. "Henry Roe Cloud, a Winnebago Indian Reformer: His Quest for American Indian Higher Education." *Kansas History* 11 (Autumn 1988): 171-184.

4498. _____. "The Idea of an Indian College or University in Twentieth Century America Before the Formation of the Navajo Community College in 1968." *Tribal College: Journal of American Indian Higher Education* 1 (Summer 1989).

4499. _____. "Native American Students: Victims of Racism." *California Aggie, University of California, Davis*, 5 June 1989.

4500. Cunningham, Bill, and S. Miller. "Racism: Assessing the Campus and Community Environment." *Journal of College Student Development* 32 (March 1991): 181.

4501. Cunningham, Jo Ann. "Black Studies Programs: Reasons for Their Success and Non-success from Inception to the Present." *National Journal of Sociology* 5 (Spring 1991): 19-41.

4502. _____. *An Investigation into the Structural Patterns of Selected New Jersey College Black Studies Programs: A National Model.* Ph.D. diss., Rutgers University, 1989. UMO # 9008803.

4503. Dalton, Michelle R. *The Long Road to Recognition: A Historical Investigation of the Activities of the Association of Colleges for Negro Youth, 1913-1934.* Ph.D. diss., University of Tennessee, 1991. UMO # 9212739.

4504. Dalton, Raymond A. *Admission, Retention, and Support Services of African-American Architecture Students: A National Survey.* Ph.D. diss., Purdue University, 1990. UMO # 9116371.

4505. Dane, Perry and others. "[Letters commenting on Ian-Honey- Lopez, "Community Ties, Race and Faculty Hiring: The Case for Professors Who Don't Think White"]." *Reconstruction* 1 (1992): 3- 21.

4506. D'Angelli, Anthony R., and Scott L. Hershberger. "African American Undergraduates on a Predominantly White Campus: Academic Factors, Social Networks, and Campus Climate." *Journal of Negro Education* 62 (Winter 1993): 67-81.

4507. Davidson, Cathy N. "'PH' Stands for Political Hypocrisy." *Academe* 77 (September-October 1991): 8-14.

4508. Davis, J. S., and K. Johus. "Changes in Low-income Freshmen Participation in College, 1966 to 1986." *Journal of Student Financial Aid* 19 (1989): 56-62.

4509. de la Torre, Adela. "Diversity, Not Quotas, for Colleges." *Los Angeles Times*, 9 March 1994.

4510. De Palma, Anthony. "As Black Ph.D.'s Taper Off, Aid for Foreigners Is Assailed." *New York Times*, 21 April 1992.

4511. _____. "Battling Bias, Campuses Face Free Speech Fight." *New York Times*, 20 February 1991.

4512. _____. "Hard-won Acceptance Spawns New Conflicts around Ethnic Studies." *New York Times*, 2 January 1991. [San Francisco State University]

4513. _____. "In Campus Debate on New Orthodoxy, A Counter Offensive." *New York Times*, 25 September 1991. [Organization of Teachers for a Democratic Culture]

4514. _____. "Massachusetts Campus is Torn by Racial Strife." *New York Times*, 18 October 1992. [University of Massachusetts, Amherst]

4515. _____. "Mississippi Slow to Act on Integrating Colleges." *New York Times*, 26 August 1992.

4516. _____. "Rare in Ivy League: Women Who Work As Full Professors." *New York Times*, 24 January 1993.

4517. _____. "Separate Ethnic Worlds Grow on Campus." *New York Times*, 18 May 1991.

4518. De Van, William A. "Toward a New Standard in Gender Discrimination: The Case of Virginia Military Institute." *William and Mary Law Review* 33 (Winter 1992): 489-542.

4519. De Witt, Karen. "College Board Scores Are Up For Second Consecutive Year." *New York Times*, 19 August 1993.

4520. Defour, D. C., and B. J. Hirsch. "The Adaptation of ack Graduate Students: A Social Network Approach." *American Journal of Community Psychology* 18 (June 1990).

4521. Dejoie, Carolyn M. "The Black Woman in Alienation in White Academia." *Negro Educational Review* 28 (January 1977): 4-12.

4522. Delgado, Richard. "Approach-avoidance in Law School Hiring: Is the Law as WASP?" *Saint Louis University Law Journal* 34 (Spring 1990): 631-642.

4523. _____. "Campus Antiracism Rules: Constitutional Narratives in Collision." *Northwestern University Law Review* 85 (Winter 1991): 343-387.

4524. Delgado, Richard, and Derrick Bell. "Minority Law Professors' Lives: The Bell-Delgado Survey." *Harvard Civil Rights-Civil Liberties Law Review* 24 (Spring 1989): 349-392.

4525. Delgado, Richard, and Jean Stefancic. "Overcoming Legal Barriers to Regulating Hate Speech on Campuses." *Chronicle of Higher Education* (11 August 1993).

4526. Dembner, Alice. "Educators Fret Over Dwindling Graduates." *Boston Globe*, 15 June 1994. [Students at New England colleges who are dropping out]

4527. _____. "Poll Finds College Students Ready to Make a Difference." *Boston Globe*, 4 September 1994.

4528. Dennis, Lawrence. "Education- The Tool of the Dominant Elite." *Social Frontier* 1 (January 1935): 11-15.

4529. *Desegregation of Public Higher Education in Tennessee*. Washington, DC: U.S. Commission on Civil Rights, 1989.

4530. Diamond, Sara. "'Politically Incorrect' Minorities." *Guardian (NYC)*, 27 March 1991. [Right-wing efforts to organize college students, The Student Forum]

4531. _____. "Readin', Writin', and Repressin'." *Z Magazine* 4 (February 1991): 44-48. [National Association on Scholars]

4532. Dickstein, Morris. "Columbia Recovered." *New York Times Magazine*, 15 May 1988. [Columbia University]

4533. Dingerson, Michael R. and others. "The Hiring of Underrepresented Individuals in Academic Administrative Positions: 1972-1979." *Research in Higher Education* 23 (1985): 115-134.

4534. "Dissident Priest Says Catholic University Shows Bias Against Blacks." *New York Times*, 23 July 1989. [Rev. George A Stallings, Jr. and Catholic University of American, Washington, D.C.]

4535. Dorsey, Carolyn. "Black Faculty at White Institutions before 1900." *Western Journal of Black Studies* 14 (Spring 1990): 1-8.

4536. Dougherty, Kevin J. "Community Colleges and Baccalaureate Attainment." *Journal of Higher Education* 63 (March-April 1992): 188-214.

4537. _____. "The Effects of Community Colleges: Aid or Hindrance to Socioeconomic Attainment?" *Sociology of Education* 60 (1987): 86-103.

4538. Douglass, Phyllis B. *A Study of Factors Associated with Attrition of Black Students at a Historically Black Four-Year College: 1985-1989*. Ph.D. diss., Temple University, 1990. [Found a 93 percent dropout rate in Coppin State College]. UMO # 9103576.

4539. Dowdy, Lewis C., Jr. *The Impact of the Philosophies of the Presbyterian Church, U.S.A., Booker T. Washington, and W. E. B. Du Bois on the Educational Program of Johnson C. Smith University*. Ph.D. diss., Rutgers University, 1989. UMO # 9008002.

4540. Drago, Edmund L. *Initiative, Paternalism, and Race Relations'. Charleston's Avery Normal Institute*. Athens, GA: University of Georgia Press, 1990.

4541. Draper, Anne, and Hal Draper. *The Dirt on California: Agribusiness and the University*. Berkeley, CA: The Independent Socialist Clubs of America, 1968.

4542. Drummond, Tammerlin, and Bettina Boxall. "Gay Rights Fight Moves on Campus." *Los Angeles Times*, 10 January 1994.

4543. D'Souza, Dinesh. *Illiberal Education. The Politics of Race and Sex on Campus*. New York, NY: Free Press, 1991.

4544. _____. "The New Segregation on Campus." *American Scholar* 60 (Winter 1991): 17-30.

4545. _____. "'P.C.' So Far." *Commentary* 92 (October 1991): 44-46.

4546. Duke, Lynne. "Malcolm X as Teacher." *Washington Post*, 19 November 1992. [The tradition of Malcolm X on college campuses]

4547. Dunn, James R. "The Shortage of Black Male Students in the College Classroom: Consequences and Causes." *Western Journal of Black Studies* 12 (Summer 1988): 73-76.

4548. Duran, C. "The Role of Libraries in American Indian Tribal College Development." *College and Research Libraries* 52 (September 1991): 395-408.

4549. Durham, Joseph T. "Quality Over Racial Identification." *Washington Post*, 13 December 1992. (letter), [Black colleges]

4550. Duster, Troy. "They're Taking Over! and Other Myths about Race on Campus." *Philosophy and Social Action* 19 (January-June 1993): 30-37.

4551. Dyer, Conrad M. *Protest and the Politics of Open Admissions: The Impact of the Black and Puerto Rican Students' Community (of City College)*. Ph.D. diss., City College of New York, 1990. UMO # 9029930.

4552. Edelman, Peter B. "Put Limits on Racist Speech." *Fulton County Daily Report*, 16 May 1989. [Questions applicability of First Amendment to racist speech]

4553. Edgcomb, Gabrielle S. *From Swastika to Jim Crow: Refugee Scholars at Black Colleges*. Krieger, 1993.

4554. Education of the States. *New Strategies for Producing Minority Teachers*. Denver, CO: Education Commission of the States, 1990.

4555. Edwards, Larry G. *Dimensions of Gender Discrimination in Oklahoma's System of Higher Education*. Ph.D. diss., University of Oklahoma, 1989. UMO # 9003668.

4556. Egar, Emmanuel E. *Development and Termination of Bishop College between 1960 to 1988*. Ph.D. diss., University of North Texas, 1990. [Black college in Texas].

4557. Ehrenberg, Ronald G., and Donna S. Rothstein. *Do Historically Black Institutions of Higher Education Confer Unique Advantages on Black Students? An Initial Analysis*. National Bureau of Economic Research, 1993.

4558. Ehrlich, Howard J. *Campus Ethnoviolence and the Policy Options*. Baltimore, MD: National Institute Against Prejudice and Violence, 1990.

4559. _____. "Ethnoviolence on the Campus." *Sociological Abstracts* supplement 167 (August 1991). 91S25048/ASA/1991/6407.

4560. Eisenman, Russell. "Academic Achievement in High School of Blacks and Whites: A Retrospective Study of Freshman College Students Who Would Not Have Been Admitted Without Open Admissions." *Mankind Quarterly* 32 (Summer 1992): 377-382.

4561. _____. "Gender and Racial Prejudice of Conservative College Women." *Psychological Reports* 68 (April 1991): 450-451.

4562. _____. "Possible Gender Bias in Ivy League and Selective Colleges." *Psychological Reports* 70 (June 1992): 970.

4563. Elain, Ada M. *The Status of Blacks in Higher Education*. Lanham, MD: 1989.

4564. Elam, Julia C., ed. *Blacks in Higher Education: Overcoming the Odds*. Lanham, MD: University Press of America, 1989.

4565. *Elements of Racism in the Darden Environment*. University of Virginia, 1992. [Charges of racism at the Darden Graduate School of Business, University of Virginia]

4566. Elmore, Charles J., and Robert T. Blackburn. "Black and White Faculty in White Research Universities." *Journal of Higher Education* 54 (1983): 1-15.

4567. Engstrom, C. M., and W. E. Sedlacek. "A Study of Prejudice Toward University Student-Athletes." *Journal of Counseling and Development* 70 (September-October 1991): 189-193.

4568. *Enhancing the Minority Presence in Graduate Education*. Washington, DC: Council of Graduate Schools, 1988.

4569. "Enrollments: Recent Ethnic Trends Vary." *The NEA 1991 Almanac of Higher Education*, p. 10. Washington, DC: National Education Association, 1991.

4570. Epps, Edgar G. "Academic Culture and the University Professor." *Academe* 75 (September-October 1989).

4571. Epps, John S. and others. "Frat Bashing." *Washington Post*, 22 May 1993. [Three letters on black fraternal organizations]

4572. Epstein, Barbara. "'Political Correctness' and Collective Powerlessness." *Socialist Review* 21 (July-December 1991): 13-35.

4573. Epstein, E. H. "Social Paradoxes of American Education." *Oxford Review of Education* 18 (1992): 201-212.

4574. Erickson, Doug. "Students: Minorities Slighted at AC." *Metro County Courier*, 7 June 1989. [Augusta College, Augusta, GA]

4575. Ervin, J. E. *Black Students' Perceptions of their Experiences at Kent State University*. Ph.D. diss., Kent State University, 1972.

4576. Ethier, Kathleen, and Kay Deaux. "Hispanics in Ivy: Assessing Identity and Perceived Threat." *Sex Roles* 22 (1990): 427-440.

4577. *Ethnoviolence on Campus: The UMBC Study*. Baltimore, MD: National Institute Against Prejudice and Violence, October 1987. [University of Maryland, Baltimore County]

4578. Evans, David L. "The Wrong Examples." *Newsweek*, 1 March 1993. [Comparative lack of male African-Americans applying for college]

4579. Faherty, William B. "Nativism and Midwestern Education: The Experience of Saint Louis University, 1832-1856." *History of Education Quarterly* 8 (1968): 447-458.

4580. *Fair and Open Environment? Bigotry and Violence College Campuses in California*. Washington, DC: U.S. Commission on Civil Rights, 1991.

4581. Fairley, Charlestine R. *A History of Clafin College, 1869- 1987*. Ph.D. diss., University of South Carolina, 1990. UMO # 9029173.

4582. Faith, Ellen S. *Strategy, Culture, and Renewal: An Interpretive Case Study of Le Moyne-Owen College, an Historically Black Institution of Higher Education*. Ph.D. diss., Harvard University, 1991. UMO # 9132337.

4583. Faithfull, Bayard. "Snowballing Tuition Fires Up Puerto Rican Students." *Guardian (NYC)*, 25 September 1991. [University of Puerto Rico]

4584. Fallows, Robert J. *A Study of Persistence of American Indian Students at a Large Southwestern University*. Ph.D. diss., Arizona State University, 1987. UMO # 8713654.

4585. Faludi, Susan. "The Naked Citadel." *New Yorker*, 5 September 1994. [A single female student at The Citadel, S.C.]

4586. Farnum, Richard A., Jr. "The American Upper Class and Higher Education, 1880-1970." in *Social Class and Democratic Leadership*, pp. 69-94. ed. Harold J. Bershady. Philadelphia, PA: University of Pennsylvania Press, 1989.

4587. _____. *Prestige in the Ivy League: Democratization and Discrimination at Penn and Columbia, 1890-1970*. Department of Sociology, University of Pennsylvania, 1980. Unpublished.

4588. _____. *Prestige in the Ivy League: Meritocracy at Columbia, Harvard and Penn, 1870-1940*. Ph.D. diss., University of Pennsylvania, 1990. [1870-1940]. UMO # 9026549.

4589. Farrell, Walter C., Jr., and Cloyzelle K. Jones. "Recent Racial Incidents in Higher Education: A Preliminary Perspective." *Urban Review* 20 (1988): 211-226.

4590. Feagin, Joe R. "The Continuing Significance of Racism: Discrimination Against Black Students in White Colleges." *Journal of Black Studies* 22 (June 1992): 546-578.

4591. Feingold, Henry L. "Investing in Themselves: The Harvard Case and the Origins of the Third American-Jewish Commercial Elite." *American Jewish History* 77 (June 1988): 530-553.

4592. Feldman, Penny H. *Recruiting an Elite; Admission to Harvard College*. New York, NY: Garland, 1987.

4593. Feron, James. "Bias Charge Upsets Manhattanville Campus." *New York Times*, 11 October 1987. [Manhattanville College, Purchase, N.Y.]

4594. Fields, Cheryl M. "Latino Leaders Fear California's Fiscal Crisis Will Slow Their Drive for Greater Access to Higher Education." *Chronicle of Higher Education*, 2 December 1992.

4595. Finn, Chester E., Jr. "The Campus: An Island of Repression in a Sea of Freedom." *Commentary* (September 1989).

4596. _____. "Why Can't Colleges Convey Our Diverse Culture's Unifying Themes?" *Chronicle of Higher Education*, 13 June 1990.

4597. "First Amendment- Racist and Sexist Expression on Campus- Court Strikes Down University Limits on Hate Speech." *Harvard Law Review* 103 (April 1990): 1397-1402.

4598. Fisk, Mark, and Jonathan Scott. "The Times on People's Park." *Lies Of Our Times: A Journal to Correct the Record* 1 (September 1990): 3-4. [Michigan State University]

4599. Fleming, Cynthia G. "Knoxville College: A History and Some Recollections of the First Fifty Years, 1875-1925." *East Tennessee Historical Society's Publications* 58-59 (1986-1987): 89-111.

4600. Fleming, Jacqueline. *Blacks in College*. San Francisco, CA: Jossey-Bass, 1984.

4601. Flint, Anthony. "Curriculum Debate Rattles Ivied Walls." *Boston Globe*, 16 September 1991. [Multiculturalism]

4602. _____. "In a Poll, Black Harvard Graduates Cite Bias." *Boston Globe*, 1 July 1990.

4603. _____. "Loss of Students Highlights RCC Woes." *Boston Globe*, 19 August 1990. [Roxbury Community College, Boston]

4604. _____. "A Multicultural Education." *Boston Globe*, 21 May 1990. [Cambridge College, Cambridge, MA]

4605. _____. "Racial Divisions Persist on N.E. Campuses." *Boston Globe*, 17 May 1992. [New England]

4606. Foderano, Lisa W. "At Vassar, Expanded Role for Blacks at Commencement." *New York Times*, 13 May 1991.

4607. Foner, Henry. "An Open Letter to Dr. Leonard Jeffries." *Jewish Currents* (October 1993).

4608. Forbes, Jack D. *Native American Higher Education: The Struggle for the Creation of D-Q University, 1960-1971*. Davis, CA: D-Q University Press, 1985.

4609. Fraga, Luis R. and others. "Hispanic Americans and Educational Policy: Limits to Equal Access." *Journal of Politics* 48 (November 1986): 850-876.

4610. Frammolino, Ralph. "College Accreditation Panel Adopts Plan On Diversity." *Los Angeles Times*, 24 February 1994. [Western Association of Schools and Colleges]

4611. _____. "Getting Grades for Diversity?" *Los Angeles Times*, 23 February 1994. [Regional accrediting associations and institutional commitment to diversity]

4612. _____. "A New Generation of Rebels." *Los Angeles Times*, 20 November 1993. [Latino college students in California]

4613. Frampton, Pamela M. *Gender and Race Effects in the Indiana and Michigan Principal Assessment Centers*. Ph.D. diss., Purdue University, 1990. UMO #9116385.

4614. Franke, Carrie. *Injustice Sheltered: Race Relations at the University of Illinois and Champaign-Urbana, 1945-1962*. Ph.D. diss., University of Illinois, 1990. UMO #9114239.

4615. Franke, Katherine. "Why Tolerate the Intolerable? Academic Institutions Shouldn't Bend Over Backwards for Hate-Mongers." *Guardian (NYC)* (16 October 1991).

4616. Frankel, Sara. "Stanford: Groping Toward Plurality." *San Francisco Examiner-Chronicle*, 18 June 1989.

4617. Franklin, John Hope, George M. Fredrickson, Jon Wiener, Gene H. Bell-Vidala, Clyde de L. Ryals, Ernst Benjamin, Barbara R. Bergman, and C. Vann Woodward. "'Illiberal Education': An Exchange." *New York Review of Books* 38 (26 September 1991): 74- 76.

4618. Franklin, V. P. "Whatever Happened to the College-Bred Negro?" *History of Education Quarterly* 24 (Fall 1984): 411-418.

4619. "Free Speech and Religious, Racial, and Sexual Harrassment." *William and Mary Law Review* 32 (Winter 1991): 207- 351 (four articles).

4620. Freedman, James O. "Bigoted Students, Doting Adults." *New York Times*, 12 October 1990. [President of Dartmouth College on racism and antisemitism in off-campus newspaper, Dartmouth Review.]

4621. "Freedom and Tenure in the Academy..." *Law and Contemporary Problems* 53 (Summer 1990): 1-418 (ten articles).

4622. Fuller, R., and R. Schoenberger. "The Gender Salary Gap: Do Academic Achievement, Internship Experience, and College Major Make a Difference?" *Social Science Quarterly* 72 (December 1991): 715-726.

4623. Futrelle, David. "Campus 'PC' Is a Paper Tiger in a Jungle of Bigotry and Laziness." *In These Times* (12 June 1991).

4624. Gabe, Li Anne C. "Entry-level Examinations and the Community College: "Cooling out" or Casting Out?" Master's thesis, Florida Atlantic University, 1990. UMO #1339795.

4625. Gale, Mary Ellen. "On Curbing Racial Speech." *Responsive Community* 1 (Winter 1990-1991): 47-58.

4626. Garrott, Carl L. *The Relationship of University French Study to Ethnocentrism-Chauvinism*. Ph.D. diss., University of Kentucky, 1985. UMO #8523913.

4627. Garza, Hisauro. "The 'Barrioization' of Hispanic Faculty." *Educational Record* (Winter 1988): 122-124.

4628. Gaudiani, Claire L. "Dirty Tricks for Scholarships." *New York Times*, 26 August 1992.

4629. Gentry, Dorothy. "Racial Harmony." *North Texas Daily*, 29 October 1989. [Blacks on campus of North Texas State University, Denton]

4630. Giovanni, Nikki. "Campus Racism 101." *Academe* 80 (May-June 1994): 19-20.

4631. _____. *Racism 101*. Morrow, 1994.

4632. Gless, Darryl L., and Barbara Herrnstein Smith, eds. *The Politics of Liberal Education*. Durham, NC: Duke University Press, 1990.

4633. Glessing, Erica. "Struggle for Black Studies Paying Off." *Santa Barbara News-Press*, 2 February 1990. [University of California, Santa Barbara]

4634. Glotzer, Richard S. *Higher Education in the American South 1660-1984: Class and Race in Institutional Development*. Ph.D. diss., University of Wisconsin, 1984.

4635. Goggin, Jacqueline. "Challenging Sexual Discrimination in the Historical Profession: Women Historians and the American Historical Association, 1890-1940." *American Historical Review* 97 (June 1992): 769-802.

4636. Goggins, Lathardus. *Central State University: The First One Hundred Years, 1887-1987*. Wilberforce, Ohio: Central State University, 1987.

4637. Goldberger, David. "Sources of Judicial Reluctance to Use Psychic Harm as a Basis for Supporting Racist, Sexist, and Ethnically Offensive Speech." *Brooklyn Law Review* 56 (Winter 1991): 1165-1212.

4638. Goldstein, Richard. "Body English." *Village Voice* (7 May 1991). [Critical discussion of proposed Collegiate Speech Protection Act of 1991]

4639. Gomes, Ralph C., and L. F. Williams, eds. *From Exclusion to Inclusion. The Long Struggle for African-American and African Studies*. Greenwood, 1992.

4640. Gomez-Cano, Gricelle E. *The Ideological Formulation of Mexican-American University Students: The Mejicano, Chicano, and Hispanic Identities*. Ph.D. diss., University of Houston, 1991. UMO #9129580.

4641. Gonzales, Phillip B. "Spanish Heritage and Ethnic Protest in New Mexico: The Anti-Fraternity Bill 0f 1933." *New Mexico Historical Review* 61 (1986): 281-299. [University of New Mexico]

4642. Goodman, Denise. "Racial Attacks Jolts U. of Maine." *Boston Globe*, 21 February 1991.

4643. Goodman, Ellen. "The Great Divide." *Boston Globe*, 2 September 1990.

4644. Goodman, Matthew. "The Alchemy of Bias." *Z Magazine* 4 (July-August 1991): 120-124. [Multicultural curriculum]

4645. Gordon, Daniel. "Inside the Stanford Mind." *Perspectives (American Historical Association)* 30 (April 1992). [New general education requirement, "Culture, Ideas, and Values"]

4646. Gordon, Larry. "Berkeley Battles the Blues." *Los Angeles Times Magazine* (13 June 1993).

4647. _____. "Chang-Lin Tien." *Los Angeles Times*, 13 September 1992. [Chancellor, UC Berkeley]

4648. Gordon, Leonard. "College Student Stereotypes of Blacks and Jews on Two Campuses: Four Studies Spanning 50 Years." *Sociology and Social Research* 7 (April 1986): 200-201. [Princeton and Arizona State universities]

4649. Gordon, Lynn D. *Gender and Higher Education in the Progressive Era*. New Haven, CT: Yale University Press, 1990.

4650. _____. "Women on Campus, 1870-1920: History to Use." *Thought and Action* 6 (Spring 1990): 5-20.

4651. Gorelick, Sherry. *City College and the Jewish Poor: Education in New York, 1800-1924*. New Brunswick, NJ: Rutgers University Press, 1981.

4652. Gourevitch, Philip. "The Jeffries Affair." *Commentary* 93 (March 1992): 34-38. [See letters about this article, July 1992, pp. 13-14]

4653. "Graduation Rates for Athletes and Other Students Who Entered College in 1985-86." *Chronicle of Higher Education* (26 May 1993). [Individual data for 298 colleges in Division I of NCAA.]

4654. Graff, Gerald and others. "'The Storm Over the University': An Exchange." *New York Review of Books* (14 February 1991): 48-49. [Reference to John Searle, "The Storm Over the University", December 6, 1990]

4655. Graglia, Lino A. "Race Norming in Law School Admissions." *Journal of Legal Education* 42 (March 1992): 97-102. [See M.A. Olivas, below]

4656. Graham, Patricia A. "Expansion and Exclusion: A History of Women in American Higher Education." *Signs* 3 (Summer 1978): 759- 773.

4657. Graham, Renee. "Racial Issues Test Students." *Boston Globe*, 3 October 1989. [Higher education in Massachusetts]

4658. Granfield, Robert. "Making It by Faking It: Working-class Students in an Elite Academic Environment." *Journal of Contemporary Ethnography* 20 (October 1991): 331-351.

4659. _____. *Making Elite Lawyers: Visions of Law at Harvard and Beyond*. Routledge, 1992.

4660. Grass, Gary. "Black Hats for the Politically Correct: Behind the PC Controversy Lurks a Conservative Propaganda Campaign." *Propaganda Review* (Fall 1991): 22-25.

4661. Gravett, Ericka. "White Students on Campus Spur Debate." *The Hilltop* (11 May 1991). [Howard University]

4662. Gray, Mary W. "The Halls of Ivy and the Halls of Justice: Resisting Sex Discrimination against Faculty Women." *Academe* 71 (1985): 33-41.

4663. Greeley, Andrew M. "Anti-Catholicism in the Academy." *Change* 9 (1977): 40-43.

4664. Green, Madeline F. *Minorities on Campus: A Handbook for Enhancing Diversity*. Washington, DC: American Council on Education, 1989.

4665. Greenawalt, Kent. "Insults and Epithets: Are They Protected Speech?" *Rutgers Law Review* 42 (Winter 1990).

4666. [Greenberg, Jack. "Greenberg Admits Wrong." *Columbia Daily Spectator*, 20 February 1990. [Columbia Law School dean admits error in attempting to regulate appearance on campus of "Professor Griff", formerly of Public Enemy rap group]

4667. Greenberg, Karen J. "The Search for a Silver Lining: The American Academic Establishment and the 'Aryanization' of German Scholarship." *Simon Wiesenthal Center Annual* 2 (1985): 115-137.

4668. Greenberg, M., and S. Zenchelsky. "The Confrontation with Nazism at Rutgers: Academic Bureaucracy and Moral Failure." *History of Education Quarterly* 30 (Autumn 1990).

4669. Greene, Victor R. "Ethnic Confrontations with State Universities, 1860-1920." in *American Education and the European Immigrant 1840-1940*, pp. 189-207. ed. Bernard J. Weiss. University of Illinois Press, 1982. [Czechs and Scandanavians]

4670. Gregoian, Vartan. "Brown Expulsion Not About Free Speech." *New York Times*, 21 February 1991. [President, Brown University]

4671. Grey, Thomas C. "Responding to Abusive Speech on Campus: A Model Statute." *Reconstruction* 1 (Winter 1990).

4672. Griffin, Ronald C. "Hill's Account: Law School, Legal Education and the Black Law Student." *Thurgood Marshall Law Review* 12 (Summer 1987): 507-523.

4673. Grimes, Paul W., and Charles A. Register. "Teacher Unions and Black Students' Scores on College Entrance Exams." *Industrial Relations* 30 (Fall 1991): 492-500.

4674. Gropper, Richard E. *Student Support Services: A Needs Identification Process for the Black, College, Student-Athlete*. Ph.D. diss., Florida International University, 1991. [Florida International University]. UMO #9129295.

4675. *Group Tensions on American Colleges, 1989*. Baltimore, MD: National Institute Against Prejudice and Violence, 1990.

4676. Grubb, W. N. "The Effects of Differentiation on Educational Attainment: The Case of Community Colleges." *Review of Higher Education* 12 (1989): 349-374.

4677. Gruhl, J., and S. Welch. "The Impact of the Bakke Decision on Black and Hispanic Enrollment in Medical and Law Schools." *Social Science Quarterly* 71 (September 1990).

4678. Grunig, L. A. "Sex Discrimination in Promotion and Tenure in Journalism Education." *Journalism Quarterly* 66 (Spring 1989): 93-100.

4679. Gugliotta, Guy. "An Impromptu 'Dream' Becomes a National Model." *Washington Post*, 16 March 1993. ["I Have a Dream Foundation", organized by Eugene M. Lang]

4680. Gurin, Patricia, and Edgar G. Epps. *Black Consciousness, Identity, and Achievement: A Study of Students in Historically Black Colleges*. New York: Wiley, 1975.

4681. Guyette, Susan, and Charlotte Heth. *Issues for the Future of American Indian Studies*. UCLA 1985,

4682. Guy-Sheftall, Beverly, and Patricia Bell-Scott. "Finding a Way: Black Women Students and the Academy." in *Educating the Majority*, pp. 47-56. eds. Carol S. Pearson and others. Collier Macmillan, 1989.

4683. Haines, Andrew W. "Minority Professors and the Myth of Sisyphus: Consciousness and Praxis within the Special Teaching Challenge in American Law Schools." *National Black Law Journal* 10 (Fall 1988): 247-297.

4684. Hall, Charles W., and Jeff Leeds. "U-Va. Upholds Its Honor Code." *Washington Post*, 4 March 1994. [Black student charges of unfairness under code]

4685. Hall, Marcia L., and Walter R. Allen. "Race Conciousness among African-American College Students." in *Black Students*, eds. Gordon L. Berry, and Joy K. Asamen. Newbury Park, CA: Sage, 1989.

4686. Hall, Patrick. "Reading, Writing, Race-and Kicking Butt." *National Catholic Reporter* (4 June 1993). [Paternalism in colleges]

4687. Ham, William T. "Harvard Student Opinion on the Jewish Question." *Nation* 115 (6 September 1922): 225-227.

4688. Hamler, Portia Y. T. "Minority Tokenism in American Law Schools." *Howard Law Review* 26 (Spring 1983): 443-599.

4689. "Handicap and Race Discrimination in Readmission Procedures." *Journal of College and University Law* 15 (Spring 1989): 431-442.

4690. Hardin, John A. *Hope versus Reality: Black Higher Education in Kentucky, 1904-1954*. Ph.D. diss., University of Michigan, 1989. UMO #9013919.

4691. Harding, Vincent. "An Open Letter to Black Students in the North." *Negro Digest* (March 1969): 5-14.

4692. Harey, Bryan, and Alan McArdle. *Coming and Going: Ten- Semester Retention and Attrition Among Students Entering in Fall 1982 and 1983.* Amherst: University of Massachusetts, Office of Institutional Research and Planning, 1989. [Includes ethnic data]

4693. Haro, Carlos Manuel. "Chicano Access to Higher Education." *Sage Race Relations Abstracts* 7 (August 1982): 1-28.

4694. Harris, Robert L., Jr. and others. *Three Essays: Black Studies in the United States.* New York: Ford Foundation, 1990.

4695. Harris, Willie J., Jr. *Black and White Students' Evaluation of Selected Social and Cultural Activities Sanctioned by Ohio University.* Ph.D. diss., Ohio University, 1989. UMO #8922892.

4696. Harrison, Eric. "For Blacks, a Crisis on Campus." *Los Angeles Times*, 1 November 1992. [The portenteous desegregative merger of Tennessee State University and the University of Tennessee, Nashville]

4697. Hart, Noah, Jr. *A Comparison of Journalistic Treatment of Student Protest Activity by Black and White Reporters for Student Newspapers at Rutgers, The State University.* Ph.D. diss., Rutgers University, 1988. UMO #8827348.

4698. Harvard-Radcliffe Black Students Association. *On the Harvard Plantation.* The Association, 22 May 1992. [A two-page statement]

4699. Harvey, Miles. "Politically Correct Is Politically Suspect." *In These Times* (25 December 1991).

4700. Haskell, Paul G. "Legal Education on the Academic Plantation." *ABA Journal* 60 (1974). [See also response by Samuel C. Thompson, Jr., same volume]

4701. Hatchett, David. "Black Public Colleges at the Crossroads." *Crisis* (June-July 1987): 20-26, 57.

4702. Hauser, Gregory F. "Social Fraternities at Public Institutions of Higher Education: Their Rights Under the First and Fourteenth Amendments." *Journal of Law and Education* 19 (Fall 1990): 433-466.

4703. Hauser, Robert M. *The Decline in College Entry among African Americans: Findings in Search of Explanations.* University of Wisconsin-Madison Center for Demography and Ecology, 1990.

4704. _____. *Measuring Adolescent Educational Transitions among African Americans, Hispanics, and Whites.* University of Wisconsin-Madison Institute for Research on Poverty, 1991.

4705. _____. *Trends in College Entry among Whites, Blacks, and Hispanics, 1972-1988.* University of Wisconsin-Madison Institute for Research on Poverty, 1991.

4706. Hawkins, Gloria V. *The Process of Implementing the Desegregation Mandate at a Traditionally Black Institution.* Ph.D. diss., University of Wisconsin, 1990. [Virginia State University]. UMO #9100140.

4707. Hawkins, Hugh. *Banding Together. The Rise of National Associations in American Higher Education.* Johns Hopkins U.P., 1992.

4708. Hawkins, L. Tiffany. "Recognizing the Nightmare: The Merger of Louisiana State University and Southern University Law Schools." *Louisiana Law Review* 50 (January 1990).

4709. Hayden, Tom. "Amid Cash Crisis, Hispanics Win a Historic Victory." *Chronicle of Higher Education* (30 June 1993). [Hunger strike by proponents of a Chicano Studies Dept. at UCLA]

4710. Hayes, Floyd W., III. "Politics and Education in America's Multicultural Society: An African-American Studies' Response to Allan Bloom." *Journal of Ethnic Studies* 17 (Summer 1989): 71-88.

4711. Haynes, Leonard L., III. "Insuring the Future of Black Colleges." *Chronicle of Higher Education* (10 August 1994): Letter.

4712. Hays, Constance L. "CUNY Barred From Punishing White Professor." *New York Times*, 5 September 1991. [Prof. Michael Levin, CCNY]

4713. Heard, Alex. "Embarrassment of Riches-Certain Riches Anyway." *Spy* (January 1990): 80-87. ["How Enormous Donations from Embarrassing Benefactors...Make Universities Behave In Enormously Embarrassing Ways."]

4714. Hechinger, Fred M. "Class War over Tuition." *New York Times*, 5 February 1974.

4715. Hekymara, Kuregly. *The Third World Movement and Its History in the San Francisco State College Strike of 1968-69.* Ph.D. diss., University of California, Berkeley, 1972.

4716. Helle, Steven. "A New-century First Amendment?" *In These Times* (26 June 1991). [The issue of free speech on campus, including racist speech]

4717. Henderson, Peter L. "The Invisible Minority: Black Students at a Southern White University." *Journal of College Student Development* 29 (July 1988): 349-355.

4718. Henry, William A., III. "Upside Down in the Groves of Academe." *Time* (1 April 1991). ["A new intolerance"]

4719. Hentoff, Nat. "The Anti-Free Speech Movement." *Village Voice* (24 April 1990). [Regulation of racist and homophobic speech on university campuses]

4720. _____. "Blues for Dr. Jeffries." *Village Voice* (1 October 1991). [Prof. Leonard Jeffries, CUNY]

4721. _____. "Civil Wars on Campus." *Village Voice* (4 May 1993). [Fighting racism and antisemitism on college campuses]

4722. _____. "The Colleges: Fear, Loathing, and Suppresion." *Village Voice* (8 May 1990). [Racist speech on college campuses]

4723. _____. "A Dissonant First Amendment Fugue." *Village Voice* (5 June 1990). [Differing views on regulating racist speech on campuses.]

4724. _____. "A Duel Between Symbols of Hate." *Village Voice* (27 August 1991). [Harvard University]

4725. _____. "Flexing Muzzles. Free Speech on Campus Is Being Attacked from An Unlikely Direction-The Left." *Playboy* (January 1990): 118-120, 203.

4726. _____. "Four Black Women Who Refused To Be Victims of Racism." *Village Voice* (9 July 1991). [Arizona State University]

4727. _____. "In the Wake of the Banished Bigot." *Village Voice* (2 April 1991). [Brown University]

4728. _____. "The Ordeal of the 'Offensive Professor'." *Village Voice* (16 April 1991). [Regulation of racist and other speech on college campuses.]

4729. _____. "P.C. Thinking Beyond the Campus: First Amendment But--." *Responsive Community* 1 (Summer 1991): 17-26.

4730. _____. "Putting the First Amendment on Trial." *Village Voice* (22 May 1990). [Punishing racist speech on college campuses]

4731. _____. "What's Happening to the ACLU?" *Village Voice* (15 May 1990). [About regulation of racist speech on college campuses.]

4732. _____. "Why Do They Hate Us?" *Village Voice* (28 May 1991). [Jewish-Black conflict at UCLA]

4733. _____. "Words that Spit in Your Face." *Village Voice* (5 November 1991). [Control of student speech at Georgetown Law Center]

4734. Hernandez, Peggy. "Afro-American Studies Show Strength." *Boston Globe*, 16 November 1990. [National]

4735. Hersh, Matthew and Wayne L. "Columbia, a Campus Divided." *New York Times*, 15 June 1990.

4736. Higginbotham, Elizabeth. "Race and Class Barriers to Black Women's College Attendance." *Journal of Ethnic Studies* 13 (Spring 1985): 89-107.

4737. *Higher Education in California*. Washington, DC: OECD Publications and Information Center, 1990.

4738. Hill, Donald K. "Law School, Legal Education, and the Black Law Student." *Thurgood Marshall Law Review* 12 (Summer 1987): 457- 505.

4739. Hill, Freddye. "The Nature and Context of Black Nationalism at Northwestern [University] in 1971." *Journal of Black Studies* (March 1975): 320-336.

4740. Hill, Retha. "Scarce Man on Campus." *Washington Post*, 21 March 1994. [African-American men]

4741. Hinds, Michael de Courcy. "Penn Won't Punish Black Students for Protesting." *New York Times*, 16 September 1993.

4742. Hinelgrin, Marea. "Students Protest Fascist Group." *Militant* (19 October 1991). [Protests against formation of a White Student Union at the University of Minnesota]

4743. Hing, Alex. "On Strike, Shut It Down!: Reminiscences of the S.F. State Strike." *East Wind* 2 (Fall/Winter 1983).

4744. *Hispanic Women: Making Their Presence on Campus Less Tenuous*. Assocation of American Colleges, 1991.

4745. "Historically Black Colleges Going North, and Thriving." *New York Times*, 9 October 1994. [Play team games in North]

4746. Hively, Robert, ed. *The Lurking Evil: Racial and Ethnic Conflict on the College Campus*. American Association of State Colleges and Universities, 1990.

4747. Holland, Dorothy C., and Margaret A. Eisenhart. "Moments of Discontent: University of Women and the Gender Status Quo." *Anthropology and Education Quarterly* 19 (June 1988): 115-138.

4748. Holmes, Steven A. "College Fund Is Threatened Over Speeches." *New York Times*, 4 May 1994. [United Negro College Fund]

4749. Hook, Sidney. "Anti-Semitism in the Academy: Some Pages of the Past." *Midstream* 24 (January 1979): 49-54.

4750. Hoole, S., and H. Ratnajeevan. "Racist Thorns in the Ivy Tower." *Los Angeles Times*, 12 June 1992. [Claremont Colleges. See Montague, below]

4751. Horne, Gerald. "Misfire." *In These Times* (20 June 1990): Letter. [Afro-American Studies]

4752. Horvitz, Eleanor F., and Benton H. Rosen. "The Jewish Fraternity and Brown University." *Rhode Island Jewish Historical Notes* 8 (1981): 294-344.

4753. Howe, Irving and others. "Race on Campus." *New Republic* (18 February 1991).

4754. Howell, Roy C. "The Mission of Black Law Schools Toward the Year 2000." *North Carolina Central Law Journal* 19 (Spring 1990): 40-55.

4755. Hudgins, John L. "The Segmentation of Southern Sociology? Social Research at Historically Black Colleges and Universities." *Social Forces* 72 (March 1994): 885-893.

4756. Hudson, Elizabeth. "Lack of Funds Threatens Building Black Students Built Brick by Brick." *Washington Post*, 28 April 1994. [Huston-Tillotson College, Austin, Texas]

4757. Huffman, Terry E. "Transculturation of Native American College Students." *Proteus* 7 (1990): 8-14.

4758. Huggins, Nathan I. *Report to the Ford Foundation on Afro- American Studies*. New York: Ford Foundation, 1985.

4759. Hunter-Gault, Charlayne. *In My Place*. Farrar, Strauss, and Giroux, 1992. [Breaking the segregation barrier at the University of Georgia in 1960-1961]

4760. Hurtado, Sylvia. *Campus Racial Climates and Educational Outcomes*. Ph.D. diss., University of California, Los Angeles, 1990. UMO #9111328.

4761. _____. "Graduate School Racial Climates and Academic Self-Concept among Minority Graduate Students in the 1970's." *American Journal of Education* 102 (May 1994): 330-351.

4762. Hustoles, Thomas P., and Walter B. Connolly, eds. *Regulating Racial Harrassment on Campus: A Legal Compendium*. Washington, DC: National Association of College and University Attorneys, 1990.

4763. Hyde, Henry J., and George M. Fishman. "The Collegiate Speech Protection Act of 1991: A Response to the New Intolerance in the Academy." *Wayne Law Review* 37 (Spring 1991): 1469-1525.

4764. Hyde, Ken. "Statistics May Show Honor [Court] Bias." *Cavalier Daily*, 22 November 1989. [University of Virginia]

4765. Hyllegard, David. *Higher Education and Desirable Work: Open Admissions and Ethnic and Gender Differences in Job Quality*. Ph.D. diss., CUNY, 1992. UMO #9218238.

4766. Hyllegard, David, and David E. Lavin. "Higher Education and Challenging Work: Open Admissions and Ethnic and Gender Differences in Job Complexity." *Sociological Forum* 7 (June 1992): 239-260.

4767. Ihle, Elizabeth. *Educated Women*. Garland, 1993. [Black women in higher education]

4768. Institute for the Study of Social Change. *The Diversity Project: An Interim Report to the Chancellor*. Berkeley: University of California, 1990.

4769. "Integration Is at Hand for Fraternity System." *New York Times*, 25 August 1991. [University of Alabama]

4770. Jackson, Derrick, III. "Black Studies: Why Harvard Should Blush." *Boston Globe*, 18 November 1990.

4771. _____. "A Flag that Divides." *Boston Globe*, 14 April 1991. [Flying a Confederate flag on Harvard campus]

4772. _____. "Racism Crashes a Party." *Boston Globe*, 22 December 1991. [Harvard University]

4773. Jackson, Diana R. *The Relationship of Racial Identity Congruence with College Environment and Ability to Deal with Racism to Black Student Academic Achievement on the Predominantly White Campus vs. the Predominantly Black Campus*. Ph.D. diss., University of Maryland, 1987. UMO #8904998.

4774. Jackson, John S. "The Political Behavior and Socio-Economic Backgrounds of Black Students: the Antecedents of Protest." *Midwest Journal of Political Science* 15 (November 1971): 661- 686.

4775. Jackson, John L. *The Student Divestment Movement: Anti- Apartheid Activism on U.S. College and University Campuses*. Ph.D. diss., Ohio State University, 1989. UMO #9001967.

4776. Jackson, Kenneth W. *A Profile of Black Faculty in Traditionally White Institutions*. Atlanta, GA: Southern Education Foundation, 1988.

4777. Jackson, Raina. "Black College Students Benefit from Legacy of 20-Year-Old Favor." *Boston Globe*, 30 July 1989. [Ruth M. Batson Educational Foundation]

4778. Jackson, Robert L. "Community Colleges Wonder Whether They Can Keep Doors Open to All." *Chronicle of Higher Education* (21 July 1993). [Community College of Philadelphia]

4779. Jacques, Jeffrey M., and Robert L. Hall. *Integration of the Black and White University: A Preliminary Investigation*. 1980. ERIC ED 212 77.

4780. James, Joy, and Ruth Farmer, eds. *Spirit, Space, and Survival: African American Women in (White) Academe*. Routledge, 1993.

4781. Jaschick, Scott. "2 Law Schools Scale Back Affirmative- Action Programs as Education Dept. Continues Scrutiny of Such Plans." *Chronicle of Higher Education* (16 December 1992). [Stanford U. and U. of Michigan]

4782. _____. "Aid Reserved for White Students Probably Won't Meet Guidelines." *Chronicle of Higher Education* (2 March 1994).

4783. _____. "Appeal Judges Throw Out Controversial Plan to Desegregate Public Colleges in Louisiana." *Chronicle of Higher Education* (5 January 1994).

4784. _____. "U.S. Issues Policy on Racial Harrassment." *Chronicle of Higher Education* (23 March 1994).

4785. _____. "Victory for Black Colleges." *Chronicle of Higher Education* (9 March 1994). [Alabama]

4786. _____. "West VA. State College Regains Black Land-Grant Status." *Chronicle of Higher Education* (27 April 1994).

4787. Jaynes, Gerald D. "Only Blacks Need Apply: African-American Studies and Intellectual Diversity in American Colleges." *Reconstruction* 1 (1991): 65-67.

4788. Jeffries, Leonard. "Text of Jeffries' July Speech." *New York City Newsday*, 19 August 1991. [Text of speech by CUNY professor Jeffries, Empire State Black Arts and Cultural Festival, Albany, NY, July 20, 1991]

4789. Jetter, Alexis. "The Hitler Caper." *Nation* (3 December 1990). [The Dartmouth Review]

4790. Johnson, David C. *Racism in the Academic Marketplace*. New York: Vantage Press, 1990.

4791. Johnson, G. D. and others. "Date Rape on a Southern Campus: Reports from 1991." *Sociology and Social Research* 76 (January 1992): 37-44.

4792. Johnson, J. H., Jr., and M. L. Oliver, eds. *Ethnic Dilemmas in Comparative Perspective: Proceedings of the Los Angeles Conference on Comparative Ethnicity*. Los Angeles: University of California, Institute for Social Science Research, 1988. [See chapter by L. Ling-Chi Wang on discrimination against Asian Americans in higher education.]

4793. Johnson, Julie. "Are Black Colleges Worth Saving?" *Time* (11 November 1991).

4794. Johnson, Kirk A. "At Wesleyan, a Day to Reflect on Racial Tension." *New York Times*, 9 May 1990.

4795. Johnson, Thomas S. "Confronting Campus Hate Speech: The First and Fourteenth Amendments Collide." *Illinois Bar Journal* 79 (December 1991): 644.

4796. Johnson, Whittington B. "The Virgil Hawkins Case: A Near Decade of Evading the Inevitable, the Demise of Jim Crow Higher Education in Florida." *Southern University Law Review* 16 (Spring 1989): 55-71.

4797. Jones, Charles H. "Equality, Dignity, and Harm: The Constitutionality of Regulating American Campus Ethnoviolence." *Wayne Law Review* 37 (Spring 1991): 1383-1432.

4798. Jones, Charisse. "What It Took to Take a Stand." *Washington Post*, 30 November 1992. [Charlayne Hunter-Gault at the U. of Ga. 1961]

4799. Jones, D. J. "The College Campus as a Microcosm of United States Society: The Issue of Racially Motivated Violence." *Urban League Review* 13 (Summer-Winter 1990).

4800. Jones, Evonne P. "The Impact of Economic, Political, and Social Factors on Recent Overt Black/White Factors in Higher Education in the United States." *Journal of Negro Education* 60 (Fall 1991): 524-537.

4801. Jones, Maxine D., and Joe M. Richardson. *Talledega College: The First Century*. Tuscaloosa: University of Alabama Press, 1990.

4802. Jordan, Mary. "Black Students Dump Campus Newspaper at Penn." *Washington Post*, 17 April 1993. [U of Pennsylvania]

4803. _____. "College Dorms Reflect Trend of Self- Segregation." *Washington Post*, 6 March 1994.

4804. _____. "In Mississippi, an Integration Uproar." *Washington Post*, 17 November 1992. [Black higher education]

4805. Jordan, Mary, and Laurie Goodstein. "Linked by Satellite, Campuses Tackle Issue of Rising Racial Tension." *Washington Post*, 19 November 1992.

4806. Joyce, Robert P. "Racial Harrassment in Education" Legal and Policy Issues." *School Law Bulletin* 21 (Fall 1990): 16-24.

4807. Juska, Sharon. "Professor Studies Racial Groups to Determine Status on Campuses." *Review (University of Delaware)* (5 May 1989). [Race and course grades]

4808. Kane, Thomas J. *College Entry by Blacks since 1970: The Role of Tuition, Financial Aid, Local Economic Conditions, and Family Background.* Ph.D. diss., Harvard University, 1991. [1973-1988]. UMO #9132088.

4809. Kanthak, Kris. "Minorities Struggle for Strong Presence at Columbia." *Columbia Daily Spectator*, 5 December 1989.

4810. Kantrowitz, Barbara, and Heather Woodin. "Diagnosis: Harrassment." *Newsweek* (26 November 1990). [Medical School, University of Iowa]

4811. Kaplin, William A. "'Hate Speech' on the College Campus: Freedom of Speech and Equality at the Crossroads." *Land and Water Law Review* 27 (Winter 1992): 243-259.

4812. Karabel, Jerome. "The Politics of Structural Change in American Higher Education: The Case of Open Admissions at the City University of New York." in *The Complete University: Break from Tradition in Three Countries*, eds. Harry Hermanns and others. Cambridge, MA: Schenkman, 1983.

4813. _____. "Status-group Struggle, Organizational Interests, and the Limits of Institutional Autonomy: The Transformation of Harvard, Yale, and Princeton, 1918-1940." *Theory and Society* 13 (1984): 1-40.

4814. Karen, D. "Achievement and Ascription in Admission to an Elite College: A Political-Organizational Analysis." *Sociological Forum* 6 (June 1991): 349-386.

4815. _____. "The Politics of Class, Race, and Gender: Access to Higher Education in the United States, 1960-1986." *American Journal of Education* 99 (February 1991): 208-237.

4816. Kaufman, Barry and others. *Outcomes of Educational Opportunity: A Study of Graduates from the City University*. New York: Office of the Deputy Chancellor of CUNY, 1982.

4817. Keller, M. J. *Trends in Financial Aid Among Blacks and Non- blacks in Maryland*. Maryland State Board of Education, 1988.

4818. Kelley, Kevin J. "Racist Death Threats Mar Vermont Campus." *Guardian (NYC)* (29 January 1992). [University of Vermont]

4819. Kennedy, Donald. *Reflections on Racial Understanding*. Office of the President, Stanford University, January 1989.

4820. Kennedy, John H. "The Law School Tenure Line." *Boston Globe*, 27 April 1990. [Female and minority hiring]

4821. Kennedy, Randall L. "In Praise of the Struggle for Diversity on Law School Faculties." *University of Chicago Legal Forum* (1991): 1-12.

4822. _____. "The Political Correctness Scare." *Loyola Law Review* 37 (Summer 1991): 231-244.

4823. _____. "Should Private Universities Voluntarily Bind Themselves to the First Amendment? No!" *Chronicle of Higher Education* (21 September 1994).

4824. Kerlow, Eleanor. *Poisoned Ivy: Power Politics and the Decline of Harvard Law School*. St. Martin's Press, 1994.

4825. Kilson, Martin L., Jr. "The Black Experience at Harvard." *New York Times*, 2 September 1973.

4826. Kimenyi, Mwangi S. "Race, Amenities, and Psychic Income." *Review of Black Political Economy* 20 (Summer 1991): 49-58. [Persisting inequalities of amenities in Southern universities, to the detriment of Black faculty.]

4827. King, J. "The Demand for Higher Education in Puerto Rico." *Economics of Education Review* 12 (September 1993).

4828. Kinnick, Mary K., and Mary F. Ricks. "The Urban Public University in the United States: An Analysis of Change, 1977- 1987." *Research in Higher Education* 31 (February 1990).

4829. Klingenstein, Susanne. *Jews in the American Academy, 1900- 1940. The Dynamics of Intellectual Assimilation*. New Haven, CT: Yale University Press, 1991.

4830. Kluge, P. F. *Alma Mater. A College Homecoming*. Addison- Wesley, 1994. [Kenyon College]

4831. Knepper, Paula R. *Student Progress in College: NLS -72 Postsecondary Education Transcript Study, 1984*. Washington, DC: U.S. Dept. of Education, Office of Educational Research and Improvement, February 1989.

4832. Koepke, Jens B. "The University of California Hate Speech Policy: A Good Heart in Ill-fitting Garb." *COMM-ENT* 12 (Summer 1990): 599-625.

4833. Kopecky, Pauline W. *A History of Equal Opportunity at Oklahoma State University*. Stillwater: Oklahoma State University, 1990.

4834. Koretz, Daniel. *Trends in the Postsecondary Enrollment of Minorities*. Santa Monica, CA: Rand Corporation, August 1990.

4835. Kors, Alan C. "Harrassment Policies in the University." *Society* 28 (May-June 1991): 22-30.

4836. Koston, R. "Robert Russa Moton and the Politics of Tuskegee, 1915-25." Master's thesis, University of Florida, 1989.

4837. Krause, Dolores R. *Factors Related to Performance of American Indian Students]*. Ph.D. diss., University of Washington, 1987. [University of Washington]. UMO #8713379.

4838. Kretzmen. "Free Speech and Racism." *Cardoza Law Review* 8 (1987).

4839. Kreuzer, Terese Loeb. "The Bidding War for Top Black Students." *Journal of Blacks in Higher Education* (Winter 1993/ 1994): 2. 114-118.

4840. Kriegel, Leonard. "A Tale of Two Leonards." *Reconstruction* 1 (1992): 142-144. [Prof. Leonard Jeffries, CUNY]

4841. Kropp, Arthur J. "Colleges Must Find Ways to Eradicate Racial Divisions." *Chronicle of Higher Education* (22 May 1992). [Written by the president of People for the American Way.]

4842. Kujovich, Gil. "Equal Opportunity in Higher Education and the Black Public Colleges: The Era of Separate But Equal." *Minnesota Law Review* 72 (1987).

4843. Kulis, Stephen S. "The Political Economy of Incorporation: Black Sociologists in Academia." *Sociological Abstracts* (August 1991): supplement 167. 91S25224/ASA/1991/6583.

4844. La Brecque, Ron. "Chicano Studies Fights for Status." *New York Times Education Life* (2 August 1992).

4845. La Noue, George R. "Race-Based Policies: A Court's Guidelines." *Chronicle of Higher Education* (8 April 1992). [The Podbersky case and race-based scholarships]

4846. La Noue, George R., and Barbara A. Lee. *Academics in Court: The Consequences of Faculty Discrimination Litigation*. Ann Arbor: University of Michigan Press, 1990.

4847. Labaton, Stephen. "For Oklahoma, Anita Hill's Story Is Open World." *New York Times*, 19 April 1993. [Law School, U. of Oklahoma]

4848. Ladd, Everett C., Jr., and Seymour M. Lipset. *The Divided Academy: Professors and Politics*. New York: McGraw-Hill, 1975.

4849. Lamar, Jake. "Whose Legacy Is It, Anyway?" *New York Times*, 9 October 1991. [College admission for "legacies"-alumni children-as a form of affirmative action.]

4850. Lamorie, Karen M. "'Why Not a Jewish Girl?': The Jewish Experience at Pembroke College in Brown University." *Rhode Island Jewish Historical Notes* 10 (November 1988): 122-140.

4851. Langan, Maria. *The Revolving Door. City Colleges of Chicago 1980-1989*. Chicago, IL: Metropolitan Opportunity Project, University of Chicago, February 1991.

4852. Lange, Ellen E. "Racist Speech on Campus: A Title VII Solution to a First Amendment Problem." *Southern California Law Review* 64 (November 1990): 105-134.

4853. Langham, Don. "University Still Plagued with Racism." *Crimson White* (18 October 1989). [University of Alabama]

4854. Larew, John. "Why Are Droves of Unqualified, Unprepared Kids Getting into Our Top Colleges?" *Washington Monthly* (June 1991). [Legacy students (children of alumni)]

4855. Lawrence, Charles R., III. "If He Hollers, Let Him Go: Regulating Racist Speech on Campus." *Duke Law Journal* (June 1990): 431-483.

4856. _____. "Minority Hiring in AALS Law Schools: The Need for Voluntary Quotas." *University of San Francisco Law Review* 20 (1986).

4857. Lawrence, Charles R., III, and Gerald Gunther. "Good Speech, Bad Speech." *Stanford Lawyer* 24 (Spring 1990). [Two views on whether universities should restrict racist expression]

4858. Lawson, Ellen. *The Three Sarahs. Documents of Antebellum Black College Women*. Lewiston, NY: Mellen, 1991.

4859. Lazere, Donald. "The Right Side of PC." *In These Times* (27 May 1992).

4860. Leatherman, Courtney. "At a Black College, Race Often Takes Precedence Over Gender." *Chronicle of Higher Education* (14 July 1993). [Spelman College]

4861. _____. "Number of Blacks Earning Ph.D's Rose 15% in Year." *Chronicle of Higher Education* (12 October 1994).

4862. _____. "West Coast Accrediting Agency Hashes Out a Policy on Racial Diversity for Campuses." *Chronicle of Higher Education* (18 November 1992).

4863. Lederman, Douglas. "Blacks Make Up Large Proportion of Scholarship Athletes Yet Their Overall Lags at Division I Colleges." *Chronicle of Higher Education* (17 June 1992).

4864. _____. "Old Times Not Forgotten." *Chronicle of Higher Education* (20 October 1993). [Race at the U. of Mississippi]

4865. Lederman, Douglas, and Christopher Shea. "The Student Press Under Fire. Editors Debate How to Diversify Staffs and Improve Coverage of Minority Groups." *Chronicle of Higher Education* (17 November 1993).

4866. Lee, Felicia R. "Minorities at Baruch Charge Neglect Despite Ethnic Mix." *New York Times*, 21 April 1990. [Bernard M. Baruch College, CUNY]

4867. _____. "Minority Issues Lie Behind Protest Over Cutting of Budget at CUNY." *New York Times*, 28 May 1990.

4868. Lee, Joe A. *A Description of the Influences of Corporate Support on Private Historically Black Four-year Colleges and Universities during the Period, 1980-1986*. Ph.D. diss., Miami University, 1990. UMO #9113507.

4869. Lee, N'Tanya. "Racism on College Campuses." *Focus (Joint Center for Political Studies)* 17 (1989).

4870. Lee, Sally J., and Jeffrey P. Brown. "Women at New Mexico State University: The Early Years, 1888-1920." *New Mexico Historical Review* 64 (1989): 77-93.

4871. Lee, Samuel T. R. "'Black Harvard' Label Patronizes Morehouse." *New York Times*, 4 October 1994.

4872. Leeds, Jeff, and Peter Baker. "Allen's Choices Make U-Va. Board All White Again." *Washington Post*, 26 February 1994.

4873. Lehrman, Karen. "Off Course." *Mother Jones* (September- October 1993). [Women's Studies programs in higher education]

4874. Leo, John. "Racism on the American College Campus." *US News and World Report* (8 January 1990).

4875. _____. "Separation Won't Solve Anything." *US News and World Report* (19 April 1993): 65.

4876. Leone, Janice. "Integrating the American Association of University Women, 1946-1949." *The Historian* 51 (May 1989): 423- 445.

4877. Leslie, C. and others. "Lessons from Bigotry 101." *Newsweek* (25 September 1989): 48-49. [Racism on campuses]

4878. _____. "A Rich Legacy of Preference." *Newsweek* (24 June 1991). [Preference in admissions for children of alumni]

4879. Lessenberry, Jack. "After a Racial Crisisl Some Painful Introspection." *New York Times*, 4 August 1993. [Olivet College]

4880. "A Lesson in Asian Disparity." *Sacramento Bee*, 9 May 1993. [Higher education in California]

4881. Lester, Julius. "Academic Freedom and the Black Intellectual." *Black Scholar* 19 (November/December 1988): 16-26.

4882. Lever, Janet, and Pepper Schwartz. *Women at Yale: Liberating a College Campus*. Indianapolis, IN: Bobbs-Merill, 1971.

4883. Levin, Michael. "The Lessons of Hate." *New York Times*, 26 September 1991. [In re: Prof Leonard Jeffries, CUNY]

4884. Levy, Renee Gearhart. "Unfinished Business." *Syracuse University Magazine* 6 (December 1989): 20-31. [Blacks in higher education]

4885. Lewis, Diane E. "Pursuit of an MBA Deemed Worthwhile for Blacks, Hispanics." *Boston Globe*, 18 November 1991.

4886. Lewis, Mark. "Colleges Take Varied Approaches to Minority Issues." *Midland Daily News*, 24 June 1989. [Ferris State University, Central Michigan University, Northwood Institute (Midland), Delta College, and Saginaw Valley State University.]

4887. Lieberman, L. and others. "Race in Biology and Anthropology: A Study of College Texts and Professors." *Journal of Research in Science Teaching* 29 (March 1992).

4888. Lindenfeld, Frank. "The Retrenchments at Cheyney University." *Humanity and Society* 13 (May 1989): 213-220.

4889. Lindgren, J. Ralph and others. *Sex Discrimination Law in Higher Education: The Lessons of the Past Decade*. Washington, DC: ASHE-ERIC Higher Education Reports, George Washington University, 1984.

4890. Lindsey, Donal F. *Indian Education at the Hampton Institute, 1877-1923*. Ph.D. diss., Kent State University, 1989. UMO #8920474.

4891. Little, Monroe H. "The Faculty of the Sixties: A Reappraisal." *Trotter Institute Review* 4 (Summer 1990): 12-15.

4892. Littlejohn, Edward J., and Leonard S. Rubinowitz. "Black Enrollment in Law Schools: Forward to the Past?" *Thurgood Marshall Law Review* 12 (Summer 1987): 415-455.

4893. Lively, Kit. "Financial Stress, Proposal for Tougher Academic Standards Challenge New York's City U. to Maintain Traditional Role." *Chronicle of Higher Education* (23 September 1992).

4894. Loo, Chalsa, and Gary Robinson. *Alienation of Ethnic Minority Students at a Predominantly White University*. Santa Cruz: University of California, 1985.

4895. Look, Jeannie. "After the S.F. State Strikes: EOP and the School of Ethinic Studies." *East West* (27 October 1988).

4896. _____. "Remembering the S.F. State Strikes." *East West* (20 October 1988).

4897. Lopez, Patrick F. *Mexican-Americans and Graduation from College*. Ph.D. diss., Harvard University, 1990. UMO #9032446.

4898. Lupo, Alan. "Cuckoo Theories." *Boston Globe*, 17 August 1991. [Leonard Jeffries and Michael Levin]

4899. Luz, Reyes Maria de la, and J. Halcon. "Racism in Academia: The Old Wolf Revisited." *Harvard Educational Review* 58 (August 1988): 299-314. [New Hispanic faculty at colleges and universities]

4900. Mabry, Marcus. "Black and Blue, Class of '89." *Newsweek* (25 September 1989): 50-51. [Racial conflict at Stanford University]

4901. _____. "A View from the Front. My Life as a Member of the PC Patrol." *Newsweek* (24 December 1990): 55. [Stanford University]

4902. MacDonald, Heather and others. "CUNY's Open Admissions Fail Miserably." *New York Times*, 15 September 1994. [Three separate letters debating issue]

4903. MacDonald, Heather. "Downward Mobility." *City Journal (NYC)* (Summer 1994). [CUNY]

4904. MacMartin, Charley. "Multiculturalism: Right Against; Left Ambivalent." *Guardian (NYC)* (27 March 1991). [University of Texas, Austin]

4905. Magner, Denise K. "Duke U. Struggles to Make Good on Pledge to Hire Black Professors." *Chronicle of Higher Education* (24 March 1993).

4906. _____. "Faculty members at Berkeley Offer Courses to Satisfy Controversial 'Diversity' Requirement." *Chronicle of Higher Education* (11 March 1992).

4907. _____. "U.S. Jury Says CUNY Erred in Ousting Black- Studies Chairman." *Chronicle of Higher Education* (19 May 1993). [Prof. Leonard Jeffries, Jr.]

4908. _____. "When Whites Teach Black Studies." *Chronicle of Higher Education* (1 December 1993).

4909. _____. "White Professor Wins Discrimination Against Black College." *Chronicle of Higher Education* (21 April 1993). [St. Augustine's College, Raleigh, N.C.]

4910. _____. "White Professors Accuse Some Black Colleges of Racism; Charges Are Strongly Denied." *Chronicle of Higher Education* (13 October 1993).

4911. *Making Good on Our Promises: Moving Beyond Rhetoric to Action. 1993.* American Association of Community Colleges Publications, P.O. Box 1737, Salisbury, MD, 21802, [Minority students in community colleges]

4912. Makofsky, Abraham. "Experience of Native Americans at a Black College: Indian Students at Hampton Institute, 1878-1923." *Journal of Ethnic Studies* 17 (Fall 1989): 31-46.

4913. Mancillas, Jorge R. "Sen. Tom Hayden and UCLA Hunger Strike." *Chronicle of Higher Education* (1 September 1993). [Creation of the Cesar Chavez Center for Interdisciplinary Instruction in Chicana and Chicano Studies at UCLA]

4914. Manegold, Catherine S. "Fewer Men Earn Doctorates, Particularly Among Blacks." *New York Times*, 18 January 1994.

4915. Mangan, Katherine S. "On New Campus in Dallas, Troubled Paul Quinn College Faces Continuing Struggle for Financial Stability." *Chronicle of Higher Education* (11 November 1992).

4916. _____. "Top Texas Court Sees No Evidence State Was Biased Against Mexican Americans." *Chronicle of Higher Education* (13 October 1993).

4917. Manshi, Charles F. *Parental Income and College Opportunity*. Washington, DC: Democratic Study Center, September 1992.

4918. Manuel, Diane. "Future's Uncertain for Black Colleges." *Boston Globe*, 31 July 1994.

4919. Manzagol, Michael. "Sins of Admissions." *California Monthly* (April 1988).

4920. Maples, Rebeka L. *A Political Analysis of Black Enrollment in Higher Education*. Ph.D. diss., Ohio State University, 1993. [1976, 1982 and 1988]. UMO #9316192.

4921. Marable, Manning. "The Quiet Death of Black Colleges." *Southern Exposure* 12 (March-April 1984): 31-39.

4922. Maraniss, David. "University Tries to Mend Racial Divisions." *Washington Post*, 7 March 1990. [University of Massachusetts, Amherst]

4923. Mardon, Steve. "Blacks Allege Bias in Arrests at New Paltz." *Poughkeepsie Journal* (1 September 1989). [State University College, New Paltz, NY]

4924. Marriott, Michel. "At Black Campus, Desegregation vs. Dismantling." *New York Times*, 29 May 1991. [Tennessee State University, Nashville]

4925. Martin, Anthony C. *The Jewish Onslaught: Dispatches from the Wellesley Battlefront*. Majority Press, 1993.

4926. Martin, Judith, and Gunther Stent. "Attack Ideas, Not People." *New York Times*, 20 March 1991. [Justification for limiting freedom of speech on college campuses in the interest of freedom of inquiry.]

4927. Martinez, Elizabeth. "Campus Racism Part II: What To Do?" *Z Magazine* 5 (September 1992): 26-29.

4928. _____. "The Politics of 'Cultural Diversity': Old Poison in New Bottles." *Z Magazine* 3 (July-August 1990): 35-40.

4929. _____. "Willie Horton's Gonna Get Your Alma Mater." *Z Magazine* 4 (July-August 1991): 126-130.

4930. Martinez, Valerie. "Latino [Scholarship] Grants Tied to Beer Sales Draw Criticism." *Long Beach Press-Telegram*, 27 September 1992. [Anheuser-Busch Co. and the National Hispanic Scholarship Fund]

4931. Massey, C. R. "Hate Speech, Cultural Diversity, and the Foundational Paradigms of Free Expression." *UCLA Law Review* 40 (October 1992): 103-198.

4932. Masters, Brooke A. "Ex-Farrakhan Aide Less Controversial Than Law Student." *Washington Post*, 25 February 1994. [Khalid Abdul Muhammad at Howard U.]

4933. _____. "Gallaudet Braving a New World." *Washington Post*, 10 March 1993. [Gallaudet University]

4934. _____. "GWU Seeks Unity in Wake of Racist Remark." *Washington Post*, 3 November 1992.

4935. _____. "A Struggle for the Heart of Howard U." *Washington Post*, 20 December 1993.

4936. Matthews, Anne. "The Campus Crime Wave." *New York Times Magazine* (7 March 1993).

4937. Maxwell, Bill. "Racism Goes to School." *Tampa Florida Sentinel Bulletin*, 9 June 1989. [Role of conservatism in encouraging racism.]

4938. Mazza, Patrick. "African Americans Describe Climate at PSU as Demoralizing, Insensitive." *Portland, OR Skanner*, 24 May 1989. [Second article of two on Portland State University]

4939. Mazza, Peter. "James Dickson Carr: First Black Graduate of Rutgers University." *Journal of the Rutgers University Libraries* 47 (December 1985).

4940. McBay, Shirley M. *The Racial Climate on the MIT Campus: A Report of the Minority Student Issues Group*. Cambridge, MA: Office of the Dean of Student Affairs, Massachusetts Institute of Technology, 1986.

4941. McCarthy, Cameron R. "Racial Resentment in American Higher Education: The Campus Scene in the '90's." *Social Alternatives* 12 (April 1993): 31-35.

4942. McCarthy, John R. *The Slavery Issue in Selected Colleges and Universities in Illinois, Ohio, Kentucky, and Indiana: 1840- 1860*. Ph.D. diss., Florida State University, 1974. UMO #7512656.

4943. McCarthy, Peggy. "Wesleyan Community Tries to Come to Grips with Racial Incidents." *Boston Globe*, 13 May 1990.

4944. McClelland, Katherine, and Carol J. Auster. "Public Platitudes and Hidden Tensions: Racial Climates at Predominantly White Liberal Arts Colleges." *Journal of Higher Education* 61 (November-December 1990).

4945. McCollum, Heather A. *Elements of Success: Effective Colleges for Blacks*. Ph.D. diss., Harvard University, 1989. UMO #9000874.

4946. McCormack, Arlene. "Improving Undergraduate Sociology Research Courses: An Example of Students Evaluating Racism in Their Own Academic Community." *Sociological Abstracts* (1989) Accession No. 89S21578.

4947. McCormick, Andy. "Black Philosophers Study Racial Problems at UD Session." *Wilmington, DE News Journal*, 5 June 1989. [University of Delaware]

4948. _____. "UD Probes Grant After Bias Charged." *Wilmington, DE News Journal*, 17 November 1989. [Charges of racism and antisemitism against Pioneer Fund, Inc., a foundation]

4949. McCormick, Richard P. *The Black Student Protest Movement at Rutgers.* New Brunswick, NJ: Rutgers University Press, 1990.

4950. McGovern, Joseph A. H., and Janice Kleinkauf. "New Paltz Students Demand Justice." *Hudson Valley Black Press*, 11 October 1989. [State University of New York at New Paltz]

4951. McGowan, D. F., and R. K. Tangri. "A Libertarian Critique of University Restrictions of Offensive Speech." *California Law Review* 79 (May 1991): 825-918.

4952. McHugh, Blanche and others, eds. *Racial Discrimination on Campus.* De Kalb, IL: Northern Illinois University, 1988.

4953. McJamerson, Evangeline M. "The Declining Participation of African-American Men in Higher Education: Causes and Consequences." *Sociological Spectrum* 11 (Janurary-March 1991): 45-65.

4954. McMillin, D. "University of Pennsylvania v. EEOC and Dixon v. Rutgers: Two Supreme Courts Speak on the Academic Freedom Privilege." *Rutgers Law Review* 42 (Summer 1990): 1089-1132.

4955. McNamara, Patricia P. *American Indians in U.S. Higher Education.* Los Angeles, CA: Higher Education Research Institute, 1984.

4956. McPherson, Michael S., and Morton O. Shapiro. *Keeping College Affordable: Government and Educational Opportunity.* Washington, DC: Brookings Books, 1991.

4957. Meece, Judith L., and Jacquelynne S. Eccles, eds. *Gender and Educational Achievement.* Lawrence Erlbaum Associates, 1994.

4958. Meisenheimer, J. R. "Black College Graduates in the Labor Market, 1979 and 1989." *Monthly Labor Review* 113 (November 1990).

4959. Melecki, Thomas G. *The Legislative Politics of State Student Financial Aid Authority Legislation in Texas: 1975 to 1989.* Ph.D. diss., University of Texas, 1991. UMO #9128306.

4960. Melendez, Sara E., and Janice Petrovich. "Hispanic Women Student in Higher Education: Meeting the Challenge of Diversity." in *Educating the Majority*, pp. 57-68. eds. Carol S. Pearson and others. Collier Macmillan, 1989.

4961. "Mentoring to Increase Minority Participation in Higher Education: The Faculty's Role." *Academe* 77 (January-February 1991): 41-55.

4962. Mercer, Joyce. "2-Year Colleges in California Hit by Biggest-Ever Enrollment Decline." *Chronicle of Higher Education* (10 March 1993).

4963. _____. "The Ambiguous Success of Desegregation at Tennessee State U." *Chronicle of Higher Education* (5 May 1993).

4964. _____. "Black Alumni Groups Spurred to Action by Supreme Court's Desegregation Decision." *Chronicle of Higher Education* (30 September 1992).

4965. _____. "A Crusader for the Survival of Historically Black Colleges." *Chronicle of Higher Education* (21 September 1994). [Elias Blake, Jr.]

4966. _____. "Fight Between 2 Universities to Open Florida's Third Law School Is Shaped by Ethnic Rivalries and Long-Time Grievances." *Chronicle of Higher Education* (28 July 1993).

4967. _____. "Marching to Save Black Colleges." *Chronicle of Higher Education* (11 May 1994). [Mississippi]

4968. _____. "Struggle in East St. Louis." *Chronicle of Higher Education* (9 February 1994). [Community College]

4969. _____. "U.S. Steps in With Plan to Desegregate State's Colleges." *Chronicle of Higher Education* (12 January 1994). [Justice Department and Mississippi]

4970. Mercer, Joyce, and Douglas Lederman. "Aftermath of a Fiery Message." *Chronicle of Higher Education* (16 March 1994). [Khalid Abdul Muhammad at Howard University]

4971. Merisotis, J. P. "Who Receives Federal Aid?" *Journal of Student Financial Aid* 17 (1987): 14-29.

4972. Merl, Jean. "Community College Cuts Protested." *Los Angeles Times*, 26 August 1992. [Los Angeles]

4973. Messer-Davidow, Ellen. "Manufacturing the Attack on Liberalized Higher Education." *Social Text* 11 (1993): 40-80.

4974. Metz, Holly. "Bad Apples, Evil Deeds." *Student Lawyer* (February 1990). [Racism in law schools and universities]

4975. Mial, Joetta M. *Pathways to a Higher Education: An Investigation of Black High School Seniors from 1971-1982.* Ph.D. diss., University of Michigan, 1989. UMO #8920589.

4976. Michelman, Frank I. "Universities, Racist Speech and Democracy in America: An Essay for the ACLU." *Harvard Civil Rights-Civil Liberties Law Review* 27 (Summer 1992): 339-370. [See Neuborne, below]

4977. Miller, Karen K. "Race, Power, and the Emergence of Black Studies in Higher Education." *American Studies* 31 (Fall 1990): 83-98. [University of California, Berkeley]

4978. Miller, S. C., and H. Hexter. *How Low-income Families Pay for College.* American Council on Education, 1985.

4979. *Minorities and Women in Higher Education in West Virginia and Civil Rights Issues in the Huntington Area.* Washington, DC: U.S. Commission on Civil Rights, 1989.

4980. *Minorities in Higher Education: 1992.* American Council on Education, 1992.

4981. "Minorities in the Education Pipeline." *Educational Record* 68-69 (Fall-Winter 1988): 1-126.

4982. "Minority Students Present Demands to Administration." *New York Times*, 3 February 1991. [University of Notre Dame]

4983. Mitchell, Robert. *The Multicultural Student's Guide to Colleges: What Every African-American, Asian-American, Hispanic, and Native-American Applicant Needs to Know About America's Top Schools.* Farrar, Strauss and Giroux, 1993.

4984. *Model Questionnaire for Campus Self-Assessments.* Baltimore, MD: National Institute Against Prejudice and Violence, n.d.

4985. Montague, Eleanor A. "Seeds of Tolerance Are Taking Root." *Los Angeles Times*, 12 June 1992. [See Hoole, above; Claremont Colleges]

4986. Montgomery, M. R. "The 'Jewish Jew'." *Boston Globe*, 16 May 1991. [Alan Dershowitz, Harvard Law School]

4987. Morgan, Joan. "Malcolm-King College: From Humble Beginnings to Calamitous Demise." *Black Issues in Higher Education* 6 (18 January 1990): 6-7.

4988. Morganthau, Tom and others. "Race on Campus: Failing the Test?" *Newsweek* (6 May 1991).

4989. Morris, Frank L. *American Minorities and International Students: Striking What Balance?* Baltimore, MD: Morgan State University, School of Graduate Studies, 1992.

4990. Morris, J. R. "Racial Attitudes of Undergraduates in Greek Housing." *College Student Journal* 25 (March 1991): 510-505.

4991. Morrow, Lance. "The Provocative Professor." *Time* (26 August 1991). [Prof. Leonard Jeffries, CUNY]

4992. Morse, David. "Prejudicial Studies. One Astounding Lesson for the University of Connecticut." *Hartford Courant*, 26 November 1989. [Long article on anti-Asian-American racism]

4993. Mortenson, Thomas G. *Attitudes of Americans Toward Borrowing to Finance Educational Expenses, 1959-1983*. Iowa City, Iowa: ACT Educational and Social Research, November 1988.

4994. _____. *Equity of Higher Educational Opportunity for Women, Black, Hispanic, and Low Income Students*. Iowa City, Iowa: ACT Educational and Social Research, 1991.

4995. _____. *Family Income, Children, and Student Financial Aid*. Iowa City, Iowa: ACT Educational and Social Research, April 1989.

4996. _____. *Pell Grant Program Changes and Their Effects on Applicant Eligiblity, 1973-74 to 1988-89*. Iowa City, Iowa: ACT Educational and Social Research, May 1988.

4997. _____. *The Reallocation of Financial Aid from Poor to Middle Income and Affluent Students*. Iowa City, Iowa: ACT Educational and Social Research, May 1990.

4998. Mortenson, Thomas G., and Zhijun Wu. *High School Graduation and College Participation of Young Adults by Family Income Backgrounds 1970 to 1989*. Iowa City, Iowa: ACT Educational and Social Research, September 1990.

4999. Moses, Yolanda T. *Black Women in Academe: Issues and Strategies*. Washington, DC: Project on the Status and Education of Women, Association of American Colleges, 1989.

5000. _____. "The Roadblocks Confronting Minority Administrators." *Chronicle of Higher Education* (13 January 1993).

5001. Mosier, Majorie. "Not All Women Are Advancing at UC." *Los Angeles Times*, 25 October 1993.

5002. Muir, Donal E. "A Comparison of 'Black' and 'White' Integration Attitudes on a Deep-South Campus: A Research Note." *Sociological Spectrum* 10 (1990).

5003. _____. "'White' Attitudes toward 'Blacks' at a Deep-South University Campus." *Sociology and Social Research* 73 (1989): 84-89. [University of Alabama]

5004. _____. "'White' Fraternity and Sorority Attitudes toward 'Blacks' on a Deep-South University Campus." *Sociological Spectrum* 11 (January-March 1991): 93-103. [University of Alabama]

5005. "The Multicultural Campus." *Academe* 76 (November-December 1990): eight articles.

5006. Munitz, B. "California State University System and First Amendment Rights to Free Speech." *Education* 112 (Autumn 1991): 4- 9.

5007. Muro, Mark. "Class Privilege." *Boston Globe*, 18 September 1981. [Legacy admissions-preference given to children of alumni, overwhelmingly white Anglo-Saxon Protestants.]

5008. Muse, Clifford L., Jr. *An Educational Stepchild: Howard University during the New Deal, 1933-1945*. Ph.D. diss., Howard University, 1989. UMO #9006617.

5009. _____. "Howard University and the Federal Government during the Presidential Administrations of Herbert Hoover and Franklin D. Roosevelt, 1928-1945." *Journal of Negro History* 76 (1991): 1-20.

5010. Muwakkil, Salim. "Black Studies Debate: Use or Lose the Canon." *In These Times* (16 May 1990).

5011. _____. "King Takes a Fall." *In These Times* (25 January 1993). ["Many black college students are denouncing Martin Luther King's vision as ineffective or worse, as complicit with white supremacy."]

5012. _____. "Michigan Brawl Could Be a Sign of Things to Come." *In These Times* (29 April 1992). [Racial conflict at Olivet College, in Olivet, Michigan]

5013. Myers, Eileen, and Phil Boas. "ASU Fraternity Gets Probation in Racial Brawl." *Tempe Daily News Tribune*, 22 June 1989. [Arizona State University]

5014. "NAACP Seeks Dormitory Space for Urban Poor." *New York Times*, 17 June 1990. [Washington and Lee University, Lexington, VA]

5015. Nagel, Elizabeth A. *Ethnic Minority Participation in Graduate Education since the Civil Rights Act of 1964: A Historiographical Study.* Ph.D. diss., Washington State University, 1990. UMO #9131083.

5016. Nasar, Sylvia. "More College Graduates Taking Low-Wage Jobs." *New York Times*, 7 August 1992.

5017. National Association of Scholars. "The Wrong Way to Reduce Campus Tensions." *New York Review of Books* (5 December 1991): 23.

5018. National Center for Education Statistics. *Trends in Racial/ Ethnic Enrollment in Higher Education: Fall 1978 Through Fall 1988.* Washington, DC: GPO, 1990.

5019. Navarrette, Ruben, Jr. "Education's Broken Promise to Minorities." *Los Angeles Times*, 14 February 1993. [Earnings gap between comparably-educated whites and nonwhites]

5020. _____. "Berkeley's Awkward Two-Step to Ensure a Racially Diverse Campus." *Los Angeles Times*, 11 October 1992.

5021. _____. *A Darker Shade of Crimson: Odyssey of a Harvard Chicano*. Bantam, 1993.

5022. Nettels, Michael T. *Black and White Students' College Performance in Majority White and Majority Black Settings.* Princeton, NJ: Educational Testing Service, 1986.

5023. Nettels, Michael T. and others. *The Causes and Consequences of College Students' Performance: A Focus on Black and White Students' Attrition Rates, Progression Rates and Grade Point Averges.* Nashville, TN: Tennessee Higher Education Commission, 1985.

5024. Nettels, Michael T., and A. Robert Thoeny, eds. *Toward Black Undergraduate Student Equality in American Higher Education.* Westport, CT: Greenwood, 1988.

5025. Neuborne, Burt. "Ghosts in the Attic: Idealized Pluralism, Community and Hate Speech." *Harvard Civil Rights-Civil Liberties Law Review* 27 (Summer 1992): 371-406. [See Michelman, above]

5026. New England Board of Higher Education. *Equality and Pluralism: Full Participation of Blacks and Hispanics in New England Higher Education.* Boston, MA: The Board, 1989.

5027. Newman, Maria. "College Officials Faulted By Rights Lawsuit Jury." *New York Times*, 18 May 1993. [CUNY and Prof. Leonard Jeffries, Jr.]

5028. _____. "Professor Winner in Suit on Speech." *New York Times*, 12 May 1993. [Prof. Leonard Jeffries, City College, CUNY]

5029. Nguyen, Alexander. "Campus Tensions: Another Year at the University." *Equity and Excellence* 26 (1993): 37-40. [Anti-Asian racism at UMass, Amherst]

5030. Nicklin, Julie L. "Financial Troubles at Small Black Colleges Raise Questions About Role of Their Trustees in Overseeing Management." *Chronicle of Higher Education* (10 March 1993). [Morris Brown College, Benedict College, a Paul Quinn College]

5031. _____. "No More Business as Usual." *Chronicle of Higher Education* (24 November 1993). [William H. Gray, III, president of the United Negro College Fund]

5032. _____. "Shaw University Regains Its Momentum." *Chronicle of Higher Education* (2 March 1994). [Raleigh, NC]

5033. _____. "Wooing Minority Alumni." *Chronicle of Higher Education* (23 February 1994).

5034. Nishida, Mo. "A Revolutionary Nationalist Perspective of the San Francisco State Strike." *Amerasia Journal* 15 (1989): 69- 79.

5035. Nixon, Harold L., and Wilma J. Henry. "White Students at the Black University: Their Experiences Regarding Acts of Racial Intolerance." *Equity and Excellence* 25 (Winter 1992): 121-123.

5036. Njeri, Itabari. "Academic Acrimony: Minority Professors Claim Racism Plays Role in Obtaining Tenure." *Los Angeles Times*, 20 September 1989.

5037. Noble, D. D. "Mental Material-The Militarization of Learning and Intelligence in United States Education." in *Cyborg Worlds. The Military Information Society*, eds. Les Levidow, and K. Robins. London: Free Association Books, 1989.

5038. Noboa-Rios, Abdin. "An Analysis of Hispanic Doctoral Recipients from U.S. Universities (1900-1973) with Special Emphasis on Puerto Rican Doctorates." *Metas* 2 (Winter 1981-82): 1-133.

5039. Noel, Peter. "Black Heart, White Hunter." *Village Voice* (27 August 1991). [Prof. Leonard Jeffries, CUNY]

5040. Nordheimer, Jon. "A College Program Ends Up in a Criminal Inquiry." *New York Times*, 5 October 1992. [Hasidic Jewish program at Rockland County Community College, NY]

5041. _____. "College Diatribe Ignites Furor on Race and Speech." *New York Times*, 29 December 1993. [Kean College, NJ]

5042. Nossiter, Adam. "Separation Down South." *Nation* (18 June 1990). [Black state universities and desegregation]

5043. "Nuturing Young Scholars: The Mission of Minority Law Teachers in the 1990's." *St. Louis University Public Law Review* 10 (1991): 145-435 (entire issue).

5044. Nyankori, J. C. O. "Postsecondary Enrollment Patterns after Court-ordered Desegregation: The Case of South Carolina." *Journal of Negro Education* 60 (Autumn 1991): 602-611.

5045. O'Brien, Eileen M. "American Indians in Higher Education." *Research Briefs (American Council on Education)* 3 (1992): 3. 1- 16.

5046. _____. "The Demise of Native American Education." *Black Issues in Higher Education* 7 (29 March 1990): 27-31.

5047. Odell, Morgan, and Jere J. Mock, eds. *A Crucial Agenda: Making Colleges and Universities Work Better for Minority Students*. Boulder, CO: Western Interstate Commission for Higher Education, 1989.

5048. Office of Minorities in Higher Education. *Minorities in Higher Education 1990*. American Council on Education, 1991.

5049. O'Haren, Maureen. "Racism at UCI: A Tenure Trap?" *Laguna News Post*, 25 May 1989. [University of California, Irvine; see below, Thomas A. Parham]

5050. Ola, Akinshiju. "Supreme Court to Mull Black Colleges' Future." *Guardian (NYC)* (14 August 1991).

5051. Olivas, Michael A. *The Dilemma of Access: Minorities in Two-Year Colleges*. Washington, DC: Howard University Press, 1979.

5052. _____. "Federal Law and Scholarships Policy: An Essay on the Office for Civil Rights, Title VI, and Racial Restrictions." *Journal of College and University Law* 18 (Summer 1991): 21-28.

5053. _____. "Legal Norms in Law School Admissions: An Essay on Parallel Universes." *Journal of Legal Education* 42 (March 1992): 103-118. [See L.A. Graglia, above]

5054. Oliver, M. L. and others. "Brown and Black in White: the Social Adjustment and Academic Performance of Chicano and Black Students in a Predominantly White University." *Urban Review* 17 (1986): 176-206.

5055. Olson, Carol, and Joe Hagy. "Achieving Social Justice: An Examination of Oklahoma's Response to Adams v. Richardson." *Journal of Negro Education* 59 (Spring 1990): 173-185.

5056. "On Freedom of Expression and Campus Speech Codes." *Academe* 78 (July-August 1982): 30-31.

5057. "Opening Academia Without Closing It Down." *New York Times*, 9 December 1990. [Multiculturalism on the campus]

5058. Oren, Dan A. "Jews at Yale-A Preliminary Examination." in *Jews in New Haven*, ed. Jonathan D. Sarna. New Haven, CT: Jewish Historical Society of New Haven, 1978.

5059. Orfield, Gary. "Executive Summary." in *The Revolving Door. City Colleges 1980-1989*, pp. i-vi. Maria Langan. Chicago, IL: Metropolitan Opportunity Project, University of Chicago,, February 1991. [Broader than title indicates]

5060. _____. "Money, Equity, and College Access." *Harvard Educational Review* 62 (Fall 1992): 337-372.

5061. Orfield, Gary, and Carole Ashkinaze. "Declining Black Access to College." in their *The Closing Door. Conservative Policy and Black Opportunity*, Ch. 6. Chicago, IL: University of Chicago Press, 1991. [Atlanta]

5062. Orfield, Gary, and Faith G. Paul. "Declines in Minority Access: A Tale of Five Cities." *Educational Review* 68 (1987- 1988).

5063. _____. *State Higher Education Systems and College Completion*. Northbrook, IL: Public Policy Research Consortium, November 1992. [2143 Ash Lane]

5064. Orlans, Harold. "Accreditation in American Higher Education: The Issue of Diversity." *Minerva* 30 (Winter 1991): 513-569.

5065. _____. "Affirmative Action in Higher Education." *Annals* 523 (September 1992): 144-158:

5066. _____. "Changing Conditions: Minority Education at Oaks College." *Thought and Action* 6 (Spring 1990): 21-34. [University of California, Santa Cruz]

5067. Ornstein, Charles. "Lawmakers Duel Over Aid to Minority Medical Students." *Chronicle of Higher Education* (17 August 1994).

5068. Orum, Lori S. *The Education of Hispanics: Status and Implications*. Washington, DC: National Council of La Raza, 1988.

5069. Oshinsky, David M., and Michael Curtis. "The Ads Should Be Rejected." *New York Times*, 11 December 1991. [Ads in college newspapers that contend the Holocaust never occurred.]

5070. Oteri, L. A., and G. D. Maloney. "Racism on Campus. The Negative Impact on Enrollment." *College and University* 65 (Spring 1990).

5071. Painter, Nell Irvin. "It's Time to Acknowledge the Damage Inflicted by Intolerance." *Chronicle of Higher Education* (23 March 1994).

5072. Palmer, Carolyn. *Violent Crimes and Other Forms of Victimization in Residence Halls*. College Administration Publications Inc., P.O. Box 15898, Asheville, NC 28813-08989, 1993.

5073. Palmer, Thomas. "Mt. Ida Suspends Officer, 2 Students After Dorm Fracas." *Boston Globe*, 31 October 1991. [Mount Ida College, Newton, MA]

5074. Parham, Thomas A. "Racism at UCI: Another View." *Laguna News Post* June 8, 1989. [University of California, Irvine]

5075. Parker, Johnny C., and Linda C. Parker. "Afirmative Action: Protecting the Untenured Minority Professor during Extreme Financial Exigency." *North Carolina Central Law Journal* 17 (Fall 1988): 119-134.

5076. Paul, Faith G. *Declining Minority Access to College in Metropolitan Chicago, 1980-1985*. Chicago, IL: Metropolitan Project, University of Chicago, 1987.

5077. _____. *Mission and Purpose: Gatekeeper to Opportunity*. Ph.D. diss., University of Chicago, 1991.

5078. "The 'PC' Struggle." *Tikkun* 6 (July-August 1991): 35-57. [Eight articles discuss 'political correctness']

5079. Pearson, Carol S. and others. *Educating the Majority: Women Challenge Tradition in Higher Education*. Collier Macmillan.

5080. Pearson, Ted. "Minorities Come Up Short at Comm Ed; Black Engineering Schools Ignored." *Chicago Reporter* 20 (July-August 1991).

5081. Pena, Mario J. *Institutional Financial Aid Policies and their Impact on Boston Puerto Rican Students' Ability to Access Higher Education*. Ph.D. diss., Harvard University, 1990. UMO #9032458.

5082. Peoples, Gerald C. *Desegregating Black Higher Education Institutions: The Case of Grambling State University*. Ph.D. diss., Kansas State University, 1990. UMO #9108405.

5083. Peoples, John A. "The Killing at Jackson State University May 1970: Reminiscences of Dr. John A. Peoples, President, Jackson State University, 1967-1984." *Vietnam Generation* 2 (1990): 55-58.

5084. Perry, Richard J., and Patricia J. Williams. "Freedom of Hate Speech." *Tikkun* 6 (July-August 1991): 55-57.

5085. Persell, Caroline H. and others. "Family Background, School Type, and College Attendance: A Conjoint System of Cultural Capital Transmission." *Sociological Abstracts* (August 1991): Supplement 167. 91S25356/ASA/1991/6715.

5086. Person, Dawn R. *The Black Student Culture of Lafayette College*. Ph.D. diss., Columbia University Teachers College, 1990. UMO #9033891.

5087. Perun, Pamela J., ed. *The Undergraduate Woman: Issues in Educational Equity*. Lexington, MA, 1982.

5088. Peters, Erskine. "Efforts of Students Should Be Encouraged, Not Berated." *Observer* (20 October 1989). [Faculty member at Notre Dame University discusses racism on his campus]

5089. Pfeiffenberger, Amy M. "Democracy at Home: The Struggle to Desegregate Washington University in the Postwar Era." *Gateway Heritage* 10 (Winter 1989-90): 14-25.

5090. Pilgrim, David. *Deception by Strategem. Segregation in Public Higher Education*. Bristol, IN: Wyndham Hall Press, 1985.

5091. Piliawsky, Monte. *Exit 13: Oppression and Racism in Academia*. Boston, MA: South End Press, 1989.

5092. Pincus, F. L., and E. Archer. *Bridges to Opportunity? Are Community Colleges Meeting the Transfer Needs of Minority Students?* New York: College Board, 1989.

5093. Pitsch, Mark. "Students Are 'Coming Back Home' To Historically Black Universities." *Education Week* (27 November 1991).

5094. Pitzl, Mary Jo. "Discipline Favored for Racism at ASU." *Arizona Republic* (19 June 1989). [600 Maricopa, AZ County residents]

5095. Platt, Anthony M. "Racism in Academia: Lessons from the Life of E. Franklin Frazier." *Monthly Review* 42 (September 1990): 29-45.

5096. Poinsett, Alex. "The Metamorphosis of Howard University." *Ebony* 27 (December 1971): 110-122.

5097. "Politics, Intellectuals, and the University." *Telos* (Winter 1990-91): 86. 103-140. [Symposium on affirmative action in higher education]

5098. Pool, Bob. "Memories of a Haven Live On at UCLA." *Los Angeles Times*, 14 May 1994. [Stevens House, refuge for minority students who were denied access to privately-rented rooms available to all other students]

5099. Poole, H. Randall. *From Black to White: The Transition of Bluefield State College from an Historically Black College to a Predominantly White Institution*. Ph.D. diss., University of Maryland, 1989. [1954-1970]. UMO #9021567.

5100. Pope-Davis, D. B., and T. M. Ottavi. "The Influence of White Racial Identity Attitudes on Racism Among Faculty Members: A Preliminary Examination." *Journal of College Student Development* 33 (September 1992): 389-394.

5101. Pottinger, Richard. "Disjunction to Higher Education: American Indian Students in the Southwest." *Anthropology and Education Quarterly* 20 (December 1989).

5102. Pouncey, Peter R. "Reflections on Black Separation at American Colleges." *Journal of Blacks in Higher Education* (Autumn 1993): 1. 57-59.

5103. Prestage, Jewel L. "The [Women's] Caucus [for Political Science] and Black Women: An Agenda for Change." *PS-Political Science and Politics* 23 (September 1990).

5104. "A Professor Flaunts His Bias." *New York Times*, 9 August 1991. [Editorial on Prof. Leonard Jeffries, Jr., CCNY]

5105. "Professor's Racial Theories Fall Wide of Mark." *New York Times*, 3 September 1991. [Five letters discuss charges of antisemitism against Prof. Leonard Jeffries, CUNY]

5106. "Professor Shouldn't Be Dismissed for Views." *New York Times*, 20 August 1991. [Four letters about Prof. Leonard Jeffries of CUNY]

5107. Pruitt, Anne S., ed. *In Pursuit of Equality in Higher Education*. Dix Hills, NY: General Hall, 1987.

5108. Puente, Teresa. "Campus Latinas Confront Prejudice." *Long Beach Press-Telegram*, 7 March 1993. [California State University]

5109. Quinn, Jane Bryant. "The New Rules for College Aid." *Newsweek* (21 September 1992).

5110. Qunitana, S. M. and others. "Meta-analysis of Latino Students' Adjustment in Higher Education." *Hispanic Journal of Behavorial Science* 13 (May 1991): 155-168.

5111. Rabinovitz, Jonathan. "For SUNY at Old Westbury, Protests and Conflict." *New York Times*, 22 March 1993. ["The flagship of racial diversity for the SUNY system?"]

5112. "Race and Sex Tied to Disparities in Professors' Pay." *New York Times*, 8 December 1991. [University of California at Berkeley]

5113. "Race on Campus." *U.S. News and World Report* (19 April 1993): 52-65.

5114. "Racial and Ethnic Issues in Higher Education." *Urban Review* (Fall 1988): 139-226.

5115. "Racial Graffiti Aimed at Friends Mar Ethnic Forum." *New York Times*, 17 November 1991. [University of California, Irvine]

5116. "Racial Harassment on Campus." *Journal of Higher Education* 63 (September-October 1992): entire issue.

5117. "Racism." *Colorado Daily*, December 6-13, 1989. [Series of six articles about racism on campus of University of Colorado, Boulder]

5118. "Racism and the Teaching of Black Studies." *Chronicle of Higher Education* (5 January 1994). [Three letters on white teachers of black studies]

5119. "Racism on Campus: Tolerating Intolerance." *Arizona Republic* (7 June 1989).

5120. "Racism Revival." *Daily Nebraskan*, 17 November 1989. [12- page "The Sower", containing a number of articles on racism.]

5121. "Racist Acts Inspire a Call for Control Over Fraternities." *New York Times*, 21 May 1989. [University of Wisconsin, Madison]

5122. "Racist Graffiti Leads to a Ban On Harrassment." *New York Times*, 17 June 1990. [Governing board of the three Arizona state universities]

5123. Ramey, Felicenne H. "Status of Minority Enrollment in California Schools of Business: U.S. Implications." *Western Journal of Black Studies* 12 (Summer 1988): 92-98.

5124. Randolph, Laura B. "Black Students Battle Racism on College Campuses." *Ebony* (December 1988): 126-130.

5125. Ransby, Barbara. *Racism in Education*. Ann Arbor: Ella Baker-Nelson Mandela Center for Anti-Racist Education, 1990. [University of Michigan, 200 W. Engineering Bldg., Ann Arbor, MI 48109-1092]

5126. Ransom, Michael R. "Gender Segregation by Field in Higher Education." *Research in Higher Education* 31 (1990): 477-494.

5127. Raymond, John. "Racist Campus Cut-Ups." *News and Review* (12 April 1984). [University of California, Santa Barbara]

5128. Reavis, Ralph. *Virginia Seminary: A Tangible Symbol of Opposition to White/Paternalism and Commitment to Self-Reliance.* Ph.D. diss., University of Virginia, 1989. [Lynchburg]. UMO #9002869.

5129. Reed, Ralph E., Jr. "Emory College and the Sledd Affair of 1902: A Case Study in Southern Honor and Racist Attitudes." *Georgia Historical Quarterly* 72 (Fall 1988): 463-492.

5130. Reed, Wornie L. "The Role of Universities in Racial Violence on Campuses." *Trotter Institute Review* 3 (Spring 1989): 3-4, 18-19. [Published by University of Massachusetts, Boston]

5131. Reeves, Garth C. "College Level Test Is Florida's Racist Shame." *Florida Photo News* (8 June 1989). [College Level Academic Skills Test (CLAST)]

5132. *Reflections on a Cherished Past: Reflections of the Ballard Normal School Experience.* Sacramento, CA: R.J. Pitts, 1980. [Macon, GA]

5133. "Regents Approve a Disputed Ban On Discrimination." *New York Times*, 18 June 1989. [University of Wisconsin system]

5134. Reich, Alice H. *The Cultural Construction of Ethnicity: Chicanos In the University.* New York: AMS Press, 1989.

5135. Reid, Alexander. "Harvard Minority Program in 20th Year." *Boston Globe*, 10 June 1990. [Harvard Medical School]

5136. Reid, Ellis E. "Earl, Bob, and Me." *Law School Record* 37 (Spring 1991): 4-9. [Afro-American lawyers at the University of Chicago Law School]

5137. Reingold, Nathan. "Refugee Mathematicians in the United States of America, 1933-1941: Reception and Reaction." in his *Science, American Style*, Rutgers University Press, 1991. [Touches on antisemitism in U.S. academic mathematics during the 1930's]

5138. *A Report of Student Concerns About Issues of Race and Racism in the School of Public Health at the University of Michigan.* Ann Arbor: School of Public Health, University of Michigan, April 1990.

5139. *Report on the University of Hawaii and the African-American Athlete.* Honolulu: Afro-American Association of Hawaii, 1991. Unpublished.

5140. Reskin, Barbara, and Deborah Merritt. "Double Minority: Empirical Evidence of a Double Standard in Law School Hiring of Minority Women." *Southern California Law Review* (September 1992).

5141. *A Resource Guide on Blacks in Higher Education.* National Association for Equal Opportunity in Higher Education, 1989.

5142. Reynolds, Tracie. "Stanford's First Black Graduate Reminisces." *Palo Alto Times Tribune*, 7 October 1989. [H.J. Benton Hamilton, Class of 1949]

5143. Rhoden, William C. "Black Student-Athletes Find Life of Privilege and Isolation." *New York Times*, 8 January 1990.

5144. Rich, Andrea L. and others. "[Three views on whether the Latino program at UCLA should become a department]." *Los Angeles Times*, 18 May 1993.

5145. Richardson, Lynda and others. "Ignoring Racial Issue Was Costly Error in Va. Beach." *Washington Post*, 18 September 1989. [Some 100,000 black college students at Greekfest '89, Labor Day weekend]

5146. Richardson, Richard C., Jr., and Louis W. Bender. *Fostering Minority Access and Achievement in Higher Education.* San Francisco, CA: Jossey-Bass, 1987.

5147. Ridenhour, Ron. "There's a Riot Going On. Racism 101 at Arizona State." *Village Voice* (26 September 1989).

5148. Ridgley, Julia. "Toward Equal Access." *Academe* 78 (September-October 1992): 13-18. [Minorities in higher education]

5149. Rivers, Eugene F. "Meritocracy and the Manipulation of Ethnic Minorities. The Epps and Evans Affairs." in *How Harvard Rules*, pp. 315-324. ed. John Trumpbour. Boston, MA: South End Press, 1989.

5150. *The Road to College. Educational Progress by Race and Ethnicity*. Boulder, CO: Western Interstate Commission for Higher Education, July 1991.

5151. Robbins, Richard. "The Future of Negro Colleges." *New South Student* (April 1966).

5152. Roberts, Darryl L. "Duke's Effort to Hire More Black Professors." *Chronicle of Higher Education* (5 May 1993).

5153. Robinson, Robert K. and others. "University of Pennsylvania v. EEOC: The Demise of Academic Freedom Privilege in the Peer Review-Process." *Labor Law Journal* 41 (June 1990): 364-369.

5154. Rochlin, Margy. "The Mathematics of Discrimination." *Los Angeles Times Magazine* (2 May 1993).

5155. Rodriguez, Adriene and others. "UCLA Law School's Faltering Commitment to the Latino Community: The New Admissions Process." *Chicano Law Review* 9 (1988): 73-96.

5156. Roebuck, Julian B., and Komanduri S. Murty. *Historically Black Colleges and Universities: Their Place in American Higher Education*. Praeger, 1993.

5157. Rogers, S. J., and E. G. Menaghan. "Women's Persistence in Undergraduate Majors: The Effects of Gender-Disproportionate Representation." *Gender and Society* 5 (December 1991): 549-564.

5158. Roiphe, Katie. "Date Rape's Other Victim." *New York Times Magazine* (13 June 1993).

5159. Rolnick, Joshua N. and others. "Anti-Semitic Ad Rallied Campus Opposition." *New York Times*, 30 December 1991. [Five letters on prohibiting the publication in college newspapers of denials that the Holocaust ever occured.]

5160. Roscoe, Wilma J., ed. *Accreditation of Historically and Predominantly Black Colleges and Universities*. Lanham, MD: University Press of America, 1989.

5161. Rose, D. C., and R. L. Sorenson. "High Tuition, Financial Aid, and Crosssubsidization: Do Needy Students Really Benefit?" *Southern Economic Journal* 59 (July 1992).

5162. Rovaris, Dereck J. *Developer of an Institution: Dr. Benjamin E. Mays, Morehouse College President, 1940-1967*. Ph.D. diss., University of Illinois at Urbana, 1990. UMO #9026309.

5163. Rubin, Brad. "Separate by Choice: Racial Segregation at Duke." *Los Angeles Times*, 17 October 1993.

5164. Rucker, Leland, and Dinah Zeiger. "Many Clergy View Boulder As Enlightened." *Colorado Daily*, 12 December 1989. [University of Colorado]

5165. Ruiz, Raul. *Alien Guests in a Strange House: Chicano Students at Harvard College*. Ph.D. diss., Harvard University, 1988. UMO #8823346.

5166. Russakoff, Dale. "Yiddish Phrase Hurled at Black Students Starts Political Correctness Debate." *Washington Post*, 1 May 1993. [Jews and Blacks at the U of Pennslyvania]

5167. Russell, L. A. "Assessing Campus Racism: The Use of Focus Groups." *Journal of College Student Development* 32 (May 1991): 271-272.

5168. Saad, Henry W. "The Case for Prohibitions of Racial Epithets in the University Classroom." *Wayne Law Review* 37 (Spring 1991): 1351-1362.

5169. Salter, John R., Jr. "Defeat Racism, Don't Censor It." *Against the Current* (May-June 1991): 32. 28.

5170. Sandalow, T. and others. "A Preliminary Report on Freedom of Expression and Campus Harrassment Codes." *Academe* 77 (May-June 1991): 23-26.

5171. Sanders, Alain L. and others. "Who's In Charge Here?" *Time* (31 December 1990). [The legality of one-race scholarships]

5172. Sanders, Danielle. "Cultural Conflicts: An Important Factor in the Academic Failure of American Indian Students." *Journal of Multicultural Counseling and Development* (April 1987).

5173. Sanders, Warren G., Jr. *Freedom of Expression and/or Freedom for Racial and Sexual Harrassment: College Campuses and "Hate-Speech" Codes.* Ph.D. diss., University of Iowa, 1992. UMO #9237004.

5174. Sanoff, Alvin P. and others. "Students Talk About Race." *U.S. News and World Report* (19 April 1993): 57-64. [University of North Carolina, Chapel Hill]

5175. Sanua, Marianne. "Stages in the Development of Jewish Life at Princeton University." *American Jewish History* 76 (1987): 391- 415.

5176. Sarnoski, Dorene R. "The Law Review Selection Process: An Analysis of Its Disparate Impact on Minority Students." *Law and Inequality* 7 (July 1989): 459-488.

5177. Savage, Reginald O. "Charges of Racism at St. Mary's College." *Chronicle of Higher Education* (27 January 1993): Letter. [Maryland]

5178. Sazama, G. W. "Has Federal Student Aid Contributed to Equality in Higher Education: A Method of Measurement." *American Journal of Economics and Sociology* 51 (April 1992): 129-146.

5179. Scannell, James J. *The Effect of Financial Aid Policies on Admission and Enrollment.* College Board Publications, 1992.

5180. Schemo, Diana J. "Anger Over List of Names Divides Blacks from their College Town." *New York Times*, 27 September 1992. [State University of New York at Oneonta]

5181. Schmidt, Peter. "Desegregation Ruling Seen Spurring Calls To Close Black Colleges." *Education Week* (3 February 1993).

5182. "School Struggles to Preserve Festival After Melee." *New York Times*, 25 June 1989. [University of California, Davis]

5183. Schwartz, Deborah R. "A First Amendment Justification for Regulating Racist Speech on Campus." *Case Western Reserve Law Review* 40 (summer 1990): 733-739.

5184. Seagears, Margaret J. *Impact of Adams v. Richardson on White Student Enrollment at Public Historically Black Colleges and Universities, 1976-1984.* Ph.D. diss., Virginia Polytechnic Institute and State University, 1988. UMO #8817418.

5185. Seale, Bobby. "Revolutionary Action on Campus and Community." *Black Scholar* (December 1969).

5186. Sedler, Robert A. "Doe v. University of Michigan and Campus Bans on Racist Speech: The View from Within." *Wayne Law Review* 37 (Spring 1991): 1325-1349.

5187. _____. "The Unconstitutionality of Campus Bans on Racist Speech: The View from Without and Within." *University of Pittsburgh Law Review* 53 (Spring 1992): 631-684.

5188. Selegue, S. M. "Campus Anti-slur Regulations: Speakers, Victims, and the First Amendment." *California Law Review* 79 (May 1991).

5189. Selvin, Paul. "The Raging Bull of Berkeley: Is Vincent Sarrich Part of a National Trend?" *Science* 251 (1991): 368-371.

5190. Shalevitz, Judith, and Joseph La Lumia. "On Campus, the Real America Now Emerges." *New York Times*, 31 May 1991. [Two separate letters on diversity in higher education]

5191. Shapiro, John T. "The Call for Campus Conduct Policies: Censorship or Constitutionally Permissible Limitations on Speech." *Minnesota Law Review* 75 (October 1990): 201-238.

5192. Shea, Christopher. "At Penn, Blacks Vent Anger at Student Paper, Triggering Debate Over Free Expression." *Chronicle of Higher Education* (28 April 1993).

5193. _____. "Dealing With Virulent Speakers." *Chronicle of Higher Education* (16 March 1994). [Esp. African-American and Jewish students on campuses]

5194. _____. "Does Student Housing Encourage Racial Separation on Campuses." *Chronicle of Higher Education* (14 July 1993).

5195. _____. "Hispanic Students, Frustrated Over Pace of Reforms on Campuses, Raise the Ante." *Chronicle of Higher Education* (13 October 1993).

5196. _____. "Protests Centering on Racial Issues Erupt on Many Campuses This Fall." *Chronicle of Higher Education* (25 November 1992).

5197. _____. "Queens College and a Measure of Diversity." *Chronicle of Higher Education* (11 May 1994). [Pigeon-holing racial classifications]

5198. _____. "Wall of Silence." *Chronicle of Higher Education* (22 June 1994). [Anti-hazing efforts in black fraternities]

5199. Sherman, Richard B. "The 'Teaching At Hampton Institute': Social Equality, Racial Integrity, and the Virginia Public Assemblage Act of 1926." *Virginia Magazine of History and Biography* 95 (1987): 275-300.

5200. Sherry, Suzanna. "Speaking of Virtue: A Republican Approach to University Regulation of Hate Speech." *Minnesota Law Review* 75 (February 1991): 933-944.

5201. Short, Thomas. "A 'New Racism' on Campus?" *Commentary* (August 1988): 46-50.

5202. Sidanius, James. "Racial Discrimination and Job Evaluation: The Case of University Faculty." *National Journal of Sociology* 3 (1989): 223-256. [University of Texas]

5203. Sidel, Ruth. *Battling Bias*. Viking, 1994. [College campuses]

5204. Siegel, Barry. "Fighting Words." *Los Angeles Times Magazine* (28 March 1993). [University of Wisconsin-Madison code against "hate-speech"]

5205. Siegel, Evan G. S. "Closing the Campus Gates to Free Expression: The Regulation of Offensive Speech at Colleges and Universities." *Emory Law Journal* 39 (Fall 1990): 1351-1400.

5206. Siegel, Jessica. "Anatomy of a Takeover." *Education Week* (2 March 1994). [New Jersey took control of Jersey City public schools in 1989]

5207. Silva, Cynthia and others. "Minority and Third World Students." in *How Harvard Rules. Reason in the Service of Empire*, pp. 303-311. ed. John Trumpbour. Boston, MA: South End Press, 1989.

5208. Silver, J. H. "African American Faculty at Traditionally White Institutions: The Impact of the Adams Case on Hiring Practices." *Urban League Review* 14 (Summer 1990): 29-38.

5209. Simpson, Janice C. "Black College Students Are Viewed as Victims of Subtle Racism." *Wall Street Journal*, 3 April 1987.

5210. Sims, Serbreina J. *Diversifying Historically Black Colleges and Universities: A New Higher Education Paradigm*. Greenwood, 1994.

5211. "Sit-In Supports Departing Official for Minorities." *New York Times*, 15 July 1990. [Cleveland State University]

5212. Slaughter, John B. "Rebuild Master Plan-for Students." *Los Angeles Times*, 22 March 1993. [California's 1960 Master Plan for Higher Education and the need to rank need-based student aid as highest priority.]

5213. Smetak, Jacqueline. "Race on Campus." *Z Magazine* 5 (July- August 1992): 5. [Iowa State University, Ames]

5214. Smith, A. Wade. "Educational Attainment as a Determinant of Social Class among Black Americans." *Journal of Negro Education* 58 (Summer 1989): 416-429.

5215. Smith, Daryl G. *The Challenge of Diversity: Involvement or Alienation in the Academy?* Washington, DC: ERIC-ASHE Research Reports, George Washington University, 1989.

5216. Smith, Gerald L. "Student Demonstrations and the Dilemma of the Black College President in 1960: Rufus Atwood and Kentucky State College." *Register of the Kentucky Historical Society* 88 (1990): 318-334.

5217. Smith, J. Clay, Jr. "Emerging Voices in the Academic State: A Bibliographic Survey of Select Writings by Minority Members of the AALS (Association of American Law Schools)." *Howard Law Journal* 33 (1990): 339-382. [1973-1988]

5218. Smolla, Rodney A. "Academic Freedom, Hate Speech, and the Idea of a University." *Law and Contemporary Problems* 53 (Summer 1990): 195-226.

5219. _____. "Rethinking First Amendment Assumptions about Racist and Sexist Speech." *Washington and Lee Law Review* 47 (Winter 1990): 171-211.

5220. Smothers, Ronald. "Mississippi's University system Going on Trial." *New York Times*, 9 May 1994. [Segregation issues]

5221. _____. "Plan to Desegregate Universities in Mississippi Is Met With Anger." *New York Times*, 23 October 1992.

5222. _____. "To Raise the Performance of Minorities, a College Increased its Standards." *New York Times*, 29 June 1994. [Georgia Institute of Technology]

5223. "Social and Cultural Tensions in the Schooling and Education of African Americans: Critical Reflections." *Urban Education* 27 (January 1993): 6 articles.

5224. Sollors, Werner and others, eds. *Blacks at Harvard: A Documentary History of African-American Experience at Harvard and Radcliffe*. NYU Press, 1993.

5225. _____. *Varieties of Black Experience at Harvard: An Anthology*. Cambridge, MA: Harvard University, Department of Afro- American Studies, 1986.

5226. Solnick, L. M. "Black College Attendance and Job Success of Black College Graduates." *Economics of Education Review* 9 (1990).

5227. South Carolina State Human Affairs Commission. *A Report on Hazing/Race Relations at the Citadel*. Columbia, SC: The Commission, 1987.

5228. Sowell, Thomas. "The New Racism on Campus." *Fortune* (13 February 1989).

5229. Spencer, Gary. "An Analysis of JAP-Baiting Humor on the College Campus." *Humor* 2 (1989): 329-348. [Jewish American Princess]

5230. Spofford, Tim. "Lynch Street: The May 1970 Slayings at Jackson State Univsity." *Vietnam Generation* 2 (1990): 59-64.

5231. St. Cloud State University. *Report of the Task Force on Racial Harrassment*. St. Cloud, MN: Minorities Studies Academic Program, 1988.

5232. St. John, Edward P., and Jay Noell. "The Effects of Student financial Aid on Access to Higher Education: An Analysis of Progress with Special Consideration of Minority Enrollment." *Research in Higher Education* 30 (December 1989).

5233. Stafford, Druicille H. *Crossing The Color Line: A Comparative Analysis of White Student Attitudes Toward Self and Minorities*. Ph.D. diss., University of Massachusetts, 1986. UMO #8612089.

5234. Stanfield, John H., II. "Private Foundations and Black Education and Intellectual Talent Development." in *Philanthropic Giving: Studies in Varieties and Goals*, ed. Richard Magat. New York: Oxford University Press, 1989.

5235. Stanley, Alessandra. "City College Professor Assailed for Remarks on Jews." *New York Times*, 7 August 1991. [Prof. Leonard Jeffries, CUNY]

5236. Staples, Brent. "Apartheid on Campus, Continued." *New York Times*, 4 July 1993.

5237. _____. "Ending Apartheid at College. First, Dismantle Segregated Housing [on Campus]." *New York Times*, 28 May 1993.

5238. _____. "Into the White Ivory Tower." *New York Times Magazine* (6 February 1994). [Black and White at the University of Chicago]

5239. Staples, Brent, and Terry Jones. "Racial Ideology and Intellectual Racism: Blacks in Academia." *Black Scholar* 15 (March-April 1984): 2-17.

5240. State Higher Education Executive Officers' Task Force on Minority Student Achievement. *A Difference of Degree: State Initiatives to Improve Minority Student Achievement*. Denver, CO: State Higher Education Executive Officers, 1987.

5241. Steele, Claude M. "Race and the Schooling of Black Americans." *Atlantic Monthly* (April 1992): 68-78.

5242. Steger, Michael. "A Cautious Approach: Racist Speech and the First Amendment at the University of Texas." *Journal of Law and Politics* 8 (Spring 1992): 609-648.

5243. Stein, Wayne J. *A History of the Tribally Controlled Community Colleges: 1968-1978*. Ph.D. diss., Washington State University, 1988. UMO #8902818.

5244. Steinberg, Stephen. *The Academic Melting Pot. Catholics and Jews in American Higher Education*. New York: McGraw-Hill, 1974.

5245. Stern, Carol S. "Colleges Must Be Careful Not to Write Bad Policies on Sexual Harrassment." *Chronicle of Higher Education* (10 March 1993).

5246. Stern, Kenneth S. *Bigotry on Campus: A Planned Response*. American Jewish Committee, 1990.

5247. Stewart, James B. *The State of Black Studies*. National Conference of Black Studies, 1985.

5248. Stewart, R. J. and others. "Alienation and Interactional Styles in a Predominantly White Environment: A Study of Successful Black Students." *Journal of College Student Development* 31 (November 1990).

5249. Stikes, C. Scully. *Black Students in Higher Education*. Carbondale: Southern Illinois University Press, 1984.

5250. Stimpson, Catharine R., and James D. Barber. "What Price 'Political Correctness'?" *Boston Globe*, 7 April 1991. [Two views]

5251. Stocker, Carol. "It All Started When Brigit Kerrigan Hung a Confederate Flag in a Harvard Window." *Boston Globe*, 10 April 1991.

5252. _____. "Jacinda Townsend Protested With a Swastika." *Boston Globe*, 10 April 1991. [Protest against hanging of a Confederate flag at Harvard]

5253. Stokes, John H. *The Impact of Desegregation on the Organizational Life of Black Colleges in the South*. Ph.D. diss., New School for Social Research, 1989. UMO #9105485.

5254. Strauss, Joseph H., and Kenneth Pepion. "Broken Promises: An American Indian Case Study." *Thought and Action* 8 (Winter 1993): 77-87. [American Indian studies program, University of Arizona]

5255. Strossen, Nadine. "Legal Scholars Who Would Limit Free Speech." *Chronicle of Higher Education* (7 July 1993).

5256. _____. "Regulating Racist Speech on Campus: A Modest Proposal." *Duke Law Journal* (June 1990): 484-573.

5257. "Student Accuses Veteran Professor of Racist Remarks." *New York Times*, 17 March 1991. [College of William and Mary]

5258. "Student at Brown Is Expelled Under a Rule Barring 'Hate Speech'." *New York Times*, 12 February 1991.

5259. Sullivan, Lisa. "Beyond Nostalgia: Notes on Black Student Activism." *Socialist Review* 20 (October-December 1990): 21-28.

5260. Sutherland, Marcia. "Black Faculty in White Academia." *Western Journal of Black Studies* 14 (Spring 1990): 17-23.

5261. Sutterlin, Rebecca, and Robert A. Kominski. *Dollars for Scholars: Postsecondary Costs and Financing*. U.S. Bureau of the Census, October 1994. [1990-1991 school year]

5262. Synnott, Marcia G. "The Admission and Assimilation of Minority Students at Harvard, Yale, and Princeton, 1900-1970." *History of Education Quarterly* 19 (1979): 285-304.

5263. Tachibana, Judy. "Minority Two-Year Transfer Rates Not Making the Grade in California." *Black Issues in Higher Education* 7 (30 August 1990): 18-19.

5264. Takagi, Dana Y. "The Retreat from Race." *Socialist Review* 22 (October-November 1992): 167-189.

5265. Takara, Kathryn W. *Opele: Report on African Americans at the University of Hawaii*. Center for Studies of Multicultural Higher Education, U. of Hawaii at Manoa, 1992.

5266. Tapscott, Richard. "Montgomery's Graduates Outpace P.G.'s in College." *Washington Post*, 9 July 1993. ["Students from wealthier suburban counties (in Maryland) fared better in college than those from less-affluent areas and inner cities."]

5267. Tashman, Billy, and Robert Neuwirth. "CUNY Under Siege." *Village Voice* (19 May 1992).

5268. Tatel, David S. *When Free Speech Becomes Harassment: Developing Effective Campus Policies*. Baltimore, MD: National Institute Against Prejudice and Violence, 1989.

5269. "A Test of Racism Produces an Uproar." *New York Times*, 17 February 1993. [Williams College]

5270. Texas Assocation of Chicanos in Higher Education. *The Mexican-Americans and Texas Higher Education*. June 1986. ERIC ED 271 283.

5271. Thelwell, Michael. "Black Studies. A Political Perspective." in *Duties, Pleasures, and Conflicts. Essays in Struggle*, pp. 130-140. Amherst: University of Massachusetts Press, 1987.

5272. _____. "Negroes with Guns." in *Duties, Pleasures, and Conflicts. Essays in Struggle*, pp. 119-129. Amherst: University of Massachusetts Press, 1987. [Cornell University, 1969]

5273. "Thirty six Years After the Hate, Black Student Triumphs." *New York Times*, 26 April 1992. [Ms. Autherine Lucy Foster, Black student who was barred from the University of Alabama for racial reasons in 1956]

5274. Thomas, Gail E. *The Access and Success of Blacks and Hispanics in U.S. Graduate and Professional Education*. Washington, DC: National Academy Press, 1986.

5275. _____. "Black College Students and Their Major Field Choice." in *In Pursuit of Equality in Higher Education*, pp. 105- 115. ed. Anne S. Pruitt. Dix Hills, NY: Garland Hall, 1987.

5276. _____. "Participation and Degree Attainment of African- American and Latino Students in Graduate Education Relative to Other Racial and Ethnic Groups: An Update from Office of Civil Rights Data." *Harvard Educational Review* 62 (Spring 1992): 45-65.

5277. Thomas, Gail E., ed. *U.S. Race Relations in the 1980's and 1990's: Challenges and Alternatives*. New York: Hemisphere Publishing, 1990. [See part 1, "Education and Race"]

5278. Thompson, Chalmer E. and others. "Cultural Mistrust and Racism Reaction Among African-American Students." *Journal of College Student Development* 31 (March 1990).

5279. Thompson, Julius E. "The Size and Composition of Alcorn A. + M. College Alumni, 1871-1930." *Journal of Mississippi History* 51 (August 1989): 219-231.

5280. Thomson, J. J. "Ideology and Faculty Selection." *Law and Contemporary Problems* 53 (Summer 1990): 155-176.

5281. Tien, Chang-Lin. "A Diverse Student Body Serves a Diverse Society." *Los Angeles Times*, 7 July 1992. [The chancellor of UC- Berkeley]

5282. Tierney, John. "For Jeffries, a Penchant for Disputes." *New York Times*, 7 September 1991. [Prof. Leonard Jeffries, Jr., CUNY]

5283. Tierney, William G. *Official Encouragement, Institutional Discouragement: Minorities in Academe-The Native American Experience*. Ablex Publishing Corp., 1992.

5284. Tifft, Susan and others. "The Search for Minorities." *Time* (21 August 1989).

5285. "A Tighter Code for Harrassment by Sex or Race." *New York Times*, 25 June 1989. [University of North Carolina, Chapel Hill]

5286. Tinto, V. *Leaving College: Rethinking the Causes and Cures of Student Attrition*. University of Chicago Press, 1987.

5287. Tokarczyk, Michelle M., and Elizabeth A. Fay, eds. *Working- Class Women in the Academy: Laborers in the Knowledge Factory*. University of Massachusetts Press, 1993.

5288. Tollett, Kenneth S., Sr. "Universal Education, Blacks and Democracy: The Expansion and Contraction of Educational Opportunities." in *Race: Twentieth-Century Dilemmas-Twenty-First-*

Century Prognoses, eds. Winston A. Van Horne, and Thomas V. Tonneson. Milwaukee: Institute on Race and Ethnicity, University of Wisconsin System, 1989.

5289. Tomasson, Robert E. "Goals for Racial Inclusion Elude Latest Crop of Young Doctors." *New York Times*, 1 April 1992.

5290. Torres-Aponte, Martine, and Kathy Mitchell. "Capital and the Corporate Canon." *Z Magazine* 3 (September 1990): 99-103. [Student movement at the University of Texas]

5291. Torry, Saundra. "Reunited in a Continuing Struggle." *Washington Post*, 9 October 1993. [Women graduates of Harvard Law School]

5292. Traub, James. *City On a Hill*. Addison-Wesley, 1994. [City College, CUNY]

5293. _____. "Class Struggle." *New Yorker* (19 September 1994). [Remedial education at the City College of New York]

5294. _____. "The Hearts and Minds of City College." *New Yorker* (7 June 1993). [Black Studies at City College, CUNY]

5295. _____. "Professor Whiff. Leonard Jeffries's 'Black Truth' Strikes Out." *Village Voice* (1 October 1991): 39-41.

5296. *Trends in Student Aid: 1984 to 1994*. College Board Publications, Box 886, NY, NY 10101-0886. Item No. 236203,

5297. Trent, William T. "Race and Ethnicity in the Teacher Education Curriculum." *Teachers College Record* 91 (Spring 1990): 361-369.

5298. "Troubled Dorm Offers Support for Minorities." *New York Times*, 8 October 1989. [University of Massachusetts, Amherst]

5299. Trow, Martin. "Class, Race, and Higher Education in America." *American Behavioral Scientist* 35 (March-June 1992): 585-605.

5300. "Trustees Allow Members to Pick Club Memberships." *New York Times*, 10 November 1991. [Vanderbilt University]

5301. Tsuang, G. W. "Assuring Equal Access of Asian Americans to Highly Selective Universities." *Yale Law Journal* 98 (January 1989).

5302. Turner, Lorenzo D. "Roosevelt College: Democratic Haven." *Opportunity* 25 (1947): 223-225.

5303. Umemoto, Karen. "'On Strike!' San Francisco State College Strike, 1968-69: The Role of Asian American Students." *Amerasia Journal* 15 (1989): 3-41.

5304. University of California Chicano/Latino Consortium. *A Report on the Status of Chicano/Latinos at the University of California*. June 1988.

5305. "University Professors Unite Against Anti-PC Onslaught." *In These Times* (9 October 1991). [Text of founding statement by Teachers for a Democratic Culture]

5306. "University Reaches Out to Blacks in Town." *New York Times*, 24 May 1989. [Madison, WI]

5307. Urban, Wayne J. "Philanthropy and the Black Scholar: The Case of Horace Mann Bond." *Journal of Negro Education* 58 (Autumn 1989).

5308. U.S. Bureau of the Census. *What's It Worth? Educational Background and Economic Status: Spring 1977*. GPO, 1990.
Current Population Reports, Series P-70, No. 21, Oct. 1990.

5309. U.S. Commission on Civil Rights. "Access to Educational Opportunity: Higher Education." in *Civil Rights Issues Facing Asian Americans in the 1990's*, Chapter 5. Washington, DC: The Commission, February 1992.

5310. _____. *The Black/White Colleges: Dismantling the Dual System of Higher Education*. Washington, DC: GPO, 1981.

5311. _____. *Briefing on Bigotry and Violence on College Campuses Before the Campus Bigotry Subcommittee*. 18 May 1989. On file at Washington DC office of the U.S. Commission on Civil Rights.

5312. U.S. Commission on Civil Rights, Kansas Advisory Committee. *Racial and Religious Tensions on Selected College Campuses*. U.S. Commission on Civil Rights, February 1992.

5313. U.S. Congress, 101st, 2nd session, House of Representatives, Committee on Education and Labor. *Hearing on the Department of Education, Office for Civil Rights Policy on Student Financial Assistance*. Washington, DC: GPO, 1991.

5314. U.S. Department of Education, Office of Planning, Budget, and Evaluation. *Debt Burden Facing College Graduates*. Washington, DC: The Department, 1991.

5315. "U.S. Mediates Students' Claims of Police Brutality." *New York Times*, 27 August 1989. [Berkeley, CA]

5316. U.S. Office for Civil Rights. *An Analysis of Black Attrition in Traditionally-Black Institutions and In All Other Institutions*. Washington, DC: U.S. Department of Education, 1981.

5317. Useem, Michael, and S. M. Miller. "Privilege and Domination: The Role of the Upper Class in American Higher Education." *Social Science Information* 14 (1975): 115-145.

5318. Vasquez, J. A., and N. Wainstein. "Instructional Responsibilities of College Faculty to Minority Students." *Journal of Negro Education* 59 (Autumn 1990).

5319. Vasquez, Jesse M. "The Co-opting of Ethnic Studies in the American University: A Critical View." *Explorations in Ethnic Studies* 11 (1988): 23-36.

5320. Verma, Gajendra K. *Inequality and Teacher Education: An International Perspective*. Falmer Press, 1993.

5321. Wake, Lloyd. "Reflections on the San Francisco State Strike." *Amerasia Journal* 15 (1989): 43-47. [1968-1969]

5322. Wald, Alan. "Racist Speech: A Problem of Power." *Against the Current* (May-June 1991): 32. 18-24.

5323. Walker, Adrian. "A Campus Divided." *Boston Globe*, 11 July 1990. [Wesleyan University]

5324. Wallace-Haymore, Denise. "Black Law Schools: The Continuing Need." *Southern University Law Review* 16 (Spring 1989): 249-280.

5325. Waltman, Jerold. "Assuring the Future of Black Colleges." *Chronicle of Higher Education* (6 July 1994).

5326. Ward, Jon A. "Race-exclusive Scholarships: Do They Violate the Constitution and Title VI of the Civil Rights Act of 1964." *Journal of College and University Law* 18 (Summer 1991): 73-103.

5327. Ward, Wanda E., and Mary M. Cross, eds. *Key Issues in Minority Education: Research Directions and Practical Implications*. Norman: University of Oklahoma Press, 1989.

5328. Warshaw, Robin. "In the Bonds of Fraternity." *Nation* (21 August 1989). [Delta Kappa Epsilon, Colgate University]

5329. Washburn, J. A. "Beyond Brown: Evaluating Equality in Higher Education." *Duke Law Journal* 43 (March 1994).

5330. Washington, Harold R. "History and the Role of Black Law Schools." *North Carolina Central Law Journal* 5 (1974).

5331. Washington, J. L. "Black Students, White Campuses, the Plight, the Promises." *Black Collegian* 19 (1988): 48-50.

5332. Washington, Valora, and William B. Harvey. *Affirmative Rhetoric, Negative Action: African-American and Hispanic Faculty at Predominantly White Institutions*. Washington, DC: School of Education and Human Development, George Washington University, 1990.

5333. Weakley, Vernon S. "Mississippi Killing Zone: An Eyewitness Account of the Events Surrounding the Murders by the Mississippi Highway Patrol at Jackson State College." *Vietnam Generation* 2 (1990): 65-74.

5334. Wechsler, Harold S. "Anti-Semitism in the Academy: Jewish Learning in American Universities, 1914-1939." *American Jewish Archives* 42 (Spring-Summer 1990): 7-21.

5335. _____. "Community and Academy: Jewish Learning at the University of California, 1870-1920." *Western State Jewish History* 18 (1986): 131-142.

5336. _____. *The Qualified Student: A History of Selective College Admission in America*. New York: Wiley, 1977.

5337. Weidemann, Celia J., and Marcie E. Kingslow. *The Involvement of Historically Black Colleges and Universities in Economic Development*. Washington, DC: Global Exchange, Inc., June 1989.

5338. Weiler, W. C. "Integrating Rank Differences into a Model of Male-Female Faculty Salary Discrimination." *Quarterly Review of Economics and Business* 30 (Spring 1990). [Higher Education in U.S.]

5339. Weinberg, H. A. "Anti-Semitism at Wellesley." *Congress Monthly* 52 (April 1985): 10-13.

5340. Weinberg, Jacob. "William Gray. Making Sure Black Minds Are Never Wasted." *Los Angeles Times*, 15 November 1992. [Historically Black colleges]

5341. Weinstein, J. "A Constitutional Roadmap to the Regulation of Campus Hate Speech." *Wayne Law Review* 38 (Fall 1991): 163-247.

5342. Weisbuch, Robert. "U-M English Department Not Biased." *Ann Arbor News*, 3 July 1989. Letter.

5343. Weiss, Bernard J. "Duquesne University: A Case Study of the Catholic University and the Urban Ethnic, 1878-1928." in *American Education and the European Immigrant 1840-1940*, ed. Weiss. University of Illinois Press, 1982.

5344. Weiss, Samuel. "Accrediting Group Defends Diversity." *New York Times*, 7 August 1991. [Middle States Association of Colleges and Schools]

5345. _____. "Are There Any Enforceable Limits On Academic Freedom of Speech." *New York Times*, 10 November 1991. [CUNY]

5346. _____. "Baruch School Losing Chief Amid Unease." *New York Times*, 5 April 1990.

5347. _____. "CUNY Teacher May Lose Post [As Departmental Chair] Over Remarks." *New York Times*, 25 October 1991. [Prof. Leonard Jeffries]

5348. Welch, Finis R. "Education and Racial Discrimination." in *Discrimination in Labor Markets*, ed. Orley Ashenfelter. Princeton, 1973.

5349. Wells, Jovita, ed. *A School for Freedom: Morristown College and Five Generations of Education for Blacks (1868-1985)*. Knoxville: East Tennessee Historical Society, 1986.

5350. Welsh, Patrick. "A Darker Shade of 'Brown'." *Washington Post*, 15 May 1994. [Black and white students at the colleges]

5351. Wennersten, John R., and Ruth E. Wennersten. "Separate and Unequal: The Evolution of a Black Land Grant College in Maryland, 1890-1930." *Maryland Historical Magazine* 72 (Spring 1977): 110- 117.

5352. Western Assocation of Schools and Colleges. *Dialogues for Diversity. Community and Ethnicity on Campus*. Phoenix, AZ: ACE/ ORYX, 1993.

5353. Western Interstate Commission for Higher Education Regional Policy Committee on Minorities in Higher Education. *From Minority to Majority: Education and the Future of the Southwest*. Boulder, CO: WICHE, 1987.

5354. "What Students Think: Racism Is a Big Issue." *New York Times*, 8 October 1989. [Based on interviews with about 300 students at 20 universities]

5355. Whiting, Albert N. *Guardians of the Flame: Historically Black Colleges, Yesterday, Today, and Tomorrow*. American Association of State Colleges and Universities, 1992.

5356. Whitten, L. A. "Infusing Black Psychology into the Introductory Psychology Course." *Teaching of Psychology* 20 (February 1993): 13-20.

5357. Wiener, Jon. "Free Speech for Campus Bigots?" *Nation* (26 February 1990).

5358. _____. "'Rape by Innuendo' at Swarthmore." *Nation* (20 January 1992).

5359. Wilkerson, Isabel. "Black Fraternities Thrive, Often on Adversity." *New York Times*, 2 October 1989.

5360. _____. "Racial Harrassment Altering Blacks' Choices on Colleges." *New York Times*, 9 May 1990.

5361. _____. "Racial Tension Erupts, Tearing a College Apart." *New York Times*, 13 April 1992. [Olivet College, Olivet, Michigan]

5362. Wilkinson, Doris Y. *A Profile of the Nation's Resources: The Academic Mission and Cultures of Traditionally Black Colleges and Universities*. Paper prepared for the Committee on the Status of Black Americans, National Research Council, Washington, D.C., 1987.

5363. Wilkins, Roger W. "A Loud Silence on Racism." *New York Times*, 8 January 1994. [College faculty, whatever their race, must show students they attack racism]

5364. Will, George F. "Academics Reaping the Whirlwind." *Washington Post*, 20 February 1994. [Critique of Western Association of Schools and Colleges diversity programs]

5365. _____. "Government Coercion, VMI's Diversity." *Washington Post*, 31 January 1993. [Virginia Military Institute in court over its all-male student body]

5366. Williams, Bruce E. "[College] Entry Rate [for Blacks] Declines." *New York Times*, 23 June 1991.

5367. Williams, John, ed. *Desegregating America's Colleges and Universities: Title VI Regulation of Higher Education*. New York: Teachers College Press, 1988.

5368. Williams, Juan. "In Search of Excellence." *Washington Post*, 20 September 1992. [Howard U.]

5369. Williams, Lea E. "Public Policies and Financial Exigencies: Black Colleges Twenty Years Later, 1965-1985." *Journal of Black Studies* 19 (December 1988): 135-149.

5370. Williams, Thomas T., and Handy Williamson, Jr. "Teaching, Research, and Extension Programs at Historically Black (1890) Land Grant Institutions." *Agricultural History* 62 (1988): 244-257.

5371. Willie, Charles V. and others, eds. *The Education of African-Americans. Vol. III of the Assessment of the Status of African-Americans*. Boston: William Monroe Trotter Institute, University of Massachusetts, 1990.

5372. Willie, Charles V., and Donald Cunnigen. "Black Students in Higher Education: A Review of Studies, 1965-1980." *Annual Review of Sociology* 7 (1981): 177-198.

5373. Wilson, Benjamin F., and Merinda D. Wilson. "Higher Education in Georgia: The Struggle for Equality." *Negro Educational Review* 30 (April-July 1979): 202-208.

5374. Wilson, Reginald. "Black Higher Education: Crisis and Promise." in *The State of Black America 1989*, ed. Janet Dewart. New York: National Urban League, 1989.

5375. _____. "Hypocrisy in Attacks on Racist Teaching." *Chronicle of Higher Education* (2 March 1994): Letter.

5376. _____. "Racism on the Campus." *New Politics* 3 (Summer 1991): 84-89.

5377. Wilson, Reginald, and Deborah J. Carter, eds. *Minorities in Higher Education*. Washington, DC: American Council on Education, 1989.

5378. Winerip, Michael. "Faculty Angst Over Diversity Courses Meets the Student Zeitgeist at UMass." *New York Times*, 4 May 1994.

5379. Wingfield, Harold L. *Affirmative Action: The Shootout Over Racism and Sexism at the University of Oregon, 1973-1975*. Ph.D. diss., University of Oregon, 1982.

5380. Winkler, Karen J. "Scholars Say Issues of Diversity Have 'Revolutionized' Field of Chicano Studies." *Chronicle of Higher Education* (26 September 1990).

5381. Witt, Stephanie L. *The Pursuit of Race and Gender Equity in American Academe*. Westport, CT: Praeger, 1990.

5382. Wolfe, Alan. "A View From the Dean's Office." *Washington Post*, 1 November 1992.

5383. Wolfe, Lee M. "Postsecondary Educational Attainment among Whites and Blacks." *American Educational Research Journal* 22 (1985): 501-525.

5384. Wolfson, Nicholas. "Free Speech Theory and Hateful Words." *University of Connecticut Law Review* 60 (Summer 1991): 1-42.

5385. Wood, Elizabeth P. *A Study of Racial Attitudes of Some White University Students: Theoretical Foundations for Developing Change Programs.* Ph.D. diss., University of Missouri, KC, 1990. UMO #9105768.

5386. Woodward, C. Vann. "Freedom and the Universities." *New York Review of Books* (18 July 1991).

5387. Woolbright, Cynthia, ed. *Valuing Diversity on Campus: A Multicultural Approach.* Association of College Unions- International, 1989.

5388. Wright, Bobby E. "American Indian Studies Programs: Surviving the '80's, Thriving in the 90's." *Journal of American Indian Education* 30 (1990): 17-24.

5389. _____. "'For the Children of the Infidels?': American Indian Education in the Colonial Colleges." *American Indian Culture and Research Journal* 12 (1988): 1-14.

5390. Wright, Patricia. "The Essential Esther." *Contact (University of Massachusetts, Amherst)* 14 (Summer 1989): 26-29. [Esther Terry, chair of the W.E.B. Du Bois Department of Afro-American Studies, University of Massachusetts, Amherst.]

5391. "Yale Students to Protest Racist Attacks on Campus." *New York Times*, 12 October 1990.

5392. Yamauchi, Joanne Sanae, and Tin-Mala. "Undercurrents, Maelstroms, or the Mainstream? A Profile of Asian Pacific- American Female Students in Higher Education." in *Educating the Majority*, pp. 69-79. eds. Carol S. Pearson and others. Collier Macmillan, 1989.

5393. Yelong, Han. "An Untold Story: American Policy Toward Chinese Students in the United States, 1949-1955." *Journal of American-East Asian Relations* (Spring 1993).

5394. Young, Anna B. *Case Studies of the Devlopment of Black Studies Programs in Selected Greater Philadelphia Institutions of Higher Learning.* Ph.D. diss., Rutgers University, 1986. [Cheyney, Lincoln, St. Joseph's, Temple, and U. of Pa.]. UMO #8709341.

5395. Young Gene C. "May 15, 1970: The Miracle at Jackson State College." *Vietnam Generation* 2 (1990): 75-81.

5396. Zayas, Luis H. and others. "So What Do the Guidance Counselors Know?" *New York Times*, 19 August 1992. three letters.

5397. Ziegler, Dhyana, and Camille Hazeur. "Challenging Racism on Campus." *Thought and Action* 5 (Fall 1989): 31-36.

5398. Zitner, Aaron. "U. of Lowell Clashes with School Paper." *Boston Globe*, 23 December 1990. [Sexual and racial harrassment by college newspaper and freedom of speech]

5399. Zomalt, Ernest E. *The Ethnic Studies Program Crisis: Conflict Resolution in a Multi-ethnic Environment 1974-1975.* Ph.D. diss., University of California, Santa Barbara, 1989. [UC, Santa Barbara]. UMO #9029588.

5400. Zweigenhaft, Richard L. "Accumulation of Cultural and Social Capital: The Differing College Careers of Prep School and Public School Graduates." *Sociological Spectrum* 13 (July-September 1993): 365-176.

5401. _____. "The Self-Monitoring of Black Students on a Predominantly White Campus." *Journal of Social Psychology* 133 (February 1993): 5-10.

EMPLOYMENT

5402. Bailey, Thomas. "Black Employment Opportunities." in *Setting Municipal Priorities 1990*, eds. Charles Brecher, and Raymond D. Horton. New York: New York University Press, 1989.

5403. Barr, Stephen. "Minority Workers Discharged at Higher Rates Than Whites." *Washington Post*, 15 December 1993. [Federal employment]

5404. Bell, Derrick A. "The Freedom of Employment Act." *Nation* (23 May 1994).

5405. Bound, John, and Richard B. Freeman. "What Went Wrong? The Erosion of Relative Earnings and Employment among Young Black Men in the 1980's." *Quarterly Journal of Economics* 107 (February 1992).

5406. Boyd, Robert L. "Black and Asian Self-Employment in Large Metropolitan Areas: A Comparative Analysis." *Social Problems* 37 (May 1990).

5407. Braun, Stephen. "Fight Over Jobs Divides Interests of Blacks, Latinos." *Los Angeles Times*, 9 August 1992. [Los Angeles]

5408. Cain, G. C., and R. E. Finnie. "The Black-White Difference in Youth Employment: Evidence for Demand-side Factors." *Journal of Labor Economics* 8 (January 1990): Part 2.

5409. Carter, Richard G. "Escaping Corporate Ghettoes." *New York Times*, 28 June 1992.

5410. Cruz, R. D. "The Industry Composition of Production and the Distribution of Income by Race and Ethnicity in Miami." *Review of Regional Studies* 21 (Summer 1991).

5411. Douglas, Marcia L. *The Myth of Meritocracy: Race, Gender, and Class in Silicon Valley.* Ph.D. diss., University of California, San Diego, 1991. UMO #9137322.

5412. Grace, Stephanie. "Report Finds Few Federal Latino Workers." *Los Angeles Times*, 23 July 1992.

5413. Hardesty, Michael, and Nina Wurgaft. "Silicon Valley: A Tale of Two Classes." *Z Magazine* 5 (September 1992): 63-65.

5414. Hernandez, Jose. *Puerto Rican Youth Employment*. Maplewood, NJ: Waterfront Press, 1983. [1976 data]

5415. Heywood, J. S., and M. S. Mohanty. "Race and Employment in the Federal Sector." *Economic Letters* 33 (June 1990).

5416. House, Ernest R., and William Madura. "Race, Gender, and Jobs: Losing Ground on Employment." *Policy Sciences* 21 (1988): 351-382.

5417. Howell, D. R., and E. N. Wolff. "Technical Change and the Demand for Skills by U.S. Industries." *Cambridge Journal of Economics* 16 (June 1992).

5418. Ihlanfeldt, K. R., and David L. Sjoquist. "Job Accessibility and Racial Differences in Youth Employment Rates." *American Economic Review* 80 (March 1990).

5419. Jaynes, Gerald D. "The Labor Market Status of Black Americans, 1939-1985." *Journal of Economic Perspectives* 4 (Autumn 1990).

5420. Knapp, M. C., and S. Y. Kwon. "Toward a Better Understanding of the Underrepresentation of Women and Minorities in Big 8 Firms." in *Advances in Public Interest Accounting*, Vol. 4. pp. 47-62. ed. C. R. Lehman. JAI Press, 1991.

5421. *The Labor Market Experience of Young African-American Men From Low-Income Families in Wisconsin*. Employment and Training Institute, University of Wisconsin-Milwaukee, P.O.Box 413, Milwaukee, Wisconsin.

5422. "Latinos in the California Economy." in *The Challenge: Latinos in a Changing California*, pp. 67-88. University of California SCR 43 Task Force. Riverside: The University of California Consortium on Mexico and the United States (UCMEXUS), 1989.

5423. Licht, Walter. *Getting Work: Philadelphia, 1840-1950*. Harvard University Press, 1992.

5424. Lichter, Daniel T. "Race, Employment Hardship, and Inequality in the American Nonmetropolitan South." *American Sociological Review* 54 (June 1989): 436-446.

5425. Margo, Robert A., and T. Aldrich Finegan. *The Decline in Black Teenage Labor Force Participation in the South, 1900-70: The Role of Schooling*. Cambridge, MA: National Bureau of Economic Research, May 1991.

5426. _____. "The Decline in Black Teenage Labor Force Participation in the South, 1900-1970: The Role of Schooling." *American Economic Review* 83 (March 1993).

5427. Meadenka, Kenneth R. "Barriers to Hispanic Employment Success in 1,200 Cities." *Social Science Quarterly* 70 (1989): 391-407.

5428. Morales, R., and Frank Bonilla, eds. *Latinos in a Changing U.S. Economy*. Sage, 1993.

5429. Newman, A. E. "Targets of Opportunity: Organizational and Environmental Determinants of Gender Integration Within the California Civil Service, 1979-1985." *American Journal of Sociology* 96 (May 1991): 1362-1401.

5430. Orfield, Gary, and Ricardo M. Tostado. *Latinos in Metropolitan Chicago: A Study of Housing and Employment*. Chicago, IL: Latino Institute, 1983.

5431. Ostrow, Ronald J. "Arms Firms Lag in Diversity at Top, Study Says." *Los Angeles Times*, 5 June 1992.

5432. Perrucci, C.C. "On Access to Employment." *Sociological Focus* 19 (1986): 215-228.

5433. Power, M., and S. Rosenberg. "Black Female Clerical Workers: Movement toward Equality with White Women?" *Industrial Relations* 32 (Spring 1993).

5434. Rawls, James J. "Gold Diggers: Indian Miners in the California Gold Rush." *California Historical Quarterly* 55 (1976): 28-45.

5435. Rosenbaum, S. A. "Safeguarding Employment for U.S. Workers: Do Undocumented Take Away Jobs?" *Chicago Law Review* 9 (1988): 175.

5436. Rothstein, Richard. "Employers, Not Schools, Fail Black Youth." *Los Angeles Times*, 18 April 1993.

5437. Santos, R., and P. Seitz. "School-to-Work Experience of Hispanic Youth." *Contemporary Policy Issues* 10 (October 1992).

5438. Schneider, M., and T. Phelan. "Blacks and Jobs: Never the Twain Shall Meet." *Urban Affairs Quarterly* 26 (December 1990).

5439. Smith, Peggie R. "Separate Identities: Black Women, Work, and Title VII." *Harvard Women's Law Journal* 14 (Spring 1991): 21- 75.

5440. Stafford, Walter W. *Closed Labor Markets: Underrepresentation of Blacks, Hispanics, and Women in New York City's Core Industries and Jobs*. New York: Community Service Society of New York, 1985.

5441. _____. *Employment Segmentation in New York City Municipal Agencies*. New York: Community Service Society, 1990.

5442. Terry, Don. "Cuts in Public Jobs May Hurt Blacks Most." *New York Times*, 10 December 1991.

5443. Thomas, R. Roosevelt, Jr. *Beyond Race and Gender. Understanding the Power of Your Total Work Force by Managing Diversity*. American Management Association, 1991.

5444. Torres, Andrea. *Human Capital, Labor Segmentation, and Inter-Minority Relative Status*. Ph.D. diss., New School for Social Research, 1988. [African-Americans and Puerto Ricans].

5445. _____. "Labor Market Segmentation: African American and Puerto Rican Labor in New York City, 1960-1980." *Review of Black Political Economy* 20 (Summer 1991): 59-77.

5446. Welch, Finis R. "The Employment of Black Men." *Journal of Labor Economics* 8 (January 1990): Part 2, 26-74.

5447. Williams, Lena. "Scrambling to Manage a Diverse Work Force." *New York Times*, 15 December 1992.

ENVIRONMENT

5448. Alexander, Nick. "Fighting Toxic Racism in Northern California." *Guardian (NYC)* (26 December 1990). [Richmond]

5449. Alston, Dana A., ed. *We Speak for Ourselves. Social Justice, Race, and Environment*. Washington, DC: Panos Institute, December 1990.

5450. Ambler, Maryjane. *Breaking the Iron Bonds: Indian Control of Energy Development*. University of Kansas Press, 1990.

5451. Anderson, David E. "Black Churches Bring Ecology Down to Earth." *National Catholic Reporter* (17 December 1993).

5452. Anderton, D. L. and others. "Environmental Equity: The Demographics of Dumping." *Demography* 31 (May 1994): 229-248.

5453. _____. "Hazardous Waste Facilities: Environment Equity Issues in Metropolitan Areas." *Evaluation Review* 18 (April 1994): 123-140.

5454. Arrandale, Tom. "When the Poor Cry NIMBY." *Governing* 6 (September 1993): 36-41.

5455. Austin, Regina, and Michael Schill. "Black, Brown, Poor and Poisoned: Minority Grassroots Environmentalism and the Quest for Eco-Justice." *Kansas Journal of Law and Public Policy* 1 (Summer 1991): 69-82.

5456. Bailey, A. J. and others. "Poisoned Landscapes: The Epidemiology of Environmental Lead Exposure in Massachusetts Children 1990-1991." *Social Science and Medicine* 39 (September 1994): 757-766.

5457. Been, Vicki. "What's Fairness Got to Do With It? Environmental Justice and the Siting of Locally Undesirable Land Uses." *Cornell Law Review* 78 (September 1993): 1001-1085.

5458. Benford, Robert D. and others. "In Whose Backyard? Concern About Siting a Nuclear Waste Facility." *Sociological Inquiry* (1993).

5459. Bennet, James. "New York Hispanic Voters and the Politics of Sludge." *New York Times*, 5 March 1993.

5460. Bernard, Mitchell S., and Carolyn L. Green. "Toxic Air Is Inner City's Silent Menace." *Los Angeles Times*, 20 July 1992. [Southern California]

5461. Broad, R. "The Poor and the Environment: Friends or Foes?" *World Development* 22 (June 1994): 811-822.

5462. Bruheze, Adri A. Albert de la. *Political Construction of Technology: Nuclear Waste in the United States, 1945-1972*. University of Twente, Department WMW-TW/RC RC r. 310, P.O. Box 217, 7500 AE Enschede, the Netherlands.

5463. Bryant, Bunyan. "Racism: A Toxic Waste." *Against the Current* no. 42 (January-February 1993): 10-12.

5464. Bryant, Pat. "Toxics and Racial Justice." *Social Policy* 20 (Summer 1989).

5465. Bullard, Robert D., ed. *Confronting Environmental Racism. Voices from the Grassroots*. South End Press, 1992.

5466. Bullard, Robert D. *Dumping in Dixie: Race, Class, and Environmental Quality*. Boulder, CO: Westview, 1990.

5467. Bullard, Robert D., and Beverly H. Wright. "Blacks and the Environment." *Humboldt Journal of Social Relations* 14 (1987): 165-184.

5468. _____. "Toxic Waste and the African American Community." *Urban League Review* 13 (Summer 1989-Winter 1989-90): 67-75.

5469. Burbank, James. "Activists of Color Are Confronting 'Environmental Racism'." *National Catholic Reporter* (11 October 1991).

5470. Chavis, Benjamin F., Jr. and others. "Bring Fair Play to Toxic Cleanup." *Los Angeles Times*, 9 February 1994.

5471. Chavis, Benjamin F., Jr. "Environmental Justice Is Social Justice." *Los Angeles Times*, 19 January 1993.

5472. _____. "Super Fraud." *Village Voice* (8 March 1994): Letter. [The Superfund and people of color]

5473. Chung, Eugene. "Racism and Sexism in the Environmental Movement." *Pacific Ties (UCLA)* (November 1990): 23.

5474. Churchill, Ward. *Struggle for the Land. Indigenous Resistance to Genocide, Ecocide and Expropriation in Contemporary North America*. Monroe, ME: Common Courage Press, 1993.

5475. Cohen, Linc. "Waste Dumps Toxic Traps for Minorities." *Chicago Reporter* 21 (April 1992).

5476. Cole, L. W. "Remedies for Environmental Racism: A View from the Field." *Michigan Law Review* 90 (June 1992): 1991-1997.

5477. Collin, Robert W. "Waste Siting Decisions and Communities of Color: A Call for Research." *Community Development Society Journal* 23 (1992): 1-10.

5478. Colten, Craig E. "Environmental Development in the East St. Louis Region, 1890-1970." *Environmental History Review* (1990).

5479. Commission for Racial Justice. *Toxic Wastes and Race in the United States: A National Report on the Racial and Socio-economic Characteristics of Communities with Hazardous Waste Sites*. United Church of Christ, 1987.

5480. Cushman, John H., Jr. "Clinton to Order Effort to Make Pollution Fairer." *New York Times*, 10 February 1994.

5481. _____. "U.S. to Weigh Blacks' Complaints About Pollution." *New York Times*, 19 November 1993.

5482. Cutter, S. L., and J. Tiefenbacher. "Chemical Hazards in Urban America." *Urban Geography* 12 (September-October 1991): 417- 430.

5483. Davis, Marcia. "Audubon Broadens Sights. D.C. Chapter Seeks More Minorities, Targets City's Environment." *Washington Post*, 7 January 1993. [National Audubon Society]

5484. Davis, Mike. "Dead West: Ecocide in Marlboro County." *New Left Review* 200 (July-August 1990): 49-73. ["Was the Cold War the Earth's worst eco-diaster in the last ten thousand years?"]

5485. Deloria, Philip. "CERT: It's Time for an Evaluation." *American Indian Law Newsletter* (September-October 1982).

5486. Di Chiro, Giovanna. "Defining Environmental Justice: Women's Voices and Grassroots Politics." *Socialist Review* 22 (October-November 1992): 93-130.

5487. Egan, Timothy. "Eskimos Learn They've Been Living Amid Secret Pits of Radioactive Soil." *New York Times*, 6 December 1992. [Alaska]

5488. "Environmental Justice." *Social Problems* 40 (February 1993): 1-124 (eight articles).

5489. Epstein, Robin. "Making the Fat Cats Chip In." *In These Times* (8 February 1993). [Louisiana]

5490. Ernst, G. J. "Racial and Economic Exploitation in the Siting of Toxic Wastes." *Bulletin of Science, Technology, and Society* 14 (1994): 28-32.

5491. Foster, S. "Race(ial) Matters: The Quest for Environmental Justice." *Ecology Law Quarterly* 20 (1993): 721-755.

5492. Frampton, George T., Jr. "Bringing Racial Diversity to the Environmental Movement." *Reconstruction* 1 (1991): 41-45.

5493. Freudenburg, W. R., and R. Gramling. "Natural Resources and Rural Poverty: A Closer Look." *Society and Natural Resources* 7 (January-February 1994): 5-22.

5494. Gedicks, Al. *The New Resource Wars. Native and Environmental Struggles Against Multi-national Corporations*. South End Press, 1993.

5495. _____. "Racism and Resource Colonialism." *Race and Class* 33 (April-June 1992): 75-81.

5496. Getlin, Josh. "Fighting Her Good Fight." *Los Angeles Times*, 18 February 1993. [Toxic dumping near Chicago's public housing project]

5497. Godsil, R. D. "Remedying Environmental Racism." *Michigan Law Review* 90 (November 1991).

5498. Head, Louis, and Michael Guerrero. "Fighting Environmental Racism." *New Solutions* 1 (Spring 1991): 38-42.

5499. Healy, Melissa. "Administration Joins Fight for 'Environmental Justice'." *Los Angeles Times*, 7 December 1993.

5500. Higgins, R. R. "Race and Environmental Equity: An Overview of the Environmental Justice Issue in the Policy Process." *Polity* 26 (Winter 1993): 281-300.

5501. Hinds, C. and others. "From the Front Lines of the Movement for Environmental Justice." *Social Policy* 22 (Spring 1992): 12- 24.

5502. Hofrichter, Richard, ed. *Toxic Struggles. The Theory and Practice of Environmental Justice*. New Society, 1994.

5503. Hurley, Andrew. "The Social Biases of Environmental Change in Gary, Indiana, 1945-1980." *Environmental Review* 12 (Winter 1988): 1-20.

5504. Irvin, Amelia. "Energy Development and the Effects of Mining on the Lakota Nation." *Journal of Ethnic Studies* 10 (Spring 1982).

5505. Jones, Jeff. "'Environmental Equity' A Base for New Coalitions?" *Guardian (NYC)* (8 January 1992).

5506. Jorgenson, Joseph, ed. *Native Americans and Energy Development II*. Cambridge, MA: Anthropology Resource Center/ Seventh Generation Fund, 1984.

5507. Kallick, D., and Charles V. Hamilton. "The Struggle for Community: Race, Class, and the Environment: An Interview with Cynthia Hamilton." *Social Policy* 21 (Autumn 1990).

5508. Kennedy, Robert F. Jr., and Dennis Rivera. "Pollution's Chief Victims: The Poor." *New York Times*, 15 August 1992.

5509. Kennedy, Sally J. *For Whose Protection? Reproductive Hazards in the United States and Britain*. University of Michigan Press, 1992.

5510. Kenworthy, Tom. "Hopis Feel their Lifeblood Draining Away." *Washington Post*, 17 November 1993. [Pollution of traditional springs by coal slurry]

5511. Krauss, Celene. "Women and Toxic Waste Protests: Race, Class, and Gender as Resources of Resistance." *Qualitative Sociology* 16 (Fall 1993): 247-262.

5512. Lawrence, R. "The Abrogation of Indian Treaties by Federal Statutes Protective of the Environment." *Natural Resources Journal* 31 (Autumn 1991): 859-886.

5513. Lee, Charles. "Evidence of Environmental Racism." *Sojourners* (February-March 1990): 23-25.

5514. _____. *Toxic Wastes and Race in the United States*. New York: United Church of Christ Commission for Racial Justice, 1987.

5515. Lee, Gary. "Clinton Executive Order Gives Boost to Mission." *Washington Post*, 17 February 1994. [Environmental problems of communities of low-income people and people of color]

5516. Lee, Pam Tau. "Environmental Justice for Asians and Pacific Islanders." *Asian Week* (13 March 1991).

5517. Lentol, Joseph R. "Let's Make a Start on Environmental Justice with Brooklyn." *New York Times*, 25 February 1994. Letter. [Greenpoint, Williamsburg, and Fort Greene area]

5518. Leonard, H. Jeffrey and others. *Environment and the Poor: Development Strategies. A Common Agenda*. Transaction Publishers, 1989.

5519. Livingstone, D. N. "The Moral Discourse of Climate: Historical Considerations on Race, Place, and Virtue." *Journal of Historical Geography* 17 (October 1991): 413-434.

5520. Lowell, Richard. *Four Attitudes Important to Environmental Education: A Study of Sub-Cultural and Socioeconomic Status Differences*. Ph.D. diss., Rutgers, The State University of New Jersey, New Brunswick, 1974.

5521. Maher, Timothy W. "Race, Class, and Trash: Whose Backyard Do We Dump In?" *Sociological Abstracts* (August 1991, Supplement 167). 91S25568/NCSA/1991/1506.

5522. Mann, Eric, and The Labor/Community WATCHDOG Organizing Committee. *L.A.'s Lethal Air*. Labor/Community Strategy Center, 14540 Haynes St., Suite 200, Van Nuys, CA 91411, 1991.

5523. Mann, Eric, and Chris Mathis. "Poor People Again Take the Toxic Brunt." *Los Angeles Times*, 10 March 1994.

5524. Marcus, Frances F. "Medical Waste Divides Mississippi Cities." *New York Times*, 24 June 1992. [Mostly black Moss Point and predominantly white Pascagoula]

5525. Martinez, Demetria. "To Explore NAFTA's Future, Visit Nogales." *National Catholic Reporter* (7 January 1994). [Arizona]

5526. Matsuoka, Jon, and Terry Kelly. "The Environmental, Economic, and Social Impacts of Resort Development and Tourism on Native Hawaiians." *Journal of Sociology and Social Welfare* 15 (December 1988): 29-44.

5527. McAdams, D. Claire. "Environmental Activism and the Intersection of Race, Class, and Gender: Patterns in Central Texas." *Sociological Abstracts* (August 1991, Supplement 167). 91S25280/ASA/1991/6639.

5528. Mohai, Paul. "Black Environmentalism." *Social Science Quarterly* 71 (1990): 744-765.

5529. Mohai, Paul, and Bunyan Bryant, eds. *Race and the Incidence of Environmental Hazards*. Westwood Press, 1992.

5530. Mydans, Seth. "Tribe Smells Sludge and Bureaucrats." *New York Times*, 20 October 1994. [Torres Martinez Desert Cahuilla, CA]

5531. Newton, Kathy C. "Beyond Ankle-biting: Fighting Environmental Discrimination Locally, Nationally, and Globally." *Workbook (Southwest Research and Information Center)* 16 (Fall 1991): 98-123.

5532. Niebuhr, Gustav. "Black Churches' Efforts on Environmentalism Praised by Gore." *Washington Post*, 3 December 1993. [Environmental racism]

5533. Paterson, Kent. "Expanding the Spectrum of U.S. Green Politics." *In These Times* (9 September 1991). [Minorities and the environmental movement]

5534. Pearson, Jessica S. *A Sociological Analysis of the Reduction of Hazardous Radiation in Uranium Mines*. National Institute for Occupational Safety and Health, 1975.

5535. Pulido, Laura. *Latino Environmental Struggles in the Southwest*. Ph.D. diss., UCLA, 1991. UMO #9213718.

5536. Purdy, Matthew. "Cost of Lead Cleanup Puts More Poor Children at Risk." *New York Times*, 25 August 1994. [N.Y.C.]

5537. *Race Poverty and the Environment* [A quarterly newsletter]

5538. "Reclaiming the Landscape, Reshaping the Movement: A Joint Issue on Environmental Racism." *Cross Roads and Forward Motion* (April 1992): entire issue.

5539. Rosen, Ruth. "Toxic Racism: Disaster in the Works." *Los Angeles Times*, 5 September 1993.

5540. Salleh, Ariel. "Class, Race, and Gender Discourse in the Ecofeminism/Deep Ecology Debate." *Environmental Ethics* 15 (Fall 1993): 225-244.

5541. Samet, M. J. and others. "Uranium Mining and Lung Cancer among Navajo Men." *New England Journal of Medicine* no. 310 (1984): 1481-1484.

5542. Schneider, Keith. "Idaho Tribe stops Nuclear Waste Truck." *New York Times*, 17 October 1991. [Shoshone-Bannock nation]

5543. _____. "Minorities Join to Fight Toxic Waste." *New York Times*, 25 October 1991. [First National People of Color Leadership Summit on the Environment]

5544. _____. "Plan for Toxic Dump Pits Blacks Against Blacks." *New York Times*, 13 December 1993. [Nuxubee County, Mississippi]

5545. _____. "The Regulatory Thickets of Environmental Racism." *New York Times*, 19 December 1993.

5546. Schwab, Margo. *Differential Exposure to Carbon Monoxide among Sociodemographic Groups in Washington, D.C.* Ph.D. diss., Clark University, 1988. UMO #8825802.

5547. *Siting of Hazardous Waste Landfills and Their Correlation with Racial and Economic Status of Surrounding Communities*. Washington, DC: U.S. General Accounting Office, 1983.

5548. Specktor, Mordicai. "Sioux Consider Nuke-dump Dollars." *Guardian (NYC)* (29 January 1992).

5549. Suro, Roberto. "Pollution-Weary Minorities Try Civil Rights Tack." *New York Times*, 11 January 1993.

5550. Swallow, S. K. and others. "Siting Noxious Facilities: An Approach that Integrates Technical, Economic, and Political Considerations." *Land Economics* 68 (August 1992): 283-301.

5551. Swinth, R. L. "The Organization of Hazardous Waste Production in the U.S.: Social and Ecological Performance." *Human Relations* 44 (1991): 147-174.

5552. Szasz, Andrew. *Ecopopulism: Toxic Waste and the Movement for Environmental Justice*. University of Minnesota Press, 1994.

5553. Tamplin, Arthur R., and John W. Gofman. *Population Control Through Nuclear Pollution*. Nelson-Hall, 1971.

5554. "Toxic Racism: Minorities Bear Brunt of Pollution." *San Francisco Examiner*, 7 April 1991. [Los Angeles]

5555. *Toxic Wastes and Race in the United States: A National Report on the Racial and Socioeconomic Characteristics of Communities with Hazardous Waste Sites*. New York: Commission for Racial Justice, United Church of Christ, 1987.

5556. Vecsey, Christopher, and Robert W. Venables, eds. *Native American Environments: Ecological Issues in American History*. Syracuse University Press, 1980.

5557. Walker, B. "Environmental Health and African Americans." *American Journal of Public Health* 81 (November 1991): 1395-1398.

5558. Walker, W. Lawrence, Sr. "NAACP Belongs in Superfund Debate." *New York Times*, 23 July 1994. Letter.

5559. Walter, Robert. "Poison in the Pacific." *Progressive* (July 1992): 32-35.

5560. Weisman, Leslie K. *Discrimination by Design: A Feminist Critique of the Man-Made Environment*. University of Illinois Press, 1992.

5561. Wheeler, David L. "When the Poor Face Environmental Risks." *Chronicle of Higher Education* (23 February 1994).

5562. Wright, R. George. "Hazardous Waste Disposal and the Problems of Stigmatic and Racial Injury." *Arizona State Law Journal* 23 (Fall 1991): 777-800.

FAMILY

5563. Abney, Lucille A. *Black Mothers' Perceptions of their Child-rearing Practices from 1945 to 1955: A Cohort of Southern Black Mothers Born in the 1930's*. Ph.D. diss., Texas Woman's University, 1991. [Galveston County, Texas]. UMO #9203109.

5564. Adams, Jacqueline. "The White Wife." *New York Times Magazine* (18 September 1994).

5565. Allen, Anita and others. "Responses to 'Where Do Black Children Belong?'." *Reconstruction* 1 (1992): 46-54. [See Bartholet, below]

5566. Anderson, Elijah. "Sex Codes and Family Life among Inner- City Youth." *Annals of the American Academy of Political and Social Science* 501 (January 1989): 59-78.

5567. Aponte, Robert. "Hispanic Families in Poverty: Diversity, Context, and Interpretation." *Families in Society* 74 (November 1993): 527-537.

5568. Aptheker, Bettina. "The Matriarchal Mirage: The Moynihan Connection in Historical Perspective." in *Women's Legacy: Essays on Race, Sex, and Class in American History*, pp. 129-151. Amherst: University of Massachusetts Press, 1982.

5569. Atkins, Elizabeth. "When Life Isn't Simply Black or White." *New York Times*, 5 June 1991. [Interracial marriage]

5570. Baca Zinn, Maxine. "Family, Feminism, and Race in America." *Gender and Society* 4 (March 1990).

5571. Bachu, Amara. *Fertility of American Women: June 1992*. U.S. Bureau of the Census,, July 1993.

5572. Balzar, John. "Biracial Families See a Road to Equality Paved with Diversity." *Los Angeles Times*, 7 October 1992. [St. Louis, MO]

5573. Bartholet, Elizabeth. *Family Bonds: Adoption and the Politics of Parenting*. Houghton Mifflin, 1993. [Transracial adoption]

5574. _____. "In Foster-Care Limbo." *Boston Globe*, 17 March 1992. [Obstacles to transracial adoption in Massachusetts]

5575. _____. "Where Do Black Children Belong? The Politics of Race Matching in Adoption." *University of Pennsylvania Law Review* 139 (May 1991): 1163-1256.

5576. Bartholet, Elizabeth, Charles Fried, and Carol S. Bevan. "Limits on Transracial Adoption Hurt Children." *New York Times*, 8 December 1993. Three letters.

5577. Bates, Douglas. *Gift Children: A Story of Race, Family, and Adoption in a Divided America*. Ticknor and Fields, 1993. [Transracial adoption]

5578. Bates, Karen G. "African Americans Got the Message Long Ago." *Los Angeles Times*, 23 June 1992. [The doctrine of personal responsibility]

5579. Bennett, Neil and others. "The Divergence of Black and White Marriage Patterns." *American Journal of Sociology* 95 (November 1989): 692-722.

5580. Berard, Yamil. "A Home for Our Children." *Long Beach Press Telegram*, 10 May 1993. [Institute for Black Parenting, Inglewood, CA; facilitates adoption of Black children by Black adoptive parents]

5581. Billingsley, Andrew. "Black Families in a Changing Society." in *The State of Black America, 1987*, pp. 97-111. New York: National Urban League, 1987.

5582. Bowser, Benjamin P. "Community and Economic Context of Black Families: A Critical Review of the Literature, 1909-1985." *American Journal of Social Psychiatry* 6 (Winter 1986): 17-46.

5583. Boyd, Robert L. "Racial Differences in Childlessness: A Centennial Review." *Sociological Perspectives* 32 (Summer 1989): 183-199.

5584. Boyd-Franklin, Nancy. "Black Family Life-Styles: A Lesson in Survival." in *Class, Race, and Sex: The Dynamics of Control*, pp. 189-199. eds. Amy Swerdlow, and Hanna Lessinger. Boston, MA: Hall, 1983.

5585. Bradbury, K. L. "The Changing Fortunes of American Families in the 1980's." *New England Economic Review* (July-August 1990).

5586. Broman, C. L. "Gender, Work-Family Roles, and Psychological Well-Being of Blacks." *Journal of Marriage and the Family* 53 (May 1991): 509-520.

5587. Brown, De Neen L. "Single Black Professionals Seek Same- With Little Success- in D.C. Area." *Washington Post*, 17 May 1994.

5588. Brown, Nancy. "'We Just Want To Be All of Who We Are'." *Los Angeles Times*, 11 January 1993. [Interracial marriages]

5589. Brown, Phil. "Black-White Interracial Marriage: A Historical Analysis." *Journal of Intergroup Relations* 16 (1989- 90): 26-36.

5590. Bumpass, L., and S. McLanahan. "Unmarried Motherhood: Recent Trends, Composition, and Black-White Differences." *Demography* 26 (May 1989).

5591. Burgess, Norma J., and Hayward D. Horton. "African American Women and Work: A Socio-Historical Perspective." *Journal of Family History* 18 (1993): 53-64.

5592. Burnham, Margaret A. "An Impossible Marriage: Slave Law and Family Law." *Law and Inequality* 5 (July 1987): 187-225.

5593. Caplan, Nathan S. and others. *The Boat People and Achievement in America. A Study of Family Life, Hard Work, and Cultural Values*. Ann Arbor: University of Michigan Press, 1989.

5594. Carter, Richard G. "Weathering Prejudice." *New York Times Magazine* (4 August 1991). [Black-White intermarriage]

5595. Cheatham, Harold E., and James B. Stewart. *Black Families: Interdisciplinary Perspectives*. New Brunswick, NJ: Transaction, 1989.

5596. Chew, Kenneth S. Y. and others. "American Children in Multiracial Households." *Sociological Perspectives* 32 (1989): 65- 85.

5597. "Childbearing Patterns among Selected Racial/ethnic Minority Groups, United States, 1990." *MMWR* 42 (1993): 398-403.

5598. Chilman, C. S. "Working Poor Families: Trends, Causes, Effects, and Suggested Policies." *Family Relations* 40 (April 1991): 191-198.

5599. Coady, Elizabeth. "Biracial Children Are Often Forced to Choose." *Long Beach Press-Telegram*, 14 September 1992.

5600. Cole, Jill C. *Perceptions of Ethnic Identity among Korean- born Adoptees and their Caucasian-American Parents*. Ph.D. diss., Columbia University, 1992. UMO #9313572.

5601. Colleran, Kevin J. "Acculturation in Puerto Rican Families in New York City." *Hispanic Research Center Research Bulletin* 7 (July-October 1984): 3-4.

5602. Comer, James P. "Black Fathers." in *Fathers and Their Families*, eds. Stanley H. Cath and others. Hillsdale, NJ: Lawrence Erlbaum Associates, 1989.

5603. _____. *Maggie's American Dream: The Life and Times of a Black Family*. New York: New American Library, 1988.

5604. Coontz, Stephanie. "The Pitfalls of 'Family Policy'." *Against the Current* no. 22 (September-October 1989): 11-18.

5605. Cortese, Anthony J.P. "Family, Culture, and Society: Educational Policy Implications for Mexican Americans." *Phylon* 49 (Spring-Summer 1992): 71-83.

5606. Cotton, Jeremiah. "The Declining Relative Economic Status of Black Families." *Review of Black Political Economy* 18 (Summer 1989).

5607. Cratty, Lark. "'It's Hard to Figure Who I Am'." *Los Angeles Times*, 21 September 1992. [Korean-born raised by Caucasian foster parents in Chicago area]

5608. Cross, William E., Jr. "Race and Ethnicity: Effects of Social Networks." in *Extended Families*, eds. M. Cochran and others. New York: Cambridge University Press, 1990.

5609. Daly, Kathleen. "Neither Conflict Nor Labeling Nor Paternalism Will Suffice: Intersections of Race, Ethnicity, Gender, and Family in Criminal Court Decisions." *Crime and Delinquency* 35 (January 1989): 136-168.

5610. Darity, William A., Jr., and Samuel L. Myers, Jr. "Does Welfare Dependency Cause Female Headship: The Case of the Black Family?" *Journal of Marriage and the Family* (November 1984): 765-779.

5611. _____. "Impacts of Violent Crime on Black Family Structure." *Contempoary Policy Issues* 8 (October 1990).

5612. Davis, A. A., and J. E. Rhodes. "African-American Teenage Mothers and Their Mothers: An Analysis of Supportive and Problematic Interactions." *Journal of Communicative Psychology* 22 (January 1994): 12-20.

5613. Davis, Angela Y., and Fania Davis. "The Black Family and the Crisis of Capitalism." *Black Scholar* (September-October 1986): 33-40.

5614. Dickson, Lynda. "The Future of Marriage and Family in Black America." *Journal of Black Studies* 23 (June 1993).

5615. Dill, Bonnie T. "Our Mothers' Grief: Racial Ethnic Women and the Maintenance of Families." *Journal of Family History* 13 (October 1988): 415-431. [19th Century]

5616. Dobie, Kathy. "Nobody's Child. The Battle Over Interracial Adoption." *Village Voice* (8 August 1989).

5617. Duke, Lynne. "Jefferson and the Question of a Slave Son." *Washington Post*, 13 April 1993. [Sally Hemings and Thomas Jefferson]

5618. Duncan, Greg J., and Saul D. Hoffman. "A Reconsideration of the Economic Consequences of Marital Dissolution." *Demography* 22 (1985).

5619. _____. "Welfare Benefits, Economic Opportunities, and Our-of-Wedlock Births among Black Teenage Girls." *Demography* 27 (November 1990).

5620. Eggebeen, David J., and Daniel T. Lichter. "Race, Family Structure, and Changing Poverty among American Children." *American Sociological Review* 56 (December 1991): 801-817.

5621. Ellwood, David T. *Poor Support: Poverty in the American Family*. Scranton, PA: Harper and Row, 1989.

5622. Ellwood, David T., and Jonathan Crane. "Family Change among Black Americans: What Do We Know?" *Journal of Economic Perspectives* 4 (Fall 1990): 65-84.

5623. Engram, E. *Science, Myth, Reality: The Black Family in One- Half Century of Research*. Westport, CT: Greenwood, 1982.

5624. Fayissa, Bichaka, and T. Fesshatzion. "Child Care Services in the Labour Force Participation and Income Distribution of Working Mothers in the U.S." *International Journal of Social Economics* 17 (1990).

5625. Felder, Henry E. *The Changing Patterns of Black Family Income, 1960-1982*. Washington, DC: Joint Center for Political Studies, 1984.

5626. Firestone, W. A. and others. "Equity in Sexuality Education: An Exploratory Study of Family Life Education in New Jersey's Rich and Poor Districts." *Educational Policy* 8 (September 1994): 289-314.

5627. Forde-Mazrui K. "Black Identity and Child Placement: The Best Interests of Black and Biracial Children." *Michigan Law Review* 92 (February 1994): 925-967.

5628. Foster, H. J. "African Patterns in the Afro-American Family." *Journal of Black Studies* 14 (December 1983): 201-232.

5629. Fowler, David H. *Modern Attitudes Towards Interracial Marriage: A Study of Legislation and Public Opinion in the Middle Atlantic and the States of the Old Northwest, 1780-1930*. New York: Garland, 1989.

5630. Funderburg, Lise. *Black, White, Other. Biracial Americans Talk About Race and Identity*. Morrow, 1994.

5631. Garfunkel, I., and S. S. McLanahan. *Single Mothers and Their Children: A New American Dilemma*. Washington, DC: Urban Institute Press, 1986.

5632. Gary, L. and others. *Stable Black Families: Final Report*. Washington, DC: Howard University Institute for Urban Affairs and Research, Mental Health Research and Developmental Center, 1983.

5633. George, Lynell. "Cross Colors." *Los Angeles Times*, 27 March 1994. [Interracial dating]

5634. Gonzales, Juan L., Jr. "The Origins of the Chicano Family in Mexico and the American Southwest." *International Journal of Sociology of the Family* 16 (Fall 1986).

5635. Gonzalez, Rosalinda M. "Chicanas and Mexican Immigrant Families 1920-1940: Women's Subordination and Family Exploitation." in *Decades of Discontent: The Women's Movement, 1920-1940*, pp. 59-83. ed. Lois Scharf. Westport, CT: Greenwood, 1982.

5636. Granger, J. M. "African American Family Policy or National Family Policy: Are They Different?" *Urban League Review* 13 (Summer-Winter 1990).

5637. Gray, S. S., and L. M. Nybell. "Issues in African-American Family Preservation." *Child Welfare* 69 (November-December 1990).

5638. Gresham, Jewell H. "The Politics of Family in America." *Nation* (24 July 1989).

5639. Griffith, Ezra E. H., and Jacqueline L. Duby. "Recent Developments in the Transracial Adoption Debate." *Bulletin of the American Academy of Psychiatry and the Law* 19 (December 1991): 339-350.

5640. Griswold del Castillo, Richard. *La Familia: Chicano Families in the Urban Southwest, 1848 to the Present*. Notre Dame, IN: University of Notre Dame Press, 1984.

5641. Hale-Benson, J. "Cultural Context for Child Care in the Black Community." in *Caring for Children: Challenge to America*, eds. J. S. Lande and others. Hillsdale, NJ: Lawrence Erlbaum Associates, 1989.

5642. Hare, Nathan, and J. Hare. *The Endangered Black Family*. San Francisco, CA: Black Think Tank, 1984.

5643. Harley, Sharon. "For the Good of Family and Race: Gender, Work, and Domestic Roles in the Black Community, 1880-1930." *Signs* 15 (1990): 336-349.

5644. Harrison, Eric. "Her Dream Becomes a Nightmare." *Los Angeles Times*, 21 September 1993. [White former grandparents-in- law get custody of two white ex-grandchildren to prevent them from living with their white mother and her black husband.]

5645. Harvey, A. R., ed. *The Black Family: An Afrocentric Perspective*. New York: Commission for Racial Justice, United Church of Christ, 1985.

5646. Heer, D. M. "Negro-White Marriage in the United States." *Journal of Marriage and the Family* 28 (1966): 262-273.

5647. Hill, Robert B. "Critical Issues for Black Families by the Year 2000." in *The State of Black America, 1989*, pp. 41-61. New York: National Urban League, 1989.

5648. _____. "Economic Forces. Structural Discrimination and Black Family Instability." *Review of Black Political Economy* 17 (1989): 5-23.

5649. Hill, Robert B. and others. *Research on African-American Families: A Holistic Perspective*. Boston, MA: William Monroe Trotter Institute, University of Massachusetts, 1989.

5650. Hodes, Martha E. *Sex Across the Color Line: White Women and Black Men in the Nineteenth Century American South*. Ph.D. diss., Princeton University, 1991. UMO #9127074.

5651. Hogan, Dennis P. and others. "Race, Kin Networks, and Assistance to Mother-headed Families." *Social Forces* 68 (March 1990).

5652. Hudson, Larry E., Jr. *"The Average Truth": The Slave Family in South Carolina, 1820-1860*. Ph.D. diss., University of Keele, 1989. Order No. BRDX92565.

5653. Hughes, Michael, and Bradley R. Hortel. "The Significance of Color Remains: A Study of Life Chances, Mate Selection, and Ethnic Consciousness among Black Americans." *Social Forces* 68 (1990): 1105-1120. [1950 and 1980]

5654. "Interracial Couples." *Ebony* 45 (August 1990): Letters.

5655. Jackson, A. W., ed. *Black Families and the Medium of Television*. Ann Arbor: University of Michigan, Bush Program in Child Development and Social Policy, 1982.

5656. Jaynes, Gerald D. *The Black Family*. Memorandum to the Committee on the Status of Black Americans, National Research Council, Washington, D.C., September 1985.

5657. Jaynes, Gerald D., and Robin M. Williams, Jr., eds. "Children and Families." in *A Common Destiny. Blacks and American Society*, pp. 509-556. Washington, DC: National Academy Press, 1989.

5658. Jensen, Leif, and Marta Tienda. "Nonmetropolitan Minority Families in the United States: Trends in Racial and Ethnic Economic Stratification, 1959-1986." *Rural Sociology* 54 (Winter 1989).

5659. Jewell, Karen S. *Survival of the Black Family: The Institutional Impact of U.S. Social Policy*. New York: Praeger, 1988.

5660. Johnson, C. M. and others. *Vanishing Dreams: Plight of America's Young Families*. Washington, DC: Children's Defense Fund, 1989.

5661. Jones, Charisse. "The Marriage Gap." *Los Angeles Times*, 28 March 1993. [Relative shortage of black men to marry black women]

5662. _____. "Role of Race in Adoptions: Old Debate Is Being Reborn." *New York Times*, 24 October 1993.

5663. Jones, Lisa. "Reckless Igging." *Village Voice* (16 June 1992).

5664. Jordan, Winthrop D., and Sheila L. Skemp, eds. *Race and Family in the Colonial South*. Jackson: University Press of Mississippi, 1987.

5665. Kiecolt, K. J., and Alan C. Alcock. "Childhood Family Structure and Adult Psychological Well-Being of Black Americans." *Sociological Spectrum* 10 (1990).

5666. Kitchen, Deborah L. *Interracial Marriage in the United States, 1900-1980*. Ph.D. diss., University of Minnesota, 1993. UMO #9321082.

5667. Kolata, Gina. "In Cities, Poor Families Are Dying of Crack." *New York Times*, 11 August 1989. [NYC]

5668. Lacey, L. J. "The White Man's Law and the American Indian Family in the Assimilation Era." *Arkansas Law Review* 40 (Fall 1986): 327-379.

5669. Langhorne, Elizabeth. "A Black Family at Monticello." *Magazine of Albemarle County History* 43 (1985): 1-16. [Hemings family]

5670. Leashore, Bogart R. *Interracial Households in 1850-1880. Detroit, Michigan.* Ph.D. diss., University of Michigan, 1979.

5671. Lee, Felicia R. "Harlem Family Battles Burden of the Past." *New York Times*, 9 September 1994. [2nd of three articles]

5672. Leigh, Wilhelmina A. "Federal Government Policies and the 'Housing Quotient' of Black American Families." *Review of Black Political Economy* 17 (Winter 1989).

5673. Lewis, J., and J. G. Looney. *The Long Struggle: Well- Functioning Working-Class Black Families.* New York: Brunner- Mazel, 1982.

5674. Lewis, Oscar. *La Vida: A Puerto Rican Family in the Culture of Poverty, San Juan and New York.* New York: Random House, 1966.

5675. Mahoney, Joan. "The Black Baby Doll: Transracial Adoption and Cultural Preservation." *UMKC Law Review* 59 (Spring 1991): 487-501.

5676. Marks, Paul G. "James McNeill Whistler's Family Secret: An Arrangement in White and Black." *Southern Quarterly* 26 (1988): 67-75.

5677. Mathabane, Mark and Gail. *Love in Black and White. The Triumph of Love over Prejudice and Taboo.* Harper/Collins, 1992.

5678. McCormick, Angela T. "Transracial Adoption: A Critical View of the Courts' Present Standards." *Journal of Family Law* 28 (April 1990): 303-318.

5679. McCrate, Elaine. "The Myth of 'Children Having Children'." *Boston Globe*, 12 October 1986.

5680. McGhee, J. D. *A Dream Denied: The Black Family in the Eighties.* Washington, DC: Research Dept., National Urban League, 1982.

5681. McGoun, W. E. "Adoption of Whites by XVIII Century Cherokees." *Journal of Cherokee Studies* 9 (1984): 37-41.

5682. McIntyre, R., and M. Hillard. "Stressed Families, Impoverished Families: Crises in the Household and in the Reproduction of the Working Class." *Review of Radical Political Economics* 24 (Summer 1992).

5683. McLoyd, Vonnie C. "The Impact of Economic Hardship on Black Families and Children: Psychological Distress, Parenting, and Socioemotional Development." *Child Development* 61 (April 1990): 311-346.

5684. Miller, Andrew T. *Looking at African-American Families: Recognition and Reaction.* Ph.D. diss., University of Pennsylvania, 1991. [Centers on 1910 data]. UMO #9200372.

5685. Moffitt, Robert. "The Effect of the U.S. Welfare System on Marital Status." *Journal of Public Economics* 41 (1990): 101-124.

5686. Morgan, S. Philip and others. "Racial Differences in Household and Family Structure at the Turn of the Century." *American Journal of Sociology* 98 (1993): 799-828.

5687. National Black Child Development Institute. *Who Will Care When Parents Don't? A Study of Black Children in Foster Care.* Washington, DC: The Institute, 1989.

5688. Nobles, Wade W. "Public Policy and the African-American Family." in *Race: Twentieth-Century Dilemmas--Twenty-first- Century Prognoses*, eds. Winston A. Van Horne, and Thomas V. Tonneson. Milwaukee: Institute on Race and Ethnicity, University of Wisconsin System, 1989.

5689. Omolade, Barbara. "The Unbroken Circle: A Historical Study of Black Single Mothers and Their Families." in *At the Boundaries of Law*, eds. Martha A. Fineman, and Nancy S. Thomadsen. Routledge, 1991.

5690. Palley, Howard A., and J. Fisher. "Societal Deprivation, the Underclass and Family Deterioration in Baltimore: A Structural Analysis." *Children and Youth Services Review* 13 (1991): 183-198.

5691. Pascoe, P. "Race, Gender, and Intercultural Relations: The Case of Interracial Marriage." *Frontiers* 12 (1991): 5-18.

5692. Paset, P. S., and R. D. Taylor. "Black and White Women's Attitudes toward Interracial Marriage." *Psychological Reports* 69 (December 1991): 753-754.

5693. Peiss, Judith. "Why Won't TV Show Jewish Couples?" *Los Angeles Times*, 2 May 1994.

5694. Peterson, Jacqueline. "Women Dreaming: The Religiopsychology of Indian-White Marriage and the Rise of Metis Culture." in *Western Women: Their Land, Their Lives*, eds. Lillian Schlissel and others. Albuquerque: University of New Mexico Press, 1988.

5695. Porterfield, Ernest. *Black and White Mixed Marriages*. Chicago, IL: Neson Hall, 1978.

5696. *Preserving Black Families: Research and Action Beyond the Rhetoric*. New York: National Association of Black Social Workers, 1986.

5697. Preston, Samuel H. and others. "African-American Marriage in 1910: Beneath the Surface of Census Data." *Demography* 29 (February 1992): 1-16.

5698. *A Proper Inheritance: Investing in the Self-Sufficiency of Poor Families*. Washington, DC: Center for Social Policy Studies, George Washington University, July 1989.

5699. Quadagno, Jill. "Race, Class, and Gender in the U.S. Welfare State: Nixon's Failed Family Assistance Plan." *American Sociological Review* 55 (1990): 11-28.

5700. Randolph, Laura B. "What Can We Do About the Most Explosive Problem in Black America: The Widening Gap Between Women Who Are Making It and Men Who Aren't." *Ebony* 45 (August 1990): 52-56.

5701. Richardson, Barbara B. *Racism and Child-rearing: A Study of Black Mothers*. Ph.D. diss., Claremont Graduate School, 1981. UMO #8114049.

5702. Robinson, Jeanne B. "Clinical Treatment of Black Families: Issues and Strategies." *Social Work* 34 (July 1989): 323-329.

5703. Rodgers, Harrell R. *Poor Women, Poor Families: The Economic Plight of America's Female-headed Households*, 2nd ed. Armonk, NY: M.E. Sharpe, 1990.

5704. Rogler, Lloyd H., and Rosemary S. Cooney. *Puerto Rican Families in New York City: Intergenerational Processes*. MapleWood, NJ: Waterfront Press, 1985.

5705. Root, Marcia P. P., ed. *Racially Mixed People in America*. Newbury Park, CA: Sage, 1992.

5706. Rosenthal, J. A. and others. "Race, Social Class, and Special Needs Adoption." *Social Work* 35 (November 1990).

5707. Ruggles, Steven. "The Origins of African-American Family Structure." *American Sociological Review* 59 (February 1994): 136-151.

5708. Ruggles, Steven, and Ron Goeken. "Race and Multigenerational Family Structure in the United States, 1900-1980." in *The Changing American Family*, eds. Scott J. South, and Stewart E. Tolnay. : Greenwood, 1992.

5709. *Running in Place: How American Families Are Faring in a Changing Economy and an Individualistic Society*. Washington, DC: Child Trends, Inc., 1994.

5710. Santana Cooney, Rosemary, and Alice Colon. "Work and Family: The Recent Struggle of Puerto Rican Females." in *The Puerto Rican Struggle*, eds. Clara E. Rodriquez and others. New York: Puerto Rican Migration Research Consortium, 1980.

5711. "Scapegoating the Black Family." *Nation* (24 July 1989): entire issue.

5712. Schwartz, Laura J. "Religious Matching for Adoption: Unraveling the Interests behind the 'Best Interests' Standard." *Family Law Quarterly* 25 (Summer 1991): 171-192.

5713. Scott, Joseph W., and Albert Black, Jr. "Deep Structures of African American Family Life: Female and Male Kin Networks." *Western Journal of Black Studies* 13 (Spring 1989): 17-24.

5714. Select Committee on Children, Youth, and Families. *U.S. Children and their Families: Current Conditions and Recent Trends*. Washington, DC: House of Representatives, 1989.

5715. Shapiro, R. J. "The Family Under Economic Stress." in *Putting Children First: A Progressive Family Policy for the 1990's*, eds. E. C. Kamarck, and W. A. Galston. Washington, DC: Progressive Policy Institute, 1990.

5716. Showmaker, Nancy. "Native American Families." in *American Families*, eds. Joseph M. Hawes, and Elizabeth I. Nybakken. : Greenwood, 1991.

5717. Simon, Rita J., and Howard Altstein. *The Case for Transracial Adoption*. American University Press, 1993.

5718. Smith, Earl. "The Black Family: Daniel Patrick Moynihan and the Image of Pathology Revisited." *Humboldt Journal of Social Relations* 14 (1987): 281-305.

5719. Smith, James P. "Poverty and the Family." in *Divided Opportunities*, eds. Gary D. Sandefur, and Marta Tienda. New York: Plenum Press, 1988.

5720. Smith, Lynn. "Salvation or Last Resort?" *Los Angeles Times*, 3 November 1993. [White adoption of black children]

5721. Smith, Patricia. "Love in Black and White." *Boston Globe*, 23 June 1991. [Racial intermarriage]

5722. Smits, David D. "'We Are Not to Grow Wild': Seventeenth- Century New England's Repudiation of Anglo-Indian Intermarriage." *American Indian Culture and Research Journal* 11 (1987): 1-31.

5723. Soto, Lourdes. "The Home Environment of Higher and Lower Achieving Puerto Rican Children." *Hispanic Journal of Behavorial Science* 10 (June 1988): 161-168.

5724. Spickard, Paul R. *Mixed Blood. Intermarriage and Ethnic Identity in Twentieth-Century America*. Madison: University of Wisconsin Press, 1989.

5725. Stuart, I. R., and L. E. Abt, eds. *Interracial Marriage: Expectations and Realities*. Grossman, 1973.

5726. Taylor, R. J. and others. "Developments in Research on Black Families: A Decade Review." *Journal of Marriage and the Family* 52 (November 1990).

5727. Thomas, Jerry. "Should White Parents Adopt Black Children?" *Chicago Tribune*, 23 June 1991.

5728. Thomas, Melvin E., and H. D. Horton. "Race, Class, and Family Structure: The Case of Family Income." *Sociological Perspectives* 35 (Autumn 1992): 433-450.

5729. Tidwell, Mike. "Romantic Notions, Old Ways of Thinking." *In These Times* (8 May 1991). [Racial intermarriage]

5730. Trent, K., and S. L. Harlan. "Household Structure among Teenage Mothers in the United States." *Social Science Quarterly* 71 (September 1990).

5731. Tucker, M. Belinda, and Claudia Mitchell-Kernan. "New Trends in Black American Interracial Marriage: The Social Structural Context." *Journal of Marriage and the Family* 52 (February 1990).

5732. U.S. Congress, 102nd, 1st session, Senate, Committee on Labor and Human Resources. *Children and Youth: The Crisis at Home for American Families: Hearing*. Washington, DC: GPO, 1991.

5733. Uyeunten, Sandra O. *Struggle and Survival: The History of Japanese Immigrant Families in California. 1907-1945*. Ph.D. diss., University of California, San Diego, 1988. UMO #8925097.

5734. *Vanishing Dreams: The Economic Plight of America's Young Families*. Washington, DC: Children's Defense Fund, 1992.

5735. Vega, W. A. "Hispanic Families in the 1980's: A Decade of Research." *Journal of Marriage and the Family* 52 (November 1990).

5736. Voydanoff, Patricia. "Economic Distress and Family Relations: A Review of the 80's." *Journal of Marriage and the Family* 52 (November 1990).

5737. Voydanoff, Patricia, and Linda C. Majka. *Families and Economic Distress*. Newbury Park, CA: Sage Publications, 1988.

5738. Walker, Harry A. "Racial Difference in Patterns of Marriage and Family Maintenance: 1890-1980." in *Feminism, Children and the New Families*, eds. Sanford M. Dornbusch, and Myra H. Strober. New York: Guilford Press, 1986.

5739. Walton, Scott. "Interracial Dating." *Long Beach Press- Telegram*, 21 October 1992.

5740. Washington, J. R. *Marriage in Black and White*. Beacon Press, 1970.

5741. Wetzel, J. R. "American Families: 75 Years of Change." *Monthly Labor Review* 113 (March 1990).

5742. Wheeler, David L. "Black Children, White Parents: the Difficult Issue of Transracial Adoption." *Chronicle of Higher Education* (15 September 1993).

5743. Wilkerson, Isabel. "Black-White Marriages Rise, But Social Acceptance Lags." *New York Times*, 2 December 1991.

5744. Wilkinson, D. Y. "Afro-Americans in the Corporation: An Assessment of the Impact on the Family." *Marriage and Family Review* 15 (1990).

5745. Williams, Lena. "For Nonwhite Dolls, A Growing Family." *New York Times*, 1 November 1990.

5746. Williams, Norma. *The Mexican American Family: Tradition and Change*. General Hall, 1990.

5747. Willie, Charles V. "Caste, Class, and Family Life Chances." in *Research in Race and Ethnic Relations*, ed. R. M. Dennis. JAI Press, 1991.

5748. _____. *A New Look at Black Families*. Dix Hills, NY: General Hall, 1988.

5749. _____. "Social Theory and Social Policy Derived from the Black Family Experience." *Journal of Black Studies* 23 (June 1993).

5750. Wilson, M. N., and T. F. J. Tolson. "Familial Support in the Black Community." *Journal of Clinical Child Psychology* 19 (December 1990).

5751. Wright, G. C. "Racism and the Availability of Family Planning Services in the U.S." *Social Forces* 56 (June 1978): 1087-1098.

5752. "You Can't Join Their Clubs." *Newsweek* (10 June 1991): 58- 59. [Six interracial couples discuss marriage]

5753. Zimmerman, Shirley L. "Myths about Public Welfare: Poverty, Family Instability, and Teen Illegitimacy." *Policy Studies Review* 8 (Spring 1989): 674-688.

5754. Zinn, Maxine Baca. "Family, Race, and Poverty in the Eighties." *Signs* 14 (Summer 1989): 856-874.

FORCED LABOR

5755. Bracey, John H., Jr., and August Meier, eds. "Peonage, Labor, and the New Deal, 1913-1939." *Papers of the NAACP*, Bethesda, MD: University Publications of America, 1990.

5756. Carper, N. Gordon. "Slavery Re-visited: Peonage in the South." *Phylon* 37 (1976): 85-99.

5757. Cvornyek, Robert L. *Convict Labor in the Alabama Coal Mines*. Ph.D. diss., Columbia University, 1993. UMO #9318231.

5758. Daniel, Pete. "Up From Slavery and Down to Peonage: The Alonzo Bailey Case." *Journal of American History* (December 1970).

5759. Fishback, Price V. "Debt Peonage in Postbellum Georgia." *Explorations in Economic History* 26 (April 1989).

5760. Katyal, N. K. "Men Who Own Women: A Thirteenth Amendment Critique of Forced Prostitution." *Yale Law Journal* 103 (December 1993).

5761. Knepper, Paul E. "Converting Idle Labor into Substantial Wealth: Arizona's Convict Lease System." *Journal of Arizona History* 31 (Spring 1990): 79-96.

5762. Lichtenstein, Alexander C. "Good Roads and Chain Gangs in the Progressive South: The Negro Convict is a Slave." *Journal of Southern History* 59 (1993): 85-110.

5763. _____. *The Political Economy of Convict Labor in the New South*. Ph.D. diss., University of Pennsylvania, 1990. [Convict- lease system, 1866-1916]. UMO #9101184.

5764. Lorch, Donatella. "Immigrants from China Pay Dearly To Be Slaves." *New York Times*, 3 January 1991. [NYC]

5765. Mancini, Matthew J. "Race, Economics, and the Abandonment of Convict Leasing." *Journal of Negro History* 63 (1978): 339-352.

5766. Morgan, Kenneth. "[British] Convict Runaways in Maryland, 1745-1775." *Journal of American Studies* 23 (1989): 253-268.

5767. Page, Catherine M. "Involuntary Servitude-A Standard at Last." *University of Toledo Law Review* 20 (Summer 1989): 1023- 1045.

5768. Roberts, Darrell. "Joseph Brown and the Convict Lease System." *Georgia Historical Review* 44 (1960).

5769. Shapiro, Karin A. *The Tennessee Coal Miners' Revolts of 1891-92: Industrialization, Politics, and Convict Labor in the Late Nineteenth-century South*. Ph.D. diss., Yale University, 1991. UMO #9315200.

5770. Stephens, Lester D. "A Former Slave and the Georgia Convict Lease System." *Negro History Bulletin* 39 (1976).

FREE BLACKS

5771. Blomberg, Belinda. *Free Black Adaptive Responses to the Antebellum Urban Environment: Neighborhood Formation and Socioeconomic Stratification in Alexandria, Virginia, 1790-1850.* Ph.D. diss., American University, 1988. UMO #8919943.

5772. Bogen, David S. "The Maryland Context of Dred Scott: The Decline in the Legal Status of Maryland Free Blacks 1776-1810." *American Journal of Legal History* 34 (October-December 1990): 381-411.

5773. Bonacich, Edna. "Abolition, the Extension of Slavery, and the Position of Free Blacks." *American Journal of Sociology* 81 (1975): 601-627.

5774. Butler, Reginald D. *Evolution of a Rural Free Black Community: Goochland County, Virginia, 1728-1832.* Ph.D. diss., Johns Hopkins University, 1989. UMO #8923661.

5775. Deal, Douglas. "A Constricted World: Free Blacks on Virginia's Eastern Shore." in *Colonial Chesapeake Society*, pp. 1680-1750. eds. Lois Green Carr and others. Chapel Hill: University of North Carolina Press, 1988.

5776. Finkelman, Paul R., ed. *Free Blacks in a Slave Society.* New York: Garland, 1989.

5777. Finkelman, Paul R. "Prelude to the Fourteenth Amendment: Black Legal Rights in the Antebellum North." *Rutgers Law Journal* 17 (Spring/Summer 1986).

5778. Fisher, John E. "The Legal Status of Free Blacks in Texas, 1836-1861." *Texas Southern Law Review* 4 (1977).

5779. Franklin, John Hope. "The Free Negro in the Economic Life of Ante-Bellum North Carolina." *North Carolina Historical Review* 19 (July and October 1942): 239-59, 359-375.

5780. _____. "Quasi-Free." *Stanford Lawyer* (Spring-Summer 1989): 10-13, 46-48.

5781. Gould, Lois V. M. *In Full Enjoyment of their Liberty: The Free Women of Color of the Gulf Ports of New Orleans, Mobile, and Pensacola, 1769-1860.* Ph.D. diss., Emory University, 1991. UMO #9127597.

5782. Higginbotham, A. Leon, Jr., and Greer C. Bosworth. "Rather than the Free: Free Blacks in Colonial and Antebellum Virginia." *Harvard Civil Rights-Civil Liberties Law Review* 26 (Winter 1991): 17-66.

5783. Horton, James O. *Free People of Color. Inside the African American Community.* Smithsonian Institution Press, 1993.

5784. _____. "Weevils in the Wheat: Free Blacks and the Constitution, 1787-1860." *This Constitution* no. 8 (1985): 4-11.

5785. Ingersoll, Thomas N. "Free Blacks in a Slave Society: New Orleans, 1718-1812." *William and Mary Quarterly* 58 (1991): 173- 200.

5786. Johnson, Whittington B. "Free Blacks in Antebellum Savannah: An Economic Profile." *Georgia Historical Quarterly* 64 (Winter 1980): 418-431.

5787. Litwack, Leon F. "The Federal Government and the Free Negro, 1790-1860." *Journal of Negro History* (October 1958).

5788. Nordmann, Christopher A. *Free Negroes in Mobile County, Alabama.* Ph.D. diss., University of Alabama, 1990. [Free Creoles of color]. UMO #9022271.

5789. Rogers, W. McDowell. "Free Negro Legislation in Georgia." *Georgia Historical Quarterly* 16 (March 1932).

5790. Smith, Dale E. *The Slaves of Liberty: Freedom in Amite County, Mississippi, 1820-1868.* Ph.D. diss., Harvard University, 1993. UMO #9331031.

5791. Whitman, Torrey S. *Slavery, Manumission, and Free Black Workers in Early National Baltimore.* Ph.D. diss., Johns Hopkins University, 1993. UMO #9327686.

5792. Wilson, Carol. *Freedom at Risk. The Kidnapping of Free Blacks in America, 1780-1865.* University Press of Kentucky, 1994.

GHETTO

5793. Aiken, Charles S. "A New Type of Black Ghetto in the Plantation South." *Annals of the Association of American Geographers* 80 (1990): 223-246. [Yazoo Delta, Mississippi]

5794. Aldrich, Howard E. "Employment Opportunities for Blacks in the Black Ghetto: The Role of White-owned Businesses." *American Journal of Sociology* 78 (1973): 1403-1425.

5795. Anderson, Elijah. "The Code of the Streets." *Atlantic Monthly* (May 1994).

5796. Applebome, Peter. "Deep South and Down Home, But It's a Ghetto All the Same." *New York Times*, 21 August 1993. [Jonestown, Mississippi]

5797. Bowser, Benjamin P. "Bayview-Hunter's Point: San Francisco's Black Ghetto Revisited." *Urban Anthropology* 17 (Winter 1988): 384-400.

5798. Caplan, Nathan S. "The New Ghetto Man: A Review of Recent Empirical Studies." *Journal of Social Issues* 26 (1970): 59-74.

5799. Casey-Leininger, Charles F. "Making the Second Ghetto in Cincinnati, Avondale, 1925-1970." Master's thesis, University of Cincinnati, 1989.

5800. Chambliss, W. J. "Policing the Ghetto Underclass: The Politics of Law and Law Enforcement." *Social Problems* 41 (May 1994): 177-194.

5801. Crane, Jonathan. *An Epidemic Model of Social Problems in Ghettos.* Ph.D. diss., Harvard University, 1988. UMO #8901672.

5802. _____. "The Epidemic Theory of Ghettos and Neighborhood Effects on Dropping Out and Teenage Childbearing." *American Journal of Sociology* 96 (March 1991).

5803. Davidson, Osha G. *Broken Heartland: The Rise of America's Rural Ghetto.* New York: Free Press, 1990.

5804. DeParle, Jason. "The Civil Rights Battle Was Easy Next to the Problems of the Ghetto." *New York Times*, 17 May 1992.

5805. Greenberg, M., and D. Schneider. "Violence in American Cities: Young Black Males Is the Answer, But What Was the Question?" *Social Science and Medicine* 39 (July 1994): 179-188.

5806. Hamovitch, Susan. "Redeveloping the Shtetl: The Buyout of Borough Park [N.Y.]." *Tikkun* 6 (March-April 1991). [Ultra- Orthodox Jewish "ghetto"]

5807. Herscher, Uri D. "The Metropolis of Ghettos." *Journal of Ethnic Studies* 4 (1976): 33-47. [Jewish ghettos]

5808. Hughes, Mark A. "Formation of the Impacted Ghetto-Evidence from Large Metropolitan Areas, 1970-1980." *Urban Geography* 11 (May-June 1990).

5809. _____. *The Limits to Location in Black Economic Mobility: An Empirical Study of the Relation between the Ghetto and Socio-economic Assimilation among Black Workers in the U.S. Metropolitan Areas*. Ph.D. diss., University of Pennsylvania, 1986.

5810. Jargowsky, Paul A. *Ghetto Poverty: The Neighborhood Distribution Framework*. Ph.D. diss., Harvard University, 1991. UMO #9211775.

5811. Jargowsky, Paul A., and David T. Ellwood. *Ghetto Poverty: A Theoretical and Empirical Framework*. Malcolm Wiener Center for Social Policy, John F, Kennedy School of Government, Harvard University, October 1990.

5812. Jencks, Christopher, and Susan E. Mayer. "The Social Consequences of Growing Up in a Bad Neighborhood." in *Inner-City Poverty in the United States*, eds. Lawrence E. Lynn, Jr., and Michael G. H. McGeary. Washington, DC: National Academy Press, 1990.

5813. Massey, Douglass, and Mitchell L. Eggers. "The Ecology of Inequality: Minorities and the Concentration of Poverty, 1970- 1980." *American Journal of Sociology* 95 (March 1990): 1153-1188.

5814. Moore, Joan W. and others. *Homeboys: Gangs, Drugs, and Prison in the Barrios of Los Angeles*. Philadelphia, PA: Temple University Press, 1978.

5815. Oliver, M., and J. Johnson. "Inter-Ethnic Conflict in an Urban Ghetto: The Case of Blacks and Latinos in Los Angeles." *Research in Social Movements, Conflict and Change* 6 (1984): 57- 94.

5816. Ortiz, Roxanne Dunbar. "The Reservation as a Social Enclave." *Development and Socioeconomic Progress* 1 (January 1981): 89-100. [Cairo]

5817. Pope, Jacqueline. "The Colonizing Impact of Public Service Bureaucracies in Black Communities." in *Race, Politics, and Economic Development: Community Perspectives*, ed. James Jennings. Verso, 1992.

5818. Savitch, Harold V. "Powerlessness in an Urban Ghetto: The Case of Political Biases and Differential Access in New York City." *Polity* 5 (Fall 1972): 17-56.

5819. Snow, David, and Peter J. Lehy. "The Making of a Black Slum-Ghetto: A Case Study of Neighborhood Transition." *Journal of Applied Behavioral Science* 16 (October-December 1980): 459-487. [Hough, Cleveland, Ohio]

5820. Tergeist, Peter. *Schwarze Bewegung und Gettoaufstände: Strukturen rassischer Gewalt in den USA*. Frankfurt: Rita G. Fischer Verlag, 1982.

5821. Trotter, Joe W., Jr. "Ghettoization vs. Proletarianization: Conceptual Problems in Afro-American Urban History." *Research in Urban Sociology* 1 (1989): 3-21.

5822. Vobejda, Barbara, At Core of the Problem Lies Absolute Isolation. *Washington Post*, 12 February 1993. [Growing segregation in Cleveland, Ohio and other cities]

5823. Wacquant, Loic J. D. "The Ghetto, The State, and the New Capitalist Economy." *Dissent* 36 (1989): 508-520.

5824. Wade, Richard C. "The Enduring Ghetto: Urbanization and the Color Line in American History." *Journal of Urban History* 17 (November 1990).

5825. Ward, David. *Poverty, Ethnicity, and the American Sicty, 1840-1925: Changing Conceptions of the Slum and the Ghetto*. New York: Cambridge University Press, 1989.

5826. Wilson, William J. *The Inner-City Ghetto: Contemporary Problems of Concentrated Urban Poverty*. New York: Knopf.

5827. _____. "Studying Inner-City Social Dislocation: The Challenge of Public Agenda Research." *American Sociological Review* 56 (1991): 1-14.

5828. Zukin, Sharon, and Bruce Haynes. "Against the 'Social Disorganization' Thesis: Community Structure in a Brooklyn Ghetto since 1945." *Sociological Abstracts* (1989). [Brownsville] Accession No. 89S21836.

GOVERNMENT AND MINORITIES

5829. Abell, J. D. "Distributional Effects of Monetary and Fiscal Policy: Impacts on Unemployment Rates Disaggregated by Race and Gender." *American Journal of Economics and Sociology* 50 (July 1991).

5830. Aguilar, Victor M. "A Case of Mismanagement: Federal Indian Policy on the Mescado Apache Indian Reservation." Master's thesis, University of Texas, El Paso, 1989.

5831. Anders, G. C. "Social and Economic Consequences of Federal Indian Policy: A Case Study of the Alaska Natives." *Economic Development and Cultural Change* 37 (January 1989).

5832. Anthony-Davis, Brenda. *Do Law Enforcement Agencies Equitably Serve and Protect All Communities? An Ethnographic Study fo Police Subculture in Tampa.* Ph.D. diss., University of South Florida, 1993. UMO #9323666.

5833. Auslander, Mary W. "Class and Race Decide New York [City] Transit Cuts." *New York Times*, 5 September 1991. letter.

5834. Barsh, Russell L., and K. Diaz-Knauf. "The Structure of Federal Aid for Indian Programs in the Decade of Prosperity, 1970-1980." *American Indian Quarterly* 8 (1984): 1-35.

5835. Bayley, David H., and Harold Mendelsohn. *Minorities and the Police: Confrontation in America.* New York: Free Press, 1969. [Denver]

5836. Bee, Robert. *The Politics of American Indian Policy.* Cambridge, MA: Schenckman, 1982.

5837. Benavidez, Max. "The City, the Riots, the Creative Response: Not a Pretty Picture." *Los Angeles Times*, 6 September 1992.

5838. "Bias Is Cited In Work Force for Congress." *New York Times*, 1 May 1994.

5839. Biolsi, Thomas. "'Indian Self-government' as a Technique of Domination." *American Indian Quarterly* 15 (1991): 23-28.

5840. Bixby, Ann K. "Public Social Welfare Expenditures, Fiscal Years 1965-1987." *Social Security Bulletin* 53 (February 1990).

5841. Bouza, Tony. "Tarnished Brass." *New York Times*, 14 October 1993. [New York City police and race, among other things]

5842. Britton, Jesse D. *Bureaucrats, Miners, and the Nez Perce Indians: Treaty-making in Washington Territory during the Civil War.* Ph.D. diss., Washington State University, 1988. UMO #8906161.

5843. Brown, Michael K. "The Segmented Welfare System: Distributive Conflict and Retrenchment in the United States, 1968-1984." in *Remaking the Welfare State*, ed. Brown. Philadelphia, PA: Temple University Press, 1988.

5844. Burt, Larry W. *Tribalism in Crisis: Federal Indian Policy, 1953-1961.* Albuquerque: University of New Mexico Press, 1982.

5845. Butts, Calvin O., 3rd and others. "Deal Openly With Racism in Subway Shooting." *New York Times*, 3 September 1994. [Three letters on shooting of black policeman by non-black policeman in NYC]

5846. Cadwalader, Sandra L., and Vine Deloria, Jr. *The Aggressions of Civilization. Federal Indian Policy Since the 1880's*. Philadelphia, PA: Temple University Press, 1984.

5847. Campbell, Walter E., III. *The Corporate Hand in an Urban Jim Crow Journey*. Ph.D. diss., University of North Carolina at Chapel Hill, 1991. [Streetcar segregation]. UMO #9135233.

5848. Capeci, Dominic J., Jr. "Walter F. White and the Savoy Ballroom Controversy of 1943." *Afro-Americans in New York Life and History* 5 (July 1981): 13-32.

5849. Castile, George P., and Robert L. Bee, eds. *State and Reservation: New Perspectives on Federal Indian Policy*. University of Arizona Press, 1992.

5850. Chamlin, Mitchell B. "A Macro Social Analysis of Change in Police Force Size, 1972-1982: Controlling for State and Dynamic Influences." *Sociological Quarterly* 30 (1989): 615-624.

5851. Christy, Mary R. "American Urban Indians: A Political Enigma-the Relationship between Phoenix Urban Indians and Phoenix City Government." Master's thesis, Arizona State University, 1979.

5852. Comment. "The Rise and Fall of the United States Commission on Civil Rights." *Harvard Civil Rights-Civil Liberties Law Review* 22 (1987).

5853. Cotterill, Robert S. "Federal Indian Management in the South, 1789-1825." *Mississippi Valley Historical Review* 20 (1933).

5854. Damrell, Joseph. "Some Observations and Interpretations of the Ojibwa Treaty Rights Struggle." *Humanity and Society* 13 (1989): 386-402.

5855. Darity, William A., Jr., and Samuel L. Myers, Jr. *Transfer Programs and the Economic Well-Being of Minorities*. Madison: Institute for Research on Poverty, University of Wisconsin, 1987.

5856. Deer, Ada. "Menominee Restoration: How the Good Guys Won." *Journal of Intergroup Relations* 3 (1974): 41-50.

5857. Deloria, Vine, Jr. *American Indian Policy in the Twentieth Century*. Norman: University of Oklahoma Press, 1985.

5858. _____. *Behind the Trail of Broken Treaties: An Indian Declaration of Independence*. Austin: University of Texas Press, 1985.

5859. _____. *A Brief History of the Federal Responsibility to the American Indian*. Washington, DC: GPO, 1979.

5860. Dotson, David D. "Why Purging the LAPD of Bias Won't Be Easy." *Los Angeles Times*, 3 April 1994.

5861. Duke, Lynne. "Law Enforcers Grapple With Diversity." *Washington Post*, 27 January 1993. [Racial discrimination and sex harassment in the federal Bureau of Alcohol, Tobacco, and Firearms]

5862. Dunn, Ashley, and Edmund Newton. "Scrutiny in Man's Death Reflects New View of Police." *Los Angeles Times*, 3 June 1993. [Michael James Bryant, an African American from Pasadena, CA]

5863. Dunne, John Gregory. "Law and Disorder in Los Angeles." *New York Review of Books* (October 10 and 24, 1991): 2 parts. [Racism in the Los Angeles police department]

5864. Durand, Roger. "Some Dynamics of Urban Service Evaluations Among Blacks and Whites." *Social Science Quarterly* (March 1976): 698-706.

5865. Edwards, Don. "Civil Rights Agency Abandoned Its Mission." *Wall Street Journal*, 3 October 1991. letter. [On the U.S. Commission on Civil Rights, see also Russell G. Redenbaugh, below]

5866. Epstein, Richard A. "Race and the Police Power: 1890 to 1937." *Washington and Lee Law Review* 46 (Fall 1989): 741-761.

5867. Escobar, Edward J. "The Dialectics of Repression: The Los Angeles Police and the Chicano Movement, 1968-1971." *Journal of American History* 79 (1993): 1483-1514.

5868. Escobar, Gabriel. "Mistrust of Police Persists in D.C.'s Latino Community." *Washington Post*, 26 November 1992.

5869. *Evolving Workforce Demographics: Federal Agency Action and Reaction*. Washington, DC: Merit Systems Protection Board, 1993.

5870. Fein, David J. "Racial and Ethnic Differences in U.S. Census Omission Rates." *Demography* 27 (May 1990).

5871. Feraca, Stephen E. *Why Don't They Give Them Guns? The Great American Indian Myth*. Lanham, MD: University Press of America, 1990.

5872. Finder, Alan, and Richard Levine. "When Wealthy Pay Less Tax Than the Other Homeowners." *New York Times*, 29 May 1990. [Black and Hispanic homeowners in NYC taxed at higher rates]

5873. Finley, Randy. *The Freedman's Bureau in Arkansas*. Ph.D. diss., University of Arkansas, 1992. UMO #9237356.

5874. Fixico, Donald L. *Termination and Relocation: Federal Indian Policy, 1945-1960*. Albuquerque: University of New Mexico Press, 1986.

5875. Fleming, Joseph E. "City of Memphis v. N.T. Greene: Before I Built a Wall I'd Ask to Know What I Was Walling In or Walling Out, and To Whom I Was Like to Give Offense." *Urban Lawyer* 21 (Fall 1989): 961-971.

5876. French, Lawrence. *The Winds of Injustice. American Indians and the U.S. Government*. Garland, 1994.

5877. Fuhrman, Susan. *Diversity Against Standardization: State Differential Treatment of Districts*. New Brunswick, NJ: Center for Policy Research in Education, Rutgers University, 1989.

5878. Galliher, Ruth A. "The Indian Agent in the United States Before 1850." *Iowa Journal of History and Politics* 14 (1916).

5879. _____. "The Indian Agent in the United States Since 1850." *Iowa Journal of History and Politics* 14 (1916).

5880. Golden, Daniel. "A Failure to Communicate." *Boston Globe Magazine* (17 February 1991). [The minority community and the police in Boston]

5881. Goshko, John M. "Foreign Service's Painful Passage To Looking More Like America." *Washington Post*, 21 April 1994. [Racial-ethnic factors in placement and promotions in U.S. foriegn service]

5882. Greenstein, Robert. "Universal and Targeted Approaches to Relieving Poverty: An Alternative View." in *The Urban Underclass*, pp. 437-459. eds. Christopher Jencks, and Paul E. Peterson. Washington, DC: Brookings Institute, 1991. [Progressive social legislation passed during the 1980's]

5883. Grinde, Donald A., Jr. "Navajo Opposition to the Indian New Deal." *Integrateducation* 19 (May-December 1981): 79-87.

5884. Grinston, Brenda. "Why Minority Cops Are Afraid to Speak Out." *Los Angeles Times*, 2 July 1991. [Black former officer who resigned from the Los Angeles police department, November 1985]

5885. Grossman, Zoltan. "A Fight for Treaty Rights." *Against the Current* 2 (May-June 1990): 29-30.

5886. _____. "Wisconsin Treaty Conflict No End in Sight." *Z Magazine* 3 (July-August 1990): 124-128. [Chippewa fishing rights in Northern Wisconsin]

5887. Hacker, Peter R. "Confusion and Conflict: A Study of Atypical Responses to Nineteenth-century Federal Indian Policies by the Citizen Band Potawatomis." *American Indian Culture and Research Journal* 13 (1989): 79-95.

5888. Hallowell, A. I. "American Indians, White and Black: The Phenomenon of Transculturalization." *Current Anthropology* 4 (April 1957): 201-217.

5889. Harman, George D. "The Indian Trust Funds, 1797-1865." *Mississippi Valley Historical Review* 21 (June 1934): 23-30.

5890. Harris, Carl V. "Reforms in Government Control of Negroes in Birmingham, Alabama, 1890-1920." *Journal of Southern History* (November 1972).

5891. Harris, Ron. "A Telling Silence in Newport." *Los Angeles Times*, 14 January 1994. [Exclusion of African Americans as participants in programs of the Resolution Trust Corporation.]

5892. Hatchett, David. "Black and Blue: Relations Between Blacks and Police Continue to Stagnate." *Crisis* 98 (December 1991): 12- 14.

5893. Hauptman, Laurence M. "Africa View: John Collier, the British Colonial Service and American Indian Policy, 1933-1945." *Historian* 48 (1986): 359-374.

5894. _____. "Learning the Lessons of History: The Oneidas of Wisconsin Reject Termination, 1943-1956." *Journal of Ethnic Studies* (1986): 31-52.

5895. Hayes, Floyd W., III "Governmental Retreat and the Politics of African-American Self-Reliant Development: Public Discourse and Social Policy." *Journal of Black Studies* 22 (March 1992): 331- 348.

5896. Heckman, J. James. "The Impact of Government on the Economic Status of Black Americans." in *The Question of Discrimination: Racial Inequality in the U.S. Labor Market*, pp. 50-80. eds. Steven Shulman, and William A. Darity. Wesleyan University Press, 1989.

5897. Hernandez, Oscar F. "Anishinabe Continue Rights Fight." *Against the Current* 6 (July-August 1991): 3-4. [Chippewa; fishing rights]

5898. Hoggart, K. "Urban Riots and Public Expenditure: New Jersey and Pennsylvania, 1962-1974." *Urban Geography* 11 (July-August 1990).

5899. Holmes, Steven A. "Federal Government Is Rethinking Its System of Racial Classification." *New York Times*, 8 July 1994.

5900. _____. "Police Poll: Satisfaction and Reserve." *New York Times*, 5 April 1991. [Black and white public opinion on police brutality]

5901. _____. "Report Criticizes Smithsonian On Hispanic Focus and Hiring." *New York Times*, 11 May 1994.

5902. _____. "U.S. Is Asked to Expand Undercover Bias Testing." *New York Times*, 26 September 1991.

5903. Hornung, Rick. *One Nation Under the Gun*. New York: Pantheon, 1992. [Mohawk resistance in upper New York State]

5904. Howe, Peter J. "Hot Line Response Varies." *Boston Globe*, 23 September 1990. [Response to calls on citizen hot line to mayor's ofice varies by race and class.]

5905. Hurtado, Albert L. "Controlling California's Indian Labor Force: Federal Administration of California Indian Affairs during the Mexican War." *Southern California Quarterly* 61 (Fall 1979): 217-238.

5906. _____. *Indian Survival on the California Frontier*. Yale University Press, 1988.

5907. Independent Commission on the Los Angeles Police Department. *Report of the Independent Commission on the Los Angeles Police Department*. Los Angeles: 1991. [Independent Commission, Suite 1919, 400 South Hope Street, Los Angeles, CA 90071-2899

5908. Jackson, Don. "Of Provocation and Dubious Justice." *Los Angeles Times*, 18 December 1992. [Race and class bias in Los Angeles policing]

5909. Jacobs. "British-Colonial Attitudes and Policies Toward the Indian in the American Colonies." in *Attitudes of Colonial Powers Toward the American Indian*, eds. H. Peckham, and C. Gibson.

5910. Jennings, Veronica T. "Montgomery Police Defend Efforts To Protect Hispanic Neighborhoods." *Washington Post*, 5 September 1993.

5911. Johnny, Ronald E. "Can Indian Tribes Afford to Let the Bureau of Indian Affairs Continue to Negotiate Permits and Leases of their Resources?" *American Indian Law Review* 16 (Spring 1991): 203-211.

5912. Johnson, Rhonda Shaw, and Peter Goonan. "Black Leaders Outraged by Police Party." *Springfield, Mass. Union-News*, 2 July 1994. ["A party given by some police officers to honor a patrolman who killed a young black man."]

5913. Johnston, David. "In Justice Dept. of the 90's, Focus Shifts from Rights." *New York Times*, 26 March 1991.

5914. Kamerman, S. B., and A. J. Kahn. "Social Services for Children, Youth and Families in the United States." *Children and Youth Services Review* 12 (1990): 1-179.

5915. Kellough, J. Edward. "Integration in the Public Workplace: Determinants of Minority and Female Employment in Federal Agencies." *Public Administration Review* 50 (September-October 1990).

5916. Kilborn, Peter T. "New York Police Force Lagging In Recruitment of Black Officers." *New York Times*, 17 July 1994.

5917. _____. "Police Profile Stays Much the Same. A Try for Diversity Meets Old Patterns." *New York Times*, 10 October 1994. [New York City]

5918. Koon, Stacey C. *Presumed Guilty: The Tragedy of the Rodney King Affair*. Regency Gateway, 1992.

5919. Krauss, Clifford. "2-Year Corruption Inquiry Finds a 'Willful Blindness' in New York's Police Department." *New York Times*, 7 July 1994. ["Highly organized networks of rogue officers...deal in drugs and prey on black and hispanic neighborhoods."]

5920. _____. "In Wake of Shooting, Bratton Appoints a Panel to Study Racial Attitudes [of NYC Police]." *New York Times*, 26 August 1994.

5921. _____. "Poll Finds a Lack of Faith in Police." *New York Times*, 19 June 1994. [New York City]

5922. "Labor Dept. Agrees to $4m Bias Settlement." *Boston Globe*, 30 September 1994. [U.S. Department of Labor settles lawsuit against itself.]

5923. Lamb, Terrence J. "Indian-Government Relations on Water Utilization in the Salt and Gila River Valleys of Southern Arizona, 1902-1914." *Indian Historian* 10 (1977): 38-45, 61-62.

5924. Landsman, Gail H. *Sovereignty and Symbol: Indian-White Conflict at Ganienkeh*. Albuquerque: University of New Mexico Press, 1988.

5925. Leonard, Paul A. *Changes in Low Income Discretionary Programs, FY81-FY89*. Washington, DC: Center on Budget and Policy Priorities, 1989.

5926. Lewis, Gregory B. "Progress Toward Racial and Sexual Equality in the Federal Civil Service?" *Public Administration Review* 48 (May-June 1988): 700-707.

5927. Little, George. "A Study of the Texas Good Neighbor Commission." Master's thesis, University of Houston, 1953.

5928. Lomax, Melanie E. "Racial Bias in Fire Department." *Los Angeles Times*, 16 April 1994.

5929. "Los Angeles Police Accused of Bias." *New York Times*, 21 December 1990. [Charges by California Department of Fair Employment and Housing]

5930. Marantz, Steve. "Data Show Black Officers Disciplined More." *Boston Globe*, 12 August 1989. [Boston]

5931. Martinez, Ruben. "1 Quake, 2 Worlds." *New York Times*, 20 January 1994. [Anglos and Latinos in the January 1994 Los Angeles earthquakes]

5932. McAllister, Bill. "Botched 'Sting' Becomes a Disaster for Inspectors." *Washington Post*, 19 May 1994.

5933. _____. "Settlement Reached in Bias Case Brought by U.S. Printing Workers." *Boston Globe*, 22 November 1990. [Bureau of Engraving and Printing U.S. Department of Treasury; reprinted from *Washington Post*.]

5934. McDonnell, Patrick J. "Black Agents' Class-Action Bias Complaint Against INS OKd." *Los Angeles Times*, 27 February 1994. [U.S. Immigration and Naturalization Service]

5935. McFadden, Robert D. "Race, Rage and New York Officers." *New York Times*, 19 September 1992. [Police officers and Mayor David N. Dinkins]

5936. McNabb, Steven. "Impacts of Federal Policy Decisions on Alaska Natives." *Journal of Ethnic Studies* 18 (Spring 1990).

5937. Merida, Kevin. "Senate Panel Upraids Hill Architect." *Washington Post*, 13 May 1994. [Charges of race and sex discrimination against U.S. Capitol Architect]

5938. Messerschmidt, Jim. *The Trial of Leonard Peltier*. Boston, MA: South End Press, 1983.

5939. Meyer, Marshall W. "Police Shootings at Minorities: The Case of Los Angeles." *Annals of the American Academy of Political and Social Science* 452 (1980): 98-110.

5940. Miller, Julie A. "Past Chief's Tenure Offers a Sober Lesson for Civil-Rights Office." *Education Week* (13 January 1993). [Office for Civil Rights, Education Department]

5941. Monk, David H., and Julie K. Underwood, eds. *Microlevel School Finance: Issues and Implications for Policy*. Cambridge, MA: Ballinger 1989.

5942. Morales, Armando. *Ando Sangrando: A Study of Mexican American Police Conflict*. La Puente, 1972.

5943. Muerty, Komanduri S. and others. "The Image of the Police in Black Atlanta Communities." *Journal of Police Science and Administration* 17 (December 1990): 250-257.

5944. Munkres, Robert L. "Congress and the Indian: The Politics of Conquest." *Annals of Wyoming* 60 (Fall 1988): 22-31.

5945. Nagel, J. H. "Psychological Obstacles to Administrative Responsibility: Lessons of the MOVE Disaster." *Journal of Policy Analysis and Management* 10 (Winter 1991).

5946. Neal, Diane, and Thomas W. Kremm. "'What Shall We Do with the Negro?' The Freedman's Bureau in Texas." *East Texas Historical Journal* 27 (1989): 23-34.

5947. Nelson, Jill. "Blue Plague." *New York Times*, 20 May 1994. [Corrupt police in Afro-American areas of New York City]

5948. Newton, Jim. "Case History." *Los Angeles Times Magazine* (27 June 1993). [Strategy of the prosecution in the second trial of four Los Angeles policemen in the Rodney G. King case.]

5949. Oberly, Jim. "Spearing Fish, Playing 'Chicken'." *Nation* (19 June 1989). [Chippewa fishing rights in Wisconsin]

5950. Officer, James E. "The American Indian and Federal Policy." in *The American Indian in Urban Society*, pp. 8-65. eds. Jack O. Waddell, and O. Michael Watson. Boston, MA: Little, Brown, 1971.

5951. Orfield, Gary. "Cutback Policies, Declining Opportunities, and the Role of Social Service Providers." *Social Service Review* 65 (December 1991): 516-530.

5952. Ozawa, M. N. "Unequal Treatment of AFDC Children by the Federal Government." *Children and Youth Services Review* 13 (1991): 257-270.

5953. "A Party for a Cleared Police Officer Stirs Up Racial Tension." *New York Times*, 24 July 1994. [Springfield, MA]

5954. Paterno, Susan. "Assistant Chief Battles Racism as Much as Fire." *Los Angeles Times*, 28 February 1993. [Hershel Clady, African-American who commands a Los Angeles County Fire Department battalion]

5955. Paulson, Howard W. "Federal Indian Policy and the Dakota Indians: 1800-1840." *South Dakota Hist.* 3 (1973): 285-309.

5956. Payne, Les. "Black Men and the Cops." *Essence* (November 1992).

5957. Pearson, Ralph L. "Charles S. Johnson and the Chicago Commission on Race Relations." *Ill. Historical Jr.* 81 (Autumn 1988): 211-220.

5958. Peres, Kenneth R. *The Political Economy of Federal Indian Policy: The Formulation and Development of the Indian Reorganization Act.* Ph.D. diss., New School for Social Research, 1989. UMO #9004583.

5959. Peroff, Nicholas C. *Menominee Drums: Tribal Termination and Restoration, 1954-1974.* Norman: University of Oklahoma Press, 1982.

5960. Phillips, George H. "The Indian Ring in Dakota Territory." *South Dakota Hist.* 2 (1972): 345-376.

5961. Porter, Robert B. "The Jurisdictional Relationship between the Iroquois and New York State: An Analysis of 25 U.S.C. s3 232, 233." *Harvard Journal on Legislation* 27 (Summer 1990): 497-577.

5962. Priest, Loring B. *Uncle Sam's Stepchildren: The Reformation of United States Indian Policy, 1865-1887.* New Brunswick, NJ: Rutgers University Press, 1942.

5963. Prucha, Francis Paul, ed. *Documents of United States Indian Policy*, 2nd ed. Lincoln: University of Nebraska Press, 1989.

5964. _____. *The Great Father: The United States Government and the American Indians*, 2 vols. Lincoln: University of Nebraska Press, 1984.

5965. _____. "Jackson's Indian Policy: A Reassessment." *Journal of American History* 56 (1969). [See Young, Mary E. below]

5966. Quindlen, Anna. "Bad and Blue." *New York Times*, 23 September 1992. [Racism among white police officers in New York City]

5967. Quinten, B. T. "Oklahoma Tribes, the Great Depression and the Indian Bureau." *Mid-America: An Historical Review* 49 (1967): 29-43.

5968. Rabinowitz, Howard N. "The Conflict between Blacks and the Police in the Urban South, 1865-1900." *Historian* 39 (November 1976).

5969. "Rally Protests Police Beating of Teen-Ager." *New York Times*, 7 August 1994. [Black officer and Hispanic teen-ager]

5970. Rapport, Sara. "The Freedman's Bureau as a Legal Agent for Black Men and Women in Georgia: 1865-1869." *Georgia Historical Quarterly* 73 (1989): 26-53.

5971. Redenbaugh, Russell G. "Rights Staff Deserves Better from Edwards." *Wall Street Journal*, 21 October 1991. [On the U.S. Commission on Civil Rights; see also Don Edwards, above.]

5972. Reed, Merl E. "Black Workers, Defense Industries, and Federal Agencies in Pennslyvania, 1941-1945." *Labor History* 27 (1986): 356-384.

5973. Reeve, Frank D. "The Government and the Navaho, 1846-1858." *New Mexico Historical Review* 14 (January 1939): 82-114.

5974. Reinhold, Robert. "Study of Los Angeles Police Finds Violence and Racism Are Routine." *New York Times*, 10 July 1991.

5975. Resnik, Judith A. "Dependent Sovereigns: Indian Tribes, States, and the Federal Courts." *University of Chicago Law Review* 56 (Spring 1989): 671-759.

5976. Ridrigues, Carl A. "When Cross-cultural Equals Double Cross." *Administration and Society* 22 (November 1990): 341-357. [Micosukee Indian nation]

5977. Rodriguez, Clara E. "Race, Culture, and Latino 'Otherness' in the 1980 Census." *Social Science Quarterly* 73 (December 1992).

5978. Rose, Jennifer. "Samoans Wrestle for Justice: Police Brutality in the South Bay Area." *Pacific Ties (UCLA)* (November 1989): 14-15.

5979. Rose, Nancy E. "Gender and Race in Government Work Programs from the 1930's to the Present." *Feminist Studies* 18 (1992).

5980. Scherro, Diana J. "Suburban [Real Estate] Taxes Are Higher for Blacks, Analysis Shows." *New York Times*, 17 August 1994.

5981. Schor, Joel. "The Black Presence in the U.S. Cooperative Extension Service Since 1945: An American Quest for Service and Equity." *Agricultural History* 60 (1986): 137-153.

5982. Seave, Paul L. "In a Dirty Job, the Dirt Coats Everything." *Los Angeles Times*, 21 June 1993. [Role of police]

5983. Sebok, A. J. "Judging the Fugitive Slave Acts." *Yale Law Journal* 100 (April 1991): 1835-1854.

5984. Serrano, Richard A. "They Hit Me, So I Hit Back." *Los Angeles Times*, 4 October 1992. [About 44 "problem officers" in the Los Angeles Police Department]

5985. Shen, Fern. "Lawsuit Says Police Force Discriminates." *Washington Post*, 1 March 1994. [Maryland Natural Resources Police]

5986. Shingles, Richard D. "Class, Status, and Support for Government Aid to Disadvantaged Groups." *Journal of Politics* 51 (November 1989).

5987. Skolnick, Jerome H., and James J. Fyfe. *Above the Law: Police and the Excessive Use of Force.* Free Press, 1993.

5988. Skolnick, Jerome H., and Fyfe James J. "Will They Do the Right Thing?" *Los Angeles Times*, 3 March 1993. [Police violence in Los Angeles]

5989. Soza, Ramona E. *Alaska Natives and Federal Indian Policy.* Ph.D. diss., University of Washington, 1988.

5990. Stefon, Frederick J. "The Irony of Termination." *Indian Historian* 11 (Summer 1978): 3-14.

5991. Streitfeld, David. "Library Taken to Task for Minority Hiring Lag." *Washington Post*, 19 March 1993. [Library of Congress]

5992. _____. "Library's Hiring Scored." *Washington Post*, 25 March 1993. [Library of Congress]

5993. Stuart, Paul H. "Financing Self-Determination: Federal Indian Expenditures, 1975-1988." *American Indian Culture and Research Journal* 14 (1990): 1-18.

5994. Stumbo, Bella. "Daryl Gates: A Portrait of Frustration." *Los Angeles Times*, August 15-16, 1982. [Long-time chief of police in Los Angeles]

5995. Sully, Langdon. "The Indian Agent: A Study in Corruption and Avarice." *American West* 10 (March 1973): 4-9.

5996. Tam, Shirley S. L. "Police Round-up of Chinese in Cleveland in 1925: A Case Study in a Racist Measure and the Chinese Response." Master's thesis, Case Western Reserve University, 1988.

5997. Taylor, Theodore W. *The Bureau of Indian Affairs.* Boulder, CO: Westview Press, 1984.

5998. *Torture, Ill-Treatment and Excessive Force by Police in Los Angeles, California.* Amnesty International, 1992.

5999. Trescott, Jacqueline. "Smithsonian Faulted For Neglect of Latinos." *Washington Post*, 11 May 1994.

6000. Turner, Alvin O. "Financial Relations between the United States and the Cherokee Nation, 1830-1870." *Journal of the West* 12 (1973): 372-385.

6001. U.S. Commission on Civil Rights. *Police Practices and the Preservation of Civil Rights.* Washington, DC: The Commission, 1980.

6002. _____. *Who is Guarding the Guardians? A Report on Police Practices*. Washington, DC: The Commission, 1981.

6003. U.S. Congress, 100th, 2nd session, Senate, Select Committee on Indian Affairs. *Oversight Hearing on Federal Acknowledgement Process*. GPO, 1988.

6004. U.S. Congress, 102nd, 1st session, House of Representatives, Committee on the Judiciary, Subcommittee on Civil and Constitutional Rights. *Police Brutality: Hearings*. GPO, 1992.

6005. U.S. Department of Justice. *The Potentiality for Racial Conflict in the Des Moines Police Department*. Washington, DC: The Department, 1989.

6006. U.S. General Accounting Office. *Job Training Partnerships Act: Racial and Gender Disparities in Services*. GAO, 1991.

6007. Vogel, Jennifer. "The Pro-Police Review Board." *Nation* (6 January 1991). [Minneapolis, MN]

6008. Wagner-Pacifici, Robin. *Discourse and Destruction: The City of Philadelphia Versus MOVE*. University of Chicago Press, 1994.

6009. Walker, Adrian, and Stephen Kurkjian. "MCAD Drops 450 Cases for Lack of Staff, Money." *Boston Globe*, 8 December 1991. [Massachusetts Commission Against Discrimination]

6010. Walker, Deward E., Jr., ed. "An Exploration of the Reservation System in North America: A Special Issue." *Northwest Anthropological Research Notes* 5 (Spring 1971).

6011. Walton, Hanes, Jr. *When the Marching Stopped: The Politics of Civil Rights Regulatory Agencies*. Albany: State University of New York Press, 1988.

6012. Weeks, Philip. *Farewell, My Nation. The American Indian and the United States, 1820-1890*. Arlington Heights, IL: Harlan Davidson, 1991.

6013. Weiner, Tim. "Citing Bias, Women May Sue the C.I.A." *New York Times*, 28 March 1994.

6014. Weyler, Rex. *Blood of the Land: The Government and Corporate War Against the American Indian Movement*. New York: Vintage Books, 1983.

6015. Wilkins, D. E. "Breaking into the Intergovernmental Matrix: The Lumbee Tribe's Efforts to Secure Federal Acknowledgment." *Publius* 23 (Autumn 1993): 123-144.

6016. Winter, Ella. "California's Little Hitlers." *New Republic* 77 (27 December 1933): 188-190. [Police and vigilantes]

6017. Wise, L. R. "Social Equity in Civil Service Systems." *Public Administration Review* 50 (September-October 1990).

6018. Wolff, Craig. "Alone, Undercover, and Black: Hazards of Mistaken Identity." *New York Times*, 22 November 1992. [Black police officer shot by a white one]

6019. Wunder, John R. "No More Treaties: The Resolution of 1871 and the Alteration of Indian Rights to Their Homelands." in *Working the Range*, ed. Wunder. Westport, CT: Greenwood, 1985.

6020. Wycliff, Don. "Black and Blue Encounters." *Criminal Justice System* 7 (Summer-Fall 1988). [Blacks and police]

6021. Zodhiates, Philip P. *Bureaucrats and Politicians: The National Institute of Education and Educational Research under Reagan*. Ph.D. diss., Harvard University, 1988. UMO #8907626.

HEALTH

6022. Abraham, Laurie. "Daily Grind of Kidney Failure Wears Down Low-Income Family." *Chicago Reporter* 18 (September 1989): 1, 3-5, 11.

6023. _____. "State's Infant Mortality Program Falling Short of '9 by 90' Goal." *Chicago Reporter* 18 (May 1989): 1,3-4,7,11. [Illinois]

6024. Acosta, P. B. and others. "Nutritional Status of Mexican- American Pre-school Children in a Border Town." *American Journal of Clinical Nutrition* 27 (1974): 1359. [San Ysidro, Calif.]

6025. Aday, L. A., and R. M. Andersen. "The National Profile of Access to Medical Care: Where Do We Stand?" *American Journal of Public Health* 74 (1984): 1331-1339.

6026. Akhter, F. "The Eugenic and Racist Premise of Reproductive Rights and Population Control." *Issues in Reproductive and Genetic Engineering* 5 (1992): 1-8.

6027. Alers, J. O. *Puerto Ricans and Health: Findings from New York City*. New York: Hispanic Research Center, Fordham University, 1978.

6028. Alford, Robert. *Health Care Politics*. Chicago, IL: University of Chicago Press, 1975.

6029. Allen, Lisa W. *Otitis Media among Puerto Ricans and Blacks: Ethnicity, Epidemiology and Family Health Cultures*. Ph.D. diss., University of Connecticut, 1988. UMO #8822907.

6030. Alters, Diane. "Crack Lures, Holds Workers to S.C. Camp." *Boston Globe*, 21 August 1989. [Edgefield, S.C.]

6031. Althaus, F. "United States Maternal Mortality Has Continued Its Decline, But Risk Remains Higher Among Minority Women." *Family Planning Perspectives* 23 (May-June 1991): 140.

6032. Altman, Lawrence K. "Many Hispanic Americans Reported in Ill Health and Lacking Insurance." *New York Times*, 9 January 1991.

6033. Alu Like. *E Ola Mau: Native Hawaiian Health Needs Study. Nutrition/Dental Task Force Report*. Honolulu: Alu Like, 1985.

6034. Amber, Robert W., and H. Bruce Dull, eds. *Closing the Gap: The Burden of Unnecessary Illness*. Oxford University Press, 1986.

6035. American Heart Association. "Cardiovascular Disease and Stroke in African-Americans and Other Racial Minorities in the United States: A Statement for Health Professionals." *Circulation* 83 (1991): 1462-1480.

6036. Amulerumarshall, O. "Substance Abuse among America's Urban Youth." *Urban League Review* 13 (Summer-Winter 1990).

6037. Anderson, G. B., and C. A. Grace. "Black Deaf Adolescents: A Diverse and Underserved Population." *Volta Review* 93 (September 1991): 73-88.

6038. Anderson, L. P. "Acculturative Stress: A Theory of Relevance to Black Americans." *Clinical Psychology Review* 11 (1991): 685-702.

6039. Anderson, R. M. and others. "Black-White Differences in Health Status: Methods or Substance?" *Milbank Memorial Fund Quarterly* 65, supplement 1 (1987): 72-99.

6040. Angel, Ronald J., and Jacqueline Lowe Worobey. "Intragroup Differences in the Health of Hispanic Children." *Social Science Quarterly* 72 (1991): 361-378.

6041. Angell, Marcia. "Privilege and Health-What Is the Connection?" *New England Journal of Medicine* 329 (8 July 1993): 126-127.

6042. Anner, John. "Feds Discriminate, but AIDS Doesn't." *Guardian (NYC)* (15 August 1990).

6043. Antonovsky, A., and J. Berstein. "Social Class and Infant Mortality." *Social Science and Medicine* 11 (1977): 453-470.

6044. Arai, Sevgi O., and King H. Holmes. "Sexually Transmitted Diseases in the AIDS Era." *Scientific American* 264 (February 1991): 62-69.

6045. Arnason, W. B. "Directed Donation: The Relevance of Race." *Hastings Center Report* 21 (November-December 1991): 13-19.

6046. Arrow, Kenneth J. "Uncertainty and the Welfare Economics of Health Care." *American Economic Review* 53 (1963).

6047. Avery, Byllye. "Black Women's Health: A Conspiracy of Silence." *Sojourners* 14 (January 1989): 15-16.

6048. Axelson, Diane E. "Women Victims of Medical Experimentation: J. Marion Sims Surgery on Slave Women, 1845- 1850." *Sage* 2 (1985): 10-13.

6049. Ayala, Victor A. *Falling through the Cracks: AIDS and the Urban "Underclass"*. Ph.D. diss., CNUY, 1991. UMO #9130291.

6050. Ayaman, John Z. "Heart Disease in Black and White." *New England Journal of Medicine* 329 (26 August 1993): 656-658.

6051. Ayaman, John Z. and others. "Racial Differences in the Use of Revascularization Procedures after Coronary Angiography." *Journal of the American Medical Association* 269 (1993): 2642- 1646.

6052. Bachman, J. G. and others. "Racial/Ethnic Differences in Smoking, Drinking, and Illicit Drug Use Among American High School Seniors, 1976-89." *American Journal of Public Health* 81 (March 1991): 372-377.

6053. Bachman, R. "An Analysis of American Indian Homicide: A Test of Social Disorganization and Economic Deprivation at the Reservation-County Level." *Journal of Research in Crime and Delinquency* 28 (November 1991): 456-471.

6054. Baer, Hans A. "The American Dominative Medical System as a Reflection of Social Relations in the Larger Society." *Social Science and Medicine* 28 (1989): 1103-1112.

6055. Bailey, E. J. "Hypertension: An Analysis of Detroit African American Health Care Treatment Patterns." *Human Organization* 50 (Autumn 1991): 287-296.

6056. Balshem, Martha. *Cancer in the Community. Class and Medical Authority*. Smithsonian Institution Press, 1993.

6057. Barden, J. C. "Failure to Meet Goals on Infant Health Is Masked by Drop in Mortality Rate." *New York Times*, 2 September 1991.

6058. Barringer, Felicity. "Whether It's Hunger or 'Misnourishment', It's a National Problem." *New York Times*, 27 December 1992.

6059. Baskerville, Dawn M. "The State of Black Health." *Black Enterprise* (July 1991): 43.

6060. Becker, Lane B. and others. "Outcome of CPR in a Large Metropolitan Area-Where Are the Survivors?" *Annals of Emergency Medicine* 20 (1991): 355-361.

6061. Becker, Lance B. and others. "Racial Differences in the Incidence of Cardiac Arrest and Subsequent Survival." *New England Journal of Medicine* 329 (26 August 1993): 600-606.

6062. Behrman, J. R. and others. "Black-White Mortality Inequalities." *Journal of Econometrics* 50 (October-November 1991): 183-204.

6063. Belsky, J. E. "Medically Indigent Women Seeking Abortion Prior to Legalization: New York City, 1969-1970." *Family Planning Perspectives* 24 (May-June 1992): 129-134.

6064. Benedict, Mary I. and others. "Racial Differences in Health Care Utilization among Children in Foster Care." *Children and Youth Services Review* 11 (1989).

6065. Berk, Marc L. and others. "The Health Care of Poor Persons Living in Wealthy Areas." *Social Science and Medicine* 32 (1991): 1097-1103.

6066. Berkman, Lisa and others. "Black/White Differences in Health Status and Mortality Among the Elderly." *Demography* 26 (November 1989).

6067. Berliner, H. "Changes in the Health Care Delivery System in New York City: 1980-1990." in *Changing U.S. Health Care*, eds. E. Ginzberg and others. Westview Press, 1993.

6068. Billings, J. and others. "Impact of Socioeconomic Status on Hospital Use in New York City." *Health Affairs* 12 (1993): 162- 173.

6069. Billings, J., and N. Teicholz. "Uninsured Patients in District of Columbia Hospitals." *Health Affairs* 9 (Winter 1990): 158-165.

6070. Bindman, A. and others. "A Public Hospital Closes: Impact on Patients' Access to Care and Health Status." *Journal of the American Medical Association* 264 (1993): 2899-2904.

6071. Black, D. and others. *Inequalities in Health: The Black Report*. New York: Penguin, 1982.

6072. "Blacks Used 'For Parts', Farrakhan Says in Speech." *New York Times*, 2 May 1994. [Black organs for whites]

6073. Bland, I. J. "Racial and Ethnic Influences: The Black Woman and Abortion." in *Psychiatric Aspects of Abortion*, pp. 171-186. ed. N.L. Stotland. Washington, DC: American Psychiatric Press, 1991.

6074. Blau, Francine, and Adam Grossberg. *Maternal Labor Supply and Child Cognitive Development*. Cambridge, MA: National Bureau of Economic Research, December 1990.

6075. *Blessed Events and the Bottom Line: Financing Maternity Care in the United States*. New York: Alan Guttmacher Institute, 1987.

6076. Bloom, B. R., and C. J. L. Murray. "Tuberculosis: Commentary on a Re-emergent Killer." *Science* no. 257 (1992): 1055-1064.

6077. Blount, M. "Surpassing Obstacles: Black Women in Medicine." *Journal of the American Medical Women's Association* 39 (1984): 192-195.

6078. Boehm, William T. and others. *Progress Toward Eliminating Hunger in America*. Washington, DC: Economics, Statistics, and Cooperatives Service, U.S. Department of Agriculture, 1980.

6079. Boney, F. Nash. "Doctor Thomas Hamilton: Two Views of a Gentleman of the Old South." *Phylon* 28 (Fall 1967): 288-292.

6080. Boone, Margaret S. *Capital Crime. Black Infant Mortality in America*. Newbury Park, CA: Sage, 1989. [Washington, DC]

6081. Brandt, A. "Racism and Research: The Case of the Tuskegee Syphilis Study." *The Hastings Center Report* 8 (1978): 21-29.

6082. "Breast Cancer Twice as Deadly in Blacks." *New York Times*, 28 September 1994.

6083. Brody, Jane E. "Research Casts Doubt On Need for Many Caesarean Births as their Rate Soars." *New York Times*, 27 July 1989.

6084. Brooks, C. H. "Social, Economic, and Biological Correlates of Infant Mortality in City Neighborhoods." *Journal of Health and Social Behavior* 21 (1980): 2-11.

6085. Brown, E. Richard and others. *Californians without Health Insurance: A Report to the California Legislature*. Berkeley: California Policy Seminar, University of California, 1987.

6086. Brown, Ian. "Who Were the Eugenicists? A Study of the Formation of an Early Twentieth-century Pressure Group." *History of Education* 17 (1988): 295-307.

6087. Brown, J. Larry, and Stanley N. Gershoff. "The Paradox of Hunger and Economic Prosperity in America." *Journal of Public Health Policy* 10 (1989): 425-435.

6088. Brown, Lawrence S., Jr., and Berry J. Primm. "Intravenous Drug Abuse and AIDS in Minorities." *AIDS and Public Policy Journal* 3 (1988): 5-15.

6089. Bryant, Sharon A. *Race Differences in Access to Needed Medical Care*. Ph.D. diss., Yale University, 1990. UMO #9122312.

6090. Buchanan, A., and K. M. Weiss. "Infant Mortality in a Mexican-American Community: Laredo, Texas, 1950-1977." *Social Biology* 38 (Fall-Winter 1991): 233-241.

6091. Burch, Thomas A. "Ethnicity and Health in Hawaii, 1975." *Hawaii Department of Health, R + S Report* 23 (August 1978).

6092. Burch, Thomas A., and Paul T. Kawaguchi. "Family Income and Health." *Hawaii Department of Health, R + S Report* 31 (January 1980).

6093. Burd, Stephen. "NIH Issues Rules Requiring Women and Minorities in Clinical Trials." *Chronicle of Higher Education* (6 April 1994).

6094. Bushnell, O. A. *The Gifts of Civilization: Germs and Genocide in Hawaii*. University of Hawaii Press, 1993.

6095. Butler, Patricia A. *Too Poor To Be Sick: Access to Medical Care for the Uninsured*. Washington, DC: American Public Health Association, 1988.

6096. Byrd, W. Michael, and Linda A. Clayton. "The African- American Cancer Crisis, Part II: A Prescription." *Journal of Health Care for the Poor and Underserved* 4 (1993): 102-116.

6097. Campbell, Gregory R. "The Changing Dimension of Native American Health: A Critical Understanding of Contemporary Native American Health Issues." *American Indian Culture and Research Journal* 13 (1989): 1-20.

6098. Caper, P. "Population-based Measures of the Quality of Medical Care." in *Health Care Quality Management for the 21st Century*, ed. J. B. Couch. Tampa, FL: American College of Physician Executives, 1991.

6099. Capitanini, Lisa. "City Losing Battle Against Epidemic in Black Communities." *Chicago Reporter* 20 (November 1991). [Sexually-transmitted diseases]

6100. Caplan, Ronald L. "The United States Health Care Crisis: A Marxian Reappraisal." *Rethinking MARXISM* 4 (Winter 1991): 94-111.

6101. Carmen, Elaine H. and others. "Inequality and Women's Mental Health: An Overview." *American Journal of Psychiatry* 138 (October 1981): 1319-1330.

6102. Carroll, D. and others. "Socio-economic Health Inequalities: Their Origins and Implications." *Psychology and Health* 8 (1993): 295-316.

6103. Catalano, R. "The Health Effects of Economic Insecurity." *American Journal of Public Health* 81 (September 1991): 1148- 1152.

6104. Chavez, L., and R. Rumbaut. *The Politics of Migrant Health Care*. University of California, San Diego, August 1985.

6105. Chen, M. "A 1993 Status Report on the Health Status of Asian Pacific Islander Americans: Comparisons with Health People 2000 Objectives." *Asian American and Pacific Islander Journal of Health* 1 (1993): 37-55.

6106. Chira, Susan. "Poverty's Toll on Health Is Plague of U.S. Schools." *New York Times*, 5 October 1991.

6107. Christmas, J. J. "Black Women and Health Care in the 80's." *Spelman Messenger* 100 (Spring 1984): 8-11.

6108. Cimons, Marlene. "New Campaign Keyed to Black Smokers." *Los Angeles Times*, 9 July 1993.

6109. Clark, V., and J. Harrell. "The Relationship among Type A Behavior, Styles Used in Coping with Racism, and Blood Pressure." *Journal of Black Psychology* 8 (1982): 89-99.

6110. Clarke, Leslie L. "The Effects of Socioeconomic Status on Infant Mortality in the United States, 1980-1984." *Sociological Abstracts* (1989). Accession No. 89S21863.

6111. Clayton, Linda A., and W. Michael Byrd. "The African- American Cancer Crisis, Part I: The Problem." *Journal of Health Care for the Poor and Underserved* 4 (1993): 83-101.

6112. Clemmitt, M. "Memories of Tuskegee Undermine Black Community's Trust in Research." *The Scientist* 5 (16 September 1991): 8-10.

6113. Cobb, W. Montague. "Surgery and the Negro Physician: Some Parallels in Background." *National Medical Association Journal* 43 (May 1951): 145-152.

6114. Cockburn, Alexander. "The Pogo Fallacy: Blaming the Genes and Not the System." *In These Times* (21 March 1990). [Race, tuberculosis, and cancer]

6115. _____. "Social Cleaning." *New Statesman and Society* (5 August 1994). [Norplant and involuntary sterilization]

6116. Cohen, Toby. "Health Care and the Class Struggle." *New York Times*, 17 November 1991.

6117. Colker, R. "An Equal Protection Analysis of United States Reproductive Health Policy: Gender, Race, Age, and Class." *Duke Law Journal* no. 2 (April 1991): 324-364.

6118. Collins, John G. "Health Characteristics by Occupation and Industry: United States, 1983-1985." *Vital Health Statistics* no. 170 (1989).

6119. "[Commentaries on Racism and Gender in Health]." *Medical Anthropology Quarterly* 8 (March 1994): 90-118.

6120. Committee on the Costs of Medical Care. *Medical Care for the American People*. University of Chicago Press, 1932.

6121. Committee on Cultural Psychiatry, Group for the Advancement of Psychiatry. *Suicide and Ethnicity in the United States*. New York: Bruner/Mazel, 1989.

6122. Community Childhood Hunger Identification Project. *A Survey of Childhood Hunger in the United States*. Washington, DC: Food Research and Action Center, 1991.

6123. Cooper, R. S. and others. "Survival Rates and Prehospital Delay during Myocardial Infarction among Black Persons." *American Journal of Cardiology* 57 (1986): 208-211.

6124. Cooper, Richard and others. "Racism, Society, and Disease." *International Journal of Health Services* 11 (1981): 39-41.

6125. Cooper, Richard, and Richard David. "The Biological Concept of Race and Its Application to Epidemiology." *Journal of Health Politics, Policy, and Law* 11 (1986): 97-116.

6126. Cope, Nancy R. "The Health Status of Black Women in the U.S.: Implications for Health Psychology and Behavioral Medicine." *Sage* 2 (Fall 1985): 20-24.

6127. Corman, Hope, and Stephen Chalkind. *The Effect of Low Birthweight on the Health, Behavior, and School Performance of School-aged Children*. National Bureau of Economic Research, 1993. [1988 data]

6128. Cormoni-Huntley, J. and others. "Race and Sex Differentials in the Impact of Hypertension in the United States." *Archives of Internal Medicine* 149 (1989): 780-788.

6129. Cornely, Paul. "Racism: The Ever-present Hidden Barrier to Health in Our Society." *American Journal of Public Health* no. 3 (1976): 146-148.

6130. Crader, D. C. "Slave Diet at Monticello." *American Antiquity* 55 (October 1990).

6131. Cramer, James C. "Trends in Infant Mortality among Racial and Ethnic Groups in California." *Social Science Research* 17 (1988): 164-189.

6132. Creighton-Zollar, Ann. "Infant Mortality by Socioeconomic Status and Race in Richmond, Virginia, 1979-1981: A Research Note." *Sociological Spectrum* 10 (1990).

6133. Crockett, Bernice N. "Health Conditions in Indian Territory 1830 to the Civil War." *Chronicle of Oklahoma* 35 (1957): 80-90. Native Americans.

6134. _____. "Health Conditions in Indian Territory from the Civil War to 1890." *Chronicle of Oklahoma* 36 (1958): 21-39. Native Americans.

6135. Crowley, J. J., and S. Simmons. "Mental Health, Race, and Ethnicity: A Retrospective Study of the Care of Ethnic Minorities and Whites in a Psychiatric Unit." *Journal of Advanced Nursing* 17 (September 1992): 1078-1087.

6136. Curran, J. W. and others. "Epidemiology of HIV Infection and AIDS in the United States." *Science* 239 (1988): 610-616.

6137. Currie, Janet, and Duncan Thomas. *Medicaid and Medical Care for Children*. National Bureau of Economic Research, 1993. [Data 1978-88]

6138. Dallek, G., and E. Brown. *The Quality of Medical Care for the Poor in Los Angeles County's Health and Hospital System*. Legal Aid Foundation of Los Angeles, 1987.

6139. Dalton, Harlon L. "AIDS in Blackface." *Daedalus* 118 (Summer 1989): 205-227.

6140. D'Antonio, Michael. *Atomic Harvest: Hanford and the Lethal Toll of America's Nuclear Arsenal*. Crown, 1994.

6141. _____. "Dying Young." *Los Angeles Times Magazine* (12 July 1992). [The national children's health crisis as viewed at Boston's Children's Hospital]

6142. Davidson, P., and E. Saunders. "Epidemiological and Clinical Comparison of Cardiovascular Disease in Black and Whites in the USA." in *Ethnic Factors in Health and Disease*, eds. J. K. Cruickshank, and D. G. Beevers. Kent: John Wright, 1989.

6143. Davis, C. G. and others. "Socioeconomic Determinants of Food Expenditure Patterns among Racially Different Low-income Households: An Empirical Analysis." *Western Journal of Agricultural Economics* 8 (1983): 183-196.

6144. Davis, Karen. "Inequality and Access to Health Care." *Milbank Quarterly* 69 (1991): 253-274.

6145. Davis, Karen, and Marsha Lillie-Blanton. *Health Care for Black Americans: Trends in Financing and Delivery*. Paper prepared for the Committee on the Status of Black Americans, National Research Council, Washington, D.C., 1987.

6146. de la Rosa, Mario. "Health Care Needs of Hispanic Americans and the Responsiveness of the Health Care System." *Health and Social Work* 14 (May 1989): 104-113.

6147. De Parle, Jason. "Lacking Plumbing, Villages in Alaska Face Health Crisis." *New York Times*, 28 November 1992.

6148. _____. "A State's Fight to Save Babies Enters Round 2." *New York Times*, 12 March 1991. [Mississippi]

6149. De Vesa, S. A., and E. L. Diamond. "Socioeconomic and Racial Differences in Lung Cancer Incidence." *American Journal of Epidemiology* 118 (1983): 818-883.

6150. *Decade of Indifference: Maternal and Child Health Trends, 1980-1990*. Children's Defense Fund, 1993.

6151. Delaney, Paul. "Fighting Myths in a Bid to Get Blacks to Consider Transplants." *New York Times*, 6 November 1991.

6152. Derickson, A. "Making Human Junk: Child Labor as a Health Issue in the Progressive Era." *American Journal of Public Health* 82 (September 1992): 1280-1290.

6153. Devaney, B. and others. "Medicaid Costs and Birth Outcomes: The Effects of Prenatal WIC Participation and the Use of Prenatal Care." *Journal of Policy Analysis and Management* 11 (Fall 1992).

6154. *Developmental, Learning, and Emotional Problems: Health of Our Nation's Children, United States, 1988*. Hyattsville, MD: National Center for Health Statistics, Scientific and Technical Information Branch, 1990.

6155. Diamond E. and others. "Harassment, Hostility, and Type A as Determinants of Cardiovascular Reactivity during Competition." *Journal of Behavioral Medicine* 7 (1982): 171-189.

6156. Dinges, Barnaby. "Black Youths Are City's Top Murder Risk." *Chicago Reporter* 19 (February 1990): 1,6-9. [Black males, ages 14-29, 1987-1989, Chicago]

6157. Diringer, Joel. "It's Indecent to Ignore Those Who Feed Us." *Los Angeles Times*, 28 June 1993. [Health problems of Latino farm workers]

6158. "Disparity is Found in Blacks' AIDS Rate." *Boston Globe*, 9 September 1994. [AIDS...reported 15 times as often in black women than in white women, and five times as frequently in black men than in whites.]

6159. Dougherty, C. J. "The Costs of Commercial Medicine." *Theoretical Medicine* 11 (December 1990): 275-286.

6160. Dowell, Michael A. "State and Local Government Legal Responsibilities to Provide Medical Care for the Poor." *Journal of Law and Health* 3 (Summer 1988): 1-45.

6161. Dreifus, Claudia. "Sterilizing the Poor." *Progressive* (December 1975): 13-18.

6162. Dressler, William W. "Lifestyle, Stress, and Blood Pressure in a Southern Black Community." *Psychosomatic Medicine* 52 (March- April 1990).

6163. Drucker, Ernest. "We Must End Crowded Housing, a TB Breeder." *New York Times*, 20 August 1993. letter.

6164. Dugger, K. "Race Differences in the Determinants of Support for Legalized Abortion." *Social Science Quarterly* 72 (September 1991): 570-587.

6165. Duleep, H. O. "Measuring Socioeconomic Mortality Differentials Over Time." *Demography* 26 (1989): 345-351.

6166. Dunkle, Margaret C. *Just What the Doctor Should Have Ordered. A Prescription for Sex-Fair Health Services*. Newton, MA: WEEA Publishing Center, 1989.

6167. Dutton, D. B. "Children's Health Care: The Myth of Equal Access." in *Better Health for Our Children: A National Strategy, Vol. IV, Background Papers*, pp. 357-440. Washington, DC: U.S. Department of Health and Human Services, 1981.

6168. _____. "Explaining the Low Use of Health Services by the Poor." *American Sociological Review* 43 (1978): 348-368.

6169. Easterbrook, Gregg. "The Doomsday Spin." *Los Angeles Times*, 9 January 1994. ["Tales of radiation tests seem to prove every citizen's worst nightmare about goverment"]

6170. Eberstadt, Nicholas. "America's Infant-mortality Puzzle." *Public Interest* (Fall 1991): 30-47.

6171. Eberstein, Issac W. "Race/Ethnicity and Infant Mortality: Determinants and Linkages." *Sociological Abstracts* Supplement 167 (August 1991) 91S25043/ASA/1991/6402.

6172. Eckholm, Erik. "Frayed Nerves of People Without Health Coverage." *New York Times*, 11 July 1994.

6173. Edelman, Marian Wright. "Children's Health and the Law: Interview." *Yale Law and Policy Review* 9 (Spring 1991): 97-109.

6174. Edwards, Karen L. and others. "African-American Psychological Health." *Journal of Ethnic Studies* 17 (Fall 1989): 1-30.

6175. Egan, Timothy. "Oregon Shakes Up Pioneering Health Plan for the Poor." *New York Times*, 22 February 1991.

6176. Ehrenreich, J., and B. Ehrenreich. *The American Health Empire: Power, Profits, and Politics*. Vintage Books, 1971.

6177. Emanuel, Irvin and others. "Poor Birth Outcomes of American Black Women: An Alternative Explanation." *Journal of Public Health Policy* 10 (1989): 299-308.

6178. Emmons, L. "Food Procurement and the Nutritional Adequacy of Diets in Low-income Families." *Journal of the American Dietetic Association* 86 (1986): 1684-1693.

6179. Essex, Max. "AIDS Pummels Minorities." *Boston Globe*, 1 December 1991.

6180. Farley, Reynolds. *An Analysis of Mortality, 1940 to the Present*. Paper prepared for the Committee on the Status of Black Americans, National Research Council, Washington, D.C., 1985.

6181. _____. *Racial Trends and Differentials in Mortality: 1940 to 1984*. Revision of 1985 Paper prepared for the Committee on the Status of Black Americans, National Research Council, Washington, D.C., 1986.

6182. Feder, J. and others. "Health." in *The Reagan Experiment*, pp. 271-305. eds. J. L. Palmer, and I. V. Sawhill. Urban Institute Press, 1982.

6183. Feinlieb, Marsha. *A Chartbook on the Health of Black Americans*. Paper prepared for the Committee on the Status of Black Americans, National Research Council, Washington, D.C.,

6184. Feldman, J. J. and others. "National Trends in Educational Differentials in Mortality." *American Journal of Epidemiology* 129 (1989): 919-933.

6185. Fennelly, K. "Barriers to Prenatal Care Among Low-income Women in New York City." *Family Planning Perspectives* 22 (September-October 1990).

6186. Ferguson, Earline R. "The Woman's Improvement Club of Indianapolis: Black Women Pioneers in Tuberculosis Work, 1903- 1938." *Indiana Magazine of History* 84 (September 1988): 237-261.

6187. Field, Christopher J. "Indigent Access to Emergency Care: The Poor Bleed Red, But the Hospitals Want Green." *New York Law School Journal of Human Rights* 8 (Spring 1991): 461-488.

6188. Fineberg, Harvey V. "The Social Dimensions of AIDS." *Scientific American* 259 (October 1988): 128-134.

6189. Finucane, T. E., and J. A. Carrese. "Racial Bias in Presentation of Cases." *Journal of General Internal Medicine* 5 (1990): 120-121.

6190. "Firearm Mortality Among Children, Youth and Young Adults 1-34 Years of Age, Trends and Current Status: United States, 1979-88." *Monthly Vital Statistics Report* 39 (1991): supplement. PHS 91-1120.

6191. Fisher, J. Walter. "Physicians and Slavery in the Antebellum Southern Medical Journal." *Journal of the History of Medicine and Allied Sciences* 23 (January 1968): 36-49.

6192. Fleshman, C. "Native American vs. All-Races Infant Mortality." *American Journal of Public Health* 82 (September 1992): 1295. [See response by S.D. Williams, 1296]

6193. Forbes, Douglas, and W. Parker Frisbie. "Spanish Surname and Anglo Infant Mortality: Differentials Over a Half-century." *Demography* 28 (November 1991): 639-660. [San Antonio, 1935-1985]

6194. Ford, Andrea. "Rights Groups Asks Review of Brotman Medical Center." *Los Angeles Times*, 20 October 1993. [Discrimination against black doctor in Brotman Medical Center, Culver City, CA]

6195. Fortune, Robert. *Chills and Fever: Health and Disease in the Early History of Alaska*. Fairbanks: University of Alaska Press, 1990.

6196. "Forum on Youth Violence in Minority Communities: Setting the Agenda for Prevention." *Public Health Reports* 106 (May-June 1991): 225-279.

6197. Fraser, Gertrude J. *Afro-American Midwives, Biomedicine and the State: An Ethnohistorical Account of Birth and Its Transformation in Rural Virginia*. Ph.D. diss., Johns Hopkins University, 1989. UMO #8923679.

6198. Freedman, Alix M. "Amid Ghetto Hunger, Many More Suffer Eating Wrong Foods." *Wall Street Journal*, 18 December 1990.

6199. French, M. T., and G. A. Zarkin. "Racial Differences in Exposure to On-the-Job Hazards." *American Journal of Public Health* 80 (January 1990).

6200. Fried, Marlene G., ed. *From Abortion to Reproductive Freedom: Transforming a Movement*. Boston, 1990.

6201. Friedman, Emily. "Health Care's Changing Face: The Demographics of the 21st Century." *Hospitals* 65 (5 April 1991): 36-40.

6202. Friedman, Samuel R. and others. "Racial Aspects of the AIDS Epidemic." *California Sociologist* 11 (Winter-Summer 1988): 55-68.

6203. Fritz, Sara. "Prescription Drug Pricing Hurting the Poor, Elderly." *Los Angeles Times*, 30 January 1994.

6204. Galishoff, Stuart. "Germs Know No Color Line: Black Health and Public Policy in Atlanta, 1900-1918." *Journal of the History of Medicine and Allied Sciences* 40 (January 1985).

6205. "Gap in Black, White Infant Deaths Growing." *Los Angeles Times*, 30 April 1994.

6206. Garcia, J. A., and R. Z. Juarez. "Utilization of Dental Health Services by Chicanos and Anglos." *Journal of Health and Social Behavior* 19 (December 1978): 428-436.

6207. Gary, Lawrence E. "Health Status of African American Men." in *African American Males*, ed. Dionne J. Jones. Transaction, 1994.

6208. Geiger, H. Jack, and David Rush. *Dead Reckoning: A Critical Review of the Department of Energy's Epidemiological Research*. Physicians for Social Responsiblity, 1992.

6209. Geronimus, A. T. and others. "Differences in Hypertension Prevalence among United States Black and White Women of Childbearing Age." *Public Health Reports* 106 (July-August 1991): 393-399.

6210. Geronimus, A. T., and J. Bound. "Black/White Differences in Women's Reproductive-Related Health Status: Evidence from Vital Statistics." *Demography* 27 (August 1990).

6211. Geronimus, A. T., and S. Korenman. "The Socioeconomic Consequences of Teen Child-bearing Reconsidered." *Quarterly Journal of Economics* 107 (November 1992).

6212. Gesler, Wilbert M., and Thomas C. Ricketts, eds. *Health in Rural North America: The Geography of Health Care Services and Delivery*. Rutgers University Press, 1991.

6213. Gibbs, Jewelle T. "Black Adolescents and Youths: An Endangered Species." *American Journal of Orthopsychiatry* 54 (1984): 6-21.

6214. _____. "Conceptual, Methodological, and Socio-cultural Issues in Black Youth Suicide: Implications for Assessment and Early Intervention." *Suicide and Life-Threatening Behavior* 18 (Spring 1988): 73-89.

6215. Gibbs, Jewelle T., and Alice M. Hines. "Factors Related to Sex Differences in Suicidal Behavior among Black Youth: Implications for Intervention and Research." *Journal of Adolescent Research* 4 (April 1989): 152-172.

6216. Gill, D. G. and others. "Health Care Provision and Distributive Justice: End Stage Renal Disease and the Elderly in Britain and America." *Social Science and Medicine* 32 (1991): 565- 578.

6217. Ginzberg, Eli, ed. *Health Services Research. Key to Health Policy*. Cambridge, MA: Harvard University Press, 1991.

6218. Gittelsohn, A. M. and others. "Income, Race, and Surgery in Maryland." *American Journal of Public Health* 81 (November 1991): 1435-1465.

6219. Glazer, Nona Y. "'Between a Rock and A Hard Place': Women's Professional Organizations in Nursing and Class, Racial and Ethnic Inequalities." *Gender and Society* 5 (September 1991): 351- 372.

6220. Gold, Allan R. "The Struggle to Make Do Without Health Insurance." *New York Times*, 30 July 1989.

6221. Goldberg, K. C. and others. "Racial and Community Factors Influencing Coronary Artery Bypass Graft Surgery Rates for All 1986 Medicare Patients." *Journal of the American Medical Association* 267 (1992): 1473-1477.

6222. Golden, Tim. "In an Urban Battle Zone, a Doctor Calls It Quits." *New York Times*, 23 June 1991. [Dr. Tyrone Medina, chief resident in emergency medicine, Lincoln Medical and Mental Health Center, South Bronx, NYC]

6223. Goldin, Claudia, and Robert A. Margo. "The Poor At Birth: Birth Weights and Infant mortality at Philadelphia's Almshouse Hospital, 1848-1873." *Explorations in Economic History* 26 (July 1989): 360-379.

6224. Golding, J. M. and others. "Stress Exposure among Mexican Americans and Non-Hispanic Whites." *Journal of Community Psychology* 19 (January 1991): 37-59.

6225. Goldstein, Richard. "The Myth of the Powerful Gay Men." *Village Voice* (20 March 1990). [AIDS and race]

6226. Gomez Gomez, E. "Sex Discrimination and Excess Female Mortality in Childhood." in *Gender, Women, and Health in the Americas*, pp. 25-42. ed. Gomez Gomez. Pan American Health Organization, 1993.

6227. Gortmaker, S. L. "Poverty and Infant Mortality in the United States." *American Sociological Review* 44 (1979): 280-297.

6228. Gray, Bradford H. *The Profit Motive and Patient Care. The Changing Accountability of Doctors and Hospitals*. Cambridge, MA: Harvard University Press, 1991.

6229. Greenberg, Michael R. "Black Male Cancer and American Urban Health Policy." *Journal of Urban Affairs* 11 (1989): 113-130. [Rejoinders, 131-139]

6230. Grey, Michael R. "Poverty, Politics, and Health: The Farm Security Administration Medical Care Program, 1935-1945." *Journal of the History of Medicine and Allied Sciences* 44 (1989): 320-350.

6231. Griffin, Minh Ly. *Health and Health Care Profile of New York City's New School Admissions, 1990-1991*. Community Service Society, 1993.

6232. Griswold del Castillo, Richard. "Health and the Mexican Americans in Los Angeles, 1850-1867." *Journal of Mexican-American History* 4 (1974).

6233. Gunther, Lenworth. "Black Health: Yesterday, Today, and Tomorrow." *Crisis* 87 (1980): 546-548.

6234. Guralnik, J. M. and others. "Educational Status and Active Life Expectancy among Older Blacks and Whites." *New England Journal of Medicine* 329 (1993): 110-116.

6235. Gussow, Zachary. *Leprosy, Racism, and Public Health: Social Policy in Chronic Disease Control*. Boulder, CO: Westview, 1989.

6236. Haan, Mary and others. "Poverty and Health: Prospective Evidence from the Alameda County Study." *American Journal of Epidemiology* 125 (1987): 989-998.

6237. _____. "Socioeconomic Status and Health: Old Observations and New Thoughts." in *Pathways to Health: The Role of Social Factors*, pp. 76-135. eds. John P. Bunker and others. Henry J. Kaiser Family Foundation, 1989.

6238. Haan, Mary, and George Kaplan. "The Contribution of Socioeconomic Position to Minority Health." in *Report of the Secretary's Task Force on black and Minority Health, Vol. II, Crosscutting Issues in Minority Health*, pp. 67-103. U.S. Department of Health and Human Services. GPO, 1985.

6239. Hale, Christiane B. *Infant Mortality: An American Tragedy*. Washington, DC: Population Reference Bureau, 1990.

6240. _____. "Infant Mortality: An American Tragedy." *Black Scholar* 21 (January-March 1990): 17-26.

6241. Hallstrom, A. and others. "Socioeconomic Status and Prediction of Ventricular Fibrillation Survival." *American Journal of Public Health* 83 (1993): 245-248.

6242. Hamid, Ansley. "From Ganja to Crack: Caribbean Participation in the Underground Economy in Brooklyn, 1976-1986: 1. Establishment of the Marijuana Economy." *International Journal of the Addictions* 26 (1991): 615-628.

6243. _____. "From Ganja to Crack: Caribbean Participation in the Underground Economy in Brooklyn, 1976-1986: 2. Establishment of the Cocaine (and Crack) Economy." *International Journal of the Addictions* 26 (1991): 729-738.

6244. _____. "The Political Economy of Crack-related Violence." *Contemporary Drug Problems* 17 (Spring 1990): 31-78.

6245. Haney, C. Allen, and Elizabeth Gear. "Black-White Differences in Cancer: A Framework for Intervention Linking Social Structure and Survival." *Sociological Practice* 9 (1991): 80-101.

6246. Hannan, E. L. and others. "Interracial Access to Selected Cardiac Procedures for Patients Hospitalized with Coronary Artery Disease in New York State." *Medical Care* 29 (1991): 430-441.

6247. Harburg, E. and others. "Socio-ecological Stress, Suppressed Hostility, Skin Color, and Black-White Male Blood Pressure: Detroit." *Psychosomatic Medicine* 35 (1973): 276-296.

6248. Harper, F. D. *Alcohol Abuse and Black America.* Alexandria, VA: Douglas Publishers, 1976.

6249. Harris, Ellen W. "Nutrition and Food Participation Programs." *Black Scholar* 21 (January-March 1990): 27-31.

6250. Harris, Hamil R. "Vaccines Don't Reach Poor Children." *Washington Post*, 17 June 1993. [Children of parents who are on Medicaid in Wash. DC]

6251. Hartman, Joan F. "The Impact of the Reagan Administration's Policy on Human Rights Relating to Health and the Family." *New York University Journal of International Law and Politics* 20 (Fall 1987): 169-191.

6252. Hasson, Gail S. *The Medical Activities of the Freedmen's Bureau in Reconstruction Alabama, 1865-1868.* Ph.D. diss., University of Alabama, 1982.

6253. "Health Care for the Poor in 1988." *Clearinghouse Review* 22 (January 1989): 981-993.

6254. "Health Policy and the Disadvantaged." *Journal of Health Politics, Policy, and Law* 15 (Summer 1990): entire issue.

6255. *Health Status of Minorities and Low Income Groups.* Washington, DC: U.S. Department of Health and Human Services, 1985.

6256. Healy, Melissa. "Charity Patients Irradiated to Gauge Effect on Soldiers." *Los Angeles Times*, 6 January 1994. [Federally-sponsored, secret research, 1960-1972]

6257. _____. "Science of Power and Weakness." *Los Angeles Times*, 8 January 1994. ["In the name of the Cold War, researchers took the disadvantaged and made them subjects of risky radiation tasks."]

6258. Helfand, Duke. "No Room to Grow." *Los Angeles Times*, 20 January 1994. [Growth of poverty and related problems in health and housing in Southern California cities]

6259. Herbert, Bob. "Tobacco Dollars." *New York Times*, 28 November 1993. [Black deaths caused by smoking]

6260. "High Rate of Caesareans Among Affluent." *New York Times*, 27 July 1989.

6261. Hilchey, Tim. "2 Studies Report Heart Care Lags for Blacks." *New York Times*, 26 August 1993. [See also article by S. Stolberg, *Los Angeles Times*, same date]

6262. Hilfiker, David. *Not All of Us Are Saints. A Doctor's Journey With the Poor.* Hill and Wang, 1994. [Poverty medicine in Wash., DC]

6263. Hilts, Philip J. "Drug Companies Warn Administration Against Vaccine Programs." *New York Times*, 2 April 1993.

6264. _____. "Growing Gap in Life Expectancies of Blacks and Whites is Emerging." *New York Times*, 9 October 1989.

6265. _____. "Life Expectancy for Blacks in U.S. Shows Sharp Drop." *New York Times*, 29 November 1990.

6266. Hine, Darlene C. *Black Women in White. Racial Conflict and Cooperation in the Nursing Profession, 1890-1950.* Bloomington: Indiana University Press, 1989.

6267. "Hispanic Health and Nutrition Examination Survey, 1982-84: Findings on Health Status and Health Care Needs." *American Journal of Public Health* 80 (December 1990): supplement, entire issue.

6268. Holian, John. "Cleveland Infant Mortality Trends and Patterns." *Sociological Abstracts* (1989). Accession No. 89S20907.

6269. Hollingsworth, J. Rogers and others. *State Intervention in Medical Care. Consequences for Britain, France, Sweden, and the United States, 1890-1970.* Ithaca, NY: Cornell University Press, 1990.

6270. Holmes, M. D. and others. "Racial Inequalities in the Use of Procedures for Iochemic Heart Disease." *Journal of the American Medical Association* 261 (1989): 3242-3243.

6271. Holmes, Samuel J. *The Negro's Struggle for Survival: A Study in Human Ecology.* Berkeley, CA, 1937.

6272. Hostetler, A. J. "Race May Affect Vein Flexibility, Team Says." *Boston Globe*, 25 June 1994. ["Veins in blacks are less flexible and more difficult to dilate..."]

6273. House, James S. and others. "Age, Socioeconomic Status, and Health." *Milbank Quarterly* 68 (1990): 383-411.

6274. Howell, Embry M. and others. "A Comparison of Medicaid and Non-Medicaid Obstetrical Care in California." *Health Care Financing Review* 12 (Summer 1991): 1-15. [October 1983]

6275. Hughes, Dana, and Elizabeth Butler. *The Health of America's Black Children.* Washington, DC: Children's Defense Fund, 1988.

6276. Hummer, Robert A. *Race and Infant Mortality in the United States: A Comprehensive Examination of Individual-level Mediating Factors.* Ph.D. diss., Florida State University, 1993. UMO #9318517.

6277. "Hunger in Black America." *Black Scholar* 21 (January-March 1990): series of articles.

6278. Hunt, J. V. and others. "Very Low Birthweight Infants at 8 and 11 Years of Age: Role of Neonatal Illness and Family Status." *Pediatrics* 82 (1988): 596-603.

6279. Hurowitz, J. C. "Toward a Social Policy for Health." *New England Journal of Medicine* 329 (1993): 130-133.

6280. Hutchinson, Earl Ofari. "Despair, Destitution Killing Off Youth." *Guardian (NYC)* (20 February 1991).

6281. Imbeault, Barbara. "Citizens Groups Rank Hawaii 51st in the Nation." *Hawaii Medical Journal* 48 (March 1989): 60-64.

6282. Institute of Medicine. *Preventing Low Birthweight.* Washington, DC: National Academy Press, 1985.

6283. Jackson, Derrick Z. "A Grim reminder of the State of African-American Health." *Boston Globe*, 7 August 1991.

6284. _____. "Miller's Mockery." *Boston Globe*, 29 December 1991. [Successful efforts by alcohol and tobacco industries to coopt Kwaanza and other Black cultural events.]

6285. _____. "Why Blacks, Latin-Americans Are At a Higher Risk for AIDS." *Boston Globe*, 18 June 1989.

6286. Jacobs, Paul. "Fallout from Nevada." *Reporter* (16 May 1957).

6287. Jason, J. and others. "Epidemiological Characteristics of Primary Homicides in the United States." *American Journal of Epidemiology* 117 (1983): 419-428.

6288. Jaynes, Gerald David, and Robin M. Williams, Jr., eds. "Black Americans' Health." in *A Common Destiny. Blacks and American Society*, pp. 391-450. Washington, DC: National Academy Press, 1989.

6289. Jennings, Veronica T. "Blacks Describe how Bias Hurt their Careers at NIH." *Washington Post*, 10 August 1993. [National Institutes of Health, Bethesda, Maryland]

6290. _____. "Racial Bias at NIH Alleged." *Washington Post*, 14 July 1993. [National Institutes of Health]

6291. Johnson, Charles. "The Status of Health Care Among Black Americans." *Journal of the National Medical Association* 83 (February 1991): 125-129.

6292. Johnson, David B. "An Overview of Ethnicity and Health in Hawaii." *Social Process in Hawaii* 32 (1989): 67-86.

6293. Johnson, Michael P. "Smothered Slave Infants: Were Slave Mothers at Fault?" *Journal of Southern History* 47 (1981): 493- 520.

6294. Johnston, Lloyd and others. *National Trends in Drug Use and Related Factors among American High School Students and Young Adults, 1975-1986.* Rockville, MD: U.S. Department of Health and Human Services, 1987.

6295. Jones, A. M. "An Econometric Investigation of Low Birth Weight in the United States." *Journal of Health Economics* 10 (May 1991).

6296. Jones, Charisse. "Hospital Faces Bias Inquiry on Allocating Rooms." *New York Times*, 19 October 1993. [Mount Sinai Medical Center, NYC]

6297. Jones, James H. *Bad Blood. The Tuskegee Syphillis Experiment*, Expanded ed. Free Press, 1992.

6298. Jones, Lowell A., ed. *Minorities and Cancer.* New York: Springer-Verlag, 1989.

6299. Jones, Rachel L. "State Budget Crisis Leaves Terminal Care for the Poor Hanging in the Balance." *Chicago Reporter* 20 (May 1991): 1,7-9. [Hospice care for Blacks and Hispanics in Chicago]

6300. Jones, Rachel L., and Lisa Capitanini. "Asthma Deaths in Chicago Double; Two-thirds of Victims Are Black." *Chicago Reporter* 21 (January 1992).

6301. Joyce, T. "The Demand for Health Inputs and their Impact on the Black Neonatal Mortality Rate in the U.S." *Social Science and Medicine* 24 (November 1987).

6302. Kallan, J. E. "Race, Intervening Variables, and Two Components of Low Birth Weight." *Demography* 30 (August 1993).

6303. Kamabahi, Jeffrey J., and Deanna B. K. Chang. "Social Control in Health and Law." *Social Process in Hawaii* 34 (1992): entire issue.

6304. Karp, Robert and others. "The Effect of Rising Food Costs on the Occurence of Malnutrition among the Poor in the United States: The Engels Phenomenon in 1983." *Bulletin, New York Academy of Medicine* 59 (October 1983).

6305. Kasiske, Bertram L. "The Effect of Race on Access and Outcome in Transplantation." *New England Journal of Medicine* 324 (31 January 1991): 302-307.

6306. Keil, J. E. and others. "Does Equal Socioeconomic Status in Black and White Men Mean Equal Risk of Mortality?" *American Journal of Public Health* 82 (1992): 1133-1136.

6307. _____. "Mortality Rates and Risk Factors for Coronary Disease in Black as Compared to White Men and Women." *New England Journal of Medicine* 329 (1993): 73-78.

6308. Keith, V. M., and D. P. Smith. "The Current Differential in Black and White Life Expectancy." *Demography* 25 (November 1988).

6309. Kennedy, J. Michael. "Medicine Bordering on Crisis." *Los Angeles Times*, 3 July 1992. [U.S.-Mexican border in Texas]

6310. Kennedy, R. D., and R. E. Deapen. "Differences Between Oklahoma Indian Infant Mortality and Other Races." *Public Health Reports* 106 (January-February 1991).

6311. Kettl, P. A., and E. O. Bixler. "Suicide in Alaska Natives, 1979-1984." *Psychiatry* 54 (1991): 55-63.

6312. Khan, Chandra C. *A Spatial Systems Approach to Nutrition Intervention: The Case of Mexican-American Children in Southwestern United States.* Ph.D. diss., Kent State University, 1990. UMO #9113537.

6313. Kilborn, Peter T. "For Hispanic Immigrants, a Higher Job- injury Risk." *New York Times*, 18 February 1992.

6314. Kipen, Howard M. and others. "Are Non-Whites at Greater Risk for Occupational Cancer?" *American Journal of Industrial Medicine* 19 (1991): 67-74.

6315. Kiple, Kenneth F., and Virginia H. Kiple. "Black Tongue and Black Men: Pellagra and Slavery in the Antebellum South." *Journal of Southern History* 43, no. 3 (1977): 411-428.

6316. Klass, Perri. "Tackling Problems We Thought We Solved." *New York Times Magazine* (13 December 1992). [Treating the children of the poor at Boston City Hospital]

6317. Kleinman, J. C. and others. "Differences in Infant Mortality by Race, Nativity Status, and Other Maternal Characteristics." *Am. Jr. Dis. Child.* 145 (1991): 194-199.

6318. Kleinman, J. C. "The Slowdown in the Infant Mortality Decline." *Paediatric and Perinatal Epidemioogy* 4 (1990): 373-381.

6319. Kleinman, J. C., and S. S. Kessel. "Racial Differences in Low Birth Weight." *New England Journal of Medicine* 317 (1987): 749-753.

6320. Klerman, Lorraine V., and Maura B. Parker. *Alive and Well? A Research and Policy Review of Health Programs for Poor Young Children.* New York: National Center for Children in Poverty, Columbia University School of Public Health, 1991.

6321. Kline, Gary. "Food as a Human Right." *Journal of Third World Studies* 10 (Spring 1993): 92-107.

6322. Kochanek, K. D. and others. "Why Did Black Life Expectancy Decline from 1984 through 1989 in the United States?" *American Journal of Public Health* 84 (June 1994): 938-944.

6323. Koday, M. and others. "Dental Decay Rates among Children of Migrant Workers in Yakima, WA." *Public Health Reports* 105 (September-October 1990).

6324. Kolata, Gina. "Deadliness of Breast Cancer In Blacks Defies Easy Answer." *New York Times*, 3 August 1994.

6325. _____. "In Medical Research Equal Opportunity Doesn't Always Apply." *New York Times*, 10 March 1991. [Ethnic and gender unrepresentativeness of sample populations used in medical research]

6326. Kolbert, Elizabeth. "New York's Medicaid Costs Surge, But Health Care for the Poor Lags." *New York Times*, 14 April 1991.

6327. Kong, Dolores. "Sex Disease Risk Higher for Minority Youth." *Boston Globe*, 29 May 1991. [Massachusetts]

6328. _____. "Social, Economic Factors Seen in Black Death Rates." *Boston Globe*, 8 December 1989. [Black males in Massachusetts]

6329. Konner, Melvin. "Still Invisible, and Dying, in Harlem." *New York Times*, 24 February 1990.

6330. Kotelchuck, M. and others. "Societal Trends that Affect Nutrition Status and Services for the Maternal and Child Health Populations." in *Background Papers for Call to Action: Better Nutrition for Mothers, Children, and Families*, pp. 23-39. ed. C. S. Sharbaugh. Washington, DC: National Center for Education in Maternal and Child Health, 1990.

6331. Krieger, Nancy. "The Making of Public Health Data: Paradigms, Politics, and Policy." *Journal of Public Health Policy* 13 (1992): 412-427.

6332. _____. "Racial and Gender Discrimination: Risk Factors for High Blood Pressure?" *Social Science and Medicine* 30 (1990): 1273-1281.

6333. Krieger, Nancy and others. "Racism, Sexism, and Social Class: Implications for Studies of Health, Disease, and Well- being." *American Journal of Preventive Medicine* 9 (November- December 1993): 82-122, supplement.

6334. Krieger, Nancy, and Elizabeth Fee. "Social Class: The Missing Link in U.S. Health Data." *International Journal of Health Services* 24 (1994): 25-44.

6335. _____. "What's Class Got To Do With It? The State of Health Data in the United States Today." *Socialist Review* 23 (1993): 59-82.

6336. La Veist, Thomas A. "Linking Residential Segregation to the Infant-Mortality Race Disparity in U.S. Cities." *Sociology and Social Research* 73 (January 1989): 90-94.

6337. _____. "The Political Empowerment and Health Status of African-Americans: Mapping a New Territory." *American Journal of Sociology* 97 (January 1992): 1080-1095.

6338. _____. "Race, Poverty, and Postneonatal Mortality in Urban Places." *Sociological Abstracts* (1989). Accession No. 89S21538.

6339. _____. "Segregation, Poverty, and Empowerment: Health Consequences for African Americans." *Milbank Quarterly* 71 (1993): 41-64.

6340. Lacey, Marc. "Solving the Ills of Black Men." *Los Angeles Times*, 1 August 1992.

6341. Langlois, Judith H. and others. "Maternal and Infant Demographics and Health Status: A Comparison of Black, Caucasian, and Hispanic Families." *Journal of Biosocial Science* 23 (1991): 91-105.

6342. Larson, L. B. and others. "Nutritional Status of Children of Mexican-American Migrant Families." *Journal of the American Dietetic Association* 64 (1974): 29. [Lower Rio Grande Valley, Texas]

6343. "Latino Health Policy." in *The Challenge: Latinos in a Changing California*, pp. 101-111. University of California SCR 43 Task Force. Riverside: The University of California Consortium on Mexico and the United States (UC MEXUS), 1989.

6344. Lazarus, E. S., and E. H. Philipson. "A Longitudinal Study Comparing the Prenatal Care of Puerto Rican and White Women." *Birth* 17 (March 1990).

6345. Leary, Warren E. "Black Hypertension May Reflect Other Ills." *New York Times*, 22 October 1991.

6346. _____. "Stress Among Blacks Is Tied to Bias." *New York Times*, 6 February 1991.

6347. _____. "Study Hints of Reason for Blacks' High Rate of Heart Disease." *New York Times*, 26 June 1994. ["Veins of blacks...less flexible and expandalbe than those of whites."]

6348. _____. "Uneasy Doctors Add Race-Conciousness to Diagnostic Tools." *New York Times*, 25 September 1990.

6349. Lederer, Susan E. "Orphans as Guinea Pigs: American Children and Medical Experiments, 1890-1930." in *In the Name of the Child: Health and Welfare, 1880-1940*, ed. Roger Cooter. Routledge, 1992.

6350. Lee, Anne S., and Everett S. Lee. "The Health of Slaves and the Health of Freedmen: A Savannah Study." *Phylon* 38 (1977): 170- 180.

6351. Lee, Felicia R. "Doctors See Gap in Blacks' Health Having a Link to Low Self-Esteem." *New York Times*, 17 July 1989.

6352. _____. "Immunization of Children [in NYC area] Is Said To Lag [Behind that of Some Third World Countries]." *New York Times*, 16 October 1991. [Algeria, El Salvador, Uganda, Cuba, Chile, North Korea, Antigua, Grenada, and Mexico]

6353. Leffall, La Salle D., Jr. "Health Status of Black Americans." *The State of Black America 1990* (January 1990): 121- 142.

6354. Leland, Mickey. "The Politics of Hunger among Blacks." *Black Scholar* 21 (January-March 1990): 2-5.

6355. Lester, D. "Mortality from Suicide and Homicide in the USA: A Regional Analysis." *Omega* 22 (1991): 219-226.

6356. Levenson, Alvin J. "Treatment of the Severely Mentally Ill Poor." *American Journal of Psychiatry* 146 (September 1989): 1232- 1233.

6357. Lewin-Epstein, N. "Determinants of Regular Source of Health Care in Black, Mexican, Puerto Rican, and Non-Hispanic White Populations." *Medical Care* 29 (June 1991): 543-557.

6358. Lieberman, E. and others. "Risk Factors Accounting for Racial Differences in the Rate of Premature Birth." *New England Journal of Medicine* 317 (1987): 743-748.

6359. Lillie-Blanton, Marsha and others. "Latina and African American Women: Continuing Disparities in Health." *International Journal of Health Services* 23 (1993): 555-584.

6360. Lindsey, Kenneth P., and Paul L. Gordon. "Involuntary Commitments to Public Mental Institutions: Issues Involving the Overrepresentation of Blacks and Assessment of Relevant Functioning." *Psychological Bulletin* 106 (September 1989): 171- 183.

6361. Link, William A. "Privies, Progressivism, and Public Schools: Health Reform and Education in the Rural South, 1909- 1920." *Journal of Southern History* 54 (November 1988): 623-642.

6362. Lipsky, Michael, and Marc A. Thibodeau. "Domestic Food Policy in the United States." *Journal of Health Politics, Policy, and Law* 15 (Summer 1990): 319-339. [Food stamps]

6363. Livingston, Ivor L. "Renal Disease and Black Americans: Selected Issues." *Social Science and Medicine* 37 (September 1993): 613-621.

6364. Logue, Barbara J. "Race Differences in Long-term Disability: Middle-Aged and Older American Indians, Blacks, and Whites in Oklahoma." *Social Science Journal* 27 (1990): 253-272. [Oklahoma, 1980 data]

6365. Looker, A. C. and others. "Iron Status: Prevalence of Impairment in Three Hispanic Groups in the U.S." *American Journal of Clinical Nutrition* 49 (1989): 553-558.

6366. Lopez, Steven. "The Empirical Basis of Ethnocultural and Linguistic Bias in Mental Health Evaluations of Hispanics." *American Psychologist* 43 (December 1988): 1095-1097. [See Malgady and others, below]

6367. Loslier, Luc. "Disparités socio-spatiale de mortalité a Porto-Rico." *Canadian Journal of Development Studies* 8 (1987): 117-132.

6368. Love, Spencie. *One Blood: The Charles R. Drew Legend and the Trauma of Race in America.* Ph.D. diss., Duke University, 1990. UMO #9028223.

6369. Love, Wallace B., and R. Palmer Howard. "Health and Medical Practice in the Choctaw Nation, 1880-1907." *Journal of the Oklahoma State Medical Association* 63 (1970): 124-128.

6370. Lowe, Linda. "Not in Cities Only: Georgia's Health Care Crisis." *Health/PAC Bulletin* 21 (Spring 1991): 9.

6371. Luder, Elisabeth and others. "Assessment of the Nutritional Status of Urban Homeless Adults." *Public Health Reports* 104 (September-October 1989).

6372. Luker, Kristin. "Dubious Conceptions: The Controversy Over Teen Pregnancy." *American Prospect* (Spring 1991): 73-83.

6373. Lundberg, O. "Causal Explanations for Class Inequality in Health: An Empirical Analysis." *Social Science and Medicine* 32 (1991): 385-394.

6374. Lunde, A. S. "Health in the United States." *Annals of the American Academy of Political and Social Science* 453 (January 1981): 28-69.

6375. Lynberg, Michele C., and Muin J. Khoury. "Contribution of Birth Defects to Infant Mortality Among Racial/Ethnic Groups, United States, 1983." *MMWR* 39 (July 1990): 1-12.

6376. Makuc, D. M. and others. "National Trends in the Use of Preventive Health Care by Women." *American Journal of Public Health* 79 (1989): 21-26.

6377. Malcolm, Andrew H. "Affluent Addicts' Road Back Begins In a Climb Past Denial." *New York Times*, 2 October 1989.

6378. _____. "Crack, Bane of Inner City, Is Now Gripping Suburbs." *New York Times*, 1 October 1989.

6379. Malgady, Robert G. and others. "Reply to 'The Empirical Basis of Ethnocultural and Linguistic Bias in Mental Health Evaluations of Hispanics'." *American Psychologist* 43 (December 1988): 1097. [See Lopez, above]

6380. Malina, R. M., and A. N. Zavaleta. "Secular Trend in Stature and Weight of Mexican American Children Between 1930 and 1970]." *American Journal of Physical Anthropology* 52 (1980): 453- 461.

6381. Mangold, William D., and Eve Powell-Griner. "Race of Parents and Infant Birthweight in the United States." *Social Biology* 38 (Spring-Summer 1991): 13-27.

6382. Manton, Kenneth G. and others. "The Black/White Mortality Crossover: Investigation from the Perspective of the Components of Aging." *Gerontologist* 19 (1979): 291-300.

6383. _____. "Health Differentials between Blacks and Whites: Recent Trends in Mortality and Morbidity." *Milbank Quarterly* 65, supplement 1 (1987): 185-187.

6384. Marc, R. D. "Socioeconomic Effects on Child Mortality in the United States." *American Journal of Public Health* 72 (1982): 539-547.

6385. Marin, Barbara V., and Gerado Marin, eds. "Hispanics and AIDS." *Hispanic Journal of Behavioral Science* 12 (May 1990): entire issue.

6386. Mariner, Wendy K. "Equitable Access to Biomedical Advances: Getting Beyond the Rights Impasse." *Connecticut Law Review* 21 (Spring 1989): 571-603.

6387. Marmot, M. G. and others. "Social/economic Status and Disease." *Annual Review of Public Health* 8 (1987): 111-135.

6388. Marshall, Mary L. "Plantation Medicine." *Bulletin of the Tulane University Medical Faculty* 3, no. 1 (1942): 45-58.

6389. Martinez-Schnell, Beverly, and Richard J. Waxweiler. "Increases in Premature Mortality Due to Homicide-United States, 1968-1985." *Violence and Victims* 4 (Winter 1989): 287-293.

6390. Martinez, Elizabeth. "Caramba, Our Anglo Sisters Just Didn't Get It." *Z Magazine* 5 (July-August 1992): 44-46. [On reproductive rights]

6391. Maugh, Thomas H., II. "Surgery Study Finds Poor at a Disadvantage." *Los Angeles Times*, 9 December 1993. [California]

6392. McBride, David. "American Medical and Intellectual Reaction to African Health Issues, 1850-1960: From Racialism to Cross- cultural Medicine." *Explorations in Ethnic Studies* 12 (1989): 1- 18.

6393. _____. "The Black-White Mortality Differential in New York State, 1900-1950: A Socio-historical Reconsideration." *Afro- Americans in New York Life and History* 14 (1990): 71-89.

6394. _____. *From TB to AIDS. Epidemics among Urban Blacks Since 1900.* Albany: State University of New York Press, 1991.

6395. _____. *Integrating the City of Medicine: Blacks in Philadelphia Health Care, 1910-1965.* Philadelphia, PA: Temple University Press, 1989.

6396. McCarthy, Claire. "A Doctor's Perspective." *Boston Globe Magazine* (10 February 1991). [Budget cuts and health care for poor people]

6397. McClain, Charles. "Of Medicine, Race, and American Law: The Bubonic Plague Outbreak of 1900." *Law and Social Inquiry* 13 (Summer 1988): 447-513. [Chinese in the U.S.]

6398. McCord, Colin, and Harold P. Freeman. "Excess Mortality in Harlem." *New England Journal of Medicine* 322 (18 January 1990): 173-177.

6399. McCormick, M. C. "Long-term Follow-up of Infants Discharged from Neonatal Intensive Care Units." *Journal of the American Medical Association* 261 (1989): 1767-1772.

6400. McCormick, M. C. and others. "Very Low Birth Weight Children: Behavior Problems and School Difficulty in a National Sample." *Journal of Pediatrics* 117 (1990): 687-693.

6401. McCracken, Robert D. "Growth and Nutritional Status of Migrant Farmworker Preschool Children: Are the Programs Working?" *Farmworker Journal* 1 (Winter 1978-79): 4-20. [Colo.]

6402. McIntosh, John L., and John F. Santos. "Suicide among Native Americans: A Compiliation of Findings." *Omega* 11 (1980- 1981): 303-316.

6403. Mclafferty S. "Health in the Inner City." *Urban Geography* 11 (May-June 1990).

6404. McNibb, S. "Native Health Status and Native Health Policy: Current Dilemmas at the Federal Level." *Arctic Anthropology* 27 (1990).

6405. McShane, Damian. "An Analysis of Mental Health Research with American Indian Youth." *Journal of Adolescence* 11 (June 1988): 87-116.

6406. Menchik, P. L. "Economic Status as a Determinant of Mortality among Black and White Older Men: Does Poverty Kill." *Population Studies* 47 (November 1993).

6407. Mendoza, Fernando S. and others. "Selected Measures of Health Status for Mexican American, Mainland Puerto Rican, and Cuban American Children." *Journal of the American Medical Association* 265 (1991): 227-232.

6408. Meyer, Madonna H. *Universalism vs. Targeting as the Basis of Social Distribution: Gender, Race, and Long-term Care in the U.S.* Ph.D. diss., Florida State University, 1991. UMO #9202308.

6409. Meyers, Alan F. and others. "School Breakfast Program and School Performance." *American Journal of Diseases of Children* 143 (October 1989).

6410. Michaels, D. "Occupational Cancer in the Black Population: The Health Effects of Job Discrimination." *Journal of the National Medical Association* 75 (1983): 1014-1018.

6411. Mickel, Richard A. *"Save the Babies": American Public Health Reform and the Prevention of Infant Mortality, 1850-1929.* Baltimore, MD: Johns Hopkins University Press, 1990.

6412. Miller, S. M. "Race in the Health of America." *Milbank Quarterly* 65 (1987): 500-531.

6413. Millner, Lois. *Maternal and Infant Health: Painful Policy Choices in Congress, 1935-1987.* Ph.D. diss., Bryn Mawr College, 1991. UMO #9126993.

6414. *Minorities in NIH Extramural Grant Programs, Fiscal Years 1982-1991.* Bethesda, MD: National Institutes of Health, 1993.

6415. Mintz, Beth. "The Role of Capitalist Class Relations in the Restructuring of Medicine." in *Bringing Class Back In*, pp. 65-81. eds. Scott G. McNall and others. Westview Press, 1991.

6416. Moldow, Gloria. *Women Doctors in Gilded-Age Washington: Race, Gender, and Professionalization.* Urbana: University of Illinois Press, 1987.

6417. Mollica, Richard F., and Mladen Milic. "Social Class and Psychiatric Inpatient Care: A Twenty-five Year Perspective." *Social Psychiatry* 21 (July 1986): 106-112.

6418. Moore, Emily. *Women and Health, United States 1980.* Washington, DC: GPO, 1980.

6419. Morgan, Dan. "How Medicaid Grew." *Washington Post*, 30 January 1994. [First of four articles]

6420. Morton, Marian J. *And Sin No More: Social Policy and Unwed Mothers in Cleveland, 1855-1990.* Ohio State University Press, 1993.

6421. Mott, Frederick D., and Multon I. Roemer. *Rural Health and Medical Care.* McGraw-Hill, 1948.

6422. Mulligan, Thomas S. "Big Dental Plan Cheats the Poor, State Audit Says." *Los Angeles Times*, 26 June 1993. [Denti Care, in California]

6423. Mullings, Leith. "Inequality and African-American Health Status: Policies and Prospects." in *Race: Twentieth-Century Dilemas--Twenty-First-Century Prognoses*, eds. Winston A. Van Horne, and Thomas V. Tonnesen. Milwaukee: Institute on Race and Ethnicity, University of Wisconsin System, 1989.

6424. Munoz, Eric. "Hospitals, Minorities Take a Beating." *New York Times*, 28 July 1989.

6425. Murphy, R. S. "At Last-a View of Hispanic Health and Nutrition Status." *American Journal of Public Health* 80 (1990): 1429-1430.

6426. Murray, Robert F., and James E. Bowman. *Genetic Variation and Disorders in Peoples of African Origin*. Baltimore, MD: Johns Hopkins University Press, 1990.

6427. Mutchler, J. E., and J. A. Burr. "Racial Differences in Health and Health Care Service Utilization in Latin Life: The Effect of Socioeconomic Status." *Journal of Health and Social Behavior* 32 (December 1991): 342-356.

6428. Muwakkil, Salim. "Living Fast, Dying Young in America's Inner Cities." *In These Times* (26 December 1990).

6429. Naierman, Naomi. *Sex Discrimination in Health and Human Development Services*. Cambridge, MA: Abt Associates, 1979.

6430. Nathalang, Matrini. *Where Did the Doctors Go? Primary Physician Office Relocation: Detroit, 1950-1980*. Ph.D. diss., University of Kentucky, 1988. UMO #8903570.

6431. National Cancer Institute. *Cancer among Blacks and Other Minorities*. Bethesda, MD: U.S. Department of Health and Human Services, 1986.

6432. National Center for Health Statistics. *Firearm Mortality Among Children and Youth*. Washington, DC: The Center, October 1989.

6433. _____. "Health Coverage by Age, Sex, Race, and Family Income: United States, 1986." *Advance Data from Vital and Health Statistics* no. 139

6434. _____. *Health Care Coverage by Sociodemographic and Health Characteristics, United States, 1984*. Washington, DC: GPO.

6435. _____. *Health Characteristics According to Family and Personal Income*. Springfield, VA: National Technical Information Service, PB 85-227411.

6436. _____. *Health Indicators for Hispanic, Black, and White Americans*. Springfield, VA: National Technical Information Service, PB 85-156956.

6437. _____. *Health, United States, 1989 and Prevention Profile*. Washington, DC: GPO, 1990.

6438. National Commission to Prevent Infant Mortality. *Death Before Life*. Washington, DC: The Commission, 1988.

6439. _____. *Troubling Trends: The Health of America's Next Generation*. Washington, DC: The Commission, 1990.

6440. National Research Council. *The Social Impact of AIDS in the United States*. National Academy Press, 1993.

6441. Navarro, Vicente. "Class and Race: Life and Death Situations." *Monthly Review* 43 (September 1991): 1-13.

6442. _____. "The Class Gap [in Mortality and Sickness Rates]." *Nation* (8 April 1991).

6443. _____. *Dangerous To Your Health. The Medical Case Crisis in the United States*. Monthly Review Press, 1993.

6444. _____. "Has Socialism Failed? An Analysis of Health Indicators Under Capitalism and Socialism." *Science and Society* 57 (Spring 1993): 6-30.

6445. _____. "Race or Class, or Race and Class." *International Journal of Health Services* 19 (1989): 311-314. [Health status of blacks in U.S.]

6446. _____. "Race or Class Versus Race and Class: Mortality Differentials in the United States." *Lancet* 336 (17 November 1990): 1238-1240.

6447. _____. "U.S. Marxist Scholarship in the Analysis of Health and Medicine." in *The Left Academy*, eds. B. Odlman, and E. Vernoff. Praeger, 1986.

6448. _____. "Why Some Countries Have National Health Insurance, Others Have National Health Services, and the United States Has Neither." *International Journal of Health Services* 19 (1989).

6449. Navarro, Vicente, ed. *Why the United States Does Not Have a National Health Program*. Baywood Publishing Co., 1992.

6450. Nazario, Sonia. "Hunger, High Food Costs Found in Inner City Area." *Los Angeles Times*, 11 June 1993. [Los Angeles]

6451. _____. "Treating Doctors for Prejudice." *Los Angeles Times*, 20 December 1993. [Teaching medical students]

6452. Neighbors, Harold W. and others. "The Influence of Racial Factors on Psychiatric Diagnosis: A Review and Suggestions for Research." *Community Mental Health Journal* 25 (Winter 1989): 301- 311.

6453. Neighbors, Harold W. "The Prevention of Psychopathology in African Americans: An Epidemiologic Perspective." *Community Mental Health Journal* 26 (April 1990).

6454. _____. "Socioeconomic Status and Psychologic Distress." *American Journal of Epidemiology* 124 (1986): 779-793.

6455. Neligh, G. "Mental Health Programs for American Indians: Their Logic, Structure and Function." *American Indian and Alaska Native Mental Health Research* 3 (Summer 1990): 7-259.

6456. Nelson, M. D., Jr. "Socioeconomic Status and Childhood Mortality in North Carolina." *American Journal of Public Health* 82 (1992): 1131-1133.

6457. Newacheck, P. W., and B. Starfield. "Morbidity and Use of Ambulatory Care Services among Poor and Non-poor Children." *American Journal of Public Health* 78 (1988): 927-933.

6458. Niehaus, J. A. "Increasing the Cost of Living: Class and Exploitation in the Delivery of Social Services to Persons with AIDS." in *Culture and AIDS*, pp. 183-204. ed. D. A. Feldman. New York: Praeger, 1990.

6459. Njeri, Itabari. "The Menace of Nihilism." *Los Angeles Times Magazine* (29 August 1993). [Violence and racism in the U.S.]

6460. Numbers, Ronald L., and Todd L. Savitt. *Science and Medicine in the Old South*. Baton Rouge: Louisiana State University Press, 1989.

6461. Odun, Maria. "Black Hospitals Work to Find a Modern Role." *New York Times*, 12 August 1992.

6462. Olmos, David R. "Prescription for Survival." *Los Angeles Times*, 10 January 1994. [Doctors of color in ethnic areas]

6463. O'Nell, Theresa D. "Psychiatric Investigations among American Indians and Alaska Natives: A Critical Review." *Culture, Medicine, and Psychiatry* 13 (March 1989): 51-87.

6464. Oparaocha, Titus E. *Differences between Blacks and Whites in the Effects of Selected Factors on Health Care Utilization*. Ph.D. diss., Howard University, 1992. UMO #9239184.

6465. O'Regan, Katherine, and Michael Wiseman. "Birth Weights and the Geography of Poverty." *Focus* 12 (Fall and Winter 1989): 16- 22.

6466. Osborne, Newton G., and Marvin D. Feit. "The Use of Race in Medical Research." *Journal of the American Medical Association* 267 (8 January 1992): 275-279.

6467. Otten, M. W., Jr. and others. "The Effect of Known Risk Factors on the Excess Mortality of Black Adults in the United States." *Journal of the American Medical Association* 263 (1990): 845-850.

6468. "Paper from the CDC-ATSDR Workshop On the Use of Race and Ethnicity in Public Health Surveillance." *Public Health Reports* 109 (January-February 1994): six articles.

6469. Pappas, Gregory. "Elucidating the Relationships between Race, Socioeconomic Status, and Health." *American Journal of Public Health* 84 (June 1994): 892-893.

6470. Pappas, Gregory and others. "The Increasing Disparity in Mortality between Socioeconomic Groups in the United States, 1960 and 1986." *New England Journal of Medicine* 329 (8 July 1993): 103-109.

6471. Paterno, Susan. "Minority Groups at Risk of Diabetes." *Los Angeles Times*, 21 July 1992.

6472. Pear, Robert. "Surgeon General Says Medicaid Enslaves Poor Pregnant Women." *New York Times*, 26 February 1994.

6473. Pearson, M. "Sociology of Race and Health." in *Ethnic Factors in Health and Disease*, eds. J. K. Cruickshank, and D. G. Beevers. Kent: John Wright, 1989.

6474. Peck, M. N. "The Importance of Childhood Socio-economic Group for Adult Health." *Social Science and Medicine* 39 (August 1994): 553-562.

6475. Pereira, J. "What Does Equity in Health Mean?" *Journal of Social Policy* 22 (January 1993): 19-48.

6476. Perez-Stable, E. J. and others. "Behavioral Risk Factors: A Comparison of Latinos and Non-Latinos in San Francisco." *American Journal of Public Health* 84 (June 1994): 971-976.

6477. Perkins, Jane. "Health Care Rights of the Poor: An Introduction." *Clearinghouse Review* 23 (November 1989): 825-831.

6478. Perrucci, R., and C. C. Perrucci. "Unemployment and Mental Health: Research and Policy Implications." in *Mental Disorder in Social Context*, pp. 237-272. ed. J. R. Greenley. Greenwich, CT: JAI Press, 1990.

6479. Petitti, D. and others. "Early Prenatal Care in Urban Black and White Women." *Birth* 17 (March 1990).

6480. Physician Task Force on Hunger in America. *Hunger in America: The Growing Epidemic*. Middleton, CT: Wesleyan University Press, 1985.

6481. _____. *Increasing Hunger and Declining Help: Barriers to Participation in the Food Stamp Program*. Harvard School of Public Health, May 1984.

6482. Pierson, C. "The Exceptional United States: First New Nation or Last Welfare State?" *Social Policy and Administration* 24 (December 1990).

6483. Pol, Louis G., and Richard K. Thomas. *The Demography of Health and Health Care*. Plenum, 1992.

6484. Polednak, Anthony P. *Racial and Ethnic Differences in Disease*. New York: Oxford University Press, 1989.

6485. Potter, L. B. "Socioeconomic Determinants of White and Black Life Expectancy Differentials, 1980." *Demography* 28 (May 1991): 303-322.

6486. Powell-Griner, Eve. "Differences in Infant Mortality among Texas Anglos, Hispanics, and Blacks." *Social Science Quarterly* 69 (1988): 452-467.

6487. Power, C. "Social and Economic Background and Class Inequalities in Health Among Young Adults." *Social Science and Medicine* 32 (1991): 411-418.

6488. Prakasa, Rao V. V. and others. "Racial Differences in Attitudes toward Euthanasia." *Euthanasia Review* 2 (Winter 1988): 260-277.

6489. Preston, Samuel H., and Michael R. Haines. *Fatal Years. Child Mortality in Late Nineteenth-Century America*. Princeton, NJ: Princeton University Press, 1991.

6490. Prieto, Dario O. "Native Americans in Medicine: The Need for Indian Healers." *Academic Medicine* 64 (July 1989): 388-389.

6491. "Prostate Cancer Diagnosed At Later Stage in Blacks." *Washington Post*, 30 November 1993.

6492. Puffer, Frank. "Access to Primary Health Care: A Comparison of the U.S. and the U.K." *Journal of Social Policy* 15 (July 1986): 293-314.

6493. Putney, Diane T. *Fighting the Scourge: American Indian Morbidity and Federal Policy, 1897-1928*. Ph.D. diss., Marquette University, 1980.

6494. Quam, L. "Post-war American Health Care: The Many Costs of Market Failure." *Oxford Review of Economic Policy* 5 (Spring 1989).

6495. Quaye, R. "The Health Care Status of African Americans." *Black Scholar* 24 (1994): 12-18.

6496. Quimby, Ernest, and Samuel R. Friedman. "Dynamics of Black Mobilization against AIDS in New York City." *Social Problems* 36 (October 1989): 403-415.

6497. Quinney, Roger E. "An Exploratory Study of the Black Homeless Population and their Medical Needs." Master's thesis, California State University, Long Beach, 1989.

6498. "Racism, Gender, Class, and Health." *Medical Anthropology Quarterly* 7 (December 1993): five articles.

6499. Ramirez, Anthony. "A Cigarette Campaign Under Fire." *New York Times*, 12 January 1990. [Cigarette-sales campaign aimed at blacks]

6500. Reed, Wornie L. and others. *The Health and Medical Care of African-Americans*. William Monroe Trotter Institute, U. of Massachusetts at Boston, 1992.

6501. Reilly, Philip R. *The Surgical Solution. A History of Involuntary Sterilization in the United States*. Baltimore, MD: Johns Hopkins University Press, 1991.

6502. Remez, L. "Infant Mortality on an Oregon Indian Reservation Is Almost 3 Times Higher Than the Overall United States Rate." *Family Planning Perspectives* 24 (May-June 1992): 138-139.

6503. A Report of the Mayor's Commission on the Future of Child Health. *The Future of Child Health in New York City*. New York: New York City Department of Health, August 1989.

6504. Rhoades, E. R. and others. "Mortality of American Indian and Alaska Native Infants." *Annual Review of Public Health* 13 (1992): 269-286.

6505. Ricciuti, H. N. "Malnutrition and Cognitive Development: Research-Policy Linkages and Current Research Directions." in *Directors of Development*, eds. Lynn Okagaki, and Robert J. Sternberg. Hillsdale, NJ: Lawrence Erlbaum, 1991.

6506. Rice, D. P. "Ethics and Equity in United States Health Care: The Data." *International Journal of Health Services* 21 (1991): 637-652.

6507. Rice, Mitchell F., and Woodrow Jones, Jr. *Public Policy and the Black Hospital: From Slavery to Segregation to Integration*. Greenwood, 1994.

6508. Ries, Peter W. "Characteristics of Persons with and without Health Care Coverage: United States, 1989." *NCHS Advance Data* no. 201 (16 May 1991).

6509. _____. "Educational Differences in Health Status and Health Care." *Vital Health Statistics* no. 179 (1991).

6510. _____. "Health Characteristics according to Family and Personal Income, United States." *Vital Health Statistics* no. 147 (1985).

6511. _____. "Health of Black and White Americans, 1985-87." *NCHS Vital Health Statistics* 10 (January 1990): 45-46.

6512. Rinehart, Sue T. "Maternal Health Care Policy: Britain and the United States." *Comparative Politics* 19 (January 1987): 193- 211.

6513. Rittenhouse, R. K. and others. "The Black and Deaf Movements in America since 1960: Parallelism and an Agenda for the Future." *American Annals of the Deaf* 136 (December 1991): 392-400.

6514. Roark, Anne C. "Blacks Most Often Named as Victims of Child Abuse." *Los Angeles Times*, 9 June 1992. [Los Angeles]

6515. Robinson, Donald. "Save Our Babies." *Parade* (30 June 1991).

6516. Rodriguez, Carlos. *The Health Care Crisis in the Latino Community*. Latino Issues Forum and Consumers Union, April 1993.

6517. Rodriguez, O., and M. Santiviago. "Hispanic Deaf Adolescents: A Multicultural Minority." *Volta Review* 93 (September 1991): 89-98.

6518. Rogers, Richard G. "Ethnic and Birth Weight Differences in Cause-Specific Infant Mortality." *Demography* 26 (May 1989).

6519. _____. "Ethnic Differences in Infant Mortality: Fact of Antifact?" *Social Science Quarterly* 70 (September 1989): 642-649.

6517. Rodriguez, O., and M. Santiviago. "Hispanic Deaf Adolescents: A Multicultural Minority." *Volta Review* 93 (September 1991): 89-98.

6518. Rogers, Richard G. "Ethnic and Birth Weight Differences in Cause-Specific Infant Mortality." *Demography* 26 (May 1989).

6519. _____. "Ethnic Differences in Infant Mortality: Fact of Antifact?" *Social Science Quarterly* 70 (September 1989): 642-649.

6520. _____. "Living and Dying in the U.S.A.: Socio- demographic Determinants of Death among Blacks and Whites." *Demography* 29 (1992): 287-303.

6521. Rogler, Lloyd H. and others. "Acculturation and Mental Health Status among Hispanics: Convergence and New Directions for Research." *American Psychologist* 46 (June 1991): 585-597.

6522. Rogler, Lloyd H. *Hispanics and Mental Health*. Melbourne, FL: Krieger, 1989.

6523. Rogot, Eugene and others. "Life Expectancy by Employment Status, Income, and Education in the National Longitudinal Mortality Study." *Public Health Reports* 107 (1992): 457-461.

6524. _____. *A Mortality Study of 1.3 Million Persons by Demographic, Social, and Economic Factors: 1979-1985 Follow-Up, U.S. National Longitudinal Mortality Study*. National Institutes of Health, 1992.

6525. Rose, Jerome C. "Biological Consequences of Segregation and Economic Deprivation: A Post-Slavery Population from Southwest Arkansas." *Journal of Economic History* 49 (June 1989): 351-360. [Cedar Grove, Arkansas]

6526. _____. *Gone to a Better Land: A Biohistory of a Rural Black Cemetery in the Post-Reconstruction South*. Fayetteville, Ark., 1985.

6527. Rose, Jerome C., and Ted A. Rothbun, eds. "Afro-American Biohistory Symposium." *American Journal of Physical Anthropology* 74 (October 1987): 177-273.

6528. Rosenbach, Margo L. *The Use of Physicians' Services By Low- income Childre*. Garland, 1993. [Medicaid]

6529. Rosenbaum, Sara. "Child Health and Poor Children." *American Behavioral Scientist* 35 (January-February 1992): 275-289.

6530. Rosenbaum, Sara, and Marilyn Sager. "Unlocking the Hospital Doors: Medical Staff Membership and Physicians Who Serve the Poor." *Yale Law and Policy Review* 9 (Spring 1991): 46-70.

6531. Rosenberg, Charles E. "Social Class and Medical Care in 19th Century America: The Rise and Fall of the Dispensary." *Bulletin of the History of Medicine* 29 (1974): 32-54.

6532. Rosenberg, Mitchell. *Children Are Hungry in Massachusetts. A Statewide Study on Childhood Hunger*. Boston: Massachusetts Community Childhood Hunger Identification Project, May 1991.

6533. Rosenberg, Terry J. "The Risk of Low Birthweight among Hispanic Women in New York City: How Important Is Descent?" *Sociological Abstracts* Accession No, 89S21680.

6534. Rosenthal, Elisabeth. "At Ailing Public Hospital in Brooklyn, Healing Mission Is Undone by Decay." *New York Times*, 28 February 1994. [Kings County Hospital]

6535. _____. "Health Problems of Inner City Poor Reach Crisis Point." *New York Times*, 24 December 1990.

6536. Rosenwaike, Ira, ed. *Mortality of Hispanic Populations. Mexicans, Puerto Ricans, and Cubans in the United States and in the Home Countries*. Westport, CT: Greenwood, 1991.

6537. Rosenwaike, Ira, and Benjamin S. Bradshaw. "Mortality of the Spanish Surname Population of the Southwest: 1980." *Social Science Quarterly* 70 (1989): 631-641.

6538. Rosenzweig, M. R., and T. P. Schultz. "Who Receives Medical Care? Income, Implicit Prices, and the Distribution of Medical Services Among Pregnant Women in the United States." *Journal of Human Resources* 26 (Summer 1991): 473-508.

6542. Ruiz, Dorothy S., ed. *Handbook of Mental Health and Mental Disorder Among Black Americans*. Westport, CT: Greenwood, 1990.

6543. Ruther, M., and A. Dobson. "Unequal Treatment and Unequal Benefits: A Reexamination of the Use of Medicare Services by Race, 1967-1976." in *Health Care Financing Review*, Washington, DC: U.S. Department of Health and Human Services, 1981.

6544. Ryan, Frank. *The Forgotten Plague. How the Battle Against Tuberculosis Was Won-and Lost*. Little, Brown, 1993.

6545. Sabatier, Renee and others. *Blaming Others: Prejudice, Race, and Worldwide AIDS*. Philadelphia, PA: New Society Publishers, 1988.

6546. Salmon, Roberto M. "The Disease Complaint at Bosque Redondo (1864-1868)." *Indian Historian* no. 9 (1976).

6547. Sardell, Alice. "Child Health Policy in the U.S.: The Paradox of Consensus." *Journal of Health Politics, Policy, and Law* 15 (Summer 1990): 271-304.

6548. Savitt, Todd L. "Black Health on the Plantation: Masters, Slaves, and Physicians." in *Science and Medicine in the Old South*, eds. Ronald L. Numbers, and Todd L. Savitt. Baton Rouge: Louisiana State University Press, 1989.

6549. _____. "Entering a White Profession." *Bulletin of the History of Medicine* (1987).

6550. _____. *Medicine and Slavery: The Diseases and Health Care of Blacks in Antebellum Virginia*. Urbana: University of Illinois Press, 1978.

6551. _____. "Slave Health and Southern Distinctiveness." in *Disease and Distinctiveness in the American South*, eds. Todd L. Savitt, and James H. Young. Knoxville: University of Tennessee Press, 1988.

6552. Savitt, Todd L., and James H. Young, eds. *Southern Disease and Southern Distinctiveness*. Knoxville: University of Tennessee Press, 1988.

6553. Schaffer, M. A., and Lia Hoagberg. "Prenatal Care Among Low-income Women." *Families in Society* 75 (March 1994): 152-159.

6554. Schaffer, R. C. "The Health and Social Functions of Black Midwives on the Texas Brazos Bottom, 1920-1985." *Rural Sociology* 56 (Spring 1991): 89-105.

6555. Schilling, R. F. and others. "Developing Strategies for AIDS Prevention Research with Black and Hispanic Drug Users." *Public Health Reports* 104 (1989): 2-11.

6556. Schlesinger, Mark, and Karl Kornebusch. "The Failure of Prenatal Care Policy for the Poor." *Health Affairs* 9 (Winter 1990): 91-111. [Medicaid]

6557. Schmidt, William E. "Lead Paint Poisons Children Despite 1971 Law on Removal." *New York Times*, 26 August 1990.

6558. Schneider, Keith. "1950 Memo Shows Worries Over Human Radiation Tests." *New York Times*, 28 December 1993.

6559. _____. "Nuclear Scientists Irradiated People In Secret Research." *New York Times*, 17 December 1993.

6560. Schneider, Ketih. "Scientists Are Sharing the Anguish Over Nuclear Experiments on People." *New York Times*, 2 March 1994.

6561. _____. "A Valley of Death for the Navajo Uranium Mines." *New York Times*, 3 May 1993.

6562. Scutt, J. A. "When Is a Women's Body Not Her Own: According to Law, When She's Pregnant." *Issues in Reproductive and Genetic Engineering* 5 (1992): 39-66.

6563. Seccombe, K. and others. "Discrepancies in Employer- sponsored Health Insurance among Hispanics, Blacks, and Whites: The Effects of Sociodemographic and Employment Factors." *Inquiry* 31 (Summer 1994): 221-229.

6564. Selik, R. M. and others. "Racial/Ethnic Differences in the Risk of AIDS in the United States." *American Journal of Public Health* 78 (1988): 1539-1577.

6565. Serafica, Felicisima and others, eds. *Mental Health of Ethnic Minorities*. Westport, CT: Praeger, 1990.

6566. Shapiro, R. S. "Medical Discrimination against Children with Disabilities: A Report of the United States Commission on Civil Rights." *Issues in Law and Medicine* 6 (Winter 1990).

6567. Shapiro, Robert and others. "The Polls: Medical Care in the United States." *Public Opinion Quarterly* 50 (1986): 418-428.

6568. Shea, S. and others. "Predisposing Factors for Severe, Uncontrolled Hypertension in an Inner-city Minority Population." *New England Journal of Medicine* 327 (1992): 776-781.

6569. Shipp, E. R. "For the Sickest Patients, an Ailing Hospital." *New York Times*, 7 April 1991. [Harlem Hospital Center, New York City]

6570. Shipp, E. R., and Mireya Navarro. "Reluctantly, Black Churches Confront AIDS." *New York Times*, 18 November 1991.

6571. Shotland, Jeffrey and others. *Full Fields, Empty Cupboards: The Nutritional Status of Migrant Farmworkers in America*. Washington, DC: Public Voice for Food and Health Policy, April 1989.

6572. Shuit, Douglas P. "Black, Poor Medicare Patients Get Worse Care." *Los Angeles Times*, 20 April 1994. [CA, PA, TX, FL, IN]

6573. _____. "Disparity in Elderly Health Care Reported." *Los Angeles Times*, 18 March 1994. [Disparities in Los Angeles County's hospitals between admissions of "rich and poor, rural and urban, and among black, Latino, and white populations" on Medicare.]

6574. _____. "Minority Doctors Skeptical of Health Reforms." *Los Angeles Times*, 1 June 1993.

6575. _____. "Poor Unlikely to Sue for Malpractice, Study Finds." *Los Angeles Times*, 13 October 1993.

6576. Shuptrine, S. C., and V. C. Grant. *Study of the AFDC- Medicaid Eligibility Process in the Southern States*. Washington, DC: Southern Governors' Association, Southern Regional Project on Infant Mortality, April 1990.

6577. Sikes, Lewright. "Medical Care for Slaves: A Preview of the Welfare State." *Georgia Historical Quarterly* 62, no. 4 (1968): 405-413.

6578. Silverman, E. R. "Study Finds Gender Disparities in Pay for Medical Researchers." *The Scientist* 8 (24 January 1994): 21.

6579. Simson, Sharon P., and Laura B. Wilson, eds. "Planning and Evaluating Minority Health Programs for the Future." *Evaluation and Program Planning* 14 (1991): 209-262. 6 articles.

6580. Singer, Merrill and others. "SIDA: The Economic, Social and Cultural Context of AIDS Among Latinos." *Medical Anthropology Quarterly* 4 (March 1990).

6581. Sipchen, Bob. "Fighting It Out on Skid Row." *Los Angeles Times*, 29 November 1992. [Alcohol in the life of an American Indian]

6582. Skidmore, Max J. "Ronald Reagan and 'Operation Coffeecup': A Hidden Episode in American Political History." *Journal of American Culture* 12 (1989): 89-96. [Campaign against health care program through social security]

6583. Smith, D. B. "The Racial Integration of Health Facilities." *Journal of Health Politics, Policy, and Law* 18 (Winter 1993): 851-870.

6584. Smith, G. D., and M. Egger. "Socioeconomic Differences in Mortality in Britain and the United States." *American Journal of Public Health* 82 (1992): 1079-1081.

6585. Smith, Patricia. "Voices of the Endangered American Black Male." *Boston Globe*, 4 September 1991.

6586. Smith, S. J. "Race and Racism: Health, Welfare, and the Quality of Life." *Urban Geography* 11 (November-December 1990): 606-616.

6587. Smith, Susan Lynn. *"Sick and Tired of Being Sick and Tired": Black Women and the National Negro Health Movement, 1915- 1950.* Ph.D. diss., University of Wisconsin, 1991.

6588. _____. "White Nurses, Black Midwives, and Public Health in Mississippi, 1920-1950." *Nursing History Review* 2 (1994): 29- 50.

6589. Snider, Dixie E., Jr. and others. "Tuberculosis and Migrant Farm Workers." *Journal of the American Medical Association* 265 (3 April 1991): 1732.

6590. Solinger, Regina A. *"Wake Up Little Susie": Single Pregnancy and Race in the Pre-Roe v. Wade Era, 1945-1965.* Ph.D. diss., CUNY, 1991. UMO #9130374.

6591. Solinger, Rickie [Regina A.]. *Wake Up Little Susie. Single Pregnancy and Race Before Roe V. Wade.* New York: Routledge, 1992.

6592. Sorlie, P. and others. "Black-White Mortality Differences by Family Income." *Lancet* 340 (1992): 346-350.

6593. Soucie, J. M. and others. "Race and Sex Discrimination in the Identification of Candidates for Renal Transplantation." *American Journal of Kidney Diseases* 19 (1992): 414-419.

6594. Spackman, D. G. "Health Care in the 90's: Making the System Work for All of Us." *Boston Bar Journal* 32 (Nov.-Dec. 1988).

6595. Specter, Michael. "Neglected for Years, TB Is Back With Strains That Are Deadlier." *New York Times*, 11 October 1992. [New York City and elsewhere in the U.S.]

6596. Spector, Paul. "Failure by the Numbers." *New York Times*, 24 September 1994. [Lag by U.S. in international comparisons of health status]

6597. Spiegel, Claire. "Uninsured Children Pay Price." *Los Angeles Times*, 23 June 1992.

6598. Spigner, Clarence. "Health, Race, and Academia in America: Survival of the Fittest?" *International Quarterly of Community Health Education* 11 (1990-91): 63-78.

6599. Sprafka, J. Michael and others. "Type A Behavior and Its Association with Cardiovascular Disease Prevalence in Blacks and Whites: The Minnesota Heart Survey." *Journal of Behavioral Medicine* 13 (February 1990).

6600. Stannard, David E. "Recounting the Fables of Savagery: Native Infanticide and the Functions of Political Myth." *Journal of American Studies* 25 (December 1991): 381-417.

6601. Staples, Clifford L. "The Politics of Employment-based [Health] Insurance in the United States." *International Journal of Health Services* 19 (1989).

6602. Starr, Paul. "Health Care for the Poor: The Past Twenty Years." in *Fighting Poverty*, pp. 106-132. eds. Sheldon H. Danzion, and Daniel H. Weinberg. Harvard University Press, 1986.

6603. Stein, Charles, and Howard Manly. "Hospital Layoffs Hit Blacks Hard." *Boston Globe*, 31 July 1994. [Massachusetts]

6604. Stolberg, Sheryl. "Fatalismo Toward Cancer." *Los Angeles Times*, 26 December 1992.

6605. _____. "Health Study Ranks Latinos Above Anglos." *Los Angeles Times*, 24 November 1993.

6606. _____. "Study Ranks Latinos Last in Health Coverage." *Los Angeles Times*, 17 February 1993.

6607. _____. "Taking It To the Streets." *Los Angeles Times Magazine* (24 October 1993). [Near TB epidemic in Los Angeles]

6608. Stout, Hilary. "Life Expectancy of U.S. Blacks Declined in 1988." *Wall Street Journal*, 9 April 1991.

6609. Strogatz, D. S. "Use of Medical Care for Chest Pain: Differences between Blacks and Whites." *American Journal of Public Health* 80 (1990): 290-294.

6610. Strong, P. M. "Black on Class and Mortality: Theory, Method, and History." *Journal of Public Health Medicine* 12 (1990): 168-180.

6611. "Study Reveals Gaps in Dental Care for Youths." *Los Angeles Times*, 27 November 1993. [1991-1992 study of 2,872 Oregon children ages 3 to 12]

6612. Sullivan, Deborah A. "Conventional Wisdom Challenged: Trends in the Infant Mortality of Minority Groups in Arizona, 1976-1986." *Research in the Sociology of Health Care* 8 (1989): 197-204.

6613. Sullivan, Louis W. "Special Report: The Status of Blacks in Medicine: Philosophical and Ethical Dilemmas for the 1980's." *New England Journal of Medicine* 309 (1983): 807-808.

6614. Susser, Mervyn. "Health as a Human Right: An Epidemiologist's Perspective on the Public Health." *American Journal of Public Health* 83 (1993): 418-426.

6615. Sutch, Richard. "The Care and Feeding of Slaves." in *Reckoning With Slavery*, pp. 231-301. eds. Paul A. David and others. New York, 1976.

6616. Syme, S. Leonard. "Social Determinants of Disease." in *Maxcy-Rosenau-Last Public Health and Preventive Medicine*, pp. 687-700. eds. Jonathan M. Last, and Robert B. Wallace. 13th ed. Appleton and Lange, 1992.

6617. Syme, S. Leonard, and L. F. Berkman. "Social Class, Susceptibility and Sickness." *American Journal of Epidemiology* 104 (1976): 1-8.

6618. Szaz, Andrew. "Industrial Resistance to Occupational Safety and Health Legislation, 1971-81." *Social Problems* 32 (1984).

6619. Thomas, James D. "Health Care of American Gypsies: Social and Medical Aspects." *Gypsy Lore Society of North America Papers of Annual Meeting* (1988): 128-138.

6620. Thomas, Stephen B. "Community Health Advocacy for Racial and Ethnic Minorities in the United States: Issues and Challenges for Health Education." *Health Education Quarterly* 17 (Spring 1990).

6621. Thomas, Stephen B., and S. C. Quinn. "The Tuskegee Syphilis Study, 1932 to 1972: Implications for HIV Education and AIDS Risk Education Programs in the Black Community." *American Journal of Public Health* 81 (November 1991): 1498-1505.

6622. Thornton, Russell. *American Indian Holocaust and Survival: A Population History since 1492.* Norman: University of Oklahoma Press, 1987.

6623. Townsend, P. and others. *Inequalities in Health.* New York: Penguin, 1990.

6624. *Trends in Infant Mortality by Cause of Death and Other Characteristics 1960-1988.* U.S. Public Health Service, 1993.

6625. Tresserras, R. and others. "Infant Mortality, Per Capita Income, and Adult Illiteracy: An Ecological Approach." *American Journal of Public Health* 82 (March 1992): 435-437.

6626. *Two Americas: Racial Differences in the U.S. 1993.* Center on Hunger, Poverty, and Nutrition Policy, Tufts University School of Nutrition, 11 Curtis Ave., Medford, MA 02155,

6627. *The Undeclared Women's Health Crisis in New York City.* New York: Public Interest Health Consortium for New York City, May 1990.

6628. "Uninsured Patients in Hospitals Are Found Far More Likely to Die." *New York Times*, 16 January 1991.

6629. U.S. Congress, 101st, 2nd session, House of Representatives, Committee on Energy and Commerce, Subcommittee on Health and the Environment. *Health Status and Needs of Minorities in the 1990's: Hearing.* Washington, DC: GPO, 1990.

6630. U.S. Congress, 101st, 2nd session, House of Representatives, Committee on the Budget, Task Force on Human Resources. *Health Care Crisis: Problems of Cost and Access for Children of Color: Hearing.* Washington, DC: GPO, 1991. [Los Angeles County, CA]

6631. U.S. Congress, 102nd, 1st session, House of Representatives, Committee on Agriculture, Subcommittee on Domestic Marketing, Consumer Relations, and Nutrition. *Hunger in America, Its Effects on Children and Families, and Implications for the Future: Hearing.* Washington, DC: GPO, 1991.

6632. U.S. Congress, 101st, 2nd session, House of Representatives, Committee on Ways and Means, Subcommittee on Human Resources. *Impact of Crack Cocaine on the Child Welfare System: Hearing*. Washington, DC: GPO, 1990.

6633. U.S. Congress, 102nd, 1st session, House of Representatives, Select Committee on Hunger. *Mississippi Revisited: Poverty and Hunger Problems and Prospects: Hearing*. Washington, DC: GPO, 1991.

6634. U.S. Congress, 101st, 2nd session, Senate, Select Committee on Indian Affairs. *Urban Indian Health Equity Bill. Hearing...* Washington, DC: GPO, 1990.

6635. U.S. Department of Agriculture. *Family Food Assistance Programs: Racial Ethnic Household Participation,July 1987*. Washington, DC: Food and Nutrition Service, Program Information Division, Data Base Monitoring Branch, 20 May 1988.

6636. U.S. Department of Health and Human Services. *Health Status of Minorities and Low-Income Groups*, 3rd ed. GPO, 1991.

6637. U.S. Department of Health and Human Services, Public Health Service. *Healthy People 2000: National Health Promotion and Disease Prevention Objectives*. Washington, DC: GPO, 1990.

6638. U.S. Department of Agriculture. *Special Supplemental Food Program for Women, Infants and Children (WIC): Racial Participation*. Washington, DC: Food and Nutrition Service, Program Information Division, Data Base Monitoring Branch, June 1988.

6639. U.S. Public Health Service. *Current Estimates from the National Health Interview Survey, 1990*. Public Health Service, Hyattsville, MD 20782,

6640. _____. *Health, United States, 1990*. Public Health Service, Hyattsville, MD 20782, [Health of minorities]

6641. Valdez, R. Burciaga, and G. Dallek. *Does the Health Care System Serve Black and Latino Communities in Los Angeles County?* Claremont, CA: Tomas Rivera Center, 1991.

6642. Velez-i, Carlos G. "The Nonconsenting Sterilization of Mexican Women in Los Angeles." in *Mexican American Women: Twice a Minority*, pp. 235-248. ed. Margarita B. Melville. St. Louis, MO: C.V. Mosby, 1980.

6643. Verbrugge, L. "Gender and Health: An Update on Hypotheses and Evidence." *Journal of Health and Behavior* 26 (1985): 156-182.

6644. Vobejda, Barbara. "Civil Rights Groups Protest Lack of Racial Data on Medical Form." *Washington Post*, 14 March 1994.

6645. Wagener, D. K., and D. W. Winn. "Injuries in Working Populations: Black-White Differences." *American Journal of Public Health* 81 (November 1991): 1408-1414.

6646. Wagner, Marsden G. "Infant Mortality in Europe: Implications for the United States." *Journal of Public Health Policy* 9 (Winter 1988): 473-484.

6647. Wagstaff, A. and others. "On the Measurement of Inequalities in Health." *Social Science and Medicine* 33 (1991): 545-557.

6648. Waitzman, N. J., and K. R. Smith. "The Effects of Occupational Class Transitions on Hypertension: Racial Disparities among Working-age Men." *American Journal of Public Health* 84 (June 1994): 945-950.

6649. Waldmann, R. J. "Income Distribution and Infant Mortality." *Quarterly Journal of Economics* 107 (November 1992).

6650. Wallace, D. "Roots of Increased Health Care Inequality in New York." *Social Science and Medicine* 31 (1990).

6651. Wallace, R., and M. T. Fullilove. "AIDS Deaths in the Bronx 1983-1988: Spatiotemporal Analysis from a Sociogeographic Perspective." *Environment and Planning A* 23 (December 1991).

6652. Wallace, S. P. "The Political Economy of Health Care for Elderly Blacks." *International Journal of Health Services* 20 (1990).

6653. Warner, David. *The Health of Mexican-Americans in South Texas*. Austin: Lyndon B. Johnson School of Public Affairs, University of Texas, 1979.

6654. Watson, Sidney D. "Reinvigorating Title VI: Defending Health Care Discrimination: It Shouldn't Be So Easy." *Fordham Law Review* 58 (April 1990): 939-978.

6655. Watts, Thomas D., and Roosevelt Wright, Jr. *Alcoholism in Minority Populations*. Springfield, IL: Charles C. Thomas, 1989.

6656. Weaver, Jerry L., and Sharon D. Garrett. "Sexism and Racism in the American Health Industry: A Comparative Analysis." *International Journal of Health Services* 8 (1978): 677-703.

6657. Weeks, John R., and Ruben G. Rumbaut. "Infant Mortality among Ethnic Immigrant Groups." *Social Science and Medicine* 33 (1991): 327-334. [San Diego area]

6658. Wegner, Eldon L., ed. "The Health of Native Hawaiians: A Selective Report on Health Status and Health Care in the 1980's." *Social Process in Hawaii* 32 (1989): entire issue.

6659. Wells-Stevens, Lyndee. "Health Care for Indigent American Indians." *Arizona State Law Journal* 20 (Winter 1988): 1105-1148.

6660. "White Men Score Highest on Medical Licensing Test." *Boston Globe*, 7 September 1994.

6661. White-Means, Shelley I., and Michael C. Thornton. "Nonemergency Visits to Hospital Emergency Rooms: A Comparison of Blacks and Whites." *Milbank Quarterly* 67 (1989).

6662. Whitman, Steve, and Vicki Legion. "Black Health in Critical Condition." *Guardian (NYC)* (20 February 1991).

6663. Whitten, David O. "Medical Care of Slaves: Louisiana Sugar Region and South Carolina Rice District." *Southern Studies* 16, no. 4 (1977): 153-180.

6664. Whittle, Jeff and others. "Racial Differences In the Use of Invasive Cardiovascular Procedures in the Department of Veterans Affairs Medical System." *New England Journal of Medicine* 329 (26 August 1993): 621-627.

6665. *WIC: A Success Story*. Washington, DC: Food Research and Action Center, January 1991.

6666. Wielawski, Irene. "Health Systems in Bind on Care for Illegal Immigrants." *Los Angeles Times*, 31 August 1993. [California]

6667. Wilcox, C. "Race, Religion, Region and Abortion Attitudes." *Sociological Analysis* 53 (Spring 1992): 97-106.

6668. Wilkerson, Isabel. "Blacks Assail Ethics in Medical Testing." *New York Times*, 3 June 1991.

6669. Wilkinson, R. G., ed. *Class and Health: Research and Longitudinal Data*. Tavistock, 1986.

6670. Wilkinson, R. G. "Income Distribution and Mortality: A 'Natural' Experiment." *Sociology of Health and Illness* 12 (1990): 391-412.

6671. Williams, David R. "The Concept of Race in Health Services Research, 1966 to 1990." *Health Services Research* 29 (August 1994): 261-274.

6672. _____. "Socioeconomic Differentials in Health: A Review and Redirection." *Social Psychology Quarterly* 53 (1990): 81-99.

6673. Williams, David R. and others. "Socioeconomic Status and Psychiatric Disorder among Blacks and Whites." *Social Forces* 71 (September 1992): 179-194.

6674. Williams, Terry. *The Cocaine Kids. The Inside Story of a Teenage Drug Ring*. Reading, MA: Addison-Wesley, 1989. [Spanish Harlem]

6675. Willis, David P. *Currents of Health Policy-Impacts on Black Americans. Health Policies and Black Americans*. New Brunswick, NJ: 1989,

6676. Wilson, L. B., and S. P. Simson. "Planning Minority Health Programs to Eliminate Health Status Disparity." *Evaluation and Program Planning* 14 (1991): 211-220.

6677. Wilson, Phill. "The Black Community Is Just Feeling Overwhelmed." *Los Angeles Times*, 22 November 1993. [AIDS]

6678. Wing, S. and others. "Socioenvironmental Characteristics Associated with the Onset of Decline of Ischemic Heart Disease Mortality in the United States." *American Journal of Public Health* 78 (1988): 923-926.

6679. Wingard, D. "the Sex Differential in Morbidity, Mortality, and Lifestyle." *Annual Review of Public Health* 5 (1988): 533-558.

6680. Winkler, A. M. "Drinking on the American Frontier." *Quarterly Journal of Studies on Alcohol* 29 (1968): 413-445.

6681. Wise, P. "Infant Mortality in the U.S." *Science for the People* 16 (March-April 1984): 23-26.

6682. Wishner, A. R. "Interpersonal Violence-related Injuries in an African-American Community in Philadelphia." *American Journal of Public Health* 81 (November 1991): 1474-1476.

6683. Wolinsky, Fredric D. and others. "Ethnic Differences in the Demand for Physician and Hospital Utilization among Older Adults in Major American Cities: Conspicuous Evidence of Considerable Inequalities." *Milbank Quarterly* 67 (1989).

6684. Woolhandler, Steffie, and D. U. Himmelstein. "Ideology in Medical Science: Class in the Clinic." *Social Science and Medicine* 28 (1989): 1205-1209.

6685. Worth, D. "Minority Women and AIDS: Culture, Race, and Gender." in *Culture and AIDS*, pp. 111-136. ed. D. A. Feldman. New York: Praeger, 1990.

6686. Wright, J. D. "Poor People, Poor Health: The Health Status of the Homeless." *Journal of Social Issues* 46 (Winter 1990): 49- 64.

6687. Yang, B. "The Economy and Suicide: A Time-Series Study of the USA." *American Journal of Economics and Sociology* 51 (January 1992).

6688. Yankauer, A. "What Infant Mortality Tells Us." *American Journal of Public Health* 80 (June 1990).

6689. Young, A. "Why the United States Does Not Have a National Health Program: The Medical-Industry Complex and Its PAC Contributions to Congressional Candidates, January 1, 1981, Through June 30, 1991." *International Journal of Health Services* 22, no. 4 (1992): 619-644.

6690. Young, Peter S. "Moving to Compensate Families in Human- Organ Market." *New York Times*, 8 July 1994.

6691. Young, Rosalie F. and others. "The Ethnic-Socioeconomic Confound in Health Sociology: Empirical Validation and Theoretical Perspective." *Sociological Abstracts.* [Original paper available from Sociological Abstracts 90S24626/ISA/1990/7557]

6692. Young, T. Kue. *The Health of Native Americans. Toward a Biocultural Epidemiology*. Oxford University Press, 1993.

6693. Young, Thomas J. "Native American Firewater Myth." *Corrective and Social Psychiatr;* 35 (April 1989).

6694. Zane, Nolan and others, eds. *Confronting Critical Health Issues of Asian and Pacific Islander Americans*. Sage, 1993.

6695. Zavaleta, Antonio N. "Federal Assistance and Mexican American Health Status in Texas." *Agenda* 11 (January-February 1981): 19-25.

6696. Zill, Nicholas, and Charlotte A. Schoenborn. *Developmental, Learning, and Emotional Problems. Health of Our Nation's Children, United States, 1988. Advance Data, No. 190*. Hyattsville, MD: National Center for Health Statistics, 1990.

6697. Zubrow, E. "The Depopulation of Native America." *Antiquity* 64 (December 1990): 754-765.

HISTORY

6698. Acuña, Rodolfo F. *A Community Under Siege: A Chronicle of Chicanos East of the Los Angeles River, 1945-1975.* Los Angeles, CA: Chicano Studies Research Center, University of California, 1984.

6699. Allen, Ernest, Jr. "The New Negro: Explorations in Identity and Social Conciousness, 1910-1922." in *1915, The Cultural Moment*, eds. Adele Heller, and Lois Rudnick. Rutgers, University Press, 1991.

6700. Allen, G. E. "Eugenics and American Social History, 1880- 1950." *Genome* 31 (1989): 885-889.

6701. Almaguer, Tomas. *Interpreting Chicano History: The World- System Approach to 19th Century California.* Berkeley: Institute for the Study of Social Change, University of California, 1977.

6702. Alvarez, Rodolfo. "The Psycho-historical and Socioeconomic Development of the Chicano Community in the United States." *Social Science Quarterly* 53 (March 1973): 920-942.

6703. Amott, Teresa, and Julie Matthaei. *Race, Gender, and Work: A Multi-Cultural History of Women in the U.S.* Boston, MA: South End Press, 1990.

6704. Anderson, Eric, and Alfred A. Moss, Jr., eds. *The Facts of Reconstruction. Essays in Honor of John Hope Franklin.* Baton Rouge: Louisiana State University Press, 1991.

6705. Anderson, Gary Clayton. *Kinsmen of Another Kind: Dakota- White Relations in the Upper-Mississippi Valley, 1650-1862.* Lincoln: University of Nebraska Press, 1984. [Southern Minnesota]

6706. Anderson-Cordova, Karen F. *Hispaniola and Puerto Rico: Indian Acculturation and Heterogeneity, 1492-1550.* Ph.D. diss., Yale University, 1990. UMO #9122259.

6707. Anderson, William L., ed. *Cherokee Removal. Before and After.* University of Georgia Press, 1992.

6708. Applebome, Peter. "A Sweetness Tempers South's Bitter Past." *New York Times*, 31 July 1994.

6709. _____. "Symbols of Old Confederacy Bring Divisions in New South." *New York Times*, 27 January 1993.

6710. Asante, Molefi K., and Mark T. Mattson. *Historical and Cultural Atlas of African Americans.* New York: Macmillan, 1990.

6711. Axtell, James L. *The European and the Indian: Essays in the Ethnohistory of Colonial North America.* New York: Oxford University Press, 1981.

6712. _____. *The Indian Peoples of Eastern America: A Documentary History of the Sexes.* New York: Oxford University Press, 1981.

6713. _____. *The Invasion Within: The Contest of Cultures in Colonial North America.* New York: 1985.

6714. Ayers, Edward L. *The Promise of the New South. Life After Reconstruction*. Oxford University Press, 1992.

6715. Bailey, Garrick, and Roberta G. Bailey. *A History of the Navajos: The Reservation Years*. Seattle: University of Washington Press, 1986. [Since 1868]

6716. Bailey, M. Thomas. *Reconstruction in Indian Territory: A Story of Avarice, Discrimination and Opportunism*. Port Washington, NY: Kennikat Press, 1972.

6717. Barreiro, Jose, ed. *Indian Roots of American Democracy*. Akwe: Kon Press, 1992.

6718. Beeson, Margaret and others. *Memories for Tomorow: Mexican- American Recollections of Yesteryear. Memorias para manana: nuestra herencia mexicana*. Detroit, MI: Ethridge, 1983. [Kansas]

6719. Berlin, Ira and others, eds. *Free At Last. A Documentary History of Slavery, Freedom, and the Civil War*. The New Press, 1992.

6720. _____. *Freedom: A Documentary History of Emancipation, 1861-1867*, Series 1, vol. 3. New York: Cambridge University Press, 1991.

6721. Berlin, Ira. "The Revolution in Black Life." in *The American Revolution*, pp. 349-382. ed. A. F. Young. De Kalb, IL: Northern Illinois University Press, 1976.

6722. Bernhard, Virginia and others, eds. *Hidden Histories of Women in the New South*. University of Missouri Press, 1994.

6723. Bernstein, Alison R. *American Indians and World War II: Toward a New Era in Indian Affairs*. University of Oklahoma Press, 1991.

6724. Bidney, D. "The Idea of the Savage in North American Ethno- history." *Journal of the History of Ideas* 15 (1954): 322-327.

6725. Biolsi, Thomas. *Organizing the Lakota: The Political Economy of the New Deal on the Pine Ridge and Rosebud Reservations*. University of Arizona Press, 1992.

6726. Blauner, Bob. *Black Lives, White Lives. Three Decades of Race Relations in America*. Berkeley: University of California Press, 1989. [1967, 1978, 1986]

6727. Blick, Jeffrey P. "English Expansion and Militarism versus Indian Resistance: Genocide, Racial Separatism and the Reservation System in Virginia (1607-1646)." *Archaeological Society of Virginia Quarterly Bulletin* 42 (1987): 28-36.

6728. Blight, David W. *Frederick Douglass' Civil War. Keeping Faith in Jubilee*. Baton Rouge: Louisiana State University Press, 1989.

6729. Boender, Debra R. *Our Fires Have Nearly Gone Out: A History of Indian-White Relations on the Colonial Maryland Frontier, 1633-1776*. Ph.D. diss., University of New Mexico, 1988. UMO #8911524.

6730. Boissevain, Ethel. "The Detribalization of the Narragansett Indians: A Case Study." *Ethnohistory* 3 (1956): 225-245. [In 1880]

6731. Bonnett, Aubrey W., and G. Llewellyn Watson, eds. *Emerging Perspectives on the Black Diaspora*. Lanham, MD: University Press of America, 1990.

6732. Brasseaux, Carl A. *Acadian to Cajun: Transformation of a People, 1803-1877*. University Press of Mississippi, 1993.

6733. Brenner, Elise M. "To Pray or to be Prey: That is the Question: Strategies for Cultural Autonomy of Masschusetts Town Indians." *Ethnohistory* 27 (1980): 135-152.

6734. Broder, David S. "History by Disney." *Washington Post*, 24 November 1993.

6735. Brown, James A. "America Before Columbia." in *Indians in American History*, pp. 19-45. ed. Frederick E. Hoxie. Arlington Heights, IL: Harlan Davidson, Inc., 1988.

6736. Brown, Philip M. "Early Indian Trade in the Development of South Carolina: Politics, Economics, and Social Mobility during the Proprietary Period, 1670-1719." *South Carolina History Magazine* 76 (1975): 118-128.

6737. Buffinton, Arthur H. "New England and the Western Fur Trade, 1629-1675." *Publications of the Colonial Study of Massachusetts, Transactions* 18 (1915-1916): 160-192.

6738. Buitrago Ortiz, Carlos. *Los origenes historicos de la sociedad precapitalista en Puerto Rico*. Rio Piedras: Hucacan, 1976.

6739. Bullard, Robert D., ed. *In Search of the New South: The Black Urban Experience in the 1970s and 1980s*. Tuscaloosa: University of Alabama Press, 1989.

6740. Burch, Sallie. "Scholars Outline Racism in Constitutional History." *Black Issues in Higher Education* 5 (15 April 1988): 16.

6741. Bynum, Victoria E. *Unruly Women. The Politics of Social and Sexual Control in the Old South*. University of North Carolina Press, 1992.

6742. Caldwell, Joe Louis. *A Social, Economic, and Political Study of Blacks in the Louisiana Delta, 1865-1880*. Ph.D. diss., Tulane University, 1989. UMO #9008725.

6743. Calloway, Colin G. "The Inter-tribal Balance of Power on the Great Plains." *Journal of American Studies* 16 (April 1982): 25-47.

6744. Calloway, Colin G., ed. *The World Turned Upside Down. Indian Voices from Early America*. St. Martin's Press, 1994.

6745. Camarillo, Albert. *Chicanos in California: A History of Mexican Americans in California*. San Francisco, CA: Boyd and Fraser, 1984.

6746. Campbell, Edward D. C. Jr, and Kym S. Rice, eds. *Before Freedom Came. African-American Life in the Antebellum South*. Charlottesville: University Press of Virginia, 1991.

6747. Carlson, Alvar W. *The Spanish-American Homeland. Four Centuries in New Mexico's Rio Arriba*. Baltimore, MD: Johns Hopkins University Press, 1990.

6748. Carrion, Arturo with others. *Puerto Rico: A Political and Cultural History*. New York: Norton, 1983.

6749. Celis, William, 3rd. "In Truth, Hispanic Groups Aim to Rewrite History." *New York Times*, 13 July 1991.

6750. Chavez, John R. *The Lost Land: The Chicano Image of the Southwest*. Albuquerque: University of New Mexico Press, 1984.

6751. Cheek, W. F. *Black Resistance before the Civil War*. Beverly Hills, CA: Glencoe Press, 1970.

6752. Chung, Sue F. "The Chinese American Citizens Alliance: An Effort in Assimilation, 1895-1965." *Chinese America: History and Perspectives* (1988): 30-57.

6753. Churchill, Ward. "Ehrenreich and Indians." *Z Magazine* 3 (November 1990): 5. [Criticism of Barbara Ehrenreich's portrayal of Indian life and history]

6754. _____. "An Unwhite Tourist's Guide to the Rocky Mountain West." *Z Magazine* 3 (September 1990): 91-98.

6755. Clayton, James L. "The Growth and Economic Significance of the Fur Trade, 1790-1890." *Minnesota History* 40 (Winter 1966): 210-220.

6756. Clines, Francis X. "The Pequots." *New York Times Magazine* (27 February 1994).

6757. Cohen, William. *At Freedom's Edge. Black Mobility and the Southern White Quest for Racial Control 1861-1915*. Baton Rouge: Louisiana State University Press, 1991.

6758. Cole, Thomas R. "Generational Equity in America: A Cultural Historian's Perspective." *Social Science and Medicine* 29 (1989): 377-383.

6759. Collier, Eugenia. "Paradox in Paradise: The Black Image in Revolutionary America." *Black Scholar* 21 (Fall 1991): 2-9.

6760. Collins, Patricia H. "Feminism in the Twentieth Century." *Black Women in America*, Vol. I, pp. 418-425.

6761. "Confederate Legacy: Reverence or Racism?" *Washington Post*, 2 August 1993. six letters. [Senate disapproval of the insignia of the United Daughters of the Confederacy]

6762. Cornell, Stephen. "Crisis and Response in Indian-White Relations: 1960-1984." *Social Problems* 32 (October 1984): 44-59.

6763. _____. "Land, Labor, and Group Formation: Blacks and Indians in the United States." *Ethnic and Racial Studies* 13 (July 1990): 368-388.

6764. Corrin, Lisa G. "Do Museums Perpetuate Cultural Bias?" *Chronicle of Higher Education* (15 June 1994).

6765. Couto, Richard A. *Lifting the Veil: A Political History of Struggle for Emancipation*. University of Tennessee Press, 1993.

6766. Covington, James W. "Florida Seminoles: 1900-1920." *Florida Historical Quarterly* 53 (1974): 181-197.

6767. Cox, Lawanda. "Lincoln and Black Freedom." in *The Historian's Lincoln: Pseudohistory, Psychohistory, and History*, ed. Gabor S. Boritt. Urbana: University of Illinois Press, 1988. [See, also, comments by Stephen B. Oates and Armstead L. Robinson, following Cox's essay.]

6768. Crosby, Alfred W., Jr. *The Columbian Exchange: Biological and Cultural Consequences of 1492*. Westport, CT, 1972.

6769. Crow, Jeffrey J. and others, eds. *Race, Class, and Politics in Southern History. Essays in Honor of Robert F. Durden*. Baton Rouge: Louisiana State University, 1990.

6770. Cutter, Charles R. *The Protector de Indios in Colonial New Mexico, 1659-1821*. Albuquerque: University of New Mexico Press, 1986.

6771. De Graaf, Lawrence B. "Recognition, Racism, and Reflections on the Writing of Western Black History." *Pacific Historical Review* 44 (1975): 22-51.

6772. De Nevi, Donald P., and Doris A. Holmes, eds. *Racism at the Turn of the Century*. San Rafael, CA: Leswing Press, 1973.

6773. Deconde, Alexander. "Endearment or Antipathy? Nineteenth Century American Attitudes towards Italians." *Ethnic Groups* 4 (1982): 131-148.

6774. Delage, Denys. *Bitter Feast: Amerindians and Europeans in Northeastern North America, 1600-64*. University of British Columbia Press, 1993. Translated by Jane Brierley.

6775. Denevan, William, ed. *The Native Population of the Americas in 1492*, 2nd ed. Madison: University of Wisconsin Press, 1992.

6776. Detweiler, Philip F. "The Changing Reputation of the Declaration of Independence: The First Fifty Years." *William and Mary Quarterly* 19 (1962): 557-574.

6777. Devens, Carol. *Countering Colonialization. Native American Women and Great Lakes Missions, 1630-1900*. University of California Press, 1992.

6778. Deverell, William, and Tom Sitton, eds. *California Progressivism Revisited*. University of California Press, 1994.

6779. Dietz, James L. *Economic History of Puerto Rico. Institutional Change and Capitalist Development*. Princeton, NJ: Princeton University Press, 1987.

6780. Dowd, Gregory E. *A Spirited Resistance. The North American Indian Struggle for Unity, 1745-1815*. Johns Hopkins, University Press, 1991.

6781. Doyle, Don H. *New Men, New Cities, New South: Atlanta, Nashville, Charleston, Mobile, 1860-1910*. Chapel Hill: University of North Carolina Press, 1990.

6782. Drake, St. Clair. *Black Folk Here and There*, vol. 1. Los Angeles: Center for Afro-American Studies, University of California, Los Angeles, 1987.

6783. Drinnon, Richard. *Facing West. The Metaphysics of Indian- Hating and Empire-Building*. Minneapolis: University of Minnesota Press, 1980.

6784. Du Bois, Ellen C., and Vicki L. Ruiz, eds. *Unequal Sisters: A Multicultural Reader in U.S. Women's History*, 2nd ed. Routledge, 1994.

6785. Du Bois, W. E. B. "Reconstruction and Its Benefits." *American Historical Review* 15 (July 1910): 781-799.

6786. Du Chateau, Andre P. "The Creek Nation on the Eve of the Civil War." *Chronicles of Oklahoma* 52 (1974): 290-315.

6787. Duany, Jorge. "Ethnicity in the Spanish Caribbean: Notes on the Consolidation of Creole Identity in Cuba and Puerto Rico, 1762-1868." *Ethnic Groups* 6 (1985): 99-124.

6788. Dunlap, David W. "A Black Cemetery Takes Its Place in History." *New York Times*, 28 February 1993. ["Negros Burial Ground" in Manhattan]

6789. Dysart, Jane E. "Another Road to Disappearance: Assimilation of Creek Indians in Pensacola, Florida during the Nineteenth Century." *Florida Historical Quarterly* 61 (July 1982): 37-48.

6790. Eckholm, Erik. "The Native-and Not So Native-American." *New York Times Magazine* (27 February 1994).

6791. Edmunds, R. David. "National Expansion from the Indian Perspective." in *Indians in American History*, pp. 159-177. ed. Frederick E. Hoxie. Arlington Heights, IL: Harlan Davidson, Inc., 1988.

6792. Elkins, Stanley M. "Racial Inferiority as the Basic Assumption." in *Ulrich Bonnell Phillips: A Southern Historian and His Critics*, eds. John David Smith, and John C. Inscoe. Westport, CT: Greenwood, 1990.

6793. Ellis, Rex M. *Presenting the Past: Education, Interpretation and the Teaching of Black History at Colonial Williamsburg*. Ph.D. diss., College of William and Mary, 1989. UMO #8923055.

6794. Engerman, Stanley L. "Toward an Explanation for the Persistence of the Myth of Black Incompetence." in *Ulrich Bonnell Phillips: A Southern Historian and His Critics*, eds. John David Smith, and John C. Inscoe. Westport, CT: Greenwood, 1990.

6795. Esper, Mark. "Tears from Wounded Knee Flow for 100 Years." *Guardian* (26 December 1990).

6796. Estrada, Leobadro F. and others. "Chicanos in the United States: A History of Exploitation and Resistance." *Daedalus* 110 (Spring 1981): 103-131.

6797. Evans, Arthur S. "The Relationship between Industrialization and White Hostility toward Blacks in Southern Cities: 1865-1910." *Urban Affairs Quarterly* 25 (1989): 322-341.

6798. Evans, David L. "Racism Resurges When Black History Isn't Learned." *Sacramento Bee*, 7 December 1988.

6799. Fabre, Genevieve, and Robert O'Meally, eds. *History and Memory in African American Culture*. Oxford University Press, 1994.

6800. Finkelman, Paul R., ed. *His Soul Goes Marching On. Responses to John Brown and Harpers Ferry Raid*. University Press of Virginia, 1994.

6801. Fitzgerald, Michael W. *The Union League Movement in the Deep South: Politics and Agricultural Change During Reconstruction*. Baton Rouge: Louisiana State University Press, 1989.

6802. Fleming, John E. "History and the Black Community." in *The State of Afro-American History: Past, Present, and Future*, ed. Darlene Clark Hine. Baton Rouge: Louisiana State University Press, 1989.

6803. Foner, Eric. "'40 Acres' Promise to Blacks Was Broken." *New York Times*, 25 October 1994. Letter.

6804. _____. "Time for a Third Reconstruction." *Nation* (1 February 1993).

6805. Foret, Michael J. *On the Marchlands of Empire: Trade, Diplomacy, and War on the Southeastern Frontier, 1733-1763*. Ph.D. diss., College of William and Mary, 1990. [Indians and Europeans]. UMO #9110050.

6806. Foster, Morris W. *"Being Comanche": The Organization and Maintenance of an American Indian Community, 1700-1986*. Ph.D. diss., Yale University, 1988. UMO #9009449.

6807. Frankel, Noralee, and Nancy S. Dye, eds. *Women in History. Gender, Class, Race, and Reform in the Progressive Era*. University Press of Kentucky, 1992.

6808. Franklin, John Hope. "African Americans and the Bill of Rights in the Slave Era." in *Crucible of Liberty*, ed. Raymond Arsenault. Free Press, 1991.

6809. _____. *The Color Line. Legacy for the Twenty-First Century*. University of Missouri Press, 1993.

6810. _____. *Race and History. Selected Essays, 1938-1988*. Baton Rouge: Louisiana State University Press, 1990.

6811. Frantz, Ronald W. "The Concept of Civilization as Enunciated by the United States Government's Indian Policy, 1824- 1876." Master's thesis, State University College, Brockport, 1985.

6812. Freeman, James M. *Hearts of Sorrow. Vietnamese-American Lives*. Stanford, CA: Stanford University Press, 1990.

6813. Frey, Sylvia R. *Water from the Rock. Black Resistance in a Revolutionary Age*. Princeton, NJ: Princeton University Press, 1991. [American Revolution]

6814. Garcia, Mario T. *Mexican Americans. Leadership, Ideology, and Identity, 1930-1960*. New Haven, CT: Yale Univeristy Press, 1989.

6815. Gilman, Rhoda R. "The Fur Trade in the Upper Mississippi Valley, 1630-1850." *Wisconsin Magazine of History* 58 (1974): 2- 18.

6816. Glasrud, Bruce A. "Enforcing White Supremacy in Texas, 1900-1910." *Red River Valley Historical Review* 4 (1979): 65-74.

6817. Goldfield, David R. *Black, White, and Southern. Race Relations and Southern Culture, 1940 to the Present*. Baton Rouge: Louisiana State University Press, 1990.

6818. Goldstein, Marcy G. *Americanization and Mexicanization: The Mexican Elite and Anglo-Americans in the Gadsden Purchase Lands, 1853-1880*. Ph.D. diss., Case Western Reserve University, 1977.

6819. Goodman, Ellen. "Voices of the Past." *Boston Globe*, 22 September 1991. [Social attitudes in century-old Pictorial History of the United States by James D. McCabe]

6820. Gotanda, N. "Origins of Racial Categorization in Colonial Virginia, 1619-1705." Master's thesis, Harvard Law School, 1980.

6821. Grimsley, Kristin D. "History Lesson for Macy's." *Washington Post*, 11 February 1994. [Black memorabilia]

6822. Grinde, Donald A., Jr. *The Iroquois and the Founding of the American Nation*. San Francisco, CA: Indian Historical Press, 1977.

6823. Griswold del Castillo, Richard. *The Treaty of Guadalupe Hidalgo: A Legacy of Conflict*. Norman: University of Oklahoma Press, 1990.

6824. Gutierrez, Ramon. "Changing Ethnic and Class Boundaries in America's Hispanic Past." in *Social and Gender Boundaries in the United States*, ed. Sucheng Chan. Lewiston, NY: Edwin Mellen Press, 1989.

6825. Hagan, William T. "How the West Was Lost." in *Indians in American History*, pp. 179-202. ed. Frederick E. Hoxie. Arlington Heights, IL: Harlan Davidson, Inc., 1988.

6826. _____. "Kiowas, Comanches, and Cattlemen, 1867-1906: A Case Study of the Failure of U.S. Reservation Policy." *Pacific Historical Review* 40 (August 1971): 333-355.

6827. Hall, Gwendolyn M. *Africans in Colonial Louisiana. The Development of Afro-Creole Culture in the Eighteenth Century*. Louisiana State University Press, 1992.

6828. Hamanaka, Sheila. *The Journey: Japanese Americans, Racism, and Renewal*. New York: Orchard Books, 1990.

6829. Hamilton, Virginia. *Many Thousands Gone. African Americans From Slavery to Freedom*. Knopf, 1993. [Written for children 8 years and up]

6830. Harmon, George D. *Sixty Years of Indian Affairs, Political, Economic, and Diplomatic, 1789-1850*. Chapel Hill: University of North Carolina Press, 1941.

6831. Harris, Leonard. "Historical Subjects and Interests: Race, Class and Conflict." in *The Year Left 2: An American Socialist Yearbook*, pp. 90-105. eds. Mike Davis and others. Verso, 1987.

6832. Harris, R. L. "Ethnic Historical Societies and the Association for the Study of Afro-American Life and History." *Journal of American Ethnic History* 13 (Winter 1994): 53-58.

6833. Hauptman, Laurence M. *The Iroquois and the New Deal*. Syracuse, NY: Syracuse University Press, 1981.

6834. _____. *The Iroquois Struggle for Survival. World War II to Red Power*. Syracuse, NY: Syracuse University Press, 1985.

6835. Hauptman, Laurence M., and James D. Wherry, eds. *The Pequots in Southern New England: The Fall and Rise of an American Indian Nation*. Norman: University of Oklahoma Press, 1990.

6836. Helmbold, Lois R. "The Depression [of the 1930's]." *Black Women in America*, pp. Vol. I, 322-331.

6837. Higginbotham, A. Leon, Jr., and Laura B. Farmelo. "Racial Justice and the Priorities of American Leadership." in *Social Class and Democratic Leadership*, pp. 276-293. ed. Harold J. Bershady. Philadelphia, PA: University of Pennsylvania Press, 1989.

6838. Himes, Joseph S. "Black-White Relations in the United States Since World War II." in *Politics of Race. Comparative Studies*, pp. 71-93. ed. Donald G. Baker. Saxon House, D.C. Heath, 1975.

6839. Hinderaker, Eric A. *The Creation of the American Frontier: Europeans and Indians in the Ohio River Valley, 1673-1800*. Ph.D. diss., Harvard University, 1991. UMO #9211694.

6840. Hogan, Willliam R. *The Texas Republic: A Social and Economic History*. Austin: University of Texas Press, 1969.

6841. Holman, Charles F., III. "Racial, Religious Hate: Is It Growing?" *Human Rights* 15 (Fall 1988).

6842. Honour, Hugh. *The Image of the Black in Western Art*, Vol. IV: From the American Revolution to World War I. Cambridge, MA: Harvard University Press, 1989.

6843. Horne, Gerald, ed. *Thinking and Rethinking U.S. History*. New York: Council on Interracial Books for Children, 1988.

6844. Horsman, Reginald. *Expansion and American Indian Policy, 1783-1812*. East Lansing: Michigan State University Press, 1967.

6845. Horton, James O. "Blacks in History and Disney's America." *Washington Post*, 5 March 1994. ["Historians should be there when Disney or anyone else practices history"]

6846. Hoxie, Frederick E. *A Final Promise: The Campaign to Assimilate the Indians, 1880-1920*. Lincoln, NE: 1984.

6847. _____. "From Prison to Homeland: The Cheyenne River Indian Reservation before World War I." *South Dakota History* 10 (Winter 1979): 1-24.

6848. Hudson, Charles M., and Carmen C. Tesser, eds. *The Forgotten Centuries: Indians and Europeans in the American South, 1521- 1704*. University of Georgia Press, 1994.

6849. Huntzicker, William E. "The 'Sioux Outbreak' in the Illustrated Press." *South Dakota History* 20 (Winter 1990): 299- 322.

6850. Hurt, R. Douglas. *Indian Agriculture in America: Prehistory to the Present*. Lawrence: University of Kansas Press, 1988.

6851. Jackson, Walter A. *Gunnar Myrdal and America's Conscience: Social Engineering and Racial Liberalism, 1938-1987*. University of North Carolina Press, 1993.

6852. Jacobs, Donald M. *While the Cabots Talked to God: Racial Conflict in Antebellum Boston: The Black Struggle, 1825-1861*. New York: P. Lang, 1990.

6853. Jacobs, Wilbur R. "Unsavory Sidelights on the Colonial Fur Trade." *New York History* 34 (April 1953): 135-148.

6854. Jaffe, A. J. Sperber, Carolyn. *The First Immigrants from Asia. A Population History of the North American Indians*. Plenum, 1992.

6855. James, C. L. R. *American Civilization*. Blackwell, 1993.

6856. Jimenez de Wagenheim, Olga. *Puerto Rico's Revolt for Independence: El Grito de Lares*. Boulder, CO: Westview, 1984.

6857. Johansen, Bruce E. *Forgotten Founders: Benjamin Franklin, the Iroquois and the Rationale for the American Revolution*. Boston, MA: Harvard Common Press, 1987 (orig. 1982).

6858. _____. "Native American Societies and the Evolution of Democracy in America 1600-1800." *Ethnohistory* 37 (Summer 1990). [See rejoinder by E. Tooker following Johansen article]

6859. Johansen, Bruce E., and Donald A. Grinde, Jr. "The Debate Regarding Native American Precedents for Democracy: A Recent Historiography." *American Indian Culture and Research Journal* 14 (1990): 61-88.

6860. Jones, Carter. *"Hope for the Race of Man": Indians, Intellectuals and the Regeneration of Modern America, 1917-1934*. Ph.D. diss., Brown University, 1991. UMO #9204889.

6861. Jones, DeWitt G. *Wade Hampton and the Rhetoric of Race: A Study of the Speaking of Wade Hampton on the Race Issue in South Carolina, 1865-1878*. Ph.D. diss., Louisiana State University, 1988. UMO #8819950.

6862. Jones, Jacqueline. *The Dispossessed: America's Underclass from the Civil War to the Present*. New York: Basic Books, 1992.

6863. Jones, Norrece T., Jr. *Born a Child of Freedom, Yet a Slave. Mechanics of Control and Strategies of Resistance in Antebellum South Carolina*. Middletown, CT: Wesleyan University Press, 1991.

6864. Josephy, Alvin M., Jr. ed. *America in 1492. The World of the Indian Peoples Before the Arrival of Columbus*. Knopf, 1992.

6865. Josephy, Alvin M., Jr. *The Civil War in the American West*. New York: Knopf, 1991. [American Indians during the Civil War]

6866. _____. "Modern America and the Indian." in *Indians in American History*, pp. 255-272. ed. Frederick E. Hoxie. Arlington Heights, IL: Harlan Davidson, Inc., 1988.

6867. Karcher, Carolyn L. "Lydia Maria Child and the Example of John Brown." *Race Traitor* no. 1 (Winter 1993): 21-44.

6868. Kardulias, P. Nick. "Fur Production as a Specialized Activity in a World System: Indians in the North American Fur Trade." *American Indian Culture and Research Journal* 14 (1990): 25-60.

6869. Katz, Stephen T. "The Pequot War Reconsidered." *New England Quarterly* 64 (1991): 206-224.

6870. Kelsey, Harry. "European Impact on the California Indians, 1530-1830." *The Americas* 41 (April 1985): 494-511.

6871. Kennedy, Randall L. "Reconstruction and the Politics of Scholarship." *Yale Law Journal* 98 (January 1989): 521-540.

6872. Kilpatrick, Jack F., and Anna G. Kilpatrick. *Shadow of Sequoia: Social Documents of Cherokees, 1862-1964*. 1965.

6873. Klarman, M. J. "How Brown Changed Race Relations: The Backlash Thesis." *Journal of American History* 81 (June 1994): 81- 118.

6874. Klos, George E. "Black Seminoles in Territorial Florida." *S. Historian* 10 (Spring 1989): 26-42.

6875. _____. "Blacks and the Seminole Removal Debate, 1821- 1835." *Florida Historical Quarterly* 68 (July 1989): 55-78.

6876. Koehler, Lyle. *A Search for Power: The "Weaker Sex" in Seventeenth-Century New England*. Urbana: University of Illinois Press, 1980.

6877. Kolchin, Peter. "The Tragic Era? Interpreting Southern Reconstruction in Comparative Perspective." in *The Meaning of Freedom*, eds. Frank McGlynn, and Seymour Drescher. University of Pittsburgh Press, 1992.

6878. Koning, Hans. *The Conquest of America. How the Indian Nations Lost Their Continent*. Monthly Review Press, 1993.

6879. _____. "Don't Celebrate 1492-Mourn It." *New York Times*, 14 August 1990.

6880. Krupperman, Karen O. *Settling with the Indians: The Meeting of English and Indian Cultures in America, 1580-1640*. Totowa, New Jersey: Rowman and Littlefield, 1980.

6881. Lancaster, Jane F. *The First Decades: The Western Seminoles from Removal to Reconstruction, 1836-1866*. Ph.D. diss., Mississippi State University, 1986. UMO #8615795.

6882. _____. *Removal Aftershock: The Seminoles' Struggles to Survive in the West, 1836-1866*. University of Tennessee Press, 1994.

6883. Larson, Robert W. *New Mexico Population: A Study of Radical Protest in a Western Tradition*. Boulder: Colorado Associated University Press, 1974.

6884. Leacock, Eleanor B., and Nancy Lurie, eds. *North American Indians in Historical Perspective*. New York: Random House, 1971.

6885. Levi-Strauss, C. "Race and History." in *Race, Science and Society*, London: Allen and Unwin, 1975.

6886. Lewis, Earl. "African Americans and the Bill of Rights." *In These Times* (18 December 1991).

6887. Liggio, Leonard P. "English Origins of Early American Racism." *Radical History Review* 3 (1976).

6888. Limanni, Anthony M. "The Growth of the Yellow-Peril Myth. Anti-Japanese Propaganda in San Francisco and California, 1885- 1915." Master's thesis, University of New Hampshire, 1989.

6889. Limerick, Patricia N. *American Frontier and Western Issues: An Historiographical Review*. Westport, CT: Greenwood, 1986.

6890. _____. "The Case of Premature Departure: The Trans- Mississippi West and American History Textbooks." *Journal of American History* 78 (March 1992): 1380-1394.

6891. Link, Martin A. *Navajo: A Century of Progress 1868-1968*. Window Rock, Arizona: The Navajo Tribe, 1968.

6892. Long, Richard A. *Black Dance: The Black Tradition in American Modern Dance*. New York: Rizzoli, 1989.

6893. Lowe, R. "The Freedmen's Bureau and Local Black Leadership." *Journal of American History* 80 (December 1993): 989- 1030.

6894. Maciel, David R., and Patricia Bueno, eds. *Aztlan: historia del pueblo chicano*, 2 vols. Mexico: Sepsetema, 1975-1976.

6895. Mancall, Peter C. *Valley of Opportunity. Economic Culture along the Upper Susquehanna, 1700-1800*. Ithaca, NY: Cornell University Press, 1991.

6896. Marino, C. "The Aboriginal Population of North America, ca. 1492: A Summary of Estimates." *International Journal of Anthropology* 5 (1990): 347-358.

6897. Martin, Joel W. *Sacred Revolt. The Muskogees' Struggle for a New World*. Boston, MA: Beacon Press, 1991.

6898. Martin, Patricia Preciado. *Images and Conversations: Mexican Americans Recall a Southwestern Past*. Tucson: University of Arizona Press, 1983. [Arizona]

6899. Martinez, Elizabeth. "Histories of the 'Sixties': A Certain Absence of Color." *Social Justice* 16 (Winter 1989).

6900. Massey, James L., and Martha A. Myers. "Patterns of Repressive Social Control in Post-Reconstruction Georgia, 1882- 1935." *Social Forces* 68 (December 1989).

6901. Matthews, Fred H. "White Community and 'Yellow Peril'." *Mississippi Valley Historical Review* 50 (March 1964): 612-633.

6902. McDermott, John D. "Wounded Knee: Centennial Voices." *South Dakota History* 20 (Winter 1990): 245-298.

6903. McGinnis, Tony. "Economic Warfare on the Northern Plains." *Annals of Wyoming* 44 (1972): 57-71.

6904. McGuire, Randall H., and Robert Paynter, eds. *The Archeology of Inequality*. Cambridge, MA: Blackwell, 1991.

6905. McLoughlin, William G. *After the Trail of Tears: The Cherokees' Struggle for Sovereignty, 1839-1880*. University of North Carolina Press, 1993.

6906. _____. *Cherokee Renascence, 1794-1833*. Princeton, NJ: Princeton University Press, 1987.

6907. _____. "Who Civilized the Cherokees?" *Journal of Cherokee Studies* 13 (1988): 55-81.

6908. McLoughlin, William G., and Walter H. Conser, Jr. "The First Man Was Red-Cherokee Responses to the Debate over Indian Origins, 1760-1860." *American Quarterly* 41 (1989): 243-264.

6909. McNickle, D'Arcy. "Indian and European: Indian-White Relations from Discovery to 1887." *Annals of the American Academy of Political and Social Science* no. 311 (1957): 1-11.

6910. _____. *Native American Tribalism. Indian Survivals and Renewals*. New York: Oxford University Press, 1973.

6911. McWilliams, Carey, and Matt S. Meier. *North From Mexico. The Spanish-speaking People of the United States*, Updated ed. Westport, CT: Greenwood, 1990.

6912. Meier, Matt S., and Feliciano Rivera. *The Chicanos: A History of Mexican Americans*. New York: Hill and Wang, 1972.

6913. Meier, Matt S., and Feliciano Rivera. *Dictionary of Mexican American History*. Westport, CT: Greenwood, 1981.

6914. Meinig, D. W. *Southwest: Three Peoples in Geographical Change, 1600-1970*. New York: Oxford University Press, 1971.

6915. Melosh, Barbara, ed. *Gender and American History Since 1890*. Routledge, 1993.

6916. Menefee, Selden C., and O. C. Cassinore. *The Pecan Shellers of San Antonio: The Problem of Underpaid and Unemployed Mexican Labor*. Washington, DC: GPO, 1940.

6917. Merrell, James H. "'The Customes of Our Country': Indians and Colonists in Early America." in *Strangers within the Realm*, eds. Bernard Bailyn, and Philip D. Morgan. University of North Carolina Press, 1991.

6918. _____. *The Indians' New World. Catawbas and Their Neighbors from European Contact through the Era of Removal*. Chapel Hill: University of North Carolina Press, 1989.

6919. _____. "The Racial Education of the Catawba Indians." *Journal of Southern History* 50 (1984): 363-384.

6920. _____. "Some Thoughts on Colonial Historians and American Indians." *William and Mary Quarterly* 46 (January 1989): 94-119.

6921. Merwin, W. S. "The Sacred Bones of Maui." *New York Times Magazine* (6 August 1989).

6922. Meyer, Melissa L. *The White Earth Tragedy: Ethnicity and Dispossession at a Minnesota Anishinabe Reservation, 1889-1920*. University of Nebraska Press, 1994.

6923. Migliorino, Ellen G. "Blacks Debate Emigration Before the Civil War." *Storia Nordamericana* 3 (1986): 93-115.

6924. Miller, Joshua. *The Rise and Fall of Democracy in Early America, 1630-1789*. Penn State University Press, 1992.

6925. Miller, Margo. "Black History in a Doll Collection." *Boston Globe*, 22 February 1991. [Wenham Museum]

6926. Miller, Randall M., and George E. Pozzetta, eds. *Shades of the Sunbelt. Essays on Ethnicity, Race, and the Urban South*. Westport, CT: Greenwood, 1988.

6927. Mirande, Alfredo. *The Chicano Experience: An Alternative Perspective*. Notre Dame, IN: University of Notre Dame Press, 1985.

6928. Moneyhon, Carl H. *The Impact of the Civil War and Reconstruction on Arkansas: Persistence in the Midst of Ruin*. Louisiana State University Press, 1993.

6929. Montejano, David. *Anglos and Mexicans in the Making of Texas, 1836-1986*. Austin: University of Texas Press, 1987.

6930. _____. "The Demise of 'Jim Crow' for Texas Mexicans, 1940-1970." *Aztlan* 16 (1985): 27-69.

6931. Moore, William Haas. *Chiefs, Agents, and Soldiers: Conflict on the Navajo Frontier, 1866-1880*. Ph.D. diss., Northern Arizona University, 1988. UMO #8907815.

6932. Morales Cabrera, Pablo. *Puerto Rico Indigena: Prehistoria y Protohistoria de Puerto Rico; Descripcion de los Usos, Costumbres, Languaje, Religion, Gobierno, Etc. del Pueblo Taino de Borinquen*. Santurce, PR: Imprenta Venezula, 1932.

6933. Morgan, Philip D. "British Encounters with Africans and African Americans, circa 1600-1780." in *Strangers Within the Realm*, eds. Bernard Bailyn, and Philip D. Morgan. University of North Carolina Press, 1991.

6934. Morgenstern, Dan. "The Night Ragtime Came to Carnegie Hall." *New York Times*, 9 July 1989. [James Reese Europe, black musician and jazz pioneer.]

6935. Morrison, Kenneth M. "Native Americans and the American Revolution: Historic Stories and Shifting Frontier Conflict." in *Indians in American History*, pp. 95-115. ed. Frederick E. Hoxie. Arlington Heights, IL: Harlan Davidson, Inc., 1988.

6936. Mulkern, John R. *The Know-Nothing Party in Massachusetts: The Rise and Fall of a People's Party*. Boston, MA: Northeastern University Press, 1990. [1854]

6937. Muwakkil, Salim. "White Supremacy's Global Scope Probed." *In These Times* (24 October 1990). [First Annual Conference on Global White Supremacy convened by the Association of African Historians, Chicago]

6938. Nabokov, Peter, ed. *Native American Testimony: A Chronicle of Indian-White Relations from Prophecy to the Present, 1492- 1992*. New York: Viking, 1991.

6939. Nash, Gary B. *Race and Revolution*. Madison, WI: Madison House, 1990. [Racism in the North in the post-Revolutionary era]

6940. _____. "Social Development." in *Colonial British America*, pp. 233-261. eds. Jack P. Greene, and J. R. Pole. Baltimore, MD: Johns Hopkins University Press, 1984.

6941. Nash, Horace D. "Blacks in Arkansas during Reconstruction: The Ex-Slave Narratives." *Arkansas Historical Quarterly* 48 (Autumn 1989): 243-259.

6942. Nieman, Donald G. *Promises to Keep: African Americans and the Constitutional Order, 1776-1989*. New York: Oxford University Press, 1990.

6943. Nobile, Philip. "Uncovering Roots." *Village Voice* (23 February 1993). [Detailed critique of the factual basis of Alex Haley's *Roots*]

6944. Nostrand, Richard L. "The Hispano Homeland in 1900." *Annals of the Association of American Geographers* 70 (1980): 382-396.

6945. O'Malley, Michael. "Specie and Species: Race and the Money Question in Nineteenth-Century America." *American Historical Review* 99 (April 1994): 369-395. [See, also, O'Malley's "Response to Nell Irvin Painter's critique, pp. 405-408]

6946. O'Reilly, Richard. *El pueblo negro de Estados Unidos: raices historicas de su lucha actual*. Havana: Editorial de Ciencias Sociales, 1984.

6947. Ortiz, Alfonso. "Indian/White Relations: A View from the Other Side of the 'Frontier'." in *Indians in American History*, pp. 1-16. ed. Frederick E. Hoxie. Arlington Heights, IL: Harlan Davidson, Inc., 1988.

6948. Oswalt, Wendell H. *Bashful No Longer: An Alaskan Eskimo Ethnohistory, 1778-1988*. Norman: University of Oklahoma Press, 1990.

6949. Owsley, Beatrice R. *Hispanic Americans: An Oral History of the American Dream*. Twayne, 1992.

6950. Pahl, Jon. *Paradox Lost. Free Will and Political Liberty in American Culture, 1630-1760*. Johns Hopkins University Press, 1992.

6951. Painter, Nell Irvin. "Thinking about the Languages of Money and Race: A Response to Michael O'Malley, 'Specie and Species'." *American Historical Review* 99 (April 1994): 396-404. [See also "Response" by O'Malley, pp. 405-408]

6952. Paredes, Raymond. "The Origins of Anti-Mexican Sentiment in the United States." *New Scholar* 6 (1977): 139-166.

6953. Parman, Donald L. "Indians of the Modern West." in *the Twentieth-Century West: Historical Interpretations*, eds. Gerald D. Nash, and Richard W. Etulain. Albuquerque: University of New Mexico Press, 1989.

6954. Paust, Jordan J. "On Human Rights: The Use of Human Rights Precepts in U.S. History and the Right to an Effective Remedy in Domestic Courts." *Michigan Journal of International Law* 10 (Spring 1989): 543-652.

6955. Pearce, R. H. *The Savages of America: a Study of the Indian and the Idea of Civilization*. Baltimore, MD, 1953.

6956. Peck, Abraham J. "That Other 'Peculiar Institution': Jews and Judaism in the Nineteenth Century South." *Modern Judaism* 7 (1987): 99-114.

6957. Perdue, Theda. "Indians in Southern History." in *Indians in American History*, pp. 137-157. ed. Frederick E. Hoxie. Arlington Heights, IL: Harlan Davidson, Inc., 1988.

6958. _____. "Native American Revitalization Movements in the Early Nineteenth-Century." in *New Worlds? The Comparative History of New Zealand and the United States*, ed. Jock Philipps. Wellington, NZ: Stout Research Centre, 1989.

6959. Perez, Nelida, and Amilcar Tirado. *Boricuas en el Norte*. New York: Centro de Estudios Portorriquena, 1986.

6960. Perlmutter, Philip. "The American Struggle with Ethnic Superiority." *Journal of Intergroup Relations* 6 (1977): 31-56.

6961. _____. *Divided We Fall: A History of Ethnic, Religious, and Racial Prejudice in America*. Ames: Iowa State University Press, 1990.

6962. Perry, Richard J. *Apache Reservation: Indigenous Peoples and the American State*. University of Texas Press, 1993.

6963. Phillips, George H. "Indians and the Breakdown of the Spanish Mission System in California." *Ethnohistory* 21 (1974): 291-302.

6964. Philp, Kenneth R., ed. *Indian Self-Rule: First-Hand Accounts of Indian-White Relations from Roosevelt to Reagan*. Salt Lake City, Utah: Howe, 1986.

6965. Pitt, Leonard M. "The Foreign Miners' Tax of 1850: A Study of Nativism and Anti-Nativism in Gold Rush California." Master's thesis, University of California, Los Angeles, 1955.

6966. "Plan to Teach U.S. History Is Said to Slight White Males." *New York Times*, 26 October 1994.

6967. Pole, J. R. *The Pursuit of Equality in American History*, 2nd ed. University of California Press, 1993.

6968. Powell, Thomas R. *The Persistence of Racism in America*. University Press of America, 1992.

6969. Poyo, Gerald E., and Gilberto M. Hinojosa, eds. *Tejano Origins in Eighteenth-Century San Antonio*. Austin: University of Texas Press, 1991.

6970. Preiswerk, Roy, and Dominique Perrot. *Ethnocentrism and History. Africa, Asia, and Indian America in Western Textbooks*. New York: NOK Publishers International, 1978.

6971. Quinn, William W., Jr. "Public Ethnohistory? Or, Writing Tribal Histories at the Bureau of Indian Affairs." *Public Historian* 10 (Spring 1988): 71-76.

6972. Quintero Rivera, Angel G. "Background to the Emergence of Imperialist Capitalism in Puerto Rico." *Caribbean Studies* 13 (1973).

6973. Rabinowitz, Howard N. *The First New South, 1865-1920*. Arlington Heights, IL: Harlan Davidson, 1992.

6974. Ransom, Roger L. *Conflict and Compromise. The Political Economy of Slavery, Emancipation, and the American Civil War*. New York: Cambridge University Press, 1989.

6975. Reed, Gerard. "The Significance of the Indian in American History." *American Indian Culture and Research Journal* 8 (1984): 1-21.

6976. Reed, Harry. *Platform for Change: The Foundations of the Northern Free Black Community: 1775-1865*. Michigan State University Press, 1994. [Boston, New York City, and Philadelphia]

6977. Richter, Daniel K. *The Ordeal of the Longhouse. The Peoples of the Iroquois League in the Era of European Colonization*. University of North Carolina Press, 1994.

6978. Riding In, James T. *Keepers of Tirawahut's Covenant: The Development and Destruction of Pawnee Culture*. Ph.D. diss., UCLA, 1991. UMO #9205968.

6979. Ripley, C. Peter, ed. *The Black Abolitionist Papers*, 5 vols. Chapel Hill: University of North Carolina Press, 1992.

6980. Rise, Eric W. "Race, Rape, and Radicalism: The Case of the Martinsville Seven, 1949-1951." *Journal of Southern History* 58 (1992): 461-490.

6981. Rister, Carl C. *The Southwestern Frontier, 1865-1881*. Cleveland, Ohio: Clark, 1928.

6982. Roberts, H. W. "The Influence of the Relations between Groups upon the Inner Life of Groups, with Special Reference to Black and White in the Southern States of the United States during the Nineteenth Century." Master's thesis, London School of Economics, 1934.

6983. Robinson, Armstead L. "The Difference Freedom Made: The Emancipation of Afro-Americans." in *The State of Afro-American History: Past, Present, and Future*, ed. Darlene Clark Hine. Baton Rouge: Louisiana State University Press, 1989.

6984. Rodriguez, O. Jaime E., ed. *The Mexican and Mexican American Experience in the 19th Century*. Bilingual Review Press, 1989.

6985. Romo, Ricardo. *East Los Angeles: History of a Barrio*. Austin: University of Texas Press, 1983.

6986. _____. "Mexican Americans in the New West." in *The Twentieth-Century West: Historical Interpretation*, eds. Gerad D. Nash, and Richard W. Etulain. Albuquerque: University of New Mexico Press, 1989.

6987. Rubio, Phil. "Civil War Reenactments and Other Myths." *Race Traitor* no. 1 (Winter 1993): 88-103.

6988. Ruiz, Vicki L., and Ellen C. Du Bois, eds. *Unequal Sisters. A Multicultural Reader in U.S. Women's History*, 2nd ed. Routledge, 1994.

6989. Ryan, Dennis P. *Beyond the Ballot Box. A Social History of the Boston Irish, 1845-1917*. Amherst: University of Massachusetts Press, 1989.

6990. Salem, Dorothy C. "World War I." *Black Women in America*, pp. Vol. II, 1284-1290.

6991. Salstrom, Paul. *Appalachia's Path to Dependency: Rethinking a Region's Economic History, 1730-1940*. University Press of Kentucky, 1994.

6992. Sanchez, George J. *Becoming Mexican-American: Ethnicity and Acculturation in Chicano Los Angeles, 1900-1943*. Ph.D. diss., Stanford University, 1989. UMO #8925947.

6993. Satz, Ronald N. "The Cherokee Trail of Tears: A Sesquicentennial Perspective." *Georgia Historical Quarterly* 73 (1989): 431-466.

6994. Scheiber, Harry N. "Race, Radicalism, and Reform: Historical Perspective on the 1879 California Constitution." *Hastings Constitutional Law Quarterly* 17 (Fall 1989): 35-80.

6995. Schneider, W. "Race and Empire: The Rise of Popular Ethnography in the Late Nineteenth Century." *Journal of Popular Culture* 11 (Summer 1977): 98-109.

6996. Schrecker, Ellen. *The Age of McCarthyism: A Brief History with Documents*. Bedford Books, 1994.

6997. Schulman, Bruce J. *From Cotton Belt to Sunbelt. Federal Policy, Economic Development, and the Transformation of the South, 1938-1980*. New York: Oxford University Press, 1990.

6998. Schultz, Duane. *Over the Earth I Come. The Great Sioux Uprising of 1862*. New York: St. Martin's Press, 1992.

6999. Schwartz, Harry. *Edmund Ruffin: Classic Fire-eater and Proslavery Crusader.* 2 vols. Ph.D. diss., City University of New York, 1990. UMO #9020807.

7000. Schwartz, Harvey. "Era of Intolerance: The Tradition of Anti-Radical Nativism in America, 1875-1920." Master's thesis, University of Washington, 1966.

7001. Scott, Anne F. *Natural Allies: Women's Associations in American History*. University of Illinois Press, 1992.

7002. Shapiro, Andrew. *We're Number One! Where America Stands-and Falls-in the New World Order*. New York, 1992.

7003. Sheehan, Bernard W. "Indian-White Relations in Early America: A Review Essay." *William and Mary Quarterly* 26 (1969).

7004. Shenkman, Richard. *Legends, Lies and Cherished Myths of American History*. Boston, MA: Hall 1990.

7005. Shipek, Florence C. "California Indian Reaction to the Franciscans." *The Americas* 41 (April 1985): 480-493.

7006. Shipler, David K. "Jefferson Is America-And America Is Jefferson." *New York Times*, 12 April 1993. [Thomas Jefferson as racist]

7007. Sider, Gerald. *Lumbee Indian Histories. Race, Ethnicity, and Indian Identity in the Southern United States*. Cambridge University Press, 1993.

7008. Smith, John David, ed. *Anti-Black Thought 1863-1925. "The Negro Problem"*, 11 volumes. Garland, 1993.

7009. Snow, Dean R. *The Iroquois*. Blackwell, 1994.

7010. Sowell, Thomas. "Assumptions vs. History in Ethnic Education." *Teachers College Record* (Fall 1981).

7011. Spicer, Edward H. *Cycles of Conquest: The Impact of Spain, Mexico, and the United States on the Indians of the Southwest, 1533-1960*. Tucson: University of Arizona Press, 1962.

7012. Standing Bear, Luther. *My People, the Sioux*. Boston: Houghton Miffin, 1928.

7013. Starna, William A. "'Public Ethnohistory' and Native- American Communities: History or Administrative Genocide?" *Radical History Review* no. 53 (Spring 1992): 126-139.

7014. Steacy, Stephen. "The Chickasaw Nation on the Eve of the Civil War." *Chronicles of Oklahoma* 49 (1971): 51-74.

7015. Steele, Ian K. *Warpaths: Invasions of North America*. Oxford University Press, 1994. [1513-1765]

7016. Stewart, Kenneth L., and Arnoldo De Leon. *Not Room Enough: Mexicans, Anglos, and Socioeconomic Change in Texas, 1850-1900*. University of New Mexico Press, 1993.

7017. Takaki, Ronald T. *Iron Cages: Race and Culture in 19th Century America*. New York: Oxford University Press, 1990 (orig. 1979). [With new epilogue]

7018. _____. "Reflections on Racial Patterns in America: An Historical Perspective." in *Ethnicity and Public Policy*, pp. 10- 16. eds. W. A. Van Horne, and T. A. Tonneson. Madison: University of Wisconsin Press.

7019. Takaki, Ronald T. *Strangers From a Different Shore. A History of Asian Americans*. Boston, MA: Little, Brown, 1989.

7020. _____. "A Tale of Two Decades: Race and Class in the 1880's and the 1980's." in *Race in America*, eds. Herbert Hill, and James E. Jones, Jr. University of Wisconsin Press, 1993.

7021. Taulbert, Clifton L. *Once Upon a Time When We Were Colored*. Tulsa, OK: Council Oaks Books, 1990. [Segregation in the Deep South]

7022. Thelen, David and others. "Perspectives: The Strange Career of Jim Crow." *Journal of American History* 75 (December 1988): 841-868.

7023. Timmons, W. H. *El Paso: A Borderlands History*. El Paso: Texas Western Press, 1990.

7024. Tingley, D. F. *The Rise of Racialistic Thinking in the United States in the Nineteenth Century*. Ph.D. diss., University of Illinois, 1953.

7025. Todorov, Tzvetan. *The Conquest of America: The Question of the Other*. Translated by Richard Howard. New York: Harper and Row, 1984.

7026. Toll, Robert G. *Blacking Up: The Minstrel Show in Nineteenth Century America*. New York: 1974.

7027. Tooker, E. "The United States Constitution and the Iroquois League." *Ethnohistory* 35 (1988): 305-336.

7028. Townsend, Kenneth W. *At the Crossroads: Native Americans and World War II*. Ph.D. diss., University of North Carolina at Chapel Hill, 1991. UMO #9135325.

7029. Trefousse, Hans L. *Historical Dictionary of Reconstruction*. Westport, CT: Greenwood, 1991.

7030. Trenton, Patricia, and Patrick T. Houlihan. *Native Americans: Five Centuries of Changing Images*. New York: H.N. Abrams, 1989. [Indians in art]

7031. Trowe, Maggie. "Did Marx, Engels Support Radical Reconstruction?" *Militant* (21 March 1994).

7032. Twombly, Robert C., and Robert H. Moore. "Black Puritan: The Negro in Seventeenth-Century Massachusetts." in *Blacks in White America Before 1865*, ed. Robert V. Haynes. New York: McKay, 1972.

7033. Tyler, S. Lyman. *Two Worlds: The Indian Encounter with the European, 1492-1509*. University of Utah Press, 1988.

7034. Usner, Daniel H., Jr. *Indians, Settlers, and Slaves in a Frontier Exchange Economy: The Lower Mississippi Valley before 1783*. 1992.

7035. Vincent, Stephen A. *African-Americans in the Rural Midwest: The Origins and Evolution of Beech and Roberts Settlements, ca. 1760-1900*. Ph.D. diss., Brown University, 1991. UMIO #9204976.

7036. Vogel, Virgil J., ed. *This Country Was Ours. A Documentary History of the American Indian*. New York: Harper and Row, 1974.

7037. Vorenberg, Michael. "Abraham Lincoln and the Politics of Black Colonization." *Journal of the Abraham Lincoln Association* 14 (Summer 1993): 23-46.

7038. Walker, Clarence E. *Deromanticizing Black History. Critical Essays and Reappraisals*. Knoxville: University of Tennessee Press, 1991.

7039. Ward, Geoffrey C. and others. *The Civil War. An Illustrated History*. New York: Knopf, 1990.

7040. Warren, Hanna R. "Reconstruction in the Cherokee Nation." *Chronicles of Oklahoma* 45 (1967): 180-189.

7041. Weatherford, Jack. *Native Roots*. New York: Crown, 1992. [American Indian history]

7042. Weber, David J. "American Westward Expansion and the Breakdown of Relations Between 'pobladores' and 'indios barbaros' on Mexico's Far Narthern Frontier, 1821-1846." *New Mexico Historical Review* 56 (July 1981): 221-238.

7043. _____. *The Mexican Frontier, 1821-1846: The American Southwest Under Mexico*. Albuquerque: University of New Mexico Press, 1982.

7044. Weeks, Philip C. *Farewell, My Nation: The American Indian and the United States 1820-1890*. Arlington Heights, IL: Harlan Davidson, Inc., 1989.

7045. _____. *The United States and the Search for the Solution to the "Indian Question" in the Nineteenth Century*. Ph.D. diss., Case Western Reserve University, 1989. UMO #9004480.

7046. Weiss, Lawrence D. *The Development of Capitalism in the Navajo Nation: A Political-Economic History*. Minneapolis, MN: MEP Publications, 1984.

7047. _____. "Modes of Production and Primitive Accumulation- Spanish New Mexico, 1600-1800." *Southwest Economy and Society* 3 (Fall 1980): 30-54.

7048. White, Richard. "Race Relations in the American West." *American Quarterly* 38 (1986): 396-416.

7049. Williams, David. *The Georgia Gold Rush: Twenty-Niners, Cherokees, and Gold Fever*. University of South Carolina Press, 1993. [Discoverty of gold in Cherokee Georgia, 1829]

7050. Williams, Vernon J., Jr. *From a Caste to a Minority: Changing Attitudes of American Sociologists Toward Afro- Americans, 1896-1945*. Westport, CT: Greenwood, 1989.

7051. Wood, Peter H. "Changing Population of the Colonial South: An Overview by Race and Region, 1685-1790." in *Powhatan's Mantle: Indians in the Colonial Southeast*, pp. 35-103. eds. Peter H. Wood and others. Lincoln: University of Nebraska Press, 1989.

7052. Wood, Peter H. and others. *Powhatan's Mantle: Indians in the Colonial Southeast*. Lincoln: University of Nebraska Press, 1989.

7053. Woodman, Harold D. "The Economic and Social History of Blacks in the Post-Emancipation South." *Trends in History* 3 (Fall 1982): 37-56.

7054. Woodward, C. Vann. "Pests of the Lower South." *New York Times*, 15 November 1991. [Predecessors of David Duke in the South]

7055. Wright, Donald R. *African Americans in the Colonial Era: From African Origins Through the American Revolution*. Arlington Heights, IL: Harlan Davidson, 1989.

7056. Wright, Gavin. "Understanding the Gender Gap: A Review Article." *Journal of Economic Literature* 29 (September 1991): 1153-1163. [Claudia D. Goldin's Understanding the Gender Gap: An Economic History of American Women (1990)]

7057. Wright, Kathleen. *The Other Americans: Minorities in American History*. Greenwich, CT, 1969.

7058. Wright, Paul. "An Examination of Factors Influencing Black Fertility Decline in the Mississippi Delta, 1880-1930." *Social Biology* 36 (Fall-Winter 1989).

7059. Wunder, John R. *Retained by the People. A History of American Indians and the Bill of Rights*. Oxford University Press, 1993.

7060. Yee, Shirley J. *Black Women Abolitionists: A Study in Activism, 1828-1860*. University of Tennessee Press, 1992.

7061. Young, Mary E. "The Exercise of Sovereignty in Cherokee Georgia." *Journal of the Early Republic* 10 (Spring 1990): 43-63.

7062. Zophy, Angela H., ed. *Handbook of American Women's History*. New York: Garland, 1990.

HOUSING

7063. "Achieving Stability in Racially Integrated Neighborhoods." *Journal of Urban Affairs* 15 (1993): 115-72 (three articles).

7064. Alba, Richard D., and John R. Logan. "Assimilation and Stratification in the Home Ownership Patterns of Racial and Ethnic Groups." *International Migration Review* 26 (Winter 1992): 1314-1341.

7065. _____. "Variations on Two Themes: Racial and Ethnic Patterns in the Attainment of Suburban Residence." *Demography* 28 (August 1991).

7066. Allen, Francis A. "Remembering Shelley v. Kraemer: Of Public and Private Worlds." *Washington University Law Quarterly* 67 (Summer 1989): 709-735.

7067. Amin, Ruhul, and A. G. Marian. "Racial Differences in Housing: An Analysis of Trends and Differentials, 1960-1978." *Urban Affairs Quarterly* 22 (1987): 363-376.

7068. Anjomani, Ardeshir and others. "Racial Succession and Residential Mobility in Dallas-Fort Worth and San Antonio." *Journal of Urban Affairs* 14 (1992): 43-60.

7069. Aoki, Keith. "Fair Housing Amendments Act of 1988." *Harvard Civil Rights-Civil Liberties Law Review* 24 (Winter 1989): 249- 263.

7070. Apgar, William C., Jr. and others. *The State of the Nation's Housing 1989*. Cambridge, MA: Joint Center for Housing Studies, Harvard University, 1989.

7071. Balington, Charles. "Montgomery Housing Plan Stirs Battles." *Washington Post*, 6 July 1993. [Politics of affordable housing in Silver Spring, Montgomery County, MD]

7072. Bates, James. "Obstacle Course. Blacks Frequently Find Frustrating Roadblocks in Trying to Buy Houses." *Los Angeles Times*, 6 September 1992. [Los Angeles County]

7073. Baylor, Ronald H. "Roads to Racial Segregation: Atlanta in the Twentieth Century." *Journal of Urban History* 15 (November 1988): 3-21.

7074. _____. "Urban Renewal, Pubic Housing, and the Racial Shaping of Atlanta." *Journal of Public History* 1 (Autumn 1989): 419-439.

7075. Bearak, Barry. "A Turf War for Urban Squatters." *Los Angeles Times*, 27 February 1994. [New York City]

7076. Bellman, Richard F., and Richard Cohn. "Housing Discrimination." *Touro Law Review* 6 (Fall 1989): 137-158.

7077. Berger, Lawrence. "Inclusionary Zoning Devices as Takings: The Legacy of the Mount Laurel Cases." *Nebraska Law Review* 70 (Spring 1991): 186-228.

7078. Bickford, Adam, and Douglas S. Massey. "Segregation in the Second Ghetto: Racial and Ethnic Segregation in American Public Housing, 1977." *Social Forces* 69 (1991): 1011-1036.

7079. Bishop, Dorn. "Fair Housing and the Constitutionality of Governmental Measures Affecting Community Ethnicity." *University of Chicago Law Review* 55 (Fall 1988): 1229-1266.

7080. Blackmar, Elizabeth. *Manhattan for Rent, 1785-1850*. Ithaca, NY: Cornell University Press, 1989.

7081. Body-Gendrot, Sophie. "Luttes de classe et luttes ethnique dans le Lower East Side a Manhattan." *Revue Francaise de Science Politique* 32 (1982): 973-999.

7082. Bohland, James R. "Indian Residential Segregation in the Urban Southwest: 1970 and 1980." *Social Science Quarterly* 63 (1982): 749-761.

7083. Bradsher, Keith. "Minorities Get More Mortgages." *New York Times*, 29 July 1994. [1993 national data]

7084. _____. "U.S., Citing Loan Bias, Bars 4 S + L Charter Changes." *New York Times*, 19 February 1994. [New Jersey and Ohio]

7085. Bratt, Rachel G. and others, eds. *Critical Perspectives on Housing*. Philadelphia, PA: Temple University Press, 1986. See Chapter 18: "The Federal Government and Equal Housing Opportunity: A Continuing Failure"

7086. Bratt, Rachel G. *Rebuilding a Low-Income Housing Policy*. Philadelphia, PA: Temple University Press, 1989.

7087. Breg, Mary H. "Reports of Discrimination Against Black Renters on the Rise." *Los Angeles Times*, 5 December 1993. [Fair Housing Foundation, California]

7088. Breger, Joseph. "Settlement Reached in Suit On Segregation in Housing." *New York Times*, 29 September 1993. [Westchester County, NY]

7089. Brenner, Joel Glenn, and Liz Spayd. "Bankers Explain Roots of Bias." *Washington Post*, 8 June 1993. [Race and mortgage money]

7090. _____. "A Pattern of Bias in Mortgage Loans." *Washington Post*, 6 June 1993. [First of three articles in series, "Separate and Unequal. Racial Discrimination in Area Home Lending," Washington, D.C. area]

7091. Bristol, Katherine G. *Beyond the Pruitt-Igoe Myth: The Development of American High-rise Public Housing, 1850-1970*. Ph.D. diss., UC Berkeley, 1991. UMO #9228582.

7092. Bullard, Robert D. "Housing Problems and Prospects for Blacks in Houston." *Review of Black Political Economy* 19 (Winter- Spring 1991): 175-194.

7093. _____. "Housing Problems and Prospects in Contemporary Houston." in *Black Dixie*, eds. Howard Beeth, and Cary D. Wintz. Texas A + M Press, 1992.

7094. _____. "Persistent Barriers in Housing Black Americans." *Journal of Applied Social Sciences* 7 (Fall-Winter 1983): 19-31.

7095. Burt, Martha R. *Over the Edge. The Growth of Homelessness in the 1980's*. Urban Institute Press, 1992.

7096. Calmore, John O. "Fair Housing vs. Fair Housing: The Problems with Providing Increased Housing Opportunities Through Spatial Deconcentration." *Clearinghouse Review* 14 (1980).

7097. _____. "To Make Wrong Right: The Necessary and Proper Aspirations of Fair Housing." *State of Black America 1989*, pp. 77-109.

7098. Canellos, Peter S. "Public-housing Ruling Puts Spotlight on Suburbs." *Boston Globe*, 28 June 1989. [Government assisted housing units in Boston metropolitan area]

7099. Canellos, Peter S., and Steve Marantz. "2nd Mortgages Boost Profits, Complaints." *Boston Globe*, 24 December 1991. [High- interest mortgages at expense of minority and poor homeowners.]

7100. Canner, G. B. and others. "Race, Default Risk and Mortgage Lending: A Study of the FHA and Conventional Loan Markets." *Southern Economic Journal* 58 (July 1991): 249-262.

7101. Canner, G. B., and Stuart A. Gabriel. "Market Segmentation and Lender Specialization in the Primary and Secondary Mortgage Markets." *Housing Policy Debate* 3 (1992): 241-329.

7102. Chacon, Ramon D. "The Beginnings of Racial Segregation: The Chinese in West Fresno and Chinatown's Role as Red Light District, 1870s-1920s." *Southern California Quarterly* 70 (Winter 1988): 371-398.

7103. Chambers, Daniel N. *Race, Housing Prices, and the Dynamics of Chicago's Housing Market, 1975-1979.* Ph.D. diss., Syracuse University, 1989. UMO #9014069.

7104. _____. "The Racial Housing Price Differential and Racially Transitional Neighborhoods." *Journal of Urban Economics* 32 (September 1992).

7105. Chandler, Mittie O. "The Influence of Blacks in State and Local Fair Housing Policy Making." *Policy Studies Review* 9 (1990): 374-388.

7106. Claiborne, William. "Boston Skirts Crisis as Projects Integrate." *Washington Post*, 28 November 1992. [Public housing]

7107. Clark, Marjorie C. *Racial Residential Segregation: Tracking Three Decades in a Single City.* Ph.D. diss., University of North Texas, 1990. [Fort Worth, Texas]. UMO #9105014.

7108. Clark, W. A. V. "Residential Segregation in American Cities: A Review and Interpretation." *Population Research and Policy Review* 5 (1986): 95-127.

7109. _____. "Residential Segregation in American Cities: Common Ground and Differences in Interpretation." *Population Research and Policy Review* 8 (May 1989). [See also, G. Galster, below]

7110. _____. "Residential Preferences and Neighborhood Racial Segregation: A Test for the Schelling Segregation Model." *Demography* 28 (February 1991): 1-20.

7111. _____. "Residential Preferences and Residential Choices in a Multiethnic Context." *Demography* 29 (August 1992): 451-466.

7112. Clay, P. "Housing Opportunity: A Dream Deferred." in *The State of Black America*, pp. 73-84. National Urban League, 1990.

7113. Clements, Mark. "What Americans Say About the Homeless." *Parade* (9 January 1994).

7114. Cloud, Cathy, and George C. Galster. "What Do We Know About Racial Discrimination in Mortgage Markets." *Review of Black Political Economy* 22 (Summer 1993): 101-120.

7115. Coate, D., and J. Vanderhoff. "Race of the Homeowner and Appreciation of Single-family Homes in the United States." *Journal of Real Estate Finance and Economics* 7 (November 1993).

7116. Coates, Robert C. "Legal Rights of Homeless Americans." *University of San Francisco Law Review* 24 (Winter 1990): 297- 362.

7117. Cohen, Nadine. "'Fairness' Outweighs 'Choice' in Public Housing." *Boston Globe*, 21 October 1994. [Boston Housing Authority]

7118. Collier, Cheryl L. "Schools, Housing, and Segregation: An Examination of School Districts in Richland and Lexington Counties of South Carolina." Master's thesis, University of South Carolina, 1989.

7119. Comptroller General of the United States. *Substandard Indian Housing Increases Despite Federal Efforts: A Change is Needed.* Washington, DC: General Accounting Office, 1978.

7120. Cooper, Phillip J. "United States v. City of Parma, Ohio: Open Housing Conflict in a Cleveland Suburb." in *Hard Judicial Choices: Federal District Court Judges and State and Local Officials*, Oxford University Press, 1988.

7121. Coulibaly, M. "Racial and Income Segregation in Low-income Housing: 1934-1992." *Review of Radical Political Economics* 25 (September 1993).

7122. Coyle, Daniel. *Hardball. A Season in the Projects.* Putnam's, 1994. [1992 Little League season in Cabrini-Green, Chicago]

7123. Cromwell, Brian A. *Pro-Integrative Subsidies and their Effect on Housing Markets: Do They Work?* Federal Reserve Bank of Cleveland, 1990.

7124. Croutch, Albert. *Housing Migratory Agricultural Workers in California, 1913-1948.* San Francisco, CA: R + E Research Associates, 1975.

7125. Cubillos, Herminia L. "Fair Housing and Latinos." *La Raza Law Journal* 2 (Fall 1988): 49-61.

7126. Cushman, John H., Jr. "Clinton Proposes Tough New Rules on Bias by Banks." *New York Times,* 9 December 1993.

7127. _____. "Fed Assails Plan to Toughen Law on Bias in Bank Loans." *New York Times,* 11 December 1993. [Federal Reserve Board]

7128. _____. "Lending-Bias Rules Create Quandary for Banks." *New York Times,* 28 November 1993. [Shawmut National Corporation, a bank holding company]

7129. Dagodag, William T. "Spatial Capital and Public Policies: The Example of Mexican-American Housing." *Professional Geographer* 26 (August 1974): 262-269. [Fresno]

7130. Darden, Joe T. "Choosing Neighbors and Neighborhoods: The Role of Race in Preference." in *Divided Neighborhoods: Changing Patterns of Racial Segregation,* ed. Gary A. Tobin. Newbury Pary, CA: Sage, 1987.

7131. _____. "The Effect of World War I on Black Occupational and Residential Segregation: The Case of Pittsburgh." *Journal of Black Studies* 18 (March 1988): 297-312.

7132. _____. "The Residential Segregation of American Indians in Metropolitan Areas of Michigan." *Journal of Urban Affairs* 6 (Winter 1984): 29-38.

7133. De Parle, Jason. "Housing Secretary Carves Out Role As a Lonely Clarion Against Racism." *New York Times,* 8 July 1993. [Henry G. Cisneros]

7134. _____. "The Shacks Disappear, But the Poverty Lives On." *New York Times,* 10 March 1991. [Sugar Ditch, Tunica, MS]

7135. _____. "An Underground Railroad from Projects to Suburbs." *New York Times,* 1 December 1993. [Black tenants leave segregated public housing in big cities for non-segregated suburban housing]

7136. Dedman, Bill. "The Color of Money." *Atlanta Journal and Atlanta Constitution,* May 1-4, 1988. [Racially-discriminatory mortgage-lending practices in Atlanta, GA.]

7137. Denton, Nancy A., and Douglas S. Massey. "Racial Identity among Caribbean Hispanics: The Effect of Double Minority Status on Residential Segregation." *American Sociological Review* 54 (October 1989): 790-808.

7138. _____. "Residential Segregation of Blacks, Hispanics, and Asians by Socioeconomic Status and Generation." *Social Science Quarterly* 69 (December 1988).

7139. Derricotte, Cheryl P. "Life Ain't Been No Crystal Stair: The Impact of Gentrification on African-American Housing Market Participation in New York City, 1980-1987." Master's thesis, Cornell University, 1989.

7140. *Desegregating Cabrini Green.* Washington, DC: U.S. Commission on Civil Rights, 1988. [Chicago]

7141. Desena, J. N. "Local Gatekeeping Practices and Residential Segregation." *Sociological Inquiry* 64 (Summer 1994): 307-321.

7142. *Efforts to Promote Housing Integration in Atrium Village and the South Suburbs.* Washington, DC: U.S. Commission on Civil Rights, 1990. [Ill.]

7143. Enriquez, Sam, and Jesse Katz. "Quake Jolts Poor Onto the Streets." *Los Angeles Times,* 30 January 1994. [Los Angeles earthquake of January 17, 1994]

7144. Fairbanks, Robert B. *Making Better Citizens: Housing Reform and the Community Development Strategy in Cincinnati, 1890-1960.* Urbana: University of Illinois Press, 1988.

7145. Farley, J. E. "Black-White Housing Segregation in the City of St. Louis: A 1988 Update." *Urban Affairs Quarterly* 26 (March 1991): 416-441.

7146. _____. "Racial Housing Segregation in St. Louis, 1980- 1990: Comparing Block and Census Tract Levels." *Journal of Urban Affairs* 15 (1993): 515-528.

7147. Farley, Reynolds. "Residential Segregation of Social and Economic Groups among Blacks, 1970-1980." in *The Urban Underclass*, eds. Christopher Jencks, and Paul E. Peterson. Washington, DC: Brookings Institution, 1991.

7148. Farley, Reynolds, and W. H. Frey. "Changes in the Segregation of Whites from Blacks During the 1980's: Small Steps Toward a More Integrated Society." *American Sociological Review* 59 (February 1994): 23-45.

7149. Feins, Judith, and Rachel G. Bratt. "Barred in Boston: Racial Discrimination in Housing." *Journal of American Planning Association* 49 (1983): 344-355.

7150. Feldstein, Mark. "Hitting the Poor Where They Live." *Nation* (4 April 1994). [House insurance and redlining practices]

7151. Fried, Marc L. "Residential Segregation: Where Do We Draw the LIne? A View of United States v. Yonkers Board of Education and Democratic Theory." *Columbia Journal of Law and Social Problems* 23 (Fall 1990): 467-485.

7152. Fuerst, J. S., and Roy Petty. "Don't Blame Architect for High-Rise Project Problems." *In These Times* (20 June 1990). [Chicago]

7153. Fuller, Elizabeth. "The Mexican Housing Problem in Los Angeles." *Sociology and Social Research* 5 (November 1920): 1-11.

7154. Gabriel, Stuart A., and Stuart S. Rosenthal. "Credit Rationing, Race, and the Mortgage Market." *Journal of Urban Economics* 29 (May 1991): 371-379.

7155. Galster, George C. "Black Suburbanization: Has It Changed the Relative Location of Races?" *Urban Affairs Quarterly* 26 (June 1991): 621-628.

7156. _____. *The Great Misapprehension: Federal Fair Housing Policy in the 80's.* Cambridge, MA: MIT Center for Real Estate Development, 1988.

7157. _____. "Neighborhood Racial Change, Segregationist Sentiments, and Affirmative Marketing Policies." *Journal of Urban Economics* 27 (May 1990).

7158. _____. "Racial Steering by Real Estate Agents: Mechanics and Motives." *Review of Black Political Economy* 19 (Summer 1990): 39-63.

7159. _____. "Racial Steering in Urban Housing Markets: A Review of the Audit Evidence." *Review of Black Political Economy* 18 (Winter 1990): 105-129.

7160. _____. "Residential Segregation in American Cities: A Further Response." *Population Research and Policy Review* 8 (March 1989). [See above, W.A.V. Clark]

7161. _____. "A Theoretical Framework for Economically Analyzing Mortgage Lending Activity in Census Tracts-Response." *Urban Affairs Quarterly* 28 (September 1992): 146-155.

7162. _____. "White Flight from Racially Integrated Neighborhoods in the 1970's: The Cleveland Experience." *Urban Studies* 27 (June 1990).

7163. Galster, George C., and Mark Keeney. "Race, Residence, Discrimination, and Economic Opportunity." *Urban Affairs Quarterly* 24 (1988): 87-117.

7164. Gillmor, Dan, and Stephen K. Doig. "Segregation Forever?" *American Demographics* 14 (January 1991): 48-51.

7165. Glazer, Nathan. "A Tale of Two Cities." *New Republic* (2 August 1993). [Critical review of Douglas S. Massey and Nancy A. Denton, American Apartheid: Segregation and the Making of the Underclass, 1993]

7166. Goel, Ankur J. "Maintaining Integration against Minority Interests: An Anti-subjugation Theory for Equality in Housing." *Urban Lawyer* 22 (Summer 1990): 369-416.

7167. Goering, John, and M. Coulibaly. "Investigating Public Housing Segregation: Conceptual and Methodological Issues." *Urban Affairs Quarterly* 25 (1989): 265-297.

7168. Goode, Victor. "Integration Versus Integration: Race, Law and Economics in the Context of Housing Discrimination." *Thurgood Marshall Law Review* 11 (1986).

7169. Green, R. D., and Joseph P. Reidy. "Accumulation, Urban Segregation and the Black Role in the U.S. Economy: A Stylized History." *Review of Radical Political Economics* 24 (Summer 1992).

7170. Greene, Liz. "Beware the Silk Gloves." *Washington Post*, 29 June 1993. [Doing something about discrimination in lending for housing]

7171. Grigsby, J. Eugene, III. "The Rise and Decline of Black Neighborhoods in Los Angeles." *CAAS Report* 12 (Spring-Fall 1989): 16-17.

7172. Grigsby, J. Eugene, III, and Mary L. Hruby. "Recent Changes in the Housing Status of Blacks in Los Angeles." *Review of Black Political Economy* 19 (Winter-Spring 1991): 211-240.

7173. Grigsby, W. G. "Housing Finance and Subsidies in the United States." *Urban Studies* 27 (December 1990).

7174. Grunwald, Michael. "Race a Key Element in Vacancy Decision." *Boston Globe*, 17 September 1994. [Boston Housing Authority procedure to fill vacancies in public housing]

7175. Gugliotta, Guy. "Housing Still Separate, Unequal in East Texas." *Washington Post*, 7 March 1994. [Beaumont]

7176. Hakken, Jon. *Discrimination Against Chicanos in the Dallas Rental Housing Market: An Experimental Extension of the Housing Market Practices Survey*. Washington, DC: Office of Policy Development and Research, U.S. Dept. of Housing and Urban Development, August 1979.

7177. Harding, Sandra. "Housing Discrimination as a Basis for Interdistrict School Desegregation Remedies." *Yale Law Journal* 93 (1983).

7178. Harney, Kenneth R. "How to Spot Subtle Forms of Loan Discrimination." *Los Angeles Times*, 1 August 1993.

7179. Harris, R. "Working Class Home Ownership in the American Metropolis." *Journal of Urban History* 17 (November 1990).

7180. Hartnett, J. J. "Affordable Housing, Exclusionary Zoning, and American Apartheid: Using Title VIII to Foster Statewide Racial Integration." *New York University Law Review* 68 (April 1993): 89-135.

7181. Hawkins, Grover G. "The Constitutional Implications of Residential Segregation and School Segregation-To Boldly Go Where Few Courts Have Gone." *Howard Law Journal* 30 (1987): 773-798.

7182. Henneberger, Melinda. "A Yonkers Street Divides in Silence: Whites, Blacks, Distrust and Blame." *New York Times*, 15 October 1992.

7183. Hernandez, Efrain, Jr. "Public Housing Desegregation [in Boston] on Steady Course." *Boston Globe*, 23 December 1991.

7184. Hernandez, Peggy. "West Roxbury Largely White, But Says Bias Isn't the Reason." *Boston Globe*, 15 September 1989.

7185. Hewitt, William L. "So Few Undesirables: Race, Residence, and Occupation in Sioux City, 1890-1925." *Annals of Iowa* 50 (Fall 1989-Winter 1990): 158-179.

7186. Higginbotham, A. Leon, Jr. and others. "De Jure Housing Segregation in the United States and South Africa: The Difficult Pursuit for Racial Justice." *University of Illinois Law Review* (Fall 1990): 763-877.

7187. Hillburg, Bill. "Overcoming Housing Barriers." *Long Beach Press-Telegram*, 14 February 1993. [History of segregation of African Americans in Long Beach, CA]

7188. Hirsch, Arnold R. "With or Without Jim Crow: Black Residential Segregation in the United States." in *Urban Policy in Twentieth-Century America*, eds. Arnold R. Hirsch, and Raymond A. Mohl. Rutgers University Press, 1993.

7189. *Housing: Chicago Style*. Washington, DC: U.S. Commission on Civil Rights, 1982.

7190. Housing Opportunities Made Equal. *Racial Steering by Racial Sales Agents in Metropolitan Richmond*. Richmond, VA: HOPE, 1980.

7191. Howe, Peter J. "A Segregated City: The Rhetoric and the Reality in Boston." *Boston Globe*, 28 June 1989.

7192. _____. "Settlement of NAACP Housing Bias Suit Raises Hopes in City." *Boston Globe*, 8 October 1989. [Boston]

7193. Hughes, M. A., and J. F. Madden. "Residential Segregation and the Economic Status of Black Workers: New Evidence for an Old Debate." *Journal of Urban Economics* 29 (January 1991).

7194. Hula, R. C. "Racial Barriers to Credit: Comment, Response." *Urban Affairs Quarterly* 28 (September 1992): 141-145.

7195. Hundley, Kristen. "A Clash of Interests in Holyoke." *Boston Globe Magazine* (2 October 1983). [Puerto Ricans and housing in Holyoke, Massachusetts]

7196. *Issues in Housing Discrimination*, 2 vols. Washington, DC: U.S. Commission on Civil Rights, 1985.

7197. Jackson, Peter. "Paradoxes of Puerto Rican Segregation in New York." in *Ethnic Segregation in Cities*, pp. 109-126. eds. Ceri Peach and others. Athens: University of Georgia Press, 1981.

7198. James, Franklin J. and others. *Discrimination, Segregation, and Minority Housing Conditions in Sunbelt Cities: A Study of Denver, Houston, and Phoenix*. Center for Public-Private Sector Cooperation, Graduate School of Public Affairs, University of Colorado-Denver, 1983.

7199. Jencks, Christopher. *The Homeless*. Harvard University Press, 1994.

7200. Jencks, Christopher, and Susan E. Mayer. "Growing Up in Poor Neighborhoods: How Much Does It Matter?" *Science* 243 (1989): 1441-1443.

7201. _____. *Residential Segregation, Job Proximity, and Black Job Opportunities: The Empirical Status of the Spatial Mismatch Hypothesis*. Evanston, IL: Center for Urban Affairs and Policy Research, Northwestern University, 1989.

7202. _____. *The Social Consequences of Growing Up in a Poor Neighborhood: A Review*. Evanston, IL: Center for Urban Affairs and Policy Research, Northwestern University, 1989.

7203. Johnson, Dirk. "Two Families Cross Color Lines to the Real World." *New York Times*, 10 June 1989. [State-aided integrated housing in Ohio]

7204. Johnston, R. J. *Residential Segregation: The State and Constitutional Conflict in American Urban Areas*. London: Academic Press, 1984.

7205. Judd, Dennis R. "Segregation Forever?" *Nation* (9 December 1991).

7206. Julian, Elizabeth K., and Michael M. Daniel. "Separate and Unequal-The Root and Branch of Public Housing Segregation." *Clearinghouse Review* 23 (October 1989): 865-876.

7207. Kaestner, Robert, and Wendy Fleischer. "Income Inequality As An Indicator of Discrimination in Housing Markets." *Review of Black Political Economy* 21 (Fall 1992): 55-80.

7208. Kaine, Timothy M. "Housing Discrimination Law in Virginia." *Virginia Bar Association Journal* 16 (Spring 1990): 15.

7209. Keating, W. Dennis. *The Suburban Racial Dilemma: Housing and Neighborhoods*. Temple University Press, 1994.

7210. Kennedy, Shawn G. "Applications to Public Housing in New York City Reach Record High." *New York Times*, 27 December 1992.

7211. Kilgannon, James. "Ethnic Residential Segregation: The Case of Asian Indians in Chicago, 1980." Master's thesis, Kansas State University, Manhattan, 1988.

7212. Kramer, Edward G., and Kenneth J. Kowalski. "An Overview of Fair Housing Litigation (2 parts)." *Practical Real Estate Lawyer* 3 (January, March 1987): 11-26, 77-88.

7213. Kraul, Chris. "Inner-City Interest." *Los Angeles Times*, 19 August 1993. [Mortgage lenders to low-income neighborhoods in California]

7214. Krmence, A. *The Influence of Housing Market Structure on Racial Transition.* Ph.D. diss., Indiana University, 1983.

7215. Kudo, Susumu. *Effects of Residential Integration and Suburban Work Location on Economic Conditions of Central City Blacks: Chicago Case Study.* Ph.D. diss., University of Illinois at Chicago, 1991. UMO #9132296.

7216. Kushner, James A. *Apartheid in America: An Historical and Legal Analysis of Contemporary Racial Segregation in the United States.* Frederick, MD: Associated Faculty Press, 1980.

7217. _____. "The Fair Housing Amendments Act of 1988: The Second Generation of Fair Housing." *Vanderbilt Law Review* 42 (May 1989): 1049-1120.

7218. Lamar, Martha and others. "Mount Laurel at Work: Affordable Housing in New Jersey, 1983-1988." *Rutgers Law Review* 41 (Summer 1989): 1197-1277.

7219. Lang, Michael H. *Homelessness and Affluence: Structure and Paradox in the American Political Economy.* New York: Praeger, 1989.

7220. Lasch-Quinn, Elisabeth. *Black Neighbors: Race and the Limits of Reform in the American Settlement House Movement, 1890- 1945.* University of North Carolina Press, 1993.

7221. Lawrence, Curtis. "Rehab Gone Awry." *Chicago Reporter* 20 (December 1991). [Chicago]

7222. Lazere, Edward B. and others. *The Other Housing Crisis: Sheltering the Poor in Rural America.* Washington, DC: Center on Budget and Policy Priorities and Housing Assistance Council, December 1989.

7223. Leavitt, J. "Women Under Fire: Public Housing Activism in Los Angeles." *Frontiers* 13 (1993): 109-130.

7224. Lee, Barrett A. and others. "Racial Differences in Urban Neighboring." *Sociological Forum* 6 (September 1991): 525-550.

7225. Lee, Barrett A., and Peter B. Wood. "The Fate of Residential Integration in American Cities: Evidence From Racially Mixed Neighborhoods, 1970-1980." *Journal of Urban Affairs* 12 (1990): 425-436.

7226. Lee, Felicia R. "On a Harlem Block, Hope Is Swallowed by Decay." *New York Times*, 8 September 1994. 1st of three articles. [129th Street between Malcolm X Blvd. and Fifth Ave.]

7227. Leigh, Wilhelmina A. "Civil Rights Legislation and the Housing Status of Black Americans: An Overview." *Review of Black Political Economy* 19 (Winter-Spring 1991): 5-28.

7228. _____. "The Social Preference for Fair Housing: During the Civil Rights Movement and Since." *American Economic Review* 78 (1988): 156-162.

7229. _____. "Trends in the Housing Status of Black Americans Across Selected Metropolitan Areas." *Review of Black Political Economy* 19 (Winter-Spring 1991): 43-64.

7230. Leigh, Wilhelmina A., and M. O. Mitchell. "Public Housing and the Black Community." *Review of Black Political Economy* 17 (Fall 1988). [See comment by P. Thompson, same issue]

7231. Leigh, Wilhelmina A., and James B. Stewart, eds. *The Housing Status of Black Americans.* New Brunswick, NJ: Transaction, 1991.

7232. Leonard, Paul A. and others. *A Place to Call Home: The Crisis in Housing for the Poor.* Washington, DC: Center on Budget and Policy Priorities, 1989.

7233. Leonard, Paul A., and Edward B. Lazere. *A Place to Call Home: The Low Income Housing Crisis in 44 Major Metropolitan Areas.* Center on Budget and Policy Priorities, 1992.

7234. Leven, C. L., and M. E. Sykuta. "The Importance of Race in Home Mortgage Loan Approvals." *Urban Affairs Quarterly* 29 (March 1994): 479-495.

7235. Levine, Hillel, and Lawrence Harmon. *The Death of an American Jewish Community. A Tragedy of Good Intentions.* New York: Free Press, 1991. [Dorchester and Mattapan, Boston]

7236. Levitas, Michael. "Homelessness in America." *New York Times Magazine* (10 June 1990).

7237. Lewis, Diane E. "Isolation Greets Suburban Blacks." *Boston Globe*, 17 January 1988. [Boston area]

7238. Lewis, Diane E., and Tom Coakley. "Suburbia Remains Challenge for Blacks." *Boston Globe*, 30 September 1990. [Boston suburbs]

7239. Lief, B. J., and S. Goering. "The Cost of Housing Discrimination and Segregation: An Interdisciplinary Social Science Statement." *Urban Affairs Annual Review* 32 (1987).

7240. "Life in the Shelters." *Los Angeles Times*, 31 January 1994. Times poll. [After Northridge earthquake]

7241. Lo, Christina. "A Housing Study of Chinatown." Master's thesis, Columbia University, 1982.

7242. Lois, Dale J. "Racial Integration in Urban Public Housing: The Method Is Legal, the Time Has Come." *New York Law School Law Review* 34 (Summer 1989): 349-384.

7243. Long, J. E., and J. B. Caudill. "Racial Differences in Home Ownership and Housing Wealth, 1970-1986." *Economic Inquiry* 30 (January 1992): 83-100.

7244. Lopez, Manuel Mariano. "Patterns of Interethnic Residential Segregation in the Urban Southwest." *Social Science Quarterly* 62 (March 1981): 50-63.

7245. Mahoney, Martha. "Law and Racial Geography: Public Housing and the Economy in New Orleans." *Stanford Law Review* 42 (May 1990): 1251-1290.

7246. Marantz, Steve. "Minority Areas Shorted on Loans, BRA Study Says." *Boston Globe*, 20 December 1989. [Boston Redevelopment Authority study of discrimination against minority neighborhoods in bank lending for purchase of homes.]

7247. Marcum, John and others. "Residential Segregation by Race in Mississippi, 1980." *Sociological Spectrum* 8 (1988): 117-131.

7248. Marcuse, Peter. "The Beginnings of Public Housing in New York." *Journal of Urban History* 12 (August 1986): 353-390.

7249. Massey, Douglas S. "The Dimensions of Residential Segregation." *Social Forces* 67 (December 1988): 281-315.

7250. Massey, Douglas S. and others. "The Effect of Residential Segregation on Black Social and Economic Well-being." *Social Forces* 66 (1987): 29-56.

7251. Massey, Douglas S., and Nancy A. Denton. "Hyper-segregation in the U.S. Metropolitan Areas: Black and Hispanic Segregation Along Five Dimensions." *Demography* 26 (August 1989).

7252. _____. "Racial Identity and the Spatial Assimilation of Mexicans in the United States." *Social Science Research* 21 (September 1992): 235-260.

7253. Massey, Douglas S., and E. Fong. "Segregation and Neighborhood Quality: Blacks, Hispanics, and Asians in the San Francisco Metropolitan Area." *Social Forces* 69 (September 1990).

7254. Massey, Douglas S., and A. B. Gross. "Explaining Trends in Racial Segregation." *Urban Affairs Quarterly* 27 (September 1991): 13-35.

7255. Massey, Douglas S., and S. M. Kanaiaupuni. "Public Housing and the Concentration of Poverty." *Social Science Quarterly* 74 (March 1993).

7256. McClain, Charles J. "In re Lee Sing: The First Residential- segregation Case." *Western Legal History* 3 (Summer-Fall 1990): 179-196.

7257. McGee, Henry W., Jr. "Affordable Housing vs. Racial Integration: L.A. Blacks Search for a New Answer to an Old Dilemma." *CAAS Report* 12 (Spring-Fall 1989): 6-9.

7258. McGraw, Dan. "Fight Ends: Texas Town Divorces Its Racist Past." *Boston Globe*, 16 August 1994. [Vidor, Texas]

7259. McGunagle, Fred. "Movement of Black Families Alters Face of West Side." *Crain's Cleveland Business* (5 June 1989). [West Side, Cleveland, Ohio]

7260. McKinney, Scott. "Change in Metropolitan Area Residential Integration, 1970-80." *Population Research and Policy Review* 8 (May 1989).

7261. McKinney, Scott, and Ann B. Schnare. *Trends in Residential Segregation by Race, 1960-1980*. Washington, DC: Urban Institute, 1986.

7262. _____. "Trends in Residential Segregation by Race, 1960- 1980." *Journal of Urban Economics* 26 (November 1989).

7263. Meyer, Eugene L. "Church's Housing Plan Hits Sore Spot in P.G." *Washington Post*, 8 August 1993. [Low-cost housing in Prince George's County, MD]

7264. Miller, Vincent P., and John M. Quigley. "Segregating by Racial and Demographic Group: Evidence from the San Francisco Bay Area." *Urban Studies* 27 (February 1990).

7265. Minehan, Cathy E. "Mortgage Study Found Race Discrimination, Not Redlining." *New York Times*, 10 September 1994, letter. [Study by Boston Federal Reserve Bank]

7266. Mohl, Raymond A. "Race and Space in the Modern City: Interstate-95 and the Black Community in Miami." in *Urban Policy in Twentieth-Century America*, eds. Arnold R. Hirsch, and Raymond A. Mohl. Rutgers University Press, 1993.

7267. Molina, Liza D. "Title VIII of the Civil Rights Act of 1968, Fair Housing Enforcement and Patterns of Residential Segregation in the City of Boston: A Critical Analysis." Master's thesis, Cornell University, 1990.

7268. Momeni, Jamshid A., ed. *Homelessness in the United States*, 2 vols. Westport, CT: Greenwood, 1989-1990.

7269. Mooney, Brian C. "Boston Sets a Slow Pace in Housing Desegregation." *Boston Globe*, 22 June 1989.

7270. Moore, John H. "Aboriginal Indian Residence Patterns Preserved in Censuses and Allotments." *Science* 207 (1980): 201- 203.

7271. Myers-Jones, Holly. *Power, Geography and Black Americans: Patterns of Black Suburbanization in the US*. Ph.D. diss., University of Washington, 1988.

7272. Nelson, Kathryn P. *Gentrification and Distressed Cities*. Madision, WI, 1988.

7273. Newburger, Harriet B. "Discrimination by a Profit- maximizing Broker in Response to White Prejudice." *Journal of Urban Economics* 26 (1989): 1-19.

7274. Newburger, Harriet B. *The Impact of Federal Housing Programs on Black Americans*. Paper prepared for the Committee on the Status of Black Americans, National Research Council, Washington, D.C., 1988.

7275. _____. *The Nature and Extent of Racial Steering Practices in U.S. Housing Markets*. Washington, DC: U.S. Department of Housing and Urban Development, Working Paper, December 1981.

7276. Nielsen, John T. "Immigration and the Low-Cost Housing Crisis: The Los Angeles Area's Experience." *Population and Environment* 11 (Winter 1989).

7277. Nishizawa, Yoshitaka. *Does Descriptive Representation Benefit Minorities? The Case of the New Haven Housing Authority*. Ph.D. diss., Yale University, 1989. UMO #9016467.

7278. North, Carol S., and Elizabeth M. Smith. "Comparison of White and Non-white Homeless Men and Women." *Social Work* 39 (November 1994): 639-647.

7279. Oliver, John, and Alfred D. Price. *Housing New York's Black Population: Affordability and Adequacy*. Albany, NY: New York African-American Institute, State University of New York, January 1988.

7280. Orfield, Gary, and Ricardo M. Tostado. *Latinos in Metropolitan Chicago: A Study of Housing and Employment*. Chicago, IL: Latino Institute, 1983.

7281. Oross, Marianne C. *The Examination of the Social, Political, and Economic Conditions Associated With Exclusionary Practices in Mount Laurel, New Jersey*. Ph.D. diss., Rutgers University, 1989. UMO #9008819.

7282. Ostrow, Ronald J. "Record Penalty Okd in Housing Discrimination Case." *Los Angeles Times*, 22 June 1993. [Michigan]

7283. *The Other Housing Crisis: Sheltering the Poor in Rural America*. Washington, DC: Center on Budget and Policy Priorities and the Housing Assistance Council, 1989.

7284. Ottensmann, J. R., and M. E. Gleeson. "The Movement of Whites and Blacks into Racially Mixed Neighborhoods-Chicago, 1960-1980." *Social Science Quarterly* 73 (September 1992): 645-662.

7285. Page, Douglas B. *Residential Segregation: A Review of the LIterature*. Washington, DC: Urban Institute, June 1988.

7286. Passell, Peter. "Redlining Under Attack. The U.S. Seeks More Loans for Minorities, But Some Economists Don't See a Problem." *New York Times*, 30 August 1994.

7287. Patrick, Deval L. "The Black and White Facts of Redlining." *Wall Street Journal*, 29 September 1994. letter.

7288. Payne, John M. "Enforcing the New Fair Housing Act." *Real Estate Law Journal* 19 (Fall 1990): 151-157.

7289. Pear, Robert. "New York [City] Admits to Racial Steering in Housing Lawsuit." *New York Times*, 1 July 1992.

7290. Pearce, Diana. "Gatekeepers and Homeseekers: Institutional Patterns in Racial Steering." *Social Problems* 26 (1979): 325-342.

7291. Pete, Gregory. "The Battle of Berkeley." *Crisis* 92 (1985): 26-31, 44-45. [Housing]

7292. Phillips, Jan. "The Political Economy of Housing Poor People." *Wisconsin Sociologist* (1988).

7293. Popkin, Susan J. and others. "Neighborhood Satisfaction of Low-income Blacks in Middle Class Suburbs." *Sociological Abstracts* (1979). Accession No. 89S 21205.

7294. Potter, Michael F. "Racial Diversity in Residential Communities: Societal Housing Patterns and a Proposal for a Racial Inclusionary Ordinance." *Southern California Law Review* 63 (May 1990): 1151-1235.

7295. Powers, William F. "Good Bank, Bad Bank?" *Washington Post*, 12 July 1993. [Minority lending in Wash, D.C. region by two banks]

7296. _____. "How Solid Are Big Banks' D.C. Loan Commitments?" *Washington Post*, 29 June 1993. [Mortgage money in the Wash, D.C. area]

7297. Reed, Veronica M. "Civil Rights Legislation and the Housing Status of Black Americans: Evidence from Fair Housing Audits and Segregation Indices." *Review of Black Political Economy* 19 (Winter-Spring 1991): 29-42.

7298. _____. "Summary of Rental Audit Studies: Select Results, 1977 to 1988." *Review of Black Political Economy* 19 (Winter- Spring 1991): 36-37.

7299. Reid, Clifford E. "The Reliability of Fair Housing Audits to Detect Racial Discrimination in Rental Housing Markets." *Journal of the American Real Estate and Urban Economics Association* 12 (Spring 1984): 86-96.

7300. "Restricting Minority Occupancy to Maintain Housing Integration." *Harvard Civil Rights-Civil Liberties Law Review* 24 (Spring 1989): 561-574. [U.S. v. Starrett City Associates]

7301. Rezendes, Michael. "Housing Integration Progresses Quietly." *Boston Globe*, 7 January 1990. [South Boston public housing]

7302. "Rights Violations Bring Texas Housing Seizure." *New York Times*, 15 September 1993. [U.S. Department of Housing and Urban Development action against Orange County Housing Authority in Vidor, Texas]

7303. Roberts, Sam. "Minorities Join a Fight on [Public Housing] Projects." *New York Times*, 15 March 1993.

7304. Robertson, William E. (Gene). "Housing for Blacks: A Challenge for Kansas City." *Review of Black Political Economy* 19 (Winter-Spring 1991): 195-209.

7305. Robinson, Carla J. "Racial Disparity in the Atlanta Housing Market." *Review of Black Political Economy* 19 (Winter-Spring 1991): 85-109.

7306. Roisman, Florence W. "The Right to Public Housing." *George Washington Law Review* 39 (1971).

7307. Roisman, Florence W., and Philip Tegeler. "Expanding Housing Opportunities through State Constitutional Law: Recent Developments." *Clearinghouse Review* 24 (August-September 1990): 343-355.

7308. _____. "Race-based Federal Claims." *Clearinghouse Review* 24 (August-September 1990): 312-342.

7309. Rosenbaum, Emily V. *Race and Ethnicity in Housing: Turnover in New York City, 1978-89.* Ph.D. diss., University of Pennsylvania, 1991. UMO #9125743.

7310. _____. "Race and Ethnicity in Housing Turnover in New York City, 1978-1987." *Demography* 29 (August 1992).

7311. Rosenbaum, James E. and others. "Social Integration of Low- income Black Adults in Middle-class White Suburbs." *Social Problems* 38 (November 1991): 448-461.

7312. Rosenblatt, Robert A. and others. "Blacks Lead in Rejections for Home Loans." *Los Angeles Times*, 6 September 1992. [Los Angeles County]

7313. _____. "Home Loan Gap. Banks Are Behind S + L's in Lending to Minorities." *Los Angeles Times*, 8 September 1992.

7314. Rossi, Peter. *Down and Out in America: The Origins of Homelessness.* Chicago, IL: University of Chicago Press, 1989.

7315. Roth, D. and others. "Gender, Racial, and Age Variations among Homeless Persons." in *Homelessness*, pp. 199-212. eds. M. J. Robertson, and M. Greenblatt. Plenum Publishing Corp., 1992.

7316. Saenz, R., and J. Vinas. "Chicano Geographic Segregation: A Human Ecological Approach." *Sociological Perspectives* 33 (Winter 1990): 465-482.

7317. Saltman, Juliet. *A Fragile Movement. The Struggle for Neighborhood Stabilization.* Westport, CT: Greenwood, 1990. [Efforts to maintain community racial integration.]

7318. _____. "Maintaining Racially Diverse Neighborhoods." *Urban Affairs Quarterly* 26 (March 1991): 416-441.

7319. _____. "Neighborhood Stabilization as a Social Movement." *Sociological Abstracts* (1989). [Stabilizing integrated neighborhoods] Accession No. 89S 21212.

7320. Sanchez, Jose R. *Housing Puerto Ricans in New York City, 1945 to 1984: A Study in Class Powerlessness.* Ph.D. diss., New York University, 1990. UMO #9025146.

7321. _____. "Residual Work and Residual Shelter: Housing Puerto Rican Labor in New York City from World War II to 1983." in *Critical Perspectives on Housing*, eds. Rachel G. Bratt and others. Philadelphia, PA: Temple University Press, 1986.

7322. Sanchez, Rene. "Poor Wait Years for Public Housing." *Washington Post*, 7 December 1992. [D.C.]

7323. Sander, Richard H. *Housing Segregation and Housing Integration: The Diverging Paths of American Cities.* Ph.D. diss., Northwestern University, 1990. UMO #9031984.

7324. Santiago, A. M. "Residential Segregation and Links to Minority Poverty: The Case of Latinos in the United States." *Social Problems* 38 (November 1991): 492-515.

7325. Schemo, Diana J. "Segregation Mars Suburban Dreams." *New York Times*, 17 March 1994. [Long Island towns]

7326. Schmidt, Peter. "Hispanics Found More Segregated in Housing Study." *Education Week* (25 March 1992).

7327. Schrender, Yda. "Labor Segmentation, Ethnic Division of Labor, and Residential Segregation in American Cities in the Early Twentieth Century." *Professional Geographer* 41 (1989): 131-143.

7328. Schuler, J. R. and others. "Neighborhood Gentrification: A Discriminant Analysis of a Historic District in Cleveland, Ohio." *Urban Geography* 13 (January-February 1992): 49-67.

7329. Schuman, Howard, and Lawrence Bobo. "Survey-Based Experiments on White Racial Attitudes toward Residential Integration." *American Journal of Sociology* 94 (September 1988): 273-299.

7330. Schwemm, Robert G., ed. *The Fair Housing Act After Twenty Years*. New Haven, CT: Yale Law School, 1989.

7331. Sege, Irene. "Two Women of Southie." *Boston Globe*, 22 September 1994. [Two black women residents of South Boston]

7332. *Segregation in Louisville and Lexington Public Housing*. Washington, DC: U.S. Commission on Civil Rights, 1988.

7333. Sexton, E. A. "Residential Location, Workplace Location, and Black Earnings." *Review of Regional Studies* 21 (Spring 1991).

7334. *A Sheltered Crisis: The State of Fair Housing in the Eighties*. Washington, DC: U.S. Commission on Civil Rights, 1983.

7335. Sherburne, Kevin P. "The Judiciary and the Ad Hoc Development of a Legal Right to Shelter." *Harvard Journal of Law and Public Policy* 12 (Winter 1989): 193-220.

7336. Shlay, A. B. and others. "Racial Barriers to Credit- Comment." *Urban Affairs Quarterly* 28 (September 1992): 126-140.

7337. Shlay, A. B., and D. Bartelt. "Race and Lending: A Rejoinder to Hula and Galster." *Urban Affairs Quarterly* 28 (September 1992): 156-158.

7338. Simon, Thomas W. "Double Reverse Discrimination in Housing: Contexualizing the Starrett City Case." *Buffalo Law Review* 39 (Fall 1991): 803-853.

7339. Singleton, David A., and C. Benjie Louis. "The Homeless: Victims of Prejudice." *New York Times*, 28 December 1989.

7340. Skidmore, Dave. "Data Show Lending Bias Unabated." *Boston Globe*, 27 October 1994. [National]

7341. Smith, Richard A. "Creating Stable Racially Integrated Communities: A Review." *Journal of Urban Affairs* 15 (1993): 115- 140.

7342. _____. "The Effects of Local Fair Housing Ordinances on Housing Segregation: Their Impact Is Small, but It's an Important Positive Change toward Integration." *American Journal of Economics and Sociology* 48 (April 1989).

7343. _____. "The Measurement of Segregation Change through Integration and Deconcentration." *Urban Affairs Quarterly* 26 (June 1991): 477-496.

7344. Smolla, Rodney. "The Unconstitutionality of Benign Programs that Discourage White Flight." *Duke Law Journal* (1981).

7345. South, Scott J., and Glenn D. Deane. "Race and Residential Mobility: Individual Determinants and Structural Constraints." *Social Forces* 72 (September 1993): 147-167.

7346. Southern Poverty Law Center. *"Move-In" Violence: White Resistance to Neighborhood Integration in the 1980's*. Atlanta, GA: The Center, 1987.

7347. Spayd, Liz, and Joel Glenn Brenner. "Area Blacks Have Worst Bank Access." *Washington Post*, 7 June 1993. [Race and mortgage money]

7348. St. John, Craig, and Nancy A. Bates. "Racial Composition and Neighborhood Evaluation." *Social Science Research* 19 (March 1990): 47-61. [Oklahoma City]

7349. Stahwra, J. M. "Rapid Black Suburbanization of the 1970's: Some Policy Considerations." *Policy Studies Journal* 18 (Winter 1990).

7350. Strazheim, M. R. "Housing Market Discrimination and Black Housing Consumption." *Quarterly Journal of Economics* 88 (1974): 19-43. [San Francisco, 1965]

7351. *A Survey of Housing Discrimination in Kansas City, Missouri*. Kansas City, MO: Kansas City Human Relations Department, 1988.

7352. Taeuber, Karl E. "Residence and Race: 1619-2019." in *Race: Twentieth-Century Dilemmas--Twenty-First-Century Prognoses*, eds. Winston A. Van Horne, and Thomas V. Tonneson. Milwaukee: Institute on Race and Ethnicity, University of Wisconsin System, 1989.

7353. Taylor, Monique M. *Home to Harlem: Black Identity and the Gentrification of Harlem*. Ph.D. diss., Harvard University, 1991. UMO #9211754.

7354. Tein, M. R. "The Devaluation of Nonwhite Community in Remedies for Subsidized Housing Discrimination." *University of Pennsylvania Law Review* 140 (April 1992).

7355. Terry, Don. "Chicago Suburb Finds Truth in Arson Rumors." *New York Times*, 14 July 1992. [Municipal officials in Chicago Heights, IL guilty of soliciting arson to evict black and poor tenants]

7356. Testa, Mark, and Paul H. Ton. "[Two letters on neighborhood segregation and integration in Chicago]." *New York Times*, 10 July 1992.

7357. Thomas, Suja A. "Efforts to Integrate Housing: The Legality of Mortgage-incentive Programs." *New York University Law Review* 66 (June 1991): 940-978.

7358. Thompson, Tracy. "District Has Nothing to Offer Families With Nowhere to Go." *Washington Post*, 27 June 1993. [Homeless families in Wash., D.C.]

7359. Timmer, Doug A. and others. *Paths to Homelessness. Extreme Poverty and the Urban Housing Crisis*. Westview, 1994.

7360. Turner, Harry. "Federal Housing Policy: Why Latinos Are Left Out in the Cold." *Nuestro* 2 (June 1978): 26-32.

7361. Tushnet, Mark V. "Shelley v. Kraemer and Theories of Equality." *New York Law School Law Review* 33 (Fall 1988): 383- 408.

7362. U.S. Commission on Civil Rights. *Issues in Housing Discrimination*. Washington, DC: GPO, 1986.

7363. _____. *A Sheltered Crisis: The State of Fair Housing in the Eighties*. Washington, DC: The Commission, 1984.

7364. U.S. Congress, 99th, 2nd session, House Committee on Housing and Community Development. *Discrimination in Federally Assisted Programs*. Washington, DC: GPO, 1987.

7365. Vacca, Carolyn, and Wanda Ellen Wakefield. "Housing Conditions as a Predictor for Riot: Rochester, New York, 1964." *Afro-Americans in New York Life and History* 15 (July 1991): 45- 61.

7366. Verhovek, Sam H. "One Man's Arrival in Town Exposes a Racial Fault Line." *New York Times*, 27 February 1993. [Vidor, TX]

7367. _____. "Under Armed Escort, Blacks Move Into White Texas Housing Project." *New York Times*, 14 January 1994. [Vidor, TX]

7368. Vise, David A., and Albert B. Crenshaw. "Fannie Mae to Expand Its Efforts On Housing Costs, Lending Bias." *Washington Post*, 10 March 1994.

7369. Wayne, Leslie. "Bailout Flop: Low-income Housing." *New York Times*, 28 December 1991. [Failure of Resolution Trust Corporation to implement program to sell affordable homes to low-income persons.]

7370. _____. "Housing Earmarked for the Poor Is Enriching Big Investors Instead." *New York Times*, 27 June 1991. [Sold by Resolution Trust Corporation in charge of resolving savings and loan crisis.]

7371. Weiker, Gregory R. "Public Policy and Patterns of Residential Segregation." *Western Law Review* 42 (1989): 651-677.

7372. White, Michael J. *American Neighborhoods and Residential Differentiation*. New York: Russell Sage Foundation, 1987.

7373. "White Supremacist Fined for Intimidation." *New York Times*, 28 July 1994. [Vidor, TX]

7374. Wienk, Ronald E. and others. *Measuring Racial Discrimination in American Housing Markets: The Housing Market Practices Survey*. Washington, DC: U.S. Department of Housing and Urban Development, 1979. [Report on 3,264 housing audits made in 1977]

7375. Wilger, Robert J. *Black-White Residential Segregation in 1980*. Ph.D. diss., University of Michigan, 1988. UMO #8907168.

7376. Wilger, Robert J., and Reynolds Farley. *Black-White Residential Segregation: Recent Trends*. Ann Arbor: Population Studies Center, University of Michigan, 1989.

7377. Wood, P. B., and B. A. Lee. "Is Neighborhood Racial Succession Inevitable? 40 Years of Evidence." *Urban Affairs Quarterly* 26 (June 1991): 610-620.

7378. Yinger, John. "Economists Know About Bias in Lending." *New York Times*, 4 September 1994, letter.

7379. Zahner, G. E. P. and others. "Psychological Consequences of Infestation of the Dwelling Unit." *American Journal of Public Health* 75 (November 1985): 1302-1307.

7380. Ziesemer, Carol and others. "Homeless Children: Are They Different from Other Low-Income Children?" *Social Work* 39 (November 1994): 658-668.

HUMOR

7381. Abramowitz, Michael. "Ethnic Joke Rails Community College." *Washington Post*, 11 September 1993. [President of Prince George's Community College makes a "Polack" joke.]

7382. Andreas, James R. "Invisible Man and the Comic Tradition." in *Approaches to Teaching Ellison's Invisible Man*, pp. 102-106. eds. Susan R. Parr, and Pancho Savery. New York: Modern Language Association of America, 1989.

7383. Apte, Mahadev L. "Ethnic Humor versus 'Sense of Humor'." *American Behavioral Scientist* 30 (1987): 27-41.

7384. _____. *Humour and Laughter and Anthropological Approach*. Ithaca, NY: Cornell University Press, 1985.

7385. Axtell, James L. "Humor in Ethnohistory." *Ethnohistory* 37 (1990): 109-125.

7386. Baker, Peter. "Gay Jokes Becoming No Laughing Matter." *Washington Post*, 21 March 1993.

7387. Barron, Milton L. "A Content Analysis of Intergroup Humor." *American Sociological Review* 15 (February 1950): 88-94.

7388. Barry, Dave. "Rads." *Washington Post Magazine* (23 January 1994). [The writer views radiation as an occasion for hilarity.]

7389. Bee, Noah. "Jewish Cartooning and Jewish Cartoonists." *Midstream* 35 (June-July 1989): 39-42.

7390. Berger, Arthur A. *An Anatomy of Humor*. Transaction, 1993.

7391. Boskin, Joseph. "Good-bye, Mr. Bones." *New York Times Magazine* (1 May 1966).

7392. Braxton, Greg. "Has Black Comedy Been Beaten Blue?" *Los Angeles Times*, 20 February 1994.

7393. Burma, John H. "Humor As a Technique in Race Conflict." *American Sociological Review* 11 (1946): 710-715.

7394. Castro, Rafaela. "Mexican Women's Sexual Jokes." *Perspectives in Mexican American Studies* 1 (1988): 129-143.

7395. Chapman, A. J., and Nicholas J. Gadfield. "Sexual Humor as Sexist Humor." *Journal of Communication* 26 (1976): 141-153.

7396. Chow, Josephine. "Sticks and Stones Will Break My Bones, but Will Racist Humor? A Look around the World at Whether Police Officers Have a Free Speech Right to Engage in Racist Humor." *Loyola of Los Angeles International and Comparative Law Journal* 14 (October 1992): 851-901.

7397. Clements, William M. "The Ethnic Joke as Mirror of Culture." *New York Folklore* 12 (1986): 87-97.

7398. Cohen, Sarah B., ed. *Jewish Wry: Essays on Jewish Humor*. Bloomington: Indiana University Press, 1987.

7399. Crew, Louie. "Tattling the Racist Laughter of Alabama Leaders, 1950-1967." *Maledicta* 10 (1988-1989): 105-114.

7400. Crisafulli, Chuck. "Today's Latino Comics Can Even Play in Peoria." *Los Angeles Times*, 6 December 1993.

7401. Davies, Christie. "Ethnic Jokes, Moral Values and Social Boundaries." *British Journal of Sociology* 33 (1982): 383-403.

7402. _____. *Ethnic Humor around the World. A Comparative Analysis*. Bloomington, IN: Indiana University Press, 1990.

7403. Denison, D. C. "The Interview: Barry Crimmins." *Boston Globe Magazine* (10 February 1991).

7404. Du Bois, W. E. B. "The Humor of Negroes." *Mark Twain Quarterly* 5 (Winter 1942-1943): 12.

7405. Easton, Nina J. "The Meaning of America." *Los Angeles Times Magazine* (7 February 1993). [Cruel humor]

7406. Ehrlich, Howard J. "Observations on Ethnic and Intergroup Humor." *Ethnicity* 6 (1979): 383-398.

7407. Epstein, Lawrence J. *A Treasury of Jewish Anecdotes*. Northvale, NJ: J. Aronson, 1989.

7408. Esar, Evan. *The Comic Encyclopedia*. Garden City, NY: Doubleday, 1978.

7409. Fernandez, Celestino, and James E. Officer. "The Lighter Side of Mexican Immigration: Humor and Satire in the Mexican Corrido." *Jr. S. W.* 31 (Winter 1989): 471-496.

7410. Friedman, Robert I. "Comics on the Stump." *Village Voice* (3 October 1989). [Jackie Mason's "comic" efforts to distract Jews in New York City from voting for David Dinkins, a black, for mayor.]

7411. Fujioka, J. M. "Abating Stereotypical Attitudes: Views on Career Paths of an Asian American Comedian." *Career Development Quarterly* 39 (June 1991): 337-340. [W. Mar]

7412. Gadfield, Nicholas J. and others. "Dynamics of Humor in Ethnic Group Relations." *Ethnicity* 6 (1979): 373-382.

7413. Garcia, Guy. "Mocking the Ethnic Beast." *Time* (28 October 1991). [Ethnic humor aimed at Hispanics by John Leguizamo]

7414. Gilstrap, Peter. "Dave Chappelle's Big Shot." *Washington Post*, 9 August 1993.

7415. Gleason, William. "'Her Laugh an Ace': The Function of Humor in Louise Erdrich's Love Medicine." *American Indian Culture and Research Journal* 11 (1987): 51-73.

7416. Goldman, M. *The Sociology of Negro Humor*. Ph.D. diss., New School for Social Research, 1960.

7417. Gray, Frances. *Women and Laughter*. University Press of Virginia, 1994.

7418. Harris, Trudier. "Moms Mabley: A Study in Humor, Role Playing, and the Violation of Taboo." *Southern Review* 24 (1988): 765-776.

7419. Hasenauer, Jim. "Using Ethnic Humor to Expose Ethnocentrism: Those Dirty DEGs." *ETC: A Review of General Semantics* 45 (Winter 1988): 351-357.

7420. Hendra, Tony. *Going Too Far*. Garden City, NY: Doubleday, 1987.

7421. Hernandez, Guillermo E. *Chicano Satire. A Study in Literary Culture*. Austin: University of Texas Press, 1991.

7422. Holt, Elvin. "A Coon Alphabet and the Comic Mask of Racial Prejudice." *Studies in American Humor* 5 (Winter 1986-1987): 207- 218.

7423. Ingrando, D. P. "Sex Differences in Response to Absurd, Aggressive, Pro-Feminist, Sexual, Sexist, and Racial Jokes." *Psychological Reports* 46 (1968): 368-370.

7424. Jaret, Charles. "It's Only a Joke: An Analysis of American Racial-Ethnic Humor." *Sociological Abstracts* (August 1991): supplement 167. 91S 25175/ASA/1991/6534.

7425. Jefferson, Margo. "Seducified by a Minstrel Show." *New York Times*, 22 May 1994. [Black shows on television]

7426. Johnson, Dirk. "With This Tough Audience, Fair-Haired Is Fair Game." *New York Times*, 3 November 1991. [Ethnic and racial jokes]

7427. Kalmar, Ivan. "Jews on the Train." *Journal of Popular Culture* 21 (1987): 139-154. [Jewish train jokes]

7428. Kanfer, Stefan. *A Summer World. The Attempt to Build a Jewish Eden in the Catskills. From the Days of the Ghetto to the Rise and Decline of the Borscht Belt*. New York: Strauss and Giroux, 1989.

7429. Kishi, Russell L. "Tiptoeing through Racial Minefield." *Los Angeles Times*, 5 October 1992.

7430. Koch, John. "Comic Stands Up for Native Americans." *Boston Globe*, 21 November 1990. [Charlie Hill, Oneida]

7431. La Fave, Lawrence, and Roger Mannell. "Does Ethnic Humor Serve Prejudice?" *Journal of Communication* 26 (Summer 1976): 116- 123.

7432. Lahr, John. "Working the Room." *New Yorker* (25 April 1994). [Jackie Mason]

7433. Limon, Jose E. "Agrinado Joking in Texas Mexican Society." *Perspectives in Mexican American Studies* 1 (1988): 109-127.

7434. Lincoln, Kenneth. *Indi'n Humor. Bicultural Play in Native America*. New York: Oxford University Press, 1991.

7435. McGhee, Paul E., and Nelda S. Duffey. "Children's Appreciation of Humor Victimizing Different Racial-Ethnic Groups." *Journal of Cross Cultural Psychology* 14 (1983): 29-40.

7436. Melzer, Richard. "New Mexico in Caricature: Images of the Territory on the Eve of Statehood." *New Mexico Historical Review* 62 (1987): 335-360.

7437. Middleton, Russell. "Negro and White Reactions to Racial Humor." *Sociometry* 22 (1959): 175-183.

7438. Mills, David. "'Race Riot'." *Washington Post*, 16 May 1993. [Paul Mooney, African-American comic]

7439. Mintz, Lawrence E., ed. *Humor in America: A Research Guide to Genres and Topics*. Westport, CT: Greenwood, 1988.

7440. Mottram, Eric. "The American Comedian as Social Critic, 1950-1970." in *Cracking the Ike Age*, ed. Dale Carter. Aarhus University Press, 1992.

7441. Nathan, Hans. *Dan Emmett and the Rise of Early Negro Minstrelsy*. Norman: University of Oklahoma Press, 1962.

7442. Nilsen, Alleen P. "Evan Mecham: Humor in Arizona Politics." *Dialogue* 22 (1989): 81-89.

7443. Norman, Michael. "Late-Night Cool." *New York Times Magazine* (1 October 1989). [Arsenio Hall]

7444. O'Connor, John J. "A Survey of Black Comedy in America." *New York Times* (9 February 1993). [A documentary for TV, "Mo' Funny: Black Comedy in America"]

7445. _____. "Taking a Pratfall on the Nastiness Threshold." *New York Times* (22 July 1990). [Andrew Dice Clay]

7446. O'Koon, Alan M. "Humor in Social Groups." Master's thesis, Bowling Green State University, 1988.

7447. Powell, C., and S. E. C. Paton, eds. *Humour in Society: Resistance and Control*. New York: St. Martin's Press, 1988.

7448. Raskin, Victor. *Semantic Mechanisms of Humour*. Dordrecht: D. Reidel, 1985.

7449. Rinder, I. D. "A Note on Humor As an Index of Minority Group Morale." *Phylon* 26 (1965): 117-121.

7450. Rosenthal, John N. "Today's Comics: No Joke." *New York Times*, 27 June 1990. [Racial and ethnic derogation by "comics"]

7451. Ross, Joe. "Why Are We Laughing? Localization of Some Southern Racist Jokes." *Tennessee Folklore Society Bulletin* 53 (1987): 130-142. [Beaufort, SC area]

7452. Saper, Bernard. "A Cognitive Behavioral Formulation of the Relation between the Jewish Joke and Antisemitism." *Humor* 4 (1991): 41-59.

7453. Sarna, J. D. "The Pork on the Fork: A Nineteenth Century Anti-Jewish Ditty." *Jewish Social Studies* 44 (Spring 1982): 169- 172.

7454. Schutz, Charles E. "The Sociability of Ethnic Jokes." *Humor* 2 (1989): 165-177.

7455. Secor, Robert. "Ethnic Humor in Early American Jest Books." in *A Mixed Race: Ethnicity in Early America*, ed. Frank Shuffelton. Oxford University Press, 1993.

7456. Sibert, Anthony, and Denise Ji-Ahnte Sibert. "'The John Larroquette Show' Confuses Racial Stereotypes With Humor." *Los Angeles Times*, 18 October 1993.

7457. Smith, Eric L. *Bert Williams. A Biography of the Pioneer Black Comedian*. Jefferson, NC: McFarland, 1992.

7458. Smoler, Fredric. "Wall Street Jokes, Vintage 1929." *American Heritage* 39 (1988): 105-109.

7459. Spalding, Henry D., ed. *Encyclopedia of Black Folklore and Humor*. Middle Village, NY: Jonathan David Publishers, 1990.

7460. "Special Issue on Native American Satiric Humor." *Studies in Contemporary Satire* 16 (1989).

7461. Takezawa, Yasuko I. "Ethnic Stereotypes in the USA: The Dynamics of Ethnic Group Images in Advertising and Jokes." *Minzokugaku-kenkyu* 52 (1988): 363-390. [In Japanese]

7462. Telushkin, Joseph. *Jewish Humor: What the Best Jewish Jokes Say About the Jews*. Morrow, 1992.

7463. Tigar, Michael. "By the Lawyers and For the Judges: An Irreverent History of the Bill of Rights." *Alabama Lawyer* 51 (March 1990): 78-80.

7464. Vallangca, Roberto V., ed. "Humor." in *Pinoys: The First Wave (1898-1941)*, pp. 30-35. Strawberry Hill Press, 1977. [Filipinos in the United States]

7465. Watkins, Mel. "He Certainly Isn't the First." *Los Angeles Times*, 3 April 1994. [Afro-American humorist Martin Lawrence]

7466. _____. *On the Real Side. Laughing, Lying, and Signifying-The Underground Tradition of African-American Humor that Transformed American Culture, From Slavery to Richard Pryor*. Simon + Schuster, 1994.

7467. Whitfield, Stephen J. "The Distinctiveness of American Jewish Humor." *Modern Judaism* 6 (1986): 145-160.

7468. Wicker, Fred W. and others. "Disparagement Humor: Dispositions and Resolutions." *Journal of Personality and Social Psychology* 39 (1980): 701-709.

7469. Wilde, Larry. *The Complete Book of Ethnic Humor*. Los Angeles, CA: Corwin Books, 1978.

7470. _____. *More, the Official Polish Jokebook*. Los Angeles, CA: Pinnacle Books, 1975.

7471. Wiley, Ralph. *Why Black People Tend to Shout*. Penguin, 1992.

7472. Williams, Elsie A. *Jackie Moms Mabley: African-American, Woman, Performer*. Ph.D. diss., University of Maryland, 1992. UMO #9234686.

7473. Williams, Lena. "After the Roast, Fire and Smoke Follow [Ted] Danson and [Whoopi] Goldberg." *New York Times*, 14 October 1993. [Racial or racist jokes?]

7474. _____. "It's Not Funny and I'm Sorry: Tacky Jokes of the Past, R.I.P." *New York Times*, 2 January 1991.

7475. Willman, Chris. "Jackie Mason: Mining the 'Politically Incorrect'." *Los Angeles Times*, 22 November 1993.

7476. Wittke, Carl. *Tambo and Bones, a History of the American Minstrel Show*. New York, 1968.

7477. Wolcott, James. "Cos Celebre." *New Yorker* (12 July 1993). [Bill Cosby and perspectives on contemporary African-American Humor]

7478. Wolff, H. A. and others. "The Psychology of Humor. Part 1: A Study of Responses to Race-Disparagement Jokes." *Journal of Abnormal and Social Psychology* 38 (1934): 345-365.

7479. Zijderveld, Anton C. "The Sociology of Humours and Laughter." *Current Sociology* 31 (Winter 1983): 1-100.

7480. Zoglin, Richard. "'Let's Get Busy!!'." *Time* (13 November 1989). [Arsenio Hall]

7481. Zolbrod, Zoe. "Aaron Freeman: Comic Contraire." *In These Times* (13 November 1991).

IMMIGRATION

7482. Abramson, Elliot M. "Reflections on the Unthinkable: Standards Relating to the Denaturalization and Deportation of Nazis and Those Who Collaborated with the Nazis during World War II." *University of Cincinnati Law Review* 57 (Spring 1989): 1311- 1350.

7483. Acosta, Frank, and Bong Hwan Kim. "Race-Baiting in Sacramento." *Los Angeles Times*, 4 May 1993. [Anti-immigrant bills in California state legislature]

7484. Altman, Ida, and James Horn, eds. *"To Make America": European Emigration to the Early Modern Period*. Berkeley, CA: University of California Press, 1991.

7485. "America's Welcome Mat Is Wearing Thin." *Business Week*, 13 July 1992. p. 119. [Harris Poll on attitudes towards immigration]

7486. Aroian, Karen J. "Subordination of Immigrants: Historical Trends and Critical Analysis." *Journal of Intergroup Relations* 19 (Spring 1992): 30-43.

7487. *A Badge of Infamy: A Petition to the United Nations on the Treatment of the Mexican Immigrant*. New York, NY: American Committee for the Protection of the Foreign Born, 1959.

7488. Bailey, Eric, and Dan Morain. "Anti-Immigration Bills Flood Legislature." *Los Angeles Times*, 3 May 1993. [Description of measures on schooling, health and welfare, and other fields]

7489. Baseler, Marilyn C. *Immigration Policies in Eighteenth Century America*. Ph.D. diss., Harvard University, 1990. UMO # 9113133.

7490. Bean, Frank D. and others, eds. *Mexican and Central American Population and U.S. Immigration Policy*. Austin, TX: Center for Mexican American Studies, University of Texas, 1989.

7491. Bean, Frank D. and others. *Opening and Closing the Doors: Evaluation Immigration Reform and Control*. Santa Monica, CA: The RAND Corporation, 1989. [Principally an analysis of the 1986 Immigration Reform and Control Act]

7492. Beirne, D. Randall. "The Impact of Black Labor on European Immigration into Baltimore's Oldtown, 1790-1910." *Maryland History Magizine* 83 (Winter 1988): 331-345.

7493. Beyer, Gregg A. "The Evolving United States Response to Soviet Jewish Emigration." *Journal of Palestine Studies* 21 (Autumn 1991): 139-156.

7494. Bole, William. "Who Helped Nazis Escape to America?" *Present Tense* 13 (1986): 6-10.

7495. Borjas, George J. "The Intergenerational Mobility of Immigrants." *Journal of Labor Economics* 11 (January 1993).

7496. Borjas, George J., and Stephen J. Trejo. "Immigrant Participation in the Welfare System." *Industrial and Labor Relations Review* 44 (January 1991): 195-211.

7497. Branigin, William. "Vietnamese Try to Buy American Dream." *Washington Post*, 19 February 1993. [Claims under Amerasian Homecoming Act of 1987]

7498. Briggs, Vernon M., Jr. "Efficiency and Equity as Goals for Contemporary U.S. Immigration Policy." *Population and Environment* 11 (Autumn 1989).

7499. Brinkley, Joel. "California's Woes on Aliens Appear Largely Self-Inflicted." *New York Times*, 15 October 1994.

7500. _____. "Chaos at the Gates." *New York Times*, 11 September 1994. [1st of 5 articles on immigration; the INS]

7501. Bryce-Laporte, Roy S. "Black Immigrants: The Experience of Invisibility and Inequality." *Journal of Black Studies* 3 (September 1972): 29-56.

7502. _____. "Voluntary Immigration and Continuing Encounters between Blacks: The Post Quincentenary Challenge." *Annals of the American Academy of Political and Social Sciences* 530 (November 1993): 28-41.

7503. Bustamante, Jorge A. "The Historical Context of the Undocumented Immigration from Mexico to the United States." *Aztlan* 3 (Fall 1972): 257-281.

7504. _____. *Mexican Immigration and the Social Relations of Capitalism*. Ph.D. diss., University of Notre Dame, 1975.

7505. Butcher, K. F. "Black Immigrants in the United States: A Comparison with Native Blacks and Other Immigrants." *Industrial and Labor Relations Review* 47 (January 1994).

7506. Calavita, Kitty. *Inside the State: The Bracero Program, Illegal Immigrants, and the INS*. Routledge, 1992.

7507. Cardenas, Gilbert. "United States Immigration Policy Toward Mexico: An Historical Perspective." *Chicano Law Review* 2 (Summer 1975): 66-91.

7508. Cardoso, Lawrence A. *Mexican Emigration to the United States, 1897-1931: Socio-Economic Patterns*. Tucson, AZ: University of Arizona Press, 1980.

7509. Castillo, Jose del, and Christopher Mitchel, eds. *La immigracion dominicana en los Estado Unidos*. Santo Domingo: Centros APEC de Educacion a Distancia, 1987.

7510. Cedillo, Gilbert. "Building Unity to Stop 'SOS'." *Against the Current* 52 (September-October 1994): 4-5. [Anti-immigrant ballot initiative in California at November 1994 election]

7511. Chan, Sucheng, ed. *Entry Denied: Exclusion and the Chinese Community in America, 1882-1943*. Philadelphia, PA: Temple University Press, 1991.

7512. Chang, Michael S. H. *From Marginality to Bimodality: Immigration, Education, and Occupational Change of Chinese Americans, 1940-1980*. Ph.D. diss., Stanford University, 1988. UMO # 8826114.

7513. Charles, Carolle. *A Transnational Dialectic of Race, Class, and Ethnicity: Patterns of Identities and Forms of Consciousness among Haitian Migrants in New York City*. Ph.D. diss., State University of New York at Binghampton, 1990. UMO # 9032541.

7514. Chavira, Ricardo. "Hatred, Fear and Vigilance." *Time*, 19 November 1990. [Anti-immigrant sentiment in San Diego, CA]

7515. Chiswick, Barry R. "The Economic Progress of Immigrants: Some Apparently Universal Patterns." in *Contemporary Economic Problems*, pp. 357-399. ed. William Fellner. : American Enterprise Institute, 1979.

7516. _____. "Jewish Immigrant Skill and Occupational Attainment at the Turn of the Century." *Explorations in Economic History* 28 (January 1991): 64-86.

7517. Chiswick, C. U. and others. "The Impact of Immigrants on the Macroeconomy." *Carnegie-Rochester Conference Series on Public Policy* 37 (December 1992). [see comment by M. H. Kosters, same issue]

7518. Cockcroft, James D. *Outlaws in the Promised Land: Mexican Immigrant Workers and America's Future*. 2nd Edition, New York, NY: Grove Press, 1988.

7519. Cohen, Melvin, and David McGowan. "The Semi-Open Door: Ideology, Aliens and the Law." *Revue Francaise d' Etudes Americaines* 15 (1990): 173-192.

7520. Commission Pro-Justice Mariel Prisoners. *The Mariel Injustice: In the Bicentennial of the United States Constitution*. Coral Gables, FL: The Commission, 1987.

7521. Comptroller-General of the United States. *Soviet Refugees: Processing and Admittance to the United States*. Washington, DC: General Accounting Office, May 1990.

7522. "Continuity and Change in Latin American Immigration." in *The Challenge: Latinos in a Changing California*, pp. 25-45. University of California SCR43 Task Force. Riverside, CA: University of California Consortium on Mexico and the United States (UCMEXUS), 1989.

7523. Cooper, Marc. "The War Against Illegal Immigrants Heats Up." *Village Voice*, 4 October 1994. [Orange County, CA]

7524. Cordasco, Francesco, ed. *Dictionary of American Immigration History*. Metuchen, NJ: Scarecrow Press, 1989.

7525. Cornelius, Wayne A. *Building the Cactus Curtain: Mexican Migration and U.S. Response, from Wilson to Carter*. Berkeley, CA: University of California Press, 1980.

7526. _____. "From Sojourners to Settlers: The Changing Profile of Mexican Migration to the U.S." in *U.S.- Mexico Relations: Labor Market Interdependence*, eds. Jorge A. Bustamante and others. : Stanford University Press, 1991.

7527. _____. "Neo-Nationalists Feed on Myopic Fears." *Los Angeles Times*, 12 July 1993.

7528. Corwin, Miles. "Packing Up and Going Back Home." *Los Angeles Times*, 4 March 1993. [Return of immigrants]

7529. Cose, Ellis. *A Nation of Strangers, Prejudice, Politics, and the Popularity of America*. Morrow, 1992.

7530. Curran, Thomas J. *Xenophobia and Immigration, 1820-1930*. Twayne, 1975.

7531. Daneshvary, Nasser, and R. Keith Schwer. "Black Immigrants in the U.S. Labor Market: An Earnings Analysis." *Review of Black Political Economy* 22 (Winter 1994): 77-98.

7532. Daniels, Roger. "Changes in Immigration Law and Nativism Since 1924." *American Jewish History* 76 (1986): 159-180.

7533. _____. *Coming to America. A History of Immigration and Ethnicity in America*. New York, NY: Harper Collins, 1990.

7534. Darling, Juanita. "Migrants' Social, Economic Ties to Mexico Stay Strong." *Los Angeles Times*, 29 November 1993.

7535. De Monaco, Mary Kim. "Disorderly Departure: An Analysis of the United States Policy toward Amerasian Immigration." *Brooklyn Journal of International Law* 15 (December 1989): 641-709.

7536. "Defusing Xenophobia: Sacramento Struggles in the Immigration-Issue Thicket." *Los Angeles Times*, 17 May 1993. (editorial).

7537. Diamond, Sara. "Blaming the Newcomers." *Z Magazine* 5 (July-August 1992): 48-51. [Undocumented immigrants]

7538. Diegmueller, Karen. "Education Bulk of Immigration Costs, Fla. Says." *Education Week*, 11 May 1994.

7539. D'Innocenzo, Michael, and Josef P. Sirefman eds. *Immigration and Ethnicity. American Society- "Melting Pot" or "Salad Bowl"?* Westport, CT: Greenwood, 1992.

7540. Dixon, Heriberto. "The Cuban-American Counterpoint: Black Cubans in the United States." *Dialectical Anthropology* 13 (1988): 227-239.

7541. Dodoo, F.N.A. *Race and Immigrant Stratification in the United States*. Ph.D. diss., University of Pennsylvania, 1988. [Black immigrants]. UMO # 8908325.

7542. Eischenbroich, Donata. *Eine Nation von Einwandern: ethnisches Bewusstsein und Integrationspolitik in den U.S.A.* Frankfurt: Campus Verlag, 1986.

7543. Emery, Garnet K. "The American Dream- for the Lucky Ones: The United States' Confused Immigration Policy." *University of Arkansas at Little Rock Law Journal* 12 (Fall 1989): 755-775.

7544. Engelberg, Stephen. "In Immigration Labyrinth, Corruption Comes Easily." *New York Times*, 12 September 1994. [Corruption in federal immigration offices]

7545. Espenshade, T. J., and C. A. Calhoun. "An Analysis of Public Opinion Toward Undocumented Immigration." *Population Research and Policy Review* 12 (1993): 189-224.

7546. Felzer, Karen. "'Could My Friend Really Be an Immigrant?'." *Los Angeles Times*, 8 February 1993.

7547. Finch, Wilbur A., Jr. "The Immigration Reform and Control Act of 1986: A Preliminary Assessment." *Social Service Review* 64 (June 1990).

7548. *Fiscal Impacts of Undocumented Aliens: Selected Estimates for Seven States*. Urban Institute, 1994.

7549. Foamante, Jorge, and Wayne Cornelius. *Flujos migratorios mexicanos hacia Estados Unidos*. Mexico City: Fondo de Cultura Economica, S.A., 1989.

7550. Freeman, James M. *Hearts of Sorrow- Vietnamese American Lives*. Stanford, CA: Stanford University Press, 1989.

7551. Freeman, Richard B. "Immigration from Poor to Wealthy Countries: Experience of the United States." *European Economic Review* 37 (April 1993).

7552. Fuchs, Lawrence H. "How Racism Has Influenced the Politics of Immigration." *Boston Globe*, 29 March 1992. [Review of Ellis Cose, A Nation of Strangers]

7553. Gabaccia, Donna, ed. *Seeking Common Ground: Multidisciplinary Studies of Immigrant Women in the United States*. Westport, CT: Greenwood, 1992.

7554. Gamio, Manuel. *Mexican Immigration to the United States*. Chicago, IL: University of Chicago Press, 1930.

7555. _____. *The Mexican Immigrant: His Life Story*. Chicago, IL: University of Chicago Press, 1931. Translated by Robert C. Jones

7556. Gemery, Henry A. "European Emigration to North America, 1700-1820: Numbers and Quasi-numbers." *Perspectives on American History* 1 (1984): 283-342.

7557. Gibney, Mark. "United States Immigration Policy and the Huddled Masses Myth." *Georgetown Immigration Law Journal* 3 (Fall 1989): 361-386.

7558. Gompers, Samuel, and Herman Guttstadt. *Some Reasons for Chinese Exclusion: Meat vs. Rice, American Manhood Against Asiatic Coolieism, Which Shall Survive?* AFL, 1901.

7559. Guerin-Gonzalez, Camille. *Cycles of Immigration and Repatriation: Mexican Farm Workers in California Industrial Agriculture, 1900-1940*. Ph.D. diss., University of California, 1985. UMO # 8604131.

7560. Gutierrez, D. G. "Sin Fronteras: Chicanos, Mexican Americans, and the Emergence of the Contemporary Mexican Immigration Debate, 1968-1978." *Journal of American Ethnic History* 10 (Summer 1991): 5-37.

7561. Hall, P. F. "The Recent History of Immigration and Immigration Restriction." *Journal of Political Economy* 21 (1913): 735-751.

7562. Halter, Marilyn. *Between Race and Ethnicity: Cape Verdean American Immigrants, 1860-1965*. University of Illinois Press, 1993.

7563. Handlin, Oscar. *Race and Nationality in American Life*. Boston, MA: Little, Brown, 1957.

7564. Hawkins, Hugh. "Removing the Wecome Mat: Changing Perceptions of the Immigrant." in *Men, Women, and Issues in American History*, Volume 2. pp. 88-113. eds. Howard H. Quint, and Milton Cantor. Homewood, IL: Dorsey Press, 1975.

7565. Helton, Arthur C. *The Implementation of the Refugee Act of 1980: A Decade of Experience*. New York, NY: Lawyers Committee for Human Rights, 1990.

7566. Henkin, Louis. "The Constitution and United States Sovereignty: A Century of Chinese Exclusion and Its Progeny." *Harvard Law Review* 100 (1987).

7567. Hoerder, Dirk, ed. *American Labor and Immigration History, 1877-1920s: Recent European Research*. University of Illinois Press, 1983.

7568. Holder, Calvin. "The Causes and Composition of West Indian Immigration to New York City, 1900-1952." *Afro-Americans in New York Life and History* 11 (January 1987): 7-28.

7569. Hondagneu, Pierrette M. *Gender and the Politics of Mexican Undocumented Immigrant Settlement*. Ph.D. diss., University of California, 1990.

7570. Hondagneu-Sotelo, Pierrette M. *Gendered Transitions: Mexican Experience of Immigration*. University of California Press, 1994.

7571. Hood, Marlowe. "Riding the Snake." *Los Angeles Times Magazine*, 13 June 1993. [Illegal immigrants from China]

7572. Hooglund, Eric, ed. *Crossing the Waters: Arabic-speaking Immigrants to the United States before 1940*. Washington, DC: Smithsonian, 1987.

7573. Huddle, D., and D. Simcox. "The Impact of Immigration on the Social Security System." *Population and Environment* 16 (September 1994): 91-98.

7574. Hunt, Linda. "U.S. Coverup of Nazi Scientists." *Bulletin of Atomic Scientists* 41 (1985): 16-24.

7575. "Immigrants and Nativism." *Los Angeles Times*, 9 August 1993. [Four letters]

7576. "Immigration Policy and the Rights of Aliens." *Harvard Law Review* 96 (April 1983): 1286-1465.

7577. Ivins, Molly. "Bordering on Hysteria." *Washington Post*, 3 February 1994. [The politics and economics of anti-illegal immigration in California but not in Texas]

7578. Jackson, Jacquelyn Johnson. "Illegal Aliens: Big Threat to Black Workers." *Ebony* 34 (April 1979): 33-40.

7579. Jackson, Jacquelyne Johnson. "Seeking Common Ground for Blacks and Immigrants." in *U.S. Immigration in the 1980s. Reappraisal and Reform*, pp. 92-103. ed. David E. Simcox. Boulder, CO: Westview, 1988.

7580. Jensen, Leif. *The New Immigration. Implications for Poverty and Public Assistance Utilization*. Westport, CT: Greenwood, 1989. [1960-1980]

7581. Johnson, Violet Mary-Ann. *The Migration Experience: Social and Economic Adjustment of British West Indian Immigrants in Boston, 1915-1950*. Ph.D. diss., Boston College, 1993. UMO # 9314170.

7582. Jones, Maldwyn A. *American Immigration*. 2nd Edition, University of Chicago Press, 1992.

7583. Kadetsky, Elizabeth. "Bashing Illegals in California." *Nation*, 17 October 1994.

7584. Kamen, Al. "When Hostility Follows Immigration." *Washington Post*, 16 November 1992. [Asian Indians in Hudson, Bergen, and Middlesex Counties, New Jersey]

7585. Kasinitz, Philip. *Caribbean New York: Black Immigrants and the Politics of Race*. Ithaca, NY: Cornell University Press, 1992.

7586. Kilborn, Peter T. "Law Fails to Stem Abuse of Migrants, U.S. Panel Reports." *New York Times*, 22 October 1992. [Immigration Reform and Control Act]

7587. King, M., and Steven Ruggles. "American Immigration, Fertility, and Race Suicide at the Turn of the Century." *Journal of Interdisciplinary History* 20 (Winter 1990).

7588. Klein, Dianne. "Majority in State Are Fed Up With Illegal Immigration." *Los Angeles Times*, 19 September 1993. [Los Angeles Times Poll of California public opinion]

7589. Kposowa, Augustine J. "The Impact of Immigration on Native Earnings in the United States, 1940 to 1980." *Applied Behavioral Science Review* 1 (1993): 1-25.

7590. Kraut, Alan M. *Silent Travelers. Genus, Genes, and the "Immigrant Menace"*. Basic Books, 1994.

7591. Kwong, Peter. "China's Human Traffickers." *Nation*, 17 October 1994. [Smugglers of Chinese to the United States]

7592. _____. "The Wages of Fear. Undocumented and Unwanted, Fouzhounese Immigrants Are Changing the Face of Chinatown." *Village Voice*, 26 April 1994. [N.Y.C.]

7593. "Labor Market Aspects of Legal Immigration Reform." *Georgetown Immigration Law Journal* 4 (Spring 1990): 249-276. [Panel discussion]

7594. Lee, Patrick. "Studies Challenge View That Immigrants Harm Economy." *Los Angeles Times*, 13 August 1993.

7595. Lee, Regina. *Through the Golden Door: Impacts of Non- Citizen Residents on the Commonwealth.* Boston, MA: Commonwealth of Massachusetts, May 1990.

7596. Lee, Sharon M. "Asian Immigration and American Race- Relations: From Exclusion to Acceptance?" *Ethnic and Racial Studies* 12 (July 1989): 368-390.

7597. Levenstein, Harvey A. "The AFL and Mexican Immigration in the 1920's: An Experiment in Labor Diplomacy." *Hispanic American Historical Review* 48 (May 1968): 106-119.

7598. Lipshultz, Robert J. *American Attitudes Toward Mexican Immigration, 1924-1952.* Master's thesis, University of Chicago, 1962.

7599. Little, Cheryl. "United States Haitian Policy: A History of Discrimination." *New York Law School Journal of Human Rights* 10, part 2 (Spring 1993): 269-324. [1963-1993]

7600. Mandel, Michael J. and others. "The Immigrants. How They're Helping to Revitalize the U.S. Economy." *Business Week*, 13 July 1992.

7601. Mann, Jim and others. "Chinese Refugees Take to High Seas." *Los Angeles Times*, 16 March 1993. [Smuggling Chinese into the U.S.]

7602. Margolis, Maxine L. and others. "Immigration Chaos Keeps U.S. in Cheap Labor." *New York Times*, 21 September 1994. [Three letters]

7603. Marston, Sallie A. "Adopted Citizens: Discourse and the Production of Meaning among Nineteenth Century American Urban Immigrants." *Transactions, Institute of British Geographers* 14 (1989).

7604. Mayo-Smith, R. "The Control of Immigration." *Political Science Quarterly* 3 (1888): 46-77, 197-225, 409-424.

7605. McDonnell, Patrick J. "Immigrant Study Cites Fiscal Gain." *Los Angeles Times*, 23 February 1994. [Study by Jeffrey S. Passel, Urban Institute]

7606. McDonnell, Patrick J., and Paul Jacobs. "FAIR at Forefront of Push to Reduce Immigration." *Los Angeles Times*, 24 November 1993. [Federation for American Immigration Reform]

7607. Meisenheimer, J. R., II. "How Do Immigrants Fare in the U.S. Labor Market?" *Monthly Labor Review* 115 (December 1992).

7608. Meusner, Jeffrey N. "Apprehending and Prosecuting Nazi War Criminals in the United States." *Nova Law Review* 15 (Spring 1991): 747-770.

7609. Miles, Jack. "Blacks vs. Browns, Immigration and the New American Dilemma." *Atlantic Monthly*, October 1992. [Los Angeles]

7610. Miller, Alan C., and Ronald J. Ostrow. "Immigration Policy Failures Invite Overhaul." *Los Angeles Times*, 11 July 1993.

7611. Miller, K. A., and B. D. Boling. "Golden Streets, Bitter Tears: The Irish Image of America During the Era of Mass Migration." *Journal of American Ethnic History* 10 (Fall-Winter 1990).

7612. Millis, Harry A. "Some of the Economic Aspects of Japanese Immigration." *American Economic Review* 5 (1915): 789-804.

7613. Muller, Thomas. "Immigration Policy and Economic Growth." *Yale Law and Policy Review* 7 (Fall-Winter 1989): 101-136.

7614. Murayama, Yuzo. *The Economic History of Japanese Immigration to the Pacific Northwest: 1890-1920*. Ph.D. diss., University of Washington, 1982.

7615. Murphy, J. P., and T. J. Espenshade. "Immigration Prism: Historical Continuities in the Kennedy-Simpson Legal Immigration Reform Bill." *Population and Environment* 12 (Winter 1990).

7616. Murphy, John C. *An Analysis of the Attitudes of American Catholics toward the Immigrant and the Negro, 1825-1925*. Washington, DC: 1940.

7617. Mydans, Seth. "A New Tide of Immigration Brings Hostility to the Surface, Poll Finds." *New York Times*, 27 June 1993.

7618. Navajas, Emma D. "Haitian Interdiction: An Overview of U.S. Policy and Practice." *Migration World Magazine* 20 (1992): 38-41.

7619. Navarrette, Ruben, Jr. "Immigration Ghosts Haunt the Hispanic Caucus." *Los Angeles Times*, 20 March 1994.

7620. Neuberger, M. J. "What's FAIR Is Foul." *Village Voice*, 17 August 1993. pp. 21-22. [Federation for American Immigration Reform]

7621. Newinger, Sheldon M. *American Jewry and United States Immigration Policy, 1881-1953*. New York, NY: Arno Press, 1980.

7622. Page, T. W. "Some Economic Aspects of Immigration before 1870: II." *Journal of Political Economy* 21 (1913): 34-55.

7623. Palmer, Ransford W. ed. *In Search of a Better Life, Perspectives on Migration from the Caribbean*. Westport, CT: Praeger, 1990.

7624. Parker, Richard A., and Louis M. Rea. "Immigration Controversy." *Los Angeles Times*, 25 August 1993. [Letter on net costs of illegal immigration]

7625. Passel, J. S., and M. Fix. "Myths About Immigrants." *Foreign Policy* 95 (Summer 1994): 151-160.

7626. Passell, Peter. "A Job-Wage Conundrum." *New York Times*, 6 September 1994. [Immigrants and employment]

7627. Pavalko, Ronald W. "Racism and the New Immigration: A Reinterpretation of the Assimilation of White Ethnics in American Society." *Sociology and Social Research* 65 (October 1980): 56-77.

7628. Pozzetta, George E., ed. *American Immigration and Ethnicity*. Garland, 1992. [20 volume set of reprinted articles]

7629. Rahming, Melvin B. *The Evolution of the West Indian's Image in the Afro-American Novel*. Millwood, NY: Associated Faculty Press, 1986.

7630. Rakowsky, Judy. "U.S. Entry Called Often Easy for Alleged Nazis, Helpers." *Boston Globe*, 23 September 1994.

7631. Ramos, George. "Bashing Illegal Immigrants Is on Today's Menu." *Los Angeles Times*, 14 December 1992.

7632. Reimers, David M. *Still the Golden Door. The Third World Comes to America*. 2nd Edition, Columbia University Press, 1992.

7633. Richardson, Chad, and Joe R. Feagin. "The Dynamics of Legalization: Undocumented Mexican Immigrants in the United States." in *Research in Political Society*, Vol. 3. pp. 179-201. ed. Richard G. Braungart. Greenwich, CT: JAI Press, 1987.

7634. Rimer, Sara. "Crammed in Tiny, Illegal Rooms, Tenants at the Margins of Survival." *New York Times*, 23 March 1992. [New York City's poorest immigrants]

7635. Ripley, Lee. "Immigrant Aid Scam Alleged." *Los Angeles Times*, 23 June 1993.

7636. Ripley, W. Z. "Race Progress and Immigration." *Annals* 34 (1909): 130-138.

7637. Romo, Ricardo. "Responses to Mexican Immigration, 1910- 1930." *Aztlan* 6 (Summer 1975): 173-194.

7638. Rubin, Jay. "Black Nativism: The European Immigrant in Negro Thought, 1830-1860." *Phylon* 39 (1978): 193-203.

7639. Salyer, Lucy E. "Captives of Law: Judicial Enforcement of the Chinese Exclusion Laws, 1891-1905." *Journal of American History* 76 (1989): 91-117.

7640. _____. *Guarding the 'White Man's Frontier': Courts, Politics, and the Regulation of Immigration, 1891-1924.* Ph.D. diss., University of California, Berkeley, 1989. [Principally Chinese immigrants]. UMO # 9006496.

7641. Schmidt, Peter. "Officials Seeking Help To Ease the Burden of Education Immigrants." *Education Week*, 23 June 1993.

7642. Shankman, Arnold. *Ambivalent Friends: Afro-Americans View the Immigrant.* Westport, CT: Greenwood, 1982.

7643. Shannon, S. M. "English in the Barrio. The Quality of Contact among Immigrant Children." *Hispanic Journal of Behavioral Sciences* 12 (August 1990).

7644. Silverstein, Stuart. "Job Market a Flash Point for Natives, Newcomers." *Los Angeles Times*, 15 November 1993. [Competition of immigrant and non-immigrant labor]

7645. Simon, Richard. "Activists for Immigrant Rights Battle Erosion of Public Support." *Los Angeles Times*, 24 November 1993.

7646. Smith, Eric J. "Citizenship Discrimination and the Frank Amendment to the Immigration Reform and Control Act." *Wayne Law Review* 35 (Summer 1989): 1523-1546.

7647. Sontag, Deborah. "Across the U.S., Immigrants Find the Land of Resentment." *New York Times*, 11 December 1992.

7648. _____. "Analysis of illegal Immigrants in New York Defies Stereotypes." *New York Times*, 2 September 1993. [Three major groups of illegal immigrants are from Ecuador, Italy, and Poland]

7649. _____. "Emigres Battling Abuse Flex Rights as Workers." *New York Times*, 15 June 1993. [Immigrants]

7650. _____. "A Fervent 'No' To Assimilation in New America." *New York Times*, 29 June 1993. [Study at Johns Hopkins University, headed by Alejandro Portes]

7651. _____. "Immigrants Swindle Their Own, Preying on Trust." *New York Times*, 25 August 1992.

7652. _____. "Reshaping New York City's Golden Door." *New York Times*, 13 June 1993. (first of six articles).

7653. Spayd, Liz. "A Daunting Economic Divide." *Washington Post*, 5 July 1993. [Immigrants in the Washington, DC area and jobs in low-paying as well as high-paying occupations]

7654. Stafford, Walter W. "Native-Born Blacks and Immigrants." *Crossroads* 36 (November 1993): 17-18.

7655. Starr, Kevin. "California Reverts to Its Scapegoating Ways." *Los Angeles Times*, 26 September 1993. [Mexican immigrants]

7656. Stolarik, Mark M. *Immigration and Urbanization: The Slovak Experience.* New York, NY: AMS Press, 1989.

7657. Stout, Angela K. *Sanctuary in the 1980s: The Dialectics of Law and Social Movement Development, 2 vols.* Ph.D. diss., University of Delaware, 1989. UMO # 9019292.

7658. Strauss, Herbert A., ed. *Jewish Immigrants of the Nazi Period in the U.S.A.: Volume 6, Essays on the History, Persecution and Emigration of German Jews.* London: K. G. Saur, 1987.

7659. Sutter, Valerie O'Connor. *The Indochinese Refugee Dilemma.* Baton Rouge, LA: Louisiana State University, 1990.

7660. Tamayo, William R. "Defending the Rights of the Undocumented: A Challenge to the Civil Rights Movement and Local Governments." *New York University Review of Law and Social Change* 16 (March 1988): 145-155.

7661. Thompson, James R. "The Black As Ironic Immigrant: Self- perception in the Early Republic." *European Contribution to American Studies* 14 (1988): 243-260.

7662. Tichenor, D. J. "The Politics of Immigration Reform in the United States, 1981-1990." *Polity* 26 (Spring 1994): 332-362.

7663. Tien, Chang-Lin. "America's Scapegoats. Immigrant-bashing Is Hurting the Native and Foreign-born Alike." *Newsweek*, 31 October 1994. [Chancellor, University of California, Berkeley]

7664. Toney, Joyce. "Similarities and Differences in the Response to Oppression among Blacks in the Diaspora." in *Immigration and Ethnicity*, eds. Michael D'Innocenzo, and Josef P. Sirefman. : Greenwood, 1992.

7665. Trueba, Henry T., and others. *Healing Multicultural America: Mexican Immigrants' Rise to Power in Rural California*. Falmer Press, 1993.

7666. Tyler, F. B. and others. "Psychosocial Characteristics of the Marginal Immigrant Latino Youth." *Youth and Society* 24 (September 1992).

7667. Vecoli, Rudolph J., and Suzanne M. Sinke, eds. *A Century of European Migrations, 1830-1930*. Champaign, IL: University of Illinois Press, 1991.

7668. Verhovek, Sam H. "Texas and California: Two Views of Illegal Aliens." *New York Times*, 26 June 1994.

7669. Vought, H. "Division and Reunion: Woodrow Wilson, Immigration, and the Myth of American Unity." *Journal of American Ethnic History* 13 (Spring 1994): 24-50.

7670. Waldinger, Roger, and G. Gilbertson. "Immigrants' Progress: Ethnic and Gender Differences among United States Immigrants In the 1980s." *Sociological Perspectives* 37 (Autumn 1994): 431-444.

7671. Weinberg, Sydney S. "The Treatment of Women in Immigration History: A Call for Change." *Journal of American Ethnic History* 11 (Summer 1992): 25-46.

7672. Weintraub, Sidney. "Illegal Immigrants in Texas: Impact on Social Services and Related Considerations." *International Migration Review* 18 (Fall 1984): 733-747.

7673. Weintraub, Sidney, and Gilberto Cardenas. *The Use of Public Services by Undocumented Aliens in Texas*. Austin, TX: Lyndon B. Johnson School of Public Affairs, University of Texas, 1984.

7674. White, G. C. *Immigration and Assimilation: A Survey of Social Thought and Public Opinion, 1882-1914*. Ph.D. diss., University of Pennsylvania, 1952.

7675. Will, George F. "Assimilation Is Not a Dirty Word." *Los Angeles Times*, 29 July 1993.

7676. Williamson, Jeffrey G. "Immigrant-Inequality Trade-Offs in the Promised Land: Income Distribution and Absorptive Capacity Prior to the Quotas." in *The Gateway: U.S. Immigration Issues and Policies*, pp. 251-288. ed. Barry R. Chiswick. Washington, DC, 1982.

7677. Winegarden, C. R., and Lay Boom Khor. "Undocumented Immigration and Income Inequality in the Native-born Population of the U.S.: Econometric Evidence." *Applied Economics* 25 (February 1993).

7678. Wtulich, Josephine. *American Xenophobia and the Slav Immigrant: A Living Legacy of Mind and Spirit*. East European Mongraphs, 1994. [1890s - 1960s]

7679. Wyman, Mark. *Round-Trip to America: The Immigrants Return to Europe, 1880-1930*. Cornell University Press, 1993.

7680. Yzaguirre, Raul. "'California Cleansing'." *Washington Post*, 18 May 1994. [Critique of California Governor Pete Wilson's anti- immigrant program]

INDUSTRY

7681. Arroyo, Laura E. "Industrial and Occupational Distribution of Chicano Workers." *Aztlan* 4 (Fall 1973): 343-382.

7682. Morefield, Richard H. "Mexicans in the California Mines, 1848-1853." *California Historical Society Quarterly* 35 (March 1956): 37-46.

7683. Paul, Rodman W. *The Mining Frontiers of the Far West, 1848- 1880*. New York, NY: Holt, Rinehart and Winston, 1963.

7684. Wagoner, Jay J. *The History of the Cattle Industry in Southern Arizona, 1540-1940*. Tuscon, AZ: University of Arizona Press, 1952.

IQ AND RACE

7685. Anderson, J. L. "Rushton Racial Comparisons: An Ecological Critique of Theory and Method." *Canadian Psychology* 32 (January 1991): 51-62. [See Rushton, below]

7686. Armelagos, George J. "Racism and Physical Anthropology: The Retreat of Scientific Racism-Review." *American Journal of Physical Anthropology* 93 (March 1994): 381-382. [See also reply by A. M. Brues, pp. 383-384]

7687. Bailey, J. Michael. "A Critique of Gordon's I.Q.- Commensurability Property." *International Journal of Sociology and Social Policy* 9 (1989): 64-74.

7688. Barker, David. "The Biology of Stupidity: Genetics, Eugenics and Mental Deficiency in the Inter-war Years." *British Journal for the History of Science* 22 (1989): 347-375.

7689. Berger, Joseph. "Professors' Theories on Race Stir Turmoil at City College." *New York Times*, 20 April 1990. [Professors Michael Levin and Leonard Jeffries, Jr., City College, CUNY]

7690. Block, N. J., and Gerald Dworkin. "I.Q.: Heritability and Inequality." *Philosophy and Public Affairs* (Summer, Fall 1974): 331-409, 40-99.

7691. Boring, E. G. "Intelligence as the Tests Test It." *New Republic* 35 (1923): 35-37.

7692. Brody, E. B., and N. Brody. *Intelligence: Nature, Determinants and Consequences*. New York, NY: Academic Press, 1976.

7693. Brooks, D. H. M. "Dogs and Slaves: Genetics, Exploitation and Morality." *Aristotelian Society* 88 (1988).

7694. Cain, D. P., and C. H. Vanderwolf. "A Critique of [J. P.] Rushton on Race, Brain Size and Intelligence." *Personality and Individual Differences* 11 (1990).

7695. Capron, Christiane, and M. Duyme. "Children's IQ and SES of Biological and Adoptive Parents in a Balanced Cross-Fostering Study." *Cahiers de Psychologie Cognitive* 11 (June 1991): 323-348.

7696. Cernovsky, Z. Z. "Intelligence and Race: Further Comments on J. P. Rushton's Work." *Psychological Reports* 68 (April 1991): 481-483. [See Rushton, below]

7697. Coughlin, Ellen K. "Class, IQ, and Heredity." *Chronicle of Higher Education*, 26 October 1994. [About Herrnstein-Murray book, The Bell Curve]

7698. De Parle, Jason. "An Architect of the Reagan Vision Plunges Into Inquiry on Race and I.Q." *New York Times*, 30 November 1990. [Charles Murray]

7699. _____. "The Most Dangerous Conservative." *New York Times Magazine*, 9 October 1994. [About Charles Murray's views on I.Q. and race, among other things]

7700. "Debate on Race and IQ Recalls Past Prejudice." *New York Times*, 26 October 1994. [Four letters]

7701. Delgado, Richard and others. "Can Science Be Inopportune? Constitutional Validity of Governmental Restrictions on Race-IQ Research." *UCLA Law Review* 31 (1983): 194-211.

7702. Duster, Troy. *Backdoor to Eugenics*. New York, NY: Routledge, 1991.

7703. Elliot, Roger. *Litigating Intelligence. IQ Tests, Special Education and Social Science in the Courtroom*. Westport, CT: Auburn House, 1987.

7704. Eysenck, Hans J. "Science, Racism, and Sexism." *Journal of Social, Political and Economic Studies* 16 (Summer 1991): 217-250.

7705. Fletcher, Ronald. *Science, Ideology, and the Media. The Cyril Burt Scandal*. New Brunswick, NJ: Transaction Publishers, 1990.

7706. Flint, Anthony. "IQ Fight Renewed. New Book Links Genes, Intelligence." *Boston Globe*, 9 August 1994. [Richard J. Herrnstein and Charles Murray, The Bell Curve: Intelligence and Class Structure in American Life]

7707. Flynn, J. R. "Race and IQ: Jensen's Case Refuted." in *Arthur Jensen: Consensus and Controversy*, eds. S. Modgil, and C. Modgil. Lewes, England: Falmer Press, 1987.

7708. Ford, Donna Y. and others. "The Coloring of IQ Testing: A New Name for an Old Phenomenon." *Urban League Review* 13 (Summer- Winter 1990): 99-111.

7709. Foster, J. "Retroviruses, Genetic Lesioning and Mental Deficiency Among Blacks: A Causal Hypothesis." *Mankind Quarterly* 31 (Fall-Winter 1990).

7710. Galloway, F. J. "Inferential Sturdiness and the 1917 Army- Alpha: A New Look at the Robustness of Educational Quality Indices as Determinants of Interstate Black-White Score Differentials." *Journal of Negro Education* 63 (Spring 1994): 251- 266.

7711. Goodman, Alan H., George J. Armelagos, and Michel-Rolph Trouillot. "The Study of Racial Differences." *Chronicle of Higher Education*, 7 September 1994. [Two letters]

7712. Greene, John C. "The American Debate on the Negro's Place in Nature, 1780-1815." in *Race, Gender, and Rank*, ed. Maryanne C. Horowitz. : University of Rochester Press, 1992.

7713. Gross, Peter, and A. Kamara. "The Dangers of Studying Racial Differences." *Chronicle of Higher Education*, 14 September 1994. [Two separate letters on article by Pat Shipman, "Facing Racial Differences- Together", in issue of August 3, 1994]

7714. Hauser, Robert M. and others. "Understanding Black-White Differences." *Public Interest* 99 (1990): 110-119. [Critique of R. J. Herrnstein, "Still an American Dilemma", Public Interest, No. 98 (1990) 3-17]

7715. Henneberg, Melinda, and others. "Head Size, Body Size and Intelligence: Intraspecific Correlations in Homo sapiens sapiens." *Homo* 36 (1985): 207-218.

7716. Herbert, Bob. "Throwing a Curve." *New York Times*, 26 October 1994. [Attacks Herrnstein and Murray's *The Bell Curve* as "a scabrous piece of racial pornography masquerading as serious scholarship"]

7717. "Heredity and Intelligence." *Cahiers de Psychologie Cognitive* 10 (December 1990): entire issue.

7718. Herrnstein, Richard J., and Charles Murray. *The Bell Curve: Intelligence and Class Structure in American Life*. Free Press, 1994.

7719. Hilliard, Asa. "Standardization and Cultural Bias Impediments to the Scientific Study and Validation of Intelligence." *Journal of Research and Development in Education* 12 (Winter 1979): 47-58.

7720. Hirsch, Jerry. "To 'Unfrock the Charlatans'." *Sage Race Relations Abstracts* 16 (May 1981): 1-65.

7721. Holt, Jim. "Anti-Social Science?" *New York Times*, 19 October 1994. [Race and IQ]

7722. Isham, W. P., and Leon J. Kamin. "Blackness, Deafness, IQ and g." *Intelligence* 17 (January-March 1993): 37-46.

7723. Itzkoff, Seymour W. *The Decline of Intelligence in America. A Strategy for National Renewal*. Praeger, 1994.

7724. Jamieson, J. W. "Arthur Jensen and the Heritablility of IQ: A Case Study in the Violation of Academic Freedom." *Mankind Quarterly* 30 (Summer 1990).

7725. _____. "Can a Mathematician Be a Social Scientist? The Case of William Shockley." *Mankind Quarterly* 30 (1989): 71-112. [Defense of Shockley's studies of IQ and race]

7726. Jamieson, J. W., ed. *Essays on the Nature of Intelligence and the Analysis of Racial Differences in the Performance of IQ Tests.* Washington, DC: Cliveden Press, 1988. [Antagonistic to idea of intellectual equality of the races]

7727. Jamieson, J. W. "'Marxian Biology' in the Western Social Sciences." *Conservative Review* 2 (February 1991): 23-26.

7728. Jensen, Arthur R. "I.Q. and Science: The Mysterious Burt Affair." *Public Interest* 105 (Autumn 1991): 93-106.

7729. _____. "Raising I.Q. without Increasing g? A Review of The Milwaukee Project: Preventing Mental Retardation in Children at Risk." *Developmental Review* 9 (September 1989).

7730. Johnson, Paul N. "'Politically Correct': The Attack on Scientific Inquiry into Heritability." *Conservative Review* 2 (April 1991): 23-26.

7731. Joynson, Robert. *The Burt Affair.* London, England: 1989. [See, also, article by editor in *Encounter*, September 1990]

7732. Kendler, H. H. "Unanswered Questions About Racism and Scientific Purpose." *American Psychologist* 46 (September 1991): 984, (letter).

7733. Kuhl, Stefan. *The Nazi Connection. Eugenics, American Racism, and German National Socialism.* Oxford University Press, 1994.

7734. Kutzik, David M. *Hereditarian I.Q. versus Human Intelligence.* Ph.D. diss., Temple University, 1990. UMO # 9022921.

7735. Layzer, David. "Nature and Nurture." *New York Times*, 23 June 1990, (letter).

7736. Levin, Michael. "Race Differences: An Overview." *Journal of Social, Political and Economic Studies* 16 (Summer 1991): 195-216.

7737. Lochlin, J. C. "Should We Do Research on Race Differences in Intelligence?" *Intelligence* 16 (January-March 1992): 1-4.

7738. Locurto, C. "The Malleability of I.Q. as Judged from Adoption Studies." *Intelligence* 14 (July-September 1990).

7739. Lowie, Robert H. "The Mind of Women and the Lower Races." *American Journal of Sociology* 12 (1907).

7740. Lynn, R. "New Evidence on Brain Size and Intelligence- Comment on Rushton and Cain and Vanderwolf." *Personality and Individual Differences* 11 (1990).

7741. Lyons, Charles H. "The Colonial Mentality: Assessments of the Intelligence of Blacks and Women in Nineteenth-century America." in *Education and Colonialism*, pp. 181-206. eds. Philip G. Altbach, and Gail P. Kelly. New York, NY: Longman, 1978.

7742. Mackintosh, N. J., and C. G. N. Mascie-Taylor. *The I.Q. Question.* London, England: HMSO, 1985. The Swann Report, Annex D, Chapter 3, pp. 126-163

7743. Martin, Michael. "Equal Education, Native Intelligence and Justice." *Philosophical Forum* 6 (Fall 1974): 29-39.

7744. McGregor, Alan, ed. *Evolution, Creative Intelligence and Intergroup Competition.* Washington, DC: Cliveden Press, 1986. [Antagonistic to idea of intellectual equality of the races]

7745. Mensh, Elaine, and Harry Mensh. *The I.Q. Mythology. Class, Race, Gender and Inequality.* Carbondale, IL: Southern Illinois University Press, 1991.

7746. Mercer, Jane R. "Latent Functions of Intelligence Testing in the Public Schools." in *The Testing of Black Students*, pp. 77- 94. ed. L. Miller. Englewood Cliffs, NJ: Prentice-Hall, 1974.

7747. Moore, Elsie G. J. "Ethnic Social Milieu and Black Children's Intelligence Test Achievement." *Journal of Negro Education* 56 (1987): 4-52.

7748. Morris, Frank L. *The Jensen Hypothesis. Social Science Research or Social Science Racism?* Los Angeles, CA: U.C.L.A. Center for Afro-American Studies.

7749. Morse, J. "A Comparison of White and Colored Children Measured by the Binet Scale of Intelligence." *Popular Science Monthly* 84 (1914): 75-79.

7750. Payette, K. A., and H. F. Clarizio. "Discrepant Team Decisions; The Effects of Race, Gender, Acheivement, and I.Q. on L.D. Eligibility." *Psychology in the Schools* 31 (January 1994): 40-48.

7751. Pearson, Roger, ed. *Race, Intelligence and Bias in Academe.* Scott-Townsend Publishers, 1992.

7752. _____. *Schockley on Eugenics and Race: The Application of Science to the Solution of Human Problems.* Scott-Townsend, 1992.

7753. Persell, Caroline H. "Genetic and Cultural Deficit Theories. Two Sides of the Same Racist Coin." *Journal of Black Studies* 12 (September 1981): 19-37.

7754. "Psychologists Protest 'Racial' Psychology." *Bulletin of the Society for the Psychological Study of Social Issues* 10 (1939): 302-304.

7755. "[Racial Differences in Intelligence]." *Mankind Quarterly* 32 (Fall-Winter 1991): 99-188. (10 articles).

7756. Ramey, C. T. "High-risk Children and I.Q.: Altering Intergenerational Patterns." *Intelligence* 16 (April-June 1992).

7757. Rees-Mogg, William. "Why Science Must Be Free to Breach Taboos." *Independent*, 10 June 1991. p. 19. [in Re: Jean P. Rushton]

7758. Rich, Spencer. "Poverty Is Blamed for 9-Point Deficit In 5- Year Olds' I.Q.s." *Washington Post*, 27 March 1993. [Study by Greg J. Duncan and colleagues]

7759. Rosenbach, J. H., and R. R. Rusch. "I.Q. and Achievement: 1930s to 1980s." *Psychology in the Schools* 28 (October 1991): 304-309.

7760. Roubertoux, Pierre, and Christiane Capron. "Are Intelligence Differences Hereditarily Transmitted?" *Cahiers de psychologie cognitive* 10 (December 1990): 555-594. [Comments, 595-714; Response, 715-721]

7761. Rury, John L. "Race, Religion, and Education: An Analysis of Black and White Scores on the 1917 Army Alpha Intelligence Test." *Journal of Negro Education* 57 (Winter 1988).

7762. Rushton, J. Philippe. "Ethnic Nepotism in Science." *Behavioral and Brain Sciences* 14 (September 1991): 526.

7763. _____. "Race, Brain Size and Intelligence- A Rejoinder to Cain and Vanderwolf." *Personality and Individual Differences* 11 (1990). [See Anderson, above]

7764. _____. "Race, Brain Size, and Intelligence: Another Reply to Cernovsky." *Psychological Reports* 68 (April 1991): 500- 502. [See Cernovsky, above]

7765. _____. *Race, Evolution, and Behavior. A Life History Perspective.* Transaction, 1994. [Contends that racial differences in behavior exist on a large scale]

7766. _____. "Racial Differences- Reply." *American Psychologist* 46 (September 1991): 983. (letter).

7767. _____. "Why We Should Study Race Differences." *Psychologische Beiträge* 32 (1990): 128-142.

7768. Samuelson, Franz. "World War I Intelligence Testing and the Development of Psychology." *Journal of the History of the Behavioral Sciences* 13 (July 1977): 274-282.

7769. Scarr, Sandra and others. "I.Q. Correlations in Transracial Adoptive Families." *Intelligence* 17 (October-December 1993): 541- 556.

7770. Scarr, Sandra. *Race, Social Class, and Individual Differences in I. Q.* Hillsdale, NJ: Lawrence Erlbaum Associates, 1981.

364 Racism in Contemporary America

7771. Scarr, Sandra, and Richard A. Weinberg. "The Nature-Nurture Problem Revisited: The Minnesota Adoption Studies." in *Methods of Family Research. Biographies of Research Projects, Vol. 1*, eds. Irving E. Sigel, and Gene Brody. Hillsdale, NJ: Lawrence Erlbaum Associates, 1989.

7772. Shipman, Pat. "Forcing Racial Differences- Together." *Chronicle of Higher Education*, 3 August 1994.

7773. _____. "Frank Discussion of Racial Differences." *Chronicle of Higher Education*, 21 September 1994, (letter).

7774. Shurkin, Joel N. *Terman's Kids. The Groundbreaking Study*. Little, Brown, 1992.

7775. Smith, Courtland L., and Kenneth L. Beals. "Cultural Correlates with Cranial Capacity." *American Anthropologist* 92 (March 1990): 193-200.

7776. Snyderman, M., and S. Rothman. *The I.Q. Controversy. The Media and Public Policy*. New Brunswick, NJ: Transaction, 1988.

7777. Stott, D. H. *Issues in the Intelligence Debate*. Windsor, Berks: NFER-Nelson, 1983.

7778. Stout, D., and S. Stuart. "E. G. Boring Review of Brigham, A Study of American Intelligence." *Social Studies of Science* 21 (February 1991): 133-142.

7779. Taylor, R. L. "Patterns of Intellectual Differences of Black, Hispanic, and White Children." *Psychology in the Schools* 28 (January 1991): 5-8.

7780. Teasdale, T. W. and others. "Intelligence and Educational Level in Adult Males at the Extremes of Stature." *Human Biology* 63 (1991): 19-30.

7781. Tuddenham, Read. "The Nature and Measurement of Intelligence." in *Psychology in the Making: Histories of Selected Research Problems*, pp. 469-525. ed. Leo Postman. New York, NY, 1963.

7782. Urban, Wayne J. "The Black Scholar and Intelligence Testing: The Case of Horace Mann Bond." *Journal of the History of Behavioral Sciences* 25 (1989): 323-334.

7783. Wenger, Morton G. "Pseudo-Egalitarianism, Class, Stratification, and the Aptitude/I.Q. Testing Controversy." *Sociological Abstracts*, 1989. Accession No. 89S21229

7784. Williams, Robert L. "Scientific Racism and I.Q.: The Silent Mugging of the Black Community." *Psychology Today*, May 1974.

7785. X, Cedric and others. *Voodoo or I.Q.: In Introduction to African Psychology*. Chicago, IL: Institute of Positive Education, 1976.

7786. Yoder, Dale. "Present Status of the Question of Racial Differences." *Journal of Educational Psychology* 19 (1928): 463- 470.

7787. Zuckerman, M. "Some Dubious Premises in Research and Theory on Racial Differences: Scientific, Social, and Ethical Issues." *American Psychologist* 45 (December 1990).

KU KLUX KLAN

7788. Alexander, Charles C. *The Ku Klux Klan in the Southwest*. Lexington, KY: University of Kentucky Press, 1965.

7789. Applebome, Peter. "Ex-Klan Members Settle Suit by Agreeing to Classes on Civil Rights." *New York Times*, 25 July 1989. [Alabama]

7790. Bagnall, Robert. "The Spirit of the Ku Klux Klan." *Opportunity* 1 (September 1923): 267.

7791. Becker, Verne. "The Counterfeit Christianity of the Ku Klux Klan." *Christianity Today* 28 (20 April 1984): 30-35.

7792. Blee, Kathleen M. *Women of the Klan. Racism and Gender in the 1920s*. Berkeley, CA: University of California Press, 1991.

7793. Carroll, Ginny. "Coming Soon: Klub K.K.K." *Newsweek*, 8 July 1991. [Reverend Thom Robb, grand wizard, Knights of the Ku Klux Klan]

7794. Carter, Dan T. "The Transformation of a Klansman." *New York Times*, 4 October 1991. [Asa (Ace) Earl Carter, "Forrest Carter"]

7795. Clark, Malcolm, Jr. "The Bigot Disclosed: 90 Years of Nativism." *Oregon Historical Quarterly* 75 (1974): 109-190. [Pages 148-182 deal with the K.K.K. in Oregon]

7796. Cole, Wendy. "Re-Enter the Dragon." *Time*, 3 October 1994. [Factions in the K.K.K.]

7797. Cook, Fred J. *The Ku Klux Klan: America's Recurring Nightmare*. Englewood Cliffs, NJ: J. Messner, 1989. [Written for young people]

7798. Curriden, Mark. "Hitting the Klan-Civility: Alabama Lawyer's Suits Cost Extremists Plenty." *ABA Journal* 75 (February 1989).

7799. Cutlip, Scott M. "Klan Made Potent Use of 'Birth of a Nation'." *New York Times*, 12 May 1994. (letter).

7800. Dees, Morris. "Remember Me By My Clients; They Make My Life Worthwhile." *Trial* 26 (April 1990): 64-69. [Victims of K.K.K. violence]

7801. Duke, Lynne. "F.B.I. Opens Probe of Alleged Ties to Man Who Confessed Role in Klan Killing." *Washington Post*, 10 September 1993. [Murder of black man, Willie Edwards, by Klan in 1957]

7802. Enders, Calvin. "White Sheets in Mecosta: The Anatomy of a Michigan Klan." *Michigan Historical Review* 14 (1988): 59-84.

7803. Escott, Paul. "White Republicanism and the Ku Klux Klan Terror: The North Carolina Piedmont during Reconstruction." in *Race, Class, and the Politics in Southern History: Essays in Honor of Robert F. Durden*, ed. Jeffrey J. Crow. Baton Rouge, LA: Louisiana State University Press, 1989.

7804. Farquhar, Michael. "Pike's Pique: Why This Statue Is a Bust." *Washington Post*, 14 March 1993. [Statue of K.K.K. leader, Albert Pike, in Washington, D.C.]

7805. Fine, Gary A. "Among Those Dark Satanic Mills: Rumors of Kooks, Cults, and Corporations." *Southern Folklore* 47 (1990): 133-146. [K.K.K.]

7806. Goetz, Stephen. "The Ku Klux Klan in New Hampshire, 1923- 1927." *History New Hampshire* 43 (Winter 1988): 244-263.

7807. Gozemba, Patricia A., and Marilyn L. Humphries. "Women in the Anti-Ku Klux Klan Movement, 1865-1984." *Women's Studies International Forum* 12 (1989): 35-40.

7808. Graaf, John de, and Alan H. Stein. "Stetson Kennedy: A Klandestine Man." *In These Times*, 11 December 1991. [An anti-K.K.K. investigator and writer]

7809. Grandolfo, Jane. "Free Speech Becomes a Burning Cross to Bear." *In These Times*, 19 August 1992. [James Stansfield, Imperial Wizard of the Texas Confederate Knights]

7810. Hentoff, Nat. "Would You Fight for the Klan's First Amendment Rights?" *Village Voice*, 9 October 1990.

7811. Holsinger, M. Paul. "The Oregon School Bill Controversy, 1922-1925." *Pacific History Review* 37 (1968): 327-342. [K.K.K. influenced state legislation to outlaw private schools]

7812. Horowitz, David A. "The Klansman as Outsider: Ethnocultural Solidarity and Antielitism in the Oregon Ku Klux Klan of the 1920s." *Pacific North West Quarterly* 80 (January 1989): 12-20.

7813. Hurst, Jack. *Nathan Bedford Forrest*. Knopf, 1993.

7814. Jenkins, William D. *Steel Valley Klan: The Ku Klux Klan in Ohio's Mahoning Valley*. Kent State University Press, 1990.

7815. Jessup, Michael M. *The Decline of the 1920s Klu Klux Klan: A Sociological Analysis*. Ph.D. diss., Southern Illinois University, 1992. UMO # 9305379.

7816. Johnson, Dirk. "Colorado Klansman Refines Message for the '90s." *New York Times*, 23 February 1992.

7817. Kallal, Edward W., Jr. *St. Augustine and the Ku Klux Klan: 1963 and 1964*. Ph.D. diss., University of Florida, 1976. [Reprinted in David J. Garrow (ed.) *St. Augustine, Florida, 1963-1964: Mass Protest and Racial Violence*. Brooklyn, NY: Carlson Publishers Inc., 1990].

7818. Kennedy, J. Michael. "Klan's Back on Old Turf in Texas." *Los Angeles Times*, 9 February 1993. [Vidor, Texas]

7819. Kennedy, Stetson. *The Klan Unmasked*. Boca Raton, FL: Florida Atlantic University Press, 1990.

7820. Kinsolving, Carey. "'The Light Came On' for Klansman." *Washington Post*, 30 January 1993. [How Tom Tarrants, former K.K.K. member in Mississippi, became an advocate of civil rights]

7821. "K.K.K. Hopes to Prove Lynchings in Rosewood Never Happened." *Long Beach Press-Telegram*, 7 March 1993. [Rosewood, Florida massacre of African-Americans in 1923]

7822. *The K.K.K. Today: A 1991 Status Report*. New York, NY: Anti-Defamation League of B'nai B'rith, 1991.

7823. "Klansman Agrees to Re-education on Races, but Not to Believing It." *New York Times*, 27 July 1989. [Alabama]

7824. *The Ku Klux Klan: A History of Racism and Violence,* 3rd edition. Southern Poverty Law Center, 1988.

7825. Lay, Shawn. *Hooded Knights on the Niagara: The Ku Klux Klan in Buffalo, New York, 1921-1925*. Ph.D. diss., Vanderbilt University, 1993. [Buffalo Klan No. 5]. UMO # 9324449.

7826. Lay, Shawn, ed. *The Invisible Empire in the West. Toward a New Historical Appraisal of the Ku Klux Klan of the 1920s*. Baltimore, MD: University of Illinois Press, 1991.

7827. Levy, Daniel S. "The Cantor and the Klansman." *Time*, 17 February 1992. [Nebraska]

7828. Lutholtz, M. William. *Grand Dragon: D. C. Stephenson and the Ku Klux Klan in Indiana*. Purdue University Press, 1991.

7829. MacLean, Nancy K. *Behind the Mask of Chivalry: Gender, Race, and Class in the Making of the Ku Klux Klan of the 1920s in Georgia*. Ph.D. diss., University of Wisconsin, 1989. UMO # 89123803.

7830. _____. "White Women and Klan Violence in the 1920s: Agency, Complicity, and Politics of Women's History." *Gender and History* 3 (Autumn 1991): 285-303.

7831. Marcotte, Paul. "Klan Cable Suit; Claims Right to Air 'Klansas City' on Public-access T.V." *ABA Journal* 75 (May 1989).

7832. Marcy, Sam. *The Klan and the Government*. New York, NY: World View Publishers, 1983.

7833. McWhorter, Diane. "Family Values and the K.K.K." *New York Times*, 1 September 1992.

7834. Miller, Gregory R. *American Run Amok: The Rhetoric of the Ku Klux Klan*. Ph.D. diss., University of Southern California, 1991. [Pre-1900].

7835. Miller, Robert M. "A Note on the Relation between the Protestant Churches and the Revival of the Ku Klux Klan." *Journal of Southern History* 22 (1956): 355-368.

7836. Moore, Leonard J. "Historical Interpretations of the 1920s Klan: The Traditional View and the Populist Revision." *Journal of Social History* 24 (Winter 1990).

7837. Nelson, Jack. *Terror in the Night: The Klan's Campaign Against the Jews*. Simon and Schuster, 1993.

7838. _____. "White Knights, Dark Hearts." *Los Angeles Times Magazine*, 10 January 1993. [Ku Klux Klan terror campaign against Mississippi's Jews in 1960s]

7839. Newton, Michael, and Judy Ann Newton. *The Ku Klux Klan. An Encyclopedia*. New York, NY: Garland, 1990.

7840. Pierson, William D. "Family Secrets: How African-American Culture Helped Shape the Early Ku Klux Klan." in *Looking South: Chapters in the Story of an American Region*, eds. Winfred B. Moore, Jr., and Joseph F. Tripp. Westport, CT: Greenwood, 1989.

7841. Quesada, Charo. "La nueva ola racista en Estados Unidos hace renacer el Klan." *Cambio* 16 (23 September 1991): 50-53. [K.K.K. violence against Hispanics]

7842. Racine, Philip N. "The Ku Klux Klan, Anti-Catholicism and Atlanta's Board of Education, 1916-1927." *Georgia Historical Quarterly* 57 (1973): 63-75.

7843. Randel, William P. *The Ku Klux Klan: A Century of Infamy*. London: 1965.

7844. Reidy, Michael J. *The Ku Klux Klan in Indiana: 1920 to 1925*. Ph.D. diss., Purdue University, 1989. Master's thesis.

7845. Ridgeway, James. "Murder Won't Out." *Village Voice*, 1 October 1991. [K.K.K. murder of Florida NAACP head, Harry T. Moore, December 25, 1951]

7846. Riley, Michael. "White and Wrong. New Klan, Old Hatred." *Time*, 6 July 1992.

7847. Rogers, Joel A. *The Ku Klux Klan Spirit*. Baltimore, MD: Black Classic Press, 1980, orig. 1923.

7848. Safianow, Allen. "'Konklave in Kokomo' Revisited." *Historian* 50 (1988): 329-347.

7849. Salley, Robert L. *Activities of the Knights of the Ku Klux Klan in Southern California, 1921-1925*. 1963.

7850. Salmony, Steven E., and Richard Smoke. "The Appeal and Behavior of the Ku Klux Klan in Object Relations Perspective." *Terrorism* 11 (1988): 247-262.

7851. Schemo, Diana J. "A Search for Tokens from Klan." *New York Times*, 11 August 1992. [Ku Klux Klan activity in Halesite, N.Y. during the 1920s]

7852. Seltzer, Rick, and Grace M. Lopes. "The Ku Klux Klan: Reasons for Support or Opposition among White Respondents." *Journal of Black Studies* 17 (1986): 91-109.

7853. Smallwood, James M. "When the Klan Rode: White Terror in Reconstruction Texas." *Journal of the West* 25 (1986): 4-13.

7854. Smith, Norman W. "The Ku Klux Klan in Rhode Island." *Rhode Island History* 37 (1978): 35-45.

7855. Stanton, Bill. *Klanwatch: Bringing the Ku Klux Klan to Justice*. New York, NY: Grove Weidenfeld, 1991.

7856. Sullivan, Joseph W. "Rhode Island's Invisible Empire: A Demographic Glimpse into the Ku Klux Klan." *Rhode Island History* 47 (May 1989): 74-82.

7857. Swinney, Everette. *Suppressing the Ku Klux Klan: The Enforcement of the Reconstruction Amendments, 1870-1877*. New York, NY: Garland, 1989.

7858. Toy, Eckard V., Jr. "The Ku Klux Klan in Tillamook, Oregon." in *The Northwest Mosaic*, pp. 106-115. eds. James A. Halseth, and Bruce A. Glasrud. : Pruett Publishing, 1977.

7859. Wade, Wyn C. *The Fiery Cross: The Ku Klux Klan in America*. New York, NY: Simon and Schuster, 1987.

7860. Wald, Kenneth D. "The Visible Empire: The Ku Klux Klan as an Electoral Movement." *Journal of Interdisciplinary History* 11 (Autumn 1980): 217-234. [Memphis, 1923]

7861. Walsh, Edward. "Birthplace of the Klan Turns Its Back on March." *Washington Post*, 26 January 1993. [Pulaski, TN]

7862. Wells, Lyn. "The Cedartown [GA] Story: The Ku Klux Klan and Labor in 'The New South'." *Labor Research Review* 8 (1986): 69-79. [1980s]

7863. Williams, Lou Falkner. *The Great South Carolina Ku Klux Klan Trials, 1871-1872*. Ph.D. diss., University of Florida, 1991. UMO # 9209092.

7864. Wolkovish-Valkavicius, William. "The Ku Klux Klan in the Nashoba Valley." *Historical Journal of Massachusetts* 18 (Winter 1990): 61-80.

7865. Zatarain, Michael. *David Duke, Evolution of a Klansman*. Gretna, LA: Pelican Publishing Co., 1990.

LABOR

7866. "After Chavez, Farm Workers Struggle." *New York Times*, 19 July 1993.

7867. Alexander, Nick. "Black Unionists Rock the House of Labor." *Guardian*, 26 February 1992. [Black Workers for Justice, NC]

7868. Almquist, Elizabeth M. "Labor Market Gender Inequality in Minority Groups." *Gender and Society* 1 (1987): 400-414.

7869. Alston, Lee J., and Joseph P. Ferrie. "Social Control and Labor Relations in the American South before the Mechanization of the Cotton Harvest in the 1950s." *Journal of Institutional and Theoretical Economics* 145 (March 1989).

7870. Alvarez, Salvador E. "The Legal and Legislative Struggle of the Farmworkers 1965-1972." *El Grito* 6 (Winter 1972-1973): 4-145.

7871. Alvirez, David. "Economic Exploitation Among the Mexican Americans in Texas and New Mexico." in *Live a New Life*, Division of Education and Cultivation of the United Methodist Church. Cincinnati, OH: United Methodist Church Publishing House, 1972.

7872. Anderson, H. Allen. "The Encomienda in New Mexico, 1598- 1680." *New Mexico Historical Review* 60 (October 1985): 353-377.

7873. Antush, John C. "Chinatown Lockout Defeated." *Against the Current* 51 (July-August 1994): 8-11. [Workers at Silver Palace Restaurant, New York City]

7874. Arnesen, Eric. "Following the Color Line of Labor: Black Workers and the Labor Movement Before 1930." *Radical History Review* 55 (Winter 1993): 53-87.

7875. _____. "Learning the Lessons of Solidarity: Work Rules and Race Relations on the New Orleans Waterfront, 1880-1901." *Labor's Heritage* 1 (1989): 26-45.

7876. _____. *Waterfront Workers of New Orleans. Race, Class, and Politics, 1863-1923*. New York, NY: Oxford University Press, 1991.

7877. Arnold, Frank. "A History of Struggle: Organizing Cannery Workers in the Santa Clara Valley." *Southwest Economy and Society* 2 (October-November 1976): 26-38.

7878. Arroyo, Luis L. "Chicano Participation in Organized Labor: The C.I.O. in Los Angeles, 1938-1950." *Aztlan* 6 (Summer 1975): 277-303.

7879. Asher, Robert. "Union Nativism and the Immigrant Response." *Labor History* 23 (Summer 1982): 325-348.

7880. Asher, Robert, and Charles Stephenson, eds. *Labor Divided. Race and Ethnicity in United States Labor Struggles, 1835-1960*. Albany, NY: State University of New York Press, 1990.

7881. Bailey, Thomas. "A Case Study of Immigrants in the Restaurant Industry." *Industrial Relations* 24 (Spring 1984): 205- 221.

7882. Baron, Harold M. "Racial Domination in Advanced Capitalism: A Theory of Nationalism and Divisions in the Labor Market." in *Labor Market Segmentation*, pp. 173-216. eds. Richard Edwards and others. Lexington, MA: Heath, 1975.

7883. Barrett, James R. "Life in 'The Jungle': An Immigrant Working-class Community on Chicago's South Side in Fiction and Fact, 1900-1910." in *Transactions of the Illinois State Historical Society....*, eds. Mary Ellen McElliot, and Patrick H. O'Neal. Springfield, IL: The Society, 1988.

7884. Beadles, N. A., and C. M. Lowery. "Union Elections Involving Racial Propaganda: The Sewell and Bancroft Standards." *Labor Law Journal* 42 (July 1991): 418-424.

7885. Berlin, Ira and others, eds. *Freedom. A Documentary History of Emancipation, 1861-1867. Series One, Volume Three. The Wartime Genesis of Free Labor: The Lower South*. New York, NY: Cambridge University Press, 1991.

7886. Bernstein, Harry. "U.F.W. of Today Sows Little Hope." *Los Angeles Times*, 30 March 1993. [United Farm Workers of America]

7887. "Black Labor Since Reconstruction." *Dollars and Sense* 18 (Summer 1976): 14-15.

7888. Boles, Frank J. *A History of Local 212 U.A.W.-C.I.O., 1937- 1949: The Briggs Manufacturing Company, Detroit, Michigan*. Ph.D. diss., University of Michigan, 1990. UMO # 9034389.

7889. Bonilla, Frank, and Ricardo Campos. "Imperialist Initiatives and the Puerto Rican Worker." *Contemporary Marxism* 5 (1982): 1-18.

7890. Boston, Thomas D. "Segmented Labor Markets: New Evidence from a Study of Four Race-Gender Groups." *Industrial and Labor Relations Review* 44 (October 1990): 99-115.

7891. Boswell, Terry E. *Race, Class and Markets: Ethnic Stratification and Labor Market Segmentation in the Metal Mining Industry, 1850-1880*. Ph.D. diss., University of Arizona, 1984. [Mexican-Americans and Chinese-American miners]. UMO # 8424915.

7892. Boxberger, Daniel L. "In and Out of the Labor Force: The Lummi Indians and the Development of the Commercial Salmon Fishery of North Puget Sound, 1880-1900." *Ethnohistory* 35 (1988): 161-190. [Internal colony]

7893. Bradbury, Katharine, and Lynne Brown. "Black Men in the Labor Market." *New England Economic Review* 32-42 (March-April 1986).

7894. Brier, Stephen B. *"The Most Persistent Unionists": Class Formation and Class Conflict in the Coal Fields and Emergence of Interracial and Interethnic Unionism, 1880-1904*. Ph.D. diss., University of California at Los Angeles, 1992. UMO # 9317430.

7895. Briggs, Cyril. "Further Notes on [the] Negro Question in Southern Textile Strikes." *Communist* 8 (July 1929).

7896. Briggs, Vernon M., Jr. and others. *The Chicano Workers*. Austin, TX: University of Texas Press, 1977.

7897. Browne, Hugh. "The Training of the Negro Laborer in the North." *Annals* 27 (1906).

7898. Burtless, Gary, ed. *A Future of Lousy Jobs? The Changing Structure of U.S. Wages*. Brookings Institute, 1990.

7899. Cantrell, Doug. "Immigrants and Community in Harlem County, 1910-1930." *Register of the Kentucky Historical Society* 86 (1988): 119-141.

7900. Cardenal, Gilbert, and Beth Ann Shelton. "Undocumented Immigrant Women in the Houston Labor Force." *California Sociologist* 5 (1982).

7901. Cargill, Jack. *Empire and Opposition: Class, Ethnicity and Ideology in the Mine-Mill Union of Grant County, New Mexico*. Master's thesis, University of New Mexico, 1979.

7902. Carll-White, Mary A. *The Role of the Black Artisan in the Building Trades and the Decorative Arts in South Carolina's Charleston District, 1760-1800*. Ph.D. diss., University of Tennessee, 1982. UMO # 8313282.

7903. Carnoy, Martin and others. *Latinos in a Changing Economy: Comparative Perspectives on the U.S. Labor Market Since 1939*. Research Foundation of the City University of New York, 1990.

7904. Casillas, Mike. "Mexican Labor Militancy in the U.S.: 1896- 1915." *Southwest Economy and Society* 4 (1978): 31-42.

7905. Casper, Ellen. *A Social History of Farm Labor in California with Special Emphasis on the United Farm Workers Union and California Rural Legal Assistance*. Ph.D. diss., New School for Social Research, 1984. UMO # 8527072.

7906. Cattan, P. "The Diversity of Hispanics in the U.S. Work Force." *Monthly Labor Review* 116 (August 1993).

7907. Cervantes, Nancy and others. "A Case of Overkill to Curb Day Laborers." *Los Angeles Times*, 25 January 1994. [Black-Latino frictions over employing workers for single days]

7908. Chacon, R. D. "Labor Unrest and Industrialized Agriculture in California: The Case of the 1933 San Joaquin Cotton Strike." *Social Science Quarterly* 65 (June 1984).

7909. Chambers, Clarke A. *California Farm Organizations: A Historical Study of the Grange, the Farm Bureau, and the Associated Farmers, 1929-1941*. Berkeley, CA: University of California, 1952.

7910. Chiswick, Barry R. "Hispanic Men: Divergent Paths in the U.S. Labor Market." *Monthly Labor Review* 111 (November 1988).

7911. Clark, Victor S. *Mexican Labor in the United States*. Washington, DC: Government Printing Office, 1908.

7912. Clines, Francis X. "An Organizer in the Spirit of Joe Hill." *New York Times*, 5 December 1993. [Francisco Chang]

7913. Cockcroft, James D. *Outlaws in the Promised Land: Mexican Immigrant Workers and America's Future*. New York, NY: Grove Press, 1986.

7914. Cornfield, D. B. "The United States Labor Movement: Its Development and Impact on Social Inequality and Politics." *Annual Review of Sociology* 17 (1991): 27-50.

7915. Coyle, Laurie and others. *Women at Farah: An Unfinished Story*. El Paso, TX: Reforma, 1979. [1972-1974 strike]

7916. Critchlow, Donald T. "Communist Unions and Racism: A Comparative Study of the Responses of the United Electrical Radio and Machine Workers and the National Maritime Union to the Black Question during World War II." *Labor History* (Spring 1976): 230- 244.

7917. Cross, Ira B. and others. *Mexican Labor in the United States*. Berkeley, CA: University of California, University of California Publications in Economics, Vol. 7, 1931-1932.

7918. Daniel, Cletus E. *Bitter Harvest: A History of California Farmworkers, 1870-1941*. Ithaca, NY: Cornell University Press, 1981.

7919. _____. *Chicano Workers and the Politics of Fairness. The F.E.P.C. in the Southwest, 1941-1945*. University of Texas Press, 1990.

7920. _____. *Labor Radicalism in Pacific Coast Agriculture*. Ph.D. diss., University of Washington, 1972.

7921. Daniels, Jo Ann, and Gloria O'Leary. *Que lejos hemos venido? How Far Have We Come? Migrant Farm Labor in Iowa, 1975*. Washington, DC: United States Commission on Civil Rights, 1976.

7922. DeBrizzi, John. "The Standard Oil Strikes in Bayonne, New Jersey, 1915-1916." *New Jersey History* 101 (1983).

7923. Defreitas, G. "Unionization among Racial and Ethnic Minorities." *Industrial and Labor Relations Review* 46 (January 1993).

7924. Delgado, Hector L. *New Immigrants, Old Unions: Organizing Undocumented Workers in Los Angeles*. Temple University Press, 1993.

7925. Denby, Charles. "Black Caucuses in the Unions." *New Politics* 7 (1968).

7926. DeParle, Jason, Last of the Manongs: Aging Voices of a Farm-Labor Fight Find an Audience. *New York Times*, 11 May 1993. [Fred Abad and Filipino farm workers in California]

7927. Deutsch, S. "Gender, Labor History, and Chicano/An Ethnic Identity." *Frontiers* 14 (1994): 1-22.

7928. Dewing, Rolland. "Desegregation of State N.E.A. Affiliate in the South." *Journal of Negro Education* (1969).

7929. Dinwoodie, D. H. "Deportation: The Immigration Service and the Chicano Labor Movement in the 1930's." *New Mexico Historical Review* 52 (July 1977): 193-206.

7930. Draper, A. "Do the Right Thing: The Desegregation of Union Conventions in the South." *Labor History* 33 (Summer 1992): 343-356.

7931. _____. "A Sisyphean Ordeal: Labor Educators, Race Relations and Southern Workers, 1956-1966." *Labor Studies Journal* 16 (Winter 1991): 3-19.

7932. Dublin, Marshall F. *1199- The Bread and Roses Union.* Ph.D. diss., Columbia University, 1988. UMO # 88275661.

7933. DuBois, W. E. B., ed. *The Negro Artisan.* Atlanta, GA: Atlanta University Press, 1902.

7934. DuBois, W. E. B., and Augustus G. Dill. *The Negro American Artisan.* Atlanta, GA: Atlanta University Press, 1912.

7935. Dulaney, W. Marvin. "The Texas Negro Peace Officers' Association: The Origins of Black Police Unionism." *Houston Review* 12 (1990): 59-78.

7936. DuPont, Patricia and others. "Black Migrant Farmworkers in New York State: Exploitable Labor." *Afro-Americans in New York Life and History* 12 (January 1988): 7-26.

7937. Farlow, Gale J. *Black Craftsmen in North Carolina before 1850.* Master's thesis. Greensboro, NC: University of North Carolina, 1979.

7938. Fehn, Bruce R. *Striking Women: Gender, Race and Class in the United Packinghouse Workers of America (U.P.W.A.), 1938-1968.* Ph.D. diss., University of Wisconsin, 1991. UMO # 9123836.

7939. Fichtenbaum, Myrna. *The Funsten Nut Strike.* New York, NY: International Publishers, 1991. [St. Louis, 1933]

7940. Fields, J., and E. N. Wolff. "The Decline of Sex Segregation and the Wage Gap, 1970-1980." *Journal of Human Resources* 26 (Fall 1991).

7941. Filippelli, Ronald L., ed. *Labor Conflict in the United States: An Encyclopedia.* New York, NY: Garland, 1990.

7942. Fink, Gary M., and Merl E. Reed, eds. *Race, Class, and Community in Southern Labor History.* University of Alabama Press, 1994.

7943. Fink, Leon, and Brian Greenberg. *Upheaval in the Quiet Zone: A History of Hospital Workers' Union, Local 1199.* Urbana, IL: University of Illinois Press, 1989.

7944. Finkelman, Paul R. "Northern Labor Law and Southern Slave Law: The Application of the Fellow Servant Rule to Slaves." *National Black Law Journal* 11 (Spring 1989): 212-232.

7945. Flaherty, Stacy A. "Boycott in Butte: Organized Labor and the Chinese Community, 1896-1897." *Montana* 37 (1987): 34-47.

7946. Flug, Michael. "Organized Labor and the Civil Rights Movement of the 1960s: The Case of the Maryland Freedom Union." *Labor History* 31 (1990): 322-346.

7947. Foner, Philip S. "Black Workers and the Labor Movement." in *The United States in Crisis: Marxist Analyses, Studies in Marxism, Vol. 4*, eds. Lajos Biro, and Marc J. Cohen. Minneapolis, MN: Marxist Educational Press 1979.

7948. Foster, James C., ed. *American Labor in the Southwest: The First 100 Years.* Tucson, AZ: University of Arizona Press, 1982.

7949. Freedman, Marcia. "The Labor Market for Immigrants in New York City." *New York Affairs* 7 (1983).

7950. Freeman, Richard B., ed. *Working Under Different Rules*. Russell Sage Foundation, 1994. ["The decline in the well-being of American workers"]

7951. Galarza, Ernesto. *Farm Workers and Agri-business in California, 1947-1960*. Notre Dame, IN: University of Notre Dame Press, 1977.

7952. _____. *Merchants of Labor: The Mexican Bracero Story*. San Jose, CA: Rosicrucian Press, 1965.

7953. _____. "The Mexican-American Migrant Worker- Culture and Powerlessness." *Integrated Education* 9 (March-April 1971): 17-21.

7954. Galvin, Miles. *The Organized Labor Movement in Puerto Rico*. Rutherford, NJ: Farleigh Dickinson University Press, 1979.

7955. Gamboa, Erasmo. *Mexican Labor and World War II: Braceros in the Pacific Northwest, 1942-1947*. Austin, TX: University of Texas Press, 1990.

7956. Garcia, Juan R. *Operation Wetback: The Mass Deportation of Mexican Undocumented Workers in 1954*. Westport, CT: Greenwood Press, 1980.

7957. Garcia y Griego, M. "The Importation of Mexican Contract Laborers to the United States, 1942-1964: Antecedents, Operation, and Legacy." in *The Border that Joins*, pp. 49-98. eds. Peter Brown, and Henry Shue. Totowa, NJ: Rowman and Littlefield, 1983.

7958. Garcia, Mario T. "Mexican American Labor and the Left: The Asociacion Nacional Mexico-Americana, 1948-1954." in *The Chicano Struggle: Analyses of Past and Present Efforts*, pp. 65-86. eds. John A. Garcia and others. Binghamton, NY, 1984.

7959. _____. "Racial Dualism in the El Paso Labor Market, 1880-1920." *Aztlan* 6 (Summer 1975): 197-218.

7960. Gardner, J. M., and D. E. Herz. "Working and Poor in 1990." *Monthly Labor Review* 115 (December 1992).

7961. Getlin, Josh. "Crusader of the Cane." *Los Angeles Times*, 7 February 1993. [Sugar cane workers in Florida]

7962. Gobel, Thomas. "Becoming American: Ethnic Workers and the Rise of the C.I.O." *Labor History* 29 (1988): 173-198.

7963. Goldfield, Michael. "Race and the C.I.O.: The Possibilities for Racial Egalitarianism during the 1930s and 1940s." *International Labor and Working-Class History* 44 (Fall 1993). [Responses by Gary Gerstle, Robert Korstad, Marshall F. Stevenson, and Judith Stein]

7964. Gomez-Quinones, Juan. *Development of the Mexican Working Class North of the Rio Bravo: Work and Culture Among Laborers and Artisans, 1600-1900*. Los Angeles, CA: Chicano Studies Center, University of California, 1982.

7965. _____. "The First Steps: Chicano Labor Conflict and Organizing 1900-1920." *Aztlan* 3 (Spring 1972): 13-49.

7966. _____. *Mexican-American Labor, 1600-1990*. University of New Mexico Press, 1994.

7967. Gonzales, Juan L., Jr. *Mexican-American Farm Workers: The California Agricultural Industry*. New York, NY: Praeger, 1985.

7968. Gottlieb, Peter. "Black Miners and the 1925-1928 Bituminous Coal Strike: The Colored Committee of Non-Union Miners." *Labor History* 28 (Spring 1987).

7969. Gould, William B., IV "Black Power in the Unions: The Impact Upon Collective Bargaining Relationships." *Yale Law Journal* 46-84 (November 1969).

7970. Graham, Glennon. *From Slavery to Serfdom: Rural Black Agriculturalists in South Carolina, 1865-1900*. Ph.D. diss., Northwestern University, 1982.

7971. Gray, James. *The American Civil Liberties Union of Southern California and Imperial Valley Agricultural Labor Disturbances, 1930, 1934*. San Francisco, CA: R & E Research Assocaites, 1977.

7972. Greenwood, L. B. "The Black Artisan in the U.S., 1890- 1930." *Review of Black Political Economy* 5 (1974): 19-44.

7973. Griffith, Barbara S. *The Crisis of American Labor: Operation Dixie and the Defeat of the C.I.O.* Philadelphia, PA: Temple University Press, 1988.

7974. Griffler, Keith P. *The Black Radical Intellectual and the Black Worker: The Emergence of a Program for Black Labor, 1918- 1938*. Ph.D. diss., Ohio State University, 1993. UMO # 9401270.

7975. Guerin-Gonzales, Camille. *Mexican Workers and American Dreams: Immigration, Repatriation, and California Farm Labor, 1900-1939*. Rutgers University Press, 1994.

7976. Haiken, Elizabeth. "'The Lord Helps Those Who Help Themselves': Black Laundresses in Little Rock, Arkansas, 1917- 1921." *Arkansas Historical Quarterly* 49 (1990): 20-50.

7977. Halker, Clark. "A History of Local 208 and the Struggle for Racial Equality in the American Federation of Musicians." *Black Music Research Journal* 8 (Fall 1988): 207-222.

7978. Halpern, Eric B. *"Black and White Unite and Fight": Race and Labor in Meatpacking, 1904-1948*. Ph.D. diss., University of Pennsylvania, 1989. UMO # 9015101.

7979. _____. "Interracial Unionism in the Southwest: Fort Worth's Packinghouse Workers, 1937-1954." in *Organized Labor in the Twentieth Century South*, pp. 152-182. ed. Robert H. Zieger.

7980. Hattam, Victoria C. "Institution and Political Change: Working-class Formation in England and the United States, 1820- 1896." *Politics and Society* 20 (1992): 133-166.

7981. Helm, Leslie. "Creating High-Tech Sweatshops." *Los Angeles Times*, 15 November 1993. [U.S. computer firms employing cheap skilled programmers the world over]

7982. Hershman, Alan. "Mexican Farmworkers in California Fields. An Interview with Alan Hershman." *Antipode* 14 (1982): 51-57.

7983. Hill, Herbert. "Anti-Oriental Agitation and the Rise of Working-Class Racism." *Trans-action* 10 (January-February 1973): 43-54.

7984. _____. "Black Dissent in Organized Labor." in *Seasons of Rebellion*, pp. 55-80. eds. Joseph Boskin, and Robert A. Rosenstone. New York, NY: Holt, Rinehart and Winston, 1972.

7985. _____. "Black Labor and the N.A.A.C.P." *Crisis* 87 (1980): 506-507.

7986. _____. "Black Workers, Organized Labor, and Title VII of the 1964 Civil Rights Act: Legislative History and Litigation Record." in *Race in America*, eds. Herbert Hill, and James E. Jones, Jr. : University of Wisconsin Press, 1993.

7987. _____. "The ILGWU Today: The Decay of a Labor Union." in *Autocracy and Insurgency in Organized Labor*, ed. Burton H. Hall. New Brunswick, NJ: Transaction Books, 1972.

7988. _____. "Myth-Making As Labor History: Herbert Gutman and the United Mine Workers of America." *International Journal of Politics, Culture and Society* 2 (Winter 1988): 132-200.

7989. _____. "Race, Ethnicity and Organized Labor: The Opposition to Affirmative Action." *New Politics* (Winter 1987): 31-82.

7990. _____. "The Racial Practices of Organized Labor- The Age of Gompers and After." in *Employment, Race, and Poverty... 1865- 1965*, pp. 365-402. eds. Arthur Ross, and Herbert Hill. New York, NY: Harcourt, Brace, and World, 1967.

7991. _____. "Racism Within Organized Labor." *Journal of Negro Education* 109-118 (1961).

7992. Hirsch, Eric L. *Urban Revolt, Ethnic Politics in the Nineteenth-Century Chicago Labor Movement*. Berkeley, CA: University of California, 1990.

7993. Hoffman, Abraham. *Unwanted Mexican Americans in the Great Depression: Repatriation Pressures, 1929-1939*. Tuscon, AZ: University of Arizona Press, 1974.

7994. Honey, Michael K. "Fighting on Two Fronts: Black Trade Unionists in Memphis in the Jim Crow Era." *Labor's Heritage* 4 (Spring 1992): 50-68.

7995. _____. *Labor and Civil Rights in the South: The Industrial Labor Movement and Black Workers in Memphis, 1929- 1945*. Ph.D. diss., Northern Illinois University, 1987. UMO # 8822365.

7996. _____. "The Popular Front in the American South: The View from Memphis." *International Labor and Working Class History* 30 (1986): 44-58.

7997. Hooler, Clarence O. *Builders of the Model T: Some Aspects of the Quality of Life and Social History of Highland Park, 1910- 1927*. Ph.D. diss., Michigan State University, 1988. UMO # 8824853.

7998. Hope, John, II. *Equality of Opportunity. A Union Approach to Fair Employment*. Washington, DC: Public Affairs Press, 1956. [United Packinghouse Workers of America]

7999. Houston, Charles H. "Foul Employment Practice on the Rails." *Crisis* (October 1949).

8000. Huntley, Horace. *Iron Ore Mines and Mine Mill in Alabama, 1933-1952*. Ph.D. diss., University of Pittsburgh, 1976.

8001. Hurston, Zora Neale. "Florida's Migrant Farm Labor." *Frontiers* 12 (1991).

8002. Hurtado, Albert L. "California Indians and the Workaday West: Labor Assimilation, and Survival." *California History* 69 (1990): 2-11.

8003. Jacobs, John. "Exploiting Farm Laborers." *Long-Beach Press- Telegram*, 15 December 1993. [Mexicans in California]

8004. Jacobson, Cardell. "Internal Colonialism and Native Americans: Indian Labor in the United States from 1871 to World War II." *Social Science Quarterly* 65 (1984): 158-171.

8005. Jaynes, Gerald D. "The Labor Market Status of Black Americans: 1939-1985." *Journal of Economic Perspectives* 4 (Fall 1990).

8006. Jensen, Joan M. "'I've Worked- I'm Not Afraid of Work': Farm Women in New Mexico, 1920-1940." *New Mexico Historical Review* 61 (January 1986): 26-52.

8007. Jimenez Montoya, Andres E. *Political Domination in the Labor Market: Racial Division in the Arizona Copper Industry*. Berkeley, CA: Institute for the Study of Social Change, 1977.

8008. _____. "The Political Formation of a Mexican Working Class in the Arizona Copper Industry, 1870-1917." *Review* 4 (Winter 1981): 535-570.

8009. Johnson, Clyde. "Red Dawn in Alabama?" *Nation*, 23 September 1991, (letter). [Blacks and Communists organize unions in Alabama during 1930s and 1940s]

8010. Joseph, Antoine. "The Formation of Class Fractions in the Gilded Age." *Ethnic and Racial Studies* 12 (1989): 490-511. [1890- 1914]

8011. Kelsey, C. "The Evolution of Negro Labor." *Annals* 21 (1903): 55-76.

8012. Kent, Ronald C. and others, eds. *Culture, Gender, Race, and U.S. Labor History*. Greenwood, 1993.

8013. Kessler-Harris, Alice. *A Woman's Wage. Historical Meanings and Social Consequences*. Lexington, KY: University Press of Kentucky, 1990.

8014. Kiang, Peter N., and Man Chak Ng. "Through Strength and Struggle: Boston's Asian American Student/Community/Labor Solidarity." *Amerasia Journal* 15 (1989): 285-293. [Garment Workers Support Committee]

8015. Kilborn, Peter T. "Wage Gap Between Sexes Is Cut In Test, but at a Price." *New York Times*, 31 May 1990. [The working-out of comparable worth in the State of Washington]

8016. Kiser, George C. "Mexican American Labor Before World War II." *Journal of Mexican American History* 2 (Spring 1972): 122- 142.

8017. Kiser, George C., and David Silverman. "Mexican Repatriation during the Great Depression." *Journal of Mexican American History* 3 (1973): 139-164.

8018. Kleinfeld, Judith, and John A. Kruse. "Native Americans in the Labor Force: Hunting for an Accurate Measure." *Monthly Labor Review* 105 (July 1982): 47-51.

8019. Kletzer, Lori G. "Job Displacement, 1979-1986: How Blacks Fared Relative to Whites." *Monthly Labor Review* 114 (July 1991): 17-25.

8020. Knouse, Stephen B. and others, eds. *Hispanics in the Workplace*. Newbury Park, CA: Sage, 1992.

8021. Kolata, Gina. "More Children Are Employed, Often Periously." *New York Times*, 21 June 1992.

8022. Korstad, Robert R. *Daybreak of Freedom: Tobacco Workers and the CIO, Winston Salem, North Carolina, 1943-1950*. Ph.D. diss., University of North Carolina, 1987. UMO # 8821486.

8023. _____. and Nelson Lichtenstein. "Opportunities Found and Lost: Labor, Radicals, and the Early Civil Rights Movement." *Journal of American History* 75 (December 1988): 786- 811.

8024. Krawczynski, Keith. *The Agricultural Labor of Black Texans as Slaves and as Freedmen*. Ph.D. diss., Baylor University, 1990.

8025. Kushnick, Louis. "The Construction of a Racialized Working Class." *Sage Race Relations Review* 17 (February 1992): 30-36. [Review essay]

8026. LaCroix, Sumner J., and Price V. Fishback. "Firm-Specific Evidence on Racial Wage Differentials and Workforce Segregation in Hawaii's Sugar Industry." *Explorations in Economic History* 26 (October 1989).

8027. Lamar, Howard R. "From Bondage to Contract: Ethnic Labor in the American West, 1600-1890." in *The Countryside in the Age of Capitalist Transformation*, eds. Stephen Hahn, and Jonathan Prude. Chapel Hill, NC: University of North Carolina Press, 1985.

8028. Laurentz, Robert. *Racial/ Ethnic Conflict in the New York City Garment Industry, 1933-1980*. Ph.D. diss., State University of New York at Binghamton, 1980.

8029. Lauriault, Robert N. "From Can't to Can't: The North Florida Turpentine Camps, 1900-1950." *Florida Historical Quarterly* 67 (1989): 310-328.

8030. Lazo, Robert. "Latinos and the AFL-CIO: The California Immigrant Workers Association as an Important New Development." *La Raza Law Journal* 4 (Spring 1991): 22-43.

8031. Ledesma, Irene. *Unlikely Strikers: Mexican-American Women in Strike Activity in Texas, 1919-1974*. Ph.D. diss., Ohio State University, 1992. UMO # 9238214.

8032. Letwin, Daniel L. *Race, Class, and Industrialization in the New South: Black and White Coal Miners in the Birmingham District of Alabama, 1878-1897*. Ph.D. diss., Yale University, 1991. UMO # 9315196.

8033. Lewis, Ronald L. "The Black Presence in the Paint-Cabin Creek Strike, 1912-1913." *West Virginia History* 46 (1985-1986): 59-71.

8034. _____. "From Peasant to Proletarian: The Migration of Southern Blacks to the Central Appalachian Coalfields." *Journal of Southern History* 55 (February 1989): 77-102.

8035. Love, R. "In Defiance of Custom and Tradition: Black Tobacco Workers and Labor Unions in Richmond, Virginia 1937- 1941." *Labor History* 35 (Winter 1994): 25-47.

8036. Maciel, David R. *Al norte del Rio Bravo. Pasado immediato, 1930-1981*. Mexico City: Siglo XXI, 1981. [History of Chicano working class]

8037. Maldonado, Edwin. "Contract Labor and the Origins of Puerto Rican Communities in the United States." *International Migration Review* 13 (Spring 1979): 103-121.

8038. Malley, Deborah De Witt. "How the Union Beat Willie Farah." *Fortune* 90 (August 1974): 164-167.

8039. Mandle, Jay R. "Continuity and Change: The Use of Black Labor after the Civil War." *Journal of Black Studies* 21 (June 1991): 414-427.

8040. Marshall, Ray. "Hunger on the Farm." *New York Times*, 25 August 1993. [The "H-2A" visa program allegedly used to lower domestic wages]

8041. Martin, Charles. "Southern Labor Relations in Transition: Gadsden, Alabama, 1930-1943." *Journal of Southern History* 47 (1981): 545-568.

8042. Martin, Philip L. and others. *Unfulfilled Promise: Collective Bargaining in California Agriculture*. Boulder, CO: Westview, 1988.

8043. Martin, Robert F. *Howard Kester and the Struggle for Social Justice in the South, 1904-1977*. Charlottesville, VA: University Press of Virginia, 1991.

8044. Mason, Phillip L. *Cultural Influences on the Art and Crafts of Early Black American Artisans (1649-1865) Towards Implications for Art Education*. Ph.D. diss., Ohio State University, 1983. UMO # 8311776.

8045. Mayo, Nathanette. "Black Workers for Justice." *Against the Current* 5 (July-August 1990): 3-5, (interview). [Founded in 1981 in Raleigh and Rocky Mount, NC]

8046. McCallum, Brenda. "Songs of Work and Songs of Worship: Sanctifying Black Unionism in the Southern Steel City." *New York Folklore* 14 (1988).

8047. McGahey, Richard, and John Jeffries. *Minorities and the Labor Market: Twenty Years of Misguided Policy*. Washington, DC: Joint Center for Political and Economic Studies, 1985.

8048. McKay, R. R. "The Impact of the Great Depression on Immigrant Mexican Labor: Repatriation of the Bridgeport, Texas, Coal Miners." *Social Science Quarterly* 65 (June 1984).

8049. McKiven, Henry Melvin, Jr. *Class, Race, and Community: Iron and Steel Workers in Birmingham, Alabama, 1875-1920*. Ph.D. diss., Vanderbilt University, 1990. UMO # 9117119.

8050. McLeod, Jonathan W. *Workers and Workplace Dynamics in Reconstruction-Era Atlanta: A Case Study*. Los Angeles, CA: U.C.L.A. Center for Afro-American Studies and the Institute for Industrial Relations, 1990.

8051. McLeod, Norman C., Jr. *Free Labor in a Slave Society: Richmond, Virginia, 1820-1860*. Ph.D. diss., Howard University, 1991. UMO # 9206388.

8052. McManus, Walter S. "Labor Market Effects of Ethnic Enclaves: Hispanic Men in the United States." *Journal of Human Resources* 25 (Spring 1990).

8053. McWilliams, Carey. *Factories in the Field: The Story of the Migratory Farm Labor in California*. Boston, MA: Little, Brown, 1934.

8054. _____. *Ill Fares the Land: Migrants and Migratory Labor in the United States*. Boston, MA: Little, Brown, 1942.

8055. Meier, August, and Elliot M. Rudwick. "Communist Unions and the Black Community: The Case of the Transport Workers Union, 1934- 1944." *Labor History* (Spring 1982): 165-197.

8056. Melendez, Edwin and others, eds. *Hispanics in the Labor Force. Issues and Politics*. Plenum, 1992.

8057. Messner, William F. *Freedmen and Ideology of Free Labor: Louisiana, 1862-1865*. Lafayette, LA: University of Southwestern Louisiana, 1978.

8058. Miller, Kelly. "The Negro as a Workingman." *American Mercury* 6 (November 1925).

8059. Miller, Marc S., ed. *Working Lives: The Southern Exposure History or Labor in the South*. New York, NY: Pantheon, 1980.

8060. Model, Suzanne. "The Effects of Ethnicity in the Workplace on Blacks, Italians, and Jews in 1910 New York." *Journal of Urban History* 16 (1989): 29-51.

8061. Molina, Charles, Jr. *Youth Labor Markets for Puerto Rican- Latin American Youth Labor in New York City*. 1978.   ERIC ED 178 762.

8062. Moody, J. Carroll, and Alice Kessler-Harris, eds. *Perspectives on American Labor History: The Problem of Synthesis*. DeKalb, IL: Northern Illinois University Press, 1989.

8063. Moore, Gilbert W. *Poverty, Class Consciousness and Race Conflict in the UAW-CIO, 1937-1955.* Ph.D. diss., Princeton University, 1978.

8064. Moreno Fraginals, Manuel and others, eds. *Between Slavery and Free Labor. The Spanish Speaking Caribbean in the Nineteenth Century.* Baltimore, MD: Johns Hopkins University Press, 1985.

8065. Morris, Richard B. "The Measure of Bondage in the Slave States." *Mississippi Valley Historical Review* 41 (1954): 219-240.

8066. Murphy, Marjorie. *Blackboard Unions. The AFT and the NEA, 1900-1980.* Ithaca, NY: Cornell University Press, 1991.

8067. Murray, David. "The Industrial Problem of the United States and the Negro's Relation to It." *Voice of the Negro* 6 (September 1904): 404-405.

8068. Nazario, Sonia. "For This Union, It's War." *Los Angeles Times*, 19 August 1993. [Justice for Janitors]

8069. Needleman, Ruth. "Women Workers: A Force for Rebuilding Unionism." *Labor Research Review* 7 (Spring 1988).

8070. Nelson, B. "Organized Labor and the Struggle for Black Equality in Mobile during World War II." *Journal of American History* 80 (December 1993): 952-988.

8071. Nkomo, Stella M., and Taylor Cox, Jr. "Factors Affecting the Upward Mobility of Black Managers in Private Sector Organizations." *Review of Black Political Economy* 18 (Winter 1990): 39-57.

8072. Noldin Valdes, Dennis. *Al Norte.* University of Texas Press, 1991. [Mexican-American workers in Midwest]

8073. Ola, Akinshiju C. "Don't Mourn- Organize the South, Say Black Workers." *Guardian*, 16 August 1989. [Black Workers for Justice]

8074. Olson, James S. "Organized Black Leadership and Industrial Unionism: The Racial Response, 1926-1945." *Labor History* (Summer 1969): 475-486.

8075. Olzak, Susan D. "Labor Unrest, Immigration, and Ethnic Conflict in Urban America, 1880-1914." *American Journal of Sociology* 94 (1989): 1303-1333.

8076. Ong, Paul M. "Race and Post-displacement Earnings among High-Tech Workers." *Industrial Relations* 30 (Fall 1991): 456-468.

8077. Ovington, Mary W. "The Negro in the Trades Unions in New York." *Annals of the American Academy of Political and Social Sciences* 27 (March 1906): 89-96.

8078. Painter, Nell Irvin. "Black Workers from Reconstruction to the Great Depression." in *Working for Democracy: American Workers from the Revolution to the Present*, eds. Paul Buhle, and Alan Dawley. : University of Illinois Press, 1985.

8079. _____. "The New Labor History and the Historical Movement." *International Journal of Politics, Culture and Society* 2 (1989): 367-370.

8080. _____. "'Social Equality', Miscegenation, Labor, and Power." in *The Evolution of Southern Culture*, ed. Numan V. Bartley. Athens, GA: University of Georgia Press, 1988.

8081. Palladino, Grace. "Forging a National Union: Electrical Workers Confront Issues of Craft, Race, and Gender, 1890-1902." *Labor's Heritage* 3 (October 1991).

8082. Park, Joseph F. "The 1930s 'Mexican Affair' at Clifton." *Journal of Arizona History* 18 (1977): 119-148. [copper strike]

8083. _____. *The History of Mexican Labor in Arizona during the Territorial Period.* Tuscon, AZ: University of Arizona Press, 1961.

8084. Perlmutter, Philip. "Intergroup Bigotry and Late Nineteenth and Early Twentieth Century Immigrant Competition, Exploitation and Succession in the United States." *Immigrants and Minorities* 6 (1987): 84-99. [Employer manipulation of ethnic differences among workers]

8085. Peterson, Joyce S. "Black Automobile Workers in Detroit, 1910-1930." *Journal of Negro History* 64 (Summer 1979): 177-190.

8086. Pichardo, Nelson A. *The Role of Community in Social Protest: Chicano Working Class Protest, 1848-1933.* Ph.D. diss., University of Michigan, 1990. UMO # 9116271.

8087. Pinchbeck, Raymond. *The Virginia Negro Artisan*. Richmond, VA: William Byrd Press, 1926.

8088. Pitts, Robert B. *Organized Labor and the Negro in Seattle*. Master's thesis, University of Washington, 1941.

8089. Popkin, S. J. and others. "Labor Market Experiences of Low- Income Black Women in Middle-Class Suburbs: Evidence from a Survey of Gautreaux Program Participants." *Journal of Policy Analysis and Management* 12 (Summer 1993).

8090. Posadas, Barbara M. "The Hierarchy of Color and Psychological Adjustment in an Industrial Environment: Filipinos, the Pullman Company, and the Brotherhood of Sleeping Car Porters." *Labor History* 23 (Summer 1982): 349-373.

8091. Prichard, Nancy L. *Paradise Found? Opportunity for Mexican, Irish, Italian, and Chinese born Individuals in Jerome Copper Mining District, 1890-1910.* Ph.D. diss., University of Colorado, 1992. UMO # 9318123.

8092. Quam-Wickham, Nancy. "Who Controls the Hiring Hall? The Struggle for Job Control in the ILWU During World War II." in *The CIO's Left-Led Unions*, pp. 47-67. ed. Steve Rosswurm. : Rutgers University Press, 1992.

8093. Quintero Rivera, Angel G. *Workers' Struggle in Puerto Rico: A Documentary History*. New York, NY: 1976.

8094. Rachleff, Peter J. "Black Richmond and the Knights of Labor." *Research in Urban Sociology* 1 (1989): 23-52. [Mid-1880s]

8095. Rankin, Bruce H., and W.W. Falk. "Earnings Differences among Workers in the South, 1989." *Sociological Abstracts* Accession No. 89S21083

8096. Raskin, A. H. "Getting Things Done." *New Yorker*, 10 December 1990. [Dennis Rivera, Local 1199, Drug, Hospital and Health Care Employees' Union, NYC]

8097. Rawick, George. *From Sundown to Sunup: The Making of the Black Community*. Westport, CT: Greenwood, 1969. [see especially last two chapters]

8098. Reidy, Joseph P. "Slavery, Emancipation, and the Capitalist Transformation of Southern Agriculture, 1850-1910." in *Agriculture and National Development*, ed. Lou Ferleger. Ames, IA: Iowa State University Press, 1990.

8099. Reisler, Mark. *By the Sweat of their Brow: Mexican Immigrant Labor in the United States, 1900-1940.* Westport, CT: Greenwood, 1976.

8100. Riccucci, Norma M. *Women, Minorities, and Unions in the Public Sector*. Westport, CT: Greenwood, 1990.

8101. Robbins, Lynn A. "Navajo Labor and the Establishment of a Voluntary Workers' Association." *Journal of Ethnic Studies* 6 (Fall 1978): 97-112.

8102. Rodriguez, C. E. "The Effect of Race on Puerto Rican Wages." in *Hispanics in the Labor Force*, eds. E. Melendez and others. New York, NY: Plenum, 1991.

8103. Roediger, David. "Labor in White Skin: Race and Working- class History." in *Reshaping the U.S. Left: Popular Struggles in the 1980s*, eds. Mike Davis, and Michael Sprinker. New York, NY: Verso, 1988.

8104. _____. "Notes on Working Class Racism." in *Within the Shell of the Old*, eds. Don Fitz, and David Roediger. : Kerr, 1990.

8105. _____. "Race and the Working-class Past in the United States: Multiple Identities and the Future of Labor History." *International Review of Social History* 38 (1993): 127-144.

8106. Rosales, Francisco A., and Daniel T. Simon. "Chicano Steel Workers and Unionism in the Midwest, 1919-1945." *Aztlan* 6 (Summer 1975): 267-275.

8107. Rose, Margaret. "From the Fields to the Picket Line: Huelga Women and the Boycott, 1965-1975." *Labor History* 31 (Summer 1990).

8108. _____. "Traditional and Nontraditional Patterns of Female Activism in the United Farm Workers of America, 1962- 1980." *Frontiers* 11 (1990).

8109. Rose, S. O. "Gender and Labor History: The Nineteenth- Century Legacy." *International Review of Social History* 38, supplement 1 (1993): 145-162.

8110. Rosenberg, David. *New Orleans Dockworkers: Race, Labor, and Unionism, 1892-1923.* Albany, NY: State University of New York Press, 1988.

8111. Rosswurm, Steve, ed. *The CIO's Left-led Unions.* Rutgers University Press, 1992.

8112. Ruiz, Vicki L. *UCAPAWA and Mexican Women Workers.* Ph.D. diss., Stanford University, 1982.

8113. Rumberger, R. W., and Martin Carnoy. "Segmentation in the U.S. Labour Market: Its Effects on the Mobility and Earnings of Whites and Blacks." *Cambridge Journal of Economics* 4 (1980): 117-132.

8114. Ryan, Roderick. "An Ambiguous Legacy: Baltimore Blacks and the CIO, 1936-1941." *Journal of Negro History* 65 (1980): 18-33.

8115. Saeger, Moe. "Fighting for the Black Belt... and More." *Z Magazine* 4 (June 1991): 48-59. [Black Workers for Justice, NC]

8116. Safa, Helen I. "Female Employment and the Social Reproduction of the Puerto Rican Working Class." *International Migration Review* 18 (Winter 1984): 1168-1187.

8117. Sainsbury, John A. "Indian Labor in Early Rhode Island." *New England Quarterly* 48 (September 1975): 378-393.

8118. Saville, Julie. "Grassroots Reconstruction: Agricultural Labour and Collective Action in South Carolina, 1860-1868." *Slavery and Abolition* 12 (December 1991): 173-181.

8119. _____. *The Work of Reconstruction: From Slave to Wage Laborer in South Carolina, 1860-1870.* Cambridge University Press, 1994.

8120. Saxton, Alexander. *The Indispensable Enemy: Labor and the Anti-Chinese Movement in California.* Berkeley, CA: University of California Press, 1971.

8121. Scarano, Francisco A. "Slavery and Free Labor in the Puerto Rican Sugar Economy: 1815-1873." *Annals of the New York Academy of Sciences* 292 (1977): 553-563.

8122. Scarborough, C. "Conceptualizing Black Women's Employment Experiences." *Yale Law Journal* 98 (May 1989).

8123. Schmidt, James D. *"Neither Slavery Nor Involuntary Servitude": Free Labor and American Law, ca. 1815-1880.* Ph.D. diss., Rice University, 1992. UMO # 9234415.

8124. Scholl, Barry. "Privatization Threatens Black City Workers." *Chicago Reporter* 20 (December 1991).

8125. Segura, Denise A. "Labor Market Stratification: The Chicano Experience." *Berkeley Journal of Sociology* 29 (1984): 57-80.

8126. _____. "Walking on Eggshells: Chicanos in the Labor Force." *Hispanics in the Workplace*, eds. Stephen B. Knouse and others. Newbury Park, CA: Sage, 1992.

8127. Semyenov, Moshe, and Yinon Cohen. "Ethnic Discrimination and the Income of Majority Group Workers." *American Sociological Review* 55 (February 1990).

8128. Semyonov, Moshe, and Yitchak Haberfeld. "Beyond Segregation: Gender and Earnings Inequality Within Job Markets." *Sociology and Social Research* 76 (October 1991): 10-13.

8129. Servin, Manuel P., and R. L. Spude. "Historical Conditions of Early Mexican Labor in the United States: Arizona- A Neglected Story." *Journal of Mexican-American History* 5 (1975): 43-56. [Metal mining]

8130. Shanker, Albert, and Herbert Hill. "Black Protest, Union Democracy and the UFT." in *Autocracy and Insurgency in Organized Labor*, ed. Burton H. Hall. New Brunswick, NJ: Transaction Books, 1972. [Exchange of views on use by United Federation of Teachers of racism in 1968]

8131. Shapiro, Herbert. "Labor and Antislavery." *NST. Nature, Society, and Thought* 2 (1989).

8132. Sherron, Philip. "Saipan Sweatshops Are No American Dream." *New York Times*, 18 July 1993.

8133. Shulman, Steven. "Racial Inequality and White Employment: An Interpretation and Test of the Bargaining Power Hypothesis." *Review of Black Political Economy* 18 (Winter 1990): 5-20.

8134. _____. "Racism and the Making of the American Working Class." *International Journal of Politics, Culture and Society* 2 (1989): 361-366.

8135. Shulman, Steven, and William A. Darity, Jr., eds. *The Question of Discrimination: Racial Inequality in the U.S. Labor Market*. Middletown, CT: Wesleyan University Press, 1989.

8136. Silverstein, Stuart. "Survey of Garment Industry Finds Rampant Labor Abuse." *Los Angeles Times*, 15 April 1994. [California-wide study]

8137. Silvestrini de Pacheco, Blanca. "Women as Workers: The Experience of Puerto Rican Women in the 1930s." in *Women Cross-Culturally: Change and Challenge*, ed. Ruby Rohrlich-Leavitt. The Hague: Mouton, 1975.

8138. Skinner, Robert E. "The Black Man in the Literature of Labor." *Labor's Heritage* 1 (1989): 50-65. [Works of Chester Himes]

8139. Sowell, David. "Racial Patterns of Labor in Postbellum Florida: Gainesville, 1870-1900." *Florida Historical Review* 63 (1985): 434-444.

8140. Squire, Madelyn C. "The National Labor Relations Act and Unions' Invidious Discrimination- A Case Review of a Would Be Constitutional Issue." *Howard Law Journal* 30 (1987): 783-798.

8141. Stahl, Ben. "The End of Segregation in Teachers Training in Delaware. Recollections of a Union Struggle 1942-1946." *Labor's Heritage* 2 (1990): 24-33.

8142. Stoddard, Ellwyn R. "Illegal Mexican Labor in the Borderlands: Institutionalized Support of an Unlawful Practice." *Pacific Sociological Review* 19 (April 1976): 175-210.

8143. Stott, Richard B. *Workers in the Metropolis: Class, Ethnicity, and Youth in Antebellum New York City*. Ithaca, NY: Cornell University Press, 1989.

8144. Streib, Gordon F. "An Attempt to Unionize a Semi-Literate Navaho Group." *Human Organization* 11 (1952): 23-31.

8145. Strough, Kelly. *The Japanese American Farm Labor Experience in the Treasure Valley during World War II: Racism, Economic Necessity, and the Failure of Political Leadership*. Master's thesis, Boise State University, 1990.

8146. Suro, Roberto. "Mexicans Come to Work, but Find Dead Ends." *New York Times*, 19 January 1992.

8147. Szymanski, Albert. "The Growing Role of Spanish Speaking Workers in the U.S. Economy." *Aztlan* 9 (1978): 177-208.

8148. Talbot, Steve. "Native Americans and the Working Class." in *Ethnicity and the Work Force*, eds. Winston A. Van Horne, and Thomas V. Tonneson. Milwaukee, WI: University of Wisconsin System, American Ethnic Studies Coordinating Committee/Urban Corridor Consortium, 1985.

8149. Tasini, Jonathan. "Grants in the Land of Cotton." *Village Voice*, 22 October 1991. [Black workers in the rural town of Waynesboro, Georgia go about organizing a union]

8150. Taylor, Paul S. *Mexican Labor in the United States*, 2 vols. New York, NY: Arno Press, 1970. [includes 8 separate works]

8151. _____. "Mexican Women in Los Angeles Industry in 1928." *Aztlan* 11 (Spring 1980): 99-131.

8152. Thomas, Cornelius C. *Black Workers at the Point of Production: Shopfloor Radicalism and Wildcat Strikes in Detroit Auto, 1955-1976*. Ph.D. diss., University of Notre Dame, 1993. UMO # 9319285.

8153. Tobin, Catherine T. *The Lowly Muscular Digger: Irish Canal Workers in Nineteenth Century America*. Ph.D. diss., University of Notre Dame, 1987. [Illinois and Michigan Canal]. UMO # 8722738.

8154. Tomaskovic-Devey, Donald. *Gender and Racial Inequality at Work: The Sources and Consequences of Employment Segregation*. ILR Press, 1993.

8155. Tomlins, C. L. "In Nat Turner's Shadow: Reflections on the Norfolk Dry Dock Affair of 1830-1831." *Labor History* 33 (Fall 1992).

8156. Trevizo, Dolores and others. "[Three articles on successful union organizing by janitors in Los Angeles]." *Against the Current* 5 (September-October 1990).

8157. Tucker, Barbara M. "Agricultural Workers in World War II: The Reserve Army of Children, Black Americans and Jamaicans." *Agricultural History* 68 (Winter 1994): 54-73.

8158. VanderVelde, Lea S. "The Labor Vision of the Thirteenth Amendment." *University of Pennsylvania Law* 138 (December 1989).

8159. Vargas, Zaragosa. *Proletarians of the North. Mexican Industrial Workers in Detroit and the Midwest, 1917-1933*. University of California Press, 1993.

8160. Walsh, Lorena S. "Plantation Management in the Chesapeake, 1620-1820." *Journal of Economic History* 49 (June 1989): 393-406.

8161. Ward, Robert D., and William W. Rogers. *Labor Revolt in Alabama: The Great Strike of 1894*. University of Alabama Press, 1965.

8162. Way, P. "Shovel and Shamrock: Irish Workers and Labor Violence in the Digging of the Chesapeake and Ohio Canal." *Labor History* 30 (Fall 1989).

8163. Weber, Devra A. "The Organization of Mexicano Agricultural Workers: The Imperial Valley and Los Angeles, 1928-1934: An Oral Approach." *Aztlan* 3 (Fall 1972): 307-347.

8164. Weiss, Lawrence D. "Industrial Reserve Army of the Southwest: Navajo and Mexican." *Southwest Economy and Society* 3 (Fall 1977).

8165. Whatley, W. C. "African-American Strikebreaking from the Civil War to the New Deal." *Social Science History* 17 (Winter 1993): 525-558.

8166. White, Carmen. "'As Soon As They Fire One of Us They Hire One O' Them': Ethnic Succession in a St. Louis Sweatshop." *City and Society* 3 (1989): 132-141.

8167. Whittaker, William G. "Samuel Gompers, Labor, and the Mexican American Crisis of 1916: The Carrizal Incident." *Labor History* 17 (Fall 1976): 551-567.

8168. Wigderson, Seth M. *The UAW in the 1950s*. 2. vols. Ph.D. diss., Wayne State University, 1989. [Touches on race]. UMO # 8922794.

8169. Wilkinson, Alec. "Big Sugar-I." *New Yorker*, 17 July 1989. [Hand-harvesting of sugar cane in South Florida by Caribbean workers, mostly from Jamaica]

8170. Wilkinson, Doris Y. "The Segmented Labor Market and African American Women from 1890-1960: A Social History Interpretation." in *Research in Race and Ethnic Relations*, Vol. 6. pp. 85-104. ed. R. M. Dennis. : JAI Press, 1991.

8171. Williams, Randall. *Hard Labor: A Report on Day Labor Pools and Temporary Employment*. Atlanta, GA: Southern Regional Council, 1988.

8172. Williams, Rhonda M., and Peggie R. Smith. "What Else Do Unions Do? Race and Gender in Local 35." *Review of Black Political Economy* 18 (Winter 1990): 59-77.

8173. Wilson, Francille R. "Black Workers' Ambivalence toward Unions." *International Journal of Politics, Culture and Society* 2 (1989): 378-381.

8174. Wilson, Joseph F. *Tearing Down the Color Bar. A Documentary History and Analysis of the Brotherhood of Sleeping Car Porters*. New York, NY: Columbia University Press, 1989. [1950-1973]

8175. "Women in the Workplace: Toward True Integration." *Sociological Perspectives* 35 (Spring 1992): entire issue.

8176. Woodruff, Nan E. "Pick or Fight: The Emergency Farm Labor Program in the Arkansas and Mississippi Delta during World War II." *Agricultural History* 64 (1990): 74-85.

8177. Worthman, Paul B. "Black Workers and Labor Unions in Birmingham, Alabama, 1897-1904." *Labor History* 10 (1969).

8178. Wright, Gavin. "The Economic Revolution in the American South." *Journal of Economic Perspectives* 1 (Summer 1987): 161- 178.

8179. Yuen, Shirley Mark, and Teresa Feng. "Coping with Unemployment, the Struggle of the PSC Garment Workers." *Asian American Resource Workshop Newsletter (Boston, MA)* (June 1986).

8180. Zamora, Emilio. *The World of Mexican Workers in Texas*. Texas A&M University Press, 1993.

8181. Zieger, Robert H., ed. *Organized Labor in the Twentieth- century South*. Knoxville, TN: University of Tennessee Press, 1991.

LAND

8182. Abel, Annie H. "Indian Reservation in Kansas and the Extinguishment of their Title." *Transactions of the Kansas State Historical Society* 8 (1903-1904): 72-109.

8183. Allen, R. H. "The Spanish Land Grant System as an Influence in the Agricultural Development of California." *Agricultural History* 9 (July 1935): 127-142.

8184. Alvarado, Jose. "Black Farmers Meet, Discuss Fight Against Massive Loss of Land." *Militant*, 6 September 1993.

8185. Amott, Teresa. "Losing Ground, Black Farmers Face Extinction." *Dollars and Sense* 147 (June 1989): 9-11.

8186. Avina, Rose H. *Spanish and Mexican Land Grants in California*. Arno, 1976.

8187. Barker, Eugene C. "Land Speculation as a Cause of the Texas Revolution." *Texas Historical Association Quarterly* 10 (July 1906): 76-95.

8188. Barsh, Russell L. "Behind Land Claims: Rationalizing Dispossession in Anglo-American Law." *Law and Anthropology* 1 (1986): 15-50.

8189. Basso, Keith H. and others. "Western Apache Ecology: From Horticulture to Agriculture." in *Anthropological Papers of the University of Arizona*, eds. Keith H. Basso, and Morris E. Opler. Tuscon, AZ: University of Arizona Press, 1971.

8190. Berry, Mary C. *The Alaska Pipeline: The Politics of Oil and Native Land Claims*. Bloomington, IN: Indiana University Press, 1975.

8191. Blavis, Patricia B. *Tijerina and the Land Grants: Mexican Americans in Struggle for Their Heritage*. New York, NY: International Publishers, 1971.

8192. Blumenthal, Walter H. *American Indians Dispossessed: Fraud in Land Cessions Forced Upon the Tribes*. Philadelphia, PA: G. S. MacManus, Co., 1955.

8193. Boston, Thomas D. "Capitalist Development and Afro-American Land Tenancy." *Science and Society* 46 (1982): 445-460.

8194. Bowden, J. J. *Private Land Claims in the Southwest*. 6 vols. Ph.D. diss., Southern Methodist University, 1969.

8195. Brodeur, Paul. *Restitution: The Land Claims of the Mashpee, Passamaquoddy, and Penobscot Indians of New England*. Boston, MA: Northeastern University Press, 1985.

8196. Brown, Loren N. "The Appraisal of the Lands of the Choctaws and Chickasaws by the Dawes Commission." *Chronicles of Oklahoma* 22 (Summer 1944): 177-191.

8197. Burton, L. "American Indian Water Rights in the Future of the Southwest." in *Water and the Future of the Southwest*, ed. Z. A. Smith. Albuquerque, NM: University of New Mexico Press, 1989.

8198. Callicott, J. Baird. "American Indian Land Wisdom? Sorting Out the Issues." *Journal of Forest History* 33 (January 1989): 35- 42. [See Cronon,below]

8199. Camp, Gregory S. "Working Out Their Own Salvation: The Allotment of Land in Severalty and the Turtle Mountain Chippewa Band 1870-1920." *American Indian Culture and Research Journal* 14 (1990): 19-38.

8200. Carlson, Alvar W. "Spanish-American Acquisition of Cropland Within the Northern Pueblo Indian Grants, New Mexico." *Ethno History* 22 (Spring 1975): 95-110.

8201. Carlson, Leonard A. "Land Allotment and the Decline of American Indian Farming." *Explorations in Economic History* 18 (1981): 128-154.

8202. Carroll, Peter F. "The Dawning of a New Era: Tribal Self- determinants in Indian Mineral Production." *Public Land Law Review* 9 (1988): 81-104.

8203. Chambers, Reid P., and Monroe E. Price. "Regulating Sovereignty: Secretarial Discretion and the Leasing of Indian Lands." *Stanford Law Review* 26 (May 1974): 1061-1096.

8204. Chandler, Alfred N. *Land Title Origins. A Tale of Force and Fraud*. New York, NY: Robert Schalkenbach Foundation, 1945.

8205. Churchill, Ward. "The Black Hills Are Not For Sale: A Summary of the Lakota Struggle for the 1868 Treaty Territory." *Journal of Ethnic Studies* 18 (Spring 1990).

8206. _____. *Indians Are Us? Culture and Genocide in Native North America*. Common Courage Press, 1994.

8207. _____. "Resisting Relocation. Dine and Hopis Fight to Keep Their Land." *Dollars and Sense* 112 (December 1985): 14-16.

8208. _____. "The Struggle for Newe Segobia." *Z Magazine* 5 (July-August 1992): 92-96. [Land of the Western Shoshone Nation]

8209. Cockburn, Alexander. "Hawaiians Want Their Land Returned." *Los Angeles Times*, 24 August 1993.

8210. Cohen, Felix S. "Original Indian Title." *Minnesota Law Review* 32 (December 1947): 28-59.

8211. Coleman, Michael C. "Problematic Panacea: Presbyterian Missionaries and the Allotment of Indians Lands in the Late Nineteenth Century." *Pacific Historical Review* 54 (May 1985): 143-159.

8212. Colley, Charles C. "The Struggle of Nevada Indians to Hold their Lands, 1847-1870." *Indian Historian* 6 (1973): 5-17.

8213. Controneo, Ross R., and Jack Dozier. "A Time of Disintegration: The Coeur D'Alene and the Dawes Act." *Western History Quarterly* 5 (1974): 405-419.

8214. Cornell, Srephen. "Land, Labour and Group Formation: Blacks and Indians in the United States." *Ethnic and Racial Studies* 13 (July 1990).

8215. Cotto, Lillian. *Land Invasion and State Responses in Puerto Rico: 1968-1976*. Ph.D. diss., Rutgers University, 1989. UMO # 9008888.

8216. Coulter, Robert T., and Steven M. Tullberg. "Indian Land Rights." in *Aggressions of Civilization: Federal Indian Policy Since the 1880s*, eds. Sandra L. Cadwalader, and Vine Deloria. Philadelphia, PA: Temple University Press, 1984.

8217. Cronon, William. *Changes in the Land: Indians, Colonists, and the Ecology of New England*. New York, NY: Hill and Wang, 1983.

8218. David, Mike. "Downwinders Challenge Mighty Uncle." *Cross Roads* 30 (April 1993): 2-6. [Western Shoshone nation attempts to regain control of its land in struggle against the U.S. government]

8219. Davis, Susan E. "Tribal Rights, Tribal Wrongs." *Nation*, 23 March 1992. [Hoopa Indians]

8220. Day, Gordon M. "The Indian as an Ecological Factor in the Northeastern Forest." *Ecology* 34 (1953): 329-346.

8221. DeParle, Jason. "Tribal Dispute Keeps Some Navajos in Squalor." *New York Times*, 16 August 1992. [Navajo-Hopi land conflict]

8222. Deutsch, Herman J. "Indian and White in the Inland Empire: The Contest for the Land, 1880-1912." *Pacific Northwest Quarterly* 47 (April 1956): 44-51.

8223. Doherty, Robert. *Disputed Waters. Native American and the Great Lakes Fishery.* Lexington, KY: University Press of Kentucky, 1990.

8224. Dozier, Jack. "The Coeur D'Alene Land Rush, 1909-1910." *Pacific Northwest Quarterly* 53 (1962): 145-150.

8225. Dubin, Corey. "Navajos Dig In at Big Mountain." *Guardian*, 16 August 1989. [Joint Use Area in northern Arizona]

8226. Dunbar Ortiz, Roxanne. *Roots of Resistance: Land Tenure in New Mexico, 1680-1980.* Los Angeles, CA: Chicano Studies Center, University of California, 1980.

8227. Ebright, Malcolm. *The Tierra Amarilla Land Grant: A History of Chicanery.* Santa Fe, NM: Center for Land Grant Studies, 1985.

8228. Edland, Roy E. "The 'Indian Problem': Pacific Northwest, 1879." *Oregon History 2* 70 (1969): 101-137.

8229. Eisinger, Chester E. "The Puritans' Justification for Taking the Land." *Essex Institute Historical Collections* 84 (April 1948): 131-143.

8230. Faiman-Silva, Sandra L. "Tribal Land to Private Land: A Century of Oklahoma Choctaw Timberland Alienation from the 1880s to the 1980s." *Journal of Forest History* 32 (October 1988): 191- 204.

8231. Flanagan, Thomas. "The Agricultural Argument and Original Appropriation: Indian Lands and Political Philosophy." *Canadian Journal of Political Science* 22 (September 1989).

8232. Fluckey, Alan R. *A History of Alaska Native Land Claims (1867-1971).* Master's thesis, University of Utah, 1979.

8233. Forde, C. Daryll. "Hopi Agriculture and Land Ownership." *Royal Anthropological Institute of Great Britain and Ireland Journal* 61 (1931): 357-405.

8234. Friedenberg, Daniel M. *Life, Liberty and the Pursuit of Land.* Prometheus Books, 1992.

8235. Frison, Theodore H. "Acquisition of Access Rights and Rights of Way on Fee, Public Domain, and Indian Lands." *Rocky Mountain Mineral Law institute Proceedings* 10 (1965): 217-259.

8236. Fuller, Craig W. *Land Rush in Zion: Opening of the Uncompahgre and Uintah Indian Reservations.* Ph.D. diss., Brigham Young University, 1990. UMO # 9033359.

8237. Furuya, Jun. *Gentlemen's Disagreement: The Controversy between the United States and Japan over the California Alien Land Law of 1913.* Ph.D. diss., Princeton University, 1989. UMO # 9002697.

8238. Gardner, Richard. *Grito! Reies Tijerina and the New Mexico Land Grant War of 1967.* Indianapolis, IN: Bobbs-Merrill, 1970.

8239. Gates, Paul W. *Fifty Million Acres: Conflicts over Kansas Land Policy, 1854-1890.* Ithaca, NY: Cornell University Press, 1954.

8240. _____, Indian Allotments Preceding the Dawes Act. in *The Frontier Challenge: Responses to the Trans-Mississippi West*, pp. 141-170. ed. John G. Clark. Lawrence, KS: University Press of Kansas, 1971.

8241. _____. "Public Land Disposal in California." *Agricultural History* 49 (January 1975): 158-178.

8242. Gibson, Michael M. "Indian Claims in the Beds of Oklahoma Watercourses." *American Indian Law Review* 4 (1976): 83-90.

8243. Gilbert, Bil. *God Gave Us This Country. Tekamthi and the First American Civil War.* New York, NY: Atheneum, 1989.

8244. Gomez, P. "The History and Adjudication of the Common Lands of Spanish and Mexican Land Grants." *Natural Resources Journal* 25 (October 1985).

8245. Graebner, Norman A. "The Public Land Policy of the Five Civilized Tribes." *Chronicles of Oklahoma* 23 (1945): 107-118.

8246. Greene, Jerome A. "The Sioux Land Commission of 1889: Prelude to Wounded Knee." *South Dakota History* 1 (1970): 41-72.

8247. Guerrero, Marianna. "American Indian Water Rights: The Blood of Life in Native North America." in *The State of Native America*, pp. 189-216. ed. M. Annette Jaimes. : South End Press, 1992.

8248. Harris, J. William. "Marx, the Market, and the Freedman: Land and Labor in Late Nineteenth-Century Georgia." in *Looking South: Chapters in the Story of an American Region*, eds. Joseph F. Tripp, and Winfred B. Moore, Jr. Westport, CT: Greenwood Press, 1989.

8249. Heritage, William. "Forestry, Past and Future, on Indian Reservations in Minnesota." *Journal of Forestry* 34 (1936): 648- 652.

8250. Hickey, Jo Ann S., and Anthony A. Hickey. "Black Farmers in Virginia, 1930-1978: An Analysis of the Social Organization of Agriculture." *Rural Sociology* 52 (1987): 75-88.

8251. Hilliard, Sam B. "Indian Land Cessions West of the Mississippi." *Journal of the West* 10 (1971): 493-510.

8252. Holford, David M. "The Subversion of the Indian Land Allotment System, 1887-1934." *Indian Historian* 8 (1975): 11-21.

8253. Hoover, Herbert T. "The Sioux Agreement of 1889 and Its Aftermath." *South Dakota History* 19 (1989): 56-94.

8254. Hunt, Jack. "Land Tenure and Economic Development on the Warm Springs Indian Reservation." *Journal of the West* 9 (January 1970): 93-109.

8255. *Indian Land Tenure, Economic Status, and Population Trends, Part 10, Supplementary Report of Land Planning Committee to National Resources Board*. Washington, DC: Goverment Printing Office, 1935.

8256. Jackson, Leroy F. "Sioux Land Treaties." *Collection of the North Dakota State Historical Society* 3 (1910): 498-528.

8257. Jacobs, Wilbur R. *Dispossessing the American Indian*. New York, NY: Scribner's, 1972.

8258. Julian, George W. "Land Stealing in New Mexico." *North American Review* 145 (1 July 1887): 2-31.

8259. Kame'eleihiwa, Lilikala (Lilikala Dorton). *Land and the Promise of Capitalism: A Dilemma for the Hawaiian Chiefs of the 1848 Mahele*. Ph.D. diss., University of Hawaii, 1986.

8260. Keckeisen, Robert J. *The Kansas "Half-breed" Lands: Contravention and Transformation of United States Indian Policy in Kansas*. Ph.D. diss., Wichita State University, 1981.

8261. Kelley, Lawrence C. "The Navaho Indians: Land and Oil." *New Mexico Historical Review* 38 (1963): 1-28.

8262. Kempers, Margot. "There's Losing and Winning: Ironies of the Maine Indian Land Claim." *Legal Studies Forum* 13 (Summer 1989): 267-299.

8263. Kickingbird, Kirke, and Karen Ducheneaux. *One Hundred Million Acres*. New York, NY: Macmillan, 1973.

8264. Kimmey, Fred M. "Christianity and Indian Lands." *Ethnohistory* 7 (Winter 1960): 44-60.

8265. Kinney, J. P. *A Continent Lost- A Civilization Won: Indian Land Tenure in America*. Baltimore, MD: Johns Hopkins University Press, 1937.

8266. Kroeber, Alfred L. "Nature of the Land- Holding Group." *Ethnohistory* 2 (Fall 1955): 303-314.

8267. Lamar, Howard R. "Land Policy in the Spanish Southwest, 1846-1891: A Study in Contrasts." *Journal of Economic History* 22 (December 1962): 498-515.

8268. Lazarus, Edward. *Black Hills/White Justice. The Sioux Nation versus the United States 1775 to the Present*. New York, NY: Harper Collins, 1991.

8269. Lazarus, Mark L., III. "An Historical Analysis of Alien Land Law: Washington Territory and State 1853-1889." *University of Puget Sound Law Review* 12 (Winter 1989): 197-246.

8270. Linton, Ralph M. "Land Tenure in Aboriginal America." in *The Changing Indian*, pp. 42-54. ed. Oliver LaFarge. Norman, OK: University of Oklahoma Press, 1942.

8271. McChesney, Fred S. "Government as Definer of Property Rights: Indian Lands, Ethnic Externalities, and Bureaucratic Budgets." *Journal of Legal Studies* 19 (June 1990): 297-335.

8272. McCluggage, Robert W. "The Senate and Indian Land Titles, 1800-1825." *Western History 2* 1 (1970): 415-425.

8273. McDonnell, Janet E. *The Disintegration of the Indian Estate: Indian Land Policy, 1913-1929*. Ph.D. diss., Marquette University, 1980.

8274. McDonnell, Janet A. *The Dispossession of the American Indian, 1887-1934*. Bloomington, IN: Indiana University Press, 1991.

8275. McGee, Leo, and Robert Boone. "Black Rural Land Decline in the South." *Black Scholar* (May 1977): 8-11.

8276. McGee, Leo, and Robert Boone, eds. *The Black Rural Landowner*. Westport, CT: Greenwood, 1979.

8277. McGregor, Davianna Pomaika'i. *Kupa'a i ka 'aina: Persistence on the Land*. Ph.D. diss., University of Hawaii, 1989. [Hawaii, 1900-1930]. UMO # 9018983.

8278. McNeil, Kurt. *Common Law Aboriginal Title: The Right of Indigenous People to Lands Occupied By Them at the Time a Territory Is Annexed to the Crown's Dominions by Settlement*. Ph.D. diss., University of Oxford, 1987. Order Number BRD-86602.

8279. Meyer, Melissa L. "'We Can Not Get a Living as We Used To': Dispossession and the White Earth Anishinaabeg, 1889-1920." *American Historical Review* 96 (April 1991): 368-394.

8280. Miller, Thomas L. *The Public Lands of Texas, 1519-1970*. Norman, OK: University of Oklahoma Press, 1972.

8281. Moore, M. R. "Native American Water Rights: Efficiency and Fairness." *Natural Resources Journal* 29 (Summer 1989).

8282. Nabokov, Peter. *Tijerina and the Courthouse Raid*. Albuquerque, NM: University of New Mexico, 1969.

8283. Nielsen, Richard A. "American Indian Land Claims: Land versus Money as a Remedy." *University of Florida Law Review* 25 (Winter 1973): 308-326.

8284. Orfield, Matthias Nordberg. *Federal Land Grants to the States with Special Reference to Minnesota*. Minneapolis, MN: University of Minnesota Studies in the Social Sciences, No. 2, 1915.

8285. Parker, Linda S. *Native American Estate: The Struggle over Indian and Hawaiian Lands*. Honolulu, HA: University of Hawaii Press, 1989.

8286. Parman, Donald L. "Inconstant Advocacy: The Erosion of Indian Fishing Rights in the Pacific Northwest, 1933-1956." *Pacific History Review* 53 (1984): 163-190.

8287. Paulson, Howard W. "The Allotment of Land in Severalty to the Dakota Indians before the Dawes Act." *South Dakota History* 1 (1971): 132-154.

8288. Pennick, Edward J. "Land Ownership and Black Economic Development." *Black Scholar* 21 (January-March 1990): 43-46.

8289. Perdue, Theda. "The Conflict Within: The Cherokee Power Structure and Removal." *Georgia Historical Quarterly* 73 (1989): 467-491.

8290. Porter, Frank W., III. "In Search of Recognition: Federal Indian Policy and the Landless Tribes of Western Washington." *American Indian Quarterly* 14 (Spring 1990): 113-132.

8291. Powell, Thomas R. "Alien Land Cases in United States Supreme Court." *California Law Review* 12 (May 1924): 259-282.

8292. Ragsdale, John W., Jr. "The Dispossession of the Kansas Shawnee." *UMKC Law Review* 58 (Winter 1990): 209-256.

8293. Ray, Roger B. "Maine Indians' Concept of Land Tenure." *Maine Historical Society Quarterly* 13 (1973): 28-51.

8294. Reeve, Frank D. "A Navajo Struggle for Land." *New Mexico Historical Review* 21 (January 1946): 1-21.

8295. Roberts, Frances C. "Politics and Public Land Disposal in Alabama's Formative Period." *Alabama Review* 22 (1969): 163-174.

8296. Rollings, Willard H. "The Pueblos of New Mexico and the Protection of Their Land and Water Rights." in *Working the Range*, ed. John R. Wunder. Westport, CT: Greenwood, 1985.

8297. Rosenthal, H. D. *Their Day in Court. A History of the Indian Claims Commission.* New York, NY: Garland, 1990. [1946- 1978]

8298. Rubenstein, Bruce A. "Justice Denied: Indian Land Frauds in Michigan, 1855-1900." *Old Northwest* 2 (1976): 131-140.

8299. Sahagun, Louis. "This Land 'Belonged to All of Us'." *Los Angeles Times*, 17 November 1993. [San Luis Valley, CO]

8300. Schulman, M. D., and B. A. Newman. "The Persistence of the Black Farmer: The Contemporary Relevance of the Lenin-Chayanov Debate." *Rural Sociology* 56 (Summer 1991): 264-283.

8301. Schweninger, Loren. "A Vanishing Breed: Black Farm Owners in the South, 1651-1982." *Agricultural History* 63 (1989): 41-60.

8302. Sells, Cato. "Land Tenure and the Organization of Agriculture on Indian Reservations in the United States." *International Review of Agricultural Economics* 77 (May 1917): 63-76.

8303. Shanahan, Donald G., Jr. "Compensation for the Loss of the Aboriginal Lands of the California Indians." *Southern California Quarterly* 57 (1975): 297-320.

8304. Silver, James W. "Land Speculation Profits in the Chicksaw Cession." *Journal of Southern History* 10 (February 1944): 84-92.

8305. Singer, Joseph W. "The Continuing Conquest: American Indian Nations, Property Law, and 'Gunsmoke'." *Reconstruction* 1 (1991): 97-103.

8306. Smith, Burton M. "Business, Politics and Indian Land Settlements on Montana, 1862-1904." *Canadian Journal of History* 20 (April 1985): 45-64.

8307. Smothers, Ronald. "For Black Farmers, Extinction Seems to Be Near." *New York Times*, 3 August 1992.

8308. Snipp, C. Matthew. "American Indians and Natural Resource Development: Indigenous Peoples' Land, Now Sought After, Has Produced New Indian-White Problems." *American Journal of Economics and Sociology* 45 (October 1986).

8309. Stauffer, Robert H. *Land Tenure in Kahana, Hawai'i, 1846- 1920.* Ph.D. diss., University of Hawaii, 1990. UMO # 9030583.

8310. Stewart, William J. "Settler, Politician, and Speculator in the Sale of the Sioux Reserve." *Minnesota History* 39 (1964): 85- 92.

8311. Suttles, Gerald D. *The Man-Made City: The Land-Use Confidence Game in Chicago.* Chicago, IL: University of Chicago Press, 1990.

8312. Sutton, Imre and others, eds. *Irredeemable America: The Indians' Estate and Land Claims.* Albuquerque, NM: University of New Mexico, 1986.

8313. Tijerina, Reies L. *Mi lucha por la Tierra.* Mexico City: Fondo de Cultura Economica, 1978.

8314. Torres, Gerald, and Kathryn Milun. "Translating Yonnondio by Precedent and Evidence: The Mashpee Indian Case." *Duke Law Journal* 625-659 (September 1990).

8315. Trafzer, Clifford E., and Richard D. Scheuerman. "'This Land Is Your Land and You Are Being Robbed Of It': Dispossession of Palouse Indian Land, 1860-1880." *Idaho Yesterdays* 29 (1986): 2-12.

8316. Treadwell, David. "Treaty Fuels New Settler, Indian Feud." *Los Angeles Times*, 23 August 1992. [Land rights of Seneca Nation in Salamanca, NY after Seneca Nation Settlement Act of 1890]

8317. Underhill, Lonnie E., and Daniel F. Littlefield, Jr. "Timber Depredations and Cherokee Legislation, 1869-1881." *Journal of Forest History* 18 (1974): 4-13.

8318. U.S. Congress, 101st 1st Session, Senate, Select Committee on Indian Affairs. *Administration of Native Hawaiian Home Lands: Joint Hearings, 3 parts*. Washington, DC: Government Printing Office, 1990. Y 4.IN2/11:S.hrg.101-555.

8319. U.S. Congress, 101st 2nd Session, House Representatives, Committee on Government Operations, Subcommittee on Government Information, Justice and Agriculture. *Decline of Minority Farming in the United States. Hearing.* Washington, DC: Government Printing Office 1991.

8320. U.S. Congress, 101st 2nd session, Senate, Select Committee on Indian Affairs. *Hawaiian Home Lands: Hearing.* Washington, DC: Government Printing Office, 1991.

8321. Veeder, William H. and others. "Water Rights: Life or Death for the American Indian." *Indian Historian* 5 (1972): 4-21.

8322. Wald, Alan. "'Land or Death' in New Mexico: Struggling Against Theft of Communal Lands." *Against the Current* 4 (March- April 1989): 3-6.

8323. Walker, Juliet E.K. "Legal Process and Judicial Challenges: Black Landownership in Western Illinois." *Western Illinois Regional Studies* 6 (1983).

8324. Weil, Richard H. "Destroying Homeland: White Earth, Minnesota." *American Indian Culture and Research Journal* 13 (1989): 69-95.

8325. Westphall, Victor. *The Public Domain in New Mexico, 1854- 1891*. Albuquerque, NM: University of New Mexico Press, 1965.

8326. White, Richard. "Indian Land Use and Environmental Change, Island County, Washington: A Case Study." *Arizona and the West* 17 (1975): 327-338.

8327. *Who Owns North Carolina?* Durham, NC: Institute for Southern Studies, 1986. [Study of 100 largest landholders in the state]

8328. Wilkinson, Charles F. "Land Tenure in the Pacific: The Context for Native Hawaiian Land Rights." *Washington Law Review* 64 (April 1989): 227-232.

8329. _____. "To Feel the Summer in the Spring: The Treaty Fishing Rights of the Wisconsin Chippewa." *Wisconsin Law Review* 3 (1991): 375-414.

8330. Williams, R. Hal. "George W. Julian and Land Reform in New Mexico, 1885-1889." *Agricultural History* 41 (January 1967): 71- 84.

8331. Wishart, David J. "The Dispossession of the Pawnee." *Annals of the Society of American Geographers* 69 (1979): 382-401.

8332. York, Frederick F. *Capitalist Development and Land in Northeastern Navajo Country, 1880s to 1980s*. Ph.D. diss., State University of New York at Binghamton, 1990. UMO # 9025837.

8333. Young, Mary E. "The Exercise of Sovereignty in Cherokee Georgia." *Journal of the Early Republic* 10 (1990): 43-63.

8334. _____. *Redskins, Ruffleshirts, and Rednecks: Indian Allotments in Alabama and Mississippi, 1830-1860*. Norman, OK: University of Oklahoma Press, 1961.

LANGUAGE

8335. Abramovitz, Mimi. "Putting an End to Doublespeak about Race, Gender, and Poverty: An Annotated Glossary for Social Workers." *Social Work* 36 (September 1991): 380-384.

8336. Adams, Karen L., and Daniel T. Brink, eds. *Perspectives on Official English: The Campaign for English as the Official Language of the U.S.A.* New York, NY: Mouton de Gruyter, 1990.

8337. Agar, M. "The Biculture in Bilingual." *Language in Society* 20 (June 1991): 167-182.

8338. Airaksinen, Timo. "The Rhetoric of Domination." in *Rethinking Power*, ed. Thomas E. Wartenberg. SUNY Press, 1992.

8339. Alegado, Dean T. "Your Accent May Be Hazardous to Your Career. The Fragrante Case." *Katipunan* (July-August 1990): 13- 14.

8340. Allan, Keith, and Kate Burridge. *Euphemism and Dysphemism. Language Used as Shield and Weapon*. New York, NY: Oxford University Press, 1991.

8341. Allen, Irving Lewis. *The City in Slang. New York Life and Popular Speech*. Oxford University Press, 1993.

8342. _____. "Sly Slurs: Mispronunciation and Decapitalization of Group Names." *Names* 36 (1988): 217-224.

8343. _____. *Unkind Words. Ethnic Labeling from Redskin to WASP*. Westport, CT: Bergin and Garvey, 1990.

8344. Aman, Reinhold. "Offensive Words in Dictionaries, IV: Ethnic, Racial, Religious and Sexual Slurs in an American and an Australian Dictionary." *Maledicta* 10 (1988-1989): 126-135.

8345. Amorose, Thomas. "The Official-Language Movement in the United States: Contexts, Issues, and Activities." *Language Problems and Language Planning* 13 (Fall 1989): 264-279.

8346. Anderson, A. B. "Comparative Analysis of Language Minorities: A Sociological Framework." *Journal of Multilingual and Multicultural Development* 11 (1990).

8347. Arington, Michele. "English-only Laws and Direct Legislation: The Battle in the States over Language Minority Rights." *Journal of Law and Politics* 7 (Winter 1991): 325-352.

8348. Armstead, Cheryl A. *Physical and Psychological Effects of Negative Statements About Blacks*. Master's thesis, Saint Louis University, 1986.

8349. Atkins, Chester G. "David Duke Message: It Can Happen Here." *Boston Globe*, 23 November 1991. [Racist language being used to support views of English Only organization]

8350. August, Diane, and Eugene E. Garcia. *Language Minority Education in the United States: Research, Policy and Practise*. Springfield, IL: Charles C. Thomas, 1988.

8351. "Avoiding Sexist Language." *Random House Webster's College Dictionary*, : Random House, 1991.

8352. Baca, L. and others. "Language Minority Students: Literacy and Educational Reform." in *Literacy. A Redefinition*, eds. Nancy J. Ellsworth and others. : Lawrence Erlbaum Associates, 1994.

8353. Bahrick, H. P. and others. "50 Years of Language Maintenance and Language Dominance in Bilingual Hispanic Immigrants." *Journal of Experimental Psychology (General)* 123 (September 1994): 264-283.

8354. Baker, Russell. "Don't Mention It." *New York Times*, 30 May 1990. [The language of race and racial depreciation]

8355. _____. "No More Mister Nice WASP." *New York Times*, 22 January 1991.

8356. Baker, Susan G. "The Continuing Struggle over Multilingualism in the Southwestern United States." *Sociological Abstracts* Supplement 167 (August 1991). 91S24917/ASA/1991/6276.

8357. Baron, Dennis. *The English-Only Question: An Offical Language for Americans?* New Haven, CT: Yale University Press, 1990.

8358. _____. "English in a Multicultural America." *Social Policy* 21 (Spring 1991): 5-14.

8359. Basso, Keith H. *Portraits of "The Whiteman": Linguistic Play and Cultural Symbols among the Western Apache*. New York, NY: Cambridge University Press, 1979.

8360. Behuniak, Peter and others. "Bilingual Education: Evaluation Politics and Practices." *Evaluation Review* 12 (October 1988): 483-509.

8361. Bender, Eric D. "The Viability of Racist Speech from High Schools to Universities: A Welcome Matriculation?" *University of Cincinnati Law Review* 59 (Winter 1991): 871-903.

8362. Berger, Joseph. "New York's Bilingual Bureaucracy Assailed as Non-English Programs Cover More Pupils." *New York Times*, 4 January 1993.

8363. Berk-Seligson, Susan. "The Importance of Linguistics in Court Interpreting." *La Raza Law Journal* 2 (Fall 1988): 14-48.

8364. "Bilingual Education." *Educational Researcher* 21 (March 1992).

8365. Billig, Michael. "The Notion of 'Prejudice': Some Rhetorical and Ideological Aspects." *Text* 8 (1988): 91-110.

8366. Brown, Claude. "The Language of Violence." *Los Angeles Times*, 24 March 1994.

8367. Brown, De Neen L. "Some Area Parents See Drawbacks in Diversity. Language Barriers Spark Concern." *Washington Post*, 23 November 1992.

8368. Buker, Eloise A. "'Lady' Justice: Power and Image in Feminist Jurisprudence." *Vermont Law Review* 15 (Summer 1990): 69- 87.

8369. Bushey, Karen. "The Maleness of Legal Language." *Manitoba Law Journal* 18 (Winter 1989): 191-212.

8370. Cadd, M. "An Attempt to Reduce Ethnocentrism in the Foreign-Language Classroom." *Foreign Language Annals* 27 (Summer 1994): 143-160.

8371. Califa, Antonio J. "Declaring English the Official Language: Prejudice Spoken Here." *Harvard Civil Rights-Civil Liberties Law Review* 293-348 (Spring 1989).

8372. Callahan, Linda F. "History: A Critical Scene in Jesse Jackson's Rhetorical Vision." *Journal of Black Studies* 24 (December 1993).

8373. Carlson, A. Cheree. "The Rhetoric of the Know-Nothing Party: Nativism as a Response to the Rhetorical Situation." *S. Communication Journal* 54 (Summer 1989): 364-383.

8374. Chen, Edward M. "Language Rights in the Private Sector." in *Language Loyalties*, pp. 269-277. ed. James Crawford. : University of Chicago Press, 1992.

8375. Citrin, Jack. "Language, Politics and American Identity." *Public Interest* no. 99 (Spring 1990): 96-109.

8376. Citrin, Jack and others. "The Official English Movement and the Symbolic Politics of Language in the United States." *Western Political Quarterly* 43 (September 1990).

8377. Clark, Gregory R., ed. *Words of the Vietnam War: The Slang, Jargon, Abbreviation, Acronyms, Nomenclature, Nicknames, Pseudonyms, Slogans, Specs, Euphemisms, Doubletalk, Chants, and Names and Places of the Era of United States Involvement in Vietnam.* Jefferson, NC: McFarland, 1986.

8378. Coleman, Wanda. "Afro-American Like Me." *Los Angeles Times Magazine*, 5 September 1993. [Colored, Negro, or Afro-American?]

8379. Comas-Diaz, Lillian, and A. M. Padilla. "The English-Only Movement: Implications for Mental Health Services." *American Journal of Orthopsychiatry* 62 (January 1992): 6-7.

8380. Comment. "Non English-speaking Persons in the Criminal Justice System: Current State of the Law." *Cornell Law Review* 61 (1976).

8381. Condor, Susan. "'Race Stereotypes' and Racist Discourse." *Text* 8 (1988): 69-89.

8382. Cordero, Laura A. "Constitutional Limitations on Official English Declarations." *New Mexico Law Review* 20 (December 1990): 17-53.

8383. Crawford, James. *Bilingual Education: History, Politics, Theory, and Practice.* Trenton, NJ: Crane Publishing Co., 1989.

8384. _____. *Hold Your Tongue. Bilingualism and the Politics of English Only.* Addison-Wesley, 1992.

8385. Crowley, Tony. *Standard English and the Politics of Language.* Urbana, Il: University of Illinois Press, 1989.

8386. Cummins, James. *Empowering Minority Students.* Sacramento, CA: California Association of Bilingual Education, 1989.

8387. D'Amato, Anthony. "Harmful Speech and the Culture of Indeterminacy." *William and Mary Law Review* 32 (Winter 1991): 329-351.

8388. *Dangerous Dialogue: Attacks on Freedom of Expression in Miami's Cuban Exile Community.* Human Rights Watch, 1992.

8389. Daniel, J. L., and Geneva Smitherman-Donaldson. "How I Got Over: Communication Dynamics in the Black Community." in *Cultural Communication and Intercultural Contact*, ed. D. Carbaugh. Hillsdale, NJ: Lawrence Erlbaum Associates, 1990.

8390. Daniels, Harvey A., ed. *Not Only English: Affirming America's Multicultural Heritage.* Urbana, IL: National Council of Teachers of English, 1990.

8391. Davila, A. and others. "Accent Penalties and the Earnings of Mexican Americans." *Social Science Quarterly* 74 (December 1993).

8392. De Avila, E. H. "Bilingualism, Cognitive Function, and Language Minority Group Membership." in *Linguistic and Cultural Influences on Learning Mathematics*, eds. Rodney Cocking, and Jose P. Mestre. Hillsdale, NJ: Lawrence Erlbaum Associates, 1990.

8393. De Groot, Joanna. "'Sex' and 'Race': The Construction of Language and Image in the Nineteenth Century." in *Sexuality and Subordination: Interdisciplinary Studies of Gender in the Nineteenth Century*, eds. Susan Mendus, and Jane Rendall. New York, NY: Routledge, 1989.

8394. De Witt, Karen. "From DeVon to LaDon, Invented Names Proclaim 'I Am'." *New York Times*, 9 January 1994. [Uniquely black names in U.S.]

8395. del Valle, Manuel. "Language Rights and Due Process- Hispanics in the United States." *Revista Juridica de la universidad Interamericana de Puerto Rico* 17 (1982).

8396. Devins, Neal. "The Rhetoric of Equality." *Vanderbilt Law Review* 44 (January 1991): 15-44.

8397. Dillon, Sam. "Report Faults Bilingual Education in New York." *New York Times*, 20 October 1994.

8398. Dundes, A. "A Study of Ethnic Slurs: The Jew and the Polack in the U.S." *Journal of American Folklore* 84 (1971): 186-203.

8399. Dunn, Ashley. "Bilingual Ballot Law Fails to Help Chinese- American Voters." *New York Times*, 14 August 1994. [New York City fails to implement federal law on bilingual ballots]

8400. _____. "A War of Words Over Language." *Los Angeles Times*, 16 November 1992. [Non-English languages in the U.S.]

8401. Dye, Gloria J. *Lakota Cultural Values and the Language of Advocacy: An Approach to Literacy in a Native Community*. Ph.D. diss., University of Michigan, 1989. [Rosebud Reservation, SD]. UMO # 9001588.

8402. Edelsky, C. *With Literacy and Justice For All: Rethinking the Social in Language and Education*. Falmer Press, 1991.

8403. Edwards, W. F. "Sociolinguistic Behavior in a Detroit Inner-City Black Neighborhood." *Language in Society* 21 (March 1992): 93-116.

8404. Ellenberg, George B. "An Uncivil War of Words: Indian Removal in the Press, 1830." *Atlanta History* 33 (Spring 1989): 50-59.

8405. Ellis, Dean S. "Speech and Social Status in America." *Social Forces* 45 (March 1967): 431-437.

8406. "English Plus: Issues in Bilingual Education." *Annals of the American Academy of Political and Social Science* 508 (March 1990): Entire issue.

8407. Escobar, Elizam. "Language, Identity and Liberation: A Critique of the Term and Concept 'People of Color'." *Left Curve* 17 (1994).

8408. Essed, Philomena. "Understanding Verbal Accounts of Racism: Politics and Heuristics of Reality Constructions." *Text* 8 (1988): 5-40.

8409. February, Vernon. *And Bid Him Sing: Essays in Literature and Cultural Domination*. London: Kegan Paul International, 1988.

8410. Feldman, Paul. "Breathing New Life Into Dying Languages." *Los Angeles Times*, 12 July 1993. [California Indian languages]

8411. Ferdman, Bernardo M. and others, eds. *Literacy Across Languages and Cultures*. SUNY Press, 1994.

8412. Fernandez, Enrique. "Loving Spanish." *Village Voice*, 4 December 1990.

8413. Fernandez, Joseph M. "Bringing Hate Crime into Focus." *Harvard Civil Rights- Civil Liberties Law Review* 26 (Winter 1991): 261-293.

8414. Fikes, Robert. *Racist and Sexist Quotations by the Rich and Famous, Past and Present*. Saratoga, CA: R&E Publishers, 1990.

8415. Fillmore, Lily Wong. "Against Our Best Interest: The Attempt to Sabotage Bilingual Education." *Language Loyalties*, pp. 367-376. ed. James Crawford. : University of Chicago Press, 1992.

8416. Fishback, Price V., and J. S. Baskin. "Narrowing the Black- White Gap in Child Literacy in 1910: The Poles of School Inputs and Family Inputs." *Review of Economics and Statistics* 73 (November 1991).

8417. Fishman, J. A. "'English only': Its Ghosts, Myths, and Dangers." *International Journal of the Sociology of Language* 74 (1988): 125-140.

8418. Forbes, Susan S., and Peter Leuros. "History of American Language Policy, Appendix A." in *U.S. Immigration and the National Interest*, Select Commission on Immigrant and Refugee Policy. Washington, DC, 30 April 1981.

8419. GAO. *Bilingual Education: Information on Limited English Proficient Students*. April 1987.

8420. Garcia Martinez, Alfonso L. "Monolinguismo y bilinguismo Puertorriqueño." *Revista del Colegio de Abogados de Puerto Rico* 50 (October-December 1989): 75-78.

8421. Gates, Henry Louis, Jr. "On the Rhetoric of Racism in the Profession." in *Literature, Language, and Politics*, ed. Betty Jean Craige. Athens, GA: University of Georgia Press, 1988.

8422. Geltman, Max. "On Learning Swahili." *National Review* (19 November 1968).

8423. George, Lynell. "Is Too Much Left Unsaid in Discussions of Race?" *Los Angeles Times*, 30 January 1994.

8424. Gimenez, Martha E. "Latino/'Hispanic'- Who Needs a Name? The Case Against a Standardized Terminology." *International Journal of Health Services* 19 (1989).

8425. Gleason, Philip. *Speaking of Diversity. Essays on the Language of Ethnicity*. John Hopkins University Press, 1992.

8426. Goldberg, David T. "A Grim Dilemma about Racist Referring Expressions." *Metaphilosophy* 17 (1986): 224-229.

8427. _____. "The Semantics of Race." *Ethnic and Racial Studies* 15 (October 1992): 543-569.

8428. Goldstein, Richard. "Notes on 'Shvartzer'." *Village Voice*, 17 October 1989. [The Jewish word for Black person or "nigger"]

8429. Goldzwig, Steven R., and G. N. Dionisopoulos. "John F. Kennedy's Civil Rights Discourse: The Evolution from 'Principled Bystander' to Public Advocate." *Communication Monographs* 56 (September 1989).

8430. Gonzalez, David. "What's the Problem with 'Hispanic'? Just Ask a 'Latino'." *New York Times*, 15 November 1992.

8431. Gonzalez, Rafael J. "Pachuco: The Birth of a Creole Language." *Perspectives in Mexican American Studies* 1 (1988): 75- 87.

8432. Goodrich, Herbert. "Conflict, Power, and Language Change." *Sociological Viewpoints* 3 (1987): 51-69.

8433. Gravlee, Jack. "A Black Rhetoric of Social Revolution." in *A New Diversity in Contemporary Southern Rhetoric*, eds. Calvin M. Logue, and Howard Dorgan. Baton Rouge, LA: Louisiana State University Press, 1987.

8434. Greenberg, and Pepzcznski. "The Effect of an Overheard Ethnic Slur on Evaluations of the Target: How to Spread a Social Disease." *Journal of Experimental Social Psychology* 21 (1985).

8435. Grimshaw, Allen D. *Conflict Talk: Sociolinguistic Investigations of Arguments in Conversations*. New York, NY: Cambridge University Press, 1989.

8436. *Guidelines on Ethnic, Racial, Sexual and Other Identification*. Los Angeles, CA: Los Angeles Times, 1993.

8437. Guy, Gregory R. "International Perspectives on Linguistic Diversity and Language Rights." *Language Problems and Language Planning* 13 (1989): 45-53. [In re: "English only"]

8438. Haederk, Michael, and Christopher Heredia. "When 'Enlightened' People Make Racist Remarks." *Los Angeles Times*, 27 May 1993.

8439. Haiman, F. S. "Sexist Speech and the First Amendment." *Communication Education* 40 (January 1991).

8440. Hall, Gwendolyn M. *Africans in Colonial Louisiana: The Development of Afro-Creole in the Eighteenth Century*. Louisiana State University Press, 1992.

8441. Halsted, Ann L. *Sharpened Tongues: The Controversy over the "Americanization" of Japanese Language Schools in Hawaii, 1919- 1927*. Ph.D. diss., Stanford University, 1989. UMO # 8912906.

8442. Hayakawa, S. I. "Bilingualism in America: English Should Be the Only Language." *U.S.A. Today* (July 1989): 32-34.

8443. Hayes-Bautista, David E., and J. Chapa. "Latino Terminology: Conceptual Bases for Standardized Terminology." *American Journal of Public Health* 77 (January 1987): 61-68.

8444. Hecht, Michael L. and others. "An Afro-American Perspective on Interethnic Communication." *Communication Monographs* 56 (December 1989).

8445. Hernandez-G., Manuel de Jesus. "Against the Tide of Linguistic Repression: Renewed Support for Bilingual Education in the State of Washington." *International Journal of the Sociology of Language* 84 (1990): 125-131.

8446. Hernandez, Peggy. "Courts' Language Barrier Seen As Threat to Justice." *Boston Globe*, 30 October 1991.

8447. Hernandez, Raymond. "Immigrants Use Diction Lessons to Counter Bias." *New York Times*, 2 March 1993.

8448. Hidalgo, Margarita. "Language Contact, Language Loyalty, and Language Prejudice on the Mexican Border." *Language in Society* 15 (June 1986): 193-220.

8449. Hirschman, Albert O. *The Rhetoric of Reaction, Perversity, Jeopardy.* Cambridge, MA: Harvard University Press, 1991.

8450. Hodulik, Patricia. "Prohibiting Discriminatory Harassment by Regulating Student Speech: A Balancing of First-Amendment and University Interests." *Journal of College and University Law* 16 (Spring 1990): 677-697.

8451. Horton, John, and José Calderon. "Language Struggles in a Changing California Community." in *Language Loyalties*, pp. 186- 194. ed. James Crawford. : University of Chicago Press, 1992. [Monterey Park, CA]

8452. Houk, James. "The Terminological Shift from 'Afro-American' to 'African-American': Is the Field of Afro-American Anthropology Being Redefined?" *Human Organization* 52 (Fall 1993): 325-328.

8453. Hurtado, Aida, and Raul Rodriguez. "Language as a Social Problem: The Repression of Spanish in South Texas." *Journal of Multilingual and Multicultural Development* 10 (1989): 401-419. [Hispanic college students of 1983 recall repression in their earlier schooling]

8454. Hutchinson, Earl Ofari. "John Singleton Needs to Learn the Power of Words." *Los Angeles Times*, 9 August 1993. [On the harm of using the word "nigger"]

8455. Ison, Paula, and Brant Seibert. "Another View of Montero v. Meyer and the English-Only Movement: Giving Language Prejudice the Sanction of Law." *Denver University Law Review* 66 (1989).

8456. Jackson, Derrick Z. "'Minor' Call, Major Gaffe." *Boston Globe*, 7 April 1991. [Abolish the word "minority" as applied to people]

8457. Jacoby, Russell. "Away With Words!" *Washington Post*, 27 February 1994. [Unmentioned social violence far more serious than talk of violent and aggressive language]

8458. Jaimes, M. Annette, and Ward Churchill. "Behind the Rhetoric: 'English Only' as Counterinsurgency Warfare." *Issues in Radical Therapy* 12 (Winter-Spring 1988): 42-51.

8459. Janmohamed, Abdul, and David Lloyd, eds. *The Nature and Context of Minority Discourse.* New York, NY: Oxford University Press, 1990.

8460. Jernudd, Bjorn H., and M. J. Shapiro. *The Politics of Language Purism.* New York, NY: Mouton de Gruyter, 1989.

8461. Jimenez, Martha. "The Educational Rights of Language--Minority Children." in *Language Loyalties*, pp. 243-251. ed. James Crawford. : University of Chicago Press, 1992.

8462. Jones, Cathy J. "Sexist Language: An Overview for Teachers and Libraries." *Law Library Journal* 82 (Fall 1990): 673-682.

8463. Jones, Lisa. "My Slave Name." *Village Voice*, 24 March 1992.

8464. Judd, Elliot L. "The English Language Amendment: A Case Study on Language and Politics." *Revista del Colegio de Abogados de Puerto Rico* 50 (October-December 1989): 115-134. [English-only Amendment]

8465. Kakutani, Michiko. "The Word Police Are Listening For 'Incorrect' Language." *New York Times*, 1 February 1993.

8466. Kalantzis, Mary and others. *Minority Language and Dominant Culture*. Philadelphia, PA: Falmer Press, 1989.

8467. Keller, Robert H., Jr. "Hostile Language: Bias in Historical Writing About American Indian Resistance." *Journal of American Culture* 9 (1986): 9-23.

8468. Kleinwachter, Wolfgang. "The Prohibition of Propaganda for War and Racism." *National Lawyers Guild Practitioner* 28-32 (Winter 1989).

8469. Krahn, H. and others. "English Language Ability and Industrial Safety among Immigrants." *Sociology and Social Research* 75 (October 1990).

8470. Krebs, Bob and others. "Latino? Hispanic? Quechua? No, American." *New York Times*, 18 November 1992. [three letters]

8471. Kurtzman, H. S. "Sex Bias in Language Stimuli." *American Psychologist* 45 (November 1990).

8472. Kurzon, Dennis. "Sexist and Nonsexist Language in Legal Texts: The State of the Art." *International Journal of the Sociology of Language* 80 (1989): 99-113.

8473. Lakoff, Robin. *Talking Power*. Basic Books, 1990.

8474. Lang, Berel. "Language and Genocide." in *Echoes from the Holocaust: Philosophical Reflections on a Dark Time*, eds. Alan Rosenberg, and Gerald E. Myers. Philadelphia, PA: Temple University Press, 1988.

8475. Lang, Kevin. "Language and Economists' Theories of Discrimination." *International Journal of the Sociology of Language* 103 (1993): 165-183.

8476. "Language and History." *History Workshop* 27 (Spring 1989): 1-65.

8477. Lardner, David F. *Dreams Reflected: The Ann Arbor King School "Black English" Case*. Ph.D. diss., University of Michigan, 1991. UMO # 9135629.

8478. Leap, William L. *American Indian English*. University of Utah Press, 1993.

8479. Lee, Felicia R. "Grappling With How to Teach Young Speakers of Black Dialect." *New York Times*, 5 January 1994.

8480. Leibold, Nora C. *Interactive Linguistic Strategies in Campaign Rhetoric: Their Use and Function*. 2 volumes. Ph.D. diss., Georgetown University, 1992. [David Duke and J. Bennett Johnson]. UMO # 9316078.

8481. "Libel and Slander: Imputation of Association with Persons of Race or Nationality as to Which There Is Social Prejudice." *American Law Review* 121 (1939).

8482. Lighter, J. E., ed. *Historical Dictionary of American Slang (Volume 1, A-G)*. Random House, 1994.

8483. Linzer, Peter. "White Liberal Looks at Racist Speech." *St. John's Law Review* 65 (Winter 1991): 187-244.

8484. Logue, Calvin M. *Eugene Talmadge. Rhetoric and Response*. Westport, CT: Greenwood, 1989.

8485. Logue, Calvin M., and Thurmon Garner. "Shift in Rhetorical Status of Blacks after Freedom." *So. Communication Journal* 54 (Fall 1988): 1-39.

8486. Love, Jean C. "Discriminatory Speech and the Tort of Intentional Infliction of Emotional Distress." *Washington and Lee Law Review* 47 (Winter 1990): 123-159.

8487. Lowe, Lydia. "Activists Target English-Only in Massachusetts." *Resist* 227 (June 1990): 6-8.

8488. Lucaites, John L., and Celeste M. Condit. "Reconstructing < Equality >: Culturetypal and Counter-Cultural Rhetorics in the Martyred Black Vision." *Communication Monographs* 57 (March 1990).

8489. Luhman, Reid. "Appalachian English Stereotypes: Language Attitudes in Kentucky." *Language in Society* 19 (September 1990): 331-348.

8490. Luvin, Tamar. "Teamsters Sue Hotel at Disney World on 'English Only' Policy." *New York Times*, 13 October 1994. [Dolphin Hotel]

8491. Macias, Reynaldo F. *Latino Illiteracy in the United States*. Tomas Rivera Center, 1988.

8492. Maggio, Rosalie. *The Bias-Free WordFinder, a Dictionary of Nondiscriminatory Language*. Beacon Press.

8493. Mahoney, Kathleen. "Language as Violence v. Freedom of Expression: Canadian and American Perspectives on Group Defamation." *Buffalo Law Review* 37 (Spring 1988): 337-373.

8494. Malveaux, Julianne. "Back Talk: Eat Those Dirty Words!" *Essence* 20 (March 1990): 146.

8495. Marriot, Michel. "Rap's Embrace of 'Nigger' Fires Bitter Debate." *New York Times*, 24 January 1993.

8496. Marshall, D. F. "The Question of an Official Language: Language Rights and the English Language Amendment." *International Journal of the Sociology of Language* 60 (1986): 7- 75.

8497. Massaro, Toni M. "Equality and Freedom of Expression: The Hate Speech Dilemma." *William and Mary Law Review* 32 (Winter 1991): 211-265.

8498. Matsuda, Mari J. "Public Response to Racist Speech: Considering the Victim's Story." *Michigan Law Review* 87 (August 1989): 2320-2381.

8499. _____. "Voices of America: Accent, Antidiscrimination Law, and a Jurisprudence for the Last Reconstruction." *Yale Law Journal* 100 (March 1991): 1329-1407.

8500. Matthews, Carolyn R. "Accent: Legitimate Nondiscriminatory Reason or Permission to Discriminate?" *Arizona State Law Journal* 23 (Spring 1991): 231-259.

8501. Maxwell, Madeline, and S. Smith-Todd. "Black Sign Language and School Integration in Texas." *Language in Society* 15 (March 1986): 81-94.

8502. Mazama, A. "An Afrocentric Approach to Language Planning." *Journal of Black Studies* 25 (September 1994): 3-19.

8503. McLean, B. "On the Revision of Scapegoat Terminolgy." *Numen* 37 (1990): 168-173.

8504. McManus, Walter S. "Labor Market Effects of Language Enclaves: Hispanic Men in the United States." *Journal of Human Resources* 25 (Spring 1990).

8505. McMinn, M. R. and others. "Does Sexist Language Reflect Personal Characteristics?" *Sex Roles* 23 (October 1990).

8506. Medicine, Beatrice. "'Speaking Indian': Parameters of Language Use among American Indians." *Focus (National Clearinghouse for Bilingual Education)*, March 1981. 1-8.

8507. Mertz, Elizabeth. "The Uses of History: Language, Ideology, and Law in the United States and South Africa." *Law and Society Review* 22 (November 1988): 661-685.

8508. Meyn, Marianne. *Lenguaje e Identidad Cultural: Un Aceramiento Teorico al Caso de Puerto Rico*. Rio Piedras, PR: Editorial Edil, 1983.

8509. Miller, Keith D. *Voice of Deliverance. The Language of Martin Luther King, Jr. and Its Sources*. New York, NY: Free Press, 1991.

8510. Minow, Martha. "Speaking and Writing against Hate." *Cardozo Law Review* 11 (July-August 1990): 1393-1408.

8511. Mishkin, Kate. "Reasonable Regulations and State Sponsored Sound." *Pace Law Review* 10 (Summer 1990): 633-659. [Ward v. Rock Against Racism]

8512. Mixon, Harold. "The Rhetoric of States' Rights and White Supremacy." in *A New Division in Contemporary Southern Rhetoric*, Calvin M. Logue, and Howard Dorgan. Baton Rouge, LA: Louisiana State University Press, 1987.

8513. Moran, Rachel F. "The Politics of Discretion: Federal Intervention in Bilingual Education." *California Law Review* 76 (December 1988): 1249-1352.

8514. Morimoto, Toyotomi. *Language and Heritage Maintenance of Immigrants: Japanese Language Schools in California, 1903-1941*. Ph.D. diss., University of California, 1989. UMO # 9000977.

8515. Morris, Michael. "From Culture of Poverty to Underclass: An Analysis of a Shift in Public Language." *American Sociologist* 20 (Summer 1989).

8516. Morris, R., and P. Wander. "Native American Rhetoric- Dancing in the Shadows of the Ghost Dance." *Quarterly Journal of Speech* 76 (May 1990).

8517. Mullen, Robert W. *Rhetorical Strategies of Black Americans*. Washington, DC: University Press of America, 1980.

8518. Muro, Mark. "Does 'WASP' Sting?" *Boston Globe*, 15 November 1990. [White Anglo Saxon Protestant]

8519. Murphy, Penny. "A Brief History of Navajo Literacy." in *Analytical Bibliography of Navajo Reading Material*, eds. Bernard Spolsky and others. Washington, DC: Bureau of Indian Affairs, 1970.

8520. Murrain, Ethel P. C. *The Mississippi Man and His Message: A Rhetorical Analysis of the Cultural Themes in the Oratory of Medgar W. Evers, 1957-1963*. Ph.D. diss., University of Southern Mississippi, 1990. UMO # 9033671.

8521. Muwakkil, Salim. "Can African-Americans Co-opt the Blackest Insult?" *In These Times*, 8 July 1992. [On being called "nigger"]

8522. Myers, Steven L. "Racial Dispute Is Set Off By Dyson With Comment." *New York Times*, 1 July 1994. [Use of "watermelon" in referring to a black woman's company]

8523. Nash, Jeffrey E. "Race and Words: A Note on the Socioliguistic Divisiveness of Race in American Society." *Sociological Inquiry* 61 (1991): 252-262.

8524. *Nativism Rekindled: A Report on the Effort to Make English Colorado's Offical Language*. Washington, DC: U.S. Commission on Civil Rights, 1989.

8525. Navarrette, Ruben, Jr. "What's in a Name? Enough to Divide a City Along Racial Lines." *Los Angeles Times*, 5 December 1993.

8526. New Jersey Supreme Court Task Force on Interpreter and Translation Services. *Equal Access to the Courts for Linguistic Minorities*. Trenton, NJ: The Supreme Court Task Force, 22 May 1985.

8527. Newcomb, John T. "Canonical Ahistoricism vs. Histories of Canons: Towards Methodological Dissensus." *South Atlantic Review* 54 (November 1989): 3-20.

8528. Nguyen, B. B. D. "Accent Discrimination and the Test of Spoken English: A Call for an Objective Assessment of the Comprehensibility of Nonnative Speakers." *California Law Review* 81 (October 1993): 1325-1363.

8529. Nieman, Donald G. "The Language of Liberation: African Americans and Equalitarian Constitutionalism, 1830-1950." in *The Constitution, Law, and American Life*, ed. Nieman. : University of Georgia Press, 1992.

8530. Njeri, Itabari. "Words to Live or Die By." *Los Angeles Times Magazine*, 31 May 1992. [Social explosion in Los Angeles]

8531. Nordheimer, Jon. "Where the Sounds of Spanish Grate." *New York Times*, 22 August 1994. [In Miami, "white working class people talk uneasily of Cubans"]

8532. Nunberg, Geoffrey. "Linguists and the Official Language Movement." *Language* 65 (September 1989).

8533. _____. "The Official English Movement: Reimagining America." in *Language Loyalties*, pp. 479-494. ed. James Crawford. : University of Chicago Press, 1992.

8534. Oboler, Suzanne. *Labeling Hispanics: Race, Class, Language, and National Origins*. Ph.D. diss., New York University, 1991. UMO # 9213194.

8535. Ogbu, John U., and Maria Matute-Bianchi. "Understanding Sociocultural Factors: Knowledge, Identity and School Adjustment." in *Beyond Language: Social and Cultural Factors in Schooling Language Minority Students*, pp. 73-142. : California State Department of Education, Bilingual Education Office, 1986.

8536. Omi, Michael. "Authoritarian Populism and Code Words: Race and the New Right." in *Social and Gender Boundaries in the United States*, ed. Sucheng Chan. Lewiston, NY: Edwin Mellen Press, 1989.

8537. Ortiz, Vilma. "Language Background and Literacy among Hispanic Young Adults." *Social Problems* 36 (April 1989): 149-164.

8538. Ovando, Carlos J. "Politics and Pedagogy: The Case of Bilingual Education. Essay Review." *Harvard Educational Review* 60 (August 1990): 341-356.

8539. Padilla, A. M. and others. "The English-only Movement: Myths, Reality, and Implications for Psychology." *American Psychologist* 46 (February 1991): 120-130.

8540. Padilla, A. M. "On the English-Only Movement." *American Psychologist* 46 (October 1991): 1090. [See also comment by J. E. Murray, 1091]

8541. Palmer, Bryan D. *Descent into Discourse: The Reification of Language and the Writing of Social History*. Philadelphia, PA: Temple University Press, 1990.

8542. Pauwels, Anne. *Non-Discriminatory Language*. Australian Government Publishing Service, 1991.

8543. Pena, Laurencio. *A Critical Analysis of Michigan's Bilingual Education Program Policy and Its Implementation*. Ph.D. diss., Michigan State University, 1991. UMO # 9208831.

8544. Perea, Juan F. "English-only Rules and the Right to Speak One's Primary Language in the Workplace." *University of Michigan Journal of Law Reform* 23 (Winter 1990): 265-318.

8545. Perez-Bustillo, Camilo. "What Happens When English Only Comes to Town? A Case Study of Lowell, Massachusetts." in *Language Loyalties*, pp. 194-201. ed. James Crawford. : University of Chicago Press, 1992.

8546. Peterson, T. R. "Reconstructing Ethnocentrism: The American Ethnic Coalition and Official English." *Howard Journal of Communications* 1 (Fall 1988): 99-112.

8547. Philogene, G. "African American as a New Social Representaion." *Journal for the Theory of Social Behaviour* 24 (June 1994): 89-110.

8548. Piatt, Bill. *Only English? Law and Language Policy in the United States*. Albuquerque, NM: University of New Mexico Press, 1990.

8549. _____. "Toward Domestic Recognition of a Human Right to Language." *Houston Law Review* 23 (1986): 885-894.

8550. Porter, Rosalie Pedalino. *Forked Tongue. The Politics of Bilingual Education*. New York, NY: Basic Books, 1990.

8551. _____. "Goals 2000 And the Bilingual Student." *Education Week*, 18 May 1994.

8552. Post, Robert C. "Racist Speech, Democracy, and the First Amendment." *William and Mary Law Review* 32 (Winter 1991): 267- 327.

8553. "Poster's 46 Slurs Ridicule Bigotry By Insulting All." *New York Times*, 24 June 1991.

8554. Potter, Jonathan, and Margaret Wetherell. "Accomplishing Attitudes: Fact and Evaluation in Racist Discourse." *Text* 8 (1988): 51-68.

8555. Pressley, Sue Anne. "'The People' Ask What's in a Name For the Navajo." *Washington Post*, 18 December 1993. [Substituting "Dine" for "Navajo"]

8556. Prewitt Diaz, Joseph O. "Assessment of Puerto Rican Children in Bilingual Education Programs in the United States." *Hispanic Journal of Behavioral Sciences* 10 (September 1988): 237-252.

8557. Quindlen, Anna. "Don't Call Me Ishmael." *New York Times*, 23 November 1991. [Using first names in order to insult]

8558. Rabino, Linda. *The Bilingual Education Program in New York City Public Schools: An Anthropological Study of Education, Language and Ethnicity*. Ph.D. diss., S.U.N.Y. Stony Brook, 1992. UMO # 9318757.

8559. Raspberry, William. "My Not So Lightly Given Name." *Washington Post*, 29 November 1993.

8560. Rebell, Michael A., and Arthur R. Block. "Otero v. Mesa County Valley School District No. 51." Chapter 8 *Educational Policymaking and the Courts*, Michael E. Rebell, and Arthur R. Block. Chicago, IL: University of Chicago Press, 1982.

8561. Riesman, D. "Democracy and Defamation: Control of Group Libel." *Columbia Law Review* 42 (1942).

8562. Riggs, F. W. "Ethnicity, Nationalism, Race, Minority: A Semantic/Onomantic Exercise." *International Sociology* 6 (September 1991): 281-306.

8563. "The Right to Full Translation of Immigration Proceedings." *Georgetown Immigration Law Journal* 4 (Spring 1990): 367-372.

8564. Rodgers, Daniel T. *Contested Truths: Keywords in American Politics Since Independence*. New York, NY: Basic Books, 1990.

8565. Rohter, Larry. "Repeal Is Likely for 'English Only' Policy in Miami." *New York Times*, 14 May 1993.

8566. _____. "Without Smiling, to Call Floridian a 'Cracker' May Be a Crime." *New York Times*, 25 August 1991.

8567. Romero, Delia W. R. *The Puerto Rican New Yorker in the New York City Schools: Did Bilingual Education Make a Difference?* Ph.D. diss., University of Massachusetts, 1987. UMO # 8710500.

8568. Ross, Thomas. "The Rhetorical Tapestry of Race: White Innocence and Black Abstraction." *William and Mary Law Review* 32 (Fall 1990): 1-40.

8569. _____. "The Rhetoric of Poverty: Their Immorality, Our Helplessness." *Georgetown Law Journal* 79 (June 1991): 1499-1548.

8570. Rothblum, E. "Avoiding Heterosexual Bias in Language." *American Psychologist* 46 (September 1991): 973-974.

8571. Sahagun, Louis. "Navajos Consider a Name Change." *Los Angeles Times*, 16 December 1993. [Dine, pronounced "di-nay"]

8572. Saldivar, Ramon. *Chicano Narrative: The Dialectics of Difference*. Madison, WI: University of Wisconsin Press, 1990.

8573. Salvino, Dana N. "The Word in Black and White: Ideologies of Race and Literacy in Antebellum America." in *Reading in America: Literature and Social History*, ed. Cathy N. Davidson. Baltimore, MD: Johns Hopkins University Press, 1989.

8574. Saravia-Shore, Marietta. *National Origin Desegregation and Bilingual Education: The Inversion of Ideology and Practice*. Ph.D. diss., Columbia University, 1986. UMO # 8919182.

8575. Sato, Charlene. "Forthcoming Linguistic Inequality in Hawaii: The Post Creole Dilemma." in *Pidginization and Creolization of Language*, eds. J. Manes, and Nicholas Wolfson. : Cambridge University Press, 1984.

8576. Schmid, Carol. *The English Only Movement: Social Bases of Support and Opposition among Anglos and Latinos*. Ph.D. diss., University of Chicago Press, 1992.

8577. Schmidt, Peter. "'English Only' Advocates Target Bill on Puerto Rico." *Education Week*, 18 October 1989. [Spanish as first language in Puerto Rico]

8578. Schneider, Edgar W. "'How To Speak Southern': An American English Dialect Stereotyped." *Amerikastudien* 31 (1986): 425-439.

8579. Schwartz, John. "Speaking Out and Saving Sounds to Keep Native Tongues Alive." *Washington Post*, 14 March 1994. [Nationwide]

8580. Shell, Marc. "Babel in America; or, the Politics of Language Diversity in the United States." *Critical Inquiry* 20 (Autumn 1993): 103-127.

8581. Short, B. "Mandating a 'Mother Tongue'. Historical and Political Foundations of the English First Movement." *Howard Journal of Communications* 1 (Fall 1988): 86-98.

8582. Sider, Gerald. "When Parrots Learn to Talk, and Why They Can't: Domination, Deception, and Self-Deception in Indian-White Relations." *Comparative Studies in Society and History* 29 (1987): 3-23.

8583. Sklarewitz, Norman. "American Firms Lash Out at Foreign Tongues." *Business and Society Review* (Fall 1992): 24-28.

8584. Smith, Tom W. "Changing Racial Labels from 'Colored' to 'Negro' to 'Black' to 'African American'." *Public Opinion Quarterly* 56 (Winter 1992): 496-514.

8585. Smitherman-Donaldson, Geneva. "Bibliographic Essay: 'A New Way of Talkin': Language, Social Change and Political Theory." *Sage Race Relations Abstracts* 14 (Febraury 1989): 5-23.

8586. Sobnosky, Matthew J. *A Critical Rhetorical Analysis of Three Responses to White Supremacy.* Ph.D. diss., University of Nebraska, 1990. UMO # 9118477.

8587. Solomon, Norman. *The Power of Babble: The Politician's Dictionary of Buzzwords and Doubletalk for Every Occasion.* Dell Publishing, 1992.

8588. Sparks, L. "Non-Sexist and Non-Racist Writing." *Area* 23 (December 1991): 289-296.

8589. Staczek, John J. "Linguistic and Cultural Heritage: Preservation of Polish-English Bilingualism in the United States." *Polish-American Studies* 46 (1989): 57-65.

8590. Stavans, Ilan. "Coming to Terms with 'Latino' and 'Hispanic'." *In These Times,* 8 July 1992.

8591. Stein, R. F. "Closing the Achievement Gap of Mexican Americans: A Question of Language, Learning Style, or Economics." *Journal of Multilingual and Multicultural Development* 11 (1990): 405-420.

8592. Strauss, Marcy. "Sexist Speech in the Workplace." *Harvard Civil Rights-Civil Liberties Law Review* 25 (Winter 1990): 1-51.

8593. Stuckless, E. R. "Reflections on Bilingual, Bicultural Education for Deaf Children: Some Concerns About Current Advocacy and Trends." *American Annals of the Deaf* 136 (July 1991): 270-272.

8594. Sunstein, Cass R. *Democracy and the Problem of Free Speech.* Free Press, 1993.

8595. _____. "Liberalism, Speech Codes and Related Problems." *Academe* 79 (July-August 1993): 14-25.

8596. Svaldi, David. *Sand Creek and the Rhetoric of Extermination: A Case Study in Indian-White Relations.* Lanham, MD.

8597. "Symposium: Communication Scholarship and Political Correctness." *Journal of Communication* 42 (Spring 1992): ten articles.

8598. Tarver, Heidi. "Language and Politics in the 1980s: The Story of U.S. English." *Politics and Society* 17 (1989).

8599. Taylor, Hanni U. *Standard English, Black English, and Bidialectalism: A Controversy.* New York, NY: P. Lang, 1989.

8600. Teitell, Conrad. "Sex Lex (part 1)." *Trial* 26 (February 1990): 73-74.

8601. _____. "Sex Lex (part 2)." *Trial* 26 (March 1990): 25-27.

8602. Tezcatlipoca, Leo Guerra. "We're Chicanos- Not Latinos or Hispanics." *Los Angeles Times,* 22 November 1993.

8603. Torrey, J. W. "Illiteracy in the Ghetto." *Harvard Educational Review* 40 (1970): 253-259.

8604. Torruellas, Rosa M. *Learning English in Three Private Schools in Puerto Rico: Issues of Class, Identity and Ideology.* Ph.D. diss., New York University, 1990. UMO # 9025150.

8605. Tremaine, Richard R. *The Ethos of Jesse Jackson in the 1984 Presidential Primaries: Rhetorical Strategies to Address Image Problems and Enhance Credibility.* Ph.D. diss., University of Minnesota, 1990. UMO # 9020274.

8606. Trueba, H. T. *Raising Silent Voices: Educating the Linguistic Minorities for the 21st Century*. Harper and Row, 1989.

8607. Twiggs, Robert D. *Pan-African Language in the Western Hemisphere*. Christopher, 1973.

8608. Twomey, Steve. "Universal Language of Intolerance." *Washington Post*, 8 February 1993.

8609. University of Missouri School of Journalism. *Dictionary of Cautionary Words and Phrases: An Excerpt from Newspaper Content Analysis Compiled by 1989 Multicultural Management Program Fellows*. Multicultural Management Program, Box 838, Columbia, MO 65205, 1991.

8610. Updike, David. "About Men. Coloring Lessons." *New York Times Magazine*, 31 July 1994. [What words to use for race?]

8611. Van Dijk, Teun A. "Cognitive and Conversational Strategies in the Expression of Ethnic Prejudice." *Text 3* no. 4 (1983): 375- 404.

8612. _____. "Principles of Critical Discourse Analysis." *Discourse and Society* 4 (April 1993): 249-283.

8613. van Dijk, Teun A. "Discourse and the Denial of Racism." *Discourse and Society* 3 (1992): 87-118.

8614. Vargas, Arturo. *Literacy in the Hispanic Community*. Washington, DC: National Council of La Raza, July 1988.

8615. Vasquez, Olga A. and others. *Pushing Boundaries: Language and Culture in a Mexicano Community*. Cambridge University Press, 1994. [Northern California school]

8616. Vass, Winifred K. *The Bantu-speaking Heritage of the United States*. Los Angeles, CA: U.C.L.A. Center for Afro-American Studies.

8617. Veltman, Calvin J. "Melting Pot U.S.A.: l'anglicisation des Hispanic-Americains." *Cahiers Quebecois de Demographie* 10 (1981): 29-48.

8618. _____. "The Status of the Spanish Language in the United States at the Beginning of the 21st Century." *International Migration Review* 24 (Spring 1990).

8619. Vetterling-Braggin, Mary, ed. *Sexist Language: A Modern Philosophical Analysis*. Totowa, NJ: Littlefield, Adams, 1981.

8620. Vientos Gaston, Nilita. "The Supreme Court of Puerto Rico and the Language Problem." *National Lawyers Guild Practitioner* 46 (Fall 1989): 104-113.

8621. Walker, Doris B. "Limiting Racist Speech in the United States vs. 'Freedom' of Speech: A Marxist View of the Apparent Constitutional Dilemma." *NST: Nature, Society, and Thought* 3 (1990): 85-96. [See comment by Herbert Aptheker, 102-104]

8622. Walker, Roger A. "Federal Bilingual, Bicultural Education: The Failure of Entitlement." *UMKC Law Review* 59 (March 1991): 769-800.

8623. Walsh, Catherine E., ed. *Literacy as Praxis: Culture, Language, and Pedagogy*. Norwood, NJ: Ablex, 1990.

8624. Walsh, Catherine E. "Literacy as Praxis: A Framework and An Introduction." in *Literacy as Praxis. Culture, Language, and Pedagogy*, ed. Catherine E. Walsh. : Ablex Publishing Co., 1991.

8625. Warren, Jenifer. "San Jose Councilwoman Stirs Racial Uproar." *Los Angeles Times*, 27 May 1993.

8626. Watrous, Peter. "Bilingual Music Is Breaking Down Cultural Barriers." *New York Times*, 2 September 1990.

8627. Watson, Robert W. "Sexism, Language and the Law Firm." *Legal Management* 8 (January-February 1989): 73-75.

8628. Watterson, K. M. "The Power of Words: The Power of Advocacy Challenging the Power of Hate Speech." *University of Pittsburgh Law Review* 52 (Summer 1991).

8629. Wellman, David. "The New Political Linguistics of Race." *Socialist Review* 16 (1986): 43-79.

8630. Wherritt, Irene, and O. Garcia. "U. S. Spanish: The Language of the Latinos." *International Journal of the Sociology of Language* 80 (1989): entire issue.

8631. White, Lucie E. "Subordination, Rhetorical Survival Skills, and the Sunday Shoes: Notes on the Hearing of Mrs. G." *Buffalo Law Review* 38 (Winter 1990): 1-58.

8632. Wibecan, Ken. "It's High Time We Expunge the Word 'Minority' and Its Concept." *Long Beach Press-Telegram*, 1 March 1993.

8633. Wilkinson, Doris Y. "Americans of African Identity." *Society* 27 (May-June 1990): 14-18.

8634. Wills, Garry. "In Praise of Censure." *Time*, 31 July 1989.

8635. Wilson, David. *The National Language of Inuit Children: A Key to Inuktitut Literacy*. Ph.D. diss., University of New Mexico, 1988. UMO # 8904899.

8636. Wilson, David B. "When Comments Are Misinterpreted as Racist." *Boston Globe*, 20 September 1989.

8637. Winch, C., and K. Sharp. "Equal Opportunities and the Use of Language: A Critique of the New Orthodoxy." *Studies in Higher Education* 19 (1994): 163-176.

8638. Wogan, P. "Perceptions of European Literacy in Early Control Situations." *Ethnohistory* 41 (Summer 1994): 407-430.

8639. Wolfram, Walt. "Re-examining Vernacular Black English." *Language* 66 (March 1990).

8640. Wolfram, Walt, and Donna Christian. *Dialects and Education: Issues and Answers*. Englewood Cliffs, NJ: Prentice Hall Regents, 1989.

8641. Wright, R. George. "Racist Speech and the First Amendment." *Mississippi College Law Review* 9 (Fall 1988): 1-28.

8642. Zeigler, Stephen M. *Conscience: The Editorial Rhetoric of Ralph McGill in the Civil Rights Era*. Ph.D. diss., Saint Louis University, 1989. UMO # 9014819.

8643. Zentalla, Ana Celia. "Returned Migration, Language, and Identity: Puerto Rican Bilinguals in Dos Worlds/Two Mundos." *International Journal of the Sociology of Language* 84 (1990): 81-100.

8644. Zentella, Ana Celia. "The Fate of Spanish in U.S.: The Puerto Rican Experience." in *The Language of Inequality*, eds. J. Manes, and Nicholas Wolfson. The Hague: Mouton 1985.

8645. _____. "Language Politics in the U.S.A.: The English- Only Movement." in *Literature, Language, and Politics*, pp. 39-53. ed. Betty Jean Craige. Athens, GA: University of Georgia Press, 1988.

8646. Zepeda, Ofelia, and Jane H. Hill. "La situation des langues indigenes aux Etats-Unis." *Diogene* 153 (January-March 1991).

8647. Zoglin, Kathryn J. "Recognizing a Human Right to Language in the United States." *Boston College Third World Law Journal* 9 (Winter 1989): 15-37.

LAW

8648. Abramson, Leslie. "Unequal Justice." *Newsweek*, July 25, 1994.

8649. Adams, James P., and William W. Dressler. "Perceptions of Injustice in a Black Community: Dimensions and Variation." *Human Relations* 41 (October 1988): 753-767.

8650. Adams, Keith. "Declarations of a Revised Constitution (Poem)." *Black Scholar* 19 (July/August, September/October 1988): 49.

8651. Addis, Adeno. "Individualism, Communitarianism, and the Rights of Ethnic Minorities." *Notre Dame Law Review* 67 (1992): 615-676.

8652. Agyeman, O. "The United States Supreme Court and the Enforcement of African-American Rights: Myth and Reality." *PS- Political Science and Politics* 24 (December 1991): 679-684.

8653. Aleinikoff, T. Alexander. "A Case for Race-consciousness." *Columbia Law Review* 91 (June 1991): 1060-1125.

8654. Allen, Peter. "Bigotry in Court: A New Report on Gender Bias Finds California Lacking." *California Lawyer* 10 (May 1990): 18.

8655. Alozie, Nicholas O. "Black Representation on State Judiciaries." *Social Science Quarterly* 69 (December 1988): 979- 986.

8656. _____. "Distribution of Women and Minority Judges: The Effects of Judicial Selection Methods." *Social Science Quarterly* 71 (June 1990).

8657. Amar, Akhil Reed. "Forty Acres and a Mule: A Republican Theory of Minimal Entitlements." *Harvard Journal of Law and Public Policy* 13 (Winter 1990).

8658. Amsterdam, Anthony G. "Thurgood Marshall's Image of the Blue-eyed Child in Brown." *New York University Law Review* 68 (May 1993): 226-236.

8659. Anastaplo, George. "Slavery and the Constitution: Explorations." *Texas Tech Law Review* 20 (June 1989): 677-786.

8660. Ansley, Frances L. "Stirring the Ashes: Race, Class and the Future of Civil Rights Scholarship." *Cornell Law Review* (1989).

8661. Applebome, Peter. "Study Faults Atlanta's System of Defending Poor." *New York Times*, 30 November 1990.

8662. Arlen, J. H. "Should Defendants' Wealth Matter?" *Journal of Legal Studies* 21 (June 1992).

8663. Armour, J. D. "Race Ipsa-Loquitur: Of Reasonable Racists, Intelligent Bayesians, and Involuntary Negrophobes." *Stanford Law Reveiw* 46 (April 1994): 781-816.

8664. Arneson, Richard J. "Is Work Special? Justice and the Distribution of Employment." *American Political Science Review* 84 (December 1990): 1127-1147. [Right to a job]

8665. Arthur, John A. "Assessing the Effects of Race on Attitudes toward the Courts." *Free Inquiry in Creative Sociology* 21 (November 1993): 127-134.

8666. Ashford, H. *A Marxist Perspective on the Fundamentals of Criminal Law*. Master's thesis, Northrop University, 1989.

8667. Au, Beth Amity. "Freedom from Fear." *Lincoln Law Review* 45 (1984). [Limiting racist speech]

8668. Austin, Regina. "Sapphire Bound!" *Wisconsin Law Review* 539- 578 (Fall 1989).

8669. Axelrod, Jill. "The Impact of the Wartime Relocation and Internment of Civilians Act on United States Constitutional Law." *Suffolk Transnational Law Journal* 13 (Fall 1989): 267-281.

8670. Bacote, Clarence A. "Negro Proscriptions, Protests, and Proposed Solutions in Georgia, 1880-1908." *Journal of Southern History* (November 1959).

8671. Baer, Judith A. "Nasty Law or Nice Ladies? Jurisprudence, Feminism, and Gender Difference." *Women and Politics* 11 (1991): 1-31.

8672. Baiamonte, John V., Jr. *Spirit of Vengence: Nativism and Louisiana Justice, 1921-1924*. Baton Rouge, LA: Louisiana State University Press, 1986. [Trying of six Italians for murder.]

8673. Bailey, Percival R. *Progressing Lawyers: A History of the National Lawyers Guild*. Ph.D. diss., Rutgers University, 1979.

8674. Ball, Milner S. "The Legal Academy and Minority Scholars." *Harvard Law Review* 103 (1990).

8675. Barnett, Martha W. "Women Practicing Law: Changes in Attitudes, Changes in Platitudes." *Florida Law Review* 42 (January 1990): 209-228.

8676. Barrow, Deborah J., and Thomas G. Walker. *A Court Divided: The Fifth Circuit Court of Appeals and the Politics of Judicial Reform*. New Haven, CT: Yale University Press, 1988.

8677. Bell, Derrick A. "After We're Gone: Prudent Speculations on America in a Post-racial Epoch." *Saint Louis University Law Journal* 34 (Spring 1990): 393-405.

8678. _____. "Civil Rights Lawyers on the Bench." *Yale Law Journal* 91 (March 1982): 826-836.

8679. _____. *Faces at the Bottom of the Well. The Permanence of Racism*. Basic Books, 1992.

8680. _____. *The Gyroscopic Effect in American Racial Reform: The Law and Race from 1940 to 1986*. Paper prepared for the Committee on the Status of Black Americans, National Research Council, Washington, DC, 1986.

8681. _____. "Learning from the 'Brown' Experience." *Black Scholar* 11 (September - October 1979): 9-16.

8682. _____. *Memorandum to the Committee on the Status of Black Americans in Response to July 31st Comments on Commissioned Paper*. Washington, DC: Paper prepared for the Committee on the Status of Black Americans, National Research Council, 1986.

8683. _____. "The Price and Pain of Racial Perspective." *Society of American Law Teachers, Equalizer* 1 (November 1986).

8684. Bell, Derrick A. and others. "Racial Reflections: Dialogues in the Direction of Liberation." *UCLA Law Review* 37 (August 1990): 1037-1100.

8685. Bell, Derrick A. "Racial Realism." *Connecticut Law Review* 24 (Winter 1992): 363-379.

8686. _____. "The Racial Preference Licensing Act: A Fable About the Politics of Hate." *ABA Journal* 78 (September 1992): 50- 55. [See Goldberg, below]

8687. _____. "Racism: A Prophecy for the Year 2000." *Rutgers Law Review* 42 (Fall 1989): 93-108.

8688. Bell, Derrick A., and Preeta Bansal. "The Republican Revival and Racial Politics." *Yale Law Review* 97 (1988).

8689. Berger, Thomas R. *A Long and Terrible Shadow: White Values, Native Rights in the Americas, 1492-1992*. University of Washington Press, 1992.

8690. Berry, Mary F. *Black Resistance/ White Law. A History of Constitutional Racism in America*. Allen Lane, 1994. Revised and updated edition

8691. Berten, David P. "Brown v. Board of Education of Topeka: An Econolegal Opinion." *Wisconsin Law Review* (1989).

8692. Berthoff, Rowland. "Conventional Mentality: Free Blacks, Women, and Business Corporations as Unequal Persons, 1820-1870." *Journal of American History* 76 (1989): 753-784.

8693. Biskupic, Joan. "For Justice [Clarence] Thomas, Work Is Refuge." *Washington Post*, 19 April 1993.

8694. Black, Charles. "The Lawfulness of the Segregation Decisions." *Yale Law Journal* 69 (1960).

8695. Blum, Bill, and Gina Lobaco. "Fighting Words at ACLU: A Decade after Skokie, Racist Speech Once Again Is Causing the ACLU to Reexamine Its Priorities While It Defends the First Amendment." *California Lawyer* 10 (February 1990).

8696. Bollinger, Lee C. "The Tolerant Society: A Response to Critics." *Columbia Law Review* 90 (May 1990): 979-1003.

8697. Bond, Julian. "A Perspective on the Present Status of Diversity in the United States." *William Mitchell Law Review* 17 (Spring 1991): 419-438.

8698. Booth, William, and Joan Biskupic. "Balancing Race and Rights in Jury Box." *Washington Post*, 11 May 1993.

8699. Boudin, Louis. "Truth and Fiction About the Fourteenth Amendment." *New York University Law Review* 16 (November 1938): 19-82.

8700. Boyarsky, Bill. "Numbers on Judiciary Don't Equal Justice for All." *Los Angeles Times*, 10 October 1993. [Overwhelming whiteness among judges in L.A. County Superior Court]

8701. Braman, Sandra. "Information and Socioeconomic Class in U.S. Constitutional Law." *Journal of Communication* 39 (1989): 163-179.

8702. Bray, Rosemary L. "Taking Sides Against Ourselves." *New York Times Magazine*, 17 November 1991. [Anita Hill and Clarence Thomas]

8703. Brennan, W. J. and others. "A Tribute to Thurgood Marshall." *Harvard Law Review* 105 (November 1991): 23-79.

8704. Brewer, Scott and others. "Colloguy: Responses to Randall Kennedy's Racial Critiques of Legal Academia." *Harvard Law Review* 103 (June 1990): 1844-1886.

8705. Brooks, Roy L. "Racial Subordination through Formal Equal Opportunity." *San Diego Law Review* 25 (November-December 1988): 879-987.

8706. Brown, Charles. "'Cancer of the Mind' Debate." *Cross Roads* 33 (July-August 1993): letter. [Outlaw racist speech?]

8707. _____. "For Outlawing Fascistic Racist Speech." *Cross Roads* 27 (January 1993). [See also letter by Charles Obler commenting on this article in No. 28 (February 1993)]

8708. Brown, Walt K. and others. "The Negative Effect of Racial Discrimination on Minority Youth in the Juvenile Justice System." *International Journal of Offender Therapy and Comparative Criminology* 34 (1990): 87-93.

8709. Brownell, Herbert, and John P. Burke. *Advising Ike. The Memoirs of Attorney General Herbert Brownell*. University of Kansas, 1993.

8710. Burns, Haywood. "Black People and the Tyranny of American Law." *Annals of the American Academy of Political and Social Science* 407 (1973).

8711. Burton, Orville. "'The Black Squint of the Law': Racism in South Carolina." in *The Meaning of South Carolina History*, eds. David R. Chesnutt, and Clyde N. Wilson. : University of South Carolina Press, 1991.

8712. Calabresi, G. "The Supreme Court 1990 Term, Foreword: Antidiscrimination and Constitutional Accountability (What the Bork-Brennan Debate Ignores)." *Harvard Law Review* 105 (November 1991): 80-151.

8713. Campisi, Jack. "The New England Tribes and Their Quest for Justice." in *The Pequots in Southern New England*, eds. Laurence M. Hauptman, and James D. Wherry. : University of Oklanhoma Press, 1990.

8714. Carleton, Francis J. *Sex Discrimination Law and Women in the Workplace: A Feminist Analysis of Legal Ideology*. Ph.D. diss., Indiana University, 1991. UMO # 9217381.

8715. Carter, Robert Lee. "From a Tiny Office on Fifth Avenue." *Washington Post*, 26 January 1993. [Memoir of Thurgood Marshall by the senior judge in the U.S. District Court for the Southern District of New York]

8716. Carter, Robert Lee. *Ghetto Lawyering: Law and Ideology in the Rise of Legal Services, 1963-1984*. Ph.D. diss., Columbia University, 1986. UMO # 8906494.

8717. Case, David S. *Alaska Natives and American Laws*. Fairbanks, AK: University of Alaska Press, 1984.

8718. Casey, J. A. "Sovereignty by Sufferance: The Illusion of Indian Tribal Sovereignty." *Cornell Law Review* 79 (January 1994): 404-454.

8719. Chato, Genvieve, and Christine Conte. "The Legal Rights of American Indian Women." in *Western Women: Their Land, Their Lives*, eds. Lillian Schissel and others. Albuquerque, NM: University of New Mexico Press, 1988.

8720. Cheyfitz, Eric. "Savage Law. The Plot Against American Indians in Johnson and Graham's Lessee v. M'Intosh and *The pioneers*." in *Cultures of United States Imperialism*, eds. Amy Kaplan, and Donald E. Pease. : Duke University Press, 1993.

8721. Chrisman, Robert, and Robert L. Allen, eds. *Court of Appeal. The Black Community Speaks Out on the Racial and Sexual Politics of Clarence Thomas vs. Anita Hill*. Ballantine, 1992.

8722. Christofferson, C. "Tribal Courts' Failure to Protect Native American Women: A Reevaluation of the Indian Civil Rights Act." *Yale Law Journal* 101 (October 1991).

8723. Clark, Kenneth B. "The Desegregation Cases: Criticism of the Social Scientists' Role." in *Prejudice and Your Child*, pp. 185-206. Boston, MA: Beacon Press, 1963.

8724. _____. "The Social Scientists and the Courts." *Social Policy* 17 (1986): 33-38.

8725. Clinton, William J. "Remarks Announcing Withdrawal of the Nomination of Lani Guinier and an Exchange with Reporters, June 3, 1993." *Weekly Compilation of Presidents Documents* 29 (7 June 1993): 1027-1029.

8726. Cobb, T. R. R. *An Inquiry into the Law of Negro Slavery in the United States of America, to which is Prefixed, An Historical Sketch of Slavery*. Negro Universities Press, 1968, orig. 1858.

8727. Cohen, Joshua, and Frank I. Michelman. "In the End, Distortion Triumphed Over Lani Guinier's Writings." *New York Times*, 13 June 1993. [See Carol Swain, below]

8728. Colbert, Douglas L. "Challenging the Challenge: Thirteenth Amendment as a Prohibition against the Racial Use of Peremptory Challenges." *Cornell Law Review* 76 (November 1990).

8729. Coleman, William T., Jr. "Three's Company: Guiner, Reagan, Bush." *New York Times*, 4 June 1993. [Civil rights law and Lani Guinier]

8730. Coliver, Sandra, ed. *Striking a Balance: Hate Speech, Freedom of Expression and Non-discrimination*. 1992.

8731. Comment. "Mexican Americans: Are They Protected by the Civil Rights Act of 1866?" *Santa Clara Law Review* 20 (1980).

8732. Conn, Stephen. "Aboriginal Rights in Alaska." *Law and Anthropology* 2 (1987): 73-91.

8733. Conyers, John, Jr. "Grand Juries: The American Inquisition." *Ramparts*, August/September 1975.

8734. Cook, Stuart W. "Toward a Psychology of Improving Justice- Research on Extending the Equality Principle to Victims of Social Injustice." *Journal of Social Issues* 46 (Spring 1990).

8735. Cooney, Mark. *Racial Discrimination in Police-Citizen Encounters: A Review of Empirical Literature*. Paper prepared for the Committee on the Status of Black Americans, National Research Council, Washington, DC.

8736. Corfman, Tom. "Minorities Press for the Bench." *Chicago Reporter*, February 1992. 21, [Chicago]

8737. Cortner, Richard C. *A "Scottsboro" Case in Mississippi: The Supreme Court and Brown v. Mississippi*. Jackson: University Press of Mississippi, 1986.

8738. Cottrol, Robert J. "A Tale of Two Cultures: Or Making the Proper Connections Between Law, Social History and the Political Economy of Despair." *San Diego Law Review* 25 (November-December 1988): 989-1025.

8739. _____. "The Thirteenth Amendment and the North's Overlooked Eqalitarian Heritage." *National Black Law Journal* 11 (Spring 1989): 198-211.

8740. Cottrol, Robert J., and Raymond T. Diamond. "The Second Amendment: Toward an Afro-Americanist Reconsideration." *Georgetown Law Journal* 80 (December 1991): 309-361.

8741. Cover, Robert M. "The Origins of Judicial Activism in the Protection of Minorities." *Yale Law Journal* 91 (1982).

8742. Crenshaw, Kimberle. "Toward a Race-conscious Pedagogy in Legal Education." *National Black Law Journal* 11 (Winter 1989): 1-14.

8743. Cullen, Holly. "Education Rights or Minority Rights?" *International Journal of Law and the Family* 7 (August 1993): 143-177.

8744. Culp, Jerome M., Jr. "Notes from California: Rodney King and the Race Question." *Denver University Law Review* 70 (1993): 199-212.

8745. _____. "Posner on Duncan Kennedy and Racial Difference: White Authority in the Legal Academy." *Duke Law Journal* 41 (April 1992): 1095-1114.

8746. _____. "Toward a Black Legal Scholarship: Race and Original Understandings." *Duke Law Journal* 39-105 (February 1991).

8747. Currie, James T. "From Slavery to Freedom in Mississippi's Legal System." *Journal of Negro History* 65 (1980).

8748. Curtis, Lynn A. "One Year Later: The Los Angeles Riots and a New National Policy." *Denver University Law Review* 70 (1993): 265-282.

8749. Danielse, Dan, and Karen Engle eds. *After Identity. A Reader in Law and Culture*. Routledge, 1994.

8750. Davis, Angela Y. "Siempre Adelante!" *National Lawyers Guild Practitioner* 46 (Spring 1989): 56-62.

8751. De Witt, Karen. "In a Color-Conscious Society, She Challenges the 'Color Blind'." *New York Times*, 18 July 1993. [Elaine R. Jones, director-counsel, NAACP Legal Defense and Educational Fund]

8752. Debo, Angie. *And Still the Waters Run: The Betrayal of the Five Civilized Tribes*. Norman, OK: University of Oklahoma Press, 1984.

8753. DeCrow, Karen. *Sexist Justice*. New York, NY: Random House, 1974.

8754. Delgado, Richard. "The Imperial Scholar Revisited: How to Marginalize Outsider Writing, 10 Years Later." *University of Pennsylvania Law Review* 140 (April 1992): 1349-1372.

8755. _____. "Norms and Normal Science: Toward a Normativity in Legal Thought." *University of Pennsylvania Law Review* 139 (1991).

8756. _____. "Pep Talks For the Poor: A Reply and Remonstrance On the Evils of Scapegoating." *Boston University Law Review* 71 (May 1991): 525-541.

8757. _____. "Recasting the American Race Problem." *Columbia Law Review* 79 (October 1991): 1389-1400.

8758. _____. "Rodrigo 7th Chronicle: Race, Democracy, and the State." *UCLA Law Review* 41 (February 1994): 721-758.

8759. _____. "Words that Wound: A Tort Action for Racial Insults, Epithets, and Name-Calling." *Harvard Civil Rights-Civil Liberties Law Review* 17 (1982): 133-181.

8760. Delgado, Richard, and Jean Stefancic. "Derrick Bell's 'Chronicle of Space Traders': Would the U.S. Sacrifice People of Color If the Price Were Right?" *University of Colorado Law Review* 62 (Spring 1991): 321-329.

8761. Deloria, Vine, Jr. *Behind the Trail of Broken Treaties: An Indian Declaration of Independence.* New York, NY: 1974,

8762. Deloria, Vine, Jr., and Clifford M. Lytle. *American Indians, American Justice.* Austin, TX: 1983,

8763. Dembitz, Nanette. "Racial Discrimination and the Military Judgement: The Supreme Court's Korematsu and Eno Decisions." *Columbia Law Review* 45 (1945).

8764. Doctorow, E. L. "A Citizen Reads the Constitution." in *America in Theory*, Leslie Berlowitz and others. New York, NY: Oxford University Press, 1988.

8765. Donovan, and Wildman. "Is the Reasonable Man Obsolete? A Critical Perspective on Self-defense and Provocation." *Loyola Los Angeles Law Review* 14 (1981).

8766. Dowdle, Michael W. "The Descent of Antidiscrimination: On the Intellectual Origins of the Current Equal Protection Jurisprudence." *New York University Law Review* 66 (October 1991): 1165-1232.

8767. Dowdy, Zachary R. "Study: Bias In the Court." *Boston Globe*, 19 September 1994. [Massachusetts court system]

8768. Duggan, Paul, and Ruben Castenada. "For 2 Jurors in Murder Case, an Unbridgeable Gap." *Washington Post*, 30 April 1994. [Black and white jurors differ over guilt of a black defendant]

8769. Durham, W. C., Jr. "Indian Law in the Continental United States: An Overview." *Law and Anthropology* 2 (1987): 93-112.

8770. Dworkin, Ronald. "Justice for Clarence Thomas." *New York Times Review of Books*, 7 November 1991.

8771. _____. "One Year Later, the Debate Goes On." *New York Times Book Review*, 25 October 1992. [Review essay of four books about the confirmation hearings for Clarence Thomas]

8772. _____. "The Reagan Revolution and the Supreme Court." *New York Review of Books*, 18 July 1991.

8773. Edelman, L. B. "Legal Ambiguity and Symbolic Structures: Organizational Mediation of Civil Rights Law." *American Journal of Sociology* 97 (May 1992): 1531-1576.

8774. Edley, Christopher, Jr. "Mr. Justice." *Boston Globe*, 30 June 1991. [The significance of the resignation of U.S. Supreme Court Justice Thurgood Marshall]

8775. Elliff, John T. *The United States Department of Justice and Individual Rights, 1937-1962.* Ph.D. diss., Harvard University, 1967.

8776. Ely, James W., Jr. "Negro Demonstrations and the Law: Danville as a Test Case." *Vanderbilt Law Review* 27 (October 1974): 927- 968.

8777. Epstein, Jason. *The Great Conspiracy Trial: An Essay on Law, Liberty and the Constitution.* New York, NY: Random House, 1970.

8778. "Excerpts from Lani Guinier's News Conference." *Washington Post*, 5 June 1993.

8779. Fede, Andrew T. *People Without Rights. An Interpretation of the Fundamentals of the Law of Slavery in the U.S. South.* Garland, 1993.

8780. Fineman, Martha A., and Nancy S. Thomadsen. *At the Boundaries of Law. Feminism and Legal Theory.* New York, NY: Routledge, 1990.

8781. Finkelman, Paul R. "Exploring Southern Legal History." *North Carolina Law Review* 64 (1985).

8782. _____. *The Law of Freedom and Bondage: A Casebook*. 1986.

8783. Finkelman, Paul R., ed. *Slave Rebels, Abolitionists, and Southern Courts: The Pamphlet Literature*. 2 vols. New York, NY: Garland, 1988.

8784. _____., ed. *Race, Law, and American History, 1700-1990*. 10 vols. Hamden, CT: Garland Publishing, 1992. [Anthology of articles]

8785. Fish, Arthur. "Hate Promotion and Freedom of Expression: Truth and Consequences." *Canadian Journal of Law and Jurisprudence* 2 (July 1989): 111-137.

8786. Fisher, Louis. "Social Influences on Constitutional Law." *Journal of Political Science* 15 (1987): 7-19.

8787. Fisher, William W., III. "Ideology, Religion, and the Constitutional Protection of Private Property." *Emory Law Journal* 39 (Winter 1990): 65-134. [Slavery]

8788. "Fitting Together the Pieces of the Puzzle: A Focus on Indian Law." *Federal Bar News Journal* 38 (March 1991): entire issue.

8789. Fitzpatrick, Peter. "Racism and the Innocence of Law." *Anatomy of Racism*, ed. David T. Goldberg. Minneapolis, MN: University of Minnesota Press, 1990.

8790. Flagg, B. J. "'Was Blind, but Now I See': White Race Consciousness and the Requirement of Discriminatory Intent." *Michigan Law Review* 91 (March 1993).

8791. Fogleson, Steven. "The Nuremberg Legacy: An Unfulfilled Promise." *Southern California Law Review* 63 (March 1990): 833- 905.

8792. Foner, Eric. "Blacks and the U.S. Constitution 1789-1989." *New Left Review, No. 183* (September-October 1990): 63-74.

8793. Forbes, Duncan. *Action on Racial Harassment: Legal Remedies and Local Authorities*. London: Legal Action Group and London Housing Unit, 1988.

8794. Ford, Andrea. "Cutbacks Will Erode Trust in Justice, Garcetti Says." *Los Angeles Times*, 19 August 1993. [Projected hiring of minority prosecutors in Los Angeles]

8795. Franklin, John Hope. "Booker T. Washington, Revisited." *New York Times*, 1 August 1991. [Appointment of Clarence Thomas to the U.S. Supreme Court]

8796. "Free Speech and Religious, Racial and Sexual Harassment." *William and Mary Law Review* 32 (Winter 1991): 207-351.

8797. Freeman, Alan. "Racism, Rights and the Quest for Equality of Opportunity: A Critical Legal Essay." *Harvard Civil Rights- Civil Liberties Law Review* 23 (1988).

8798. Freeman, Jo. "From Protection to Equal Opportunity: The Revolution in Women's Legal Status." *Women, Politics and Change*, eds. Louise A. Tilly, and Patricia Gurin. : Russell Sage Foundation, 1990.

8799. Freilich, Robert H. and others. "Reagan's Legacy: A Conservative Majority Rules on Civil Rights, Civil Liberties and State and Local Government Issues." *Urban Lawyer* 21 (Fall 1989): 633-731.

8800. Friedelbaum, Stanley H., ed. *Human Rights in the States. New Directions in Constitutional Policymaking*. Westport, CT: Greenwood, 1988.

8801. Frug, M. J. "A Postmodern Feminist Legal Manifesto." *Harvard Law Review* 105 (March 1992): 1045-1075. [see also responses, 1076-1105]

8802. Fukurai, Hiroshi and others. "Cross-sectional Jury Representaion or Systematic Jury Representation? Simple Random and Cluster Sampling Strategies in Jury Selection." *Journal of Criminal Justice* 19 (1991): 31-48.

8803. _____. *Race and the Jury. Racial Disfranchisement and the Search for Justice*. Plenum, 1992.

8804. _____. "Where Did Black Jurors Go? A Theoretical Synthesis of Racial Disenfranchisement in the Jury System and Jury Selection." *Journal of Black Studies* 22 (December 1991): 196-215.

8805. Gaines, Ernest J. *A Lesson Before Dying*. Knopf, 1993. [A novel about racist justice in Louisiana]

8806. Gale, Mary Ellen. "Reimagining the First Amendment: Racist Speech and Equal Liberty." *St. John's Law Review* 65 (Winter 1991): 119-185.

8807. Galloway, Russell W. *Justice for All? The Rich and Poor in Supreme Court History, 1790-1990*. Carolina Academic, 1991.

8808. Garrow, David. "History Lesson for the Judge." *Washington Post*, 20 June 1993. [In Roe v. Wade; see Ruth Bader Ginsberg, below]

8809. Gates, Henry Louis, Jr. "Statistical Stigmata." *Cardoza Law Review* 11 (July-August 1990): 1275-1289.

8810. Gatewood, Willard B., Jr. "The Perils of Passing: The McCrarys of Omaha." *Nebraska History* 71 (1990): 64-70.

8811. Gellman, Susan. "'Sticks and Stones Can Put You in Jail, but Can Words Increase Your Sentence?' Constitutional and Policy Dilemmas of Ethnic Intimidation Laws." *UCLA Law Review* 39 (1991): 333-396.

8812. "Gender, Race and the Politics of Supreme Court Appointments: The Import of the Anita Hill/Clarence Thomas Hearings." *Southern California Law Review* (March 1992): 25 articles.

8813. Genovese, Eugene D. "Critical Legal Studies as Radical Politics and World View." *Yale Journal of Law and the Humanities* 3 (Winter 1991).

8814. Gerber, Scott D. "The Jurisprudence of Clarence Thomas." *Journal of Law and Politics* 8 (Winter 1992): 107-141.

8815. Gillespie, Veronica M., and Gregory L. McClinton. "The Civil Rights Restoration Act of 1987. A Defeat for Judicial Conservatism." *National Black Law Journal* 12 (Spring 1990): 61- 72.

8816. Ginsberg, Ruth Bader. "The Case Against the Case." *Washington Post*, 20 June 1993. [On Roe v. Wade; see David Garrow, above]

8817. Goings, Kenneth W. *The NAACP Comes of Age. The Defeat of Judge John J. Parker*. Bloomington, IN: Indiana University Press, 1990.

8818. Goldberg-Ambrose, Carole. "Not Strictly Racial: A Response to Indians as Peoples." *UCLA Law Review* 39 (October 1991): 169- 190. [See also David Williams, below]

8819. Goldberg, Stephanie B. "The Law, a New Theory Holds, Has a White Voice." *New York Times*, 17 July 1992.

8820. _____. "Who's Afraid of Derrick Bell?" *ABA Journal* 78 (September 1992): 56-59. [See Bell, above]

8821. Goodman, James E. *Stories of Scottsboro*. Ph.D. diss., Princeton University, 1990. UMO # 9012715.

8822. _____. *Stories of Scottsboro*. Pantheon, 1994.

8823. Gotanda, Neil. "A Critique of Our Constitution is Color Blind." *Stanford Law Review* 44 (November 1991): 1-68.

8824. Graham, Barbara L. "Judicial Recruitment and Racial Diversity on State Courts: An Overview." *Judicature* 74 (June-July 1990).

8825. Grant, J. A. C. "Testimonial Exclusion Because of Race: A Chapter In the History of Intolerance in California." *UCLA Law Review* 17 (1970): 192-201.

8826. Gray, Jerry. "Panel Says Courts Are 'Infested With Racism'." *New York Times*, 5 June 1991. [Report by New York State Judicial Commission on Minorities]

8827. Green, George N. "The Felix Longoria Affair." *Journal of Ethnic Studies* 19 (Fall 1991): 23-49. [Three Rivers, Texas, 1949]

8828. Greenberg, Jack. *Crusaders in the Courts*. Basic Books, 1994.

8829. Grey, T. C. "Civil Rights vs. Civil Liberties: The Case of Discriminatory Verbal Harassment." *Social Philosophy and Policy* 8 (Spring 1991): 81-107.

8830. Grinde, Donald A., Jr., and Bruce E. Johansen. *Exemplar of Liberty: Native America and the Evolution of Democracy*. University of California, American Indian Studies Center, 1991.

8831. Guinier, Lani. "What I Would Have Told the Senate." *Washington Post*, 13 June 1993.

8832. Hager, Philip. "Confidence in Court System Dips." *Los Angeles Times*, 11 December 1992. [California-wide public opinion poll sponsored by state Judicial Council]

8833. _____. "Efforts Being Increased to Expand Juries Diversity." *Los Angeles Times*, 3 August 1992.

8834. Hall, Kermit L., ed. *Race Relations and the Law in American History: Major Historical Interpretations*. New York, NY: Garland, 1987.

8835. Hardwick, John. "The Schism between Minorities and the Critical Legal Studies Movement: Requiem for a Heavyweight?" *Boston College Third World Law Journal* 11 (Winter 1991): 137- 164.

8836. Hardy, James D. "The Banality of Slavery." *Southern Studies* 25 (1986): 187-195.

8837. Harper, Conrad K. "Integrate the Federal Bench." *New York Times*, 22 February 1991. [New York City]

8838. Harring, Sidney L. "Crazy Snake and the Creek Struggle for Sovereignty: The Native American Legal Culture and American Law." *American Journal of Legal History* 34 (October 1990): 365-380.

8839. Harris, Angela P. "Race and Essentialism in Feminist Legal Theory." *Stanford Law Review* 42 (February 1990).

8840. Hayes, John Charles. "The Tradition of Prejudice versus the Principle of Equality: Homosexuals and Heightened Equal Protection Scrutiny after Bowers v. Hardwick." *Boston College Law Review* 31 (March 1990): 375-475.

8841. Hazard, Geoffrey C., Jr. and others. "[Letters commenting on Randall Kennedy "Justice Brennan: Why No Black Law Clerks?"]." *Reconstruction* 1 (1992): 153-157.

8842. Henderson, Lynne. "Law's Patriarchy." *Law and Society Review* 25 (1991): 411-444.

8843. Henderson, Thelton. "The Law and Civil Rights: The Justice Department in the South." *New University Thought* 3 (1963): 36-45.

8844. Hentoff, Nat. "Fired by the NAACP for Sticking to Its Principles." *Village Voice*, 23 November 1993. [Anthony Griffin, attorney in Texas]

8845. _____. *Free Speech for Me But Not for Thee: How the Left and Right Relentlessly Censor Each Other*. Harper Collins, 1992.

8846. _____. "The Perennial Face of Fascism." *Village Voice*, 20 October 1992. [Interference with free speech from right and left]

8847. _____. "'The Right To Be a Bigot'." *Village Voice*, 4 August 1992. [On hate crimes]

8848. _____. "'This Is the Hour of Danger for the First Amendment'." *Village Voice*[Critique of St. Paul ordinance against cross burnings and the like]

8849. Higginbotham, A. Leon. "The Case of the Missing Black Judges." *New York Times*, 29 July 1992.

8850. Higginbotham, A. Leon, Jr. "An Open Letter to Clarence Thomas from a Federal Judicial Colleague." *University of Pennsylvania Review* 140 (January 1992): 1005-1028.

8851. _____. "Race, Sex, Education and Missouri Jurisprudence: Shelley v. Kraemer in a Historical Perspective." *Washington University Law Quarterly* 67 (Summer 1989): 673-708.

8852. _____. "Racism in American and South African Courts: Similarities and Differences." *New York University Law Review* 65 (June 1990): 479-588.

8853. [Higginbotham, A. Leon , Issue Dedicated to]. *University of Pennsylvania Law Review* 142 (December 1993): 7 articles.

8854. Higginbotham, A. Leon, Jr., and Laura B. Farmelo. "Racial Justice and the Priorities of American Leadership." in *Social Class and Democratic Leadership: Essays in Honor of E. Digby Baltzell*, ed. Harold J. Bershady. Philadelphia, PA: University of Pennsylvania Press, 1989.

8855. Higginbotham, A. Leon, Jr., and Barbara K. Kopytoff. "Property First, Humanity Second: The Recognition of the Slave's Human Nature in Virginia Civil Law." *Ohio State University Law Journal* 50 (1989).

8856. Higginbotham, A. Leon, Jr., and Barbara K. Kopytoff. "Racial Purity and Interracial Sex in the Law of Colonial and Antebellum Virginia." *Georgetown Law Journal* 77 (August 1989): 1967-2030.

8857. Hobbs, Steven H. "From the Shoulders of [Charles H.] Houston: A Vision for Social and Economic Justice." *Howard Law Journal* 32 (Fall 1989): 505-547.

8858. Hockett, Jeffrey D. "Justice Robert H. Jackson and Segregation: A Study of the Limitations and Proper Basis of Judicial Action." *Supreme Court Historical Society Yearbook* (1989): 52-67.

8859. Hoerder, Dirk. "Immigrants, Labor and the Higher Courts from 1877 to the 1920s." *Storia Nordamericana* 4 (1987): 3-29.

8860. Hoff, Joan. *Unequal Before the Law. A Legal History of U.S. Women*. New York, NY: New York University Press, 1990.

8861. Hoffer, Peter C. *The Law's Conscience: Equitable Constitutionalism in America*. Chapel Hill, NC: University of North Carolina Press, 1990. [Deals with Brown v. Board of Education, among other things]

8862. Hoffman, Jan. "New York Casts for Solutions to Gaping Holes in Juror Net." *New York Times*, 26 September 1993. [Blacks and Hispanics greatly underrepresented in jury pools]

8863. Hogin, Bradley R. "Equal Protection, Democratic Theory, and the Case of the Poor." *Rutgers Law Journal* 21 (Fall 1989): 1-66.

8864. Holley, Dannye, and Thomas Kleven. "Minorities and the Legal Profession: Current Platitudes, Current Barriers." *Thurgood Marshall Law Review* 12 (Summer 1987): 299-345.

8865. Holmes, Malcolm D. and others. "Judges' Ethnicity and Minority Sentencing: Evidence concerning Hispanics." *Social Science Quarterly* 74 (September 1993): 496-506.

8866. Holmes, Steven A. "Some Workers Lose Right to File Suit for Bias At Work." *New York Times*, 18 March 1994. [Some large employers compel workers to resort to binding arbitration rather than litigation]

8867. Holtzman, Elizabeth. "United States Involvement with Nazi War Crimes." *New York Law School of International and Comparative Law* 11 (Fall 1990): 337-345.

8868. Hornung, Rick. "The Black Avenger. The Troubled Soul of Alton Maddox." *Village Voice*, 21 November 1989.

8869. Horwitz, Morton J. "The Meaning of the Bork Nomination in American Constitutional History." *University of Pittsburgh Law Review* 50 (Winter 1989): 655-666.

8870. _____. *The Transformation of American Law, 1870-1960. The Crisis of Legal Orthodoxy*. Oxford University Press, 1992.

8871. Houseman, Alan W. "Poverty Law Development and Options for the 1990s." *Clearinghouse Review* 24 (May 1990): 2-16.

8872. Howard-Pitney, David. *The Afro-American Jeremiad: Appeals for Justice in America*. Philadelphia, PA: Temple University Press, 1990.

8873. Howington, Arthur F. *According to the Law: The Treatment of Slaves and Free Blacks in the State and Local Courts of Tennessee*. New York, NY: Garland, 1989.

8874. Isaac, Katherine. *Civics for Democracy*. Center for the Study of Responsive Law, 1992.

8875. Jackson, Derrick Z. "Hardly a Lynch Victim." *Boston Globe*, 16 October 1991. [Clarence Thomas]

8876. Jackson, Donald W. *Even the Children of Strangers: Equality Under the U.S. Constitution*. University Press of Kansas, 1992.

8877. Jensen, Erik M. "The Imaginary Connection between the Great Law of Peace and the United States Constitution: Reply to Professor Schaaf." *American Indian Law Review* 15 (Summer 1990): 295-308.

8878. Johansen, Bruce E., and Donald A. Grinde, Jr. "The Debate Regarding Native American Precedents for Democracy: A Recent Historiography." *American Indian Culture and Research Journal* 14 (1990): 61-88.

8879. Johnson, Alex M., Jr. "The New Voices of Color." *Yale Law Journal* 100 (1991): 2007-2063.

8880. _____. "'Racial Critique of Legal Academia': A Reply in Favor of Context." *Stanford Law Review* 43 (November 1990): 137-165. [See Randall Kennedy, below]

8881. Jones. "An Argument for Federal Protection against Racially Motivated Crimes: 18 USC SS 241 and the Thirteenth Amendment." *Harvard Civil Rights-Civil Liberties Review* 21 (1986).

8882. Jones, Elaine R. "Broder v. Guinier." *Washington Post* (20 June 1993). [Analysis of continuing racism in gaining full representation for African-Americans]

8883. Joseph, Joel D. *Black Mondays: Worst Decisions of the Supreme Court*. Bethesda, MD: National Press, 1987.

8884. Justice, William Wayne. "The New Awakening: Judicial Activism in a Conservative Age." *Southwestern Law Journal* 43 (October 1989): 657-676.

8885. Kaine, Timothy M. "Race, Trial Strategy and Legal Ethics." *University of Richmond Law Review* 24 (Spring 1990): 361-383.

8886. Kairys, David. "Prejudicial Restraint: Race and the Supreme Court." *Tikkun* 7 (May-June 1992): 37-43. [See Randall Kennedy, below]

8887. Kancewick, Mary, and Eric Smith. "Subsistence in Alaska: Towards a Native Priority." *UMKC Law Review* 59 (Spring 1991): 645-677.

8888. Kaufman, Natalie H. *Human Rights Treaties and the Senate: A History of Opposition*. Chapel Hill, NC: University of North Carolina Press, 1990.

8889. Kelsey, Frederick T. "Gender based Peremptory Challenges and the New York State Constitution." *Touro Law Review* 8 (Fall 1991): 91-139.

8890. Kemerer, Frank R. *William Wayne Justice: A Judicial Biography*. University of Texas Press, 1991.

8891. Kennebeck, Edwin. *Juror Number Four: The Trial of Thirteen Black Panthers as Seen from the Jury Box*. New York, NY: Norton, 1973.

8892. Kennedy, Randall L. "Competing Conceptions of Racial Discrimination: A Response to Cooper and Graglia." *Harvard Journal of Law and Public Policy* 14 (Winter 1991): 93-101.

8893. _____. "Grand Marshall." *Nation*, 12 August 1991. [On Thurgood Marshall]

8894. _____. "Indiscriminate Indictments." *Tikkun* 7 (May 1992): 43-44, 87-88. [See Kairys, above]

8895. _____. "Justice Brennan: Why No Black Law Clerks?" *Reconstruction* 1 (1991): 63-64.

8896. _____. "Martin Luther King's Constitution: A Legal History of the Montgomery Bus Boycott." *Yale Law Journal* 98 (April 1989): 999-1068.

8897. _____. "Racial Critiques of Legal Academia." *Harvard Law Review* 102 (June 1989): 1745-1819.

8898. Kennedy, Stetson. *Jim Crow Guide: The Way It Was*. Boca Raton, FL: Florida Atlantic Univeristy Press, 1990.

8899. Kerruish, Valerie. *Jurisprudence as Ideology*. New York, NY: Routledge, 1991.

8900. King, Patricia. "On the Backs of Black Women: Judge Thomas, the Self-made Man." *Radical America* 24 (January-March 1990): 9- 14.

8901. Klare, Karl. "The Quest for Industrial Democracy and the Struggle Against Racism: Perspectives from Labor Law and Civil Rights Law." *Oregon Law Review* 61 (1982): 157-200.

8902. Klarman, M.J. "An Interpretive History of Modern Equal Protection." *Michigan Law Review* 90 (November 1991): 213-318.

8903. Kly, Yussuf N. *International Law and the Black Minority in the U.S.* Atlanta, GA: Clarity, 1985.

8904. Korey, William. *The Promises We Keep. Human Rights, the Helsinki Process and American Foreign Policy*. St. Martin's Press, 1993.

8905. Korsmo, Fae L. *Empowerment or Termination? Native Rights and Resource Regimes in Alaska and Swedish Lapland*. Ph.D. diss., University of New Mexico, 1992. UMO # 9315933.

8906. Kousser, J. Morgan. "Before Plessy, Before Brown: The Development of the Law of Racial Integration in Louisiana and Kansas." in *Toward a Usable Past*, eds. Paul Finkelman, and Stephen E. Gottlieb. : University of Georgia Press, 1991.

8907. Kull, Andrew. *The Color-Blind Constitution*. Harvard University Press, 1992.

8908. Kurtz, Howard. "A Revisionist's Nightmare." *Washington Post*, 10 June 1993. [David Brock, author of *The Real Anita Hill*]

8909. Kushner. "Apartheid in America." *Howard Law Review* 22 (1979): 675-682.

8910. Lahav, P. "The Eichmann Trial, the Jewish Question, and the American-Jewish Intelligentsia." *Boston University Law Review* 72 (May 1992): 555-578.

8911. Lammers, John C. "The Accommodation of Chinese Immigrants in Early California Courts." *Sociological Perspectives* 31 (October 1988): 446-465.

8912. Langum, David G. *Law and Community on the Mexican California Frontier: Anglo-American Expatriates and the Clash of Legal Traditions, 1821-1846*. Norman, OK: University of Oklahoma Press, 1987.

8913. Lazarus, Edward. *Black Hill/ White Justice. The Sioux Nation Versus the United States, 1775 to the Present*. New York, NY: Harper Collins, 1992.

8914. Leach, Carol A. *The Relationship of Judges' Gender to Decision-making in the State and Federal Courts*. Ph.D. diss., Southern Illinois University, 1990. UMO # 9129847.

8915. Leadership Conference on Civil Rights. "Without Justice." *Black Law Journal* 8 (Spring 1983): 29-59. [Attorney General of the U.S.]

8916. LeBlanc, Lawrence. *The United States and the Genocide Convention*. Durham, NC: Duke University Press, 1991.

8917. Lewin, Tamara. "Hate-Crime Law Is Focus of Case On Free Speech." *New York Times*, 1 December 1991. [St. Paul, MN]

8918. Lewis, Neil A. "2 Years After His Bruising Hearing, Justice Thomas Still Shows the Hurt." *New York Times*, 27 November 1993. [Supreme Court Justice Clarence Thomas]

8919. _____. "Black Judge's Success Story Begins in Cold Attic." *New York Times*, 19 July 1991. [A. Leon Higginbotham, Jr.]

8920. _____. "Justice Thomas Calls for Responsibility." *New York Times*, 17 May 1994. [U.S. Supreme Court Justice Clarence Thomas]

8921. Liebman, James S. "Implementing Brown in the Nineties: Political Reconstruction, Liberal Recollection, and Litigatively Enforced Legislative Reform." *Virginia Law Review* 76 (April 1990): 349-435.

8922. Lindner, Charles L. "Judicial L.A.: South Africa Without the Formality." *Washington Post*, 14 March 1993. [Lack of black judges in Los Angeles courts]

8923. _____. "Lesson of the King Case: The Risk of Shuttle Justice." *Los Angeles Times*, 25 April 1993. [Change of venue and minority concerns about fairness]

8924. Lipschultz, Sybil. "Social Feminism and Legal Discourse: 1908-1923." *Yale Journal of Law and Feminism* 2 (Fall 1989): 131- 160.

8925. Lively, Donald E. *The Constitution and Race*. New York, NY: Praeger, 1992.

8926. Lopez, Gerald P. *Rebellions Lawyering. One Chicano's Vision of Progressive Law Practice*. Westview Press, 1992.

8927. _____. "Training Future Lawyers to Work with the Politically and Socially Subordinated: Anti-Generic Legal Education." *West Virginia Law Review* 92 (1990).

8928. Lopez, Jerry. [Gerald P.] "The Idea of a Constitution in the Chicano Tradition." *Journal of Legal Education* 37 (1987).

8929. Luban, David. "Difference Made Legal: The Court and Dr. King." *Michigan Law Review* 87 (August 1989): 2152-2224.

8930. Lucas, Malcolm M. "A Supreme Comedian? The Chief Justice Denies Charges of Racism." *California Lawyer* 10 (January 1990): 28.

8931. Lyman, Stanford M. "The Race Question and Liberalism: Casuistries in American Constitutional Law." *International Journal of Politics, Culture and Society* 5 (1991): 183-247.

8932. Lyons, Oren and others. *Exiled in the Land of the Free. Democracy, Indian Nations, and the U.S. Constitution*. Santa Fe, NM: Clear Light Publishers, 1993.

8933. MacCoun, Robert J. "The Emergence of Extralegal Bias during Jury Deliberation." *Criminal Justice and Behavior* 17 (September 1990): 303-314.

8934. MacKenzie, Melody K., ed. *Native Hawaiian Rights Handbook*. Honolulu,: Native Hawaiian Legal Corporation, 1991.

8935. Maggs, Peter B. "Access to Justice for the Consumer in the U.S.A." *Journal of Consumer Policy* 13 (March 1990).

8936. Magnarella, Paul J. "Justice in a Culturally Pluralistic Society: The Cultural Defense on Trial." *Journal of Ethnic Studies* 19 (Fall 1991): 65-84.

8937. Malveaux, Julianne. "One Nation, With Liberty and Justice for the Few." *Los Angeles Times*, 3 July 1991.

8938. Mann, Coramae Rickey. *Unequal Justice. A Question of Color*. Indiana University Press, 1993.

8939. Margolick, David. "Idea of Jury of Peers is Questioned: Must a Jury Reflect the Population?" *New York Times*, 17 February 1992.

8940. Marshall, Thurgood. "Interview." *Ebony* 46 (November 1990): 44-49.

8941. Martin, Charles. "The Civil Rights Congress and Southern Black Defendants." *Georgia Historical Quarterly* 71 (Spring 1987): 25-52.

8942. Martin, Gordon A., Jr. "On Leaving Roxbury." *Boston Globe*, 12 June 1994. [The former presiding justice of Roxbury District Court discusses his 11-year term]

8943. Matsuda, Mari J. "Legal Sanctions against Racial Speech Working in Many Democratic Nations. Why Not Here?" *ACLU Open Forum* 5 (September/October 1990).

8944. _____. "Public Response to Racist Speech: Considering the Victim's Story." *Michigan Law Review* (August 1989).

8945. _____. "Voices of America: Accent, Antidiscrimination Law, and a Jurisprudence for the Last Reconstruction." *Yale Law Journal* 100 (March 1991): 1329-1408.

8946. McClelland, Katherine, and C. Hunter. "The Perceived Seriousness of Racial Harassment." *Social Problems* 39 (February 1992).

8947. McConnell, Michael W. "Trashing Natural Law." *New York Times*, 16 August 1991. [In re: Judge Clarence Thomas' nomination to the Supreme Court]

8948. McCrea, Carrie. "From Griggs to Wards Cover: The Blurring of Disparate Impact and Disparate Treatment under Title VII of the 1964 Civil Rights Act." *California Western Law Review* 26 (Spring 1990): 449-474.

8949. McDonald, Janis L. "The Republican Revival: Revolutionary Republicanism's Relevance for Charles Sumner's Theory of Equality and Reconstruction." *Buffalo Law Review* 38 (March 1990): 465-514.

8950. McDonald, Laughlin, and John A. Powell. *The Rights of Racial Minorities: The Basic ACLU Guide to Racial Minority Rights, 2nd Edition, completely revised and updated.* Southern Illinois University Press, 1993.

8951. McKanna, Clare V., Jr. "Four Hundred Dollars Worth of Justice: The Trial and Execution of Indian Joe, 1892-1893." *Journal of San Diego History* 33 (1987): 197-212. [Jose Gabriel]

8952. _____. "Life Hangs in the Balance: The U.S. Supreme Court's Review of Ex Parte Gon-Shay-Ee." *Western Legal History* 3 (1990): 197-211.

8953. McMillan, Penelope. "Grand Juries' Racial Makeup Under Challenge." *Los Angeles Times*, 12 October 1993. [Los Angeles County]

8954. Medhurst, Martin. "The First Amendment vs. Human Rights: A Case Study in Community Sentiment and Argument From Definition." *Western Journal of Speech Communication* 46 (1982): 1-19.

8955. Meier, Kenneth J., and Thomas M. Holbrook. "'I Seen My Opportunities and I Took 'Em': Political Corruption in the American States." *Journal of Politics* 54 (February 1992): 135- 155. [Touches on issue of racial targeting of prosecution]

8956. Meltzner, Michael, and Victor Navasky, eds. *The "Trial" of Bobby Seales*. New York, NY: Prism Books, 1970.

8957. Menkel-Meadow, Carrie, and Shari Seidman Diamond. "The Content, Method and Epistemology of Gender in Sociological Studies." *Law and Society Review* 25 (May 1991): 221-238.

8958. Merkel, Philip L. "At the Crossroads of Reform: The First Fifty Years of American Legal Aid, 1876-1926." *Houston Law Review* 27 (January 1990): 1-44.

8959. Merry, S. E. "Law as Fair, Law as Help- The Texture of Legitimacy in American Society." in *New Directions in the Study of Justice, Law, and Social Control*, New York, NY: Plenum, 1990.

8960. Middleton, Stephen. *The Black Laws in the Old Northwest. A Documentary History*. Greenwood, 1992.

8961. _____. "Cincinnati and the Fight for the Law of Freedom in Ohio, 1830-1856." *Locus* 4 (Fall 1991): 59-73.

8962. Miller, G. P. "Rights and Structure in Constitutional Theory." *Social Philosophy and Policy* 8 (Spring 1991).

8963. "Minnesota Supreme Court Task Force for Gender Fairness in the Courts: Final Report." *William Mitchell Law Review* 15 (Autumn 1989): 825-948.

8964. Minow, Martha. "From Class Action to Miss Saigon: The Concept of Representation in Law." *Cleveland State Law Journal* 39 (1991): 269-300.

8965. _____. "Justice Engendered." *Harvard Law Review* 101 (November 1987): 10-96.

8966. _____. "Putting Up and Putting Down: Tolerance Reconsidered." *Osgood Hall Law Journal* 28 (Summer 1990): 409-448.

8967. Mirande, Alfredo. *Gringo Justice*. Notre Dame, IN: University of Notre Dame Press, 1987.

8968. Morales, Alfonso. "Law, Culture and Social Inequality in Historical New Mexico." *Sociological Abstracts* Accession No. 89S21608 (1989).

8969. Morrison, Toni. *Race-ing Justice, En-gendering Power. Essays on Anita Hill, Clarence Thomas, and the Construction of Social Reality*. Pantheon, 1992.

8970. Morsch, J. "The Problem of Motive in Hate Crimes: The Argument Against Presumptions of Racial Motivation." *Journal of Criminal Law and Criminology* 82 (Autumn 1991): 659-689.

8971. Murray, Pauli, ed. *States' Laws on Race and Color...* Cincinnati, OH: Women's Division of Christian Service, Board of Missions and Church Extension, Methodist Church, 1951.

8972. Muwakkil, Salim. "Black Reaction to [Clarence] Thomas is Complex." *In These Times*, 23 October 1991.

8973. Nash, A. E. Keir. "Reason of Slavery: Understanding the Judicial Role in the Peculiar Institution." *Vanderbilt Law Review* 32 (January 1979).

8974. Nedelsky, Jennifer. "The Protection of Property in the Origins and Development of the American Constitution." in *To Form a More Perfect Union*, eds. Herman Belz and others. : University Press of Virginia, 1992.

8975. Neuman, G. L. "The Lost Century of American Immigration Law (1776-1875)." *Columbia Law Review* 93 (December 1993): 1833-1901.

8976. Newman, Roger K. *Hugo Black: A Biography*. Pantheon, 1994.

8977. Newton, Jim. "Judge Attacks Reiner Over Removal from Denny Case." *Los Angeles Times*, 27 August 1992. [Removal of black judge in case involving black defendants]

8978. _____. "L.A. Trials Show 'Blind Justice' Is Hard to Achieve." *Los Angeles Times*, 24 October 1993.

8979. _____. "Prospective King Jurors Get Bias Questionnaire." *Los Angeles Times*, 4 February 1993. [Rodney G. King, who was beaten by Los Angeles police]

8980. _____. "Riot's Shadow Hangs Over King Jury Selection." *Los Angeles Times*, 31 January 1993. [In re: forthcoming trial of Rodney G. King in Los Angeles]

8981. Newton, N. J. "Status of Native American Tribal Indians under United States Law." *Law and Anthropology* 1 (1986): 51-91.

8982. Niedermeyer, Deborah. "'The True Interests of a White Population': The Alaska Indian Country Decisions of Judge Matthew P. Deady." *New York University Journal of International Law and Politics* 21 (1988): 195-257.

8983. Noel, Peter. "Ordeal By Suspicion. The Making of a Hostile Witness." *Village Voice*, 18 January 1994. [Crown Heights, N.Y.C.]

8984. Norman, David L. and others. "In Honor of Brown versus Board of Education." *Yale Law Journal* 93 (May 1984): 983-1012.

8985. Nossiter, Adam. "The Case That Refuses to Die." *Nation*, 12 March 1990. ["legal lynching in Louisiana", Gary Tyles]

8986. Nunn, Kenneth B. "Rights Held Hostage: Race, Ideology and the Peremptory Challenge." *Harvard Civil Rights-Civil Liberties Law Review* 28 (Winter 1993): 63-118.

8987. O'Brien, Sharon. "Cultural Rights in the United States: A Conflict of Values." *Law and Inequality: A Journal of Theory and Practice* 5 (July 1987): 267-358.

8988. O'Connell, Robert M. "The Elimination of Racism from Jury Selection: Challenging the Peremptory Challenge." *Boston College Law Review* 32 (March 1991): 433-485.

8989. Odum, Maria. "Money Shortage Seen as Hindering Indian Justice." *New York Times*, 4 October 1991. [Tribal courts]

8990. Okamura, Raymond Y. "Campaign to Repeal the Emergency Detention Act." *Amerasia Journal* 2 (1974): 71-111.

8991. Olsen, Frances. "Feminism and Critical Legal Theory: An American Perspective." *International Journal of the Sociology of the Law* 18 (May 1990): 199-215.

8992. "[On Thurgood Marshall]." *Stanford Law Review* 44 (Summer 1992): entire issue.

8993. O'Neil, Robert M. "Hateful Messages That Force Free Speech to the Limit." *Chronicle of Higher Education*, 16 February 1994.

8994. Park, David. "Can the No State Action Shibboleth Legitimize the Racist Use of Peremptory Challenges in Civil Actions?" *John Marshall Law Review* 23 (Winter 1990): 271-283.

8995. Patterson, Orlando. "Race, Gender and Liberal Fallacies." *New York Times*, 20 October 1991. [Clarence Thomas]

8996. Pegues, Robert L., Jr. *A Documentary Research of the Role of the School Superintendent in School Federal Court Trials: Four Major Large Ohio Cities, 1964-1984*. Ph.D. diss., Kent State University, 1989. UMO # 9015879.

8997. Peller, Gary. "The Discourse of Constitutional Degradation." *Georgetown Law Review* 81 (December 1992): 313-342. [See Tushnet, below]

8998. _____. "Race Consciousness." *Duke Law Journal* 4 (September 1990): 758-847.

8999. Perry, Barbara A. *A Representative Supreme Court? The Impact of Race, Religion, and Gender on Appointments*. Westport, CT: Greenwood, 1991.

9000. Pincus, Samuel N. *The Virginia Supreme Court, Blacks and the Laws, 1870-1902*. Garland, 1990.

9001. Pitts, Bruce. "Eliminating Hate: A Proposal for a Comprehensive Bias Crime Law." *Law and Psychology Review* 14 (Spring 1990): 139-151.

9002. "Politics, Values, and the [Clarence] Thomas Nomination." *PS: Political Science and Politics* 25 (September 1992): 6 articles.

9003. Post, Deborah W. "Race, Riots and the Rule of Law." *Denver University Law Review* 70 (1993): 237-264.

9004. Quan, D. "Asian Americans and Law: Fighting the Myth of Success." *Journal of Legal Education* 38 (December 1988): 619-628.

9005. Quinn, William W., Jr. "Federal Acknowledgment of American Indian Tribes: The Historical Development of a Legal Concept." *American Journal of Legal History* 34 (October 1990): 331-364.

9006. Ragsdale, John W., Jr. "Indian Reservations and the Preservation of Tribal Culture: Beyond Wardship to Stewardship." *UMKC Law Review* 59 (Spring 1991): 503-554.

9007. Ramirez, Deborah A. "Excluded Voices: The Disenfranchisement of Ethnic Groups from Jury Service." *Wisconsin Law Review* (1993): 761-809.

9008. Rapport, Sara. "The Freedmen's Bureau as a Legal Agent for Black Men and Women in Georgia: 1865-1868." *Georgia Historical Quarterly* 73 (Spring 1989): 26-53.

9009. Raskin, Jamin B. "A Precedent for Arab-Americans?" *Nation*, 4 February 1991. [Korematsu v. United States (1944)]

9010. Reidinger, Paul. "Sue U.: From Classroom to Courtroom." *ABA Journal* 76 (February 1990).

9011. "Responses to the Minority Critiques of the Critical Legal Studies Movement." *Harvard Civil Rights-Civil Liberties Law Review* 22 (Spring 1987): 297-447.

9012. Richards, David A. J. *Conscience and the Constitution: History, Theory, and Law of the Reconstruction Amendments*. Princeton University Press, 1993.

9013. Riegel, Stephen J. "The Persistent Career of Jim Crow: Lower Federal Courts and the 'Separate but Equal Doctrine', 1865- 1896." *American Journal of Legal History* 28 (January 1984).

9014. Robinson, Donald. "Constitutional Legacy of Slavery." in *The Challenge to Racial Stratification*, ed. Matthew Holden, Jr. : Transaction, 1993.

9015. Robinson, Walter S., Jr. "The Legal Status of the Indian in Colonial Virginia." *Virginia Magazine of History and Biography* 61 (1953): 249-259.

9016. Rollenhagen, Mark. "Black Staffers Increasing at Federal Court." *Cleveland Plain Dealer*, 29 July 1991. [U.S. District Court for the Northern District of Ohio]

9017. Ronda, James P. "Red and White at the Bench: Indians and the Law in Plymouth County, 1680-1691." *Essex Institute Historical Collection* 110 (1974): 200-215.

9018. Rosenberg, Gerald N. *The Hollow Hope. Can Courts Bring About Social Change?* Chicago, IL: University of Chicago Press, 1991.

9019. Rosenthal, H. *Their Day in Court: A History of the Indian Claims Commission.* Ph.D. diss., Kent State University, 1976.

9020. Rusco, Elmer R. "Early Nevada and Indian Law." *Western Legal History* 2 (Summer/Fall 1989): 163-190.

9021. Ryan, J. Brendan. "Different Voices, Different Choices? The Impact of More Women Lawyers and Judges on the Justice System." *Judicature* 74 (October-November 1990): 138-146.

9022. Sabin, J. I. "Clio and the Court Redux: Toward a Dynamic Mode of Interpreting Reconstruction Era Civil Rights Laws." *Columbia Journal of Law and Social Problems* 23 (1990).

9023. Saks, Eva. "Representing Miscegenation Law." *Raritan* 8 (1988): 39-69. [Pre-Civil War]

9024. Sanders, Douglas. "Collective Rights." *Human Rights Quarterly* 13 (August 1991): 368-386.

9025. Savage, David S., and Ronald J. Ostrow. "Women, Minorities Outpace White Men for Judgeships." *Los Angeles Times,* 11 January 1994. [First year of Clinton administration]

9026. Savage, Mark. "Native Americans and the Constitution: The Original Understanding." *American Indian Law Review* 16 (Spring 1991): 57-118.

9027. Scales-Trent, Judy. "Law: Oppression and Resistance." *Black Women in America* I 701-705.

9028. Schafran, Lynn H. "Gender Bias in the Courts: An Emerging Focus for Judicial Reform." *Arizona State Law Journal* 21 (Spring 1989): 237-273.

9029. _____. "Gender and Justice: Florida and the Nation." *Florida Law Review* 42 (January 1990): 181-208.

9030. Schwartz, Paul H. "Equal Protection in Jury Selection? The Implementation of Batson v. Kentucky in North Carolina." *North Carolina Law Review* 69 (September 1991): 1533-1577.

9031. Scruggs, Frank, and Deborah H. Wagner. "Where the Injured Fly for Justice: A Summary of the Report and Recommendations of the Florida Supreme Court Racial and Ethnic Bias Study Commission." *Florida Bar Journal* 65 (March 1991): 10-16.

9032. Seematter, Mary E. "Trials and Confessions: Race and Justice in Antebellum St. Louis." *Gateway Heritage* 12 (Fall 1991): 36-47.

9033. *Selected Administration of Justice Issues Affecting American Indians in Oklahoma.* Washington, DC: U.S. Commission on Civil Rights, 1989.

9034. Sereny, Gitta. "John Demjanjuk and the Failure of Justice." *New York Times Review of Books,* 8 October 1992.

9035. Shattuck, Petra T., and Jill Norgren. *Partial Justice: Federal Indian Law in a Liberal Constitutional System.* Berg, 1991.

9036. Sheldon, Charles H. "Representativeness of the Washington Judiciary: Ethnic and Gender Considerations." *Washington State Bar News* 43 (November 1989): 31.

9037. Sheppard, Tyron J., and Richard Nevins. "Constitutional Equality-Reparations at Last." *University of West Los Angeles Law Review* 105-125 (1991).

9038. Sherwin, Richard K. "Law, Violence, and Illiberal Belief." *Georgetown Law Journal* 78 (August 1990): 1785-1835.

9039. Simons, James. "The Austin Law Commune: A Condensed History." *National Lawyers Guild Practitioner* 47 (Spring 1990): 45-50.

9040. Singer, Joseph W. "Sovereignty and Property." *Northwestern University Law Review* 86 (Fall 1991): 1-56. [American Indians]

9041. Sipchen, Bob. "Ready to Fight." *Los Angeles Times,* 20 December 1992. [Johnnie L. Cochran, Jr., lawyer, Los Angeles]

9042. *Slave Rebels, Abolitionists, and Southern Courts.* New York, NY: 1988. 2 vols.

9043. Smith, Christopher E. *Courts and the Poor.* Nelson-Hall, 1991.

9044. Smith, Gaddis. "Black Seamen and the Federal Courts, 1789- 1860." in *Ships, Seafaring, and Society: Essays in Maritime History*, ed. Timothy J. Runyan. Detroit, MI: Wayne State University Press, 1987.

9045. Smith, J. Clay, Jr. "Justice and Jurisprudence and the Black Lawyer." *Notre Dame Law Review* 69 (1994): 1077-1114.

9046. Smith, Steven D. "The Restoration of Tolerance." *California Law Review* 78 (March 1990): 305-356.

9047. Smothers, Ronald. "Cursed and Praised, Retiring Judge Recalls Storm." *New York Times*, 8 November 1991. [Judge Frank M. Johnson, Jr. of Alabama]

9048. _____. "Georgia Agreement Promises to Add Black Judges." *New York Times*, 19 June 1992.

9049. Songer, Donald R., and Reginald S. Sheehan. "Who Wins on Appeal? Upperdogs or Underdogs in the United States Courts of Appeals." *American Journal of Political Science* 36 (February 1992): 235-258. [Upperdogs]

9050. Spann, Girardeau A. *Race against the Court: The Supreme Court and Minorities in Contemporary America*. New York, NY: New York University Press, 1993.

9051. Spohn, C. "The Sentencing Decisions of Black and White Judges: Expected and Unexpected Similarities." *Law and Society Review* 24 (1990): 1197-1216.

9052. Stephens, Beth. "Hypocrisy on [International Human] Rights." *New York Times*, 24 June 1993.

9053. Strauss, David A. "Discriminatory Intent and the Taming of Brown." *University of Chicago Law Review* 56 (Summer 1989): 935- 1015.

9054. Strebeigh, Fred. "Defining Law on the Feminist Frontier." *New York Times Magazine*, 6 October 1991. [Catharine A. MacKinnon, University of Michigan Law School]

9055. Strickland, Rennard. *Fire and Spirits: Cherokee Law from Clan to Court*. Norman, OK: University of Oklahoma Press, 1975.

9056. _____. "Genocide-at-Law: An Historic and Contemporary View of the Native American Experience." *University of Kansas Law Review* 34 (1986): 713-755.

9057. Strossen, Nadine. "'Hate Crimes': The ACLU's Position." *Washington Post*, 6 March 1993.

9058. Sunstein, Cass R. *After the Rights Revolution. Reconceiving the Regulatory State*. Cambridge, MA: Harvard University Press, 1990.

9059. "Symposium: Brown v. Board of Education and Its Legacy: A Tribute to Justice Thurgood Marshall." *Fordham Law Journal* 61 (October 1992): 10 articles.

9060. "Symposium Honoring Judge A. Leon Higginbotham, Jr." *Law and Inequality* 9 (August 1991): VI-496.

9061. "Symposium Honoring Justice Thurgood Marshall." *Georgetown Law Journal* 80 (August 1992): 2003-2130.

9062. "Symposium: National Conference on Minority Bar Passage: Bridging the Gap Between Theory and Practice." *Thurgood Marshall Law Review* 16 (Summer 1991): entire issue.

9063. "Symposium: The Future of Civil Rights Law." *Harvard Journal of Law and Public Policy* 14 (Winter 1991): entire issue.

9064. Taborn, Virginia. "Law and the Black Experience." *National Black Law Journal* 11 (Spring 1989): 267-279.

9065. Tagupa, William E. "Native Hawaiian Reparations: An Ethnic Appeal to Law, Conscience and the Social Sciences." *Journal of Ethnic Studies* 5 (Spring 1977).

9066. Tanford, J. Alexander. "Racism in the Adversary System: The Defendant's Use of Peremptory Challenges." *Southern California Law Review* 63 (May 1990): 1015-1060.

9067. Tarrow, Norma. "United States of America Human Rights Education: Alternative Conceptions." in *Socialisation of School Children and Their Education for Democratic Values and Human Rights*, pp. 183-203. ed. Hugh Starkey. Berwyn, PA: Swets and Zeitlinger, 1991.

9068. Thomas, Clarence W. "Black Americans Based Claim for Freedom on Constitution." *San Diego Union and Tribune*, 6 October 1987. B7, [Critique of Thurgood Marshall's view of the Founding Fathers]

9069. _____. "The Higher Law Background of the Privileges and Immunities Clause of the Fourteenth Amendment." *Harvard Journal of Law and Public Policy* 12 (1989).

9070. _____. "Toward a 'Plain Reading' of the Constitution- The Declaration of Independence in Constitutional Interpretation." *Howard Law Journal* 30 (1987).

9071. Toobin, Jeffrey. "The Burden of Clarence Thomas." *New Yorker*, 27 September 1993. [Justice Thomas's first two years on the U.S. Supreme Court]

9072. Torres, G. "The Evolution of American Culture: The Problematic Place of Race and the Right to Have Rights." *Law and Inequality* 9 (August 1991): 457-467.

9073. Torry, Saundra. "D.C. Law Firms Lack Diversity, Survey Says." *Washington Post*, 2 April 1993.

9074. _____. "Many With Legal Needs Avoid the Court System." *Washington Post*, 6 February 1994. [American Bar Association survey]

9075. _____. "Study of Bias In Courts Splits Judges." *Washington Post*, 28 February 1994. [U.S. Court of Appeals for the District of Columbia Circuit]

9076. Tribe, Laurence H., and Michael C. Dorf. *On Reading the Constitution*. Cambridge, MA: Harvard University Press, 1991.

9077. Tushnet, Mark V. "The Degradation of Constitutional Discourse." *Georgetown Law Review* 81 (December 1992): 251-312; 343-350. [See Peller, above]

9078. _____. "Justice Brennan, Equality, and Majority Rule." *University of Pennsylvania Law Review* 139 (May 1991): 1357-1372.

9079. Tushnet, Mark V., and K. Lezin. "What Really Happened in Brown v. Board of Education." *Columbia Law Review* 91 (December 1991): 1867-1930.

9080. "The Urban Crisis: The Kerner Commission Report Revisited." *North Carolina Law Review* 71 (June 1993): 1289-1785. 16 articles

9081. U.S. Commission on Civil Rights. *Mexican Americans and Administration of Justice in the Southwest*. Washington, DC: Government Printing Office, 1970.

9082. Utah Task Force on Gender and Justice. "Report to the Utah Judicial Council, March 1990." *Journal of Contemporary Law* 16 (Fall 1990).

9083. Wahl, Jenny Bourne. "The Bondsman's Burden: An Economic Analysis of the Jurisprudence of Slaves and Common Carriers." *Journal of Economic History* 53 (September 1993): 495-526.

9084. Walton, Lamont M. "Beyond Civility: Bigotry and Sexism in the Law." *Michigan Bar Journal* 69 (September 1990).

9085. Wambaugh, Byron L. "Has Integration Been Achieved?" *Southern University Law Review* 17 (Fall 1990): 235-251.

9086. Wasby, Stephen L. "Civil Rights and the Supreme Court: A Return of the Past." in *The Challenge to Racial Stratification*, ed. Matthew Holden, Jr. : Transaction, 1993.

9087. Watson, Alan. *Slave Law in the Americas*. Athens, GA: University of Georgia Press, 1989.

9088. Watson, Larry D. *The Quest for Order: Enforcing Slave Codes in Revolutionary South Carolina, 1760-1800*. Ph.D. diss., University of South Carolina, 1980.

9089. Weaver, Harold D. *The Law and Education for Minority Groups in Seventeen Southern States*. Ph.D. diss., Pennsylvania State University, 1945. UMO # 0000791.

9090. West, Cornel. "The Role of Law in Progressive Politics." *Vanderbilt Law Review* 43 (November 1990): 1797-1806.

9091. West, Robin. "Toward an Abolitionist Interpretation of the Fourteenth Amendment." *West Virgina Law Review* 94 (Fall 1991): 111-155.

9092. Weyranch, Walter O., and Maureen A. Bell. "Autonomous Lawmaking: The Case of the 'Gypsies'." *Yale Law Journal* 103 (November 1993): 323-399.

9093. White, Edward L., III. *Another Look at Our Founding Fathers and Their Product: A Response to Justice Thurgood Marshall*. Ph.D. diss., University of Florida, 1989.

9094. _____. "Another Look at Our Founding Fathers and Their Product: A Response to Justice Thurgood Marshall." *Notre Dame Journal of Law, Ethics and Public Policy* 4 (Winter 1989): 73-130.

9095. White, Forrest R. "Brown Revisited." *Phi Delta Kappan* 76 (September 1994): 12-20.

9096. White, John V. "Reactions to Oppression: Jurisgenesis in the Jurispathic State." *Yale Law Journal* 100 (June 1991): 2727- 2746.

9097. White, Vilbert L. "Charles Houston and Black Leadership of the 1930s and 1940s." *National Black Law Journal* 11 (Fall 1990): 331-347.

9098. Whitman, Mark, ed. *Removing a Badge of Slavery: The Record of Brown v. Board of Education*. Markus Wiener, 1993.

9099. Wibecan, Ken. "L.A. Trials Show Power of Racism in Just-Us System." *Long Beach Press-Telegram*, 22 February 1993.

9100. Wilkinson, Charles F. "Indian Tribes and the American Constitution." in *Indians in American History*, pp. 117-134. ed. Frederick E. Hoxie. Arlington Heights, IL: Harlan Davidson Inc., 1988.

9101. Williams, David C. "The Borders of the Equal Protection Clause: Indians as Peoples." *U.C.L.A. Law Review* 38 (April 1991): 759-870. [See Goldberg-Ambrose and David C. Williams, Oct. 1991]

9102. _____. "Sometimes Suspect: A Response." *U.C.L.A. Law Review* 39 (October 1991): 191-212. [See above, Goldberg-Ambrose]

9103. Williams, Patricia J. *The Alchemy of Race and Rights*. Cambridge, MA: Harvard University Press, 1991.

9104. _____. "Clarence Thomas: A Fiction of Individualism." *Radical America* 24 (January-March 1990): 17-19.

9105. _____. "Fetal Fictions: An Exploration of Property Archetypes in Racial and Gendered Contexts." *Florida Law Review* 42 (January 1990): 81-94.

9106. _____. "Lani, We Hardly Knew You. How the Right Wing Created a Monster Out of a Civil Rights Advocate and Bill Clinton Ran in Terror." *Village Voice*, 15 June 1993. [Lani Guinier]

9107. _____. "Spirit-Murdering the Messenger: The Discourse of Fingerpointing as the Law's Response to Racism." *Miami Law Review* 42 (1987).

9108. Williams, Robert A., Jr. "The Algebra of Federal Indian Law: The Hard Trail of Decolonizing and Americanizing the White Man's Jurisprudence." *Wisconsin Law Review* (1986).

9109. _____. *The American Indian in Western Legal Thought. The Discourses of Conquest*. New York, NY: Oxford University Press, 1990.

9110. Wilson, Carol. *Freedom at Risk: The Kidnapping of Free Blacks in America, 1780-1865*. Ph.D. diss., West Virginia University, 1991. UMO # 9203873.

9111. Wilson, Joan Hoff. *Law, Gender, and Injustice: A Legal History of U.S. Women*. New York, NY: N.Y.U. Press, 1991.

9112. Wilson, Margaret. "The Last Nail in the Coffin for Indian Tribal Sovereignty." *Utah Law Review* (Summer 1991): 675-704. [Duro v. Reina]

9113. Windham, Joseph E. *Bondage, Bias and the Bench: An Historical Analysis of Maryland Court of Appeals Cases Involving Blacks, 1830-1860*. Ph.D. diss., Howard University, 1990. UMO # 9134079.

9114. "Wisconsin Hate Crime Law To Apply in LaCrosse Case." *Pacific Citizen*, 30 November 1990. p. 1.

9115. Wise, Arthur E. *The Constitution and Equality: Wealth, Geography, and Educational Opportunity.* Ph.D. diss., University of Chicago, 1967.

9116. _____. "The Constitution and Equal Educational Opportunity." in *The Quality of Inequality: Urban and Suburban Public Schools*, pp. 27-46. ed. Charles U. Daly. Chicago, IL: University of Chicago Center for Policy Study, 1968.

9117. Wong, Doris Sue. "Witnesses Detail Racial, Ethnic Bias in Courts." *Boston Globe*, 6 December 1991. [Testimony before Massachusetts Supreme Judicial Court's Commission to study racial and ethnic bias in the courts]

9118. Wontat, Donald. "A Firm Focus on Diversity." *Los Angeles Times*, 14 April 1994. [Arnelle and Hastie, an Afro-American owned law firm serving principally corporate clients]

9119. Wunder, John R. "Chinese in Trouble." *Western Historical Quarterly* 17 (1985).

9120. _____. "Law and the Chinese on the Southwest Frontier, 1850s-1902." *Western Legal History* 2 (Summer/Fall 1989): 139-158.

9121. Yamamoto, Eric Y. "Korematsu Revisited-Correcting the Injustice of Extraordinary Government Excess and Lax Judicial Review: Time for a Better Accommodation of National Security Concerns and Civil Liberties." *Santa Clara Law Review* 1 (1986).

9122. Young, Mary E. "Racism in Red and Black: Indians and Other Free People of Color in Georgia Law, Politics, and Removal Policy." *Georgia Historical Quarterly* 73 (Fall 1989): 492-518.

9123. Zion, J. W. "Aboriginal Rights: The Western United States of America." *Law and Anthropology* 2 (1987): 195-211.

9124. Ziontz, Alvin J. "IR and R Section, Are You Listening?" *Human Rights* 16 (Winter 1989): 30. [Problems of American Indians Committee]

9125. Zweig, Gail R. "Sex Discrimination: The Continuing War Over How to Acheive Equality." *Annual Survey of American Law* 561-596 (Summer 1988).

LIBRARIES

9126. American Library Association, President's Committee on Library Services to Minorities. *Equity at Issue: Library Service to the Nation's Four Major Minority Groups*. Chicago, IL: American Library Association, 1986.

9127. Ball, Patricia B. H. *African American Male Library Administrators in Public and Academic Libraries*. Ph.D. diss., University of Pittsburgh, 1992. UMO # 9319153.

9128. Broderick, Dorothy M. "Steps for Fighting Racism." *American Libraries* (February 1989): [letter]

9129. Bundy, Mary Lee. *Activism in American Librarianship, 1962- 1973*. New York: 1987.

9130. Carmichael, James V., Jr. "The Social Responsibility of Professional Groups." *Chornicle of Higher Education* 16 March 1994. [Anti-racism by American Library Association in past years]

9131. Chabran, Richard. "Latino Reference Arrives." *American Libraries* (May 1987): 384-388.

9132. Chabran, Richard, and Lillian Castillo-Speed. *Latinos and the University of California Libraries*. 19 November 1988.

9133. Chadley, O. A. "Addressing Cultural Diversity in Academic and Research Libraries." *College and Research Libraries* 53 (May 1992): 206-214.

9134. Fisher, Edith M. *Modern Racism in Academic Librarianship towards Black Americans: A California Study*. Ph.D. diss., University of Pittsburgh, 1991. UMO # 9209576.

9135. Freiband, S. J. "Multicultural Issues and Concerns in Library Education." *Journal of Education and Library Information Science* 33 (Fall 1992): 287-294.

9136. Ginnette, Elinor Des Verney, ed. *Black Bibliophiles and Collectors: Preservers of Black History*. Washington, D.C.: Howard University Press,

9137. Gladwell, Malcolm. "6 Days a Week, the Library Is Closed." *Washington Post*, 6 April 1993. [Class basis of library openings and closings. Also, data on recent U.S. reading trends]

9138. Glaviano, Cliff, and R. Errol Lam. "Academic Libraries and Affirmative Action: Approaching Cultural Diversity in the 1990s." *College and Research Libraries* 51 (November 1990): 513-523.

9139. Guerena, Salvador. "The Chicano Intellectual Tradition: Towards the Fifth Century." *UC Mexus News* No. 25 (Fall 1989): 2-4.

9140. Gunn, Arthur C. "A Black Woman Wants To Be a Professional." *American Libraries* (February 1989): 154-157. [Virginia Proctor Powell Florence, first Black woman to complete professional library education.]

9141. Haro, Roberto. "The Development of Library Programs for Hispanics in America: 1962-1973." in *Activism in American Librarianships, 1962-1973*, Mary Lee Bunday, and Frederick J. Stielow, eds. Westport, CT: Greenwood, 1987.

9142. Hildenbrand, S. "A Historical Perspective on Gender Issues in American Librarianship." *Canadian Journal of Information Science* 17 (September 1992): 18-28.

9143. Jenkins, Betty L. "A White Librarian in a Black Harlem." *Library Quarterly* 60 (1990): 216-231. [Ernestine Rose]

9144. Josey, E. J., and Marva L. De Loach. "Library Services to Ethnic Communities." *Ethnic Forum* 7 (1987): 17-35.

9145. Lee, D. R. "Faith Cabin Libraries: A Study of Alternative Library Service in the Segregated South, 1932-1960." *Libraries and Culture* 26 (Winter 1991): 167-182.

9146. McPheeters, Annie L. *Library Service in Black and White: Some Personal Recollections, 1921-1980*. Metuchen, NJ: Scarecrow Press, 1988. [Atlanta-Fulton Public Library]

9147. Roff, Sandra. "The Accessibility of Libraries to Blacks in 19th Century Brooklyn, New York." *Afro-Americans in New York Life and History* 5 (July 1981): 7-12.

9148. Sherpell, Brenda K. *Racial and Gender Integration Patterns of Professional Librarians in Texas Academic Libraries, 1972- 1992*. Ph.D. diss., Texas Woman's University, 1992. UMO # 9300204.

9149. Smith, Elizabeth M. "Racism: It Is Always There." *Library Journal* 113 (1 November 1988): 35-39.

9150. Speller, Benjamin F., Jr., ed. *Educating Black Librarians*. Jefferson, NC: McFarland, 1991.

9151. Warner, Robert M. *Point of Intersection: The University Library and the Pluralistic Campus Community*. Ann Arbor, MI: University of Michigan Library, 1988.

LITERATURE

9152. Abarry, Abu. "The African-American Legacy in American Literature." *Journal of Black Studies* 20 (June 1990).

9153. Andrews, Bert, and Paul Carter Hansen. *In the Shadow of the Great White Way: Images from the Black Theatre*. NY: Thunder's Mouth Press, 1989.

9154. Anthony, Booker T. *The Individual and Tradition in the Fiction of Ernest J. Gaines*. Ph.D. diss., Ohio State University Press, 1988. [Racism in the rural South]. UMO # 8820246.

9155. Appiah, Kwame Anthony. "The Conservation of Race." *Black American Literature Forum* 23 (Spring 1989): 37-60.

9156. Asian American Student Alliance. *Quarry*. Santa Cruz: Asian American Student Alliance of the University of California at Santa Cruz, 1987. [Anthology]

9157. Asian Pacific Islander Student Alliance. *Seaweed Soup*. Santa Cruz: Asian Pacific Islander Student Alliance, University of California at Santa Cruz, 1989. [Anthology]

9158. Asian Women United of California. *Making Waves: An Anthology of Writings By and About Asian American Women*. Boston, MA: Beacon Press, 1990.

9159. Awkward, Michael. "Race, Gender, and the Politics of Reading." *Black American Literature Forum* 22 (Spring 1988): 5-7.

9160. Bailey, Frankie Y. *Out of the Woodpile. Black Characters in Crime and Detective Fiction*. Westport, CT: Greenwood, 1991.

9161. Baker, Houston A., Jr., and Patricia Redmond, eds. *Afro- American Literary Study in the 1990's*. Chicago, IL: University of Chicago Press, 1989.

9162. Ball, A. F. "Cultural Preference and the Expository Writing of African-American Adolescents." *Written Communication* 9 (October 1992): 501-532.

9163. Ballard, Elizabeth L. *Red-Tinted Landscape: The Poetics of Indian Removal in Major American Texts of the Nineteenth Century*. Ph.D. diss., University of Oklahoma, 1989. UMO # 8921066.

9164. Baraka, Amiri. "Straight No Chaser." *Z Magazine* 5 (October 1992): 89-92.

9165. Bernstein, Richard. "Looking Inside That Outsider, Othello the Moor." *New York Times*, 16 June 1991.

9166. Bess, Reginald. "A. W. Amo: First Great Black Man of Letters." *Journal of Black Studies* 19 (1989): 387-393.

9167. Braxton, Joanne M., and Andree Nicola McLaughlin, eds. *Wild Woman in the Whirlwind. Afra-American Culture and the Contemporary Literary Renaissance*. New Brunswick, NJ: Rutgers University Press, 1989.

9168. Breslauer, Jan. "On the Staging of Diversity." *Los Angeles Times*, 20 June 1993. [Old Globe Theatre, San Diego]

9169. _____. "Seeking the Sources of Hatred." *Los Angeles Times*, 8 July 1992. [God's Country, a play about Neo-Nazis in the Pacific Northwest]

9170. Breslin, James E. B. "Ezra Pound and the Jews." *San Jose Studies* 12 (1986): 37-45.

9171. Brown, Carrie. "Life on the Color Line: Charles Waddell Chesnutt." *Timeline* 5 (October-November 1988): 2-13.

9172. Bruce-Novoa, Juan,ed. *Retrospace: Collected Essays on Chicano Literature*. Houston, TX: Arte Publico, 1990.

9173. Bruxvoort, Harold J. *An Analysis of the Fiction of Charles W. Chesnutt*. Ph.D. diss., Drake University, 1988. UMO # 8825167.

9174. Burns, Judy, and Jill MacDougall. "An Interview with Gayatri Spivak." *Women and Performance* 5 (1990): 80-92.

9175. Carter, Paul, and Bert Andrews. *In the Shadow of the Great White Way: Images from the Black Theatre*. Thunder's Mouth Press, 1989.

9176. Chock, Eric, and Darrell H. Y. Lum, eds. *The Best of Bamboo Ridge: The Hawaii Writers' Quarterly*. Honolulu: Bamboo Ridge Press, 1986.

9177. Chum, Gloria. "The High Note of the Barbarian Reed Pipe: Maxine Hong Kingston." *Journal of Ethnic Studies* 19 (Fall 1991): 85-94.

9178. Coleman, James W. *Blackness and Modernism: The Literary Development of John Edgar Wideman*. Jackson: University Press of Mississippi, 1989.

9179. Collins, Glenn. "Recreating Black Vaudville, Without Removing the Warts." *New York Times*, 28 June 1990.

9180. Costanzo, Angelo, and Christine A. Loveland, eds. "Ethnic Concerns in the United States." *Proteus* 7 (Spring 1990): entire issue.

9181. DePalma, Anthony, Huck Finn's Voice Is Heard As Twain Meets Black Youth. *New York Times*, 7 July 1992.

9182. DeVries, Hilary. "A Black Theatre Group Faces New Hurdles." *New York Times*, 7 January 1990. [Negro Ensemble Company]

9183. _____. "Theatre's Godfather Reaches Entr'acte." *New York Times June 30, 1991*[Lloyd Richards, Yale University]

9184. Dezell, Maureen. "The Tug of Warrior." *Boston Globe*, 23 September 1994. [Differing evaluations of the dramatization of Maxine Hong Kingston's books]

9185. Diamant, Anita. "A Vision of the Street." *Boston Globe Magazine*, 2 February 1992. [Novelist Ann Petry]

9186. Dixon, Bob. *Catching Them Young: Sex, Race and Class in Children's Fiction*. 1970. [See Chapter 3: Racism, all things white and beautiful]

9187. Domkin Ellen, and Susan Clement, eds. *Upstaging Big Daddy: Directing Theater As If Gender and Race Matter*. University of Michigan Press, 1993.

9188. Doyle, Laura. *Bordering on the Body. The Racial Matrix of Modern Fiction and Culture*. Oxford University Press, 1994.

9189. Duany, Jorge. "Hispanics in the United States: Cultural Diversity and Identity." *Caribbean Studies* 22 (1989): 1-35.

9190. Dunbar, Paul Laurence. *The Collected Poetry of Paul Laurence Dunbar Edited by Joanne M. Braxton*. University Press of Virginia, 1993.

9191. Ehrlich, Gretel. *Heart Mountain*. NY: Viking, 1988. [Novel]

9192. Ellis, R. J. "Mark Twain and the Ideology of Southern Slavery." in *Slavery and Other Forms of Unfree Labor*, ed. Leonie J. Archer. NY: Routledge, 1988.

9193. Engle, Ron, and Tice Miller, eds. *The American Stage. Social and Economic Issues from the Colonial Period to the Present*. Cambridge: U. P., 1993.

9194. Epturoy, Annie O., and J. A. Surpegui. "Chicano Literature: Introduction and Bibliography." *American Studies International* 28 (1990): 48-82.

9195. Evans, Charles T. *In Defence of Huckleberry Finn; Anti- racism Motifs in Huckleberry Finn and a Review of Racial Criticism in Twain's Work*. Ph.D. diss., Rice University, 1988. UMO # 8900231.

9196. Fabre, Genevieve, ed. *European Perspectives on Hispanic Literature of the United States*. Houston, TX: Arte Publico, 1988.

9197. Fecher, Charles A., ed. *The Diary of H. L. Mencken*. NY: Knoff, 1989. [Contains antisemetic and antiblack comments by Mencken]

9198. Fecher, Charles A. *Mencken: A Study of His Thought*. [A defense of Henry L. Mencken against charges of antisemitism. By 1989, Fecher had changed his mind. See The Diary of H. L. Mencken(1989).]

9199. Fishkin, Shelley F. "Race and Culture at the Century's End: A Social Context for Puddin'head Wilson." *Essays in Arts and Sciences* 19 (May 1990): 1-27.

9200. Flowers, Sandra H. *A Poetics of the Poetry, Drama, and Fiction Associated with Afro-American Cultural and Revolutionary Nationalism, 1963-72*. Ph.D. diss., Emory University, 1989. UMO # 8924680.

9201. Foley, Barbara. "Race and Class in Radical African-American Fiction of the Depression Years." *NST: Nature, Society, and Thought* 3 (1990): 305-324.

9202. Foster, M. Marie Booth. *Southern Black Creative Writers, 1829-1953: Bio-Bibliographies*. Westport, CT: Greenwood, 1988.

9203. Fox-Genovese, Elizabeth. "Between Individualism and Fragmentation: American Culture and the New Literary Studies of Race and Gender." *American Quarterly* 42 (1990): 7-34.

9204. Fraden, Reva. *Blueprints for a Black Federal Theatre, 1935- 1939*. Cambridge University Press, 1994.

9205. Franklin, H. Bruce. "The Literature of the American Prison." *Massachusetts Review* 18 (1977): 51-78.

9206. Fried, Lewis and others, eds. *Handbook of American-Jewish Literature. An Analytical Guide to Topics, Themes, and Sources*. Westport, Ct: Greenwood, 1988.

9207. Fromm, Harold. "Real Life, Literary Criticism, and the Perils of Bourgeoisification." *New Literary History* 20 (Autumn 1988): 49-64.

9208. Gates, Henry Louis, Jr. "'African American Criticism'." in *Redrawing the Boundaries*, eds. Stephen Greenblatt, and Giles Gunn. : Modern Language Association, 1991.

9209. _____. "'Authenticity' or the Lesson of Little Tree." *New York Times Book Review*, 24 November 1991. [Can one or should one be able to tell the race or ethnicity of an author from the writing alone?]

9210. _____. "Canon-formation, Literary History, and the Afro- American Tradition: From the Seen to the Told." in *Afro-American Literary Study in the 1990's*, eds. Houston A. Baker, Jr., and Patricia Redmond. Chicago: University of Chicago Press, 1989.

9211. Gates, Henry Louis, Jr., ed. *Reading Black, Reading Feminist. A Critical Anthology*. NY: New American Library, 1990.

9212. Gates Henry Louis, Jr. "Why the 'Mule Bone' Debate Goes On." *New York Times*, 10 February 1991. [Play by Langston Hughes and Zora Neale Hurston]

9213. George, Lynell. "Walter Mosley's Street Stories." *Los Angeles Times Magazine*, 22 May 1994. [Mystery writer of stories set in Los Angeles]

9214. Gillespie, C. S. and others. "A Look at the Newbery Medal Books from a Multicultural Perspective." *Reading Teacher* 48 (September 1994): 48-51.

9215. Gillman, Susan. *Dark Twins: Imposture and Identity in Mark Twain's America*. Chicago, IL: University of Chicago Press, 1989.

9216. Gillman, Susan, and Forrest G. Robinson, eds. *Mark Twain's Pudd'nhead Wilson: Race, Conflict and Culture*. Durham, NC: Duke University Press, 1990.

9217. Glazer, Mark. *A Dictionary of Mexican American Proverbs*. Westport, CT: Greenwood, 1987.

9218. Goldensohn, Barry. "[Ezra] Pound and Antisemitism." *Yale Review* 75 (1986): 399-421.

9219. Gounard, Jean-Francois. *The Racial Problem in the Works of Richard Wright and James Baldwin*. Westport, CT: Greenwood, 1991.

9220. Grauerholz, Elizabeth, and B. A. Pescosolido. "A Note on the Renegotiation of Hegemony: Cultural Crisis and Images of Blacks in Children's Picture Books, 1938-1986." Sociological Abstracts, Accession No. 89521433.

9221. Greenblatt, Stephen. "The Best Way to Kill Our Literary Inheritance Is to Turn It into a Decorous Celebration of the New World Order." *Chronicle of Higher Education* (12 June 1991). [See Will, below]

9222. Grigsby, John L. "The Poisonous Snake in the Garden: Racism in the Agrarian Movement." *CLA Journal* 34 (September 1990): 32- 43.

9223. Grimsted, David. "Anglo-American Racism and Phyllis Wheatley's 'Sable Veil', 'Lengthened Chain', and 'Knitted Heart'." in *Women in the Age of the American Revolution*, eds. Ronald Hoffman, and Peter J. Albert. Charlottesville: University Press of Virginia, 1989.

9224. Hanson, Elizabeth S. *The American Indian in American Literature: A Study in Metaphor*. Lewiston, NY: Edwin Mullen, 1988.

9225. Harris, Ruby M. *A Survey and Content Analysis of the Black Experience as Depicted in Contemporary Fiction for Children*. Ph.D. diss., Boston College, 1989. UMO # 8922284.

9226. Hay, Samuel A. *African American Theatre. An Historical and Critical Analysis*. Cambridge University Press, 1994.

9227. Hemp, Paul, Beyond Winnie the Pooh. *Boston Blobe*, 5 May 1992. [Minority market for children's books]

9228. Henry, William A., III. "When East and West Collide." *Time*, 14 August 1989. [Asian-American playwright David Henry Hwang]

9229. Howard, Elizabeth F. "Books About Black Children A 'Basic Need'." *Education Week*, 14 March 1990.

9230. Jackson, Byden. *The History of Afro-American Literature, Vol. 1*. Baton Rouge, LA: Louisiana State University Press, 1989.

9231. Jeyifous, Abiodum. "Black Critics on Black Theater in America." *Drama Review* 18 (September 1974): 37-39.

9232. Johnson, Dianne A. *For the Children of the Sun: What We Say to Afro-American Youth through Story and Image*. Ph.D. diss., Yale University, 1988. UMO # 8917696.

9233. Joyce, Donald F. "Reflections on the Changing Publishing Objectives of Secular Black Book Publishers, 1900-1986." in *Reading in America: Literature and Social History*, ed. Cathy N. Davidson. Baltimore MD: Johns Hopkins University Press, 1989.

9234. Joyce, Joyce A., Henry Louis Gates, Jr., and Houston A. Baker, Jr. *New Literary History* 18 (1987): 335-384. [Black literary criticism]

9235. Judy, Ronald A. T. *Forming the American Canon: African Arabic Slave Narratives and the Vernacular*. Ph.D. diss., University of Minnesota Press, 1993.

9236. Kanellos, Nicolas. *A History of Hispanic Theater in the United States: Origins to 1940*. Austin: University of Texas Press, 1990.

9237. Kelly, Kevin. "Oleanna Enrages - and Engages." *Boston Globe*, 4 May 1992. [Play by David Mauret]

9238. _____. "[Tazewell] Thompson Tackles the Traditions of the Theater." *Boston Globe*, 24 February 1991.

9239. Kendrick, Dolores. *The Women of Plums: Poems in the Voices of Slave Women*. NY: Morrow, 1989.

9240. Klamer, Arjo and others, eds. *The Consequences of Economic Rhetoric*. NY: Cambridge University Press, 1988.

9241. Kohl, Herbert. "Learning from Life." *Nation* (23 September 1991). [Discussion of Chelsea House Publishers' 40-volume series, Black Americans of Achievement, written for young people]

9242. Kostelantz, Richard. *Politics in the African-American Novel. James Weldon Johnson, W. E. B. DuBois, Richard Wright, and Ralph Ellison*. Westport, CT: Greenwood, 1991.

9243. Krupat, Arnold. *The Voice in the Margin: Native American Literature and the Canon*. Berkeley: University of California Press, 1989.

9244. Labor, Earle and others, eds. *The Letters of Jack London*. 3 Volumes. Stanford, CA: Stanford University Press, 1988. [Contains many expressions of racism]

9245. LaCapra, Dominick, ed. *The Bounds of Race Perspectives on Hegemony and Resistance*. Ithaca, NY: Cornell University Press, 1991.

9246. Lahr, John. "Under the Skin." *New Yorker*, 28 June 1993. [Anna Deavere Smith and her "Twilight": Los Angeles 1992]

9247. Lauter, Paul. *Canons and Context*. NY: Oxford University Press, 1991.

9248. Lenz, Gunter H., ed. *History and Tradition in Afro-American Culture*. Frankfurt: Campus, 1984.

9249. Leong, Russell C. "Poetry within Earshot: Notes on an Asian American Generation 1968-1978." *American Journal* 15 (1989): 165- 193.

9250. Little, Jonathan D. *Definition through Difference: The Tradition of Black-White Miscegenation in American Fiction*. Ph.D. diss., University of Wisconsin, Madison, 1989. UMO # 8915545.

9251. Lomeli, Francisco A., ed. "Hispanic Literature in the United States: Theoretical and Critical Approaches." *Discurso* 7 (1990): 5-140, special issue.

9252. Lopez Gonzalez, Arabia and others, eds. *Mujer y literatura mexicana y chicaca: Culturas en contacto, II*. Mexico City: Colegio de Mexico, 1990.

9253. Lorant, Laurie. *Herman Melville and Race: Themes and Imagery*. Ph.D. diss., New York University, 1972.

9254. MacCann, Dormarse C. *The White Supremacy Myth in Juvenile Books about Blacks, 1830-1900*. Ph.D. diss., University of Iowa, 1988. UMO # 8913203.

9255. Maccoby, Hyam. "The Anti-Semitism of T. S. Eliot." *Midstream* 19 (1973): 68-79.

9256. Maddox, Lucy. *Removals: Nineteenth-Century American Literature and the Politics of Indian Affairs*. Oxford University Press, 1991.

9257. Mathews, Jay. "'Golden Gate's' David Henry Hwang: Burning Bridges." *Washington Post*, 30 January 1994.

9258. Matthews, Victoria Earle. "The Value of Race Literature." *Massachusetts Review* 27 (1986): 159-191. [1895]

9259. Max, Daniel. "McMillan's Millions." *New York Times Magazine*, 9 August 1992. [Terry McMillan]

9260. Mayberry, Katherine J. "White Feminists Who Study Black Writers." *Chronicle of Higher Education* (16 October 1994).

9261. McCaskill, Barbara Ann. *To Rise Above Race: Black Women Writers and their Readers, 1859-1939*. Ph.D. diss., Emory University, 1988.

9262. McCraw, William. "Fascist of the Last Hour." *San Jose Studies* 12 (1986): 46-57. [Ezra Pound]

9263. McDowell, Deborah E., and Arnold Rampersad, eds. *Slavery and the Literary Imagination*. Baltimore, MD: Johns Hopkins University Press, 1989.

9264. McDowell, Edwin. "Black Writers Gain Audiences and Visibility in Publishing." *New York Times*, 12 February 1991.

9265. McKay, Claude. *Harlem Glory. A Fragment of Aframerican Life*. Chicago, IL: Charles H. Kerr, 1990. [A novel]

9266. Melhem, D. H. *Heroism in the New Black Poetry: Introduction and Interviews*. Lexington: University Press of Kentucky, 1989.

9267. Meves, Antonio. "La marginacion del negro en la literatura puertorriquena." *Revista/Review Interamericana* 18 (1988): 112-119.

9268. Miller, R. Baxter. *The Art and Imagination of Langston Hughes*. Lexington: University Press of Kentucky, 1989.

9269. Mills David. "Simply Wonderful." *Washington Post*, 6 October 1993. [Black plays]

9270. Morrison, Toni. *Playing in the Dark. Whiteness and the Literary Imagination*. Cambridge, MA: Harvard University Press, 1992.

9271. Mosley, Walter. "Heroes in Black, Not White." *New York Times*, 15 June 1994. [Author of detective novels]

9272. Multicultural Literature, IV. *ADE Bulletin* 91 (Winter 1988): 29-62. [Mexican-American and Puerto Rican writers]

9273. Murphy, J. S. "Some Thoughts About Class, Caste, and the Canon." *Teachers College Board* 93 (Winter 1991): 265-280.

9274. Muslin, H. L. "The Jew in Literature: The Hated Self." *Israel Journal of Psychiatry and Related Sciences* 27 (1990).

9275. Nelson Salvino, Dana. *Problems of Knowing Constructions of "Race" in American Literature, 1638-1867*. Ph.D. diss., Michigan State University, 1989. UMO # 8923887.

9276. Njeri, Itabari. "A Mirror on Our Fires." *Los Angeles Times*, 14 June 1992. [Anna Deavere Smith, performance artist of racial conflict]

9277. Nuernbery, Susan M. *The Call of Kind: Race in Jack London's Fiction*. Ph.D. diss., University of Massachusetts, 1990. UMO # 9022729.

9278. Oberon Garcia, Claire. "Emotional Baggage in a Course on Black Writers." *Chronicle of Higher Education* (27 July 1994).

9279. Osborne, Stephen D. *Indian-Hating in American Literature, 1682-1857*. Ph.D. diss., University of Washington, 1989. UMO # 9006983.

9280. Otis, Lauren. "Contemporary Urban Fiction: Racially Myopic, or The New Racial Realism." *Crisis* 96 (November 1989): 12-13, 47-48.

9281. Pao, Angela. "The Critic and the Butterfly: Sociocultural Contexts and the Reception of David Henry Hwang's M. Butterfly." *Amerasia Journal* 18 (1992): 1-16.

9282. Pearson, Michael. "The Double Bondage of Racism in Walker Percy's Fiction." *Mississippi Quarterly* 41 (September 1988): 479-495.

9283. Pease, Donald E. "New Americanists: Interventions into the Canon." *boundary 2* 17 (March 1990): 1-37.

9284. Perkins, Kathy A., ed. *Black Female Playwrights. An Anthology of Plays before 1950*. Bloomington: Indiana University Press, 1989.

9285. "Play Helps Town Look at Racists." *New York Times*, 23 November 1990. ["The Foreigner" by Larry Shue, in Metaline Falls, Washington]

9286. Rainey, Kenneth T. "Race and Reunion in Nineteenth-Century Reconciliation Drama." *American Transcendental Quarterly* 2 (June 1988): 155-169. [After Civil War]

9287. Rans, Geoffrey. "Inaudible Man: The Indian in the Theory and Practice of White Fiction." *Canadian Review of American Studies* 8 (September 1877): 103-116.

9288. Rath, Sura P. "Romanticizing the Tribe: Stereotypes in Literary Portraits of Tribal Cultures." *Diogenes* 148 (December 1989): 61-77.

9289. Reilly, J. "Under the White Gaze: Jim Crow, the Nobel, and the Assault on Toni Morrison." *Monthly Review* 45 (April 1994): 41-46.

9290. Reynolds, Craig A. *Afro-American Experiential Poetry*. Ph.D. diss., University of Maryland, 1989. UMO # 8924221.

9291. Rindo, Ronald J. *Fallen Rainbow Over the Promised Land; Federal Indian Policy and American Frontier Fiction, 1819-1830*. Ph.D. diss., University of Wisconsin - Milwaukee, 1989. UMO # 9003106.

9292. Robles, Al. "Hanging on To the Carabao's Tail." *Amerasia Journal* 15 (1989): 195-218. [On and of Asian American poetry]

9293. Rocard, Macienne, and Edward G. Brown, Jr. *The Children of the Sun: Mexican-Americans in the Literature of the United States*. Tucson: University Press of Arizona, 1989.

9294. Rose, Lloyd. "Rollin': The Unsung Vaudevillians." *Washington Post*, 16 November 1993. [Black vaudevillians]

9295. Rothstein, Mervyn. "Festival Sets Goal For Black Theater: New Togetherness." *New York Times*, 17 August 1989. [1988 National Black Theater Festival, Winston-Salem, N. C.

9296. Rubenstein, Roberta. *Boundaries of the Self: Gender, Culture, Fiction*. Urbana: University of Illinois Press, 1987.

9297. Ruoff, A. La Vonne Brown, and Jerry W. Ward, Jr., eds. *Redefining American Literary History*. NY: Modern Language Association of America, 1990.

9298. Sampson, Henry T. *The Ghost Walks: A Chronological History of Blacks in Show Business, 1865-1910*. Metuchen, NJ: Scarecrow Press, 1988.

9299. San Juan, E., Jr. *Carlos Bulosan and the Imagination of the Class Struggle*. Quezon City: University of the Philippines Press, 1972.

9300. _____. "Mapping the Boundaries: The Filipino Writer in the U. S. A." *Journal of Ethnic Studies* 19 (March 1991): 117-131.

9301. _____. "Race and Literary Theory: From Difference to Contradiction." *Proteus* 7 (March 1990): 32-36. [Touches on racism]

9302. Sanders, Leslie C. *The Development of Black Theater in America: From Shadows to Selves*. Baton Rouge: Louisiana State University Press, 1988.

9303. Saxton, Alexander. "The Racial Trajectory of the Western Hero." *Amerasia Journal* 11 (1984): 67-79.

9304. Scharina, Richard G. *From Class to Caste in American Drama. Political and Social Themes Since the 1930's*. Westport, CT: Greenwood, 1991.

9305. Shirley, Carl R., and Paula W. Shirley. *Understanding Chicano Literature*. Columbia: University of South Carolina Press, 1988.

9306. Skloot, Robert. "Theatrical Images of Genocide." *Human Rights Quarterly* 12 (May 1990): 185-201.

9307. Slapin, Beverly, and Doris Seale, eds. *Through Indian Eyes. The Native Experience in Books for Children*. New Society Publishers, 1992. [3rd edition]

9308. Smith, Beverly B. *The Ecology of Nativism in the American Theatre, 1917-1929: A Semiotic Study*. Ph.D. diss., Kent State University, 1992. UMO # 9300375.

9309. Snead, James. "Racist Traces in Postmodernist Theory and Literature." *Critical Quarterly* 33 (March 1991): 31-39.

9310. Sohn, Hongeal. *Literature and Society: African-American Drama and American Race Relations.* Ph.D. diss., University of Iowa, 1993. UMO # 9334661.

9311. Sollors, Werner, and Maria Diedrich, eds. *The Black Columbiad. Defining Moments in African American Literature and Culture.* Harvard University Press, 1994.

9312. Suhl, Isabelle. "Doctor Doolittle--The Great White Father." *Interracial Books for Children* 2 (1968).

9313. Sundquist, Eric J. *To Wake the Nations. Race in the Making of American Literature.* Harvard University Press, 1992.

9314. Swann, Brian, and Arnold Krupat, eds. *Recivering the Word. Essays in Native American Literature.* Berkley: University of California Press, 1990.

9315. Tate, Claudia. "Laying the Floor: Or, The History of the Formation of the Afro-American Canon." *Book Research Quarterly* 3 (Summer1987): 60-78.

9316. Tedesco, John L. "The White Character in Black Drama, 1955- 1970: Description and Rhetorical Function." *Communication Monograph* 45 (1978): 64-74.

9317. Thelwell, Michael. "Modernist Fallacies and the Responsibility of the Black Writer." in *Duties, Pleasures, and Conflicts. Essays in Struggle*, pp. 218-232. Amherst: University of Massachusetts Press, 1987.

9318. Tongchinsub, Helen J. *The Treatment of American Indians, Asian Americans, and Hispanic Americans in Selected Literature Anthologies Used in Grades Seven through Twelve Published since 1980.* Ph.D. diss., University of Pittsburgh, 1988. UMO # 8911387.

9319. Torres, Luis A. *From Imitation to Diversification: Nineteenth Century California Pre-Chicano Poetry.* Ph.D. diss., University fo Washington, 1989. UMO # 9013824.

9320. Turner, Lorenzo D. "Walt Whitman and the Negro." *Chicago Jewish Forum* 15 (September 1953).

9321. Vandell M. "Using Multicultural Literature to Confront Racism and Conflict." *Reading Teacher* 44 (February 1991): 368.

9322. Wall, Cheryl A., ed. *Changing Our Own Words. Essays on Criticism, Theory, and Writing by Black Women.* New Brunswick, NJ: Rutgers University Press, 1989.

9323. Warren, Kenneth W. *Black and White Strangers. Race and American Literary Realism.* Universtiy of Chicago Press, 1993.

9324. Will, George F. "Literary Politics: 'The Tempest'? It's 'Really' About Imperialism. Emily Dickinson's Poetry? Masturbation." *Newsweek*, 22 April 1991. [See Greenblatt, above]

9325. Willis, Susan. *Specifying Black Women Writing the American Experience.* Madison: University of Wisconsin Press, 1989.

9326. Wilson, August. "How to Write a Play Like August Wilson." *New York Times*, 10 March 1991.

9327. _____. "I Want a Black Director." *New York Times*, 26 September 1990. [Written by a Black playwright]

9328. Wilson, Christopher P. *White Collar Fictions: Class and Social Representation in American Literature, 1885-1925.* Athens: University of Georgia Press, 1992.

9329. Wong, Sau-Ling Cynthia. *Reading Asian American Literature. From Necessity to Extravagance.* Princeton University Press, 1994.

9330. Yardley, Jonathan. "A Case for Colorblind Leadership." *Washington Post*, 28 December 1992.

9331. Young, Joseph A. *Black Novelist as White Racist: The Myth of Black Inferiority in the Novels of Oscar Micheaux.* NY: Greenwood Press, 1989.

9332. Yuill, Phyllis J. *Little Black Sambo: A Closer Look: A History of Helen Bannerman's 'The Story of 'Little Black Sambo' and Its Popularity/Controversy in the United States.* NY: Council on Interracial Books for Children, 1976.

9333. Zafar, Rafia M. *White Call, Black Response: Adoption, Subversion, and Transformation in American Literature from the Colonial Era to the Age of Abolition.* Ph.D. diss., Howard University, 1989. UMO # 8926201.

9334. Zill, Nicholas, and Marianne Winglee. *Who Reads Literature? The Future of the United States as a Nation of Readers.* Calvin John, MD: Seves Locks Press, 1990.

LOCALITY -- ALABAMA

9335. Applebome, Peter. "In Selma, Everything and Nothing Changed." *New York Times*, 2 August 1994.

9336. Chestnut, J.L., Jr. *Black in Selma*. Toronto: Harper and Collins, 1990.

9337. Fitto, Alston III. *Selma: Queen City of the Blackbelt*. Selma, Alabama: Clairmont Press, 1989.

9338. Fly, Jerry W., and George R. Reinhart. "Racial Separation during the 1970s: The Case of Birmingham." *Social Forces* 58 1255- 1262.

9339. Kelley, Robin D. G. *Hammer and Hoe, Alabama Communists During the Great Depression*. Chapel Hill: University of North Carolina Press, 1990.

9340. Morris Aldon D. "Birmingham Confrontation Reconsidered: An Analysis of the Dynamics and Tactics of Mobilization." *American Sociological Review* 58 (October 1993): 621-636. [1963]

9341. Smothers, Ronald. "Alabama Town Is Torn Again By Racial Strife." *New York Times*, 6 October 1992. [Fort Deposit, Lowndes County]

9342. U.S. Commission on Civil Rights, Alabama Advisory Committee. *Crisis and Opportunity: Race Relations in Selma*. U.S. Commission on Civil Rights, December 1991.

9343. Wilson, B. M. "Structural Imperatives Behind Racial Change in Birmingham, Alabama." *Antipode* 24 (July 1992): 171-202.

LOCALITY -- ALASKA

9344. Berger, Thomas R. *Village Journey. The Report of the Alaska Native Review Commission*. NY: Hill and Wang, 1985.

9345. Case, David S. "Subsistence and Self-Determination: Can Alaska Natives Have a More Effective Voice?" *University of Colorade Law Review* 60 (September 1989): 1009-1035.

9346. Jones, Dorothy Knee. *The Status of Women in Alaska*. Alaska Commission on Human Rights, 1977.

9347. Jorgensen, Joseph G. *Oil Age Eskimos*. Berkeley: University of California Press, 1990.

9348. Kanazawa, Tooru J. *Sushi and Sourdough*. Seattle: University of Washington Press, 1989. [Fictionalized memoir of first Japanese settlers in Alaskan and Pacific Northwest frontier.]

9349. Karpoff, J. M., and E. M. Rice. "Structure and Performance of Alaska Native Corporations." *Contemporary Policy Issues* 10 (July 1992)

9350. Niedermeyer, Deborah. "The True Interests of a White Population: The Alaska Indian Country Decisions of Judge Matthew P. Deady." *New York University Journal of International Law and Politics* 21 (September 1988): 195-257.

9351. Osborn, Kevin. *The Peoples of the Arctic*. NY: Chelsea House, 1990. [Inuit and Aleuts]

9352. Overstreet, Everett L. *Black on a Background of White: A Chronicle of Afro-Americans' Involvement in America's Last Frontier*. Fairbanks, Alaska: Alaska Black Caucus, 1988.

9353. Spencer, Hal. "As Isolationism and Racism Intersect." *New York Times*, 23 October 1987. [Anchorage, Alaska]

9354. Steltzer, Ulli. *Inuit. The North in Transition*. Chicago, IL: University of Chicago Press, 1985.

9355. Thalpa, Megh P. *Gender and Ethnic Inequality in Alaska: Changes in Educational and Occupational Attainment, 1970-80*. Ph.D. diss., Stanford University, 1989. UMO # 8912943.

9356. Torrey, Barbara. *Slaves of the Harvest: The Story of the Tribe of Aleuts*. Tanadgusix Corporation, 1978.

LOCALITY -- ARIZONA

9357. Dimas, Pete R. *Progress and a Mexican-American Community's Struggle for Existence: Phoenix's Golden Gate Barrio.* Ph.D. diss., Arizona State University, 1991.

9358. Koenenn, Connie. "A Bridge Between Two Worlds." *Los Angeles Times*, 9 May 1994. [The Hopi Nation]

9359. Officer, James E. "Historical Factors in Interethnic Relations in the Community of Tuscon." *Arizoniana* (Fall 1960): 12-16.

LOCALITY -- ARKANSAS

9360. Gordon, Fon Louise. *The Black Experience in Arkansas, 1880- 1920.* Ph.D. diss., University of Arkansas, 1989, UMO # 8925689.

9361. Graves, John W. *The Arkansas Negro and Segregation 1890- 1903.* Master's thesis, University of Arkansas, Fayetteville, 1967.

9362. _____. "Jim Crow in Arkansas: A Reconsideration of Urban Race Relations in the Post-Reconstruction South." *Journal of Southern History* 55 (August 1989): 421-448.

9363. _____. *Town and Country: Race Relations in an Urban- Rural Context, Arkansas,1865-1905.* Fayetteville: University of Arkansas Press, 1990.

9364. Hendrickson, Paul. "Orval Faubus and the Shadow of History." *Washington Post*, 25 January 1993. [Former governor of Arkansas who defied desegregation in 1957]

9365. Holmes, Steven A. "Race Relations in Arkansas Reflect Gains for Clinton, But Raise Questions." *New York Times*, 3 April 1992.

9366. Shaw, Wendy. *Poverty in Arkansas since World War II.* Master's thesis, University of Arkansas, Fayetteville, 1990.

9367. Spitzberg, Irving J., Jr. *Racial Politics in Little Rock, 1954-1964.* NY: Garland, 1989.

9368. Sylva, Michael F. Black Populations in Arkansas. Master's thesis, University of Arkansas, Fayetteville, 1981.

LOCALITY -- CALIFORNIA

9369. Acuna, Rodolfo F. *A Community Under Siege: A Chronicle of Chicanos East of the Los Angeles River, 1945-1975*. Chicano Studies Research Center, UCLA.

9370. Alarcon, Evelina. "The Los Angeles Rebellion." *Political Affairs* (June 1992).

9371. Aubry, Larry. "I See an Erosion of Values, an Erosion of Caring." *Los Angeles Times*, 28 March 1994. [South Central Los Angeles]

9372. Benson, Todd. "The Consequences of Reservation Life: Native Californians on the Round Valley Reservation, 1871-1884." *Pacific Historical Review* 60 (1991): 221-244.

9373. Broussard, Albert S. *Black San Francisco: The Struggle for Racial Equality in the West, 1900-1954*. University Press of Kansas, 1993.

9374. Burchell, Robert A. "The Faded Dream: Inequity in Northern California in the 1860s and 1870s." *Journal of American Studies* 23 (1989): 215-234.

9375. Cain, Bruce E., and D. Roderick Kiewiet. *Minorities in California*. Pasadena: California Institute of Technology, 1986.

9376. California, State of, Fair Employment Practice Commission. *Negroes and Mexican American in South and East Los Angeles*. January 1968.

9377. Carlton, Robert L. *Blacks in San Diego County 1850-1900*. Master's thesis, San Diego State University, 1977.

9378. Childs, John Brown. "Preparing for the 'Big One'." *Z Magazine* 5 (July 1992): 56-58. [Los Angeles uprising of April-May 1992]

9379. *Civil Liberties in Crisis: Los Angeles During the Emergency*. ACLU of Southern California, 1992.

9380. Cohen, Nathan ed. *The Los Angeles Riots: A Socio- Psychological Study*. Praeger, 1970. [Watts Riot]

9381. Conot, Robert. *Rivers of Blood, Years of Darkness*. Bantam Books, 1967. [Watts Riot]

9382. Corwin, Miles. "How Good a Student is L.A.?" *Los Angeles Times*[The aftermath of riots in Miami and Los Angeles]

9383. Daniels, Douglas H. *Pioneer Urbanites, A Social and Cultural History of Black San Francisco*. Berkley: University of California Press, 1991.

9384. Davis, Mike. *City of Quartz: Excavating the Future in Los Angeles*. NY: Verso, 1990.

9385. _____. "Ignore Riot Mythology and Deal with Real L.A." *Los Angeles Times*, March 1993.

9386. _____. "The L.A. Inferno. April 30 [1992]." *Socialist Review* 22 (January-March 1992): 57-80.

9387. _____. "Who Killed Los Angeles? Part Two: The Verdict is Given." *New Left Riview* 199 (May 1993): 29-54.

9388. Deverell, William, and Tom Sitton, eds. *California Progressivism Revisited*. University of California Press, 1994.

9389. Dunn, Ashley, and Shaun Hubler. "Unlikely Flash Point for Riots." *Los Angeles Times*, 5 July 1992. [Origins of Los Angeles riot of 1992 in some of the more stable neighborhoods of the city.]

9390. Easton, Nina J. "Bringing It All Back Home." *Los Angeles Times*, 26 October 1992. [Crenshaw area, Los Angeles]

9391. *Ethnic Antagonisms in Los Angeles*. UCLA Los Angeles County Social Survey, 1992.

9392. Fisher, J. *A History of the Political and Social Development of the Black Community in California 1850-1950*. Ph.D. diss., State University of New York at Stony Brook, 1971.

9393. Fong, Timothy P. *The First Suburban Chinatown: The Remaking of Monterey Park, California*. Temple University Press, 1994.

9394. Frakes, George E., and Curtis B. Solberg, eds. *Universities in California History*. NY: Random House, 1971.

9395. Garcia, Mikel, and Jerry Wright. "Race Consciousness in Black Los Angeles, 1886-1915." *CAAS Reports* 12 (Spring-Fall 1989): 4-5.

9396. George, Lynell. *No Crystal Stair. African Americans in the City of Angels*. Verso, 1992.

9397. Georges, Kathi, and Jennifer Joseph, eds. *The Verdict Is In*. Manic D Press, 1993. [Rodney King beating case in Los Angeles]

9398. Gooding-Williams, Robert, ed. *Reading Rodney King/ Reading Urban Uprising*. Routledge, 1993.

9399. Granberry, Michael. "A Tribe's Battle for Its identity." *Los Angeles Times*, 13 March 1994. [Juaneno Band of Mission Indians]

9400. Griswold del Castillo, Richard. "Southern California Chicano History: Regional Origins and National Critique." *Aztlan* 19 (Spring 1988/1990): 109-124.

9401. Gwynn, Douglas B. and others. *California Rural Poor: Trends, Correlates and Policies*. Davis, CA: The California Institute of Rural Studies, University of California, 1989.

9402. Haas, Mary L. *The Barrios of Santa Ana: Community, Class, and Urbanization, 1850-1947*. Ph.D. diss., University of California, 1985. UMO # 8527418.

9403. Haitman, Diane. "Can the Arts Heal L.A.?" *Los Angeles Times*, 6 September 1992.

9404. Harris, Scott. "'Little India'." *Los Angeles Times*, 1 September 1992. [Artesia, CA]

9405. Hayes-Bautista, David E. *No Longer a Minority: Latinos and Social Policy in California*. UCLA Chicano Studies Research Center, 1992.

9406. Hicks, Joe, Antonio Villaraigosa, and Angela Oh. "Los Angeles Rebellion and Beyond." *Against the Current* 40 (September- October 1992): 44-48.

9407. Hillburg, Bill. "Long Beach Pioneer Recalls 'Chills' She Felt from Racism." *Long Beach Press-Telegram*, 7 February 1993.

9408. _____. "Pioneering Blacks Came to L.B. Seeking New Life." *Long Beach Press-Telegram*, 1 February 1993.

9409. _____. "Racism Was 'Tradition' in Long Beach." *Long Beach Press- Telegram*, 7 February 1993.

9410. Horne, Gerald. "Hell in the City of Angels: 1965 and 1992." *Guild Practitioner* 49 (Summer 1992): 65-72.

9411. Hubler, Shaun. "Tears, No Love, for Inner City." *Los Angeles Times*, 9 August 1992. [Los Angeles and its suburbs]

9412. Katz, Jesse. "Latino Gang Carnage Is Part of an Invisible War." *Los Angeles Times*, 12 July 1992. [Los Angeles]

9413. Kissinger, C. Clark. "L.A. Revisited: A Riot Recast as Rebellion." *National Catholic Reporter*, 18 September 1992.

9414. Klein, Norman M., and Martin J. Schliesh, eds. *Twentieth- Century Los Angeles: Power, Promotion, and Social Conflict*. Claremont, CA: Regina Books, 1990.

9415. Kotkin, Joel. "Perilous Illusions About Los Angeles." *Los Angeles Times*, 14 June 1992. [Interpretations of Los Angeles riots of April 30, 1992]

9416. "Latino Settlements in California." in *The Challenge: Latinos in a Changing California*, University of California SCR 43 Task Force. Riverside, CA: The University of California Consortium on Mexico and the United States (UCMEXUS), 1989.

9417. Madhubuti, Haki R., ed. *Why L.A. Happened. Implications of the '92 Los Angeles Rebellion*. Third World Press, 1993.

9418. Marin, Marguerite V. *Social Protest in an Urban Barrio: A Study of the Chicano Movement, 1966-1974*. Lanham, MD: University Press of America, 1991. [East Los Angeles]

9419. Matsumoto, Valerie. *Farming the Home Place. A Japanese American Community in California, 1919-1982*. Cornell University Press, 1994.

9420. Maxted, Julia, and Abebe Zegeye. "Race, Class and Polarization in Los Angeles." in *Exploitation and Exclusion: Race and Class in Contemporary U.S. Society*, eds. Abebe Zegeye and others. London: Hans Zell, 1991.

9421. McBroome, Delores N. *Parallel Communities: African Americans in California's East Bay, 1850-1963*. Ph.D. diss., University of Oregon, 1991. UMO # 9125224.

9422. McWilliams, Carey. *Southern California: An Island on the Land*. Gibbs Smith, 1990.

9423. Mills, David. "Korean Images of a Torn L.A." *Washington Post*, 14 November 1992.

9424. Monroy, Douglas G. *Thrown Among Strangers. The Making of Mexican Culture in Frontier California*. Berkeley, CA: University of California Press, 1990.

9425. Morefield, Richard. *The Mexican Adaptation in American California, 1846-1875*. San Francisco, CA: R & E Research Associates, 1971.

9426. Morrison, Peter A., and Ira S. Lowry. *A Riot of Color: The Demographic Setting of Civil Disturbance in Los Angeles*. Rand, 1993.

9427. Ong, Paul M., and S. Hee. *Losses in the Los Angeles Civil Unrest: April 29 to May 1, 1992*. Los Angeles, CA: Center for Pacific Rim Studies, University of California, 1993.

9428. Pastor, Manuel. *Latinos and the Los Angeles Uprising: The Economic Context*. Claremont, CA: Tomas Rivera Center, 1993.

9429. Reinhold, Robert. "California Is Proving Ground For Multiracial Vision in U.S." *New York Times*, 16 June 1990.

9430. _____. "Los Angeles Dream Is Dying for Some, Thriving for Others." *New York Times*, 28 August 1989.

9431. Rodriguez, Luis J. *Always Running: A Memoir of La Vida Loca, Gang Days in Los Angeles*. Curbstone, 1992.

9432. Rustin, Bayard. "The Watts 'Manifesto' and the McCone Report." in *Racism in California*, eds. Roger Daniels, and Spencer C. Olin, Jr. : Macmillan, 1972.

9433. Rutten, Tim. "A New Kind of Riot." *New York Review of Books*, 11 June 1992. [Los Angeles, April 30, 1992]

9434. Sanchez, George J. *Becoming Mexican American. Ethnicity, Culture and Identity in Chicano Los Angeles, 1900-1945*. Oxford University Press, 1993.

9435. Sears, David O., and John B. McConahay. *The Politics of Violence: The New Urban Blacks and the Watts Riot*. Houghton Mifflin, 1973.

9436. Sipchen, Bob. "A Riot by Any Other Name." *Los Angeles Times*, 3 August 1992. [Los Angeles events, April 29-30, 1992]

9437. Stall, Bill, and Ralph Frammolino. "Perceptions of Inequity Cloud State Tax System." *Los Angeles Times*, 11 October 1993.

9438. Starr, Kevin. *Material Dreams: Southern California Through the 1920s*. New York, NY: Oxford University Press, 1990.

9439. Taylor, Paul S. "Foundations of California Rural Society." *California Historical Society Quarterly* 29 (September 1945): 193-228.

9440. Torres, Vicki. "Foot Soldiers Add Violent Twist to Asian Street Gangs." *Los Angeles Times*, 15 August 1993. [Southern California]

9441. Tyler, Bruce M. *Black Radicalism in Southern California, 1950-1982*. Ph.D. diss., UCLA, 1983. UMO # 8322041.

9442. UCLA Ethnic Studies Center. *Ethnic Groups in Los Angeles: Quality of Life Indicators*. Los Angeles, CA: University of California Press, 1987.

9443. Vallee, Victor, and Rodolfo D. Torres. "Latinos in a 'Post- Industrial' Disorder." *Socialist Review* 23 (1994): 1-28.

9444. "The Verdict and the Violence." *High Performance* (September 1992): entire issue. [Articles on the Los Angeles riots of April- May 1992]

9445. Weibel-Orlando, Joan. *Indian Country, L.A.: Maintaining Ethnic Community in Complex Society*. University of Illinois Press, 1991.

LOCALITY -- COLORADO

9446. Blea, Irene I. *Bessemer: A Sociological Perspective of a Chicano Barrio.* Ph.D. diss., University of Colorado, 1980.

9447. Cummins, Densil H. *Social and Economic History of Southwestern Colorado, 1860-1948.* Ph.D. diss., University of Texas, 1951.

LOCALITY -- DISTRICT OF COLUMBIA

9455. Abbott, Carl. "Dimensions of Regional Change in Washington, D.C." *American Historical Review* 95 (December 1990): 1367-1393.

9456. DeWitt, Karen. "The Nation's Capital Eagerly Awaits Urban Remedies." *New York Times*, 25 April 1993.

9457. Fitzpatrick, Sandra, and Maria R. Goodwin. *A Guide to Black Washington: A Directory of Places of Black Historic and Cultural Significance in Washington*. NY: Hippocrene Books, 1989.

9458. Harrigan, John J. *Negro Leadership in Washington, D.C.* Ph.D. diss., Georgetown University, 1971.

9459. Jaffe, Harry S., and Tom Sherwood. *Dream City. Race, Power, and the Decline of Washington, D.C.* Simon and Schuster, 1994.

9460. Johnson, Haynes. *Dusk at the Mountain: The Negro, the Nation, and the Capital*. Garden City, NY: Doubleday, 1963.

9461. May, Lee. "Socially, Color Line Is Still Drawn in Nation's Capital." *Los Angeles Times*, 17 January 1989.

9462. Willoughby, John. "For D.C., the Worst of Times." *Against the Current* 2 (May-June 1990): 23-28.

LOCALITY -- DELAWARE

9456. Hornstein, Robert, and Daniel Atkins. "Poverty Amidst Plenty in 1992." *Against the Current* No. 40 (September-October 1992): 26-30.

LOCALITY -- FLORIDA

9457. Clary, Mike, Deep South, Deep Trouble. *Los Angeles Times*, 17 June 1992. [Cross City, FL]

9458. Crooks, James B. *Jacksonville after the Fire, 1901-1919: A New South City*. U. of North Florida Press, 1991.

9459. Evans, Arthur S., Jr, and David Lee. *Pearl City, Florida. A Black Community Remembers*. Gainesville: University Presses of Florida, 1990.

9460. Greenbaum, Susan D. *Afro-Cubans in Ybor City: A Centennial History*. Tampa, FL: 1986.

9461. Landers, Jane L. *Black Society in Spanish St. Augustine, 1784-1821*. Ph.D. diss., University of Florida, 1988.

9462. Maingot, Anthony P. "Relative Power and Strategic Ethnicity in Miami." in *Perspectives in Immigrant and Minority Education*, pp. 36-48. eds. Ronald J. Samuda, and Sandra L. Woods. Lanham, MD: University Press of America, 1983.

9463. Portes, Alejandro, and Alex Stepick. *City on the Edge: The Transformation of Miami*. University of California Press, 1993.

9464. Schafer, Daniel L. "A Class of People Neither Freeman nor Slaves: From Spanish to American Race Relations in Florida, 1821- 1861." *Journal of Social History* 26 (Spring 1993): 587-609.

9465. Schmalz, Jeffrey. "Trial Forces Miami to Confront Its Legacy of Racial Tensions." *New York Times*, 13 November 1989.

LOCALITY -- GEORGIA

9466. Applebome, Peter. "Flood Threatens to Wash Away Dreams." *New York Times*, 16 July 1994. [Blacks in Albany, GA]

9467. Binder, Wolfgang, ed. *America's My Home: Interviews with Young Blacks from Georgia*. NY: Lang, 1984.

9468. Brundage, W. Fitzhugh. "The Darien Insurrection of 1899: Blacks Protest during the Nadir of Race Relations." *Georgia Historical Quarterly* 74 (Summer 1990): 234-253.

9469. Bryant, Jonathan M. *A Country Where Plenty Should Abound: Race, Law, and Markets in Greene County, Georgia, 1850-1885*. Ph.D. diss., U. of Georgia, 1992. UMO # 9316311.

9470. Gottlieb, Martin with Peter Applebome. "Ways of Older South Linger in City of Clarence Thomas's Boyhood." *New York Times*, 8 August 1991. [Savannah, GA]

9471. Greene, Melina F. *Praying for Sheetrock*. Cambridge, MA: Addison-Wesley, 1991. [McIntosh County, GA]

9472. K'Meyer, Tracy E. *Koinonia Farm: Building the Beloved Community in Postwar Georgia*. Ph.D. diss., U of North Carolina, 1993. UMO # 9324060.

9473. Kuhn, Clifford M. and others. *Living Atlanta. An Oral History of the City, 1914-1948*. Athens: University of Georgia Press, 1990.

9474. Shadron, Virginia. *Popular Protest and Legal Authority in Post-World War II Georgia: Race, Class, and Gender Politics in the Rosa Lee Ingram Case*. Ph.D. diss., Emory University, 1991. UMO # 9127621.

LOCALITY -- HAWAII

9475. Abrams, Garry. "The Liberation of Hawaii?" *Los Angeles Times*, 17 January 1993.

9476. Bartey, Beth, and David Farber. *The First Strange Place: Men and Women in Hawaii During World War II*. NY: Free Press, 1992.

9477. Bartey, Beth, and Farber David. "Hotel Street: Prostitution and the Politics of War." *Radical History Review* No. 52 (Winter 1992): 54-77. [Hawaii's vice district during World War II]

9478. Halloran, Richard. "Rare Storm Over Race Disturbs a Melting Pot." *New York Times*, 26 December 1990. [Hawaii]

9479. Holmes, T. Michael. *The Specter of Communism in Hawaii*. U of Hawaii Press, 1994. [1947-1953]

9480. Keaulana, Kimo Alama, and Scott Whitney. "Ka wai kau wai o Maleka water from America: The Intoxication of the Hawaiian People." *Contemporary Drug Problems* 17 (Summer 1990): 161-194.

9481. Kirch, Patrick V. *Anahulu: The Anthropology of History in the Kingdom of Hawaii. Vol II: The Archeology of History*. U of Chicago Press, 1992.

9482. Limerick, Patricia N. "The Multicultural Islands." *American Historical Review* 97 (February 1992): 121-135.

9483. Merrill, Christopher. "A Little Justice in Hawai'i." *Nation* (5 September 1994). [Kaho'olawe island]

9484. Nordyke, Eleanor C. "Blacks in Hawai'i: A Demographic and Historical Perspective." *Hawaiian Journal of History* 22 (1988): 241-255.

9485. Nordyke, Eleanor C., and Richard K. C. Lee. "The Chinese in Hawai'i: A Historical and Demographic Perspective." *Hawaiian Journal of History* 23 (1989): 196-216.

9486. Peterson, Jonathan. "Honolulu Sets Pattern as Capital of Diversity." *Los Angeles Times*, 19 January 1994.

9487. Pukui, Mary Kawena and others. *Nana I Ke Kumu, Look to the Source*. Vol. 2. Hui Hanai: Queen Lili'uokalani Children's Center, 1972.

9488. Reinhold, Robert. "A Century After Queen's Overthrow, Talk of Sovereignty Shakes Hawaii." *New York Times*, 8 November 1992.

9489. Sahlins, Marshall. *Anahulu: The Anthropology of History in the Kingdom of Hawaii. Vol. I: Historical Ethnography*. U of Chicago Press, 1992.

9490. Scruggs, Marc. "Anthony D. Allen: A Prosperous American of African Descent in Early 19th Century Hawaii." *Hawaiian Journal of History* 26 (1992): 55-93.

9491. Spriggs, Matthew. "The Hawaiian Transformation of Ancestral Polynesian Society: Conceptualizing Chiefly States." in *State and Society*, pp. 57-73. eds. John Gladhill and others. : Unwin Hyman, 1988.

9492. Stephan, C. W. "Ethnic Identity among Mixed-Heritage People in Hawaii." *Symbolic Interaction* 14 (Autumn 1991): 261-178.

9493. Tate, Merze. "Slavery and Racism as Deterrents to the Annexation of Hawaii 1854-1855." *Journal of Negro History* 47 (1962): 1-18.

LOCALITY -- ILLINOIS

9494. Capitanini, Lisa, and James Ylisela, Jr. "City and Edison Fiddle While Blackout Threat Grows." *Chicago Reporter* 20 (July- August 1991).

9495. Casuso, Jorge, and Eduardo Cauracho. *Hispanics in Chicago*. Chicago, IL: The Chicago Reporter and the Community Renewal Society, 1985.

9496. Hartmann, D. J. "Racial Change in the Chicago Area, 1980- 1987." *Sociology and Social Research* 74 (April 1990).

9497. Mier, Robert. *Social Justice and Local Development*. Sage, 1993. [Chicago in the 1980's]

9498. Nuevo Kerr, Louis Ano. "Mexican Chicago: Chicano Assimilations Aborted, 1939-1954." in *The Ethnic Frontier*, eds. Melvin G. Holli, and Peter d'A Jones. Grand Rapids, Michigan: Erdmans, 1977.

9499. Padilla, Felix M. *Puerto Rican Chicago*. Notre Dame, IN: University of Notre Dame Press, 1987.

9500. Powers, Ron. *Far From Home. Life and Loss in Two American Towns*. NY: Random House, 1991. [Cairo, IL and Kent, CT]

9501. Washington, Laura S., and Curtis Lawrence. "West Side Losses in Clout City." *Chicago Reporter* 19 (December 1990). [Chicago]

9502. Wilkerson, Isabel. "The Tallest Fence: Feelings on Race in a White Neighborhood." *New York Times*, 21 June 1992. [Chicago's Mount Greenwood and Roseland sections, two miles apart]

LOCALITY -- INDIANA

9503. Catlin, Robert A. *Racial Politics & Urban Planning: Gary, Indiana, 1980-1989*. University Press of Kentucky, 1993.

9504. Leininger, Julie. *Chicanos in South Bend : Some Historical Narratives*. Notre Dame, IN: Centro de Estudios Chicanos e Investigaciones Sociales Inc., 1977.

9505. Thornbrough, Emma Lou. *The Negro in Indiana before 1900*. Indiana University Press, 1993.

LOCALITY -- IOWA

9506. Dykstra, Robert R. *Bright Radical Star: Black Freedom & White Supremacy on the Hawkeye Frontier*. Harvard University Press, 1993. [1833 to ca. 1880]

9507. Hull, Jon D. "A White Person's Town?" *Time*, 23 December 1991. [Dubuque, Iowa]

9508. McCormick, John, and Vern E. Smith. "Can We Get Along?" *Newsweek*, 9 November 1992. [Dubuque, Iowa]

LOCALITY -- KANSAS

9509. Frehill-Rowe, Lisa M. "Postbellum Race Relations & Rural Land Tenure : Migration of Black & White to Kansas & Nebraska, 1870-1890." *Social Forces* 72 (September 1993): 77-92.

9510. Gordon, Jacob U. *Narratives of African Americans in Kansas, 1870-1992 : Beyond the Exodust Movement*. Edwin Mellen Press, 1993.

9511. Woods, Randall B. "Integration, Exclusion, or Segregation : The Color Line in Kansas, 1878-1900." *Western Historical Quarterly* 14 (1983).

LOCALITY -- KENTUCKY

9512. Smothers, Ronald. "Livable City Ponders Its Outburst of Anger & Unrest." *New York Times*, 27 October 1994. [Black community in Lexington, KY]

9513. Thomas, Herbert A., Jr. "Victims of Circumstance : Negroes in a Southern Town, 1865-1880." *Register of the Kentucky Historical Society*, 71 (1973): 253-271. [Lexington]

LOCALITY -- LOUISIANA

9514. Espina, Marina E. *Filipinos in Louisiana*. New Orleans, LA: Laborde & Sons, 1988.

9515. Hanger, Kimberly S. *Personas de varias clases y colores : Free People of Color in Spanish New Orleans, 1769-1803*. Ph.D. diss., University of Florida, 1991. UMO # 9201999.

9516. Hirsch, Arnold R., and Joseph Logsdon, eds. *Creole New Orleans. Race & Americanization*. Louisiana State University Press, 1992.

9517. Rankin, David C. "The Impact of the Civil War on the Free Colored Community of New Orleans." *Perspectives in American History* 11 (1977-78): 377-416.

9518. Rinanelli, Marco, and Postwan Sheryl L., eds. *The 1891 New Orleans Lynching and U.S.-Italian Relations. A Look Back*. Peter Lang, 1992.

9519. Vandel, G. "Black Violence in Post-Civil War Louisiana." *Journal of Interdisciplinary History* 25 (Summer 1994): 45-64.

LOCALITY -- MARYLAND

9520. Beyers, Dan. "Memories." *Washington Post Magazine*, 22 November 1992. [Twenty-five years of Columbia, MD a planned community.]

9521. Mc Dougall, Harold A. *Black Baltimore : A New Theory of Community*. Temple University Press, 1993.

9522. McElvey, Kay N. *Early Black Dorchester, 1776-1870 : A History of the Struggle of African-Americans in Dorchester County, Maryland, To Be Free to Make their Own Choices*. Ph.D. diss., University of Maryland, 1991. [749 pp.]. UMO # 9133192.

9523. Phillips, Christopher W. *"Negroes and Other Slaves" : The African-American Community of Baltimore, 1790-1860*. Ph.D. diss., University of Georgia, 1992. UMO # 9235467.

LOCALITY -- MASSACHUSETTS

9524. Chancer, Lynn S. "New Bedford, Massachusetts, March 3, 1983-March 22, 1984 : The 'Before and After' of a Group Rape." *Gender & Society* 1 (September 1987): 239-260.

9525. Gorov, Lynda. "Not All Hostilities Race-based, Say Many in Southie." *Boston Globe*, 23 July 1994. [South Boston, MA]

9526. Graham, Renee. "Complaints Renewed on Inequities of Life in Boston's Minority Areas." *Boston Globe*, 21 May 1991.

9527. Hohler, Bob. "5 Years After Riots, Lawrence's Hispanics Feel Betrayed, Angry." *Boston Globe*, 13 August 1989. [Mass.]

9528. Kahn, Joseph P. "Wellesley's Town Limits." *Boston Globe*, 16 April 1991. [Black and white in the Boston suburb]

9529. Kiang, Peter N. "The New Mix in Boston's Melting Pot." *Boston Globe*, 24 July 1994. [Hispanics and Asians]

9530. Lewis, Diane E. "Cambridge Image Gets a Tarnishing." *Boston Globe*, 21 September 1989. [Racism in Cambridge, Mass. civic affairs]

9531. Mandell, Daniel R. *Behind the Frontier : Indian Communities in Eighteenth-Century Massachusetts.* Ph.D. diss., University of Virginia, UMO # 9237457.

9532. "Menino Calls Race Relations the Overriding Issue for City." *Boston Globe*, 19 September 1994. [Boston mayor]

9533. Rezendes, Michael. "Tarnished Healer." *Boston Globe Magazine*, 20 May 1990. [Boston Mayor Ray Flynn and the city's Black population]

9534. Ribadeneira, Diego, and Renee Graham. "Life Here Is About Surviving." *Boston Globe*, 11 June 1989. [First of three articles, "Roxbury. A Community in Crisis."]

9535. Stapp, Carol B. *Afro-Americans in Antebellum Bostom: An Analysis of Probate Records*. Garland, 1993.

LOCALITY -- MICHIGAN

9536. Levine, David A. *Internal Combustion. The Races in Detroit, 1915-1926*. Westport, CT: Greenwood, 1976.

9537. Marable, Manning. "GM Devastates Flint's Black Community." *Guardian*, 14 March 1990.

9538. McGehee, Scott, and Susan Watson, eds. *Blacks in Detroit: A Report of Articles from the Detroit Free Press*. Detroit, MI: Detroit Free Press, 1980.

9539. Sawyer, Marcia R. *Surviving Freedom: African-American Farm Housholds in Cass County. Michigan, 1832-1880*. Ph.D. diss., Michigan State University, 1991. UMO # 9134163.

9540. Thomas, Frances S., ed. *The State of Black Michigan: 1990*. East Lansing, MI: Urban Affairs Program, Michigan State University, 1990.

9541. Thomas, Richard W. *Life for Us Is What We Make It. Building Black Community in Detroit*. Bloomington, IN: Indiana University Press, 1992.

LOCALITY -- MISSISSIPPI

9542. Applebome, Peter. "A Tragedy Is Transformed Into a 'Miracle' in a Mississippi Town." *New York Times*, 3 January 1994. [Smithdale]

9543. Archer, Chalmers, Jr. *Growing Up Black in Rural Mississippi*. Walker and Co., 1992.

9544. Booth, William. "30 Years in the Life of Jackson, Miss." *Washington Post*, 11 February 1994.

9545. Carpenter, Barbara, ed. *Ethnic Heritage in Mississippi*. University Press of Mississippi, 1992.

9546. Chevigny, Bell Gale. "The Fruits of Freedom Summer." *Nation*, 8 August 1994. [Mississippi]

9547. _____. "Still It's a Fight for Power." *Nation*, 22 August 1994. [Community organizing in Mississippi]

9548. Cobb, James C. *The Most Southern Place on Earth. The Mississippi Delta & the Roots of Regional Identity*. Oxford University Press, 1993.

9549. Connolly, Michael B. *Reconstruction in Kemper County, Mississippi*. Master's thesis, Old Dominion University, 1989. UMO # MA 1339500.

9550. Dunbar, Anthony P. *Delta Time*. New York: Pantheon, 1990. [Mississippi Delta]

9551. Kennedy, Randall L. "'Keep the Nigger Down!' The Age of Segregation in Mississippi." *Reconstruction* 1 (1991): 115-123. [Review discussion of Neil McMillen, *Dark Journey: Black Mississippians in the Age of Jim Crow*]

9552. McMillen, Neil R. *Dark Journey: Black Mississippians in the Age of Jim Crow*. Urbana, IL: University of Illinois Press, 1989.

9553. O'Dell, John H. "Life in Mississippi: An Interview with Fanny Lou Hamer." *Freedomways* 5 (Spring 1965): 231-241.

9554. Salvaggio, D. W. "Mississippi Travelin': A Teacher's Portrait of the South with Continued Racism." *Education* 111 (Summer 1991): 568-572.

9555. Sidey, Hugh. "Sad Song of the Delta." *Time*, 24 June 1991.

9556. Smith, Mary J. *A Study of Race and Community in the New South: Washington County Mississippi, 1920-1940*. Master's thesis, Louisiana University, 1987.

9557. Taulbert, Clifton L. *Once Upon a Time When We Were Colored*. Tulsa, OK: Council Oak Books, 1989. [Glen Allan, MS]

9558. Wilkie, Curtis. "When Races Came Together in Mississippi." *Boston Globe*, 19 September 1994. [War on Poverty since 1960s]

9559. Williams, James L. *Civil War & Reconstruction in the Yazoo Mississippi Delta, 1863-1875*. Ph.D. diss., University of Arizona, 1992. UMO # 9309026.

9560. Woods, W. Leon. *The Travail of Freedom : Mississippi Blacks, 1862-1870.* Ph.D. diss., Princeton University, 1979. UMO # 8003797.

LOCALITY -- MISSOURI

9561. Bourgois, Philippe. "If You're Not Black You're White: A History of Ethnic Relations in St. Louis." *City and Society* 3 (1989): 106-131.

9562. Fellman, Michael. "Emancipation in Missouri." *Missouri Historical Review* 83 (1988): 36-56.

9563. Greene, Lorenzo J. and others. *Missouri's Black Heritage*. St. Louis, MO: Forum Press, 1980.

9564. Jones-Sneed, Frances M. *The Bottom of Heaven: A Social & Cultural History of African Americans in Three Creek, Boone County, Missouri*. Ph.D. diss., University of Missouri, 1991. UMO # 9220818.

9565. Lederer, Katherine. *Many Thousands Gone: Springfield's Lost Black History*. Springfield, MO: K. Lederer, 1986.

9566. Rynearson, Ann M. *Hiding Within the Melting Pot: Mexican Americans in St. Louis*. Ph.D. diss., Washington University, 1980. UMO # 8103699.

LOCALITY -- MONTANA

9567. Emmons, David M. *The Butte Irish: Class and Ethnicity in an American Mixing Town, 1875-1925*. Urbana, IL: University of Illinois Press, 1989.

9568. Lang, William L. "The Nearly Forgotten Blacks On Last Chance Gulch, 1900-1912." in *Montana Vistas*, ed. Robert R. Swartout, Jr. : University Press of America, 1981.

9569. Richards, Paul. "Martin Luther King Day: 48 down, 2 To Go." *In These Times* (20 February 1991). [Successful movement in Montana to declare Martin Luther King, Jr. Day as holiday]

9570. Rosenblatt, Roger. "Their Finest Minute." *New York Times Magazine* (3 July 1994). [Billings, Montana fights racism]

LOCALITY -- NEBRASKA

9571. Frehill-Rowe, Lisa M. "Postbellum Race Relations & Rural Land Tenure: Migration of Blacks & Whites to Kansas & Nebraska, 1870-1890." *Social Forces* 72 (September 1993): 77-92.

LOCALITY -- NEVADA

9672. Au, Beth Amity. *Home Means Nevada: The Chinese in Winnemusca, Nevada, 1870-1950, a Narrative History*. Master's thesis, UCLA, 1993.

9673. Davis, Mike. "Racial Caldron in Las Vegas." *Nation*, 6 July 1992.

LOCALITY -- NEW HAMPSHIRE

9574. Cunningham, Valerie. "The First Blacks of Portsmouth." *Historical New Hampshire* 44 (1989): 180-201.

9575. Kahn, Joseph P. "Pride, or Prejudice." *Boston Globe*, 6 December 1990. [Racism in New Hampshire]

LOCALITY -- NEW JERSEY

9576. Cumbler, John T. *A Social History of Economic Decline: Business, Politics, and Work in Trenton.* New Brunswick, NJ: Rutgers University Press, 1989.

9577. Hodges, Graham R. *African Americans in Monmouth County During the Age of the American Revolution.* Lincroft, NJ: Monmouth County Park System, 1990.

9578. _____. *Black Resistance in Colonial and Revolutionary Bergen County, NJ.* Hackensack, NJ: Bergen County Historical Society, 1989.

9579. Lazare, Daniel. "Collapse of a City." *Dissent* 38 (Spring 1991): 267-275. [Camden, NJ]

9580. Lee, Helen Jackson. *Nigger in the Window.* Garden City, NY: Doubleday, 1978.

9581. Smith, Anna Burtill. "Reminiscences of Colored People of Princeton, New Jersey." *Princeton Recollector* 3 (Winter 1977).

9582. Wright, Giles R. *Afro-Americans in New Jersey: A Short History.* Trenton, NJ: New Jersey Historical Commision, Department of State, 1988.

LOCALITY -- NEW MEXICO

9583. Billington, Monroe. "A Profile of Blacks in New Mexico on the Eve of Statehood." *Password* 32 (1987): 55-66.

9584. Espinosa, J. Manuel, ed. *The Pueblo Indian Revolt of 1696 and the Franciscan Missions in New Mexico: Letters of the Missionaries and Related Documents.* Norman: University of Oklahoma Press, 1988.

9585. Gutierrez, Ramon. *When Jesus Came, the Corn Mother Went Away: Marriage, Sexuality, and Power in New Mexico, 1500-1846.* Stanford, CA: Stanford University Press, 1991.

9586. Heath, Jim F., and Frederick M. Nunn. "Negroes and Discrimination in Colonial New Mexico: Don Pedro Bautista Pino's Startling Statements of 1812 in Perspective." *Phylon* 31,4 (1970): 372-378.

9587. Hordes, Stanley M. "The Inquisition and the Crypto-Jewish Community in Colonial New Spain and New Mexico." in *Cultural Encounters*, eds. Mary E. Perry, and Anne J. Cruz. : University of California Press, 1991.

9588. U.S. Commision on Civil Rights, New Mexico State Advisory Committee. *Survey of Political Participation, Employment and Demographic Characteristics of Eleven Countries in Southern New Mexico.* 2 vols., November 1983. Eric ED 254 387-254 388

9589. Zeleny, Carolyn. *Relations Between the Spanish-Americans and Anglo-Americans in New Mexico: A Study in Conflict and Accomodation in a Dual-Ethnic Situation.* New York: Arno, 1974.

LOCALITY -- NEW YORK

9590. Bavor, Sherrie L. "Development of New York's Puerto Rican Community." *Bronx County Historical Society Journal* 25 (1988): 1- 9.

9591. Bilotta, James D. "Reflections of an African American on His Life in the Greater Buffalo Area, 1930s-1960s." *Afro-American NY Life & History* 13 (July 1989): 47-55.

9592. Castle, Musette S. "A Survey of the History of African Americans in Rochester, New York: 1800-1860." *Afro-American NY Life & History* 13 (July 1989): 7-32.

9593. *Cause for Alarm: The Condition of Black and Latino Males in New York City*. New York: Federation of Protestant Welfare Agencies, 1991.

9594. Chira, Susan. "New York's Poorest Neighborhoods Bear the Brunt of Social Programs." *New York Times*, 16 July 1989. [NYC]

9595. Cooper, Andrew W. "The Two Nations of Crown Heights." *New York Times*, 6 January 1993. [NYC]

9596. "Crown Heights: Behind the Lines." *Village Voice*, 15 December 1992. [Four articles on New York City ethnic/racial crisis]

9597. Dao, James, Casino Issue Hotly Divides Mohawks As New York Reservation Arms Itself. *New York Times*, 22 March 1993. [St. Regis Mohawk Reservation]

9598. Epstein, Jason. "The Tragical History of New York." *New York Review of Books*, 9 April 1992.

9599. Farber, Samuel. "Forgetting Race in New York." *Against the Current* no. 34 (September-October 1991): 41-45. [Critique of Jim Sleeper, The Closest of Strangers: Liberalism and the Politics of Race in New York (1990)]

9600. Farley, Eva L. *The Underside of Reconstruction New York: The Struggle over the Issue of Black Equality*. Garland, 1993.

9601. Finder, Alan. "Majority in New York Poll Finds Quality of Life in City Is Eroding." *New York Times*, 8 October 1993.

9602. Finkelman, R. Paul. "The Protection of Black Rights in Seward's New York." *Civil War History* 34 (1988): 211-234.

9603. Fisher, Ian. "In the Williamsbridge Section of the Bronx, the Races Mix but Don't Mingle." *New York Times*, 2 January 1993.

9604. Foote, Thelma W. *Black Life in Colonial Manhattan, 1664- 1786*. Ph.D. diss., Howard University, 1991. UMO # 9211680.

9605. Getlin, Josh. "Rage and Atonement." *Los Angeles Times*, 29 August 1993. [Black and White in Crown Heights, N.Y.]

9606. Goodfried, Joyce D. *Before the Melting Pot. Society and Culture in Colonial New York City, 1664-1730*. Princeton, NJ: Princeton University Press, 1992.

9607. Greenberg, Cheryl L. *Or Does It Explode? Black Harlem in the Great Depression*. New York: Oxford University Press, 1991.

9608. _____. "The Politics of Disorder: Reexamining Harlem's Riots of 1935 & 1943." *Journal of Urban History* 18 (August 1992): 395-441.

9609. Herring, Paul W. B. *Selected Aspects on the History of the African-American in the Mohawk & Upper Hudson Valley, 1633-1940*. Ph.D. diss., SUNY, Binghampton, 1992. UMO # 9300980.

9610. Hodges, Graham R. "Black Revolt in New York City & the Neutral Zone: 1775-83." in *New York in the Age of the Constitution, 1775-1800*, eds. Paul A. Gilje, and William Pencak. : Farleigh Dickinson University Press, 1992.

9611. Jackson, Peter. *A Social Geography of Puerto Ricans in New York*. Ph.D. diss., Oxford University, 1981.

9612. Lorini, Alessandra. *Public Rituals, Race Ideology & the Transformation of Urban Culture: The Making of the New York African-American Community, 1825-1918*. Ph.D. diss., Columbia University, 1991. UMO # 9209862.

9613. Marcus, Grania B. "A Forgotten People: Discovering the Black Experience in Suffolk County, Chapter V: Daily Life." *Long Island Historical Journal* 1 (Fall 1988): 17-34.

9614. Martinucci, Suzanne. "Why New York." *Crisis* 96 (November 1989): 20-22. [Antiblack action in NYC]

9615. McCormick, John, and Peter McKillop. "The Other Suburbia." *Newsweek*, 26 June 1989. [Poverty in Suffolk County, NY]

9616. McDowell, Winston. "Race and Ethnicity during the Harlem Jobs Campaign, 1932-1935." *Journal of Negro History* 69 (1984): 134-146.

9617. McFadden, Robert D. and others. *Outrage. The Story Behind the Tawana Brawley Hoax*. New York: Bantam Books, 1990.

9618. Mollenkopf, John F., and Manuel Castells, eds. *Dual City. Restructuring New York*. New York: Foundation, 1991.

9619. New York City Department of City Planning. *The Puerto Rican New Yorkers - Part II: Socioeconomic Characteristics and Trends 1970-1980*. New York: The Department, 1985.

9620. New York Mayor's Commission. *The Report of the Mayor's Commission on Black New Yorkers*. New York: The Commission, 1988.

9621. Palmer, Brian. "There Goes the Neighborhood." *Village Voice*, 27 August 1991. [Canarsie, NYC]

9622. Pollack, Andy. "Koch Goes But the Crisis Stays." *Against the Current* 2 (May-June 1990): 18-22.

9623. "Race Rage: a Special Report." *Village Voice*, 29 May 1990. [Series of articles on racial conflict in New York city]

9624. Rieder, J. "Placing Canarsie." *Sociological Forum* 7 (June 1992): 337-354.

9625. Rodriguez, C. E. "Racial Classification among Puerto Rican Men and Women in New York." *Hispanic Journal of Behavioral Science* 12 (November 1990).

9626. Shipp, E. R. "Canarsie's Long-Held Racial Anxieties Resurface." *New York Times*, 8 August 1991.

9627. Torgovnick, Marianna De Marco. "On Being White, Female, and Born in Bensonhurst." *Partisan Review* 57 (Summer 1990): 456-466.

9628. Walker, George E. *The Afro-American in New York City, 1827-1860*. Garland, 1993.

9629. Wasserman, Miriam. *The School Fix, NYC, USA*. New York: Simon & Schuster, Clarion, 1970.

9630. Watkins, Ralph. "A Survey of the African American Presence in the History of the Downstate New York Area." *Afro-American NY Life & History* 15 (1991): 53-79. [New York City since Dutch times]

LOCALITY -- NORTH CAROLINA

9631. *Black/White Perceptions - Race Relations in Greensboro*. Washington, D.C.: U.S. Commission on Civil Rights, 1980.

9632. Bontemps, Anna A. *A Social History of Black Culture in Colonial North Carolina*. Ph.D. diss., University of Illinois, 1989. UMO # 8916216.

9633. Flowers, Linda. *Throwed Away: Failure of Progress in North Carolina*. Knoxville: University of Tennessee Press, 1990.

9634. Furuseth, Owen J., and Wayne A. Walcott. "Defining Quality of Life in North Carolina." *Social Science Journal* 27 (1990).

9635. Gavins, Raymond. "Behind a Veil: Black North Carolinians in the Age of Jim Crow." in *W.J. Cash and the Minds of the South*, ed. Paul G. Escot. : L.S.U. Press, 1992.

9636. _____. "The Meaning of Freedom: Black North Carolina in the Nadir, 1880-1900." in *Race, Class, and Politics in Southern History: Essays in Honor of Robert F. Durden*, ed. Jeffrey J. Crow. Baton Rouge: Louisiana State University Press, 1989.

9637. _____. "North Carolina Folklore and Song in the Age of Segregation: Toward Another Meaning of Survival." *North Carolina Historical Review* 66 (October 1989): 412-442.

9638. Gilmore, Glenda E. *Gender & Jim Crow: Women & the Politics of White Supremacy in North Carolina*. Ph.D. diss., University of North Carolina, Chapel Hill, 1992. UMO # 9234961.

9639. Hanchett, Thomas W. *Sorting Out the New South City: Charlotte and Its Neighborhoods*. Ph.D. diss., University of North Carolina, UMO # 9324043.

9640. Kilborn, Peter T. "Blacks Make Boycott Hurt a Small Town." *New York Times*, 18 August 1994. [Battleboro, N.C.]

9641. Riley, Michael. "The Legacy of Segregation." *Time*, 25 June 1990. [Greensboro, NC]

9642. Spencer, Buffy. "North Carolina: Laboratory for Racism and Repression." *Outfront*, August 1976.

9643. U.S. Commission on Civil Rights, North Carolina Advisory Committee. *Black-White Perceptions: Race Relations in Greensboro: A Report*. Washington, D.C.: The Commission, 1980.

9644. Wetmore, Ruth Y. "The Role of the Indian in North Carolina History." *North Carolina Historical Review* 56 (April 1979): 162- 176.

LOCALITY -- NORTH DAKOTA

9645. Harris, James J. "An Overview of the North Dakota Indian Economy." *North Dakota Quarterly* 44 (1976): 52-66. [1887-1976]

LOCALITY -- OHIO

9646. Bigglestone, William E. *They Stopped in Oberlin: Black Residents and Visitors of the Nineteenth Century*. Scottsdale, Ariz: Innovation Group, 1981.

9647. Cheek, William, and Aimee Lee Cheek. "Culture and Kinship: John Mercer Langston in Cincinnati: 1840-1843." *Queen City Heritage* 47 (Spring 1989): 3-22.

9648. Dougal, April S. *The Toledo Young Men's Christian Association: A Case Study in Urban Segregated Institutions*. Master's thesis, Ohio State University, 1990.

9649. O'Malley, Michael. "Lawyer Lashes Out at Citywide Bigotry." *Cleveland Plain Dealer*, 18 July 1991. [Avery S. Friedman]

9650. *Race Relations in Toledo: A Summary Report of a Community Forum*. Washington, D.C.: Commission on Civil Rights, 1989.

9651. Sawrey, Robert D. *Dubious Victory. The Reconstruction Debate in Ohio*. University Press of Kentucky, 1992.

9652. *The State of Black Cleveland 1990*. Cleveland: The Urban League, July 1990.

LOCALITY -- OKLAHOMA

9653. Moore, John H. "The Myskoke National Question in Oklahoma." *Science and Society* 52 (1988). [Creek Indians]

LOCALITY -- OREGON

9654. Egan, Timothy. "150 Years Later, Indians Cope With the Bitter Results of Settlement." *New York Times*, 1 June 1993.

9655. Thoele, Mike. "Black Island in a Sea of White." *Eugene Register-Guard*, 31 January 1993. [History of African-American settlement in Eugene, Oregon]

LOCALITY -- PENNSYLVANIA

9656. Anderson, Elijah. *Streetwise. Race, Class, and Change in an Urban Community*. Chicago, IL: University of Chicago Press, 1990. [Philadelphia]

9657. Banner-Holey, Charles P. *To Do Good and To Do Well: Middle-Class Blacks & the Depression. Philadelphia, 1929-1941*. Garland, 1993.

9658. Bulter, Ernest W., and Helen M. Butler. *Neighbors of the 2100 Block: A Philadelphia Story*. Pitman, NJ: Webb Press, 1986.

9659. Glasco, Lawrence. "Double Burden: The Black Experience in Pittsburgh." in *City at the Point*, ed. Samuel P. Hays. Pittsburgh, PA: University of Pittsburgh Press, 1989.

9660. Gray, David J. "Shadows of the Past: The Rise & Fall of Prejudice in An American City." *American Journal of Economics and Sociology* 50 (1991): 33-44. [Scranton, PA since the 1930s]

9661. Lane, Roger. *William Dorsey's Philadelphia and Ours. On the Past and Future of the Black City in America*. New York: Oxford University Press, 1991.

9662. Nash, Gary B., and Jean R. Soderlund. *Freedom by Degrees: Emancipation in Pennsylvania and Its Aftermath*. New York: Oxford University Press, 1990.

9663. Oblinger, Carl D. *New Freedoms, Old Miseries: The Emergence and Disruption of Black Communities in Southeastern Pennsylvania, 1780-1860*. Ph.D. diss., Lehigh University, 1988. UMO # 8901884.

9664. O'Brien, Patrick M. *MOVE: News Coverage of Confrontations, Philadelphia, 1978-1987*. Ph.D. diss., University of Iowa, 1992. UMO # 9236992.

9665. Rose, Dan. *Black American Streeet Life. South Philadelphia, 1969-1971*. Philadelphia: University of Pennsylvania Press, 1987.

9666. Stains, Laurence R. "The Latinization of Allentown, Pa." *New York Times Magazine*, 15 May 1994. [Puerto Ricans]

LOCALITY -- SOUTH CAROLINA

9667. Bellardo, Lewis J. *A Social and Economic History of Fairfield County, South Carolina, 1865-1871.* Ph.D. diss., University of Kentucky, 1979. UMO # 8011110.

9668. Black, Chris. "Racism With No Apologies at a Carolina Bar." *Boston Globe*, 10 October 1989. [North Augusta, SC]

9669. Buhler Wilkerson, K. "Caring in Its Proper Place: Race and Benevolence in Charleston, SC, 1813-1930." *Nursing Research* 41 (January-February 1992): 14-20.

9670. Harrison, Eric. "S.C. County Mirrors Gulf Between Races in the South." *Los Angeles Times*, 28 November 1993. [Williamsburg County]

9671. Hill, Walter Byron. *Family, Life, and Work Culture: Black Charleston, South Carolina, 1880 to 1910.* Ph.D. diss., University of Maryland, 1989. UMO # 8924164.

9672. Jenkins, Wilbert L. *Chaos, Conflict & Control: The Responses of the Newly-freed Slaves in Charleston, South Carolina to Emancipation and Reconstruction, 1865-1877* 2 vols. Ph.D. diss., Michigan State University, UMO # 9216316.

9673. Marchio, James. "Nativism in the Old South: Know-Nothingism in Antebellum South Carolina." *S. Historian* 8 (Spring 1987): 39- 53.

9674. Morgan, Philip D. "Black Life in Eighteenth-Century Charleston." *Perspectives in American History* 1 (1984).

9675. Vernon, Amelia W. *African Americans at Mars Bluff, South Carolina.* Louisiana State University Press, 1994.

LOCALITY -- SOUTH DAKOTA

9676. Biolsi, Thomas. *Organizing the Lakota: The Political Economy of the New Deal on the Pine Ridge and Rosebud Reservations*. University of Arizona Press, 1992.

LOCALITY -- TENNESSEE

9677. Ash, Stephen V. *Civil War, Black Freedom, and Social Change in the Upper South: Middle Tennessee, 1860-1870.* 2 vols. Ph.D. diss., University of Tennessee, 1983.

9678. Carriere, Marius, Jr. "Blacks in Pre-Civil War Memphis." *Tennessee Historical Quarterly* 48 (Spring 1989): 3-14.

9679. Hoffochwelle, Mary S. *Rebuilding the Rural Southern Community: Reformers, Schools, and Homes in Tennessee, 1914-1929.* Ph.D. diss., Vanderbilt University, 1993.

9680. McBride, William G. *Blacks and the Race Issue in Tennessee Politics, 1865-1876.* Ph.D. diss., Vanderbilt University, 1989.

9681. Smothers, Ronald. "City Seeks to Grow by Disappearing." *New York Times*, 18 October 1993. [Memphis into Shelby County, TN]

LOCALITY -- TEXAS

9682. Amin, Julius. "Black Lubbock: 1955 to the Present." *West Texas Historical Association Year Book* 65 (1989): 24-35.

9683. Beeth, Howard. "Houston & History, Past and Present: A Look at Black Houston in the 1920s." *Southern Studies* 25 (Summer 1986): 172-181.

9684. Beeth, Howard, and Cary D. Wintz, eds. *Black Dixie: AfroTexan History & Culture in Houston.* Texas A & M University, 1992.

9685. Benson, Nettie L. "Texas Viewed from Mexico, 1820-1834." *Southwestern Historical Quarterly* 90 (1987): 219-291.

9686. Bullard, Robert D., ed. "Blacks in Heavenly Houston." in *In Search of the New South: The Black Urban Experience in the 1070s and 1980s,* pp 16-44. Tuscaloosa, AL.: University of Alabama Press, 1989.

9687. _____. *Invisible Houston: The Black Experience in Boom and Bust.* College Station: Texas A & M University Press, 1987.

9688. Calvert, Robert A., and Arnoldo de Leon. *The History of Texas.* Arlington Heights, IL: 1990.

9689. Christian, Carole E. "Joining the American Mainstream: Texas's Mexican Americans during World War I." *Southwestern Historical Quarterly* 92 (April 1989): 559-595.

9690. "Chuy Ramirez: Innovation Needed." *Pharr Press,* 10 May 1979. [Recalls Chicano progress during past 30 Years; Texas]

9691. Colby, Ira C. *The Freedmen's Bureau in Texas and Its Impact on the Emerging Social Welfare System and Black-White Social Relations, 1865-1885.* Ph.D. diss., University of Pennsylvania, 1984. UMO # 8418265.

9692. Crouch, Barry A. *The Freedman's Bureau and Black Texas.* Austin,TX: University of Texas Press, 1992.

9693. De León, Arnoldo. *Mexican Americans in Texas.* Harlan Davidson, 1993.

9694. _____. *The Tejano Community, 1836-1900.* Albuquuerque, NM: University of New Mexico Press, 1981.

9695. _____. "The Tejano Experience in Six Texas Regions." *West Texas Historical Association Year Book* 65 (1989): 36-49.

9696. _____. "Texas Mexicans: Twentieth-century Interpretation." in *Texas through Time,* eds. Walter L. Buenger, and Robert A. Calvert. : Texas A & M University Press, 1991.

9697. Dyer, James, and others. "Social Distance among Racial Ethnic Groups in Texas: Some Demographic Correlates." *Social Science Quarterly* 70 (September 1989).

9698. Faulk, Odie B. *The Last Years of Spanish Texas, 1778-1821.* The Hague: Mouton, 1964.

9699. Foley, Douglas E. and others. *From Peónes to Politicos: Class and Ethnicity in a South Texas Town, 1900-1987*, Revised ed. Austin: University of Texas Press, 1988.

9700. Foley, Douglas E. *Learning Capitalist Culture, Deep in the Heart of Tejas*. Philadelphia: University of Pennsylvania Press, 1990.

9701. Goldberg, Robert A. "Racial Change of the Southern Periphery: The Case of San Antonio, Texas, 1960-1965." *Journal of Southern History* 49 (August 1983): 349-374.

9702. Graf, LeRoy P. *The Economic History of the Lower Rio Grande Valley, 1820-1875*. Ph.D. diss., Howard University, 1942.

9703. Harrington, James C. "Deep in the Heart of America's Third World." *Los Angeles Times*, 28 February 1993. [Human rights on the South Texas border]

9704. Haynes, Kingsley. *Colonias in the Lower Rio Grande Valley of South Texas*. Austin: Lyndon B. Johnson School of Public Affairs, University of Texas, 1977.

9705. Jackson, Charles C. *A Southern Black Community Comes of Age. Black San Antonio in the Great Depression, 1930-1941*. Master's thesis, Texas A & M University, 1989.

9706. Long, Jeff. *Duel of Eagles: The Mexican and U.S. Fight for the Alamo*. New York: Morrow, 1990.

9707. Maril, Robert Lee. *Living on the Edge of America. At Home on the Texas-Mexico Border*. Texas A & M University Press, 1992.

9708. Marten, James. "What Is To Become of the Negro? White Reaction to Emancipation in Texas." *Mid-America* 73 (April-July 1991): 115-133.

9709. Montejano, David. *Anglos and Mexicans in the Making of Texas, 1836-1986*. Austin: University of Texas Press, 1987.

9710. Montejano-Enriquez, David. *The Making of a Racial Order: A Journey Through Mexican Texas, 1848-1930*. Ph.D. diss., Yale University, 1977.

9711. Orum, Anthony M. *Power, Money, and the People: The Making of Modern Austin*. Austin: Texas Monthly, 1987.

9712. Poyo, Gerald E., and Gilberto M. Hinojosa, eds. *Tejano Origins in Eighteenth-Century San Antonio*. University of Texas Press, 1991.

9713. Richardson, C. F. "Houston's Colored Citizens: Activities and Conditions among the Negro Population." *Southern Studies* 25 (Summer 1986): 182-186.

9714. Saenz, Rogelio, and John K. Thomas. "Minority Poverty in Nonmetropolitan Texas." *Rural Sociology* 56 (1991): 204-223.

9715. Shinn, Vara D. *Social and Economic Status of the Mexican in Texas Since 1910*. Master's thesis, University of Chicago, 1930.

9716. Smallwood, James M. *Time of Hope, Time of Despair: Black Texans During Reconstruction*. Port Washington, NY: Kennekat Press, 1981.

9717. So Relle, James M. "Race Relations in 'Heavenly Houston', 1919-45." in *Black Dixie*, eds. Howard Beeth, and Cary D. Wintz. : Texas A & M University Press, 1992.

9718. Spurlin, Virginia L. *The Corners of Waco: Black Professionals in Twentieth Century Texas*. Ph.D. diss., Texas Tech University, 1991. UMO # 9129412.

9719. Wintz, Cary D. "The Emergence of a Black Neighborhood: Houston's Fourth Ward, 1865-1915." in *Religion and the Life of the Nation: American Recoveries*, ed. Rowland A. Sherrill. Urbana, IL: University of Illinois Press, 1990.

9720. Xie, Jinjing. *The Black Community in Waco, Texas: A Study of Place, Family, and Work, 1880-1900*. Master's thesis, Baylor University, 1988.

LOCALITY -- VERMONT

9721. Daley, Yvonne. "Nazi Flag Display Stirs Furor in Vt." *Boston Globe*, 6 January 1991. [Springfield, VT]

9722. Haviland, William A., and Marjory W. Power. *The Original Vermonters: Native Inhabitants, Past and Present*. Hanover, N.H.: University Press of New England, 1981.

LOCALITY -- VIRGINIA

9723. Brown, Kathleen M. *Gender and the Genesis of a Race and Class System in Virginia, 1630-1750*. Ph.D. diss., University of Wisconsin - Madison, 1990. UMO # 9127487.

9724. De Laney, Theodore C., Jr. "Aspects of Black Religious and Educational Development in Lexington, Virginia, 1840-1928." *Proceedings of the Rockbridge Historical Society* 10 (1980-89): 139-151.

9725. Epperson, Terrence W. *"To Fix a Perpetual Brand": The Social Construction of Race in Virginia, 1675-1750*. Ph.D. diss., Temple University, 1991. UMO # 9120790.

9726. Hartzell, Lawrence L. "The Exploration of Freedom in Black Petersburg, Virginia, 1865-1902." in *The Edge of the South*, eds. Edward L. Ayers, and John C. Willis. : University Press of Virginia, 1991.

9727. Henderson, William D. *The Unredeemed City: Reconstruction in Petersburg, Virginia, 1865-1874*. Washington, D.C.: University Press of America, 1977.

9728. Hoffman, Steven J. *Behind the Facade: The Constraining Influence of Race, Class, and Power on the Elites in the City- building Process, Richmond, Virginia, 1870-1920*. Ph.D. diss., Carnegie Mellon University, 1993. UMO # 9331094.

9729. Holton, Woody. *The Revolt of the Ruling Class: The Influence of Indians, Merchants, and Laborers on the Virginia Gentry's Break with England*. Ph.D. diss., Duke University, 1990. UMO # 9028216.

9730. Lewis, Earl. *In Their Own Interests: Race, Class, and Power in Twentieth-Century Norfolk, Virginia*. Berkeley: University of California Press, 1990.

9731. McGraw, Marie T. "Richmond Free Blacks and African Colonization, 1816-1832." *Journal of American Studies* 21 (1987): 207-224.

9732. Morgan, Lynda J. *Emancipation in Virginia's Tobacco Belt, 1850-1870*. University of Georgia Press: 1992.

9733. Morrow, Lance. "Prince Edward and the Past." *Time*, 20 November 1989. [Race relations in Prince Edward County, Virginia]

9734. Newby, Cassandra L. *"The World Was All before Them": A Study of the Black Community in Norfolk, Virginia, 1861-1884*. Ph.D. diss., College of William & Mary, 1992. UMO # 9304506.

9735. Pincus, Samuel N. *The Virginia Supreme Court, Blacks, and the Law, 1870-1902*. New York: Garland, 1990.

9736. Plunkett, Michael. *African-American Sources in Virginia: A Guide to Manuscripts*. Charlottesville: University Press of Virginia, 1990.

9737. Rachleff, Peter J. "Members in Good Standing': Richmond's Community of Former Slaves, 1865-1873." *Virginia Cavalcade* 39 (1989): 148-157.

9738. Rountree, Helen C. "The Indians of Virginia: A Third Race in a Biracial State." in *Southeastern Indians Service the Removal Era*, pp. pp. 27-48. Athens: University of Georgia Press, 1979.

9739. Schwarz, Philip J. "'A Sense of Their Own Power': Self- Determination in Recent Writings on Black Virginians." *Va. Mag. of History and Biography* 97 (July 1989): 279-310.

9740. Sidbury, James. *Gabriel's World: Race Relations in Richmond, Virginia, 1750-1810.* Ph.D. diss., John Hopkins University, 1991. UMO # 9132730.

9741. Tripp, Steve E. *Restive Days: Race and Class Relations in Lynchburg, Virginia, 1858-1872.* Ph.D. diss., Carnegie Mellon University, 1990. UMO # 9107575.

LOCALITY -- WASHINGTON

9742. Franklin, Joseph. *All Through the Night: The History of Spokane Black Americans, 1860-1940*. Fairfield, WA: Ye Galleon Press, 1989.

9743. Nomura, Gail M. "Within the Law: The Establishment of Filipino Leasing Rights on the Yakima Indian reservation." *American Journal* 13 (1986-87): 99-117. [Washington]

9744. "Political Turmoil in Northwest Follows Racial Slur." *New York Times*, 8 May 1994. [Anti-Chinese remarks in state of Washington]

9745. Taylor, Quintard. "Black Urban Development - Another View: Seattle's Central District, 1910-1940." *Pacific Historical Review* 58 (1989): 429-448.

9746. U.S. Commission on Civil Rights. *Hearing...: American Indian Issues in the State of Washington*. Vol. I. Washington, D.C.: GPO, 1977.

9747. White, Sid, and J. E. Solberg, eds. *People of Washington: Perspectives on Cultural Diversity*. Pullman: Washington State University Press, 1989.

LOCALITY -- WEST VIRGINIA

9748. Trotter, Joe W., Jr. *Coal, Class, and Color. Blacks in Southern West Virginia, 1915-1932*. Urbana, IL: University of Illinois Press, 1990.

9749. Wade, Howard P. *Black Gold and Black Folk: A Case Study of McDowell County, West Virginia's Black Migrants, 1890-1940*. Ph.D. diss., University of Miami, 1990. UMO # 9104420.

LOCALITY -- WISCONSIN

9750. Norman, Jack. "Congenial Milwaukee: A Segregated City." in *Unequal Partnerships: The Political Economy of Urban Redevelopment in Postwar America*, ed. Gregory D. Squires. New Brunswick, NJ: Rutgers University Press, 1989.

LOCALITY -- WYOMING

9751. Guenther, Todd R. "'Y'All Call Me Nigger Jim Now, but Someday You'll Call Me Mr. James Edwards': Black Success on the Plains of the Equality State." *Annals of Wyoming* 61 (Fall 1989): 20-40.

9752. Lamb, David. "Home On the Range - Where Blacks Are Finding a Haven." *Los Angeles Times*, 8 April 1993. [Blacks in Wyoming]

9753. Shalinsky, Audrey C. "Indian-White Relations as Reflected in Twentieth Century Wyoming Town Celebrations." *Heritage of the Great Plains* 21 (1988): 21-34.

MASS MEDIA

9754. Addis, Adeno. "'Hell Man, They Did Invent Us': The Mass Media, Law, and African Americans." *Buffalo Law Review* 41 (Spring 1993): 523-626.

9755. Adelson, Andrea. "How Television Is Cultivating New Ways of Looking at Blacks." *New York Times*, 7 February 1991.

9756. Agboaye, Elrikioya. *Media Agenda-building Effect: Analysis of American Public Apartheid Activities, Congressional and Presidential Policies on South Africa, 1976-1988.* Ph.D. diss., University of North Texas, 1989. UMO #9016152.

9757. Ajaye, Franklyn. "'Apartheid TV' Afects Viewers' Lives." *Los Angeles Times*, 16 November 1992. [Black shows and white shows on prime-time television]

9758. Aksoy, A., and K. Robins. "Hollywood for the 21st Century: Global Competition for Critical Mass in Image Markets." *Cambridge Journal of Economics* 16 (March 1992.

9759. Akudinobi, Jude G. *Under the Sign of Darkness: The Africa Film in the 80's.* Ph.D. diss., University of Southern California, 1988.

9760. Aleiss, Angela M. "American Indian Filmmakers Ignored." *Los Angeles Times*, 25 June 1992.

9761. _____. *From Adversaries to Allies: The American Indian in Hollywood Films, 1930-1950.* Ph.D. diss., Columbia University, 1991. UMO #9209781.

9762. Alexander, A. and others, eds. *Media-Economics: Theory + Practice*. Lawrence Erlbaum Associates, 1993.

9763. Alexander, Elizabeth. "Life in the 'Jet' Stream." *Voice Literary Supplement* (March 1994). [Jet magazine]

9764. Alexander, Nick. "Bay Area Gets Black-run Public TV." *Guardian (NYC)* (25 September 1991). [KMTP-TV, San Francisco, CA]

9765. Allain, Mathe. "They Don't Even Talk Like Us: Cajun Violence in Film and Fiction." *Journal of Popular Culture* 23 (Summer 1989): 65-75.

9766. Alligood, D. L. "When the Medium Becomes the Message: A Proposal for Prinicipal Media Liability for the Publication of Racially Exclusionary Real Estate Advertisiments." *UCLA Law Review* 40 (October 1992): 199-252.

9767. Altheide, David L. "The Impact of Television News Formats on Social Policy." *Journal of Broadcasting and Electronic Media* 35 (Winter 1991): 3-21.

9768. American Psychological Association. *Big World, Small Screen: The Role of Television in American Society*. Lincoln: University of Nebraska Press, 1992.

9769. Ansen, David and others. "The Battle for Malcolm X." *Newsweek* (26 August 1991). [Spike Lee's projected film on Malcolm X]

9770. Applebome, Peter. "On the Past and Future of a Politician: Was [David] Duke Made for TV, or Made by It?" *New York Times*, 20 November 1991.

9771. "Arab-Americans Protest 'True Lies'." *New York Times*, 16 July 1994. [Arnold Schwarzenegger film]

9772. Armstrong, G. B. and others. "TV Entertainment, News, and Racial Perceptions of College Students." *Journal of Communication* 42 (Summer 1992): 153-178.

9773. Aronowitz, Stanley. "Working-class Culture in the Electronic Age." in *Cultural Politics in Contemporary America*, pp. 135-150. eds. Ian H. Angus, and Sut Jhally. New York: Routledge, 1989.

9774. Asante, Molefi K. "Television and Black Consciousness." *Journal of Communication* 26 (Autumn 1976): 137-141.

9775. Astroff, Roberta. "Communication and Contemporary Colonialism: Broadcast Television in Puerto Rico." *Studies in Latin American Popular Culture* 6 (1987): 11-26.

9776. Auster, Albert. "'Funny You Don't Look Jewish': The Image of Jews on Television." *Television Quarterly* 26 (1993): 65-74.

9777. Austin, Sydney B. "AIDS and Africa: United States Media and Racist Fantasy." *Cultural Critique* 14 (Winter 1989-1990): 129-152.

9778. Avisar, Ilan. *Screening the Holocaust. Cinema's Images of the Unimaginable*. Bloomington: Indiana University Press, 1988.

9779. Backes, Mike. "'Sun' Doesn't Perpetuate Stereotypes." *Los Angeles Times*, 7 June 1993. [Denial that film, Rising Sun, is anti-Asian]

9780. Bagdikian, Ben H. *The Media Monopoly*, 3rd Edition ed. Boston, MA: Beacon Press, 1990.

9781. Baker, Ronald L. "Ritualized Violence and Local Journalism in the Devlopment of a Lynching Legend." *Fabula* 29 (1988): 317- 325.

9782. Baraka, Amiri. "Selling Out Malcolm and His Memory." *Washington Post*, 22 November 1992. [Review of "Malcolm X" film, made by Spike Lee.]

9783. Barker, Martin. *Comics: Ideology, Power, and the Critics*. New York: Manchester University Press, 1989.

9784. Barnes, Dawn C. *Portraits of Interracial Romance and Sexuality in Holllywood Cinema: 1965-1975*. Ph.D. diss., University of Maryland, 1992. UMO #9304299.

9785. Barrile, Leo G. "Television's 'Bogeyclass?': Status, Motives and Violence in Crime Drama Characters." *Sociological Viewpoints* 2 (1986): 39-56.

9786. Bass, Charlotta. *Forty Years: Memoirs from the Pages of a Newspaper*. Los Angeles, CA: Bass Publishers, 1960. [Los Angeles Sentinel, an African American publication]

9787. Bataille, Gretchen M., and C. L. P. Silet. "Economic and Psychic Exploitation of American Indians." *Explorations in Ethnic Studies* 6 (July 1993): 8-21.

9788. Bates, Karen G. "'They've Gotta Have Us'. Hollywood's Black Directors." *New York Times Magazine* (14 July 1991).

9789. _____. "Unshackle Race From Sitcom Safety." *Los Angeles Times*, 1 September 1992.

9790. Bayles, Martha. "Television: The Problem with Post- Racism." *New Republic* (5 August 1985).

9791. Benjamin, Playthell. "Farrakhan Returns to TV Land." *Village Voice* (24 April 1990).

9792. _____. "Spike Lee's Oeuvre. Is He Doing the Right Thing?" *African Community* 2-3 (December 1990-January 1991): 8-11.

9793. Berardi, Gayle K., and Thomas W. Segady. "The Development of African-American Newspapers in the American West: A Sociohistorical Perspective." *Journal of Negro History* 75 (Summer-Fall 1990): 96-111.

9794. Berger, Joseph. "Forum for Bigotry and Racist Hate? Fringe Groups on Public-Access TV." *New York Times*, 23 May 1993.

9795. Berlant, Lauren. "Race, Gender, and Nation in The Color Purple." *Critical Inquiry* 14 (Summer 1988): 831-859.

9796. Berman, Marshall. "Close to the Edge: Reflections on Rap." *Tikkun* 8 (March-April 1993): 13-18, 75-78.

9797. Bernstein, Richard. "The Arts Catch Up With a Society in Disarray." *New York Times*, 3 September 1990. [Racism and diversity on stage and in the streets]

9798. _____. "Hollywood Seeks a White Audience For New Black Films." *New York Times*, 17 July 1991.

9799. Berry, Gordon L., and Claudia Mitchell-Kernan, eds. *Television and the Socialization of the Minority Child*. New York: Academic Press, 1982.

9800. Berry, Jason. "Duke's Disguise." *New York Times*, 16 October 1991. [Contends that press has failed to expose facts about the pro-Nazi past of David Duke.]

9801. _____. "Louisiana Hateride." *Nation* (9 December 1991). [David Duke's free ride on the mass media]

9802. "The Best Political Action Newsletters from Around the County-Workplace, Civil Rights, Environment, Policy, Health, Peace." *Social Policy* 20 (Winter 1990).

9803. *Bigotry and Cable TV: Legal Issues and Community Responses*. Baltimore, MD: National Institute Against Prejudice and Violence, April 1988.

9804. Binder, A. "Constructing Racial Rhetoric: Media Depictions of Harm in Heavy Metal and Rap Music." *American Sociological Review* 58 (December 1993): 753-767.

9805. Blades, Ruben. "The Politics Behind the Latino's Legacy." *New York Times*, 19 April 1992. [In the mass media]

9806. Bobo, J. "Black Women's Responses." *Jump Cut* 33 (February 1988): 43-51. ["The Color Purple" film]

9807. Bogle, Donald. *Blacks in American Films and Television: Illustrated Encyclopedia*. New York: Garland, 1988.

9808. _____. *Toms, Coons, Mulattoes, Mammies, and Bucks. An Interpretative History of Blacks in American Films*, New expanded ed. New York: Continuum, 1989.

9809. Bramlett-Solomon, S. "Southern vs. Northern Newspaper Coverage of the Dime Store Demonstration Movement: A Study of News Play and News Source Diversity." *Mass Comm. Review* 15 (1988): 24-30.

9810. Bratt, Larry. "Menace II the Mind." *Washington Post*, 11 July 1993. ["For a generation of Black men in prison, television is the dangerous drug of choice."]

9811. Braxton, Greg. "As Robert Townsend Sees It." *Los Angeles Times*, 3 August 1993. [African American film maker]

9812. _____. "A 'Different' Take on the L.A. Riots." *Los Angeles Times*, 13 August 1992.

9813. _____. "KNBC Shows Commitment to Latinos." *Los Angeles Times*, 14 March 1994. [Los Angeles television station]

9814. _____. "Laughz N the Hood." *Los Angeles Times*, 6 August 1992. [Black comics on HBO television]

9815. _____. "Where More Isn't Better." *Los Angeles Times*, 4 October 1992. [Blacks on television]

9816. Breslauer, Jan. "Out of the Woods?" *Los Angeles Times*, 27 September 1992. [The East West Players, "oldest Asian-American theatre company in the U.S.]

9817. Brooks, Dwight E. *Consumer Markets and Consumer Magazines: Black America and the Culture of Consumption, 1920-1960*. Ph.D. diss., University of Iowa, 1991. UMO #9136901.

9818. Brown, G., and L. Sweet. "Hollywood Shuffle." *Monthly Film Bulletin* 55 (April 1988): 99-100. [Robert Townsend on changing black stereotypes]

9819. Brown, K. F. "The Oklahoma Eagle, a Study of Black Press Survival." *Howard Journal of Communication* 1 (June 1988): 1-11. [Tulsa]

9820. Browne, Nick. "Race: The Political Unconscious in American Film." *East-West Film Journal* 6 (January 1992): 80-92.

9821. Brownlow, Kevin. *Behind the Mask of Innocence: Sex, Violence, Prejudice Crime-Films of Social Conscience in the Silent Era*. New York: Knopf, 1991.

9822. Brownstein, Ronald. "The New York Times on Nazism (1933-1939)." *Midstream* 26 (April 1980): 14-19.

9823. Bullard, Linda M. and others. "Mailbag: A Deaf Ear to 'South Central'." *Los Angeles Times*, 2 May 1994. [Eight letters differing with paper's television critic on the "South Central" show and related matters]

9824. Burd, G. "Minorities in Reporting Texts: Before and After the 1968 Kerner Report." *Mass Comm. Review* 15 (1988): 45-60.

9825. Byrd, Joann. "Handcuffed in Georgetown." *Washington Post*, 26 December 1993. [Newspaper coverage of race and crime]

9826. Campbell, Edward D., Jr. *The Celluloid South. Hollywood and the Southern Myth*. University of Tennessee Press, 1981.

9827. Canby, Vincent. "Black Films: Imitation of Life?" *New York Times*, 8 February 1991.

9828. _____. "Spike Lee Tackles Racism in 'Do the Right Thing'." *New York Times*, 30 June 1989.

9829. _____. "Spike Lee Riffs About an Artist, Not a Genius." *New York Times*, 26 August 1990. [Mo' Better Blues]

9830. Cantor, Louis. *Wheelin' on Beale: How WDIA-Memphis Became the Nation's First All-Black Radio Station and Created the Sound that Changed America*. Pharos, 1992.

9831. Caputi, J., and H. Vann. "Questions of Race and Place." *Cineaste* 15 (1987): 16-21.

9832. Carliss, Richard. "Boyz of New Black City." *Time* (17 June 1991). [Black films of ghetto life]

9833. _____. "A Man. A Legend. A What!?" *Time* (23 September 1991). [Rush Limbaugh, right-wing talk-radio host]

9834. Carmody, Deirdre. "Magazines Try to Fill a Void in Minority Hiring." *New York Times*, 18 July 1994.

9835. Carr, C. "Talk Show." *Village Voice* (12 November 1991). [Robbie McCauley's dialogues on racism]

9836. Carr, Jay. "Film in Black and White." *Boston Globe*, 28 April 1991. [Interview with Black director Bill Duke]

9837. _____. "From Harvard to Hollywood." *Boston Globe*, 22 March 1990. [Reginald Hudlin]

9838. _____. "New Visibility for Blacks on Screen." *Boston Globe*, 23 June 1991.

9839. _____. "Spike Lee Takes the Fever's Measure." *Boston Globe*, 2 June 1991. [Film: Jungle Fever]

9840. Carter, Bill. "Black Americans Hold a TV Mirror Up to Their Life." *New York Times*, 27 August 1989. [A black crew makes a 1-hour network show, "Black and White in America."]

9841. _____. "Bryant Gumbel. Forecast for 'Today': Cloudy." *New York Times Magazine* (10 June 1990).

9842. _____. "In the Huxtable World, Parents Knew Best." *New York Times*, 26 April 1992. ["The Cosby Show" after eight years]

9843. Carton, Paul. "Mass Media Culture and the Breakdown of Values among Inner-City Youth." *Future Choices* 2 (Winter 1991): 11-21.

9844. Cerone, Daniel. "TV Not Representative of Society, Study Finds." *Los Angeles Times*, 16 June 1993.

9845. Cha-Jua, Sundiata K. "Mississippi Burning: The Burning of Black Self-Activity." *Radical History Review* no. 45 (Fall 1989): 125-136.

9846. Chang, Gordon H. "'Superman is About to Visit the Relocation Centers' and the Limits of Wartime Liberalism." *Amerasia Journal* 19 (1993): 37-60.

9847. Cherry, David L. "Attention to Black People's P.O.W.E.R. in the Major Metropolitan Press." *Journal of Black Studies* 21 (June 1991): 387-397.

9848. Chow, Crystal. "60 Years on the Siver Screen." *Rice* (September 1988): 10-22. [Asian Americans]

9849. Chrisman, Robert. "What Is the Right Thing? Notes on the Deconstruction of Black Ideology." *Black Scholar* 21 (March-May 1990): 53-57. [Spike Lee's Do the Right Thing]

9850. Chua, Lawrence. "Eastern Standard." *Village Voice* (1 August 1989). [The 12th Asian American International Film Festival]

9851. Chung, Richard. "Hollywood and Asian Americans." *Hokubei Mainichi*, February 7-9, 1990.

9852. Churchill, Ward. "Categories of Stereotyping of American Indians in Film." in *Fantasies of the Master Race*, pp. 231-241. Monroe, ME: Common Courage Press, 1992.

9853. _____. *Fantasies of the Master Race. Literature, Cinema and the Colonization of American Indians*, ed. M. Annette Jaimes. Monroe, ME: Common Courage Press, 1992.

9854. _____. "Lawrence of South Dakota." *Z Magazine* 4 (June 1991): 76. [Kevin Costner and Dances With Wolves film]

9855. Cirino, Robert. *Don't Blame the People*. New York: Vantage, 1972.

9856. Clay, Phillip L. "The Search for Voice: Ideology and Perspective in the Black Community." in *Social, Political, and Economic Issues in Black America*, vol. 4. pp. 119-146. ed. Wornie L. Reed. Boston: William Monroe Trotter Institute, University of Massachusetts at Boston, 1990.

9857. Collier, Aldore. "Fighting the Power in Hollywood." *Ebony* 45 (August 1990): 106-110.

9858. Committee for Cultural Studies. *PBS and the American Worker*. New York: City University of New York, June 1990.

9859. Cooper, Arnold. "'Protection to All, Discrimination to None':The Parsons Weekly Blade, 1892-1900." *Kansas History* 9 (1986): 58-71.

9860. Cooper, Kenneth J. "Hispanic Caucus Shows Its New-found Clout." *Washington Post*, 2 October 1993.

9861. Cortes, C. "Italian-Americans in Film: From Immigrants to Icons." *Melus* 14 (1987): 107-126.

9862. Cortes, Carlos E. "To View a Neighbor: The Hollywood Textbook on Mexico." in *Images of Mexico in the United States*, San Diego: Center for U.S.-Mexican Studies, University of California, 1989.

9863. Cose, Ellis. *The Quiet Crisis: Minority Journalists and Newsroom Opportunity*. Berkeley, CA: Institute for Journalism Education, 1985.

9864. Cottle, Simon. *TV News, Urban Conflict, and the Inner City*. Pinter Publishers, 1993.

9865. Coward, John M. *The Newspaper Indian: Native Americans and the Press in the Nineteenth Century*. Ph.D. diss., University of Texas, 1989. UMO #8920688.

9866. Cox, Ted. "TV News in Chicago Fuels Racial Anxiety." *Chicago Reporter* 20 (January 1991): 3-5.

9867. Cripps, Thomas. *Making Movies Black: The Hollywood Message Movie from World War II to the Civil Rights Era*. Oxford University Press, 1993.

9868. Crouch, Stanley. "Death Among the Ruins." *Washington Post*, 27 February 1994. ["Sugar Hill," a film with Wesley Snipes]

9869. _____. "Menace, Anyone?" *Washington Post*, 27 June 1993. [Film: "Menace II Society"]

9870. Cruz, Robert. "Integration Slow On Comic Strip Row." *Chicago Reporter* 18 (July-August 1989). [Three Chicago newspapers]

9871. Cudd, Mike, and Clay Steinman. "White Racism + The Cosby Show." *Jump Cut* 37 (July 1992): 5-14.

9872. D'Adderio, Mercedes. "Grappling With a 'Lie That Tells Us the Truth'." *Los Angeles Times*, 22 March 1993. ["Falling Down," a film starring Michael Douglas]

9873. Dargis, Manohla. "Double Vision. Ethan and Joel Coen on Jews, Hollywood, and Barton Fink." *Village Voice* (13 August 1991).

9874. _____. "To Live and Die in L.A.?" *Village Voice* (20 November 1990). [The institutional racism of promoting black-made films]

9875. Dates, Jannette L., and William Barlow, eds. *Split Image: African Americans in the Mass Media*. Washington, DC: Howard University Press, 1990.

9876. Dauphin, Gary. "Paint the Whites' House Black." *Village Voice* (3 May 1994). [704 Hauser, a TV sitcom of African-American characters]

9877. Davis, Chester. "A Brief History of Blacks on Television." *African Commentary* 2-3 (December 1990-January 1991): 17-20.

9878. Davis, Henry V. *The Black Press: From Mission to Commercialism, 1827-1927*. Ph.D. diss., University of Michigan, 1990. UMO #9023538.

9879. Davis, Thulani and others. "We've Gotta Have It." *Village Voice* (20 June 1989): 67-78. ["Spike Lee and a New Black Cinema"]

9880. Day, Barbara. "Film Brings Tuskegee Tragedy to Light." *Guardian (NYC)* (22 May 1991). [A documentary film about experimenting with black men who, in the 1930's, had been infected with syphilis.]

9881. De Nicolo, David. "Once Larry, Now Laurence." *New York Times*, 8 August 1993. [Laurence Fishburne, African-American actor]

9882. de Vries, Hilary. "Eddie Murphy, Straight Up." *Los Angeles Times*, 28 June 1992.

9883. Demeter, John, and Holly Sklar. "'Dark' and White." *Z Magazine* 3 (May 1990): 15.

9884. Diawara, M. "Le spectateur noir face au cinema dominant: tours et detours de l'identification." *CinemAction* 46 (January 1988): 93-101.

9885. Dickerson, Sandra A. *Is Sapphire Still Alive: The Image of Black Women in Television Situation Comedies in the 1990's*. Ph.D. diss., Boston University, 1991. UMO #9202864.

9886. "'Do the Right Thing': Issues and images." *New York Times*, 9 July 1989. [Exploration of issues in Spike Lee's Do the Right Thing by Mary S. Campbell, Henry L. Gates, Jr., Nathan Glazer, Alvin F. Poussaint, Burton B. Roberts, Paul Schrader, Betty Shabazz, and others]

9887. Dodd, D. K. and others. "Content Analysis of Women and Racial Minorities as News Magazine Cover Persons." *Journal of Social Behavior and Personality* 3 (1988): 231-236.

9888. Douglas, Kirk. "My Son Is the Villain, Not the Hero, of Urban Drama." *Los Angeles Times*, 22 March 1993. ["Falling Down", a film starring the writer's son, Michael Douglas]

9889. Dowd, Maureen. "He's Never Been Happier, or More Glum." *New York Times*, 28 June 1992. [Eddie Murphy]

9890. Downing, John D. H. "'The Cosby Show' and American Racial Discourse." in *Discourse and Discrimination*, pp. 46-73. eds. Geneva Smitherman-Donaldson, and Teun A. van Dijk. Detroit, MI: Wayne State University Press, 1988.

9891. Doyle, James. "Huck and Mookie." *Reconstruction* 1, no. 2 (1990): 29-37. [Analysis of Spike Lee's film, Do the Right Thing]

9892. Du Brow, Rick. "Changes Behind the Camera Are Overdue." *Boston Globe*, 28 September 1991. [Lack of Black studio executives and TV officials]

9893. Dubin, Zan. "NEA Funding Called Unfair to Minorities." *Los Angeles Times*, 5 August 1992. [National Endowment for the Arts]

9894. Dutka, Elaine. "Asian-American: Rising Furor Over 'Rising Sun'." *Los Angeles Times*, 28 July 1993. [Film]

9895. Dyson, Michael E. "Growing Up Under Fire: Boyz n the Hood and the Agony of the Black Man in America." *Tikkun* 6 (September- October 1991): 74-78.

9896. _____. "The Politics of Black Masculinity and the Ghetto in Black Film." in *The Subversive Imagination: Artists, Society, and Social Responsibility*, ed. Carol Becker. Routledge, 1994.

9897. Easton, Nina J. "Black Female Directors Coming Up Against an Invisible Wall in Hollywood." *Springfield (Mass.) Union-News*, 16 November 1991.

9898. Ehrenstein, D. "The Color of Laughter." *American Film* 14 (September 1988): 8-11. [Bill Cosby and Eddie Murphy]

9899. Eichelberger, Hubert L. *"A Brief History of Black Stereotypes in Film: 1902 to Blaxploitation 1973", Chapter 1 in his Toward An Understanding of the Significance of Blacks in Commercial TV Advertising and Fostered Behavioral Attitudes.* Ph.D. diss., Emory University, 1990. UMO #9113989.

9900. Ely, Melvin Patrick. *The Adventures of Amos 'N' Andy. A Social History of An American Phenomenon*. New York: Free Press, 1990.

9901. Engleberg, Stephen. "A New Breed of Hired Hands Cultivates Grassroots Anger." *New York Times*, 17 March 1993. [Rise of business and other groups to stimulate phone calls to public officials]

9902. Entman, Robert M. *The Images of Blacks on Chicago's Local TV News Programs*. Chicago, IL: Human Relations Foundation, Chicago Community Trust, 1991.

9903. _____. "Modern Racism and the Images of Blacks in Local Television News." *Critical Studies in Mass Communication* 7 (December 1990): 332-345.

9904. Ettema, James S. "Press Rites and Race Relations: A Study of Mass-Mediated Ritual." *Critical Studies in Mass Communication* 7 (December 1990): 309-331.

9905. Ettema, James S., and David Protess. *Uncovering Race: Press Coverage of Racial Issues in Chicago*. Evanston, IL: Institute for Modern Communications, Northwestern University, 1989.

9906. Evenson, Debra. "Women's Rights and the Media." *National Lawyers Guild Practitoner* 48 (Winter 1991): 18-21.

9907. Faber, R. J. and others. "Televised Portrayals of Hispanics: A Comparison of Ethnic Perceptions." *International Journal of Intercultural Relations* 11 (1987): 155-169.

9908. Fair, J. E., and R. J. Astrolff. "Constructing Race and Violence: United States News Coverage and the Signifying Practices of Apartheid." *Journal of Communication* 41 (Autumn 1991): 58-74.

9909. Falk, Gerhard. "The Reaction of the German-American Press to Nazi Persecutions, 1933-1941." *Journal of Reform Judaism* 32 (1985): 12-23.

9910. Feingold, Michael. "Stage Fright. The Dumbing of American Theater." *Village Voice* (13 August 1991).

9911. Fernandez, Enrique. "Paper Chase." *Village Voice* (7 May 1991). [Problems of Latinos working on newspapers and magazines]

9912. Fine, Joyce. "American Radio Coverage of the Holocaust." *Simon Wiesenthal Center Annual* 5 (1988): 145-165.

9913. Flores, Caraballo Eliut D. *The Politics of Culture in Puerto Rican Television: A Macro-Micro Study of English vs. Spanish Language Television Usage*. Ph.D. diss., University of Texas, 1991. UMO #9200623.

9914. "Focus on Racism in the Media." *Extra* (July-August 1992): entire issue.

9915. Fox, David J. "Disney Will Alter Song in 'Aladdin'." *Los Angeles Times*, 10 July 1993. [Arab-American criticism of song as racist]

9916. _____. "A Slimmer Year for Black Films." *Los Angeles Times*, 17 August 1992.

9917. Fraser, C. Gerald. "Fans Mourn Loss of an Interracial Soap Opera." *New York Times*, 5 March 1991. ["Generations"]

9918. Fraser, Laura. "The Tyranny of the Media Correct, the Assault on the New McCarthyism." *Extra!* (May-June 1991).

9919. Freedman, Samuel G. "Love and Hate in Black and White." *New York Times*, 2 June 1991. [Spike Lee's film, Jungle Fever]

9920. Fregoso, Rosa Linda. *The Bronze Screen: Chicana and Chicano Film Culture*. University of Minnesota Press, 1993.

9921. _____. "The Representation of Cultural Identity in Zoot Suit (1981)." *Theory and Society* 22 (October 1993): 659-674.

9922. French, Desiree. "In Search of a Voice for Blacks in Film." *Boston Globe*, 22 March 1990. [Claude Taylor and Toni Cade Bambara]

9923. French, Mary Ann. "Great Expectations." *Washington Post*, 25 July 1993. [John Singleton, African-American film maker]

9924. Friedman, Lester D., ed. *Unspeakable Images. Ethnicity and the American Cinema*. Baltimore, MD: University of Illinois Press, 1991.

9925. Friedman, Milton. "Stereotypes in the Media." *San Francisco Chronicle*, 9 May 1988.

9926. Fusco, Coco. "'All We Need Is Ganas?'." *Village Voice* (5 December 1989). [Treatment of Hispanics in recent films]

9927. Gaines, J. "The Scar of Shame: Skin Color and Caste in Black Silent Melodrama." *Cinema Journal* 26 (Summer 1987): 3-21.

9928. Galbraith, Jane. "Group Takes 'Rising Sun' Protest Public." *Los Angeles Times*, 7 April 1993. [Anti-Japanism in movie based on Michael Crichton's novel, Rising Sun]

9929. Gardner, C., and M. Henry. "Racism, Anti-racism and Access Television: The Making of 'Open Door'." *Screen Education* no. 31 (Summer 1979).

9930. Gates, Henry Louis, Jr. "'Jungle Fever' Charts Black Middle-Class Angst." *New York Times*, 23 June 1991.

9931. _____. "Niggaz With Latitude." *New Yorker* (21 March 1994). [Allen and Albert Hughes]

9932. _____. "TV's Black World Turns-But Stays Unreal." *New York Times*, 12 November 1989.

9933. Georgakas, Dan, and Miriam Rosen, eds. "The Arab Image in American Film and Television." *Cineaste* 17 (1989): 1-24.

9934. George, Nelson. "Box Office Riot." *Village Voice* (26 March 1991). ["New Jack City" film]

9935. _____. "The Ebony Agenda." *Village Voice* (6 June 1989). [Ebony magazine]

9936. _____. "New Jack L.A." *Village Voice* (21 April 1992). [Blacks in and around the Hollywood scene]

9937. Gerson, W. M. "Mass Media Socialization Behavior Negro- White Differences." *Social Forces* 45 (1966).

9938. Gilbert, Matthew. "Mo' Better Crossover." *Boston Globe*, 21 October 1990. [Spike Lee]

9939. Gilliam, Dorothy. "Diversity in the Newsroom." *Boston Globe*, 11 April 1991. [Minority employment in newspaper industry.]

9940. _____. "Honored to Serve." *Washington Post*, 31 July 1993. [Newly-elected president of the National Association of Black Journalists]

9941. _____. "Newspapers Still Behind the Times." *Washington Post*, 16 April 1994. [American Society of Newspaper Editors report showing slowdown in "hiring of journalists of color."

9942. Ginsburg, Carl. *Race and the Media: The Enduring Life of the Moynihan Report*. New York: Institute for Media Analysis, 1989.

9943. Gist, Marilyn E. "Minorities in Media Imagery: A Social Cognitive Perspective of Journalistic Bias." *Newspaper Research Journal* 11 (Summer 1990): 52-63.

9944. Givens, Robin. "Why Are Black Actresses Having Such a Hard Time in Hollywood?" *Ebony* (June 1991).

9945. Glaberson, William. "As Minority Journalists Meet, An Example of White Power." *New York Times*, 29 July 1994.

9946. _____. "At a Meeting of Minority Journalists, Two Starting Points on Political Correctness." *New York Times*, 1 August 1994.

9947. _____. "Hiring of Minority Journalists Has Slowed, Survey Says." *New York Times*, 15 April 1994.

9948. _____. "New York Press Had Its Blind Spots, Too, In Disorders of 1991." *New York Times*, 22 July 1993. [Crown Heights, Brooklyn Violence]

9949. _____. "Press." *New York Times*, 18 July 1994. [Earl Caldwell, veteran black journalist]

9950. Glicksman, M. "Bed-Stuy BBQ." *Film Comment* 25 (July-August 1989): 12-16, 18. [Spike Lee, "Do the Right Thing"]

9951. Goldsen, Rose. *Television, The Product Is You*. New York: McGraw-Hill, 1977.

9952. Goldstein, Patrick. "The Mission Beyond Hollywood." *Los Angeles Times*, 31 May 1992. [Director John Singleton]

9953. Gomes, Ralph C., and L. F. Williams. "Race and Crime: The Role of the Media in Perpetuating Racism and Classism in America." *Urban League Review* 14 (Summer 1990): 57-70.

9954. Good, P. "Is Network News Slighting the Minorities?" *TV Guide* (5 March 1977).

9955. Goodman, Walter. "Missing Middle-Class Black in TV News." *New York Times*, 22 May 1990.

9956. Graham, A. "Real to Reel." *Listener* 122 (2 November 1989): 10-11. [Spike Lee, "Do the Right Thing"]

9957. Gray, Herman. "Race Relations as News." *American Behavioral Scientist* 30 (March-April 1987).

9958. _____. "Television, Black Americans, and the American Dream." *Critical Studies in Mass Communication* 6 (December 1989): 376-386.

9959. Green, Mark. *Still Invisible*. New York City Department of Consumer Affairs, August 1992. [Omission of minorities from advertisements for expensive fashion, beauty, and cosmetic products]

9960. Greenberg, Bradley S., and J. E. Brand. "Minorities and the Mass Media: 1970s to 1990s." in *Media Effects. Advances in Theory and Research*, pp. 273-314. eds. J. Bryant, and D. Zillmann. Lawrence Erlbaum Associates, 1994.

9961. Greenberg, James. "Did Hollywood Sit on 'Fences' [Over Hiring a Black Director]?" *New York Times*, 27 January 1991.

9962. _____. "In Hollywood, Black Is In." *New York Times*, 4 March 1990.

9963. "Gregory Hines." *African Commentary* 2-3 (December 1990- January 1991): 22-27. [Interview by Martha Grier]

9964. Grimes, William. "Can a Film Be Both Racist and Classic?" *New York Times*, 27 April 1994. ["The Birth of a Nation"]

9965. _____. "Should Only Blacks Make Movies About Blacks?" *New York Times*, 28 March 1994.

9966. Guerrero, Ed. *Framing Blackness: The African American Image in Film*. Temple University Press, 1993.

9967. _____. "Framing Blackness: The African American Image in the Cinema of the Nineties." *Cineaste* 20 (1993): 24-31.

9968. _____. "The Slavery Motif in Recent Popular Cinema." *Jump Cut* 33 (February 1988): 52-59.

9969. Guinier, Lani. "A Challenge to Journalists on Racial Dialogue." *Extra!* 6 (November-December 1993): 7-9.

9970. Gunther, Marc. "Black Producers Add a Fresh Nuance." *New York Times*, 26 August 1990.

9971. Gussow, Mel. "Striding Past Dragon Lady and No.1 Son." *New York Times*, 3 September 1990. [Asian-American actors]

9972. Hall, Carla. "Back from a Different World." *Washington Post*, 8 May 1993. [Debbie Allen, African-American choreographer, dancer, actress, and film director]

9973. _____. "Love in Black and White. Hollywood's Take on Interracial Dating." *Washington Post*, 20 December 1992.

9974. Hamamoto, Darrell Y. *Monitored Peril. Asian Americans and the Politics of TV Representation.* University of Minnesota Press, 1994.

9975. Hammer, Joshua. "Must Blacks Be Buffoons?" *Newsweek* (26 October 1992). [Prime-time television]

9976. Hammer, Joshua, and Howard Manly. "Where Black is Gold." *Newsweek* (2 December 1991). [African-American Culture in the mass media]

9977. Hansen, Miriam. *Babel and Babylon: Spectatorship in American Silent Film.* Cambridge, MA: Harvard University Press, 1991. [Intolerance, by D.W. Griffith, following the making of Birth of a Nation]

9978. Hardy, James Earl. "New and Improved. Monti Sharp, Raising the Standard for Black Roles in Soaps." *Washington Post*, 5 September 1993.

9979. Harrison, Barbara Grizzuti. "The Importance of Being Oprah [Winfrey]." *New York Times Magazine* (11 June 1989).

9980. Hartigan, Patti. "Casting Calls." *Boston Globe*, 19 August 1990. [Racial diversity on the American stage]

9981. _____. "Director Wants to See Roles for All Races." *Boston Globe*, 6 December 1991. [Clinton Turner Davis, stage director]

9982. Hartigan, Paul. "Taking on Racism with Opera." *Boston Globe*, 17 January 1992.

9983. Harwood, Richard. "'Diversity' Comes Home." *Washington Post*, 27 November 1993. [Efforts to desegregate the U.S. newspaper labor force]

9984. Heiman, Andrea. "Diversity Seen as the Ticket to Boost Movie Attendance." *Los Angeles Times*, 12 June 1993.

9985. Hentoff, Nat. "Did Breslin's Punishment Fit the Crime?" *Village Voice* (29 May 1990). [Jimmy Breslin, columnist for Newsday]

9986. _____. "The Insatiable Lust to Suppress Speech." *Village Voice* (13 March 1990). [Andy Rooney of CBS]

9987. _____. "Just Who Is a Bigot?" *Village Voice*, 29 March 1994. [Discussion about radio-talk-show host Bob Grant on WABC]

9988. Hilburn, Robert. "The Rap Is: Justice." *Los Angeles Times*, 31 May 1992. [Ice Cube]

9989. Hill, George H. and others. *Black Women in Television: An Illustrated History and Bibliography.* New York: Garland, 1990.

9990. Hill, George H. *From Claire and Weezie to Julia and Beulah: Black Women on TV: Historical Perspective and Bibliography.* Angwin, CA: Daystar Publishing Co., 1987.

9991. Hines, Judith D. *The Next Step: Toward Diversity in the Newspaper Business*. Reston, VA: Amerian Newspaper Publishers Association Foundation and the Poynter Institute for Media Studies, 1991.

9992. Hinson, Hal. "When Injustice Gets Under the Skin." *Washington Post*, 10 July 1993. ["Nothing But a Man", film made in 1964 abourt Black life in Birmingham, Alabama]

9993. "History of the Office of Censorship." Frederick, MD: University Publications of America, 1987. 3 Microfilm reels.

9994. Hoberman, J. "Our Troubling Birth Rite. The Library of Congress Moves to Suppress American Movie History." *Village Voice* (30 November 1993). ["The Birth of a Nation"]

9995. Hoffman, Paul D. "Minorities and Ethnics in the Arizona Press: Arizona Newspaper Portrayals during American Involvement in World War I." *Locus* 1 (1989): 69-91.

9996. Holly, Ellen. "Why the Furor Over 'Miss Saigon' Won't Fade." *New York Times*, 26 August 1990. [A black access-writer discusses non-traditional casting and its problems.]

9997. "The Holocaust and the American Media." *Dimensions (Anti- Defamation League International Center for Holocaust Studies)* 4 (1989): 4-27.

9998. Hooks, Bell, and Anuradha Singwaney. "Mississippi Masala." *Z Magazine* 5 (July-August 1992): 41-43. [Review of film made by Mira Nair]

9999. Horowitz, Bruce. "Can Ads Help Cure Social Ills?" *Los Angeles Times*, 2 June 1992.

10000. _____. "More Advertisers Are Tailoring TV Spots to Ethnicity of Viewers." *Los Angeles Times*, 3 May 1994.

10001. _____. "Nike Does It Again. Film Targets Blacks With a Spin on 'Family Values'." *Los Angeles Times*, 25 August 1992.

10002. _____. "Riots Wake Up Some Ad Shops." *Los Angeles Times*, 16 June 1992. [Very small representation of minorities in Los Angeles advertising industry.]

10003. Horowitz, Joy. "Black Acresses Are Still Waiting for Star Roles." *New York Times*, 29 May 1991. [Hollywood]

10004. Houston, Paul. "Survey Cites Conservative 'Vocal Minority'." *Los Angeles Times*, 16 July 1993. [Radio talk shows]

10005. Hoynes, William, and David Croteau. *All the Usual Suspects: MacNeil/Lehrer and Nightline*. New York: Fairness and Accuracy in Reporting (FAIR), May 1990. [Selection of guests from a narrow social and racial range]

10006. Hruska, Bronwen, and Graham Rayman. "On the Outside, Looking In." *New York Times*, 21 February 1993. [African-American women film directors]

10007. Huck, Karen F. *White Minds and Black Bodies in the War for Democracy: Race, Representation, and the Reader in "Life" Magazine, 1938-1946*. Ph.D. diss., University of Utah, 1993. UMO #9325716.

10008. Hughes, Langston. *The Return of Simple*. Hill and Wang, 1994.

10009. Hunt, Barbara Ann. *The Use of Television by the Reverend Jesse Louis Jackson, 1968-1978*. Ph.D. diss., Northwestern University, 1988. UMO #8902649.

10010. Hutton, Frankie P. *The Antebellum Black Press and the Quest for Inclusion: Ideals and Messages of Social Responsiblity, Morality, Class and Style*. Ph.D. diss., Rutgers, The State University of New Jersey, 1990. UMO #9123284.

10011. _____. *The Early Black Press in America, 1820s to 1860's*. Greenwood, 1992.

10012. "In the Black." *Village Voice* (4 June 1991): 69-90. [Special section on Black film]

10013. Iwata, Edward. "Asian Movies Take Flight." *Los Angeles Times*, 13 May 1993. [Asian Americans in the movie industry]

10014. Jabara, A. and others. "The Arab Image in American Film and Television." *Cineaste* 17, supplement 1-4 (1989): eight articles.

10015. Jackson, Don. "Blacks Making Inroads Outside of Networks." *Los Angeles Times*, 26 October 1992.

10016. Jackson, Elizabeth K. *Contemporary Black Film, Television, and Video Makers: A Survey Analysis of Producers.* Ph.D. diss., Northwestern University, 1989. UMO #8913980.

10017. James, Cathy L. *Soap Opera Mythology and Racial-ethnic Social Change: An Analysis of African-American, Asian/Pacific- American and Mexican/Hispanic-American Storylines during the 1980's.* Ph.D. diss., University of California, San Diego, 1991. UMO #9137324.

10018. Jenkins, Mark. "Black in the Saddle." *Washington Post*, 9 May 1993. [Interview with film-director Mario Van Peebles on African Americans in the Old West

10019. Johnson, Kirk A. "Media Images of Boston's Black Community." *Trotter Institute Review* 4 (Spring 1990): 10-16. [Newspapers, television, and radio]

10020. Johnson, Leola A. *The Social Affilations of Black Journalists.* Ph.D. diss., University of Minnesota, 1990. UMO #9107434.

10021. Jojola, Ted. "Corn, or What We Indians Call Maize." *Village Voice* (5 December 1989). [Treatment of Native Americans in recent films]

10022. Jones, Alex S. "Black Journalists Seeking New Gains in the Newsroom." *New York Times*, 17 August 1989.

10023. _____. "An Editorial Stirs a Newsroom Feud." *New York Times*, 21 December 1990. [Many members of Philadelphia Inquirer news staff accuse paper of publishing a racist editorial.

10024. _____. "Editors Report Gains in 1990 in Minority Journalist Hiring." *New York Times*, 12 April 1991.

10025. _____. "Editors Take On Clnflicts of News Staff Diversity." *New York Times*, 9 April 1992.

10026. _____. "'Sense of Muscle' for Black Journalists." *New York Times*, 21 August 1989. [National Association of Black Journalists]

10027. Jones, Charisse. "When Culture Crosses Over." *Los Angeles Times*, 13 December 1992. [Mainstreaming Afro-American culture]

10028. Jones, Felecia G. *The Black Audience and Black Entertainment Television.* Ph.D. diss., University of Georgia, 1989. UMO #9003410.

10029. _____. "The Black Audience and the BET Channel." *Journal of Broadcasting and Electronic Media* 34 (Fall 1990): 477-486.

10030. Jones, G. William. *Black Cinema Treasures. Lost and Found.* University of North Texas Press, 1991.

10031. Jones, Jacquie. "Lee and the Black-film 'Boom'." *In These Times* (26 June 1991). [Spike Lee]

10032. Jones, Lisa. "The Defiant Ones. A Talk with Film Historian Donald Bogle." *Village Voice* (4 June 1991): 69, 88.

10033. _____. "Girls on the Strip." *Village Voice* (10 March 1992). [About the work of Barbara Brandon, first black woman cartoonist to be nationally syndicated.]

10034. Kaplan, Janice L. "Cartooning a Black Tableau." *Washington Post*, 12 August 1993. [Comic books by African Americans]

10035. Katz, Jon. "Can the Media Do the Right Thing?" *Rolling Stone* (28 May 1992).

10036. Katz, William Loren. "Movies Discover Black Cowboys and Cavalry." *New York Times*, 2 June 1993, letter.

10037. Kaufman, Joanne. "Passion Plays. The Actress Forges Art From the Ashes of Racial Conflict." *Washington Post*, 15 April 1993. [Anna Deavere Smith]

10038. Kaufman, Michael T. "In a New Film, Spike Lee Tries To Do the Right Thing." *New York Times*, 25 June 1989. ["[In Do the Right Thing] I wanted to generate discussion about racism because too many people have their head in the sand about racism...Racism is the most pressing problem in the United States..."]

10039. Keller, Gary D., ed. *Chicano Cinema: Research, Reviews, and Resources*. Tempe, AZ: Bilingual Review/Press, Arizona State University, Hispanic Research Center, 1985.

10040. Kifner, John. "Mississippi In '64: Fact Vs. Fantasy." *New York Times*, 6 July 1994. ["Freedom On My Mind", a film about SNCC in Mississippi]

10041. Kirby, Jack T. *Media-made Dixie: The South in the American Imagination*, Revised ed. Athens: University of Georgia Press, 1986.

10042. Kissel, Howard. "'Nothing Jewish'." *Present Tense* 17 (January-February 1990): 46-50. [Portrayal of Jews in Hollywood films]

10043. Klotman, Phyllis R., ed. *Screenplays of the African American Experience*. Bloomington: Indiana University Press, 1991.

10044. Kneeland, Douglas E. "Minorities Are No Minor Concern." *Chicago Tribune*, 25 October 1990. [Possible racism in running obituary stories on Sammie Davis, Jr. and Jim Henson]

10045. Kolbert, Elizabeth. "And Now, All-Ideology TV, With All Talk Conservative." *New York Times*, 27 November 1993. [National Empowerment Television]

10046. _____. "From 'Beulah' to 'Oprah': The Evolution of Black Images on TV." *New York Times*, 15 January 1993.

10047. _____. "Racial Gap in Television Viewing Habits Widens." *New York Times*, 5 April 1993.

10048. Koppes, Clayton R., and Gregory D. Black. "Blacks, Loyalty, and Motion-picture Propaganda in World War II." *Journal of American History* 73 (September 1986): 383-403.

10049. Kray, S. "Orientalization of an Almost White Woman: The Interlocking Effects of Race, Class, Gender, and Ethnicity in American Mass Media." *Critical Studies in Mass Communication* 10 (December 1990): 349-366.

10050. Kubey, Robert, and Mihaly Csikszentmihalyi. *Television and the Quality of Life: How Viewing Shapes Everyday Experience*. Hilldale, NJ: Lawrence Erlbaum Associates, 1990.

10051. Kurtz, Howard. "Diverse Views of the News." *Washington Post*, 2 March 1993. [Los Angeles Times minority staff criticizes content of paper]

10052. _____. "The Inside Story Of an Outsider." *Washington Post*, 15 June 1993. [African-American reporter on the Washington Post, 1986-1990 who wrote Volunteer Slavery; see Jill Nelson, below]

10053. Lacher, Irene. "Heroes of a Different Color." *Long Beach Press-Telegram*, 14 November 1993. [Comic-book super heroes of various ethnicities and genders]

10054. Landini, Ann L. *The "Cherokee Phoenix": The Voice of the Cherokee Nation, 1828-1834*. Ph.D. diss., University of Tennessee, 1990. UMO #9030717.

10055. Landsman, Gail H. "Indian Activism and the Press: Coverage of the Conflict at Ganienkeh." *Anthropological Quarterly* 60 (July 1987): 101-113.

10056. Lawrence, David, Jr. "Broken Ladders, Revolving Doors: The Need for Pluralism in the Newsroom." *Newspaper Research Journal* 11 (Summer 1990): 18-23.

10057. "Le cinema noir americain." *CinemAction* 46 (January 1988): 1-205.

10058. Ledbetter, James. "The News in Black and White." *Village Voice* (3 May 1994). [A black journalist leaves the New York Daily News]

10059. Lee, Martin A., and Norman Solomon. *Unreliable Sources: A Guide to Detecting Bias in News Media*. Lyle Stuart, 1990.

10060. Lee, Moonlake Lee. "The Camera's Slanted Eye on the East: How Asians Are Portrayed on American Television." B.A. Thesis, Rutgers College, 1992.

10061. Lee, Spike. *Do the Right Thing*. New York: Fireside, 1989.

10062. Lee, Spike, and Lisa Jones. *Mo' Better Blues*. New York: Simon and Schuster, 1990.

10063. Leiby, Richard. "White Like Me." *Washington Post*, 1 August 1993. [Journalists]

10064. Leidholdt, Alexander S. *The "Virginian-Pilot" Newspaper's Role in Moderating Norfolk, Virginia's 1958 School Desegregation Crisis.* Ph.D. diss., Old Dominion U., 1991. UMO #9216101.

10065. Leland, John. "Rap and Race." *Newsweek* (29 June 1992).

10066. Leland, John, and Donna Foote. "A Bad Omen for Black Movies?" *Newsweek* (29 July 1991). [Violence in movie houses]

10067. Lentz, Richard. *Symbols, the News Magazines, and Martin Luther King.* Baton Rouge: Louisiana State University Press, 1989.

10068. Lester, P. M. "African-American Photo Coverage in 4 United States Newspapers, 1937-1990." *Journalism Quarterly* 71 (Summer 1994): 380-394.

10069. Levin, Doron P. "Black Journalists Tell of Facing New Job Pressures." *New York Times*, 22 August 1992.

10070. Levine, R. M. "We're On the Team, but We're Not Playing." *TV Guide* (18 July 1981).

10071. _____. "Why 'Unconscious Racism' Persists." *TV Guide* (25 July 1981).

10072. Levy, Joe. "Blues for Generation X." *Village Voice* (30 June 1992). [Sister Souljah's rap talk]

10073. Lew, Julie. "Hollywood's War On Indians Draws To a Close." *New York Times*, 7 October 1990.

10074. Lewis, Lisa A. *Gender Politics and MTV: Voicing the Difference.* Philadelphia, PA: Temple University Press, 1990.

10075. Lichter, S. R., and L. S. Lichter. "Does Television Shape Ethnic Images." *Media and Values* 43 (Spring 1988): 5-8. [Students at high school in Howard Beach, N.Y. two months before a white killing of a black man.]

10076. Lieb, Rebecca. "Nazi Hate Movies Continue to Ignite Fierce Passions." *New York Times*, 4 August 1991.

10077. Liebler, C. M. "Beyond Kerner: Ethnic Diversity and Minority Journalists." *Mass Comm. Review* 15 (1988): 32-44. [1987 data]

10078. Lieh, T. "Protest at the Post: Converage of Blacks in the Washington Post Magazine." *Mass Comm. Review* 15 (1988): 61-68.

10079. Lipstadt, Deborah E. "Finessing the Truth: The Press and the Holocaust." *Dimensions* 4 (1989): 10-14.

10080. Loewen, James W. "Teaching Race Relations from Feature Films." *Teaching Sociology* 19 (January 1991): 82-86.

10081. Lott, Bernice. "Sexist Discrimination As Distancing Behavior. 2. Primetime Television." *Psychology of Women* 13 (September 1989).

10082. Lubiano, Wahneema. "But Compared to What? Reading Realism, Representation, and Essentialism in School Daze, Do the Right Thing, and the Spike Lee Discourse." *Black American Literature Forum* 25 (Summer 1991): 253-282.

10083. Lusanne, Clarence. "Rap, Race, and Rebellion." *Z Magazine* 5 (September 1992): 36-37.

10084. Lutz, Hartmut. "'Indians' and Native Americans in the Movies: A History of Stereotypes, Distortions, and Displacements." *Visual Anthropology* 3 (1990): 31-48.

10085. Lyman, Stanford M. "Race, Sex, and Servitude: Images of Blacks in American Cinema." *International Journal of Politics, Culture, and Society* 4 (Fall 1990): 49-77.

10086. Maciel, David R. "Braceros, Mojados, and Alambristras: Mexican Immigration to the United States in Contemporary Cinema." *Hispanic Journal of Behavorial Science* 8 (1986): 369-385.

10087. Marable, Manning. "Liberation Radio Shut Down." *Guardian (NYC)* (2 August 1989). [Dewayne Readus, Springfield, IL Station WTRA-FM, low-power.]

10088. Marchetti, Gina. *Romance and the "Yellow Peril." Race, Sex, and Discursive Strategies in Hollywood Fiction*. University of California Press, 1994. [Films about Asians and interracial sexuality]

10089. Marinaccio, James. "In a Sea of Black Filmmakers, Charles Lane Tests the Waters." *American Visions* (August 1991): 42-43.

10090. Marriott, Michel. "Harsh Rap Lyrics Provoke Black Backlash." *New York Times*, 15 August 1993.

10091. _____. "Raw Reactions to a Film on Racial Tension." *New York Times*, 3 July 1989. [Spike Lee's Do the Right Thing]

10092. Martindale, Carolyn. "Coverage of Black Americans in Four Major Newspapers, 1950-1989." *Newspaper Research Journal* 11 (Summer 1990): 96-112.

10093. _____. *The White Press and Black America*. Westport, CT: Greenwood, 1986.

10094. Martinez, Thomas M., and Jose Peralez. "Chicanos and the Motion Picture Industry." *La Raza* 1 (1971).

10095. Matabane, Paula W. "Television and the Black Audience: Cultivating Moderate Perspectives on Racial Integration." *Journal of Communication* 38 (1988): 21-31.

10096. Matthews, Dakin. "Artistic Differences? Yes; Racism? No." *Los Angeles Times*, 6 December 1993. [Casting a play]

10097. Mayer, Egon. "When Rape Makes News." *New York Times*, 17 June 1989. letter. [And when it does not]

10098. McChesney, Robert W. "Crusade against Mammon: Father Harney, WLWL, and the Debate over Radio in the 1930's." *Journalism History* 14 (Winter 1987): 118-130.

10099. McDougall, Harold A. "Jesse Jackson, the Media, and the New Civil Rights Movement." *Mississippi College Law Review* 9 (Fall 1988).

10100. McDowell, Jeanne. "He's Got to Have It His Way." *Time* (17 July 1989). [Spike Lee and Do the Right Thing film]

10101. McFadden, Robert D. and others. *Tawana: The Brawley Hoax and America's Racial Agony*. New York: Bantam, 1990.

10102. McGarry, Richard G. "Evaluating Inter-ethnic Conflict in the Press: A Linguistic Model." Master's thesis, University of Florida, 1989.

10103. McGee, Celia. "An Actress's Journey to an Unexpected Place." *New York Times*, 5 December 1993. [Charlayne Woodard]

10104. *Media Bias Detector*. New York: FAIR: Fairness and Accuracy in Reporting, 1991.

10105. Meisler, Andy. "The Ever-expanding Realm of Queen Latifah." *New York Times*, 9 January 1994.

10106. Mendoza, Manuel. "Latinos Awaiting Place on TV." *Boston Globe*, 18 September 1994. [Reprinted from Dallas News]

10107. Meyer, Sylvan, and Walter Spearman. *Racial Crisis and the Press*. Atlanta, GA, 1960.

10108. Michaelson, Judith. "The Talk of the Town? It's White." *Los Angeles Times*, 22 August 1993. [Absense of minority radio talk show hosts except on weekends in Los Angeles]

10109. _____. "Talk Radio: At the Mike, If Not White Lean Right." *Los Angeles Times*, 23 August 1993. [Nationwide]

10110. Miller, Kerby. "A Study of the Extent of Scientific Influence upon Popular Opinions of Race and the American Negro: Derived from an Examination of Popular Magazine Articles from 1935 to 1966." Unpublished paper, Department of History, University of California, Berkeley, 1967.

10111. Miller, Randall M., ed. *Ethnic Images in American Film and Television*. Philadelphia, PA: Balch Institute, 1978.

10112. _____. *The Kaleidoscopic Lens. How Hollywood Views Ethnic Groups*. Englewood, NJ: Jerome S. Ozer, 1989.

10113. Miskin, Al. "Mediations." *Middle East Report* 19 (July- August 1989): 33. [U.S. mass media use of anti-Arab stereotypes]

10114. Moore, Michael. "'Roger' and I, Off to Hollywood and Home to Flint." *New York Times*, 15 July 1990. [Maker of film documentary, "Roger and Me", about General Motors and unemployed workers]

10115. Morris, Sarah P. "Television." *Black Women in America, II*, pp. 1148-1153.

10116. Mosco, V., and J. Wasko, eds. *The Political Economy of Information*. Madison: University of Wisconsin Press, 1988.

10117. Muro, Mark. "Show's Values Gain Respect." *Boston Globe*, 19 April 1992. [Commentaries on "The Cosby Show" upon completion of its eight-year run.]

10118. Murphy, Eddie, and Reginald Hudlin, On 'Boomerang' and Issues of Black and White. *Los Angeles Times*, 20 July 1992.

10119. Murphy, James E., and Sharon M. Murphy. *Let My People Know: American Indian Journalism, 1828-1978*. Norman: University of Oklahoma Press, 1981.

10120. *Muted Voices: Frustration and Fear in the Newsroom*. National Association of Black Journalists, 1993.

10121. Muwakkil, Salim. "Hip-hop Racism, or Another Rum Rap?" *In These Times* (5 February 1992).

10122. Mydans, Seth. "Spanish-Language TV Called Biased." *New York Times*, 24 July 1989. [Class-biased conflict among various Hispanic groups in U.S.]

10123. _____. "TV Unites, and Divides, Hispanic Groups." *New York Times*, 27 August 1989.

10124. Myrick, H., ed. *In Search of Diversity: Symposium on Minority Audiences and Programming Research*. Washington, DC: Corporation for Public Broadcasting, 1981.

10125. National Commission on Working Women. *Unequal Picture: Black, Hispanic, Asian, and Native American Characters on Television*. Washington, DC, 1989.

10126. Nelson, Jill. *Volunteer Slavery: My Authentic Negro Experience*. Noble Press, 1993. [African-American reporter on the Washington Post, 1986-1990; see Howard Kurtz, above]

10127. Newberger, Carolyn. "Intolerance Is the Real Message of 'The Lion King'." *Boston Globe*, 27 June 1994. [Film]

10128. Newhagen J.E. "Media Use and Political Efficacy: The Suburbanization of Race and Class." *Journal of the American Society for Information Science* 45 (July 1994): 386-394.

10129. Nobile, Philip. "The Invisible Man." *Village Voice* (8 October 1991). [Scarcity of Black men on commercial TV in New York City]

10130. Noriega, Chon A. "Citizen Chicano: The Trials and Titillations of Ethnicity in the American Cinema, 1935-1962." *Social Research* 58 (Summer 1991): 413-438.

10131. _____. *Road To Aztlan: Chicanos and Narrative Cinema*. Ph.D. diss., Stanford University, 1991. UMO #9206833.

10132. Nutter, Jeanne D. *Coverage of Marcus Garvey by the New York "Age" and the New York "Times": A Comparative Historical Analysis*. Ph.D. diss., Howard University, 1991. UMO #9239183.

10133. O'Brien, Sally. "Writer Defends Report on Jogger Case." *Guardian (NYC)* (21 November 1990). [Racism and rape]

10134. O'Brien, Tom. *The Screening of America. Movies and Values from Rocky to Rainman*. New York: Continuum, 1990.

10135. O'Connor, John J. "Blacks on TV: Scrambled Signals." *New York Times*, 27 October 1991.

10136. _____. "The Curse of Incessant Cursing." *New York Times*, 31 July 1994. [Black comics]

10137. _____. "On TV, Less Separate, More Equal." *New York Times*, 29 April 1990.

10138. Omi, Michael. "In Living Color: Race and American Culture." in *Cultural Politics in Contemporary America*, pp. 111- 122. eds. Ian H. Angus, and Sut Jhally. New York: Routledge, 1989.

10139. Orenstein, Peggy. "Spike's Riot." *Mother Jones* (September 1989). [Spike Lee and "Do the Right Thing"]

10140. Ortizano, Giacoma L. "Visibility of Blacks and Whites in Magazine Photographs." *Journalism Quarterly* 66 (Autumn 1989).

10141. Pacheco, Patrick. "The Hudlin Brothers Set Out To Prove Black Is Bountiful." *New York Times*, 26 July 1992. [Black movie- makers]

10142. "Papers, Advertisers Attacked Over Racial Bias." *News Media and the Law* 15 (Spring 1991): 39-40.

10143. Pareles, Jon. "On Rap, Symbolism and Fear." *New York Times*, 2 February 1992.

10144. Parenti, Michael. "The Media Are the Mafia: Italian- American Images and the Ethnic Struggle." *Monthly Review* (March 1979): 20-26.

10145. Park, Jeana H. "Portrayal of Store Owner Seen as Volatile Stereotype." *Los Angeles Times*, 22 March 1993. ["Falling Down", a film starring Michael Douglas]

10146. Patterson, Pat. "Race and the Media in the 1980's." in *The State of Black America 1982*, pp. 239-263. ed. James D. Williams. New York: National Urban League, 14 January 1982.

10147. Payne, Les. "Desegregation in the City Room: 20 Years After Kerner." in *Kerner Plus 20*, Washington, DC: National Association of Black Journalists, 1988.

10148. Pearl, Jonathan M. *Jewish Themes in Prime-time Network Television Dramatic Programs, 1953-1986*. Ph.D. diss., New York University, 1988. UMO #8825046.

10149. Pearl, Jonathan M., and Judith Pearl. "As Others See Us. Jews on TV." *Moment* 15 (October 1990): 38-43, 58.

10150. Pease, Edward C. "Minority News Coverage in the Columbus Dispatch." *Newspaper Research Journal* 10 (Spring 1989): 17-37.

10151. _____. *Still the Invisible People: Job Satisfaction of Minority Journalists at U.S. Daily Newspapers*. Ph.D. diss., Ohio University, 1991. UMO #9131131.

10152. Pease, Ted, and J. Frazier Smith. *The Newsroom Barometer. Job Satisfaction and the Impact of Racial Diversity at U.S. Daily Newspapers*. Athens, Ohio: Bush Research Center, E.W. Scripps School of Journalism, July 1991.

10153. Pease, Ted, and Guido H. Stempel, III. "Surviving to the Top: Views of Minority Newspaper Executives." *Newspaper Research Journal* 11 (Summer 1990).

10154. Perkins, Kathy A. "Theater." *Black Women in America II*, pp. 1161-1165.

10155. Perry, Bruce. "The History That Isn't On the Screen." *Washington Post*, 22 November 1992. [Review of "Malcolm X" film, made by Spike Lee]

10156. Pettit, Arthur G. *Images of the Mexican American in Fiction and Film*. Texas A + M University Press, 1980.

10157. Philips, Chuck. "The Uncivil War." *Los Angeles Times*, 19 July 1992. [Rap music]

10158. Pickering, M. "Race, Gender, and Broadcast Comedy: The Case of the BBC's Kentucky Minstrels." *European Journal of Communication* 9 (September 1994): 311-334.

10159. Pierce, Chester M. and others. "An Experiment in Racism." *Education and Urban Society* (November 1977): 61-87. [Blacks in TV commercials]

10160. Pierre, Robert E., and Veronica T. Jennings. "'Chasm' Splits Whites, Blacks in Newsroom." *Washington Post*, 25 July 1993. [Survey by the National Association of Black Journalists]

10161. Pilmer, W. "Scarlett and the Blacks." *Listener* 122 (30 November 1989): 20-21.

10162. Poindexter, Paula, and Carolyn A. Stroman. "Blacks and Television: A Review of Research Literature." *Journal of Broadcasting* 24 (1981): 103-122.

10163. Press, Andrea L. *Women Watching Television. Gender, Class, and Generation in the American Television Experience*. Philadelphia: University of Pennsylvania Press, 1991.

10164. Preston, William, Jr. and others. *Hope and Folly: The United States and UNESCO, 1945-1985*. Minneapolis: University of Minnesota Press, 1989.

10165. Pristin, Terry. "A Matter of 'Honor'." *Los Angeles Times*, 21 May 1993. [Criticism of recent Latino films as depicting violent culture]

10166. _____. "'Substanial Barriers' to Minority Writers, Survey Finds." *Los Angeles Times*, 15 June 1993. [Film and TV]

10167. Puette, William J. *Media Portrayals of Organized Labor: The Limits of American Liberalism*. Ph.D. diss., University of Hawaii, 1989. UMO #9019002.

10168. Puga, Ana. "Minority Journalists Gather in Atlanta." *Boston Globe*, 28 July 1994. ["Unity", joint conference of black, Hispanic, Native American, + Asian journalists]

10169. Puig, Claudia. "KMPC Deejay Fired Over 'Racist' Skit." *Los Angeles Times*, 24 September 1992.

10170. "Racial, Indecent Broadcasts before FCC." *News Media and the Law* 14 (Winter 1990): 42-44.

10171. "Racism in the Media." *EXTRA!* (July-August 1992). [Published by FAIR-Fairness and Accuracy in Reporting]

10172. Rainer, Peter. "'Falling Down' Trips Over Its Own Hate." *Los Angeles Times*, 15 March 1993. [Film starring Michael Douglas]

10173. Ravo, Nick. "Ernest Dickerson Would Rather Be Called Director." *New York Times*, 18 April 1993. [African-American film cameraman and director]

10174. Raybon, Patricia. "A Case of 'Severe Blues'." *Newsweek* (2 October 1989). [Anti-black bias in Mass Media]

10175. Reed, Ishmael. "Tuning Out Network Bias." *New York Times*, September 1991.

10176. Reid, Mark A. *Black Oriented Film (1961-1977): Film Form, Black Culture, Ideological Content*. Ph.D. diss., University of Iowa, 1988. UMO #8815127.

10177. _____. *Redefining Black Film*. University of California Press, 1993.

10178. Reid, Tim. "A Tale of Two Cultures." *Los Angeles Times, TV Times*, 20 February 1994. [African-American TV actor-producer]

10179. Ribadeneira, Diego. "Hispanic Are Cast in Negative Light in Media, Groups Says." *Boston Globe*, 21 July 1994. [National Council of La Raza]

10180. Rich, Frank. "Public Stages." *New York Times Magazine* (7 November 1993). [Ted Danson in blackface]

10181. Richard, Alfred C., Jr. *Censorship and Hollywood's Hispanic Image*. Greenwood, 1993.

10182. Richards, C. "Anti-racist Initiatives." *Screen* 27 (September-October 1986): 74-79.

10183. Richardson, Marilyn. "What Price Glory?" *Reconstruction* 1, no. 2 (1990): 40-41. [Analysis of film Glory, a portrayal of black soldiers in the Civil War.]

10184. Richie, Rob, and Jim Naureckas. "Lani Guinier. 'Quota Queen' or Misquoted Queen?" *EXTRA!* 6 (July-August 1993): 5.

10185. Rickey, Carrie. "Spike Lee Gains World Status." *Boston Globe*, 25 May 1989. [His film, "Do the Right Thing"]

10186. Ridgeway, James. "Rightward Ho! Talk Radio's Journey to the End of Night." *Village Voice* (14 June 1994).

10187. Rigsby, Enrique Du Bois. *A Rhetorical Clash with the Established Order: An Analysis of Protest Strategies and Perceptions of Media Responses, Birmingham, 1963*. Ph.D. diss., University of Oregon, 1990. UMO #9111135.

10188. Roberts, C. "The Presentation of Blacks in Television Newscasts." *Journalism Quarterly* 52 (1975).

10189. Robertson, Nan. *The Girls in the Balcony: Women, Men and the New York Times*. New York: Random House, 1992. [Sexism at the New York Times]

10190. Robinson, Gene S. "Television Advertising and Its Impact on Black America." *The State of Black America 1990* (January 1990): 157-171.

10191. Rodriguez, Luis J. "Rappin' in the 'Hood." *Nation* (12 August 1991). [Unlicensed or pirate radio]

10192. Roefs, Wim, and Eileen Waddell. "Kenneth Campbell in Black and White." *In These Times* (23 October 1991). [Blacks in journalism in the South]

10193. Rogin, Michael P. "Making America Home: Racial Masquerade and Ethnic Assimilation in the Transition to Talking Pictures." *Journal of American History* 79 (December 1992): 1050-1077.

10194. Rohter, Larry. "Bias Law Casts Pall Over New Orleans Mardi Gras." *New York Times*, 2 February 1992.

10195. Rose, Jennifer. "Asian Women on Television: Still Typecast into Dead End Roles." *Philippine-American Journal* 1 (Winter 1989): 7-9.

10196. Rose, Lloyd. "He's Gotta Have It: Spike's 'X'." *Washington Post*, 22 November 1992. [Review of "Malcolm X" film, made by Spike Lee]

10197. Ross, Michael E. "At Newsstands, Black Is Plentiful." *New York Times*, 26 December 1993. [Magazine on black themes]

10198. Ross, Stephen J. "Cinema and Class Conflict: Labor, Capital, the State and American Silent Film." in *The Wilson Era: Essays in Honor of Arthur S. Link*, eds. John M. Cooper, Jr., and Charles E. Neu. Arlington Heights, IL, 1990.

10199. Ross, Steven J. "Struggles for the Screen: Workers, Radicals, and the Political Uses of Silent Film." *American Historical Review* 96 (April 1991): 333-367.

10200. Rothenberg, Randall. "Blacks Are Found To Be Still Scarce in Advertisements in Major Magazines." *New York Times*, 23 July 1991.

10201. Rothstein, Mervyn. "From Cartoons to a Play About Racism in the 60's." *New York Times*, 14 August 1991. [Lynda Barry's The Good Times Are Killing Me]

10202. Roudevitch, M. "Black Cartoon: Mickey est-il negre?" *CinemAction* 46 (January 1988): 79-81.

10203. Rubin, Bernard, ed. *Small Voices and Great Trumpets: Minorities and the Media*. New York: Praeger, 1980.

10204. Rule, Sheila. "Young Black Film Makers Face the Aftermath of Success." *New York Times*, 11 August 1994.

10205. Russell, Margaret M. "Race and the Dominant Gaze: Narratives of Law and Inequality in Popular FIlm." *Legal Studies Forum* 15 (Summer 1991): 243-254. [Birth of a Nation]

10206. Ryan, Charlotte. "A Study of National Public Radio." *EXTRA!* 6 (April-May 1993): 18-21, 26.

10207. Sampson, Henry T. *Blacks in Black and White: A Source Book on Black Films*. Metuchen, NJ, 1977.

10208. Sanders, Bob Ray. "Black Stereotypes on T.V.: 25 Years of 'Amos 'n' Andy'." *New American Movement* (February 1975).

10209. Savan, Leslie. "Bash and Cash." *Village Voice* (25 February 1992). [Anti-Japanese themes in U.S. advertising]

10210. _____. "Shortsheeting David Duke." *Village Voice* (26 November 1991). [The mass-media campaign against David Duke in Louisiana]

10211. Scardino, Albert. "Black Papers Retain a Local Niche." *New York Times*, 24 July 1989. [Atlanta Daily World and others]

10212. Scheinin, Richard. "Angry Over 'Aladdin'. Arabs Decry Film's Stereotypes." *Washington Post*, 10 January 1993.

10213. Schiller, Herbert. *Culture, Inc.: The Corporate Takeover of Public Expression*. New York: Oxford University Press, 1989.

10214. Shaw, David. "The Media and the LAPD: From Coziness to Conflict." *Los Angeles Times*, 24 May 1992. [Los Angeles Police Department]

10215. Shenitz, Bruce. "When Race Plays a Role." *New York Times*, 26 August 1990.

10216. Shirley, Don. "Taking a 'Maiden' Voyage." *Los Angeles Times*, 25 January 1994. [Wanda De Jesus and Jimmy Smits; two actors discuss Latino issues and humanity on the stage]

10217. Shohat, Ella. "Ethnicities-in-Relation: Towards a Multi- Cultural Reading of American Cinema." in *Ethnicity and American Cinema*, ed. Lester D. Friedman. University of Illinois Press, 1990.

10218. Siegel, Ed. "Life After 'Cosby'." *Boston Globe*, 19 April 1992.

10219. _____. "Of TV, Race and Romance." *Boston Globe*, 17 November 1991. [Portrayal on television of interracial romance]

10220. Singer, Eleanor. "The Polls-A Review: NBC's R.A.C.E.!" *Public Opinion Quarterly* 54 (Winter 1990): 605-608.

10221. Slee, Amruta. "Black Cowboys Ride Again." *New York Times*, 21 March 1993. [Western films]

10222. Sloan, Kay. *Loud Silents: Origins of the Social Problem Film*. Urbana: University of Illinois Press, 1988.

10223. Sloan, William D. "The Black Media, 1865-Present: Liberal Crusaders or Defenders of Tradition?" in his *Perspectives on Mass Communication History*, Hillsdale, NJ: Lawrence Erlbaum, 1991.

10224. Smith, Patricia. "Blaxploitation Was Beautiful." *Boston Globe*, 4 September 1994.

10225. _____. "A Daughter's Tale." *Boston Globe*, 15 March 1992. [Film director-writer Julie Dash and the making of "Daughters of the Dust," a film about Gullah people.]

10226. _____. "Voices Struggling to Be Heard." *Boston Globe*, 1 September 1991. [Black women film directors]

10227. _____. "Waiting for Professor Lee." *Boston Globe*, 26 January 1992. [Spike Lee at Harvard University]

10228. Spearman, Walter, and Sylvan Meyer. *Racial Crisis and the Press*. Atlanta, GA: Southern Regional Council, 1960.

10229. Stahl, Lori. "Pressing the Point: Minorities Protest News Media Images." *Dallas Morning News*, 28 October 1990.

10230. Stamets, Bill. "Marlon Riggs: In his Own Image." *In These Times* (22 April 1992). [Black film-maker]

10231. Stayton, Richard. "The Storm Over 'Oleanna'." *Los Angeles Times*, 30 January 1994. [Racism and sexism in a staging of David Mamet's play.]

10232. Steenland, Sally. *Unequal Picture: Black, Hispanic, Asian, and Native American Characters on Television*. Washington, DC: National Commission on Working Women of Wider Opportunities, 1989.

10233. Still, Lawrence A., ed. *The End of Rhetoric, the Beginning of Action, I-II: A Report of the First and Second Black Careers in Communications Conference*. Washington, DC: School of Communications, Howard University, 1973.

10234. Stone, Alan A. "Glory: A Failure of Reconstruction." *Reconstruction* 1, no. 2 (1990): 42-48. [Analysis of film Glory, a portrayal of black soldiers in the Civil War.]

10235. _____. "Jungle Fever." *Reconstruction* 1 (1992): 147- 152. [Spike Lee's films]

10236. Stone, C. Sumner. "Journalism Schools' Students and Faculty in the Year of Kerner Plus 20." in *Kerner Plus 20*, Washington, DC: National Association of Black Journalists, 1988.

10237. Stone, V. A. "Trends in the Status of Minorities and Women in Broadcast News." *Journalism Quarterly* 65 (Summer 1988): 288- 293.

10238. Streich, Birgit. "Propaganda Business: The Roosevelt Administration and Hollywood." *Humboldt Journal of Social Relations* 16 (1990): 43-65. [The economics of anti-fascist films]

10239. Stroman, Carolyn A. *The Mass Media and Black Americans*. Paper prepared for the Committee on the Status of Black Americans, National Research Council, Washington, D.C., 1986.

10240. _____. "Television's Role in the Socialization of African American Children and Adolescents." *Journal of Negro Education* 60 (Summer 1991): 314-327.

10241. Sullivan, Jim. "Pop's New Voices of Rage." *Boston Globe*, 22 December 1991. [Hate messages from rappers]

10242. Sumner, David E. "A Clash over Race: Tennessee Governer Ellington versus CBS, 1960." *Journalism Quarterly* 68 (Autumn 1991): 541-550.

10243. _____. *The Local Press and the Nashville Student Movement, 1960*. Ph.D. diss., University of Tennessee, 1989. UMO #9009116.

10244. Sun, Shirley. "For Asians Denied Asian Roles, 'Artistic Freedom' Is No Comfort." *New York Times*, 26 August 1990.

10245. Tabor, Mary B.W. "Encouraging 'Those Who Would Speak Out With Fresh Voice' through the Federal Communications Commission's Minority Ownership Policies." *Iowa Law Review* 76 (March 1991): 609-639.

10246. Taibbi, Mike, and Anna Sims-Phillips. *Unholy Alliances. Working the Tawana Brawley Story*. San Diego, CA: Harcourt Brace Jovanovich, 1989.

10247. Tajima, Renee. "'I Just Hope We Find a Nip in This Building Who Speaks English'." *Village Voice* (5 December 1989). [Treatment of Asian Americans in recent films]

10248. Takahashi, Dean. "The L.A. Riots and Media Preparedness." *Editor and Publisher* (23 May 1992). [On the Los Angeles Times by one of its reporters]

10249. Tassy, Elaine. "'Sankofa' Takes a Different Route to Theaters." *Los Angeles Times*, 25 January 1994. [Problems of marketing a different kind of film targeted at African-American audiences]

10250. Taylor, Ella. *Prime-Time Families: Television Culture in Postwar America*. Berkeley: University of California Press, 1989.

10251. Terry, Don. "In Week of an Infamous Rape [of a White Woman], 28 Other Victims [All Black or Hispanic] Suffer." *New York Times*, 29 May 1989.

10252. Terry, Wallace. "Don't Be Afraid To Fail." *Parade* (17 November 1991). [Debbie Allen]

10253. Tesser, Neil. "Latinos Lag in News History." *Chicago Reporter* 21 (March 1992). [Chicago news media]

10254. Thibodeau, Ruth. "From Racism to Tokenism: The Changing Face of Blacks in New Yorker Cartoons." *Public Opinion Quarterly* 53 (Winter 1989).

10255. Thompson, Julius E. *The Black Press in Mississippi, 1865- 1985*. University Press of Florida, 1993.

10256. Thompson, Shirley E. "Film." *Black Women in America, I*, pp. 428-433.

10257. Tierney, John. "Racial Unrest Fuels Physical Attacks on Journalists." *New York Times*, 21 May 1990. [New York City]

10258. Toplin, Robert B. "From Slavery to Freedom: The View through Film and TV Drama." in *The State of Afro-American History: Past, Present, and Future*, ed. Darline Clark Hine. Baton Rouge: Louisiana State University Press, 1989.

10259. Traub, James. "A Counter-Reality Grows in Harlem. Tuning in to The Gary Byrd Show." *Harper's* 283 (August 1991): 69-76. [Black radio talk show]

10260. Traube, Elizabeth G. "Transforming Heroes: Hollywood and the Demonization of Women." *Public Culture* 3 (Spring 1991): 1-29.

10261. Trevino, Jesus S. "Latinos Are Imprisoned by TV's Color Barrier, Too." *Los Angeles Times*, 15 June 1992.

10262. Turner, Patricia A. *Ceramic Uncles and Celluloid Mommies.* Anchor, 1994. [Racist stereotypes]

10263. _____. "Tainted Glory: Truth and Fiction in Contemporary Hollywood." *Trotter Institute Review* 4 (Spring 1990): 5-9. [Central part of article deals with film, "Glory", 1990]

10264. "TV's Black World." *New York Times*, 3 December 1989, letter.

10265. Tyler, Bruce M. "Racist Art and Politics at the Turn of the Century." *Journal of Ethnic Studies* 15 (1988): 85-103. [Birth of a Nation film]

10266. U.S. Commission on Civil Rights. *Window Dressing on the Set: Women and Minorities in Television.* Washington, DC: GPO, 1977.

10267. "U.S. Media and the Palestinians." *American-Arab Affairs* (Spring 1989): 68-93.

10268. Van Dijk, Teun A. *Racism and the Press.* New York: Routledge, 1991.

10269. Van Peebles, Mario, and Melvin Van Peebles. "For 'New Jack City', It's the Same Old Story." *New York Times*, 31 March 1991. [Son and father, both film-makers, discuss the state of black film-making in the U.S.]

10270. Vidman, N., and M. Rokeach. "Archie Bunker's Bigotry: A Study in Selective Perception and Exposure." *Journal of Communication* (Winter 1974): 36-47.

10271. Vincent, Richard C. and others. "Sexism on MTV: The Portrayal of Women in Rock Videos." *Journalism Quarterly* 64 (1987): 750-754, 941.

10272. Vincent, Ted. "The Crusader Monthly's Black Nationalist Support for the Jazz Age." *Afro-Americans in New York Life and History* 15 (July 1991): 63-76.

10273. Vizenor, Gerald. *Crossbloods. Bone Counts, Bingo, and Other Reports.* Minneapolis: University of Minnesota Press.

10274. Walker, Jimmie. "Black Shows Should Have as Much Dramatic License as White Shows." *Los Angeles Times*, 26 October 1992.

10275. Wallace, Michele. "'I Don't Know Nothin' 'Bout Birthin' No Babies." *Village Voice* (5 December 1989). [Treatment of blacks in recent films]

10276. Ward, Renee. "Black Films, White Profits." *Black Scholar* 13-24 (May 1976).

10277. Waters, Enoch P. *American Diary: A Personal History of the Black Press.* Chicago, IL: Path Press, 1987.

10278. Waters, Harry F. "Another Kind of Superhero." *Newsweek* (18 August 1993). [African-American comic books]

10279. Watrous, Peter. "When the Queen Speaks, People Listen." *New York Times*, 25 August 1991. [Queen Latifah]

10280. Wechsler, Pat. "Brooklyn's Fresh Filmmaker." *Washington Post*, 2 April 1993. [Leslie Harris, African-American film director]

10281. Weigel, Russell H. and others. "Race Relations on Prime Time Television." *Journal of Personality and Social Psychology* 39 (1980): 884-893.

10282. Weinstein, Steve. "New TV Riot Poll Sets Off Debate." *Los Angeles Times*, 6 June 1992. [TV news directors believe TV coverage of Los Angels rioting contributed to rioting in other cities.]

10283. "What Does TV Do for Racial Understanding?" *Los Angeles Times*, 20 September 1993. [Seven replies]

10284. White, A. "Keeping Up with the Joneses." *Film Comment* 25 (July-August 1989): 9-11. [Racism and imperialism in "Indiana Jones" films]

10285. Whittler, T. E., and J. Dimeo. "Viewers' Reactions to Racial Cues in Advertising Stimuli." *Journal of Advertising Research* 31 (December 1991): 37-46.

10286. Wibecan, Ken. "2 Beating Incidents Treated as Differently As Black and White." *Long Beach Press-Telegram*, 8 June 1992.

10287. _____. "Are Media Stirring Up More Riots?" *Long Beach Press-Telegram*, 15 February 1993. [Reference is to Los Angeles riot of April-May 1992]

10288. _____. "Minority Identification By Media Is Rank Racism." *Long Beach Press-Telegram*, 15 June 1992.

10289. Wicker, Tom. "Made by the Media." *New York Times*, 8 December 1991. [David Duke]

10290. Wilkerson, Isabel. "Black Life on TV: Realism or Stereotypes?" *New York Times*, 15 August 1993.

10291. Wilkes, Robert E., and Humberto Valencia. "Hispanics and Blacks in Television Commercials." *Journal of Advertising* 18 (1989): 19-25.

10292. Williams, Christopher C. "A Black Network Makes Its Move." *New York Times*, 17 September 1989. [Black Entertainment Television, a cable network]

10293. Williams, Lena. "Minority Journalists Question Reporting on Los Angeles Riots." *New York Times*, 28 June 1992.

10294. Wilson, Clint C., II. *Black Journalists in Paradox. Historical Perspectives and Current Dilemmas.* Westport, CT: Greenwood, 1991.

10295. Wilson, Harry L. "Media Treatment of Black Candidates: The 1989 Virginia Gubernatorial Campaign." *Virginia Social Science Journal* 26 (Winter 1991): 82-90.

10296. Wimmer, K. A. "Deregulation and the Market Failure in Minority Programming: The Socioeconomic Dimensions of Broadcast Reform." *Comm/Ent* 8 (Spring/Summer 1986): 329-480.

10297. "A Window on the Fast-Growing Audience of Asian- Americans." *New York Times*, 22 March 1993. [Publication of A. Magazine]

10298. Winkel, F. W. "Crime Reporting in Newspapers-An Exploratory Study of the Effects of Ethnic References in Crime News." *Social Behaviour* 5 (June 1990).

10299. Withall, Keith. "How Not To Tackle Racism on TV." *Race and Class* 31 (January-March 1990): 49-61.

10300. Wolcott, James. "Blows and Kisses." *New Yorker* (13 November 1993). [Ethnicity, race, and racism on television]

10301. Woll, Allen L. *Ethnic and Racial Images in American Film and Television.* New York, 1987.

10302. Wolseley, Roland E. *The Black Press, U.S.A.: Voice of Today*, 2nd ed. Ames: Iowa State University Press, 1989.

10303. Wurtzel, Elizabeth. "Fight the Power." *New Yorker* (28 September 1992). [Racial aspects of rap]

10304. Yang, Jeff. "Anything but the Girl." *Village Voice* (4 October 1994). [TV series, All-American Girl, about Asian Americans]

10305. Yearwood, Gladstone L. "The Hero in Black Film: An Analysis of the Film Industry and Problems in Black Cinema." *Wide Angle: A Film Quarterly of Theory, Criticism, and Practice* 5 (1982).

10306. Zamora, Del, Donald Zuckerman, and Kevin Benson. "Frida's Story: Artistic Choice or Cultural Catastrophe?" *Los Angeles Times*, 10 August 1992. [Two contrasting articles on casting a non-Latina actress as a Mexican artist]

10307. Ziegler, Dhyana, and Alisa White. "Women and Minorities on Network Television News: An Examination of Correspondents and Newsmakers." *Journal of Broadcasting and Electronic Media* 34 (Spring 1990).

MIGRATION

10308. Aderno, Malaika, ed. *Up South. Stories, Studies and Letters of This Century's African-American Migration*. New Press, 1993.

10309. Ashton, Guy T. "Migration and the Puerto Rican Support System." *R. Interam* 12 (Summer 1982): 228-242.

10310. Baerga, M. D., and L. Thompson. "Migration in a Small Semiperiphery: The Movement of Puerto Ricans and Dominicans." *International Migration Review* 24 (Winter 1990).

10311. Beale, Calvin L. "Migration Patterns of Minorities in the United States." *American Journal of Agricultural Economics* 55 (1973): 938-946.

10312. Belanger, Alain, and Andrei Rogers. "The Internal Migration and Spatial Redistribution of the Foreign-born Population in the United States: 1965-1970." *International Migration Review* 26 (Winter 1992).

10313. Bonilla, Frank, and Ricardo Campos. "Evolving Patterns of Puerto Rican Migration," in *The Americas in the International Division of Labor*, ed. Steve Sanderson. New York: Holmes and Meier, 1985.

10314. Campos, E. "The Process of Migration and the Social Structure of Puerto Rican Society." in *Sourcebook on the New Immigration to the United States*, ed. Roy S. Bryce-Laporte. New Brunswick, NJ: Transaction Books, 1979.

10315. Carlson, Shirley J. "Black Migration to Pulaski County, Illinois, 1860-1900." *Illinois Historical Journal* 80 (1987): 37- 46.

10316. Cebula, R. J., and W. J. Belton. "Voting with One's Feet: An Empirical Analysis of Public Welfare and Migration of the American Indian, 1985-1990." *American Journal of Economics and Sociology* 53 (July 1994): 273-280.

10317. Cohen, William. *At Freedom's Edge. Black Mobility and the Southern White Quest for Racial Control 1861-1915*. Baton Rouge: Louisiana State University Press, 1991.

10318. Cohn, D'Vera, and Rene Sanchez. "Migration From D.C. Is Booming." *Washington Post*, 28 April 1994.

10319. Corwin, Miles. "L.A.'s Loss: 'Black Flight'." *Los Angeles Times*, 13 August 1992. [Blacks moving to suburbs out of Los Angeles]

10320. Covington, James W. "Migration of Seminoles into Florida, 1700-1820." *Florida Historical Quarterly* 46 (1968).

10321. Cromartie, John, and Carol Stack. "Reinterpretation of Black Return and Nonreturn Migration to the South, 1975-1980." *Geographical Review* 79 (July 1989): 297-310.

10322. De Witt, Karen. "Wave of Suburban Growth Is Being Fed by Minorities." *New York Times*, 15 August 1994.

10323. _____. "Black Journeys" Many Travelers Along Many Roads." *New York Times*, 27 February 1994. [Migration]

10324. Devlin, George A. *South Carolina and Black Migration, 1865-1940: In Search of the Promised Land*. New York: Garland, 1990.

10325. Flores, Juan, ed. *Divided Arrival: Narratives of the Puerto Rican Migration 1920-1950*. New York: Centro de Estudios Puertorriquenos, 1988.

10326. Gill, Flora. *The Economics of the Black Exodus*. Ph.D. diss., Stanford University, 1974.

10327. Goodwin, E. Marvin. *Black Migration in America from 1915 to 1960: An Uneasy Exodus*. Lewiston, NY: Mellen, 1990.

10328. Gottlieb, Peter. *Making Their Own Way: Southern Blacks' Migration to Pittsburgh, 1916-30*. Urbana: University of Illinois Press, 1987.

10329. Gregg, Robert S. *Sparks from the Anvil of Oppression: Philadelphia's African Methodists and the Great Migration, 1890- 1930*. Ph.D. diss., University of Pennsylvania, 1989. UMO #8922507.

10330. Grossman, James R. *Land of Hope. Chicago, Black Southerners, and the Great Migration*. Chicago, IL: University of Chicago Press, 1989.

10331. Hardy, Charles A., III. *Race and Opportunity: Black Philadelphia during the Era of the Great Migration, 1916-1930. Two Volumes*. Ph.D. diss., Temple University, 1989. UMO #9007353.

10332. Harrison, Alferdteen, ed. *Black Exodus. The Great Migration from the American South*. Jackson: University Press of Mississippi, 1991.

10333. History Task Force, Center de Estudios Puertorriquenos. *Labor Migration Under Capitalism: The Puerto Rican Experience*. New York: Monthly Review Press, 1978.

10334. _____. *Sources for the Study of Puerto Rican Migration 1879-1930*. New York: Research Foundation of the City University of New York, 1982.

10335. Jett, Stephen C. "The Navajo in the American Southwest." in *To Build in a New Land*, ed. Allen G. Noble. Johns Hopkins University Press, 1992.

10336. Joe, J. "Forced Relocation and Assimiliation: Dillon Myer and the Native American." *Amerasia Journal* 13 (1986-1987): 161- 165.

10337. Johnson, J.H., Jr. "Recent African American Migration Trends in the United States." *Urban League Review* 14 (Summer 1990): 39- 56.

10338. Johnston, Allan. "Being Free: Black Migration and the Civil War." *Australasian Journal of Asian Studies* 6 (1987): 3-21.

10339. Klos, George E. "Blacks and the Seminole Removal Debate 1821-1835." *Florida Historical Quarterly* 68 (1989): 55-78.

10340. Lapp, Michael. *Managing Migration: The Migration Division of Puerto Rico and Puerto Ricans in New York City, 1948-1968*. Ph.D. diss., Johns Hopkins University, 1991. UMO #9113690.

10341. _____. "The Migration Division of Puerto Rico and Puerto Ricans in New York City, 1948-1969." in *Immigration in New York*, eds. William Pencak and others. Balch Institute Press, 1991.

10342. Larson, Tom. "The Effect of Discrimination and Segregation on Black Male Migration." *Review of Black Political Economy* 20 (Winter 1992): 53-73.

10343. Lemann, Nicholas. "Pro + Con: The Underclass and the Great Migration." *Public Interest* no. 105 (Autumn 1991): 107-113.

10344. _____. *The Promised Land. The Great Black Migration and How It Changed America*. New York: Knopf, 1991.

10345. Lemann, Nicholas, and H. Rogie Rogosin. "How to Read the Black Migration to the North." *New York Times*, 27 June 1991. [Two separate letters; see M. Duneier, above]

10346. Letwin, Daniel. *Black Migration: 1940-1970*. Paper prepared for the Committee on the Status of Black Americans, National Research Council, Washington, D.C., 1986.

10347. Lewis, Ronald L. "From Peasant to Proletarian: The Migration of Southern Blacks to the Central Appalachian Coalfields." *Journal of Southern History* 55 (1989): 77-102.

10348. Maldonado-Denis, Manuel. *The Emigration Dialectic: Puerto Rico and the U.S.A.*, Tr. by Roberto S. Crespi. New York: International, 1980.

10349. _____. "Puerto Rican Emigration: Proposals for Its Study." *Contemporary Marxism* no. 5 (Summer 1982).

10350. Maldonado, R. "Why Puerto Ricans Migrated to the U.S. in 1947-1973." *Monthly Labor Review* 99 (1976): 7-18.

10351. Margo, Robert A. "The Effect of Migration on Black Incomes: Evidence from the 1940 Census." *Economic Letters* 31 (December 1989).

10352. McCoy, Clyde, and James Brown. "Appalachian Migration to Midwestern Cities." in *The Invisible Minority: Urban Appalachians*, eds. W. Philliber, and C. McCoy. Lexington: University of Kentucky Press, 1981.

10353. McGreevy, John T. *American Catholics and the African- American Migration, 1919-1970.* Ph.D. diss., Stanford University, 1992. UMO #9234135.

10354. McHugh, Kevin E. "Hispanic Migration and Population Redistribution in the United States." *Professional Geographer* 41 (November 1989).

10355. Melendez, E. "Puerto Rican Migration and Occupational Selectivity, 1982-1988." *International Migration Review* 28 (Spring 1994): 49-67.

10356. Miles, Robert, and Victor Satzewich. "Migration, Racism and 'Postmodern' Capitalism." *Economy and Society* 19 (1990): 334- 358.

10357. Morales, Julio, Jr. *Puerto Rican Poverty and the Migration to Elsewhere: Waltham, Massachusetts: A Case Study.* Ph.D. diss., Brandeis University, 1979. UMO #8012759.

10358. _____. *Puerto Rican Poverty and Migration.* New York: Praeger, 1986.

10359. Nodin Valdes, Dennis. *El Pueblo Mexicano en Detroit y Michigan: A Social History.* Wayne State University Press, 1982.

10360. Obermiller, P., and W. Philliber, eds. *Too Few Tomorrows: Urban Appalachians in the 1980's.* Boone, NC: Appalachian Consortium Press, 1987.

10361. O'Hare, William P. and others. *Blacks On the Move: A Decade of Demographic Change.* Joint Center for Political Studies, 1982.

10362. Orser, W. Edward. "Secondhand Suburbs: Black Pioneers in Baltimore's Edmondson Village, 1955-1980." *Journal of Urban History* 16 (May 1990).

10363. Ortiz, Vilma. "Changes in the Characteristics of Puerto Rican Migrants from 1955 to 1980." *International Migration Review* 20 (Fall 1986): 612-628.

10364. Oszuscik, Philippe. "African-Americans in the American South." in *To Build in a New Land*, ed. Allen G. Noble. Johns Hopkins University Press, 1992.

10365. Rodgers, Lawrence R. *The Afro-American Great Migration Novel.* Ph.D. diss., University of Wisconsin, Madison, 1989. UMO #8915557.

10366. Saenz, Rogelio. "Interregional Migration Patterns of Chicanos: The Core, Periphery, and Frontier." *Social Science Quarterly* 72 (March 1991): 135-148.

10367. Schneider, M., and T. Phelan. "Black Suburbanization in the 1980's." *Demography* 30 (May 1993).

10368. Sheridan, Richard B. "From Slavery in Missouri to Freedom in Kansas: The Influx of Black Fugitives and Contrabands into Kansas, 1854-1865." *Kansas History* 12 (1989): 28-47.

10369. Soderlund, Jean R. "Black Importation and Migration into Southeastern Pennsylvania, 1682-1810." *Proceedings of the American Philosophical Society* 133 (1989): 144-153.

10370. Tolnay, Stewart E., and E. M. Beck. "Racial Violence and Black Migration in the American South, 1910 to 1930." *Sociological Abstracts* supplement 167 (August 1991) 91S25480/ASA/1991/6839.

10371. Trotter, Joe W., Jr. *The Great Migration in Historical Perspective*. Bloomington, IN: Indiana University Press, 1991.

10372. Vedder, Richard K., and others. "Demonstrating their Freedom: The Post-Emancipation Migration of Black Americans." in *Research in Economic History*, vol. 10. pp. 213-239. ed. Paul J. Uselding. JAI Press, 1986.

10373. Vobejda, Barbara. "Poor Americans Are Seen Fleeing Some States as Immigrants Move In." *Washington Post*, 12 September 1993.

10374. Weiss, Kenneth R. "Migration by Blacks From the South Turns Around." *New York Times*, 11 June 1989.

10375. Wilson, Leslie E. *Dark Spaces: An Account of Afro-American Suburbanization, 1890-1950*. Ph.D. diss., CUNY, 1992. UMO #9218286.

10376. Wright, Giles R. "Oral History and the Writing of Afro- American History: The Great Migration Experience (1915-1930)." *Journal of the Afro-American Historical and Genealogical Society* 10 (1989): 6-13.

MILITARY

10377. Allen, Robert L. *The Port Chicago Mutiny. The Story of the Largest Mass Mutiny Trial in U.S. Naval History*. New York: Warner Books, 1989.

10378. Angrist, Joshua D. *Economic Analysis of the Vietnam Era Draft Lottery*. Ph.D. diss., Princeton University, 1989. UMO #9007151.

10379. Anner, John. "Coloring the Peace Movement." *Guardian (NYC)* (6 February 1991). [People of color in movement against the Persian Gulf War]

10380. Applebome, Peter. "Arab-Americans Fear a Land War's Backlash." *New York Times*, 20 February 1991. [Persian Gulf War]

10381. Appy, Christian G. *Working-class War: American Combat Soldiers and Vietnam*. University of North Carolina Press, 1993.

10382. Badillo, Gilbert, and G. David Curry. "The Social Incidence of Vietnam Casualties: Social Class or Race?" *Armed Forces and Society* 2 (May 1976): 397-406.

10383. Baldwin, Mary F. *Developing a Climate of Equal Opportunity in Large Systems: A Case Study of the United States Navy's Equal Opportuity Race Relations Program*. Ph.D. diss., University of Massachusetts, 1993. UMO #8310264.

10384. Barkalow, Carol. *In the Men's House: An Inside Account of Life in the Army by One of West Point's First Female Graduates*. New York: Poseidon Press, 1990.

10385. Barsh, Russell L. "American Indians in the Great War." *Ethnohistory* 38 (Summer 1991): 276-303.

10386. Bartling, Carl A., and Mickey R. Dansby. "Assessment of Commitment to Equal Opportunity Goals in the Military." *Journal of Psychology* 124 (1990): 699-709.

10387. Bennett, B. Kevin. "The Jacksonville Mutiny." *Military Law Review* 134 (Fall 1991): 157-172.

10388. Berlin, Ira and others, eds. *Freedom: A Documentary History of Emancipation, 1861-1867. Series II, Vol. I: The Black Military Experience*. New York: Cambridge University Press, 1983.

10389. Bernstein, Alison R. *American Indians and World War II*. Norman: University of Oklahoma Press, 1991.

10390. _____. *Walking in Two Worlds: American Indians and World War Two*. Ph.D. diss., Columbia University, 1986. UMO #8610742.

10391. Billingsley, Andrew. "Enlists GI Joe as a Black Role Model." *Los Angeles Times*, 19 February 1993.

10392. Billington, Monroe. "Black Soldiers at Ford Selden, New Mexico, 1866-1891." *New Mexico Historical Review* 62 (1987): 65- 79.

10393. _____. "Civilians and Black Soldiers in New Mexico Territory, 1866-1900: A Cross-cultural Experience." *Military History of the Southwest* 19 (1989): 71-82.

10394. Bishop, Katherine. "Schools Resist Call(s) of the Military." *New York Times*, 4 February 1991. [Nearly all-Black Oakland Technical High School, California]

10395. Bullard, R. L. "Some Characteristics of the Negro Volunteer." *Journal of the Military Service Institution* 29 (1901): 29-39.

10396. Burk, Robert F. "Cold War, Limited War, and Limited Equality: Blacks in the U.S. Armed Forces, 1945-1970." in *The Foreign and Domestic Dimensions of Modern Warfare: Vietnam, Central America, and Nuclear Strategy*, ed. Howard Jones. Tuscaloosa: University of Alabama Press, 1988.

10397. Bussey, Charles. *Firefight at Yechon: Courage + Racism in the Korean War*. Riverside, NJ: Brassey's Defence Publishers, 1991.

10398. Butler, John S. "Inequality in the Military: An Examination of Promotion Time for Black and White Enlisted Men." *American Sociological Review* (October 1976): 807-818.

10399. _____. *Inequality in the Military: The Black Experience*. Saratoga, CA: Century Twenty One, 1980.

10400. Butler, John S., and K. L. Wilson. "The American Soldier: Race Relations and the Military." *Social Science Quarterly* 59 (December 1978): 451-467.

10401. Butler, Michael R., and Edward M. McNertney. "The Allocation of Death in the Vietnam War: Comment." *Southern Economic Journal* 55 (1989): 1029-1035. [See also reply by Brian L.Giff and Robert D. Tollison, 1034-1035]

10402. Carlisle, David K. "Soldierly Conduct." *New York Times Book Review* (30 July 1989): letter. [Maj. General Maxwell D. Taylor encouraged the continuation of discriminatory practices when he was superintendent of West Point, 1946-1949.]

10403. Carranoc, Lynwood, and Estle Beard. *Genocide and Vendetta: The Round Valley Wars in Northern California]*. Norman: University of Oklahoma Press, 1981.

10404. Carroll, John M., ed. *The Black Military Experience in the Amerian West*. New York: Liveright, 1971.

10405. Cashion, Robert T. "The Role of the Texas Rangers in the Mexican War." *E.C. Barksdale Student Lectures* 10 (1987-88): 268- 302.

10406. Chama, J. Richard. "Arresting 'Tailhook': The Prosecution of Sexual Harassment in the Military." *Military Law Review* 140 (Spring 1993): 1-64.

10407. Cheatham, Harold E. *Gender and Racial Equity in U.S. Military Occupational Distribution*. Patrick Air Force Base, FL: Final Report to Defense Equal Opportunity Management Institute, 30 September 1988.

10408. Cheatham, Harold E., and Susan R. Seem. "Occupation Equity: A Black and White Portrait of Women in the United States Military." *Review of Black Political Economy* 19 (Summer 1990): 65-78.

10409. Chomsky, Carol. "The United States-Dakota War Trials: A Study in Military Injustice." *Stanford Law Review* 43 (November 1990): 13-98.

10410. Christian, Garna L. "The Brownsville Raid's 168th Man: The Court-Martial of Corporal Knowles." *S.W. Historical Quarterly* 93 (July 1989): 45-59.

10411. Christopher, Renny T. *The Vietnam War/the American War: Images and Representaions in Euro-American and Vietnamese Exile Narratives*. Ph.D. diss., University of California, Santa Cruz, 1992. UMO #9302961.

10412. Cimprich, John, and Robert C. Mainfort, Jr. "The Fort Pillow Massacre: A Statistical Note." *Journal of American History* 76 (1989): 830-837.

10413. Clines, Francis X. "When Black Soldiers Were Hanged: A War's Footnote." *New York Times*, 7 February 1993. [Disproportionately large number of executions of black soldiers during World War II.]

10414. Congressional Budget Office. *Social Representation in the U.S. Military*. Washington, DC: CBO, October 1990.

10415. Cortright, David. "Black GI Resistance During the Vietnam War." *Vietnam Generation* 2 (1990): 57-64.

10416. Daniels, Lee A. "With Military Set to Thin Ranks, Blacks Fear They'll be Hurt Most." *New York Times*, 7 August 1991.

10417. Daula, Thomas and others. "Inequality in the Military: Fact or Fiction?" *American Sociological Review* 55 (October 1990): 714-718.

10418. Davis, Benjamin O., Jr. *Benjamin O. Davis, Jr. American. An Autobiography*. Washington, DC: Smithsonian Institution Press, 1991.

10419. De Parle, Jason. "In One City, 2 Campuses Worlds Apart on [Persian Gulf] War." *New York Times*, 22 February 1991. [Xavier and Tulane universities, New Orleans, LA]

10420. _____. "War, Class, Divisions and Burden of Service." *New York Times*, 13 November 1990.

10421. De Rose, David J. "Soldados Razos: Issues of Race in Vietnam War Drama." *Vietnam Generation* 1 (1989): 38-55.

10422. De Vergee, Winston W. *Assignment in Hell*. New York: Vantage Press, 1991. [Black marine in World War II]

10423. Donaldson, Gary A. *The History of African-Americans in the Military: Double V*. Melbourne, FL: Krieger, 1991.

10424. Dorn, Edwin. *Who Defends America?* Washington, DC: Joint Center for Political and Economic Studies, 1989.

10425. Doyle, Susan B. *Intercultural Dynamics of the Bozeman Trail Era: Red, White, and Army Blue on the Northern Plains, 1863-1868*. Ph.D. diss., University of New Mexico, 1991. UMO #9136262.

10426. Duncan, Russell, ed. *Blue-Eyed Child of Fortune. The Civil War Letters of Colonel Robert Gould Shaw*. University of Georgia Press, 1992.

10427. Edwards, J. E. and others. "Hispanic Representation in the Federal Government: Lessons from the Navy's Equal Opportunity Enhancement Program." in *Hispanics in the Workplace*, eds. Stephen B. Knouse and others. Newbury Park, CA: Sage, 1992.

10428. Firestone, J. M. "Occupational Segregation: Comparing the Civilian and Military Work Force." *Armed Forces and Society* 18 (Spring 1992): 363-382.

10429. "First Black Combat Pilot Finally Gets Recognition." *Long Beach Press-Telegram*, 12 October 1992. [Reprinted from Chicago Tribune]

10430. Fletcher, Marvin E. *America's First Black General: Benjamin O. Davis, Sr., 1880-1970*. Lawrence: University Press of Kansas, 1989.

10431. _____. *The Black Soldier and Officer in the United States Army, 1891-1917*. Columbia University Press, 1974.

10432. Flynn, George Q. "Selective Service and American Blacks During World War II." *Journal of Negro History* 69 (1984): 14-25.

10433. Foust, Brady, and Howard Botts. "Age, Ethnicity, and Class in the Viet Nam War: Evidence from the Casualties File." *Vietnam Generation Newsletter* 3 (December/January 1991-1992): 22-31.

10434. Fowler, Arlen L. *The Black Infantry in the West, 1869- 1891*. Westport, CT: Greenwood, 1971.

10435. Franco, Jere. "Bringing Them In Alive: Selective Service and Native Americans." *Journal of Ethnic Studies* 18 (Fall 1990): 1-27.

10436. _____. *Patriotism on Trial: Native Americans in World War II*. Ph.D. diss., University of Arizona, 1990. UMO #9024503.

10437. Franklin, John Hope. "Their War and Mine." *Journal of American History* 77 (1990): 576-579. [World War II]

10438. Fuchs, Richard L. *An Unerring Fire: The Massacre of Fort Pillow*. Fairleigh Dickinson University, 1994.

10439. Gaines, W. Craig. *The Confederate Cherokees. John Drew's Regiment of Mounted Rifles*. Baton Rouge: Louisiana State University Press, 1989.

10440. Gatewood, Willard B., Jr. "Alonzo Clifton McClennan: Black Midshipman from South Carolina, 1873-1874." *South Carolina Historical Magazine* 89 (1988): 24-39.

10441. Gill, Gerald. "From Maternal Pacifism to Revolutionary Solidarity: African-American Women's Opposition to the Vietnam War." in *Sights on the Sixties*, ed. Barbara L. Tischler. Rutgers University Press, 1992.

10442. Glatthaar, Joseph T. "Black Glory: The African-American Role in Union Victory." in *Why the Confederacy Lost*, ed. Gabor S. Boritt. : Oxford University Press, 1992.

10443. _____. *Forged in Battle. The Civil War Alliance of Black Soldiers and White Officers*. New York: Free Press, 1989.

10444. Greene, Jerome A., ed. *Lakota and Cheyenne: Indian Views of the Great Sioux War, 1876-1877*. University of Oklahoma Press, 1994.

10445. Gropman, Alan. "Benjamin O. Davis, Jr.: History on Two Fronts." in *Makers of the United States Air Force*, ed. John L. Frisbee. Washington, DC: Pergamon-Brassey's, 1989.

10446. Grusky, Sara. "The Changing Role of the U.S. Military in Puerto Rico." *Social and Economic Studies* 36 (1987): 37-76.

10447. Guttridge, Leonard F. *Military. A History of Naval Insurrection*. Naval Institute Press, 1992. [Includes material relating to racial disturbances on the Constellation]

10448. Hairell, Keith R. *The Battle of Fort Pillow and Its Significance in 1864*. Master's thesis, Sam Houston State University, 1981.

10449. Halloran, Richard. "Military Recruiting Hurt By Tight Labor Market." *New York Times*, 1 August 1989.

10450. Hayles, Robert, and Ronald W. Perry. "Racial Equality in the American Naval Justice System: An Analysis of Incarceration Differentials." *Ethnic and Racial Studies* 4 (January 1981): 44-55.

10451. Hedges, Chris. "Harlem's Guard Troops Complain of Treatment." *New York Times*, 23 February 1991. [Persian Gulf War]

10452. Holm, Tom. "Fighting a White Man's War: The Extent and Legacy of American Indian Participation in World War II." *Journal of Ethnic Studies* 9 (Summer 1981): 69-81.

10453. _____. "Forgotten Warriors: American Indian Servicemen in Vietnam." *Vietnam Generation* 1 (1989): 56-68.

10454. Holmes, Malcolm D., and John S. Butler. "Status Inconsistency, Racial Separation, and Job Satisfaction: A Case Study of the Military." *Sociological Perspectives* 30 (April 1987): 201-224.

10455. Hooker, Richard D., Jr. "Affirmative Action and Combat Exclusion: Gender Roles in the U.S. Army." *Parameters* 19 (1989): 36-50.

10456. Hope, Richard O. "Blacks in the U.S. Military: Trends in Participation." in *Race: Twentieth-Century Dilemmas--Twenty- first-Century Prognoses*, eds. Winston A. Van Horne, and Thomas V. Tounesen. Milwaukee: Institute on Race and Ethnicity, University of Wisconsin System, 1989.

10457. Jackson, Derrick Z. "A Slow Seller in Roxbury." *Boston Globe*, 10 February 1991. [Blacks in Boston and the Persian Gulf War]

10458. Jakeman, Robert J. *Jim Crow Earns His Wings: The Establishment of Segregated Flight Training at Tuskegee, Alabama, 1934-1942*. Ph.D. diss., Auburn University, 1988. UMO #8918798.

10459. Janowitz, Morris, and Charles Moskos, Jr. "The Military Establishment: Racial Composition of the Volunteer Armed Forces." *Society* 12 (May-June 1975): 37-42.

10460. Johnson, Charles, Jr. *African American Soldiers in the National Guard: Recruitment and Deployment During Peacetime and War*. Greenwood Press, 1992.

10461. _____. *Black Soldiers in the National Guard, 1877-1949*. Ph.D. diss., Howard University, 1976.

10462. Johnson, R. J., and H. B. Kaplan. "Psychological Predictors of Enlistment in the All-Voluntary Armed Forces: A Life-Event-History Analysis." *Youth and Society* 22 (March 1991): 291-317.

10463. Jones, Rachel L. "80 Percent of Chicago-Area Recruits Are Minorities." *Chicago Reporter* 20 (January 1991): 1, 6-9.

10464. Joseph, Richard. "Injustice Taints the 'Just War'." *New York Times* (2 March 1991). [Social injustices in the US and the Persian Gulf War]

10465. Kaplan, Amy. "Black and Blue on San Juan Hill." in *Cultures of United States Imperialism*, pp. 219-236. eds. Amy Kaplan, and Donald E. Pease. Duke University Press, 1993. [Black soldiers in the American empire]

10466. Kaplan, Fred. "Class, Racial Imbalances Mark Volunteer Military." *Boston Globe*, 6 December 1990.

10467. Karst, Kenneth L. "The Pursuit of Manhood and the Desegregation of the Armed Forces." *UCLA Law Review* 38 (February 1991): 499-581.

10468. King, William M. "'Our Men in Vietnam': Black Media as a Source of the Afro-American Experience in Southeast Asia." *Vietnam Generation* 1 (1989): 94-117.

10469. King, William M., ed. "A White Man's War: Race Issues and Vietnam." *Vietnam Generation* 1 (March 1989): entire issue.

10470. Knouse, Stephen B. "Racial, Ethnic, and Gender Issues in the Military." *International Journal of Intercultural Relations* 15 (1991): entire issue.

10471. Knox, Margaret L. "The New Indian Wars. A Growing Movement Is Gunning for Tribal Treaties, Reservations and Rights." *Los Angeles Times Magazine* (7 November 1993). [Wars against Indians]

10472. Kohn, Richard H., ed. *The United States Military under the Constitution of the United States, 1789-1989*. New York University Press, 1991.

10473. Kraft, Scott. "Black Like Me: Troops in Somalia." *Los Angeles Times*, 29 January 1993. [African-American soldiers in Somalia]

10474. Kryder, D. "The American State and the Management of Race Conflict in the Workplace and in the Army, 1941-1945." *Polity* 26 (Summer 1994): 601-634.

10475. Lacayo, Richard. "Why No Blue Blood Will Flow." *Time* (26 November 1990). [Economic class in the military during possible Persian Gulf war.]

10476. Lancaster, John, and Barton Gullman. "Marines Say Racial Numbers Back Mundy; Validity in Dispute." *Washington Post*, 16 November 1993. [Do black Marine Corps officers shoot, swim, or navigate as well as white officers?]

10477. Lane, Linda R. "The Military." *Black Women in America II*, pp. 791-797.

10478. Laskowsky, Henry J. "Alamo Bay and the Gook Syndrome." *Vietnam Generation* 1 (1989): 130-139.

10479. Lawton, Millicent. "Downsized Military Curtails Job Options For Some Graduates." *Education Week* (10 June 1992).

10480. Lemus, Rienzi B. "The Enlisted Men in Action, or the Colored American Soldier in the Philippines." *Colored American Magazine* 5 (May 1902): 46-54.

10481. Levy, Peter B. "Blacks and the Vietnam War." in *The Legacy. The Vietnam War in the American Imagination*, pp. 209-232. ed. D. Michael Shafer. Beacon Press, 1990.

10482. Luckett, Perry D. "The Black Soldier in Vietnam War Literature and Film." *War, Literature and, the Arts* 1 (1989): 1- 27.

10483. MacGregor, Morris J., and Bernard C. Nalty, eds. *Blacks in the United States Armed Forces: Basic Documents*. Scholarly Resources, 1977.

10484. Mahon, John K. "Anglo-American Methods of Indian Warfare, 1676-1794." *Mississippi Valley Historical Review* 45 (1958): 254- 275.

10485. Marable, Manning. "Peace and the Color Line: Toward a Third World Peace Studies Curriculum." in *Politics of Education*, eds. Susan J. O'Malley and others. Albany: State University of New York Press, 1990.

10486. May, Robert E. "Invisible Man: Blacks and the U.S. Army in the Mexican War." *Historian* 49 (1987): 463-477.

10487. McGuire, Phillip. "Desegregation of the Armed Forces: Black Leadership, Protest and World War II." *Journal of Negro History* 68 (1983): 147-158.

10488. _____. *He, Too, Spoke for Democracy: Judge Hastie, World War II, and the Black Soldier*. Westport, CT: Greenwood, 1988.

10489. Miller, Sherman N. "Should the Military Underwrite Teacher's Salaries?" *Cleveland Call and Post*, 17 May 1990. [Call for investment "in the neighborhoods supplying a disproportionate amount of the foot soldiers for America's Military Industrial Complex."]

10490. Modell, John and others. "World War II in the Lives of Black Americans: Some Findings and an Interpretation." *Journal of American History* 76 (1989): 838-848.

10491. Moffat, Susan. "Draft Rift Lingers 50 Years Later." *Los Angeles Times*, 12 March 1993. [Japanese Americans who refused to fight in U.S. armed forces during World War II]

10492. Moffat, Susan, and Susan Essayan. "'Go For Broke' Regiment Reflects on Bias Struggle." *Los Angeles Times*, 24 March 1993. [42nd Regimental Combat Team and the Japanese-American 100th Infantry Batallion, World War II]

10493. Moore, B. L. "African-American Women in the United States Military." *Armed Forces and Society* 17 (Spring 1991): 363-384.

10494. Morin, Raul. *Among the Valiant*. Los Angeles, CA: Borden Publishing Co., 1963. [Mexican Americans in U.S. military during World War II.]

10495. Moskos, Charles C., Jr. "The American Combat Soldier in Vietnam." *Journal of Social Issues* 31 (Fall 1985): 25-38.

10496. _____. "How Do They Do It?" *New Republic* (5 August 1991). [Race relations in the U.S. Army]

10497. Moskos, Charles C., Jr., and John S. Butler. *Blacks in the Military Since World War II*. Paper prepared for the Committee on the Status of Black Americans, National Research Council, Washington, D.C.: 1987.

10498. Murphy, Wanda H. *A Comparison of Black and White Daily Newspapers' Editorial Opinions Regarding a Selected Set of Events Related to the U.S. Involvement in the Vietnam War*. Master's thesis, Michigan State University, 1978.

10499. Musicant, Ivan. *The Banana Wars: A History of United States Military Intervention in Latin America from the Spanish- American War to the Invasion of Grenada*. New York: Macmillan, 1990.

10500. Muwakkil, Salim. "Religious Bullying, Racism Corrode Troop Relations." *In These Times* (20 February 1991). [Persian Gulf War]

10501. Mydans, Seth. "Children Rejected in Vietnam Find a Sad Sanctuary in U.S." *New York Times*, 28 May 1991. [American children of U.S. servicemen]

10502. Nalty, Bernard C. "The Black Servicemen and the Constitution." in *The United States Military under the Constitution of the United States, 1789-1989*, ed. Richard H. Kohn. NYU Press, 1991.

10503. _____. "A Record of Valor: Black Soldiers before Independence." *American Visions* 3 (1988): 18-23.

10504. "Navy Rejects Request to Overturn '44 Courts-Martial of 258 Blacks." *New York Times*, 9 January 1994.

10505. Noel, Peter. "FBI Probes Racism at N.Y. Navy Bases." *Village Voice* (23 July 1991). [See letter by C.H. Gnerbich, in Village Voice, August 6, 1991]

10506. An Observer. "The Gulf War and the Wounds of Race." *Reconstruction* 1 (1991): 6-10.

10507. Olsen, Frederick H. *The Navy and the White Man's Burden: Naval Administration of American Samoa*. Ph.D. diss., Washington University, 1976.

10508. Perry, Ronald W. "The Justice System and Sentencing: The Importance of Race in the Military." *Criminology* (August 1977): 225-234.

10509. Petras, James, and C. Davenport. "Prestigious Publications and Public Relevance: Vietnam War and Black Protest in the ASR and ASPR." *Crime, Law, and Social Change* 17 (March 1992): 107- 122. [American Sociological Review and American Political Science Review]

10510. Poe, S. C. "Human Rights and the Allocation of United States Military Assistance." *Journal of Peace Research* 28 (May 1991): 205-216.

10511. Potts, E. Daniel, and Annette Potts. "The Deployment of Black American Servicemen Abroad during World War Two." *Australian Journal of Politics and History* 35 (1989): 92-96.

10512. "Racial, Ethnic, and Gender Issues in the Military." *International Journal of Intercultural Relations* 15 (1991): entire issue (7 articles).

10513. Ramirez, Richard, and Madeleine Adamson. "The GI Bill of Goods: Minorities and the Military." *Minority Trendsletter* 1 (Fall 1988): 8-10.

10514. Redkey, Edwin S., ed. *A Grand Army of Black Men: Letters from African American Soldiers in the Union Army, 1861-1865*. Cambridge University Press, 1992.

10515. Reese, Joan. "Two Enemies to Fight: Blacks Battle for Equality in Two World Wars." *Colorado Heritage* (1990): 2-17.

10516. Reza, H. G. "Blacks' Battle in Military Likened to Gays'." *Los Angeles Times*, 14 June 1993.

10517. Rhodes, Charles D. "The Utilization of Native Troops in Our Foreign Possessions." *Journal of the Military Service Institution of the United States* 30 (1902): 1-22.

10518. Rishell, Lyle. *With a Black Platoon in Combat: A Year in Korea*. Texas A + M University Press, 1993.

10519. Rodriguez Beruff, Jorge. "Puerto Rico and the Militarization of the Caribbean, 1979-1984." *Contemporary Marxism* no. 10 (1985): 68-91.

10520. Rosenfeld, Megan. "Divided Over a Dream: A Monumental Battle." *Washington Post*, 27 January 1993. [Proposed Black Revolutionary War Patriots Memorial, to be built in D.C.]

10521. Rosenfeld, Paul, and Amy Culbertson. "Hispanics in the Military." in *Hispanics in the Workplace*, eds. Stephen B. Knouse and others. Newbury Park, CA: Sage, 1992.

10522. Rothwell, Bruce A. *Equal Promotion Opportunity and the Air Force: A Review of the Line Officer Promotion System*. Ph.D. diss., University of Alabama, 1991. UMO #9130259.

10523. Russell, James W. *Who Dies in Vietnam?* Master's thesis, University of Wisconsin, 1968.

10524. Sandler, Stanley. *Segregated Skies. All-Black Combat Squadrons of World War II*. Blue Ridge Summit, PA: Smithsonian Institution Press, 1992.

10525. Scharnhorst, Gary. "From Soldier to Saint: Robert Gould Shaw and the Rhetoric of Racial Justice." *Civil War History* 34 (December 1988): 308-322.

10526. Schexnider, Alvin J. "Blacks in the Military: The Victory and the Challenge." *State of Black America* (1988): 115-128.

10527. Schilz, Thomas F. "Plight of the Tonkawas, 1875 to 1898." *Chronicles of Oklahoma* 64 (1986): 68-87. [Former scouts for US Army; ended up losing all their lands]

10528. Schmitt, Eric. "Japanese-American Proves Marine Bias." *New York Times*, 2 January 1994.

10529. _____. "Marines Find Racial Disparity in Officer Programs." *New York Times*, 20 November 1992.

10530. Scott, William R. *The Sons of Sheba's Race: African Americans and the Italo-Ethiopian War, 1935-1941*. Indiana University Press, 1993.

10531. Seaman, Louis L. "Native Troops for Our Colonial Possessions." *North American Review* 171 (1900): 847-860.

10532. "Seeking 'Fair Deal' for a Black Cadet." *New York Times*, 31 January 1994. [Expulsion of Johnson C. Whittaker from the U.S. Military Academy in 1882]

10533. Segal, D. R., and V. Verdugo. "Demographic Trends and Personnel Policies as Determinants of the Racial Composition of the Volunteer Army." *Armed Forces and Society* 20 (Summer 1994): 619-632.

10534. Shafer, D. Michael. "The Vietnam-Era Draft: Who Went, Who Didn't and Why It Matters." in *The Legacy. The Vietnam War in the American Imagination*, pp. 57-79. ed. D. Michael Shafer. Beacon Press, 1990.

10535. Silberman, Neil A. "The Pequot Massacres." *MHQ: The Quarterly Journal of Military History* 1 (1989): 74-81.

10536. Simpson, Brooks D. "'The Doom of Slavery': Ulysses S. Grant, War Aims, and Emancipation, 1861-1863." *Civil War History* 36 (1990): 36-56.

10537. Smith, Sherry L. *The View from Officers' Row: Army Perceptions of Western Indians*. Tucson: University of Arizona Press, 1990.

10538. Stanfield, John H., II. "The Dilemma of Conscientious Objection for Afro-Americans." in *The New Conscientious Objection*, eds. Charles C. Moskos, Jr., and John W. Chambers, II. Oxford University Press, 1993.

10539. Steele, Matthew F. "The 'Color Line' in the Army." *North American Review* 186 (June 1907).

10540. Stiepsu, Judith H. *Arms and the Enlisted Woman*. Philadelphia, PA: Temple University Press, 1989.

10541. Stillwell, Paul, ed. *The Golden Thirteen. Recollections of the First Black Naval Officers*. Naval Institute Press, 1993.

10542. Sturdvant, Sandra P., and Brenda Stolzfus. *Let the Good Times Roll: Prostitution and the U.S. Military in Asia*. The New Press, 1993.

10543. Taulbert, Clifton L. *The Last Train North*. Tulsa, Oklahoma: Council Oak Books, 1992.

10544. Thomas, Joyce. *The 'Double V' Was for Victory: Black Soldiers, the Black Protest, and World War II*. Ph.D. diss., Ohio State University, 1993. UMO #9401367.

10545. Thomas, Patricia J., ed. *Women in the Navy*. Lawrence Erlbaum Associates, 1994.

10546. Thorne, Christopher. "Britain and the Black G.I.'s." *Sunday Times Magazine* (1973): 58-66.

10547. Trujillo, Charley. *Chicanos: Soladados in Vietnam*. San Jose, CA: Chusma House Publications, 1990.

10548. Tye, Larry. "All-Volunteer Force No Mirror of Society." *Boston Globe*, 2 February 1991.

10549. U.S. Congress, 102nd, 2nd session, House of Representatives, Committee on the Armed Services. *Gender Discrimination in the Military: Hearings...* Washington, DC: GPO, 1992.

10550. _____. *Women in the Military: The Tailhook Affair and the Problem of Sexual Harrassment Report*. Washington, DC: GPO, 1992.

10551. U.S. Department of Defense. *Black Americans in Defense of Our Nation: A Pictorial Documentary of the Black American Male and Female Participation and Involvement in the Military Affairs of the United States of America*. Washington, DC: GPO, 1991.

10552. U.S. Department of Defense. Office of the Inspector General. *The Tailhook Report: The Official Inquiry into the Events of Tailhook '91*. St. Martin's, 1993.

10553. Vahsen, Penny. "Blacks in White Hats." *U.S. Naval Institute Proceedings* 113 (1987): 65-70. [Naval Academy]

10554. Voelz, Peter M. *Slave and Soldier: The Military Impact of Blacks in the Colonial Americas*. Garland, 1993.

10555. Walker, Richard P. "The Swastika and the Lone Star: Nazi Activity in Texas POW Camps." *Military History of the Southwest* 19 (1989): 39-70.

10556. Ward, John W. "The Use of Native Troops in Our New Possessions." *Journal of the Military Service Institution of the United States* 31 (1902): 793-805.

10557. Warner, J. T. "Military Recruiting Programs during the 1980's: Their Success and Policy Issues." *Contemporary Policy Issues* 8 (October 1990).

10558. Weaver, John D. *The Brownsville Raid*. Texas A + M University Press, 1992 reprint.

10559. Weddle, Kevin J. "Ethnic Discrimination in Minnesota Volunteer Regiments during the Civil War." *Civil War History* 35 (1989): 239-259.

10560. White, Bruce. "The American Indian as Soldier, 1890-1909." *Canadian Review of American Studies* 7 (1976): 15-25.

10561. Wilbekim, Emil. "World War II's Black Pilots Fought on Two Fronts." *New York Times*, 21 April 1991.

10562. Wilkerson, Isabel. "Blacks Wary of Their Big Role in Military." *New York Times*, 25 January 1991.

10563. Willis, John M. *Who Died in Vietnam? An Analysis of the Social Background of Vietnam War Casualties*. Ph.D. diss., Purdue University, 1975. UMO #7607155.

10564. Ybarra, Lea. "Perceptions of Race and Class among Chicano Vietnam Veterans." *Vietnam Generation* 1 (1989): 69-93.

10565. Zeitlin, Maurice and others. "Death in Vietnam: Class, Poverty, and the Risks of War." *Politics and Society* 3 (Spring 1973): 313-328.

10566. Zollo, Richard P. "General Francis S. Dodge and His Brave Black Soldiers." *Essex Institute Historical Collections* 122 (1986): 181-206.

MINORITIES IN CONFLICT

10567. Abel, Annie H. *The Slaveholding Indians*. Cleveland, OH: Arthur H. Clark, 1915-1919.

10568. Anderson, James. "Black-Latino Inmate Feud Spilling Into Streets." *Long Beach Press-Telegram*, 17 April 1994. [Los Angeles County's Peter J. Pitchess Honor Rancho in Castaic]

10569. Anderson, Robert L. "The End of An Idyll." *Florida Historical Quarterly* 42 (1963): 35-47. [Blacks and Indians]

10570. Andrews, Thomas F. "Freedmen in Indian Territory: A Post- Civil War Dilemma." *Journal of the West* 4 (1965).

10571. Barrett, Wayne. "Mapmaker, Mapmaker, Make Me a Map." *Village Voice* (6 August 1991). ["How the Beastly Politics of Redistricting Pits Minorities Against One Another [in New York City]"]

10572. Bateman, Rebecca B. "Africans and Indians: A Comparative Study of the Black Carib and Black Seminole." *Ethnohistory* 37 (1990): 1-24.

10573. _____. *'We're Still Here': History, Kinship, and Group Identity among the Seminole Freedmen in Oklahoma*. Ph.D. diss., Johns Hopkins University, 1991. UMO #9113641.

10574. Boyd, Christopher. "Blacks Nurture Boycott in Miami." *Boston Globe*, 21 January 1991.

10575. Braund, Kathryn E. Holland. "The Creek Indians, Blacks, and Slavery." *Journal of Southern History* 57 (November 1991): 601-636.

10576. Britter, Thomas A. *The History of the Seminole Negro- Indian Scouts*. Master's thesis, Hardin-Simmons University, 1990.

10577. Chang, Edward T. "Building Minority Coalitions: A Case Study of Korean and African Americans." *Korea Journal of Population and Development* 21 (July 1992): 37-56.

10578. Chang, Jeff. "Race, Class, Conflict, and Empowerment: On Ice Cube's 'Black Korea'." *Amerasia Journal* 19 (1993): 87-107.

10579. Chavira, Ricardo and others. "Browns vs. Blacks." *Time* (29 July 1991). [Latinos and Afro-Americans]

10580. Coleman, Wanda. "Blacks, Immigrants, and America." *Nation* (15 February 1993). [African-Americans and Asians]

10581. Conciatore, Jacqueline, and Roberto Rodriguez. "Blacks and Hispanics: A Fragile Alliance." *Black Issues in Higher Education* 7 (11 October 1990): 12-15.

10582. Davis, Mike. "The Sky Falls on Compton." *Nation* (19 September 1994). [Latinos and African Americans]

10583. Deal, J. Douglas. *Race and Class in Colonial Virginia: Indians, Englishmen, and Africans on the Eastern Shore during the Seventeenth Century*. Garland, 1993.

10584. Dyer, James and others. "Social Distance among Racial and Ethnic Groups in Texas: Some Demographic Correlates." *Social Science Quarterly* 70 (1989): 607-616.

10585. Ellman, Yisrael. "Arab Americans and American Jews." *New Outlook* 35 (March-April 1992): 39-41.

10586. Forbes, Jack D. *Africans and Native Americans. The Language of Race and the Evolution of Red-Black Peoples*. University of Illinois Press, 1994.

10587. _____. *Apache, Navajo and Spaniard*. University of Oklahoma Press, 1960.

10588. _____. *Black Africans and Native Americans: Color, Race and Caste in the Evolution of Red-Black Peoples*. Oxford: Basil Blackwell, 1988.

10589. _____. "Hispano-Mexican Pioneers of the San Francisco Bay Region: An Analysis of Racial Origins." *Aztlan* 14 (Spring 1983): 175-189.

10590. _____. "The Manipulation of Race, Caste, and Identity: Classifying Afroamericans, Native Americans and Red-Black People." *Journal of Ethnic Studies* 17 (Winter 1990): 1-51.

10591. _____. "Mustees, Half-Breeds and Zambos in Anglo North America: Aspects of Black-Indian Relations." *American Indian Quarterly* 7 (1983): 57-83.

10592. Glanz, Rudolf. "Jews and Chinese in America." *Studies in Judaica Americana*, New York, 1970.

10593. Gleason, Philip. "Minorities (Almost) All: The Minority Concept in American Social Thought." *American Quarterly* 43 (September 1991): 392-424.

10594. Gonzalez, David. "A Storm in Williamsburg as Two Ethnic Groups Clash." *New York Times*, 17 November 1990. [Hispanics and Jews, Brooklyn]

10595. Graham, Hugh D. "Race, Language, and Social Policy: Comparing the Black and Hispanic Experience in the United States." *Population and Environment* 12 (Autumn 1990).

10596. Halliburton, R., Jr. "Black Slave Control in the Cherokee Nation." *Journal of Ethnic Studies* 3 (1975): 23-35.

10597. _____. "Black Slavery Among the Cherokees." *American Hist. Illus.* 11 (1976): 12-19.

10598. Hernandez, Sandra, and Jean Merl. "Melee Erupts Between Black, Latino Students." *Los Angeles Times*, 19 February 1994. [Paramount High School, Los Angeles County]

10599. Holmes, Steven A. "Minority Leaders See a Clash of Hues In a Rainbow Coalition." *New York Times*, 16 June 1991.

10600. _____. "Survey Finds Minorities Resent One another Almost as Much as They Do Whites." *New York Times*, 3 March 1994.

10601. Hudson, Charles M., ed. "Red, White, and Black. Symposium on Indians in the Old South." *Southern Anthropological Society. Proceedings* no. 5 (1971).

10602. Hutchinson, Earl Ofari. "Black-Latino Clashes Shatter Solidarity Myth." *Guardian (NYC)* (25 September 1991).

10603. _____. "Fighting the Wrong Enemy." *Nation* (4 November 1991). [Blacks and Koreans]

10604. James, Parthena L. "Reconstruction in the Chickasaw Nation: The Freedman Problem." *Chronicles of Oklahoma* 45 (1967): 44-57.

10605. Jeltz, Wyatt F. "The Relations of Negroes and Choctaw and Chickasaw Indians." *Journal of Negro History* 33 (1948): 24-37.

10606. Johnson, James H., Jr., and Melvin L. Oliver. "Interethnic Minority Conflict in Urban America: The Effects of Economic and Social Dislocations." *Urban Geography* 10 (September-October 1989).

10607. Johnston, James H. "Documentary Evidence of Relations of Negroes and Indians." *Journal of Negro History* 14 (1929).

10608. Katz, Jesse. "Clashes Between Latino, Black Gangs Increase." *Los Angeles Times*, 26 December 1993. [Southern California]

10609. Katz, William Loren. "Black and Indian Cooperation and Resistance to Slavery." *Freedomways* 17 (1977): 164-174.

10610. _____. *Black Indians: A Hidden Heritage*. New York: Atheneum, 1988.

10611. Kearney, Reginald. *Afro-American Views of Japanese, 1900- 1945*. Ph.D. diss., Kent State University, 1992.

10612. Kerrigan, Colm. "Irish Temperance and U.S. Anti-Slavery: Father Mathew and the Abolitionists." *History Workshop Journal* no. 31 (Spring 1991): 104-119.

10613. Klos, George E. "Black Seminoles in Territorial Florida." *Southern Historian* 10 (1989): 26-42.

10614. Kurtz, Howard. "Hughes Remarks Anger Hispanics." *Washington Post*, 22 February 1994. [African-American criticism of Hispanics in Washington, D.C.]

10615. Lee, Gary, and Roberto Suro. "Latino-Black Rivalry Festers in Cities." *Washington Post*, 13 October 1993.

10616. Lee, John H. "Diary of a War of Attrition in Volatile Urban Dispute." *Los Angeles Times*, 2 July 1991. [Black-Korean conflict in Los Angeles]

10617. Lew, Walter K. "Black Korea." *Amerasia Journal* 19 (1993): 171-174.

10618. Littlefield, Daniel F., Jr., and Mary Ann Littlefield. "The Beams Family: Free Blacks in Indian Territory." *Journal of Negro History* 49 (1976): 16-35.

10619. Martin, Douglas. "Korean Store Owners Join Forces, Seeking Ties, Opportunity and Clout." *New York Times*, 22 March 1993. [Korean-American Grocers Association of New York]

10620. Martinez, Elizabeth. "When No Dogs or Mexicans Are Allowed..." *Z Magazine* 4 (January 1991): 37-42. [Latinos and Black Americans]

10621. McClain, Paula D., and Albert K. Karnig. "Black and Hispanic Socioeconomic and Political Competition." *American Political Science Review* 84 (June 1990).

10622. McLaughlin, William G. "Red Indians, Black Slavery and White Racism: America's Slaveholding Indians." *American Quarterly* 26 (1974): 367-385.

10623. Meyer, Josh. "Peace Plan Elusive as County Jails Race War Continues." *Los Angeles Times*, 17 January 1994. [Latinos and African-Americans in the Pitchess Honor Rancho, Castaic, CA]

10624. _____. "Prisoners Are Segregated After Brawl." *Los Angeles Times*, 11 January 1994. [Black and Latino prisoners in the Pitchess Honor Rancho, Los Angeles County]

10625. Mohl, Raymond A. "On the Edge: Blacks and Hispanics in Metropolitan Miami since 1959." *Florida Historical Quarterly* 69 (July 1990): 37-56.

10626. Mydans, Seth. "Korean Shop Owners Fearful of Outcome of Beating Trial." *New York Times*, 10 April 1993. [Los Angeles]

10627. Nakano, Erich. "Building Common Ground-The Liquor Store Controversy." *Amerasia Journal* 19 (1993): 167-170. [Korean-owned liquor stores in South Central Los Angeles]

10628. Palmie, Stephan. "Spics or Spades? Racial Classification and Ethnic Conflict in Miami." *Amerikastudien/American Studies* 34 (1989): 211-221.

10629. Porter, Kenneth W. "Negroes and the Fur Trade." *Minnesota History* 15 (December 1934): 421-433.

10630. _____. "Negroes and Indians on the Texas Frontier, 1831-1876." *Journal of Negro History* 41 (1956): 185- 214, 285-310.

10631. _____. "Negroes and the Seminole War, 1835- 1842." *Journal of Southern History* 30 (1964): 427-450.

10632. _____. "Notes Supplementary to 'Relations between Negroes and Indians'." *Journal of Negro History* 18 (1933).

10633. _____. "Relations between Negroes and Indians Within the Present Limits of the United States." *Journal of Negro History* 18 (1932).

10634. Radzialowski, Thaddeus C. "The History of Relations between the Blacks and the Polish Ethnic Group in the United States of America." in *American Polonia: Past and Present*, eds. Hieronim Kubiak and others. Wroclaw: Polish Academy of Sciences, 1988.

10635. Roberts, Sam. "Hispanic Population Outnumbers Blacks in Four Cities as Nation's Demographics Shift." *New York Times*, 9 October 1994.

10636. _____. "Reshaping of New York City Hits Black-Hispanic Alliance." *New York Times*, 28 July 1991.

10637. Robles, Jennifer. "Captive Grocery Market Pits Blacks Against Arabs." *Chicago Reporter* 18 (November 1989).

10638. Rodriguez, Antonio H., and Carlos A. Chavez. "The Rift Is Exposed; Let's Bridge It:" *Los Angeles Times*, 24 July 1992. [Tension between Latino and African-Americans in Los Angeles]

10639. Rohter, Larry. "As Hispanic Presence Grows, So Does Black Anger." *New York Times*, 20 June 1993. [Miami, Florida]

10640. Romo, Harriet D., ed. *Latinos and Blacks in the Cities: Policies for the 1990's*. Austin, Texas: Office of Publications, Depr. LBC, LBJ School of Public Affairs, UT-Austin, 1990.

10641. Rose, Harold M. "Blacks and Cubans in Metropolitan Miami's Changing Economy." *Urban Geography* 10 (September-October 1989).

10642. Sefton, James E. "Black Slaves, Red Masters, White Middlemen: A Congressional Debate of 1852." *Florida Historical Quarterly* 51 (1972): 113-128.

10643. Shah, H., and M. C. Thornton. "Racial Ideology in United States Mainstream News Magazine Coverage of Black-Latino Interaction, 1980-1992." *Critical Studies in Mass Communication* 11 (June 1994): 141-161.

10644. Shankman, Arnold. "'Asiatic Ogre' or 'Desirable Citizen'? The Image of Japanese Americans in the Afro-American Press, 1867- 1933." *Pacific Historical Review* 46 (1977): 567-587.

10645. Smith, C. Calvin. "The Opressed Opressors: Negro Slavery Among the Choctaw Indians of Oklahoma." *Red River Valley Hist. Review* 2 (1975): 240-254.

10646. "So Where Are the Cooler Heads as Latinos, Blacks Square Off?" *Los Angeles Times*, 26 July 1992. [Editorial about situation in Los Angeles]

10647. Speck, Frank G. "Negroes and the Creek Nation." *Southern Workman* 37 106-110.

10648. Stepick, Alex. "The Haitian Informal Sector in Miami." *City and Society* 5 (June 1991): 10-22.

10649. Stern, Norton B. "The King of Temecula, Louis Wolf." *Western States Jewish History* 22 (1990): 99-111. [Jews and American Indians]

10650. Tobar, Hector. "Coming Together in Anger and Charity." *Los Angeles Times*, 11 June 1992. [Black-Latino unity after the Los Angeles riots]

10651. Tong, Soo Chung. "Animosity between Black and Asians Must Go." *Koreatown* (January-March 1984).

10652. Torres, Vicki. "Hate Crimes Ruin a Dream Neighborhood." *Los Angeles Times*, 29 November 1992. [Latino attacks on African Americans in Azusa, CA]

10653. Usner, Daniel H., Jr. *Indians, Settlers, and Slaves in a Frontier Exchange Economy: The Lower Mississippi Valley Before 1783*. Chapel Hill: University of North Carolina Press, 1992.

10654. Weinstein, Henry. "Tensions Escalate Between Leaders of Blacks, Latinos." *Los Angeles Times*, 11 July 1992. [In Los Angeles]

10655. Wilkerson, Isabel. "Black Mediator Serves As a Bridge to Koreans." *New York Times*, 2 June 1993. [Chicago]

10656. Willis, William S. "Divide and Rule: Red, White, and Black in the Southeast." *Journal of Negro History* 48 (1963): 157-176.

10657. Willson, Walt. "Freedmen in Indian Territory During Reconstruction." *Chronicles of Oklahoma* 49 (1971): 230-244.

10658. Woodson, Carter G. "Relations of Negroes and Indians in Massachusetts." *Journal of Negro History* (1920).

10659. Wrone, David R. "The Cherokee Act of Emancipation." *Journal of Ethnic Studies* 1 (1973): 87-90.

10660. Yi, Jeongduk. *Social Order and Contest in Meanings and Power: Black Boycotts against Korean Shopkeepers in Poor New York City Neighborhoods.* Ph.D. diss., CUNY, 1993. UMO #9325168.

10661. Young, Mary E. "Racism in Red and Black: Indians and Other Free People of Color in Georgia Law, Politics, and Removal Policy." *Georgia Historical Quarterly* 73 (Fall 1989): 492-518.

MULTICULTURALISM

10662. Abarry, Abu Shardow, ed. "Afrocentricity." *Journal of Black Studies* 21 (December 1990): entire issue.

10663. Abell, Creed W. and others. "A Statement of Academic Concern." *Daily Texan*, 18 July 1990. 2.

10664. Adams, Russell L. "Neophytes in Afrocentrism." *Washington Post*, 9 September 1993. [Critique of District of Columbia schools' handling of a proposed Afrocentric curriculum]

10665. Adelman, Clifford. *Tourists in Our Own Land*. U.S. Education Department, 1992.

10666. Adler, Jerry and others. "African Dreams." *Newsweek* (23 September 1991). [Afrocentrism]

10667. "Africentrism and Multiculturalism: Conflict or Consonance?" *Journal of Negro Education* 61 (Summer 1992): 235- 418.

10668. "Afrocentricity." *Journal of Black Studies* 21 (December 1990): entire issue.

10669. Aguero, Kathleen, ed. *Daily Fare: Essays from the Multicultural Experience*. University of Georgia Press, 1993.

10670. Alexander, Nick. "California Bound in Textbook Controversy." *Guardian (NYC)* (14 August 1991).

10671. Allen, Norm. "Black Athena: An Interview with Martin Bernal." *Free Inquiry* 10 (Spring 1990).

10672. *Alternatives to Afrocentrism*. Manhattan Institute, Center for the New American Community, 1994.

10673. *The American Tapestry: Educating a Nation, a Guide to Infusing Multiculturalism into American Education*. Alexandria, VA: National Association of State Boards of Education, October 1991.

10674. "The Americas Before and After 1492: Current Geographical Research." *Annals of the Association of American Geographers* 82 (September 1992): entire issue.

10675. Anderson, Martin. *Imposters in the Temple*. Simon and Schuster, 1992.

10676. Anderson, Peggy. "The Myth of Hellenism." *Guardian (NYC)* (13 March 1987).

10677. Anderson, Rasmus B. *Life Story*. Madison, WI, 1917.

10678. Anderson, Sara F. P. *Teaching Biology-related Social Issues: A Multi-disciplinary Approach for High School Students*. Ph.D. diss., University of Maryland, 1982. UMO #8308731.

10679. Appleby, Joyce. "Recovering America's Historic Diversity: Beyond Exceptionalism." *Journal of American History* 79 (September 1992): 419-431.

10680. Appleby, Joyce and others. *Telling the Truth About History*. Norton, 1994.

10681. Asante, Molefi Kete. "The Afrocentric Idea in Education." *Journal of Negro Education* 60 (Spring 1991): 170-180.

10682. Asante, Molefi Kete and others. "Afrocentrism in a Multicultural Democracy." *American Visions* (August 1991): 20-26.

10683. Asante, Molefi K., and Diane Ravitch. "Multiculturalism: An Exchange." *American Scholar* 60 (Spring 1991): 267-276.

10684. Ascher, Marcia. *Ethnomathematics: A Multicultural View of Mathematical Ideas*. Brooks-Cole, 1991.

10685. Auster, Lawrence. "America: Multiethnic, Not Multicultural." *Academic Questions* 4 (Fall 1991): 72-84.

10686. Axtell, James L. "Moral Reflections on the Columbian Legacy." *History Teacher* 25 (August 1992): 407-425.

10687. Bailey, Marlon M., and Michael Boulden. "The Challenges of 'Radical' Afrocentrism." *Chronicle of Higher Education* (27 April 1994). [Two letters criticize Christie Farnham Pope's March 30 piece critical of Afrocentrism]

10688. Baines, John. "Was Civilization Made in Africa?" *New York Times Book Review* (11 August 1991): 12-13.

10689. Balakian, Anna. "[Letter to the Editor]." *Chronicle of Higher Education* (4 March 1992): B7.

10690. Bamber, Linda. "Class Struggle." *Women's Review of Books* (February 1990).

10691. Banks, James A. "African American Scholarship and the Evolution of Multicultural Education." *Journal of Negro Education* 61 (Summer 1992): 273-286.

10692. _____. *Multicultural Education*. Allyn and Bacon, 1988.

10693. Barber, Benjamin R. *An Aristocracy for Everyone: The Politics of Education and the Future of America*. Ballantine Books, 1993.

10694. _____. "Global Multiculturalism." *World Policy Journal* 10 (Spring 1993).

10695. Barra, Allen, and Ty Burr. "Oliver Stone's Re-creation of the Kennedy Assassination Is Inspired Propaganda. But Is America Buying It?" *Entertainment* (17 January 1992): 16.

10696. Barreiro, José. "Challenging the Eurocentric Notion." in *Indian Roots of Democracy*, pp. xii-xvi. Ithaca, NY: Northeast Indian Quarterly, 1988.

10697. Bauer, Dale M. "The Other 'F' Word: The Feminist in the Classroom." *College English* (April 1990).

10698. Bedard, Marcia, and Beth Hartung. "'Blackboard Jungle' Revisited." *Thought and Action* (Spring 1991).

10699. Bellah, Robert N. "Citizenship, Diversity, and the Search for the Common Good." in *"The Constitution of the People": Reflections on Citizens and Civil Society*, ed. Robert E. Calvert. University Press of Kansas, 1991.

10700. Bellow, Saul. "Papuans and Zulus." *New York Times*, 10 March 1994.

10701. Bennett, William J. "Is Our Culture in Decline?" *Education Week* (7 April 1993).

10702. Bercovitch, Sacvan and others. "Commemorating 1492." *Tikkun* 7 (September-October 1992): 58-62.

10703. Berlowitz, Marvin J. "Multicultural Education: Fallacies and Alternatives." in *Racism and the Denial of Human Rights: Beyond Ethnicity*, eds. Berlowitz, and Ronald S. Edari. Minneapolis, MN: MEP Publications, 1984.

10704. Bernal, Martin. "'Black Athena' Author Responds to Critics." *Chronicle of Higher Education* (11 May 1994): letter.

10705. _____. "On the Transmission of the Alphabet into the Aegean before 1400 B.C." *Bulletin of the American Schools of Oriental Research* 267 (1987): 1-19.

10706. _____. "Response to Dr. John Ray." *Journal of Mediterranean Archeology* 3 (1990): 118-119.

10707. Bernal, Martha E., and George P. Knights, eds. *Ethnic Identity: Formation and Transmission Among Hispanics and Other Minorities*. SUNY Press, 1993.

10708. Bernstein, Richard. *Dictatorship of Virtue. Multiculturalism and the Battle for America's Future*. Knopf, 1994.

10709. Bernstein, Richard, and Louis Menand. "'The Culture Wars': An Exchange." *New York Review of Books* (3 November 1994).

10710. Bhabha, Homi. "Race and the Humanities: The 'Ends' of Modernity?" *Public Culture* 4 (Spring 1992).

10711. Bishop, Alan J. "Western Mathematics: The Secret Weapon of Cultural Imperialism." *Race and Class* 32 (October-December 1990): 50-65.

10712. "[Blacks and Multiculturalism.]" *Black Scholar* 23 (1993): selected articles.

10713. Blanch, Mary C. *Culture As a Control Mechanism in Schools*. Ph.D. diss., University of Utah, 1989. UMO #9003705.

10714. Blaut, J. M. *The Colonizer's Model of the World. Geographical Diffusionism and Eurocentric History*. Guilford Publications, 1993.

10715. Bloom, Lisa. "Constructing Whiteness: Popular Science and National Geographic in the Age of Multiculturalism." *Configurations* 2 (January 1994).

10716. Bok, Derek. "Worrying about the Future." *Harvard Magazine* (May-June 1991).

10717. Bowersock, G. W. "[Review of Black Athena, vol. 1]." *Journal of Interdisciplinary History* 19 (1989).

10718. Branhaw, Brocht. "Hellenomania." *Liverpool Classical Monthly* 14 (April 1989): 57-58.

10719. Bredemeier, B. J. L. "And Ain't I a Woman? Toward a Multicultural Approach to Gender and Morality." *Quest* 44 (August 1992): 179-209.

10720. Brennan, T. "PC and the Decline of the American Empire." *Social Policy* 22 (Summer 1991): 16-32. [PC: "Political Correctness"]

10721. Brettschneider, Marla. "Multiculturalism, 'JAP Baiting', and the Irrational." *Israel Horizons* 41 (Summer-Fall 1993): 14, 16.

10722. Broun, Elizabeth. "Foreword." in *The West as America: Reinterpreting Images of the Frontier, 1820-1920*, Smithsonian Institution Press, 1991.

10723. Buenker, John D., and Lorman A. Ratner, eds. *Multiculturalism in the United States. A Comparative Guide to Acculturation and Ethnicity*. Westport, CT: Greenwood, 1992.

10724. Buhanan, Barbara S. *Describing Cultural Diversity: A Comparison of Research Strategies*. Ph.D. diss., University of Arizona, 1987. UMO #8803248.

10725. Burdick, Susan E. *Gender, Culture and Classroom Interactions*. Ph.D. diss., Michigan State University, 1987. UMO #8714309.

10726. Burkart, Walter. "The Orientalizing Revolution Near Eastern Influence on Greek Culture in the Early Archaic Age." Translated by Margaret E. Pinder, and Walter Burkart. Harvard University Press, 1993.

10727. Buttlar, Lois, comp. "Multicultural Education: A Guide to Reference Sources." *Ethnic Forum* 7 (1987): 77-96.

10728. Cain, William. "An Interview with Irving Howe." *American Literary History* 1 (Fall 1989): 554-564.

10729. California Joint Committee for Review of the Master Plan for Higher Education. *California Faces...California's Future Education for Citizenship in a Multicultural Democracy*. Sacramento, CA, March 1989.

10730. Caraway, Nancie. "Holes in the Melting Pot." *In These Times* (16 September 1992). [Critical review of Arthur M. Schlesinger, Jr., The Disuniting of America].

10731. Carby, Hazel V. "The Multicultural Wars." *Radical History Review* no. 54 (Fall 1992): 7-18.

10732. Carnochan, W. B. *The Battleground of the Curriculum: Liberal Education and American Experience.* Stanford University Press, 1993.

10733. Carrier, James G. "Occidentalism: The World Turned Upside- Down." *American Ethnologist* 19 (May 1992): 195-212.

10734. Carruthers, J. H. "Outside Academia: Bernal's Critique of Black Champions of Ancient Egypt." *Journal of Black Studies* 22 (June 1992): 459-476.

10735. Cekola, Anna, and Len Hall. "Ethnic Backgrounds in the Foreground." *Los Angeles Times*, 6 December 1992. [Multicultural clubs at Trabuco Hills High School, Orange County, CA]

10736. Centeno-Rodriguez, Migdalia. *Cultural Sensitivity in the Corporate World.* Ph.D. diss., Pennsylvania State University, 1989. UMO #9007835.

10737. "The Challenge of 'Black Athena'." *Arethusa* (Fall 1989): special issue.

10738. Cheney, Lynne V. *Telling the Truth. A Report on the State of the Humanities in Higher Education.* National Endowment for the Humanities, September 1992.

10739. Chicago Cultural Studies Group. "Critical Multiculturalism." *Critical Inquiry* 18 (Spring 1992): 530-555.

10740. Chin, Daryl. "Multiculturalism and Its Masks: The Art of Identity Politics." *Performing Arts* 14 (January 1991): 1-15.

10741. Clewell, Beatriz C. and others. *Breaking the Barriers. Helping Female and Minority Students Succeed in Mathematics and Science.* Jossey-Bass, 1992.

10742. Cochran, Connie E. *Cultural Awareness of Elementary Teachers in the City of Camden Public Schools.* Ph.D. diss., Temple University, 1987. UMO #8812560.

10743. Cohen, Richard. "From Pluralism...To Multiculturalism." *Washington Post*, 19 May 1994. [Contends that certain aspects of a national culture can be superior to those of other cultures]

10744. "College Art Association Looks at Ways to Encourage 'Pluralism' in Its Annual-Meeting Program." *Chronicle of Higher Education* (8 April 1992): A9.

10745. "Columbus on Trial." *Social Justice* 19 (Summer 1992): 8 articles.

10746. Commissioner's Task Force on Minorities. *A Curriculum of Inclusion.* New York State Education Dept., 1989.

10747. Conner, Constance. "Is Multiculturalism Enough?" *Women's Studies* 20 (1992): 209-215.

10748. "A Conversation with Radin Palous." *Humanities* (March- April 1992): 9.

10749. Conzen, Kathleen N. and others. "The Invention of Ethnicity: A Perspective from the USA." *Altreitalie* 3 (1990): 37-62.

10750. Cooper, Kenneth J. "Broadening Horizons. Afrocentrism Takes Root in Atlanta Schools." *Washington Post*, 26 November 1992.

10751. Corner, T., ed. *Education in Multicultural Societies.* Croom Helm, 1984.

10752. Costrell, Robert. "The Mother of All Curriculums." *Brookline Citizen* (15 March 1991).

10753. Coughlin, Ellen K. "In Multiculturalism Debate, Scholarly Book on Ancient Greece Plays Controversial Part." *Chronicle of Higher Education* (31 July 1991).

10754. Coulson, R. "Arbitration and Cultural Diversity." *Arbitration Journal* 47 (March 1992): 2-4.

10755. "Cracking the Cultural Consensus." *Society* 29 (November- December 1991): 5-44, eight articles.

10756. Craige, Betty Jean. *Laying the Ladder Down: The Emergence of Cultural Holism.* University of Massachusetts Press, 1992.

10757. _____. "The Pursuit of Truth Is Inherently Disruptive and Anti-Authoritarian." *Chronicle of Higher Education* (6 January 1993). [See Lynne V. Cheney, above]

10758. _____. *Reconnection: Dualism to Holism in Literary Study.* University of Georgia Press, 1988.

10759. "Cultural Diversity in Education." *Journal of Teacher Education* 43 (March-April 1992): six articles.

10760. Cummins, James. "From Multicultural to Anti-Racist Education: An Analysis of Programmes and Policies in Ontario." in *Minority Education*, eds. Tove Skuttnab-Kangas, and James Cummins. Multilingual Matters Ltd., 1988.

10761. "The Curse of Columbus." *Race and Class* 33 (January-March 1992): entire issue.

10762. D'Ambrosio, U. "Ethnomathematics and Its Place in the History and Pedogogy of Mathematics." in *Schools, Mathematics and Work*, pp. 15-25. ed. M. Harris. Sussex, England: Falmer Press, 1991.

10763. Darder, Antonia. *Critical Pedagogy, Cultural Democracy, and Biculturalism: The Foundation for a Critical Theory of Bicultural Education.* Ph.D. diss., Claremont Graduate School, 1989.

10764. Darron, George H., Jr. *Class, Culture, and Perception: Photographing to Reveal an Intercultural Process.* Ph.D. diss., Boston University, 1989. UMO #9005503.

10765. Dei, G. J. S. "Afrocentricity: A Cornerstone of Pedagogy." *Anthropology and Education Quarterly* 25 (March 1994): 3-28.

10766. Denning, Michael. "The Academic Left and the Rise of Cultural Studies." *Radical History Review* no. 54 (1992): 21-47.

10767. Dershowitz, Alan M. "Harvard Witch Hunt Burns the Incorrect at the Stake." *Los Angeles Times*, 22 April 1992. A11 (Washington edition).

10768. Dickman, Howard, ed. *The Imperiled Academy*. Transaction, 1993.

10769. Diehl, Joanne Feit. "[Letter to the Editor]." *New York Times*, 25 May 1985. section 7.

10770. Diggins, John Patrick. *The Rise and Fall of the American Left*. Norton, 1992.

10771. "[Discussion of Black Athena]." *Journal of Mediterranean Archeology* 3 (June 1990): 52-110.

10772. "Diversity: It's More than Race of Culture." *Quill* (May 1992): entire issue.

10773. Duban, James. "A Modest Proposal: Stick to Writing in E306 at UT." *Austin American-Statesmen*, 26 August 1990. H3.

10774. Egan, Timothy. "Teaching Tolerance in Workplaces: A Seattle Program Illustrates Limits." *New York Times*, 8 October 1993. [Employees of the Washington State Ferry System]

10775. "Egyptian History Revised." *Journal of African Civilization* 4 (November 1982): special section. [Some material on black aspects of the subject]

10776. Ehrenreich, Barbara. "Cultural Baggage." *New York Times Magazine* (5 April 1992).

10777. Ellis, John M. "Political Correctness and Reason." *California Academic Review* (Fall 1991).

10778. Ellsworth, Elizabeth. "Why Doesn't This Feel Empowering? Working through the Repressive Myths of Critical Pedagogy." *Harvard Educational Review* (August 1989).

10779. Elshtain, Jean B. "Education Beyond Politics." *Partisan Review* (June 1992).

10780. Epstein, Kitty Kelly, and William F. Ellis. "Oakland Moves to Create Its Own Multicultural Curriculum." *Phi Delta Kappan* (April 1992): 635-638.

10781. Erickson, Joseph L. "Letter to the Editor." *Long Beach Union*, 13 September 1993. [Letter on "the dangerous doctrine of multiculturalism".]

10782. Escoffier, Jeffrey. "The Limits of Multi-Culturalism." *Socialist Review* 21 (July-December 1991): 61-73.

10783. *Etiquette of the Undercaste*. Smithsonian Institution, 1992.

10784. Feldman, K. D. "Multicultural Education and Anthropology: The Rise of Civilization as a Foundation Course." *Human Organization* 51 (Summer 1992): 185-186.

10785. Fish, Stanley. "There's No Such Thing As Free Speech and It's a Good Thing Too." *Boston Review* (February 1992).

10786. Flint, Anthony. "Black Academics Split on Afrocentrism." *Boston Globe*, 27 September 1994.

10787. Foote, Thelma W. "The Black Intellectual, Recent Curricular Reforms, and the Discourse of Collective Identity." *Radical History Review* no. 56 (Spring 1993): 51-57.

10788. Fortunati, Vita. "Multicultural Education and the Challenge of Ethnic Studies and Feminism: An Italian Perspective." *Yale Journal of Law and the Humanities* 6 (Winter 1994): 99-104.

10789. Foster, Lawrence, and Patricia Hergog, eds. *Defending Diversity: Contemporary Philosophical Perspectives on Pluralism and Multiculturalism*. University of Massachusetts Press, 1994.

10790. Fox, Robert E. "Afrocentrism and the X Factor." *Transition* no. 57

10791. Frideres, James S., ed. *Multiculturalism and Intergroup Relations*. Westport, CT: Greenwood, 1989. [Canada, Israel, U.S.A.]

10792. Fullinwider, R. K. "Multicultural Education." *University of Chicago Legal Forum* (1991): 75-100.

10793. Gabler, Neal. "The Dark Side of the American Dream." *Los Angeles Times*, 14 June 1992. [Moral relativism and multiculturalism]

10794. Gaines, Joseph H. *Music As Socio-cultural Behavior: Implications for Cross-cultural Education-A Case Study*. Ph.D. diss., Teachers College, Columbia University, 1989. UMO #9002533.

10795. Garcia, J., and S. L. Pugh. "Multicultural Education in Teacher Preparation Programs: A Political or an Educational Concept." *Phi Delta Kappan* 74 (November 1992): 214-219.

10796. Garcia, Mario T. "Multiculturalism and American Studies." *Radical History Review* no. 54 (1992): 49-56.

10797. Gardner, Jane F. "The Debate on Black Athena." *Classical Review* 41 (1991).

10798. Gates, Henry Louis, Jr. "The Debate [About Multiculturalism] Has Been Miscast From the Start." *Boston Globe Magazine* (13 October 1991).

10799. _____. "A Liberalism of Heart and Spine." *New York Times*, 27 March 1994.

10800. _____. *Loose Canons. Notes on the Culture Wars*. Oxford University Press, 1992.

10801. _____. "Multicultural Madness." *Tikkun* 6 (November- December 1991): 55-58.

10802. _____. "Multiculturalism and Its Discontents." *Black Scholar* 24 (1994): 16-17.

10803. Gates, Henry Louis, Jr., and Donald Kagan. "Whose Culture Is It Anyway?" *New York Times*, 4 May 1991. [Two contrasting views]

10804. Genovese, Eugene D. "Heresy, Yes-Sensitivity, No." *New Republic* (15 April 1991): 30-35.

10805. Geyer, Michael. "Multiculturalism and the Politics of General Education." *Critical Inquiry* 19 (Spring 1993): 499-533.

10806. Giannaris, Constantine. "Rocking the Cradle." *New Statesman* (10 July 1987).

10807. Gibson, Margaret A. "Approaches to Multicultural Education in the United States: Some Conceptions and Assumptions." *Anthropology and Education Quarterly* 15 (1984): 94-119.

10808. Gilbert, Sandra M., and Susan Gubar. "[Letter to the Editor]." *New York Review of Books* (16 August 1990).

10809. Gilligan, Carol. *In a Different Voice: Psychological Theory and Women's Development*. Harvard University Press, 1982.

10810. Glazer, Nathan. "Where Is Multiculturalism Leading Us?" *Phi Delta Kappan* 75 (December 1993): 319-323.

10811. Gleason, Philip. "Immigration and American Catholic Higher Education." in *American Education and the European Immigrant 1840-1940*, pp. 161-175. ed. Bernard J. Weiss. University of Illinois Press, 1982.

10812. Godwin, Gail. "One Woman Leads to Another." *New York Times*, 28 April 1985. section 7.

10813. Gomez-Pena, Guillermo. "The Multicultural Paradigm: An Open Letter to the National Arts Community." *High Performance* (September 1989): 18-27.

10814. Goonatilake, Susantha. "The Son, the Father, and the Holy Ghosts." *Economic and Political Weekly* (5 August 1989).

10815. Goot, M. "Multiculturalists, Monoculturalists and the Many In between: Attitudes to Cultural Diversity and Their Correlates." *Australian and New Zealand Journal of Sociology* 29 (August 1993): 226-250.

10816. Gow, David. "The Unknown Quantity." *Guardian (NYC)* (3 November 1987). [Anti-racist mathematics]

10817. Graening, John J. *An Evaluation of a Secondary Mathematics Teacher Education Program Emphasizing School Experiences in Contrasting Cultural Settings*. Ph.D. diss., Ohio State University, 1971. UMO #7204503.

10818. Graff, Gerald. *Beyond the Culture Wars. How Teaching the Conflicts Can Revitalize American Education*. Norton, 1992.

10819. Grant, Carl A. and others. "The Literature on Multicultural Education: Review and Analysis." *Educational Studies* 12 (1986): 47-71.

10820. Grant, Carl A. *Research and Multicultural Education: From the Margins to the Mainstream*. Falmer Press, 1992.

10821. Gray, Mary W. and others. *Statement on the 'Political Correctness' Controversy*. AAUP, 1991.

10822. Gray, Paul. "The Trouble With Columbus." *Time* (7 October 1991).

10823. _____. "Whose America?" *Time* (8 July 1991): 13-20.

10824. Greene, Linda S., and Robert H. Bork. "The Next-to-Last Word on Political Correctness." *New York Times*, 11 December 1993.

10825. Greene, M. "Diversity and Inclusion: Toward a Curriculum for Human Beings." *Teachers College Record* 95 (Winter 1993): 211- 221.

10826. Grele, Ronald J., ed. *Subjectivity and Multiculturalism in Oral History. International Annual of Oral History, 1990*. Greenwood, 1992.

10827. Gress, David. "The Case against Martin Bernal." *New Criterion* (December 1989).

10828. Gribben, Alan. "Politicizing English 306." *Austin American-Statesmen*, 23 June 1990. A14.

10829. Griffin, Jasper. "Who Are These Coming to the Sacrifice." *New York Review of Books* (15 June 1989).

10830. Hacker, Andrew. "'Diversity' and Its Dangers." *New York Review of Books* (7 October 1993). [Essay-review of six books]

10831. Hall, Edith. "When Is a Myth Not a Myth? Bernal's 'Ancient Model'." *Arethusa* 25 (1992): 181-201. [Also, Bernal's reply, 203- 214]

10832. Hall, Jonathan. "Black Athena: A Sheep in Wolf's Clothing? " *Journal of Mediterranean Archeology* 3 (1990): 247-254.

10833. Hanhan, Sara E. F. *The Young Child's View of Human Diversity: An Exploration*. Ph.D. diss., University of North Dakota, 1984. UMO #8425322.

10834. Harding, Sandra. "Is Science Multicultural? Challenges, Resources, Opportunities." *Configurations* 2 (May 1994). [Followed by comments of four writers]

10835. Harris, Marvin. *Why Nothing Works: The Anthropology of Daily Life*. Simon and Schuster, 1981.

10836. Hart D'avalos, Armando. "500 Years Since Columbus's Voyage." *Militant* (1 November 1991). [Cuban minister of culture]

10837. Hauser, Mary E. *Cultural Transmission in a Multicultural Elementary School*. Ph.D. diss., UC Santa Barbara, 1990. UMO #9130089.

10838. Hayes-Bautista, David E. "Academe Can Take the Lead in Binding Together the Residents of Multicultural Society." *Chronicle of Higher Education* (28 October 1992).

10839. _____. *Redefining California: Latino Social Engagement in a Multicultural Society*. Chicano Studies Research Center, UCLA, 1992.

10840. Henson, Scott, and Tom Philpott. "Charge of the Right Brigade against Multicultural Education." *Guardian (NYC)* (16 October 1991).

10841. _____. "The Right Declares a Culture War." *Humanist* 52 (March-April 1992): 10-16, 46.

10842. Hett, E. Jane. *The Development of an Instrument to Measure Global Mindedness*. Ph.D. diss., University of San Diego, 1991. UMO #9123938.

10843. Hill, Patrick J. "Multiculturalism: The Crucial Philosophical and Organizational Issues." *Change* 23 (July-August 1991): 38-47.

10844. Himmelfarb, Gertrude. "Conversation with Historian Gertrude Himmelfarb." *Humanities* (May-June 1991): 4-12, 34. Wash, D.C.: National Endowment for the Humanities.

10845. Hirsch, E. D., Jr. *The Aims of Interpretation*. University of Chicago Press, 1976.

10846. *History-Social Science Framework for California Public Schools: Kindergarten through Grade Twelve*. California State Department of Education, 1988.

10847. Hodge, Michael E. *Voices from Beneath the Veil: Toward an Afrocentric Sociology of African Americans*. Ph.D. diss., University of Florida, 1992. UMO #9331150.

10848. Hodgkinson, Keith. "Eurocentric World Views-The Hidden Curriculum of Humanities Maps and Atlases." *Multicultural Teaching* 5 (Spring 1987).

10849. _____. "Standing the World on its Head: A Review of Eurocentrism in Humanities Maps and Atlases." *Teaching History* no. 62 (January 1991): 19-23.

10850. Hofstadter, Richard, and Walter P. Metzger. *The Development of Academic Freedom in the United States*. Columbia University Press, 1955.

10851. Holcomb, Billie D. *The Cultural Impact of Shorthand*. Ph.D. diss., University of Oklahoma, 1970. UMO #7022986.

10852. Hook, Eleanor. *The Experience of the Transfer of Cultural Meaning in Visual Arts*. Ph.D. diss., Union Institute, 1990. UMO #9107759.

10853. Hook, Sidney. "Communists, McCarthy and American Universities." *Minerva* (Autumn 1987).

10854. Horne, Gerald. "Afrocentric Curriculum Should Right Narrow Nationalism." *Guardian (NYC)* (20 February 1991).

10855. Horwitz, Sari, and Cindy Loose. "Afrocentric Program Gets Go-Ahead." *Washington Post*, 4 September 1993. [Webb Elementary School, Wash. D.C.]

10856. Houghton, John W. *Culture and Currency: Cultural Bias in Monetary Theory and Policy*. Westview, 1991.

10857. Howe, Irving. "The Value of the Canon." *New Republic* (18 February 1991).

10858. Howe, K. R. "Liberal Democracy, Equal Educational Opportunity, and the Challenge of Multiculturalism." *American Educational Research Journal* 29 (Autumn 1992): 455-470.

10859. Huber, Bettina J. "Today's Literature Classroom: Findings from the MLA's 1990 Survey of Upper-Division Courses." *ADE Bulletin* (Spring 1992): 48-53.

10860. Hughes, Clarence E. *Cultural Pluralism versus Cultural Assimilationism as a Suggested Perspective for Social Studies Education*. Ph.D. diss., University of Missouri, KC, 1974.

10861. Hughes, Robert. *Culture of Complaint. The Fraying of America*. Oxford University Press, 1993.

10862. _____. "Making the World Safe for Elitism." *Washington Post*, 27 June 1993. ["Multiculturalism in Art Equals Middlebrow Kitsch"]

10863. Hurlbert, C. Mark, and Samuel Totten, eds. *Social Issues in the English Classroom*. National Council of Teachers of English, 1992. [Includes discussion of racism]

10864. Hustveldt, Lloyd. *Rasmus Bjorn Anderson, Pioneer and Scholar*. Northfield, MN: Norwegian American Historical Assoc., 1966.

10865. Hutchinson, Earl Ofari. "Some Africanists Play Into Enemy Hands." *Guardian (NYC)* (6 May 1992).

10866. Hwang, D. H. "Evolving a Multicultural Tradition." *MELUS* 16 (Fall 1989-1990): 16-19.

10867. Hymowitz, Kay S. "Multiculturalism Is Anti-Culture." *New York Times*, 25 March 1993.

10868. "The Identity in Question." *October* 61 (Summer 1992): entire issue.

10869. "The Inclusive University: Multicultural Perspectives in Higher Education." *American Behavioral Scientist* 34 (November- December 1990): entire issue.

10870. Ingulli, Elaine D. "Transforming the Curriculum: What Does the Pedagogy of Inclusion Mean for Business Law." *American Business Law Journal* 28 (Winter 1991): 605-647.

10871. "Is Duke 'Politically Correct'?" *Duke: A Magazine for Alumni and Friends* (August-September 1991): 23. [Paid advertisement]

10872. Jackson, Kenneth T. "Too Many Have Let Enthusiasm Outrun Reason." *Boston Globe Magazine* (13 October 1991): 27-32.

10873. Jarvis, S. R. "Brown and the Afrocentric Curriculum." *Yale Law Journal* 101 (April 1992).

10874. Jean, Clinton M. *Behind the Eurocentric Veil: The Search for African Realities*. Amherst: University of Massachusetts Press, 1992.

10875. Jennings, James, and Illene Carver. "Are Today's Teachers Being Prepared for Diversity? An Analysis of School Catalogues." *Trotter Institute Review* (Winter/Spring 1992): 4-7.

10876. Johnson, Alex M., Jr. "The New Voice of Color." *Yale Law Journal* (May 1991).

10877. Johnson, Sylvia T., ed. "Africentrism and Multiculturalism: Conflict or Consonance." *Journal of Negro Education* 61 (Summer 1992).

10878. Jones, Bruce A. "Multicultural Education, Racism and Reason for Caution." *Black Issues in Higher Education* 7 (22 November 1990): 96.

10879. Jones, Judith H. *The Development of an Educational Program and an Analysis of Its Effectiveness in Altering Racial Attitudes of Mid-level Managers in a Public Agency*. Ph.D. diss., University of North Carolina, 1991. UMO #9135276.

10880. Jorde, Doris M. *An Ethnographic Study of an Urban High School: Science in the School Culture*. Ph.D. diss., UC Berkeley, 1984. UMO #8512870.

10881. Joseph, G. G. "Foundations of Eurocentrism in Mathematics." in *Schools, Mathematics and Work*, ed. M. Harris. Sussex, England: Falmer Press, 1991.

10882. Joughin, Louis, ed. "The 1915 Declaration of Principle." in *Academic Freedom and Tenure: A Handbook of the American Association of University Professors*, University of Wisconsin Press, 1969.

10883. Kalantzis, Mary, and William Cope. "Multiculturalism May Prove to Be the Key Issue of Our Epoch." *Chronicle of Higher Education* (4 November 1992).

10884. Kang, Jaime M. *Incorporating Diversity into Early Childhood Education: A Multicultural Approach*. Ph.D. diss., Southern Baptist Theological Seminary, 1991. UMO #9205773.

10885. Katz, Stephen T. "The Problems of Europocentrism and Evolutionism in Marx's Writings on Colonialism." *Political Studies* 38 (December 1990): 672-686.

10886. Kauffman, L. A. "The Diversity Game." *Village Voice* (31 August 1993). [Teaching about multiculturalism in business]

10887. Keats, Brian E. *The Effects of an Afro-American History Course on the Racial Attitudes of High School Students*. Ph.D. diss., University of Wisconsin, 1989. UMO #8923379.

10888. Keller, Gary D. and others, eds. *Curriculum Resources in Chicano Studies*. Tempe, AZ: Bilingual Review/Press, 1989.

10889. Kelly, David H. "Egyptians and Ethiopians: Color, Race, and Racism." *Classical Outlook* 68 (Spring 1991): 77-82.

10890. Kempton, Murray. "Another Case of Multiculturalism." *New York Review of Books* (9 April 1992). [Changing literary canons and organized criminals]

10891. Kennedy, Randall L. "Racial Critiques of Legal Academia." *Harvard Law Review* (June 1989).

10892. King, Joyce E. "Dysconscious Racism: Ideology, Identity, and the Miseducation of Teachers." *Journal of Negro Education* 60 (1991): 133-146.

10893. Klein, Kerwin L. "Frontier Tales: The Narrative Construction of Cultural Borders in Twentieth-Century California." *Comparative Studies in Society and History* 34 (July 1992): 464-490.

10894. Kohl, Herbert. "The Politically Correct Bypass Multiculturalism and the Public Schools." *Social Policy* 22 (Summer 1991): 33-41.

10895. Kramer, Rita. *Ed School Follies: The Miseducation of America's Teachers*. Free Press, 1991.

10896. Krauthammer, Charles. "Westward Hokum: Political Correctness Comes to the Smithsonian." *Washington Post*, 31 May 1991. A19.

10897. Kukathas, Chandran. "Are There Any Cultural Rights?" *Political Theory* 20 (February 1992): 105-139.

10898. Kuper, Adam. *The Chosen Primate. Human Nature and Cultural Diversity*. Harvard University Press, 1994.

10899. Kymlicka, Will. "The Rights of Minority Cultures. Reply to Kukathas." *Political Theory* 20 (February 1992): 140-146.

10900. La Pointe, Clare. *Cross-cultural Learning: The Relationships between Cultures, Learning Styles, Classroom Environments, and Teaching Procedures*. Ph.D. diss., UCLA, 1990. UMO #9014728.

10901. Ladson Billings, G. "Beyond Multicultural Illiteracy." *Journal of Negro Education* 60 (Spring 1991): 147-157.

10902. Lambropoulos, Vasiclis. *The Rise of Eurocentrism. Anatomy of Interpretation*. Princeton University Press, 1992.

10903. Landers, Robert K. "Conflict Over Multicultural Education." *Editorial Research Reports* (3 November 1990): 682- 695.

10904. Lawton, Millicent. "Differing on Diversity." *Education Week* (1 December 1993).

10905. Lazare, Daniel. "The Cult of Multiculturalism." *Village Voice* (7 May 1991).

10906. Lazere, Donald. "Back to Basics: A Force for Oppression or Liberation?" *College English* (January 1992).

10907. Leach, Edmund. "Aryan Warlords in Their Chariots." *London Review of Books* (2 April 1987).

10908. Leff, Lisa. "Diversity Tests Schools. Area Educators Struggle to Balance Curriculum." *Washington Post*, 28 November 1992.

10909. Lefkowitz, Mary. "Afrocentrism Poses a Threat to the Rationalist Tradition." *Chronicle of Higher Education* (6 May 1992).

10910. _____. "Confronting False Theories in the Classroom." *Chronicle of Higher Education* (19 January 1994). [Criticizes some Afrocentric propositions]

10911. _____. "Not Out of Africa." *New Republic* 206 (10 January 1992): 29-36. [Also, letter by Bernal and reply, March 9, 1992, pp. 4-5]

10912. Lejeune, Catherine. "The Challenge Facing America over the Chicano Identity Question in Light of the Quincentenary Celebration of 1992." *North Dakota Quarterly* 60 (Winter 1992): 174-179.

10913. Levine, George and others. *Speaking for the Humanities*. American Council of Learned Societies, 1989.

10914. Levine, Molly M., ed. "The Challenge of Black Athena." *Arethusa* (Fall 1989): symposium.

10915. _____. "Classical Scholarship-Anti-Black and Anti- Semitic?" *Bible Review* 6 (June 1990).

10916. Levine, Molly M. "Multiculturalism and the Classics." *Arethusa* 25 (1992): 215-220.

10917. _____. "The Use and Abuse of Black Athena." *American Historical Review* 97 (April 1992): 440-460. [Review article]

10918. Levine, Paul. "War No More." *Nation* (8 February 1993).

10919. Lippard, Lucy R. "Sniper's Nest. Showing the Right Thing for a Change." *Zeta Magazine* 2 (November 1989): 79-81. [Account of conference, "Show the Right Thing", on "multicultural film and video exhibition".]

10920. Liu, T. P. "Race and Gender in the Politics of Group Formation: A Comment on Notions of Multiculturalism." *Frontiers* 12 (1991).

10921. Locke, Don C. *Increasing Multicultural Understanding. A Comprehensive Model*. Sage, 1992.

10922. Loewen, James W. "Columbus in History and High School." *Akwe: kon Journal* 9 (Spring 1992): 28-36.

10923. _____. *The Truth About Columbus*. The New Press, 1992.

10924. Lowenthal, David. "History Becomes 'Heritage' in Race Question." *Perspectives* (January 1994): 17-18. [History and Afrocentricity]

10925. Lynch, James and others, eds. *Cultural Diversity and the Schools. 4 vols*. Falmer Press, 1992.

10926. MacDonald, Heather. "The Sobol Report: Multiculturalism Triumphant." *New Criterion* (January 1992).

10927. Malamud, Martha A. "[Review of Bernal, vol. 1]." *Criticism* 1 (1989): 317-322.

10928. Manning, Stuart. "Frames of Reference for the Past: Some Thoughts on Bernal, Truth and Reality." *Journal of Mediterranean Archeology* 3 (1990): 255-274.

10929. Marable, Manning. "Blueprint for Black Studies and Multiculturalism." *Black Scholar* 22 (Summer 1992): 30-35.

10930. _____. "Columbus Myth at the Heart of Racism." *Guardian (NYC)* (16 October 1991).

10931. _____. "Multicultural Democracy." *Cross Roads: Contemporary Political Analysis and Left Dialogue* 11 (June 1991): 8-11.

10932. _____. "Multicultural Democracy: Toward a New Strategy for Progressive Activism." *Z Magazine* (November 1991).

10933. Marriott, Michel. "Afrocentrism: Balancing or Skewing History?" *New York Times*, 11 August 1991.

10934. _____. "As a Discipline Advances, a Debate on Scholarship." *New York Times*, 11 August 1991. [Afrocentrism]

10935. Martin, Frank. "The Egyptian Ethnicity Controversy and the Sociology of Knowledge." *Journal of Black Studies* 14 (March 1984): 295-325.

10936. Martin, Jeannie. "The Development of Multiculturalism." in *Report to the Minister for Immigration and Ethnic Affairs*, vol. II. pp. 120-160. Canberra: Australian Govt. Printer, 1983.

10937. _____. "Multiculturalism and Feminism." in *Intersexions: Gender/Class/Culture/Ethnicity*, eds. Gillian Bottomby and others. Sydney: Allen + Unwin, 1991.

10938. Martin, Judith. "Free Speech? Put a Sock In It." *Washington Post*, 13 March 1994.

10939. Massero, Toni Marie. *Constitutional Literacy: A Core Curriculum for a Multicultural Nation*. Duke University Press, 1993.

10940. Mathews, David. "A Symposium on Freedom and Ideology: The Debate about Political Correctness." *Civic Arts Review* (Winter 1992).

10941. Matsuda, Mari J. "Looking to the Bottom: Critical Legal Studies and Reparations." *Harvard Civil Rights-Civil Liberties Law Review* (Spring 1987).

10942. Mattai, P. R. "Rethinking the Nature of Multicultural Education: Has It Lost Its Focus or Is It Being Misued?" *Journal of Negro Education* 61 (Winter 1992): 65-77.

10943. Matthews, Anne. "Deciphering Victorian Underwear and Other Seminars." *New York Times Magazine* (10 February 1991).

10944. Maxcy, Spencer J. *Three Conceptions of "Cultural Pluralism" and their Bearings upon Education*. Ph.D. diss., Indiana University, 1972. UMO #7311973.

10945. McCart, Carol L. *Using a Cultural Lens to Explore Faculty Perceptions of Academic Freedom*. Ph.D. diss., Pennsylvania State University, 1991. UMO #9127379.

10946. McCarthy, C. "Multicultural Approaches to Racial Inequality in the United States." *Oxford Review of Education* 17 (1991): 301-316.

10947. _____. "Race and Education in the United States: The Multicultural Solution." *Interchange* 21 (1990).

10948. McConnell, Michael W. "Multiculturalism, Majoritarianism, and Educational Choice: What Does Our Constitutional Tradition Have to Say?" *University of Chicago Legal Forum* (1991): 123-152.

10949. McIntosh, Peggy. "Seeing Our Way Clear: Feminist Re-Vision of the Academy." in *Proceedings of the Eighth Annual GLCA Women's Studies Conference*, ed. Katherine Loring. Rochester, IN: Great Lakes Colleges Association Women's Studies Program, 1983.

10950. McKenna, F. R. "The Myth of Multiculturalism." *Journal of American Indian Education* 21 (November 1981): 1-9.

10951. McLaren, Peter L. "Collisions with Otherness: Multiculturalism, the Politics of Difference, and the Ethnographer as Nomad." *American Journal of Semiotics* 9 (1992): 121-148.

10952. Melmyk, Mary F. *The Effects of Teachers' Social Distance Scores on Teacher-Student Interactions in Relation to the Gender and Ethnic Background of Students*. Ph.D. diss., University of Hawaii, 1990. UMO #9107041.

10953. Menand, Louis. "The Culture Wars." *New York Review of Books* (6 October 1994). [Review-essay on Richard Bernstein, Dictatorship of Virtue]

10954. _____. "Lost Faculties." *New Republic* (July 9 and 16, 1990).

10955. _____. "What Are Universities For? The Real Crisis on Campus Is One of Identity." *Harper's* (December 1991).

10956. Meyer, P., and S. McIntosh. "The U.S.A. Today Index of Ethic Diversity." *International Journal of Public Opinion Research* 4 (Spring 1992): 56-57.

10957. Milkman, Ruth. "Women's History and the Sears Case." *Feminist Studies* (Summer 1986).

10958. Mohanty, Chandra Talpade. "On Race and Voice: Challenges for Liberal Education in the 1990's." *Cultural Critique* 14 (Winter 1989-1990).

10959. Mohanty, S. P. "Us and Them: On the Philosophical Bases of Political Criticism." *Yale Journal of Criticism* 2 (1989).

10960. Moore, Mavor. "The Politics of Multiculture." *Journal of Arts Management and Law* 20 (Spring 1990): 5-15.

10961. Morris, Sarah P. "Greece and the Levant: A Response to Martin Bernal's Black Athena." *Journal of Mediterranean Archeology* 3 (1990).

10962. Morrow, Victoria P. *Bicultural Education: An Instance of Cultural Politics*. Ph.D. diss., University of Colorado, 1978. UMO #7903077.

10963. Morton, Patricia. *Disfigured Images: The Historical Assault on Afro-American Women*. Praeger, 1991.

10964. Muhly, James D. "Black Athena versus Traditional Scholarship." *Journal of Mediterranean Archeology* 3 (1990): 83- 100.

10965. _____. "Where the Greeks Got their Gifts." *Washington Post Book World* (21 July 1991).

10966. "The Multicultural Curriculum: Educationally and Socially Correct." *Jewish Affairs* 21 (July-August 1991): 3-4.

10967. "Multiculturalism and Beyond: Race and Poverty: Education and Ethnicity." *Contention: Debates in Society, Culture and Science* 2 (Fall 1992): special section.

10968. "Multiculturalism and the Language Arts." *Language Arts* 70 (March 1993): entire issue.

10969. "Multiculturalism As A Fourth Force in Counseling." *Journal of Counseling and Development* 70 (September-October 1991): entire issue.

10970. "Multiculturalism: The New Racism." *LA Weekly* (June 5-11, 1992): 12-32 (6 articles).

10971. Mura, David. "Strangers in the Village." in *The Graywolf Annual Five: Multicultural Literacy*, St. Paull, MN: Graywolf Press, 1988.

10972. Murray, Jeffrey. "Cartographic Propaganda-How the Map Became the Message." *Geographical Magazine* 59 (May 1987).

10973. Murray, Kathleen. "The Unfortunate Side Effects of 'Diversity Training'." *New York Times*, 1 August 1993.

10974. Myers, Linda James. *Understanding an Afrocentric World View: Introduction To am Optimal Psychology*. Dubuque, Iowa: Kendall/Hunt, 1988.

10975. Myers, Steven Lee. "Few Teachers [in NYC] Are Using 'Rainbow' Curriculum." *New York Times*, 6 December 1992.

10976. Nash, Gary B. and others. "Multiculturalism and Education." *Contention: Debates in Society, Culture, and Science* 1 (Spring 1992): 1-58 (entire issue).

10977. NCSS Task Force on Ethnic Studies Curriculum Guidelines. *Curriculum Guidelines for Multicultural Education*. National Council for the Social Studies, 1991. [Adopted by NCSS Board of Directors, 1976, revised 1991]

10978. "The New World." *Boston Globe Magazine* (13 October 1991). [A special issue on multiculturalism]

10979. *New York State United Teachers 1991 Education Opinion Survey*. Delmar, NY: Fact Finders, Inc., 1991.

10980. New York State Social Studies Review and Development Committee. *One Nation, Many People: A Declaration of Cultural Interdependence*. Albany, NY: The State Education Department, June 1991.

10981. Newfield, Christopher. "What Was Political Correctness? Race, the Right, and Managerial Democracy in the Humanities." *Critical Inquiry* 19 (Winter 1993): 308-336.

10982. Nieto, Sonia. *Affirming Diversity. The Sociopolitical Context of Multicultural Education*. New York: Routledge, 1992.

10983. Nobile, Vince and others. "White Professors, Black History: Forays into the Multicultural Classroom." *Perspectives* 31 (September 1993): 1, 7-19. [Six historians debate some issues]

10984. Noble, Allen G., ed. *To Build In a New Land. Ethnic Landscapes in North America*. Johns Hopkins University Press, 1992. [22 essays]

10985. O'Connor, Alan. "The Problem of American Cultural Studies." *Critical Studies in Mass Communication* 6 (1989): 404- 461.

10986. Ogbu, John U. "Understanding Cultural Diversity and Learning." *Journal for the Education of the Gifted* 17 (Summer 1994): 355-383.

10987. Oliver, Jennings P. *The Relationship between the Racial Attitudes of White College Freshman and Sophomores as Influenced by Exposure to Multicultural Education Practices*. Ph.D. diss., Kansas State University, 1991. UMO #9201021.

10988. Olneck, Michael R. "The Recurring Dream: Symbolism and Ideology in Intercultural and Multicultural Education." *American Journal of Education* 98 (February 1990).

10989. Olsen, Laurie. "Whose Culture Is This? Whose Curriculum Will It Be?" *California Perspectives* (Fall 1991).

10990. Ortiz de Montellano, Bernard. "Afrocentric Creationism." *Creation/Evolution* 29 (Winter 1991-92): 1-8.

10991. _____. "Avoiding Egyptocentric Pseudoscience: Colleges Must Help Set Standards for Schools." *Chronicle of Higher Education* (25 March 1992).

10992. _____. "Multicultural Pseudoscience: Spreading Scientific Illiteracy among Minorities-Part I." *Sceptical Inquirer* 16 (Fall 1991): 46-50.

10993. Paine, Charles. "Relativism, Radical Pedagogy, and the Ideology of Paralysis." *College English* (October 1989).

10994. Palmer, Thomas. "Academia Retooling American Image." *Boston Globe*, 30 June 1991. [Conference on "Embracing our Multicultural Future: Institutions for All of America's People"]

10995. Parens, J. "Multiculturalism and the Problem of Patricularism." *American Political Science Review* 88 (March 1994): 169-184.

10996. Patai, Daphne. "The Struggle for Feminist Purity Threatens the Goals of Feminism." *Chronicle of Higher Education* (5 February 1992): B1.

10997. Patterson, Orlando. "Black Like All of Us. Celebrating Multiculturalism Diminishes Blacks' Role in American Culture." *Washington Post*, 7 February 1993.

10998. _____. "Rethinking Black History." *Harvard Educational Review* 41 (August 1971).

10999. Patterson, Thomas C. "Another Blow to Eurocentrism." *Monthly Review* 40 (December 1988).

11000. "'PC' Debate Shows No Signs of Passing." *Academe* (November-December 1991): 8.

11001. Pellicani, Luciano. "The Cultural War between East and West." *Telos* no. 89 (Fall 1991): 127-132. [Translated by Florindo Volpacchio]

11002. Peradotto, John. "Letter to the Editor." *Chronicle of Higher Education* (4 September 1991).

11003. Perry, Ruth. "Historically Correct." *Women's Review of Books* (February 1992).

11004. Perry, Theresa, and James W. Fraser, eds. *Freedom's Plow. Teaching in the Multicultural Classroom.* Routledge, 1993.

11005. Peskind, Jennifer. *An Ethnographic Study of the Instructional Culture of Introductory College Chemistry.* Ph.D. diss., Ohio State University, 1990. UMO #9105093.

11006. Pfister, Joel. "The Americanization of Cultural Studies." *Yale Journal of Criticism* 4 (1991): 199-229.

11007. Phelps, Christopher. "The Second Time as Farce: The Right's 'New McCarthyism'." *Monthly Review* 43 (October 1991): 39- 57.

11008. "Pilgrims and Other Imperialists." *Wall Street Journal*, 17 May 1991. A14. [Editorial]

11009. Piper-Mandy, Erylene L. *The Talented 100th: Issues in Ethnicity and Education.* Ph.D. diss., UC Irvine, 1990. UMO #9117258.

11010. Platt, Anthony M. "Defenders of the Canon: What's Behind the Attack on Multiculturalism?" *Social Justice* 19 (Summer 1992): 122-140.

11011. Pohlman, Bruce E. *Ethnicity, Class, and Culture: Multicultural Education in the Rural Northwest.* Ph.D. diss., UC, Berkeley, 1989. [Native Americans]. UMO #9021567.

11012. Poliakoff, Michael. "Roll Over Aristotle: Martin Bernal and His Critics." *Academic Questions* (Summer 1991): 14.

11013. "The Political Correctness/Multiculturalism Controversy." *Humanist* (March-April 1992): 4 articles.

11014. Pollack, Andy. "Labor and the Fight for Diversity." *Against the Current* no. 36 (January-February 1992): 13-19. [Class and multiculturalism]

11015. Pollard, William R. *Gender Roles and Gender Stereotypes in Cross-Cultural Education.* Ph.D. diss., University of Pennsylvania, 1985. UMO #8515438.

11016. Pope, Christie Farnham. "The Challenge Posed by Radical Afrocentrism." *Chronicle of Higher Education* (30 March 1994). [White professor teaching black history]

11017. "Postponement of Course Raises Academic Freedom Issues." *MLA Newsletter* (Spring 1991): 6-7.

11018. Pounder, Robert L. "Black Athena 2: History Without Rules." *American Historical Review* 97 (April 1992): 461-464. [Review article]

11019. Prince, Hugh B. "The Mosaic and the Melting Pot." *New York Times*, 23 September 1991.

11020. _____. "Multiculturalims: Myths and Realities." *Phi Delta Kappan* 74 (November 1992): 208-213.

11021. Pringle, Peter D. *An Effectiveness Evaluation of the Orange County Cultural Awareness Training Program.* Master's thesis, California State U., Long Beach, 1988. UMO #1333871.

11022. Quindlen, Anna. "Goodbye, Diorama History." *New York Times*, 23 June 1991.

11023. Rabasa, Jose. *Inventing America: Spanish Historiography and Formation of Eurocentrism.* University of Oklahoma Press, 1993.

11024. Ramaga, P. V. "Relativity of the Minority Concept." *Human Rights Quarterly* 14 (February 1992): 104-119.

11025. Rauch, Jonathan. *Kindly Inquisitors. The New Attacks on Free Thought.* University of Chicago Press, 1993.

11026. Ravitch, Diane. "Multiculturalism: E Pluribus Plures." *American Scholar* 59 (Summer 1990): 337-354.

11027. Ravitch, Diane, and Arthur Schlesinger, Jr. "NY Should Teach History, Not Ethnic Cheerleading." *Newsday*, 29 June 1990. Viewpoints section, 77.

11028. Ray, John. "An Egyptian Perspective." *Journal of Mediterranean Archeology* 3 (1990): 80-81.

11029. _____. "Levant Ascendant." *Times Literary Supplement* (18 October 1991).

11030. Reinhold, Robert. "Class Struggle. Cowgirls and the Bantu Migration: In Its Controversial New Textbooks, California Is Rewriting History." *New York Times Magazine* (29 September 1991).

11031. Renji, Judith. *Going Public: Schooling for a Diverse Democracy.* New Press, 1993.

11032. _____. "Whose Religion? Intolerances Old and New." *OAS Magazine of History* 6 (Summer 1991): 18-24.

11033. Rex, John. "The Concept of a Multi-cultural Society." *New Community* 14 (Autumn 1987): 218-229.

11034. Reyes, Maria de la Luz, and Lamela A. McCullum, eds. "Diversity and Literacy in Schools: Issues for Urban Society." *Education and Urban Society* 24 (February 1992): 171-291.

11035. Rilloraza, Frances A. *Multicultural Education In Service Programs in Large School Districts in California Having Substantial Minority Enrollment.* Ph.D. diss., University of the Pacific, 1979. UMO #8016795.

11036. Robbins, B. "Othering the Academy: Professionalism and Multiculturalism." *Social Research* 58 (Summer 1991): 355-372.

11037. Robinson, Carla J. "United States: The Real World of Political Correctness." *Race and Class* 35 (January-March 1994): 73-79.

11038. Rodriguez, Richard. "Slouching Towards Los Angeles. Removing the Blindfold, the 'Cities of Angels' Begin to See Themselves as One." *Los Angeles Times*, 11 April 1993.

11039. Rohter, Larry. "Battle Over Patriotism Curriculum." *New York Times*, 15 May 1994. [Lake County, FL school board orders teaching of U.S. culture as superior]

11040. Romero, Gloria J., and Lourdes Arguelles, eds. "Culture and Conflict in the Academy: Testimonies from a War Zone." *California Sociologist* 14 (Winter/Summer 1991): entire issue.

11041. Roseberry, William. "Multiculturalism and the Challenge of Anthropology." *Social Research* 59 (Winter 1992): 841-858.

11042. Rothenberg, Paula S. *Racism and Sexism: An Integrated Study*. St. Martin's Press: 1988.

11043. Rountree, E. L. "Multiculturalism and the Hiring Process." *Perspectives* 30 (May-June 1992).

11044. Ryan, Alan. "Invasion of the Mind Snatchers." *New York Review of Books* (11 February 1993). [Review essay]

11045. Said, Edward W. *Culture and Imperialism*. Knopf, 1993.

11046. San Juan, E., Jr. "Multiculturalism vs. Hegemony: Ethnic Studies, Asian Americans, and U.S. Racial Politics." *Massachusetts Review* 32 (Fall 1991): 467-478.

11047. Santamaria, Ulysses, and Kristin Couper. "The Making of the Multiracial Society in the United States: Strategies and Perspectives." *Social Science Information* 24 (1985): 145-159.

11048. Schlesinger, Arthur M., Jr. "A Dissent on Multicultural Education." *Partisan Review* 58 (Fall 1991): 630-634.

11049. _____. *The Disuniting of America: Reflections on a Multicultural Society*. Whittle Books, 1991.

11050. Schmitz, Betty. *Core Curriculum and Cultural Pluralism: A Guide for Campus Planners*. Association of American Colleges, 1992.

11051. Schoen, David and others, eds. *Multicultural Teaching in the University*. Praeger, 1993.

11052. "School Board Will Recognize Other Cultures, but as Inferior." *New York Times*, 13 May 1994. [Lake County, FL]

11053. "School to Test 'Afrocentric' Study Approach." *Cleveland Plain Dealer*, 30 August 1993. [All Saints Prepatory Academy, Louisville, KY]

11054. Schwartz, Barry, ed. *Educating for Civic Responsibility in a Multicultural World*. Swarthmore College Bookstore, 1993.

11055. Scott, Joan W. "The Campaign Against Political Correctness: What's Really at Stake." *Radical History Review* no. 54 (1992): 59-79. [Originally published in Change, Nov. 1991]

11056. _____. "Multiculturalism and the Politics of Identity." *October* 61 (Summer 1992).

11057. Searle, John. "The Storm over the University." *New York Review of Books* (6 December 1990): 34-42.

11058. Segal, Daniel, ed. *Crossing Cultures. Essays in the Displacement of Western Civilization*. Tucson: University of Arizona Press, 1992.

11059. Seigel, Fred. "The Cult of Multiculturalism." *New Republic* (18 February 1991).

11060. Semons, Maryann. *The Salience of Ethnicity at a Multiethnic Urban High School*. Ph.D. diss., UC Berkeley, 1987. UMO #8814059.

11061. Shachtman, Marc. "Learning and Losing: The Need for a Balance in Political Views." *Oberlin Forum* (October 1990).

11062. Shils, Edward. *The Academic Ethic: The Report of a Study Group of the International Council on the Future of the University*. University of Chicago Press, 1983.

11063. Shohat, Ella, and Robert Stam. *Unthinking Eurocentrism. Towards a Multi-Cultural Film Theory*. Routledge, 1994.

11064. Siebers, Tobin. "The Ethics of Anti-Ethnocentrism." *Michigan Quarterly Review* (Winter 1993): 41-70.

11065. Singer, Toba. "Multiculturalism." *Militant* (20 September 1993). [Critique of Malcolm X for Beginners on the role of women]

11066. Sipchen, Bob. "Are We One Nation, Indivisible? Were We Ever?" *Los Angeles Times*, 13 April 1993.

11067. _____. "Divided We Stand?" *Los Angeles Times*, 13 April 1993. [Multiculturalism]

11068. Sirota, K. L. and others. "Ethnic Diversity and the Classroom Climate: The Effect on Attitudes Toward Others in the Multicultural Classroom." in *Research in Inequality and Social Conflict*, Vol. 2. pp. 223-242. eds. Michael N. Dobkowski, and I. Wallimann. JAI Press, 1992.

11069. Sleeter, Christine, ed. *Empowerment through Multicultural Education*. SUNY Press, 1991.

11070. Smith, Albert Joseph, Jr. *The Relationship of Teachers Preparedness in Multicultural Education to Levels of Ethnic Awareness and Multicultural Exposure Among Elementary School Certificate Personnel*. Ph.D. diss., University of Washington, 1983. UMO #8312175.

11071. Sobol, Thomas. "Reading, Writing-and Iroquois Politics." *Time* (11 November 1991).

11072. Somekawa, Ellen, and Elizabeth A. Smith. "Theorizing the Writing of History of 'I Can't Think Why It Should Be So Dull For a Great Deal of It Must Be Invention'." *Journal of Social History* (Fall 1988).

11073. Stage, Frances K., and Kathleen Manning. *Enhancing the Multicultural Campus Environment: A Cultural Brokering Approach*. Jossey-Bass, 1993.

11074. "Statement on Professional Ethics." *American Association of University Professors Policy Documents and Reports*, AAUP, 1990.

11075. Stearns, Peter N. *Meaning Over Memory: Recasting the Teaching of Culture and History*. University of North Carolina Press, 1993.

11076. Steele, Shelby. "Nothing Is Ever Simply Black and White." *Time* (12 August 1991). [Interview by Sylvester Monroe]

11077. Sternhell, Carol. "Life in the Mainstream: What Happens When Feminists Turn Up on both Sides of the Courtroom?" *Ms.* (July 1986).

11078. Stimpson, Catharine R. "Multiculturalism: A Big Word at the [University] Presses." *New York Times Book Review* (22 September 1991).

11079. Stoffle, C. J., and P. A. Tarin. "No Place for Neutrality: The Case for Multiculturalism." *Library Journal* 119 (July 1994): 46-50.

11080. Stotsky, Sandra. "Multicultural Education in the Brookline Public Schools: The Deconstruction of an Academic Curriculum." *Network News and Views* (October 1991).

11081. Sue, D. W. and others. "Multicultural Counseling Competencies and Standards: A Call to the Professions." *Journal of Counseling and Development* 70 (March-April 1992): 477-486.

11082. Sullivan, Andrew. "Racism 101: A Crash Course on Afro- centrism." *New Republic* (26 November 1990): 20-21.

11083. Sullivan, Robert. "Trouble in Paradigms." *Museum News* (January-February 1992): 41-44.

11084. Suzuki, Bob. *An Asian American Perspective on Multicultural Education: Implications for Practice and Research*. NAAPAE Occasional Papers, 1980.

11085. Swartz, E. "Multicultural Education: Disrupting Patterns of Supremacy in School Curricula, Practices, and Pedagogy." *Journal of Negro Education* 62 (Autumn 1993): 493-506.

11086. Szulc, Tad. "The Greatest Danger We Face." *Parade* (25 July 1993). [Critical of multiculturalism]

11087. Takaki, Ronald T., and Linda Chavez. "Are the Multicultural Experiments Working? Two Views." *Washington Post Book Review* (1 August 1993).

11088. Tate, Greg. "History: The Colorized Version, or Everything You Learned in School Was Wrong." *Village Voice* 28 (March 1989).

11089. Taylor, Charles. *Multiculturalism*, expanded ed. Princeton University Press, 1994.

11090. Taylor, D. M. "The Social Psychology of Racial and Cultural Diversity: Issues of Assimilation and Multiculturalism." in *Bilingualism, Multiculturalism, and Second Language Learning*, ed. Allan G. Reynolds. Hillsdale, NJ: Lawrence Erlbaum Associates, 1991.

11091. Taylor, John. "Are You Politically Correct?" *New York* (21 January 1991): 32-40.

11092. Thelin, John R. "The Curriculum Crusades and the Conservative Backlash." *Change* 24 (January-February 1992): 17-23.

11093. Thernstrom, Abigail. "E Pluribus Plura-Congress and Bilingual Education." *Public Interest* 60 (Summer 1990): 3-22.

11094. Thernstrom, Stephan. "The Columbus Controversy." *American Educator* (Spring 1992).

11095. _____. "McCarthyism Then and Now." *Academic Questions* (Winter 1990-1991): 14-16.

11096. Thiederman, Sondra. *Profiting in America's Multicultural Marketplace. How to Do Business Across Cultural Lines*. New York: Lexington Books, 1992.

11097. Thornton, Leslie J., II. *Cross Cultural Psychiatry: Multicultural Education in Psychiatric Residency Programs*. Ph.D. diss., University of Michigan, 1987. UMO #8720354.

11098. Trice, H., and Morand D. "Cultural Diversity: Subcultures and Countercultures in Work Organizations." in *Studies in Organizational Sociology: Essays in Honor of Charles K. Warriner*, pp. 69-106. ed. G. Miller. JAI Press, 1991.

11099. Turner, Terence. "Anthropology and Multiculturalism: What is Anthropology that Multiculturalists Should Be Mindful of It?" *Cultural Anthropology* 8 (November 1993): 411-429.

11100. "Twisted History." *Newsweek* (23 December 1991): 46-49.

11101. "U. of Texas's Postponement of Controversial Writing Course Kindles Debate Over Role of Outsiders in Academic Policy." *Chronicle of Higher Education* (20 February 1991): A18.

11102. "Universities Learning Hard Lessons in Race Relations." *Los Angeles Times*, 4 January 1992.

11103. Van Brakel, J. "The Ethnocentricity of Colour." *Behavioral and Brain Sciences* 15 (March 1992): 53.

11104. Verhovek, Sam H. "A New York Panel Urges Emphasizing Minority Cultures." *New York Times*, 20 June 1991.

11105. "Voters Defeat Proponents of America-First Curriculum." *New York Times*, 7 October 1994. [Lake County, FL]

11106. Vyas, H. V. "Theory Construction in Multicultural Education: Problems and Prospects." *Journal of Multilingual and Multicultural Development* 13, no. 3 (1992): 261-268.

11107. Wallach, Alan. "Revisionism Has Transformed Art History, but Not Museums." *Chronicle of Higher Education* (22 January 1992): B2.

11108. Wallerstein, Immanuel. "Culture as the Ideological Battleground of the Modern World System." in his *Geopolitics and Geoculture*, Cambridge University Press, 1991.

11109. Walzer, Michael. *What It Means To Be An American*. Marsilio Books, 1992.

11110. Watts, Steven. "The Idiocy of American Studies: Post- structuralism, Language, and Politics in the Age of Self- Fulfillment." *American Quarterly* 43 (December 1991): 625-660.

11111. Wenze, Gloria T. *Multiethnic Education for White Ethnic Children in a Scranton, Pennsylvania Elementary School*. Ph.D. diss., University of New Mexico, 1984. UMO #8501202.

11112. West, Cornel. "Minority Discourse and the Pitfalls of Canon Formation." *Yale Journal of Criticism* 1 (Fall 1987): 193- 202.

11113. "When Worlds Collide. How Columbus's Voyages Transformed Both East and West." *Newsweek* (Fall/Winter 1991): entire issue.

11114. Whitney, Gleaves. "Is the American Academy Racist?" *University Bookman* 30 (1990): 4-15.

11115. "Whose Culture?" *Educational Leadership* 49 (December 1991- January 1992): entire issue.

11116. Wildavsky, Aaron. "Finding Universalistic Solutions to Particularistic Problems: Bilingualism Resolved through a Second Language Requirement for Elementary Schools." *Journal of Policy Analysis and Management* 11 (1992): 310-314.

11117. Williams, Elizabeth R. *Cultural Prejudice: How They View Themselves and Others.* Ph.D. diss., Boston University, 1986. UMO #8617535.

11118. Wolfe, Alan. "The Myth of the Free Scholar." *Center Magazine* (July 1969).

11119. Woodward, C. Vann. "Freedom and the Universities." *New York Review of Books* (18 July 1991): 32-37.

11120. Wortham, Anne. "Afrocentrism Isn't the Answer for Black Students in American Society." *Executive Educator* 14 (September 1992): 23-25.

11121. Yang, Jo. "Clouding the Human Mind." *Pacific Ties* (October 1990): 18-19. [Eurocentrism]

11122. Yurco, Frank. "Were the Ancient Egyptians Black or White?" *Biblical Archaelogy Review* 15 (September-October 1989): 24-29.

NATIONALISM

11123. Abraham, Kinfe. *Politics of Black Nationalism: From Harlem to Soweto*. Africa World, 1991.

11124. Allen, Ernest, Jr. "Afro-American Identity: Reflections on the Pre-Civil War Era." *Contributions in Black Studies* 7 (1985- 86): 45-93.

11125. _____. "Black Nationalism on the Right." *Soulbook* 1 (Winter 1964): 7-19.

11126. _____. "Theoretical Remarks on Afro-American Cultural Nationalism." *Journal of Ethnic Studies* 2 (Summer 1974): 1-10.

11127. Anaya, Rudolfo A., and Francisco Lomeli, eds. *Aztlan: Essays on the Chicano Homeland*. Albuquerque: University of New Mexico Press, 1989.

11128. Blaut, James. *Imperialism and thd Puerto Rican Nation*. New York: Federacion Universitaria Socialista Puertorriquena, 1977.

11129. Bracey, John H., Jr. "Black Nationalism Since Garvey." in *Key Issues in the Afro-American Experience*, pp. 259-279. eds. Nathan I. Huggins and others. New York: Harcourt Brace Jovanovich, 1971.

11130. Butler, R. E. *On Creating a Hispanic America: A Nation Within a Nation?* Washington, DC: Center for Inter-American Security, 1985.

11131. Carrion, Juan M. "The Origins of Puerto Rican Nationalism: Precocity and Limitations of the Nineteenth Century Independence Movement." in *Rethinking the Nineteenth Century: Contradictions and Movements*, ed. Francisco O. Ramirez. Westport, CT: Greenwood, 1988.

11132. Cazemajou, Jean, ed. *Les minorites hispaniques en Amerique du Nord (1960-1980): conflits ideologiques et echanges culturels*. Presses Universitaues de Bordeaux, 1985.

11133. Cohen, Sharon. "Separatist Sentiment Grows Among Blacks." *Cleveland Plain Dealer*, 1 August 1993. [Nationwide]

11134. Cunnigen, Donald. "Malcolm X's Influence on the Black Nationalist Movement of Southern Black College Students." *Western Journal of Black Studies* 17 (Spring 1993): 32-43.

11135. Deloria, Vine, Jr., and Clifford M. Lytle. *The Nations Within: The Past and Future of American Indian Sovereignity*. New York: Pantheon Press, 1984.

11136. Dudley, Michael K., and Keoni K. Agard. *A Hawaiian Nation II: A Call for Hawaiian Sovereignty*. Honolulu: Na Kane Oka Malo, 1990.

11137. Dunbar Ortiz, Roxanne. "Land and Nationhood: The American Indian Struggle for Self-Determination and Survival." *Socialist Review* (May-August 1982): 63-64.

11138. Dyer, Brainerd. "The Persistence of the Idea of Negro Colonization." *Pacific Historical Review* 12 (1943): 53-66.

11139. Dyson, Michael E. "[Comment on Gary Peller, "Race Against Integration"]." *Tikkun* 6 (January-February 1991): 67-69.

11140. _____. "Malcolm X and the Revival of Black Nationalism." *Tikkun* 8 (March-April 1993): 45-48.

11141. Edsall, Thomas B. "[Comment on Gary Peller, "Race Against Integration"]." *Tikkun* 6 (January-February 1991): 69-70.

11142. Fernandez, Ronald. *Los Macheteros: The Wells Fargo Robbery and the Violent Struggle for Puerto Rican Independence.* New York: Prentice-Hall, 1987.

11143. Forman, James. *Self-determination: An Examination of the Question and Its Application to the African-American People*, Revised ed. Washington, DC: Open Hand Pub., 1984.

11144. Gethers, Soloman P. "Black Nationalism and Human Liberation." *Black Scholar* 1 (May 1976): 43-50.

11145. Glazer, Nathan. "[Comment on Gary Peller, "Race Against Integration"]." *Tikkun* 6 (January-February 1991): 66-67.

11146. Goldfield, Michael. "The Decline of the Communist Party and the Black Question in the U.S.: Harry Haywood's Black Bolshevik." *Review of Radical Political Economics* 12 (Spring 1980): 44-63.

11147. Herod, Agustina. *Afro-American Nationalism.* New York, 1986.

11148. Hicks, Dixie C. *Marcus Garvey and Pan-Africanism.* Ph.D. diss., Memphis State University, 1992. UMO #9239617.

11149. Holden, Mathew, Jr. *The Politics of the Black 'Nation'.* New York: Chandler, 1973.

11150. Hornick, Michael S. *Nationalist Sentiment in Puerto Rico from the American Invasion until the Foundation of the Partido Nacionalista 1898-1922.* Ph.D. diss., State University of New York at Buffalo, 1972. UMO #73-05122.

11151. Johnson, Troy R. *The Indian Occupation of Alacatraz Island: Indian Self-determination and the Rise of Indian Activism.* Ph.D. diss., UCLA, 1993. UMO #9321905.

11152. Jones, Lynne. "Nationalism and the Self." *New Politics* 4 (Summer 1993): 111-120.

11153. Kamara, Mohammed B. *Toward an African-American Critical Pedagogy for Liberation.* Ph.D. diss., University of North Carolina at Greensboro, 1992. UMO #9314586.

11154. Karenga, Maulana. "A Dialogue with Karenga." *Emerge* (January 1992): 11-12. [Interview]

11155. Klehr, Harvey, and William Thompson. "Self-Determination in the Black Belt: Origins of a Communist Policy." *Labor History* 30 (1989): 354-366.

11156. Klor de Alva, J. Jorge. "Aztlan, Borinquen and Hispanic Nationalism in the United States." in *Aztlan: Essays on the Chicano Homeland*, pp. 135-171. eds. Rudolfo A. Anaya, and Francicso A. Lomeli. Albuquerque, NM: Academia/El Norte, 1989.

11157. Lichtenstein, William, and David Winkhurst. "Red Alert in Puerto Rico." *Nation* (30 June 1979): 780-782.

11158. Liden, Harold. *History of the Puerto Rican Independence Movement, 19th Century*, vol. 1. Maplewood, NJ: Waterfront, 1981.

11159. Lightfoot, Claude. "Negro Nationalism and the Black Muslims." *Political Affairs* 41 (July 1962): 3-20.

11160. Lively, Adam. "Continuity and Radicalism in American Black Nationalist Thought, 1914-1929." *Journal of American Studies* 18 (August 1994): 207-235.

11161. Lopez, Jose, ed. *Puerto Rican Nationalism: A Reader.* Chicago, IL: Editorial Coqui, 1971.

11162. Marable, Manning. "Black Nationalism in the 1970's: Through the Prism of Race and Class." *Socialist Review* 10 (March- June 1980): 57-108.

11163. _____. "The Third Reconstruction: Black Nationalism in a Revolutionary America." *Social Text* 4 (Fall 1981): 3-27.

11164. McCall, Nathan. "Can Farrakhan Play a Garvey." *African Commentary* 1 (June 1990): 23-25.

11165. McKelvey, Charles. "The Influence of Black Nationalism on Martin Luther King." *Sociological Abstracts* supplement 167 (August 1991) 91S25283/ASA/1991/6642.

11166. Miles, Robert. "Recent Marxist Theories of Nationalism and the Issue of Racism." *British Journal of Sociology* 38 (1987): 24- 43.

11167. Morgan, Ken. "Nation of Islam." *Militant* (16 May 1994): letter.

11168. "Nationalism and Ethnic Particularism." *Tikkun* 7 (November-December 1992): 49-56. [Michael Walzer, Jean Bethke Elshtain, Gail Kligman, Bogdan Denitch, Todd Gitlin, and Marshall Berman]

11169. Obadele, Imari Abuhakari. *Foundations of the Black Nation: A Textbook of Ideas Behind the New Black Nationalism and the Struggle for Land in America*. Detroit, MI: House of Songhay, 1975.

11170. _____. *Free the Land! The True Story of the RNA 11 in Mississippi*. Washington, DC: House of Songhay, 1984.

11171. Ortiz, Roxanne Dunbar. "Land and Nationhood. The American Indian Struggle for Self-Determination and Survival." *Socialist Review* 12 (May-August 1982): 105-120.

11172. Perdue, Theda. *Nations Remembered: An Oral History of the Five Civilized Tribes, 1865-1907*. Westport, CT: Greenwood, 1980.

11173. Pico, Isabel. "Los estudiantes universitarios de la decada del trienta: del nacionalismo cultural al nacionalismo politico." *Revista de Ciencias Sociales* 24 (1985): 516-552.

11174. Pinkney, Alphonso. *Red, Black, and Green: Black Nationalism in the United States*. New York: Cambridge University Press, 1976.

11175. "Puerto Rico: Class Struggle and National Liberation." *Latin American Perspectives* 3 (Summer 1976): entire issue.

11176. Quintero Rivera, Angel G. "Notes on Puerto Rican National Development: Class and Nation in a Colonial Context." *Marxist Perspectives* 3 (Spring 1980): 10-30.

11177. _____. *Puerto Rico: Identidad Nacional y Clases Sociales*. Rio Piedras, PR: Ediciones Huracan, 1979.

11178. Ramirez-Barbot, Jaime. *A History of Puerto Rican Radical Nationalism, 1920-1965*. Ph.D. diss., Ohio State University, 1973. UMO #7326892.

11179. Ruffing, Lorraine Turner. "The Navajo Nation: A History of Dependence and Underdevelopment." *Review of Radical Political Economics* 11 (Summer 1979): 25-43.

11180. Sales, William W., Jr. *Malcolm X and the Organization of Afro-American Unity: A Case Study in Afro-American Nationalism*. Ph.D. diss., Columbia University, 1991. UMO #9202742.

11181. San Juan, E., Jr. "Critique of the New Politics of Racism/ Nationalism in the United States." *Nature, Society, and Thought* 5 (October 1992): 307-319.

11182. Seijo Bruno, Mini. *La insurreccion nacionalista en Puerto Rico, 1950*. Rio Piedras: Editorial Edil, 1989.

11183. Stampp, Kenneth M. "One Alone? The United States and National Self-Determination." in *Lincoln, the War President*, ed. Gabor S. Boritt. : Oxford University Press, 1992.

11184. Steele, Richard W. "The War on Intolerance: The Reformation of American Nationalism, 1939-1941." *Journal of American Ethnic History* 9 (Autumn 1989).

11185. Tani, E., and Kae Sera. *False Nationalism/False Internationalism: Class Contradictions in Armed Struggle*. Chicago, IL: Seeds Beneath the Snow Publications, 1985.

11186. Tate, Gayle T. "Black Nationalism: An Angle of Vision." *Western Journal of Black Studies* 12 (Spring 1988): 40-48.

11187. Tolbert, Richard C. "A New Brand of Black Nationalism." *Negro Digest* 16 (August 1967): 20-23.

11188. Trotsky, Leon. *On Black Nationalism and Self- Determination*. New York: Pathfinder, 1978.

11189. Turner, James. "The Sociology of Black Nationalism." *Black Scholar* 1 (December 1969).

11190. U.S. Congress, 97th, 1st session, House of Representatives, Committee on the Judiciary, Subcommittee on Administrative Law and Governmental Relations. *Cherokee Nation of Oklahoma: Hearings...* Washington, DC: GPO, 1982.

11191. Van Horne, Winston A. "Integration or Separation: Beyond the Philosophical Wilderness Thereof." in *Race: Twentieth-Century Dilemmas--Twenty-first-Century Prognoses*, eds. Van Horne, and Thomas V. Tonneson. Milwaukee: Institute on Race and Ethnicity, University of Wisconsin System, 1989.

11192. Vandermeer, John, and Perfecto Ivette. "The Politics of Neo-Colonialism: The Case of the Puerto Rican 15." *Against the Current* 4 (July-August 1989): 5-8. [Puerto-Rican nationalist movement]

11193. Walters, W. Ronald. "White Racial Nationalism in the United States." *Urban League Review* 13 (Summer 1989-Winter 1989-90): 141-164.

11194. Warmecke, A. M. and others. "The Roots of Nationalism: Nonverbal Behavior and Xenophobia." *Ethology and Sociobiology* 13 (July 1992): 267-282.

11195. White, Fran. "[Clarence] Thomas Hearings Showed that Nationalists Just Don't Get It." *Guardian (NYC)* (18 December 1991).

11196. Woodmansee, John J., and Richard D. Tucker. "A Scale of Black Separatism." *Psychological Reports* 27 (December 1970): 855- 858.

11197. Young, Mary E. "The Cherokee Nation: Mirror of the Republic." *American Quarterly* 33 (Winter 1981): 502-524.

11198. Yuval-Davis, Nira. "Nationalism and Racism." *Cahiers de recherche sociologique* 20 (1993): 183-202.

11199. Ziontz, Alvin J. "Recent Government Attitudes toward Indian Tribal Autonomy and Separatism in the United States." in *Ethnic Groups and the State*, ed. Paul Brass. Totowa, NJ: Barnes and Noble, 1985.

OCCUPATIONS

11200. Berger, Ruth. "Promoting Minority Access to the Profession." *Social Work* 34 (July 1989): 346-349.

11201. Bolster, William Jeffrey. *African-American Seamen: Race, Seafaring Work, and Atlantic Maritime Culture, 1750-1860.* Ph.D. diss., Johns Hopkins University, 1992. UMO #9216542.

11202. _____. "'To Feel Like a Man': Black Seamen in the Northern States, 1800-1860." *Journal of American History* 76 (March 1990).

11203. Booker, Linnette. *Blacks in Public Relations: Their Past, Present and Future.* Master's thesis, Point Park College (Pa.), 1989.

11204. Broussard, Albert S. "McCants Stewart: The Struggles of a Black Attorney in the Urban West." *Oregon Historical Quarterly* 89 (Summer 1988): 157-179.

11205. Calderon, J-C. "There Are Signs of Hope." *New York Times*, 27 October 1991. [Letter on people of color in architecture]

11206. Cappell, Charles L. "The Status of Black Lawyers." *Work and Occupations* 17 (1990): 100-121.

11207. "The Career and Life Experiences of Black Professionals." *Journal of Organizational Behavior* 11 (November 1990): entire issue.

11208. Carlson, S. M. "Trends in Race/Sex Occupational Inequality: Conceptual and Measurement Issues." *Social Problems* 39 (August 1992): 268-290.

11209. Cheatham, Harold E. "Africentricity and Career Development of African Americans." *Career Development Quarterly* 38 (June 1990).

11210. Cirino-Gerena, Gabriel. "A Job Analysis of the Work of Puerto Rican Lawyers during their First Six Years of Practice." *The Bar Examiner* 59 (November 1990): 5-8.

11211. Cohn, D'Vera, and Barbara Vobejda. "Few Blacks Reach Top in Private Sector, Census Finds." *Washington Post*, 18 January 1993.

11212. Collins, Sharon M. "Blacks on the Bubble: The Vulnerability of Black Executives in White Corporations." *Sociological Quarterly* 34 (August 1993): 429-447.

11213. Day, Anthony. "A Shift in Composition." *Los Angeles Times*, 3 April 1994. [Asian and Asian-American musicians in U.S. symphony orchestras]

11214. Elliott, R. T. "More on the Status of Black CPA's." *Journal of Accounting* 170 (December 1990).

11215. Fabricant, Florence. "More Blacks Join the Ranks Of Top Chefs." *New York Times*, 20 October 1993.

11216. Farr, James. "A Slow Boat to Nowhere: The Multiracial Crews of the American Whaling Industry." *Journal of Negro History* 68 (1983): 159-170.

11217. Fiorentine, R., and S. Cole. "Why Fewer Women Become Physicians: Explaining the Premed Persistence Gap." *Sociological Forum* 7 (1992).

11218. Fossett, M.A., and others. "Racial Occupational Inequality, 1940-1980: A Research Note on the Impact of the Changing Regional Distribution of the Black Population." *Social Forces* 68 (1989): 415-427.

11219. Glaberson, William. "New Pressure on Minority Journalists." *New York Times*, 7 March 1994.

11220. Glazer, Nona Y. "Between a Rock and a Hard Place: Women's Professional Organizations in Nursing and Class, Racial, and Ethnic Inequalities." *Gender and Society* 5 (September 1991): 351- 372.

11221. Harmon, Amy. "Study Finds Few Latinos in Top [Corporate] Jobs." *Los Angeles Times*, 5 March 1993. [Study by Hispanic Association on Corporate Responsibility]

11222. Hartigan, Patti. "Stage Still Seen as an Elitist White Domain." *Boston Globe*, 7 January 1991.

11223. Hartigan, Patti, and Diane E. Lewis. "The Fine Arts: A World Without Color." *Boston Globe*, 6 January 1991. [Series of articles on absence of persons of color in Boston-area fine arts]

11224. Henwood, K. "Resisting Racism and Sexism in Academic Psychology: A Personal/Political View." *Feminism and Psychology* 4 (February 1994): 41-62.

11225. Hesseltine, William B., and Louis Kaplan. "Negro Doctors of Philosophy in History." *Negro History Bulletin* 6 (December 1942): 59, 67.

11226. Hewitt, William L. "So Few Undesirables: Race, Residence, and Occupation in Sioux City, 1890-1925." *Annals of Iowa* 50 (1989): 158-179.

11227. Hine, Darlene Clark. *Black Women in White. Racial Conflict and Cooperation in the Nursing Profession*. Bloomington: Indiana University Press, 1989.

11228. _____. "Nursing." *Black Women in America II*, pp. 887- 891.

11229. Horovitz, Bruce. "And Now, a Job From a Sponsor." *Los Angeles Times*, 13 April 1993. [Employment of minorities in Los Angeles advertising agencies]

11230. Horton, Lois E., and James O. Horton. "Race, Occupation and Literacy in Reconstruction Washington, D.C." in *Toward a New South?*, eds. Orville Burton, and Robert C. McMath. Westport, CT: Greenwood, 1982.

11231. Hudson, Jill. "The Dead End On the Runway." *Washington Post*, 28 March 1994. [Black fashion models]

11232. Irwin, James R. "Farmers and Laborers: A Note on Black Occupations in the Postbellum South." *Agricultural History* 64 (Winter 1990): 53-60.

11233. Jackson, J. H. "Trials, Tribulations, and Triumphs of Minorities in Psychology: Reflections at Century's End." *Professional Psychology* 23 (April 1992): 80-86.

11234. Jones, Edward W., Jr. "Black Managers: The Dream Deferred." *Harvard Business Review* (May-June 1986): 84-93.

11235. Kahn, Eve M. "Renewed Hope for Black Architects." *New York Times*, 9 April 1992.

11236. Kane, Tim D. "Structural Change and Chicano Employment in the Southwest, 1950-1970: Some Preliminary Observations." *Aztlan* 4 (Fall 1973): 383-398.

11237. Kashefi, M. "Occupational Transformation in the United States, 1950-1980: Involvement with Data, People, and Things." *Sociology and Social Research* 76 (January 1992).

11238. Kernfoxworth, M. "Status and Roles of Minority PR Practitioners." *Public Relations Review* 15 (Autumn 1989).

11239. Kurtz, Howard. "Minority Journalists Make Push for Newsroom Empowerment." *Washington Post*, 14 August 1993.

11240. Larber, J. "Can Women Physicians Ever Be True Equals in the American Medical Profession?" in *Current Research on Occupations and Professions*, vol. 6. pp. 25-40. eds. H. Z. Lopata, and J. A. Levy. Greewich, CT: JAI Press, 1991.

11241. Lecca, Pedro J., and Thomas D. Watts. *Pathways for Minorities Into the Health Professions.* Lanham, MD: University Press of America, 1989.

11242. Lee, Gary. "Breaking the Color Barrier in PR." *Washington Post*, 1 February 1993. [Public Relations industry in Wash., D.C.]

11243. Leo, John. "Tribalism in the Newsroom?" *U.S. News and World Report* (4 December 1994).

11244. Lewis, William Gilbert. *Toward Representative Bureaucracy: An Assessment of Black Representation in Police Bureaucracies.* Ph.D. diss., New York University, 1988. UMO #8825080.

11245. Malitz, Nancy. "Ethnic Voices Call the Tune In the Cities." *New York Times*, 6 February 1994. [Classical music institutions and inner cities]

11246. Marina, D., and A. R. Viraida. "Minority Involvement in Psychoanalysis." in *History of the Division of Psychoanalysis of the American Psychological Association*, pp. 153-155. eds. Roger C. Lane, and M. Meisels. Lawrence Erlbaum Associates, 1994.

11247. McRae, M. B., and R. T. Carter. "Occupational Profiles of Blacks in Management: Implications for Career Counseling." *Journal of Employment Counseling* 29 (March 1992): 2-4.

11248. Menciner, Stephanie. "Separate Tables." *Washington Post*, 13 December 1992. [Absence of Black waiters in Washington's fanciest restaurants]

11249. Mitchell, B. N., and V. L. Flintall. "The Status of the Black CPA-20 Year Update." *Journal of Accounting* 170 (August 1990).

11250. Murayama, Yuzo. "Occupational Advancement of Japanese Immigrants and Its Economic Implications: Experience in the State of Washington, 1903-1925." *Japanese Journal of American Studies* no. 3 (1989): 141-153.

11251. Oldfield, J. R. "A High and Honorable Calling: Black Lawyers in South Carolina, 1868-1915." *Journal of American Studies* 23 (December 1989): 395-406.

11252. Olzak, Susan D. "Causes of Shifts in Occupational Segregation of the Foreign-Born: Evidence from American Cities, 1870-1880." *Social Forces* 68 (1989): 593-620. [Blacks and White immigrants]

11253. Ouroussoff, Nicolai. "After a Moment in the Sun, Eclipsed Again." *New York Times*, 6 October 1991. [Black architects]

11254. Perkins, Linda M. "The History of Blacks in Teaching: Growth and Decline Within the Profession." in *American Teachers: Histories of a Profession at Work*, ed. Donald Warren. New York: Macmillan, 1989.

11255. Putney, Martha S. *Black Sailors: Afro-American Merchant Seaman and Whaleman Prior to the Civil War.* Westport, CT: Greenwood, 1987.

11256. Rhodes, Jane, and Carolyn Calloway-Thomas. "Journalism." *Black Women in America, I*, pp. 662-666.

11257. Rothstein, Edward. "Black Composers Seek To Emerge as a Force In Classical Music." *New York Times*, 14 April 1994.

11258. _____. "Racism Is Only Part Of the Story." *New York Times*, 25 April 1993. [African Americans in classical music]

11259. Schmidt, Fred H. "Job Caste in the Southwest." *Industrial Relations* 9 (October 1969): 100-110.

11260. Schmitz, Susanne, and Paul E. Gabriel. "The Impact of Changes in Local Labor Market Conditions on Estimates of Occupational Segregation." *Review of Black Political Economy* 27 (Summer 1992): 45-58.

11261. Schwarz, K. Robert. "Black Maestros On the Podiums, But No Pedestal." *New York Times*, 11 October 1992. [Conditions of symphony orchestras]

11262. Scott, Joan W. "Gender and the Profession of History: American Women Historians, 1884-1984." *Daedalus* (Fall 1987): 93- 118.

11263. Shrestha, Nanda R., and De Witt Davis, Jr. "Minorities in Geography: Some Disturbing Facts and Policy Measures." *Professional Geographer* 41 (1989): 410-421.

11264. Sidanius, J. and others. "Consensual Racism and Career Track: Some Implications of Social Dominance Theory." *Political Psychology* 12 (December 1991): 691-722.

11265. Smith, J. Clay, Jr. *Emancipation. The Making of the Black Lawyer, 1844-1944*. University of Pennsylvania Press, 1993.

11266. Snipp, C. Matthew, and M. Tienda. "Mexican American Occupational Mobility." *Social Science Quarterly* 65 (June 1984).

11267. Sokoloff, Natalie J. "Are Professions Becoming Desegregated? An Analysis of Detailed Professional Occupations by Race and Gender." *Sociological Abstracts* (1989) Accession No. 89S21729.

11268. _____. *Black Women and White Women in the Professions*. Routledge, 1992.

11269. Staples, Brent. "Beyond Tokenism in the Newsroom." *New York Times*, 20 September 1993.

11270. Story, Rosalyn M. *And So I Sing: African-American Divas of Opera and Concert*. New York: Warner Books, 1990.

11271. Thomas, Susan Gregory. "Can a Black Woman Make It in the White World of Dealing Art?" *Washington Post*, 20 June 1993.

11272. Travis, Jack. *African American Architects in Current Practice*. Princeton Architectural Press, 1991. [About 35 African- American architects]

11273. Vartabedian, Ralph. "Aerospace Careers in Low Orbit." *Los Angeles Times*, 16 November 1992. [Asians charge glass ceiling in industry]

11274. Verhovek, Sam H. "Black Journalists Look to Advance." *New York Times*, 23 July 1993.

11275. Walker, E. George. "Make Room for Black Classical Music." *New York Times*, 3 November 1991. [Black composers of classical music; by a Black composer.]

11276. Walters, Donna K. H. "For Minority Lawyers, It's Who You Know, Bar Survey Suggests." *Los Angeles Times*, 1 March 1994. [October 1993 survey by American Bar Association's Converence of Minority Partners in Majority/Corporate Law Firms]

11277. Welkos, Robert W. "Against the Odds." *Los Angeles Times*, 6 September 1992. [About Stephanie Allain, African American vice president of production at Columbia Pictures]

11278. Wharton, Amy S. "Gender Segregation in Private Sector, Public Sector, and Self-Employed Occupations, 1950-1981." *Social Science Quarterly* 70 (1989): 923-940.

11279. Willox-Blau, Pamela. "Toward Cultural Integration: the Career Development of Black Musicians and the Symphony Orchestra." *Journal of Arts Management and Law* 20 (Spring 1990): 17-35.

11280. Worthman, Paul B. "Working-Class Mobility in Birmingham, Alabama, 1880-1914." in *Anonymous Americans*, ed. Tamara Hareven. Englewood Cliffs, NJ: Prentice-Hall, 1971.

OPPRESSION

11281. Acuna, Rodolfo F. "Bird in a Cage: Subjugation of the Chicano in the U.S." in *The Reinterpretation of American History and Culture*, eds. William H. Cartwright, and Richard L. Watson, Jr. Washington, DC: National Council for the Social Sciences, 1974.

11282. Almaguer, Tomas. "Class, Race, and Chicano Oppression." *Socialist Revolution* (July-September 1975): 71-99.

11283. _____. "Historical Notes on Chicano Oppression: The Dialectics of Racial and Class Domination in North America." *Aztlan* 5 (Spring 1974).

11284. Baldwin, James. "Psychology of Oppression." in *Contemporary Black Thought*, ed. A. Vandi. Beverly Hills, CA: Sage, 1980.

11285. Britton, A., and M. Maynard. *Sexism, Racism, and Oppression*. Blackwell, 1984.

11286. Buckley, Thomas. "Suffering the Cultural Construction of Others." *American Indian Quarterly* (Fall 1989).

11287. Johnson, Robert C. "The Political Economy of Criminal Oppression." *Black Scholar* 8 (1977): 14-22.

11288. Ramazanoglu, Caroline. *Feminism and the Contradictions of Oppression*. New York: Routledge, 1989.

11289. Staples, Robert. "To Be Young, Black, and Oppressed." *Black Scholar* (December 1975): 2-9.

11290. Talbot, Steve. *Roots of Oppression: The American Indian Question*. New York: International Publishers, 1981.

11291. West, Cornel. "Marxist Theory and the Specificity of Afro- American Oppression." in *Marxism and the Interpretation of Culture*, eds. Cary Nelson, and Lawrence Grossberg. Urbana: University of Illinois Press, 1988.

PHILOSOPHY

11292. "African-American Perspective and Philosophical Traditions." *Philosophical Forum* 24 (Fall-Spring 1992-1993): entire triple issue.

11293. Ashby, Stephen M. *Hermeneutic of Suspicion and the Scapegoat: Toward Ontological Understanding*. Ph.D. diss., Bowling Green State University, 1992. UMO #9237690.

11294. Bracken, H. "Essence, Accident and Race." *Hermathena* 116 (Winter 1973): 91-96.

11295. _____. "Philosophy and Racism." *Philosophia* 8 (1978): 241-260.

11296. Frye, Charles A. *From Egypt to Don Juan: The Anatomy of Black Philosophy*. Lanham, MD: University Press of America, 1988.

11297. Goldberg, David T. "Racism and Rationality: The Need for a New Critique." *Philosophy of the Social Sciences* 20 (September 1990): 317-350.

11298. _____. *Racist Culture: Philosophy and the Politics of Meaning*. Blackwell, 1993.

11299. Harris, Leonard. "The Legitimation Crisis in American Philosophy: Crisis Resolution from the Standpoint of the Afro- American Tradition of Philosophy." *Social Science Information* 26 (March 1987): 57-75.

11300. Harris, Leonard, ed. *Philosophy Born of Struggle-Anthology of Afro-American Philosophy from 1917*. Kendall/Hunt Publishing Co., 1983.

11301. Immerwahr, John. "Hume Revised Racism." *Journal of the History of Ideas* 53 (July-September 1992): 481-486.

11302. Immerwahr, John, and Michael Burke. "Race and the Modern Philosophy Course." *Teaching Philosophy* 16 (March 1993): 21-34.

11303. Jones, Rhett. "Time, Social Psychology and Black Thought." *Afro-American Journal of Philosophy* 1 (1983): 35-48.

11304. Karenga, Maulana. "Black Studies and the Problematic of Paradigm: The Philosophical Dimension." *Journal of Black Studies* 18 (June 1988): 395-414.

11305. Kly, Yussuf N. *The Black Book: The True Political Philosophy of Malcolm X*. Clarity Press, 1986.

11306. Locke, Alain L. *Race Contacts and Interracial Relations: Lectures on the Theory and Practice of Race*, ed. Jeffrey C. Stewart. Harvard University Press, 1992.

11307. McGrary, Howard, Jr., and Bill E. Lawson. *Between Slavery and Freedom. Philosophy and American Slavery*. Indiana University Press, 1992.

11308. Mecklin, J. M. "The Philosophy of the Color Line." *American Journal of Sociology* 19 (1913): 343-357.

11309. Pittman, John, ed. "African-American Perspectives and Philosophical Traditions." *Philosophical Forum* 24 (Fall-Spring 1992-93): entire issue.

11310. Sniderman, Paul M. and others. "Racism and Liberal Democracy." *Politics and the Individual* 3 (1993): 1-28.

11311. Stewart, Jeffrey C., ed. *The Critical Temper of Alain Locke: A Selection of His Essays on Art and Culture*. New York: Garland, 1983.

11312. Uebel, Thomas E. "Scientific Racism in the Philosophy of Science: Some Historical Examples." *Philosophical Forum* 22 (Fall 1990): 1-18.

11313. Varet, Gilbert. *Racisme et philosophie*. Paris: Editions Denoel, 1973.

11314. Washington, Johnny. *A Journey into the Philosophy of Alain Locke*. Greenwood, 1994.

11315. West, Cornel. "The Black Underclass and Black Philosophers." in *Prophetic Thought in Postmmodern Times*, pp. 143-157. Monroe, Maine: Common Courage Press, 1993.

11316. Yu, Yuh-Chao. "The Ideal of Equality in America." *Sino- American Relations* 14 (Winter 1988): 65-95.

PLANNING

11317. Bauman, John F. "The Paradox of Post-war Urban Planning: Downtown Revitalization versus Decent Housing for All." in *Two Centuries of American Planning*, ed. Daniel Schaffer. London: Mansell, 1988.

11318. Bayor, Ronald H. "Roads to Racial Segregation: Atlanta in the Twentieth Century." *Journal of Urban History* 15 (1988): 3-21.

11319. Galster, George C., and Edward W. Hill, eds. *The Metropolis in Black and White. Place, Power, and Polarization*. New Brunswick, NJ: Transaction Publishers, 1992.

11320. Giloth, Robert, and J. Betancur. "Where Downtown Meets Neighborhood: Industrial Displacement in Chicago, 1978-87." *Journal of American Planning Association* 54 (Summer 1988): 279- 290.

11321. Grant, Nancy L. *TVA and Black Americans. Planning for the Status Quo*. Philadelphia, PA: Temple University Press, 1989.

11322. Hall, Peter. "The Turbulent Eighth Decade: Challenges to American City Planning." *Journal of the American Planning Association* 55 (1989): 275-282.

11323. Hoch, Charles, ed. "Power, Planning and Conflict." *Journal of Architectural and Planning Research* 7 (Winter 1990): 271-350 (entire issue).

11324. Hoch, Charles. "Racism and Planning." *American Planning Association Journal* 59 (Autumn 1993): 451-460.

11325. Power, Garrett. "The Advent of Zoning." *Planning Perspectives* 4 (1989): 1-13.

11326. Randolph, Robert, ed. *Proceedings of the First Minority Planning Conference*. Gary, IN: Afro-American Studies Dept., Division of Arts and Sciences, 1976.

11327. Wachs, Martin, ed. *Ethics in Planning*. New Brunswick, NJ: Center for Urban-Policy Research, 1985.

PLURALISM

11328. Akam, Everett H. *Pluralism and the Search for Community: The Social Thought of American Cultural Pluralists*. Ph.D. diss., University of Rochester, 1990. UMO #9021084.

11329. Appleton, N. *Cultural Pluralism in Education: Theoretical Foundations*. Longmans, 1983.

11330. Baron, Salo W. "Is America Ready for Ethnic Minority Rights?" *Jewish Social Studies* 46 (1984): 189-214. [National cultural self-determination]

11331. Bourne, Jenny. "Cheerleaders and Ombudsmen: The Sociology of Race Relations in Britain." *Race and Class* 21 (Spring 1980).

11332. Buelens, Gert. "Beyond Ethnicity?" *Journal of American Studies* 23 (1989): 315-320.

11333. Bullivaint, Brian M. *Pluralism, Cultural Maintenance and Evolution*. Clevedon, Avon: Multilingual Matters, 1984.

11334. Cazemajou, Jean, and Jean-Pierre Martin. *La crise du melting-pot: ethnicite et identite aux 'Etats-Unis de Kennedy a Reagan*. Paris: Editions Aubier-Montaigne, 1983.

11335. Cervantes, Fred A. "Chicanos Within the Political Economy: Some Questions Concerning Pluralist Ideology Representation and the Economy." *Aztlan* 7 (Fall 1976): 337-345.

11336. Cortese, Anthony J. P. *Ethnic Ethics: The Restructuring of Moral Theory*. Albany: State University of New York Press, 1990.

11337. Emihovich, Catherine, ed. "Toward Cultural Pluralism: Redefining Integration in American Society." *Urban Review* 20 (Spring 1988): 1-72.

11338. Fuchs, Lawrence H. *The American Kaleidoscope: Pluralism and the Civic Culture*. Middletown, CT: Wesleyan University Press, 1989.

11339. Gerber, David A. *The Making of an American Pluralism: Buffalo, New York, 1825-60*. Urbana: University of Illinois Press, 1989.

11340. Gleason, Philip. "The Melting Pot: Symbol of Fusion or Confusion." *American Quarterly* 16 (1964): 20-46.

11341. Gordon, Edmund W. "Human Diversity and Pluralism." *Educational Psychologist* 26 (Spring 1991): 99-108.

11342. Hall, Stuart. "Pluralism, Race and Class in Caribbean Society." in *Race and Class in Post-Colonial Society*, pp. 150- 182. ed. UNESCO. Paris: UNESCO, 1977.

11343. Hord, Frederick. "African Americans, Cultural Pluralism and the Politics of Culture." *West Virginia Law Review* 91 (Summer 1989): 1047-1065.

11344. Jordan, Grant. "The Pluralism of Pluralism: An Anti- Theory?" *Political Studies* 38 (June 1990): 286-301.

11345. Kochman, T. "Cultural Pluralism: Black and White Styles." in *Cultural Communication and Intercultural Context*, pp. 219-224. ed. D. Carbaugh. Hillsdale, NJ: Lawrence Erlbaum Associates, 1990.

11346. Lambert, Wallace E., and Donald M. Taylor. *Coping with Cultural and Racial Diversity in Urban America*. Westport, CT: Praeger, 1990.

11347. Marger, Martin. "Factors of Structural Pluralism in Multiethnic Societies: A Comparative Case Study." *International Journal of Group Tensions* (Spring 1989): 52-68. [Black-white relations in U.S. and Catholic-Protestant relations in Northern Ireland]

11348. Matthews, Fred H. "The Revolt against Americanism: Cultural Pluralism and Cultural Relativism as an Ideology of Liberation." *Canadian Review of American Studies* 1 (Spring 1970): 4-31.

11349. Norgren, Jill, and Serena Nanda. *American Cultural Pluralism and Law*. Westport, CT: Praeger, 1988.

11350. O'Brien, Sharon. "Cultural Rights in the United States: A Conflict of Values." *Law and Inequality* 5 (July 1987): 267-358.

11351. Payton, Robert L. and others. *A Melting Pot or a Nation of Minorities*, ed. W. Lawson Taitte. Austin: University of Texas Press, 1986.

11352. Pearson, Maggie. "The Politics of Ethnic Minority Health Studies." *Radical Community Medicine* no. 16 (Winter 1983-84): 34- 44.

11353. Rabinowitz, Howard N. "Race, Ethnicity, and Cultural Pluralism in American History." in *Ordinary People + Everyday Life*, pp. 23-49. eds. James B. Gardner, and George R. Adams. Nashville, TN: American Association for State and Local History, 1983.

11354. Radhakrishnan, R. "Culture as Common Ground: Ethnicity and Beyond." *Massachusetts Review* 14 (Summer 1987): 5-20.

11355. Ramirez, Albert. "From Monolithic to Pluralistic Systems: Asymmetric/Unequal Power Analysis." *Proteus* 7 (1990): 43-49.

11356. Roback, J. "Plural But Equal: Group Identity and Voluntary Integration." *Social Philosophy and Policy* 8 (Spring 1991): 60- 80.

11357. San Juan, E., Jr. "The Cult of Ethnicity and the Fetish of Pluralism." *Cultural Critique* 18 (Spring 1991): 215-229.

11358. Saxton, Alexander. "Nathan Glazer, Daniel Moynihan and the Cult of Ethnicity." *Amerasia Journal* 4 (Summer 1977): 141-150.

11359. Singer, Beth J. "The Democratic Solution to Ethnic Pluralism." *Philosophy and Social Criticism* 19 (April 1993): 97- 114.

11360. "Toward Cultural Pluralism: Redefining Integration in American Society." *Urban Review* 20 (Spring 1988): entire issue.

11361. Tuckman, G. "Pluralism and Disdain: American Culture Today." in *America at Century's End*, pp. 340-360. ed. Alan Wolfe. Berkeley: UC Press, 1991.

11362. Van den Berghe, Pierre L. "Pluralism." in *Handbook of Social and Cultural Anthropology*, pp. 959-978. ed. J. Honigman. Rand Mc Nally, 1973.

11363. Warren, Wilson J. *The Limits of New Deal Social Democracy: Working-class Structural Pluralism in Midwestern Meatpacking, 1900-1955*. Two volumes. Ph.D. diss., University of Pittsburgh, 1992. UMO #9317970.

11364. Young, Crawford. *The Politics of Cultural Pluralism*. Madison: University of Wisconsin Press, 1976.

11365. Young, Crawford, ed. *The Rising Tide of Cultural Pluralism*. University of Wisconsin Press, 1993.

11366. Zunz, Oliver. "The Genesis of American Pluralism." *Tocqueville Review* 9 (1987-88): 201-219.

POLITICS AND RACISM

11367. Abourezk, James. *Advise and Dissent: Memories of South Dakota and the U.S. Senate*. Chicago, IL: Lawrence Hill Books, 1989.

11368. Abramowitz, Michael. "P.G.'s Political Shift. Young Blacks Move In to Seats of Power." *Washington Post*, 18 February 1994. [Prince George's County, MD]

11369. Abrams, Douglas C. "Irony of Reform: North Carolina Blacks and the New Deal." *North Carolina Historical Review* 66 (April 1989): 149-178.

11370. Abrams, Kathryn. "Raising Politics Up: Minority Political Participation and Section 2 of the Voting Rights Act." *New York University Law Review* 63 (June 1988): 449-531.

11371. Abramson, Paul R., and William Claggett. "Race-related Differences in Self-reported and Validated Turnout in 1986." *Journal of Politics* 51 (1989): 397-408.

11372. Abron, Jonina M. "The Legacy of the Black Panther Party." *Black Scholar* 17 (1986): 33-37.

11373. Adams, Ron J. "Whose Vote Counts? Minority Vote Dilution and Election Rights." *Washington University Journal of Urban and Contemporary Law* 35 (Summer 1989): 219-235.

11374. *Al Filo/At the Cutting Edge: The Empowerment of Chicago's Latino Electorate*. Chicago, IL: Latino Institute, 1986.

11375. Alkalimat, Abdul. "Bibliography Essay: Jesse Jackson: The Politics of Opportunity or Opportunism?" *Sage Race Relations Abstracts* 14 (November 1989): 3-15.

11376. Altemeyer, B. *Enemies of Freedom: Understanding Right-wing Authoritarianism*. San Francisco, CA, 1988.

11377. _____. *Right-wing Authoritarianism*. Winnipeg, 1981.

11378. Anbinder, Tyler. *Nativism and Slavery. The Northern Know Nothings and the Politics of the 1850's*. Oxford University Press, 1992.

11379. Anders, Evan M. *Bosses Under Siege: The Politics of South Texas During the Progressive Era*. Ph.D. diss., University of Texas, 1978. UMO #7910923.

11380. Anderson, Susan. "Black Leadership Gap. Eyes on the Prizes, Not the People." *Nation* (16 October 1989) 9).

11381. _____. "Black Power on Trial." *New Politics* 3 (Summer 1990): 5-15.

11382. Anthony, Earl. *Spitting in the Wind: The True Story Behind the Violent Legacy of the Black Panther Party*. Malibu, CA: Roundtable Publishing Co., 1990.

11383. Apple, Michael W. "Redefining Equality: Authoritarian Populism and Conservative Restoration." *Teachers College Record* 90 (1988): 167-184. [See pp. 185-195 for Response and Rejoinder]

11384. Applebome, Peter. "Black Conservatives: Minority Within a Minority." *New York Times*, 13 July 1991.

11385. _____. "The 'Bubba' Stereotype Is Vanishing As a Region Becomes More Moderate." *New York Times*, 1 March 1992. [Black and white voting in the South]

11386. _____. "From Atlanta to Birmingham, Blur of Progress and Stagnation." *New York Times*, 3 August 1994.

11387. _____. "Georgia District Ruling is Test for Racial Politics." *New York Times*, 19 September 1994. [Gerrymander or racial justice in drawing electoral district boundaries]

11388. _____. "In Alabama, Blacks Battle for the Authority to Govern." *New York Times*, 31 January 1992.

11389. _____. "Louisiana Showdown. Duke vs. Edwards." *New York Times*, 10-11 November 1991. 2 articles.

11390. _____. "Road Still Tough for Black Candidates." *New York Times*, 14 August 1990.

11391. Arian, Asher and others. *Changing New York City Politics*. New York: Routledge, 1991.

11392. Arrington, T. S., and T. G. Watts. "The Election of Blacks to School Boards in North Carolina." *Western Political Quarterly* 44 (December 1991).

11393. Arthur, Paul. "Diasporan Intervention in International Affairs: Irish America as a Case Study." *Diaspora* 1 (1991): 143- 162.

11394. "Asian Americans in Politics? Rarely." *New York Times*, 3 June 1993.

11395. Auspitz, Josiah L. "Blacks, Tokenism and the G.O.P." *New York Times*, 9 July 1993.

11396. Bai, Su Sun. "Affirmative Pursuit of Political Equality for Asian Pacific Americans: Reclaiming the Voting Rights Act." *University of Pennsylvania Law Review* 139 (January 1991): 731-767.

11397. Bailey, Michael S. *The Role of Black Mayors in the Agenda Politics of American Cities*. Ph.D. diss., Ohio State University, 1990. UMO #9105071.

11398. Baker, Stephen C., and Paul Kleppner. "Race War Chicago Style: The Election of a Black Mayor, 1983." *Research in Urban Policy* 2, no. 13 (1986): 215-238.

11399. Ball, Howard. "Racial Vote Dilution: Impact of the Reagan DOJ and the Burger Court on the Voting Rights Act." *Publius* 16 (1986): 29-48. [DOJ=Department of Justice]

11400. Ball, Thomas E. *Julian Bond vs. John Lewis: On the Campaign Trail with John Lewis and Julian Bond*. Atlanta, GA: W.H. Wolfe, 1988.

11401. Barker, Lucius J. "Black Americans and the Politics of Inclusion." *PS* 16 (Summer 1983): 500-507.

11402. Barker, Lucius J., ed. *Black Electoral Politics. Participation, Performance, Promise. The National Political Science Review*, Vol. 2. New Brunswick, NJ: Transaction, 1990.

11403. _____. *Ethnic Politics and Civil Liberties. National Political Science Review*, Vol. 3. New Brunswick, NJ: Transaction, 1991.

11404. Bartels, Larry M., and C. Anthony Broh. "The 1988 Presidential Primaries." *Public Opinion Quarterly* 53 (1989): 563- 589.

11405. Bates, Timothy, and Darrell L. Williams. "Racial Politics: Does It Pay?" *Social Science Quarterly* 74 (September 1993): 507- 522.

11406. Bayes, Jane H. *Minority Politics and Ideologies in the United States*. Novato, CA: Chandler and Sharp, 1982.

11407. _____. "Women and Public Administration: A Comparative Perspective." *Women and Politics* 11 (1991): 111-132.

11408. Bayor, Ronald H. "Models of Ethnic and Racial Politics in the Urban Sunbelt South." in *Searching for the Sunbelt*, ed. Raymond A. Mohl. University of Tennessee Press, 1990.

11409. _____. "Race, Ethnicity, and Political Change in the Urban Sunbelt South." in *Shades of the Sunbelt: Essays on Ethnicity, Race, and the Urban South*, eds. Randall M. Miller, and George E. Pozzetta. Boca Raton: Florida Atlantic University Press, 1989.

11410. Beatty, Bess. *A Revolution Gone Backward: The Black Response to National Politics, 1876-1896*. Westport, CT: Greenwood, 1987.

11411. Beeghley, L. "Social Structure and Voting in the United States: A Historical and International Analysis." in *Perspectives on Social Problems*, Vol. 3. pp. 265-288. eds. J. A. Holstein, and G. Miller. JAI Press, 1992.

11412. Bell, Derrick. "The Referendum: Democracy's Barrier to Racial Equality." *Washington Law Review* (1978).

11413. Bell, Derrick, and Preeta Bansal. "The Republican Revival and Racial Politics." *Yale Law Journal* 97 (July 1988): 1609-1621.

11414. Benjamin, Playthell. "The Attitude Is the Message. Louis Farrakhan Pursues the Middle Class." *Village Voice* (15 August 1989).

11415. _____. "GOP Goes the Weasel. Tony Brown Stands Up for Republicans." *Village Voice* (20 August 1991).

11416. Bennett, L. "Harold Washington and the Black Urban Regime." *Urban Affairs Quarterly* 28 (March 1993): 423-440.

11417. Bennett, Stephen E. "Left Behind: Exploring Declining Turnout among Noncollege Young Whites, 1964-1988." *Social Science Quarterly* 72 (June 1991): 314-333.

11418. Bennett, Stephen E., and David Resnick. "The Implications of Nonvoting for Democracy in the United States." *American Journal of Political Science* 34 (August 1990): 771-802.

11419. Berke, Richard L. "Republicans Make Strong Gains From Appeals to Hispanic Voters." *New York Times*, 5 July 1993.

11420. Berlet, Chip. *Right Woos Left: Populist Party, La Rouchian, and Other Neo-fascist Overtures to Progressives, And Why They Must Be Rejected*. Cambridge, MA: Political Research Associates, 7 October 1992.

11421. Berry, Jeffrey M. and others. "The Political Behavior of Poor People." in *The Urban Underclass*, pp. 357-372. eds. Christopher Jencks, and Paul E. Peterson. Washington, DC: Brookings Institution, 1991.

11422. Black, Earl, and Merle Black. *The Vital South: How Presidents Are Elected*. Cambridge, MA: Harvard U.P., 1992.

11423. "Black Electoral Success in 1989." *PS-Political Science and Politics* 23 (June 1990): 9 articles.

11424. *Black Power in Chicago: A Documentary Survey of the 1983 Mayoral Democratic Primary*, Vol. 1. Chicago, IL: People's College Press, 1983.

11425. *Blacks and the 1984 Republican National Convention*. Washington, DC: Joint Center for Political Studies, 1988.

11426. *Blacks and the 1988 Democratic National Convention*. Washington, DC: Joint Center for Political Studies, 1988.

11427. Bleifuss, Joel. "PR is PC." *In These Times* (23 October 1991). [Proportional representation and minority representation]

11428. Block, Sam. "Never Turn Back: An Interview with Sam Block." *Southern Exposure* 15 (1987): 37-50. [Registering black voters in Greenwood, MS, in SNCC, 1962]

11429. Bobo, Lawrence. "Attitudes toward the Black Political Movement: Trends, Meaning, and Effects on Racial Policy Preferences." *Social Psychology Quarterly* 51 (December 1988): 287-302.

11430. Bobo, Lawrence, and Franklin D. Gilliam. "Race, Sociopolitical Participation, and Black Empowerment." *American Political Science Review* 84 (1990): 377-394.

11431. Boice, L. and others. "Blacks and the Republican Party: The 20 Percent Solution." *Political Science Quarterly* 107 (Spring 1992): 63-80.

11432. Bond, Julian. "Where We've Been, Where We're Going: A Vision of Racial Justice in the 1990's." *Harvard Civil Rights- Civil Liberties Law Review* 25 (Summer 1990): 273-285.

11433. Boneparthe. "The Image of Women in American Government Textbooks." *Teaching Political Science* 7 (1980).

11434. Bonney, Norman. "Race and Politics in Chicago in the Daley Area." *Race* 15 (1974): 329-350.

11435. Bowser, Benjamin P. "Social Significance of the Jesse Jackson Campaign." *Sage Race Relations Abstracts* 10 (May 1985): 34-45.

11436. Boyarsky, Bill. "Redistricting Takes On New Urgency." *Los Angeles Times*, 3 July 1991.

11437. Bradley, Bill. "No More Race Politics, Mr. President." *Harper's* 283 (September 1991): 17. [From a speech delivered by the New Jersey senator on the Senate floor, July 10, 1991]

11438. Brantley, Daniel. "Gandhi and Black America, 1930s-1940s." *Political Science Review* 25 (1986): 82-89. [India]

11439. Brinkley, Alan. "The Problem of American Conservatism." *American Historical Review* 99 (April 1994): 409-429. [See also critique by Susan M. Yohn and Leo P. Ribuffo, pp. 430-449: and response by Brinkley, pp. 450-452]

11440. Broussard, Albert S. "The Politics of Despair: Black San Franciscans and the Political Process, 1920-1940." *Journal of Negro History* 69 (1984): 26-37.

11441. Brown, J. K. "The Nineteenth Amendment and Women's Equality." *Yale Law Journal* 102 (June 1993).

11442. Brown, Peter. *Minority Party: Why Democrats Face Defeat in 1992 and Beyond*.

11443. Browning, Rufus P. and others, eds. *Racial Politics in American Cities*. New York: Longman, 1990. [Chicago, Boston, Atlanta, Birmingham, New Orleans, Miami, San Antonio, Denver]

11444. Browning, Rufus P., and Dale R. Marshall. "Black and Hispanic Power in City Politics: A Forum." *PS-Political Science and Politics* 19 (Summer 1986): 573-640.

11445. Buckley, Stephen. "'Cumulative Voting' Is Ordered." *Washington Post*, 6 April 1994. [Worcester County, Maryland]

11446. Bullock, Charles S., III. "Misinformation and Misperceptions: A Little Knowledge Can Be Dangerous." *Social Science Quarterly* 72 (December 1991): 834-839. [See also B. Grofman, below]

11447. _____. "Turnout in Municipal Elections." *Policy Studies Review* 9 (Spring 1990): 539-549. [Six cities, 1976-1986]

11448. Bullock, Charles S., III, and S. A. Macmanus. "Structural Features of Municipalities and the Incidence of Hispanic Council Members." *Social Science Quarterly* 71 (December 1990): 665-681.

11449. Burleigh, Nina. "Hazards of [David] Duke in Louisiana." *Guardian (NYC)* (6 November 1991).

11450. Burman, S. "The Illusion of Progress: Race and Politics in Atlanta, Georgia." *Ethnic and Racial Studies* 2 (1979): 441-454.

11451. Butler, Katharine I., and Richard Murray. "Minority Vote Dilution Suits and the Problem of Two Minority Groups: Can a Rainbow Coalition Claim the Protection of the Voting Rights Act?" *Pacific Law Journal* 21 (April 1990): 619-689.

11452. Button, James W. "The Outcomes of Contempoary Black Protest and Violence." in *Violence in America*, Vol. 1. ed. Ted Robert Gurr. Newbury Park, CA: Sage, 1989.

11453. Button, James W., and Richard K. Scher. "The Election and Impact of Black Officials in the South." in *Public Policy and Social Institutions*, ed. Harrell R. Rogers, Jr. Greenwich, CT: JAI Press, 1984.

11454. Byng, Michelle D. *A New Face in the Structure of Community Power: The Black Political Elite of Richmond, Virginia*. Ph.D. diss., University of Virginia, 1992. UMO #9237488.

11455. Cagan, Leslie, and Susan Hibbard. "Doing the Right Thing?: Leftists Active in the Dinkins' Mayoral Campaign." *Radical America* 22 (November-December 1988): 7-21.

11456. Cain, Bruce. "The Contemporary Context of Ethnic and Racial Politics in California." in *Racial and Ethnic Politics in California*, eds. Bryan O. Jackson, and Michael B. Preston. Berkeley: IGS Press, Institute of Governmenal Studies, University of California, 1991.

11457. Cantrell, Gregg. "Racial Violence and Reconstruction Politics in Texas, 1867-1868." *Southwestern Historical Quarterly* 93 (1990): 333-355.

11458. Cantrell, Gregg, and D. Scott Barton. "Texas Populists and the Failure of Biracial Politics." *Journal of Southern History* 55 (November 1989): 659-692.

11459. Carmines, G., and James A. Stinson. *Issue Evolution: Race and the Transformation of American Politics*. Princeton, NJ: Princeton University Press, 1989.

11460. Carter, Dan T. *When the War Was Over: The Failure of Self- Reconstruction in the South, 1865-1867*. Baton Rouge: Louisiana State University Press, 1985.

11461. Carter, Hodding. "Not the End." *New York Times*, 18 November 1991. [After the Nov. 1991 defeat of David Duke in Louisiana]

11462. Carter, Stephen L. "Nativism and Its Discontents." *New York Times*, 8 March 1992. [On Patrick Buchanan's racial and related views]

11463. Cavanagh, Thomas E. *The Impact of the Black Electorate*. Washington, DC: Joint Center for Political Studies, 1984.

11464. Cavanagh, Thomas E., ed. *Manuscript Prepared for the Panel on Political Participation*. Committee on the Status of Black Americans, National Research Council, Washington, D.C., 1987.

11465. Champagne, Duane. *Strategies and Conditions of Political and Cultural Survival in American Indian Societies*, Revised ed. Cambridge, MA: Cultural Survival Inc., 1989.

11466. Chandhuri, Joyotpaul. "Indians and the Social Contract." *National Political Science Review* 1 (1989): 190-200. [Political behavior of American Indians]

11467. Chavez, Linda. *Out of the Barrio: Toward a New Politics of Hispanic Assimilation*. New York: Basic Books, 1992.

11468. Chen, Marion and others. "Empowerment in New York Chinatown: Our Work as Student Interns." *Amerasia Journal* 15 (1989): 299-303.

11469. Cherian, Anila and others. "'Third Worldism': Reactionary Politics in Progressive Disguise." *Radical America* 24 (January- March 1990): 69-71.

11470. Christopher, Maurice. *America's Black Congressmen*. New York: Cromwell, 1971.

11471. Citrin, Jack and others. "White Reactions to Black Candidates: When Does Race Matter?" *Public Opinion Quarterly* 54 (1990): 74-96.

11472. Clark, W. A. V., and Peter A. Morrison. "Gauging Hispanic Voting Strength: Paradoxes and Pitfalls." *Population Research and Policy Review* 11 (1992).

11473. Clarke, Stuart A. "Fear of a Black Planet. Race Identity Politics, and Common Sense." *Socialist Review* 21 (July-December 1991): 37-59.

11474. Clement, Audrey Rose. *The Congressional Black Caucus: Its Representational Role*. Ph.D. diss., Temple University, 1993. UMO #9332780.

11475. Clemente, Frank, and Frank Watkins, eds. *Keep Hope Alive, Jesse Jackson's 1988 Presidential Campaign: A Collection of Major Speeches, Issue Papers, Photographs and Campaign Analysis*. Boston, MA: South End Press, 1990.

11476. Cloward, Richard A., and Francis Fox Piven. "Race and the Democrats." *Nation* (9 December 1991).

11477. Clymer, Adam. "A Daughter of Slavery Makes the Senate Listen." *New York Times*, 23 July 1993. [African-American Sen. Carol Moseley Braun attacks attempted approval of Confederate flag.]

11478. Cohler, Larry. "Republican Racist." *New Republic* (September 18 and 25, 1989). [David Duke]

11479. Cohodas, Nadine. *Strom Thurmond and the Politics of Southern Change*. Simon and Schuster, 1993.

11480. Coleman, Mary D. *Legislators, Law and Public Policy: Political Change in Mississippi and the South since Connor v. Johnson*. Ph.D. diss., University of Wisconsin, 1990. UMO #9027490.

11481. Conyers, James E., and Walter L. Wallace. *Black Elected Officials: A Study of Black Americans Holding Governmental Office*. New York: Russell Sage Foundation, 1976.

11482. Cooper, Kenneth J. "The Black Caucus's Odd Man In." *Washington Post*, 1 September 1993. [Republican congressman Gary Franks and the Congressional Black Caucus]

11483. Cooper, Marc. "The Trouble With Jesse [Jackson]." *Village Voice* (21 April 1992). [Democratic party politics and the 1992 presidential campaign]

11484. Corfman, Tom. "Voting Rights Act Arms Latinos for Congressional Remap Fight." *Chicago Reporter* 20 (May 1991): 3-6. [Chicago and suburbs]

11485. Cornell, Stephen. *The Return of the Native. American Indian Political Resurgence*. New York: Oxford University Press, 1988.

11486. Coughlin, Dan. "Smoking Guns." *Village Voice* (21 April 1992). [U.S. Congressmen from Harlem who support tobacco companies.]

11487. Cox, Stephanie Ann. *Minority Political Participation in North Carolina*. Raleigh: North Carolina Human Relations Council, North Carolina Dept. of Administration, 1983.

11488. Cruse, Harold W. and others. "Doubting Thomas." *Tikkun* 6 (September-October 1991): 23-30. [Issues involved in the nomination to the U.S. Supreme Court of Clarence Thomas]

11489. Cruse, Harold W. "New Black Leadership Required." *New Politics* II (Winter 1990): 43-47.

11490. Cruz, Takash P., and Joaquin Avila. *Latino Political Particpation in Rural California*. Davis, CA: The California Institute of Rural Studies, 1989.

11491. Danigelis, Nicholas L. "Black Political Participation in the United States: Some Recent Evidence." *American Sociological Review* 43 (October 1978): 756-771.

11492. D'Antonio, Michael. "Bedeviling the GOP." *Los Angeles Times Magazine* (29 November 1992). [The Religious Right in the GOP]

11493. Davidson, Chandler. "The Impetus for Realignment in the South: Class and Race in Texas Politics." *Sociological Abstracts* (1989) Accession No. 89S21342.

11494. Davidson, Chandler, ed. *Minority Vote Dilution*. Washington, DC: Howard University Press, 1990, orig. 1984. [Contains new postscript]

11495. Davidson, Chandler. *Race and Class in Texas Politics*. Princeton, NJ: Princeton University Press, 1990.

11496. Davidson, Chandler, and Bernard Grofman, eds. *Quiet Revolution in the South. The Impact of the Voting Rights Act, 1965-1990*. Princeton University Press, 1994.

11497. Davis, John F. "Playing Pigmentation Politics." *Village Voice* (12 September 1989). [Racial issues in mayoral elections in New York City and Chicago]

11498. Davis, Marilyn A. *Political Participation in Georgia's Fifth Congressional District: An Analysis of Racial and Socioeconomic Voting Patterns, 1946 to 1978*. Ph.D. diss., Atlanta University, 1979. UMO #9113632.

11499. Davis, Theodore J., Jr. "African-Americans' Educational Characteristics and Political Representation in Mississippi." *Southeastern Political Review* 21 (Winter 1993): 133-151.

11500. Davison, Donald L., and Michael A. Krassa. "Blacks, Whites, and the Voting Rights Act: The Poltics of Contextual Change." *Midsouth Political Science Journal* 12 (Summer 1991): 3- 22.

11501. Dawson, Michael C. *Behind the Mule: Race and Class in African-American Politics*. Princeton University Press, 1994.

11502. De Bates, Estelle. "What [David] Duke Vote Reveals About U.S. Politics." *Militant* (1 November 1991).

11503. de la Garza, Rodolfo O. "'And Then There Were Some...': Chicanos as National Political Actors, 1967-1980." *Aztlan* 15 (Spring 1984): 1-24.

11504. de la Garza, Rodolfo O. and others. *Latino Voices: Mexican, Puerto Rican, and Cuban Perspectives on American Politics*. Westview Press, 1993.

11505. Decker, Cathleen. "Activists Moving to Forge a New Conservative Creed." *Los Angeles Times*, 4 July 1992.

11506. Delaney, Paul. "'Black and Conservative' Takes Many Different Tones." *New York Times*, 22 December 1991.

11507. Delgado, Richard. "Zero-based Racial Politics and an Infinity-based Response: Will Endless Talking Cure America's Racial Ills?" *Georgetown Law Journal* 80 (June 1992): 1879-1890.

11508. Devoual, Regina. "Beyond Ballots and Boycotts. Claiborne County, Mississippi." *Dollars and Sense* no. 79 (September 1982): 14-16.

11509. Diamond, Sara. "Patriots on Parade." *Z Magazine* 5 (September 1992): 20-22. [National Coalition to Reform Money and Taxes]

11510. Dinkins, Davis N. "This City Is Sick of Violence: Dinkins's Speech Against Hate." *New York Times*, 12 May 1990. Text of speech, "An Affirmation of Tolerance and Respect," delivered by New York City Mayor Dinkins on May 11, 1990.]

11511. "District of Columbia: The State of Controversy." *Catholic University Law Review* 39 (Winter 1990): entire issue.

11512. Domhoff, G. William. *The Power Elite and the State: How Policy Is Made in America*. Hawthorne, NY: Aldine de Gruyter, 1990.

11513. Drago, Edmund L. *Black Politicians and Reconstruction in Georgia*. Baton Rouge: Louisiana State University Press, 1982.

11514. Duncan, James R. *Rufus Brown Bullock, Reconstruction, and the "New South," 1834-1907: An Exploration into Race, Class, Party and the Corruption of the American Creed*. Ph.D. diss., University of Georgia, 1988. UMO #8910411.

11515. Dyer, Brainerd. "One Hundred Years of Negro Suffrage." *Pacific Historical Review* 37 (1968): 1-20.

11516. Dyson, Michael E. "Bill Cosby and the Politics of Race." *Zeta Magazine* 2 (September 1989): 26-30.

11517. Eatwell, Roger, and Noel O'Sullivan, eds. *The Nature of the Right. European and American Politics and Political Thought Since 1789*. London: Pinter, 1989.

11518. Edds, Margaret. *Claiming the Dream: The Victorious Campaign of Douglas Wilder of Virginia*. Chapel Hill, NC: Algonquin Books of Chapel Hill, 1990.

11519. _____. *Free at Last: What Really Happened When Civil Rights Came to Southern Politics*. Bethesda, MD: Adler and Adler, 1987.

11520. Edgar, D. "Reagan's Hidden Agenda: Racism and the New American Right." *Race and Class* 22 (Winter 1981): 221-238.

11521. Edsall, Thomas B. "Conflicting Trends Seen in Whites' Willingness to Vote for Blacks." *Washington Post*, 19 December 1993.

11522. _____. "In Mississippi Delta, House Race Is as Complex as Black and White." *Washington Post*, 14 March 1993.

11523. _____. "Willie Horton's Message." *New York Review of Books* (13 February 1992).

11524. Edsall, Thomas B., and Mary D. Edsall. *Chain Reaction: The Impact of Race, Rights, and Taxes on American Politics*. New York: Norton, 1991.

11525. Ellison, Christopher G., and David A. Gay. "Black Political Participation Revisited: A Test of Compensatory, Ethnic Community, and Public Arena Models." *Social Science Quarterly* 70 (1989): 101-119.

11526. Engstrom, Richard L. and others. "Cumulative Voting as a Remedy for Minority Vote Dilution: The Case of Alamogordo, New Mexico." *Journal of Law and Politics* 5 (Spring 1989): 469-497.

11527. Engstrom, Richard L. "When Blacks Run for Judge: Racial Divisions in the Candidate Preferences of Louisiana Voters." *Judicature* 73 (August-September 1989): 87.

11528. Epstein, Barbara. *Political Protest and Cultural Revolution. Nonviolent Direct Action in the 1970s and 1980s*. Berkeley: University of California Press, 1991.

11529. Erie, Steven P. *Rainbow's End. Irish-Americans and the Dilemmas of Urban Machine Politics, 1840-1985*. Berkeley: University of California Press, 1988.

11530. Ervin, A. M. "The Emergence of Native Alaskan Political Capacity, 1959-1971." *Musk-Ox* 19 (1976): 3-15.

11531. Everett, Kevin D. *Opportunity and Action: The Dynamics of American Protest*. Ph.D. diss., University of North Carolina, 1993. [902 protest demonstrations in Atlanta, Richmond, Minneapolis, and Wash. DC, 1961-1983]. UMO #9324018.

11532. Falcon, Angelo. "Black and Latino Politics in New York City: Race and Ethnicity in a Changing Urban Context." in *Latinos and the Political System*, pp. 171-194. ed. F. Chris Garcia. Notre Dame, IN: University of Notre Dame Press, 1988.

11533. _____. "Puerto Ricans and the 1989 Mayoral Election in New York City." *Hispanic Journal of Behavorial Science* 11 (August 1989): 245-258.

11534. Federici, Michael P. *The Challenge of Populism. The Rise of Right-Wing Democratism in Postwar America*. Praeger, 1991.

11535. Feldman, S. M. "Whose Common Good? Racism in the Political Community." *Georgetown Law Journal* 80 (June 1992): 1835-1878.

11536. Filer, J. E. and others. "Voting Laws, Educational Policies, and Minority Turnout." *Journal of Law and Economics* 34 (October 1991): 371-394.

11537. Finder, Alan. "Party, Described as Cult, Seeks Role in Primary." *New York Times*, 9 September 1989. [New Alliance Party]

11538. Fineman, Howard and others. "The New Politics of Race." *Newsweek* (6 May 1991).

11539. Fisher, James A. "The Political Development of the Black Community in California, 1850-1950." *California Historical Society Quarterly* 50 (September 1971): 256-266.

11540. Fitch, Robert. "Making New York City Safe for Plutocracy." *Nation* (11 December 1989).

11541. Fitzgerald, Michael W. "'To Give Our Votes to the Party': Black Political Agitation and Agricultural Change in Alabama, 1865-1870." *Journal of American History* 76 (1989): 589-605.

11542. Flake, Floyd. "How to Undo a Century of Racism in Politics." *New York Times*, 11 July 1993. Letter. [Race and electoral redistricting]

11543. Foner, Eric. *Freedom's Lawmakers. A Directory of Black Officeholders during Reconstruction*. Oxford University Press, 1993.

11544. Formisano, Ronald P. "The Edge of Caste: Colored Suffrage in Michigan, 1827-1861." *Michigan History* (Spring 1972).

11545. Foster, E. C. "A Time of Challenge: Afro-Mississippi Political Developments Since 1965." *Journal of Negro History* 68 (1983): 185-200.

11546. Foster, Michele. "The Politics of Race: Through the Eyes of African-American Teachers." *Journal of Education* 172 (1990): 123-141.

11547. Frankel, L. M. "National Representation for the District of Columbia: A Legislative Solution." *University of Pennsylvania Law Review* 139 (June 1991): 1659-1710.

11548. Franklin, Jimmie L. *Back to Birmingham. Richard Arrington Jr. and His Times*. Tuscaloosa: University of Alabama Press, 1989. [Mayor of Birmingham]

11549. Frederick, David C. "John Quincy Adams, Slavery, and the Disappearance of the Right of Petition." *Law and History Review* 9 (Spring 1991): 113-155.

11550. Fremon, David K. "Minority Candidates Fall Short in 91: Hispanics Look Ahead to Ward Remap." *Chicago Reporter* 20 (April 1991).

11551. _____. "Race and Class Influence City Vote Totals." *Chicago Reporter* 19 (December 1990). [Chicago elections of Nov. 6, 1990]

11552. French, Mary Ann. "Don't Kill the Messenger." *Washington Post*, 23 January 1994. [Malcolm X's message]

11553. Friedman, Robert I. "The Israel Lobby's Blacklist." *Village Voice* (4 August 1992). [American Israel Public Affairs Committee]

11554. Frisby, Michael K. "The New Black Politics." *Boston Globe Magazine* (14 July 1991).

11555. _____. "Race Tactic Deplored, But Seen as Effective." *Boston Globe*, 16 October 1991. [As used by Clarence Thomas in search of confirmation as U.S. Supreme Court justice.]

11556. _____. "Without Jackson, Black Vote Is Wild Card." *Boston Globe*, 6 August 1991.

11557. Fujiyama, Rodney M. *The Social Backgrounds of Hawaii's Legislators*. University of Hawaii: Senior Honors Thesis, 1967.

11558. Fulani, Lenora B. "African-Americans Can't Win Justice in the Two-Party System." *New York Times*, 11 August 1992. Letter.

11559. "The Future of Voting Rights After Shaw v. Reno." *Michigan Law Review* 92 (December 1993): three articles.

11560. Gabel, Peter. "Ending Coercive Deference." *Tikkun* 7 (September-October 1992): 16-19. [See Peller and Crenshaw]

11561. Gage, Matilda Joslyn and others. *History of Woman Suffrage*. Salem, NH: Ayer Co., 1985 reprinted.

11562. Garcia, F. Chris, ed. *Latinos and the Political System*. Notre Dame, IN: University of Notre Dame Press, 1988.

11563. Garcia, F. Chris and others. "Studying Latino Politics: The Development of the Latino National Political Survey." *PS- Political Science and Politics* 22 (December 1989).

11564. Garcia, Ignacio M. *Armed with a Ballot: The Rise of La Raza Unida Party in Texas*. University of Arizona: Master's thesis, 1990. UMO #MA1339668.

11565. _____. *United We Win: The Rise and Fall of La Raza Unida Party*. Tucson: MASRC, University of Arizona, 1989.

11566. Garcia, John A. "Chicano Politics in the 1980s and Beyond: A Review of the Literature in the Decade of the Hispanics." *National Political Science Review* 1 (1989): 180-189.

11567. _____. "The Voting Rights Act and Hispanic Political Representation in the Southwest." *Publius* 16 (1986): 41-66.

11568. Garr, Daniel. "Planning, Politics and Plunder: The Missions and Indian Pueblos of Hispanic California." *Southern California Quarterly* 54 (1972): 291-312.

11569. Garrow, David J. "Black Voting in South Carolina." *Review of Black Political Economy* 9 (1978): 60-78.

11570. Gerson, Jeffrey N. *Building the Brooklyn Machine: Irish, Jewish and Black Political Succession in Central Brooklyn, 1919- 1964*. Ph.D. diss., City University of New York, 1990. UMO #9029935.

11571. Geschwender, James A., and Rhonda F. Levine. "Class Struggle and Political Transformation in Hawaii, 1946-1960." *Research in Political Sociology* 2 (1986): 243-268.

11572. Gibeau, Dawn. "Political Religious Strife Brings Steamy Sabah to Boiling Point." *National Catholic Register* (20 September 1991).

11573. Gilliam, F. D., and K. J. Whitley. "Race, Class, and Attitudes Toward Social Welfare Spending: An Ethnic Interpretation." *Social Science Quarterly* 70 (March 1989).

11574. Gilliam, Jerry. "Latino Caucus Gains Clout in Legislature as Population Shifts." *Los Angeles Times*, 29 November 1993. [California]

11575. Glaser, James M. *The Paradox of Black Participation and Other Observations on Black Activism, 1952-1984*. Paper prepared for the Committee on the Status of Black Americans, National Research Council, Washington, D.C., 1987.

11576. _____. *Race, Campaign Politics, and the Realignment in the South*. Ph.D. diss., University of California, Berkeley, 1991. UMO #9203572.

11577. Goldberg, Barry. "Race, Class, and History." *New Politics* 4 (Winter 1993): 50-68.

11578. Goldfield, Michael. "The Color of Politics in the United States: White Supremacy as the Main Explanation for the Peculiarities of American Politics from Colonial Times to the Present." in *The Bounds of Race*, pp. 104-133. ed. Dominick La Capra. Cornell University Press, 1991.

11579. Goldman, Robert M. *"A Free Ballot and a Fair Count." The Department of Justice and the Enforcement of Voting Rights in the South, 1877-1893*. New York: Garland, 1990.

11580. Goldstein, Richard. "The Myth of the Jewish Vote." *Village Voice* (28 April 1992). [Democratic party presidential primary election in New York City, April 1992]

11581. Gomes, Ralph C., and Linda F. Williams, eds. *From Exclusion to Inclusion. The Long Struggle for African-American Political Power*. Westport, CT: Greenwood, 1991.

11582. Gomez-Quinones, Juan. *Chicano Politics: Reality and Promise, 1940-1990*. Albuquerque: University of New Mexico Press, 1990.

11583. _____. *Roots of Chicano Politics, 1600-1940*. University of New Mexico Press, 1994.

11584. Gonzalez, David. "Hispanic Voters Struggle to Find the Strength in Their Numbers." *New York Times*, 26 May 1991.

11585. Gonzales, Moishe. "Race vs. Gender: The Post-Modern Politics of the Thomas Confirmation Hearing." *Telos* no. 89 (Fall 1991): 121-126.

11586. Goodgame, Dan. "Why Bigotry Still Works At Election Time." *Time* (25 November 1991).

11587. Gray, H. "African-American Political Desire and Seductions of Contemporary Cultural Politics." *Cultural Studies* 7 (October 1993): 364-373.

11588. Gray, Jerry. "In New Jersey, the Candidates Make a Radio Show the Issue." *New York Times*, October 1926. [Two candidates for U.S. senator discuss racism]

11589. Green, Charles St. Clair, and Basil Wilson. *The Struggle for Black Empowerment in New York City: Beyond the Politics of Pigmentation*. New York: Praeger, 1989.

11590. Green, Donald P., and Lisa M. Waxman. "Direct Threat and Political Tolerance: An Experimental Analysis of the Tolerance of Blacks toward Racists." *Public Opinion Quarterly* 51 (Summer 1987): 149-165.

11591. Green, Elna C. "Those Oppposed: The Antisuffragists in North Carolina, 1900-1920." *North Carolina Historical Review* 65 (1990): 315-333. [White supremacy and the women's vote]

11592. Green, James. "The Making of Mel King's Rainbow Coalition: Political Changes in Boston, 1963-1983." *Radical America* 17/18 (1983-1984): 9-33.

11593. Green, John C. and others. "Faith and Election: The Christian Right in Congressional Campaigns 1978-1988." *Journal of Politics* (1993).

11594. Green, Marci, and Bob Carter. "'Races' and 'Race-makers': The Politics of Racialization." *Sage Race Relations Abstracts* 13 (1988): 4-30.

11595. Green, Paul M., and Melvin G. Holli. *Bashing Chicago Traditions: Harold Washington's Last Campaign*. Grand Rapids, MI: Eerdmans, 1989.

11596. Greenhouse, Linda. "Justics Plan to Delve Anew Into Race and Voting Rights." *New York Times*, 11 July 1993.

11597. Greer, Edward. *Big Steel: Black Politics and Corporate Power in Gary, Indiana*. New York: Monthly Review Press, 1979.

11598. Grimshaw, William J. *Bitter Fruit: Black Politics and the Chicago Machine, 1931-1991*. University of Chicago Press, 1992.

11599. Grofman, Bernard. "Multivariate Methods and the Analysis of Racially Polarized Voting: Pitfalls in the Use of Social Science by the Courts." *Social Science Quarterly* 72 (December 1991): 826-833. [See also C. S Bullock, above]

11600. _____. "Straw Men and Stray Bullets: A Reply." *Social Science Quarterly* 72 (December 1991): 840-843. [See also C.S. Bullock, above]

11601. Grofman, Bernard, and Chandler Davidson, eds. *Controversies in Minority Voting: The Voting Rights Act in Perspective*. Brookings Institution, 1992.

11602. Grofman, Bernard, and Lisa R. Handley. "Identifying and Remedying Racial Gerrymandering." *Journal of Law and Politics* 8 (Winter 1992): 345-404.

11603. _____. "The Impact of the Voting Rights Act on Black Representation in Southern State Legislatures." *Legislative Studies Quarterly* 16 (February 1991): 111-128.

11604. _____. "Minority Population Proportion and Black and Hispanic Congressional Success in the 1970s and 1980s." *American Politics Quarterly* 17 (October 1989).

11605. Gross, Jane. "Diversity Hinders Asians' Power in the U.S." *New York Times*, 25 June 1989.

11606. Guerra, Fernando J. *Ethnic Politics in Los Angeles: The Emergence of Black, Jewish, Latino and Asian Officeholders, 1960- 1989*. Ph.D. diss., University of Michigan, 1990. UMO #9034430.

11607. Guerra, Sandra. "Voting Rights and the Constitution: The Disenfranchisement of Non-English Speaking Citizens." *Yale Law Journal* 97 (June 1988): 1419-1437.

11608. Guinier, Lani. "Keeping the Faith: Black Voters in the Post-Reagan Era." *Harvard Civil Rights-Civil Liberties Law Review* 24 (Spring 1989): 393-435.

11609. _____. "Second Proms and Second Primaries: The Limits of Majority Rule." *Boston Review* (September-October 1992).

11610. _____. "The Triumph of Tokenism: The Voting Rights Act and the Theory of Black Electoral Success." *Michigan Law Review* 89 (1991).

11611. _____. *The Tyranny of the Majority*. Free Press, 1994.

11612. Gurin, Patricia and others. *Hope and Independence. Blacks' Response to Electoral and Party Politics*. New York: Russell Sage Foundation, 1989. [Black opinion on Jesse Jackson's 1984 presidential-primary campaign.]

11613. Gutow, Steve. "Suggested Reading For Jews In 1994." *Jewish Community Chronicle* (29 December 1993). [Pat Robertson's The New World Order and its antagonistic statements about Jews.]

11614. Hacker, Andrew. "The Blacks and Clinton." *New York Review of Books* (28 January 1993).

11615. Hackey, R. B. "Competing Explanations of Voter Turnout among American Blacks." *Social Science Quarterly* 73 (March 1992): 71-89.

11616. Hagen, Michael G. *Blacks and Liberalism*. Paper prepared for the Committee on the Status of Black Americans, National Research Council, Washington, D.C., 1988.

11617. _____. *Racial Differences in Voter Registration and Turnout*. Paper prepared for the Committee on the Status of Black Americans, National Research Council, Washington, D.C., 1988.

11618. _____. *The Salience of Racial and Social Welfare Issues*. Paper prepared for the Committee on the Status of Black Americans, National Research Council, Washington, D.C.

11619. Hagerty, Randy L. *The Political Assimilation of Mexican Immigrants in the American Southwest*. Ph.D. diss., University of Illinois, 1991. [West Texas]. UMO #9210824.

11620. Haller, M. H. "Policy Gambling, Entertainment, and the Emergence of Black Politics: Chicago from 1900 to 1940." *Journal of Social History* 24 (Summer 1991): 719-740.

11621. Hamilton, Charles V. "On Parity and Political Empowerment." in *The State of Black America 1989*, ed. Janet Dewart. New York: National Urban League, 1989.

11622. Hamilton, D. C., and Charles V. Hamilton. "The Dual Agenda of African American Organizations Since the New Deal: Social Welfare Policies and Civil Rights." *Political Science Quarterly* 107 (Autumn 1992): 435-452.

11623. Handley, Lisa R. *The Quest for Minority Voting Rights: The Evolution of a Vote Dilution Standard and Its Impact on Minority Representation*. Ph.D. diss., George Washington University, 1991. UMO #9202882.

11624. Hanks, Lawrence J. *Black Voter Mobilization Since 1960*. Paper prepared for the Committee on the Status of Black Americans, National Research Council, Washington, D.C., 1986.

11625. _____. *The Struggle for Black Political Empowerment in Three Georgia Counties*. Knoxville: University of Tennessee Press, 1987.

11626. Hardy, Thomas. "Hispanic District Becomes Longer Shot." *Chicago Tribune* (23 June 1991). [Chicago area]

11627. Hardy-Fanta, Carol. *Latina Women, Latino Men, and Political Participation in Boston: La Chispa que prende*. Ph.D. diss., Brandeis University, 1991. UMO #9129521.

11628. _____. *Latina Politics, Latino Politics: Gender, Culture, and Political Participation in Boston*. Temple University Press, 1993.

11629. Harrington, Michael. "Old Left, New Left, What's Left?: An Interview with Michael Harrington." *Radical America* 22 (November- December 1988): 47-59. [See comments on race, 60-64]

11630. Harris, Frederick C. and others. "Who's Registered and Who's Not: Targeting Voter Registration in Chicago." *Policy Studies Review* 9 (Spring 1990): 575-581. [Race and ethnicity, 1989]

11631. Harris, Kirk E. *The Paradox of African-American Mayoral Leadership and the Persistence of Poverty in the African-American Community*. Ph.D. diss., Cornell University, 1992. UMO #9300688.

11632. Harrison, T. M. and others. "Images versus Issues in the 1984 Presidential Election: Differences between Men and Women." *Human Communication Research* 18 (December 1991): 209-227.

11633. Hartmann-Laugs, Petra S. *Die politische Integration der Mexiko-Amerikaner: eine Analyse mexikoamerikanischen Wahlverhaltens in der Jahren 1960-1974 unter Berücksichtigung soziökonomischer Variablen*. Bern, Switzerland: Verlag Peter Lang, 1980.

11634. Hartmann, Susan M. *From Margin to Mainstream: American Women in Politics Since 1960*. Philadelphia, 1989.

11635. Hatch, Roger D. "Jesse Jackson's Presidential Campaign: A Religious Assessment." *Soundings* 70 (1987): 379-405.

11636. Hauptman, Laurence M. *Contemporary Iroquois and the Struggle for Survival. From World War II to the Emergence of Red Power*. Syracuse, NY: Syracuse University Press, 1985.

11637. Hawking, James E. *Political Education in the Harold Washington Movement*. Ph.D. diss., Northern Illinois University, 1991. UMO #9202935.

11638. Hawks, Joanne V. "A Challenge to Racism and Sexism: Black Women in Southern Legislatures, 1965-1986." *Sage* 5 (Fall 1988): 20-23.

11639. Heath, G. Louis. *Of the Pigs: The History and Literature of the Black Panther Party*. Metuchen, NJ: Scarecrow Press, 1976.

11640. Heilig, Peggy, and Robert J. Mundt. "Changes in Representational Equity: The Effect of Adopting Districts." *Social Science Quarterly* 64 (June 1983): 393-397.

11641. Hendricks, Wanda A. *The Politics of Race: Black Women in Illinois, 1890-1920*. Ph.D. diss., Purdue University, 1990. UMO #9104644.

11642. Henig, Jeffrey R. "Race and Voting: Continuity and Change in the District of Columbia." *Urban Affairs Quarterly* 28 (June 1993): 544-570. [1978-1990]

11643. Henig, Jeffrey R., and Dennis E. Gale. "The Political Incorporation of Newcomers to Racially Changing Neighborhoods." *Urban Affairs Quarterly* 22 (March 1987): 399-419.

11644. Henry, Charles P. "Big Philanthropy and the Funding of Black Organizations." *Review of Black Political Economy* 9 (Winter 1979): 174-190.

11645. _____. *Culture and African American Politics*. Bloomington: Indiana University Press, 1990.

11646. _____. "The Role of Race in the Bradley-Deukmejian Campaign." *Critical Perspectives of Third World America* 1 (Fall 1983): 40-55.

11647. Hentoff, Nat. "Dinkins: No Arab Americans Need Apply." *Village Voice* (5 December 1989). [Politics in NYC]

11648. _____. "'I Am to Black People As the Pope Is To White People'." *Village Voice* (21 May 1991). [About Louis Farrakhan]

11649. _____. "Stereotyping New York's Jews." *Village Voice* (12 December 1989). [Arab Americans and Jews in New York City politics.]

11650. Hernandez, Antonia. "Working for the Latino Cause With Soft-spoken Determination." *Los Angeles Times*, 13 December 1992. [President and general counsel of Mexican American Legal Defense and Education Fund]

11651. Hernandez, Efrain, Jr., and Adrian Walker. "Hispanic Gains Don't Translate Into Power." *Boston Globe*, 24 March 1991. [Lawrence and elsewhere in Massachusetts]

11652. Hero, Rodney E. "Hispanics in Urban Government and Politics-Some Findings, Comparisons and Implications." *Western Political Quarterly* 43 (1990): 403-414.

11653. _____. *Latinos and the U.S. Political System: Two- Tiered Pluralism*. Temple U.P., 1992.

11654. _____. "Multiracial Coalitions in City Elections Involving Minority Candidates: Some Evidence from Denver." *Urban Affairs Quarterly* 25 (1989): 342-351.

11655. Herring, Cedric. "Racially Based Changes in Political Alienation in America." *Social Science Quarterly* 72 (March 1991): 123-134.

11656. Herring, Mary. "Legislative Responsiveness to Black Constituents in Three Deep South States." *Journal of Politics* 52 (August 1990): 740-758. [AL, GA, and LA]

11657. Higginbotham, Evelyn B. "In Politics to Stay: Black Women Leaders and Party Politics in the 1920's." in *Women, Politics, and Change*, eds. Louise A. Tilly, and Patricia Gurin. Russell Sage Foundation, 1990.

11658. Hine, Darlene Clark. *Black Victory: The Rise and Fall of the White Primary in Texas*. KTO Press, 1979.

11659. Hirsch, Arnold R. "Chicago: The Cook County Democratic Organization and the Dilemma of Race, 1931-1987." in *Snowbelt Cities: Metropolitan Politics in the Northeast and Midwest since World War II*, ed. Richard M. Bernard. Bloomington: Indiana University Press, 1990.

11660. _____. "Race and Politics in Modern New Orleans: The Mayoralty of Dutch Morial]." *Amerikastudien* 35 (1990): 461-484.

11661. Hitchens, Christopher. "Minority Report." *Nation* (16 December 1991). [Political implications of David Duke's movement]

11662. Hochschild, Jennifer L. *The Politics of the Estranged Poor*. Princeton, NJ: Department of Politics, Princeton University, February 1990.

11663. _____. "The Politics of the Estranged Poor." *Ethics* 101 (April 1991): 560-578.

11664. _____. *What's Fair? American Beliefs about Distributive Justice*. Cambridge, MA: Harvard University Press, 1981.

11665. Holland, Ronando W. *The Key to Black Politics*. Ph.D. diss., Duke University, 1989. [Marcus Garvey, Martin Luther King, Jr., and Jesse Jackson]. UMO #9002051.

11666. Holli, Melvin G., and Paul M. Green. *Bashing Chicago Traditions. Harold Washington's Last Campaign*. Grand Rapids, MI: Eerdmans, 1989.

11667. Holmes, Steven A. "Must Democrats Shift Signals on Blacks to Win the Presidency?" *New York Times*, 10 November 1991.

11668. Holt, Wythe. *Virginia's Constitutional Convention of 1901- 1902*. Garland, 1990. [Disfranchisement of Blacks]

11669. Hornsby, Alton, Jr. "The Negro in Atlanta Politics." *Atlanta Historical Bulletin* 21 (Spring 1977).

11670. Hornung, Rick. "The Making of a Revolutionary. Coltrane Chimurenga and the Struggle for Black Leadership in New York." *Village Voice* (9 October 1990).

11671. Huckfeldt, Robert, and Carol W. Kohfeld. *Race and the Decline of Class in American Politics*. Urbana: University of Illinois Press, 1989.

11672. Hunter, T. P. "A Different View of Progress: Minority Women in Politics." *Journal of State Government* 64 (April-June 1991): 48-52.

11673. Hurns, Walter M. *Post-Reconstruction Municipal Politics in Jackson, Mississippi*. Ph.D. diss., Kansas State University, 1989. UMO #8924326.

11674. Hutchinson, Earl Ofari. "Why the Surprise on [Clarence] Thomas' Conservatism?" *Guardian (NYC)* (28 August 1991).

11675. Huth, Tom. "Free Elections in Utah!" *New York Times*, 24 November 1990. [Navajo voting in Aneth, Utah]

11676. Inniss, Leslie B. *The Relationship between Class Level and Political Attitudes among Black Americans: 1974-1977, 1982, and 1987*. Ph.D. diss., University of Texas, 1990. UMO #9105573.

11677. Inter-University Program for Latino Research. *Latino Voices: Mexican, Puerto Rican and Cuban Perspectives on American Politics*. Westview Press, 1993.

11678. Ireland, Doug. "Reich-Wing Republican." *Village Voice* (29 October 1991). [David Duke]

11679. Issacharoff, S. "Polarized Voting and the Public Process: The Transformation of Voting Rights Jurisprudence." *Michigan Law Review* 90 (June 1992): 1833-1891.

11680. Jackson, David. "Double Vision." *Chicago Magazine* (October 1989). [Racial issues in Chicago]

11681. Jackson, Derrick Z. "A [White] Leadership Vacuum." *Boston Globe*, 20 November 1991.

11682. Jackson, Jesse L. "Statehood for New Columbia." *Zeta Magazine* 2 (September 1989): 25. [Wash. D.C.]

11683. Jacoby, Tamar. "The Devastating Power of Racial Belligerence." *Alicia Patterson Foundation Reporter* 14 (1991). [Sonny Carson, NYC]

11684. Jaynes, Gerard D., and Robin M. Williams, Jr., eds. "Black Political Participation." in *A Common Destiny. Blacks and American Society*, pp. 205-268. Washington, DC: National Academy Press, 1989.

11685. Jennings, James. "New Urban Racial and Ethnic Conflicts in United States Politics." *Sage Race Relations Abstracts* 17 (August 1992): 3-36.

11686. _____. *The Politics of Black Empowerment: The Transformation of Black Activism in Urban America*. Detroit, MI: Wayne State University Press, 1990.

11687. Jennings, James, and Mel King, eds. *Black Politics in Boston*. Cambridge, MA: Schenkman, 1986.

11688. Jennings, James, and Monte Rivera, eds. *Puerto Rican Politics in Urban America*. Westport, CT: Greenwood Press, 1984.

11689. Johnson, David R. and others, eds. *The Politics of San Antonio: Community, Progress and Power*. Lincoln: University of Nebraska Press, 1983.

11690. Johnson, Roberta Ann. "The Prison Birth of Black Power." *Journal of Black Studies* 5 (1975): 395-414.

11691. Jones, Charles E. "The Political Repression of the Black Panther Party 1966-1971: The Case of the Oakland Bay Area." *Journal of Black Studies* 18 (June 1988): 415-434.

11692. Jones, Elaine R. "In Peril: Black Lawmakers." *New York Times*, 11 September 1994. ["Court decisions only David Duke could love"]

11693. Juarez Robles, Jennifer. "Mayor Daley Quiet On Racial Issues; Rips 'Foreign Press'." *Chicago Reporter* 18 (July-August 1989).

11694. Judis, John B. "The Conservative Crackup." *American Prospect* (Fall 1990).

11695. Kahn, Joseph P. "Black and Right." *Boston Globe*, 20 August 1991. [Glenn Loury]

11696. Kand, K. Connie. "South Korean Politics Remain a Passion in L.A." *Los Angeles Times*, 13 December 1992.

11697. Kantor, Paul. "The Political Economy of Business Politics in U.S. Cities: A Developmental Perspective." *Studies in American Political Development* 8 (1990): 303-316.

11698. Kapur, Sudarshan. *Gandhi and the Afro-American Community, 1919-1955: A Study of the Image and Influence of the Gandhian Movement in the Black Communities of America before the Coming of Martin Luther King, Jr.* Ph.D. diss., Iliff School of Theology and University of Denver, 1989. UMO #8924293.

11699. Karlan, Pamela S. "Maps and Misreadings: The Role of Geographic Compactness in Racial Vote Dilution Litigation." *Harvard Civil Rights-Civil Liberties Law Review* 24 (Winter 1989): 173-248.

11700. _____. "Undoing the Right Thing: Single-member Offices and the Voting Rights Act." *Virginia Law Review* 77 (February 1991): 1-45.

11701. Karnig, Albert K., and Paula D. McClain, eds. *Urban Minority Administrators: Politics, Policy, and Style*. Westport, CT: Greenwood, 1988.

11702. Karnow, Stanley. "Apathetic Asian Americans? Why Their Success Hasn't Spilled Over Into Politics." *Washington Post*, 29 November 1992.

11703. Keiser, Richard A. "Explaining African-American Political Empowerment: Windy City Politics from 1900 to 1983." *Urban Affairs Quarterly* 29 (September 1993): 84-116. [Chicago]

11704. Kelleher, Richard V. *The Black Struggle for Political and Civil Rights in Broward County, 1943-1989*. Florida Atlantic University: Master's thesis, 1990. UMO #MA1339847.

11705. Kelley, Robin D. G. "The Left." *Black Women in America I*, pp. 708-714.

11706. Kendrick, Ann. *A Comparison of the Core Economic Beliefs of Blacks and Whites*. Paper prepared for the Committee on the Status of Black Americans, National Research Council, Washington, D.C., 1988.

11707. _____. *The Dynamics of Black Electoral Participation*. Paper prepared for the Committee on the Status of Black Americans, National Research Council, Washington, D.C., 1986.

11708. Keyes, Alan. "To Be Republican, Gifted, and Black." *Boston Globe*, 7 July 1991. [Black conservatism]

11709. Kibbe, David C., and Kenneth Bain. "Patron Politics in McAllen, Texas." *Nation* (26 September 1981).

11710. Kilson, Martin L, Jr. "Black Politicians: A New Power." *Dissent* (August 1971): 333-345.

11711. _____. *Report on Black Politics in Comparative Perspective*. Paper prepared for the Committee on the Status of Black Americans, National Research Council, Washington, D.C., 1987.

11712. _____. "The Weakness of Black Politics: Cursed by Factions and Feuds." *Dissent* 34 (1987): 523-529. [NYC]

11713. Kincaid, John. "Beyond the Voting Rights Act: White Responses to Black Political Power in Tchula, Mississippi." *Publius* 16 (Fall 1986).

11714. King, Mae C. "Oppression and Power: The Unique Status of the Black Women in the American Political System." *Journal of Social and Behavioral Sciences* 23 (Spring 1977): 146-160.

11715. King, Patricia and others. "The Ongoing Struggle Over Clarence Thomas." *Reconstruction* 1 (1992): 58-81.

11716. Kleiman, Michael B. "Trends in Racial Differences in Political Efficacy: 1952 to 1972." *Phylon* (June 1976): 159-162.

11717. Klein, Joe. "Bubba Is Back." *Newsweek* (26 September 1994). [Redrawing of congressional districts in Georgia]

11718. Koppel, Martin. "New Alliance Party Woos Perot Followers." *Militant* (24 January 1994).

11719. Korobkin, Russell. "The Politics of Disfranchisement in Georgia." *Georgia Historical Quarterly* 74 (Spring 1990): 20-58. [1906]

11720. Kousser, J. Morgan. "How to Determine Intent [of Reapportionment]: Lessons from L.A." *Journal of Law and Politics* 7 (Summer 1991): 591-732.

11721. Kramer, Michael. "Rumblings on the Left." *Time* (13 December 1993). [Jesse Jackson and Bill Clinton]

11722. Kurtz, Michael L., and Morgan D. Peoples. *Earl K. Long: The Sage of Uncle Earl and Louisiana Politics*. Baton Rouge: Louisiana State University Press, 1991.

11723. Kuttner, Robert. "Ron Brown's Party Line." *New York Times Magazine* (3 December 1989). [Black chairman of the Democratic party]

11724. Ladd, Everett C. *Negro Political Leadership in the South*. Ithaca, NY: Cornell University Press, 1966.

11725. Ladner, Joyce A. "What Black Power Means to Negroes in Mississippi." in *Transformation of Activism*, ed. August Meier. New Brunswick, NJ: Transaction, 1973.

11726. Landry, David M., and Joseph B. Parker, eds. *Mississippi Government and Politics in Transition*. Dubuque, Iowa: Kendall and Hunt, 1976.

11727. Lawrence, D. G. "The Collapse of the Democratic Majority: Economics and Vote Choice since 1952." *Western Political Quarterly* 44 (December 1991): 797-820.

11728. Lawson, Steven F. *Running for Freedom: Civil Rights and Black Politics in America since 1941*. Philadelphia, PA: Temple University Press, 1990.

11729. Ledbetter, Billy D. "White Texans' Attitudes Toward the Political Equality of Negroes, 1865-1870." *Phylon* 40 (September 1979): 253-263.

11730. Lee, Felicia R. "For Blacks, Loss by Dinkins Spotlights Painful Racial Gap." *New York Times*, 4 November 1993. [N.Y.C.]

11731. Lee, James F., ed. *Contemporary Southern Politics*. Baton Rouge: Louisiana State University Press, 1988.

11732. Leighley, J. E., and J. Negler. "Socioeconomic Class Bias in Turnout, 1964-1988: The Voters Remain the Same." *American Political Science Review* 86 (September 1992): 725-736.

11733. Lemann, Nicholas. "Race, Reform and Urban Voters." *New York Times*, 4 November 1993. [Black and white mayors in large cities]

11734. Lerner, Michael. "Fascist Winds Return. Stopping David Duke and Patrick Buchanan. A Strategy for the 1990s." *Tikkun* 7 (January-February 1992): 37-42.

11735. Lesher, Dave. "Few Votes, No Voice, No Clout." *Los Angeles Times*, 11 December 1993. [Latinos in Santa Ana, CA]

11736. Levinson, Sanford. "Democratic Politics and Gun Control." *Reconstruction* 1 (1992): 137-141.

11737. Lewis, Anthony. "'America Be On Guard'." *New York Times*, 18 November 1991. [David Duke in the future]

11738. Lewison, Edwin R. *Black Politics in New York City*. Twayne, 1974.

11739. Lichter, S. R. and others. *The Video Campaign: Network Coverage of the 1988 Primaries*. Washington, DC: American Enterprise Institute for Public Policy Research, 1988.

11740. Limerick, Patricia N. "Some Advice to Liberals on Coping With Their Conservative Critics." *Chronicle of Higher Education* (4 May 1994).

11741. Lipset, Seymour M. "Are American Jews Drifting to the Right?" *Israeli Democracy (Ramat Aviv)* (Spring 1989): 39-42.

11742. Lisio, Donald J. *Hoover, Blacks, and Lily-whites: A Study of Southern Strategies*. Chapel Hill: University of North Carolina Press, 1985.

11743. Liu, Edward. "'Hop Sing' Policy Blunts Promises." *Los Angeles Times*, 24 January 1993. [Absence of Asian-Americans in high Clinton administration positions]

11744. Llorens, James L. *Black Empowerment in State Legislatures: The Impact of Black Representation on Public Welfare Expenditures in the American States, 1970-1988*. Ph.D. diss., Louisiana State U., 1992. UMO #9301078.

11745. Loewen, James W. "Racial Bloc Voting and Political Mobilization in South Carolina." *Review of Black Political Economy* 19 (Summer 1990): 23-37.

11746. Logan, Andy. "Around City Hall. Fighting the Power." *New Yorker* (11 September 1989). [Race and politics in New York City]

11747. _____. "In the Spirit of La Guardia." *New Yorker* (21 February 1994). [African-Americans and NYC mayor Rudolph Giuliani]

11748. Longoria, Thomas, Jr., and others. "Mexican American Voter Registration and Turnout: Another Look." *Social Science Quarterly* 71 (June 1990): 356-361.

11749. Lopach, James J. and others. *Tribal Government Today: Politics on Montana Indian Reservations*. Boulder, CO: Westview Press, 1989.

11750. Luebke, Paul. "The Social and Political Bases of a Black Candidate's Coalition: Race, Class and Ideology in the 1976 North Carolina Primary Election." *Politics and Society* 9 (1979): 239-261.

11751. Lusanne, Clarence. *African Americans At the Crossroads. The Restructuring of Black Leadership and the 1992 Elections*. South End Press, 1994.

11752. Luskin, R. C. and others. "How Minority Judges Fare in Retention Elections." *Judicature* 77 (May-June 1994): 316-321.

11753. Lyall, Sarah. "Blacks in Hempstead Fight Lack of Political Clout." *New York Times*, 5 July 1989. [Long Island, New York]

11754. Lynch, Robert N. "Women in Northern Paiute Politics." *Signs* 11 (Winter 1986): 352-366.

11755. Lynn, Frank. "Council Gerrymandering Is Reversed." *New York Times*, 24 March 1991. [New York City Council]

11756. Mackey, Eric M. *The Impact of Race, Industrialization and Modernization on Electoral Change in the South, 1940-1984*. Ph.D. diss., University of Michigan, 1990. UMO #9023597.

11757. Maganini, Stephen. "Southeast Asian Refugees More Involved in Politics." *Long Beach Press-Telegram*, 3 January 1994.

11758. Major, Reginald. *A Panther Is a Black Cat*. New York: Morrow, 1971.

11759. "Mandela, Massachusetts. Boston's Black Independence Movement." *Dollars and Sense* no. 124 (March 1987): 10-12, 22.

11760. Marable, Manning. *Black American Politics*. New York: Methuen, 1985.

11761. _____. *Black American Politics From the Washington Marches to Jesse Jackson*. Verso, Revised ed., 1993.

11762. _____. "Black Power in Chicago: An Historical Overview of Class Stratification and Electoral Politics in a Black Urban Community." *Review of Radical Political Economics* 17 (September 1985): 157-182.

11763. _____. "Black Politics and the Challenges for the Left." *Monthly Review* 41 (April 1990): 22-31.

11764. _____. "Conservatives Gobble Up 'Oreo' Ideology." *Guardian (NYC)* (18 July 1990).

11765. _____. *The Crisis of Color and Democracy. Essays on Class and Power*. Monroe, ME: Common Courage Press, 1992.

11766. _____. "'In an Hour of Great Crisis' The Gary Black Political Convention of 1972." *Guardian (NYC)* (12 February 1992).

11767. _____. "A New Black Politics." *The Progressive* 54 (August 1990): 18-23.

11768. _____. *Race, Reform, and Rebellion. The Second Reconstruction in Black America, 1945-1990*, Revised second ed. Jackson: University Press of Mississippi, 1991.

11769. _____. "Toward Black American Empowerment. Violence and Resistance in the African-American Community in the 1990s." *African Commentary* 2 (May 1990): 16-21.

11770. Marshall, Dale R. "The Continuing Significance of Race: The Transformation of American Politics." *American Political Science Review* 84 (June 1990).

11771. _____. *Racial Politics in American Cities*. New York, 1990.

11772. Marshall, Ronald J. *Black Participation in Presidential Elections, 1964-1984*. Howard University: Master's thesis, 1990.

11773. Marshall, Thurgood. "The Rise and Collapse of the 'White Democratic Primary'." *Journal of Negro Education* 26 (Spring 1957).

11774. Marston, Linda L. *Race, Class and Presidential Politics: Social Group Support for Jesse Jackson in 1984*. Ph.D. diss., University of Massachusetts, 1989. UMO #8917376.

11775. Martinez, Elizabeth. "'Chingon Politics' Die Hard: Reflections on the First Chicano Activists Reunion." *Z Magazine* 3 (April 1990): 46-50.

11776. Martinez, Frank. "Chicano Participation in Oregon Poor People's Conference." *Regeneracion* 1 (1970): 4.

11777. Mathews, Jay. "Color-Coded Congressmen." *Newsweek* (21 September 1992). [Redrawing congressional districts]

11778. McAdam, Douglas, and Kelly Moore. "The Politics of Black Insurgency, 1930-1975." in *Violence in America*, vol. 1. ed. Ted Robert Gurr. Newbury Park, CA: Sage, 1989.

11779. McCarthy, G. Michael. "Smith vs. Hoover: The Politics of Race in West Tennessee." *Phylon* 39 (1978): 154-168.

11780. McCarthy, John T. *Black Power Ideologies: An Essay in African-American Political Thought*. Temple U.P.

11781. McConnell, Scott. "The Making of the Mayor." *Commentary* (February 1990): 29-38. [David Dinkins, New York City]

11782. McCorisle, Mac. "Gantt versus Helms: Toward the New Progressive Era?" *Reconstruction* 1 (1991): 18-24. [Harvey Gantt and Jesse Helms, N.C.]

11783. McCrary, Peyton. "Racially Polarized Voting in the South: Quantitative Evidence from the Courtroom." *Social Science History* 14 (1990): 507-531.

11784. McCrary, Peyton, and J. Gerald Hebert. "Keeping the Courts Honest: The Role of Historians as Expert Witnesses in Southern Voting Rights Cases." *Southern University Law Review* 16 (Spring 1989): 101-128.

11785. McDonald, Laughlin. "The Quiet Revolution in Minority Voting Rights." *Vanderbilt Law Review* 42 (May 1989): 1249-1297.

11786. McGehee, Elizabeth. *White Democracy, Racism, and Black Disfranchisement: North Carolina in the 1830s*. College of William and Mary: Master's thesis, 1989.

11787. McLemee, Scott. "The New Face of Fascism." *Against the Current* no. 36 (January-February 1992): 3-5. [David Duke]

11788. McMillen, Neil R. "Black Enfranchisement in Mississippi: Federal Enforcement and Black Protest in the 1960s." *Journal of Southern History* (1977).

11789. McNickle, Chris. *To Be Mayor of New York: The Transfer of Political Power from the Irish to the Jews and the Decline of the Political Machine in New York City, 1881-1977*. Ph.D. diss., University of Chicago, 1989.

11790. McPherson, James A. "Out of Many. A Few." *Reconstruction* 1 (1991): 83-87. [See Jim Sleeper, below]

11791. McQuiston, John T. "Democrats and Blacks in Conflict." *New York Times*, 4 July 1994. [Nassau County, NY]

11792. McTighe, Michael J. "Jesse Jackson and the Dilemmas of a Prophet in Politics." *Journal of Church and State* 32 (Summer 1990): 585-607.

11793. Meyer, Gerald. *Vito Marcantonio. Radical Politicion, 1902- 1954*. Albany: State University of New York Press, 1989.

11794. Meyerson, Harold. "A Politics in America? Populism, Race, and Apathy." *Dissent* 38 (Winter 1991): 37-41.

11795. Michelman, Frank I. "Conceptions of Democracy in American Constitutional Argument: Voting Rights." *Florida Law Review* 41 (Summer 1989): 443-490.

11796. Miller, Alton, ed. *Climbing a Great Mountain: Selected Speeches of Harold Washington*. Chicago, IL: Bonus Books, 1988.

11797. Miller, Alton. *Harold Washington: The Mayor, The Man*. Chicago, IL: Bonus Books, 1989.

11798. Miller, B. "Who Shall Rule and Govern? Local Legislative Delegation, Racial Politics, and the Voting Rights Act." *Yale Law Journal* 102 (October 1992): 105-204.

11799. Miller, Warren E., and Santa A. Traugott. *American National Election Studies Data Sourcebook, 1952-1986*. Cambridge, MA: Harvard University Press 1989.

11800. Mohl, Raymond A. "Ethnic Politics in Miami, 1960-1986." in *Shades of the Sunbelt: Essays on Ethnicity, Race, and the Urban South*, eds. Randall M. Miller, and George E. Pozzetta. Boca Raton: Florida Atlantic University Press, 1989.

11801. Mollenkopf, John F. *A Phoenix in the Ashes*. Princeton U.P., 1992. [New York City politics]

11802. Momayezi, Nasser. "The Growing Political Power of Minorities in the United States: The Case of Mexican Americans in Texas." *Southeastern Political Review* 21 (Spring 1993): 309-326.

11803. Monroy, Douglas G. "Like Swallows at the Old Mission: Mexicans and the Racial Politics of Growth in Los Angeles in the Interwar Period." *Western Historical Quarterly* 14 (1983): 435-458.

11804. Moreland, Lawrence W. and others, eds. *Blacks in Southern Politics*. Westport, CT: Praeger, 1987.

11805. Morley, Jefferson. "Bush and the Blacks: An Unknown Story." *New York Review of Books* (16 January 1992).

11806. Morris, Lorenzo, ed. *The Social and Political Implications of the 1984 Jesse Jackson Presidential Campaign*. Westport, CT: Praeger, 1990.

11807. Morrison, Minion K. C. *Black Political Mobilization*. Albany: State University of New York, 1987.

11808. _____. "Federal Aid and Afro-American Political Power in Three Mississippi Towns." *Publius* 17 (1987): 97-111.

11809. _____. "Intragroup Conflict in African-American Leadership: The Case of Tschula. Mississippi." *Comparative Studies in Society and History* 32 (October 1990): 701-717.

11810. Moseley-Braun, Carol. "Raw Racism Gets a Black Eye in the Senate." *National Catholic Reporter*, 13 August 1993. [Extracts from speech on floor of the U.S. Senate]

11811. Moseley, Samuel A. *Poverty Politics and Political Transformation in North Carolina: A Comparative Case Study of Three Cities*. Ph.D. diss., Ohio State University, 1989. UMO #9014460.

11812. Moss, E. Yvonne. "Black Political Participation: The Search for Power." in *Social, Political, and Economic Issues in Black America*, vol. 4. pp. 83-117. ed. Wornie L. Reed. Boston: William Monroe Trotter Institute, University of Massachusetts at Boston, 1990.

11813. Munoz, Carlos, Jr. "Chicano Politics: The Current Conjuncture." *The Year Left*, vol. 2.

11814. Munoz, Carlos, Jr. *Youth, Identity, Power: The Chicano Generation*. New York: Verso, 1989.

11815. Muwakkil, Salim. "Black Empowerment: Recasting 'Uncle Tom'." *In These Times* (21 November 1990). [Booker T. Washington's contemporary advocates]

11816. _____. "Black Politicians Seek Broader Base by Dropping Confrontational Style." *In These Times* (18 October 1989).

11817. _____. "[Congressional] Black Caucus Wins Influence, Visibility." *In These Times* (21 June 1989).

11818. _____. "Follow What Leader?" *In These Times* (22 February 1993). [Congressional Black Caucus]

11819. Nash, Gary B. *Race, Class, and Politics: Essays on American Colonial and Revolutionary Society*. Urbana: University of Illinois Press, 1986.

11820. Naughton, Jim, and Stephen Buckley. "Blacks in Prince George's Assess Burgeoning Power, Dreams." *Washington Post*, 25 October 1992.

11821. Navarro, Vicente. "The Rainbow and the Democratic Party." *New Politics* 2 (Summer 1989): 20-26.

11822. Neilson, Melany. *Even Mississippi*. University: University of Alabama Press, 1989. [The 1982 and 1984 Congressional campaigns of Robert Clark in Mississippi]

11823. Nelson, Albert J. *Emerging Influentials in State Legislatures: Women, Blacks, and Hispanics*. New York: Praeger, 1991.

11824. Nessen, Joshua. "The Battle for New York City." *Z Magazine* 4 (September 1991): 71-78.

11825. "The New Alliance Party: A Study in Deception." *ADL Research Report* (February 1990): 1-13.

11826. Noel, Peter. "Death of a Movement. How New York's Black Activists Won and Lost the Struggle for a United Front." *Village Voice* (18 August 1992). [Since 1987]

11827. O'Brien, Sharon. *American Indian Tribal Governments*. Norman: University of Oklahoma Press, 1989.

11828. O'Hare, William P. "City Size, Racial Composition, and Election of Black Mayors Inside and Outside the South." *Journal of Urban Affairs* 12 (1990): 307-313.

11829. Oliphant, Thomas. "An Evil to Confront." *Boston Globe*, 23 October 1991. [Prospect of election of David Duke as governor of Louisiana]

11830. Olsen, Marvin. "The Social and Political Participation of Blacks." *American Sociological Review* 35 (1970): 682-697.

11831. Oreskes, Michael. "Bush at G.O.P. High in Black Approval, Poll Finds." *New York Times*, 13 April 1990.

11832. _____. "The Civil Rights Act]0f 1964], 25 Years Later: A Law that Shaped a Realignment." *New York Times*, 2 July 1989. [Effect of the law on politics]

11833. Orfield, Gary. "Race and the Liberal Agenda: The Loss of the Integrationist Dream, 1965-1974." in *The Politics of Social Policy in the United States*, pp. 313-356. eds. Margaret Weire and others. Princeton, NJ: Princeton University Press, 1988.

11834. Orfield, Gary, and Carole Ashkinaze. *The Closing Door: Conservative Policy and Black Opportunity*. Chicago, IL: University of Chicago Press, 1991. [Atlanta]

11835. Ornelas, Carlos and others. *Decolonizing the Interpretation of the Chicano Political Experience*. Los Angeles: UCLA Chicano Studies Center, 1975.

11836. Ortiz, Isidro D. "The Political Economy of Chicano Urban Politics." *Plural Societies* 11 (1980): 41-54.

11837. Orum, Anthony M. "A Reappraisal of the Social and Political Participation of Negroes." *American Journal of Sociology* 72 (1966): 32-46.

11838. Painter, Nell Irvin. "Race Relations, History, and Public Policy: The Alabama Vote Fraud Cases of 1985." in *America in Theory*, eds. Leslie Berlowitz and others. New York: Oxford University Press, 1988.

11839. Parker, Frank R. *Black Votes Count. Political Empowerment in Mississippi After 1965*. Chapel Hill: University of North Carolina Press, 1990.

11840. _____. "Protest, Politics, and Litigation: Political and Social Change in Mississippi, 1965 to Present." *Mississippi Law Journal* 57 (December 1987): 677-704.

11841. Payton, Brenda. "Looking for a Post-Gulf Role." *Nation* (1 July 1991). [Black antiwar movement]

11842. Peller, Gary, and Kimberle Crenshaw. "Running from Race." *Tikkun* 7 (September-October 1992): 13-16. [Democratic Party in 1992 presidential elections. See Gabel, above]

11843. Penn, Lisha B. *The Quest of Virginia Blacks for Suffrage: 1619-1965*. Virginia State University: Master's thesis, 1990.

11844. Perry, Bruce, ed. *Malcolm X. The Last Speeches*. New York: Pathfinder Press, 1989.

11845. Perry, H. L. "Pluralist Theory and National Black Politics in the United States." *Polity* 23 (Summer 1991): 549-566.

11846. Peterson, Iver. "Indians in West Turning to Voting Rights Tool that Aided Blacks in South." *New York Times*, 5 July 1986. [Crow and Northern Cheyenne Indians, in Big Horn County, Montana]

11847. Peterson, Jonathan. "Blame, Not Excuses, for Rioters." *Los Angeles Times*, 6 August 1992. [Black neo-conservatives on the Los Angeles riots of April-May 1992]

11848. Petrin, Ronald A. "Ethnicity and Urban Politics: French- Canadians in Worcester, 1895-1915." *Historical Journal of Massachusetts* 15 (June 1987): 141-153.

11849. Pettigrew, Thomas F., and D. Alston. *Tom Bradley's Campaign for Governor: The Dilemma of Race and Political Strategies*. Washington, DC: Joint Center for Political Studies, 1988.

11850. Phelps, Christopher. "The Second Time as Farce: The Right's New McCarthyism." *Monthly Review* 43 (October 1991): 39- 57.

11851. Phillips, Kevin. *Boiling Point: Republicans, Democrats and the Decline of Middle Class Prosperity*. Random House, 1993.

11852. _____. "Down and Out. Can the Middle Class Rise Again?" *New York Times Magazine* (10 January 1993).

11853. Pierammunzi, C. A., and J. D. Hutcheson. "Deracialization in the Deep South: Mayoral Politics in Atlanta." *Urban Affairs Quarterly* 27 (December 1991): 192-201.

11854. Pohlmann, Marcus D. *Black Politics in Conservative America*. New York: Longman, 1989.

11855. Polionard, J. L. and others. "Representation and Policy: Appointments of Mexican Americans to Boards and Commissions." *Social Science Journal* 28 (1991): 259-266.

11856. Pollack, Andy. "The Unmasking of Mayor Dinkins." *Against the Current* no. 48 (January-February 1994): 15-19.

11857. Potts, Nancy J. "Unfilled Expectations: The Erosion of Black Political Power in Chattanooga, 1865-1911." *Tennessee Historical Quarterly* 49 (Summer 1990): 112-128.

11858. Powell, Kimberly A. *The 1984 and 1988 Presidential Campaigns of Jesse Jackson*. Northern Illinois University: Master's thesis, 1989.

11859. Powledge, Fred. "George Bush Is Whistling 'Dixie'." *Nation* (14 October 1991). [President Bush and racism]

11860. Prager, Jeffrey. "American Political Culture and the Shifting Meaning of Race." *Ethnic and Racial Studies* 10 (1987): 62-81.

11861. Pratt, Geronimo j-jaga, and Mumia Abu-Jamal. "The Black Panthers: Interviews with Geronimo Ji-jaga Pratt and Mumia Abu- Jamal." *Race and Class* 35 (July-September 1993): 9-26.

11862. Preston, Michael B. "Political Change in the City-Black Politics in Chicago." in *Diversity, Conflict, and State Politics*, pp. 178-196. ed. Peter F. Nardulli. Urbana: University of Illinois Press, 1989.

11863. Price, Edward. "The Black Voting Rights Issue in Pennsylvania, 1780-1900." *Pennsylvania Magazine of History and Biography* 100 (July 1976).

11864. Prysby, Charles L. "Attitudes of Southern Democratic Party Activists toward Jesse Jackson: The Effects of the Local Context." *Journal of Politics* 51 (May 1989): 305-318.

11865. Puddington, Arch. "Clarence Thomas and the Blacks." *Commentary* 93 (February 1992): 28-33.

11866. Quintero Rivera, Angel G. "The Development of Social Classes and Political Conflicts in Puerto Rico." in *Puerto Rico and Puerto Ricans*, eds. Adalberto Lopez, and James Petras. Cambridge, MA: Schenkman, 1974.

11867. "A Racist Anti-Semitic Neo-Nazi Sprints Now for the Mainstream." *Texas Observer* (January 17 and 31, 1992). [Special double issue on David Duke]

11868. Rae, N. C. "Class and Culture: American Political Cleavages in the 20th Century." *Western Political Quarterly* 45 (September 1992): 629-650.

11869. Ragsdale, Bruce A., and Joel D. Treese. *Black Americans in Congress, 1870-1989*. Washington, DC: GPO, 1990.

11870. Raines, Howell. "Alabama Bound." *New York Times Magazine* (3 June 1990). [Race, politics, and economics in the state.]

11871. Raskin, Jamin B. "Domination, Democracy, and the District: The Statehood Problem." *Catholic University Law Review* 39 (Winter 1990). [District of Columbia]

11872. Raspberry, William. "Motor Voter and the 'Them' Problem." *Washington Post*, 19 March 1993. [On opposition to a bill facilitating voter registration]

11873. "Recent Advances in Black Electoral Politics." *PS- Political Science and Politics* 23 (1990): 141-162 (eight articles).

11874. Reed, Adolph, Jr. "All for One and None for All." *Nation* (28 January 1991): 86-92. [Louis Farrakhan and Black leadership]

11875. _____. "The Black Urban Regime: Structural Origins and Constraints." *Comparative Urban and Community Research* 1 (1988): 138-189.

11876. Reed, Adolph, Jr., and Julian Bond. "Equality: Why We Can't Wait." *Nation* (9 December 1991). [A critical discussion of Thomas B. Edsall and Mary D. Edsall, Chain Reaction: The Impact of Race, Rights, and Taxes on American Politics]

11877. Reed, Christopher R. "A Century of Civics and Politics: The Afro-Americans of Chicago." *Illinois Issues* (July 1987): 32- 36.

11878. Reiss, Matthew. "Ron Daniels: Not Just Another Pope of Hope." *Village Voice* (15 September 1992). [Former executive director of the Rainbow Coalition]

11879. Remnick, David. "The Situationist." *New Yorker* (5 September 1994). [Marion Barry and Wash. D.C. politics]

11880. Retana, Robert G. "Preservation of Minority Group Voting Strength as Justification for Deviation from One Person-One Vote Standard." *La Raza Law Journal* 3 (Spring 1990): 51-82. [Garza v. County of Los Angeles]

11881. *Reversing Political Powerlessness for Black Voters in South Carolina: Will Single-Member Election Districts Lead to Political Segregation?* Washington, DC: U.S. Commission on Civil Rights, 1991.

11882. Rhodes, Carroll. "Enforcing the Voting Rights Act in Mississippi through Litigation." *Mississippi Law Journal* 57 (December 1987): 705-737.

11883. Rich, Wilbur C. *Coleman Young and Detroit Politics: From Social Activist to Power Broker.* Detroit, MI: Wayne State University Press, 1989.

11884. Richter, William L. "'The Revolver Rules the Day!': Colonel DeWitt C. Brown and the Freedman's Bureau in Paris, Texas, 1867-1868." *Southwestern Historical Quarterly* 93 (1990): 303-332.

11885. Riddlesperger, James W., Jr., and James D. King. "Elitism and Presidential Appointments." *Social Science Quarterly* 70 (1989): 902-910.

11886. Ridenhour, Ron. "Keeping [David] Duke's Secrets." *Lies Of Our Times* 1 (October 1990): 9. [Lack of coverage of Louisiana white supremacists by mass media.]

11887. Ridgeway, James. "Here He Comes, Mr. America." *Village Voice* (9 October 1990). [David Duke]

11888. _____. "The Racist Sucker Punch. Why White People Vote the Way They Do." *Village Voice* (21 May 1991).

11889. _____. "White Blight. David Duke Worms Ahead." *Village Voice* (4 July 1989).

11890. Riley, Michael. "The Duke of Louisiana." *Time* (4 November 1991). [David Duke]

11891. Rivlin, Gary. *Fire On the Prairie. Chicago's Harold Washington and the Politics of Race.* New York: Holt, 1992.

11892. Roberts, Lawrence E. "Women in Populism, 1888-1892." *Heritage of the Great Plains* 2-3 (Summer 1990): 15-27.

11893. Roberts, Sam. "Can Politics Get To the Roots of Racial Strife?" *New York Times*, 20 May 1990. [New York City]

11894. _____. "Gerrymandering in the Name of Equality." *New York Times*, 17 June 1991. [Redistricting New York City]

11895. _____. "The Role Race Plays in Politics." *New York Times*, 2 August 1993. [New York City]

11896. Rogers, A. "Towards a Geography of the Rainbow Coalition, 1983-1989." *Environment and Planning-D-Society + Space* 8 (December 1990): 409-426.

11897. Rogers, Rebecca A. *Voting Patterns of Hispanics in Texas, 1960-1984.* College of William and Mary: Master's thesis, 1989.

11898. Rosales, Rodolfo. *The Rise of Chicano Middle Class Politics in San Antonio, 1955 to 1985*. Ph.D. diss., University of Michigan, 1991. UMO #9208638.

11899. Rubin, Lawrence. "American Jewish Concerns in the US Presidential Election." *Analysis (Institute of Jewish Affairs)* no. 4 (October 1992).

11900. Rush, Mark E. *Does Redistricting Make a Difference? Partisan Representation and Electoral Behavior*. Johns Hopkins University Press, 1993.

11901. Russell, Kathy and others. *The Color Complex. The Politics of Skin Color Among African Americans*. Harcourt Brace Jovanovich, 1992.

11902. Russo, Andrew. *The Lyndon Larouche Political Movement*. San Jose State University: Master's thesis, 1989. UMO #MA1339646.

11903. Rutten, Tim. "Politicians Sow Double Standards on Race." *Los Angeles Times*, 9 July 1992.

11904. Salces, Luis M., and Peter W. Colby. "Manana will Be Better: Spanish-American Politics in Chicago." *Illinois Issues* (February 1980): 19-21.

11905. Saltzstein, Grace H. "Black Mayors and Police Policies." *Journal of Politics* 51 (August 1989).

11906. Sawer, Mary R. "Gifts and Grievances of Black Elected Officials." *Journal of State Government* 61 (1988): 49-51.

11907. Scadron, S. Michael. "Cumulative Voting in Action." *Washington Post*, 13 July 1993, letter. [How to abolish congressional districts, elect candidates at-large, and attain unparalleled representativeness]

11908. Scheuerman, William E., and Sidney Plotkin. *Private Interests, Public Spending. Balanced Budget Conservatism and the Fiscal Crisis*. South End Press, 1993.

11909. Schmidt, Peter. "Ark. Law Forcing Districts to Shift To Ward-Based School Board Races." *Education Week* (14 September 1994). [Applies to "school districts that are at least 10 percent minority."]

11910. Schockley, E. E. "Voting Rights Act Section 2: Racially Polarized Voting and the Minority Community's Representation of Choice." *Michigan Law Review* 89 (February 1991).

11911. Schonbach, Morris. *Native American Fascism during the 1930s and 1940s: A Study of Its Roots, Its Growth, and Its Decline*. New York: Garland, 1985.

11912. Schulte, Steven C. "Indians and Politicians: The Origins of a 'Western' Attitude toward Native Americans in Wyoming 1868- 1906." *Annals of Wyoming* 56 (Spring 1984): 2-11.

11913. Schwenk, Katrin. "The Death of Mayor Washington: Political Race Wars Relived." *Amerikastudien/American Studies* 34 (1989): 203-209. [Harold Washington, Chicago]

11914. Scott, Maurice, Jr. *Panther Genesis*. Nashville, TN: Aurora Press, 1970.

11915. Senese, Guy B. *Self-Determination and the Social Education of Native Americans*. New York: Praeger, 1991.

11916. Shapiro, A. L. "Challenging Criminal Disenfranchisement under the Voting Rights Act: A New Strategy." *Yale Law Journal* 103 (November 1993).

11917. Sharpton, A. "Also Spoke Reverend Sharpton." *Village Voice* (4 October 1994): letter. [Analysis of his vote in 1992 and 1994 elections in New York]

11918. Shogan, Robert. "Congressional Black Caucus Renounces Farrakhan Pact." *Los Angeles Times*, 3 February 1994.

11919. Shriver, Donald W., Jr. "A Struggle for Justice and Reconciliation: Forgiveness in the Politics of the American Black Civil Rights Movement, 1955-68." *Studies (Ireland)* 78 (1989): 136-150.

11920. Silcox, Harry C. "The Black 'Better Class' Political Dilemma: Philadelphia Prototype Isaiah C. Wears." *Pennsylvania Magazine of History and Biography* 113 (1989): 45-66.

11921. Silverblatt, Ronnie, and Robert J. Amann. "Race, Ethnicity, Union Attitudes, and Voting Predilections." *Industrial Relations* 30 (Spring 1991): 271-285.

11922. Simms-Maddox, Margaret J. *The Development of the Black Elected Democrats of Ohio (BEDO) into a Viable State Legislative Caucus.* Ph.D. diss., Ohio State University, 1991. UMO #9130556.

11923. Sinsheimer, Joseph A. "The Freedom Vote of 1963: New Strategies of Racial Protest in Mississippi." *Journal of Southern History* 55 (May 1989): 217-244.

11924. Skelton, George. "Voters of Asian Heritage Slow to Claim Voice." *Los Angeles Times*, 19 August 1993. [California]

11925. Skerry, Peter N. *The Ambivalent Minority: Emergent Styles of Mexican-American Politics.* 2 vols. Ph.D. diss., Harvard University, 1991. [Los Angeles and San Antonio]. UMO #9132041.

11926. Skocpol, Theda. "Sustainable Social Policy: Fighting Poverty Without Poverty Programs." *American Prospect* (Summer 1990).

11927. Sleeper, Jim. *The Closest of Strangers. Liberalism and the Politics of Race in New York.* New York: Norton, 1990.

11928. _____. "Demagoguery in America: Wrong Turns in the Politics of Race." *Tikkun* 6 (November-December 1991): 43-50, 92.

11929. _____. "Racial Politics Reconsidered: A Response to Walker and McPherson." *Reconstruction* 1 (1991): 88-92.

11930. Smith, J. Owens and others. *Blacks and American Government: Politics, Policy, and Social Change.* Dubuque, Iowa: Kendall/Hunt, 1987.

11931. Smith, Kenneth L. "The Radicalization of Martin Luther King, Jr.: The Last Three Years." *Journal of Ecumenical Studies* 26 (1989): 270-288.

11932. Smith, Robert C. "Financing Black Politics: A Study of Congressional Elections." *Review of Black Political Economy* 17 (Summer 1988).

11933. Smith, Robert C., and Joseph P. McCormick, II. "The Challenge of a Black Presidential Candidacy." *New Directions* (April 1984).

11934. Smith, Tom W. "Liberal and Conservative Trends in the United States since World War II." *Public Opinion Quarterly* 54 (Winter 1990): 479-507.

11935. Smothers, Ronald. "Blacks Say G.O.P. Ballot Challenges Are Tactic to Harass Minority Voters." *New York Times*, 25 October 1992. [Helena, Arkansas]

11936. _____. "Helped by New Districts, Blacks Make Big Gains in Mississippi Legislature." *New York Times*, 9 August 1992.

11937. _____. "In South Carolina, a Tale of Campaign Trickery." *New York Times*, 19 April 1992. [Example of a white political strategist who "shamelessly exploit[ed] racial differences and racism in the pursuit of victory."]

11938. _____. "Racially Divisive Campaign in Memphis." *New York Times*, 2 October 1991.

11939. Snedeker, George. "Capitalism, Racism, and the Struggle for Democracy: The Political Sociology of Oliver C. Cox." *Socialism and Democracy* 7 (Fall-Winter 1988): 75-95.

11940. Sonenshein, Raphael J. "Can Black Candidates Win Statewide Elections?" *Political Science Quarterly* 105 (Summer 1990).

11941. _____. "The Dynamics of Biracial Coalitions: Crossover Politics in Los Angeles." *Western Political Quarterly* 42 (June 1989): 333-354.

11942. _____. *Politics in Black and White. Race and Power in Los Angeles.* Princeton University Press, 1993.

11943. Spiegel, Claire, and K. Connie Kang. "The Fast Rocky Rise of Jay Kim." *Los Angeles Times*, 27 October 1993. [Jay C. Kim's election to Congress, erroneously called first Asian American elected]

11944. Squires, Gregory D. *Chicago: Race, Class and the Response to Urban Decline.* Philadelphia, PA: Temple University Press, 1987.

11945. Stanley, Harold M. *Voter Mobilization and the Politics of Race: The South and Universal Suffrage, 1952-1984*. New York: Praeger, 1987.

11946. "Statistical and Demographic Issues Underlying Voting Rights Cases." *Evaluation Review* 15 (December 1991): 8 articles.

11947. Stavis, Morton. "A Century of Struggle for Black Enfranchisement in Mississippi: From the Civil War to the Congressional Challenge of 1965-and Beyond." *Mississippi Law Journal* 57 (December 1987): 591-676.

11948. Steele, James. "Congressional Black Caucus At a Turning Point." *CrossRoads* no. 28 (February 1993): 22-25.

11949. Steinberg, Stephen. "Shifting the Focus of Blame." *New Politics* 38 (Summer 1991): 96-100. [Review of Jim Sleeper, The Closest of Strangers]

11950. Stekler, Paul J. "Electing Blacks to Office in the South- Black Candidates, Bloc Voting, and Racial Unity Twenty Years after the Voting Rights Act." *Urban Lawyer* 17 (1985): 473-487.

11951. Stephenson, Grier. "The Supreme Court, the Franchise, and the Fifteenth Amendment: The First Sixty Years." *UMKC Law Review* 57 (Fall 1988): 47-65.

11952. Stokes, Geoffrey. "Run Jesse Run." *Village Voice* (6 November 1990). [Harvey Gantt and Jesse Helms in election for U.S. senator from North Carolina]

11953. Stone, Clarence N. *Regime Politics: Governing Atlanta, 1946-1988*. Lawrence: University of Kansas Press, 1989.

11954. Strong, James. "Racism and the D.C. Mayor's Race." *African Commentary* 1 (June 1990): 26-28.

11955. Suro, Roberto. "[David] Duke Softens Past in Louisiana Race." *New York Times*, 24 September 1991.

11956. _____. "Hispanic Politicians Seek a Recipe for Raw Numbers." *New York Times*, 12 April 1992.

11957. _____. "In Dallas, Race Is At the Heart of City Politics." *New York Times*, 10 September 1989.

11958. _____. "When Minorities Start Becoming Majorities." *New York Times*, 23 June 1991. [Texas]

11959. Swain, Carol M. *Black Faces. Black Interests. The Representation of African Americans in Congress*. Harvard U.P., 1993.

11960. _____. "Black-Majority Districts: A Bad Idea." *New York Times*, 3 June 1993.

11961. Tapscott, Richard. "More Potent Black Caucus Emerges in MD Assembly." *Washington Post*, 4 April 1994.

11962. Tashman, Billy. "Class and Caste Swing the Vote." *Village Voice* (1 June 1993). [Analysis of local school board elections in New York City]

11963. Tate, Katherine T. and others. *The 1984 National Black Election Study Sourcebook*. Ann Arbor: Institute for Social Research, University of Michigan, 1988.

11964. Tate, Katherine T. *Black Politics as a Collective Struggle: The Impact of Race and Class in 1984*. Ph.D. diss., University of Michigan, 1989. UMO #8920624.

11965. _____. "Black Political Participation in the 1984 and 1988 Presidential Elections." *American Political Science Review* 85 (December 1991): 1159-1176.

11966. _____. *From Protest to Politics: The New Black Voters in American Elections*. Harvard U.P., 1993. [1984 and 1988 elections]

11967. Teixeira, Ruy A. *The Disappearing American Voter*. Brookings Institution, 1992.

11968. Terborg-Penn, Rosalyn. "Suffrage Movement." *Black Women in America II*, pp. 1124-1128.

11969. Terkildsen, N. "When White Voters Evaluate Black Candidates: The Processing Implications of Candidate Skin Color, Prejudice, and Self-monitoring." *American Journal of Political Science* 37 (November 1993): 1032-1053.

11970. Terry, Don. "Blacks Started Dinkins' Bid In a Symbolic River-Crossing." *New York Times*, 17 September 1989. [David N. Dinkins, successful black candidate in NYC mayoral Democratic Party primary election]

11971. _____. "Blacks See Old Hate Behind [David] Duke's New Strength." *New York Times*, 9 November 1991.

11972. Theilmann, John, and Al Wilhite. "Differences in Campaign Funds: A Racial Explanation." *Review of Black Political Economy* 15 (Summer 1986): 45-58.

11973. _____. *Discrimination and Congressional Campaign Contributions*. Praeger, 1991.

11974. Thelwell, Michael. "The August 28th [1963] March on Washington. The Castrated Giant." in *Duties, Pleasures, and Conflicts. Essays in Struggle*, pp. 57-73. Amherst: University of Massachusetts Press, 1987.

11975. _____. "'God Aint Finished with Us Yet.' Jesse Jackson and the Politics of the 1980s." in *Duties, Pleasures, and Conflicts. Essays in Struggle*, pp. 235-258. Amherst: University of Massachusetts Press, 1987.

11976. Thelwell, Michael, and Lawrence Guyot. "The Politics of Necessity and Survival in Mississippi." in *Duties, Pleasures, and Conflicts. Essays in Struggle*, pp. 87-107. Amherst: University of Massachusetts Press, 1987.

11977. Thomas, Clarence W. "No Room At the Inn: The Loneliness of the Black Conservative." *Policy Review* no. 58 (Fall 1991): 72-78. [Written in 1987]

11978. Thometz, Carol E. *The Decision-Makers: The Power Structure of Dallas*. Dallas, TX: Southern Methodist University Press, 1963.

11979. Thompson, James P., III. *The Impact of Jesse Jackson Campaigns on Local Black Political Mobilization in New York City, Atlanta, and Oakland*. Ph.D. diss., City University of New York, 1990. UMO #9029983.

11980. Tilly, Chris. "The Politics of the 'New Inequality'." *Socialist Review* 20 (January-March 1990): 103-120.

11981. Tobar, Hector. "No Strength in Numbers for L.A.'s Divided Latinos." *Los Angeles Times*, 1 September 1992.

11982. Tobias, Henry J., and Charles E. Woodhouse, eds. *Minorities and Politics*. Albuquerque: University of New Mexico Press, 1969.

11983. Tomasky, Michael. "Feels Like a Freeze Out." *Village Voice* (30 July 1991). [Redistricting of NYC City Council]

11984. Travis, Dempsey T. *"Harold": The People's Mayor: An Authorized Biography of Mayor Harold Washington*. Chicago, IL: Urban Research Press, 1989.

11985. Trebay, Guy. "A Bend in the River." *Village Voice* (14 April 1992). [Seeking Bill Clinton votes among Blacks in Mississippi]

11986. Troutt, David Dante. "When Restoring Black Rights Is Discriminatory." *Los Angeles Times*, 4 July 1993. [Voting rights and congressional reappointment in North Carolina]

11987. Tuckel, Peter, and Richard Masiel. "Voter Turnout Among European Immigrants to the United States." *Journal of Interdisciplinary History* 24 (Winter 1994).

11988. Tumulty, Karen. "New Voices Shake Up the House." *Los Angeles Times*, 5 July 1993. [Women and minorities in the U.S. House of Representatives]

11989. Tushnet, Mark V. "Principles, Politics, and Constitutional Law." *Michigan Law Review* 88 (October 1989): 49-81.

11990. "Tutela Delays Seeking State Loan." *Cleveland Plain Dealer*, 6 August 1987. [Analysis of results of August 4th operating levy election]

11991. Twomey, Steve and others. "[A series of articles on statehood for the District of Columbia]." *Washington Post Magazine* (4 July 1993).

11992. Tye, Larry. "Blacks Winning Office. Many Local Successes in U.S., But Statewide Posts Elusive." *Boston Globe*, 26 December 1990.

11993. _____. "In South, Ballot Box Inequality Lingers On." *Boston Globe*, 23 July 1990.

11994. Uhlander, Carole J. "Political Participation of Ethnic Minorities in the 1980s." *Political Behavior* 11 (September 1989): 195-231. [California]

11995. _____. "Turnout in Recent American Presidential Elections." *Political Behavior* 11 (1989): 57-79. [1980 and 1984]

11996. Umoja, A. A. *The Impact of the Black Mayor on Municipal Spending*. Ph.D. diss., University of Georgia, 1990. UMO #9107238.

11997. Underwood, James L. *The Constitution of South Carolina. Vol. IV: The Struggle for Political Equality*. University of South Carolina Press, 1993. [Voting rights since the Civil War]

11998. Underwood, Katherine. *Process and Politics: Multiracial Electoral Coalition Building and Representation in Los Angeles' Ninth District, 1949-1962*. Ph.D. diss., UC San Diego, 1992. [Edward Roybal]. UMO #9312130.

11999. University of Iowa and Libraries. *The Right Wing Collection of the University of Iowa Libraries, 1918-1977*. Glen Rock, NJ, 1978.

12000. U.S Commission on Civil Rights, South Carolina Advisory Committee. *Reversing Political Powerlessness for Black Voters in South Carolina: Will Single-Member Election Districts Lead to Political Segregation?* Washington, DC: The Commission, 1991.

12001. "U.S. District Court Upholds 'Gerrymander' for Blacks." *New York Times*, 3 August 1994. [Louisiana and North Carolina]

12002. Verhovek, Sam H. "Black Republican Candidates find Niche in the New Order." *New York Times*, 7 October 1994.

12003. Vigil, Maurillio E. *Hispanics in American Politics: The Search for Political Power*. Lanham, MD: University Press of America, 1987.

12004. Villarreal, Roberto E., and Norma G. Hernandez, eds. *Latinos and Political Coalitions. Political Empowerment for the 1990s*. Westport, CT: Greenwood, 1991.

12005. Waldinger, Roger, and Thomas Bailey. "The Continuing Significance of Race: Racial Conflict and Racial Discrimination." *Politics and Society* 19 (September 1991).

12006. Walker, Laura. "Liberalism and Racial Politics in New York." *Reconstruction* 1 (1991): 77-82. [See Jim Sleeper, above]

12007. Wallace, David T. *The Quest for Black Voting Rights...1864-1896*. University of Cincinnati: Master's thesis, 1989.

12008. Walters, Ronald W. *Black Presidential Politics in America: A Strategic Approach*. Albany: State University Press of New York, 1988.

12009. _____. "Black Politics: Mobilization for Empowerment." in *Race: Twentieth-Century Dilemmas--Twenty-first-Century Prognoses*, eds. Winston Van Horne, and Thomas V. Tonneson. Milwaukee: Institute on Race and Ethnicity, University of Wisconsin System, 1989.

12010. Walton, Hanes, Jr. "Democrats and African Americans: The American Idea." in *Democrats and the American Idea*, ed. Peter B. Kovler. Center for National Policy, 1992.

12011. Warren, Nagueyalti. "Pan-African Cultural Movements: From Baraka to Karenga." *Journal of Negro History* 75 (Winter, Spring 1990): 16-28.

12012. Watson, Denton L. *Lion in the Lobby. Clarence Mitchell's Struggle for the Passage of Civil Rights Laws*. New York: Morrow, 1990.

12013. Watts, Jerry G. "Clinton and Blacks: Evading Race." *New Politics* 4 (Winter 1993): 17-21.

12014. _____. "Somewhere Over the Rainbow: Reflections on Black Politics in the Age of Jackson." *Soundings* 70 (1987): 407- 434. [Jesse Jackson]

12015. Weed, Amy S. "Getting Around the Voting Rights Act: The Supreme Court Sets the Limits of Racial Voting Discrimination in the South." *Boston College Third World Law Journal* 10 (Spring 1990): 381-404.

12016. Weeks, O. Douglas. "The Texas-Mexicans and the Politics of South Texas." *American Political Science Review* 24 (August 1930).

12017. Wei, William. *The Asian American Movement*. Temple University Press, 1993.

12018. Welch, Susan, and L. S. Foster. "The Impact of Economic Conditions on the Voting Behavior of Blacks." *Western Political Quarterly* 45 (March 1992): 221-236.

12019. Welch, Susan, and Lee Sigelman. "A Black Gender Gap?" *Social Science Quarterly* 70 (1989): 120-133.

12020. Wells David I. "Our Ethnic Cleansing." *New York Times*, 11 July 1993, letter. [Race and electoral redistricting]

12021. Wesley, Charles H. "Negro Suffrage in the Period of Constitution-Making, 1787-1865." *Journal of Negro History* (April 1947).

12022. West, Cornel. "Nihilism in Black America." *Dissent* 38 (Spring 1991): 221-226.

12023. Wheeler, Majorie S. *New Women of the New South: The Leaders of the Woman Suffrage Movement in the Southern States*. Oxford U.P., 1993.

12024. White, John. *Black Leadership in America. From Booker T. Washington to Jesse Jackson*, 2nd ed. White Plains, NY: Longmans, 1990.

12025. "Whither the Rainbow?" *Nation* (18 December 1989). [An exchange of letters on Jesse Jackson and the Rainbow Coalition]

12026. Wilkerson, Isabel. "With No Unifying Force, Political Power for Blacks Ebbs in Chicago." *New York Times*, 30 May 1991.

12027. Wilkins, Roger W. "Free at Last?" *Modern Maturity* 37 (April- May 1994): 27,31,33.

12028. Williams, Eddie N. "Persistent Racism: A Challenge for the 21st Century." *Focus (Joint Center for Political Studies)* (November-December 1989).

12029. Williams, Eddie N., and Milton D. Morris. "Racism and Our Future." in *Race in America*, eds. Herbert Hill, and James E. Jones, Jr. University of Wisconsin Press, 1993.

12030. Williams, Juan. "The Seduction of Segregation and Why King's Dream Still Matters." *Washington Post*, 16 January 1994.

12031. Williams, Linda F. "Significant Trends in Black Voter Attitudes." *Black Scholar* 17 (1986): 24-27.

12032. Williams, Loretta J. "Domestic Destabilization on Dred Scott and African-American Elected Leaders." *Z Magazine* 4 (July- August 1991): 30-34.

12033. Wills, Garry. "David Duke's Addictive Politics." *Time* (1 October 1990).

12034. _____. "The Golden Blade." *New York Review of Books* (13 February 1992). [Pat Buchanan]

12035. Wilson, William J. "Race-Neutral Policies and the Democratic Coalition." *American Prospect* (Spring 1990).

12036. Winant, Howard. "Postmodern Racial Politics in the United States: Difference and Inequality." *Socialist Review* 20 (January- March 1990): 121-147.

12037. Wintz, Cary D. "The Emergence of a Black Neighborhood." in *Urban Texas: Politics and Development*, eds. Char Miller, and Heywood Sanders. College Station: Texas A + M University Press, 1990. [Houston]

12038. Wirls, Daniel. "Reinterpreting the Gender Gap." *Public Opinion Quarterly* 50 (1986): 316-330.

12039. Wolfenstein, Eugene V. *The Victims of Democracy: Malcolm X and the Black Revolution*. London: Free Association Books, 1990.

12040. Wolfley, Jeanette. "Jim Crow, Indian Style: The Disfranchisement of Native Americans." *American Indian Law Review* 16 (Spring 1991): 167-202.

12041. Woodson, Robert L., Jr. "The Wages of Blaming Racism for Everything." *Los Angeles Times*, 21 November 1993.

12042. Workman, Andrew. *The Rejection of Accommodation by Mississippi's Black Public Elite, 1946-1954*. University of North Carolina: Master's thesis, 1989.

12043. Wright, John S. "To the Battle Royal: Ralph Ellison and the Quest for Black Leadership in Postwar America." in *Recasting America. Culture and Politics in the Age of Cold War*, ed. Lary May. Chicago: University of Chicago Press, 1989.

12044. Wright, Ted A. *A Case Study and Theoretical Analysis of the Problem of Power for American Indian and Alaska Native Tribes*. Ph.D. diss., Pennsylvania State University, 1990. [Indian Self-Determination and Education Assistance Act]. UMO #9104994.

12045. Yuen, Ying Chen. "Riding the Dragon." *Village Voice* (31 October 1989). [Politics in New York's Chinatown]

12046. Zax, J. S. "Election Methods and Black and Hispanic City Council Membership." *Social Science Quarterly* 71 (June 1990).

12047. Zucker, Bat-Ami. "The Role of the Supreme Court in the Decline and Fall of the White Primary in the South, 1921-1953." *Amerikastudien* 32 (1987): 493-506.

PUBLIC OPINION

12048. "31% of Young White Adults Show Anti-Black Views." *Los Angeles Times*, 12 June 1993.

12049. Applebome, Peter. "Racial Divisions Persist 25 Years After King Killing." *New York Times*, 4 April 1993.

12050. Berke, Richard L. "U.S Voters Focus on Selves, Poll Says." *New York Times*, 21 September 1994. ["People are less inclined to express concerns for the plight of blacks"]

12051. Bobo, Lawrence. *Race in the Minds of Black and White Americans*. Paper prepared for the Committee on the Status of Black Americans, National Research Council, Washington, D.C., 1987.

12052. _____. *Racial Attitudes and the Status of Black Americans: A Social Psychological View of Change since the 1940s*. Paper prepared for the Committee on the Status of Black Americans, National Research Council, Washington, D.C., 1987.

12053. _____. "Running the R.A.C.E.?" *Public Opinion Quarterly* 55 (Spring 1991): 131-134.

12054. Carmines, Edward G., and Richard A. Champagne, Jr. "The Changing Content of American Racial Attitudes: A Fifty Year Portrait." *Research in Micropolitics* 3 (1990): 187-208.

12055. Case, Charles E., and Andrew M. Greeley. "Attitudes toward Racial Equality." *Humboldt Journal of Social Relations* 16 (1990): 67-94. [Poll data, 1965-1980]

12056. Citizens League Research Institute. *Race Relations in Greater Cleveland: A Report on the Attitudes, Opinions, and Experiences of Greater Cleveland*. The Institute, 1991.

12057. Citrin, Jack and others. "American Identity and the Politics of Ethnic Change." *Journal of Politics* 52 (November 1990): 1124-1254.

12058. Corbett, Michael. "Changes in Noneconomic Political Attitudes of Southern and Northern Youth, 1970s to 1980s." *Journal of Youth and Adolesence* 17 (June 1988): 197-210.

12059. Danigelis, Nicholas L., and S. J. Cutler. "Cohort Trends in Attitudes About Law and Order: Who's Leading the Conservative Wave?" *Public Opinion Quarterly* 55 (Spring 1991): 24-49.

12060. Davis, James A., and Tom W. Smith. *General Social Surveys, 1972-1990: Cumulative Codebook*. Chicago, IL: National Opinion Research Center, 1990.

12061. de la Garza, Rodolfo O. "Researchers Must Heed New Realities When They Study Latinos in the U.S." *Chronicle of Higher Education* (2 June 1993).

12062. De Leon, Arnoldo. *White Racial Attitudes Towards Mexicans in Texas, 1821-1900*. Ph.D. diss., Texas Christian University, 1974.

12063. DeParle, Jason. "For Some Blacks, Social Ills Seem to Follow White Plans." *New York Times*, 11 August 1991.

12064. Dippie, Brian W. *The Vanishing American. White Attitudes and U.S. Indian Policy*. Middleton, CT: Wesleyan University Press, 1982.

12065. Dowden, Frieda S. *Age, Education, Contact and Racial Attitudes of White Americans*. Ph.D. diss., University of Maryland, 1990. UMO #9030893.

12066. Firebaugh, Glenn, and Kenneth E. Davis. "Trends in Antiblack Prejudice, 1972-1984: Region and Cohort Effects." *American Journal of Sociology* 94 (1988): 257-272.

12067. Fossett, M. A., and K. J. Kiecolt. "The Relative Size of Minority Populations and White Racial Attitudes." *Social Science Quarterly* 70 (December 1989).

12068. Glaser, James M. "Back to the Black Belt: Racial Environment and White Racial Attitudes in the South." *Journal of Politics* 56 (February 1994): 21-41.

12069. Gratus, J. *The Great White Lie: Slavery, Emancipation, and Changing Racial Attitudes*. New York: Monthly Review Press, 1973.

12070. Groskind, Fred. "Public Reactions to Poor Families: Characteristics that Influence Attitudes toward Assistance." *Social Work* 36 (September 1991): 446-453. [1986 data]

12071. Harris, Louis. *The Unfinished Agenda on Race in America*. New York: NAACP Legal Defense and Educational Fund, 1989.

12072. Herring, Cedric. "Convergence, Polarization, or What? Racially Based Changes in Attitudes and Outlooks, 1964-1984." *Sociological Quarterly* 30 (1989): 267-281. [Relative importance of race]

12073. Hill, Robert B. "The Polls and Ethnic Minorities." *Annals* (March 1984): 155-166.

12074. Hobbs, Michael A. "Racial Relations Worsening here, 55% Say in Poll." *Cleveland Plain Dealer*, 7 June 1989. [Cuyahoga County (Cleveland), Ohio]

12075. Hochschild, Jennifer L. "The Political Contingency of Public Opinion, or What Shall We Make of the Declining Faith of Middle- Class African Americans." *PS-Political Science and Politics* 27 (March 1994): 35-38.

12076. Howe, Peter J. "Poll: Case Hurt Race Relations." *Boston Globe*, 21 January 1990. [Carol Stewart murder case in Boston]

12077. Jackson, James S., ed. *Life in Black America*. Sage, 1991. [Data from the National Survey of Black Americans]

12078. Jaynes, Gerald David, and Robin M. Williams, Jr., eds. "Racial Attitudes and Behavior." in *A Common Destiny. Blacks and American Society*, Washington, DC: National Academy Press, 1989.

12079. Jorgenson, David E., and Christabel Jorgenson. "Age and White Racial Attitudes: National Surveys, 1972-1989." *Sociological Spectrum* 12 (January-March 1992): 21-34.

12080. Kagay, Michael T. "Poll on Doubt of Holocaust Is Corrected." *New York Times*, 8 July 1994. [New Roper poll to correct 1992 Roper poll; see below, Tom W. Smith, 1994]

12081. Kegay, Michael. "Poll Finds Most Blacks Reject Farrakhan's Ideas as Theirs." *New York Times*, 5 March 1994.

12082. Kellogg, Peter J. *Northern Liberals and Black America: a History of White Attitudes, 1936-1952*. Ph.D. diss., Northwestern University, 1971.

12083. Kifner, John. "Pollster Finds Error on Holocaust Doubts." *New York Times*, 20 May 1994. [Roper firm acknowledges erroneous interpretation of poll of public knowledge about the Holocaust.]

12084. Kluegel, James R. "Trends in Whites' Explanations of the Black-White Gap on Socioeconomic Status, 1977-1989." *American Sociological Review* 55 (1990): 512-525.

12085. Lesher, Dave. "O.C. Residents Call Migrants a Burden." *Los Angeles Times*, 22 August 1993. [Poll of Orange County, CA residents on legal and illegal immigrants]

12086. Lichtblau, Eric, and Carla Rivera. "Most Asians Think Well of O.C., and Vice Versa." *Los Angeles Times*, 20 August 1993. [Orange County, CA]

12087. Lipset, Seymour M., and William Schneider. "Racial Equality in America." *New Society* 44 (April 1978): 128-131.

12088. Luttbeg, Norma R., and Michael D. Martinez. "Demographic Differences in Opinion, 1956-1984." *Research in Micropolitics* 3 (1990): 83-117.

12089. Mahnic, Eric. "Blacks, Latinos Express Sense of Isolation." *Los Angeles Times*, 13 May 1993. [Public-opinion poll in Los Angeles]

12090. McKay, Emily G. *Recent Hispanic Polls: A Summary of Results*. Washington, DC: Hispanic Policy Development Project, February 1984.

12091. Merrimar, W. Richard, and Edward G. Carmines. "The Limits of Liberal Tolerance: The Case of Racial Policies." *Polity* 20 (1988): 518-526.

12092. Morgan, Thomas. "Race Relations Getting Worse, Many in Poll Say." *New York Times*, 27 June 1990. [New York City]

12093. Munkres, Robert L. "Broken Hand and the Indians: A Case Study of Mid-19th Century White Attitudes." *Annals of Wyoming* 50 (Spring 1978): 157-171.

12094. *New York City Intergroup Relations Survey*. American Jewish Committee, 1992.

12095. "Poll Finds Most Believe Holocaust." *Boston Globe*, 2 July 1994. [Gallup Poll, January 1994]

12096. Popkin, Samuel L. *The Reasoning Voter: Communication and Persuasion in Presidential Campaigns*. Chicago, IL: University of Chicago Press, 1991.

12097. "The Public Views the Police." *New York Times*, 5 April 1991.

12098. Ransford, H. E., and B. J. Palisi. "Has There Been a Resurgence of Racist Attitudes in the General Population?" *Sociological Spectrum* 12 (July-September 1992): 231-256.

12099. Roberts, Sam. "Private Opinions on Public Opinion: Question Is, What Is the Question?" *New York Times*, 21 August 1991. [Deals with race and public opinion polls, among other things.]

12100. Roper, Burns W. "Racial Tensions Are Down." *New York Times*, 26 July 1990. [Compares 1990 poll with 1978 poll]

12101. Rucinski, D. "Rush to Judgment: Fast Reaction Polls in the Anita Hill-Clarence Thomas Controversy." *Public Opinion Quarterly* 57 (Winter 1993): 575-592.

12102. Schuman, Howard. "Changing Racial Norms in America." *Michigan Quarterly Review* 30 (Summer 1991): 460-477. [Since 1980s]

12103. Seib, Gerald F., and Joe Davidson. "Whites, Blacks, Agree On Problems; The Issue Is How to Solve Them." *Wall Street Journal*, 29 September 1994.

12104. Shapiro, R. Y., and J. T. Young. "Public Opinion Toward Social Welfare Policies: The United States in Comparative Perspective." in *Research in Micropolities: Public Opinion*, Vol. 3. ed. S. Long. Greenwich, CT: JAI Press, 1990.

12105. Shingles, Richard D. "Class, Status, and Support for Government Aid to Disadvantaged Groups." *Journal of Politics* 51 (November 1989): 933-962.

12106. Sigelman, Lee, and Susan Welch. *Black Americans' Views of Racial Inequality: The Dream Deferred*. New York: Cambridge University Press, 1991.

12107. Smith, A. Wade. "Problems and Progress in the Measurement of Black Public Opinion." *American Behavioral Scientist* 30 (March-April 1987).

12108. Smith, Robert C., and Richard Seltzer. *Race, Class, and Culture: A Study in Afro-American Mass Opinion*. SUNY Press, 1992.

12109. Smith, Tom W. *Holocaust Denial: What the Survey Data Reveal*. American Jewish Committee, 1994. [See above, Michael R. Kagey]

12110. _____. "Liberal and Conservative Trends in the United States since World War II." *Public Opinion Quarterly* 54 (Winter 1990): 479-507.

12111. Sniderman, Paul M., and Thomas Piazza. *The Scar of Race*. Harvard University Press, 1993.

12112. Steeh, C., and Howard Schuman. "Young White Adults: Did Racial Attitudes Change in the 1980s?" *American Journal of Sociology* 98 (September 1992): 340-367.

12113. Stinson, James A. *Public Opinion in America: Moods, Cycles, and Swings*. Boulder, CO: Westview, 1991.

12114. "Study Finds Whites Still Hold Racial Stereotypes." *Boston Globe*, 9 January 1991. [General Social Survey, National Opinion Research Center]

12115. Suro, Roberto. "Poll Finds Hispanic Desire to Assimilate." *New York Times*, 15 December 1992.

12116. Terkel, Studs. *Race. How Blacks and Whites Think and Feel About the American Obsession*. New York: New Press, 1992.

12117. Turner, Castellano B., and William J. Wilson. "Dimensions of Racial Ideology: A Study of Urban Black Attitudes." *Journal of Social Issues* (Spring 1976): 139-152.

12118. Wallace, Amy. "Riots Changed Few Attitudes, Poll Finds." *Los Angeles Times*, 3 September 1992. [Some responses in Los Angeles about beliefs regarding differential inborn intelligence of various racial-ethnic groups.]

12119. "Who's In and Who's Out." *Ebony* 45 (August 1990): 128-132. [Poll of national samples of African Americans]

12120. Wood, Floris, ed. *An American Profile: Opinions and Behavior, 1972-1989: Opinion Results on 300 High-interest Issues Derived from the General Social Survey Conducted by the National Opinion Research Center*. Detroit, MI: Gale, 1990.

12121. Zia, Helen. "The Ms. Survey Results: How You Feel about Race." *Ms.* (May-June 1992): 20-22.

RACISM -- DEFINING

12122. Alston, Lee J. "Race Etiquette in the South: The Role of Tenancy." in *Research in Economic History*, Vol. 10. ed. Paul J. Uselding. Greenwich, CT: JAI Press, 1986.

12123. Alter, Jonathan. "Degrees of Discomfort. Is Homophobia Equivalent to Racism." *Newsweek* (12 March 1990).

12124. Applebome, Peter. "At The Heart of Anguish on Getting Past Racism." *New York Times*, 30 May 1990. [Shelby Steele]

12125. Baird, Robert M., and Stuart E. Rosenbaum, eds. *Bigotry, Prejudice, and Hatred. Definition, Causes, and Solution*. Buffalo, NY: Prometheus Books, 1992.

12126. Banton, Michael. "The Idiom of Race: A Critique of Presentism." in *Research in Race and Ethnic Relations*, eds. C. B. Marett, and C. Leggon. Greenwich, CT: JAI Press, 1980.

12127. _____. "The Relationship between Racism and Antisemitism." *Patterns of Prejudice* 26 (1992): 17-27.

12128. Banton, Michael, and Jeffrey Prager. "Interpreting United States Racial Ideology: A Debate." *Ethnic and Racial Studies* 10 (1987): 466-472.

12129. Blackman, Yvette H. "Racism Alive, Thriving in U.S." *Long Beach Press-Telegram*, 14 February 1994.

12130. Boas, Franz. "Human Faculty as Determined by Race." *Proceedings of the American Association for the Advancement of Science* 43 (1894): 301-327.

12131. _____. "Race Problems in America." *Science* no. 29 (1909): 838-849.

12132. Bonilla, Frank. "Ethnic Orbits: The Circulation of Capitals and People." *Contemporary Marxism* no. 10 (1985).

12133. Brewer, J. D. "Competing Understandings of Common Sense Understanding: A Brief Comment on 'Common Sense Racism'." *British Journal of Sociology* 35 (1984): 66-74.

12134. Brown, Tony. "Why Japanese Get Away with Racism in U.S." *Los Angeles Sentinel*, 6 April 1990.

12135. Cacas, Samuel. "Racism Isn't Just Black and White." *Daily Californian*, 1 September 1988.

12136. Carlton, Eric. "Race, Massacre and Genocide: An Exercise in Definitions." *International Journal of Sociology and Social Policy* 10 (1990): 80-93.

12137. Carr, Jay. "On the Racism of Colorblindness." *The Eighties* 5 (Winter 1985): 66-96.

12138. Center for the Study of Sport in Society. *Youth Attitudes on Racism*. Northeastern University, October 1990.

12139. Dadisman, M. "Racism in America: The Struggle Will Define Us." *Human Rights* 19 (Autumn 1992): 15.

12140. Darden, Joe T. "Blacks and Other Racial Minorities: The Significance of Color in Inequality." *Urban Geography* 10 (November-December 1989).

12141. Davis, F. James. *Who Is Black? One Nation's Definition*. University Park: Penn State Press, 1991.

12142. Dos Santos, Joel R. *O que e racismo*. Sao Paulo: Livraria Brasiliense Editora, 1980.

12143. Farley, Reynolds. "Blacks, Hispanics, and White Ethnic Groups: Are Blacks Uniquely Disadvantaged?" *American Economic Review* 80 (May 1990).

12144. "Forum [on the Concept of Ethnicity]." *Journal of American Ethnic History* 12 (Autumn 1992): 3-90, four articles.

12145. Froman, Robert. *Racism*. New York: Dell, 1972. [Racism against nonblacks]

12146. Genoves, S. "The Myth of Racism." in *Aggression and War. Their Biological and Social Bases*, eds. J. Grobel, and R. A. Hinde. New York: Cambridge University Press, 1989.

12147. Giraud, Michel. "The Distracted Look: Ethnocentrism, Xenophobia or Racism?" *Dialectical Anthropology* 12 (1987): 413- 419.

12148. Glaude, E. S. "An Analysis of the Cress Theory of Color Confrontation." *Journal of Black Studies* 22 (December 1991): 284- 293.

12149. Gloor, Pierre-Andre. "A propos de la xenophobie et du racisme." *Anthropologie* 84 (1980): 583-601.

12150. Goldberg, David T., ed. *Anatomy of Racism*. Minneapolis: University of Minnesota Press, 1990.

12151. Goldberg, David T. "Racism and Rationality: The Need for a New Critique." *Philosophy of the Social Sciences* 20 (September 1990): 317-350.

12152. _____. "The Semantics of Race." *Ethnic and Racial Studies* 15 (October 1992): 543-569.

12153. Gomberg, P. "Patriotism Is Like Racism." *Ethics* 101 (October 1990).

12154. Gotanda, Neil. "Asian American Rights and the 'Miss Saigon Syndrome'." in *Asian-Americans and the Supreme Court*, pp. 1087- 1103. ed. Hyung-chan Kim. Greenwood. ["Racism against Asian Americans really does exist."]

12155. Green, Marci, and Bob Carter. "'Races' and 'Race Makers': The Politics of Racialization." *Sage Race Relations Abstracts* 13 (May 1988).

12156. Hacker, Andrew. "Playing the Racial Card." *New York Review of Books* (24 October 1991).

12157. _____. *Two Nations. Black and White, Separate, Hostile, Unequal*. New York: Scribner's, 1992.

12158. Hagan, William T. "Full Blood, Mixed Blood, Genetic, and Ersatz: The Problem of Indian Identity." *Arizona West* 27 (Winter 1985): 309-326.

12159. Haker, Andrew. "On Inequality, Race and a Nation Divided." *Boston Globe*, 29 March 1992. [Interview]

12160. Hamanaka, Sheila. *The Journey: Japanese Americans, Racism, and Renewal*. New York: Orchard Books, 1990.

12161. Hayes-Bautista, David E., and Gregory Rodriguez. "Latinos Are Redefining Notions of Racial Identity." *Los Angeles Times*, 13 January 1993.

12162. Hollister, Frederick J. "Skin Color and Life Chances of Puerto Ricans." *Caribbean Studies* 9 (1969): 87-94.

12163. Holmes, Steven A. "Behind a Dark Mirror: Traditional Victims Give Vent to Racism." *New York Times*, 13 February 1994.

12164. Hong, Kate. "The Flip Side of Racism." *KoreAm Journal* (9 August 1990): 13.

12165. Houston, Velina H. "Defining Race: A View of Biological Truth for Multiracial Persons." *Multi-racial Asian Times 1990* 11- 14. [Newsletter of American League, Santa Monica, CA]

12166. Jacoby, Jeff. "Racism Now the Exception." *Boston Globe*, 23 August 1994.

12167. Jacoby, Susan. "The 'Logic' of Racism." *Present Tense* 17 (March-April 1990): 12-13.

12168. Jennings, James. "The Foundation of American Racism: Defining Bigotry, Racism, and Racial Hierarchy." *Trotter Institute Review* 4 (Fall 1990): 12-16.

12169. Kaufman, Jonathan. "The Color Line." *Boston Globe Magazine* (18 June 1989). [First of two articles]

12170. Kleinpenning, G., and L. Hagendorn. "Forms of Racism and the Cumulative Dimension of Ethnic Attitudes." *Social Psychology Quarterly* 56 (March 1993): 21-36.

12171. Lacy, Michael G. *Toward a Rhetorical Conception of Civil Racism*. Ph.D. diss., University of Texas, 1992. UMO #9239293.

12172. Lee, Sharon M. "Racial Classification in the U.S. Census 1890-1990." *Ethnic and Racial Studies* 16 (January 1993): 75-94.

12173. Liu, Tessie. "Teaching the Differences among Women from a Historical Perspective: Rethinking Race and Gender as Social Categories." *Women's Studies International Forum* 14 (1991): 265- 276.

12174. Lowy, Richard. "Yuppie Racism: Race Relations in the 1980s." *Journal of Black Studies* 21 (June 1991): 445-464.

12175. Martinez, Elizabeth. "There's More to Racism than Black and White." *Z Magazine* 3 (November 1990): 48-52. [Chicano movement]

12176. Mathews, Thomas. *The Question of Color in Puerto Rico*. San Juan: University of Puerto Rico, Institute of Caribbean Studies, 1968.

12177. Mazunder, Sucheta. "Racist Responses to Racism: The Aryan Myth and South Asians in the United States." *South Asia Bulletin* 9 (1989): 47-55.

12178. Memmi, Albert. *Le racisme: Description, Definition, Traitment*. Paris: Gallimard, 1982.

12179. Miller, William H. *The Concept of Race: A Methodology for the Exploration of the Use of Race in Policy Development*. Ph.D. diss., Saint Louis University, 1991. UMO #9131015.

12180. Mintz, Sidney W. "Groups, Group-boundaries and the Perception of 'Race'." *Comparative Studies in Society and History* 13 (1971): 437-450.

12181. Morin, Richard. "Racism on the Left and Right." *Washington Post*, 6 March 1994.

12182. Muga, David A. "Native Americans and the Nationalities Question." *NST. Nature, Society, and Thought* 1 (Fall 1987).

12183. Muir, Donal E. "Race: The Mythic Root of Racism." *Sociological Inquiry* 63 (Summer 1993): 339-350.

12184. Nelson, William Javier. "Racial Definition: Background for Divergence." *Phylon* 47 (Winter 1987): 318-326.

12185. Nye, William P. "The Emergent Idea of Race: A Civilization-Analytic Approach to Race and Racialism in the United States." *Theory and Society* 5 (May 1978): 345-372.

12186. Pico de Hernandez, Isabel. "The Quest for Race, Sex and Ethnic Equality in Puerto Rico." *Caribbean Studies* 14 (1975): 127-141.

12187. "The Politics of Ethnic Construction: Hispanic, Chicano, Latino." *Latin American Perspectives* 19 (Autumn 1992): 5 articles.

12188. Prager, Jeffrey. "American Political Culture and the Shifting Meaning of Race." *Ethnic and Racial Studies* 10 (January 1987): 62-81.

12189. Puddington, Arch. "Is White Racism the Problem?" *Commentary* 94 (July 1992): 31-36.

12190. Quindlen, Anna. "All of These You Are." *New York Times*, 28 June 1992.

12191. Ramirez, Albert. "Racism toward Hispanics: The Culturally Monolithic Society." in *Eliminating Racism: Profiles in Controversy*, pp. 137-157. eds. P. A. Katz, and D. A. Taylor. New York: Plenum, 1988.

12192. Reinsch, Paul S. "The Negro Race and European Civilization." *American Journal of Sociology* 11 (1905): 147-167.

12193. Reynolds, L. T. "A Retrospective on Race: The Career of a Concept." *Sociological Focus* 25 (February 1992): 1-14.

12194. Riaklin, E. "The Colours and Dresses of Racism in America." *International Journal of Social Economics* 17 (1990).

12195. Riggs, F. W. "Ethnicity, Nationalism, Race, Minority: A Semantic/Onomantic Exercise. Part 2." *International Sociology* 6 (December 1991): 443-464.

12196. Rodriguez, Clara E., and H. Cordera Guzman. "Placing Race in Context." *Ethnic and Racial Studies* 15 (October 1992): 523-542.

12197. Ross, Andrew. "Ballots, Bulets, or Batman: Can Cultural Studies Do the Right Thing?" *Screen* 31 (Spring 1990): 26-44. [Racism]

12198. Roth, Byron M. "Social Psychology's 'Racism'." *Public Interest* no. 98 (Winter 1990): 26-36.

12199. Royce, Anna Peterson. *Ethnic Identity: Strategies of Diversity*. Bloomington: Indiana University Press, 1982.

12200. Sheehan, Henry. "When Asians are Caucasians." *Boston Globe*, 19 August 1990.

12201. Skillings, J. H., and J. E. Dobbins. "Racism As a Disease: Etiology and Treatment Implications." *Journal of Counseling and Development* 70 (September-October 1991): 206-212.

12202. Sniderman, Paul M. and others. "The New Racism." *American Journal of Political Science* 35 (May 1991): 423-447.

12203. Stannard, David E. "On Racism and Genocide." in his *American Holocaust. Columbus and the Conquest of the New World*, Oxford U.P., 1992.

12204. Stein, Judith. "Defining the Race, 1890-1930." in *The Invention of Ethnicity*, ed. Werner Sollors. New York: Oxford University Press, 1989.

12205. Stepan, Nancy Leys, and Sander L. Gilman. "Appropriating the Idioms of Science: The Rejection of Scientific Racism." in *The Bounds of Race*, pp. 72-103. ed. Dominick La Capra. Cornell U. Press, 1991.

12206. "Stranded, for Security's Sake." *New York Times*, 27 August 1994. ["Bridgeport Residents Cry Racism as Mall Limits Bus Service"]

12207. Taguieff, Pierre-Andre. "Les Presuppositions definitionnelles d'un indefinissable: le racisme." *Mots* no. 8 (1984).

12208. Tanaka, Togo. "How to Survive Racism in America's Free Society." in *Voices Long Silent: An Oral Inquiry into the Japanese American Evacuation*, eds. A. Hansen, and Betty E. Mitson. Fullerton, CA, 1974.

12209. Thomas, Gail E. "Puritans, Indians, and the Concept of Race." *New England Quarterly* 48 (March 1975): 3-27.

12210. Thomas, Gail E. "Discerning the Posture of American Race Relations in the 1980s: Competitive versus Paternalistic?" *Sociological Spectrum* 9 (1989): 1-21.

12211. Williams, Lena. "Growing Black Debate on Racism: When Is It Real, When An Excuse?" *New York Times*, 5 April 1992.

12212. Williams, Vernon J., Jr. *From a Caste to a Minority: Changing Attitudes of American Sociologists toward Afro- Americans, 1896-1945*. Westport, CT: Greenwood, 1989.

12213. Winkler, Karen J. "The Significance of Race." *Chronicle of Higher Education* (11 May 1994). [The meanings of race in black communities]

12214. Yeboah, Samuel K. *The Ideology of Racism*. London: Hansib, 1988.

12215. Zack, Naomi. *Race and Mixed Race*. Temple University Press, 1993.

RACISM -- EXPORTING

12216. Borstelmann, Thomas. *Apartheid's Reluctant Uncle. The United States and Southern Africa in the Early Cold War*. Oxford U.P., 1993.

12217. Boyle, Francis A. "The Hypocrisy and Racism Behind the Formulation of U.S. Human Rights Foreign Policy." in his *Defending Civil Resistance Under International Law*, chapter 7. Dobbs Ferry, NY: Transnational Publishers, 1987.

12218. Brantley, Daniel. "Black Americans as Participants in the Foreign Service." *Crisis* 93 (1986): 30-33.

12219. Chapman, Gregory D. "Taking Up the White Man's Burden: Tennesseans in the Philippine Insurrection, 1899." *Tennessee Historical Quarterly* 47 (Spring 1988): 27-40.

12220. Colenbrander, Sarah. *Commerce, Race, and Diplomacy: Henry Shelton Sanford and the American Recognition of the International Association of the Congo*. University of Montana: Master's thesis, 1989.

12221. Drinnon, Richard. *Facing West: The Metaphysics of Empire- Building and Indian-Hating*. Minneapolis: University of Minnesota Press, 1980.

12222. Hambleton, James R. *Mask of Hypocrisy: Wilsonian Racism and Germanophobia in the United States. Dictatorship of Haiti, the Formative Years, 1915-1918*. San Jose State University: Master's thesis, 1991.

12223. Hellwig, David J. "The Afro-American Press and Woodrow Wilson's Mexican Policy, 1913-1917." *Phylon* 48 (1987): 261-270.

12224. Hero, Alfred O. "American Negroes and U.S. Foreign Policy: 1937-1967." *Journal of Conflict Resolution* 8 (June 1969): 220- 251.

12225. Hunt, Alfred N. *Haiti's Influence on Antebellum America*. Baton Rouge, LA, 1988.

12226. Kaplan, Amy. "'Left Alone with America': The Absence of Empire in the Study of American Culture." in *Cultures of United States Imperialism*, pp. 3-21. eds. Amy Kaplan, and Donald E. Pease. Duke U. Press, 1993.

12227. Kaplan, Amy, and Donald E. Pease, eds. *Cultures of United States Imperialism*. Duke U. Press, 1993.

12228. Kennedy, P. W. "Race and American Expansion in Cuba and Puerto Rico, 1895-1905." *Journal of Black Studies* 1 (1971): 306- 316.

12229. Krenn, Michael L. "'Their Proper Share': The Changing Role of Racism in U.S. Foreign Policy since World War One." *Nature, Society, and Thought* 4 (January-April 1991): 57-79.

12230. Lash, William H., III. "Unwelcome Imports: Racism, Sexism, and Foreign Investment." *Michigan Journal of International Law* 13 (Fall 1991): 1-42.

12231. Lauren, Paul G. *Power and Prejudice: The Politics and Diplomacy of Racial Discrimination*. Boulder, CO: Westview, 1988.

12232. Le Melle, Tilden J. "Race, International Relations, U.S. Foreign Policy, and the African Liberation Struggle." *Journal of Black Studies* 3 (1972): 95-109.

12233. Lewis, Gordon K. "The Imperialist Ideology and Mentality: America Stands At the Top of the World." *Caribbean Affairs* 1 (1988): 209-230.

12234. Marks, George P., III, ed. *The Black Press Views American Imperialism (1898-1900)*. New York: Arno Press, 1971.

12235. Mendez Gonzalez, Rosalinda. "Class Struggles, 'Operation Wetback' and 'Operation Guatemala': The Cold War Objectives of Domestic Racism." in *Research in Political Economy*, vol. 10. ed. Paul Zarembka. Greenwich, CT: JAI Press, 1987.

12236. Michaels, Walter B. "Anti-Imperial Americanism." in *Cultures of United States Imperialism*, pp. 365-391. eds. Amy Kaplan, and Donald E. Pease. Duke U. Press, 1993. [Anti-imperialism and racial identity]

12237. Miller, Stuart Creighton. *"Benevolent Assimilation." The American Conquest of the Philippines, 1899-1903*. Yale U.P., 1982.

12238. Noer, Thomas J. *Cold War and Black Liberation: The United States and White Rule in Africa, 1948-1968*. Columbia: University of Missouri Press, 1985.

12239. Panella, Frank. *Lebensraum and Manifest Destiny: A Comparative Study in the Justification of Expansion*. Washington, DC, 1950.

12240. Pease, Donald E. "New Perspectives on U.S. Culture and Imperialism." in *Cultures of United States Imperialism*, pp. 22- 37. eds. Amy Kaplan, and Donald E. Pease. Duke U. Press, 1993.

12241. Plummer, Brenda G., and Donald R. Culverson. "Black Americans and Foreign Affairs: A Reassessment." *Sage Race Relations Abstracts* 12 (February 1987): 21-31.

12242. Redding, J. Sanders. *An American in India: A Personal Report on the India Dilemma and the Nature of Her Conflicts*. Indianapolis, IN: Bobbs-Merrill, 1954.

12243. Richardson, Henry J., III. "The International Implications of the Los Angeles Riots." *Denver University Law Review* 70 (1993): 213-236.

12244. Roberts, Alden E. "Racism Sent and Received: Americans And Vietnamese View One Another." *Research in Race and Ethnic Relations* 5 (1988): 75-97.

12245. Schwabe, Klaus. "The Global Role of the United States and Its Imperial Consequences, 1898-1973." in *Imperialism and After: Continuities and Discontinuities*, pp. 13-33. eds. Wolfgang J. Mommsen, and Jurgen Osterhammel. Allen and Unwin, 1986.

12246. Shenton, James P. "Imperialism and Racism." in *Essays in American Historiography*, eds. Donald Sheehan, and H. C. Syrett. Columbia U. Press, 1960.

12247. Simpson, Christopher. *The Splendid Blond Beast. Money, Law, and Genocide in the Twentieth Century*. Grove Press, 1993.

12248. Wald, Priscilla. "Terms of Assimilation. Legislating Subjectivity in the Emerging Nation." in *Cultures of United States Imperialism*, pp. 59-84. eds. Amy Kaplan, and Donald E. Pease. Duke U. Press, 1993.

12249. White, Philip V. "Race Against Time: The Role of Racism in U.S. Foreign Relations." in *Impacts of Racism on White Americans*, pp. 177-189. eds. Benjamin P. Bowser, and Raymond G. Hunt. Beverly Hills, CA: Sage, 1981.

12275. Demo, David H., and M. Hughes. "Socialization and Racial Identity among Black Americans." *Social Psychology Quarterly* 53 (December 1990).

12276. Dukes, R. L. "Ethnic and Gender Differences in Self- Esteem." *Youth and Society* 22 (March 1991): 318-338.

12277. Ellis, G. W. "The Psychology of American Race Prejudice." *Journal of Race Development* 5 (1915): 297-315.

12278. Eysenck, Hans J. "The Causes and Cures of Prejudice-A Reply." *Personality and Individual Differences* 11 (1990). [See Ray, below]

12279. French, Mary Ann. "Subtle Shades Of the Rainbow." *Washington Post*, 7 February 1994. [About Shurlee Taylor Haizlip and the role of color in African American life]

12280. Fulani, Lenora B., ed. *The Psychopathology of Everyday Racism and Sexism*. New York: Harrington Park Press, 1988.

12281. Gilman, S. L. "Freud, Race, and Gender." in *Psychoanalysis, Feminism, and the Future of Gender*, pp. 137-162. eds. J. H. Smith, and A. M. Mahfowz. Johns Hopkins University Press, 1994.

12282. Goleman, Daniel. "Data Show Low Esteem Lingers in Black Youth." *New York Times*, 31 August 1987.

12283. Griffith, Ezra E. H. and others, eds. *Racial and Ethnic Identity. Psychological Development and Creative Expression*. Routledge, 1994.

12284. Group for the Advancement of Psychiatry. *Us and Them: The Psychology of Ethnonationalism*. New York: Brunner/Mazel, 1987.

12285. Helms, Janet E., ed. *Black and White Racial Identity: Theory, Research, and Practice*. New York: Greenwood, 1990.

12286. Houston, Lawrence N. *Psychological Principles and the Black Experience*. Lanham, MD: University Press of America, 1990.

12287. Hughes, Michael, and David H. Demo. "Self-Perceptions of Black Americans: Self-esteem and Personal Efficacy." *American Journal of Sociology* 95 (July 1989): 132-159.

12288. Iheanacho, S. O. "Minority Self-Concept: A Research Review." *Journal of Instructional Psychology* 15 (March 1988): 3- 11.

12289. Jackson, Gerald. "The Origin and Development of Black Psychology: Implications for Black Studies and Human Behavior." *Studia Africana* 1 (September 1979).

12290. Jamison, Charles N., Jr. "Racism, the Hurt That Men Won't Name." *Essence* (November 1992).

12291. Kaplan, M. S., and G. Marks. "Adverse Effects of Acculturation: Psychological Distress among Mexican American Young Adults." *Social Science and Medicine* 31 (1990).

12292. King, Joyce E. "Dysconscious Racism: Ideology, Identity, and the Miseducation of Teachers." *Journal of Negro Education* 60 (1991): 133-147.

12293. Lawrence, Charles R., III "The Id, the Ego, and Equal Protection: Reckoning with Unconscious Racism." *Stanford Law Review* 39 (January 1987).

12294. Longres, John F., Jr. "Racism and Its Effects on Puerto Rican Continentals." *Social Casework* 55 (February 1974): 67-75.

12295. Lynch, Frederick R. "Race Unconsciousness and the White Male." *Society* 29 (January-February 1992): 30-35.

12296. Mabry, Marcus, and Patricia Rogers. "Bias Begins at Home." *Newsweek* (5 August 1991).

12297. Mills, Bette D. *Emotional Reactions of African-Americans to Viewing Racist Incidents*. Ph.D. diss., University of Maryland, 1990. UMO #9110331.

12298. Neal, Fannie Allen. "Confronting Prejudice and Discrimination: Personal Recollections and Observations." in *Opening Doors*, eds. Harry J. Knopke and others. University of Alabama Press, 1991.

12299. Newby, Robert G. "Racial Acts Stem From Resentment." *Detroit News*, 11 August 1989.

12300. Nobles, Wade W. "African (Black) Psychology: Transformed and Transforming." *Sage Race Relations Abstracts* 11 (February 1986): 4-48.

12301. Ostow, Mortimer. "A Psychoanalytic Approach to the Problems of Prejudice, Discrimination, and Persecution." in *Opening Doors*, eds. Harry J. Knopke and others. University of Alabama Press, 1991.

12302. Outlaw, Marpessa Dawn. "Mixed Like Me. Scrapping Mulatto Myths." *Village Voice* (24 September 1991).

12303. Phinney, Jean S. "Ethnic Identity in Adolescents and Adults: Review of Research." *Psychological Bulletin* 108 (November 1990).

12304. Pierce, Chester M. "Offensive Mechanisms." in *The Black Seventies*, ed. Floyd B. Barbour. Boston, MA: Porter Sargent, 1970.

12305. Ponterotto, Joseph G. "Racial/Ethnic Minority Research in the Journal of Counseling Psychology: A Content Analysis and Methodological Critique." *Journal of Counseling Psychology* 35 (October 1988): 410-418. [1976-1986]

12306. Ray, J. J. "Racial Extremism and Normal Prejudice: A Comment." *Personality and Individual Differences* 11 (1990). [See Eysenck, above]

12307. Sampson, Edward E. *Celebrating the Other: A Dialogic Account of Human Nature*. Westview Press, 1993.

12308. Taylor, Jerome. "Relationship between Internalized Racism and Marital Satisfaction." *Journal of Black Psychology* 16 (Spring 1990): 45-53.

12309. Tuch, Steven A. "Race Differences in the Antecedents of Social Distance Attitudes." *Sociology and Social Research* 72 (April 1988): 181-184.

12310. Watts, R. J. "Elements of a Psychology of Human Diversity." *Journal of Community Psychology* 20 (April 1992): 116- 131.

12311. Wells, Elmer E. *The Mythical Negative Black Self-Concept*. Ph.D. diss., University of New Mexico, 1971.

12312. Wright, Bobby E. *The Psychopathic Racial Personality and Other Essays*. Chicago, IL: Third World Press, 1985.

RACISM -- SCHOLARLY

12313. Adotevi, Stanislas. "Ethnology and the Repossession of the World." *Discourse* 11 (1989): 19-46.

12314. Barkan, Elazar. *The Retreat of Scientific Racism. Changing Concepts of Race in Britain and the United States between the World Wars*. New York: Cambridge U.P., 1991.

12315. _____. "Mobilizing Scientists Against Nazi Racism, 1933-1939." in *Bones, Bodies, Behavior. Essays on Biological Anthropology*, ed. G. W. Stocking. Madison: University of Wisconsin Press, 1988.

12316. Barsh, Russel L. "Are Anthropologists Hazardous to Indians' Health." *Journal of Ethnic Studies* 15 (1988): 1-38.

12317. Beckwith, Jonathan R. "The Science of Racism." in *How Harvard Rules. Reason in the Service of Empire*, pp. 243-247. ed. John Trumpbour. Boston, MA: South End Press, 1989.

12318. Bernal, Martin. *Black Athena: The Afroasiatic Roots of Classical Civilization. Volume I: The Fabrication of Ancient Greece, 1785-1985*. New Brunswick, NJ: Rutgers University Press, 1987.

12319. Blauner, Robert, and David Wellman. "Toward the Decolonization of Social Research." in *The Death of White Sociology*, pp. 310-330. ed. Joyce A. Ladner. New York: Vintage, 1973.

12320. Bradford, Phillips Verner, and Harvey Blume. *Ota Benga. The Pygmy in the Zoo*. St. Martin's press, 1992. [1904-1906]

12321. Cernovsky, Z. Z. "Race and Brain Weight: A Note on J.P. Rushton's Conclusions." *Psychological Reports* 66 (February 1990).

12322. Dalal, Farhad. "The Racism of Jung." *Race and Class* 29 (Winter 1988): 1-22.

12323. Degler, Carl N. *In Search of Human Nature. The Decline and Revival of Darwinism in American Social Thought*. New York: Oxford University Press, 1991.

12324. Evans, Ross A. "Psychology's White Face." *Social Policy* 1 (March-April 1971): 54-58.

12325. Fairchild, Halford H. "Scientific Racism: The Cloak of Objectivity." *Journal of Social Issues* 47 (1991): 101-115.

12326. Fong, Melanie, and Larry O. Johnson. "The Eugenics Movement: Some Insights Into the Institutionalization of Racism." *Issues in Criminology* 9 (Fall 1974): 89-115.

12327. Giraud, Michel. "Ethnologie et racisme: le cas des études afro-américaines." *Ethnologie francaise* 18 (1988): 153-157.

12328. Goggin, Jacqueline. "Countering White Racist Scholarship: Carter G. Woodson and the Journal of Negro History." *Journal of Negro History* 68 (1983): 355-375.

12329. Graham, S. "Most of the Subjects Were White and Middle Class: Trends in Published Research on African Americans in Selected APA Journals, 1970-1989." *American Psychologist* 47 (May 1992): 629-639.

12330. Greene, J. C. "The American Debate on the Place of the Negro in Nature: 1780-1815." *Journal of the History of Ideas* 15 (1954): 384-396.

12331. Haghighat, Chapour. *Le racisme "scientifique": offensive contre l'egalite sociale...* Paris: Collin Science libre, 1988.

12332. Helms, Janet E. "Eurocentrism Strikes in Strange Ways and In Unusual Places." *Counseling Psychologist* 17 (October 1989): 643-647.

12333. Horsman, Reginald. "Scientific Racism and the American Indian in the Mid-Nineteenth Century." *American Quarterly* 27 (1975): 152-168.

12334. Hughes, Everett M. "Ethnocentric Sociology." *Social Forces* 40 (1961): 1-4.

12335. Hyatt, Marshall. *Franz Boas, Social Activist: The Dynamics of Ethnicity*. Westport, CT: Greenwood, 1990. [Critique of racism in U.S. social science]

12336. Jackson, Derrick Z. "The Force of Words." *Boston Globe*, 11 August 1989. [Analysis of racist language used by a university professor.]

12337. Jarausch, Komad H. "The Perils of Professionalism: Lawyers, Teachers, and Engineers in Nazi Germany." *German Studies Review* 9 (1986): 107-137.

12338. Kan, Sergei. "Why the Aristocrats were 'Heavy' or How Ethnopsychology Legitimized Inequality Among the Tlingit." *Dialectical Anthropology* 14 (1989).

12339. Killian, Lewis M. "Working for the Segregationist Establishment." *Journal of Applied Behavioral Science* 25 (1989): 487-498. [Florida, 1954]

12340. Leslie, C. and others. "Scientific Racism: Reflections on Peer Review, Science and Ideology." *Social Science and Medicine* 31 (1990).

12341. Livingstone, D. N. "Science and Society: Nathaniel S. Shaler and Racial Ideology." *Transactions, Institute of British Geographers* no. 9 (1984).

12342. Lorimer, Douglas A. "Theoretical Racism in Late-Victorian Anthropology, 1870-1900." *Victorian Studies* 31 (1988): 405-430.

12343. Lurie, E. "Louis Agassiz and the Rise of Man." *Isis* 45 (1954): 227-242.

12344. Mabee, Carleton. "Margaret Mead's Approach to Controversial Public Issues: Racial Boycott in the AAAS." *Historian* 48 (1986): 191-208. [Amer. Assoc. for the Advancement of Science]

12345. Mazunder, Sucheta. "Racist Responses to Racism: The Aryan Myth and South Asians in the United States." *South Asia Bulletin* 9 (1989): 47-55.

12346. Mehler, Barry A. "Foundation for Fascism: The New Eugenic Movement in the United States." *Patterns of Prejudice* 23 (Winter 1989-90): 17-25.

12347. _____. *A History of the American Eugenics Society, 1921-1940*. Ph.D. diss., University of Illinois, 1988. UMO #8823199.

12348. _____. "The New Eugenics: Academic Racism in the US Today." *Science for the People* 15 (May-June 1983).

12349. Murphy, J. "A Most Respectable Prejudice: Inequality in Educational Research and Policy." *British Journal of Sociology* 41 (March 1990).

12350. Novick, Peter. *That Noble Dream: The "Objectivity Question" and the American Historical Profession*. New York: Cambridge University Press, 1988.

12351. Remy, Anselme. "Anthropology: For Whom and What?" *Black Scholar* (April 1976): 12-16.

12352. Rogin, Michael P. "Liberal Society and the Indian Question." *Politics and Society* 1 (1971): 269-312.

12353. Rosaldo, Renato. *Culture and Truth: The Remaking of Social Analysis*. Beacon Press, 1989. [Critique of American cultural anthropology]

12354. Ross, Edward A. "The Causes of Race Superiority." *Annals* 18 (1901): 67-89.

12355. Roth, B. M. "Social Science and Black/White. 3. Social Psychology's Racism." *Public Interest* no. 98 (Winter 1990).

12356. Salloch, Erika. "Traces of Fascist Ideology in American Professional Journals, 1933-1945" in *Teaching German in America: Prolegomena to a History*, pp. 253-270. eds. David P. Benseler and others. Madison: University of Wisconsin Press, 1988.

12357. Senecal, Michael D. *American Psychology and the Comparison of Races, 1890-1937*. University of South Carolina: Master's thesis, 1989.

12358. Skutnabb-Kangas, Tove. "Legitimating or Delegitimating New Forms of Racism: The Role of Researchers." *Journal of Multilingual and Multicultural Development* 11 (1990): 77-100.

12359. Smith, Courtland L., and Kenneth L. Beals. "Cultural Correlates with Cranial Capacity." *American Anthropologist* 92 (March 1990).

12360. Smith, John David, ed. *Anti-Black Thought 1863-1925. "The Negro Problem"*. Garland, 1992. [11-volume anthology of racist writings]

12361. Stanfield, John H., III, ed. *A History of Race Relations Research. First Generation Recollections*. Sage, 1993.

12362. _____. *Race and Ethnicity in Research Methods*. Sage, 1993.

12363. Stuart, Paul H. "The Kingsley House Extension Program: Racial Segregation in a 1940s Settlement Program." *Social Science Review* 66 (March 1992): 112-120.

12364. Sue, D. W., and S. Sue. ""Ethnic Minorities" Resistance to Being Researched." *Professional Psychology* 3 (1972): 11-18.

12365. Suzuki, Peter T. "When Black Was White: Misapplied Anthropology in Wartime America." *Man and Life* 12 (January-June 1986): 1-13.

12366. Talbot, Steve. "The Meaning of Wounded Knee 1973: Indian Self-government and the Role of Anthropology." in *The Politics of Anthropology*, pp. 227-258. eds. G. Huizer, and B. Mannheim. The Hague: Mouton, 1979.

12367. Turner, James, and W. Eric Perkins. "Toward a Critique of Social Science." *Black Scholar* (April 1976): 2-11.

12368. UNESCO. *Racism, Science, and Pseudo-science*. Paris: UNESCO, 1983.

12369. Vogel, Virgil J. "The Blackout of Native American Cultural Achievements." *American Indian Quarterly* 11 (1987): 11-35.

RACISM -- TESTING

12370. Smith, Susan J. "Race and Racism." *Urban Geography* 10 (November-December 1989).

12371. Tjosvold, Ida J. *Moral Reasoning Regarding Minorities: An Alberta Test*. University of Calgary: Master's thesis, 1988.

RACISM -- THEORY

12372. Allahar, Anton L. "When Black First Became Worth Less." *International Journal of Comparative Sociology* 34 (January-April 1993): 39-55.

12373. Allen, Theodore W. *The Invention of the White Race. Vol I: Racial Oppression and Social Control.* Routledge, 1993.

12374. Andersen, Margaret L. "American Race Relations 1970-1975: A Critical Review of the Literature." *Sage Race Relations Abstracts* 2 (November 1976): 1-34.

12375. Anthias, Floya. "Race and Class Revisited-Conceptualizing Race and Racisms." *Sociological Review* 38 (February 1990).

12376. Aptheker, Herbert. "White Chauvinism: The Struggle Inside the Ranks." in his *The Unfolding Drama: Studies in U.S. History*, pp. 120-129. New York: International Publishers, 1978.

12377. Balibar, Etienne. "Gibt es einen 'neuen Rassismus?'." *Das Argument* 31 (May-June 1989): 369-380.

12378. Balibar, Etienne, and Immanuel Wallerstein. *Race, Nation and Class. Ambiguous Identities*, Translated by Chris Turner. New York: Verso, 1991.

12379. Banton, Michael. "The Nature and Causes of Racism and Racial Discrimination." *International Sociology* 7 (March 1992): 69-84.

12380. _____. "The Race Relations Problematic." *British Journal of Sociology* 42 (March 1991): 115-130.

12381. Barkan, Elazar. *The Retreat of Scientific Racism: Changing Concepts of Race in Britain and the United States between the World Wars*. Cambridge U.P., 1992.

12382. Baron, Harold M. "Racism Transformed: The Implications of the 1960s." *Review of Radical Political Economics* 17 (Fall 1985): 10-33.

12383. Bauman, Zygmunt. "Racism, Anti-Racism and Moral Progress." *Arena Journal* no. 1 (1993).

12384. Bell, Derrick. "Racism: A Prophecy for the Year 2000." *Rutgers Law Review* 42 (Autumn 1989).

12385. _____. "White Superiority in America: Its Legal Legacy, Its Economic Costs." *Villanova Law Review* 33 (September 1988): 767-779.

12386. Billig, Michael. "The Notion of 'Prejudice': Some Rhetorical and Ideological Aspects." *Text* 8 (1988): 91-110.

12387. _____. "Prejudice and Tolerance." in *Ideological Dilemmas*, pp. 100-123. eds. Billig and others. London: Sage, 1988.

12388. Birrell, Susan. "Racial Relations Theories and Sport: Suggestions for a More Critical Analysis." *Sociology of Sport Journal* 6 (1989): 212-227.

12389. Blakey, Michael. *Race, Racism, and the American Way*. Monthly Review Press, 1993.

12390. Blaut, J. M. "The Theory of Cultural Racism." *Antipode* 24 (October 1992): 289-299. [See Harvey, below]

12391. Bogardus, E. *A Forty-year Racial Distance Study*. University of Southern California, 1967.

12392. Bonacich, Edna. "Capitalism and Racial Oppression: In Search of Consciousness." in *Race, Class and Urban Change*, vol. 1. pp. 181-194. ed. Jerry Lembcke. Greenwich, CT: JAI Press, 1989.

12393. _____. "Racism in Advanced Capitalist Society: Comments on William J. Wilson's The Truly Disadvantaged." *Journal of Sociology and Social Welfare* 16 (December 1989): 41-55.

12394. Boyd, D. A. C. "The Historical Materialist-Symbolist Theory of Race Discrimination." *Social and Economic Studies* 36 (June 1987): 123-143.

12395. Breitman, George. *Race Prejudice. How It Began, When It Will End*. New York: Pathfinder, 1971.

12396. Case, Charles E. and others. "Social Determinants of Racial Prejudice." *Sociological Perspectives* 32 (1989): 469-483.

12397. Cherry, Robert. "Shifts in Radical Theories of Inequality." *Review of Radical Political Economics* 20 (Summer and Fall 1988): 184-189.

12398. Christian, Barbara. "The Race for Theory." *Cultural Critique* 6 (Spring 1987): 51-63. [Questions concept of "minority."]

12399. Clegg, Sue. "Theories of Racism." *International Socialism* no. 37 (Winter 1988): 93-117.

12400. Cole, Mike. "'Race' and Class or 'Race', Class, Gender and Community?: A Critical Appraisal of the Racialised Fraction of the Working-class Thesis." *British Journal of Sociology* 40 (1989): 118-129. [Critique of Robert Miles]

12401. Conzen, Kathleen N. and others. "The Invention of Ethnicity: A Perspective from the USA." *Journal of American Ethnic History* 12 (Fall 1992): 3-63.

12402. Cook, Anthony E. "Cultural Racism and the Limits of Rationality in the Saga of Rodney King." *Denver University Law Review* 70 (1993): 297-312.

12403. Coughlin, Ellen K. "Sociologists Examine the Complexities of Racial and Ethnic Identity in America." *Chronicle of Higher Education* (24 March 1993).

12404. Cox, Oliver C. *Race Relations: Elements and Social Dynamics*. Detroit, MI: Wayne State University Press, 1976.

12405. Crenshaw, Kimberle, and Gary Peller. "Reel Time/Real Justice." *Denver University Law Review* 70 (1993): 283-296.

12406. Cress-Welsing, Frances. *The Isis Papers: The Keys to the Colors*. Chicago, IL: Third World Press.

12407. Degler, Carl N. "Racism in the United States: An Essay Review." *Journal of Southern History* 47 (February 1992).

12408. Dumont, L. "Caste, Racism and Stratification." in *Symbolic Anthropology: A Reader in the Study of Symbols and Meanings*, eds. J. L. Dolgin and others. New York: Columbia University Press, 1977.

12409. Duster, Troy. "The Structure of Privilege and Its Universe of Discourse." *American Sociologist* 2 (1976): 73-78.

12410. Dyson, Michael E. "Melanin Madness." *Emerge* (February 1992).

12411. Essed, Philomena. *Understanding Everyday Racism. An Interdisciplinary Theory*. London: Sage, 1991. [U.S. and Netherlands]

12412. Farley, Reynolds. *Racial Conflict in the United States: The Melting Pot and the Color Line*. Population Studies Center, University of Michigan, 1991.

12413. Feagin, Joe R., and Hernan Vera. *White Racism. The Basics*. Routledge, 1994.

12414. Fein, Helen. "Genocide-A Sociological Perspective." *Current Sociology* 38 (Spring 1990): entire issue.

12415. Fernando, Suman. "Racism and Xenophobia." *Innovation* 6 (1993): 9-19.

12416. Fichtenbaum, Rudy. "A Critique of the Segmentation Theory of Racial Discrimination." *NST: Nature, Society, and Thought* 3 (1990): 389-400.

12417. Finot, Jean. *Race Prejudice*, Translated by Florence Wade- Evans. Miami, FL, 1969, orig. 1906.

12418. Flew, Antony. "Three Concepts of Racism: 'Anti-racism', Prejudice (and Worse)." *Encounter* 75 (July-August 1990): 63-66.

12419. Fontette, Francois de. *Le racisme*, 4th ed. Paris: Presses Universitaires de France, 1981.

12420. Frankel, Charles and others. *La science face au racisme*. Paris: Fayard, 1981.

12421. Fucciool, John J. *Colonized Outcaste Ethnic Groups in American Society*. Ph.D. diss., City University of New York, 1990. [Afro-Americans and Puerto Ricans]. UMO #9020758.

12422. Fuchs, Stephan A., and Charles E. Case. "Prejudice as Lifeform." *Sociological Inquiry* 59 (1989): 310-317.

12423. Gay, Kathlyn. *Bigotry*. Hillsdale, NJ: Enslow Publishers, 1989. [Written for young people]

12424. Goldberg, Barry, and Colin Greer. "American Visions, Ethnic Dreams: Public Ethnicity and the Sociological Imagination." *Sage Race Relations Abstracts* 15 (February 1990): 5-60.

12425. Goleman, Daniel. "As Bias Crime Seems to Rise, Scientists Study Roots of Racism." *New York Times*, 29 May 1990.

12426. Gordon, Leonard. "Racial Theorizing: Is Sociology Ready to Replace Polemic Causation Theory with a New Polemic Model?" *Sociological Perspectives* 32 (1989): 129-136.

12427. Guillaumin, Colette. *L'Ideologie raciste. Genese et language actuel*. Paris: Mouton, 1972.

12428. _____. "Race and Nature: The System of Marks." *Feminist Issues* 8 (Fall 1988): 25-44.

12429. Hall, Stuart. "Race, Articulation and Societies Structured in Dominance." in *Sociological Theories: Race and Colonialism*, pp. 305-345. ed. UNESCO. Paris: UNESCO, 1980.

12430. Hanke, Lewis. *Aristotle and the American Indians: A Study in Race Prejudice in the Modern World*. Indiana U.P., 1959.

12431. Harvey, David. "Postmodern Morality Plays." *Antipode* 24 (October 1992): 300-336. [See Blaut, above]

12432. Jackman, Mary R., and M. Crane. "Some of My Friends Are Black...: Interracial Friendship and Whites' Racial Attitudes." *Public Opinion Quarterly* 50 (1986): 459-486.

12433. Jackman, Mary R., and M. J. Muha. "Education and Intergroup Attitudes: Moral Enlightenment, Superficial Democratic Commitment, or Ideological Refinement?" *American Sociological Review* 49 (1984): 751-769.

12434. Jackson, P. "Social Geography: Race and Racism." *Progress in Human Geography* 9, no. 1 (1985).

12435. Jaroff, Leon. "Teaching Reverse Racism." *Time* (4 April 1994). [Black superiority over whites based on melanin]

12436. Jenness, Doug. "Origins of the Myth of Race." *Militant* (21 February 1992): 9-12.

12437. Jones, Clifton R. "Sociological Research in Racial Theory, 1960-1988." *International Journal of Group Tensions* 20 (Spring 1990): 91-98.

12438. Judis, John B. "Reviewing Reasons for Racial Tensions." *In These Times* (16 May 1990).

12439. Karenga, Maulana. "Racism Subtle in America." *Daily Forty-Niner (California State University, Long Beach)*, 1 March 1990. [Interview by Axel Koester; Part 1]

12440. Kennedy, Randall L. "Racial Critiques of Legal Academia." *Harvard Law Review* 102 (June 1989): 1745-1819.

12441. _____. "Still a Pigmentocracy." *New York Times*, 21 July 1993. ["Stark lines of racial hierarchy can be seen in virtually every index of well-being and power"]

12442. Leiman, Melvin. "The Political Economy of Racism: Radical Perspectives and New Directions." *Insurgent Sociologist* 14 (Fall 1987): 73-110.

12443. Leonardo, Micaela di. "Boyz on the Hood." *Nation* (17 August 1992). [Review article on four books on race.]

12444. Levinson, Arlene. "Racism: A Particularly Human Condition." *Riverside Press-Enterprise*, 15 August 1993. [About Johnny Lee Clary's theory]

12445. Lock, Margaret. "The Concept of Race: An Ideological Construct." *Transcultural Psychiatric Review* 30 (1993): 203-227.

12446. Lopez, D., and Y. Espiritu. "Panethnicity in the United States: A Theoretical Framework." *Ethnic and Racial Studies* 13 (April 1990).

12447. Lyman, Stanford M. *Militarism, Imperialism, and Racial Accommodation. An Analysis and Interpretation of the Early Writings of Robert E. Park*. University of Arkansas Press, 1992.

12448. McLaren, Peter L., and Michael Dantley. "Leadership and a Critical Pedagogy of Race: Cornel West, Stuart Hall, and the Prophetic Tradition." *Journal of Negro Education* 59 (Winter 1990).

12449. Memmi, Albert. *Le Racisme*. Gallimard, 1982.

12450. Miles, Robert. "Class, Race and Ethnicity: A Critique of Cox's Theory." *Ethnic and Racial Studies* 3 (April 1980): 169-187. [Oliver C. Cox]

12451. _____. "The Contradictions of Racism." in *Rescue 43: Xenophobia and Exile*, University of Copenhagen. Munksgaard, 1993.

12452. _____. *Racism*. London: Routledge, 1989.

12453. _____. "Racism, Ideology, and Disadvantage." *Social Studies Review* 5 (March 1990): 148-151.

12454. _____. *Racism after 'Race Relations'*. London: Routledge, 1993.

12455. Moghadam, Val. "Against Eurocentrism and Nativism: A Review Essay on Samir Amin's Eurocentrism and Other Texts." *Socialism and Democracy* no. 9 (Fall-Winter 1989): 81-104.

12456. Molnar, Alex, and others. "Contemporary Issues: The Resurgence of Racism." *Educational Leadership* 47 (October 1989). [Six articles]

12457. Monaghan, Peter. "'Critical Race Theory' Questions Role of Legal Doctrine in Racial Inequity." *Chronicle of Higher Education* (23 June 1993).

12458. Muga, David A. "The Marxist Problematic As a Model Interdisciplinary Approach to Ethnic Studies." *Journal of Ethnic Studies* 17 (Winter 1990): 53-80.

12459. Muir, Donal E. "Race: The Mythic Root of Racism." *Sociological Inquiry* 63 (Summer 1993): 339-350.

12460. Olender, Maurice, ed. *Le racisme: mythes et sciences*. Brussels: Editions Complexe, 1981.

12461. Omi, Michael, and Howard Winant. *Racial Formation in the United States From the 1960s to the 1990s*, Second ed. Routledge, 1994.

12462. Padilla, Yolanda C. "Social Science Theory on the Mexican- American Experience." *Social Science Review* 64 (June 1990).

12463. Patterson, Orlando. *Ethnic Chauvinism: The Reactionary Impulse*. New York: Stein and Hill, 1977.

12464. Persons, Stow. *Ethnic Studies at Chicago, 1905-45*. Urbana: University of Illinois Press, 1987.

12465. Phelps, E. "The Statistical Theory of Racism and Sexism." *American Economic Review* 62 (1972): 659-661.

12466. Pierre-Charles G. "Racialism and Sociological Theories." in *Sociological Theories: Race and Colonialism*, pp. 69-83. ed. UNESCO. Paris: UNESCO, 1980.

12467. Platt, Tony. "E. Franklin Frazier Reconsidered." *Social Justice* 16 (Winter 1989).

12468. Prager, Jeffrey. "American Racial Ideology as Collective Representation." *Ethnic and Racial Studies* 5 (January 1982): 99- 119.

12469. _____. "White Racial Privilege and Social Change: An Examination of Theories of Racism." *Berkeley Journal of Sociology* (1972-73): 117-150.

12470. "Race, Class, and Gender." *Gender and Society* 6 (September 1992): 8 articles.

12471. Raspberry, William. "Black America's Burden." *Boston Globe*, 28 July 1994. [Supports contention of Urban League's Hugh B. Price that it is paranoid to think that "racism accounts for all that plagues us."]

12472. Rex, John. "Racialism and the Urban Crisis." in *Race, Science, and Society*, pp. 262-300. ed. Leo Kuper. New York: Columbia University Press, 1975.

12473. Reynolds, Vernon and others, eds. *The Sociobiology of Ethnocentrism: Evolutionary Dimensions of Xenophobia, Discrimination, Racism and Nationalism*. London: Croom Helm, 1987.

12474. Rogers, Wylie S. *The Political Economy of Black Inequality: An Exploratory Analysis*. Ph.D. diss., University of Illinois, Chicago, 1989. UMO #9003746.

12475. "Roots of the Anti-Busing Movement." *Dollars and Sense* no. 19 (September 1976): 14-16. [Three neighborhoods in Boston]

12476. Rose, Steven. "The Sociobiology of Ethnocentrism." *Sage Race Relations Abstracts* 14 (November 1989): 16-18.

12477. Ross, E. A. "The Causes of Race Superiority." *Annals* 18 (1901).

12478. San Juan, E., Jr. "Problems in the Marxist Project of Theorizing Race." *Rethinking MARXISM* 2 (Summer 1989): 58-80.

12479. _____. "Theorizing Anti-Racist Struggle." *Against the Current* no. 34 (September-October 1991): 27-33.

12480. Saxton, Alexander. "Historical Explanations of Racial Inequality." *Marxist Perspectives* (Summer 1979): 146-168.

12481. Sidanius, J. and others. "A Comparison of Symbolic Racism Theory and Social Dominance Theory as Explanations for Racial Policy Attitudes." *Journal of Social Psychology* 132 (June 1992): 377-396.

12482. Smedley, Audrey. *Race in North America: Origin and Evolution of a World View*. Westview Press, 1993.

12483. Snedeker, George. "Capitalism, Racism, and the Struggle for Democracy: The Political Sociology of Oliver C. Cox." *Socialism and Democracy* no. 7 (Fall-Winter 1988): 75-95.

12484. Sniderman, Paul M. and others. "Policy Reasoning and Political Values: The Problem of Racial Equality." *American Journal of Political Science* 28 (1984): 75-94.

12485. Sniderman, Paul M., and P. E. Tetlock. "Reflections on American Racism." *Journal of Social Issues* 42 (1986): 173-187.

12486. _____. "Symbolic Racism: Problems of Motive Attribution in Political Analysis." *Journal of Social Issues* 42 (1986): 129- 150.

12487. Solomos, John, and L. Back. "Conceptualizing Racisms: Social Theory, Politics and Research." *Sociology* 28 (February 1994): 143-162.

12488. Squires, Gregory D. *Capital and Communities in Black and White: The Intersections of Race, Class, and Uneven Development*. SUNY Press, 1994.

12489. Taguieff, Pierre-Andre, ed. *Face au racisme*, 2 vols. Editions La Decouverte, 1991.

12490. Takaki, Dana Y. "The Retreat from Race." *Socialist Review* 22 (October-December 1992): 167-189.

12491. Tatum, B. D. "Talking About Race, Learning About Racism: The Application of Racial Identity Development Theory in the Classroom." *Harvard Educational Review* 62 (Spring 1992): 1-24.

12492. Taylor, Marulee C. "Fraternal Deprivation and Competitive Racism: A Second Look." *Sociology and Social Research* 65 (October 1980): 37-55.

12493. Thompson, Richard H. *Theories of Ethnicity: A Critical Appraisal*. Westport, CT: Greenwood, 1989.

12494. Tidwell, Billy J. "More than a Moral Issue: The Costs of American Racism in the 1990s." *Urban League Review* 14 (Winter 1990-1991): 9-28.

12495. Torres, Gerald. "Critical Race Theory: The Decline of the Universalist Ideal and the Hope of Plural Justice-Some Observations and Questions of an Emerging Phenomenon." *Minnesota Law Review* 75 (February 1991): 993-1007.

12496. Walker, E. Clarence. "How Many Niggers Did Karl Marx Know? Or, a Peculiarity of the Americans." in *Deromanticizing Black History: Critical Essays and Reappraisals*, Walker. University of Tennessee Press, 1991.

12497. Washington, Robert E. "Brown Racism and the Formation of a World System of Racial Stratification." *Sociological Abstracts* (1989). Accession No. 89S21798.

12498. West, Cornel. "Learning to Talk of Race." *New York Times Magazine* (2 August 1992).

12499. _____. "The New Cultural Politics of Difference." in *Out There*, eds. Russell Ferguson and others. MIT Press, 1991.

12500. Williams, J. C. "Dissolving the Sameness/Difference Debate: A Post-Modern Path Beyond Essentialism in Feminist and Critical Race Theory." *Duke Law Journal* no. 2 (April 1991): 296- 323.

12501. Wilson, C. E. "Black Power and the Myth of Black Racism." *Liberation* 11 (September 1966).

12502. Wilson, William J. "The Declining Significance of Race." *Society* 15 (January/February 1978).

12503. Winant, Howard. *Racial Conditions: Politics, Theory, Caomparisons*. University of Minnesota Press, 1994.

12504. Wolf, Eric R. "Perilous Ideas: Race, Culture, People." *Current Anthropology* 35 (February 1994): 1-12.

12505. Wolpe, Harold. "Class Concepts, Class Struggle and Racism." in *Theories of Race and Ethnic Relations*, pp. 110-130. eds. John Rex, and D. Mason. New York: Cambridge University Press, 1986.

12506. Yeboah, Samuel K. *The Ideology of Racism*. London: Hansib, 1988.

12507. Zegeye, Abebe and others, eds. *Exploitation and Exclusion: Race and Class in Contemporary US Society*. London: Hans Zell, 1991.

RACIST GROUPS

12508. Aho, James A. *The Politics of Righteousness: Idaho Christian Patriotism*. University of Washington Press, 1990.

12509. Anderson, Eric. *Skinheads: From Britain to San Francisco via Punk Rock*. Washington State University: Master's thesis, 1987.

12510. Anti-Defamation League. *Shaved for Battle*. New York: ADL, 1987. [Skinheads in U.S.]

12511. Applebome, Peter. "Skinhead Violence Grows, Experts Say." *New York Times*, 18 July 1993.

12512. Bacigal, Ronald J., and M. I. Bacigal. "When Racists and Radicals Meet." *Emory Law Journal* 38 (Fall 1989): 1145-1187.

12513. Barkun, Michael. "Millenarian Aspects of 'White Supremacist' Movements." *Terrorism and Political Violence* 1 (1989): 409-434.

12514. Bates, Eric. "New Blood for the Old Order." *Southern Exposure* 17 (1989): 53-54.

12515. Bayor, Ronald H. "Klans, Coughlinites, and Aryan Nations: Patterns of American Anti-Semitism in the Twentieth Century." *American Jewish History* 76 (1986): 181-196.

12516. Behar, Richard. "Warlocks, Whitches and Swastikas." *Time* (29 October 1990). [Clifton, NJ]

12517. Bellant, Russ. *Old Nazis, The New Right, and the Republican Party. Domestic Fascist Networks and U.S. Cold War Politics*. Boston, MA: South End Press, 1992.

12518. Bleifuss, Joel. "In the Shadows." *In These Times* (9 October 1991). [Stirrings on the far right wing]

12519. Bole, William. "Who Helped Nazis Escape to America?" *Present Tense* 13 (1986): 6-10.

12520. Bridges, Tyler. *The Rise of David Duke*. University of Mississippi Press, 1994.

12521. Canedy, Susan. *America's Nazis: A Democratic Dilemma. A History of the German American Bund*. Menlo Park, CA: Markgraf, 1990.

12522. Chavez, Linda. "The World View of a Radical Racist." *New America* (December 1975).

12523. Coates, James R. *Armed and Dangerous: The Rise of the Survivalist Right*. New York: Noonday Press, 1987.

12524. Cohen, Richard. "Generation of Bigots." *Washington Post*, 23 July 1993. ["A generation of bigots is coming of age" in the U.S.]

12525. Coplon, Jeff. "The Skinhead Reich." *Utne Reader* (May-June 1989): 80-89. [Reprinted, in part, from Rolling Stone]

12526. Corcoran, James. *Bitter Harvest. Gordon Kahl and the Posse Comitatus: Murder in the Heartland*. New York: Viking, 1990.

12527. de Vise, Daniel. "Fisher's Passage to Intolerance." *Long Beach Press-Telegram*, 26 July 1993. [Christopher Fisher, organizer of the Fourth Reich Skinheads, Long Beach, California]

12528. Dees, Morris. "Young, Gullible and Taught to Hate." *New York Times*, 25 August 1993. [Skinheads]

12529. Dees, Morris, and Steve Fiffer. *Hate on Trial. The Case Against America's Most Dangerous Neo-Nazi*. Villard, 1993. [Tom Metzger]

12530. Diamond, S. A. "The Years of Waiting: National Socialism in the United States, 1922-1933." *American Jewish Historical Quarterly* 59 (March 1970): 256-271.

12531. Diamond, Sara. "'Populists' Tap Resentment of the Elite." *Guardian (NYC)* (3 July 1991).

12532. Dobie, Kathy. "Long Day's Journey Into White." *Village Voice* (28 April 1992). [Skingirls from the American Front, a leading skinhead group]

12533. Eisenman, Russell. "Student Attitudes toward David Duke Before and After Seeing the Film 'Who is David Duke'." *Bulletin of the Psychonomic Society* 31 (January 1993): 37-38.

12534. "Evers-Case Suspect Tied to Bias Unit." *New York Times*, 30 October 1991. [Phinehas Priesthood, apparently a racist organization]

12535. Flynn, Kevin, and Gary Gerhardt. *The Silent Brotherhood. Inside America's Racist Underground*. New York: Free Press, 1989.

12536. Franklin, James L. "Idaho Says An Emphatic No To Hate." *Boston Globe*, 23 November 1989. [Neo-Nazi groups in Idaho and other far Western states]

12537. Freed, David and others. "Southland Is Ripe Turf for White Hate Groups." *Los Angeles Times*, 25 July 1993. [Extensive article on Southern California]

12538. Friar, Jerome. "White Patriots." *Society* 25 (1987): 87-93.

12539. Garland, Terri. "All in the Family." *Los Angeles Times Magazine* (15 August 1993). [Photos of the lives of white supremacists]

12540. Grossman, Zoltan. "Treaty Support Grows in Face of Right- Wing Violence." *Guardian (NYC)* (31 May 1989). [Fishing treaty rights of Chippewa Indians]

12541. Hamm, Mark S. *American Skinheads: The Criminology and Control of Hate Crimes*. Praeger, 1993.

12542. *Hate Groups in Michigan: A Sham or a Shame*. Washington, DC: U.S. Commission on Civil Rights, 1982.

12543. Haygood, Wil. "David Duke and the Politics of Fear." *Boston Globe*, 28 March 1991.

12544. Hendrickson, Paul. "The Wilderness of Idaho. In the Land of the Big Sky, There's Plenty of Room for Extremists." *Washington Post*, 27 October 1992. [Aryan Nations and similar groups]

12545. Hixson, William B., Jr. *Search for the American Right Wing. An Analysis of the Social Science Record, 1955-1987*. Princeton, NJ: Princeton U.P., 1992.

12546. Hoppes, Karen E. *William Dudley Pelley and the Silvershirt Legion: A Case Study of the Legion in Washington State, 1933- 1942*. Ph.D. diss., CUNY, 1992. UMO #9304674.

12547. Howell, S. E. "Racism, Cynicism, Economics, and David Duke." *American Politics Quarterly* 22 (April 1994): 190-207.

12548. *In the Face of Hate*. Jennifer Covert, 724 13th Avenue, #304, Olympia, WA 98501. A 30-minute video about neo-Nazi violence.

12549. Iudica, Doreen. "Police Fear Skinheads Gaining Foothold." *Boston Globe*, 11 August 1991. [White Youth League, Massachusetts]

12550. Jones, Tamara. "Hate From America's Heartland." *Los Angeles Times*, 7 September 1993. [How American Nazi propagandist supplies Nazi material to users in Germany]

12551. Jordan, Robert A. "Skinheads: An Alert." *Boston Globe*, 22 July 1989. [Massachusetts]

12552. Kazin, Michael. "The Grass-Roots Right: New Histories of U.S. Conservatism in the Twentieth Century." *American Historical Review* 97 (February 1992): 136-155.

12553. Koshan, James C. *White Power: The Neo-Nazi Movement in the United States, 1959-1989.* Indiana University of Pennslyvania: Master's thesis, 1988.

12554. Kuhl, Stefan. *The Nazi Connection. Eugenics, American Racism, and German National Socialism.* Oxford U.P., 1993.

12555. Lang, Susan S. *Extremist Groups in America.* New York: F. Watts, 1990. [Written for young people]

12556. Langer, Elinor. "The American Neo-Nazi Movement Today." *Nation* (16 July 1990): 82-108.

12557. Lee, Gretchen. "Arab Americans in St. Louis Feel Sting of Bigotry." *In These Times* (24 April 1991).

12558. Lewin, Tamara. "For U.S. Nazi Hunters, a Mixed Year." *New York Times*, 6 July 1992.

12559. Lewis, Anthony. "It Can Happen Here." *New York Times*, 11 November 1991. [David Duke and Nazism in the U.S.]

12560. Louisiana Coalition Against Racism and Nazism. *Collection, 1982-1990.* Amistad Research Center, Tulane University, [Collection of printed materials about David Duke]

12561. Lutz, Chris. *They Don't All Wear Sheets: A Chronology of Racist and Far Right Violence, 1980-1986.* Atlanta, GA: Center for Democratic Renewal, 1987.

12562. Marcus, Frances F. "White-Supremacist Group Fills a Corner in Duke Campaign." *New York Times*, 14 November 1991. [National Association for the Advancement of White People]

12563. Martin, J. Malcolm. *Herrenrasse.* Spes in Deo Publications, 21661 HWY 550 Montrose, CO 81401-8713, 1994. [Novel about a racist group]

12564. Martinez, Thomas M., and John Guinther. *Brotherhood of Murder.* New York: McGraw-Hill, 1988. [The Order]

12565. Marty, Martin E. "Skinheads: When Violence Feeds on Chaos." *Los Angeles Times*, 25 July 1993.

12566. Maurer, David J. "The Black Legion: A Paramilitary Fascist Organization of the 1930s." in *For the General Welfare: Essays in Honor of Robert H. Bremner*, eds. Frank Annunziata and others. New York: Peter Lang, 1989.

12567. Mills, David. "Don't Think Twice, It's All White." *Washington Post*, 16 May 1993. [William L. Pierce, a racist writer]

12568. Misukiewicz, Claude. "The Seeds of Hatred. Radical Right Gains Ground in the Farm Belt." *Dollars and Sense* no. 144 (March 1989): 20-22.

12569. Montague, Alan. "U.S. Far Right Extremist Groups in 1987." *Patterns of Prejudice* 22 (1988): 31-35.

12570. "Montana City Reacts Early to Subdue Racist Organizations." *New York Times*, 20 February 1994. [Billings]

12571. Moore, Jack B. *Skinheads, Shaved for Battle: A Cultural History of American Skinheads.* Bowling Green State U. Press, 1993.

12572. Mullen, Faith E. *Ten Years of Hate: A Fantasy Theme Analysis of the White Supremacy Rhetoric of Robert C. Miles.* Ph.D. diss., University of Nebraska, 1991. UMO #9211478.

12573. "Neo-Nazi Skinheads: A 1990 Status Report." *Terrorism (NY)* 13 (May-June 1991): 243-275. [State-by-state data]

12574. Newton, Jim. "Skinheads Get Prison for Bombings, Plot." *Los Angeles Times*, 14 January 1994. [Fourth Reich Skinheads]

12575. Novick, Michael. "L.A. Nazi Leader Found Guilty in Cross- burning." *Guardian (NYC)* (13 November 1991). [Tom Metzger, head of White Aryan Resistance]

12576. _____. "Nazi Confab Poses as Black History Event." *Guardian (NYC)* (12 February 1992). [Los Angeles]

12577. _____. "Racist Terror." *In These Times* (5 December 1990): letter. [In Portland, Oregon and elsewhere, organized by Tom and John Metzger and others]

12578. Olson, Craig S. *Spark Without Flame: The German Library of Information, a Nazi Propaganda Agency in the United States, 1936- 1941*. University of North Dakota: Master's thesis, 1991.

12579. Palmer, Brian. "Food, Folks, and Fear." *Village Voice* (23 July 1991). [Celebrating the Fourth of July with David Duke]

12580. Phelps, Christopher. "Skinheads: The New Nazism." *Against the Current* no. 22 (September-October 1989): 3-6.

12581. Platte, Mark, and Michael Connelly. "Supremacist Group a Mystery to Hate Crime Experts." *Los Angeles Times*, 17 July 1993. [Fourth Reich Skinheads]

12582. Platte, Mark, and Roxana Kopetman. "'It's Almost Like There Are 2 Sides to Him." *Los Angeles Times*, 23 July 1993. [Evolution of a white supremacist in Long Beach, CA]

12583. "A Racist Anti-Semitic Neo-Nazi Sprints Now for the Mainstream." *Texas Observer* (January 17 and 31, 1992). [Special double issue on David Duke]

12584. Reed, Julia. "His Brilliant Career." *New York Review of Books* (9 April 1992). [David Duke]

12585. Rees, Philip. *Biographical Dictionary of the Extreme Right Since 1890*. New York: Simon and Schuster, 1991.

12586. Rider, Andrea. "Conduct Unbecoming a Racist." *Spy* (September 1991). [David Duke]

12587. Rose, Douglas, ed. *The Emergence of David Duke and the Politics of Race*. University of North Carolina Press, 1992.

12588. Ryan, Michael. "Haters Can Change." *Parade* (15 September 1991). [David Waughtal, former member of Christian Identity and other neo-Nazi groups.]

12589. Seymour, Cheri. *The Committee of the States: Inside the Radical Right*. Excalibur Press Kirkland, WA 98034, 1993.

12590. Simpson, Christopher. *Blowback: America's Systematic Recruitment of Nazis and Its Disastrous Effect on Our Domestic and Foriegn Policy*. Grove Weidenfeld: 1987.

12591. Singlaub, John K., and Malcolm McConnell. *Hazardous Duty*. New York: Summit Books, 1991. [Touches on the World Anti- Communist League]

12592. Singular, Stephen. *Talked to Death. The Life and Murder of Alan Berg*. New York: Morrow, 1987.

12593. _____. *Talked to Death. The Murder of Alan Berg and the Rise of the Neo-Nazis*. Berkeley, 1989.

12594. "Skinheads: 'People Want to Feel Connected'." *Los Angeles Times*, 2 August 1993. [Nine different views]

12595. *Skinheads Target the Schools*. New York: ADL, June 1990.

12596. *Sounds of Hate: Neo-Nazi Rock Music from Germany*. ADL, 1992.

12597. Suall, Irwin, and David Lowe. "The Hate Movement Today: A Chronicle of Violence and Disarray." *Terrorism* 10 (1987): 345- 364.

12598. _____. "Shaved for Battle-Skinheads Target America's Youth." *Political Communication and Persuasion* 5 (1988): 139-144.

12599. Sullivan, Robert. "Tom Metzger: Skinhead Guru." *Zeta Magazine* 2 (September 1989): 5. [Letter]

12600. Toy, Eckard V., Jr. "Right-Wing Extremism from the Ku Klux Klan to the Order, 1915 to 1988." in *Violence in America*, Vol. 1. ed. Ted Robert Gurr. Newbury Park, CA: Sage, 1989.

12601. _____. "Silver Shirts in the Northwest: Politics, Prophecies, and Personalities in the 1930s." *Pacific North West Quarterly* 80 (October 1989): 139-146.

12602. Waldron, Ann. *Hodding Carter. The Reconstruction of a Racist*. Chapel Hill, NC: Algonquin Books of Chapel Hill, 1993.

12603. *WAR '87*. Fallbrook, CA: White Aryan Resistance, 1987.

12604. *When Hate Groups Come to Town: A Handbook of Effective Community Responses*, 2nd ed. Atlanta, GA: Center for Democratic Renewal.

12605. Wilkerson, Isabel. "Seeking a Racial Mix, Dubuque Finds Tension." *New York Times*, 3 November 1991. [Dubuque, Iowa chapter of National Assocation of White People]

12606. Young, Thomas J. "Violent Hate Groups in Rural America." *International Journal of Offender Therapy and Comparative Criminology* 34 (April 1990): 15-21.

12607. *Young and Violent: The Growing Menace of America's Neo-Nazi Skinheads*. Anti-Defamation League, 1988.

12608. Zatarain, Michael. *David Duke: Evolution of a Klansman*. Gretna, LA: Pelican Publishing Co., 1990.

12609. Zeskind, Leonard. *The "Christian Identity" Movement: Analyzing Its Theological Rationalization for Racist and Anti- Semitic Violence*. Atlanta, GA: Center for Democratic Renewal, 1987.

RACIST THOUGHTWAYS

12610. Caudill, E. "Racism and Darwinism." in *Darwinism in the Press: The Evolution of an Idea*, Caudill. Lawrence Erlbaum Associates NJ Hillsdale. 1990.

12611. Dovidio, John F., and Samuel L. Gaerton. "Changes in the Expression and Assessment of Racial Prejudice." in *Opening Doors*, eds. Harry J. Knopke and others. University of Alabama Press, 1991.

12612. Goldberg, David T., ed. *Anatomy of Racism*. Minneapolis: University of Minnesota Press, 1990.

12613. Hoxie, Frederick E. "The Curious Story of Reformers and the Amerian Indians." in *Indians in American History*, pp. 205- 228. ed. Hoxie. Arlington Heights, IL: Harlan Davidson, Inc., 1988.

12614. Hu, Arthur. "Asian Americans: Model Minority or Double Minority." *Amerasia Journal* 15 (1989): 243-257.

12615. Jackman, Mary R. *The Velvet Glove: Paternalism and Conflict in Gender, Class, and Race Relations*. University of California Press, 1994.

12616. "Le neo-racisme." *Apres-demain* (April 1983): 3-31.

12617. Montero, Oscar. "El prejudicio racial en Puerto Rico y las maniobras del critico." *Hispamerica: Revista de Literatura* 17 (April 1988): 111-115.

12618. Pareles, Jon. "There's a New Sound in Pop Music: Bigotry." *New York Times*, 10 September 1989.

12619. Pettigrew, Thomas F. "Advancing Racial Justice: Past Lessons for Future Use." in *Opening Doors*, eds. Harry J. Knopke and others. University of Alabama Press, 1991.

12620. Pico, Isabel, and Idsa Alegra. *El texto libre de prejuicios sexuales y raciales*. Rio Piedras, Puerto Rico: Centro de Investigaciones Sociales, 1983.

12621. Rowse, T. "Paternalism's Changing Reputation." *Mankind* 18 (1988): 57-73.

12622. Sartorius, Rolf, ed. *Paternalism*. Minneapolis: University of Minnesota Press, 1984.

RECREATION

12623. Applebome, Peter. "Tourism Enriches an Island Resort, But Hilton Head Blacks Feel Left Out." *New York Times*, 2 September 1994.

12624. Ball, Edward. "A Mardi Gras of One's Own." *Village Voice* (9 March 1993). [Racial segregation in Mardi Gras]

12625. Butsch, Richard, ed. *For Fun and Profit: The Transformation of Leisure into Consumption.* Philadelphia, PA: Temple University Press, 1990.

12626. Coates, James R. *Recreation and Sport in the African- American Community of Baltimore, 1890-1920.* Ph.D. diss., University of Maryland, 1991. UMO #9205044.

12627. Delehanty, Randolph S. *San Francisco Parks and Playgrounds, 1839 to 1990: The History of a Public Good in One North American City.* Two volumes. Ph.D. diss., Harvard University, 1992. UMO #9307543.

12628. Gruesser, John C. "Afro-American Travel Literature and Africanist Discourse." *Black American Literature Forum* 24 (Spring 1990): 5-20.

12629. Hutchison, Ray. "A Critique of Race, Ethnicity, and Social Class in Recent Leisure-Recreation Research." *Journal of Leisure Research* 20 (1988): 10-30.

12630. Koehler, David H., and Margaret T. Wrightson. "Inequality in the Delivery of Urban Services: A Reconsideration of the Chicago Parks." *Journal of Politics* 49 (1987): 80-99.

12631. McGuire, F. A. and others. "Race, Class, and Leisure Activity Preferences: Marginality and Ethnicity Revisited." *Journal of Leisure Research* 26 (1994): 158-173.

12632. Meyer, Eugene L. "An Odd Venue for a Voting Rights Issue." *Washington Post*, 12 October 1993. [Highland Beach, founded in 1893 as "the first black resort in the United States"]

12633. Mjagky, Nina. *History of the Black YMCA in America, 1853- 1946.* Ph.D. diss., University of Cincinnati, 1990. UMO #9108753.

12634. Mladenka, Kenneth R. "The Distribution of an Urban Public Service: The Changing Role of Race and Politics." *Urban Affairs Quarterly* 24 (1989): 556-583. [Park and recreation services in Chicago]

12635. Nasaw, David. *Going Out: The Rise and Fall of Public Amusements.* Basic Books, 1994.

12636. Philipp, S. F. "Race and Tourism Choice: A Legacy of Discrimination." *Annals of Tourism Research* 21 (1994): 479-488.

12637. Sloan, Gene. "Mapping Travel Habits of Blacks." *USA Today*, 29 April 1993.

12638. Stewart, Jocelyn Y. "Forgotten Oasis of Freedom." *Los Angeles Times*, 2 March 1994. [Val Verdem, the "Black Palm Springs"]

12639. Taylor, Dorceta E. *Determinants of Leisure Participation: Explaining the Different Rates of Participation in African- Americans, Italians, and Other Whites in New Haven.* Ph.D. diss., Yale University, 1991. UMO #9136199.

12640. Williams, Lena. "Blacks, on Vacation, Going Side by Side." *New York Times*, 5 July 1989.

RELIGION

12641. Aho, James A. *The Politics of Righteousness: Idaho Christian Patriotism*. University of Washington Press, 1990.

12642. Alho, Olli. *The Religion of the Slaves: A Study of the Religious Tradition and Behaviour of Plantation Slaves in the United States, 1835-1860*. Helsinki: Finnish Academy of Science and Letters, 1976.

12643. Alvis, Joel L., Jr. *Religion and Race: Southern Presbyterians, 1946-1983*. University of Alabama Press, 1994.

12644. Angell, Stephen W. *Bishop Henry McNeal Turner and African- American Religion in the South*. Knoxville: University of Tennessee Press, 1992.

12645. Axtell, James L. "The European Failure to Convert the Indians: An Autopsy." in *Papers of the Sixth Algonquin Conference*, pp. 272-290. ed. William Cowan. Ottawa: National Museum of Canada, 1975.

12646. Ayers, B. Drummond, Jr. "Cardinal Forbids Mass by Black Priest." *New York Times*, 25 June 1989. [Black charges of racism against Roman Catholic Church in the U. S.]

12647. Baer, Hans A. "Black Mainstream Churches: Emancipatory or Accommodative Responses to Racism and Social Stratification in American Society?" *Review of Religious Research* 30 (1988): 162- 176.

12648. _____. *The Black Spiritual Movement. A Religious Response to Racism*. University of Tennessee Press, 1984.

12649. _____. "The Juxtaposition of Protest and Accommodation in African American Religion." in *Research in the Social Scientific Study of Religion*, vol. 3. pp. 181-200. eds. M. L. Lynn, and D. O. Moberg. Greenwich, CT: JAI Press, 1991.

12650. Bailey, Kenneth K. "The Post Civil War Racial Separations in Southern Protestantism: Another Look." *Church History* 46 (1977): 453-75.

12651. Barboza, Steven. *American Jihad. Islam After Malcolm X*. Doubleday, 1994.

12652. Barkun, Michael. *Religion and the Racist Right. The Origins of the Christian Identity Movement*. University of North Carolina Press, 1994.

12653. Bastide, Roger. "Color, Racism and Christianity." in *Color and Race*, ed. John Hope Franklin. Boston, MA: Houghton Mifflin, 1968.

12654. Battle, V. DuWayne. "The Influence of Al-Islam in America on the Black Community." *Black Scholar* 19 (January 1988): 33-41.

12655. Becnel, Thomas. *Labor, Church, and the Sugar Establishment: Louisiana, 1887-1976*. Baton Rouge: Louisiana State University Press, 1980.

12656. Bellah, Robert N., and Frederick E. Greenspahn, eds. *Uncivil Religion: Interreligious Hostility in America*. NY Crossroad: 1987.

12657. ben-Jochannan, Yosef. *The Black Man's Religion*. NY: Alekebu-Lon Boods Association, 1972.

12658. _____. *We the Black Jews*. NY: Alekebu-Lan Books Association, 1949.

12659. Berg, Phillip L. "Racism and the Puritan Mind." *Phylon* 36 (1975): 1-7.

12660. Berke, Richard L. "Christian Right Defies Categories. Survey Discloses Diversity in Politics and Religion." *New York Times*, 22 July 1994.

12661. Boles, John B., ed. *Masters and Slaves in the House of the Lord: Race and Religion in the American South, 1740-1870*. Lexington: University Press of Kentucky, 1988.

12662. Briggs, Kenneth. "Hispanics' Role in Tomorrow's Church Unclear." *National Catholic Reporter*, 14 July 1989.

12663. Brightman, Robert. "Toward a History of Indian Religion: Religious Changes in Native Societies." in *New Directions in American Indian History*, ed. Colin G. Calloway. Norman: University of Oklahoma Press, 1988.

12664. Cadena, Gilbert R. "A Socio-religious History of Chicanos and the Catholic Church." *Sociological Abstracts accession No. 89S21305* (1989).

12665. Caldwell, Erskine. *Deep South, Memory and Observation*. Athens: University of Georgia Press, 1980.

12666. Cantor, David. *The Religious Right: The Assault on Tolerence and Pluralism in America*. Anti-Defamation League, June 1994.

12667. Carvajal, Doreen. "Trying to Halt 'Silent Exodus'." *Los Angeles Times*, 9 May 1994. [Drift of younger Korean-Americans from traditional churches]

12668. Castillo, Edward D. "Indian Account of the Decline and Collapse of Mexico's Hegemony over the Missionized Indians of California." *American Indian Quarterly* 13 (1989): 391-408.

12669. "Catholic Indians Confront 2 Traditions." *New York Times*, 17 August 1992.

12670. Charles, Allan D. "Black-White Relations in an Antebellum Church in the Carolina Upcountry." *South Carolina Historical Magazine* 89 (1988): 218-226. [Union County, 1818-1865]

12671. "The Church and Racism: Toward a More Fraternal Society." *Catholic Lawyer* 32 (Fall 1988): 273-300. [Vatican Document issued by the Pontifical Justice and Peace Commission]

12672. Clines, Francis X. "Prison Has the Body, but Allah Has the Spirit." *New York Times*, 2 July 1992. [Black Muslims in the Fishkill Correctional Facility, NY]

12673. Cohen, Debra Nussbaum. "Jews Attend Services Less Than Christians, Survey Says." *Washington Post*, 2 October 1993. [The Tobin-Berger study]

12674. Coleman, Michael C. "Not Race, But Grace: Presbyterian Missionaries and American Indians, 1837-1893." *Journal of American History* 67 (June 1980): 41-60.

12675. Colvin, Richard Lee. "Mixed Blessings." *Los Angeles Times*, 23 August 1993. [Missionaries and the Navajos]

12676. Cone, James H. *Martin and Malcolm and America. A Dream or a Nightmare*. Maryknoll, NY: Orbis Books, 1991.

12677. Conwill, Giles. "African-American: A Rite Whose Time Has Come." *National Catholic Reporter*, 25 August 1989.

12678. _____. "Toussaint or Not To Saint, That is the Question." *National Catholic Reporter*, 3 April 1992. [On the canonizing of Black saints]

12679. Cook, Anthony E. "Beyond Critical Legal Studies: The Reconstructive Theology of Dr. Martin Luther King." *Harvard Law Review* 103 (March 1990): 985-1044.

12680. Cortes, Carlos E., ed. *Church Views of the Mexican American*. NY: Arno, 1974. [Several works]

12681. Creel, Margaret W. *A Peculiar People: Slave Religion and Community Culture Among the Gullahs*. New York University Press: 1988.

12682. Crummell, Alexander. *Africa and America; Addresses and Discourses*. Negro Universities Press: 1969 repr.

12683. Czuchlewski, Paul E. "Liberal Catholicism and American Racism, 1924-1960." *Records of the American Catholic Historical Society of Philadelphia* 85 (1974): 144-162.

12684. Dart, John. "Pentacostal Fellowship to Form Racially Mixed Organization." *Los Angeles Times*, 22 January 1994.

12685. Davies, Alan. *Infected Christianity: A Study of Modern Racism*. Kingston: McGill-Queen's University Press, 1988.

12686. Davis, Cyprian. "Black Catholics in Nineteenth Century America." *U. S. Catholic Historian* 5 (1986): 1-17.

12687. Davis, Cyprian. *The History of Black Catholics in the United States*. NY: Crossroad/Continuum, 1990.

12688. Deck, Allan. *The Second Wave: Hispanic Ministry and the Evangelization of Cultures*. NY: Paulist Press, 1989.

12689. Dolan, Jay P., and Allan Fiqueroa Deck, eds. *Hispanic Catholic Culture in the U. S.: Issues and Concerns*. University of Notre Dame Press, 1994. [Latino Catholic communities since 1965]

12690. Dolan, Jay P., and Gilberto M. Hinojosa, eds. *Mexican Americans and the Catholic Church, 1900-1965*. University of Notre Dame Press, 1994.

12691. Dolan, Jay P., and Jamie R. Vidal, eds. *Puerto Rican and Cuban Catholics in the U. S., 1900-1965*. University of Notre Dame Press, 1994. [Especially NY]

12692. Dorgan, Howard. "Response of the Main-Line Southern White Protestant and Pulpit to Brown vs. Board of Education, 1954- 1965." in *A New Diversity in Contemporary Southern Rhetoric*, eds. Calvin M. Logue, and Howard Dorgan. Baton Rouge: Louisiana State University Press, 1987.

12693. Duke, Lynne. "At Core of the Nation of Islam: Confrontation." *Washington Post*, 21 March 1994.

12694. DuPree, Sherry S. *Biographical Dictionary of African- American Holiness-Pentecostals: 1880-1990*. Vol. I. Washington, D.C.: Middle Atlantic Regional Press, 1990.

12695. Dvorak, Katherine L. *An African-American Exodus. The Segregation of the Southern Churches*. Brooklyn, NY: Carlson Publishing Inc., 1990.

12696. Dye, Peggy. "Peace and the Sword." *Village Voice*, 12 June 1990. [Rev. Calvin O. Butts, III and the Abyssinian Baptist Church, Harlem]

12697. Emerson, T. E., and P. S. Cross. "The Sociopolitics of the Living and the Dead: The Treatment of Historic and Prehistoric Remains in Contemporary Midwest America." *Death Studies* 14 (1990).

12698. Evans, Linda J. *Abolitionism in the Illinois Churches, 1830-1865*. Ph.D. diss., Northwestern University, 1981.

12699. Fair, Harole L. *Southern Methodists on Education and Race, 1900-1920*. Ph.D. diss., Vanderbilt University, 1971.

12700. Farrakhan, Louis. *A Torchlight for America*. Chicago, IL: FCN Publishing, 1993.

12701. Feigelman, W. and others. "The Social Characteristics of Black Catholics." *Sociology and Social Research* 75 (April 1991): 133-143.

12702. Felder, Cain Hope, ed. *Stony the Road We Trod: African- American Biblical Interpretation*. Fortress Press, 1991.

12703. Felder, Cain Hope. *Troubling Biblical Waters. Race, Class, Family*. Maryknoll, NY: Orbis Books, 1990. [Blacks in the Bible]

12704. Findlay, James F., Jr. *Church People in the Struggle: The National Council of Churches and the Black Freedom Movement, 1950-1970.* Oxford University Press, 1993.

12705. _____. "Religion and Politics in the Sixties: The Churches and the Civil Rights Act of 1964." *Journal of American History* 77 (June 1990).

12706. Finkelman, Paul R., ed. *Religion and Slavery.* NY: Garland, 1989.

12707. "First Order of Black Nuns Heeds Call for 165th Year." *Los Angeles Times*, 12 March 1994.

12708. Fitzpatrick, Joseph P. "The Hispanic Poor in the American Catholic Middle-class Church." *Thought* 63 (1988): 189-200.

12709. Foley, Albert S. "Adventures in Black Catholic History: Research and Writing." *U. S. Catholic Historian* 5 (1986): 103- 118.

12710. _____. "Adventures in Black Catholic History: Research and Writing." *U. S. Catholic Historian* 5 (1986): 103-118.

12711. Foley, Albert S. *The Catholic Church and the Washington Negro.* Ph.D. diss., University of North Carolina, 1950.

12712. Fox-Genovese, Elizabeth, and Eugene D. Genovese. "The Divine Sanction of the Social Order: Religious Foundations of the Southern Slaveholders; World View." *Journal of the American Academy of Religion* 55 (1987): 211-133.

12713. Francis, Mark R. *Liturgy in a Multicultural Community.* The Liturgical Press, 1991.

12714. Franklin, James L. "Emerging Calls for Change.Black Catholics, Criticism of Church Are Growing." *Boston Globe*, 3 August 1989.

12715. _____. "In Boston, Black Recruits Stay Within the Church." *Boston Globe*, 3 August 1989. [Roman Catholic Church]

12716. _____. "Scholar Examines Black Viewpoint on Bible." *Boston Globe*, 8 September 1991.

12717. Freedman, Samuel G. *Upon This Rock. The Miracles of a Black Church.* Harper Collins, 1993. [Saint Paul Community Baptist Church, East New York, Brooklyn]

12718. Garcia Leduc, Jose M. *La Inglesia y el claro catolico de Puerto Rico (1800-1873): Su proyeccion social, economica y politica.* Ph.D. diss., Catholic University of America, 1990.

12719. Gaustad, Edwin S. *A Religious History of America, Revised Edition.* NY: Harper Collins, 1990.

12720. Genovese, Eugene D. "Black Plantation Preachers in the Slave South." *Southern Studies* 2 (Fall and Winter 1991): 203-229.

12721. Genovese, Eugene D., and Elizabeth Fox-Genovese. "The Religious Ideals of Southern Slave Society." *Georgia Historical Quarterly* 70 (1986): 1-16.

12722. Giago, Tom. "Indian Rituals Bypass Racism to Revile Religion." *National Catholic Reporter* (1 November 1991).

12723. Gilkes, Cheryl T. "Religion." *Black Women in America, II* 967-72.

12724. Goodstein, Laurie. "Religion's Changing Face." *Washington Post*, 28 March 1994. ["More churches depicting Christ as Black"]

12725. Gordon-McCutchan, R. C. "The Battle for Blue Lake: A Struggle for Indian Religious Rights." *Journal of Church and State* 33 (Autumn 1991): 785-797.

12726. Granger, James R. *A Black Man's Bible.* Washington, D. C.: Uraeus Publications, 1990.

12727. Greenberg, Gershon. "American Catholics during the Holocaust." *Simon Wiesenthal Center Annual* 4 (1987): 175-201.

12728. Greene, Carole Norris. "I Don't Want to Call It Schism." *National Catholic Reporter*, 26 May 1989. [Blacks in the Roman Catholic Church]

12729. Gregg, Robert. *Sparks from the Anvil of Oppression: Philadelphia's African Methodists and Southern Migrants, 1890- 1940.* Temple University Press, 1994.

12730. Haddad, Yvonne. *The Muslims of America*. NY: Oxford University Press, 1991.

12731. Hageman, Alice L. and others eds. *Sexist Religion and Women in the Church: No More Silence*. NY: Association Press 1974,

12732. Hall, John R. *Gone from the Promised Land: Jonestown in American Cultural History*. New Brunswick, NJ: Transaction Books, 1987.

12733. Hamilton, Denise. "Latino Members Avenged by Plan to Evangelize Chinese at Church." *Los Angeles Times*, 27 February 1994. [St. Thomas Aquinas Catholic Church, Monterey Park, CA]

12734. Hanke, Lewis. "Pope Paul III and the American Indians." *Harvard Theological Review* 30 (1937): 65-102.

12735. Harding, Vincent. "Religion and Resistance among Antebellum Negroes, 1800-1860." in *The Making of Black America, Vol. 1*, eds. August Meier, and Elliot M. Rudwick. NY: Atheneum, 1969.

12736. Haynes, Leonard L., III. *The Negro Community Within American Protestantism 1819-1844*. Boston, MA: Christopher Publishing House, 1953.

12737. Heady, Brown. "First Americans and the First Amendment: American Indians for Religious Freedom." *Southern Illinois University Law Journal* 13 (Summer 1989): 945-974.

12738. Hedges, Chris. "For Mainline Protestantism the Inner City Grows Remote." *New York Times*, 31 May 1990. [New York City]

12739. Hennelly, Robert. "Shtetl Without Pity. Dissent Is Dangerous at an Upstate Hasidic Village Where the Religious and Political Leadership Are One." *Village Voice*, 21 December 1993. [Kiryas Joel, NY]

12740. Henry, Sarah. "Marketing Hate." *Los Angeles Times Magazine*, 12 December 1993. [White supremacist Church of the Creator]

12741. Higginbotham, Evelyn B. *Righteous Discontent: The Women's Movement in the Black Baptist Church, 1880-1920*. Harvard University Press, 1993.

12742. Hildebrand, Reginald F. *Methodism and the Meaning of Freedom: Missions to Southern Blacks during the Era of Emancipation and Reconstruction*. Ph.D. diss., Princeton University, 1991.

12743. Holifield, E. Brooks. "The Penurious Preacher? Nineteenth- century Clerical Wealth: North and South." *Journal of the American Academy of Religion* 58 (1990): 17-36. [Touches on slaveholding by southern clergy]

12744. Hutchison, William R., ed. *Between the Times. The Travail of the Protestant Establishment in America, 1900-1960*. NY: Cambridge University Press, 1989.

12745. Jackson, Derrick Z. "Desegregating Sundays." *Boston Globe*, 26 October 1994. ["Sunday morning is the most segregated morning in the One-Nation-Under-God United States"]

12746. James, Portis P. *The Real McCoy, African-American Invention and Innovation, 1619-1930*. Washington, D. C.: Smithsonian Institution Press, 1989.

12747. Johnson, Paul E., ed. *African-American Christianity. Essays in History*. University of California Press, 1994.

12748. Jones, Charisse. "Black Baptists Gather to Rally the Faithful Against Social Ills." *New York Times*, 7 September 1993.

12749. Jones, Elias F. "The Quest for Authentic Identity." *Journal of Religious Thought* 44 (Winter-Spring 1988): 35-49.

12750. Jones, Major J. *The Color of God: The Concept of God in Afro-American Thought*. Macon, GA: Mercer University Press, 1987.

12751. Kater, John L., Jr. "Experiment in Freedom: The Episcopal Church and the Black Power Movement." *Historical Magazine of the Protestant Episcopal Church* 48 (1979): 67-81.

12752. Key, Oren W. "Evangelists Knocking, Knocking at Hispanic Doors." *National Catholic Reporter*, 14 July 1989.

12753. Kirkpatrick, Lee A. "Fundamentalism, Christian Orthodoxy, and Intrinsic Religious Orientation as Predictors of Discriminatory Attitudes." *Journal for the Scientific Study of Religion* 32 (September 1993): 256-268.

12754. Kly, Yussuf N. "The African-American Muslim Minority, 1776- 1900." *Journal (Institute of Muslim Minority Affairs)* 10 (1989): 152-160.

12755. LaFarge, John. *Interracial Justice: A Study of the Catholic Doctrine of Race Relations*. NY: America Press, 1937.

12756. Lawrence, Curtis. "Minority Churches [in Chicago] Slow to Join AIDS Fight." *Chicago Reporter* (June 1992).

12757. Lee, Martha F. *The Fall of America: The Nation of Islam and the Millennium*. Ph.D. diss., University of Calgary, 1986.

12758. Lefevre, Patricia. "Bishop Sees Racism as 'Iron Curtain'." *National Catholic Reporter*, 24 November 1989. [On the ignoring by the U.S. Catholic Church of "Brothers and Sisters to Us: A Pastoral Letter on Racism in our Day", 1979]

12759. Lienesch, Michael. *Redeeming American Piety and Politics in the New Christian Right*. University of North Carolina Press, 1994.

12760. Lincoln, C. Eric, and Lawrence H. Mamiija. *The Black Church in the African American Experience*. Durham NC: Duke University Press, 1990.

12761. Lincoln, C. Eric. "The American Muslim Mission in the Context of American Social History." in *The Muslim Community in North America*, pp. 224-231. eds. Earle H. Waugh and others. : University of Alberta Press, 1983.

12762. _____. *The Black Muslims in America*. 3rd ed. William B. Eerdmans, 1993.

12763. Lippy, Charles H., and Peter W. Williams, eds. *Encyclopedia of the American Religious Experience: Studies of Traditions and Movements, 3 vols*. NY: Scribner's, 1988.

12764. Little, Lawrence S. *A Quest for Self-Determination: The African Methodist Episcopal Church during the Age of Imperialism: 1884-1916*. Ph.D. diss., Ohio State University, 1993.

12765. Loescher, Frank S. *The Protestant Church and the Negro: A Pattern of Segregation*. NY: Association Press, 1948.

12766. Loftin, John D. "Anglo-American Jurisprudence and the Native American Tribal Quest for Religious Freedom." *American Indian Culture and Research Journal* 13 (1989): 1-52.

12767. Long, Jana. "Coming of Age Islamic." *Washington Post*, 9 May 1993. [Difficulties of an African-American woman becoming and remaining a Muslim]

12768. Luker, Ralph E. *The Social Gospel in Black and White: American Racial Reforms, 1885-1912*. Chapel Hill: University of North Carolina Press, 1991.

12769. Mackinley, Peter W. "The New England Puritan Attitude toward Black Slavery." *Old-Time New England* 63 (1973): 81-88. [1641-1776]

12770. MacRobert, Iain. *The Black Roots and White Racism of Early Pentacostalism in the U.S.A.* Basingstoke: Macmillan, 1988.

12771. *Many Rains Ago. A Historical and Theological Reflection on the Role of the Episcopate in the Evangelization of African American Catholics*. Washington, D.C.: U.S. Catholic Conference, 1990.

12772. Marsh, Clifton E. *From Black Muslims to Muslims: The Transition from Separatism to Islam, 1930-1980*. Scarecrow, 1984.

12773. Martin, Sandy D. *Black Baptists and African Missions; The Origins of a Movement, 1880-1915*. Macon, GA: Mercer University Press, 1989.

12774. Mathews, Donald G. "Religion and Slavery: The Case of the American South." in *Anti-Slavery, Religion and Reform; Essays in Memory of Roger Anstey*, pp. 207-232. eds. Christine Bolt, and Seymour Drescher. Folkestone, England: Dawson, 1980.

12775. Maxwell, Carol J. C. "White Like Them: Asian Refugees in a White Christian Congregation." *City and Society* 3 (1989): 153- 164. [St. Louis, MO]

12776. Mc Cray, Walter A. *The Black Presence in the Bible, 2 vols*. P.O. Box 5369, Chicago, Il 60680: Black Light Fellowship, 1991.

12777. Mc Loughlin, William G. "Cherokee Slaveholders and Baptist Missionaries, 1845-860." *Historian* 45 (February 1983): 147-166.

12778. McCarthy, Tim. "Apache Tribe Lives New Vision in Fight to Save Mountain." *National Catholic Reporter*, 2 August 1991. [San Carolos Apache, Mount Graham]

12779. McCloud, Aminah B. *African American Islam*. Routledge, 1995.

12780. McLoughlin, William G. *Cherokees and Missionaries, 1789- 1839*. New Haven, CT: Yale University Press, 1984.

12781. _____. "Indian Slaveholders and Presbyterian Missionaries, 1837-1861." *Church History* 42 (1973): 535-551.

12782. McMahon Eileen M. *What Parish Are You From? A Study of the Chicago Irish Parish Community and Race Relations, 1916-1970*. Ph.D. diss., Loyola University of Chicago, 1989. [St. Sabina Parish].

12783. Mickels, Marilyn W. *Black Catholic Protest and the Federated Colored Catholics, 1917-1933*. NY: 1988.

12784. Moen, M. C. "From Revolution to Evolution: The Changing Nature of the Christian Right." *Sociology of Religion* 55 (Autumn 1994): 345-358.

12785. Montgomery, William E. *Under Their Own Vine and Fig Tree: The African-American Church in the South, 1865-1900*. Louisiana State University Press, 1993.

12786. "Mormons Oust First Indian in the Hierarchy." *New York Times*, 5 September 1989.

12787. Mosley, William. *What Color Was Jesus*. Chicago, Il: African World Press, 1987.

12788. Mueller, J. J. and others. *Valuing Our Differences: The History of African-American Catholics in the United States*. P.O. Box 539, Dubuque, IA 52001: 1993.

12789. Murray, Hugh. "What About the Nation of Islam's Historical Ties to Fascism." *New York Times*, 23 February 1994. [letter]

12790. Murray, Peter C. "The Racial Crisis in the Methodist Church." *Methodist History* 26 (1987): 3-14.

12791. Nash, Gary B. "New Light on Richard Allen: The Early Years of Freedom." *William and Mary Quarterly* 36 (1989): 332-340.

12792. Nelson, William E., Jr. *The Role of the Black Church in Politics*. Paper prepared for the Committee on the Status of Black Americans, National Research Council, Washington, D.C., 1987.

12793. Newman, Mark. *Getting Right with God; Southern Baptists and Race Relations, 1945-1980*. Ph.D. diss., University of Mississippi, 1993.

12794. Newman, Harvey K. "Black Clergy and Urban Regimes: The Role of Atlanta's Concerned Black Clergy." *Journal of Urban Affairs* 16 (1994): 23-34.

12795. _____. "Piety and Segregation: White Protestant Attitudes toward Blacks in Atlanta, 1865-1905." *Georgia Historical Quarterly* 63 (1979): 238-251.

12796. Newman, Richard, ed. *Black Preacher to White America. The Collected Writings of Lemuel Haynes, 1774-1833*. Brooklyn, NY: Carlson Publishing Co., 1990.

12797. Noel, Peter. "For the Love of Street Money." *Village Voice*, 23 November 1993. [Al Sharpton in New Jersey]

12798. _____. "The 'Sins' of Father Lucas." *Village Voice*, 9 June 1992. [Catholic priest in Harlem]

12799. Ocha, Stephen J. *Desegregating the Altar: The Josephites and the Struggle for Black Priests, 1871-1960*. Baton Rouge: Louisiana State University Press, 1990.

12800. Oleksa, Michael. *Orthodox Alaska: A Theology of Mission*. St. Vladimit's Seminary Press, 1993.

12801. Osborne, William A. *The Segregated Convent: Race Relations and American Catholics*. NY: Herder and Herder, 1967.

12802. Ostling, Richard N. "Strains On the Heart." *Time*, 19 November 1990. [Black churches]

12803. Paris, Peter J. *The Social Teaching of the Black Churches*. Philadelphia, PA: Fortress Press, 1985.

12804. Phillips, Romeo E. "White Racism in Black Church Music." *Negro History Bulletin* 36 (1973): 17-20.

12805. Pillar, James J. "The Catholic Church's Ministry to the Choctaws of Mississippi in the Nineteenth Century." *Journal of Mississippi History* 50 (November 1988): 287-315.

12806. Pitts, Walter F. *Old Ship of Zion. The Afro-Bapitst Ritual in the African Diaspora*. Oxford University Press, 1992.

12807. Pontifical Commission Institia et Pax. *The Church and Racism. Towards a More Fraternal Society*. Vatican City: 1988.

12808. Pope John Paul II. "False Idol." *In These Times*, 13 December 1993. [Criticizes certain aspects of capitalism, socialism, and communism]

12809. Pope John Paul II. "It Must Be Understood that Jews Who For 2000 Years Were Dispersed Among the Nations of the World, Had Decided to Return to the Land of their Ancestors. This is Their Right." *Parade*, 3 April 1994. [Interview by Ted Szulc]

12810. Pulido, Alberto L. *Race Relations within the American Catholic Church: An Historical and Sociological Analysis of Mexican American Catholics*. Ph.D. diss., University of Notre Dame, 1989.

12811. Raboteau, Albert J. "Black Catholics and Afro-American Religious History: Autobiographic Reflections." *U.S. Catholic Historian* 5 (1986): 119-127.

12812. Raboteau, Albert J. and others, eds. "The Black Church: Continuity within Change." in *Altered Landscapes: Christianity in America: 1935-1985*, ed. David W. Lotz. Grand Rapids, MI: William B. Eerdmans, 1989.

12813. Raboteau, Albert J. "Down at the Cross: Afro-American Spirituality." *U.S. Catholic Historian* 8 (1989): 33-38.

12814. _____. "Martin Luther King, Jr., and the Tradition of Black Religious Protest." in *Religion and the Life of the Nation: American Recoveries*, eds Rowland A. Sherrill. Urbana: University of Illinois Press, 1990.

12815. Ramos, Moises Rosa. *Analysis of the Church in Puerto Rico*. Church and Theology Project of the National Ecumenical Movement of Puerto Rico, 1985.

12816. Raskin, Jamin B. "Interview with Marie Robinson." *Z Magazine* 3 (July-August 1990): 140-144. [A member of the Nation of Islam in Washington, D.C.]

12817. Reimers, David M. *White Protestantism and the Negro*. NY: Oxford University Press, 1965.

12818. Rhodes, John. "An American Tradition: The Religious Persecution of Native Americans." *Montana Law Review* 52 (Winter 1991): 13-72.

12819. Sandoval, Moises. *On the Move: A History of the Hispanic Church in the United States*. Orbis, 1990.

12820. Schuchter, Arnold. "Slavery and the Churches." in *Reparations*, Phildelphia, PA: Lippincott, 1970.

12821. Sharps, Ronald L. "Black Catholics in the United States: A Historical Chronology." *U.S. Catholic Historian* 12 (Winter 1994): 119-141.

12822. Sherkat, D. E., and Christopher G. Ellison. "The Politics of Black Religious Change: Disaffiliation from Black Mainline Denominations." *Social Forces* 70 (December 1991): 431-454.

12823. "Should Jews Fear the 'Christian Right'?" *New York Times*, 2 August 1994. [Advertisement on op-ed page]

12824. Singer, Merrill. "The Social Context of Conversion to a Black Religious Sect." *Review of Religious Research* 30 (1988): 177-192.

12825. Smith, Edward D. *Climbing Jacob's Ladder: The Rise of Black Churches in Eastern American Cities, 1740-1877*. Washington, D.C.: Smithsonian Institution Press, 1988.

12826. Smith, Patricia. "Role Models for Troubled Youth." *Boston Globe*, September 1991. [Nation of Islam in Boston]

12827. Smith, Warren Thomas. *John Wesley and Slavery*. Nashville, TN: Abingdon, Press, 1986.

12828. Snay, Mitchell. "American Thought and Southern Distinctiveness: The Southern Clergy and the Sanctification of Slavery." *Civil War History* 35 (December 1989): 311-328.

12829. Sontag, Deborah. "Canonizing a Black: Saint or Uncle Tom?" *New York Times*, 23 February 1992. [Pierre Toussaint]

12830. Spaights, E. "Racial Prejudice Toward Blacks Among White Churchgoers." *Psychology* 28 (1991): 1-10.

12831. Sparks, Randy Jay. *A Mingled Yarn: Race and Religion in Mississippi, 1800-1876*. Ph.D. diss., Rice University, 1988.

12832. _____. "Mississippi's Apostle of Slavery: James Smylie and the Biblical Defense of Slavery." *Journal of Mississippi History* 51 (May 1989): 89-106.

12833. Stammer, Larry B. "Christian Cleric Argues That Jesus Was Black." *Los Angeles Times*, 27 March 1993. [Archbishop George A. Stallings, Jr., founder of the Imani Temple of the African American Catholic Congregation]

12834. _____. "Conservative Trend Found in Younger Priests." *Los Angeles Times*, 21 February 1994.

12835. Stead, Robert. "Traditional Lakota Religion in Modern Life." in *Sioux Indian Religion: Tradition and Innovation*, eds. Raymond J. Demallie, and Douglas R. Parks. Norman: University of Oklahoma Press, 1988.

12836. Sullivan, Robert. "An Army of the Faithful." *New York Times Magazine*, 1925. [The Christian Coalition and the Republican Party]

12837. Sumner, David E. *The Episcopal Church's Involvement in Civil Rights, 1943-1973*. Ph.D. diss., University of the South, 1983.

12838. Swift, David E. *Black Prophets of Justice, Activist Clergy Before the Civil War*. Baton Rouge: Louisiana State University Press, 1989.

12839. Swoboda, Frank. "EEOC's Emerging Religious Harassment Guidelines Worry Employers, Others." *Washington Post*, 30 January 1994.

12840. Taylor, Clarence. *The Black Churches of Brooklyn from the Early 19th Century to the Civil Rights Movement*. Ph.D. diss., CUNY, 1992.

12841. _____. *The Black Churchgoers of Brooklyn*. Columbia University Press, 1994.

12842. Taylor, R. and others. "Black Americans' Perceptions of the Socio-Historical Role of the Church." *Journal of Black Studies* 18 (1987): 123-138.

12843. Terrell, John U. *The Arrow and the Cross: A History of the American Indian and the Missionaries*. Santa Barbara, CA: Capra Press, 1979.

12844. Terry, Don. "Black Muslims Enter Islamic Mainstream." *New York Times*, 3 May 1993.

12845. _____. "Ministry of Hope, Message of Hate." *New York Times*, 3 March 1994. [First of three articles on the Nation of Islam]

12846. Terry, Sara. "Resurrecting Hope." *Boston Globe Magazine*, 17 July 1994. ["Members of Boston's Black clergy are taking their ministry to the streets."]

12847. Thomas, Gail E. "Puritans, Indians, and the Concept of Race." *New England Quarterly* 48 (1975): 3-27.

12848. Tobin, Gary A., and Gabriel Berger. *Synagogue Affiliation: Implications for the 1990's*. Cohen Center for Modern Jewish Studies, Brandeis University, 1993.

12849. Trousdale, Ann M. "A Submission Theology for Black Americans: Religion and Social Action in Prize-winning Children's Books About the Black Experience in America." *Research in the Teaching of English* 24 (May 1990).

12850. Turner, Richard B. "The Ahmadiyya Mission to Blacks in the United States in the 1920's." *Journal of Religious Thought* 44 (Winter-Spring 1988): 50-66.

12851. Tyler, Lyon G. "Drawing the Color Line in the Episcopal Diocese of South Carolina, 1876 to 1890: The Role of Edward McCrady, Father and Son." *South Carolina Historical Magazine* 91 (1990): 107-124.

12852. Unsworth, Tim. "U.S. Seminarians: Dedicated and Different." *National Catholic Reporter*, 6 May 1994. [Catholic seminaries]

12853. Vecsey, Christopher, ed. *Religion in Native North America*. Moscow: University of Idaho Press, 1990.

12854. Vidal, Jamie R. "The American Church and the Puerto Rican People." *U.S. Catholic Historian* 9 (1990): 119-135.

12855. Washington, Joseph R., Jr. *Race and Religion in Mid- Nineteenth Century America, 1850-1877: Protestant Parochial Philanthropists*. Lewiston, NY: E. Mellen Press, 1989.

12856. Watts, Jill M. *"Shout the Victory": The History of Father Divine and the Peace Mission Movement, 1879-1942*. Ph.D. diss., University of California, Los Angeles, 1989.

12857. Weeks, Louis B. "Racism, World War I, and the Christian Life: Francis J. Grimke in the Nation's Capital." *Journal of Presbyterian History* 51 (1973): 471-488.

12858. West, Cornel. *Prophesy Deliverence! Toward a Revolutionary Afro-American Christianity*. Philadelphia, PA: Westminster Press, 1982.

12859. White, Ronald C. *Liberty and Justice for All: Racial Reform and the Social Gospel (1877-1925)*. San Francisco, CA: Harper and Row, 1990.

12860. White, Shane. *Somewhat More Independent. The End of Slavery in New York City, 1770-1810*. Athens: University of Georgia Press, 1991.

12861. Wilcox, Clyde. *God's Warriors: The Christian Right in Twentieth-Century America*. Johns Hopkins University Press, 1992.

12862. Wilcox, Clyde, and L. Gomez. "Religion, Group Identification, and Politics among American Blacks." *Sociological Analysis* 51 (Fall 1990): 271-285.

12863. Wilkerson, Isabel. "White Priest Embraces Blacks' Spiritual Roots." *New York Times*, 27 July 1989. [Rev. Michael Pfleger, pastor of St. Sabina Catholic Church, Chicago]

12864. Wills, David W. "Beyond Commonality and Plurality: Persistent Racial Polarity in American Religion and Politics." in *Religion and American Politics: From the Colonial Period to the 1980's*, ed. Mark A. Noll. NY: Oxford University Press, 1990.

12865. Wills, David A. "An Enduring Distance: Black Americans and the Establishment." in *Between the Times: The Travail of the Protestant Establishment in America, 1900-1960*, ed. William T. Hutchison. NY: Cambridge University Press, 1989.

12866. Wills, Garry. *Under God. Religion and American Politics*. NY: Simon and Schuster, 1990.

12867. Wilmore, Gayrand S. *African American Religious Studies: An Interdisciplinary Anthology*. Durham, NC: Duke University Press, 1989.

12868. _____. *Black Religion and Black Radicalism: Am Interpretation of the Religious History of Afro-American People, 2nd Edition.* Maryknoll, NY: Orbis, 1983.

12869. Wilson, Basil, and Charles Green. "The Black Church and the Struggle for Community Empowerment in New York City." *Afro- Americans in New York Life and History* 12 (1988): 51-79.

12870. Wilson, William J. "Slavery, Paternalism and White Hegemony." *American Journal of Sociology, 81* 5 (1976): 1190-1198.

12871. Winston, Sanford. "Indian Slavery in the Carolina Region." *Journal of Negro History* 19 (October 1934).

12872. Wolcott, Roger T., and Dorita F. Bolger comps. *Church and Social Action: A Critical Assessment and Bibliographical Survey.* NY: Greenwood Press, 1990.

12873. Wood, Betty. "James Edward Oglethorpe, Race and Slavery: A Reassessment." in *Oglethorpe in Perspective: Georgia's Founder after Two Hundred Years*, eds. Phinizy Spalding, and Harvey J. Jacobson. Tuscaloosa: University of Alabama Press, 1989.

12874. Wood, Forrest G. *The Arrogance of Faith: Christianity and Race in America from the Colonial Era to the Twentieth Century.* NY: Knopf, 1990.

12875. Wood, Peter H. "Indian Servitude in the Southeast." in *Handbook of North American Indians, Vol. 4,: History of Indian- White Relations*, ed. Witcomb E. Washburn. Washington, D.C.: 1988.

12876. _____. "Slave Resistance in Colonial South Carolina." in *Atlantic American Societies*, eds. Alan L. Karros, and J. R. McNeill. : Routledge, 1992.

12877. Woodrum, E., and A. Bell. "Race, Politics, and Religion in Civil Religion among Blacks." *Sociological Analysis* 49 (1989): 353-367.

12878. Wright, Gavin. "The Economics and Politics of Slavery and Freedom in the U.S. South." in *The Meaning of Freedom*, eds. Frank McGlynn, and Seymour Drescher. : University of Pittsburgh Press, 1992.

12879. _____. "What Was Slavery." *Social Concept* 6 (1991): 29- 51.

12880. Yacovone, Donald. "The Transformation of the Black Temperance Movement, 1827-1854: An Interpretation." *Journal of the Early Republic* (1988): 281-297.

12881. Yinger, J. Milton. *Black Americans and Predominantly White Churches.* Paper prepared for the Committee on the Status of Black American National Research Council, Washington, D.C., 1986.

12882. Yoshida, Ryo. *A Socio-historical Study of Racial/Ethnic Identity in the Inculturated Religious Expression of Japanese Christianity in San Francisco, 1877-1924.* Ph.D. diss., Graduate Theological Union, 1989.

12883. Yusuf, Imtiyaz. "Islam in America: A Historical-Social Perspective." *Hamdard Isoamicus (Pakistan)* 12 (1989): 79-86.

12884. Zielinski, Martin A. *Doing the Truth: The Catholic Interracial Council of New York, 1945-1965.* Ph.D. diss., Catholic University of America, 1989.

12885. _____. "Working for Interracial Justice: The Catholic Interracial Council of New York, 1934-1964." *U.S. Catholic Historian* 7 (1988): 232-262.

SCIENCE AND TECHNOLOGY

12886. American Association for the Advancement of Science. *Puerto Ricans in Science and Biomedicine.* 1981.

12887. Andrews, R. "American Indians in Science..." *The Scientist* 6 (16 March 1992): 1.

12888. Barlour, George E. "Early Black Flyers of Western Pennsylvania." *Western Pennsylvania Historical Magazine* 69 (April 1986): 95-119.

12889. Beane, De Anna Banks. *Mathematics and Science: Critical Filters for the Future of Minority Students.* Wasnington, D.C.: The Mid-Atlantic Equity Center, 1988.

12890. Benner, Yvonne E., and Michelle L. Aldrich. *Puerto Rican Scientists and Engineers: A Directory.* Washington, D.C.: American Association for the Advancement of Science, April 1979.

12891. "Black Students and the Mathematics, Science, and Technology Pipeline: Turning the Trickle Into a Flood." *Journal of Negro Education* 59 (Summer 1990): entire issue.

12892. Carmichael, J. W.,Jr., and John P. Sevenair. "Preparing Minorities for Science Careers." *Issues in Science and Technology* 7 (Spring 1991): 55-60. [Xavier University]

12893. Clewell, Beatriz C., and Bernice Anderson. *Women of Color in Mathematics, Science and Engineering: A Review of the Literature.* Washington, D.C.: Center for Women Policy Studies.

12894. Closs, M. P. *Native American Mathematics.* Austin: University of Texas Press, 1986.

12895. Congressional Task Force on Woman, Minorities and the Handicapped in Science and Technology. *Changing America: The New Face of Science and Engineering.* Washington, D.C.: 1988.

12896. Dickinson, S. L. J. "Equal Opportunity Employment." *Scientist* 5 (2 September 1991): 6-10.

12897. Dix, Linda S., ed. *Minorities: Their Underrepresentation and Career Differentials in Science and Engineering, Proceedings of a Workshop.* Washington, D.C.: National Academy Press, 1987.

12898. Fechter, Alan. "The Black Scholar: An Endangered Species." *Review of Black Political Economy* 19 (Fall 1990): 49-59. [Mathematics, Science, and Engineering]

12899. Forde, Frank and others. *Black Makers of History: The Real McCoy: The A-Z of Black People in Science and Technology.* London: Bookplace, 1988.

12900. Frankel, Mark S. "Multicultural Science." *Chronicle of Higher Education* (10 November 1993).

12901. Gill, Dawn, and Les Levidow, eds. *Anti-Racist Science Teaching.* London: Free Association Books, 1987.

12902. Haberfeld, Yitchak, and Yehouda Shenhav. "Are Women and Blacks Closing the Gap? Salary Discrimination in American Science during the 1970's and 1980's." *Industrial and Labor Relations Review* 44 (October 1990): 68-82.

12903. Harding, Sandra, ed. *The 'Racial' Economy of Science: Toward a Democratic Future*. Indiana University Press, 1993.

12904. Hunt, Linda. *Secret Agenda: The United States Government, Nazi Scientists, and Project Paperclip, 1945-1990*. St. Martin's Press, 1991.

12905. Hunter, M. "Racist Relics: An Ugly Blight on Our Botanical Nomenclature." *The Scientist* 5 (25 November 1991): 13. [See following comment by E. Garfield]

12906. Irigaray, Luce. "Is the Subject of Science Sexed?" *Cultural Critique* 1 (Fall 1985): 73-88.

12907. James, Portia P. *The Real McCoy: African-American Invention and Innovation, 1619-1930*. Washington, D.C.: Smithsonian Institution, 1989.

12908. Johnson, Robert C., Jr. "Science, Technology, and Black Community Development." *Trotter Institute Review* 5 (Winter/Spring 1991)

12909. Karwatka, Dennis. "Against All Odds." *American Heritage of Invention and Technology* 6 (Winter 1991): 50-55. [Jan Matzeliger]

12910. Kass-Simon, Gabriele, and Patricia Farnes, eds. *Women of Science: Righting the Record*. Bloomington: Indiana University Press, 1990.

12911. Kennedy, J. Michael. "Ways Sought to Lead Poor onto Information Highway." *Los Angeles Times*, 11 January 1994.

12912. Kidwell, Clar S. "Native Knowledge in the Americas." *Osiris* 1 (1985): 209-228. [Science and technology]

12913. Koertge, Noretta. "Are Feminists Alienating Women From the Sciences?" *Chronicle of Higher Education*, 14 September 1994.

12914. Lohr, Steve. "Data Highway Ignoring Poor, Study Charges." *New York Times*, 24 May 1994. [Information highway]

12915. McDade, Laurie A. "Knowing the 'Right Stuff': Attrition, Gender, and Scientific Literacy." *Anthropology and Education Quarterly* 19 (June 1988): 93-114.

12916. Nappi, Chiara R. "Women in Science: Why So Few?" *Forum for Applied REseardh and Public Policy* 6 (Spring 1991): 98-101.

12917. Noble, David F. *A World Without Women. The Christian Clerical Culture of Western Science*. Knopf, 1992.

12918. Oakes, Jeannie. *Lost Talent: The Underparticipation of Women, Minorities, and Disabled Persons in Science*. Santa Monica, CA: The Rand Corporation, 1990.

12919. Olson, Richard. "Historical Reflections on Feminist Critiques of Science: The Scientific Background to Modern Feminism." *History of Science* 28, part 2 (June 1990)

12920. Patterson, Rosalyn. "Black Women in the Biological Sciences." *Sage* 6 (Fall 1989): 8-14.

12921. Pearson, Willie, Jr. "The Flow of Black Scientific Talent: Leaks in the Pipeline." *Humbolt Journal of Social Relations* 14 (1987): 44-61.

12922. Pearson, Willie, Jr, and LaRue C. Pearson. "Baccalaureate Origins of Black American Scientists: A Cohort Analysis." *Journal of Negro Education* 54 (1985): 24-34.

12923. Person-Lynn, Kwaku. "Is African American Studies Obsolete? " *Los Angeles Times*, 1 February 1994. [Role of science and technology]

12924. Sammons, Vivian, ed. *Blacks in Science*. NY: Hemisphere Publishing Corp., 1989.

12925. Smith, Elaine M. "Science." *Black Women in America* II 1015-1018.

12926. Tashman, Billy. "Demise of the Fittest. The Sorry State of Science Education in [New York] City Schools." *Village Voice*, 28 January 1992.

12927. Task Force on Women, Minorities, and the Handicapped in Science and Tachnology. *Changing America: The New Face of Science and Engineering*. Washington, D.C.: Task Force on Women, Minorities, and the Handicapped in Science and Technology, 1988.

12928. Tilghman, Shirley M. "Science vs. the Female Scientist." *New York Times*, 25 January 1993.

12929. _____. "Science vs. Women--A Radical Solution." *New York Times*, 26 January 1993.

12930. Valverde, Leonard A. "Underachievement and Underrepresentation of Hispanics in Mathematics and Mathematics- Related Careers." *Journal fro Research in Mathematics Education* 15 (1984): 123-133.

12931. *Viewing Science and Technology Through a Multicultural Prism*. American Association for the Advancement of Science, 1993.

12932. Wharton, David E. *A Struggle Worthy of Note: The Engineering and Technological Education of Black Americans*. Greenwood, 1993.

12933. "Women Scientists Lagging in Industry Jobs." *New York Times*, 18 January 1994.

12934. Wycliff, Don. "Blacks' Advance Slow in Science Careers." *New York Times*, 8 June 1990.

SEXISM

12935. Adelson, Leslie A. "Racism and Feminist Aesthetic: The Provocation of Anne Duden's 'Opening of the Mouth'." *Signs* 13 (Winter 1988): 234-252.

12936. Almquist, Elizabeth M. *Minorities, Gender, and Work*. Lexington, MA: Heath, 1979.

12937. Andolsen, Barbara H. *Daughters of Jefferson, Daughters of Bootblacks*. Macon, GA: Mercer University Press, 1986. [Racism in the feminist movement]

12938. Backhouse, Constance, and David H. Flaherty, eds. *Challenging Times. The Women's Movement in Canada and the United States*. McGill: Queen's University Press, 1992.

12939. Bader, Eleanor J. "NOW Confronts Racism." *New Directions for Women* (November-December 1990).

12940. Bakken, Gordon M. "Constitutional Convention Debates in the West: Racism, Religion, and Gender." *Western Legal History* 3 (Summer-Fall 1990): 212-244.

12941. Banks, Taunya Lovell, and Leonard Gross. "Gender Bias in the Classroom." *Southern Illinois University Law Journal* 14 (Spring 1990): 527-543.

12942. Berger, Leslie. "Women's Panel Finds Ingrained Sexism in LAPD." *Los Angeles Times*, 19 October 1993.

12943. Bertaux, N. E. "The Roots of Today's Women's Jobs and Men's Jobs: Using the Index of Dissimilarity to Measure Occupational Segregation by Gender." *Explorations in Economic History* 28 (October 1991): 433-459.

12944. Bonvillain, Nancy. "Gender Relations in Native North America." *American Indian Culture and Research Journal* 13 (1989): 1-28.

12945. Brenner, Johanna. "The Best of Times, the Worst of Times: U.S. Feminism Today." *New Left Review* 200 (July-August 1993): 101-159.

12946. Brooks-Higginbotham, Evelyn. "The Problems of Race in Women's History." in *Coming to Terms: Feminism, Theory and politics*, ed. Elizabeth Weed. NY: Routledge, 1989.

12947. Brown, Judith O. and others. "The Failure of Gender Equality: An Essay in Constitutional Dissonance." *Buffalo Law Review* 36 (Fall 1987): 573-644.

12948. Browne, Kingsley R. "Title VII as Censorship: Hostile- Environment Harassment and the First Amendment." *Ohio State Law Journal* 52 (April 1991): 481-550.

12949. Buchanan, Brenda, and Jennifer Wriggins. "Thoughts on Gender Law and Language." *Maine Bar Journal* 5 (July 1990): 230- 232.

12950. Buck, J. L. "Nonsexist Language: Successes, Neologisms, and Barbarisms." *Teaching of Psychology* 17 (October 1990).

12951. Bunch, C. "Women's Rights as Human Rights: Toward a Re- vision of Human Rights." *Human Rights Quarterly* 12 (November 1990).

12952. Canon, Lynn W. and others. "Race and Class Bias in Qualitative Research on Women." *Gender and Society* 2 (1988): 449- 462.

12953. Collins, Patricia H. *Black Feminist Thought: Knowledge, Consciousness, and the Politics of Empowerment*. Boston, MA:: Unwin Hyman, 1990.

12954. _____. *The Social Construction of Black Feminist Thought: An Essay in the Sociology of Knowledge*. Cincinnati, OH: Department of Afro-American Studies, University of Cincinnati, 1987.

12955. _____. "The Social Construction of Black Feminist Thought." *Signs* 14 (Summer 1989): 745-773.

12956. Collins, Patricia H., and Margaret L. Andersen, eds. *An Inclusive Curriculum: Race, Class, and Gender in Sociological Instruction*. Washington, D.C.: American Sociological Association, 1987.

12957. Coriden, James A., ed. *Sexism and Church Law: Equal Rights and Affirmative Action*. NY: Paulist Press, 1977.

12958. Crenshaw, Kimberle. "Demarginalizing the Intersection of Race and Sex: A Black Feminist Critique of Antidiscrimination Doctrine, Feminist Theory and Antiracist Politics." in *Feminism in the Law. Theory, Practice, and Criticism*, ed. R. M. Sos. Chicago, IL: University of Chicago Law School, 1989.

12959. Currie, Janet. *Gender Gaps in Benefits Coverage*. National Bureau of Economic Research, 1993.

12960. Deberg, Betty A. *Ungodly Women: Gender and the First Wave of American Fundamentalism*. Minneapolis, MN: Fortune Press, 1990.

12961. Degh, Linda. "Beauty, Wealth, and Power: Career Choices for Women in Folktales, Fairytales and Modern Media." *Fabula* 30 (1989): 43-62.

12962. DeHart, Jane Sherman, and Linda K. Keber. "Gender and Equality in the American Experience." in *Making America*, ed. Luther S. Luedtke. : University of North Carolina Press, 1992.

12963. Dickinson, Leslie K. "Gender Bias in the U. S. Bankruptcy Code." *Family Conciliation Courts Review* 31 (October 1993): 437- 460.

12964. Dobrowolsky, Alexander Z., and Richard F. Devlin. "The Big Mac Attack; A Critical Affirmation of Mac Kinnon's Unmodified Theory of Partiarchal Power." *McGill Law Journal* 36 (April 1991): 575-608.

12965. Donahue, John J., III. "Prohibiting Sex Discrimination in the Workplace: An Economic Perspective." *University of Chicago Law Review* (Fall 1989): 1337-1368.

12966. Duclos, Nitya. "Lessons of Difference: Feminist Theory on Cultural Diversity." *Buffalo Law Review* 38 (Spring 1990).

12967. Dummett, Ann. "Racism and Sexism: A False Analogy." *New Blackfriars (Oxford)* 56 (November 1975): 484-492.

12968. Dyson, Michael E. "2 Live Crew." *Z Magazine* 4 (January 1991): 76-78.

12969. Erickson, Nancy S. "Final Report: Sex Bias in the Teaching of Criminal Law." *Rutgers Law Review* 42 (Winter 1990).

12970. Estrich, Susan. "Sex at Work." *Stanford Law Review* 43 (April 1991): 813-861. [Sexual harassment in workplace]

12971. Faludi, Susan. *Backlash: The Undeclared War Against American Women*. NY: Crown, 1991.

12972. Fender, Janet. "Education and the Woman Engineer." in *Technology of Our Times*, ed. Frederick Su. Bellingham, WA: S.P.I.E., 1990.

12973. Fernandez Cintron, Celia, and Marcia Rivera Quintero. "Bases de la Sociedad Sexista en Puerto Rico." *Revista Interamericana* 4 (Summer 1974): 239-245.

12974. Ficarrotto, Thomas J. "Racism, Sexism, and Erotophobia: Attitudes of Heterosexuals Toward Homosexuals." *Journal of Homosexuality* 19 (1990).

12975. "Final Report of the Massachusetts Gender Bias Study: Gender Bias in Courthouse Interactions." *Massachusetts Law Review* 74 (June 1989).

12976. Finot, Jean. *Problems of the Sexes, Translated by Mary J. Safford.* NY: 1913.

12977. Folbre, Nancy. "How Does She Know? Feminist Theories of Gender Bias in Economics." *History of Political Economy* 25 (Spring 1994).

12978. Folbre, Nancy, and Marjorie Abel. "Women's Work and Women's Households: Gender Bias in the U.S. Census." *Social Research* 56 (1989): 545-569.

12979. French, Mary Ann. "War of the Words." *Washington Post*, 15 August 1993. [Women-hating in hip-hop]

12980. Fulani, Lenora B. *The Psychopathology of Everyday Racism and Sexism.* NY: 1988.

12981. Gabriel, Susan L., and Isaiah Smithson, eds. *Gender in the Classroom: Power and Pedagogy.* Urbana: University of Illinois Press, 1990.

12982. Gannon, L. and others. "Sex Bias in Psycholgical Research: Progress or Complacency?" *American Psychologist* 47 (March 1992): 389-396.

12983. "Gender Bias Study of the Court System in Massachusetts." *New England Law Review* 24 (Spring 1990): 745-856. [Report of the Massachusetts Supreme Judicial Court]

12984. Gladwell, Malcolm. "Pythagorean Sexism." *Washington Post*, 14 March 1993. [Men are not better at mathematics than women]

12985. Gooley, Ruby Lee. *Race and Gender Consciousness amony Black Women in America.* Ph.D. diss., University of Michigan, 1989.

12986. Gordon, Suzanne, and Judith Shindul-Rothschild. "Nurses Have Had It With Sexism." *Los Angeles Times*, 7 December 1993.

12987. Graci, Joseph P. "Are Foreign Language Textbooks Sexist? An Exploration of Modes of Evaluation." *Foreign Language Annals* 22 (October 1989).

12988. Greenbaum, Marc D. "Report of the Gender Bias Study of the Supreme Judicial Court." *Suffolk University Law Review* 23 (Fall 1989): 575-683. [Massachusetts]

12989. Griffith, Mary Ellen. "Sexism, Language, and the Law." *West Virginia Law Review* 91 (Fall 1988): 125-151.

12990. Grillo, R., and S. M. Wildman. "Obscuring the Importance of Race: The Implication of Making Comparisons between Racism and Sexism (or Other Isms)." *Duke Law Journal* No. 2 (April 1991): 397-412.

12991. Guillaumin, Colette. "Sexism, a Right-wing Constant of Any Discourse: A Theoretical Note." in *The Nature of the Right: A Feminist Analysis of Order Patterns*, pp. 21-25. ed. Gill Seidel. Amsterdam: Benjamins, 1988.

12992. Hacker, Sally. *Doing It the Hard Way: Investigations of Gender and Technology.* Unwin Hyman, 1990.

12993. Halewood, Michael. "Men, Sex, and Power." *University of Toronto Faculty of Law Review* 48 (Spring 1990): 329-333.

12994. Hogan, J. D., and V. S. Sexton. "Women and the American Psychological Association." *Psychology of Women Quarterly* 15 (December 1991): 623-634.

12995. Hooks, Bell. "Feminism and Racism. The Struggle Continues." *Z Magazine* 3 (July-August 1990): 41-43.

12996. _____. "Reflections on Race and Sex." *Zeta Magazine* 2 (July-August 1989): 57-61.

12997. Horowitz, Maryanne C., ed. *Race, Class, and Gender in Nineteenth-Century Culture.* Rochester, NY: University of Rochester Press, 1991.

12998. Hrdy, S. B. "Sex Bias in Nature and History: A Late 1980's Reexamination of the Biological Origins Argument." in *Yearbook of Physical Anthropology, vol. 33*, ed. E. J. E. Szathwary. NY: Wiley-Liss, 1990.

12999. Hubler, Shaun, and Stuart Silverstein. "Women's Pay in State Lags 31% Behind Men's." *Los Angeles Times*, 29 December 1992. [California]

13000. Hughes, Marija M., Comp. *The Sexual Barrier: Legal, Medical, Economic and Social Aspects of Sex Discrimination*. Washington, D.C.: Hughes Press, 1977.

13001. Hurtado, Aida. "Reflections of White Feminism: A Perspective from a Woman of Color." in *Social and Gender Boundaries in the United States*, ed. Sucheng Chou. Lewiston, NY: Edwin Mellen Press, 1989.

13002. Jacobsen, J. P. "Sex Segregation at Work: Trends and Predictions." *Social Science Journal* 31 (1994): 153-170.

13003. Jarrell, Robin. *Women and Children First: The Forced Sterilization of Native American Women.* Ph.D. diss., Wellesley College, Undergraduate Thesis, 1988.

13004. Jones, Lisa. "The Invisible Ones." *Village Voice*, 12 November 1991. [Black feminism and Emma Mae Martin, sister of Supreme Court Justice Clarence Thomas]

13005. Katzenstein, M. F. "Feminism Within American Institutions: Unobtrusive Mobilization in the 1980's." *Signs* 16 (Autumn 1990).

13006. Kaufman, Michael T. "This Hall Outlives Its Famous." *New York Times*, 3 April 1993. [Sexism and racism in the Hall of Fame for Great Americans, Bronx, N.Y.]

13007. Kenneally, James J. "Sexism, the Church, Irish Women." *Eire-Ireland* 21 (1986): 3-16.

13008. Lasson, K. "Feminism Awry: Excesses in the Pursuit of Rights and Trifles." *Journal of Legal Education* 42 (March 1992): 1-30.

13009. Le Moncheck, Linda. *Dehumanizing Women: Treating Persons as Sex Objects*. Totowa, N.J.: Rowan and Allanheld, 1985.

13010. Lee See, Letha A. "Tensions between Black Women and White Women: A Study." *Affilia* 4 (1989): 31-45.

13011. Levine, Bettijane. "Behind the 'Lani Guinier Mask'." *Los Angeles Times*, 7 December 1993.

13012. Lewis, Diane K. "A Response to Inequality: Black Women, Racism and Sexism." *Signs* 3 (Winter 1977): 339-361.

13013. Lewontin, R. C. "Women Versus the Biologists." *New York Review of Books*, 7 April 1994.

13014. Loftus, E. F. and others. "Money, Sex, and Death: Gender Bias in Wrongful Death Damage Awards." *Law and Society Review* 25 (1991): 263-286.

13015. Loiacono, Stephanie. "Blacks and the Women's Movement." *Crisis* 96 (November 1989): 26-27, 45-46.

13016. Long, Stewart, and Andrew M. Gill. "The Gender Gap in Wages of Illegal Aliens." *Social Science Journal* 26 (Winter 1989).

13017. Lott, Bernice. "Sexist Discrimination as Distancing Behavior: I. A Laboratory Demonstration." *Psychology of Women Quarterly* 11 (1987): 47-58.

13018. _____. "Sexist Discrimination As Distancing Behavior. II. Primetime Television." *Psychology of Women Quarterly* 13 (September 1989): 341-355.

13019. MacKinnon, Catherine A. "Reflections on Sex Equality under Law." *Yale Law Journal* 100 (March 1991): 1281-1328.

13020. Maltz, Earl M. "The Constitution and Nonracial Discrimination: Alienage, Sex, and Framers' Ideal of Equality." *Constitutional Commentary* 7 (Summer 1990): 251-282.

13021. Matarese, Linda B. and others. "A Survey of Gender Bias among Corporate/Securities Lawyers: Does It Exist?" *Journal of the Legal Profession* 14 (1989): 49-72.

13022. Mills, Linda G. "A Calculation for Bias: How Malingering Females and Dependent Housewives Fare in the Social Security Disability System." *Harvard Women's Law Journal* 16 (Spring 1993): 211-232A.

13023. Morgan, Joan. "A Blackwoman's Side to the [Mike] Tyson Trial." *Village Voice*, 3 March 1992.

13024. Moynihan, Maria. *Court Conduct Handbook*. Boston, MA: Committee for Gender Equality, July 1990. [Guide to non-sexist treatment of female court personnel]

13025. Muwakkil, Salim. "Censorship and Sensibility." *In These Times*, 4 July 1990. [The issue of censoring rap group expressions on women and other topics]

13026. Nain, Gemma Tang. "Black Women, Sexism, and Racism: Black or Antiracist Feminism?" *Feminist Review* 37 (1991): 1-22.

13027. National Center for the Study of Collective Bargaining and the Professions, comp. *Sex Discrimination in Higher Education and the Professions*. NY: Baruch College, CUNY, 1989.

13028. Nilsen, Alleen P. and others. *Sexism and Language*. Urbana, IL: National Coucil of Teachers of English, 1977.

13029. O'Sullivan, Chris. "Race and Rape." *In These Times*, 8 April 1992.

13030. Painter, Nell Irvin. "Race, Gender, and Class in 'The Mind of the South': Cash's Maps of Sexuality and Power." in *W.J. Cash and the Minds of the South*, ed. Paul Escott. : Louisiana State University Press, 1992.

13031. Pico, Isabel and others. *Machismo y educacion en Puerto Rico*. San Juan, Puerto Rico: Comision para el Mejoramiento de los Derechos de la Mujer, 1979.

13032. Posner, Richard A. "An Economic Analysis of Sex Discrimination Laws." *University of Chicago Law Review* 56 (Fall 1989): 1311-1335.

13033. Puta, Manfred. "Male Chauvinism." *Notes and Queries* 36 (September 1989): 360-361.

13034. Rabinovitz, Jonathan. "New York Tribe Ponders Women's Vote." *New York Times*, 26 December 1992. [Shinnecock nation, Long Island]

13035. Rasky, Susan F. "A Rare Glimpse of Sexism in Economics." *Chronicle of Higher Education*, 27 January 1993.

13036. Raspberry, William. "Foulmouthed Trash." *Washington Post*, 30 July 1993. [Contempt for Black somen by some Black rap artists]

13037. Ravitch, Diane. "What Gender Bias?" *Washington Post*, 21 November 1993.

13038. Reid, P. Trotman, and J. Clayton. "Racism and Sexism at Work." *Social Justice Research* 5 (1992).

13039. Reskin, Barbara F., and Patricia A. Roos. *Job Queues, Gender Queues: Explaining Women's Inroads Into Male Occupations*. Philadelphia, PA: Temple University Press, 1991.

13040. Rhode, Deborah L. "Occupational [Gender] Inequality." *Duke Law Journal* 1207-1241 (December 1988).

13041. Richards, Evelleen. "Darwin and the Descent of Women." in *The Wider Domain of Evolutionary Thought*, pp. 57-111. eds. D. Oldroyd, and J. Langham. Dordrecht, Holland, 1983.

13042. Rodriguez, Clara E. "On the Declining Interest in Race." *Women's Studies Quarterly* 16 (Fall-Winter 1988): 18-32.

13043. Rose, Gillian. *Feminism and Geography: The Limits of Geographic Knowledge*. University of Minnesota Press, 1993.

13044. Ross, J. L., and M. M. Upp. "Treatment of Women in the U.S. Social Security System, 1970-1988." *Social Security Bulletin* 56 (Fall 1993).

13045. Rothenberg, P., ed. *Racism and Sexism: An Integrated Study*. NY St. Martin's Press.

13046. Sanders, Rickie. "Integrating Race and Ethnicity into Geographic Gender Studies." *Professional Geographer* 42 (May 1990).

13047. Saporta, Sol. "Linguistic Taboos, Code-words, and Women's Use of Sexist Language: A Double Bind." *Maledicta* 10 (1988-1989): 163-166.

13048. Savage, David G. "Supreme Court Bars Sex Bias in Jury Selection." *Los Angeles Times*, 20 April 1994.

13049. Schafran, Lynn H. "Update: Gender Bias in the Courts. Despite Progress, Problems Persist." *Trial* 27 (July 1991).

13050. Scott, Joan Wallach. "Gender: A Useful Category of Historical Analysis" pp. 28-50 in Her, Gender and the Politics of History. NY: Columbia University Press, 1988.

13051. Shemlow, Mary V. *Coping with Sexism in the Military*. NY: Rosen Publishing Group, 1990.

13052. Shoop, Julie J. "Report Finds Gender Bias in California Courts." *Trial* 26 (July 1990): 104-105.

13053. Shweder, Richard A. "The Crime of White Maleness." *New York Times*, 18 August 1991.

13054. Sidanius, Jim. "The Interface Between Racism and Sexism." *Journal of Psychology* 127 (May 1993): 311-322.

13055. Simons, Jargaret A. "Racism and Feminism: A Schism in the Sisterhood." *Feminist Studies* 5 (1979): 384-401.

13056. Smith, Althea, and Abigail J. Stewart. "Approaches to Studying Racism and Sexism in Black Women's Lives." *Journal of Social Issues* 39 (1983): 1-15.

13057. Solomon, Irvin D. *Feminism and Black Activism in Contemporary America: An Ideological Assessment*. Westport, CT: Greenwood, 1989.

13058. Stacey, Judith. "Sexism By a Subtler Name? Postindustrial Conditions and Postfeminist Consciousness." *Socialist Review* 96 (November-December 1987): 7-30.

13059. Stewart, M. W. and others. "Sexist Language and University Academic Staff: Attitudes, Awareness and Recognition of Sexist Language." *New Zealand Journal of Educational Studies* 25 (1990).

13060. Stone, Lorraine. "Neoslavery--Surrogate Motherhood Contracts v. the Thirteenth Amendment." *Law and Inequality: A Journal of Theory and Practice* (July 1988): 63-73.

13061. Suardiaz, Debra E. *Sexism in the Spanish Language*. Ph.D. diss., University of Washington, Master's thesis, 1973.

13062. Sugarman, David B., and M. A. Straus. "Indicators of Gender Equality for American States and Regions." *Social Indicators Research* 20 (June 1988): 229-270.

13063. Tamez, Elsa. *Against Machismo*. Meyer Stone/Crossroad/ Continuum, 1987.

13064. Taylor, Hazel. "Sexism and Racism: Partners of Oppression." *Cassoe Newsletter* (May-June 1983): 5-8.

13065. Thalmann, Rita. "Sexism and Racism." in *The Nature of the Right: A Feminist Analysis of Order Patterns*, pp. 153-160. ed. Gill Seidel. Amsterdam: Benjamins, 1988.

13066. Torry, Saundra. "Taking Steps to Cure Gender Bias in the Courtroom." *Washington Post*, 29 March 1993.

13067. "A Tradition of Women in the Law." *New York University Law Review* 66 (December 1991): entire issue.

13068. Trescott, Martha M. "Women in the Intellectual Development of Engineering: A Study in Persistence and Systems Thought." in *Women of Science: Righting the Record*, pp. 147-187. eds. Gabriele Kass-Simon, and Patricia Farnes. : Indiana University Press, 1990.

13069. Truman, G. E., and J. J. Barondi. "Gender Differences in the Information Systems Managerial Ranks: An Assessment of Potential Discriminatory Practices." *MIS Quarterly* 18 (June 1994): 129-142.

13070. U.S. Congress, 102d, 2nd session, House of Representatives, Committee on Ways and Means, Subcommittee on Social Security. *Women and Social Security: Families are Changing, the*

Workplace is Changing. Should Social Security Change Too? Hearing.... Washington, D.C.: GPO, 1992.

13071. Utaumi, K. "Inequalities for Women in the California Divorce Law." *Journal of Divorce and Remarriage* 16 (1991).

13072. Valdes, Alisa. "Fighting For a Place in a Man's World." *Boston Globe,* 12 April 1992. [Sexism at Berklee College of Music, Boston]

13073. Wagner, Sally R. "The Iroquois Confederacy: A Native American Model for Non-sexist Men." *Changing Men* 19 (Spring/ Summer 1988): 32-34.

13074. Wallace, Michele. *Black Macho and the Myth of the Superwoman.* NY Dial Press: 1979.

13075. _____. "When Black Feminism Faces the Music, and the Music is Rap." *New York Times,* 29 July 1990.

13076. Walters, Donna K. H. "Barriers Still Persist, Women Lawyers say." *Los Angeles Times,* 19 March 1994. [Los Angeles]

13077. Waters, Robert C. "Gender Bias in Florida's Justice System." *Florida Bar Journal* 64 (May 1990): 10-16.

13078. Weinstein, Henry. "Federal Court Survey Finds Gender Bias in 9th Circuit." *Los Angeles Times,* 22 August 1993. [U.S. Court of Appeals for the 9th Circuit]

13079. Welch, Susan, and Lee Sigelman. "A Gender Gap Among Hispanics? A Comparison with Blacks and Anglos." *Western Political Quarterly* 45 (March 1992): 181-200.

13080. Wigeman, Bobyn. *Negotiating the Masculine: Configurations of Race and Gender in American Culture.* Ph.D. diss., University of Washington, 1988.

13081. Wilcox, Clyde. "Black Women and Feminism." *Women and Polotics* 10 (1990): 65-84.

13082. Williams, Delores S. "The Color of Feminism; Or, Speaking the Black Woman's Tongue." *Journal of Religious Thought* 43 (1986): 42-58.

13083. Williams, Patricia J. "Fetal Fictions: An Exploration of Property Archetypes in Racial and Gendered Contexts." in *Race in America,* eds/ Herbert Hill, and James E. Jones, Jr. : University of Wisconsin Press, 1993.

13084. _____. "On Being the Object of Property." *Signs* 14 (Autumn 1988).

13085. Williams, Robert A., Jr. "Gendered Checks and Balances: Understanding the Legacy of White Patriarchy in an American Indian Cultural Context." *Georgia Law Review* 24 (Summer 1990): 1019-1044.

13086. Wolf, Naomi. *The Beauty Myth: How Images of Beauty Are Used Against Women.* NY: Morrow, 1991.

13087. "Women and Rights." *Dissent* (Summer 1991): 369-405, six articles.

SLAVERY

13088. Abzug, Robert H. *New Perspectives on Race and Slavery in America*. Lexington, KY: 1986.

13089. Alegria, Ricardo E. "Los origenes de la esclavitud negra en Puerto Rico." *Revista del instituto do cultura puertorriquena* 16, no. 61 (1973): 3-7.

13090. Allen, Theodore. "Slavery, Racism and Democracy." *Monthly Review* 29 (March 1978): 57-63.

13091. Archer, Leonie J., ed. *Slavery and Other Forms of Unfree Labour*. NY: Routledge, 1988.

13092. "Atlantic Slave Trade: Scale, Structure, and Supply." *Journal of African History* 30 (1989).

13093. Baralt, Guillermo Antonio. *Esclavos rebeldes: conspiraciones y sublevaciones de esclavos en Puerto Rico(1795- 1873)*. Rio Piedras: Ediciones Huracan, 1982.

13094. _____. *Slave Conspiracies and Uprisings in Puerto Rico, 1796-1848*. Ph.D. diss., University of Chicago, 1977.

13095. Bender, Thomas, ed. *The Antislavery Debate. Capitalism and Abolitionism As a Problem in Historical Interpretation*. University of California Press, 1992.

13096. Berlin, Ira. "How the Slaves Freed Themselves." *Washington Post*, December 1992.

13097. _____. "The Slave Trade and the Development of Afro- American Society in English Mainland North America, 1619-1775." *Southern Studies* 2 (Fall and Winter 1991): 335-349.

13098. Berlin, Ira, and Philip D. Morgan, eds. *Cultivation and Culture. Labor and the Shaping of Slave Life*. University Press of Virginia, 1993.

13099. _____. "The Slaves' Economy: Independent Production by Slaves in the Americas." *Slavery and Abolition* 12 (1991): entire issue.

13100. Berlin, Ira, and Philip D. Morgan, Eds. *The Slaves' Economy: Independent Production by Slaves in the Americas*. Frank Cass, 1991.

13101. Bertelsen, Kevin J. *Indian Slavery in Colonial Virginia and South Carolina*. Master's thesis, College of William and Mary, 1985.

13102. Botkin, B. A. *Lay My Burden Down: A Folk History of Slavery*. Athens: University of Georgia Press, 1989, reprint.

13103. Braund, Kathryn E. Holland. "The Creek Indians, Blacks and Slavery." *Journal of Southern History* 57 (November 1991): 601- 636.

13104. Briggs, Winstanley. "Slavery in French Colonial Illinois." *Chicago History* 18 (1989): 66-81.

13105. Bromberg, Alan B. *Slavery in the Virginia Tobacco Factories, 1800-1860*. Ph.D. diss., University of Virginia, 1968.

13106. Campbell, Randolph B. *An Empire for Slavery. The Peculiar Institution in Texas, 1821-1865*. Baton Rouge: Louisiana State University Press, 1989.

13107. "Capitalism and Slavery." *Social Concepts* 6 (December 1991): (3 articles).

13108. Chaplin, J. E. "Slavery and the Principle of Humanity: A Modern Idea in the Early Lower South." *Journal of Social History* 24 (Winter 1990).

13109. Clark, Elizabeth B. "Matrimonial Bonds: Slavery and Divorce in Nineteenth-Century America." *Law and History Review* 8 (Spring 1990): 25-54.

13110. Clayton, Ronnie W. *Mother Wit. The Ex-slave Narratives of the Louisiana Writers' Project.* NY: Peter Lang, 1990.

13111. Clemmer, Richard O. "Land Use Patterns and Aboriginal Rights, Northern and Eastern Nevada: 1858-1971." *Indian Historian* 7 (Winter 1974): 24-41, 47-49.

13112. Coldham, Peter W. *Emigrants in Chains: A Social History of Forced Emigration to the Americas, 1607-1776.* Baltimore, MD: 1992.

13113. Coll y Cuehi, Cayetano. *Historia de la Esclavitud en Puerto Rico.* San Juan, Puerto Rico: Publicacion de la Sociedad de Autores Puertorriquenos, 1969. [Edited by Isabel Cuehi Coll}

13114. Crouch, Barry A. "Booty Capitalism and Capitalism's Booty: Slaves and Slavery in Ancient Rome and South America." *Slavery and Abolition* 6 (1985): 3-24.

13115. Curet, Jose. *From Slave to Liberto: A Study on Slavery and Its Abolition in Puerto Rico, 1840-1880.* Ph.D. diss., Columbia University, 1980. UMO # 8016913.

13116. Deyle, Steven. "'By Farr the Most Profitable Trade': Slave Trading in British Colonial North America." *Slavery and Abolition* 10 (1989): 107-125.

13117. _____. "The Irony of Liberty: Origins of the Domestic Slave Trade." *Journal of the Early American Republic* 12 (1992): 37-62.

13118. Diaz Soler, Luis M. *La historia de la esclavitud negra en Puerto Rico.* 2nd ed. Rio Piedras, Puerto Rico: University of Puerto Rico Press, 1965.

13119. Dillon, Merton L. *Slavery Attacked. Southern Slaves and Their Allies, 1619-1865.* Baton Rouge: Louisiana State University Press, 1990.

13120. Donald, Leland. "Paths Out of Slavery on the Aboriginal North Pacific Coast of North America." *Slavery and Abolition* 10 (1989): 1-22.

13121. Douglas, Robert L. "Myth or Truth: A White and Black View of Slavery." *Journal of Black Studies* 19 (1989): 343-360. [Stanley M. Elkins and John W. Blassingame]

13122. Drago, Edmund L., ed. *Broke by the War: Letters of a Slave Trader.* University of South Carolina Press, 1991.

13123. Duncan, John D. "Indian Slavery." in *Race Relations in British North America, 1697-1783,* eds. Bruce A. Glasrud, and Alan M. Smith. Chicago, IL, 1982.

13124. Eaklor, Vicki L. *American Antislavery Songs. A Collection and Analysis.* Westport, CT: Greenwood, 1988.

13125. Ekberg, Carl J. "Black Slavery in Illinois, 1720-1765." *Western Illinois Regional Studies* 12 (1989): 5-19.

13126. Eltis, David. "Europeans and the Rise and Fall of African Slavery in the Americas: An Interpretation." *American Historical Review* 98 (December 1993): 1399-1423.

13127. _____. "Labour and Coercion in the English Atlantic World from the Seventeenth to the Early Twentieth Centuries." *Slavery and Abolition* 14 (April 1993): 207-26.

13128. Fernandez Mendez, Eugenio. *Las encomiendas y esclavitud de los indios de Puerto Rico (1508-1550), 3rd Edition.* Rio Piedras, Puerto Rico: Editorial Edil, 1970.

13129. Fields, Barbara J. "Slavery, Race and Ideology in the United States of America." *New Left Review* No. 181 (May-June 1990): 95-119.

13130. Figueroa, Luis A. *Facing Freedom: The Transition from Slavery to Free Labor in Guayama, Puerto Rico, 1860-1898.* Ph.D. diss., University of Wisconsin, 1991. UMO # 9209305.

13131. Finkelman, Paul R. "A Covenant with Death: Slavery and the U.S. Constitution." *American Visions* 1 (1986): 21-27.

13132. Finkleman, Paul R., ed. *Articles on American Slavery, 18 volumes*. NY: Garland, 1990.

13133. _____. *Colonial Southern Slavery*. NY: Garland, 1989.

13134. Finkleman, Paul R. "Slavery and the Northwest Ordinance: A Study in Ambiguity." *Journal of the Early Republic* 6 (1986): 343- 370.

13135. _____. "Slavery at the Philadelphia Convention." *This Constitution* No. 18 (1988): 25-30. [1787]

13136. Flinter, Jorge. "La esclavitud negra en Puerto Rico hacia 1830." *Revista del instituto de cultura puertorriquena* 16, no. 61 (1973): 8-17.

13137. Fogel, Robert W. *Without Consent or Contract. The Rise and Fall of American Slavery*. NY: Norton, 1990.

13138. Forbes E. "African Resistance to Enslavement: The Nature and the Evidentiary Record." *Journal of Black Studies* 23 (September 1992): 39-59.

13139. Grindle, David J. "Manumission: the Weak Link in Georgia's Law of Slavery." *Mercer Law Review* 41 (Winter 1990): 701-722.

13140. Hall, Kermit L., ed. *The Law of American Slavery: Major Historical Interpretations*. NY: Garland, 1987.

13141. Halliburton, R., Jr. "Origins of Black Slavery among the Cherokees." *Chronicles of Oklahoma* 52 (1974-1975): 483-496.

13142. Harrold, Stanley. "John Brown's Forerunners: Slave Rescue Attempts and the Abolitionists, 1841-1851." *Radical History Review* No. 55 (Winter 1993): 89-110.

13143. Huggins, Nathan I. "The Deforming Mirror of Truth: Slavery and the Master Narrative of American History." *Radical History Review* No. 49 (Winter 1991): 25-48. [See, also, responses by Peter H. Wood, Peter Dimock, and Barbara Clark Smith, 49-59.]

13144. Ifill, Max B. *The African Diaspora: A Drama of Human Exploitation*. Port-of Spain, Trinidad: Economic and Business Research, 1986.

13145. Jones, Norrece T., Jr. *Born a Child of Freedon, Yet a Slave: Mechanisms of Control and Strategies of Resistance in Antebellum South Carolina*. Middletown, CT: Wesleyan University Press, 1990.

13146. Katz, Jonathan. *Resistance at Christiana: The Fugitive Slave Rebellion, Christiana, Pennsylvania, September 11, 1851, A Documentary Account*. Crowell, 1974.

13147. Kolchin, Peter. *Unfree Labor: American Slavery and Russian Serfdom*. Cambridge, MA: Belknap Press of Harvard University Press, 1987.

13148. Littlefield, Daniel C. "The Slave Trade to Colonial South Carolina: A Profile." *South Carolina Historical Magazine* 91 (1990): 68-99.

13149. Lowrie, Samuel H. *Culture Conflict in Texas, 1821-1835*. NY: Columbia University Press, 1932.

13150. Lyman, Stanford M. "Asians, Blacks, Hispanics, Amerinds: Confronting Vestiges of Slavery." in *Rethinking Today's Minorities*, ed. Vincent N. Parrillo. : Greenwood, 1991.

13151. Magnaghi, Russell M. "The Role of Indian Slavery in Colonial St. Louis." *Missouri Historical Society Bulletin* 31 (1975): 264-272.

13152. Malouf, C., and A. A. Malouf. "The Effects of Spanish Slavery on the Indians of the Intermountain West." *Southwestern Journal of Anthropology* 1 (1945): 378-391.

13153. Mazrui, Ali A., and Bethwell Ogot. "Who Should Pay for Slavery." *World Press Review* 40 (August 1993): 22-23. [Reparations]

13154. McDonald, Roderick A. *The Economy and Material Culture of Slaves*. Louisiana State University Press, 1993.

13155. McDonnell, Lawrence T. "Money Knows No Master: Market Relations in the American Slave Community." in *Developing Dixie: Modernization in a Traditional Society*, eds. Winifred B. More, and Joseph F. Tripp. Westport, CT: Greenwood, 1988.

13156. McGary, Howard J., Jr., and Bill E. Lawson. *Between Slavery and Freedom: Philosophy and American Slavery*. Indiana University Press, 1993.

13157. McKinley, Catherine. "Infanticide and Slave Women." *Black Women in America* I 607-609.

13158. Meaders, Daniel E. *Fugitive Slaves and Indentured Servants before 1800*. Ph.D. diss., Yale University, 1990. UMO # 9034221.

13159. Miller, John Chester. *The Wolf by the Ears. Thomas Jefferson and Slavery*. Charlottesville: University Press of Virginia, 1991.

13160. Miller, Randall M. "The Fabric of Control--Slavery in Antebellum Southern Textile Mills." *Business History Review* 55 (1981): 471-490.

13161. Morgan, Philip D. "Slave Life in Piedmont Virginia, 1720- 1800." in *Colonial Chesapeake Society*, eds. Lois Green Carr and others. Chapel Hill: University of North Carolina Press: 1988.

13162. Morris, Christopher. "An Event in Community Organization: The Mississippi Slave Insurrection Scare of 1835." *Journal of Social History* 22 (1988): 93-111.

13163. Moss, R. S. *Slavery on Long Island: Its Rise and Decline During the Seventeenth through the Nineteenth Centuries*. Ph.D. diss., St. John's University, 1985.

13164. Nash, Gary B. "From 1688 to 1788: Slavery and Freedom in Pennsylvanis." in *States of Progress: Germans and Blacks in America over 300 Years...*, ed. Randall M. Miller. Phidldelphia, PA: German Society of Pennsylvania, 1989.

13165. Nordstrom, Carl. "The New York Slave Code." *Afro-American New York Life and History* 4 (January 1980): 7-25.

13166. Oakes, James. "The Political Significance of Slave Resistance." *History Workshop Journal* no. 22 (1986): 89-107.

13167. _____. *Slavery and Freedom. An Interpretation of the Old South*. NY Knopf: 1990.

13168. Olwell, Robert A. *Authority and Resistance: Social Order in a Colonial Slave Society, the South Carolina Lowcountry, 1739- 1782*. Ph.D. diss., John's Hopkins University, 1991. UMO # 9132700.

13169. Owen, Christopher H. *Sanctity, Slavery, and Segregation: Methodists and Society in Nineteenth Century Georgia*. Ph.D. diss., Emory University, 1991. UMO # 9204818.

13170. Owens, Leslie H. "The African in the Garden: Reflections about New World Slavery and Its Loneliness." in *The State of Afro-American History: Past, Present, and Future*, ed. Darlene Clark Hine. Baton Rouge: Louisiana State University Press, 1989.

13171. Parish, Peter J. *Slavery: History and Historians*. NY: Harper and Row, 1989.

13172. Pearson, Edward A. *From Stono to Vesey: Slavery, Resistance and Ideology in South Carolina, 1739-1822*. Ph.D. diss., University of Wisconsin, 1992. UMO # 9304173.

13173. Perdue, Theda. *Slavery and the Evolution of Cherokee Society, 1540-1866*. University of Tennessee Press, 1979.

13174. Phillips, Christopher W. *Negroes and Other Slaves: The African-American Community of Baltimore, 1790-1860*. Ph.D. diss., University of Georgia, 1992. UMO # 9235467.

13175. Phillips, William D., Jr. *Slavery from Roman Times to the Early Transatlantic Trade*. Minneapolis: University of Minnesota Press, 1985.

13176. Poole, Stafford and Douglas J. Slawson. *Church and Slave in Perry County, Missouri, 1818-1865*. Lewiston, PA: E. Mellen Press, 1986.

13177. Pritchett, Jonathan B., and R. M. Chamberlain. "Selection in the Market for Slaves: New Orleans, 1830-1860." *Quarterly Journal of Economics* 108 (May 1993).

13178. Ramos-Mattei, Andres. "Las condiciones de vida del esclavo en Puerto Rico: 1840-1873." *Anuario de Estudios Americanos (Spain)* 43 (1986): 377-390.

13179. Ransom, Roger L. *Conflict and Compromise: The Political Economy of Slavery, Emancipation, and the American Civil War.* NY: Cambridge University Press, 1989.

13180. Ransom, Roger L., and Richard Sutch. "Capitalists without Capital: The Burden of Slavery and the Impact of Emancipation." *Agricultural History* 62 (Summer 1988): 133-160.

13181. Reidy, Joseph P. "Slavery, Emancipation and the Capitalist Transformation of Southern Agriculture, 1850-1910." in *Agriculture and National Development*, ed. Lou Ferleger. : Iowa State University Press, 1990.

13182. Ripley, C. Peter and others, eds. *Witness for Freedom. African American Voices on Race, Slavery, and Emancipation*. University of North Carolina Press, 1993. [89 documents from 5-volume Black Abolitionist papers]

13183. Roberts, Diane. *The Myth of Aunt Jemimah. Representations of Race and Religion*. Routledge, 1994. [The history of white women's encounter with slavery and its aftermath]

13184. Schafer, Judith K. *Slavery, the Civil Law, and the Supreme Court of Louisiana*. Louisiana State University Press, 1994.

13185. Schweninger, Loren. "John Carrothers Stanly and the Anomaly of Black Slaveholding." *North Carolina Historical Review* 67 (1990): 159-192. [1774-1840]

13186. Shaffer, Ralph E. and others, eds. *Which Path to Freedom? The Black Anti-slavery Debate, 1815-1860*. Pomona, CA: School of Arts, California State Polytechnic University, 1986.

13187. Shaw, Robert B. *A Legal History of Slavery in the United States*. Potsdam, NY: Northern, 1991.

13188. Slaughter, Thomas P. *Bloody Dawn: The Christiana Riot and Racial Violence in the Antebellum North*. NY: Oxford University Press, 1992.

13189. Smith, Raymond T. "Race, Class, and Gender in the Transition of Freedom." in *The Meaning of Freedom*, eds. Frank McGlynn, and Seymour Drescher : University of Pittsburgh Press, 1992.

13190. Soderlund, Jean R. *Quakers and Slavery: A Divided Spirit*. Princeton, NJ: Princeton University Press, 1985.

13191. Stakeman, Randolph. "Slavery in Colonial Maine." *Maine Historical Society Quarterly* 27 (1987): 58-81.

13192. Starna, William A., and Ralph Watkins. "Northern Iroquoian Slavery." *Ethnohistory* 38 (Winter 1991): 34-57.

13193. _____. "Northern Iroquoian Slavery." *Ethnohistory* 38 (January 1991): 34-57.

13194. Starobin, Robert S., ed. *Blacks in Bondage. Letters of American Slaves*. Preiceton, NJ: Markus Wiener, 1991.

13195. Stevenson, Brenda E. "Slavery." *Black Women in America* II 1045-1070.

13196. Stewart, James B. *William Lloyd Garrison and the Challenge of Emancipation*. Arlington Heights, IL: Harlan Davidson, 1992.

13197. Stradling, David. *Morality, Economy and Political Philosophy: Determining the Factors in the Decline of Slavery in New Jersey, 1783-1814*. Master's thesis: Colgate University, 1990.

13198. Styron, William. "Slavery's Pain, Disney's Gain." *New York Times*, 4 August 1994.

13199. Sunseri, Alvin R. "Indian Slave Trade in New Mexico, 1846- 1861." *Indian Historian* 6 (1973): 20-22.

13200. Sutch, Richard. "The Breeding of Slaves for Sale and the Westward Expansion of Slavery, 1850-1860." in *Race and Slavery in the Western Hemisphere*, pp. 173-210. eds. Stanley L. Engerman, and Eugene D. Genovese. : Princeton University Press, 1975.

13201. Tadman, Michael. *Speculators and Slaves: Masters, Traders, and Slaves in the Old South*. Madison: University of Wisconsin Press, 1990.

13202. Thomas, Laurence M. *Vessels of Evil: American Slavery and the Holocaust*. Temple University Press, 1993.

13203. Thompson, Thomas M. *National Newspaper and Legislative Reactions to Louisiana's Deslondes Slave Revolt of 1811*. Master's thesis: Tulane University, 1990.

13204. "Transatlantic Slave Trade." *Social Science History* 13 (1989): 341-438.

13205. Vaughn, Alden T. "The Origins Debate: Slavery and Racism in Seventeenth-Century Virginia." *Virginia Magazine of History and Biography* 97 (July 1989): 311-354.

13206. Venet, Wenly H. *Neither Ballots Nor Bullets: Women Abolitionists and the Civil War*. Charlottesville: University Press of Virginia, 1992.

13207. Walker, James W. St G. "Blacks as American Loyalists: The Slaves' War for Independence." *Historical Reflections* 2 (1975): 51-67.

13208. Westfall, William. "Antislavery as a Racist Outlet: A Hypothesis." *International Social Science Revies* 61 (Winter 1986): 3-11.

13209. White, Deborah G. "Female Slaves: Sex Roles and Status in the Antebellum Plantation South." *Journal of Family History* 8 (Fall 1983): 248-261.

SOCIALISM AND RACISM

13210. Andrews, E. F. "Socialism and the Negro." *International Socialist Review* 5 (1905): 125-153.

13211. Barsh, Russell L. "Contemporary Marxist Theory and Native American Reality." *American Indian Quarterly* 12 (1988): 187-211.

13212. Boyd, Herb. "Blacks and the American Left." *Crisis* (February 1988): 22-31.

13213. Cresswell, Stephen. "Red Mississippi: The State's Socialist Party, 1914-1920." *Journal of Mississippi History* 50 (August 1988): 153-171.

13214. Gorman, Robert A. "Black Neo-Marxism in Liberal America." *Rethinking Marxism* 2 (Winter 1989): 118-140.

13215. Grigsby, Daryl. *For the People. Black Socialists in the United States, Africa and the Caribbean.* San Diego, CA: Asante Publications, 1989.

13216. Gunn, John Walker. "Socialism and the Negro." *Appeal to Reason*, 18 September 1915.

13217. Harris, Abram L. *Race, Radicalism, and Reform: Selected Papers.* New Brunswick, NJ: Transaction Publication, 1989. [Darity, William A., Jr., ed.]

13218. Shawki, Ahmed. "Black Liberation and Socialism in the United States." *International Socialism* (July 1990).

13219. Solomon, Mark I. *Red and Black: Communism and Afro-Americans, 1929-1935.* NY: Garland, 1988.

13220. Vidrine, E. "Negro Locals." *International Socialist Review* 5 (January 1905): 389-405.

13221. Washington-Bolder, Jacqueline. *American Socialism: Its Origin, Nature and Impact on the Black Working Class and the Socio-economic Development of the United States.* Ph.D. diss., Howard University, 1975.

13222. Zamora, Emilio, Jr. "Chicano Socialist Labor Activity in Texas, 1900-1920." *Aztlan* 6 (Summer 1975): 221-236.

SPORTS

13223. Alexander, A. *Status of Minority Women in the Association of Intercollegiate Athletics for Women*. Master's thesis, Temple University, 1978.

13224. Anderson, Dave. "Community Relations, Yankee Style." *New York Times*, 19 July 1994. [Racist remarks by official of Yankee baseball team]

13225. Anderson, Torben. *Race Discrimination by Major League Baseball Fans*. Ph.D. diss., University of Washington, 1988. [Baseball-card pricing and All-Star voting; see Nardinelli and Regoli, below]. UMO # 8911601.

13226. Araton, Harvey and Filip. *The Financial Rise and Moral Decline of the Boston Celtics*. NY: Harper Collins, 1992.

13227. Banks, Michael A. *Black Athletes in the Media, 2 vols*. Ph.D. diss., CUNY, 1993. UMO #9325068.

13228. Beran, Janice S. "Diamonds in Iowa: Blacks, Buxton, and Baseball." *Journal of Negro History* 75 (Summer, Fall 1990): 81- 95.

13229. Berkow, Ira. "A Black Star Long, Long Ago." *New York Times*, 24 November 1990. [Charles Gregory, first Black college All-American basketball player at Columbia University, 1931]

13230. _____. "Players Find Glory Replaced by Reality." *New York Times*, 3 April 1992. [Former college basketball players and their post-college careers]

13231. _____. "Schott Punished for Wrong Thing." *New York Times*, 4 February 1993. [Marge Schott, part-owner of Cincinnati Reds baseball team]

13232. Berryman, Jack W. "Early Black Leadership in Collegiate Football." in *Education in Massachusetts: Selected Essays*, eds. Michael F. Konig, and Martin Kaufman. Westfield, MA: Westfield State College, 1989.

13233. Bierman, J. A. "The Effect of Television Sports Media on Black Male Youth." *Sociological Inquiry* 60 (Autumn 1990): 413- 427.

13234. Blum, Debra E. "Black Coaches vs an NCAA Rule." *Chronicle of Higher Education*, 10 November 1993.

13235. _____. "Few Black Sports Administrators Have Been Hired by Colleges." *Chronicle of Higher Education*, 14 September 1994.

13236. _____. "Forum Examines Discrimination Against Black Women in College Sports." *Chronicle of Higher Education*, 21 April 1993.

13237. Boulding, D. C. *Participation of the Negro in Selected Amateur and Professional Athletics from 1935 to 1955*. Master's thesis: University of Wisconsin, Madison, 1957.

13238. Boyle, R. H. "A Minority Group: The Negro Baseball Player." in *Sport: Mirror of American Life*, pp. 100-134. ed. Boyle. Boston: Little, Brown, 1963.

13239. Braddock, Jomills Henry, II. *Institutional Discrimination: A Study of Managerial Recruitment in Professional Football*. National Football League Players Association, 1980.

13240. _____. "Sport and Race Relations in American Society." *Sociological Spectrum* 9 (1989): 53-76.

13241. "Breaking the Greens' Color Line." *Boston Globe*, 17 August 1991. [Racial exclusion by private golf clubs]

13242. Brown, E. and others. "Wage and Nonwage Discrimination in Professional Basketball: Do Fans Affect It?" *American Journal of Economics and Sociology* 50 (July 1991): 333-346.

13243. Brown, R. W., and R. T. Jewell. "Is There Customer Discrimination in College Basketball? The Premium Fans Pay for White Players." *Social Science Quarterly* 75 (June 1994): 401-413.

13244. Burdekin, R. C. K., and T. L. Idson. "Customer Preferences, Attendance and the Racial Structure of Professional Basketball Teams." *Applied Economics* 23, Part b (January 1993).

13245. Cahn, Susan K. *Coming or Strong: Gender and Sexuality in Women's Sport, 1900-1960, 2 vols.* Ph.D. diss., University of Minnesota, 1990. UMO # 9100929.

13246. Callahan, Tom. "Exacting Obedience, Offering Disrespect." *Washington Post*, 7 February 1993. [Racism in baseball}

13247. Capeci, Dominic J., Jr., and Martha Wilkerson. "Multifarious Hero: Joe Louis, American Society, and Race Relations during World Crisis, 1935-1945." in *The Sporting Image: Readings in American Sport History*, ed. Paul J. Zingg. Lanham, MD: University Press of America, 1988.

13248. Captain, G. "Enter Ladies and Gentlemen of Color: Gender, Sport, and the Ideal of African American Manhood and Womanhood during the Late 19th and Early 20th Centuries." *Journal of Sport History* 18 (Spring 1991): 81-102.

13249. Cattau, Daniel. "Baseball Strikes Out With Black Fans." *Chicago Reporter* 20 (April 1991).

13250. Chalk, Ocania. *Black College Sport*. NY: Dodd Mead, 1976. [History of Black athletes in colleges]

13251. Chamlin, Mitchell B., and Bruce J. Arneklev. "Macro-social Determinants of the Racial Composition of Major League Baseball Teams." *Sociological Focus* 26 (February 1993): 65-79.

13252. Christl, Cliff. "Chapter 220 and Athletics." *Milwaukee Journal*, 15 January 1989. [City-suburban desegregation and Black high school students on predominantly white teams.]

13253. Chu, Donald B., and J. O. Segrave. "Leadership Recruitment and Ethnic Stratification in Basketball." *Journal of Sport and Social Issues* 5 (Fall/Winter 1980): 13-22.

13254. Cole, Lewis. *Never Too Young to Die: The Death of Len Bias*. NY: Pantheon, 1989.

13255. Costa, D. Margaret, and Jane A. Adair. "Sports." *Black Women in America, II* 1099-1102.

13256. Davis, J. E. "Baseball's Reluctant Challenge: Desegregating Major League Spring Training Sites, 1961-1964." *Journal of Sports History* 19 (Summer 1992).

13257. Davis, Laurel R. "The Articulation of Difference: White Preoccupation with the Question of Racially Linked Genetic Differences among Athletes." *Sociology of Sport Journal* 7 (1990): 179-187.

13258. Denlinger, Ken. "America's Sports Still Lag in Race." *Washington Post*, 7 February 1993.

13259. Diaz, Jaime. "In Golf, Integration is More Than 9-Iron Away." *New York Times*, 5 August 1991.

13260. _____. "Racism Issue Shakes World of Golf." *New York Times*, 29 July 1990.

13261. Dixon, Phil with Hannigan, Patrick J. *The Negro Baseball Leagues: A Photographic History. 1992*. Ameron Ltd., P.O. Box 1200, Mattituck, NY 11952.

13262. Early, Gerald. "Baseball and African-American Life." in *Baseball. An Illustrated History*, Geoffrey C. Ward, and Ken Burns. : Knopf, 1994.

13263. Edwards, Harry. "Beyond Symptoms: Unethical Behavior in American Collegiate Sport and the Problem of the Color Line." *Journal of Sport and Social Issues* 9 (Summer-Fall 1985): 3-13.

13264. _____. "Sport Within the Veil: The Triumphs, Tragedies and Challenges of Afro-American Involvement." *Annals of the American Academy of Political and Social Sciences* 445 (September 1979): 116-128.

13265. Eitzen, Stanley D. *Black Athletes in American Society Since 1940: Continuity and Change in Racial Barriers to Equal Participation*. Paper prepared for the Committee on the Status of Black Americans, National Research Council, Washington, D.C., 1986.

13266. Eitzen, Stanley D., and David Furst. "Racial Bias in Women's Collegiate Volleyball." *Journal of Sport and Social Issues* 13 (1989): 46-57.

13267. Fainaru, Steve. "Blacks At Fenway." *Boston Globe*, 4 August 1991. [The Boston Red Sox and the race issue]

13268. Foley, Douglas E. "The Great American Football Ritual: Reproducing Race, Class, And Gender Inequality." *Sociology of Sport Journal* 7 (1990): 111-135.

13269. Frey, Darcy. "The Last Shot." *Harper's Magazine* (April 1993). [Basketball life in a Coney Island housing project]

13270. Gammons, Peter. "Minority Hiring Problem Needs Reasonable Solution." *Boston Globe*, 15 November 1991. [Scarcity of minority front-office employees in organized baseball]

13271. Gaston, John. "The Destruction of the Young Black Male: The Impact of Popular Culture and Organized Sports." *Journal of Black Studies* 16 (June 1986): 369-384.

13272. George, John P. "The Virtual Disappearance of the White Male Sprinter in the United States: A Speculative Essay." *Sociology of Sport Journal* 11 (March 1994): 70-78.

13273. George, Nelson. "B-Ball Buppie." *Village Voice*, May 1989. [Michael Jordan and commercial endorsements]

13274. _____. *Elevating the Game: Black Men and Basketball*. NY: Harper Collins, 1992.

13275. Gonzalez Echevarria, R. "The Cuban Baseball Crisis." *New York Times*, 6 April 1992. [The threat of genuine multiculturalism in American professional baseball]

13276. Green, Robert L. and others. "Black Athletes: Educational, Economic, and Political Considerations." *Journal of Non-White Concerns* 3 (October 1974): 6-38.

13277. Greenberg, Henry B. ("Hank"). *Hank Greenberg: The Story of My Life (Edited by Ira Berkow)*. NY: Times Books, 1989. [Touches on antisemitism against Greenberg, major league baseball player]

13278. Greene, Linda S. "Reaching Beyond Personal Slurs to Public Policy. Major League Baseball Must Address and Then End Its Institutional Racism." *New York Times*, 13 December 1992.

13279. Guttmann, Allen. "Black Athletes." in *A Whole New Ball Game: An Interpretation of American Sports*, Guttmann. Chapel Hill: University of North Carolina Press, 1988.

13280. Haberman, John. "Crossover Dreams--and Nightmares." *Boston Globe*, 21 August 1994. [Black identity and sport in America]

13281. Harris, Othello. "Race, Sport and Social Support." *Sociology of Sport Journal* 11 (March 1994): 40-50.

13282. _____. *Sport and Race: A Comparison of the Social and Academic Worlds of Black and White Student Athletes*. Ph.D. diss., University of Maryland, 1989. UMO # 8924161.

13283. Holway, John. *Black Diamonds: Life in the Negro Leagues from the Men Who Lived It*. Westport, CT: Meckler, 1989.

13284. _____. *Blackball Stars: Negro League Pioneers*. Westport, CT: Meckler, 1988.

13285. Hoose, Phillip M. "A New Pool of Talent." *New York Times Magazine*, 29 April 1990. [Black swimmers]

13286. Hughes, Raymond. *Desegregating the Holy Day: Football, Blacks, and the Southeastern Conference*. Ph.D. diss., Ohio State University, 1991. UMO # 9130489.

13287. Hunter, David W. *A Comparison of Anaerobic Power between Black and White Adolescent Males*. Ph.D. diss., Ohio State University, 1988. [Forty-yard dash]. UMO # 8907241.

13288. Jackson, Bo, and Dick Schaap. *Bo Knows Bo: The Autobiography of a Ballplayer*. Garden City, NY: Doubleday, 1990.

13289. Jackson, Derrick Z. "Grades Before Sport." *Boston Globe*, 27 October 1991. [Robert Smith, ex-football player at Ohio State University]

13290. _____. "Stereotypes Carry the Ball on New Year's Day." *Boston Globe*, 7 January 1990. [Network television's animalistic characterization of Black football players]

13291. Jenkins, Thomas H. "Social Forces and Ecology of Institutions in the Social Production of Professional Boxers: A Study of Ethnic Succession and Social Change." *Sociological Abstracts* (1989). [1890-1949] Accession No. 89S20910.

13292. Jennings, Kenneth M. "The Race and Ethnic Issue." in *Balls and Strikes, The Money Game in Professional Baseball*, Kenneth M. Jennings. Westport, CT: Praeger, 1990.

13293. Jennings, Kenneth M., and F. McLaughlin. "Wage and Performance Discrimination: The Situation Facing Hispanics and Blacks in Major League Baseball." *Journal of Behavaioral Economics* 18 (Winter 1989).

13294. Johnson, N. R., and D. P. Marple. "Racial Discrimination in Professional Basketball: An Empirical Test." *Sociological Focus* 6 (1973): 6-18.

13295. Jones, Gregg A. and others. "Racial Discrimination in College Football." *Social Science Quarterly* 68 (1987): 70-83.

13296. Kahn, Lawrence M. "Discrimination in Professional Sports: A Survey of the Literature." *Industrial and Labor Relations Review* 44 (1991): 395-418.

13297. _____. "The Effects of Race on Professional Football Players' Compensation." *Industrial and Labor Relations Review* 45 (January 1992): 295-310.

13298. Koch, James, and C. W. VanderHill. "Is There Discrimination in the 'Black Man's Game'?" *Social Science Quarterly* 69 (March 1988): 83-94. [NBA]

13299. Koostra, Paul and others. "The Unequal Opportunity for Equal Ability Hypothesis: Racism in the National Football League." *Sociology of Sport Journal* 10 (September 1993): 241-255.

13300. Lapchick, Richard E. *Five Minutes to Midnight: Race and Sport in America in the 1990's*. Lanham, MD: University Press of America, 1991.

13301. _____. *Pass to Play: Student Athletes and Academics*. Washington, D.C.: National Education Association, 1989.

13302. Lapchick, Richard E., and J. P. Brown. *1992 Racial Report Card*. Center for the Study of Sport in Society, 1992.

13303. Lapchick, Richard E., and John B. Slaughter. *The Rules of the Game: Ethics in College Sport*. Macmillan 1989.

13304. Lapchick, Richard E., and D. Stucky. *The Racial Report Card: Race in the NBA, NFL, and MLB*. Center for the Study of Sport in Society, 1991.

13305. Lavoie, Marc, and Wilbert M. Leonard, II. "Salaries, Race/ Ethnicity, and Pitchers in Major League Baseball: A Correlation and Comment." *Sociology of Sport Journal* 7 (December 1990): 394- 398.

13306. Leonard, Wilbert M., II. and others. "Performance and Characteristics of White, Black, and Hispanic Major League Baseball Players: 1955-1984." *Journal of Sport and Social Issues* 12 (Spring-Fall 1988): 31-43.

13307. Leonard, Wilbert M., II. "Salaries and Race/Ethnicity in Major League Baseball: The Pitching Component." *Sociology of Sport Journal* 6 (June 1989): 152-162.

13308. Levine, Peter. *Ellis Island to Ebbets Field. Sport and the American Jewish Experience*. Oxford University Press, 1992.

13309. Levy, Scott J. "Tricky Ball: [James] "Cool Papa' Bell and Life in the Negro Leagues." *Gateway Heritage* 9 (Spring 1989): 26- 35.

13310. Lewis, Carl with Jeffrey Marx. *Inside Track: My Professional Life in Amateur Track and Field*. NY Simon and Schuster: 1990.

13311. Lipsyte, Robert. "Blacks on the [Basketball] Court; Why Not on Campus?" *New York Times*, 27 March 1992.

13312. MacMillan, Jackie. "Going to Extremes on Stanley." *Boston Globe*, 26 August 1990. [Jerome Stanley, Black basketball players' agent]

13313. Mathisen, J. A., and G. S. Mathisen. "The Rhetoric of Racism in Sport: Tom Brokaw Revisited." *Sociology of Sport Journal* 8 (June 1991): 168-177.

13314. McRae, F. Finley. "Hidden Traps Beneath the Placid Greens, A History of Blacks in Golf." *American Visions* (April 1991).

13315. Medoff, Marshall. "Baseball Attendance and Fan Discrimination." *Journal of Behavioral Economics* 15 (Spring- Summer 1986): 149-155.

13316. Miller, Patrick. "With the Same Traits of Courage...The Early Afro-American Experience in Sports." *Proteus* 3 (1986): 60- 66.

13317. Mullen, Phil, and Mark Clark. "Blacks in Baseball: An Historical Perspective, 1867-1988." in *Cooperstown Symposium on Baseball and the American Culture*, ed. Alvin L. Hall. : Meckler, 1991.

13318. Muwakkil, Salim. "Overachiever vs. Underclass: A Black Athlete's Obligation." *In These Times*, 11 September 1991. [Michael Jordan]

13319. Naison, Marta. "Doing the Right Thing: Youth, Sports, and Race in Brooklyn, USA." *Reconstruction* 1 (1991): 68-71.

13320. Nardinelli, C., and C. Simon. "Customer Racial Discrimination in the Market for Memorabilia: The Case of Baseball." *Quarterly Journal of Economics* 105 (August 1990). [Baseball cards; see Anderson, above, and Regoli, below.]

13321. Newton, Edmund. "Tournament of Roses to Add 5 Minorities." *Los Angeles Times*, 30 November 1993.

13322. Ostenby, Peter M. *Other Games, Other Glory: The Memphis Red Sox and the Trauma of Integration, 1948-1955*. Master's thesis, University of North Carolina, 1989.

13323. Pascal, Anthony M., and Leonard A. Rapping. *Racial Discrimination in Organized Baseball*. Santa Monica, CA: Rand Corporation, 1970.

13324. Pattnayak, S. R., and J. Leonard. "Racial Segregation in Major League Baseball, 1989." *Sociology and Social Research* 76 (October 1991): 3-9.

13325. Pennington, Richard. *Breaking the Ice: The Racial Integration of Southwest Conference Football*. Jefferson, NC: McFarland, 1987.

13326. Phillipps, John C. "The Integration of Central Positions in Baseball: The Black Shortstop." *Sociology of Sport Journal* 8 (1991): 161-167.

13327. Plaschke, Bill. "Cincy Takes Schott to the Heart." *Los Angeles Times*, 1 May 1993. [Marge Schott, principal owner of the Cincinnati Reds baseball team, makes racially derogatory remarks]

13328. Purdy, D. A. and others. "A Reexamination of Salary Discrimination in Major League Baseball by Race/Ethnicity." *Sociology of Sport Journal* 11 (March 1994): 60-69.

13329. "Racial Minorities and Big-time U.S. Team Sports." *Qualitative Sociology* 15 (1992): review essays.

13330. Rainville, R. E., and McCormick E. "Extent of Covert Racial Prejudice in Pro Football Announcers' Speech." *Journalism Quarterly* 54 (1978): 20-26.

13331. Reed, Wornie L. "Blacks in Golf." *Trotter Institute Review* 5 (Winter/Spring 1991): 19-23.

13332. _____. "Sports Notes. The Minimal Pay of College Athletes." *Trotter Institute Review* 3 (Spring 1989): 17-18. [Published by University of Massachusetts, Boston]

13333. Regoli, B. "Racism in Baseball Card Collecting." *Human Relations* 44 (March 1991): 255-264. [See Andersen and Nardinelli, above]

13334. Rhoden, William C. "N.C.A.A.'s Smoke and Morrors." *New York Times*, 11 January 1992. [Black college athletes]

13335. Riess, Steven A. "Race and Ethnicity in American Baseball, 1900-1919." in *The Sporting Image: Readings in American Sport History*, pp. 247-266. ed. Paul J. Zingg. Lanham, MD: University Press of America, 1988.

13336. _____. "Sport, Race, and Ethnicity in the American City, 1870-1950." in *Immigration and Ethnicity*, eds. Michael D'Innocenzo, and Josef P. Sirefman : Greenwood, 1992.

13337. Roberts, Randy, and James S. Olson. *Winning Is the Only Thing. Sports in America since 1945*. Baltimore, MD: Johns Hopkins University Press, 1989.

13338. Sage, George H. *Power and Ideology in American Sport: A Critical Perspective*. Human Kinetics, 1990.

13339. Sailes, G. A. "The Myth of Black Sports Supremacy." *Journal of Black Studies* 21 (June 1991): 480-487.

13340. Samson, Jacques, and M. Yerles. "Racial Differences in Sports Performances [in the U.S.]." *Canadian Journal of Sport Sciences* 13 (June 1988): 109-116.

13341. Sandomir, Richard. "Baseball Segregation Victims Still Cannot Claim the Glory." *New York Times*, 15 March 1993. [Exploitation of former Negro Baseball Leaguers]

13342. Schneider, John J., and Stanley D. Eitzen. "Racial Segregation by Professional Football Positions, 1960-1985." *Sociology and Social Research* 70 (1986): 259-261.

13343. Scully, Gerald W. "Discrimination: The Case of Baseball." in *Government and the Sports Business*, pp. 221-274. ed. R. Nott. : Brookings Institution, 1974.

13344. Sellers, R. M. "Racial Differences in the Predictors for Academic Achievement of Student-Athletes in Division I Revenue- Producing Sports." *Sociology of Sport Journal* 9 (March 1992): 48- 59.

13345. Sexton, Joe. "Rough Road for Blacks in the NHL." *New York Times*, 25 February 1990. [National Hockey League]

13346. Shapiro, Leonard. *Big Man on Campus, John Thompson and the Georgetown Hoyas*. NY: Holt, 1991.

13347. Shropshire, Kenneth L. *Agents of Opportunity. Sports Agents and Corruption in Collegiate Sports*. Philadelphia: University of Pennsylvania Press, 1990.

13348. Silverman, Buddy R. S. *The Jewish Athletes Hall of Fame*. NY: Shapolsky Publishers, 1989.

13349. Smith, Claire. "Baseball Failing in Minority Hiring, Officials Say." *New York Times*, 28 September 1991. [Hiring for management, not playing, positions]

13350. _____. "Baseball's Angry Man." *New York Times Magazine*, 13 October 1991. [William D. (Bill) White, Black president of National League]

13351. _____. "Belated Tribute to Baseball's Negro Leagues." *New York Times*, 13 August 1991.

13352. _____. "No Prejudice in Pinstripes, the Yanks Maintain." *New York Times*, 26 February 1993. [Absence of Blacks and Hispanics in Yankee front-office jobs]

13353. Smith, Earl, and Monica A. Seff. "Race, Positions Segregation and Salary Equity in Professional Baseball." *Journal of Sport and Social Issues* 13 (1989): 92-110.

13354. Smith, Sam. *The Jordan Rules*. NY: Simon and Shuster, 1992. [Michael Jordan]

13355. Smith, Thomas G. "Outside the Pale: The Exclusion of Blacks from the National Football League, 1946-1954." *Journal of Sport History* 15 (1988): 255-281.

13356. Sommers, Paul M., ed. *Diamonds Are Forever. The Business of Baseball*. Washington, D.C.: Brookings Institution, 1992.

13357. Sperber, Murray. *College Sports Inc. The Athletic Department vs. The University*. NY: Holt, 1990.

13358. Spivey, Donald, and Thomas E. Jones. "Intercollegiate Athletic Servitude: A Case Study of the Black Illini Student Athletes, 1931-1967." in *The Sporting Image: Readings in American Sporting Image*, ed. Paul J. Zingg. Lanham, MD: University Press of America, 1988.

13359. Starr, Mark and others. "Baseball's Black Problem." *Newsweek*, 19 July 1993. [Organized baseball's estrangement from the African-American community]

13360. Sulek, Robert P. *Academic Support Services for College Basketball Programs: A Case Study of Indiana University during Coach Bob Knight's Tenure (1972-present)*. Ph.D. diss., Harvard University, 1989. UMO #9000884.

13361. Valenti, John and Ron Naelerio. *Swee'pea and Other Playground Legends. Tales of Drugs, Violence, and Basketball*. NY: Michael Kesend Publishing, 1990.

13362. Vanfossen, Beth E. and others. "Social Mobility Opportunities through Sports Participation by Race and Gender." *Sociological Abstracts* (1989). [High school] Accession No. 89S21786.

13363. Wacquant, Loic J. D. "The Social Logic of Boxing in Black Chicago: Toward a Sociology of Pugilism." *Sociology of Sport Journal* 9 (September 1992): 221-254.

13364. Waldman, Steven, and Clara Bingham. "Sports, Race and Politics." *Newsweek*, 17 August 1992. [The racial education of Jack Kemp and Bill Bradley]

13365. Wartberg, Steve. *Winning is an Attitude. A Season in the Life of John Chaney and the Temple Owls*. NY: St. Martin's Press, 1991.

13366. Watson, Tom. "The American Way of Golf." *New York Times*, 17 June 1991. [Discrimination in golf-club membership]

13367. Whitney, Stu, and Bob Kourtakis. *Behind the Green Curtain: The Sacrifice of Ethics and Academics in Michigan State Football's Rise to National Prominence*. Grand Rapids, MI: Masters Press, 1990.

13368. Wiggins, David K. "The Future of College Athletics Is at Stake: Black Athletes and Racial Turmoil on Three Predominantly White University Campuses, 1968-1972." *Journal of Sport History* 15 (1988): 304-333. [University of California, Berkeley, Syracuse University, and Oregon State University]

13369. _____. "Great Speed but Little Stamina. The Historical Debate Over Black Athletic Superiority." *Journal of Sport History* 16 (1989): 158-185.

13370. _____. "Prized Performers, But Frequently Overlooked Students: The Involvement of Black Athletes in Intercollegiate Sports on Predominantly White University Campuses, 1890-1972." *Research Quarterly for Exercise and Sport* 62 (June 1991): 164- 177.

13371. Williams, R., and Z. Youssef. "Consistency of Football Coaches in Stereotyping the Personality of Each Position's Player." *International Journal of Sport Psychology* 3 (1972): 3- 13.

13372. Wilson, Wayne. *Racial Hiring Practices of Los Angeles Area Sports Organizations*. Amateur Athletic Foundation of Los Angeles, December 1992.

13373. Wolff, Alexander, and Armen Keteyian. *Raw Recruits*. NY: Pocket Books, 1991. [Black athletes in higher education]

13374. Yetman, Norman R., and Forrest J. Berghorn. "Racial Participation and Integration in Intercollegiate Basketball: A Longitudinal Perspective." *Sociology of Sport Journal* 10 (September 1993): 301-314. [1948-1990]

13375. Zimbalist, Andrew. *Baseball and Billions: A Probing Look Inside the Big Business of Our National Pastime*. Basic Books, 1993.

STEREOTYPES

13376. Abrahamse, Allan F. and others. *Beyond Stereotypes: Who Becomes a Single Teenage Mother*. Santa Monica, CA: Rand 1988.

13377. Abrams, D. and others. "Social Identity and the Handicapping Functions of Stereotypes: Children's Understanding of Mental and Physical Handicap." *Human Relations* 43 (November 1990).

13378. Albert, Alexa A., and Judith R. Porter. "Children's Gender-Role Stereotypes: A Sociological Investigation of Psychological Models." *Sociological Forum* 3 (Spring 1988): 184- 210.

13379. Alexandro, Francis W. "Stereotyping as a Method of Exploitation in Film." *Black Scholar* (May 1976): 26-29.

13380. Aoki, Guy, and Philip W. Chung. "'Rising Sun', Hollywood and Asian Stereotypes." *Los Angeles Times*, 3 May 1993. [Anti- Asian stereotypes]

13381. Applebome, Peter. "Arabs in U.S. Feel Separated by Other Gulfs." *New York Times*, 10 February 1991.

13382. Arkel, Dik van. "The Growth of the Anti-Jewish Stereotype: An Attempt at a Hypothetical-Deductive Method of Historical Research." *International Review of Social History* 10 (1985): 170- 306.

13383. Aucoin, Don. "Street Stereotypes." *Boston Globe*, 18 May 1990. [Black youth]

13384. Baker, Bob. "Stereotype That Won't Go Away." *Los Angeles Times*, 31 May 1992. [Young Black males]

13385. Bardwell, Jill R. and others. "Relationship of Parental Education, Race, and Gender to Sex Role Stereotyping in Five- Year-Old Kindergartners." *Sex Roles* 15 (September 1986): 275-281.

13386. Barnett, Marguerite Ross. "Nostalgia as Nightmare: Blacks and American Popular Culture." *Crisis* 89 (1982): 42-45.

13387. Barr, Alwyn. "African Americans in Texas: From Stereotypes to Diverse Roles." in *Texas Through Times*, eds. Walter L. Buenger, and Robert A. Calvery. : Texas A and M University Press, 1991.

13388. Bar-Tal, Daniel and others. *Stereotyping and Prejudice: Changing Conceptions*. NY: Springer-Verlog, 1989.

13389. Bartholomaus, Craig W. Of One Blood: The Nineteenth Century African-American Literary Response to Racial Stereotyping Ph.D. diss., University of Colorado, 1991. UMO #9206597.

13390. Bataille, Gretchen M., and Charles L. P. Silet. *The Pretend Indians: Images of Native Americans in the Movies*. Ames: Iowa State University Press, 1980.

13391. Berg, C. R. "Stereotyping in Films in General and of the Hispanic in Particular." *Howard Journal of Communications* 2 (Summer 1990): 236-300.

13392. Bergen, David J., and John E. Williams. "Sex Stereotypes in the United States Revisited: 1972-1988." *Sex Roles* 24 (April 1991): 413-424.

13393. Blum, Justin. "Some See Pride, Others Hatred." *Washington Post*, 30 June 1993. [Flying the Confederate battle flag]

13394. Brenson, Michael. "Black Images, American History." *New York Times*, 20 April 1990. [Racial stereotypes in the history of U.S. Paintings, drawings, and sculpture]

13395. Britt, Brian. "Georgia Rallies 'Round the Flag." *Nation*, 5 April 1993. [St. Andrew's Cross of the Confederate battle banner]

13396. Brott, Armin A. "Not All Men Are Sly Foxes." *Newsweek*, 1 June 1992.

13397. Bryant, Z. Lois and others. "Race and Family Structure Stereotyping: Perceptions of Black and White Nuclear Families and Stepfamilies." *Journal of Black Psychology* 15 (Fall 1988): 1-16.

13398. Burnham, Margaret A. "Stereotypes and Suspicion." *Boston Globe*, 14 July 1994. [Anti-Black stereotypes]

13399. Campbell, Donald T. "Stereotypes and Perceptions of Group Differences." *American Psychologist* 22 (1967): 812-829.

13400. Canellos, Peter S. "Stitching up an Identity." *Boston Globe*, 15 June 1991. [Problems of distributing Black dollar]

13401. Carr, Norma. *The Puerto Ricans in Hawaii: 1900-1958.* Ph.D. diss., University of Hawaii, 1989. [see, esp., chapter 9]. UMO #9019003.

13402. Carranza, E. Lou. "Stereotypes about Mexican Americans." *San Jose Studies* 19 (Winter 1993): 34-43.

13403. Chikoma. "The Neglect of the Black Intellectual." *African Commentary* 1 (November 1989): 38-39.

13404. Chupa, Anna M. *Anne, the White Woman in Contemporary African-American Fiction: Archetypes, Stereotypes and Characterizations.* NY: Greenwood Press, 1990.

13405. Clifton, James A., ed. *The Invented Indian: Iconoclastic Essays.* New Brunswick, NJ: Transaction,, 1990.

13406. Coatsworth, John H., and Carlos Rico, eds. *Images of Mexico in the United States.* La Jolla, CA: Center for U.S.- Mexican Studies, University of California, San Diego, La Jolla California 92093, 1989.

13407. Cohen, N. W. "Antisemitic Imagery: The Nineteenth Century Background." *Jewish Social Studies* 47 (Summer-Fall 1985): 307- 312.

13408. Devine, Patricia G. "Automatic and Controlled Processes in Prejudice: The Role of Stereotypes and Personal Beliefs." in *Attitude Structure and Function*, eds. Anthony R. Pratkanis and others. Hillsdale, NJ: Lawrence Erlbaum Associates, 1989.

13409. _____. "Stereotypes and Prejudice: Their Automatic and Controlled Components." *Journal of Personality and Social Psychology* 56 (January 1989): 5-18.

13410. Devine, Patricia G., and S. M. Baker. "Measurement of Racial Stereotype Subtyping." *Personality and Social Psychology Bulletin* 17 (February 1991): 44-50.

13411. Diab, Lufty N. "Factors Affecting Studies of National Stereotypes." *Journal of Social Psychology* 59 (1963): 29-40.

13412. Dillow, Gordon. "Dolls Like Me." *Los Angeles Times*, 2 December 1993. [Ethnically-appropriate dolls]

13413. "Does 'Aladdin' Stereotype Arabs/ Children Say Yes--and No." *Los Angeles Times*, 14 June 1993.

13414. Dorman, James H. "Ethnic Stereotyping in American Popular Culture: The Depiction of American Ethnics in the Cartoon Periodicals of the Gilded Age." *Amerikastudien/American Studies* 30 (1985): 489-507.

13415. _____. "Shaping the Popular Image of Post- Reconstruction American Blacks: The 'Coon Song' Phenomenon of the Gilded Age." *American Quarterly* 40 (December 1988): 450-471. [1865-1896]

13416. Dorris, Michael. "Noble Savages? We'll Drink to That." *New York Times*, 21 April 1992. [Cultural expoloitation of Native Americans].

13417. Doten, Patti. "Palestinians In a New Light. Out of the Intifadah, Truer Views of a People." *Boston Globe*, 27 June 1989. [Boston area]

13418. Drummond, Tammerlin. "Fight Against Stereotypes Is an Education for Muslim." *Los Angeles Times*, 20 September 1992. [Tustin, CA]

13419. Dubin, Steven C. "Symbolic Slavery: Black Representations in Popular Culture." *Social Problems* 34 (1987): 122-140.

13420. DuBois, Rachel D. "Our Enemy--The Stereotype." *Progressive Education* 12 (March 1935): 146-150.

13421. Dworkin, Anthony G., and Rosalind J. Dworkin. "Interethnic Stereotypes of Acculturating Asian Indians in the United States." *Plural Societies* 18 (July 1988): 61-70.

13422. Eagly, Alice H., and Antonio Mladinic. "Gender Stereotypes and Attitudes Toward Women and Men." *Personality and Social Psychology Bulletin* 15 (December 1989).

13423. Ehrlich, Howard J. "Stereotyping and Negro-Jewish Stereotypes." *Social Forces* 41 (1962): 171-176.

13424. Elrich, Marc. "The Stereotype Within. Why My Students Don't Buy Black History Month." *Washington Post*, 13 February 1994.

13425. Falkenberg, Loren. "Improving the Accuracy of Stereotypes within the Workplace." *Journal of Management* 16 (1990): 107-118. [Gender]

13426. Farsy, Fouad A. Al-. "Cultural Stereotyping and Foreign Policy." *American-Arab Affairs* 31 (Winter 1989-90): 1-10.

13427. Fernandez, Raul. "The Political Economy of Stereotypes." *Aztlan* 1 (Fall 1970): 39-45.

13428. Firestone, David. "Attacking the Stereotypes in Toyland." *Los Angeles Times*, 31 December 1993.

13429. Fiske, S. T. and others. "Social Science Research on Trial: Use of Sex Stereotyping Research in "Price Waterhouse v. Hopkins"." *American Psychologist* 46 (October 1991): 1061-1070.

13430. Fitzpatrick, Robert B. "Stereotyping in the Workplace: Evidence of Discrimination?" *Trial* 26 (January 1990).

13431. Forster, Imogen. "Stereotypes: Mainly for the Very Young: Racism in Children's Books." *Artage* No. 11 (Winter 1985).

13432. Fouquette, Danielle A. "Largely Latino High School Fights Ethnic Stereotyping." *Los Angeles Times*, 13 April 1993.

13433. Fowler, Don D. "Images of American Indians, 1492-1892." *Halcyon* 12 (1990): 75-100. [Stereotypes]

13434. Franklin, Stephen. "Area's Muslims Battling Against 'False Stereotypes'." *Chicago Tribune*, 3 September 1993.

13435. "French Canadian Stereotype Bids Farewell to His Public." *New York Times*, 14 February 1993. [Portland, Maine]

13436. Garcia, Guy. "Burying the Frito Bandito Once and For All." *New York Times*, 30 January 1994. [Films]

13437. Gardner, and Taylor. "Ethnic Stereotypes: Their Effects on Person Perception." *Canadian Journal of Psychology* 22 (1968).

13438. Garlick, Barbara and others, eds. *Stereotypes of Women in Power. Historical Perspectives and Revisionist Views*. Greenwood, 1992.

13439. Gecord, P. E. "Stereotyping and Favorableness in the Perception of Negro Faces." *Journal of Abnormal and Social Psychology* 59 (1959): 309-314.

13440. George, Nelson. "Beige Is Fine." *Village Voice*, 29 August 1989. [Black models in advertising]

13441. Gibbs, Jewelle T. "10 Myths About Young Black Males." *Boston Globe*, 17 November 1991.

13442. Gilman, Sander L. *Difference and Pathology: Stereotypes of Sexuality, Race and Madness*. Ithaca, NY: Cornell University Press, 1985.

13443. Goings, Kenneth W. "Memorabilia." *Black Women in America* II 781-782.

13444. Goodman, L. E., and M. J. Goodman. "Particularly amongst the Sunburnt Nations: The Persistence of Sexual Stereotypes of Race in Bio-Science." *International Journal of Group Tensions* 19 (1989): 221-243, 365-384.

13445. Gorchev, Leila. "When Will It Be Okay to Be an Arab?" *Washington Post*, 27 December 1992.

13446. Green, Rayna. "The Pocahontas Peoples: The Image of Indian Women in American Culture." *Massachusetts Review* 16 (1976): 698- 714.

13447. Halstein, J. A. "Melville's Stereotypical Treatment of Jews." *Journal of Reform Judaism* 28 (Fall 1981): 40-51.

13448. Hamilton, D., and T. Trolier. "Stereotypes and Stereotyping: An Overview of the Cognitive Approach." in *Prejudice, Discrimination and Racism*, pp. 127-163. eds. John F. Dovidio, and S.L. Gaertner. Orlando, FL: Academic Press, 1986.

13449. Hamilton, Marsha. "The Image of Arabs in the Sources of American Culture." *Choice* 28 (April 1991): 1271-1281.

13450. Hanson, Jeffery R., and Linda P. Rouse. "Dimensions of Native American Stereotyping." *American Indian Culture and Research Journal* 11 (1987): 33-58.

13451. Harris, Scott. "P.C. Police Beware: Some Take Pride in Stereotypes." *Los Angeles Times*, 30 December 1993. [Pictures on sweat shirts]

13452. Harrison, Eric. "Georgia Flag's Rebel Emblem Assumes Olympian Proportions." *Los Angeles Times*, 11 February 1993.

13453. Hassell, Malve von. "Issei Women: Stereotypes, Silences, and Fields of Power." *Feminist Studies* 18 (1992).

13454. Havig, Alan. "Richard F. Outcault's 'Pore Lil'Mose': Variations on the Black Stereotype in American Comic Art." *Journal of American Culture* 11 (1988): 33-41.

13455. Hawley, Sandra M. "The Importance of Being Charley Chan." in *America Views China*, eds. Jonathan Goldstein and others. : Lehigh University Press, 1991.

13456. Hay, Elizabeth. *Sambo Sahib. The Story of Little Black Sambo and Helen Bannerman*. Savage, MD: Barnes and Noble, 1981.

13457. Herzfeld, M. "The Practice of Stereotypes." *Homme* 32 (January-March 1992): 67-78. [In French]

13458. Herzog, E. "Social Stereotypes and Social Research." *Journal of Social Issues* 20 (1970): 109-125.

13459. Hewitt, William L. "Blackface in the White Mind: Racial Stereotypes in Sioux City, Iowa, 1874-1910." *Palimpsest* 71 (Summer 1990): 68-79.

13460. Hohler, Bob. "A Window on Racism." *Boston Globe*, 20 June 1991. ["Black Americana, one of the hottest commodities on the country's antique market." Indian Summer Antiques, Jaffrey, NH]

13461. Horwitz, Sari. "Pulling Together Against Racial Stereotypes." *Washington Post*, 25 July 1993. [Wilson High School, Washington, D.C.]

13462. James, Caryn. "Embrace the Stereotype; Kiss the Movie Goodbye." *New York Times*, 27 January 1991.

13463. Jen, Gish. "Challenging the Asian Illusion." *New York Times*, 11 August 1991. [Stereotypes of Asian-Americans]

13464. Johnson, Darrell L. *Sport Stereotyping: The Effect of Phenotypical Characteristics on Perceptions of Factors Contributing to Success in Men's Collegiate Basketball.* Ph.D. diss., University of Alabama, 1991. UMO #9130240.

13465. Johnson, S. D. "Anti-Arabic Prejudice in Middletown." *Psychological Reports* 70 (June 1992): 811-818.

13466. Jones, Lisa. "Blaxploitation!" *Village Voice*, 5 June 1990. [Black women as they are portrayed in Blaxploitation films]

13467. _____. "A Doll Is Born." *Village Voice*, 26 March 1991. [White and Black dolls]

13468. Jones, M. "Stereotyping Hispanics and Whites: Perceived Differences in Social Roles as a Determinant of Ethnic Stereotypes." *Journal of Social Psychology* 131 (August 1991): 469-476.

13469. Jones, R. S. P. and others. "The Social Effects of Stereotypes Behavior." *Journal of Mental Deficiency Research* 34 (June 1990).

13470. Josefowitz Siegel, Rachael. "Antisemitism and Sexism in Stereotypes of Jewish Women." *Women and Therapy* 5 (1986): 249- 257.

13471. Kang, K. Connie. "Separate, Distinct--and Equal." *Los Angeles Times*, 20 August 1993. [Asian American stereotypes]

13472. Karlins, Marian and others. "On the Fading of Social Stereotypes: Studies in Three Generations of College Students." *Journal of Personality and Social Psychology* 13 (1969): 1-16.

13473. Kenneally, Christopher. "Disparaging Americans in Name of 'Americana'." *Boston Globe*, 8 October 1989. [Sale of stereotypical knick-knacks portraying Black people]

13474. Kosmitzki, C. and others. "Do National Stereotypes Apply Equally to Individual Members of Social Minority and Majority Groups?" *Journal of Social Psychology* 143 (June 1994): 395-398.

13475. LaDuke, B. "Yolanda Lopeza; Breaking Chicana Stereotypes." *Feminist Studies* 20 (Spring 1994): 117-132.

13476. Langum, David G. "Californios and the Image of Indolence." *Western Historical Quarterly* 9 (April 1978): 181-196.

13477. Lawson, Carol. "Stereotypes Unravel, But Not Too Quickly, In New Toys for 1993." *Los Angeles Times*, 11 February 1993.

13478. Laycock, Douglas. "Vicious Stereotypes in Polite Society." *Constitutional Commentary* 8 (Summer 1991): 395-407.

13479. Lee, Felicia R. "An Editor Sees Asian-American Identity as a Work in Progress." *New York Times*, 10 October 1993.

13480. Lee, Thea. "Trapped on a Pedestal. Asian Americans Confront Model-Minority Stereotypes." *Dollars and Sense* No. 154 (March 1990): 12-15.

13481. Lemons, J. Stanley. "Black Stereotypes as Reflected in Popular Culture, 1880-1920." *American Quarterly* (Spring 1977): 102-116.

13482. Leonard, Rebecca, and Don C. Locke. "Communication Stereotypes in the 1980's: How Do Blacks and Whites See Themselves and Each Other?" *Educational and Psychological Research* 8 (Spring 1988): 73-82.

13483. Leschin, Luisa and others. "'Latins' Look at Cultural Archetypes." *Los Angeles Times*, 29 June 1992.

13484. Levy, David W. "Racial Stereotypes in Antislavery Fiction." *Phylon* 31 (1970): 265-279.

13485. LiPuma, Edward. "Capitalism and the Crimes of Mythology: An Interpretation of the Mafia Mystique." *Journal of Ethnic Studies* 17 (Summer 1989): 1-21.

13486. Louie, Vivian. "For Asian Americans, a Way to Fight a Maddening Stereotype." *New York Times*, 8 August 1993. [Alleged Asian-American lack of assertiveness]

13487. Loynd, Ray. "'Margins': Reflections of Racial Stereotyping." *Los Angeles Times*, 11 February 1993. [Review of play]

13488. Luhman, Reid. "Appalachian English Stereotypes: Language Attitudes in Kentucky." *Language in Society* 19 (September 1990).

13489. Maassen, Gerard H., and Martyn P. M. DeGoede. "Stereotype Measurement and Comparison between Categories of People." *Internatilnal Journal of Public Opinion Research* 5 (Fall 1993): 278-284.

13490. Mabry, Marcus, and Rhonda Adams. "A Long Way From 'Aunt Jemina'." *Newsweek*, 14 August 1989.

13491. Macaulay, Jacqueline. "Stereotyping Child Welfare." *Society* (January-February 1977): 47-51.

13492. MacCann, Dormarse. and others. "Picture Books About Blacks: An Interview with Opal Moore." *Wilson Library Bulletin* 65 (June 1991): 25-28.

13493. Macrae, C. N., and J. W. Sheperd. "Stereotypes and Social Judgements." *British Journal of Social Psychology* 28 (December 1989).

13494. Martin, C. L. and others. "The Development of Gender Stereotype Components." *Child Development* 61 (December 1990): 1891-1904.

13495. Martin, C. L., and J. K. Little. "The Relation of Gender Understanding to Children's Sex-Type Preferences and Gender Stereotypes." *Child Development* 61 (October 1990).

13496. Martinez, Thomas M. "Advertising and Racism: The Case of the Mexican-American." *El Grito* 2 (Summer 1969): 3-13.

13497. Maykovich, Minako K. "Reciprocity in Racial Stereotypes: White, Black, and Yellow." *American Journal of Sociology* 77 (March 1972): 876-897.

13498. Mazon, Mauricio. "Illegal Alien Surrogates: A Psycho- historical Interpretation of Group Stereotyping in Time of Economic Stress." *Aztlan* 6 (Summer 1975): 305-324.

13499. McKibben, Gordon. "A Cartoon Stereotype that Touched a Racial Nerve." *Boston Globe*, 20 January 1992.

13500. McMillen, Liz. "The Power of Rumor." *Chronicle of Higher Education*, 23 March 1994. ["Legends that circulate among Black men and women"]

13501. Michalak, Laurence. "Hollywood's Arabs: 'Exotic and Evil'." *Guardian (NYC)* (8 November 1989).

13502. Mieder, Wolfgang. "'The Only Good Indian Is a Dead Indian': History and Meaning of a Proverbial Stereotype." *Journal of American Folklore* 106 (1993): 38-60.

13503. Miller, Arthur G., ed. *The Eye of the Beholder: Contemporary Issues in Stereotyping*. NY: Praeger, 1982.

13504. Miller, LaMar P., and Joshua P. Bogin. "Rid American Sports of Racial Stereotypes." *New York Times (letter)*, 10 November 1991.

13505. Monkawa, David. "For Years, Asians Have Been Seen as the Enemy." *Los Angeles Times*, 8 November 1993.

13506. Monroe, Suzanne S. *Images of Native American Female Protagonists in Children's Literature, 1928-1988*. Ph.D. diss., University of Arizona, 1988. UMO #8906391.

13507. Montgomery, M. R. "Redrawing the Native American Image." *Boston Globe*, 28 February 1991. [School and college exploitation of identity with Indian names and insignia]

13508. Morgan, Joan. "Black Attack!" *Village Voice*, 16 January 1990. [Black women in fashion magazines]

13509. Morris, Madeline. "Stereotypic Alchemy: Transformative Stereotypes and Antidiscrimination Law." *Yale Law and Policy Review* 7 (Fall-Winter 1989): 251-273.

13510. Morsy, Soheir A. "The Bad, the Ugly, the Super-rich, and the Exceptional Moderate; U.S. Popular Images of the Arabs." *Journal of Popular Culture* 20 (1986): 13-29.

13511. Muldoon, James. "The Indian as Irishman." *Essex Institute Historical Collections* 111 (1975): 267-289.

13512. Natanson, Nicholas A. *Politics, Culture, and the FSA Black Image.* Ph.D. diss., 2 vols. University of Iowa, 1988. [Farm Security Administration documentary photography, 1935-1942]. UMO #8913272.

13513. "The Negro Stereotype." *Newsweek*, 3 April 1967. p.59.

13514. Nesdale, A. R. *Ethnic Stereotypes and Children.* Richmond, California: Clearing House on Migration Issues, 1987.

13515. Oakes, Penelope J. and others. *Stereotyping and Social Reality.* Blackwell, 1994.

13516. Obidinski, Eugene. "Pride, Prejudice, and the Stereotypes of the Polonia." in *American Polonia: Past and Present*, eds. Hieronim Kubiak and others. Wroclaw: Polish Academy of Sciences, 1988.

13517. O'Connor, John J. "They're Funny, Lovable, Heroic--and Jewish." *New York Times*, 15 July 1990. [Jewish characters on TV]

13518. _____. "This Jewish Mom Dominates TV, Too." *New York Times*, 14 October 1993.

13519. Olds, Madelin J. *The Rape Complex in the Postbellum South.* Ph.D. diss., Carnegie-Mellon University, 1989. UMO #8918063.

13520. Ow, Jeffrey A. "Mutant Asian Racism: A Look at Asian Stereotypes in Marvel Comics." *Slant* (November 1992). [UC Berkeley's Asian Pacific news magazine]

13521. Owen, Jean V. "Women in Manufacturing: Engendering Change." *Cost Engineering* 35 (August 1993): 11-14. [Stereotypes about women engineers]

13522. Pakes, Fraser. "See with the Stereotypic Eye: The Visual Image of the Plains Indians." *Native Studies Review* 1 (1985): 1- 31.

13523. Park, Jeanne. "Eggs, Twinkies and Ethnic Stereotypes." *New York Times*, 20 April 1990. [An Asian-American high school student discusses stereotypes]

13524. Petroni, F. A. "Uncle Toms: White Stereotypes in the Black Movement." *Human Organization* 29 (1970): 260-266.

13525. Porter, James. "To Reduce the Ignorance Upon Which Stereotypes Feed Is Becoming an Indreasingly Urgent Matter." *(London) Times Educational Supplement*, 21 March 1980.

13526. Poskocil, Art. "Encounters Between Blacks and White Liberals: The Collision of Stereotypes." *Social Forces* (March 1977): 715-727.

13527. Powell, R. R., and J. Garcia. "What Research Says...About Stereotypes." *Science and Children* 25 (1988): 21-23.

13528. Preiswerk, Roy, and Dominique Perrot, Stereotypes. in *Ethnocentrism and History*, pp. 173-190. NY: NOK Publishers International, 1978.

13529. Press, Marcia. *That Black Man-White Woman Thing: Images of an American Taboo.* Ph.D. diss., Indiana University, 1989. UMO #8925196.

13530. Prothro, E. T. "Studies in Stereotypes: V. Familiarity and the Kernel of Truth Hypothesis." *Journal of Social Psychology* 41 (1955): 3-10.

13531. Razran I. "Ethnic Dislikes and Stereotypes: A Laboratory Study." *Journal of Abnormal and Social Psychology* 45 (1950): 7- 27.

13532. Reed, Wornie L. "Consequences of Racial Stereotyping." *Trotter Institute Review* 4 (Spring 1990): 17-18.

13533. Rollka, Bodo. "Anmerkungen zur stereotypen Rezeption der schwarzen Minorität Amerikas in der alten und neuen Welt." *Amerikastudien* 31 (1986): 413-424.

13534. Rosenbery, Howard. "Bigotry on TV; The Stain Still Lingers." *Los Angeles Times*, 16 December 1992. [Ethnic stereotypes]

13535. Rosenberg, Howard. "Stereotypes of Arabs a TV Fixture." *Los Angeles Times*, 9 June 1993.

13536. Rothbell, Gladys W. *The Case of the Jewish Mother: A Study in Stereotyping.* Ph.D. diss., SUNY Stonybrook, 1989. UMO #9317915.

13537. Rubin, Diana. "The Lost Action Heroine." *Washington Post*, 15 July 1993. [Stereotypes in children's fiction]

13538. Sabbagh, Suba J. *Sex, Lies and Stereotypes: The Image of Arabs in American Popular Fiction.* Washington, D.C.: American- Arab Anti-Discrimination Committee, 1990.

13539. Saenger, G., and S. Flowerman. "Stereotypes and Prejudical Attitudes." *Human Relations* (1954).

13540. Sailes, G. A. "An Investigation of Campus Stereotypes: The Myth of Black Athletic Superiority and the Dumb Jock Stereotype." *Sociology of Sport Journal* 10 (March 1993): 88-97.

13541. Schaff, Adam. *Stereotypen und das menschliche Handeln.* Vienna: Europa-Verlag, 1980.

13542. Schroeder, Jeanne L. "Feminism Historicized: Medieval Misogynist Stereotypes in Contemporary Feminist Jurisprudence." *Iowa Law Review* 75 (July 1990): 1135-1217.

13543. Sennett, Richard. "The Identity Myth." *New York Times*, 30 January 1994.

13544. Serrano, Richard A. "Anti-Muslim Fervor in Jersey City Grows in Signs of Frustration." *Los Angeles Times*, 26 June 1993.

13545. Shaheen, Jack G. "Arab Caricatures Deface Disney's 'Aladdin'." *Los Angeles Times*, 21 December 1992.

13546. _____. "Image-Makers Need to Catch Up With Reality." *Los Angeles Times*, 22 September 1993. [Hollywood's portrayal of Palestinians as stereotypes]

13547. _____. "The 'Ugly Arab': A U.S. Racist Stereotype." *Boston Globe*, 26 August 1990.

13548. Sharbach, Sarah E. *Stereotypes of Latin America, Press Images, and U.S. Foreign Policy, 1920-1933.* Garland, 1993.

13549. Sharpe, Lora. "Dolls In All the Colors of a Child's Dream." *Boston Globe*, 22 February 1991.

13550. Shohat, Ella. "Gender in Hollywood's Orient." *Middle East Report* No. 162 (January-February 1990): 40-42.

13551. Simmons, William S. "Cultural Bias in the New England Puritans' Perception of Indians." *William and Mary Quarterly* 38, 3rd series (January 1981): 56-72.

13552. Slotkin, Richard. "Narratives of Negro Crime in New England, 1675-1800." *American Quarterly* 25 (1973): 3-31.

13553. Smith, Patricia. "Proud to Be Black." *Boston Globe*, 10 February 1991. [White Kids With Soul]

13554. Smith, Tom W., and James A. Davis. *Ethnic Images.* National Opinion Research Center, University of Chicago, 1991.

13555. Sontag, Deborah. "Muslims in the United States Fear an Upsurge in Hostility." *New York Times*, 7 March 1993.

13556. Staples, Brent. "Aunt Jemima Gets a Makeover." *New York Times*, 19 October 1994.

13557. _____. "Spike Lee's Blacks: Are They Real People?" *New York Times*, 2 July 1989.

13558. Stark, Evan. "The Myth of Black Violence." *New York Times*, 18 July 1990.

13559. Stedman, Raymond W. *Shadows of the Indian: Stereotypes in American Culture.* Norman: University of Oklahoma Press, 1982.

13560. Stephan, Walter G., and David Rosenfield. "Racial and Ethnic Stereotypes." in *In the Eye of the Beholder: Contemporary Issues in Stereotyping*, ed. Arthur G. Miller. NY: Praeger, 1982.

13561. "Stereotypes: Structure, Function and Process." *British Journal of Social Psychology* 33 (March 1994): entire issue.

13562. "The Stereotyping Habit: Young People Try To Fight It." *Los Angeles Times*, 30 November 1992.

13563. Stevenson, Thomas H. "How Are Blacks Portrayed in Business Ads?" *Industrial Marketing Management* 20 (August 1991): 193-199.

13564. Stoffle, C. J. "Minority Stereotypes." *Library Journal* 115 (October 15, 1990).

13565. Struth, Susan. "Permissible Sexual Stereotyping versus Impermissible Sexual Stereotyping: A Theory of Causation." *New York Law School Law Review* 34 (Winter 1989): 679-710.

13566. Thurber, Cheryl. *'Dixie': The Cultural History of a Song and Place*. Ph.D. diss., University of Mississippi, 1993. UMO #9326121.

13567. Trebay, Guy. "The Color of Money." *Village Voice*, 25 February 1992. [Ethnic dolls]

13568. U.S. Congress, 101st, 2nd session., House of Representatives, Select Committee on Children, Youth, and Families. *Beyond the Stereotypes: Women, Addiction, and Perinatal Substance*. Washington, D.C.: GPO, 1990.

13569. U.S. Congress, 94th, 2nd session. Senate Select Committee to Study Governmental Operations with Respect to Intelligence Activities. *Final Report--Book III, Supplementary Detailed Staff Reports on Intelligence Activities and the Rights of Americans*. GPO, 1976.

13570. Vinacke, W. Edgar. "Stereotying among National-Racial Groups in Hawaii: A Study in Ethnocentrism." *Journal of Social Psychology* 30 (November 1949): 265-291.

13571. Watanabe, Teresa. "'Rising' Laughter." *Los Angeles Times*, 30 November 1993. [Japanese response to stereotypes of Japanese in American movies]

13572. Weinberg, Marvin L. "Sexual Stereotyping." *Case and Comment* 94 (January-February 1989).

13573. Whitehead, Neil L., and Brian R. Ferguson. "Deceptive Stereotypes About Tribal Warfare." *Education Week*, 10 November 1993.

13574. Wiggins, William H., Jr. "Boxing's Sambo Twins: Racial Stereotypes in Jack Johnson and Joe Louis Newspaper Cartoons, 1908 to 1938." *Journal of Sport History* 15 (1988): 242-254.

13575. Wilkinson, Doris Y. "The Doll Exhibit: A Psycho-Cultural Analysis of Black Female Role Stereotypes." *Journal of Popular Culture* 21 (1987): 19-29.

13576. Williams, David P., III. *The Contribution of Selectively Focused Print Coverage to the Negative Stereotyping of a Challenging Group*. Ph.D. diss., Arizona State University, 1987. [University Microfilms Order No. 8722039, The Black Panther Party]

13577. Williams, John A. "Italian-American Identity, Old and New: Stereotypes, Fashion and Ethnic Revival." *Folklife Center News* 11 (Fall 1989): 4-7.

13578. Willis, Gwendolyn. *Stereotyping in T.V. Programming: Assessing the Need for Multicultural Education in Teaching Scriptwriting*. Ph.D. diss., University of Pittsburgh, 1990. UMO #9028425.

13579. Wilson, Wayne, ed. *Gender Stereotyping in Televised Sports*. Amateur Athletic Foundation of Los Angeles, August 1990.

13580. Wroblewski, Roberta, and A. C. Huston. "Televised Occupational Stereotypes and Their Effects on Early Adolescents: Are They Changing?" *Journal of Early Adolescence* 7 (Fall 1987): 283-297. [Sex-related]

13581. Wuthnow, Robert. "Anti-Semitism and Stereotyping." in *In the Eye of the Beholder: Contemporary Issues in Stereotyping*, ed. Arthur G. Miller. NY: Praeger, 1982.

13582. Yun, Grace, ed. *A Look Beyond the Model Minority Image: Critical Issues in Asian America*. NY: Minority Rights Group, 1989.

13583. Zuckerman, M. and others. "The Vocal Attractiveness Stereotype: Replication and Elaboration." *Journal of Nonverbal Behavior* 14 (Summer 1990).

SURVEILLANCE

13584. Abe, Frank. "Study Points to JACL Collaboration with U.S." *Rafu Shimpo* (4 April 1990). [Japanese American Citizens League]

13585. Adams, James P. "AIM and the F.B.I." *Christian Century* (2 April 1975).

13586. _____. "AIM, the Church, and the F.B.I.: The Douglas Durham Case." *Christian Century* 92 (14 May 1975): 437-439.

13587. Altiers, Diane. "Shhhhh...Some Firms Are Busy Spying On Our Nation's Social Activists." *Boston Globe*, 9 July 1989.

13588. American Friends Service Committee. *The Police Threat to Political Liberties*. Washington, DC: AFSC, 1979.

13589. Amnesty International. *Proposal for a Commission of Inquiry into the Effect of Domestic Intelligence Activities on Criminal Trials in the United States of America*. New York: Amnesty International, 1980.

13590. Armstrong, Gregory. *The Dragon Has Come: The Last Fourteen Months in the Life of George Jackson*. New York: Harper and Row, 1974.

13591. Ault, Ulrika E. "The FBI's Library Awareness Program: Is Big Brother Reading Over Your Shoulder?" *New York University Law Review* 65 (December 1990): 1532-1565.

13592. Baker, Nancy V. *Conflicting Loyalties: Law and Politics in the Attorney General's Office, 1789-1990*. Lawrence: University Press of Kansas, 1992.

13593. Bari, Judi. "For F.B.I., Back to Political Sabotage?" *New York Times*, 23 August 1990.

13594. Bass, Paul. "No Haven, Connecticut." *In These Times* (9 May 1990). [Role of FBI in the 1969 murder in New Haven, CT of Black Panther Alex Rackley]

13595. Bates, Tom. "The Government's Secret War on the Indian." *Oregon Times* (February-March 1976).

13596. Becker, Theodore, and Vernon G. Murray, eds. *Government Lawlessness in America*. New York: Oxford University Press, 1971.

13597. Belknap, Michal R. *Cold War Political Justice*. Greenwood Press, 1977.

13598. _____. "The Mechanics of Repression: J. Edgar Hoover, the Bureau of Investigation and the Radicals 1917-1925." *Crime and Social Justice* (Spring-Summer 1977).

13599. _____. "Secrets of the Boss's Power: Two Views of J. Edgar Hoover." *Law and Social Inquiry* 14 (Autumn 1989).

13600. Bergman, Lowell, and David Weir. "Revolution on Ice: How the Black Panthers Lost the FBI's War of Dirty Tricks." *Rolling Stone* (9 September 1976).

13601. Berlet, Chip. "Hurting the 'Green Menace': the Environmental Movement Has Become the Target of Domestic Covert Operations." *Humanist* 51 (July-August 1991): 24-31.

13602. Berman, Jerry L. "FBI Charter Legislation: The Case for Prohibiting Domestic Intelligence Investigations." *Journal of Urban Law* 55 (1985).

13603. Berman, Jerry L., and Morton H. Halperin, eds. *The Abuses of Intelligence Agencies*. Washington, DC: Center for National Security Studies, 1975.

13604. Bernstein, Carl. "The CIA and the Media." *Rolling Stone* (20 October 1977).

13605. Berry, Jason. "'Intelligence' Abuses by the IRS." *Nation* 224 (January 1977): 9-13.

13606. Biskind, Peter. "Political Prisoners U.S.A." *Seven Days* (8 September 1978).

13607. Booth, William. "Florida Senate Unveils Records of Probe Styled on McCarthyism." *Washington Post*, 3 July 1993. [Florida Legislative Investigative Committee, 1956-1964]

13608. Boyer, Edward J. "Past Haunts Ex-Panther in New Life." *Los Angeles Times*, 24 May 1994. [Julius C. Butler]

13609. Broadwater, Jeff. *Eisenhower and the Anti-Communist Crusade*. Chapel Hill: University of North Carolina Press, 1992.

13610. Bryant, Pat. "Justice in the Movement." *Southern Exposure* 8 (Summer 1980). [Community Relations Service of the U.S. Justice Department]

13611. Burkholders, Steve. "Red Squads on the Prowl/Still Spying After All These Years." *Progressive* (October 1988).

13612. Burton, Shirley, and Kellee Green. "Defining Disloyalty: Treason, Espionage, and Sedition Prosecutions, 1861-1946." *Prologue* 21 (1989): 215-221.

13613. Cannon, Lou. "Black Agents Accuse INS of Racial Bias." *Washington Post*, 10 December 1992. [Immigration and Naturalization Service]

13614. Carson, Clayborne. *Malcolm X: The FBI File*. Carroll and Graf, 1991.

13615. Centers of Southern Struggle. "FBI Files on Selma, Memphis, Montgomery, Albany, and St. Augustine." University Publications of America, 1988. 21 microfilm reels.

13616. Charms, Alexander. *Cloak and Gavel. FBI Wiretaps, Bugs, Informers, and the Supreme Court*. University of Illinois Press, 1992.

13617. Chevigny, Paul. *Cops and Rebels*. New York: Pantheon, 1972.

13618. Churchill, Ward. "In the Spirit of Crazy Horse." *Z Magazine* 3 (April 1990): 90-93.

13619. Churchill, Ward, and Jim Vander Wall. "COINTELPRO-AIM." in their *The COINTELPRO Papers*, pp. 231-302. Boston, MA: South End Press, 1990.

13620. _____. "COINTELPRO-Black Liberation Movement." in their *The COINTELPRO Papers*, pp. 91-164. Boston, MA: South End Press, 1990.

13621. _____. *The COINTELPRO Papers: Documents from the FBI's Secret Wars against Domestic Dissent*. Boston, MA: South End Press, 1990.

13622. _____. "COINTELPRO-Puerto Rican Independence Movement" in their *The COINTELPRO Papers*, pp. 63-90. Boston, MA: South End Press, 1990.

13623. Clark, Wayne A. *An Analysis of the Relationship Between Anti-Communism and Segregationist Thought in the Deep South, 1948-1964*. Ph.D. diss., University of North Carolina, 1976.

13624. Cohen, Marc J. "Taiwan Government Agents in the U.S." *Covert Action Information Bulletin* 34 (Summer 1990): 55-58.

13625. COINTELPRO. "The Counterintelligence Program of the FBI." Scholarly Resources, 1978. 30 microfilm reels.

13626. "A Collective Dedication. Ten Years After the Murder of Fred Hampton." *Keep Strong* (Dec. 1979-Jan, 1980): 41-65.

13627. Committee to End the Marion Lockdown. *Can't Jail the Spirit: Political Prisoners in the U.S.* Chicago, IL, 1989.

13628. Connolly, Ed. "Scandals of the State Militias." *Nation* (18 March 1991).

13629. Criley, Richard. *The FBI v. the First Amendment*. First Amendment Foundation, 1313 West 8th St., Suite 313, Los Angeles, CA 90017, 1991. [The FBI's war against Frank Wilkinson and the National Committee Against Repressive Legislation.]

13630. Curry, Richard O., ed. *Freedom at Risk: Secrecy, Censorship, and Repression in the 1980's.* Philadelphia, PA: Temple University Press, 1988.

13631. Curti, Merle. *The Roots of American Loyalty*. Columbia U.P., 1946.

13632. Davis, David Brion, ed. *The Fear of Conspiracy: Images of Un-American Subversion from the Revolution to the Present*. Ithaca, NY: Cornell University Press, 1971.

13633. Davis, James K. *Spying on America: The FBI's Domestic Counterintelligence Program*. Praeger, 1992.

13634. Debo, Dan. "COINTELPRO Lives On: The Unending Ordeal of Dhoruba Moore." *New Studies on the Left* 14 (Spring-Summer 1989).

13635. Diamond, Sigmund. *Compromised Campus. The Collaboration of Universities with the Intelligence Community. 1945-1955*. Oxford U.P., 1992.

13636. _____. "Informed Consent and Survey Research: The FBI and the University of Michigan Survey Research Center." in *Surveying Social Life: Papers in Honor of Herbert H. Hyman*, ed. Hubert J. O'Gorman. Middletown, CT: Wesleyan University Press, 1988.

13637. Dolan, Maura. "FBI Policy on Homosexuals at Issue in Ex- Agent's Suit." *Los Angeles Times*, 26 November 1993.

13638. Donner, Frank. *Protectors of Privilege: Red Squads and Police Repression in Urban America*. Berkeley: University of California Press, 1990.

13639. _____. "The Theory and Practice of American Political Intelligence." *New York Review of Books* (22 April 1971).

13640. Edwards, Don. "Reordering the Priorities of the FBI in Light of the End of the Cold War." *St. John's Law Review* 65 (Winter 1991): 59-84.

13641. Egan, Timothy. "13 Unsolved Deaths Feed Indian Mistrust of FBI." *New York Times*, 18 April 1993.

13642. Ellis, C. M. D. *"Negro Subversion": The Investigation of Black Unrest and Radicalism by Agencies of the United States Government, 1917-1920.* 2 vols. Ph.D. diss., University of Aberdeen (Scotland), 1984. Order No. BRDX 86269.

13643. "Ex-FBI Agent Exposes Use of Informants to Destroy the BPP." *Freedom Magazine* 18 (January 1985).

13644. "F.B.I. Agents Lose Challenge to Blacks' Promotion." *New York Times*, 19 September 1993.

13645. "FBI File on the Black Panther Party, North Carolina." Scholarly Resources, 1988. 2 microfilm reels.

13646. "FBI Files on Homosexual Groups Public." *News Media and the Law* 13 (Winter 1989): 15-16. [California]

13647. "FBI Harassment of Black Americans." *Bilalian News* (January 1980).

13648. "FBI Settles Suit that Alleged Bias." *New York Times*, 10 August 1990.

13649. Fine, David. "Federal Grand Jury Investigations of Political Dissidents." *Harvard Civil Rights-Civil Liberties Law Review* 7 (1972).

13650. Flaherty, David H. *Protecting Privacy in Surveillance Societies. The Federal Republic of Germany, Sweden, France, Canada, and the United States*. Chapel Hill: University of North Carolina Press, 1990.

13651. "Florida Reviews An Era of Fear." *New York Times*, 4 July 1993. [Sweeping surveillance of civil rights leaders and others during 1960s]

13652. Foerstel, Herbert N. *Surveillance in the Stacks. The FBI's Library Awareness Program*. Westport, CT: Greenwood, 1991.

13653. Fried, Joseph P. "Intelligence Pact Broken By Police, a Judge Rules." *New York Times*, 22 July 1989. [New York City]

13654. Friedman, Robert I. *The False Prophet: Rabbi Meir Kahane, From FBI Informant to Knesset Member*. Lawrence Hill Books, 1990.

13655. _____. "The Origins of Black/Jewish Hatred in New York." *Village Voice* (10 April 1990). [Role of FBI in fomenting Black-Jewish conflict in NYC during 1960's.]

13656. "The Future of Espionage." *Queen's Quarterly* 100 (Summer 1993): 269-414, entire issue.

13657. Gandy, Oscar H. ,. Jr. "The Surveillance Society: Information Technology and Bureaucratic Social Control." *Journal of Communication* 39 (1989): 61-76.

13658. Garrow, David J. "FBI Political Harassment and FBI Historiography: Analyzing Informants and Measuring the Effects." *Public Historian* 10 (Fall 1988): 5-18.

13659. Gelbspan, Ross. *Break-ins, Death Threats and the FBI: The Covert War Against the Central America Movement*. Boston: South End, 1991.

13660. _____. "COINTELPRO in the '80s: The 'New' FBI." *Covert Action Information Bulletin* 31 (Winter 1989).

13661. Gibson, James L. "The Policy Consequences of Political Intolerance: Political Repression during the Vietnam War Era." *Journal of Politics* 51 (1989): 13-35.

13662. Giese, Paula. "Profile of an Informer." *Covert Action Information Bulletin* 24 (Summer 1985). [Douglas Durham]

13663. Glaberson, William. "College's C.I.A. Ties Cause Furor, and Soul Searching." *New York Times*, 20 June 1991. [Rochester Institute of Technology]

13664. Goldstein, Robert J. "An American Gulag? Summary Arrest and Emergency Detention of Political Dissidents in the United States." *Columbia Human Rights Law Review* 17 (1978).

13665. Gordon, Diana R. *The Justice Juggernaut. Fighting Street Crime, Controlling Citizens*. New Brunswick, NJ: Rutgers University Press, 1990.

13666. Group, David J. *The Legal Repression of the American Communist Party, 1946-1961: A Study in the Legitimation of Coercion*. Ph.D. diss., University of Massachusetts, 1979.

13667. Haines, Gerald K., and David A. Langbart. *Unlocking the Files of the FBI: A Guide to Its Records and Classification System*. Scholarly Resources, 1993.

13668. Halperin, Morton H. "The FBI and the Civil Rights Movement." *First Principle* 4 (September 1978).

13669. Halperin, Morton H. and others. "The FBI's Vendetta against Martin Luther King, Jr." in *The Lawless State. The Crimes of the U.S. Intelligence Agencies*, pp. 61-89. New York: Penguin, 1976.

13670. Heinstreet, Leslie. "Earth First! and COINTELPRO." *Z Magazine* 3 (July-August 1990): 19-26.

13671. Hentoff, Nat. "Police Abuse of the Gorgeous Mosaic." *Village Voice* (10 July 1990). [Police spying on the New York City Civil Rights Coalition]

13672. _____. "Public Meetings and Police Spies in New York." *Village Voice* (3 July 1990).

13673. Hentschel, K. "A Postscript on Einstein and the FBI." *Isis* 81 (June 1990).

13674. Hill, Herbert. "The CIA in National and International Labor Movements." *International Journal of Politics, Culture, and Society* 6 (Spring 1993): 405-407.

13675. Hirschorn, Michael W. "Newly Released Documents Provide Rare Look at How FBI Monitors Students and Professors." *Chronicle of Higher Education* (10 February 1988).

13676. Hoover, Karl D. *The German-Hindu Conspiracy in California, 1913-1918*. Ph.D. diss., University of California, Santa Barbara, 1989. UMO #9014699.

13677. Hougan, Jim. *Spooks: The Haunting of America-the Private Use of Secret Agents*. New York: Morrow, 1978.

13678. Hyman, Harold M. *To Try Men's Souls: Loyalty Tests in American History*. University of California Press, 1959.

13679. Ichinokuchi, Tad. *John Aiso and the M.I.S.: Japanese- American Soldiers in the Military Intelligence Service, World War II*. Los Angeles, CA: MIS Club of Southern California, 1988.

13680. "Informe sobre discrimen y persecucion por razones politicas: la practica gubernamental de mantener listas, ficheros y expedientes de ciudadanos por razon de su ideologia politica." *Revista del Colegio de Abogados de Puerto Rico* 51 and 52 (October-December 1990 and January-March 1991): 1-162 and 163- 315. 2 parts

13681. Jayko, Margaret, ed. *FBI on Trial. The Victory in the Socialist Workers Party Suit Against Government Spying*. New York: Pathfinder, 1988. [Contains complete text of court decision by U.S. District Judge Thomas P. Griesa, pp. 19-133.]

13682. Johnston, David. "FBI Agent to Quit Over Her Treatment in a Sex Harassment Case." *New York Times*, 11 October 1993.

13683. _____. "FBI Chief Is Balancing On Very Slippery Track." *New York Times*, 18 August 1989. [Racial discrimination inside the FBI]

13684. _____. "FBI Hoping to Erase Poor Image on Racism." *New York Times*, 19 October 1990.

13685. _____. "FBI Promises Gains to Blacks in a Settlement." *New York Times*, 22 April 1992. [Black FBI agents who had charged discrimination by the agency.]

13686. _____. "Study Finds Job Complaints Widespread at FBI." *New York Times*, 19 June 1991. [Includes charges of racial discrimination]

13687. Johnston, Hugh. "The Surveillance of Indian Nationalists in North America, 1908-1918." *BC Studies* 78 (1988): 3-27.

13688. Judd, Stephen G. "The CIA and the University: A Problem of Power." *International Journal of Intelligence and Counterintelligence* 6 (Fall 1993): 339-358.

13689. Kahn, Robert. "New Documents Detail FBI Spying on Refugee Advocates." *National Catholic Reporter*, 13 March 1992.

13690. Kennedy, Stetson. "Florida's Christmas Murders." *New York Times*, 3 December 1991. [Possible role of FBI in covering up murder of NAACP leader in Florida.]

13691. Kim, Illsoo. "The Role of the KCIA in the Community." in *New Urban Immigrants: The Korean Community in New York*, pp. 233- 237. Princeton University Press, 1981. [Korean Central Intelligence Agency]

13692. King, Colbert I. "The Sessions Record: A Different View." *Washington Post*, 25 January 1993. [William Sessions, FBI Director, and his policies on minorities and women in the organization]

13693. Kornweibel, Theodore, Jr. "Black on Black: The FBI's First Negro Informants and Agents and the Investigation of Black Radicalism During the Red Scare." *Criminal Justice History* 8 (1987): 121-136.

13694. Kovel, Joel. "Was J. Edgar Hoover Gay?" *Z Magazine* 3 (November 1990): 103-106.

13695. Kraft, Stephanie. "An Uncharted Agency." *Valley Advocate* (24 July 1989). [FBI's surveillance activities]

13696. Kumamoto, Bob. "The Search for Spies: American Counterintelligence and the Japanese American Community 1931- 1942." *Amerasia Journal* 6 (Fall 1979): 45-75.

13697. Kunstler, William M. "The Ordeal of Leonard Peltier." *Covert Action Information Bulletin* (Summer 1985).

13698. Kurtz, Michael L. "Political Corruption and Organized Crime in Lousiana: The FBI Files on Earl Long." *Louisiana History* 29 (1988): 229-252.

13699. Laffoley, Steven. "The Techniques of Freedom: The FBI's 'Responsibilities Program' and the Rise of Liberal Anti-Communism in the United States, 1951-1955." Master's thesis, Saint Mary's University, Canada, 1991.

13700. Lawrence, Ken. *The New State Repression*. Chicago, IL: International Network Against the New State Repression, 1985.

13701. Levin, Murray B. *Political Hysteria in America: The Democratic Capacity for Repression*. New York: Basic Books, 1971.

13702. Linfield, Michael. *Freedom Under Fire. U.S Civil Liberties in Times of War*. Boston, MA: South End Press, 1990.

13703. Lumumba, Chokwe. "Short History of the U.S. War on the RNA." *Black Scholar* (January-February 1981).

13704. Lundy, J. "Police Undercover Agents." *George Washington Law Review* 37 (March 1969): 634-668.

13705. Lyman, Stanley D. *Wounded Knee 1973. A Personal Account*. Lincoln: University of Nebraska Press, 1991.

13706. Lyon, David. *The Electronic Eye: The Rise of Surveillance Society*. University of Minnesota Press: 1994.

13707. Malcolm X. "FBI Surveillance file." Scholarly Resources, 1978. 2 microfilm reels.

13708. Marsh, Dave, and Phyllis Pollack. "Wanted for Attitude." *Village Voice* (10 October 1989). [FBI censorship of record album by hip-hop black group, N.W.A. ("Niggers with Attitude")]

13709. Marx, Gary T. "Some Reflections on Undercover: Recent Developments and Enduring Issues." *Crime, Law, and Social Change* 18 (September 1992).

13710. _____. "Thoughts on a Neglected Category of Social Movement Participant: The Agent Provocateur and the Informant." *American Journal of Sociology* 80 (1974): 402-442.

13711. Masotti, Louis H., and Jerome R. Corsi. *Shoot-Out in Cleveland: Black Militants and the Police: July 23, 1968*. Praeger, 1969.

13712. McGee, Jim. "Gathering Intelligence for the ADL." *Washington Post*, 19 October 1993.

13713. Merrill Ramrez, Marie A. *The Other Side of Colonialism: COINTELPRO Activities in Puerto Rico in the 1960's*. Ph.D. diss., University of Texas, 1990. UMO #9031660.

13714. Michak, Don. "The FBI's Race Problem Heats Up." *Nation* (12 August 1991).

13715. Military Intelligence Service of Northern California and National Japanese American Historical Society. *The Pacific War and Peace: Americans of Japanese Ancestry in Military Intelligence Service, 1941 to 1952*. NJAHS, 1991.

13716. Mills, Ami Chen. *CIA Off Campus: A Do-It-Yourself Handbook*. Chicago, IL: Bill of Rights Foundation, 1990.

13717. "Mississippi Is Ordered to Open Anti-Rights Files." *New York Times*, 30 July 1989. [Mississippi Sovereignty Commission, 1956-1973]

13718. Moore, Dhoruba. "Strategies of Repression Against the Black Movement." *Black Scholar* 12 (1981): 10-16.

13719. Morgan, Patricia. *Shame of a Nation: A Documented Story of Police-State Terror Against Mexican-Americans in the U.S.A*. Los Angeles Committee for Protection of the Foreign Born, 1954.

13720. Mott, Patrick. "Mystery Tour." *Los Angeles Times*, 13 August 1992. [The FBI and Freedom of Information access to files about John Lennon.]

13721. Movement Support Network. "Harassment Update: Chronological List of FBI and Other Harassment Incidents." 6th ed. New York: Center for Constitutional Rights/National Lawyers Guild Anti-Repression Project, 1987.

13722. Neufield, Russell. "COINTELPRO in Puerto Rico." *Quash: Newsletter of the National Lawyers Guild Grand Jury Project* (August-September 1982).

13723. Newton, Huey P. *War Against the Panthers: A Study of Repression in America.* Ph.D. diss., University of California, Santa Cruz, 1980.

13724. Noakes, John. "Enforcing the Domestic Tranquility: Aliens and the Establishment of the (Federal) Bureau of Investigation." *Sociological Abstracts* supplement 167 (August 1991). 91S25333/ASA/1991/6692.

13725. Northcott, Karen. *The FBI in Indian Communities.* Minneapolis, MN: American Friends Service Committee, 1979.

13726. "Officers in Puerto Rico Aimed to Kill, Panel Hears." *New York Times*, 28 November 1991. ["A group of Federal officials and Puerto Rican police officers whose aim was to kill advocates of independence for the island."]

13727. Okihiro, Gary Y. *Cane Fires: The Anti-Japanese Movement in Hawaii.* Philadelphia, PA: Temple University Press, 1991. [Touches on surveillance of Japanese Americans by U.S. military intelligence since 1918.]

13728. O'Reilly, Kenneth. "The FBI and the Origins of McCarthyism." *Historian* 45 (May 1983).

13729. _____. "The FBI and the Politics of the Riots, 1964- 1968." *Journal of American History* 75 (1988): 91-114.

13730. _____. *McCarthy Era Blacklisting of School Teachers, College Professors, and Other Public Employees. The FBI Responsibilities Program File and the Dissemination of Information Policy File.* Bethesda, MD: University Publications of America, 1990.

13731. Ostrow, Ronald J. "Coretta King, at FBI Headquarters, Backs Sessions, Assails Hoover." *Los Angeles Times*, 17 February 1993. [William S. Sessions, FBI Director, and J. Edgar Hoover, past FBI Director]

13732. O'Tolle, George. *The Private Sector: Rent-a-Cops, Private Spies, and the Police-Industrial Complex.* New York: Norton, 1978.

13733. Parenti, Michael. "Creeping Fascism." *Society* 9 (June 1972): 4-8.

13734. _____. "Law and Order: The Repression of Dissent." in his *Democracy for the Few*, 3rd ed. Chapter 9, New York: St. Martin's Press, 1980.

13735. Poveda, Tony G. *Lawlessness and Reform: The FBI in Transition.* Pacific Grove, CA: Brooks/Cole, 1990.

13736. Rapp, Burt. *Deep Cover: Police Intelligence Operations.* Boulder, CO: Paladin Press, 1989.

13737. Rauf, M. Naeem. "Recent Developments in Wire-tap Law." *Criminal Law Quarterly* 31 (March 1989): 208-239.

13738. Reed, Merl E. "The FBI, MOWM, and CORE, 1941-1946." *Journal of Black Studies* 21 (June 1991): 465-479. [MOWM=March on Washington Movement]

13739. Rhoda, Heather. "FBI Ups Psychological Warfare against Activists." *Guardian (NYC)* (28 August 1991).

13740. Robins, Natalie. *Alien Ink. The F.B.I.'s War on Freedom of Expression.* New York: Morrow, 1992.

13741. Rohde, Stephen F. "Criminal Syndicalism: The Repression of Radical Political Speech in California." *Western Legal History* 3 (Summer-Fall 1990): 309-339.

13742. Rossi, Luigi. "La comunita italo-americano, antifascisti e servizi segreti statunitensi durante il seconda conflitto mondiale." *Sociologia* 24 (1990): 211-243.

13743. Russett, Bruce, and Alfred Stepan, eds. *Military Force and American Society*. New York: Harper and Row, 1973.

13744. Ryan, Jeffrey R. *The Conspiracy that Never Was: United States Government Surveillance of Eastern European American Leftists, 1942-1959*. Ph.D. diss., Boston College, 1990. UMO #9015811.

13745. Salmond, John A. *The Conscience of a Lawyer: Clifford J. Durr and American Civil Liberties, 1899-1975*. University of Alabama Press, 1990.

13746. Sayer, Ian, and Douglas Botting. *America's Secret Army. The Untold Story of the Counter Intelligence Corps*. New York: Franklin Watts, 1989.

13747. Sciolino, Elaine. "Bumpy Ride for CIA in Effort to Hire Minorities." *New York Times*, 4 November 1991.

13748. Seigle, Larry. "Washington's Fifty-Year Domestic Contra Operation." *New International* 6 (1987): 157-204. [Socialist Workers Party]

13749. Sessions, William S. "Constitutional Protections in FBI Investigations." *Kentucky Law Review* 78 (January 1990): 393-401.

13750. _____. "FBI Initiatives in Equal Opportunity and Violent Crime." *Crisis* 99 (April-May 1992): 24-27. [By the director of the FBI]

13751. Shenon, Philip. "FBI Suspends Veteran [Hispanic] Agent, Provoking Furor." *New York Times*, 5 March 1990.

13752. Simmons, Jerold. *Operation Abolition: The Campaign to Abolish the House Un-American Activities Committee, 1938-1965*. New York: Garland, 1989.

13753. Smist, Frank J., Jr. *Congress Oversees the United States Intelligence Community, 1947-1989*. Knoxville: University of Tennessee Press, 1990.

13754. Smith, Baxter. *Secret Documents Exposed: FBI Plot Against the Black Movement*. New York: Pathfinder, 1974.

13755. Smith, Vern E. "Old Enemies, New Questions." *Newsweek* (23 July 1990). [The killing of NAACP field secretary Medgar Evans in Jackson, MS]

13756. Smothers, Ronald. "Legacy of Innuendo Splits a State Anew." *New York Times*, 1 October 1989. [Mississippi Sovereignty Commission]

13757. Snyder, Robert E. "Spying on Southerners: The FBI and Erskine Caldwell." *Georgia Historical Quarterly* 72 (1988): 248- 281.

13758. Stevens, Don, and Jane Stevens. *South Dakota: The Mississippi of the North or Stories Jack Anderson Never Told You*. Custer, SD, 1977.

13759. Stone, Nancy-Stephanie. *A Conflict of Interest: The Warren Commission, the FBI, and the CIA*. Ph.D. diss., Boston College, 1987. UMO #8904001.

13760. Talbert, Roy, Jr. *Negative Intelligence. The Army and the American Left, 1917-1941*. Jackson: University Press of Mississippi, 1991.

13761. Tasang, Daniel C. "My CIA File." *Our Right to Know* (Autumn 1988). [Librarian]

13762. Theoharis, Athan. "Conservative Politics and Surveillance: The Cold War, the Reagan Administration, and the FBI." in *Freedom at Risk: Secrecy, Censorship, and Repression in the 1980's*, ed. Richard O. Curry. Philadelphia, PA: Temple University Press, 1988.

13763. Theoharis, Athan, ed. *The "Do Not File" File [of the FBI]*. Bethesda, MD: University Publications of America, 1990.

13764. _____. *FBI Wiretaps, Bugs, and Break-Ins. The National Security Electronic Surveillance Card File and the Surreptitious Entries File*. Bethesda, MD: University Publications of America, 1990.

13765. Theoharis, Athan. "FBI Wiretapping: A Case Study of Bureaucratic Autonomy." *Political Science Quarterly* 107 (Spring 1992): 101-122.

13766. _____. "How the F.B.I. Gaybaited [Adlai] Stevenson." *Nation* 250 (7 May 1990).

13767. Theoharis, Athan, ed. *The J. Edgar Hoover Official and Confidential File.* Bethesda, MD: University Publications of America, 1990.

13768. _____. *The Louis Nichols Official and Confidential File and the Clyde Tolson Personal File [of the FBI].* Bethesda, MD: University Publications of America, 1990.

13769. Tolbert, Emory J. "Federal Surveillance of Marcus Garvey and the U.N.I.A." *Journal of Ethnic Studies* 14 (1987): 25-46.

13770. Tompkins, Stephen G. "Army Spied on MLK Jr., Family." *Long Beach Press-Telegram*, 21 March 1993.

13771. Turner, Patricia A. "Reel Blacks. A Kinder, Gentler FBI." *Trotter Institute Review* 4 (Spring 1990): 19-20.

13772. U.S. Congress, 92nd, 1st session, House of Representatives, Committee on Internal Security. *The Black Panther Party: Its Origins and Development as Reflected in Its Official Newspaper, The Black Panther-Community News Service.* Washington, DC: GPO, 1971.

13773. U.S. Congress, 94th, 2nd session. *The FBI's Covert Program to Destroy the Black Panther Party.* Washington, DC: GPO, 1976.

13774. U.S. Congress, 92nd, 1st session, House of Representatives, Committee on Internal Security. *Gun Barrel Politics: The Black Panther Party, 1966-1971.* Washington, DC: GPO, 1971.

13775. Vartabedian, Ralph. "Jobless in the Name of Security." *Los Angeles Times*, 11 July 1993. [Workers discharged by Pentagon as security risks]

13776. Wakeman, F. "American Police Advisers and the Nationalist Chinese Secret Service, 1930-1937." *Modern China* 18 (April 1992): 107-137.

13777. Wannall, W. Raymond. "The FBI's Domestic Intelligence Operations: Domestic Security in Limbo." *Journal of Intelligence and Counterintelligence* 4 (Winter 1990): 443-473.

13778. Washburn, Patrick S. "J. Edgar Hoover and the Black Press in World War II." *Journalism History* 13 (1986): 26-33.

13779. Watson, Bruce W. and others, eds. *United States Intelligence. An Encyclopedia.* New York: Garland, 1990.

13780. Weiner, Tim. "C.I.A. Is working to Overcome Sex and Race Bias, Chief Says." *New York Times*, 21 September 1994.

13781. "Who Are the Real Terrorists?" *Akwesasne Notes* (Late Fall 1976).

13782. Wilkerson, Frank. *The Era of Libertarian Repression--1948- 1973: From Congressman to President, with Substantial Support from the Liberal Establishment.* Akron, Ohio: University of Akron Press, 1974.

13783. Wirtz, James J. "Constraints of Intelligence Collaboration: The Domestic Dimension." *International Journal of Intelligence and Counterintelligence* 6 (Spring 1993): 85-99.

13784. Wohlforth, Tim. "My Secret Life, By the FBI: Files of an American Leftist." *In These Times* (2 October 1991).

13785. Woon-Ha, Kim. "The Activities of the South Korean Central Intelligence Agency in the United States." in *Counterpoint Perspectives on Asian America*, pp. 140-145. ed. Emma Gee. Asian American Studies Center, UCLA, 1976.

13786. Zoccino, Nanda. "Ex-FBI Informer Describes Terrorist Role." *Los Angeles Times*, 26 January 1976.

TESTS

13787. Acevedo, Mary A. "Assessment Instruments for Minorities." *ASHA Reports Series (American Speech-Language-Hearing- Association)* no. 16 (December 1986): 46-51. [Spanish-language populations]

13788. Baird, Leonard L. "Do Students Think Admissions Tests Are Fair? Do Tests Affect Their Decisions?" *Research in Higher Education* 26 (1987): 373-388.

13789. Barrett, Laurence I. "Cheating on the Tests." *Time* (3 June 1991). [Race-norming]

13790. Barsh, Russell L. "Measuring Human Rights: Problems of Methodology and Purpose." *Human Rights Quarterly* 15 (February 1993): 87-121.

13791. Beere, Carole A. *Sex and Gender Roles. A Handbook of Tests and Measures.* Westport, CT: Greenwood, 1990.

13792. Bernstine, Daniel O. "Minority Law Students and the Bar Examination: Are Law Schools Doing Enough?" *Bar Examiner* 58 (August 1989): 10-16.

13793. Blits, Jan H. and others. "Symposium: Race-Norming." *Society* 27 (March-April 1990). [Five articles]

13794. Blits, Jan H., and Linda S. Gottfredson. "Employment Testing and Job Performance." *Public Interest* no. 98 (1990): 18- 25. [Race-norming]

13795. Bracey, Gerald W. "S.A.T. Scores: Miserable or Miraculous? " *Education Week* (21 November 1990).

13796. Bracken, B. A., and T. A. Fagan, eds. "Intelligence: Theories and Practices." *Journal of Psychoeducational Assessment* 8 (September 1990): entire issue.

13797. Brazziel, William F. "Improving SAT Scores: Pros, Cons, Methods." *Journal of Negro Education* 57 (Winter 1988): 81-93.

13798. Buckley, Stephen. "Montgomery [MD] Test Scores Soar for Black, Latino Students." *Washington Post*, 18 May 1993. [Both groups passed writing test "at rates comparable to white and Asian students"]

13799. Burnstein, Paul, and Susan Pitchford. "Social-Scientific and Legal Challenges to Education and Test Requirements in Employment." *Social Problems* 37 (May 1990).

13800. Cameron, Robert G. *The Common Yardstick: A Case for the SAT.* New York: College Entrance Examination Board, 1989.

13801. Carlson, Paul E., and Thomas M. Stephens. "Cultural Bias and Identification of Behaviorally Disordered Children." *Behavioral Disorders* 11 (May 1986): 191-199.

13802. Carranza, E. L. "Scale for the Measurement of Attitude Toward Chicanos: A Research Note." *Hispanic Journal of Behavorial Science* 14 (May 1992).

13803. Carter, Robert T., and Jane L. Swanson. "The Validity of the Strong Interest Inventory with Black Americans: A Review of the Literature." *Journal of Vocational Behavior* 36 (April 1990).

13804. Christian, Edward B. *A Survey of Trust and Intimacy Attitudes in Social Relationships.* Ph.D. diss., Temple University, 1990. UMO #9103563.

13805. "Civil Rights--Disparate-impact Doctrine-Court Prohibits Awarding Scholarships on the Basis of Standardized Tests that Discriminatorily Impact Woman." *Harvard Law Review* 103 (January 1990): 806-811.

13806. "The Class of 1990: A Selective Statistical Portrait of SAT Test Takers." *Black Issues in Higher Education* 7 (13 September 1990): 6-7.

13807. Cole, Beverly P. "Testing Blacks Out of Education and Employment." *Crisis* 91 (1984): 8-12.

13808. Crawford, Samuel D., and Robert H. Bentley. "An Inner-City 'IQ' Test." in *Black Language Reader*, pp. 80-83. eds. Bentley and Crawford. Scott Foresman, 1973.

13809. Crocker, Linda and others. "Test Anxiety and Standardized Achievement Test Performance in the Middle School Years." *Measurement and Evaluation in Counseling and Development* 20 (January 1988): 149-157.

13810. Crouse, James, and Dale Trusheim. *The Case Against the SAT.* Chicago, IL: University of Chicago Press, 1988.

13811. Dana, Richard D. "Culturally Diverse Groups and MMPI Interpretation." *Professional Psychology: Research and Practice* 19 (October 1988): 490-495.

13812. Davidson, Jeanette R. *Evaluation of an Education Model for Race/Ethnic Sensititve Social Work and Critique of the White Racial Identity Attitude Scale.* Ph.D. diss., University of Texas, Arlington, 1991. UMO #9217628.

13813. Dometrius, Nelson C., and Lee Sigelman. "Teacher Testing and Racial-Ethnic Representation in Public Education." *Social Science Quarterly* 69 (March 1988): 70-82.

13814. Drew, David, and John Gray. "The Black-White Gap in Examination Results: A Statistical Critique of a Decade's Research." *New Community* 17 (1991): 159-172.

13815. Einspruch, Eric L. *An Examination of Selection Bias in the Florida College Level Academic Skills Test.* Ph.D. diss., University of Miami, 1988. UMO #8827961.

13816. Emsellem, Maurice. "Racial and Ethnic Bariers to the Legal Profession: The Case Against the Bar Examination." *New York State Bar Journal* 61 (April 1989): 42.

13817. Fair Test. *Standardized Tests and Our Children: A Guide to Testing Reform.* Fair Test, 1990.

13818. Figueroa, Richard A. "Psychological Testing of Linguistic- Minority Students: Knowledge Gap and Regulations." *Exceptional Children* 56 (October 1989).

13819. Fiske, Edward B. "Steady Gains Achieved by Blacks on College Admission Test Scores." *New York Times*, 23 September 1987.

13820. *From Gatekeeper to Gateway: Transforming Testing in America.* Boston, MA: National Commission on Testing and Public Policy, Boston College, 1990.

13821. Gamache, Le Ann M. "Fairness in Testing." *Bar Examiner* 60 (May 1991): 29-34.

13822. Gelb, Steven A. and others. "Rewriting Mental Testing History: The View from the American Psychologist." *Sage Race Relations Abstracts* 11 (May 1986).

13823. "Gender Gap Continues to Close on S.A.T.'s." *New York Times*, 25 August 1994. ["Black women improve their test scores more than any other group."]

13824. Giffin, Margaret E. "Personal Research on Testing, Selection, and Performance Appraisal." *Public Personnel Management* 18 (Summer 1989): 127-137.

13825. Gifford, Bernard R., ed. *Policy Perspectives on Educational Testing.* Kluwer, 1993.

13826. Gifford, Bernard R. "The Political Economy of Testing and Opportunity Allocation." *Journal of Negro Education* 59 (Winter 1990).

13827. Gifford, Bernard R., ed. *Test Policy and Test Performance: Education, Language, and Culture.* Boston, MA: Kluwer Academic Publishers, 1989.

13828. _____. *Test Policy and the Politics of Allocation: The Workplace and the Law.* Boston, MA: Kluwer, 1989.

13829. Halpin, G. and others. "An Investigation of Racial Bias in the Peabody Picture Vocabulary Test-Revised." *Educational and Psychological Measurement* 50 (Spring 1990).

13830. Hamilton, Denise. "Test Your Diversity IQ." *Los Angeles Times*, 16 May 1994. Supplement: "Work Force Diversity".

13831. Helms, Janet E. "Why Is There No Study of Cultural Equivalence in Standardized Cognitive Ability Testing." *American Psychologist* 47 (September 1992): 1083-1101.

13832. Hood, Stafford, and Laurence Parker. "Meaningful Minority Participation in the Development and Validation of Certification Testing Systems: A Comparison of the Certification Testing Systems of Illinois and Pennsylvania." in *Advances in Program Evaluation*, Vol. 1, Part A. pp. 247-280. ed. R. E. Stake. Greenwich, CT: JAI Press, 1991.

13833. _____. "Minorities, Teacher Testing, and Recent U.S. Supreme Court Holdings: A Regressive Step." *Teachers College Record* 92 (Summer 1991).

13834. Hubin, David R. *The Scholastic Aptitude Test: Its Development and Introduction, 1900-1948.* Ph.D. diss., University of Oregon, 1988. UMO #8903812.

13835. Huebner, E. Scott, and Tammy Dew. "An Evaluation of Racial Bias in a Life Satisfaction Scale." *Psychology in the Schools* 30 (October 1993): 305-309. [Students' Life Satisfaction Scale]

13836. Johnson, Alex M., Jr., and others. "School Psychologists' Use of Techniques for Nonbiased Assessment." *College Student Journal* 21 (Winter 1987): 334-339.

13837. Johnson, Dirk. "Study Says Small Schools Are Key to Learning." *New York Times*, 21 September 1994. [SAT and ACT scores, 1994]

13838. Jones, Reginald L. *Psychological Assessment of Minority Group Children: A Casebook.* Berkeley, CA: Cobb and Henry, 1988.

13839. Kaufman, Karen and others. "Maladjustment in Statistical Minorities within Ethnically Unbalanced Classrooms." *American Journal of Community Psychology* 18 (1990): 757-765. [Teacher- administered adjustment rating scale]

13840. Kelman, W. "Concepts of Discrimination in General Ability Job Testing." *Harvard Law Review* 104 (April 1991): 1157-1248.

13841. Klein, Stephen P. "Bar Examinations: Ignoring the Thermometer Does Not Change the Temperature." *New York State Bar Journal* 61 (October 1989): 28.

13842. Lewin, M., and C. L. Wild. "The Impact of the Feminist Critique on Tests, Assessment, and Methodology." *Psychology of Women Quarterly* 15 (December 1991): 581-596.

13843. Madaus, George F. "The Effects of Important Tests on Students." *Phi Delta Kappan* 73 (November 1991): 226-231.

13844. Madaus, George F. *From Gatekeeper to Gateway: Transforming Testing in America.* National Commission on Testing and Public Policy, 1990.

13845. McLean, J. E., and C. R. Reynolds. "Analysis of WAIS-R Factor Patterns by Sex and Race." *Journal of Clinical Psychology* 47 (July 1991): 548-557.

13846. Miller, J., and A. Lopes. "Bias Produced by Fast Guessing in Distribution-based Tests of Race Models." *Perception of Psychophysics* 50 (December 1991): 584-590.

13847. Miller-Jones, D. "Culture and Testing." *American Psychologist* 44 (1989): 360-366.

13848. Milofsky, Carl. *Testers and Testing: The Sociology of School Psychology.* New Brunswick, NJ: Rutgers University Press, 1990.

13849. Morris, R., and V. Carstairi. "Which Deprivation? A Comparison of Selected Deprivation Indexes." *Journal of Public Health Medicine* 13 (November 1991): 318-326.

13850. Moss, Kary L. "Standardized Tests as a Tool of Exclusion: Improper Use of the SAT in New York." *Berkeley Women's Law Journal* 4 (1989): 230-244.

13851. Muhammad, Ahvay. *Toward the Development of a Measure of Black Identity*. Ph.D. diss., University of Rochester, 1991. UMO #9128773.

13852. National Research Council. *Fairness in Employment Testing: Validity Generalization, Minority Issues, and the General Aptitude Test Battery*. Washington, DC: National Academy Press, 1989.

13853. Neill, Monty. "Assessment and the 'Educational Impact Statement'." *Education Week* (23 September 1992).

13854. Nettels, Michael T., ed. *The Effect of Assessment on Minority Student Participation*. San Francisco, CA: Jossey-Bass, 1990.

13855. Noel, Peter. "Are You a Racist? Racist Quotient Questionnaire." *Village Voice* (11 February 1992): 34-35.

13856. _____. "Getting On the Bias. Readers Sound Off On the Racism Quotient Test." *Village Voice* (9 March 1993). [See Noel, "Are You a Racist?", Villiage Voice, February 11, 1992]

13857. Owen, David. *None of the Above: Behind the Myth of Scholastic Aptitude*. Boston, MA: Houghton Mifflin, 1985.

13858. Payne, Dinah and others. "Between a Rock and a Hard Place: The Issue of Fairness in Testing." *Labor Law Journal* 41 (May 1990).

13859. *The Prices of Secrecy: The Social, Intellectual, and Psychological Costs of Current Assessment Practice*. Cambridge, MA: Educational Technology Center, Harvard Graduate School of Education, 1990.

13860. "Race-Norming." *Society* 27 (1990): 4-25 (five articles).

13861. Raven, J. "The Raven Progressive Matrices: A Review of National Norming Studies and Ethnic and Socioeconomic Variation Within the United States." *Journal of Educational Measurement* 26 (Spring 1989).

13862. Riccucci, Norma M. "Merit Equity, and Test Validity: A New Look at an Old Problem." *Administration Society* 23 (May 1991): 74-93.

13863. Richardson, Tina. *A Semi-Projective Approach to the Assessment of Racial Consciousness in White Americans*. Ph.D. diss., University of Maryland, 1991. UMO #9205117.

13864. Rosser, Phyllis and others. *Gender Bias in Testing. Current Debates. Future Priorities*. New York: Ford Foundation, May 1991.

13865. Sabinani, H. B., and Joseph G. Ponterotto. "Racial/Ethnic Minority-specific Instrumentation in Counseling Research: A Review, Critique, and Recommendations." *Measurement and Evaluation in Counseling and Development* 24 (January 1992): 161- 187.

13866. Shanker, Albert. "Making School Count." *New York Times*, 24 March 1991.

13867. Shapiro, Martin M. and others. "Minimizing Unnecessary Racial Differences in Occupational Testing." *Valparaiso University Law Review* 23 (Winter 1989): 213-265.

13868. Shepard, Lorrie A. "Negative Policies for Dealing with Diversity: When Does Assessment and Diagnoses Turn Into Sorting and Segregation?" in *Literacy for a Diverse Society: Perspectives, Practices, and Policies*, ed. Elfrieda Hiebert. New York: Teachers College Record, 1991.

13869. Simon, Rita J., and Mona J. E. Dannier. "Gender, Race, and the Predictice Value of the LSAT." *Journal of Legal Education* 40 (December 1990): 525-532. [Law School Admission Test]

13870. Solorzano Bernat, Gloria. *Chicano Racial Attitude Measure (CRAM): Effects of a Bilingual-Bicultural Education, and Further Standardization*. Ph.D. diss., University of Arizona, 1978. UMO #7908361.

13871. Stenross, Barbara, and Steven P. Wilcox. "Do Preemployment Tests Always Hurt Minorities? The Case of Nonwhite Employment in Law Enforcement." *Sociological Practice Review* 1 (August 1990): 105-108.

13872. Stewart, Donald M. "Don't Believe Those Myths!" *College Digest* 2 (1989): special issue. [The S.A.T. and minority students]

13873. Stone, B. J., and B. E. Gridley. "Test Bias of a Kindergarten Screening Battery: Predicting Achievement for White and Native American Elementary Students." *School Psychology Review* 20 (1991): 132-139.

13874. Tenopyr, Mary L. "Fairness in Employment Testing." *Society* 27 (March-April 1990): 17-20.

13875. *Testing in American Schools: Asking the Right Questions.* Office of Technology Assessment, Washington, DC 20510-8025, February 1992.

13876. Towers, Karen R. L. *Intercultural Sensitivity Survey: Construction and Initial Validation.* Ph.D. diss., University of Iowa, 1990. UMO #9112496.

13877. Utley, C. A. and others. "Policy Implications of Psychological Assessment of Minority Children." in *Interactive Assessment*, pp. 445-469. eds. H. C. Haywood, and D. Tzuriel. Springer-Verlag, 1992.

13878. Valencia, Richard R., and Sofia Aburto. "The Uses of Abuses of Educational Testing: Chicanos as a Case in Point." in *Chicano School Failure and Success: Research and Policy Agenda for the 1990s*, pp. 203-251. ed. Valencia. Falmer Press, 1991.

13879. Viadero, Debra. "Proposal to Adjust NAEP Scores for Diversity Mulled." *Education Week* (9 March 1994).

13880. Wainer, Howard. "How Accurately Can We Assess Changes in Minority Performance on the SAT?" *American Psychologist* 43 (October 1988): 774-778.

13881. Weiss, John G. and others. *Standing Up To the SAT*. New York: Arco, 1989.

13882. Wigdor, Alexander K., and Wedell R. Garner, eds. *Ability Testing: Uses, Consequences, and Controversies*. Washington, DC: National Academy Press, 1982.

13883. Wilgoren, Jodi, and Richard O'Reilly. "Scoring of School Tests Found to Be Inaccurate." *Los Angeles Times*, 10 April 1994. [California Learning Assessment System]

13884. Wong, Ken. "Orientals Complain of Job Bias." *East/West* (16 September 1970).

UNDOING PERSONAL RACISM

13885. Aptheker, Bettina. "'Strong Is What We Make Each Other': Unlearning Racism within Women's Studies." *Women's Studies Quarterly* 9 (1982): 13-16.

13886. Barnard, William A., and Mark S. Benn. "Belief Congruence and Prejudice Reuction in an Interracial Contact Setting." *Journal of Social Psychology* 128 (February 1988): 125-134.

13887. Boven, Theo van. "Advances and Obstacles in Building Understanding and Respect between People of Diverse Religions and Beliefs." *Human Rights Quarterly* 13 (November 1991): 437-449.

13888. Bullard, Sara. "Tolerance Begins in the Home." *New York Times Education Life* (10 January 1993).

13889. Butler, David L. *The Reducation of Racial Prejudice through the Use of Vicarious Experiences.* Ph.D. diss., University of Michigan, 1982. UMO #8304430.

13890. Corvin, Sue A., and Fred Wiggins. "An Antiracism Training Model for White Professionals." *Journal of Multicultural Counseling and Development* 17 (July 1989): 105-114.

13891. Daubman, K. A. "Reducing Racism: A Reply." *Psychological Science* 2 (November 1991): 429 (letter).

13892. Derman-Sparks, Louise and others. *Anti-Bias Curriculum: Tools for Empowering Young Children.* Washington, DC: National Association for the Education of Young Children, 1989.

13893. Deuchler, Jason C. "Race, Hate and My New Bike." *New York Times*, 6 May 1992. [Oak Park, IL]

13894. Eisenberg, N. "The Development of Prosocial Values." in *Social and Moral Values*, eds. Eisenberg and others. Hillsdale, NJ: Lawrence Erlbaum Associates, 1989.

13895. Epperson, Sharon. "Familiarity Breeds Kinship at Racial Awareness Camp." *Boston Globe*, 17 August 1989. [Anytown project, National Conference of Christians and Jews.]

13896. Ford, Clyde W. *We Can All Get Along. 50 Steps You Can Take to Help End Racism.* DTP Trade Paperbacks, 1994.

13897. Gaertner, S. L. and others. "How Does Cooperation Reduce Intergroup Bias?" *Journal of Personality and Social Psychology* 59 (October 1990).

13898. George, Lynell. "Better Left Unsaid?" *Los Angeles Times*, 30 January 1994. [Discussing racial matters]

13899. Goleman, Daniel. "New Way to Battle Bias: Fight Acts, Not Feelings." *New York Times*, 16 July 1991.

13900. _____. "Psychologists Find Ways To Break Racism's Hold." *New York Times*, 5 September 1989.

13901. Hallinan, Maureen T., and Ruy A. Teixeira. "Opportunities and Constraints: Black-White Differences in the Formation of Interracial Friendships." *Child Development* 58 (October 1987): 1358-1371.

13902. Hayes, Mellody. "'Dear Dad: No One Race Is Perfect'." *Los Angeles Times*, 6 December 1993.

13903. Henley, Barbara, and Mary Smith Arnold. "Unlearning Racism: A Student Affairs Agenda for Professional Development." *Journal of College Student Development* 31 (March 1990).

13904. Janofsky, Michael. "Victims of Bias Try to Guide Skinheads Off Road of Hate." *New York Times*, 1 January 1994. [Fourth Reich Skinheads of Orange County, CA; See Newton, below]

13905. Jarivs, Brian. "Against the Great Divide." *Newsweek* (3 May 1993).

13906. Jarriett, Olga S. *Assessment of Racial Preferences and Racial Identification of Black and White Kindergarten Children in Non-racial And Bi-racial Settings.* Ph.D. diss., Georgia State University, 1980. UMO #8027104.

13907. Johnson, Rhoda E. "Making a Stand for Change: A Strategy for Empowering Individuals." in *Opening Doors*, eds. Harry J. Knopke and others. University of Alabama Press, 1991.

13908. King, Edith. "Recent Experimental Strategies for Prejudice Reduction in American Schools and Classrooms." *Journal of Curriculum Studies* 18 (1986): 331-338.

13909. Lee, Felicia R. "Exploring Mine Field of Racism." *New York Times*, 31 July 1993.

13910. Mansnerus, Laura. "Worlds Apart." *New York Times Education Life* (5 August 1990).

13911. McConahay, John B. "Reducing Racial Prejudice in Desegregated Schools." in *Effective School Desegregation: Equity, Quality, and Feasibility*, pp. 35-53. ed. Willis D. Hawley. Beverly Hills, CA: Sage, 1981.

13912. McWhirter, J. Jeffries and others. "Anytown: A Human Relations Experience." *Journal of Specialists in Group Work* 13 (September 1988): 117-123.

13913. Neal, Fannie Allen. "Confronting Prejudice and Discrimination. Personal Recollections and Observations." in *Opening Doors*, pp. 26-39. eds. Harry J. Knopke and others. University of Alabama Press, 1991.

13914. Newton, Jim. "A Three-Day Assault on Skinheads' Hatred." *Los Angeles Times*, 31 December 1993. [Attempts to educate members of the Fourth Reich Skinheads, California, out of their individual racism; See Janofsky, above]

13915. Njeri, Itabari. "The Conquest of Hate." *Los Angeles Times Magazine* (25 April 1993). [National Coalition Building Institute]

13916. Paley, Vivian Gussin. *You Can't Say You Can't Play*. Harvard University Press, 1992.

13917. Peters, William. *A Class Divided. Then and Now*, Expanded ed. New Haven, CT: Yale University Press, 1987.

13918. Piliavin, J. A., and H. W. Charng. "Altruism: A Review of Recent Theory and Research." *Annual Review of Sociology* 16 (1990).

13919. Ponterotto, Joseph G., and Paul B. Pederson. *Preventing Prejudice. A Guide for Counselors and Educators*. Sage, 1993.

13920. Quicke, John C. "Prejudice Elimination as an Educational Aim." *British Journal of Educational Studies* 39 (February 1991): 45-58.

13921. Roper, Larry D. *Relationships Among Levels of Social Distance, Dogmatism, Affective Reactions and Interracial Behaviors in a Course on Racism*. Ph.D. diss., University of Maryland, 1988. UMO #8827113.

13922. Smith, A. "Social Influence and Antiprejudice Training Programs." in *Social Influence Processes and Prevention*, eds. J. Edwards and others. New York: Plenum, 1990.

13923. Smith, Darryl F. *Enhancing Self-efficacy for Cross-racial Communication among College Students*. Ph.D. diss., University of North Carolina, Chapel Hill, 1990. UMO #9106145.

13924. Teltsch, Kathleen. "Reacting to Rising Violence, Schools Introduce 'Fourth R': Reconciliation." *New York Times*, 26 December 1990.

13925. Weinstein, Gerald. "Design Elements for Intergroup Awareness Training." *Journal for Specialists in Group Work* 13 (May 1988): 96-103.

13926. Whetstone, Lauren M. *An Evaluation of Prejudice Reduction Programs for Children.* Ph.D. diss., Claremont Graduate School, 1991. UMO #9135396.

13927. Wilson, David L. "Diversity on a Disk." *Chronicle of Higher Education* (19 January 1994). ["Multimedia package to foster racial and ethnic sensitivity"]

13928. "Workshop Tries to Teach Pupils How Not to Hate." *New York Times*, 21 October 1992. [Wilson High School, Washington, DC]

UNEMPLOYMENT

13929. Abell, J. D. "Defense Spending and Unemployment Rates: An Empirical Analysis Disaggregated by Race and Gender." *American Journal of Economics and Sociology* 51 (January 1992): 27-42.

13930. Aspen Institute. *Closing the Gap for U.S. Hispanic Youth: Public/Private Strategies*. Lanham, MD: University Press of America, 1989.

13931. Badgett, M. V. Lee. *Racial Differences in Unemployment Rates and Employment Opportunities*. Ph.D. diss., University of California, Berkeley, 1990.

13932. _____. "Rising Black Unemployment: Changes in Job Stability Or in Employability?" *Review of Black Political Economy* 22 (Winter 1994): 55-75.

13933. Bluestone, Barry. "Deindustrialization and Unemployment in America." *Review of Black Political Economy* 17 (Fall 1988).

13934. Boisjoly, J., and Greg J. Duncan. "Job Losses Among Hispanics in the Recent Recession." *Monthly Labor Review* 117 (June 1994): 16-23.

13935. Bullock, Paul. *Hard-Core Unemployment and Poverty in Los Angeles*. GPO, 1966.

13936. De Freitas, Gregory. "Ethnic Differentials in Unemployment Among Hispanic Americans." in *Hispanics in the U.S. Economy*, eds. G. Borjas, and M. Tienda. New York: Academic Press, 1985.

13937. Deanda, R. M. "Unemployment and Underemployment Among Mexican-Origin Workers." *Hispanic Journal of Behavorial Sciences* 16 (May 1994): 163-175.

13938. Dilts, D. A. and others. "Unemployment-Which Persons Burden-Men or Women, Black or White." *Ethnic and Racial Studies* 12 (January 1989).

13939. Folson, Franklin. *Impatient Armies of the Poor: the Story of Collective Action of the Unemployed 1808-1942*. Nivot, CO: University Press of Colorado, 1990.

13940. Fox, Stephen R. *Unemployment among Black Youths: A Content Analysis of Congressional Hearings, 1961-1982*. Ph.D. diss., Virginia Commonwealth University, 1989. UMO #9006094.

13941. Holzer, Harry J. "Can We Solve Black Youth Unemployment?" *Challenge* 31 (November-December 1988).

13942. Horton, Hayward D., and B. Lundy-Allen. "The Demography of Mega-Depression: Race and Unemployment in Rural Economics." *Sociological Abstracts* supplement 164 (June 1991). [Iowa] 91S24740/RSS/1991?2378.

13943. Hunter, Herbert M. "African American Youth Unemployment: Current Trends and Future Prospects." *Urban League Review* 14 (Summer 1990): 71-89.

13944. Inverarity, J., and R. Grattet. "Institutional Responses to Unemployment: A Comparison of U.S. Trends, 1948-1985." *Contemporary Crises* 13 (December 1989).

13945. Kates, Nick and others. *The Psychosocial Impact of Unemployment*. Washington, DC: American Psychiatric Press, 1990.

13946. Kimenyi, Mwangi S. "Immigration and Black-White Unemployment Rates in the United States." *Konjunkturpolitik* 35 (1989).

13947. Kletzer, Lori G. "Job Displacement, 1979-86: How Blacks Fared Relative to Whites." *Monthly Labor Review* 114 (July 1991): 17-25.

13948. Kliman, Andrew J. *Rising Joblessness among Black Male Youth, 1950-1980: A Regional Analysis.* Ph.D. diss., University of Utah, 1988. UMO #8909951.

13949. Lafer, G. "Minority Unemployment, Labor Market Segmentation, and the Failure of Job-Training Policy in New York City." *Urban Affairs Quarterly* 28 (December 1992): 206-235.

13950. Leana, C. R., and D. C. Feldman. "Gender Differences in Responses to Unemployment." *Journal of Vocational Behavior* 38 (February 1991): 78-91.

13951. Lichter, Daniel T. "Race and Underemployment: Black Employment Hardships in the Rural South." in *The Rural South in Crisis*, pp. 181-197. ed. Lionel J. Beaulieu. Boulder, CO: Westview, 1988.

13952. Mar, Don. "Vacancies, Unemployment, and Black and White Wage Earnings: 1956-1983." *Review of Black Political Economy* 21 (Summer 1992): 33-44.

13953. Mar, Don, and Paul M. Ong. "Race and Rehiring in the High- Tech Industry." *Review of Black Political Economy* 22 (Winter 1994): 43-54. [Silicon Valley]

13954. Moore, T. S. "Racial Differences in Postdisplacement Joblessness." *Social Science Quarterly* 73 (September 1992): 674- 689.

13955. Mydans, Seth. "The Young Face of Inner City Unemployment." *New York Times*, 22 March 1992. [Los Angeles]

13956. Ong, Paul M. "Race and Post-Displacement Earnings among High-Tech Workers." *Industrial Relations* 30 (Fall 1991): 456-468.

13957. O'Reagan, K. M. "The Effect of Social Networks and Concentrated Poverty on Black and Hispanic Youth Unemployment." *Annals of Regional Science* 27 (December 1993): 327-342.

13958. Rolison, Garry L. "Nonemployment of Black Men in Major Metropolitan Areas." *Sociological Inquiry* 63 (Summer 1993): 318- 329.

13959. Spaights, Ernest, and H. Dixon. "Black Youth Unemployment: Issues and Problems." *Journal of Black Studies* 16 (June 1986): 385-396.

13960. Stratton, L. S. "Racial Differences in Men's Unemployment." *Industrial and Labor Relations Review* 46 (April 1993).

13961. Tidwell, Billy J. "The Unemployment Experience of African- Americans: Some Important Correlates and Consequences." *The State of Black America 1990* (January 1990): 213-223.

13962. Tinker, George E., and Loring Bush. "Native American Unemployment: Statistical Games and Coverups." in *Racism and the Underclass*, pp. 119-144. eds. George W. Shepard, Jr., and David Penna. Greenwood, 1991.

13963. Ullah, P. "The Association between Income, Financial Strain and Psychological Well-being among Unemplyed Youths." *Journal of Occupational Psychology* 63 (December 1990).

13964. Vedder, R. G., and L. Gallaway. "Racial Differences in Unemployment in the United States, 1890-1990." *Journal of Economic History* 52 (September 1992).

13965. Wellington, Alison J. *Employment Effects of the Minimum Wage on Youths and Changes in the Wage Gap by Gender and Race: 1976-1985.* Ph.D. diss., University of Michigan, 1990. UMO #9034542.

13966. Williams, Donald R. "Job Characteristics and the Labor Force Participation Behavior of Black and White Male Youth." *Review of Black Political Economy* 18 (Fall 1989): 5-24.

13967. Williams, Roger C. "An Estimate of Black Gross Job Losses Due to Reduced Defense Expenditures." *Review of Black Political Economy* 22 (Winter 1994): 31-41.

13968. Winegarden, C. R., and Lay Boon Khor. "Undocumented Immigration and Unemployment of U.S. Youth and Minority Workers: Economic Evidence." *Review of Economics and Statistics* 73 (February 1991): 105-112.

VIOLENCE VS. MINORITIES

13969. Amann, Peter H. "Vigilante Fascism: The Black Legion as an American Hybrid." *Comparative Studies in Society and History* 25 (July 1983): 490-524.

13970. Applebome, Peter. "Mississippi Hearing in Evers Slaying Could Raise Searing Issues on Rights." *New York Times*, 15 October 1992. [Inquiry into 1963 assassination of Medgar Evers.]

13971. "Asia Bashing: Bias against Orientals Increases with Rivalry of Nation's Economics." *Wall Street Journal*, 28 November 1986.

13972. Asian American Resource Workshop. *To Live in Peace: Responses to Anti-Asian Violence in Boston*. Boston, MA: October 1987.

13973. Assael, Shaun. "Marky Mark's Rap Sheet. Doing Time for Bias Crime." *Village Voice* (16 February 1993).

13974. Baker, Ray Stannard. "What Is a Lynching? A Study of Mob Justice, South and North." *McClure's Magazine* 24 (February 1905).

13975. Balasing, Michael John. "Anti-Asian Violence in the United States 1980-1990: The Facts of an Unfinished Agenda." Senior thesis, Princeton University, 1990.

13976. Barnes, Arnold, and Paul H. Ephros. "The Impact of Hate Violence on Victims: Emotional and Behavioral Responses to Attacks." *Social Work* 39 (May 1994): 247-251.

13977. Beck, E. M. and others. "The Gallows, the Mob and the Vote: Lethal Sanctioning of Blacks in North Carolina and Georgia, 1882 to 1930." *Law and Society Review* 23 (1989).

13978. Beck, E. M., and Stewart E. Tolany. "The Killing Fields of the Deep South. The Market for Cotton and the Lynching of Blacks, 1882-1930." *American Sociological Review* 55 (August 1990).

13979. Beck, E. M., and Stewart E. Tolnay. "White Cotton and Black Death: The Lynching of Blacks and the Price of Cotton in the American South, 1882-1930: A Cautious Second Look." *Sociological Abstracts* (1989). Acession no. 89S20989.

13980. Becklund, Laurie. "Firebombings Destroy Project's Racial Harmony." *Los Angeles Times*, 15 September 1992. [Targeted at black residents in Boyle Heights, Los Angeles]

13981. Bederman, Gail. "'Civilization', the Decline of Middle- Class Manliness, and Ida B. Wells's Antilynching Campaign (1892- 94)." *Radical History Review* no. 52 (Winter 1992).

13982. Belknap, Michal R. *Federal Law and Southern Order: Racial Violence and Constitutional Conflict in the Post-Brown South*. Athens: University of Georgia Press, 1987.

13983. _____. "The Vindication of Burke Marshall: The Southern Legal System and the Anti-Civil Rights Violence of the 1960's." *Emory Law Journal* 93 (1987).

13984. Bernstein, Iver. *The New York City Draft Riots. Their Significance for American Society and Politics in the Age of the Civil War*. New York: Oxford University Press, 1989.

13985. *Bigotry and Violence in Illinois*. Washington, DC: U.S. Commission on Civil Rights, 1988.

13986. *Bigotry and Violence in Georgia*. Washington, DC: U.S. Commission on Civil Rights, 1989.

13987. *Bigotry and Violence in Minnesota*. Washington, DC: U.S. Commission on Civil Rights, 1989.

13988. *Bigotry and Violence in Rhode Island*. Washington, DC: U.S. Commission on Civil Rights, 1990.

13989. Blew, Robert W. "Vigilantism in Los Angeles, 1835-1874." *Southern California Quarterly* 54 (Spring 1972): 11-30.

13990. Booth, William. "Black Survivors of 1923 Massacre Seek Compensation from Florida." *Washington Post*, 26 February 1994.

13991. _____. "Rosewood. 70 Years Ago, a Town Disappeared In a Blaze Fueled by Racial Hatred. Not Everyone Has Forgotten." *Washington Post*, 30 May 1993. [Rosewood, FL]

13992. Brown, Richard M. "Southern Violence-Regional Problem of National Nemesis? Legal Attitudes Toward Southern Homicide in Historical Perspective." *Virginia Law Review* 32 (1979).

13993. Brundage, W. Fitzhugh. "The Darien 'Insurrection' of 1899: Black Protest During the Nadir of Race Relations." *Georgia Historical Quarterly* 74 (1990): 234-253.

13994. _____. *Lynching in the New South: Georgia and Virginia, 1880-1930*. Ph.D. diss., Harvard University, 1988. UMO #8908954.

13995. _____. *Lynching in the New South: Georgia and Virginia, 1880-1930*. University of Illinois Press, 1993.

13996. Cameron, James. *A Time for Terror: A Survivor's Story*. Baltimore, MD: Black Classic Press, 1994 (orig. 1982).

13997. Capeci, Dominic J., Jr. "The Lynching of Cleo Wright: Federal Protection of Constitutional Rights during World War II." *Journal of American History* 72 (March 1986): 859-887.

13998. Capeci, Dominic J., Jr., and Martha Wilkerson. "The Detroit Rioters of 1943: A Reinterpretation." *Michigan Historical Review* 16 (Spring 1990): 49-72.

13999. "Catholic Racism Pulled the Trigger on Yusef Hawkins." *National Catholic Register* (8 September 1989).

14000. Caughey, John W. "Their Majesties the Mob." *Pacific Historical Review* 26 (1957): 217-234.

14001. _____. *Their Majesties the Mob*. Chicago: University of Chicago Press, 1960. [Vigilantism against Mexican Americans]

14002. Center for Democratic Renewal. *They Don't All Wear Sheets: A Chronology of Racist and Far Right Violence--1980-1986*. Atlanta, GA: National Council of the Churches of Christ in the USA, 1987.

14003. Chadbourn, James H. *Lynching and the Law*. Chapel Hill: University of North Carolina Press, 1933.

14004. Chalk, Frank, and Kurt Jonassohn. *The History and Sociology of Genocide. Analyses and Case Studies*. New Haven, CT: Yale University Press, 1990.

14005. *The Chinese Massacre at Rock Springs, Wyoming Territory, September 2, 1885*. Boston, MA: Franklin Press, Rand Avery and Co., 1886.

14006. Churchill, Ward. "The New Genocide-A Hidden Holocaust in the State of Native American Environments." in *Research in Inequality and Social Conflict*, vol. 1. eds. I. Wallimann, and Michael N. Dobkowski. Greenwich, CT: JAI Press, 1989.

14007. Clary, Mike. "Dream Turns to Tragedy." *Los Angeles Times*, 2 February 1993. [Murder of 19-year-old Luyen Phan Nguyen in Coral Springs, Florida]

14008. Clinansmith, Michael S. "The Black Legion: Hooded Americanism in Michigan." *Michigan History* 55 (Fall 1971).

14009. *Collected Works of Ida B. Wells-Barnett*. New York: Oxford University Press, 1990.

14010. "Combating Racial Violence: A Legislative Proposal." *Harvard Law Review* 101 (April 1988): 1270-1286.

14011. Comment. "Racially Motivated Violence and Intimidation: Inadequate State Enforcement and Federal Civil Rights Remedies." *Journal of Criminal Law and Criminology* 75 (1984).

14012. "Compilation of Racial Attacks on [Asian] Indians, Part 1." *APAC Alert* 7 (October 1988): 3-4. [Monthly report]

14013. Couch, Barry A. "A Spirit of Lawlessness: White Violence, Texas Blacks, 1865-1868." *Journal of Social History* 18 (Winter 1984).

14014. Crane, Paul, and Alfred Larson. "The Chinese Massacre." *Annals of Wyoming* 12 (January, April 1940): 47-55, 153-160.

14015. Culberson, William C. *Vigilantism in America: A Political Analysis of Private Violence.* Ph.D. diss., Claremont Graduate School, 1988. UMO #8900997.

14016. _____. *Vigilantism. Political History of Private Power in America.* Westport, CT: Greenwood, 1990.

14017. Dauphine, James G. "The Knights of the White Camelia and the Election of 1868: Louisiana's White Terrorists: a Benighting Legacy." *Louisiana History* 30 (Spring 1989): 173-190.

14018. Davis, Jack E. "Shades of Justice: The Lynching of Jesse James Payne and Its Aftermath." Master's thesis, University of South Florida, 1989.

14019. _____. "'Whitewash' in Florida: The Lynching of Jesse James Payne and Its Aftermath." *Florida Historical Quarterly* 68 (1990): 277-298.

14020. Davis, Mike. "Behind the Orange Curtain." *Nation* (31 October 1994). [Violence against Mexican-Americans and African Americans in Orange County, CA]

14021. de Guzman, Mila. "Facing a Hostido '90s: Anti-Asian Violence." *Katipunan* (September 1990): 13-14.

14022. De Santis, J.P. *For the Color of His Skin. The Murder of Yusef Hawkins and the Trial of Bensonhurst.* New York: Piharos Books, 1991.

14023. Downey, Dennis B., and Raymond M. Hyser. *No Crooked Death: Coatesville, Pennsylvania, and the Lynching of Zachariah Walker.* Urbana: University of Illinois Press, 1990.

14024. Edgerton, Carol. "Racist Terror Ties Up Chippewa Fishing Rights." *Guardian (NYC)* (10 April 1991).

14025. Ehrlich, Howard J. "Studying Workplace Ethnoviolence." *International Journal of Group Tensions* 19 (1989): 69-80.

14026. Ehrlich, Howard J., and Barbara E. K. Larcom. "Ethnoviolence in the Workplace." *CSERV Bulletin* 3 (1994). [Center for the Study of Ethnic and Racial Violence]

14027. Ellement, John. "Hate Crimes Often Result in Injuries, Report Finds." *Boston Globe*, 27 January 1991. [Criminal History Systems Board, Boston]

14028. Ellis, Mary L. *"Rain Down Fire": The Lynching of Sam Hose.* Ph.D. diss., Florida State University, 1992. UMO #9306031.

14029. Escobar, Gabriel. "Family's Tragedy Is Korean Merchants' Call to Action." *Washington Post*, 17 August 1993. [Racist attacks on Koreans in Wash., D.C.]

14030. *The Ethnoviolence Project: Pilot Study.* Baltimore, MD: National Institute Against Prejudice and Violence, October 1986.

14031. Ferrell, Claudine L. *Nightmare and Dream: Antilynching in Congress, 1917-1921.* New York: Garland, 1989.

14032. Fine, Sidney. *Violence in the Model City. The Cavanagh Administration, Race Relations, and the Detroit Riot of 1967.* Ann Arbor: University of Michigan Press, 1989.

14033. Finnegan, Terence R. *"At the Hands of Parties Unknown": Lynching in Mississippi and South Carolina, 1881-1940.* Ph.D. diss., University of Illinois, Urbana-Champaign, 1993. UMO #9329027.

14034. Formwalt, Lee W. "Petitioning Congress for Protection: A Black View of Reconstruction at the Local Level." *Georgia Historical Quarterly* 73 (Summer 1989): 305-322.

14035. Franklin, Vincent P. "The Philadelphia Race Riot of 1918." *Pennsylvania Magazine of History and Biography* 99 (1975): 336- 350.

14036. Friend, Llerena B. "W.P. Webb's Texas Rangers." *Southwestern Historical Quarterly* 74 (January 1971): 293-323.

14037. Gastil, Raymond D. "Violence." in *Encyclopedia of Southern Culture*, eds. Charles R. Wilson, and William Ferris. Chapel Hill: University of North Carolina Press, 1989.

14038. Gilje, Paul A. *The Road to Mobacracy: Popular Disorder in New York City, 1763-1834.* Chapel Hill: University of North Carolina Press, 1987.

14039. Godshalk, David R. *In the Wake of Riot: Atlanta's Struggle for Order, 1899-1919.* Ph.D. diss., Yale University, 1992. [Atlanta Race Riot of 1906]. UMO #9306946.

14040. Guillemin, Jeanne. "American Indian Resistance and Protest." in *Violence in America*, Vol. 1. ed. Robert Gurr. Newbury Park, CA: Sage, 1989.

14041. Hackney, Sheldon. "Southern Violence." *American Historical Review* 74 (1969).

14042. Hair, William I. *Carnival of Fury: Robert Charles and the New Orleans Race Riot of 1900.* Baton Rouge: Louisiana State University Press, 1986.

14043. *Hate Crimes in Los Angeles County 1989. A Report to the Los Angeles County Board of Supervisors.* Los Angeles, CA: Los Angeles County Commission on Human Relations, February 1990.

14044. Haygood, Wil. "The Four Girls." *Boston Globe Magazine* (3 February 1991). [Four Black girls who were killed in a racist bombing in Birmingham, Alabama, Sept. 15, 1963]

14045. _____. "Surviving a Night of Terror." *Boston Globe* [Varnado, LA, June 1965].

14046. Hepworth, Joseph T., and Stephen G. West. "Lynchings and the Economy: A Time-Series Reanalysis of Hovland and Sears (1940)." *Journal of Personality and Social Psychology* 55 (August 1988): 239-247.

14047. Hines, Mary E. *Death At the Hands of Persons Unknown: The Geography of Lynching in the Deep South, 1882 to 1910.* Ph.D. diss., Louisiana State University, 1992. [AL, GA, LA, and MS]. UMO #9302902.

14048. Hogan and Hartson Attorneys and Washington D.C. Lawyers Committee for Civil Rights Under Law. *Striking Back at Bigotry: Remedies under Federal and State Law for Violence Motivated by Racial, Religious and Ethnic Prejudice and 1988 Supplement.* Baltimore, MD: National Institute Against Prejudice and Violence, 1986, 1988.

14049. Horne, Gerald. "Race Backwards: Genes, Violence, Race and Genocide." *Covert Action Quarterly* 43 (Winter 1992-93): 29-35.

14050. Howard, Walter T. "In the Shadow of Scottsboro: The 1937 Robert Hinds Case." *Gulf Coast Historical Review* 4 (1988): 64-81. [Florida]

14051. _____. "Vigilante Justice and National Reaction: The 1937 Tallahassee Double Lynching." *Florida Historical Quarterly* 67 (1988): 32-51.

14052. Hutton, Mary M. B. *The Rhetoric of Ida B. Wells: The Genesis of the Anti-Lynch Movement.* Ph.D. diss., Indiana University, 1975.

14053. Hynes, Charles J., and Bob Drury. *Incident at Howard Beach. The Case for Murder.* New York: Putnam's, 1990.

14054. *Incidents of Bigotry and Violence in Essex County.* Washington, DC: U.S. Commission on Civil Rights, 1988. [NJ]

14055. "Incidents of Housing Violence (January 1989 to March 1990)." in *Terror in Our Neighborhoods*, Montgomery, AL: The Klanwatch Project of the Southern Poverty Law Center, May 1990. [Nationwide cases of violence against Black and other people who moved into "white" neighborhoods]

14056. Ingalls, Robert P. "Lynching and Establishment Violence in Tampa, 1858-1935." *Journal of Southern History* 53 (1987): 613- 644.

14057. Jennings, Veronica T. "Man Tells Jury of 'Hunting' Blacks." *Washington Post*, 29 October 1992.

14058. _____. "MD. Latinos Alarmed at Attacks." *Washington Post*, 1 September 1993. [Montgomery, MD]

14059. Justice, Blair. *Detection of Potential Community Violence*. Washington, DC: Office of Law Enforcement Assistance, U.S. Department of Justice, 1968. [Texas]

14060. Kaplan, David A. "Film About a Fatal Beating Examines a Community." *New York Times*, 16 July 1989. ["Who Killed Vincent Chin?" Documentary about anti-Asian racism.]

14061. Kateri Hernandez, Tonya. "Bias Crimes: Unconscious Racism in the Prosecution of Racially Motivated Violence." *Yale Law Journal* 99 (January 1990): 845-864.

14062. Kleg, Milton, and Peter H. Martorella. "Hate Group Education: Confronting Ethnoviolence." *CSERV Bulletin* 3 (1994): 12-26. [Center for the Study of Ethnic and Racial Violence]

14063. Knowlton, Clark S. "Violence in New Mexico: A Sociological Perspective." *California Law Review* 58 (October 1970): 1054-1084.

14064. Kovaleski, Serge F., and Cindy Loose. "Fear Behind the Counter." *Washington Post*, 10 September 1993. [Murders of Asian and other storekeepers in the District of Columbia]

14065. Lamon, Lester C. "Racial Civil Disorders, 1860-1917." in *Encyclopedia of Black America*, eds. W. A. Low, and Virgil Clift. New York: McGraw-Hill, 1981.

14066. Laurie, Clayton D. "'The Chinese Must Go': The United States Army and the Anti-Chinese Riots in Washington Territory, 1885-1886." *Pacific Northwest Quarterly* 81 (January 1990): 22-29.

14067. _____. "Civil Disorder and the Military in Rock Springs, Wyoming: The Army's Role in the 1885 Chinese Massacre." *Montana* 40 (Summer 1990): 44-59.

14068. Lee, Virginia N., and Joseph M. Fernandez. "Legislative Responses to Hate-motivated Violence: The Massachusetts Experience and Beyond." *Harvard Civil Rights-Civil Liberties Law Review* 25 (Summer 1990): 287-340.

14069. Legters, Lyman H. "The American Genocide." *Policy Studies Journal* 16 (Summer 1988): 768-777. [White-Indian relations]

14070. Los Angeles County Board of Supervisors. *Hate Crime in Los Angeles County 1988*. Los Angeles, CA: The Board, February 1989.

14071. Lucas, Thomas A. "Men Were Too Fiery for Much Talk: The Grinnell Anti-Abolitionist Riot of 1860." *Palimpsest* 68 (1987): 12-21.

14072. Massey, James L., and Martha A. Myers. "Patterns of Repressive Social Control in Post-Reconstruction Georgia, 1882- 1935." *Social Forces* 68 (1989): 458-488.

14073. Mastromarino, Mark A. "Teaching Old Dogs New Tricks: The English Mastiff and the Anglo-American Experience." *Historian* 49 (1986): 10-25. [To hunt and kill Native Americans]

14074. McKanna, Clare V., Jr. "The Treatment of Indian Murders in San Diego, 1850-1900." *Journal of San Diego History* 36 (Winter 1990): 65-77.

14075. Miller, Robert M. "The Protestant Churches and Lynching." *Journal of Negro Education* 42 (1957): 18-31.

14076. Mixon, Gregory L. *The Atlanta Riot of 1906*. Ph.D. diss., University of Cincinnati, 1989. UMO #9003217.

14077. National Organization of Black Law Enforcement Executives (NOBLE). *Racial and Religious Violence: A Law Enforcement Guidebook*. Washington, DC: NOBLE, March 1986.

14078. New York Governor's Task Force. *Governor's Task Force on Bias Related Violence: Final Report*. Albany, NY: Division of Human Rights, 1988.

14079. Newman, Maria. "Victim of Bias Attack, 14, Wrestles With His Anger." *New York Times*, 9 January 1992. [Bronx, NYC]

14080. Newton, Michael, and Judy Ann Newton. *Racial and Religious Violence in America. A Chronology*. New York: Garland, 1990.

14081. North Carolinians against Racist and Religious Violence. *1988 Report: Bigoted Violence and Hate Groups in North Carolina*. Durham, NC: NCARRV, 1989.

14082. Nossiter, Adam. "A Slain Student's Trust in America." *New York Times*, 23 October 1992. [Yoshihiro Hattori, Japanese exchange student]

14083. O'Brien, Gail W. "Return to 'Normalcy': Organized Racial Violence in the Post World War II South." in *Violence in America*, Vol. 1. ed. Ted Robert Gurr. Newbury Park, CA: Sage, 1989.

14084. O'Donnell, Santiago. "Attacks on Asian Merchants May Be Bias Crimes." *Washington Post*, 24 February 1994. [D.C.]

14085. Olson, Bruce A. *The Houston Light Guards: Elite Cohesion and Social Order in the New South, 1873-1940*. Ph.D. diss., University of Houston, 1989. UMO #9016778.

14086. Olzak, Susan D. *The Dynamics of Ethnic Competition and Conflict*. Stanford University Press, 1993.

14087. Palmer, Brian. "Tempest in Teaneck." *Village Voice* (10 July 1990). [Aftermath of killing of black 16-year old Phillip C. Pannell by white policemen in Teaneck, N.J.]

14088. Pena, Albert. "Racist Monument." *Regeneracion* 1, no. 5 (1970): 1. [Texas Rangers]

14089. *Perceptions of Hate Group Activity in Georgia*. Washington, DC: U.S. Commission on Civil Rights, 1982.

14090. Peterson, Iver. "Vandalism Raises the Specter of Racial Hatred in Glen Ridge." *New York Times*, 11 June 1994. [N.J.]

14091. Pinderhughes, Howard. "The Anatomy of Racially Motivated Violence in New York City: A Case Study of Youth in Southern Brooklyn." *Social Problems* 40 (November 1993): 478-492.

14092. Pinkney, Alphonso. *The American Way of Violence*. New York: Vintage, 1972.

14093. Pittman, Walter E. "The Mel Chatham Affair: Interracial Murder in Mississippi in 1889." *Journal of Mississippi History* 43 (1981).

14094. Quindlen, Anna. "A Changing World." *New York Times*, 20 May 1990. [The white Bensonhurst killing of Yusuf Hawkins]

14095. "Racially-motivated Violence and Intimidation: Inadequate State Enforcement and Federal Civil Rights Remedies." *Journal of Criminal Law and Criminology* 75 (1984): 103-137.

14096. Reynolds, Donald E. "Vigilante Law During the Texas Slave Panic of 1860." *Locus* 2 (1990): 173-186.

14097. Roberts, Sam. "Once Again, Racism Proves To Be Fatal in New York City." *New York Times*, 3 September 1989. [Murder of Yusef K. Hawkins, in Bensonhurst]

14098. Rohter, Larry. "Compensation in Attack Divides Florida Leaders." *New York Times*, 14 March 1994. [Proposal to compensate African Americans for destruction by white mob in 1923]

14099. Samora, Julian and others. *Gunpowder Justice: A Reassessment of the Texas Rangers*. Notre Dame, IN: University of Notre Dame Press, 1979.

14100. Sanger, David E. "After Gunman's Acquittal, Japan Struggles to Understand America." *New York Times*, 25 May 1993. [Fatal shooting of Yoshihiro Hattori near Baton Rouge, LA]

14101. Senechal, Roberta. *The Sociogenesis of a Race Riot: Springfield, Illinois, in 1908*. Urbana: University of Illinois Press, 1990.

14102. Slaughter, Thomas P. *Bloody Dawn. The Christiana Riot and Racial Violence in the Antebellum North*. New York: Oxford University Press, 1991. [1851]

14103. Solomon, Alisa. "Meanwhile in Brooklyn." *Village Voice* (20 November 1990). [Anti-Palestinian attacks]

14104. Staples, Robert. "Black Male Genocide: A Final Solution to the Race Problems in America." *Black Scholar* 18 (May-June 1987): 2-11.

14105. Stocker, Carol, and Barbara Carton. "Guilty...of Being Black." *Boston Globe*, 7 May 1992. [Harassment of Black men in Boston area]

14106. Storti, Craig. *Incident at Bitter Creek: The Story of the Rock Springs Chinese Massacre*. Ames: Iowa State University Press, 1990.

14107. Strickland, Rennard. "Genocide-at-Law: An Historic and Contemporary View of the Native American Experience." *University of Kansas Law Review* 34 (1986).

14108. Svaldi, David. *Sand Creek and the Rhetoric of Extermination: A Case Study in Indian-White Relations*. University Press of America, 1989.

14109. Taylor, John. "The Rosewood Massacre." *Esquire* (July 1994). [Race riot by white mob in Rosewood, Florida in 1923]

14110. *They Don't All Wear Sheets: A Chronology of Racist and Far Right Violence: 1980-1986*. Center for Democratic Renewal (The Division for Church and Society of the National Council of Churches of Christ in the U.S.A.), 1987.

14111. Tolnay, Stewart E., and E. M. Beck. "Black Flight: Lethal Violence and the Great Migration, 1900-1930." *Social Science History* 14 (Fall 1990): 347-370.

14112. _____. "Black Lynchings: The Power Threat Hypothesis Revisited." *Social Forces* 67 (March 1989): 605-623. [1889-1931; see also commentaries]

14113. Turner, R. H. "Race Riots Past and Present: A Cultural- Collective Behavior Approach." *Symbolic Interaction* 17 (Autumn 1994): 309-324.

14114. U.S. Commission on Civil Rights. *Intimidation and Violence. Racial and Religious Bigotry in America*. Washington, DC: The Commission, January 1983.

14115. _____. *Intimidation and Violence. Racial and Religious Bigotry in America*. Washington, DC: The Commission, 1990.

14116. U.S. Congress, 96th, 2nd session, House of Representatives, Committee on the Judiciary, Subcommittee on Crime. *Increasing Violence Against Minorities: Hearings...* Washington, DC: GPO, 1981.

14117. U.S. Congress, 97th, 1st session, House of Representatives, Committee on the Judiciary, Subcommittee on Crime. *Racially Motivated Violence. Hearing...* Washington, DC: GPO, 1983.

14118. Vandal, Gilles. "'Bloody Caddo': White Violence against Blacks in a Louisiana Parish, 1865-1876." *Journal of Social History* 25 (Winter 1991): 373-388.

14119. Vyzralek, Frank E. "Murder in Masquerade: A Commentary on Lynching and Mob Violence in North Dakota's Past, 1882-1931." *North Dakota History* 57 (Winter 1990): 20-29.

14120. Wallace, Michael. "The Uses of Violence in American History." *American Scholar* 40 (Winter 1970-1971).

14121. Ware, Lowry. "The Burning of Jerry: The Last Slave Execution by Fire in South Carolina?" *South Carolina Historical Magazine* 91 (1990): 100-106.

14122. Washington Lawyers' Committee for Civil Rights Under Law. *Civil and Criminal Remedies for Racially and Religiously Motivated Violence in Maryland, Virginia and the District of Columbia*. Washington, DC, June 1983.

14123. Webb, Walter P. *The Texas Rangers: A Century of Frontier Defense.* Boston: Houghton Miffin, 1935. [See above, Julian Samora and others]

14124. Weiss, J. C. "Ethnoviolence: Violence Motivated by Bigotry." in *Encyclopedia of Social Work,* 1990 Supplement. pp. 307-319. ed. L. Ginsberg. 18th ed. Silver Spring, MD: National Association of Social Workers, 1990.

14125. Wells, Ida B. *On Lynchings.* Salem, NH: Ayer Co., 1987.

14126. Werner, John M. *Reaping the Bloody Harvest: Race Riots in the United States During the Age of Jackson, 1824-1849.* New York: Garland, 1989.

14127. Wexler, C., and Gary T. Marx. "When Law and Order Works: Boston's Innovative Approach to the Problem of Racial Violence." *Crime and Delinquency* 32 (1986): 205-223.

14128. "White Landlords, Robbing Negro Tenants, Let Loose Arkansas Reign of Terror." *Appeal to Reason* (14 February 1920). [Massacre of black farmers in Elaine, Arkansas in 1919]

14129. Wolf, C. "Constructions of a Lynching." *Sociological Inquiry* 62 (Winter 1992): 83-97.

14130. Wong, William. "Anti-Asian Violence." *Forum* (June 1989).

14131. Wright, George C. *Racial Violence in Kentucky 1865-1940, Lynchings, Mob Rule, and "Legal Lynchings".* Baton Rouge: Louisiana State University Press, 1990.

14132. Wunder, John R. "Anti-Chinese Violence in the American West, 1850-1910." in *Law for Elephant, Law for the Beaver*, eds. John McLaren and others. Ninth Judicial Circuit Historical Society, 1992.

14133. _____. "South Asians, Civil Rights, and the Pacific Northwest: The 1907 Bellingham anti-Indian Riot and Subsequent Citizenship and Deportation Struggles." *Western Legal History* 4 (Winter-Spring 1991): 59-68.

14134. Young, Thomas J. "Violent Hate Groups in Rural America." *International Journal of Offender Therapy and Comparative Criminology* 34 (April 1990): 15-21.

14135. Zangrando, Robert L. *The NAACP Crusade against Lynching, 1909-1950.* Philadelphia, PA: Temple University Press, 1980.

14136. Zarbin, Earl. "The Whole Was Done So Quietly: The Phoenix Lynchings of 1879." *Journal of American History* 4 (1980).

14137. Zia, Helen. "Another American Racism." *New York Times*, 12 September 1991. [Violence against Asian-Americans]

14138. Ziglar, William. "The Decline of Lynching in America." *International Social Science Review* 63 (Winter 1988): 14-25.

WEALTH AND INCOME

14139. Alejo, Francisco J. "Poder, propriedad y distribucion: el papel del Estado." *El Trimestre Economico* 50 (January-March 1983): 19-47.

14140. America, Richard F., ed. *The Wealth of Races. The Present Values of Benefits from Past Injustices*. Westport, CT: Greenwood, 1990.

14141. Andic, Faut M. *Distribution of Family Incomes in Puerto Rico: A Case Study of the Impact of Economic Development on Income Distribution*. Rio Piedras, PR: University of Puerto Rico, Institute of Caribbean Studies, 1964.

14142. Andic, Faut M., and A. J. Mann. "Secular Tendencies in the Inequality of Earnings in Puerto Rico." *Review of Social Economy* 34 (April 1976): 13-21.

14143. Barringer, Felicity. "Rich-Poor Gulf Widens Among Blacks." *New York Times*, 25 September 1992.

14144. _____. "White-Black Disparity in Income Narrowed in '80s, Census Shows." *New York Times*, 24 July 1992.

14145. Birnbaum, Howard, and Rafael Weston. "Home Ownership and the Wealth Position of Black and White Americans." *Review of Income and Wealth* 20 (March 1974): 103-118. [Data from 1967 Survey of Economic Opportunity]

14146. Blau, Francine D., and John W. Graham. "Black-White Differences in Wealth and Asset Composition." *Quarterly Journal of Economics* 105 (1990): 321-329.

14147. Bonacich, Edna. "Inequality in America: The Failure of the American System for People of Color." *Sociological Spectrum* 9 (1989): 77-101.

14148. Bradford, William D. *Wealth, Assets, and Income of Black Households*. Paper prepared for the Committee on the Status of Black Americans, National Research Council, Washington, D.C., 1987.

14149. Brimmer, Andrew F. "Building Wealth and Assets." *Black Enterprise* (July 1991): 31-34. [In Black Community]

14150. _____. "Income and Wealth." *Ebony* 42 (August 1987): 42- 48.

14151. Browne, Robert S. "The Economic Case for Reparations to Black America." *American Economic Review* 62 (May 1972): 39-46.

14152. _____. "Wealth Distribution and Its Impact on Minorities." *Review of Black Political Economy* 4 (1974).

14153. Burchell, Robert A. "Opportunity and the Frontier: Wealth- Holding in Twenty-Six Northern Californian Countries, 1848-1880." *Western Historical Quarterly* 18 (1987): 177-196.

14154. Cao Garcia, Ramon J. "Distribucion del ingreso en Puerto Rico: Unos comentarios y un nuevo analisis." *Revista de ciencias sociales* 21 (September-December 1979): 321-359.

14155. Chand, Krishan. *Education, Income and Natives*. September 1979. [Alaska Natives] ERIC ED 215 835.

14156. Christensen, Kimberly. "Political Determinants of Income Changes for African-American Women and Men." *Review of Radical Political Economics* 24 (Spring 1992): 52-70.

14157. Coalition on Human Needs. *How the Poor Would Remedy Poverty: Interviews with Low Income People in Washington, D.C.* Washington, DC: The Coalition, 1986.

14158. Crosby, Faye J. and others. "Changing Patterns of Income among Blacks and Whites Before and After Executive Order 11246." *Social Justice Research* 5 (1992).

14159. de Vise, Pierre. *The Geography of Wealth and Poverty in Suburban America: 1979 to 1987*. Chicago, IL: Office of Public Relations, Roosevelt University, 1989.

14160. Driessen, P. "The Race Factor in Social Security." *Review of Black Political Economy* 17 (Fall 1988).

14161. Felder, Henry E. *The Changing Patterns of Black Family Income 1960-1982*. Washington, DC: Joint Center for Political and Economic Studies, 1984.

14162. Ferrie, Joseph P. "The Wealth Accumulation of Antebellum European Immigrants to the U.S., 1840-60." *Journal of Economic History* 54 (March 1994): 1-33.

14163. Flanagan, Sharon P. "The Georgia Cherokees Who Remained: Race, Status, and Property in the Chattahoochie Community." *Georgia Historical Quarterly* 73 (Fall 1989): 584-609.

14164. Goldscheider, F. K., and C. Goldscheider. "The Intergenerational Flow of Income: Family Structure and the Status of Black Americans." *Journal of Marriage and the Family* 53 (May 1991): 499-508.

14165. Gonzalez, Gilbert G. "Factors Relating to Property Ownership of Chicanos in Lincoln Heights, Los Angeles." *Aztlan* 2 (Fall 1971): 107-143.

14166. Gould, Richard A. "The Wealth Quest Among the Tolowa Indians of Northwestern California." *Proceedings of the American Philosophical Society* 110 (1966): 67-89.

14167. Greenstein, Robert, and Scott Baranick. *Drifting Apart: New Findings on Growing Income Disparaties between the Rich, the Poor and the Middle Class*. Center on Budget and Policy Priorities, 1990.

14168. Greenwood, D. T., and E. N. Wolff. "Changes in Wealth in the United States, 1962-1983: Savings, Capital Gains, Inheritance, and Lifetime Transfers." *Journal of Population Economics* 5 (1992).

14169. Hamilton, Richard F., and James D. Wright. *The State of the Masses*. New York: Aldine, 1986.

14170. Haslag, J. H., and L. L. Taylor. "A Look at Long-Term Developments in the Distribution of Income." *Federal Reserve Bank of Dallas Economic Review* 1st Quarter (1993).

14171. Helyar, John. "The Big Hustle: Atlanta's Two Worlds: Wealth and Poverty, Magnet and Mirage." *Wall Street Journal*, 29 February 1989.

14172. Herscovici, S. "The Distribution of Wealth in Nineteenth Century Boston: Inequality among Natives and Immigrants, 1860." *Explorations in Economic History* 30 (July 1993).

14173. Hubler, Shaun. "'80s Failed to End Economic Disparity, Census Shows." *Los Angeles Times*, 17 August 1992. [By ethnic group]

14174. Jones, Alice Hanson. "The Wealth of Women, 1774." in *Strategic Factors in Nineteenth Century American Economic History*, eds. Claudia Goldin, and Hugh Rockoff. University of Chicago Press, 1992.

14175. Kroch, E. "Recent Real Income and Wage Trends in the United States." *Federal Reserve Bank of New York Quarterly Review* 16 (Summer 1991).

14176. Lehrer, Evelyn, and Marc Nerlove. "The Impact of Female Work on Family Income Distribution: Black-White Differentials." *Review of Income and Wealth* 27 (December 1981): 423-431.

14177. Leigh, J. P. "Distribution of Lifetime Income Allowing for Varying Mortality Rates among Women, Men, Blacks, and Whites." *Journal of Economic Issues* 26 (December 1992).

14178. Levy, Frank S., and Richard C. Michel. *The Economic Future of American Families: Income and Wealth Trends*. Lanham, MD: University Press of America, 1990.

14179. _____. *Providing for the Future: Income and Wealth Prospects for America's Middle Class*. Washington, DC: Urban Institute, 1990.

14180. Long, J. E., and S. B. Caudill. "Racial Differences in Homeownership and Housing Wealth, 1970-1986." *Economic Inquiry* 30 (January 1992).

14181. Maldonado, Rita M. "Education, Income Distribution and Economic Growth in Puerto Rico." *Review of Social Economy* 34 (April 1976).

14182. Mann, Arthur J. "Economic Development, Income Distribution, and Real Income Levels: Puerto Rico, 1953-1977." *Economic Development and Cultural Change* 33 (April 1985): 485- 502.

14183. _____. "The Federal System and Income Distribution: The Case of Puerto Rico." *Public Finance Quarterly* 4 (July 1976): 339-366.

14184. Metzler, William H. "Mexican Americans and the Acquisitive Syndrome." *Journal of Mexican-American History* 3 (1973): 1-12.

14185. Nasar, Sylvia. "Even Among the Well-Off, the Richest Get Richer." *New York Times*, 5 March 1992.

14186. _____. "Those Born Wealthy or Poor Usually Stay So, Studies Say." *New York Times*, 18 May 1992.

14187. Oliver, Melvin L., and Thomas M. Shapiro. "Race and Wealth." *Review of Black Political Economy* 17 (1989): 5-25.

14188. _____. "Wealth of a Nation: A Reassessment of Asset Inequality in America Shows at Least One Third of Households are Asset-Poor." *American Journal of Economics and Sociology* 49 (April 1990): 129-151.

14189. Passell, Peter. "Forces in Society, and Reaganism, Helped Dig Deeper Hole for Poor." *New York Times*, 17 July 1989. [1979- 1987]

14190. Perelman, S., and P. Pestieau. "Inheritance and Wealth Composition." *Journal of Population Economics* 5 (1992).

14191. Pope, Polly. "Trade in the Plains: Affluence and Its Effects." *Kroeber Anthrop. Soc. Papers* 34 (1966): 53-61.

14192. Quadagno, Jill. *The Color of Welfare: How Racism Undermined the War on Poverty*. Oxford University Press, 1994.

14193. Reich, Michael. "Black-White Income Differences." in *The Imperiled Economy*, Vol. 2. eds. Robert Cherry and others. New York: Union for Radical Political Ecnomics, 1988.

14194. Robinson, B. "Disparity in Present Value Net Social Security Wealth." *Black Scholar* 24 (1994): 19-30.

14195. Santiago, K. Antonio. "La concentracion y la centralizacion de la propriedad en Puerto Rico, 1898-1929." *Homines* 8 (January 1984): 129-156.

14196. Sawhill, Isabel V. "Poverty in the U.S.: Why Is It So Persistent?" *Journal of Economic Literature* 26 (September 1988): 1073-1119.

14197. Schweninger, Loren. *Black Property Owners in the South, 1790-1915*. Urbana: University of Illinois Press, 1990.

14198. _____. "Prosperous Blacks in the South, 1790-1880." *American Historical Review* 95 (February 1990): 31-56. [References to many other studies and sources of information.]

14199. Smith, P. K. "Recent Patterns in Downward Income Mobility: Sinking Boats in a Rising Tide." *Social Indicators Research* 31 (March 1994).

14200. Soltow, Lee. "A Century of Personal Wealth Accumulation." in *The Economics of Black America*, eds. Harold G. Vatter, and T. Palm. Harcourt Brace Jovanovich, 1972.

14201. Tidwell, Billy J. "Black Wealth: Facts and Fiction." *State of Black America* (1988): 193-210.

14202. Tilly, Chris. "Regenerating Inequality: The Distribution of U.S. Family Income and Individual Earnings in the 1980s." in *The Imperiled Economy*, Vol. 2. eds. Robert Cherry and others. New York: Union for Radical Political Economics, 1988.

14203. U.S. Bureau of the Census. *Money Income and Poverty Status 1989: Advance Data from the March 1990 Current Population Survey*. Washington, DC: GPO, 1990.

14204. Weisskopf, Richard. "Income Distribution and Economic Growth in Puerto Rico, Argentina, and Mexico." *Review of Income and Wealth* 16 (December 1970): 303-332.

WHITES

14205. "Abolish the White Race-By Any Means Necessay." *Race Traitor* no. 1 (Winter 1993): 1-8.

14206. Alba, Richard D. *Ethnic Identity: The Transformation of White America*. New Haven, CT: Yale University Press, 1990.

14207. Alberts, William E. "The White Magic of Systemic Racism." *Crisis* 85 (1978): 295-308.

14208. Applebome, Peter. "'65 Rights Act Now a Tool for Whites." *New York Times*, 8 August 1989. [Mississippi and Alabama]

14209. Ash, Stephen V. "Poor Whites in the Occupied South, 1861- 1865." *Journal of Southern History* 57 (1991): 39-62.

14210. Bolsterli, Margaret J. *Born in the Delta. Reflections on the Making of a Southern White Sensibility*. Knoxville: University of Tennessee Press, 1991.

14211. Bolton, Charles C. *The Failure of Yeoman Democracy: Poor Whites in the Antebellum South*. Ph.D. diss., Duke University, 1989. [NC and MS]. UMO #9006726.

14212. _____. *Poor Whites of the Antebellum South: Tenants and Laborers in Central North Carolina and Northeast Mississippi*. Duke University Press, 1994.

14213. Bowser, Benjamin P., and Raymond G. Hunt, eds. *Impacts of Racism on White Americans*. Newbury Park, CA: Sage, 1981.

14214. Campbell, Will D. "The World of the Redneck." *Christianity and Crisis* 24 (1974): 111-118.

14215. Carey, Art. "What's Right with White Guys? Here Are 10 Good Points." *Long Beach Press-Telegram*, 2 June 1993.

14216. Carter, R. T. "The Relationship between Racism and Racial Identity among White Americans: An Exploratory Investigation." *Journal of Counseling and Development* 69 (September-October 1990).

14217. Cecil-Fronsman, Bill. *Common Whites: Class and Culture in Antebellum North Carolina*. University Press of Kentucky, 1992.

14218. Davis, Jefferson, Mrs. "The White Man's Problem." *Arena* 23 (January 1900): 1-41.

14219. Dunbar Ortiz, Roxanne. "One or Two Things I Know about Us: 'Okies' in American Culture." *Radical History Review* no. 59 (Spring 1994): 4-34.

14220. Ehrenreich, Barbara. "Welfare: A White Secret." *Time* (16 December 1991). [Whites constitute 61 percent of population receiving welfare.]

14221. Evans, Arthur S. "The Relationship Between Industrialization and White Hostility Toward Blacks in Southern Cities: 1865-1910." *Urban Affairs Quarterly* 25 (December 1989).

14222. Fellman, Michael. "Getting Right With the Poor White." *Canadian Review of American Studies* 18 (1987): 527-539.

14223. Flynt, J. Wayne. *Dixie's Forgotten People: The South's Poor Whites*. Bloomington: Indiana University Press, 1979.

14224. _____. *Poor But Proud: Alabama's Poor Whites*. Tuscaloosa: University of Alabama Press, 1989.

14225. _____. "Spindle, Mine, and Mule: The Poor White Experience in Post-Civil War Alabama." in *From Civil War to Civil Rights*, ed. Sarah Woolfolk Wiggins. Tuscaloosa: University of Alabama Press, 1987.

14226. Fowlkes, Diane L. *White Political Women: Paths from Privilege to Empowerment*. Knoxville: University of Tennessee Press, 1992.

14227. Frankenberg, Ruth A. E. "Growing Up White: Feminism, Racism and the Social Geography of Childhood." *Feminist Review* 45 (Autumn 1993): 51-84.

14228. _____. *White Women, Race Matters: The Social Construction of Whiteness*. Ph.D. diss., University of California, Santa Cruz, 1988. UMO #8905621.

14229. Fraser, James W. "Two Who Said 'No' to Whiteness: Boston Public Schools, 1962-1975." *Race Traitor* no. 1 (Winter 1993): 9- 20. [Evelyn Morash and Mary Ellen Smith]

14230. George, John P., Jr. *"With Friends Like That...": The Role of the White Upper Class in the Etiology of Southern Racism, 1790-1975*. Ph.D. diss., Mississippi State University, 1990. UMO #9131236.

14231. Giles, Michael W., and Arthur S. Evans. "The Power Approach to Intergroup Hostility." *Journal of Conflict Resolution* 30 (1986): 469-486.

14232. Harrington, Walt. *Crossings: A White Man's Journey Into Black America*. HarperCollins, 1993. [See below, Charrisse Jones]

14233. Helms, Janet E. "Toward a Model of White Racial Identity Inventory." in *Black and White Racial Identity: Theory, Research, and Practice*, ed. Janet E. Helms. Westport, CT: Greenwood, 1990.

14234. Hoffman, Michael A., II. *They Were White and They Were Slaves: The Untold History of the Enslavement of White in Early America*. Dresden, NY: Wiswell Ruffin House, 1991.

14235. Hurst, John. "Invisible Poor-Whites." *Los Angeles Times*, 11 July 1992. [California]

14236. Ibidunni, A. O. and others. "Do White Leaders Denounce White Racism?" *New York Times*, 2 February 1994. [Three letters]

14237. Jacobs, Sally. "White Males: Only Ethnic Group That's Not in Vogue." *Long Beach Press-Telegram*, 29 November 1992.

14238. Jelen, Ted G. "The Impact of Home Ownership on Whites' Racial Attitudes." *American Politics Quarterly* 18 (April 1990).

14239. Jones, Charisse. "Unsentimental Journey." *Los Angeles Times*, 9 February 1993. [Interview with Walt Harrington, a white man who toured Black America.]

14240. Jones, Rachel L. "Striving for Success Doesn't Make Us 'White'." *Boston Globe*, 6 September 1994.

14241. Katz, Irvin, and R. Glen Hass. "Racial Ambivalence and American Value Conflict: Correctional and Priming Studies of Dual Cognitive Structures." *Journal of Personality and Social Psychology* 55 (December 1988): 893-905.

14242. Kinder, Donald R. "The Continuing American Dilemma: White Resistance to Racial Change 40 Years after Myrdal." *Journal of Social Issues* 42 (1986): 151-171.

14243. Kivisto, Peter, ed. *The Ethnic Enigma: The Salience of Ethnicity for European-origin Groups*. Philadelphia, PA: Balch Institute, 1989.

14244. Kluegel, James R. "Trends in Whites' Explanations of the Black-White Gap in Socioeconomic Status, 1977-1989." *American Sociological Review* 55 (1990): 512-525.

14245. Kornblum, William, and James Beshers. "White Ethnicity: Ecological Dimensions." in *Power, Culture, and Place: Essays on New York City*, ed. John F. Mollenkopf. New York: Russell Sage Foundation, 1988.

14246. Lee, Valerie E. "Responses of White Students to Ethnic Literature: One Teacher's Experience." *Reader* 15 (Spring 1986): 24-33.

14247. Leonardo, Micaela di. "Racial Fairy Tales." *Nation* (9 December 1991).

14248. Lieberson, Stanley, and Mary C. Waters. "The Ethnic Responses of Whites: What Causes Their Instability, Simplification, and Inconsistency." *Social Forces* 72 (December 1993): 421-450.

14249. Locke, Hubert G. *The Care and Feeding of White Liberals*. New York: Newman Press, 1970.

14250. Lott, Eric. "White Like Me. Racial Cross-Dressing and the Construction of American Whiteness." in *Cultures of United States Imperialism*, pp. 474-495. eds. Amy Kaplan, and Donald E. Pease. Duke University Press, 1993.

14251. Michaels, Walter B. "The Souls of White Folk." in *Literature and the Body: Essays on Populations and Persons*, ed. Elaine Scarry. Baltimore, MD: Johns Hopkins University Press, 1988.

14252. Miller, Mark and others. "White Male Paranoia." *Newsweek* (29 March 1993): 48-54.

14253. "Mountain People as an Urban Minority." *Washington Post*, 27 December 1993. [Reference to 1992 Cincinnati ordinance outlawing discrimination against Appalachians]

14254. Njeri, Itabari. "Facing Up to Being White." *Los Angeles Times*, 28 December 1989.

14255. Ownby, Ted, ed. *Black and White Cultural Interaction in the Antebellum South*. University Press of America, 1993.

14256. Pasternak, Judy. "Bias Blights Life Outside Appalachia." *Los Angeles Times*, 29 March 1994. [White underclass in Cincinnati, Ohio]

14257. Patin, Thomas. "White Mischief: Metaphor and Desire in a Misreading of Navajo Culture." *American Indian Culture and Research Journal* 15 (1991): 75-89.

14258. Patterson, Tim. "1992: Caucasian Year in Review." *CrossRoads* no. 28 (February 1993): 30.

14259. Pettigrew, Thomas F. "Racism and the Health of White Americans: A Social Psychological View." in *Racism and Mental Health*, eds. Charles V. Willie and others. Pittsburgh, PA: University of Pittsburgh Press, 1973.

14260. Rice, T. W. "Partisan Change Among Native White Southeners, 1965-1982." *American Politics Quarterly* 22 (April 1994).

14261. Rodgers, Raymond, and Jimmie N. Rodgers. "The Evolution of the Attitude of Malcolm X Toward Whites." *Phylon* 44 (June 1983): 108-115.

14262. Royko, Mike. "Bigotry Thrives, As Foolish as Ever." *Chicago Tribune*, 2 January 1992. [On anti-Italian American ideology]

14263. Segrest, Mab. *Memoir of a Race Traitor*. South End Press, 1993. [An anti-racist white person in Alabama and elsewhere in South]

14264. Sobel, Mechal. "All Americans Are Part African: Slave Influence on 'White' Values." in *Slavery and Other Forms of Unfree Labour*, ed. Leonie J. Archer. New York: Routledge, 1988.

14265. Solinger, R. "The Girl Nobody Loved: Psychological Explanations for White Single Pregnancy in the Pre-Roe v. Wade Era, 1945-1965." *Frontiers* 11 (1990).

14266. Solomon, C. M. "Are White Males Being Left Out?" *Personnel Journal* 70 (November 1991): 88-95.

14267. Tatum, B. D. "Teaching White Students About Racism: The Search for White Allies and the Restoration of Hope." *Teachers College Record* 95 (Summer 1994): 462-476.

14268. Tilove, Jonathan. "Poor and White: 'The Last Scapegoat'." *Springfield [MA] Union-News*, 8 September 1994. [Lower Price Hill, Cincinnati, OH]

14269. Tuch, Steven A., and Marylee C. Taylor. "Whites' Opinions about Insitutional Constraints on Racial Equality." *Sociology and Social Research* 70 (1986): 268-271.

14270. Tucker, F. *The White Conscience: An Analysis of the White Man's Mind and Conduct*. New York: Ungar, 1968.

14271. Wallace, Amy. "Whites Face a New Fear: Being Judged by Color." *Los Angeles Times*, 15 June 1992.

14272. Walters, W. Ronald. "White Racial Nationalism in the United States." *Without Prejudice* 1 (Fall 1987).

14273. Ware, Vron. *Beyond the Pale: White Women, Racism and History*. Verso, 1992.

14274. Waters, Mary C. *Ethnic Options. Choosing Identities in America*. Berkeley: University of California Press, 1990.

14275. Watrous, Peter. "White Singers and Black Style Pop Bonanza." *New York Times*, 11 March 1990.

14276. "The White Issue." *Village Voice* (18 May 1993). [Articles on whites and whiteness]

14277. Whittaker, Elvi. *The Mainland Haole: The White Experience in Hawaii*. New York: Columbia University Press, 1986.

WOMEN OF COLOR

14278. Acosta-Belen, Edna, ed. *The Puerto Rican Woman: Perspectives on Culture, History, and Society*. New York: Praeger, 1986.

14279. "African American Women In Defense of Ourselves." *New York Times*, 17 November 1991. 53. [Condemns appointment of Clarence Thomas to U.S. Supreme Court]

14280. "The African-American Woman: Complexities in the Midst of a Simplistic World View." *Journal of Black Studies* 20 (December 1989): entire issue.

14281. Albers, Patricia, and Beatrice Medicine, eds. *The Hidden Half: Studies of Plains Indian Women*. Lanham, MD: University Press of America, 1983.

14282. Alexander, Adele L. *Ambiguous Lives. Free Women of Color in Rural Georgia, 1789-1879*. University of Arkansas Press, 1981.

14283. Ali, Sharazad. *The Blackman's Guide to Understanding the Blackwoman*. Civilized Publications, 1989. [See Haki Madhubuti, below]

14284. Allen, Paula G., ed. *Spider Woman's Granddaughters. Traditional Tales and Contemporary Writing by Native American Women*. Boston, MA: Beacon Press, 1989.

14285. Allen, Ruth A. "Mexican Peon Women in Texas." *Sociology and Social Research* 16 (December 1931): 131-142.

14286. Andolsen, Barbara H. *Daughters of Jefferson, Daughters of Bootblacks: Racism and American Feminism*. Macon, GA: Mercer University Press, 1986.

14287. Antell, Judith A. *American Indian Women Activists*. Ph.D. diss., University of California, Berkeley, 1990. UMO #9103626.

14288. Anzaldua, Gloria, ed. *Making Face, Making Soul, Haceino Caras: Creative and Critical Perspectives by Women of Colour*. San Francisco, 1990.

14289. Aponte, Carmen I. *A Descriptive Profile: Puerto Rican Females in New York and New Jersey*. Ph.D. diss., Ohio State University, 1985. UMO #8602970.

14290. Armitage, Susan H., and Deborah G. Wilbert. "Black Women in the Pacific Northwest: A Survey and Research Prospectus." in *Women in Pacific Northwest History: An Anthology*, ed. Karen J. Blair. Seattle: University of Washington, 1988.

14291. "Asian Women Battling To Avoid Type-Casting." *New York Times*, 23 January 1994.

14292. Asian Women United of California, ed. *Making Waves. An Anthology of Writings by and about Asian American Women*. Boston, MA: Beacon Press, 1989.

14293. Azize, Yamile. *La mujer en la lucha. Historia del feminismo en Puerto Rico 1898-1930*. San Juan, Puerto Rico: Editorial Cultural, 1985.

14294. _____. *La mujer en Puerto Rico. Ensayos de investigacion*. Editorial Huracan, 1987.

14295. _____. *Luchas de la mujer en Puerto Rico: 1898-1919*. San Juan, Puerto Rico: Fraficor, 1979.

14296. Azize, Yamila. "The Roots of Puerto Rican Feminism: The Struggle for Universal Suffrage." *Radical America* 23 (January-February 1989): 70-79.

14297. Bataille, Gretchen M., ed. *Native American Women. A Biographical Dictionary*. Garland, 1992.

14298. Better, Shirley J. *Black Working Women: Role Perception, Role Status, and Life Satisfaction*. Ph.D. diss., University of California, Los Angeles, 1987. UMO #8803670.

14299. Biola, Heather. "The Black Washerwoman in Southern Tradition." *Tennessee Folklore Society Bulletin* 45 (1979): 17-27.

14300. "Black Panther Sisters Talk About Women's Liberation." *The Movement* (September 1969).

14301. Blackwelder, Julia K. "Race, Ethnicity, and Women's Lives in the Urban South." in *Shades of the Sunbelt*, eds. Randall M. Miller, and George E. Pozzetta. Westport, CT: Greenwood, 1988.

14302. Blea, Irene I. *La Chicana and the Intersection of Race, Class and Gender*. Westport, CT: Praeger, 1991.

14303. Blicksilver, Edith. *The Ethnic American Woman: Problems, Protests, Lifestyle*. Dubuque, Iowa: Kendall/Hunt, 1978.

14304. Bonvillain, Nancy. "Gender Relations in Native North America." *American Indian Culture and Research Journal* 13 (1989): 1-28.

14305. Boyd, Julia. *In the Company of My Sisters: Black Women and Self-Esteem*. Dutton, 1994.

14306. Brewer, Rose M. "Black Women and Feminist Sociology: The Emerging Perspective." *American Sociologist* 20 (1989): 57-70.

14307. Brown, Judith K. "Economic Organization and the Position of Women Among the Iroquois." *Ethnohistory* 17 (1970): 151-167.

14308. Brun, Nancy. *Shedding Light on Women's Work and Wages: Consequences of Protective Legislation*. Ph.D. diss., New School for Social Research, 1988. UMO #9030684.

14309. Burgess, Norma J. "Gender Roles Revisited: The Development of the Women's Place Among African American Women in the United States." *Journal of Black Studies* 24 (June 1994): 391-401.

14310. Burnham, Dorothy. "The Life of the Afro-American Woman in Slavery." *International Journal of Women's Studies* 1 (July-August 1978): 363-377.

14311. Camacho, Roseanne V. *Woman Born of the South: Race, Region and Gender in the Work of Lillian Smith*. Ph.D. diss., Brown University, 1991. UMO #9204836.

14312. Caraway, Nancie. *Segregated Sisterhood. Racism and the Politics of American Feminism*. Knoxville: University of Tennessee Press, 1992.

14313. Castaneda, Antonia I. "Women of Color and the Rewriting of Western History: The Discourse, Politics, and Decolonization of History." *Pacific Historical Review* 61 (November 1992): 501-533.

14314. Castenada, Antonia I. "Gender, Race, and Culture: Spanish- Mexican Women in the Historiography of Frontier California." *Frontiers* 11 (1990).

14315. Chametzky, Jules, ed. *Black Writers Redefine the Struggle: A Tribute to James Baldwin*. Amherst, MA: Institute for Advanced Studies in the Humanities, University of Massachusetts, 1989.

14316. Clinton, Catherine. "Mammy." *Black Women in America II*, pp. 744-747.

14317. Collier-Thomas, Bettye. "National Council of Negro Women." *Black Women in America II*, pp. 853-864.

14318. Collins, Patricia H. "Learning from the Outsider Within: The Sociological Significance of Black Feminist Thought." *Social Problems* 33 (1986): 814-832.

14319. _____. "The Social Construction of Black Feminist Thought." *Signs* 14 (Summer 1989): 745-773.

14320. Comas-Diaz, Lillian. "Feminism and Diversity in Psychology: The Case of Women of Color." *Psychology of Women Quarterly* 15 (December 1991).

14321. _____. "Mainland Puerto Rican Women: A Sociocultural Approach." *Journal of Community Psychology* 16 (January 1988): 21- 31.

14322. Commission on Civil Rights of Puerto Rico. *La Iqualdad de Derechos y Opportunidades de la Mujer Puertorriquena*. San Juan: The Commission, 1972.

14323. "Common Grounds and Crossroads: Race, Ethnicity and Class in Women's Lives." *Signs* 14 (Summer 1989): entire issue.

14324. Cordova, Teresa, ed. *Chicana Voices: Intersections of Class, Race, and Gender*. University of New Mexico Press, 1993.

14325. Cox, Cherise. "Anything Less Is Not Feminism: Racial Difference and the WMWM." *Law and Critique* 1 (Autumn 1990): 237- 248. [WMWM=White Middle Class Women's Movement]

14326. Crawford, Vicki L., and others, eds. *Women in the Civil Rights Movement. Trailblazers and Torchbearers, 1941-1965*. Brooklyn, NY: Carlson Publishing Inc., 1990.

14327. Cunningham, James S., and Nadja Zalokar. "The Economic Progress of Black Women, 1940-1980: Occupational Distribution and Relative Wages." *Industrial and Labor Relations Review* 45 (April 1992): 540-555.

14328. David, Hilda B. *The African-American Women of Edisto Island: 1850-1920*. Ph.D. diss., Emory University, 1990. UMO #9027901.

14329. Demirturk, Emine L. *The Female Identity in Cross-Cultural Perspectives: Immigrant Women's Autobiographies*. Ph.D. diss., University of Iowa, 1986.

14330. Deutsch, Sarah J. *Culture, Class, and Gender: Chicanas and Chicanos in Colorado and New Mexico, 1900-1940*. 2 vols. Ph.D. diss., Yale University, 1985. UMO #8601080.

14331. Dobie, Kathy. "Black, Female, and Muslim." *Village Voice* (28 May 1991).

14332. Du Bois, Ellen C., and Vicki L. Ruiz, eds. *Unequal Sisters. A Multicultural Reader in U.S. Women's History*. Routledge, 1990.

14333. Du Bois, W. E. B. "The Work of Negro Women in Society." *Spelman Messenger* 18 (February 1902): 1-3.

14334. Dugger, Karen. "Social Location and Gender-Role Attitudes: A Comparison of Black and White Women." *Gender and Society* 2 (December 1988): 425-448.

14335. Dysart, Jane E. "Mexican Women in San Antonio, 1830-1860: The Assimilation Process." *Western Historical Quarterly* 7 (October 1976).

14336. Emanuel, Irvin and others. "Poor Birth Outcomes of American Black Women: An Alternative Explanation." *Journal of Public Health Policy* 10 (1989): 299-308.

14337. Essed, Philomena. *Everyday Racism: Reports from Women of Two Cultures*. Claremont, CA: Hunter House, 1989. [U.S.A. and Netherlands]

14338. Etter-Lewis, Given. *My Soul is My Own. Oral Narratives of African American Women in the Professions*. Routledge, 1993.

14339. Ferguson, Earline Rae. "The Women's Improvement Club of Indianapolis: Black Women Pioneers in Tuberculosis Work, 1903- 1938." *Indiana Magazine of History* 84 (September 1988): 237-261.

14340. Figueroa, Loida. "El papel historico y social de la mujer en el Caribe hispanico, especialmenti en Puerto Rico." *Atenea* 6 (1986): 149-170.

14341. Fosu, Augustin K. "Trends in Relative Earnings Gains by Black Women: Implications for the Future." *Review of Black Political Economy* 17 (Summer 1988): 31-46.

14342. Frankel, Noralee, and Nancy S. Dye, eds. *Gender, Class, Race, and Reform in the Progressive Era*. University Press of Kentucky, 1991.

14343. Garcia, Alma M. "The Development of Chicana Feminist Discourse, 1970-1980." *Gender and Society* 3 (June 1989): 217-238.

14344. Garnett, Cynthia M. "African-American Women and the Issue of Abortion." *African Commentary* 1 (November 1989): 18-20.

14345. Gilkes, C. T. "'Liberated to Work Like Dogs': Labeling Black Women and Their Work." in *The Experience and Meaning of Work in Women's Lives*, eds. Hildreth Y. Grossman, and Nia L. Chester. Hillsdale, NJ: Lawrence Erlbaum Associates, 1989.

14346. Gilmore, Glenda E. *Gender and Jim Crow: Women and the Politics of White Supremacy in North Carolina, 1896-1920*. Ph.D. diss., University of North Carolina at Chapel Hill, 1992. UMO #9234961.

14347. Graymont, Barbara. "Indian Women Played Tribal Role." *New York Times*, 12 January 1993. letter. [Long Island Shinnecock]

14348. Guy-Sheftall, Beverly. *Daughters of Sorrow. Attitudes Toward Black Women, 1880-1920*. Brooklyn, NY: Carlson Publishing Inc., 1990.

14349. Hammonds, Evelynn. "Never Meant to Survive: A Black Woman's Journey." in *Politics of Education*, eds. Susan G. O'Malley and others. Albany: State University of New York Press, 1990. [Interview]

14350. Harley, Sharon. "When Your Work is Not Who You Are: The Development of a Working-Class Consciousness among Afro-American Women." in *Gender, Class, Race, and Reform in the Progressive Era*, pp. 42-55. eds. Noralee Frankel, and Nancy S. Dye. University of Kentucky Press, 1991.

14351. Hart, Jamie, Elsa Barkley Brown, and N. H. Goodall. "Black Women in the United States: A Chronology." *Black Women in America II*, pp. 1309-1332.

14352. Hartado, Aida. "Relating to Privilege: Seduction and Rejection in the Subordination of White Women and Women in Color." *Signs* 14 (Summer 1989): 833-855.

14353. Haynes, Elizabeth R. "Negroes in Domestic Service in the United States." *Journal of Negro History* 8 (October 1923): 384- 442.

14354. Helmbold, Lois R. "Downward Occupational Mobility during the Great Depression: Urban Black and White Working Class Women." *Labor History* 29 (Spring 1988): 135-172.

14355. Hernandez, Aileen C. *National Women of Color Organizations*. New York: Ford Foundation, 1991.

14356. Higginbotham, Evelyn B. "African-American Women's History and the Metalanguage of Race." *Signs* 17 (Winter 1992): 251-274.

14357. _____. "Beyond the Sound of Silence: Afro-American Women's History." *Gender and Society* 1 (1989): 50-67.

14358. Hine, Darlene Clark, ed. *Black Women in American History. From Colonial Times Through the Nineteenth Century*, 4 vols. Brooklyn, NY: Carlson Publishing Inc., 1990. [96 articles]

14359. _____. *Black Women in American History. The Twentieth Century*, 4 vols. Brooklyn, NY: Carlson Publishing Inc., 1990. [70 articles]

14360. _____. *Black Women's History. Theory and Practice*, 2 vols. Brooklyn, NY: Carlson Publishing Inc., 1990.

14361. Hine, Darlene Clark. "Lifting the Veil, Shattering the Silence: Black Women's History in Slavery and Freedom." in *The State of Afro-American History: Past, Present, and Future*, ed. Hine, Darlene Clark. Baton Rouge: Louisiana State University Press, 1989.

14362. _____. "Rape and the Inner Lives of Black Women in the Middle West: Preliminary Thoughts on the Culture of Dissemblance." *Signs* 14 (Summer 1989): 912-920.

14363. _____. "We Specialize in the Wholly Impossible: The Philanthropic Work of Black Women." in *Lady Bountiful Revisited: Women, Philanthropy, and Power*, ed. Kathleen D. McCarthy. New Brunswick, NJ: Rutgers U.P., 1990.

14364. Holleran, Philip M., and Margaret Schwartz. "Another Look at Comparable Worth's Impact on Black Women." *Review of Radical Political Economy* 16 (Winter 1988): 97-102.

14365. Hooks, Bell. "Black Students Who Reject Feminism." *Chronicle of Higher Education* (13 July 1994).

14366. _____. *Sisters of the Yam. Black Women and Self- recovery*. South End Press, 1993.

14367. Horton, James O. "Freedom's Yoke: Gender Conventions Among Antebellum Free Blacks." *Feminist Studies* 12 (Spring 1986): 51- 76.

14368. "Immigrant Women." *Journal of American Ethnic History* 8 (Spring 1989): entire issue.

14369. Ione, Carole. *Pride of Family. Four Generations of American Women of Color*. New York: Summit, 1991.

14370. Iwataki, Miya. "The Asian Women's Movement-A Retrospective." *East Wind* 2 (Spring-Summer 1983): 35-41.

14371. James, Stanlie M., ed. *Theorizing Black Feminisms: The Visionary Pragmatism of Black Women*. Routledge, 1993.

14372. Jameson, Elizabeth. "Toward a Multicultural History of Women in the Western United States." *Signs* 13 (1988): 761-791.

14373. Jennings, Thelma. "'Us Colored Women Had to Go Through a Plenty': Sexual Expolitation of African-American Slave Women." *Journal of Women's History* 1 (Winter 1990): 45-74.

14374. Jewell, Karen S. *From Mammy to Miss America and Beyond: Cultural Images and the Shaping of U.S. Social Policy*. Routledge, 1993.

14375. Jewell, Terri L., ed. *The Black Women's Gumbo Ya-Ya: Quotations by Black Women*. Freedom, CA: The Crossing Press, 1993.

14376. Jones, Adrienne Lash. *Jane Edna Hunter. A Case Study of Black Leadership 1910-1950*. Brooklyn, NY: Carlson Publishing Inc., 1990. [Cleveland, Ohio]

14377. _____. "Young Women's Christian Association." *Black Women in America II*, pp. 1299-1303.

14378. Jones, Beverly W. *Quest for Equality. The Life and Writings of Mary Eliza Church Terrell, 1863-1954*. Brooklyn, NY: Carlson Publishing Inc., 1990.

14379. Jones, Jacqueline. "My Mother Was Much of a Woman': Black Women, Work, and Family Under Slavery, 1830-1860." *Feminist Studies* 8 (Summer 1982): 235-269.

14380. _____. "Race, Sex, and Self-evident Truths: The Status of Slave Women during the Era of the American Revolution." in *Women in the Age of the American Revolution*, eds. Ronald Hoffman, and Peter J. Albert. Charlottesville: University Press of Virginia, 1989.

14381. Ladner, Joyce A. "Black Women As Doers: The Social Responsibility of Black Women." *Sage* 6 (Summer 1989).

14382. "Latina Policy Issues." in *The Challenge: Latinos in a Changing California*, University of California SCR 43 Task Force. Riverside: The University of California Consortium on Mexico and the United States (UCMEXUS), 1989.

14383. Lee, Mary Paik. *Quiet Odyssey: A Pioneer Korean Woman in America*, ed. Sucheng Chan. Seattle: University of Washington Press, 1990.

14384. Leslie, Kent A. "Amanda America Dickson: An Elite Mulatto Lady in Nineteenth-Century Georgia." in *Southern Women: Histories and Identities*, eds. Virginia Bernhard and others. University of Missouri Press, 1992.

14385. Leslie, Paul L. *Black Southern Professional Women: Struggles and Contributions. 3 vols.* Ph.D. diss., Boston University, 1991. UMO #9105309.

14386. Leslie, Virginia K. A. *Woman of Color, Daughter of Privilege: Amanda America Dickson, 1849-1893*. Ph.D. diss., Emory University, 1990. UMO #9027922.

14387. Levy, Anita. *Other Women. The Writing of Class, Race, and Gender, 1832-1898*. Princeton, NJ: Princeton University Press, 1991.

14388. Lim, Shirley Geok-lin and others, eds. *The Forbidden Stitch: An Asian Women's Anthology*. Corvallis, OR: Calyx Books, 1989.

14389. Ling, Susie. "The Mountain Movers: Asian American Women's Movement in Los Angeles." *Amerasia Journal* 15 (1989): 51-67.

14390. Locke, Mamie E. "From Three-fifths to Zero: Implications of the Constitution for African-American Women, 1787-1870." *Women and Politics* 10 (1990): 33-46.

14391. Lum, Joann, and Peter Kwong. "Surviving in America. The Trials of a Chinese Immigrant Woman." *Village Voice* (31 October 1989).

14392. Lyles, Barbara D. "The Black Woman: Person or Non-Person." *Crisis* (May 1975): 163-166.

14393. Mabee, Carleton. "Sojourner Truth, Bold Prophet: Why Did She Never Learn to Read?" *New York History* 69 (January 1988): 55- 77.

14394. Mack-Williams, Voloria Kibibi. C. *Hard Workin' Women: Class Divisions and African American Women's Work in Orangeburg, South Carolina, 1880-1940*. Ph.D. diss., State University of New York at Binghamton, 1991. UMO #9110794.

14395. Madhubuti, Haki R., ed. *Confusion By Any Other Name: Essays Exploring the Negative Impact of 'The Blackman's Guide to Understanding the Blackwoman'*. Chicago, IL: Third World Press, 1990. [See Sharazad Ali, above]

14396. Malson, Micheline R. and others, eds. *Black Women in America. Social Science Perspective*. Chicago, IL: University of Chicago Press, 1990.

14397. Mann, Susan A. "Slavery, Sharecropping, and Sexuality Inequality." *Signs* 14 (Summer 1989): 775-798.

14398. Marshall, S. E. "Equity Issues and Black-White Differences in Women's ERA Support." *Social Science Quarterly* 71 (June 1990).

14399. Matsuda, Mari J. ""When the First Quail Calls: Multiple Consciousness as Jurisprudential Method" (Speech presented at Yale Law-School Conference on Women of Color and the Law, April 6, 1988)." *Women's Rights Law Reporter* 11 (Spring 1989): 7-10.

14400. May, Mary. "Meeting in Deep South, NARW Focuses on Racism." *National Catholic Reporter* (28 July 1989). [National Assembly of Religious Women]

14401. Mays, V. M., and Lillian Comasdiaz. "Feminist Therapy with Ethnic Minority Populations: A Closer Look at Blacks and Hispanics." in *Feminist Psychotherapies*, eds. M. A. Dutton Douglas, and L. E. A. Walker. Norwood, NJ: Ablex, 1988.

14402. McCann, Carole R. *Race, Class and Gender in U.S. Birth Control Politics, 1920-1945*. Ph.D. diss., University of California, Santa Cruz, 1987. UMO #8810866.

14403. McClain, Paula D. "Black Females and Lethal Violence: Has Time Changed the Circumstances under Which They Kill." *Omega: Journal of Death and Dying* 13 (1982): 13-25.

14404. _____. "Cause of Death-Homicide: A Research Note on Black Females as Homicide Victims." *Victimology* 7 (1982): 204- 212.

14405. Medicine, Beatrice. "Native American (Indian) Women: A Call for Research." *Anthropology and Education Quarterly* 19 (June 1988): 86-92.

14406. Morales, R., and Paul M. Ong. "Immigrant Women in Los Angeles." *Economic and Industrial Democracy* 12 (February 1991).

14407. Morton, Patricia. *Disfigured Images. The Historical Assault on Afro-American Women*. Westport, CT: Greenwood, 1991.

14408. Moses, T. Yolanda. *Black Women in Academe: Issues and Strategies*. Washington, DC: Project on the Status and Education of Women, Association of American Colleges, 1989.

14409. Murray, Carolyn B., and G. B. Stahly. "Some Victims Are Derogated More Than Others." *Western Journal of Black Studies* 11 (Winter 1987): 177-180.

14410. Muwakkil, Salim. "Men Not the Only Victims of Problems Vexing Blacks." *In These Times* (20 December 1989).

14411. Nakano, Mei. *Japanese American Women: Three Generations, 1890-1990*. San Francisco, CA: National Japanese American Historical Society, 1990.

14412. _____. "Japanese American Women: Three Generations." *History News* 45 (March-April 1990): 10-13.

14413. Neverdon-Morton, Cynthia. *Afro-American Women of the South and the Advancement of the Race, 1895-1925*. Knoxville: University of Tennessee Press, 1988.

14414. Nicola-McLaughlin, Andree, and Zala Chandler. "Black Women on the Frontline: Unfinished Business of the Sixties." in *Politics of Education*, eds. Susan G. O'Malley and others. Albany: State University of New York Press, 1990.

14415. Norton, Eleanor Holmes. "Black Women as Women." *Social Policy* 3 (July/August 1972): 2-3.

14416. Nsiah-Jefferson, Laurie. "Reproductive Laws, Women of Color, and Low-income Women." *Women's Rights Law Reporter* 11 (Spring 1989): 14-39.

14417. Osburn, Katherine M. B. *"And As the Squaws Are a Secondary Consideration": Southern Ute Women under Directed Culture Change, 1887-1934*. Ph.D. diss., University of Denver, 1993. [Dawes Act]. UMO #9317066.

14418. Oshana, Maryann. "Native American Women in Westerns: Reality and Myth." *Frontiers: A Journal of Women's Studies* 6 (Fall 1981).

14419. Parkhurst, Jessie W. "The Role of the Black Mammy in the Plantation Household." *Journal of Negro History* 23 (July 1938): 349-369.

14420. Perkins, Carol O. *Pragmatic Idealism: Industrial Training, Liberal Education and Women's Special Needs. Conflict and Continuity in the Experience of Mary McLeod Bethune and Other Black Women Educators, 1900-1930*. Ph.D. diss., Claremont Graduate School and San Diego University, 1987. UMO #8709295.

14421. Powlishta, K. K. and others. "Gender, Ethnic, and Body Type Biases: The Generality of Prejudice in Childhood." *Developmental Psychology* 30 (July 1994): 526-536.

14422. Redfern, Bernice. *Women of Color in the United States*. New York, 1989.

14423. Ries, Paula, and Anne J. Stone, eds. *The American Woman 1992-93: A Status Report*. Norton, 1992.

14424. Riley, Glenda. "American Daughters: Black Women in the West." *Montana* 38 (Spring 1988): 14-27.

14425. Roberts, D. E. "Punishing Drug Addicts Who Have Babies: Women of Color, Equality, and the Right of Privacy." *Harvard Law Review* 104 (May 1991): 1419-1483.

14426. Rouse, Jacqueline A. "Atlanta's African-American Women's Attack on Segregation, 1900-1920." in *Gender, Class, Race, and Reform in the Progressive Era*, eds. Noralee Frankel, and Nancy S. Dye. University Press of America, 1991.

14427. Salem, Dorothy C. *African American Women. A Biographical Dictionary*. Garland, 1992.

14428. _____. "National Association of Colored Women." *Black Women in America II*, pp. 842-851.

14429. _____. *To Better Our World. Black Women in Organized Reform, 1890-1920*. Brooklyn, NY: Carlson Publishing Inc., 1990.

14430. Sanchez Korrol, Virginia E. "Survival of Puerto Rican Women in New York Before World War II." in *The Puerto Rican Struggle*, pp. 47-57. eds. Clara E. Rodriquez and others. New York: Puerto Rican Migration Research Consortium, 1980.

14431. Scales-Trent, Judy. "Black Women and the Constitution: Finding Our Place, Asserting Our Rights." *Harvard Civil Rights- Civil Liberties Law Review* 24 (1989): 9-44.

14432. Schafer, Ann E. *The Status of Iroquois Women*. Master's thesis: University of Pa., 1941.

14433. Schwalm, Leslie A. *The Meaning of Freedom: African- American Women and their Transition from Slavery to Freedom in Lowcountry South Carolina*. Ph.D. diss., University of Wisconsin, 1991. [1840-1867]. UMO #9133415.

14434. Schweninger, Loren. "Property-Owning Free African-American Women in the South, 1800-1870." *Journal of Women's History* 1 (1990): 13-44.

14435. Scott, Anne Firor. "Most Invisible of All: Black Women's Voluntary Association." *Journal of Southern History* 56 (1990): 3- 22.

14436. Scott, Barbara Marbien. *The Making of a Middle-class Black Woman: A Socialization for Success.* 2 vols. Ph.D. diss., Northwestern University, 1988. UMO #8902697.

14437. Sears, Richard. "Working Like a Slave: Views of Slavery and the Status of Women in Antebellum Kentucky." *Register of the Ky. Hist. Society* 87 (Winter 1989): 1-19.

14438. Shebala, Markey. "Progress Made for Navajo Women." *Navajo Times* (5 January 1984).

14439. Shepard, Gloria. *The Rape of Black Women during Slavery.* Ph.D. diss., State University of New York at Albany, 1988. UMO #8805389.

14440. Shoemaker, Nancy. *Negotiators of Change. Historical Perspectives on Native American Women.* Routledge, 1994.

14441. _____. "The Rise or Fall of Iroquois Women." *Journal of Women's History* 2 (Winter 1991): 39-57.

14442. Shortridge, Barbara G. *Atlas of American Women*. New York: Macmillan, 1987.

14443. Simms, Margaret C. *The Choices that Young Black Women Make: Education, Employment, and Family Formation*. Washington DC: Joint Center for Political Studies, 1988. Wellesley Working Paper #190

14444. Smith, Y. R. "Women of Color in Society and Sport." *Quest* 44 (August 1992): 228-250.

14445. Snipp, C. Matthew, and I. A. Aytac. "The Labor Force Participation of American Indian Women." in *Female Labor Force Participation and Development*, pp. 189-212. eds. I. Sirageldin and others. Greenwich, CT: JAI Press, 1990.

14446. Soderlund, Jean R. "Black Women in Colonial Pennsylvania." *Pennsylvania Magazine of History and Biography* 107 (January 1983): 49-68.

14447. Soldatenko, Maria A. *The Everyday Lives of Latina Garment Workers in Los Angeles: The Convergence of Gender, Race, Class and Immigration*. Ph.D. diss., UCLA, 1992. UMO #9317055.

14448. Taeuber, Cynthia M., ed. *Statistical Handbook on Women in America*. Phoenix, AZ: Oryx, 1991.

14449. Taosie, R. "Changing Women: The Cross-currents of American Indian Feminine Identity." *American Indian Culture and Research Journal* 12 (1988): 1-37.

14450. Taylor, Kristin Clark. *The First to Speak: A Woman of Color Inside the White House*. Doubleday, 1993.

14451. Thompson, Mildred. *Ida B. Wells-Barnettt. An Exploratory Study of an American Black Woman, 1893-1930.* Brooklyn, NY: Carlson Publishing Inc., 1990.

14452. Thurber, Cheryl. "The Development of the Mammy Image and Mythology." in *Southern Women: Histories and Identity*, eds. Virginia Bernhard and others. University of Missouri Press, 1992.

14453. Tucker, Susan. *Telling Memories among Southern Women: Domestic Workers and their Employers in the Segregated South*. Baton Rouge: Louisiana State University Press, 1988.

14454. Wagner, Sally R. "The Iroquois Influence on Women's Rights." *Akwe: kon Journal* 9 (Spring 1992): 4-15.

14455. Waldman, Elizabeth. "Profile of the Chicana. A Statistical Fact Sheet." in *Mexican Women in the United States. Struggles Past and Present*, pp. 195-204. eds. Magdalena Mora, and Adelaida R. Del Castillo. Los Angeles: Chicano Studies Research Center, University of California, 1980.

14456. Walker, Alice. "What Can the White Man...Say to the Black Woman?" *Nation* (22 May 1989).

14457. Ward, Janie Victoria. "Racial Identity Formation and Transformation." in *Making Connections: The Relational Worlds of Adolescent Girls at Emma Willard School*, , 1989.

14458. Wilcos, Clyde. "Black Women and Feminism." *Women and Politics* 10 (1990): 65-84.

14459. Wilkinson, Doris. "Minority Women: Socio-Cultural Issues." in *Women and Psychotherapy*, pp. 285-304. eds. Annette Brodsky, and Rachel Haremustin. New York: Guilford Press, 1980.

14460. Williams, Delores. "The Color of Feminism; or, Speaking the Black Woman's Tongue." *Journal of Religious Thought* 43 (1986): 42-58.

14461. Winkler, Karen J. "The Rise of Black Feminist Thought." *Chronicle of Higher Education* (30 March 1994).

14462. Winston, Judith A. "An Antidiscrimination Legal Construct that Disadvantages Working Women of Color." *Clearinghouse Review* 25 (1991): 403-419.

14463. Woo, Merle. *Our Common Cause: Freedom Organizing in the Eighties*. Latham, NY: Kitchen Table: Women of Color Press, 1988.

14464. Wright, Michelle D. "African American Sisterhood: The Impact of the Female Slave Population on American Political Movements." *Western Journal of Black Studies* 15 (Spring 1991): 32-45.

14465. Yamanaka, K., and Katherine McClelland. "Earning the Model- Minority Image: Diverse Strategies of Economic Adaptation by Asian-American Women." *Ethnic and Racial Studies* 17 (January 1994): 79-114.

14466. Yung, Judith. *Unbinding the Feet, Unbinding their Lives: Social Change for Chinese Women in San Francisco, 1902-1945*. Ph.D. diss., University of California, Berkeley, 1990. UMO #9103942.

14467. Zalokar, Nadja. *The Economic Status of Black Women: An Exploratory Investigation*. Washington, DC: U.S. Commission on Civil Rights, 1990.

14468. Zamberana, Ruth E. "A Walk Into Two Worlds: Women of Color and Their Special Struggles." *Social Welfare* 1 (Spring 1986): 10- 12.

GENERAL

14469. Abraham, Sameer Y., and Nabeel Abraham, eds. *Arabs in America: An Overview. The Arab World and Arab Americans: Understanding a Neglected Minority*. Detroit, MI: Center for Urban Studies, Wayne State University, 1981.

14470. Alba, Richard D., ed. *Ethnicity and Race in the USA. Toward the Twenty-First Century*. New York: Routledge, 1988.

14471. Allen, W. B. "Black and White Together: A Reconsideration." *Social Philosophy and Policy* 8 (Spring 1991): 172-195.

14472. Bates, Karen G. "Why I Envy South Africa." *Los Angeles Times*, 18 May 1994. [Racial realities in U.S. and S. Africa]

14473. Bean, Frank D., and Marta Tienda. *The Hispanic Population of the United States*. New York: Russell Sage Foundation, 1990.

14474. Bennett, Claudette E. *The Black Population in the United States: March 1990 and 1989*. Washington DC: GPO, 1991.
Current Population Reports, Population Characteristics, Series P-20, No. 448.

14475. Binkley, Kenneth M. *Racial Traits of American Blacks*. Springfield, IL: Charles C. Thomas, 1989.

14476. "Black America in the 1980's." *Humboldt Journal of Social Relations* 14 (Fall-Winter-Spring-Summer 1987): entire issue.

14477. Blea, Irene I. *Toward a Chicano Social Science*. New York: Praeger, 1988.

14478. Bonacich, Edna. "Inequality in America: The Failure of the American System for People of Color." *Sociological Spectrum* 9 (1989): 77-101.

14479. Boston, Thomas D. "A Common Destiny: How Does It Compare to the Classic Studies of Black Life in America?" *American Economic Review* 80 (May 1990).

14480. _____. "The History of African-American Economic Thought and Policy." *American Economic Review* 81 (May 1991): 303- 306.

14481. Buhle, Mari Jo and others, eds. *The Encyclopedia of the American Left*. New York: Garland, 1990.

14482. Bullard, Robert D., ed. *In Search of the New South: Black Progress in An Era of Change*. Tuscaloosa: University of Alabama Press, 1989.

14483. Cashmore, E. Ellis. *Dictionary of Race and Ethnic Relations*, 2nd ed. London: Routledge and Kegan Paul, 1988.

14484. Churchill, Ward. "Critical Issues in Native North America." *Copenhagen* 1989 (IWGIA).

14485. _____. "I Am Indigenist. Notes on the Ideology of the Fourth World." in *Struggle for the Land*, pp. 403-451. Monroe, ME: Common Courage Press, 1993.

14486. Clark, Kenneth B. "Unfinished Business: The Toll of Psychic Violence." *Newsweek* (11 January 1993).

14487. Clayton, Lawrence A., ed. *The Hispanic Experience in North America. Sources for Study in the United States*. Ohio State U. P., 1993.

14488. Collin, Robert W., and Robin A. Morris. "Racial Inequality in American Cities: An Interdisciplinary Critique." *National Black Law Journal* 11 (Spring 1989): 177-197.

14489. Cross, William E., Jr. *Shades of Black. Diversity in African-American Identity*. Philadelphia, PA: Temple University Press, 1991.

14490. Crouch, Stanley. *Notes of a Hanging Judge. Essays and Reviews, 1979-1989*. New York: Oxford University Press, 1990.

14491. Crummell, Alexander. *Destiny and Race: Selected Writings, 1840-1898*, ed. Wilson Jeremiah Moses. University of Massachusetts Press, 1992.

14492. Darity, William A., Jr. "Racial Inequality in the Managerial Age: An Alternative Vision to the NRC Report." *American Economic Review* 80 (May 1990).

14493. Delaney, Paul. "The Deep South, 30 Years Later." *New York Times*, 23 February 1992.

14494. Delgado, Richard. "Pep Talks for the Poor: A Reply and Remonstrance on the Evils of Scapegoating." *Boston University Law Review* 71 (May 1991): 525-544.

14495. Dewart, Janet, ed. *The State of Black America 1991*. New York: National Urban League, 1991.

14496. DiMaggio, Paul, and Francie Ostrower. "Participation in the Arts by Black and White Americans." *Social Forces* 68 (March 1990).

14497. Early, Gerald, ed. *Lure and Loathing. Essays on Race, Identity, and Ambivalence of Assimilation*. Penguin Press: 1993.

14498. Edwards, Audrey, and Craig K. Polite. *Children of the Dream: The Psychology of Black Success*. Doubleday, 1992.

14499. Ellis, Trey. "Remember My Name." *Village Voice* (13 June 1989). [On naming and re-naming black people in the U.S.]

14500. Ernst, Friedhelm. *"Arab-Americans" in Nordamerika: eine Literaturstudie zur Geschichte und zu gegenwärtigen Strukturen und Problemen arabischer Einwanderungs-"communities"*. West Berlin: Das Arabische Buch Vertriebs, 1986.

14501. Ertel R. and others. *En Marge. Les minorités aux Etats- Unis*. Paris: Maspero, 1974.

14502. Farley, Reynolds. "The Common Destiny of Blacks and Whites: Observations about the Social and Economic Status of the Races." in *Race in America*, eds. Herbert Hill, and James E. Jones, Jr. University of Wisconsin Press, 1993.

14503. Garcia, Juan R. and others, eds. *In Times of Challenge: Chicanos and Chicanas in American Society*. Houston, TX: Mexican American Studies Program, University of Houston, 1988.

14504. Garwood, Alfred N., ed. *Black Americans: A Statistical Sourcebook, 1991*, 2nd ed. Numbers and Concepts, Suite E4-221, 2525 Araphoe Ave., Boulder, CO 80302.

14505. Gonzalez, David. "The Afro-Amerasians, Tangled Emotions Surface." *New York Times*, 17 November 1992.

14506. Guess, Jerry M. "Race. The Challenge of the 90's." *Crisis* 96 (November 1989): 28-33.

14507. Hacker, Andrew. "Trans-National America." *New York Review of Books* (22 November 1990). [Review essay]

14508. Harding, Vincent. "Responsibilities of the Black Scholar to the Community." in *The State of Afro-American History: Past, Present and Future*, pp. 277-284. ed. Darline Clark Hine. Baton Rouge: LSU Press, 1986.

14509. Hauser, Robert M. and others. "Understanding Black-White Differences." *Public Interest* no. 99 (Spring 1990). [See rejoinder by R.J. Herrnstein in same issue]

14510. Herrnstein, R. J. "Social Science and Black/White. Still an American Dilemma." *Public Interest* no. 98 (Winter 1990).

14511. Hill, Herbert, and James E. Jones, Jr., eds. *Race in America. The Struggle for Equality.* University of Wisconsin Press, 1992.

14512. Hirschman, Charles, and Ellen P. Kraly. "Racial and Ethnic Inequality in the United States, 1940 and 1950: The Impact of Geographic Location and Human Capital." *International Migration Review* 24 (Spring 1990).

14513. Hochschild, Jennifer L. "Equal Opportunity and the Estranged Poor." *Annals of the American Academy of Political and Social Science* no. 501 (January 1989): 43-55.

14514. Hofmann, Suellyn M. *Strengthening the Web of Oppression: A Study of Racism and Sexism in the Literature of Adult Education.* Ph.D. diss., Florida State University, 1988. UMO #8825740.

14515. Hooks, Bell, pseud. [Watkins, Gloria]. *Black Looks. Race and Representation.* Boston, MA: South End Press, 1993.

14516. Hooks, Bell, pseud. [Watkins, Gloria], and Cornel West. *Breaking Bread. Insurgent Black Intellectual Life.* Boston, MA: South End Press, 1991.

14517. Horton, Carrell P., and Jessie Carney Smith. *Statistical Record of Black America, 1990.* Detroit, MI: Gale, 1990.

14518. Jackson, James S., ed. *Life in Black America.* Newbury Park, CA: Sage, 1991.

14519. Jacob, Evelyn, and Cathie Jordan, eds. *Minority Education: Anthropological Perspectives.* Ablex, 1993.

14520. Jaimes, M. Annette, ed. *The State of Native America. Genocide, Colonization, and Resistance.* Boston, MA: South End Press, 1992.

14521. Jaynes, Gerald D., and Robin M. Williams, Jr., eds. *A Common Destiny. Blacks and American Society.* Washington, DC: National Academy Press, 1989.

14522. Jiobu, Robert M. *Ethnicity and Inequality.* Albany: State University of New York Press, 1990. [1980 Census data]

14523. Killian, Lewis M. "Race Relations and the Nineties: Where Are the Dreams of the Sixties?" *Social Forces* 69 (1990): 1-13.

14524. Knopke, Harry J. and others, eds. *Opening Doors: Perspectives on Race Relations in Contemporary America.* University of Alabama Press, 1991.

14525. Landry, Bart. "The Enduring Dilemma of Race in America." in *America at Century's End*, pp. 185-207. ed. Alan Wolfe. Berkeley: UC Press, 1991.

14526. Leigh, David J. "Malcolm X and the Black Muslim Search for Ultimate Reality." *Ultimate Reality and Meaning* 13 (March 1990): 33-49.

14527. Lester, Julius. "Black and White Together." *Salmagundi* 81 (1989): 174-181.

14528. Lieberson, Stanley, and Mary C. Waters. *From Many Strands. Ethnic and Racial Groups in Contemporary America.* New York: Russell Sage Foundation, 1990.

14529. Lusanne, Clarence. *Pipe Dream Blues. Racism and the War on Drugs.* Boston, MA: South End Press, 1991.

14530. Majors, Richard, and Janet M. Billson. *Cool Pose: The Dilemmas of Black Manhood in America.* Lexington Books, 1992.

14531. Marable, Manning. *The Crisis of Color and Democracy. Essays on Race, Class and Power.* Monroe, ME: Common Courage Press, 1992.

14532. Marable, Virginia M. *Cross-cultural Symbolism of Color.* Ph.D. diss., United States International University, 1991. UMO #9123779.

14533. Margo, Robert A. "What Is the Key to Black Progress?" in *Second Thoughts*, ed. Donald N. McCloskey. Oxford University Press, 1993.

14534. Martin, B. L. "From Negro to Black to African American: The Power of Names and Naming." *Political Science Quarterly* 106 (Spring 1991): 83-108.

14535. McCarus, Ernest, ed. *The Development of Arab-American Identity*. University of Michigan Press, 1994.

14536. McGee, Henry W., Jr. "Afro-American Resistance to Gentrification and the Demise of Integrational Ideology in the United States." *Urban Lawyer* 23 (Winter 1991): 25-44.

14537. McKee, Jesse O., ed. *Ethnicity in Contemporary America: A Geographical Appraisal*. Dubuque, Iowa: Kendall/Hunt, 1985.

14538. Menchaca, Martha. "Chicano-Mexican Cultural Assimilation and Anglo-Saxon Cultural Dominance." *Hispanic Journal of Behavorial Science* 11 (1989): 203-231.

14539. Miah, Malik. "Does Race Still Matter?" *Against the Current* no. 50 (May-June 1994): 42-44. [Review of Cornel West's Race Matters]

14540. Miller, Randall M., and George E. Pozzetta, eds. *Shades of the Sunbelt: Essays on Ethnicity, Race, and the Urban South*. Boca Raton: Florida Atlantic University Press, 1989.

14541. "Minorities, Equality, and America's Future." *Journal of State Governments* 61 (March-April 1988): entire issue.

14542. Mintz, Sidney W. "Panglosses and Pollyannas; or, Whose Reality Are We Talking About?" in *The Meaning of Freedom*, eds. Frank McGlynn, and Seymour Drescher. University of Pittsburgh Press, 1992.

14543. Mintz, Sidney W., and Richard Price. *The Birth of African- American Culture: An Anthropological Perspective*, Revised cd. Beacon, 1992.

14544. Muehlberger, Robert J. "Class Characteristics of Hispanic Writing in the Southeastern United States." *Journal of Forensic Sciences* 34 (March 1989): 371-376.

14545. Muwakkil, Salim. "Race, Class and Candor." *In These Times* (22 May 1991).

14546. Nadeau, Richard and others. "Innumeracy about Minority Populations [in the U.S.]." *Public Opinion Quarterly* 57 (Fall 1993): 332-347. [Overestimating the number of minorities]

14547. O'Hare, William P. and others. "African Americans in the 1990s." *Population Bulletin* 46 (July 1991): entire issue.

14548. Oommen, T. K. "Race, Ethnicity, and Class: An Analysis of Interrelations." *International Social Science Journal* 46 (February 1994): 83-94.

14549. Partes, A., and C. Truelove. "Making Sense of Diversity: Recent Research on Hispanic Minorities in the United States." *Annual Review of Sociology* 13 (1987): 359-385.

14550. Patterson, Orlando. "Toward a Future that Has No Past: Reflections on the Fate of Blacks in America." *Public Interest* no. 27 (1972): 25-62.

14551. Perez Firmat, Gustavo. *Life on the Hyphen: The Cuban- American Way*. University of Texas Press, 1994.

14552. Piper, Adrian. "Xenophobia and Kantian Rationalism." *Philosophical Forum* 24 (Fall-Spring 1992-1993).

14553. Ploski, Harry A., and James Williams, eds. *The Negro Almanac: A Reference Work on the Afro-American*, 5th ed. Detroit, MI: Gale, 1990.

14554. Price, Daniel O. *Changing Characteristics of the Negro Population*. Washington, DC: GPO, 1969.

14555. Prothrow-Stith, Deborah, and Michaele Weissman. *Deadly Consequences: How Violence Is Destroying Our Teenage Population and a Plan to Begin Solving the Problem*. Harper Collins, 1992.

14556. Reed, Adolph, Jr. "Steele Trap." *Nation* (4 March 1991). [Critique of Shelby Steele, The Content of Our Character: A New Vision of Race in America]

14557. Reed, Wornie L., ed. "Critique of the NRC Study: A Common Destiny: Blacks and American Society." Vol. VI of the *Assessment of the Status of African-Americans*, Boston, MA: William Monroe Trotter Institute, University of Massachusetts Press at Boston, 1990.

14558. Robeson, Paul, Jr. *Paul Robeson, Jr. Speaks to America*. Rutgers U.P., 1993.

14559. Rodgers, Harrell R. *The Cost of Human Neglect*. M.E. Sharpe, 1982.

14560. Rostkowski, Joelle. *Le renouveau indien aux Etats-Unis*. Paris: Editions l'Harmattan, 1986.

14561. Schick, Frank L., and Renee Schick, eds. *Statistical Handbook on U.S. Hispanics*. Phoenix, AZ: Oryx, 1991.

14562. Seltzer, Richard, and Robert C. Smith. "Color Differences in the Afro-American Community and the Differences They Make." *Journal of Black Studies* 21 (March 1991): 279-285.

14563. Sen, A. "On the Darwinian View of Progress." *Population and Development Review* 19 (March 1993).

14564. Sigelman, Lee, and Susan Welch. *Black Americans' Views of Racial Inequality: The Dream Deferred*. New York: Cambridge University Press, 1991.

14565. Simpson, Janice C. "Tidings of Black Pride and Joy." *Time* (23 December 1991). [Kwanzaa]

14566. Sindab, Jean. "U.S. Racism: On the Rise and On the Rampage." *Link* no. 6 (1989). [Published by the Programme to Combat Racism of the World Council of Churches]

14567. Skerry, Peter N. *Mexican Americans: The Ambivalent Minority*. Free Press, 1992.

14568. Small, Christopher. *Music of the Common Tongue: Survival and Celbration in Afro-American Music*. London: John Calder, 1989.

14569. Snipp, C. Matthew. *American Indians: The First of This Land*. New York: Russell Sage Foundation, 1989. [Analysis of 1980 Census data on American Indians]

14570. _____. "Sociological Perspectives on American Indians." *Annual Review of Sociology* 18 (1992): 351-372.

14571. "Special Report on Race and Black America." *Los Angeles Times*, 8 September 1991.

14572. Staples, Brent. "On Denouncing Racism. Why Are Some Blacks Accountable for All?" *New York Times*, 19 October 1991.

14573. Steinberg, Stephen. "The Politics of Memory." *New Politics* 3 (Winter 1991): 64-70.

14574. Stewart, James B. "The Rise and Fall of Negro Economics: The Economic Thought of George Edmund Haynes." *American Economic Review* 81 (May 1991): 311-314.

14575. Stiffarm, Lenore, and Phil Lane, Jr. "The Demography of Native North America." in *The State of Native America*, ed. M. Annette Jaimes. South End Press, 1992.

14576. Stokes, Curtis. "Tocqueville and the Problem of Racial Inequality." *Journal of Negro History* 75 (Winter, Spring 1990): 1-15.

14577. Suro, Roberto. "Generational Chasm Leads to Cultural Turmoil for Young Mexicans in U.S." *New York Times*, 20 January 1992.

14578. Takaki, Ronald T. "Reflections on Racial Patterns in America." in *From Different Shores: Perspectives on Race and Ethnicity in America*, pp. 26-37. ed. Takaki. New York, 1987.

14579. Thomas, Gail E., ed. *U.S. Race Relations in the 1980s and 1990s: Challenges and Alternatives*. New York: Hemisphere, 1990. [Conference on the 20th anniversary of the Kerner Commission]

14580. Thomas, Melvin E. "Race, Class, and Personal Income: An Empirical Test of the Declining Significance of Race Thesis." *Social Problems* 40 (August 1993): 328-342.

14581. Tucker, William H. *The Science and Politics of Racial Research*. University of Illinois Press, 1994.

14582. Tuma, Elias H. "The Palestinians in America." *The Link* 14 (1981): 1-14.

14583. Van Deburg, William L. *New Day in Babylon. The Black Power Movement and American Culture, 1965-1975*. University of Chicago Press, 1992.

14584. Weatherford, Willis D., and Charles S. Johnson. *Race Relations: Adjustment of Whites and Negroes in the United States*. New York: Negro Universities Press, 1969 repr.

14585. Webster, Yehudi O. *The Racialization of America*. New York St. Martin's Press: 1992.

14586. West, Cornell. *Race Matters*. Beacon Press, 1993.

14587. Weyr, Thomas. *Hispanic USA: Assimilation or Separation*. New York: Harper and Row, 1988.

14588. Whittier, T. E. and others. "Stregth of Ethnic Affiliation: Examining Black Identification with Black Culture." *Journal of Social Psychology* 131 (August 1991): 461-468.

14589. Woodford, John. "The Malcolmized Moment." *Against the Current* no. 51 (July-August 1994).

14590. Woods, Paula L., and Felix H. Liddell. *I, Too, Sing America: The African-American Book of Days*. Workman Publishing, 1993.

14591. Young, Alford A., Jr. "The 'Negro Problem' and the Character of the Black Community: Charles S. Johnson, E. Franklin Frazier, and the Constitution of a Black Sociological Tradition, 1920-1935." *National Journal of Sociology* 7 (Summer 1993): 95- 133.

BIBLIOGRAPHIES

14592. Abahsain, M. M., comp. "Arabs in Popular Fiction Published in the U.S.A. (1919-1973): An Annotated Bibliography." *Journal of the College af Arts, King Saud University* 14 (1987): 71-89.

14593. Abrash, Barbara, and Catherine Egan, eds. *Mediating History. The MAP Guide to Independent Video by and About African American, Asian American, Latino, and Native American People.* New York University Press, 1993.

14594. Aby, Stephen H., and Martha J. McNamara, comps. *The IQ Debate. A Selective Guide to the Literature.* Westport, CT: Greenwood, 1991.

14595. Acosta-Belen, Edna, comp. "The Literature of the Puerto Rican Migration in the United States: An Annotated Bibliography." *ADE Bulletin* 91 (Winter 1988): 56-62.

14596. Alkalimat, Abdul. "Bibliographic Essay: Black Marxism in the White Academy: The Contours and Contradictions of an Emerging School of Black Thought." *Sage Race Relations Abstracts* 13 (November 1988): 3-19.

14597. Allen, Walter R., comp. *Black American Families, 1965- 1984: A Classified Selectively Annotated Bibliography.* Greenwood, 1986.

14598. Amaro, Hortensia and others, comps. "Contemporary Research on Hispanic Women: A Selected Bibliography of the Social Science Literature." *Psychology of Women Quarterly* 11 (December 1987): 523-532.

14599. *An Annotated Bibliography on Selected Fair Housing Issues.* Washington, DC: U.S. Commission on Civil Rights, 1986.

14600. Baca Zinn, Maxine. "Mexican Heritage Women: A Bibliographic Essay." *Sage Race Relations Abstracts* 9 (August 1984): 1-12.

14601. Bataille, Gretchen M., and Kathleen M. Sands, comps. *American Indian Women: A Guide to Research.* Garland, 1991.

14602. Baucham, Rosalind G., comp. *African American Organizations. A Selective Bibliography.* Garland, 1994.

14603. Beck, David, comp. *The Chicago American Indian Community, 1893-1988: Annotated Bibliography and Guide to Sources in Chicago.* Chicago, IL: NAES College Press, 1988.

14604. Bennett, James, ed. *Control of the Media in the United States: An Annotated Bibliography.* Garland, 1992.

14605. Bowser, Benjamin P. "Race and US Foreign Policy. A Bibliographic Essay." *Sage Race Relations Abstracts* 12 (February 1987): 4-20.

14606. Boyce, Byrl N., and Sidney Turoff, comps. *Minority Groups and Housing: A Bibliography, 1950-1970.* Morristown, NJ: General Learning Press, 1972.

14607. Burkett, Randall K. and others, eds. *Black Biography, 1790-1950. A Cumulative Index. 3 volumes*. Alexandria, VA: Chadwyck-Healey, 1991.

14608. Camarillo, Albert, comp. *Latinos in the United States: A Historical Bibliography*. ABC-CLIO, 1986.

14609. Castillo-Speed, Lillian. "Chicana Studies: A Selected List of Materials since 1980." *Frontiers* 11 (1990).

14610. Cevallos, Elena A., comp. *Puerto Rico*. Santa Barbara, CA: Clio Press, 1985.

14611. Cheung, King-kok, and Stan Yogi, comps. *Asian American Literature: An Annotated Bibliography*. New York: Modern Language Association of America, 1988.

14612. Churchill, Ward, and Jim Vander Wall. "Bibliography." in their *The COINTELPRO Papers*, pp. 420-438. Boston, MA: South End Press, 1990.

14613. Consortium for Research on Black Adolescence, comp. *Black Adolescence: Current Issues and Annotated Bibliography*. Boston, MA: Hall, 1990.

14614. Davis, James J., comp. "Foreign Language Study and Afro- Americans: An Annotated Bibliography, 1931-1988." *Journal of Negro Education* 58 (Autumn 1989).

14615. Davis, Lenwood G., comp. *The Black Family in the United States: A Revised, Updated, Selectively Annotated Bibliography*. Greenwood, 1986.

14616. _____. *The Black Woman in American Society: A Selected Annotated Bibliography*. Boston, MA: Hall, 1975.

14617. Dunmore, Charlotte J., comp. *Black Children and their Families: A Bibliography*. San Francisco, CA: R and E Research Associates, 1976.

14618. Floyd, Nubra E., ed. *The Minority Student in Higher Education: An Annotated Bibliography*. 1982.
ERIC ED 237 042.

14619. Fong, Rowera, and Noreen Mokuau. "Not Simply 'Asian Americans': Periodical Literature Review on Asians and Pacific Islanders." *Social Work* 39 (May 1994): 298-305. [Great gaps in social work periodical literature]

14620. Fowlie-flores, Fay, comp. *Annotated Bibliography of Puerto Rican Bibliographies*. Westport, CT: Greenwood, 1990.

14621. Gabaccia, Donna, comp. *Immigrant Workers in the United States*. Westport, CT: Greenwood, 1989.

14622. Garcia, F. Chris and others, comps. *Latinos and Politics: A Selected Research Bibliography*. Austin: Center for Mexican American Studies of the University of Texas Press, 1990.

14623. Garcia-Ayvens, Francisco, ed. *Chicano Anthology Index: A Comprehensive Author, Title, and Subject Index to Chicano Anthologies, 1965-1987*. Berkeley: Chicano Studies Library Publications Unit, University of California, 1990.

14624. Garcia-Ayvens, Francisco, and Richard Chabran, eds. *Chicano Periodical Index: A Cumulative Index to Selected Periodicals, 1979-1981*. Boston, MA: Hall, 1983.

14625. Geary, James W., comp. "Blacks in Northern Blue: A Select Annotated Bibliography of Afro-Americans in the Union Army and Navy During the Civil War." *Bulletin of Bibliography* 45 (1988): 183-193.

14626. Goldman, N., comp. "Bibliography of Multi-Cultural Film and Video." *Sightlines* 24 (Fall 1991).

14627. Goldstein, R. J. "Political Repression in Modern American History (1870-Present): A Selective Bibliography." *Labor History* 32 (Autumn 1991): 526-550.

14628. Gray, John, comp. *Blacks in Film and Television. A Pan- African Bibliography of Films, Filmmakers, and Performers*. Westport, CT: Greenwood, 1990.

14629. Green, Marci, and Bob Carter. "Bibliographic Essay: 'Races' and 'Race-Makers': The Politics of Racialization." *Sage Race Relations Abstracts* 13 (May 1988): 4-30.

14630. Green, Rayna, comp. *Native American Women: A Bibliography*. OHOYO, Inc.: OHOYO Resource Center, 2301 Midwestern Parkway, Suite 214 Wichita Falls, TX 76308, 1981.

14631. Hall, Kermit L., comp. *A Comprehensive Bibliography of American and Consititutional History Supplement, 1980-1987*, 2 vols. Millwood, NY: Kraus International Publications, 1991.

14632. Ham, Debra Newman, ed. *The African-American Mosaic: A Library of Congress Resource Guide for the Study of Black History and Culture*. GPO, 1994.

14633. Harrison, Cynthia and others, comps. *Women in American History: A Bibliography*, 2 vols. Santa Barbara, CA: ABC-Clio, 1979, 1985.

14634. Hirsch, Jerry. "[Bibliography "documenting the triumph of racism in the scientific establishment"]." *Sage Race Relations Abstracts* 6 (May 1981): 40-65.

14635. Hubbard, Dolan and others, comps. "Studies in Afro- American Literature: An Annual Annotated Bibliography 1988." *Callaloo* 12 (Fall 1989): 680-740.

14636. Kaiser, Ernest D., ed. *The Kaiser Index to Black Resources, 1948-1986*, 5 vols. Brooklyn, NY: Carlson Publishing Co., 1992. [174,000 entries]

14637. Kim, Hyung-chan. *Asian American Studies. An Annotated Bibliography and Research Guide*. Westport, CT: Greenwood, 1989.

14638. Kinloch, Graham, comp. *Race Ethnic Relations: An Annotated Bibliography*. New York: Garland, 1984.

14639. Koehler, Lyle, comp. "Native Women of the Americas: A Bibliography." *Frontiers* 6 (Fall 1981): 73-101.

14640. Lam, R. Errol, and Kalman S. Szekely, comps. "Blacks in Television: A Selective, Annotated Bibliography." *Journal of Popular Film and Television* 14 (1987): 176-183.

14641. Lamy, Bernhard. "La Recherche récente sur le racisme dans la sociologie americaine et britannique. Une Analyse bibliographigue." *Societes Contemporaines* 1 (March 1990): 113-136.

14642. Littlefield, Daniel F., Jr. and James W. Parins, comps. *A Bibliography of Native American Writers, 1772-1924*. Metuchen, NJ: Scarecrow Press, 1985.

14643. MacDonald, John S., and Leatrice MacDonald. "The Black Family in the Americas: A Review of the LIterature." *Sage Race Relations Abstracts* 3 (February 1978): 1-42.

14644. Maddock, Stella, and Tony Duncan, comps. *Institutional Racism: A Selective Guide to the Literature*. Derbyshire Library Service, Great Britain, 1984.

14645. McIntosh, J. L., comp. *Suicide among U.S. Racial/Ethnic Minorities, 1984-1988: A Comprehensive Bibliography*. Monticello, IL: Vance, 1988.

14646. Meier, Matt S., comp. *Bibliography of Mexican American History*. Westport, CT: Greewood, 1984.

14647. _____. *Mexican-American Biographies: A Historical Dictionary, 1836-1987*. Westport, CT: Greewood, 1988.

14648. Mickens, Ronald, comp. "Black Women in Science and Technology: A Selected Bibliography." *Sage* 6 (Fall 1989): 54.

14649. Nilsen, Don L. F. *Humor Scholarship. A Research Bibliography*. Greenwood, 1993.

14650. Nordquist, Joan, comp. *The Homeless in America: A Bibliography*. Santa Cruz, CA: Reference and Research Services, 1988.

14651. Omatsu, Glenn, comp. "Violence against Asian Americans." *Amerasia Journal* 13 (1986-87): 213-214.

14652. Omi, Michael, and Howard Winant. "Bibliographic Essay: Racial Theory in the Post-war United States: A Review and Critique." *Sage Race Relations Abstracts* 12 (May 1987): 3-44.

14653. Orfabea, Gregory. "On Arab Americans: A Bibliographical Essay." *American Studies International* 27 (1989): 26-41.

14654. *Prejudice and Violence: An Annotated Bibliography of Selected Materials on Ethnoviolence*, 2nd ed. Baltimore, MD: National Institute Against Prejudice and Violence, April 1989.

14655. "Racial Harrassment/Hate Speech Bibliography." *Journal of Higher Education* 63 (September-October 1992).

14656. Redfern, Bernice, comp. *Women of Color in the United States: A Guide to the Literature*. New York: Garland, 1989.

14657. Rice, Mitchell, and Woodrow Jones, Jr., comps. *Health of Black Americans from Post-Reconstruction to Integration, 1871- 1960. An Annotated Bibliography of Contemporary Sources*. Westport, CT: Greenwood, 1990.

14658. Singerman, Robert, comp. *Judaica Americana*, 2 vols. Westport, CT: Greenwood, 1990. [Up to 1900]

14659. Smith, J. Clay, Jr. "The 'Lynching' at Howard Beach: An Annotated Bibliographic Index." *National Black Law Journal* 12 (Spring 1990): 29-60.

14660. St. Clair, Diane, comp. "Bibliography on Repression." *Black Scholar* 12 (1981): 85-90.

14661. Stevenson, Rosemary M., comp. *Index to Afro-American Reference Resources*. Westport, CT: Greenwood, 1988.

14662. Theoharis, Athan. *The FBI. An Annotated Bibliography and Research Guide*. Garland, 1994.

14663. Timberlake, Andrea and others, comps. *Women of Color and Southern Women: A Bibliography of Social Science Research, 1975 to 1988*. Memphis, TN: Center for Research on Women, Memphis State University, 1988.

14664. _____. *Women of Color and Southern Women: A Bibliography of Social Science Research, 1975 to 1988. Annual Supplement, 1990*. Memphis, TN: Center for Research on Women, Memphis State University, 1991.

14665. Valk, Barbara G., ed. *Borderline: A Bibliography of the United States-Mexico Borderlands*. Los Angeles: Latin American Center Publications, University of California, 1988.

14666. Van Scoy, Holly, and Thomas Oakland. "Minority Group Literature in Psychology and Education Journals: 1952-1973." *Journal of Black Studies* 22 (December 1991).

14667. Vertinsky, P. A., comp. "Sport History and Gender Relations, 1983-1993. Bibliography." *Journal of Sport History* 21 (Spring 1994): 25-58.

14668. Vivo, Paquita, comp. *Puerto Rican Migration: The Return Flow La Migracion Puertorriquena: El Reflujo a la Isla*. 1982. ERIC ED 221 635.

14669. Waldman, Carl. *Who Was Who in Native American History: Indian and Non-Indians from Early Contacts through 1900*. New York: Facts on File, 1990.

14670. Watts, Tim J., comp. *Politics of Hate: White Extremist Groups in the 1980s, a Bibliography*. Vance Bibliographies, 1989.

14671. *Women's Annotated Legal Bibliography*. New York: Benjamin N. Cardoza School of Law, Yeshiva University, 1984.

AUTHOR INDEX

Numbers refer to entries, not pages.

Aaron, Hank, 609
Aaron, Henry J., 3134
Abahsain, M.M., 14592
Abarry, Abu Shardow, 9152, 10662
Abbott, Carl, 9448
Abbott, Devon I., 4281
Abe, Frank, 13584
Abel, Annie H., 8182, 10567
Abel, E.L., 2520
Abel, Emily, 4282
Abel, Marjorie, 12978
Abell, Creed W., 10663
Abell, J.D., 5829, 13929
Abelon, R.P., 12268
Abernathy, Ralph D., 610, 1459
Abney, D., 2231
Abney, Lucille A., 5563
Abourezk, James, 11367
Abraham, Kinfe, 11123
Abraham, Laurie, 6022-6023
Abraham, Nabeel, 14469
Abraham, Sameer Y., 14469
Abrahamse, Allan F., 13376
Abramovitz, Mimi, 3135, 8335
Abramowitz, Michael, 7381, 11368
Abrams, D., 13377
Abrams, Douglas C., 11369
Abrams, Garry, 9475
Abrams, Kathryn, 11370
Abrams, Sheila, 4283
Abramson, Elliot M., 7482
Abramson, Jeffrey, 2232
Abramson, Leslie, 8648
Abramson, Paul R., 11371
Abramson, P.R., 2202
Abramson, Theodore, 4052
Abrash, Barbara, 14593
Abron, Jonina M., 11372
Abt, L.E., 5725

Abu-Jamal, Mumia, 2233, 11861
Aburto, Sofia, 13878
Aby, Stephen H., 14594
Abzug, Robert H., 2782, 13088
Acevedo, Mary A., 13787
Achenbach, James, 4284
Acker, James R., 2234-2235
Acosta, Frank, 7483
Acosta, P.B., 6024
Acosta-Belen, Edna, 14278, 14595
Acuna, Rodolfo F., 1717, 4285, 6698, 9369, 11281
Adair, Jane A., 13255
Adamo, Mark, 611
Adams, David W., 3456
Adams, Frank, 612
Adams, George R., 11353
Adams, Jacqueline, 5564
Adams, James P., 8649, 13585-13586
Adams, Karen L., 8336
Adams, Keith, 8650
Adams, Rhonda, 13490
Adams, Robert H., 1140
Adams, Ron J., 11373
Adams, Russell L., 10664
Adams, Terry K., 3136
Adamson, Madeleine, 10513
Aday, L.A., 6025
Addis, Adeno, 8651, 9754
Adelman, Clifford, 4286, 10665
Adelman, David C., 1460
Adelson, Andrea, 9755
Adelson, Leslie A., 12935
Aderno, Malaika, 10308
Adinarayansih, S.P., 12259
Adler, David, 2850
Adler, Jerry, 933, 1079, 4287, 10666
Adotevi, Stanislas, 12313
Adrogue, Sofia, 1

Agar, M., 8337
Agard, Keoni K., 11136
Agassi, J., 466
Agboaye, Elrikioya, 9756
Agee, M.L., 3137
Aguero, Kathleen, 10669
Aguilar, Victor M., 5830
Aguirre, Adalberto, Jr., 4290-4291
Aguirre, B.E., 2839
Agyeman, O., 8652
Aho, James A., 12508, 12641
Aiken, Charles S., 5793
Ailes, Roger, 2554
Airaksinen, Timo, 8338
Ajaye, Franklyn, 9757
Akam, Everett H., 11328
Akbar, Na-im, 12260
Akemann, Charles, 5
Akhter, F., 6026
Aksoy, A., 9758
Akudinobi, Jude G., 9759
Alarcon, Evelina, 9370
Alba, Richard D., 7064-7065, 14206, 14470
Albers, Patricia, 14281
Albert, Alexa A., 13378
Albert, Bill, 2079
Albert, Michael, 421
Albert, Peter J., 1461, 9223, 14380
Alberts, John B., 3458
Alberts, William E., 14207
Albizu Campos, Pedro, 1986
Albonetti, Celesta A., 2236-2237
Alcock, Alan C., 5665
Aldred, Lisa, 613
Aldrich, Howard E., 1252, 5794
Aldrich, Michelle L., 12890
Alegado, Dean T., 8339
Alegra, Idsa, 12620
Alegria, Ricardo E., 13089
Aleinikoff, T. Alexander, 8653
Aleiss, Angela M., 9760-9761
Alejo, Francisco J., 14139
Alers, J.O., 6027
Alexander, A., 9762, 13223
Alexander, Adele L., 14282
Alexander, Charles C., 7788
Alexander, Elizabeth, 9763
Alexander, James S., 3459
Alexander, Jeffrey C., 467
Alexander, Karl L., 3668, 4292
Alexander, L., 2840
Alexander, Nick, 5448, 7867, 9764, 10670
Alexander, William S., 4293
Alexandro, Francis, W., 13379
Alexis, M., 2841
Alford, Robert, 6028
Alho, Olli, 12642
Ali, Sharazad, 14283
Alkalimat, Abdul, 4294, 11375, 14596

Allahar, Anton L., 12372
Allain, Mathe, 9765
Allan, Keith, 8340
Allen, Anita, 5565
Allen, Anita L., 4296
Allen, Charlotte, 3460
Allen, Derek B., 2238
Allen, Ernest, Jr., 6699, 11124-11126
Allen, Francis A., 7066
Allen, G.E., 6700
Allen, Irving Lewis, 8341-8343
Allen, Joyce E., 1141, 3138
Allen, Lisa W., 6029
Allen, Norm, 10671
Allen, Paula G., 14284
Allen, Peter, 8654
Allen, R.H., 8183
Allen, Robert L., 4297, 8721, 10377
Allen, Ruth A., 14285
Allen, Theodore W., 12373, 13090
Allen, Walter R., 3139, 4298-4302, 4685,
    14597
Allen, W.B., 14471
Allen-Meares, Paula, 3461
Alleyne, Mervyn, 378
Alligood, D.L., 9766
Allsup, Carl, 1924
Almaguer, Tomas, 3425-3426, 6701, 11282-
    11283
Almeida, Deirdre A., 4303
Almquist, Elizabeth M., 7868, 12936
Alozie, Nicholas O., 8655-8656
Alston, Dana A., 5449, 11849
Alston, Denise, 4304
Alston, Lee J., 7869, 12122
Altbach, Philip G., 3817, 4305, 7741
Altemeyer, B., 11376-11377
Alter, Jonathan, 468, 469, 12123
Alterman, Eric, 470, 4306
Alters, Diane, 6030
Althaus, F., 6031
Althauser, Robert, 1718
Altheide, David L., 9767
Altiers, Diane, 13587
Altman, Ida, 7484
Altman, Lawrence K., 6032
Altschuler, D.M., 2239
Altstein, Howard, 5717
Alvarado, Jose, 8184
Alvarez, Rodolfo, 6702
Alvarez, Salvador E., 7870
Alvarez Gonzalez, Jose J., 1389, 1462
Alvirez, David, 3041, 7871
Alvis, Joel L., Jr., 12643
Amaker, Norman C., 1463
Aman, Reinhold, 8344
Amann, Peter H., 13969
Amann, Robert J., 11921
Amar, Akhil Reed, 8657

Amaro, Hortensia, 14598
Amber, Robert W., 6034
Ambler, Marjane, 2103, 5450
Ambrecht, Biliana C.S., 2104
Ambrose, David M., 2842
Amenia, Richard F., 3140
America, Richard F., 14140
Amin, Julius, 9682
Amin, Ruhul, 7067
Ammar, Marie B., 3463
Amorose, Thomas, 8345
Amott, Teresa, 3141, 6703, 8185
Amsden, Charles, 2189
Amsterdam, Anthony, 2241
Amsterdam, Anthony G., 8658
Amulerumarshall, O., 6036
Anastaplo, George, 8659
Anaya, Rudolfo A., 11127, 11156
Anbinder, Tyler, 11378
Anctil, Pierre, 1719
Anders, Evan M., 11379
Anders, Gary C., 2105, 3142, 5831
Andersen, Margaret L., 12374, 12596
Andersen, R.M., 6025
Anderson, A.B., 8346
Anderson, Bernice, 12893
Anderson, D.K., 3780
Anderson, Dave, 13224
Anderson, David E., 5451
Anderson, Elijah, 4308, 5566, 5795, 9656
Anderson, Elizabeth, 4309
Anderson, Eric, 3998, 6704, 12509
Anderson, Gary Clayton, 6705
Anderson, G.B., 6037
Anderson, George Edward, 6
Anderson, H. Allen, 7872
Anderson, J.L., 7685
Anderson, James, 10568
Anderson, James D., 3464-3465
Anderson, Kristi, 1390
Anderson, L.P., 6038
Anderson, Martin, 4310, 10675
Anderson, Peggy, 10676
Anderson, Rasmus B., 10677
Anderson, R.M., 6039
Anderson, Robert L., 10569
Anderson, Sara F.P., 10678
Anderson, Susan, 11380-11381
Anderson, Talmadge, 7, 4311
Anderson, T.L., 2106
Anderson, Torben, 13225
Anderson, William L., 6707
Anderson-Cordova, Karen F., 6706
Anderton, D.L., 5452, 5453
Andic, Faut M., 14141-14142
Andolsen, Barbara H., 12937, 14286
Andreas, James R., 7382
Andrew, Loyd D, 4312
Andrews, Bert, 9153, 9175

Andrews, Donald R., 3466
Andrews, E.F., 13210
Andrews, M., 1720
Andrews, R., 12887
Andrews, Thomas F., 10570
Andrews, William L., 614
Angel, G., 1868
Angel, Ronald J., 6040
Angell, Marcia, 6041
Angell, Stephen W., 12644
Angle, J., 3143
Angrist, Joshua D., 10378
Angus, David, 3991
Angus, Ian H., 9773, 10138
Anjomani, Ardeshir, 7068
Anner, John, 6042, 10379
Annis, R.C., 12263
Annunziata, Frank, 12566
Ansen, David, 9769
Ansley, Frances L., 1464, 4313, 8660
Antell, Judith A., 14287
Anthias, Floya, 1721, 12375
Anthony, Booker T., 9154
Anthony, Earl, 11382
Anthony-Davis, Brenda, 5832
Antonovsky, A., 6043
Antush, John C., 7873
Anzaldua, Gloria, 14288
Aoki, Guy, 13380
Aoki, Keith, 7069
Apess, William, 615
Apgar, William C., Jr., 7070
Aponte, Carmen I., 14289
Aponte, R., 3144
Aponte, Robert, 5567
Appiah, Kwame Anthony, 9155
Apple, Michael W., 3468, 4149, 11383
Applebome, Peter, 2242-2247, 2536-2537,
    3203, 3469-3470, 4314-4319, 5796, 6708,
    6709, 7789, 8661, 9335, 9466, 9470, 9542,
    9770, 10380, 11384-11390, 12049, 12124,
    12511, 12623, 13381, 13970, 14208
Appleby, Joyce, 10679, 10680
Appleton, N., 11329
Appy, Christian G., 10381
Apte, Mahadev L., 7383-7384
Apter, Andrew, 379
Aptheker, Bettina, 5568, 13885
Aptheker, Herbert, 422-424, 936, 12376
Aquirre, Adalberto, Jr., 2248
Arai, Sevgi O., 6044
Araton, Harvey, 13226
Archambault, David L., 4320
Archbold, Douglas A., 2538
Archer, Chalmers, Jr., 9543
Archer, E., 5092
Archer, Leonie J., 9192, 13091, 14264
Arcinega, Tomas, 4321-4322
Arguelles, Lourdes, 11040

Arian, Asher, 11391
Arias, M. Beatriz, 2539, 3471
Arington, Michele, 8347
Arkel, Dik van, 13382
Arkin, Daniel J., 2540
Arlen, J.H., 8662
Armelagos, George J., 7686, 7711
Armendariz, Albert, 2845
Armitage, Susan H., 14290
Armor, David J., 2541, 3472
Armour, J.D., 8663
Armour-Thomas, E., 3473
Armstead, Cheryl A., 8348
Armstrong, G.B., 9772
Armstrong, Gregory, 13590
Armstrong, Liz S., 2542
Arnason, W.B., 6045
Arneklev, Bruce J., 2249, 13251
Arnesen, Eric, 7874-7876
Arneson, Richard J., 8664
Arnez, Nancy L., 3474
Arnold, Frank, 7877
Arnold, Mary Smith, 13903
Arnold, R.A., 2250
Aroian, Karen J., 7486
Aronowitz, Stanley, 1722, 9773
Arrandale, Tom, 5454
Arries, Jonathan F., 3475
Arrington, T.S., 11392
Arrow, Kenneth, 2846-2847, 6046
Arroyo, Laura E., 7681
Arroyo, Luis L., 7878
Arsenault, Raymond, 6808
Arthur, John A., 2251, 8665
Arthur, Paul, 11393
Aruri, Naseer H., 4323
Arvanites, Thomas M., 2252
Asamen, Joy K., 3502, 4359, 4685
Asante, Molefi K., 380, 4324, 6710, 9774, 10681-10683
Ascher, Carol, 3476
Ascher, Marcia, 10684
Asgill, E.O., 381
Ash, Stephen V., 9677, 14209
Ashby, Stephen M., 11293
Ashe, Arthur, 616
Ashenfelter, Orley, 2847, 3108, 5348
Asher, Robert, 7879, 7880
Ashford, H., 8666
Ashkinaze, Carole, 5061, 11834
Ashley, Mary Ellen, 4325
Ashmore, Harry S., 1465
Ashraf, J., 4326
Ashton, Guy T., 10309
Assael, Shaun, 13973
Astroff, Roberta, 9775
Astrolff, R.J., 9908
Athans, Mary C., 474
Athill, Diana, 617

Atkins, Chester G., 8349
Atkins, Daniel, 1
Atkins, Elizabeth, 5569
Atwood, Barbara Ann, 1268
Au, Beth Amity, 8667, 9572
Aubry, Larry, 9371
Aucoin, Don, 13383
Augenbraun, Harold, 618, 1269
August, Diane, 8350
Ault, Ulrika E., 13591
Auslander, Mary W., 5833
Auspitz, Josiah L., 11395
Austen, Ralph, 937
Auster, Albert, 9776
Auster, Carol J., 4944
Auster, Lawrence, 10685
Austin, B.W., 2848
Austin, Regina, 5455, 8668
Austin, Roy L., 1723
Austin, Sydney B., 9777
Avalos, M., 4329
Avery, Byllye, 6047
Avery, Sheldon, 619
Avila, Joaquin, 11490
Avina, Rose H., 8186
Avisar, Ilan, 9778
Avorn, Jerry, 4330
Awkward, Michael, 9159
Axelrod, Jill, 8669
Axelson, Diane E., 6048
Axtell, James L., 6711-6713, 7385, 10686, 12645
Ayala, Victor A., 6049
Ayaman, John Z., 6050-6051
Ayers, B. Drummond, Jr., 4332, 12646
Ayers, David John, 4331
Ayers, Edward L., 6714, 9726
Ayres, Ian, 2849
Aytac, I.A., 14445
Azares, Tania, 4333
Azize, Yamile, 14293-14296

Baca, L., 8352
Baca Zinn, Maxine, 5570, 14600
Bacchi, C., 8
Bachman, J.G., 6052
Bachman, R., 6053
Bachman, Ronet, 2253
Bachu, Amara, 5571
Bacigal, M.I., 12512
Bacigal, Ronald J., 12512
Back, L., 12487
Backes, Mike, 9779
Backhouse, Constance, 12938
Bacote, Clarence A., 8670
Bader, Eleanor J., 12939
Badgett, M.V. Lee, 9, 2850, 13931-13932
Badillo, Gilbert, 10382
Badwound, Elgin, 4334

Baer, Hans A., 6054, 12647-12649
Baer, Judith A., 8671
Baerga, M.D., 10310
Bagdikian, Ben H., 9780
Bagnall, Robert, 7790
Bahr, M.W., 3479
Bahrick, H.P., 8353
Bai, Su Sun, 11396
Baiamonte, John V., Jr., 8672
Baida, A.H., 4335
Baier, Paul R., 2543
Bailey, A.J., 5456
Bailey, David T., 1724
Bailey, E.J., 6055
Bailey, Eric, 7488
Bailey, Frankie Y., 9160
Bailey, Garrick, 6715
Bailey, J. Michael, 7687
Bailey, Jerry D., 273
Bailey, Kenneth K., 12650
Bailey, Lynn R., 2190
Bailey, M. Thomas, 6716
Bailey, Marlon M., 10687
Bailey, Michael S., 1635, 11397
Bailey, Percival R., 8673
Bailey, Roberta G., 6715
Bailey, T., 3103
Bailey, Thomas, 2851, 5402, 7881, 12005
Bailyn, Bernard, 6917, 6933
Bain, Kenneth, 11709
Baines, John, 10688
Bains, Lee E., 1466
Bair, J.H., 4336
Baird, Keith E., 416
Baird, Leonard L., 13788
Baird, Robert M., 12125
Baird, Susan, 425
Baithorpe, Robin B., 1467
Baker, Bob, 13384
Baker, David, 2248
Baker, Donald G., 6838
Baker, Donald P., 3480-3481
Baker, Houston A., Jr., 9161, 9210, 9234
Baker, Karin, 2254
Baker, Lee D., 426-427
Baker, Lillian, 2191
Baker, Nancy V., 13592
Baker, Peter, 1468, 4872, 7386
Baker, R. Scott, 2544
Baker, Ray Stannard, 13974
Baker, Ronald L., 9781
Baker, Russ W., 3482
Baker, Russell, 8354-8355
Baker, S.M., 13410
Baker, Stephen C., 11398
Baker, Susan G., 8356
Bakken, Gordon M., 12940
Balakian, Anna, 10689
Balandier, G., 1987

Balasing, Michael John, 13975
Baldus, David C., 2255
Baldwin, James, 938, 968, 11284
Baldwin, Lewis V., 1469
Baldwin, M., 3145
Baldwin, Mary F., 10383
Balibar, Etienne, 12377-12378
Balington, Charles, 7071
Balkwell, J.W., 2256
Ball, A.F., 9162
Ball, Edward, 12624
Ball, Howard, 11399
Ball, Milner S., 8674
Ball, Patricia B.H., 9127
Ball, Thomas E., 11400
Ballard, Elizabeth L., 9163
Balshem, Martha, 6056
Balzar, John, 5572
Bamber, Linda, 10690
Bane, Mary Jo, 1270
Banks, James A., 4046, 10691-10692
Banks, Michael A., 13227
Banks, Sandy, 3484-3485, 3584
Banks, Taunya Lovell, 12941
Banner-Haley, Charles P., 1725, 9657
Bansel, Preeta, 8688, 11413
Banton, Michael, 475, 12126-12128, 12379-
  12380
Barak, Gregg, 2257
Baraka, Amiri, 9164, 9782
Baralt, Guillermo Antonio, 13093-13094
Baranick, Scott, 14167
Baratz, Joan C., 4337, 12250
Baratz, Stephen S., 12250
Barbalet, J.M., 1391
Barber, Benjamin R., 10693-10694
Barber, James D., 5250
Barber, William J., 4338
Barbezat, D.A., 10
Barbour, Floyd B., 12304
Barboza, Steven, 12651
Barcelo, Cosme J., 3146
Barden, J.C., 6057
Bardwell, Jill R., 13385
Bari, Judi, 13593
Baris, Jay G., 1143
Barkalow, Carol, 10384
Barkan, Elazar, 12314-12315, 12381
Barkan, Steven, 1470
Barker, David, 7688
Barker, Eugene C., 8187
Barker, Lucius J., 11401-11403
Barker, Martin, 9783
Barker, Rodney, 2258
Barksdale, Marcellus C., 1471
Barkun, Michael, 12513, 12652
Barlour, George E., 12888
Barlow, Andrew, 1472, 4339
Barlow, William, 620, 9875

Barnard, William A., 13886
Barnes, Arnold, 13976
Barnes, Dawn C., 9784
Barnes, Robin, 11
Barnett, Marguerite Ross, 2539, 3486, 13386
Barnett, Marilyn F., 2545
Barnett, Martha W., 8675
Barnett, Stephen R., 4340
Baron, Dennis, 8357-8358
Baron, Harold M., 3427, 3487, 7882, 12382
Baron, Salo W., 11330
Barondi, J.J., 13069
Barr, Alwyn, 13387
Barr, Stephen, 5403
Barra, Allen, 10695
Barreiro, Jose, 6717, 10696
Barrera, Mario, 1726-1727, 1925, 1988
Barrett, James R., 7883
Barrett, Laurence I., 13789
Barrett, Paul M., 2546
Barrett, Wayne, 10571
Barrile, Leo G., 9785
Barringer, Felicity, 2852, 6058, 14143-14144
Barringer, Herbert R., 3147
Barron, Milton L., 7387
Barrow, Clyde W., 4341
Barrow, Deborah J., 8676
Barry, Dave, 7388
Barsh, Russell Lawrence, 1271, 5834, 8188, 10385, 12316, 13211, 13790
Bar-Tal, Daniel, 13388
Bartel, Virginia B., 2547
Bartels, Larry M., 11404
Bartelt, D., 7337
Bartey, Beth, 9476-9477
Bartholet, Elizabeth, 5573-5576
Bartholomaus, Craig W., 13389
Bartholomew, Amy, 1392
Bartlett, Katharine T., 4342
Bartlett, Robin, 12
Bartley, Numan V., 8080
Bartling, Carl A., 10386
Barton, D. Scott, 11458
Baruch, Chad, 4343
Baseler, Marilyn C., 7489
Baskerville, Dawn M., 6059
Baskin, J.S., 8416
Bass, Charlotta, 9786
Bass, Paul, 13594
Basso, Keith H., 8189, 8359
Bastide, Roger, 12653
Bastrain, Lisa D., 2521
Basu, T.K., 1926
Bataille, Gretchen M., 9787, 13390, 14297, 14601
Batchelor, John E., 2548
Bateman, Rebecca B., 10572-10573
Bates, Douglas, 5577
Bates, Eric, 12514

Bates, James, 7072
Bates, Joseph H., 2549
Bates, Karen G., 5578, 9788-9789, 12261, 14472
Bates, Nancy A., 7348
Bates, Steve, 3488-3489
Bates, Timothy, 1144-1150, 2107, 2943, 11405
Bates, Tom, 13595
Batson, Ruth M., 2550
Batten, Laura, 1272
Battle, V. DuWayne, 12654
Baucham, Rosalind G., 14602
Bauer, Dale M., 10697
Bauleke, Howard, 1443
Bauman, John F., 11317
Bauman, Mark K., 939
Bauman, Zygmunt, 12383
Bavor, Sherrie L., 9590
Baxter, Brent L., 2259
Baxter, Tom, 4344
Bayes, Jane H., 11406-11407
Bayles, Martha, 9790
Bayley, David H., 5835
Baylor, D.E., 13
Baylor, Timothy J., 1927
Bayor, Ronald H., 7073-7074, 11318, 11408-11409, 12515
Bays, Martha D., 2853
Beadles, N.A., 7884
Beady, C., 2551
Beale, Calvin L., 10311
Beale, Lewis, 4345
Beals, Kenneth L., 7775, 12359
Beals, Melba Patillo, 621
Bean, Frank D., 7490-7491, 14473
Beane, De Anna Banks, 12889
Bearak, Barry, 7075
Beard, Estle, 10403
Bearden, Russell, 2192
Beardsley, Richard K., 1928
Beatty, Bess, 11410
Beaty, Jonathan, 2260
Beauford, E. Yvonne, 3148
Beaulieu, Lionel J., 3148, 13951
Beck, David, 14603
Beck, E.M., 10370, 13977-13979, 14111-14112
Beck, Nicholas, 3490
Becker, Carol, 9896
Becker, Lance B., 6060-6061
Becker, Theodore, 13596
Becker, Verne, 7791
Beckham, Edgar F., 4346
Becklund, Laurie, 13980
Beckwith, Jonathan R., 12317
Becnel, Thomas, 12655
Bedard, Marcia, 10698
Bederman, Gail, 13981
Bee, Noah, 7389
Bee, Robert, 1989, 5836, 5849

Beeghley, L., 11411
Been, Vicki, 5457
Beer, William R., 14, 206
Beere, Carole A., 13791
Beeson, Margaret, 6718
Beeth, Howard, 7093, 9683-9684, 9717
Beevers, D.G., 6142, 6473
Behar, Richard, 12516
Behrman, J.R., 6062
Behuniak, Peter, 8360
Beifuss, Joan T., 1473
Beirne, D. Randall, 7492
Bejin, A., 428
Belanger, Alain, 10312
Belknap, Michal R., 1474, 13597-13599,
    13982-13983,
Bell, A., 12877
Bell, Derrick A., 15-17, 622, 1475-1476, 2261,
    2552, 2854, 3428, 3492, 4347-4348, 4524,
    5404, 8677-8688, 11412-11413, 12384-
    12385
Bell, F.A., 809
Bell, Malcolm, Jr., 383
Bell, Maureen A., 9092
Bell, Muriel, 383
Bellah, Robert N., 10699, 12656
Bellant, Russ, 476, 12517
Bellardo, Lewis J., 9667
Bellman, Richard F., 2855, 7076
Bellow, Saul, 10700
Bell-Scott, Patricia, 4349, 4682
Bell-Vidala, Gene H., 4617
Belsky, J.E., 6063
Belton, W.J., 10316
Belz, Herman, 18-19, 8974
Benavidez, Max, 5837
Bender, Eric D., 4350, 8361
Bender, Eugene I., 940
Bender, Leslie, 2856
Bender, Louis W., 5146
Bender, Mike, 2857
Bender, Thomas, 13095
Benedict, Mary I., 6064
Benezet, Louis T., 4351
Benford, Robert D., 5458
Benitez-Nazario, Jorge A., 1990
Benjamin, Ernst, 4617
Benjamin, Gerald, 3493
Benjamin, Lois, 1477, 1728
Benjamin, Playthell, 941, 9791-9792, 11414-
    11415
Benjamin, Stacy E., 2262
Ben-Jochannan, Yosef, 942, 12657-12658
Benmayor, Rina, 3494
Benn, Mark S., 13886
Benner, Yvonne E, 12890
Bennet, James, 5459
Bennett, B. Kevin, 10387
Bennett, Claudette E., 14474

Bennett, Clifford T., 4278
Bennett, Gerald G., 3149
Bennett, James, 14604
Bennett, L., 11416
Bennett, Neil, 5579
Bennett, Rob, 2553
Bennett, Stephen E., 11417-11418
Bennett, William J., 10701
Bennett-Alexander, Dawn D., 20
Benokraitis, Nina, 21
Benseler, David P., 12356
Benson, Kevin, 10306
Benson, Nettie L., 9685
Benson, Todd, 9372
Benstock, Shari, 689
Bentley, Robert H., 13808
Beran, Janice S., 13228
Berard, Yamil, 5580
Berardi, Gayle K., 9793
Berberoglu, Berch, 1729
Bercovitch, Sacvan, 10702
Bereman, M.A., 4352
Berends, Mark, 3711
Berg, C.R., 13391
Berg, Phillip L., 12262, 12659
Berg, S. Carol, 3495
Bergen, David J., 13392
Berger, Arthur A., 7390
Berger, Elmer, 623
Berger, Gabriel, 12848
Berger, Joseph, 22, 3496-3497, 4353-4355,
    7689, 8362, 9794
Berger, Lawrence, 7077
Berger, Leslie, 12942
Berger, Ruth, 11200
Berger, Thomas R., 8689, 9344
Berghorn, Forrest J., 13374
Bergman, Barbara R., 4617
Bergman, Lowell, 13600
Bergmann, Werner, 477-478
Berk, Marc L., 6065
Berk, Richard A., 2263
Berke, Richard L., 11419, 12050, 12660
Berkman, L.F., 6617
Berkman, Lisa, 6066
Berkow, Ira, 13229-13231
Berk-Seligson, Susan, 8363
Berlant, Lauren, 9795
Berlet, Chip, 538, 11420, 13601
Berlin, Ira, 624, 6719-6721, 7885, 10388,
    13096-13100
Berliner, H., 6067
Berlowitz, Leslie, 8764, 11838
Berlowitz, Marvin J., 1846, 10703
Berman, Jerry L., 13602-13603
Berman, Marshall, 9796
Berman, Paul, 943-944, 4356-4357
Bernal, Martha E., 1273, 3498, 10707
Bernal, Martin, 10704-10706, 12318

Bernard, Mitchell S., 5460
Bernard, Richard M., 11659
Bernasconi, Robert, 1393
Berne, Robert, 3499-3500
Bernhard, Virginia, 6722, 14384, 14452
Bernstein, Alison R., 4358, 6723, 10389-10390
Bernstein, Carl, 13604
Bernstein, David, 1478
Bernstein, Harry, 7886
Bernstein, Iver, 13984
Bernstein, Michael, 2850
Bernstein, Richard, 23, 9165, 9797-9798,
    10708-10709
Bernstein, Sharon, 3501
Bernstine, Daniel O., 13792
Berry, Bertice B., 2858
Berry, Gordon L., 3502, 4359, 4685, 9799
Berry, Jason, 9800-9801, 13605
Berry, Jeffrey M., 11421
Berry, J.W., 12263
Berry, Mary C., 8190
Berry, Mary F., 8690
Berryman, Jack W., 13232
Bershady, Harold J., 540, 4586, 6837, 8854
Berstein, J., 6043
Bertaux, N.E., 12943
Bertelsen, Kevin J., 13101
Berten, David P., 8691
Berthoff, Rowland, 8692
Berube, Michael, 4360
Besharov, Douglas J., 1274
Beshers, James, 14245
Bess, Reginald, 9166
Betancur, J., 11320
Beth, Loren, 625
Betsey, Charles L., 24, 1151
Betten, Neil, 2859
Better, Shirley J., 14298
Bettis, P.J., 1479
Bevan, Carol S., 5576
Beyer, Eric, 4361
Beyer, Gregg A., 7493
Beyers, Dan, 9520
Bhabha, Homi, 10710
Bianchi, Suzanne M., 1275, 1759
Bick, Abraham, 946
Bickel, Robert N., 3503
Bickford, Adam, 7078
Biddle, Frederic M., 1152
Bidney, D., 6724
Bierman, J.A., 13233
Bigelow, Donovan R., 25
Bigglestone, William E., 9646
Bikales, William G., 947
Bilbao, Elena, 3504
Billig, Michael, 8365, 12386-12387
Billings, J., 6068-6069
Billingsley, Andrew, 3150, 5581, 10391
Billington, Monroe, 9583, 10392-10393

Billson, Janet M., 1341, 14530
Billy, Bahe, 2108
Bilotta, James D., 9591
Binder, A., 9804
Binder, Wolfgang, 1991, 9467
Bindman, A., 6070
Bingham, Clara, 13364
Binkley, Kenneth M., 14475
Biola, Heather, 14299
Biolsi, Thomas, 5839, 6725, 9676
Bird, Van S., 1730
Birnbaum, Howard, 14145
Birnbaum, Jesse, 2265
Biro, Lajos, 7947
Birrell, Susan, 12388
Bishop, Alan J., 10711
Bishop, David, 4364
Bishop, Dorn, 7079
Bishop, J.A., 3145
Bishop, Katherine, 479, 10394
Biskind, Peter, 13606
Biskupic, Joan, 2860, 8693, 8698
Bivins, Karin C., 3505
Bixby, Ann K., 5840
Bixler, E.O., 6311
Bjork, Lars G., 4365
Black, Albert, Jr., 26, 5713
Black, Charles, 8694
Black, Chris, 2555, 3506, 9668
Black, D., 6071
Black, Donald, 2861
Black, Earl, 11422
Black, Elias, 4366
Black, Gregory D., 10048
Black, Merle, 11422
Black Horse, Francis D., 2266
Blackburn, McKinley L., 3151-3152
Blackburn, Robert T., 4566
Blackett, R.J.M., 627
Blackman, Margaret B., 628
Blackman, Yvette H., 12129
Blackmar, Elizabeth, 7080
Blackwelder, Julia K., 3153, 14301
Blades, Ruben, 9805
Blair, Karen J., 14290
Blair, Philip M., 2862
Blakely, Edward J., 3234
Blakely, J.H., 132
Blakeney, Ronnie A.F., 951
Blakey, M.L., 839
Blakey, Michael, 12389
Blalock, Hubert M., Jr., 1731
Blanch, Mary C., 10713
Blanchard, F., 27
Blanchard, Tsvi, 952
Bland, I.J., 6073
Blank, R., 2556
Blau, Francine D., 6074, 14146
Blauner, Robert, 953, 6726, 12319

Blaut, J.M., 10714, 11128, 12390
Blavis, Patricia B., 8191
Blea, Irene I., 9446, 14302, 14477
Blecker, Robert, 2267
Blee, Kathleen M., 7792
Bleifuss, Joel, 11427, 12518
Blew, Robert W., 13989
Blick, Jeffrey P., 6727
Blicksilver, Edith, 14303
Blight, David W., 6728
Blits, Jan H., 13793-13794
Bloch, Farrell, 1480
Block, Arthur R., 250, 8560
Block, N.J., 7690
Block, Sam, 11428
Block, W., 2863
Block, W.E., 28
Blomberg, Belinda, 5771
Bloom, B.R., 6076
Bloom, Lisa, 10715
Blount, M., 6077
Bluestone, Barry, 3154, 13933
Blum, Bill, 8695
Blum, Debra E., 4373-4376, 13234-13236
Blum, Justin, 13393
Blumberg, Rhonda L., 1481
Blume, Harvey, 12320
Blume, Howard, 2557, 3507-3510
Blumenthal, Walter H., 8192
Blumrosen, Alfred W., 29, 2864
Boas, Franz, 12130-12131
Boas, Phil, 4377, 5013
Bobo, J., 9806
Bobo, Lawrence, 30, 2558, 7329, 11429-11430,
    12051-12053
Bock, W.B., 3412
Bodayla, Stephen D., 1394
Bodenhamer, David J., 18, 2268
Bodinger-De Uriarte, Christina, 2269
Body-Gendrot, Sophie, 7081
Boehm, William T., 6078
Boelhower, William, 629
Boender, Debra R., 6729
Bogardus, E., 12391
Bogas, K.L., 2865
Bogen, David S., 4378, 5772
Boggs, Stephen T., 3511
Bogin, Joshua P., 13504
Bogle, Donald, 9807-9808
Bogle, Kathryn H., 630
Bohara, A.K., 71, 2866
Bohing, Edward A., 2867
Bohland, James R., 7082
Boice, L., 11431
Boisjoly, J., 13934
Boissevain, Ethel, 6730
Bojar, Karen, 2559
Bok, Derek, 10716
Bok, Marcia, 1482

Bole, William, 7494, 12519
Boles, Frank J., 7888
Boles, John B., 12661
Bolger, Dorita F., 12872
Bolick, Clint, 1483
Boling, B.D., 7611
Bollinger, Lee C., 8696
Bolster, William Jeffrey, 11201-11202
Bolsterli, Margaret J., 14210
Bolt, Christine, 12774
Bolton, Charles C., 14211-14212
Bonacich, Edna, 31-32, 1732-1733, 3155, 3429,
    4379, 5773, 12392-12393, 14147, 14478
Bond, George C., 2976
Bond, Horace Mann, 3512
Bond, Julian, 1484, 8697, 11432, 11876
Boneparth, E., 1154
Boney, F. Nash, 6079
Bonilla, Frank, 1992-1993, 1997, 3156, 4380,
    5428, 7889, 10313, 12132
Bonner, Thomas N., 4381
Bonnett, Aubrey W., 6731
Bonney, Norman, 11434
Bontemps, Anna A., 9632
Bonvillain, Nancy, 12944, 14304
Booker, Linnette, 11203
Boone, Margaret S., 6080
Boone, Robert, 8275-8276
Boor, M., 4336
Booth, William, 631, 8698, 9544, 13607,
    13990-13991
Boozer, M.A., 3513
Boring, E.G., 7691
Boritch, H., 2270
Boritt, Gabor S., 6767, 10442, 11183
Borjas, George J., 7495-7496, 13936
Bork, Robert H., 10824
Borrego, John G., 1929
Borstelmann, Thomas, 12216
Borunda, Mario R., 4383
Bosch, Norma, 1395
Boskin, Joseph, 7391, 7984
Bosma, Boyd, 2560
Boston, Thomas D., 1734, 7890, 8193, 14479-
    14480
Boswell, Terry E., 2868, 7891
Bosworth, Greer C., 5782
Botkin, B.A., 13102
Botting, Douglas, 13746
Bottomby, Gillian, 10937
Bottomore, Tom, 1735
Botts, Howard, 10433
Boudin, Louis, 8699
Boulard, Garry, 4384-4385
Boulden, Michael, 10687
Boulding, D.C., 13237
Bound, John, 3158-3159, 5405, 6210
Boundy, Kathleen, 3514
Bourgois, Philippe, 9561

Bourne, Jenny, 11331
Bouza, Anthony V., 2271
Bouza, Tony, 5841
Boven, Theo van, 13887
Bowden, J.J., 8194
Bowditch, Christine, 3515
Bowen, E.J., 33
Bowen, James S., 2869
Bowers, Cynthia, 1930
Bowersock, G.W., 10717
Bowman, James E., 6426
Bowman, Jeffrey H., 2417
Bowser, Benjamin P., 3441, 5582, 5797,
    11435, 12249, 14213, 14605
Boxall, Bettina, 4542
Boxberger, Daniel L., 7892
Boxhill, B.R., 1792
Boxill, Bernard R., 1485, 3160
Boyarsky, Bill, 8700, 11436
Boyce, Byrl N., 14606
Boyd, Christopher, 10574
Boyd, D.A.C., 12394
Boyd, Herb, 954, 13212
Boyd, Julia, 14305
Boyd, Robert L., 1155-1156, 5406, 5583
Boyd, William L., 3516
Boyd-Franklin, Nancy, 5584
Boyer, Edward J., 13608
Boyer, Ernest L., 4386
Boyer, Paul, 4387
Boyer, Peter J., 2272
Boyer, W.W., 1994
Boyes-Watson, Carolyn F., 34
Boykin, A. Wade, 12264
Boyle, Francis A., 12217
Boyle, R.H., 13238
Boyle, Susan C., 1736
Boynton, Robert S., 4388
Bracey, Derek, 632
Bracey, Gerald W., 3517, 13795
Bracey, John H., Jr., 633, 1486, 2870-2871,
    5755, 11129
Bracken, B.A., 13796
Bracken, H., 11294-11295
Brackman, Harold D., 955
Bradbury, Katharina L., 1737
Bradbury, Katharine, 7893
Bradbury, K.L., 5585
Braddock, Jomills Henry II, 2561, 3518, 13239-
    13240
Braden, William, 1277
Bradford, Phillips Verner, 12320
Bradford, Sarah, 634
Bradford, William D., 14148
Bradley, Ann, 3519-3520
Bradley, Bill, 11437
Bradshaw, Benjamin S., 6537
Bradsher, Keith, 7083-7084
Brady, Patricia, 3521

Braeman, John, 1487
Braham, Peter, 429
Braham, Randolph L., 480
Braiman, Eva, 4389
Braithwaite, J., 2273
Braman, Sandra, 8701
Bramlett-Solomon, S., 635, 9809
Branch, Taylor, 956
Brand, J.E., 9960
Brandt, A., 6081
Brandt, Godfrey L., 430
Branhaw, Brocht, 10718
Branigin, William, 7497
Brantley, Daniel, 11438, 12218
Brass, Paul, 11199
Brasseaux, Carl A., 6732
Bratt, Larry, 9810
Bratt, Rachel G., 7085-7086, 7149, 7321
Braun, Stephen, 2562, 5407
Braund, Kathryn E. Holland, 10575, 13103
Braungart, Richard G., 7633
Braungart, Richard S., 109
Braverman, William A., 481
Braxton, Greg, 7392, 9811-9815
Braxton, Joanne M., 636, 9167
Bray, Rosemary L., 637, 8702
Brazier, Arthur M., 2109
Brazzell, Johnetta C., 4390-4391
Brazziel, William F., 13797
Brecher, Charles, 3493, 5402
Bredbenner, Candice D., 1396
Bredemeier, B.J.L., 10719
Breg, Mary H., 7087
Breger, Joseph, 7088
Breiter, Toni, 3146, 3161
Breitman, George, 12395
Breneman, E.R., 2626
Brennan, T., 10720
Brennan, W.J., 8703
Brenner, Aaron, 35
Brenner, Elise M., 6733
Brenner, Joel Glenn, 7089-7090, 7347
Brenner, Johanna, 12945
Brenner, Robert, 2110
Brenner, Scott C., 2563
Brenson, Michael, 13394
Brent, Jonathan, 957
Breslauer, Jan, 9168-9169, 9816
Breslin, James E.B., 9170
Breslin, Jimmy, 958
Brett, Armand George, 36
Brettschneider, Marla, 10721
Brew, Sarah L., 1931
Brewer, J.D., 12133
Brewer, M.B., 2705
Brewer, Rose M., 14306
Brewer, Scott, 8704
Brez Stein, Colman, Jr., 3522
Bridge, George S., 2274

Bridges, Larry D., 3162
Bridges, Roger, 1488
Bridges, Tyler, 12520
Brier, Stephen B., 7894
Briggs, Carl M., 3523
Briggs, Cyril, 7895
Briggs, Kenneth, 12662
Briggs, Vernon M., Jr., 2872, 3163, 7498, 7896
Briggs, Winstanley, 13104
Brigham, J.C., 4392
Brighouse, Harry, 4393
Bright, S.B., 2275
Brightman, Robert, 12663
Brimmer, Andrew, F., 1157, 3164, 14149-14150
Brink, Daniel T., 8336
Brinkley, Alan, 11439
Brinkley, Joel, 7499-7500
Brint, Steven, 4394
Brisbane, Robert H., 1932
Brisbay, Erin, 4395
Bristol, Katherine G., 7091
Britt, Brian, 13395
Britter, Thomas A., 10576
Britton, A., 11285
Britton, Jesse D., 5842
Broad, R., 5461
Broadwater, Jeff, 13609
Brock, Jacobus, 1397
Broden, F. Clinton, 3524
Broder, David S., 2564, 6734
Broderick, Dorothy M., 9150
Brodeur, Paul, 8195
Brodin, Mark S., 2873
Brodsky, Annette, 14459
Brody, E.B., 7692
Brody, Gene, 7771
Brody, Jane E., 6083
Brody, N., 7692
Broh, C. Anthony, 11404
Broman, C.L., 5586
Bromberg, Alan B., 13105
Bromwich, David, 4396
Brooks, C.H., 6084
Brooks, D.H.M., 2874, 7693
Brooks, Dwight E., 9817
Brooks, Homer, 1978
Brooks, Nancy Rivera, 1158
Brooks, Roy L., 37, 2565, 8705
Brooks-Gunn, J., 3525
Brooks-Higginbotham, Evelyn, 12946
Brott, Armin A., 13396
Brough, C.H., 4397
Broun, Elizabeth, 10722
Broussard, Albert S., 638, 9373, 11204, 11440
Brown, A.W., 639
Brown, Carrie, 9171
Brown, Charles, 3165, 8706-8707

Brown, Cherie, 482
Brown, Claude, 8366
Brown, Clyde, 168
Brown, Darryl, 4398
Brown, De Neen L., 3526, 4399-4400, 5587, 8367
Brown, E., 6138, 13242
Brown, E. Richard, 6085
Brown, Edward G., Jr., 9293
Brown, Elaine, 640
Brown, Elsa Barkley, 14351
Brown, G., 9818
Brown, George H., 3527
Brown, Ian, 6086
Brown, Irene A., 3166
Brown, J. Larry, 6087
Brown, James, 10352
Brown, James A., 6735
Brown, Jeffrey P., 4870
Brown, J.K., 11441
Brown, J.P., 13302
Brown, Judith K., 14307
Brown, Judith O., 12947
Brown, K., 3528
Brown, Kathleen M., 9723
Brown, Ken, 1159
Brown, Kevin, 2566
Brown, K.F., 9819
Brown, Lawrence S., Jr., 6088
Brown, Linda B., 3529
Brown, Loren N., 8196
Brown, Lynne, 7893
Brown, Michael K., 5843
Brown, Nancy, 5588
Brown, Oscar, Sr., 641
Brown, Peter, 7957, 11442
Brown, Phil, 5589
Brown, Philip M., 6736
Brown, Richard D., 642
Brown, Richard M., 13992
Brown, R.W., 13243
Brown, Sara A., 1278
Brown, Shirley V., 4401-4402
Brown, Tony, 2567, 12134
Brown, Walt K., 2875, 8708
Browne, Hugh, 7897
Browne, Joseph L., 3530
Browne, Kingsley R., 12948
Browne, Nick, 9820
Browne, R.S., 3215
Browne, Robert S., 3167, 14151-14152
Brownell, Herbert, 8709
Browning, J., 1916
Browning, Rufus P., 11443-11444
Brownlow, Kevin, 9821
Brownstein, Alan E., 4403
Brownstein, P.J., 2239
Brownstein, Ronald, 1489, 2276, 2568, 9822
Brubaker, William R., 1398

Bruce, Dickson C., Jr., 384, 643
Bruce-Novoa, Juan, 9172
Bruck, David I., 2277
Brueggemann, John F., 1738
Bruheze, Adri A. Albert de la, 5462
Brumberg, Stephan F., 3531
Brumble, H. David III, 644
Brun, Nancy, 14308
Brundage, W. Fitzhugh, 9468, 13993-13995
Bruxvoort, Harold J., 9173
Bryan, Dianetta G., 1490
Bryan, Paul E., 12265
Bryant, Bunyan, 5463, 5529
Bryant, Flora R., 645
Bryant, J., 9960
Bryant, John, 1160
Bryant, Jonathan M., 9469
Bryant, Pat, 5464, 13610
Bryant, Sharon A., 6089
Bryant, Z. Lois, 13397
Bryce-Laporte, Roy S., 7501, 7502, 10314
Bryden, David P., 38, 4404
Bryk, Anthony, 3886
Buchanan, A., 6090
Buchanan, Brenda, 12949
Buchsbaum, Tamar, 4405
Buck, J.L., 12950
Buckley, Stephen, 11445, 11820, 13798
Buckley, Thomas, 11286
Buckley, William F., 483
Buelens, Gert, 11332
Buenger, Walter L., 9695, 13387
Buenker, John D., 10723
Bueno, Patricia, 6894
Buffinton, Arthur H., 6737
Buhanan, Barbara S., 10724
Buhle, Mari Jo, 14481
Buhle, Paul, 8078
Buhler Wilkerson, K., 9669
Buitrago Ortiz, Carlos, 6738
Buker, Eloise A., 8368
Bullard, Linda M., 9823
Bullard, R.L., 10395
Bullard, Robert D., 2876, 5465-5468, 6739, 7092-7094, 9686-9687, 14482
Bullard, Sara, 13888
Bullivaint, Brian M., 11333
Bullock, Charles S., III, 2569, 2747, 11446-11448
Bullock, Paul, 13935
Bulter, Ernest W., 9658
Bumpass, L., 5590
Bunch, C., 12951
Bunch, Kenyon D., 4407
Bunday, Mary Lee, 9140
Bundy, Mary Lee, 9128
Bunker, John P., 6237
Bunzel, John H., 39-40, 4408-4410
Burbank, James, 5469

Burch, Sallie, 6740
Burch, Thomas A., 6091-6092
Burchell, Robert A., 9374, 14153
Burd, G., 9824
Burd, Stephen, 6093
Burdekin, R.C.K., 13244
Burdick, Susan E., 10725
Burgess, Norma J., 5591, 14309
Burk, Robert F., 1491, 10396
Burkart, Walter, 10726
Burke, Fred G., 3532
Burke, John P., 8709
Burke, Michael, 11302
Burke, William T., III, 4411
Burkett, Randall K., 14607
Burkholders, Steve, 13611
Burleigh, Nina, 11449
Burlew, A. Kathleen H., 12266
Burma, John H., 7393
Burman, George, 2877
Burman, S., 11450
Burner, Eric R., 646, 1492
Burnham, Dorothy, 14310
Burnham, Margaret A., 5592, 13398
Burns, Haywood, 1493, 8710
Burns, James MacGregor, 1494
Burns, Judy, 9174
Burns, Ken, 13262
Burns, Michael M., 41
Burns, Stewart, 1494-1495
Burnside, Jacqueline G., 4412
Burnstein, Paul, 13799
Buron, L., 3252
Burr, J.A., 6427
Burr, Ty, 10695
Burridge, Kate, 8340
Burstein, Paul, 42-43, 2878-2879
Burt, Larry W., 2111, 5844
Burt, Martha R., 7095
Burtless, Gary, 3151, 7898
Burton, L., 8197
Burton, Orville, 8711, 11230
Burton, Shirley, 13612
Busby, Margaret, 385
Bush, G.M., 12267
Bush, Loring, 13962
Bushey, Karen, 8369
Bushnell, O.A., 6094
Buss, Fran L., 3169
Buss, William, 2880
Bussey, Charles, 10397
Bustamante, Jorge A., 7503-7504, 7526
Butchart, Ronald E., 3533-3534
Butcher, K.F., 7505
Butler, Amy C., 3535
Butler, Anne M., 2278
Butler, David L., 13889
Butler, Elizabeth, 6275
Butler, Helen M., 9658

Butler, John S., 10398-10400, 10454, 10497
Butler, Katharine I., 11451
Butler, Michael R., 10401
Butler, Patricia A., 6095
Butler, R.E., 11130
Butler, Reginald D., 5774
Butler, Richard J., 1496, 3170
Butsch, Richard, 12625
Butterfield, Bruce D., 44
Butterfield, Fox, 647, 4413-4414
Buttlar, Lois, 10727
Button, James W., 1497-1498, 11452-11453
Butts, Calvin O., 3rd, 5845
Byars, Lauretta F., 3536
Byng, Michelle D., 11454
Bynum, Victoria E., 6741
Byrd, Joann, 9825
Byrd, Veronica, 1161
Byrd, W. Michael, 6096, 6111
Byrne, J. Peter, 4415
Byrne, J.M., 2279
Byrnes, Deborah A., 431

Caban, Pedro A., 1995-1996
Cabranes, Jose A., 1399
Cacas, Samuel, 12135
Cadd, M., 8370
Cadena, Gilbert R., 12664
Cadet, Marc V., 4416
Cadwalader, Sandra L., 5846, 8216
Cagan, Leslie, 11455
Cage, Mary C., 960, 4417-4420
Cahan, E.D., 3537
Cahn, Susan K., 13245
Cain, Bruce, 9375
Cain, D.P., 7694
Cain, G.C., 5408
Cain, William E., 3127-3128, 10728
Calabrese, Raymond L., 3538
Calabresi, G., 8712
Calabresi, Massimo, 4421-4422
Calavita, Kitty, 7506
Calderon, Garcia, 1739
Calderon, J-C., 11205
Calderon, José, 8451
Caldwell, Erskine, 12665
Caldwell, Janet, 432
Caldwell, Joe Louis, 6742
Calhoun, C.A., 7545
Calhoun, Emily, 2881
Califa, Antonio J., 8371
Calitri, Ronald, 3540
Callahan, Linda F., 8372
Callahan, Tom, 13246
Callicott, J. Baird, 8198
Calloway, Colin G., 6743-6744, 12663
Calloway-Thomas, Carolyn, 11256
Calmore, John O., 7096-7097
Calvert, Robert A., 9688, 9695

Calvert, Robert E., 1400, 10699
Calvery, Robert A., 13387
Calvo, Janet M., 1401
Calvo Buezas, Tomas, 1933
Camacho, Annie M., 3541
Camacho, Eduardo, 1740
Camacho, Roseanne V., 14311
Camarillo, Albert, 6745, 14608
Camayd-Freixas, Yohel, 3542
Cambridge, Alrick X., 433
Camburn, E., 4424
Cameron, J.W., 3543
Cameron, James, 13996
Cameron, Kathleen A., 2532
Cameron, Robert G., 13800
Cameron, Samuel, 2280
Cameron, Stephen, 3544
Cammack, Mark, 4425
Camp, Gregory S., 8199
Camp, William E., 2570
Campano, F., 3171
Campbell, Bruce A., 1741
Campbell, Donald T., 12268-12269, 13399
Campbell, Edward D.C., Jr., 6746, 9826
Campbell, Gregory R., 6097
Campbell, James, 648
Campbell, Patricia B., 2882
Campbell, Randolph B., 13106
Campbell, Walter E., III, 5847
Campbell, Will D., 14214
Campisi, Jack, 8713
Campos, E., 10314
Campos, Ricardo, 1993, 1997, 3156, 7889,
    10313
Campos Tapia, Javier, 1934
Canady, John E., Jr., 2571
Canby, Vincent, 9827-9829
Canedy, Susan, 12521
Canellos, Peter S., 7098-7099, 13400
Canner, G.B., 7100-7101
Cannon, Lou, 13613
Cannon, Lynn W., 1742, 1908
Canny, Nicholas, 1998
Canon, Lynn W., 12952
Cantor, David, 12666
Cantor, Louis, 9830
Cantor, Milton, 7564
Cantrell, Doug, 7899
Cantrell, Gregg, 11457-11458
Cao Garcia, Ramon J., 14154
Capeci, Dominic J., Jr., 5848, 13247, 13997-
    13998
Caper, P., 6098
Capitanini, Lisa, 3545, 6099, 6300, 9494
Caplan, Nathan S., 5593, 5798
Caplan, Ronald L., 6100
Cappell, Charles L., 11206
Capron, Christiane, 7695, 7760
Captain, G., 13248

Caputi, J., 9831
Caranese, A.V., 4431
Caraway, Nancie, 10730, 14312
Carbaugh, D., 8389, 11345
Carby, Hazel V., 10731
Card, David, 3546-3547, 4432
Cardenal, Gilbert, 7507, 7673, 7900
Cardenas, Jose, 3548
Cardoso, Lawrence A., 7508
Carey, Art, 14215
Cargal, James M., 977
Cargill, Jack, 7901
Carleton, Francis J., 8714
Carlisle, David K., 10402
Carliss, Richard, 9832-9833
Carll-White, Mary A., 7902
Carlson, A. Cheree, 8373
Carlson, Alvar W., 6747, 8200
Carlson, Leonard A., 8201
Carlson, Paul E., 13801
Carlson, Shirley J., 10315
Carlson, S.M., 11208
Carlton, Eric, 12136
Carlton, Robert L., 9377
Carmen, Elaine H., 6101
Carmichael, James V., Jr., 9129
Carmichael, Joel, 485
Carmichael, J.W., Jr., 12892
Carmines, Edward G., 12054, 12091
Carmines, G., 11459
Carmody, Deirdre, 9834
Carnochan, W.B., 10732
Carnoy, Martin, 2862, 7903, 8113
Carpenter, Barbara, 9545
Carpenter-Stevenson, Sandy, 3550
Carper, N. Gordon, 5756
Carr, C., 9835
Carr, Jay, 9836-9839, 12137
Carr, Leslie G., 2573
Carr, L.G., 2572
Carr, Lois Green, 5775, 13161
Carr, Norma, 13401
Carr, Raymond, 1999
Carranoc, Lynwood, 10403
Carranza, E. Lou, 13402, 13802
Carrasquillo, Angela L., 1279
Carrera, John W., 3685
Carrese, J.A., 6189
Carrico, Richard L., 2281
Carrier, James G., 10733
Carriere, Marius, Jr., 9678
Carrington, B., 3066
Carrion, Arturo , 6748
Carrion, Juan M., 1743, 11131
Carroll, D., 6102
Carroll, Ginny, 7793
Carroll, James, 486
Carroll, James R., 1162
Carroll, John M., 649, 10404

Carroll, Peter F., 8202
Carroll-Seguin, Rita, 3232
Carruthers, J.H., 10734
Carson, Clayborne, 650, 1499-1503, 13614
Carson, Emmett D., 1744, 3172
Carstairi, V., 13849
Carter, Bill, 1163, 9840-9842
Carter, Bob, 11594, 12155, 14629
Carter, Dale, 1232, 1607, 7440
Carter, Dan T., 7794, 11460
Carter, Deborah J., 4434, 5377
Carter, Edward C., II, 1402
Carter, G.L., 1504
Carter, George E., 47
Carter, Hodding, 3551, 11461
Carter, Paul, 9175
Carter, R.T., 3552
Carter, Richard G., 5409, 5594
Carter, Robert Lee, 1505, 8715-8716
Carter, Robert T., 1745, 13803
Carter, R.T., 11247, 14216
Carter, S.L., 2883, 4435
Carter, Stephen L., 48-49, 11462
Carton, Barbara, 14105
Carton, Paul, 9843
Cartwright, William H., 11281
Carvajal, Doreen, 487, 12667
Carver, Illene, 10875
Cary, Jean M., 3553
Cary, Lorene, 3554
Casas, J. Manuel, 12270
Case, Charles E., 12055, 12396, 12422
Case, David S., 8717, 9345
Casebeer, Linda S., 2574
Casey, J.A., 8718
Casey-Leininger, Charles F., 5799
Cashion, Robert T., 10405
Cashman, Sean D., 1506
Cashmore, E. Ellis, 14483
Casillas, Mike, 7904
Caskey, J.P., 1164
Casper, Ellen, 7905
Cass, Julia, 653
Cassell, Frank A., 4110
Casserly, Michael, 2575
Cassinore, O.C., 6916
Casso, H.G., 142
Castaneda, Antonia I., 14313
Castaneda, Ruben, 2884
Castells, Manuel, 9618
Castenada, Antonia I., 14314
Castenada, Ruben, 8768
Castile, George P., 5849
Castillo, Edward D., 12668
Castillo, Jose del, 7509
Castillo-Speed, Lillian, 9131, 14609
Castle, Musette S., 9592
Castro, Rafaela, 7394
Castro, Raymond, 3173

Casuso, Jorge, 9495
Catalano, R., 6103
Cataldo, Everett F., 3555
Cater, Sandy, 1280
Cath, Stanley H., 5602
Catlin, Robert A., 9503
Cattan, P., 7906
Cattau, Daniel, 13249
Caudill, E., 12610
Caudill, J.B., 7243
Caudill, S.B., 14180
Caughey, John W., 14000-14001
Cauracho, Eduardo, 9495
Cavaliere, Frank J., 4411
Cavanagh, Thomas E., 11463-11464
Cavenaugh, David N., 1281
Cazanave, Noel, 50
Cazemajou, Jean, 11132, 11334
Cazenave, N.A., 1282
Cebula, R.J., 10316
Cecelski, David S., 3556-3557
Cecil-Fronsman, Bill, 14217
Cedillo, Gilbert, 7510
Cekola, Anna, 10735
Celis, William, 3rd, 651, 2576-2579, 2885,
    3558-3560, 4436-4438, 6749
Cellini, Joseph, 488
Centeno-Rodriguez, Migdalia, 10736
Cernovsky, Z.Z., 7696, 12321
Cerone, Daniel, 9844
Cervantes, Fred A., 11335
Cervantes, Nancy, 7907
Cesaire, Aime, 2000
Cevallos, Elena A., 14610
Chabotar, K.J., 2580
Chabran, Richard, 9130-9131, 14624
Chacon, Maria, 4440
Chacon, R.D., 7908
Chacon, Ramon D., 7102
Chadbourn, James H., 14003
Chadley, O.A., 9132
Chafetz, Gary, 2581
Chaikind, Stephen, 4441
Chait, Richard P., 4442
Cha-Jua, Sundiata K., 9845
Chalfant, John, 3562
Chalk, Frank, 14004
Chalk, Ocania, 13250
Chalkind, Stephen, 6127
Chall, Jeanne S., 3563
Chama, J. Richard, 10406
Chamberlain, Marian K., 51, 4443
Chamberlain, R.M., 13177
Chambers, Clarke A., 7909
Chambers, Daniel N., 7103-7104
Chambers, John W., II, 10538
Chambers, Julius L., 1507-1508
Chambers, Raymond M., 4444
Chambers, Reid P., 8203

Chambers, T., 1283
Chambliss, W.J., 5800
Chametzky, Jules, 14315
Chamlin, Mitchell B., 5850, 13251
Champagne, Duane, 11465
Champagne, Richard A., Jr., 12054
Chan, Sucheng, 1965, 4445, 6824, 7511, 8536,
    14383
Chancer, Lynn S., 9524
Chand, Krishan, 14155
Chandhuri, Joyotpaul, 11466
Chandler, Alfred N., 8204
Chandler, Mittie O., 2582, 7105
Chandler, Robert J., 1509
Chandler, Zala, 14415
Chandras, Kan V., 4446
Chang, David, 52
Chang, Deanna B.K., 6303
Chang, Edward C., 4447
Chang, Edward T., 10577
Chang, Gordon H., 9846
Chang, Grace, 3175
Chang, Jeff, 10578
Chang, Michael S.H., 7512
Chao, Suzie, 4450
Chapa, J., 8443
Chapa, Jorge, 3564
Chapelle, Tony, 1165
Chaplin, J.E., 13108
Chapman, A.J., 7395
Chapman, Bernadine S., 3565
Chapman, Gregory D., 12219
Chappell, David L., 1510
Charen, Mona, 2283
Charles, Allan D., 12670
Charles, Carolle, 7513
Charms, Alexander, 13616
Charng, H.W., 13918
Chasan, Alice, 4451
Chase, J.T., 1486
Chateauvert, Melinda, 3566
Chato, Genvieve, 8719
Chavez, Carlos A., 10638
Chavez, F.R., 3567
Chavez, Jerome A., 489
Chavez, John R., 6750
Chavez, Linda, 53, 6104, 11087, 11467, 12522
Chavez, Margaret M., 2886
Chavez, Stephanie, 490, 3485, 3568-3572
Chavira, Ricardo, 3573, 7514, 10579
Chavis, Benjamin F., Jr., 5470-5472
Cheatham, Harold E., 5595, 10407-10408,
    11209
Cheek, Aimee Lee, 652, 9647
Cheek, W.F., 6751
Cheek, William, 652, 9647
Cheekoway, Marjorie B., 2583
Chen, Edward M., 8374
Chen, Li-Ju, 3848

Chen, M., 6105
Chen, Marion, 11468
Chenetier, Marc, 629
Cheney, Lynne V., 10738
Chepyator-Thomson, Jepkorir R., 3574
Cherian, Anila, 11469
Cherlin, A.J., Jr., 1388
Cherry, David L., 54, 9847
Cherry, Robert, 961, 2887, 2888, 12397, 14193, 14202
Chesnutt, David R., 397, 8711
Chestam, H.E., 4452
Chester, Nia L., 14345
Chestnut, J.L., Jr., 653, 9336
Cheung, King-kok, 14611
Chevigny, Bell Gale, 9546-9547
Chevigny, Paul, 13617
Chew, Kenneth S.Y., 1284, 5596
Cheyfitz, Eric, 2001, 8720
Chiara, Susan, 3575
Chiasson, L., 2193
Chideya, Faroi, 4453
Childs, John Brown, 9378
Chilman, C.S., 5598
Chimezie, Amuzie, 3577
Chin, Daryl, 10740
Chin, Do-lin, 2284
Chira, Susan, 1289, 2584-2585, 3578-3582, 4454, 6106, 9594
Chiswick, Barry R., 7515-7516, 7676, 7910
Chiswick, C.U., 7517
Chock, Eric, 9176
Chocolate, Deborah N., 386
Chomsky, Carol, 10409
Chong, Dennis, 1511-1512
Chou, Sucheng, 13001
Chow, Crystal, 9848
Chow, Josephine, 7396
Chrisman, Robert, 8721, 9849
Chriss, B., 3583
Christensen, John W., 1290
Christensen, Kimberly, 3176, 14156
Christgau, Robert, 962
Christian, Barbara, 12398
Christian, Carole E., 9689
Christian, Donna, 8640
Christian, Edward B., 13804
Christian, Garna L., 10410
Christian-Smith, Linda K., 4149
Christl, Cliff, 13252
Christmas, J.J., 6107
Christofferson, C., 8722
Christopher, Maurice, 11470
Christopher, Renny T., 10411
Christy, Marian, 654
Christy, Mary R., 5851
Christy, Ralph D., 4455
Chu, Donald B., 13253
Chu, Henry, 3584

Chua, Lawrence, 9850
Chubb, John E., 3585
Chujo, Ken, 3586
Chum, Gloria, 9177
Chung, Eugene, 5473
Chung, Philip W., 13380
Chung, Richard, 9851
Chung, Sue F., 6752
Chunn, Eva Wells, 3587
Chupa, Anna M., 13404
Churaman, Charlotte V., 4456
Churchill, Ward, 2002-2006, 2285, 4457-4458, 5474, 6753-6754, 8205-8208, 8458, 9852-9854, 13618-13622, 14006, 14484-14485, 14612
Chused, Richard H., 4459
Chuun, Eva Wells, 2796
Ciaramitaro, Bridget, 2112
Cimons, Marlene, 6108
Cimprich, John, 10412
Cintron Ortiz, Rafael, 3588
Cirino, Robert, 9855
Cirino-Gerena, Gabriel, 11210
Citrin, Jack, 8375-8376, 11471, 12057
Claggett, William, 11371
Clague, Monique W., 4460
Claiborne, William, 7106
Clair, R.T., 1166
Clarizio, H.F., 7750
Clark, Benjamin F., Sr., 1523
Clark, E. Culpepper, 2586, 4461
Clark, Elizabeth B., 13109
Clark, Gregory R., 8377
Clark, Hunter R., 672
Clark, Joe, 3591
Clark, John G., 8240
Clark, Kenneth B., 655, 2587, 8723-8724, 14486
Clark, Leroy D., 1524
Clark, Malcolm, Jr., 7795
Clark, Marjorie C., 7107
Clark, Mark, 13317
Clark, Truman R., 2007
Clark, V., 6109
Clark, Victor S., 7911
Clark, W.A.V., 2588-2589, 7108-7111, 11472
Clark, Wayne A., 13623
Clarke, David A., 4462
Clarke, Donald, 656
Clarke, Leslie L., 6110
Clarke, R., 2752
Clarke, Stuart A., 11473
Clary, Mike, 2286, 9457, 14007
Claudio, Rafael R., 3592
Claussen, Cheryl, 2889
Clay, Camille A., 4464
Clay, P., 7112
Clay, Phillip L., 9856
Clayson, Dennis E., 539

Clayton, Constance, 3593
Clayton, Cornell W., 4465
Clayton, J., 13038
Clayton, James L., 6755
Clayton, Lawrence A., 14487
Clayton, Linda A., 6096, 6111
Clayton, Ronnie W., 13110
Clayton, Susan D., 55, 65
Clegg, Sue, 12399
Clement, Audrey Rose, 11474
Clement, Susan, 9187
Clemente, Frank, 11475
Clements, Mark, 7113
Clements, William M., 7397
Clemmer, Richard O., 13111
Clemmitt, M., 6112
Clewell, Beatriz C., 10741, 12893
Clift, Virgil, 14065
Clifton, James A., 657, 13405
Clinansmith, Michael S., 14008
Clines, Francis X., 2287, 6756, 7912, 10413,
    12672
Clinton, Catherine, 14316
Clinton, William J., 8725
Closs, M.P., 12894
Cloud, Cathy, 2890, 7114
Cloutier, Norman R., 3430
Cloward, Richard A., 11476
Clymer, Adam, 11477
Clymer, K.J., 491
Coady, Elizabeth, 5599
Coakley, Jay, 4466
Coakley, Tom, 3594-3595, 7238
Coate, D., 7115
Coate, S., 56
Coates, James R., 12523, 12626
Coates, Robert C., 7116
Coatsworth, John H., 13406
Cobas, Jose A., 3431
Cobb, James C., 1525, 9548
Cobb, T.R.R., 8726
Cobb, W. Montague, 6113
Cobbs, Lewis, 3596
Cochran, Connie E., 10742
Cochran, M., 5608
Cochran, Thomas, 1167
Cock, Jacklyn, 4358
Cockburn, Alexander, 6114-6115, 8209
Cockcroft, James D., 7518, 7913
Cockerham, W.C., 12271
Cocking, Rodney, 8392
Codije, Corinn, 658
Codina, George E., 12272
Cohen, Adam, 4467
Cohen, Cynthia P., 1291-1292
Cohen, Deborah, 1293, 3597
Cohen, Debra Nussbaum, 963, 12673
Cohen, Dov, 4468
Cohen, Felix S., 8210

Cohen, Joshua, 8727
Cohen, Kitty O., 964
Cohen, Laurie P., 2288
Cohen, Linc, 5475
Cohen, Marc J., 7947, 13624
Cohen, Melvin, 7519
Cohen, Muriel, 2590-2592, 3598-3599
Cohen, Nadine, 7117
Cohen, Naomi W., 492-494
Cohen, Nathan, 9380
Cohen, N.W., 13407
Cohen, Richard, 495, 965-966, 2289-2290,
    10743, 12524
Cohen, Robert, 4469
Cohen, Ronald, 3600
Cohen, Sarah B., 7398
Cohen, Sharon, 11133
Cohen, Steven F., 2291
Cohen, Steven M., 496
Cohen, Toby, 6116
Cohen, William, 6757, 10317
Cohen, Yinon, 8127
Cohler, Larry, 497, 11478
Cohn, Bob, 57, 326
Cohn, D'Vera, 10318, 11211
Cohn, Richard, 2855, 7076
Cohodas, Nadine, 11479
Coil, Suzanne M., 3177
Colbert, Douglas L., 2292, 8728
Colburn, David R., 1526, 2593
Colby, Ira C., 9691
Colby, Peter W., 11904
Coldham, Peter W., 13112
Cole, Beverly P., 3601, 13807
Cole, Charles E., 3602
Cole, Jill C., 5600
Cole, Johnnetta B., 4470-4471
Cole, Lewis, 729, 13254
Cole, L.W., 5476
Cole, Mike, 3603, 12400
Cole, S., 11217
Cole, Stephen, 4472
Cole, Thomas R., 6758
Cole, Wendy, 7796
Coleman, James S., 3604-3605
Coleman, James W., 9178
Coleman, L., 1168
Coleman, Mary D., 11480
Coleman, Michael C., 3606-3608, 8211, 12674
Coleman, Wanda, 8378, 10580
Coleman, William T., Jr., 8729
Colenbrander, Sarah, 12220
Coliver, Sandra, 4473, 8370
Colker, R., 6117
Coll y Cuehi, Cayetano, 13113
Colleran, Kevin J., 5601
Colley, Charles C., 8212
Collier, Aldore, 9857
Collier, Cheryl L., 7118

Collier, Eugenia, 6759
Collier-Thomas, Bettye, 14317
Collin, Robert W., 5477, 14488
Collins, Donald E., 1403
Collins, Glenn, 9179
Collins, John G., 6118
Collins, Patricia H., 6760, 12953-12956,
    14318-14319
Collins, Sharon M., 58, 1746, 11212
Collins, Timothy, 3609
Collison, Michele N-K, 4474-4477
Collo, Martin J., 2008, 3178
Colon, Alan K., 4478
Colon, Alice, 5710
Colon Morera, Jose J., 2009
Colon-Tarrats, Nelson L., 3610
Colten, Craig E., 5478
Colvin, Richard Lee, 12675
Comas-Diaz, Lillian, 8379, 14401, 14320-14321
Combs, M., 2293
Combs, Ron, 2594
Comer, J., 2293
Comer, James P., 1294, 3611-3613, 5602-5603
Conable, Charlotte W., 4480
Conarroe, Joel, 4481
Conciatore, Jacqueline, 10581
Condit, Celeste M., 8488
Condor, Susan, 8381
Cone, James H., 12676
Conklin, Paul, 4483
Conley, Darlene J., 4484
Conn, Stephen, 8732
Connell, R.W., 3617
Connelly, Michael, 12581
Conner, Constance, 10747
Connolly, Catherine R., 2891
Connolly, Ed, 13628
Connolly, Michael B., 9549
Connolly, Walter B., 4762
Conot, Robert, 9381
Conover, P.J., 1404
Conrad, Cecilia A., 3181
Conrad, Clifton F., 4485-4486
Conrad, John P., 2294
Conroy, Sarah B., 659
Conser, Walter H., Jr., 6908
Constantine, J.M., 4487
Conte, Christine, 8719
Conti, Gina, 4488-4489
Controneo, Ross R., 8213
Conway, Claire, 2854
Conwill, Giles, 12677-12678
Conyers, James E., 11481
Conyers, John, Jr., 2295, 8733
Conzen, Kathleen N., 10749, 12401
Cook, Anthony E., 12402, 12679
Cook, Blanche Wiesen, 2951, 4490
Cook, Fred J., 7797
Cook, S., 1168

Cook, Stuart W., 8734
Cookson, P.W., 3618
Cooney, Mark, 2892, 8735
Cooney, Rosemary S., 5704
Coontz, Stephanie, 5604
Cooper, Andrew W., 9595
Cooper, Arnold, 660, 9859
Cooper, Christine G., 2893
Cooper, Donald G., 2595
Cooper, Eric, 3619
Cooper, John M., Jr., 10198
Cooper, Kenneth J., 9860, 10750, 11482
Cooper, Marc, 7523, 11483
Cooper, Peter, 1297
Cooper, Phillip J., 7120
Cooper, Richard, 6124-6125
Cooper, R.S., 6123
Cooper, Sandra E., 4490
Cooper, Wayne, F., 661
Cooter, Roger, 6349
Cope, Nancy R., 6126
Cope, William, 10883
Coplon, Jeff, 12525
Copp, D., 3182
Corbett, Michael, 12058
Corcoran, James, 12526
Cordasco, Francesco, 1748, 7524
Cordero, Laura A., 8382
Cordova, Teresa, 14324
Corevan, James, 498
Corfman, Tom, 60, 2296, 8736, 11484
Coriden, James A., 12957
Corman, Hope, 6127
Cormoni-Huntley, J., 6128
Cornelison, Alice, 3620
Cornelius, Janet D., 1527, 3621
Cornelius, Wayne A., 7525-7527, 7549
Cornell, Stephen, 2113, 6762-6763, 8214,
    11485
Cornely, Paul, 6129
Corner, T., 10751
Cornfield, D.B., 7914
Cornwall, Richard R., 2894
Corrado Guerrero, Rafael, 3183
Corrin, Lisa G., 6764
Corsi, Jerome R., 13711
Cortes, C., 9861
Cortes, Carlos E., 9862, 12680
Cortese, Anthony J.P., 61, 5605, 11336
Cortez, Albert, 4219
Cortner, Richard C., 8737
Cortright, David, 10415
Corvin, Sue A., 13890
Corwin, Miles, 7528, 9382, 10319
Cosca, C., 3818
Cose, Ellis, 62-63, 1935, 7529, 9863
Costa, D. Margaret, 13255
Costanzo, Angelo, 9180
Costrell, Robert, 10752

Cotterill, Robert S., 5853
Cottle, Simon, 9864
Cotto, Lillian, 8215
Cotton, Jeremiah, 2895, 3184-3186, 5606
Cottrol, Robert J., 8738-8740
Couch, Barry A., 14013
Couch, J.B., 6098
Coughlin, Dan, 11486
Coughlin, Ellen K., 7697, 10753, 12403
Coulibaly, M., 7121, 7167
Coulon, John R., 3622
Coulson, R., 10754
Coulter, Robert T., 8216
Coulton, Claudia J., 3187
Couper, Kristin, 11047
Courlander, Harold, 662
Couto, Richard A., 1528, 6765
Cover, Robert M., 8741
Covington, James W., 6766, 10320
Covington, Jeanette, 2297
Cowan, William, 12645
Coward, John M., 9865
Cowden, Jonathan A., 2633
Cox, Cherise, 14325
Cox, Lawanda, 6767
Cox, Oliver C., 967, 12404
Cox, Stephanie Ann, 11487
Cox, Taylor, Jr., 8071
Cox, Ted, 9866
Coyle, Daniel, 7122
Coyle, Laurie, 7915
Crabb, Beth, 2298
Crader, D.C., 6130
Craige, Betty Jean, 8421, 8645, 10756-10758
Crain, Robert L., 2596-2598
Cramer, James C., 6131
Crane, Jonathan, 5622, 5801-5802
Crane, M., 12432
Crane, Paul, 14014
Cranor, Carl, 2896
Cratty, Lark, 5607
Crawford, Elizabeth M., 2357
Crawford, James, 8374, 8383-8384, 8415,
    8451, 8461, 8533, 8545
Crawford, Samuel D., 13808
Crawford, Vicki L., 1529, 14326
Cray, Robert E., Jr., 3188
Creel, Margaret W., 12681
Creighton-Zollar, Ann, 6132
Crenshaw, Albert B., 7368
Crenshaw, Kimberle, 2897-2898, 8742, 11842,
    12405, 12958
Crespi, Roberto S., 10348
Cresswell, Stephen, 13213
Cress-Welsing, Frances, 12406
Crew, Louie, 7399
Criley, Richard, 13629
Cripps, Thomas, 9867
Crisafulli, Chuck, 7400

Crist, Alan N., 4492
Cristobal, Hope Alvarez, 1936
Critchlow, Donald T., 7916
Critzer, John W., 247
Crocker, Jennifer, 12273
Crocker, Linda, 13809
Crockett, Bernice N., 6133-6134
Crockett, Norman L., 919
Cromartie, John, 10321
Cromwell, Adelaide M., 387, 1749
Cromwell, Brian A., 7123
Cronin, Mary E., 1298
Cronon, William, 8217
Crooks, James B., 9458
Crosby, Alfred W., Jr., 6768
Crosby, Faye J., 27, 55, 64-65, 2212, 2899,
    14158
Cross, Dorothy, 4493
Cross, Harry, 2900
Cross, Ira B., 5327
Cross, P.S., 12697
Cross, Robert D., 4494
Cross, Theodore, 4495-4496
Cross, William E., Jr., 5608, 12274, 14489
Croteau, David, 10005
Crouch, Barry A., 9692, 13114
Crouch, Stanley, 9868-9869, 14490
Crouse, James, 13810
Croutch, Albert, 7124
Crow, Jeffrey J., 6769, 7803, 9636
Crow Dog, Mary, 663
Crowley, J.J., 6135
Crowley, Tony, 8385
Crowther, Edward R., 3624
Cruickshank, J.K., 6142, 6473
Crum, Steven J., 4497-4499
Crummell, Alexander, 12682, 14491
Cruse, Harold W., 968, 11488-11489
Crutchfield, Robert D., 2274
Cruz, Anne J., 9587
Cruz, Laura, 1170
Cruz, R.D., 5410
Cruz, Robert, 9870
Cruz, Takash P., 11490
Cruz, Wilfredo, 2114-2115
Csikszentmihalyi, Mihaly, 10050
Cuban, Larry, 3625
Cubillos, Herminia L., 7125
Cuciti, Peggy, 3189
Cudd, Mike, 9871
Cudjoe, Selwyn R., 969
Culberson, William C., 14015-14016
Culbertson, Amy, 10521
Cullen, Holly, 8743
Culp, Jerome M., Jr., 2901, 8744-8746
Culver, J.H., 2299
Culverson, Donald R., 12241
Cumbler, John T., 9576
Cummings, Eric, 2300

Cummings, L.L., 135
Cummins, Densil H., 9447
Cummins, James, 8386, 10760
Cunnigen, Donald, 5372, 11134
Cunningham, Bill, 664, 4500
Cunningham, James S., 14327
Cunningham, Jo Ann, 4501-4502
Cunningham, Valerie, 9574
Curet, Jose, 13115
Curran, Jeanne, 66
Curran, J.W., 6136
Curran, Thomas J., 7530
Curriden, Mark, 7798
Currie, James T., 8747
Currie, Janet, 6137, 12959
Curry, Barbara K., 67
Curry, G. David, 2301, 10382
Curry, Richard O., 13630, 13762
Curry-Swann, Lynne, 2902
Curti, Merle, 13631
Curtis, Lynn A., 8748
Curtis, Michael, 499, 5069
Cushman, John H., Jr., 5480-5481, 7126-7128
Cutler, S.J., 12059
Cutlip, Scott M., 7799
Cutter, Charles R., 6770
Cutter, S.L., 5482
Cvornyek, Robert L., 5757
Czuchlewski, Paul E., 12683

D'Adderio, Mercedes, 9872
Dadisman, M., 12139
Dagodag, William T., 7129
Dagum, Camilo, 3190
Dahlback, Olof, 2903
Dajani, Souad, 500
Dalal, Farhad, 12322
D'Alessio, Stewart J., 501
Daley, Yvonne, 9721
Dallek, G., 6138, 6641
Dalton, Harlon L., 6139
Dalton, Michelle R., 4503
Dalton, Raymond A., 4504
Daly, Charles U., 3626, 9116
Daly, Kathleen, 2302, 5609
D'Amato, Anthony, 8387
D'Ambrosio, U., 10762
Damrell, Joseph, 5854
Dana, Richard D., 13811
Dane, Perry, 4505
Daneshvary, Nasser, 7531
Danforth, John C., 68
D'Angelli, Anthony R., 4506
Daniel, Cletus E., 69, 7918-7920
Daniel, J.L., 8389
Daniel, Leon, 3191
Daniel, Michael M., 7206
Daniel, Pete, 5758
Daniels, Douglas H., 9383

Daniels, George M., 1171
Daniels, Harvey A., 8390
Daniels, Jo Ann, 7921
Daniels, Lee A., 10416
Daniels, Roger, 2194, 7532-7533, 9432
Danielse, Dan, 8749
Danigelis, Nicholas L., 11491, 12059
Dannier, Mona J.E., 13869
Dansby, Mickey R., 10386
Dansicker, A.M., 70
Dantley, Michael, 12448
D'Antonio, Michael, 6140-6141, 11492
Danziger, Sheldon H., 3192-3194, 6602
Dao, James, 9597
Dardanoni, V., 1751
Darden, Joe T., 3195-3196, 7130-7132, 12140
Darder, Antonia, 10763
Dargis, Manohla, 9873-9874
Darity, William A., 350, 665, 2303, 3067,
       3158, 3197, 3432-3433, 5610-5611, 5855,
       5896, 8135, 14492
Darling, Juanita, 3627, 7534
Darling-Hammond, Linda, 3552, 3628-3631
Darnell, Frank, 3632
Darron, George H., Jr., 10764
Dart, John, 12684
Dash, Steven, 2599
Datcher-Loury, Linda, 3633
Dates, Jannette L., 9875
Daubman, K.A., 13891
Daula, Thomas, 10417
Dauphin, Gary, 9876
Dauphine, James G., 14017
Davenport, C., 10509
Davenport, Suzanne, 3995
David, Hilda B., 14328
David, Linda, 874
David, Mike, 8218
David, Paul A., 6615
David, Richard, 6125
Davidson, Cathy N., 4507, 8573, 9233
Davidson, Chandler, 1530, 11493-11496, 11601
Davidson, Howard A., 1292
Davidson, Jeanette R., 13812
Davidson, Joe, 12103
Davidson, Osha G., 5803
Davidson, P., 6142
Davidson-Podgorny, G., 2706
Davies, Alan, 12685
Davies, Christie, 7401-7402
Davies, Mark, 666
Davies, Susan, 4425
Davila, A., 71, 2866, 3198, 8391
Davis, A.A., 5612
Davis, Angela Y., 5613, 8750
Davis, Benjamin O., Jr., 667, 10418
Davis, C.G., 6143
Davis, Charles T., 668
Davis, Chester, 9877

Davis, Christopher H., 72
Davis, Cyprian, 12686-12687
Davis, David Brion, 13632
Davis, De Witt, Jr., 11263
Davis, D.S., 970
Davis, F. James, 12141
Davis, Fania, 5613
Davis, Frank Marshall, 669
Davis, Gwenn, 670
Davis, Henry V., 9878
Davis, J.S., 4508
Davis, Jack E., 14018-14019
Davis, James A., 12060, 13554
Davis, James J., 14614
Davis, James K., 13633
Davis, J.E., 13256
Davis, Jefferson, Mrs., 14218
Davis, John A., 2304
Davis, John F., 11497
Davis, Karen, 6144-6145
Davis, Kenneth E., 12066
Davis, Laurel R., 13257
Davis, Lenwood G., 14615-14616
Davis, Leroy, Jr., 671
Davis, M., 3292
Davis, Marcia, 5483
Davis, Marilyn A., 11498
Davis, Martha F., 2904
Davis, Michael D., 672
Davis, Mike, 5484, 6831, 8103, 9384-9387,
    9573, 10582, 14020
Davis, Ray, 434
Davis, Susan E., 8219
Davis, Theodore J., Jr., 11499
Davis, Thulani, 9879
Davison, Donald L., 11500
Dawes, Robyn M., 3199
Dawidowicz, L.S., 502
Dawkins, Marvin P., 3518
Dawley, Alan, 8078
Dawson, Michael C., 11501
Day, Anthony, 11213
Day, Barbara, 9880
Day, Dawn, 1299
Day, Gordon M., 8220
de Albuquerque, Klaus, 2012
De Avila, E.H., 8392
De Bates, Estelle, 11502
De Bona, Joseph, 2600
De Fina, Robert H., 3390
De Freitas, Gregory, 13936
De Graaf, Lawrence B., 6771
De Groot, Joanna, 8393
de Guzman, Mila, 14021
De Hoog, Ruth H., 12251
De Jong, David H., 3634
de la Garza, Rodolfo O., 11503-11504, 12061
De La Rosa, Denise, 3635
de la Rosa, Mario, 6146

De La Rosa Salazar, Denise, 3334
de la Torre, Adela, 4509
De Laney, Theodore C., Jr., 9724
De Leon, Arnoldo, 3636, 4178, 7016, 9688,
    9693-9696, 12062
De Maille, Raymond J., 2116
De Monaco, Mary Kim, 7535
De Nevi, Donald P., 6772
De Nicolo, David, 9881
De Palma, Anthony, 3637, 4510-4517, 9181
De Parle, Jason, 1755, 2305, 3203-3204, 3638,
    5804, 6147-6148, 7133-7135, 7698-7699,
    7926, 8221, 10419-10420, 12063
De Rose, David J., 10421
De Santis, J.P., 3639, 14022
De Van, William A., 4518
De Vergee, Winston W., 10422
De Vesa, S.A., 6149
de Vise, Daniel, 12527
de Vise, Pierre, 14159
De Vitis, Joseph L., 4230
De Vore, Donald E., 3640
de Vries, Hilary, 9882
De Witt, Karen, 2601, 4519, 8394, 8751,
    10322-10323
De Young, A.J., 3641
Deal, Douglas, 5775
Deal, J. Douglas, 10583
Deale, Frank, 73
Deanda, R.M., 13937
Deane, Glenn D., 7345
Deapen, R.E., 6310
Dearden, I.F.M., 2905
Deaux, Kay, 4576
Deberg, Betty A., 12960
Debo, Angie, 8752
Debo, Dan, 13634
Debouzy, Marianne, 1438
DeBrizzi, John, 7922
Deck, Allan, 12688
Deck, Allan Fiqueroa, 12689
Decker, Cathleen, 11505
Deconde, Alexander, 6773
DeCrow, Karen, 8753
Dedman, Bill, 7136
Deeb, Norma Jean, 2602
Deer, Ada, 5856
Deere, Beth, 2834
Dees, Morris, 1531, 7800, 12528-12529
Defeis, Elizabeth F., 2306
Defour, D.C., 4520
Defreitas, G., 7923
Degh, Linda, 12961
Degler, Carl N., 12323, 12407
DeGoede, Martyn P.M., 13489
DeHart, Jane Sherman, 12962
Dehavenson, Anna Lou, 3201
Dei, G.J.S., 10765
Dejoie, Carolyn M., 4521

Del Castillo, Adelaida R., 14455
del Valle, Manuel, 2013, 2907, 8395
Delage, Denys, 6774
Delaney, Elizabeth A., 673
Delaney, Paul, 6151, 11506, 14493
Delaney, Sarah, 673
Delany, B., 3642
Delatorre, A., 1902
Delehanty, Randolph S., 12627
DeLeon, Arnoldo, 3202
Delgado, Hector L., 7924
Delgado, Richard, 74, 1532, 1753, 4522-4525,
    7701, 8754-8760, 11507, 14494
Deloria, Philip, 5485
Deloria, Vine, Jr., 3643, 5846, 5857-5859,
    8216, 8761-8762, 11135
Demallie, Raymond J., 12835
Dembitz, Nanette, 8763
Dembner, Alice, 75, 4526-4527
Demeter, John, 9883
Demirturk, Emine L., 14329
Demo, David H., 12275, 12287
DeMott, Benjamin, 1754
Denard, Carolyn, 674
Denby, Charles, 7925
Denevan, William, 6775
Denison, D.C., 7403
Denlinger, Ken, 13258
Denning, Michael, 10766
Dennis, Homer, 1739
Dennis, Lawrence, 4528
Dennis, R.M., 5747, 8170, 12254
Dennis, Thomas, 12252
Dent, David J., 3644
Dentler, Robert A., 3645
Denton, Nancy A., 1836, 7137-7138, 7251-
    7252
Denton, Virginia L., 3646-3647
Derickson, A., 6152
Derman-Sparks, Louise, 435, 13892
Derricotte, Cheryl P., 7139
Dershowitz, Alan M., 76, 503-504, 10767
Desena, J.N., 7141
Detlefsen, Robert R., 1533-1534
Detweiler, Philip F., 6776
Deuchler, Jason C., 13893
Deutsch, Claudia H., 3649
Deutsch, Herman J., 8222
Deutsch, J., 2307
Deutsch, M.E., 2308
Deutsch, S., 7927
Deutsch, Sarah J., 14330
Devaney, B., 6153
Devens, Carol, 6777
Deverell, William, 6778, 9388
Devine, Patricia G., 13408-13410
Devins, Neal, 77, 8396
Devlin, George A., 10324
Devlin, Richard F., 12964

Devoual, Regina, 11508
DeVries, Hilary, 675-676, 9182-9183
Dew, Tammy, 13835
Dewart, Janet, 1937-1939, 3389, 5374, 11621,
    14495
Dewing, Rolland, 7928
DeWitt, Karen, 9449
Dex, Shirley, 2908
Dexter, L.A., 2014
Deyle, Steven, 13116-13117
Dezell, Maureen, 9184
Dhand, Harry, 3651
Di Chiro, Giovanna, 5486
Diab, Lufty N., 13411
Diamant, Anita, 9185
Diamond, E.L., 6149, 6155
Diamond, Raymond T., 3652, 8740
Diamond, S.A., 12530
Diamond, Sara, 4530-4531, 7537, 11509, 12531
Diamond, Sigmund, 13635-13636
Diamond, Stanley, 2909
Diawara, M., 9884
Diaz, Jaime, 13259-13260
Diaz Soler, Luis M., 13118
Diaz-Knauf, K., 5834
Dickens, Nicole P., 2603
Dickerson, Sandra A., 9885
Dickinson, Leslie K., 12963
Dickinson, S.L.J., 3653, 12896
Dickman, Howard, 1654, 10768
Dickson, Lynda, 4466, 5614
Dickstein, Morris, 4532
Didion, Joan, 2309
Diedrich, Maria, 9311
Diegmueller, Karen, 3654, 7538
Diehl, Joanne Feit, 10769
Dietz, James L., 2015, 6779
Diffie, Bailey W., 2016
Diffie, Justine W.F., 2016
Diggins, John Patrick, 10770
Dill, Augustus G., 7934
Dill, Bonnie T., 5615
Dillon, Merton L., 13119
Dillon, Sam, 3655, 8397
Dillow, Gordon, 13412
Dilts, D.A., 13938
DiMaggio, Paul, 14496
Dimas, Pete R., 9357
Dimeo, J., 10285
Dingerson, Michael R., 78, 4533
Dinges, Barnaby, 6156
Dinkins, Davis N., 11510
Dinnerstein, Leonard, 505, 972
D'Innocenzo, Michael, 7539, 7664, 13336
Dinwoodie, D.H., 7929
Dionisopoulos, G.N., 8429
Dippie, Brian W., 12064
DiPrete, T.A., 1785
Diringer, Joel, 6157

Dittmer, John, 1535
Dix, Linda S., 12897
Dixon, Bob, 9186
Dixon, H., 13959
Dixon, Heriberto, 7540
Dixon, Phil, 13261
Dobbins, J.E., 12201
Dobie, Kathy, 5616, 12532, 14331
Dobkowski, Michael N., 506, 2829, 11068, 14006
Dobrowolsky, Alexander Z., 12964
Dobson, A., 6543
Doctorow, E.L., 8764
Dodd, D.K., 9887
Dodoo, F.N.A., 3205, 7541
Doherty, Julian C., 3206
Doherty, Robert, 8223
Doig, Stephen K., 7164
Dolan, Jay P., 12689-12691
Dolan, Maura, 2310, 13637
Dolgin, J.L., 12408
Dometrius, Nelson C., 13813
Domhoff, G. William, 11512
Domkin, Ellen, 9187
Donahue, John J., III, 12965
Donald, Leland, 13120
Donaldson, Gary A., 10423
Donato, R., 2605
Donelan, Richard W., 3656
Donnelly, Samuel J.M., 2311
Donner, Frank, 13638-13639
Donohue, J.J., 2913
Donohue, John, Jr., III, 1536-1537
Dononhue, J.J., 3068
Dorf, Michael C., 9076
Dorgan, Howard, 8433, 8512, 12692
Dorman, James H., 13414-13415
Dorn, Edwin, 10424
Dornbusch, Sanford M., 5738
Dornfeld, Maude, 2385
Dorris, Michael, 13416
Dorsey, Carolyn, 4535
Dos Santos, Joel R., 12142
Doten, Patti, 13417
Dotson, David D., 5860
Dougal, April S., 9648
Dougherty, C.J., 6159
Dougherty, Kevin J., 4536-4537
Douglas, Kirk, 9888
Douglas, M.A. Dutton, 14401
Douglas, Marcia L., 5411
Douglas, Robert L., 13121
Douglass, Phyllis B., 4538
Dove, Dorothy E.N., 3657
Dovidio, John F., 12611, 13448
Dowd, Gregory E., 1940, 6780
Dowd, Maureen, 9889
Dowden, Frieda S., 12065
Dowdle, Michael W., 8766

Dowdy, Lewis C., Jr., 4539
Dowdy, Zachary R., 8767
Dowell, Michael A., 6160
Downey, Dennis B., 14023
Downing, John D.H., 9890
Doyle, Anne M., 3658
Doyle, Don H., 6781
Doyle, James, 9891
Doyle, Laura, 9188
Doyle, Susan B., 10425
Dozier, Jack, 8213, 8224
Drago, Edmund L., 3659, 4540, 11513, 13122
Drake, St. Clair, 677, 6782
Draper, A., 7930-7931
Draper, Alan, 1538
Draper, Anne, 4541
Draper, Hal, 4541
Drazen, Shelley M., 3660
Dreier, P., 2117
Dreifus, Claudia, 6161
Drescher, Seymour, 3216, 6877, 12774, 12878, 13189, 14542
Dressler, William W., 6162, 8649
Drew, David, 13814
Driessen, P., 14160
Drinnon, Richard, 6783, 12221
Drucker, Ernest, 6163
Drummond, Tammerlin, 4542, 13418
Drury, Bob, 14053
D'Souza, Dinesh, 4543-4545
Du Bois, Ellen C., 6784, 6988, 14332
Du Bois, W.E.B., 1405, 3129, 6785, 7404, 7933-7934, 14333
Du Brow, Rick, 9892
Du Chateau, Andre P., 6786
Duany, Jorge, 6787, 9189
Duany, Luis, 1358
Duban, James, 10773
Duberman, Martin B., 678
Dubin, Corey, 8225
Dubin, Steven C., 13419
Dubin, Zan, 9893
Dublin, Marshall F., 7932
DuBois, Rachel D., 13420
Duby, Jacqueline L., 5639
Ducheneaux, Karen, 8263
Duclos, Nitya, 12966
Dudley, David Lewis, 679
Dudley, Michael K., 11136
Dudziak, Mary L., 1539, 2606-2607
Duffey, Nelda S., 7435
Duffy, Bernard K., 507
Dugas, Carroll J., 2608
Duggan, Paul, 8768
Dugger, Karen, 6164, 14334
Duin, Virginia, 3207
Duits, T., 2917
Duke, Lynne, 974, 1540, 4546, 5617, 5861, 7801, 12693

Dukes, R.L., 12276
Dulaney, W. Marvin, 1541, 7935
Duleep, H.O., 6165
Dull, H. Bruce, 6034
Dummett, Ann, 12967
Dumont, L., 12408
Dunbar, Anthony P., 9550
Dunbar, Leslie W., 278, 975
Dunbar, Paul Laurence, 9190
Dunbar, Stephen B., 3902
Dunbar Ortiz, Roxanne, 8226, 11137, 14219
Duncan, Greg J., 3208, 5618-5619, 13934
Duncan, James R., 11514
Duncan, John D., 13123
Duncan, Kevin C., 3209
Duncan, Russell, 10426
Duncan, Tony, 14644
Dundes, A., 8398
Dunham, Katherine, 680
Dunkle, Margaret C., 6166
Dunlap, David W., 6788
Dunmore, Charlotte J., 14617
Dunn, Ashley, 5862, 8399-8400, 9389
Dunn, James R., 4547
Dunne, Bill, 2312
Dunne, John Gregory, 5863
Dunne, John R., 2609
Dunson, Bruce H., 2901
DuPont, Patricia, 7936
DuPree, Sherry S., 12694
Duran, C., 4548
Duran, Joseph D., 2914
Durand, Roger, 5864
Durham, Joseph T., 4549
Durham, W.C., Jr., 8769
Dusenberry, Verne, 3210
Duster, Troy, 4550, 7702, 12409
Dutka, Elaine, 9894
Dutton, D.B., 6167-6168
Duyme, M., 7695
Dvorak, Katherine L., 12695
Dworkin, Anthony G., 13421
Dworkin, Gerald, 7690
Dworkin, Ronald, 8770-8772
Dworkin, Rosalind J., 13421
Dye, Gloria J., 8401
Dye, Nancy S., 6807, 14342, 14350, 14426
Dye, Peggy, 12696
Dyer, Brainerd, 11138, 11515
Dyer, Conrad M., 4551
Dyer, James, 9697, 10584
Dykstra, Robert R., 9506
Dysart, Jane E., 6789, 14335
Dyson, Michael E., 681, 1941, 9895-9896,
    11139-11140, 11516, 12410, 12968

Eagles, Charles W., 1499
Eagly, Alice H., 13422
Eakin, Paul J., 682-683

Eaklor, Vicki L., 13124
Early, Gerald, 13262, 14497
Easterbrook, Gregg, 6169
Eastman, Dale, 1172
Easton, Nina J., 7405, 9390, 9897
Eatwell, Roger, 11517
Eber, Linda, 508-509
Eberhard, D.R., 3662
Eberstadt, Nicholas, 6170
Eberstein, Issac W., 6171
Ebright, Malcolm, 8227
Eccles, Jacquelynne S., 4957
Echewa, Willie W., 3663
Eckford, Elizabeth, 2610
Eckholm, Erik, 6172, 6790
Edari, Ronald S., 1846, 10703
Edds, Margaret, 11518-11519
Edelman, J.B., 8773
Edelman, Marian Wright, 6173
Edelman, Peter B., 1300, 3213, 4552
Edelsky, C., 8402
Edgar, D., 11520
Edgcomb, Gabrielle S., 4553
Edgerton, Carol, 14024
Edin, Kathryn, 3269
Edland, Roy E., 8228
Edley, Christopher, Jr., 8774
Edmond, Alfred, Jr., 1173
Edmond, Beverly C., 79
Edmunds, R. David, 6791
Edmundson, William A., 2313
Edsall, Mary D., 11524
Edsall, Thomas B., 11141, 11521-11524
Edwards, Audrey, 2611-2612, 14498
Edwards, Don, 5865, 13640
Edwards, Ellen, 1174
Edwards, Harry, 13263-13264
Edwards, J., 13922
Edwards, J.E., 10427
Edwards, Jeffrey B., 2119
Edwards, John, 80-81
Edwards, Karen L., 6174
Edwards, Larry G., 4555
Edwards, Ralph, 3664
Edwards, Richard, 7882
Edwards, W.F., 8403
Edwards, William J., 684
Egan, Catherine, 14593
Egan, Timothy, 5487, 6175, 9654, 10774,
    13641
Egar, Emmanuel E., 4556
Egerton, John, 3665
Eggebeen, David J., 5620
Egger, M., 6584
Eggers, M.L., 3214
Eggers, Mitchell L., 3300, 5813
Ehrenberg, Ronald G., 10, 4557
Ehrenreich, Barbara, 6176, 10776, 14220
Ehrenreich, J., 6176

Ehrenstein, D., 9898
Ehrlich, Gretel, 9191
Ehrlich, Howard J., 4558-4559, 7406, 13423, 14025-14026
Eichelberger, Hubert L., 9899
Eichorn, D., 4017
Eickhoff, Harold W., 976
Einspruch, Eric L., 13815
Eischenbroich, Donata, 7542
Eisenberg, N., 13894
Eisenhart, Margaret A., 4747
Eisenman, Russell., 4560-4562, 12533
Eisenstein, Z., 82
Eisinger, Chester E., 8229
Eitzen, Stanley D., 13265-13266, 13342
Ekberg, Carl J., 13125
Ekland-Olson, Sheldon, 2314
Ekstrom, Ruth B., 3887
Elain, Ada M., 4563
Elam, Julia C., 4564
Eleazer, R.B., 3666
Elias, Robert, 2315
Eliza Colon, Sylvia M., 2017
Elkins, Stanley M., 6792
Ellement, John, 14027
Ellenberg, George B., 8404
Elliff, John T., 8775
Elliot, Jeffrey, 685
Elliot, Roger, 3667, 7703
Elliott, R.T., 11214
Elliott, Stuart, 1175
Ellis, C.M.D., 13642
Ellis, Dean S., 8405
Ellis, Deborah, 241, 3037
Ellis, G.W., 12277
Ellis, John M., 10777
Ellis, Joseph V., 977
Ellis, Mary L., 14028
Ellis, R.J., 9192
Ellis, Rex M., 6793
Ellis, Trey, 14499
Ellis, Walter, 820
Ellis, William F., 10780
Ellison, Christopher G., 2120, 11525, 12822
Ellison, J., 665, 3215, 3432
Ellison, Mary, 2915
Ellman, Yisrael, 10585
Ellsworth, Elizabeth, 10778
Ellsworth, Nancy J., 3714, 8352
Ellwood, David T., 1270, 3265, 5621-5622, 5811
Elmore, Charles J., 4566
Elrich, Marc, 13424
Elshtain, Jean B., 10779
Eltis, David, 13126-13127
Ely, James W., Jr., 18, 2593, 8776
Ely, Melvin Patrick, 9900
Emanuel, Irvin, 6177, 14336
Emerson, Michael O., 1756

Emerson, T.E., 12697
Emery, Garnet K., 7543
Emi, Frank, 2195
Emihovich, Catherine, 11337
Emmons, David M., 9567
Emmons, L., 6178
Emsellem, Maurice, 13816
Enders, Calvin, 7802
Engelberg, Stephen, 7544
Engels, Chris, 83
Engerman, Stanley L., 3216, 6794, 13200
England, Paula, 2916
Engle, Karen 8749
Engle, Ron, 9193
Engleberg, Stephen, 9901
Engram, E., 5623
Engstrom, C.M., 4567
Engstrom, Richard L., 11526-11527
Enriquez, Sam, 7143
Entman, Robert M., 9902-9903
Entwisle, Doris R., 3668
Ephros, Paul H., 13976
Epp, Charles R., 1568
Epperson, Sharon, 13895
Epperson, Terrence W., 9725
Epps, Edgar G., 4570, 4680
Epps, John S., 4571
Epps, P., 3669
Epstein, Barbara, 4572, 11528
Epstein, E.H., 4573
Epstein, Jason, 8777, 9598
Epstein, Joyce, 2613-2614
Epstein, Kitty Kelly, 10780
Epstein, Lawrence J., 7407
Epstein, Richard A., 1542, 5866
Epstein, Robin, 5489
Epturoy, Annie O., 9194
Erdoes, Richard, 663
Erhogbe, Edward O., 388
Erickson, Doug, 4574
Erickson, Joseph L., 10781
Erickson, Nancy S., 12969
Erie, Steven P., 11529
Ernst, Friedhelm, 14500
Ernst, G.J., 5490
Ertel, R., 14501
Ervin, A.M., 11530
Ervin, J.E., 4575
Esar, Evan, 7408
Escobar, Edward J., 5867
Escobar, Elizam, 8407
Escobar, Gabriel, 5868, 14029
Escoffier, Jeffrey, 10782
Escot, Paul G., 9635
Escott, Paul, 7803, 13030
Eskew, Glenn T., 1543
Espenshade, T.J., 7545, 7615
Esper, Mark, 6795
Espina, Marina E., 9514

Espinosa, D.J., 84
Espinosa, J. Manuel, 9584
Espinosa, Ruben, 3671
Espinoza, Leslie G., 85
Espiritu, Y., 12446
Essayan, Susan, 10492
Essed, Philomena, 8408, 12411, 14337
Essex, Max, 6179
Estrada, Leobadro F., 6796
Estrich, Susan, 12970
Etaugh, C., 2917
Ethier, Kathleen, 4576
Ettema, James S., 9904-9905
Etter-Lewis, Given, 14338
Etulain, Richard W., 6953, 6986
Evans, Arthur S., Jr, 3434, 6797, 9459, 14221, 14231
Evans, Charles T., 9195
Evans, Christopher, 3672
Evans, David L., 4578, 6798
Evans, Linda J., 12698
Evans, M.O., 3673
Evans, Ross A., 12324
Evanzz, Karl, 687
Evenson, Debra, 9906
Evera, S. Van, 3057
Everett, Kevin D., 11531
Exum, William H., 86
Eysenck, Hans J., 7704, 12278
Ezorsky, Gertrude, 87-88

Faber, R.J., 9907
Fabre, Genevieve, 6799, 9196
Fabricant, Florence, 11215
Fadaei-Tehrani, R., 2316
Fagan, J., 2317
Fagan, T.A., 13796
Faherty, William B., 4579
Faiman-Silva, Sandra L., 8230
Fainaru, Steve, 13267
Fainstein, Norman Q., 1757-1758, 3217
Fainstein, Susan S., 3217
Fair, Harole L., 12699
Fair, J.E., 9908
Fairbanks, Robert B., 7144
Fairchild, H.H., 3674
Fairchild, Halford H., 12325
Fairley, Charlestine R., 4581
Faith, Ellen S., 4582
Faithfull, Bayard, 4583
Falcon, Angelo, 11532-11533
Falk, Gerhard, 9909
Falk, W.W., 3218, 3343, 8095
Falkenberg, Loren, 13425
Fallows, Robert J., 4584
Faludi, Susan, 4585, 12971
Farber, David, 89, 9476-9477
Farber, M.A., 3675
Farber, Samuel, 9599

Farhi, Paul, 1176
Farkas, George, 3676-3677
Farley, Eva L., 9600
Farley, J.E., 7145-7146
Farley, Reynolds, 1759, 3139-3220, 3268, 6180-6181, 7147-7148, 7376, 12143, 12412, 14502
Farlow, Gale J., 7937
Farmelo, Laura B., 6837, 8854
Farmer, James, 1544
Farmer, Ruth, 4780
Farnes, Patricia, 12910, 13068
Farnum, Richard A., Jr., 4586-4588
Farquhar, Michael, 7804
Farr, James, 11216
Farrakhan, Louis, 979-980, 12700
Farrell, John A., 510
Farrell, Walter C., Jr., 4589
Farsy, Fouad A. Al-, 13426
Fass, Paula S., 3678
Fatemi, Khosrow, 3221
Faulk, Odie B., 9698
Fava, Eileen M., 2615
Fay, Elizabeth A., 5287
Fayer, Steve, 1573
Fayissa, Bichaka, 3225, 5624
Feagin, Joe R., 21, 1760, 1800, 2918, 4590, 7633, 12413, 12253
Feagins, Ken, 90
February, Vernon, 8409
Fecher, Charles A., 9197-9198
Fechter, Alan, 12898
Fede, Andrew T., 8779
Feder, J., 6182
Federici, Michael P., 11534
Fee, Elizabeth, 6334-6335
Feeley, M.M., 2318
Fehn, Bruce R., 7938
Feierman, Steven, 389
Feigelman, W., 12701
Fein, David J., 5870
Fein, Helen, 511, 12414
Feinberg, Renee, 3222
Feinberg, W.E., 92, 3331
Feiner, Susan, 2919, 3435
Feingold, Henry L., 512, 4591
Feingold, Michael, 9910
Feinlieb, Marsha, 6183
Feins, Judith, 7149
Feit, Marvin D., 6466
Felder, Cain Hope, 12702-12703
Felder, Henry E., 5625, 14161
Feldman, D.A., 6458, 6685
Feldman, D.C., 13950
Feldman, Egal, 513
Feldman, J.J., 6184
Feldman, K.D., 10784
Feldman, Paul, 8410
Feldman, Penny H., 4592

Feldman, S.M., 11535
Feldstein, Mark, 7150
Felice, Lawrence G., 3679
Fellman, Michael, 9562, 14222
Fellner, William, 7515
Felson, R.B., 2491
Felzer, Karen, 7546
Fender, Janet, 12972
Fendrich, James M., 688, 1406
Feng, Teresa, 8179
Fenier, Susan, 2888
Fennelly, K., 6185
Fenyo, Mario D., 3680
Feraca, Stephen E., 93, 5871
Ferdman, Bernardo M., 8411
Ferguson, Brian R., 13573
Ferguson, Earline Rae, 6186, 14339
Ferguson, Ronald F., 3681
Ferguson, Russell, 12499
Ferleger, Lou, 3223-3224, 8098, 13181
Fernandez, Celestino, 7409
Fernandez, Enrique, 8412, 9911
Fernandez, Ferdinand F., 2920
Fernandez, Joseph M., 8413, 14068
Fernandez, Raul, 13427
Fernandez, Roberto M., 4011
Fernandez, Ronald, 11142
Fernandez Cintron, Celia, 12973
Fernandez Mendez, Eugenio, 13128
Fernando, Suman, 12415
Feron, James, 4593
Ferrell, Claudine L., 14031
Ferrie, Joseph P., 7869, 14162
Ferris, William, 14037
Fessehatzion, Tekie, 3225, 5624
Feuchtwang, Stephen, 433
Feuer, M.J., 981
Ficarrotto, Thomas J., 12974
Fichtenbaum, Myrna, 7939
Fichtenbaum, Rudy, 12416
Ficocelli-Lepore, Sandra, 2616
Field, Christopher J., 6187
Field, Hubert S., 2921
Fields, Barbara J., 13129
Fields, Cheryl M., 4594
Fields, J., 7940
Fife, Brian L., 2617
Fife, M.D., 94
Fiffer, Steve, 1531, 12529
Figueroa, Loida, 14340
Figueroa, Luis A., 13130
Figueroa, Richard A., 13818
Fikes, Robert, 8414
Filbert, M. Shanara, 2319
Filer, J.E., 11536
Filippatos, Parisis, 1545
Filippelli, Ronald L., 7941
Fillmore, Lily Wong, 8415
Finch, Wilbur A., Jr., 7547

Finder, Alan, 95-96, 5872, 9601, 11537
Findlay, James F., Jr., 12704-12705
Fine, David, 13649
Fine, Gary A., 7805
Fine, Joyce, 9912
Fine, Sidney, 14032
Fineberg, Harvey V., 6188
Finegan, T. Aldrich, 5425-5426
Fineman, Howard, 11538
Fineman, Martha A., 5689, 8780
Finger, John R., 1407
Fingerhut, L.A., 2320
Fink, Gary M., 7942
Fink, Leon, 7943
Finkenbine, Roy E., 3682
Finkleman, Paul R., 1546, 5766-5777, 6800,
    7944, 8781-8784, 8906, 9602, 12706,
    13131-13135
Finklen, Myra, 4337
Finley, Randy, 5873
Finley, Stephanie A., 2618
Finn, Chester E., Jr., 97, 4595-4596
Finn, Peter, 2321
Finnegan, Terence R., 14033
Finnie, R.E., 5408
Finot, Jean, 12417, 12976
Finucane, T.E., 6189
Fiorentine, R., 11217
Firebaugh, Glenn, 12066
Firestone, David, 13428
Firestone, J.M., 10428
Firestone, W.A., 3684, 5626
First, Joan M., 3685
Fiscus, Ronald J., 98
Fish, Arthur, 8785
Fish, John, 2121
Fish, Stanley, 10785
Fishback, Price V., 3686, 5759, 8026, 8416
Fisher, Edith M., 9133
Fisher, G.M., 3226
Fisher, Ian, 9603
Fisher, J., 5690, 9392
Fisher, J. Walter, 6191
Fisher, James A., 11539
Fisher, John E., 5778
Fisher, Louis, 8786
Fisher, Robert, 2122-2123
Fisher, William W., III, 8787
Fishkin, Shelley F., 9199
Fishman, George M., 4763
Fishman, J.A., 8417
Fisk, Mark, 4598
Fiske, Edward B., 13819
Fiske, S.T., 13429
Fiss, Owen, 1547
Fitch, Robert, 11540
Fite, Gilbert C., 2124
Fits, Don, 455
Fitto, Alston, III, 9337

Fitz, Don, 8104
Fitzgerald, Michael W., 1177, 6801, 11541
Fitzpatrick, Joseph P., 2019, 3687, 12708
Fitzpatrick, Peter, 8789
Fitzpatrick, Robert B., 13430
Fitzpatrick, Sandra, 9450
Fitzsimmons, William, 4450
Fix, M., 7625
Fixico, Donald L., 1761, 5874
Flacks, D., 1408
Flagg, B.J., 8790
Flaherty, David H., 12938, 13650
Flaherty, Stacy A., 7945
Flake, Floyd, 11542
Flanagan, Sharon P., 14163
Flanagan, Thomas, 8231
Flanders, Todd R., 1548
Flanigan, Daniel J., 2322-2323
Fleischer, Wendy, 7207
Fleming, Cynthia G., 1549-1550, 4599
Fleming, Jacqueline, 4600
Fleming, John E., 6802
Fleming, Joseph E., 5875
Fleshman, C., 6192
Fletcher, Arthur A., 100
Fletcher, Marvin E., 10430-10431
Fletcher, Ronald, 7705
Flew, Antony, 12418
Flicker, Barbara, 2922, 3688
Flint, Anthony, 4601-4605, 7706, 10786
Flintall, V.L., 11249
Flinter, Jorge, 13136
Floerchinger, Teresa D., 2923
Flores, Caraballo, Eliut D., 9913
Flores, Estevan T., 3689
Flores, Henry, 2125
Flores, Juan, 10325
Flowerman, S., 13539
Flowers, Linda, 9633
Flowers, Ronald B., 2324-2325
Flowers, Sandra H., 9200
Floyd, Nubra E., 14618
Fluckey, Alan R., 8232
Flug, Michael, 1551, 7946
Fly, Jerry W., 9338
Flynn, George, Q., 10432
Flynn, J.R., 7707
Flynn, Kevin, 12535
Flynn, Michael S., 1178
Flynn, Sarah, 1573
Flynt, J. Wayne, 514, 14223-14225
Foamante, Jorge, 7549
Foderaro, Lisa W., 1304, 2924, 4606
Foehrenbach, Josie, 3690
Foerstel, Herbert N., 13652
Fogel, Norman, 589
Fogel, Robert W., 13137
Fogg, Neal, 3386
Fogleson, Steven, 8791

Folbre, Nancy, 12977-12978
Foley, Albert S., 12709-12711
Foley, Barbara, 9201
Foley, Douglas E., 3691, 9699-9700, 13268
Follett, R.S., 101
Folson, Franklin, 13939
Foner, Eric, 6803-6804, 8792, 11543
Foner, Henry, 4607
Foner, Philip S., 7947
Fong, E., 7253
Fong, Melanie, 12326
Fong, Rowera, 14619
Fong, Timothy P., 9393
Fontette, Francois de, 12419
Foote, Donna, 10066
Foote, Thelma W., 9604, 10787
Forbath, Jean, 1762, 3228
Forbes, Douglas, 6193
Forbes, Duncan, 8793
Forbes, E., 2020, 13138
Forbes, Jack D., 2021, 4608, 10586-10591
Forbes, Susan S., 8418
Ford, Andrea, 6194, 8794
Ford, Clyde W., 13896
Ford, Donna Y., 7708
Ford, Michael D., 3692
Ford, Royal, 1305
Forde, C. Daryll, 8233
Forde, Frank, 12899
Forde-Mazrui K., 5627
Fordham, Signithia M., 3693-3698
Foret, Michael J., 6805
Forman, James, Jr., 102, 11143
Formisano, Ronald P., 2619, 11544
Formwalt, Lee W., 14034
Forst, Brian, 2326
Forster, Imogen, 13431
Fort, Vincent D., 1552
Fortunati, Vita, 10788
Fortune, Robert, 6195
Forward, Susan, 3053
Fossett, M.A., 11218, 12067
Foster, E.C., 11545
Foster, Edward M., 1763
Foster, H.J., 5628
Foster, J., 7709
Foster, James C., 319, 7948
Foster, Lawrence, 10789
Foster, Lorn, 1912
Foster, L.S., 12018
Foster, M. Marie Booth, 9202
Foster, Michele, 11546
Foster, Morris W., 6806
Foster, Peter, 436
Foster, S., 5491
Fosu, Augustin K., 103, 14341
Fouquette, Danielle A., 3699, 13432
Foust, Brady, 10433
Fowler, Arlen L., 10434

Fowler, David H., 5629
Fowler, Don D., 13433
Fowler, G.A., 2925
Fowlie-flores, Fay, 14620
Fowlkes, Diane L., 14226
Fox, David J., 9915-9916
Fox, James G., 2327
Fox, Robert E., 10790
Fox, Stephen R., 2196, 13940
Fox-Genovese, Elizabeth, 689, 9203, 12712, 12721
Fraden, Reva, 9204
Frady, Marshall, 690
Fraga, Luis R., 4609
Frakes, George E., 9394
Frammolino, Ralph, 4610-4612, 9437
Frampton, George T., Jr., 5492
Frampton, Pamela M., 4613
Francis, Mark R., 12713
Franck, Michael, 2926
Franco, Jere, 3700, 10435-10436
Frank, Nyle C., 3701
Franke, Carrie, 4614
Franke, Katherine, 4615
Frankel, Charles, 12420
Frankel, David M., 3311
Frankel, L.M., 11547
Frankel, Mark S., 12900
Frankel, Noralee, 6807, 14342, 14350, 14426
Frankel, Sara, 4616
Frankenberg, Ruth A.E., 14227-14228
Franklin, H. Bruce, 9205
Franklin, James L., 12536, 12714-12716
Franklin, Jimmie L., 11548
Franklin, John Hope, 4617, 5779-5780, 6808-6810, 8795, 10437, 12653
Franklin, Joseph, 9742
Franklin, Raymond, 1764, 3436
Franklin, Stephen, 13434
Franklin, Vincent P., 2126, 14035
Franklin, V.P., 4618
Frantz, Douglas, 3702
Frantz, Ronald W., 6811
Frase, M.J., 3846
Fraser, C. Gerald, 9917
Fraser, Gertrude J., 6197
Fraser, James W., 11004, 14229
Fraser, Laura, 9918
Fraser, Nancy, 1409
Fratoe, Frank A., 1179
Frazier, C.E., 2328
Frederick, David C., 11549
Frederick, Kenneth L., 2927
Fredrickson, George M., 1765, 4617
Freed, David, 12537
Freedman, Alix M., 6198
Freedman, James O., 4620
Freedman, Marcia, 7949
Freedman, Samuel G., 3703, 9919, 12717

Freeman, Alan, 8797
Freeman, Harold P., 6398
Freeman, James M., 6812, 7550
Freeman, Jo, 1620, 8798
Freeman, Richard B., 2329, 2901, 3158-3159, 5405, 7551, 7950
Fregoso, Rosa Linda, 9920-9921
Frehill-Rowe, Lisa M., 9509, 9571
Freiband, S.J., 9134
Freilich, Robert H., 1553, 8799
Freiling, Harald, 515
Freitag, Sandra, 173
Fremon, David K., 11550-11551
French, Desiree, 9922
French, Lawrence, 5876
French, Mary Ann, 691, 1306, 9923, 11552, 12279, 12979
French, M.T., 6199
French, S., 104
Freshman, C., 2928
Freudenburg, W.R., 5493
Freudmann, Lillian C., 516
Freund, J., 428
Frey, Darcy, 13269
Frey, Sylvia R., 6813
Frey, W.H., 7148
Friar, Jerome, 12538
Frias, Albert, 2929
Frickey, P.P., 89, 2022
Frideres, James S., 10791
Fried, Charles, 105-106, 5576
Fried, Joseph P., 13653
Fried, Lewis, 859, 9206
Fried, Marc L., \7151
Fried, Marlene G., 6200
Friedelbaum, Stanley H., 8800
Friedenberg, Daniel M., 8234
Friedly, Michael, 692
Friedman, Emily, 6201
Friedman, Lawrence, 2330
Friedman, Lester D., 9924, 10217
Friedman, Milton, 9925
Friedman, Murray, 982
Friedman, Robert I., 7410, 11553, 13654-13655
Friedman, Robert J., 983-984
Friedman, Samuel R., 6202, 6496
Friend, Llerena B., 14036
Frisbee, John L., 10445
Frisbie, W. Parker, 6193
Frisby, Michael K., 11554-11556
Frison, Theodore H., 8235
Fritz, Sara, 6203
Frolik, Joe, 3704
Froman, Robert, 12145
Fromm, Harold, 9207
Frug, M.J., 8801
Frye, Charles A., 11296
Frye, Hardy, 2127
Fucciool, John J., 12421

Fuchs, Lawrence H., 7552, 11338
Fuchs, Richard L., 10438
Fuchs, Stephan A., 2930, 12422
Fuerst, J.S., 2620, 7152
Fuhrman, Susan, 5877
Fujioka, J.M., 7411
Fujiyama, Rodney M., 11557
Fukuda, Yoshiaki, 2197
Fukurai, Hiroshi, 8802-8804
Fulani, Lenora B., 11558, 12280, 12980
Fuller, Craig W., 8236
Fuller, Elizabeth, 7153
Fuller, R., 4622
Fullilove, M.T., 6651
Fullinwider, R.K., 10792
Fullwood, Sam, III, 1942-1943
Fultz, Michael, 3899
Funderburg, Lise, 5630
Funk, Nanette, 107
Furst, David, 13266
Furuseth, Owen J., 9634
Furuya, Jun, 8237
Fusco, Coco, 9926
Futrelle, David, 4623
Fyfe, James J., 5987-5988

Gabaccia, Donna, 7553, 14621
Gabe, J., 3705
Gabe, Li Anne C., 4624
Gabe, T., 3229
Gabel, Peter, 11560
Gabler, Neal, 985, 10793
Gabor, Thomas, 2460
Gabriel, Paul E., 11260
Gabriel, Stuart A., 7101, 7154
Gabriel, Susan L, 12981
Gadfield, Nicholas J., 7395, 7412
Gaertner, S.L., 13448, 13897
Gaerton, Samuel L., 12611
Gage, Matilda Joslyn, 11561
Gaines, Ernest J., 8805
Gaines, J., 9927
Gaines, Joseph H., 10794
Gaines, Kevin K., 1766
Gaines, W. Craig, 10439
Gaiter, Leonce, 1767
Galanis, Diane E., 693
Galarza, Ernesto, 7951-7953
Galbraith, Jane, 9928
Gale, Dennis E., 11643
Gale, Mary Ellen, 4625, 8806
Galenson, David W., 1496, 3170
Galishoff, Stuart, 6204
Gallart, Maria A., 3504
Gallaway, L., 13964
Gallegos, Bernardo P., 3706-3707
Gallen, David, 694, 708
Galliher, Ruth A., 5878-5879
Gallman, Robert E., 3230

Gallman, Vanessa, 1768
Galloway, F.J., 7710
Galloway, Russell W., 8807
Galst, Liz, 1554
Galster, George C., 108, 2582, 2890, 2931,
    7114, 7155-7163, 11319
Galston, W.A., 5715
Galvan, Armando, 2621
Galvin, Miles, 7954
Gamache, Le Ann M., 13821
Gambino, Ferruccio, 695
Gamboa, Erasmo, 7955
Gamio, Manuel, 7554-7555
Gammons, Peter, 13270
Gamoran, Adam, 3708-3712
Gamson, William A., 109
Gandara, Patricia, 3713
Gandy, Oscar H., Jr., 13657
Gannon, L., 12982
Gans, Herbert J., 986, 1672, 1769-1771, 1892
Garcia, Alma M., 14343
Garcia, Eugene E., 3714, 8350
Garcia, F. Chris, 11532, 11562-11563, 14622
Garcia, Guy, 7413, 13436
Garcia, Ignacio M., 11564-11565
Garcia, J., 10795, 13527
Garcia, John A., 1944, 6206, 7958, 11566-
    11567
Garcia, Juan R., 7956, 14503
Garcia, Luis T., 110
Garcia, Mario T., 696, 1410, 1426, 2023,
    6814, 7958-7959, 10796
Garcia, Mikel, 9395
Garcia, O., 8630
Garcia, Richard A., 1772-1773
Garcia, Velia, 2331
Garcia Leduc, Jose M., 12718
Garcia Martinez, Alfonso L., 8420
Garcia y Griego, M., 7957
Garcia-Ayvens, Francisco, 14623-14624
Gardner, C., 9929
Gardner, J.M., 7960
Gardner, James B., 11353
Gardner, Jane F., 10797
Gardner, John, 2932
Gardner, Richard, 8238
Garfinkel, I., 5631
Garibaldi, Antoine, 111
Garland, Terri, 12539
Garlick, Barbara, 13438
Garman, D., 202
Garner, Thurmon, 8485
Garner, Wedell R., 13882
Garnett, Cynthia M., 437, 14344
Garr, Daniel, 11568
Garreau, Joel, 1180
Garrett, P., 1340
Garrett, Robert, 112
Garrett, Romeo B., 390

Garrett, Sharon D., 6656
Garrott, Carl L., 4626
Garrow, David, 8808
Garrow, David J., 697-698, 755, 1555-1560,
11569, 13658
Garvey, John, 3715
Garwood, Alfred N., 14504
Gary, L., 5632
Gary, Lawrence E., 6207
Garza, Hisauro, 4627
Gasper, Michele C., 920
Gastil, Raymond D., 14037
Gaston, John, 13271
Gates, Henry Louis, Jr., 668, 699-701, 987-
988, 1945, 8421, 8809, 9208-9212, 9234,
9930-9932, 10798-10803
Gates, Paul W., 8239-8241
Gatewood, Willard B., Jr., 1774, 8810, 10440
Gaudiani, Claire L., 4628
Gaustad, Edwin S., 12719
Gautier-Mayoral, Carmen, 2024, 3231
Gavins, Raymond, 9635-9637
Gay, David A., 11525
Gay, Judith, 3953
Gay, Kathlyn, 12423
Gear, Elizabeth, 6245
Geary, James W., 14625
Gecord, P.E., 13439
Gedicks, Al, 5494-5495
Gee, Emma, 2046, 13785
Geiger, H. Jack, 6208
Gelb, Joyce, 989
Gelb, Steven A., 13822
Gelbspan, Ross, 13659-13660
Gellman, Susan, 8811
Geltman, Max, 8422
Gemery, Henry A., 7556
Genova, W., 2622
Genoves, S., 12146
Genovese, Eugene D., 8813, 10804, 12712,
12720-12721, 13200
Gentile, Nancy J., 2198
Gentry, Dorothy, 4629
Georgakas, Dan, 9933
George, John P., Jr., 13272, 14230
George, Lynell, 1775, 5633, 8423, 9213, 9396,
13898
George, Nelson, 1181, 1307, 2332, 9934-9936,
13273-13274, 13440
George, R.P., 1561
Georges, Kathi, 9397
Georges-Abeyle, Daniel E., 2333
Gephart, Martha A., 1776
Gerber, David A., 547, 11339
Gerber, J., 3718
Gerber, Scott D., 8814
Gerhardt, Gary, 12535
Geronimus, A.T., 6209-6211
Gershman, Carl, 990

Gershoff, Stanley N., 6087
Gerson, Jeffrey N., 11570
Gerson, W.M., 9937
Gerstacker, Friedrich, 3437
Geschwender, James A., 3232, 11571
Geske, T.G., 3719
Gesler, Wilbert M., 6212
Gethers, Soloman P., 11144
Getlin, Josh, 702-703, 5496, 7961, 9605
Getz, Lynne M., 3720-3721
Gewertz, Catherine, 2933, 3722-3723
Geyer, Michael, 10805
Gholar, Cheryl R., 3724
Giago, Tom, 12722
Giannaris, Constantine, 10806
Gibbs, Jewelle T., 6213-6215, 13441
Gibeau, Dawn, 11572
Gibney, Mark, 7557
Gibson, C., 5909
Gibson, James L., 13661
Gibson, Margaret A., 3725-3727, 3869, 3941,
4021, 4186, 10807
Gibson, Michael M., 8242
Giese, Paula, 13662
Giffin, Margaret E., 13824
Gifford, Bernard R., 13825-13828
Gilbert, Bil, 8243
Gilbert, Matthew, 9938
Gilbert, Sandra M., 10808
Gilbertson, G., 7670
Giles, Michael W., 14231
Giles, Robert W., 2623
Gilhousen, M.R., 3728
Gilje, Paul A., 9610, 14038
Gilkes, Cheryl T., 12723, 14345
Gill, Andrew M., 2934, 13016
Gill, Dawn, 3729, 12901
Gill, D.G., 6216
Gill, Flora, 10326
Gill, Gerald, 10441
Gill, W., 3730
Gillespie, C.S., 9214
Gillespie, Veronica M., 8815
Gilliam, Dorothy, 2624, 9939-9941
Gilliam, F.D., 11573
Gilliam, Frank, 1777
Gilliam, Franklin D., 11430
Gilliam, Jerry, 11574
Gilligan, Carol, 10809
Gillispie, Mark, 3731
Gillman, Susan, 9215-9216
Gillmor, Dan, 7164
Gilman, Rhoda K., 6815
Gilman, Sander L., 12205, 13442
Gilman, S.L., 12281
Gilmore, Glenda E., 9638, 14346
Giloth, Robert, 11320
Gilstrap, Peter, 7414
Gimenez, Martha E., 3233, 8424

Ginger, Ann Fagan, 704, 2935
Gingerich, Ronald, 1989
Ginnette, Elinor Des Verney, 9135
Ginsberg, Benjamin, 517
Ginsberg, L., 14124
Ginsberg, Rick, 4058
Ginsberg, Ruth Bader, 8816
Ginsburg, Carl, 9942
Ginzberg, Eli, 6067, 6217
Giovanni, Nikki, 4630-4631
Giraud, Michel, 992, 12147, 12327
Giroux, Henry A., 1722
Gist, Marilyn E., 9943
Gite, Lloyd, 2128
Gittelsohn, A.M., 6218
Gittens, Joan, 1308
Givens, Robin, 9944
Glaberson, William, 113, 9945-9949, 11219,
    13663
Glackman, Howard, 114
Gladhill, John, 9491
Gladwell, Malcolm, 9136, 12984
Glanz, Rudolf, 10592
Glasco, Lawrence, 1778, 9659
Glaser, James M., 11575-11576, 12068
Glasgow, Douglas S., 1779
Glasrud, Bruce A., 6816, 7858, 13123
Glasser, T.L., 1411
Glatthaar, Joseph T., 10442-10443
Glaude, E.S., 12148
Glaviano, Cliff, 115, 9137
Glazer, Mark, 9217
Glazer, Nathan, 518, 991-992, 7165, 10810,
    11145
Glazer, Nona Y., 6219, 11220
Gleason, Philip, 8425, 10593, 10811, 11340
Gleason, William, 7415
Gleeson, M.E., 7284
Glenn, Charles L., Jr., 2625, 2753, 3732-3733
Glennon, Robert J., 1562
Gless, Darryl L., 4632
Glessing, Erica, 4633
Glick, Mark A., 1856
Glicksman, M., 9950
Glock, Charles Y., 519
Gloor, Pierre-Andre, 12149
Glotzer, Richard S., 4634
Glover, Danny, 2334
Glover, Glenda, 1182
Gluck, Sherna Berger, 3494
Gobel, Thomas, 7962
Godshalk, David R., 14039
Godsil, R.D., 5497
Godwin, Gail, 10812
Goeken, Ron, 5708
Goel, Ankur J., 7166
Goering, John, 1563, 7167
Goering, S., 7239
Goertz, Margaret E., 2731

Goetz, Judith P., 2626
Goetz, Stephen, 7806
Gofman, John W., 5553
Goggin, Jacqueline, 705-706, 2937, 4635,
    12328
Goggins, Lathardus, 4636
Goings, Kenneth W., 8817, 13443
Gold, Allan R., 6220
Goldberg, Barry, 11577, 12424
Goldberg, David T., 438, 1309, 8426-8427,
    8789, 11297-11298, 12150-12152, 12612
Goldberg, J.J., 993
Goldberg, K.C., 6221
Goldberg, M.Z., 2335
Goldberg, Robert A., 9701
Goldberg, Stephanie B., 8819-8820
Goldberg-Ambrose, Carole, 8818
Goldberger, David, 4637
Golden, Daniel, 664, 2025, 5880
Golden, R.M., 2414
Golden, Tim, 6222
Goldensohn, Barry, 9218
Goldfield, David R., 1564, 6817
Goldfield, Michael, 7963, 11146, 11578
Goldfrank, W.L., 3444
Goldin, Claudia, 6223, 14174
Golding, J.M., 6224
Goldman, M., 7416
Goldman, N., 14626
Goldman, Peter, 707
Goldman, Robert M., 11579
Goldman, Roger, 708
Goldscheider, C., 14164
Goldscheider, F.K., 14164
Goldsen, Rose, 9951
Goldsmith, Donna J., 1310
Goldsmith, Kory, 2627
Goldsmith, William W., 3234
Goldstein, Jonathan, 13455
Goldstein, Marcy G., 6818
Goldstein, Morris, 116
Goldstein, Naomi, 1311
Goldstein, Patrick, 9952
Goldstein, Paul J., 2336
Goldstein, Richard, 994-995, 4638, 6225, 8428,
    11580
Goldstein, Robert J., 13664, 14627
Goldstock, Ronald, 2337
Goldzwig, Steven R., 8429
Goleman, Daniel, 1312, 12282, 12425, 13899-
    13900
Golub, Jennifer L., 996
Gomberg, P., 12153
Gomes, Ralph C., 4639, 9953, 11581
Gomez, Jewelle, 709
Gomez, L., 12862
Gomez, P., 8244
Gomez Gomez, E., 6226
Gomez-Cano, Gricelle E., 4640

Gomez-Pena, Guillermo, 10813
Gomez-Quinones, Juan, 7964-7966, 11582-11583
Gomillion, Charles G., 710
Gompers, Samuel, 7558
Gonzales, Juan L., Jr., 5634, 7967
Gonzales, Manuel G., 1780
Gonzales, Moishe, 11585
Gonzales, Phillip B., 4641
Gonzalez, David, 711, 3734, 8430, 10594, 11584, 14505
Gonzalez, Fernando, 391
Gonzalez, Gilbert G., 3735, 14165
Gonzalez, Henry S., 1183
Gonzalez, Rafael J., 8431
Gonzalez, Rosalinda M., 5635
Gonzalez Casanova, Pablo, 2026
Gonzalez Echevarria, R., 13275
Good, P., 9954
Goodall, N.H., 14351
Goode, Victor, 3736
Goodfried, Joyce D., 9606
Goodgame, Dan, 11586
Goodheart, Lawrence B., 712
Gooding-Williams, Robert, 9398
Goodlad, John, 3631
Goodman, Alan H., 7711
Goodman, Denise, 2938, 4642
Goodman, Ellen, 4643, 6819
Goodman, James E., 8821-8822
Goodman, L.E., 13444
Goodman, Matthew, 4644
Goodman, M.J., 13444
Goodman, Walter, 9955
Goodman-Draper, Jacqueline, 2129
Goodrich, Herbert, 8432
Goodrich, Linda S., 3737
Goodson, Martia G., 713
Goodstein, Laurie, 520, 4805, 12724
Goodwin, A.L., 3552
Goodwin, E. Marvin, 10327
Goodwin, Maria R., 9450
Gooley, Ruby Lee, 12985
Goonan, Peter, 5912
Goonatilake, Susantha, 10814
Goot, M., 10815
Gopaul-McNicol, Sharon-Ann, 3738
Gorchev, Leila, 13445
Gordon, Charles, 1412
Gordon, Daniel, 4645
Gordon, Diana R., 13665
Gordon, Edmund W., 4239, 11341
Gordon, Fon Louise, 9360
Gordon, Jacob U., 9510
Gordon, Larry, 4646-4647
Gordon, Leonard, 4648, 12426
Gordon, Linda, 1409
Gordon, Lynn D., 4649-4650
Gordon, Paul L., 6360

Gordon, Suzanne, 12986
Gordon, William M., 2628
Gordon-McCutchan, R.C., 12725
Gore, Al, 2130
Gorelick, Sherry, 4651
Gorham, Lucy, 1787
Gorin, Stephen, 117
Gorman, H.J.O., 2956
Gorman, Robert A., 13214
Gorov, Lynda, 9525
Gortmaker, S.L., 6227
Goshko, John M., 5881
Gotanda, Neil, 6820, 8823, 12154
Gotfredson, Michael R., 2338
Gottesman, Jill, 490
Gottfredson, Denise C., 3739
Gottfredson, Linda S., 13794
Gottlieb, Martin, 711, 714, 9470
Gottlieb, Peter, 7968, 10328
Gottlieb, Stephen E., 3740, 8906
Gottschalk, Peter, 3194, 3235
Gouke, Cecil G., 2939
Gould, Lois V.M., 5781
Gould, Richard A., 14166
Gould, William B., IV, 2940, 7969
Gouldner, Helen, 3741
Gounard, Jean-Francois, 9219
Gourevitch, Philip, 4652
Gourse, Leslie, 715
Govan, Reginald C., 1565-1566
Gove, Samuel K., 273
Gover, Kevin, 1704-1705
Gow, David, 10816
Gozemba, Patricia A., 7807
Graaf, John de, 7808
Grace, C.A., 6037
Grace, Stephanie, 5412
Graci, Joseph P., 12987
Grady, Michael K., 3743
Graebner, Norman A., 8245
Graening, John J., 10817
Graf, LeRoy P., 9702
Graff, Gerald, 4654, 10818
Graglia, Lino A., 2941-2942, 4655
Graham, A., 9956
Graham, Barbara L., 8824
Graham, Glennon, 7970
Graham, Hugh D., 1567, 10595
Graham, John W., 14146
Graham, Patricia A., 4656
Graham, Renee, 2629, 4657, 9526, 9534
Graham, S., 12329
Gramling, R., 5493
Granberry, Michael, 9399
Grandolfo, Jane, 7809
Granfield, M., 1227
Granfield, Robert, 4658-4659
Granger, James R., 12726
Granger, J.M., 5636

Grant, Carl A., 2630, 3744, 4149, 10819-10820
Grant, J.A.C., 8825
Grant, Linda M., 2631
Grant, Nancy L., 11321
Grant, Twala M., 3745
Grant, V.C., 6576
Grass, Gary, 4660
Grattet, R., 13944
Gratton, Brian, 3242
Gratus, J., 12069
Grauerholz, Elizabeth, 9220
Graves, A., 2079
Graves, John W., 9361-9363
Gravett, Ericka, 4661
Gravlee, Jack, 8433
Gray, Bradford H., 6228
Gray, C. Boyden, 3746
Gray, David J., 9660
Gray, Frances, 7417
Gray, H., 11587
Gray, Herman, 9957-9958
Gray, James, 7971
Gray, Jerry, 3747, 8826, 11588
Gray, John, 13814, 14628
Gray, Linda C., 921
Gray, Mary W., 4662, 10821
Gray, P.A., 2131
Gray, Paul, 10822-10823
Gray, S.S., 5637
Graymont, Barbara, 14347
Gree, Gordon, 3237
Greeley, Andrew M., 4663, 12055
Green, Carolyn L., 5460
Green, Charles, 12869
Green, Charles St. Clair, 11589
Green, Charles W., 2632
Green, Donald P., 2633, 11590
Green, Elna C., 11591
Green, George N., 8827
Green, James, 11592
Green, John C., 11593
Green, K.C., 2634
Green, Kellee, 13612
Green, Madeline F., 4664
Green, Marci, 11594, 12155, 14629
Green, Mark, 9959
Green, Paul M., 11595, 11666
Green, Rayna, 13446, 14630
Green, R.D., 7169
Green, Robert L., 13276
Green, Shelley, 1184
Green, Stephen G., 299
Greenawalt, Kent, 4665
Greenbaum, Marc D., 12988
Greenbaum, Susan D., 9460
Greenberg, Bradley S., 9960
Greenberg, Brian, 7943
Greenberg, Cheryl L., 997, 3238, 9607-9608
Greenberg, Gershon, 12727

Greenberg, Henry B. ("Hank"), 13277
Greenberg, Jack, 1946, 2339, 4666, 8828
Greenberg, James, 9961-9962
Greenberg, Karen J., 4667
Greenberg, M., 4668, 5805
Greenberg, Michael R., 6229
Greenblatt, M., 7315
Greenblatt, Stephen, 9208, 9221
Greenburgh, Deborah M., 118
Greene, Carole Norris, 12728
Greene, Dwight L., 2340
Greene, Jack P., 6940
Greene, J.C., 12330
Greene, Jerome A., 8246, 10444
Greene, John C., 7712
Greene, Kathanne W., 119
Greene, Linda S., 10824, 13278
Greene, Liz, 7170
Greene, Lorenzo J., 716, 9563
Greene, M., 10825
Greene, Melina F., 9471
Greene, R., 1781
Greene, Victor R., 4669
Greenfeld, Helaine, 2635
Greenhouse, Linda, 11596
Greenley, J.R., 6478
Greenspahn, Frederick E., 12656
Greenspan, Stanley G., 3748
Greenstein, Robert, 5882, 14167
Greenwood, D.T., 14168
Greenwood, Janette T., 1782
Greenwood, L.B., 7972
Greer, Colin, 439, 12424
Greer, Edward, 11597
Greer, James L., 3798
Gregg, Robert S., 10329, 12729
Gregorian, Vartan, 4670
Gregory, S., 1783
Greider, Katherine, 717
Grele, Ronald J., 10826
Gresham, Jewell H., 3413, 5638
Gress, David, 10827
Grey, M.A., 3749
Grey, Michael R., 6230
Grey, T.C., 8829
Grey, Thomas C., 4671
Gribben, Alan, 10828
Gridley, B.E., 13873
Griffin, Jasper, 10829
Griffin, Minh Ly, 6231
Griffin, Peter B., 120
Griffin, Ronald C., 4672
Griffith, Barbara S., 7973
Griffith, David, 3239
Griffith, Ezra E.H., 5639, 12283
Griffith, Mary Ellen, 12989
Griffith, Stephanie, 3750
Griffler, Keith P., 7974
Grigsby, Daryl, 13215

Grigsby, J. Eugene, III, 7171-7172
Grigsby, John L., 9222
Grigsby, W.G., 7173
Grillo, R., 12990
Grim, Valerie, 2132
Grimes, Paul W., 4673
Grimes, William, 9964-9965
Grimshaw, Allen D., 8435
Grimshaw, Patricia, 2027
Grimshaw, William J., 11598
Grimsley, Kristin D., 6821
Grimsted, David, 9223
Grinde, Donald A., Jr., 5883, 6822, 6859,
    8830, 8878
Grindle, David J., 13139
Grinston, Brenda, 5884
Griswold del Castillo, Richard, 1784, 5640,
    6232, 6823, 9400
Groarke, Leo, 121
Grobel, J., 12146
Grofman, Bernard, 1530, 11496, 11599-11604
Gropman, Alan, 10445
Gropper, Richard E., 4674
Groskind, Fred, 12070
Gross, A.B., 7254
Gross, Jane, 3751-3753, 11605
Gross, Leonard, 12941
Gross, Michael P., 4320
Gross, Peter, 7713
Grossberg, Adam, 6074
Grossberg, Lawrence, 11291
Grossman, Deidre A., 122
Grossman, Hildreth Y., 14345
Grossman, James R., 10330
Grossman, Joel P., 1568
Grossman, Zoltan, 5885-5886, 12540
Group, David J., 13666
Grove, Lloyd, 718
Grown, Caren, 2943
Grubb, W.N., 4676
Gruesser, John C., 12628
Gruhl, J., 4677
Grunig, J.E., 2944
Grunig, L.A., 2944, 4678
Grunwald, Michael, 7174
Grusky, D.B., 1785
Grusky, Sara, 10446
Gubar, Susan, 10808
Guenther, Todd R., 9751
Guerena, Salvador, 9138
Guerin-Gonzalez, Camille, 7559, 7975
Guerra, Fernando J., 11606
Guerra, Sandra, 11607
Guerrero, Andre L., 3754
Guerrero, Ed, 9966-9968
Guerrero, Marianna, 8247
Guerrero, Michael, 5498
Guess, Jerry M., 14506
Gugliotta, Guy, 3240-3241, 3755, 4679, 7175

Guidry, William B, 123
Guilfoyle, Michael H., 2341
Guillaumin, Colette, 12427-12428, 12991
Guillemin, Jeanne, 14040
Guiney, Ellen, 3756
Guinier, Lani, 719, 8831, 9969, 11608-11611
Guinther, John, 12564
Gullman, Barton, 10476
Gunn, Arthur C., 9139
Gunn, Giles, 9208
Gunn, John Walker, 13216
Gunther, Gerald, 4857
Gunther, Lenworth, 6233
Gunther, Marc, 9970
Gup, Ted, 3757
Guralnik, J.M., 6234
Gurin, Patricia, 1390, 4680, 8798, 11612,
    11657
Gurr, Robert, 14040
Gurr, Ted Robert, 11452, 11778, 12600, 14083
Gurwitt, Rob, 2636
Gussow, Mel, 9971
Gussow, Zachary, 6235
Gutierrez, D.G., 7560
Gutierrez, Henry J., 2637
Gutierrez, Ramon, 6824, 9585
Gutow, Steve, 11613
Guttmann, Allen, 13279
Guttridge, Leonard F., 10447
Guttstadt, Herman, 7558
Guy, Gregory R., 8437
Guyette, Susan, 4681
Guyot, Lawrence, 11976
Guy-Sheftall, Beverly, 4682, 14348
Guzman, H. Cordera, 12196
Gwynn, Douglas B., 9401
Gyant, LaVerne, 1569

Haan, Mary, 6236-6238
Haas, Mary L., 9402
Haber, Carole, 3242
Haberfeld, Yitchak, 2946, 3243, 8128, 12902
Haberman, John, 13280
Hacker, Andrew, 124-125, 998, 2947, 10830,
    11614, 12156-12157, 14507
Hacker, Peter R., 5887
Hacker, Sally, 12992
Hackey, R.B., 11615
Hackney, Sheldon, 14041
Haddad, Yvonne, 12730
Hadreas, Peter, 126
Haederk, Michael, 8438
Haertel, Edward H., 3758
Hagan, J., 2342
Hagan, William T., 3244, 6825-6826, 12158
Hagedorn, Leah E., 521
Hageman, Alice L., 12731
Hagen, Michael G., 11616-11618
Hagen, Susan M., 1570

Hagendorn, L., 12170
Hager, Philip, 8832-8833
Hagerty, Randy L., 11619
Haggard-Gibson, Nancy J., 999
Haghighat, Chapour, 12331
Hagy, Joe, 5055
Hahn, Stephen, 8027
Haiken, Elizabeth, 7976
Haiman, F.S., 8439
Haines, Andrew W., 4683
Haines, Gerald K., 13667
Haines, Herbert H., 1571
Haines, Michael R., 6489
Hair, William I., 14042
Hairell, Keith R., 10448
Haitman, Diane, 9403
Haizlip, Shirlee Taylor, 720
Haker, Andrew, 12159
Hakken, Jon, 2948, 7176
Halcon, J., 4899
Hale, Christiane B., 6239-6240
Hale-Benson, J., 5641
Halewood, Michael, 12993
Haley, R.B., 127
Halker, Clark, 7977
Hall, Alvin L., 13317
Hall, Burton H., 7987, 8130
Hall, Carla, 9972-9973
Hall, Charles W., 4684
Hall, Edith, 10831
Hall, Gwendolyn M., 6827, 8440
Hall, John R., 12732
Hall, Jonathan, 10832
Hall, Kermit L., 1572, 2593, 8834, 13140, 14631
Hall, Len, 10735
Hall, Linda B., 2951
Hall, Marcia L., 4685
Hall, P.F., 7561
Hall, Patrick, 4686
Hall, Peter, 11322
Hall, Robert L., 4779
Hall, Sidney G., III, 522
Hall, Stuart, 11342, 12429
Hall, Thomas D., 2133
Haller, M.H., 11620
Halliburton, R., Jr., 10596-10597, 13141
Hallinan, Maureen T., 2638, 3759, 13901
Halloran, Richard, 9478, 10449
Hallowell, A.I., 5888
Hallstrom, A., 6241
Halperin, Morton H., 13603, 13668-13669
Halpern, Eric B., 7978-7979
Halpern, Stanley, 1000-1001
Halpin, G., 13829
Halseth, James A., 7858
Halsted, Ann L., 8441
Halstein, J.A., 13447
Halter, Marilyn, 7562

Halvorsen, Kate, 3760
Ham, Debra Newman, 14632
Ham, William T., 4687
Hamamoto, Darrell Y., 9974
Hamanaka, Sheila, 6828, 12160
Hambleton, James R., 12222
Hamid, Ansley, 6242-6244
Hamid, Kazi A., 2068
Hamilton, Charles V., 128, 721, 5507, 11621-11622
Hamilton, David, 3245
Hamilton, D.C., 11622
Hamilton, Denise, 12733, 13830
Hamilton, Kenneth M., 922
Hamilton, Marsha, 13449
Hamilton, Richard F., 14169
Hamilton, Virginia, 6829
Hamilton, D., 13448
Hamler, Portia Y.T., 4688
Hamm, Mark S., 12541
Hamm, Roger, 3761
Hammer, Joshua, 9975-9976
Hammonds, Evelynn, 14349
Hamovitch, Susan, 5806
Hampden, Brenda S., 129
Hampton, Henry, 1573
Han, Shin-Kap, 1238
Hanchett, Thomas W., 3762, 9639
Hancock, Lynell, 3763-3769
Handler, J., 3246
Handley, Lisa R., 11602-11604, 11623
Handlin, Oscar, 3438, 7563
Handy, John W., 1185, 2134
Haney, C. Allen, 6245
Haney-Lopez, Ian, 130
Hanft, Laura, 76
Hanger, Kimberly S., 9515
Hanhan, Sara E.F., 10833
Hanke, Lewis, 12430, 12734
Hankin, Joseph N., 131
Hanks, Lawrence J., 11624-11625
Hanley, Robert, 2639, 3770
Hanna, Judith L., 2640
Hannan, E.L., 6246
Hansberry, Lorraine, 1313
Hansell, S., 2551
Hansen, A., 12208
Hansen, Arthur A., 2199-2200
Hansen, Chris, 2641
Hansen, Miriam, 9977
Hansen, Paul Carter, 9153
Hanson, Elizabeth S., 9224
Hanson, Jeffery R., 13450
Hanushek, Eric A., 3771
Harber, C., 440
Harburg, E., 6247
Hardesty, Michael, 5413
Hardin, Bristow, 3439
Hardin, John A., 4690

Harding, Sandra, 10834, 12903
Harding, Vincent, 1574, 4691, 12735, 14508
Hardwick, John, 8835
Hardy, Charles A., III, 10331
Hardy, James D., 8836
Hardy, James Earl, 9978
Hardy, Kenneth A., 2350
Hardy, Richard J., 1626
Hardy, Thomas, 11626
Hardy-Fanta, Carol, 11627-11628
Hare, B.R., 1314
Hare, J., 5642
Hare, Nathan, 5642
Haremustin, Rachel, 14459
Hareven, Tamara, 11280
Harey, Bryan, 4692
Harlan, S.L., 5730
Harley, Sharon, 1786, 3088, 5643, 14350
Harloe, Michael, 3443
Harlow, Caroline Wolf, 2343
Harman, George D., 5889
Harmon, Amy, 11221
Harmon, George D., 6830
Harmon, Lawrence, 7235
Harney, Kenneth R., 7178
Haro, Carlos Manuel, 4693
Haro, Roberto, 9140
Harp, Lonnie, 3772
Harper, Conrad K., 8837
Harper, F.D., 6248
Harrell, J., 6109
Harrigan, John J., 9451
Harriman, Helga H., 3248
Harring, Sidney L., 8838
Harrington, Charles C., 2539
Harrington, James C., 9703
Harrington, Michael, 11629
Harrington, Oliver W., 722
Harrington, Walt, 14232
Harris, Abram L., 1187, 13217
Harris, Angela P., 8839
Harris, Carl V., 3773, 5890
Harris, Clarissa M., 1575
Harris, D.A., 2344
Harris, Donald J., 3249
Harris, Ellen W., 6249
Harris, Fred R., 1918, 3136, 3245
Harris, Frederick C., 11630
Harris, Frederick W., 1315
Harris, Hamil R., 3774, 6250
Harris, J. William, 8248
Harris, James J., 9645
Harris, Kirk E., 11631
Harris, Leonard, 6831, 11299-11300
Harris, Louis, 12071
Harris, M., 10762, 10881
Harris, Marvin, 10835
Harris, Othello, 13281-13282
Harris, R., 7179

Harris, R.L., 6832
Harris, Robert L., Jr., 4694
Harris, Ron, 2345, 5891
Harris, Ruby M., 9225
Harris, Scott, 9404, 13451
Harris, Trudier, 7418
Harris, Willie J., Jr., 4695
Harrison, Alferdteen, 10332
Harrison, Barbara Grizzuti, 9979
Harrison, Bennett, 1188, 1787
Harrison, Cynthia, 14633
Harrison, Eric, 2346, 2642, 4696, 5644, 9670, 13452
Harrison, T.M., 11632
Harrold, Stanley, 13142
Hart, Jamie, 14351
Hart, Jordana, 3775-3776
Hart, Noah, Jr., 4697
Hart, Thomas, 3777
Hart D'avalos, Armando, 10836
Hartado, Aida, 14352
Harter, Kevin, 3778
Harth, Erica, 2201
Hartigan, Patti, 9980-9981, 11222-11223
Hartigan, Paul, 9982
Hartman, C.A., 2949
Hartman, Joan F., 6251
Hartmann, D., 2950
Hartmann, D.J., 9496
Hartmann, Susan M., 11634
Hartmann-Laugs, Petra S., 11633
Hartnett, J.J., 7180
Hartung, Beth, 10698
Hartzell, Lawrence L., 9726
Harvey, A.R., 5645
Harvey, David, 12431
Harvey, E.B., 132
Harvey, J.T., 3250
Harvey, James J., 4106
Harvey, Miles, 4699
Harvey, William B., 344, 3779, 5332
Harwood, Richard, 9983
Hasenauer, Jim, 7419
Hasenfeld, Y., 3246
Haskell, Paul G., 4700
Haskell, Thomas L., 2951
Haskins, R., 4019
Haslag, J.H., 14170
Hass, R. Glen, 14241
Hassell, Malve von, 13453
Hasson, Gail S., 6252
Hatch, Roger D., 11635
Hatchett, David, 1186, 4701, 5892
Hathorn, Clay, 3251
Hattam, Victoria C., 7980
Haupt, Peter I., 523
Hauptman, Lawrence M., 5893-5894, 6833-6835, 8713, 11636
Hauser, Gregory F., 4702

Hauser, Mary E., 10837
Hauser, Robert M., 3780, 4703-4705, 7714, 14509
Haveman, R., 3252
Haveman, Robert H., 1316-1317
Havig, Alan, 13454
Haviland, William A., 9722
Haw, K.F., 3781
Hawes, Joseph M., 5716
Hawking, James E., 11637
Hawkins, Darnell F., 2348-2350, 12254
Hawkins, Gloria V., 4706
Hawkins, Grover G., 7181
Hawkins, Hugh, 4707, 7564
Hawkins, J.A., 441
Hawkins, L. Tiffany, 4708
Hawkins, Steve, 2351
Hawks, Joanne V., 11638
Hawley, Sandra M., 13455
Hawley, W., 2698
Hawley, Willis D., 2643, 2754, 13911
Hax, Elizabeth R., 3782
Hay, Elizabeth, 13456
Hay, Samuel A., 9226
Hayakawa, S.I., 8442
Hayashi, Haruo, 2202
Hayden, Robert C., 2550
Hayden, Tom, 4709
Hayes, Cheryl D., 1318
Hayes, Constance L., 3783
Hayes, Floyd W., III, 3784, 4710, 5895
Hayes, John Charles, 8840
Hayes, Mellody, 13902
Hayes-Bautista, David E., 3253, 8443, 9405, 10838-10839, 12161
Haygood, Wil, 133, 723, 12543, 14044-14045
Hayles, Robert, 10450
Haynes, Bruce, 5828
Haynes, Elizabeth R., 14353
Haynes, Kingsley, 9704
Haynes, Leonard L., III, 4711, 12736
Haynes, Robert V., 7032
Hays, Constance L., 4712
Hays, Kristen L., 3785
Hays, Samuel P., 9659
Haywood, Harry, 1788
Haywood, H.C., 3667, 13877
Hazard, Geoffrey C., Jr., 8841
Hazeur, Camille, 5397
Head, Louis, 5498
Headley, Bernard D., 2049, 2352-2353
Heady, Brown, 12737
Healy, Melissa, 5499, 6256-6257
Heard, Alex, 4713
Heath, G. Louis, 11639
Heath, Jim F., 9586
Hebert, J. Gerald, 11784
Hechinger, Fred M., 4714
Hecht, Michael L., 8444

Heckman, James J., 134, 1537, 2952, 3254, 3544, 5896
Hedges, Chris, 10451, 12738
Hee, S., 9427
Heer, D.M., 5646
Heevitt, William L., 2953
Heidkind, Jürgen, 3206
Heilbrun, Alfred B., Jr., 2354
Heilig, Peggy, 11640
Heilman, M.E., 135
Heiman, Andrea, 9984
Heinstreet, Leslie, 13670
Heinz, Martha C., 1319
Heise, Michael R., 2644
Heisler, Barbara S., 1413, 1789
Hekymara, Kuregly, 4715
Helfand, Duke, 6258
Helle, Steven, 4716
Heller, Adele, 6699
Heller, Celia, 441, 1002
Heller, Kirley A., 3786
Hellwig, David J., 1005, 12223
Helm, Leslie, 7981
Helmbold, Lois R., 6836, 14354
Helms, Janet E., 1745, 12285, 12332, 13831, 14233
Helton, Arthur C., 7565
Helyar, John, 14171
Hemenway, Robert, 724
Hemeryck, Sondra, 1576
Hemmings, Annette B., 3787
Hemp, Paul, 1189-1190, 9227
Henderson, Al, 2135
Henderson, Alexa B., 1191
Henderson, Jacquie, 1577
Henderson, Lynne, 8842
Henderson, Peter L., 4717
Henderson, Ronald, 2645
Henderson, Thelton, 8843
Henderson, William C., 2355
Henderson, William D., 9727
Hendra, Tony, 7420
Hendrick, Clyde, 2706
Hendrick, Irving G., 3788
Hendricks, Wanda A., 725, 11641
Hendrickson, Paul, 9364, 12544
Henig, Jeffrey R., 2646, 11642-11643
Henig, Robin M., 726
Hening, Jeffrey R., 3789
Henkin, Louis, 7566
Henley, Barbara, 13903
Henneberger, Melinda, 7182, 7715
Hennelly, Robert, 12739
Hennessy, M., 442
Henrikson, Markku, 2029
Henriques, Diana B., 1192
Henry, Annie B., 3790
Henry, Charles P., 11644-11646
Henry, M., 9929

Henry, Sarah, 12740
Henry, William A., III, 136, 1004, 4718, 9228
Henry, Wilma J., 5035
Henson, Scott, 10840-10841
Hentoff, Nat, 137, 524-526, 727, 1002, 1005-
    1011, 1029, 2356, 3791-3792, 4719-4733,
    7810, 8844-8848, 9985-9987, 11647-11649,
    13671-13672
Hentschel, K., 13673
Henwood, K., 11224
Hepworth, Joseph T., 14046
Herbert, Bob, 1012, 1947, 2647, 3793, 6259,
    7716
Herbert, Gayle, 3794
Heredia, Christopher, 8438
Hergog, Patricia, 10789
Heritage, William, 8249
Hermanns, Harry, 4812
Hernandez, Aileen C., 14355
Hernandez, Antonia, 11650
Hernandez, Efrain, Jr., 7183, 11651
Hernandez, Guillermo E., 7421
Hernandez, Jose, 5414
Hernandez, Norma G., 12004
Hernandez, Oscar F., 5897
Hernandez, Peggy, 3795, 4094, 4734, 7184,
    8446
Hernandez, Raymond, 8447
Hernandez, Sandra, 10598
Hernandez-G., Manuel de Jesus, 8445
Hero, Alfred O., 12224
Hero, Rodney E., 11652-11654
Herod, Agustina, 11147
Herring, Cedric, 1578, 1810, 11655, 12072
Herring, Mary, 11656
Herring, Paul W.B., 9609
Herrnstein, Richard J., 7718, 14510
Herscher, Uri D., 5807
Herscovici, S., 14172
Hersh, Matthew, 4735
Hershberger, Scott L., 4506
Hershman, Alan, 7982
Hertzberg, Arthur, 527
Hertzberg, Hazel W., 3255
Herz, D.E., 7960
Herzfeld, M., 13457
Herzog, E., 13458
Hess, Debra, 728
Hess, G. Alfred, Jr., 2648, 3796-3799
Hesseltine, William B., 11225
Heth, Charlotte, 1761, 4681
Hett, E. Jane, 10842
Heuterman, T.H., 1414
Hevies, Gregory N., 3800
Hewitt, William L., 7185, 11226, 13459
Hexter, H., 4978
Heywood, J.S., 2954, 5415
Hibbard, Susan, 11455
Hickerson, Harold, 2030

Hickey, Anthony A., 8250
Hickey, Jo Ann S., 2137-2138, 8250
Hicks, Desiree F., 3801
Hicks, Dixie C., 11148
Hicks, Joe, 9406
Hicks, Jonathan P., 138, 2955
Hidalgo, Margarita, 8448
Hiebert, Elfrieda, 13868
Higginbotham, A. Leon, Jr., 5782, 6837, 7186,
    8849-8852, 8854-8856
Higginbotham, Elizabeth, 4736
Higginbotham, Evelyn B., 11657, 12741,
    14356-14357
Higgins, R.R., 5500
Hilburn, Robert, 9988
Hilchey, Tim, 6261
Hildebrand, Reginald F., 12742
Hildenbrand, S., 9141
Hilfiker, David, 6262
Hill, Donald K., 4738
Hill, Edward W., 11319
Hill, Freddye, 4739
Hill, Gary D., 2357
Hill, George H., 9989-9990
Hill, Herbert, 139, 169, 655, 1013-1014, 1140,
    1476, 1507, 1585, 1611, 2727, 7020, 7983-
    7991, 8130, 12029, 13083, 13674, 14502,
    14511
Hill, Jane H., 8646
Hill, Ned, 2582
Hill, Norbert S., Jr., 4458
Hill, Patrick J., 10843
Hill, Retha, 3802, 4740
Hill, Robert B., 1790-1791, 2956, 5647-5649,
    12073
Hill, R.P., 1320
Hill, T.E., 140
Hill, Walter Byron, 9671
Hillard, David, 729
Hillard, M., 5682
Hillburg, Bill, 7187, 9407-9409
Hilliard, Asa, 7719
Hilliard, Sam B., 8251
Hillson, Jon, 2649
Hilts, Philip J., 6263-6265
Himes, Joseph S., 6838
Himmelfarb, Gertrude, 10844
Himmelstein, D.U., 6684
Hinde, R.A., 12146
Hinderaker, Eric A., 6839
Hinds, C., 5501
Hinds, Michael de Courcy, 1193, 2650, 4741
Hine, Darlene Clark, 730, 3465, 6266, 6802,
    6983, 10258, 11227-11228, 11658, 13170,
    14358-14363, 14508
Hinelgrin, Marea, 4742
Hines, Alice M., 6215
Hines, Judith D., 9991
Hines, Mary E., 14047

Hing, Alex, 4743
Hinkle, Don, 731
Hinojosa, Gilberto M., 6969, 9712, 12690
Hinson, Hal, 9992
Hirsch, Arnold R., 7188, 7266, 9516, 11659-
    11660
Hirsch, B.J., 4520
Hirsch, B.T., 2957
Hirsch, E.D., Jr., 10845
Hirsch, Eric L., 7992
Hirsch, Herbert, 529
Hirsch, Jerry, 7720, 14634
Hirschi, Travis, 2338
Hirschman, Albert O., 8449
Hirschman, Charles, 1333, 14512
Hirschorn, Michael W., 1015, 13675
Hitchens, Christopher, 11661
Hively, Robert, 4746
Hixson, William B., Jr., 12545
Hoadley, Diane L., 2958
Hoagberg, Lia, 6553
Hobbs, Michael A., 12074
Hobbs, Richard S., 732
Hobbs, Steven H., 8857
Hoberman, J., 9994
Hoch, Charles, 11323-11324
Hochbaum, Martin, 1128
Hochschild, Jennifer L., 1792, 11662-11664,
    12075, 14513
Hockett, Jeffrey D., 8858
Hodes, Martha E., 5650
Hodge, Michael E., 10847
Hodges, Graham R., 9577-9578, 9610
Hodgkinson, Keith, 10848-10849
Hodulik, Patricia, 8450
Hoerder, Dirk, 7567, 8859
Hoff, Joan, 8860
Hoffer, Peter C., 8861
Hoffman, Abraham, 7993
Hoffman, Charles, 2358
Hoffman, Emily P., 2959, 3256-3257
Hoffman, Jan, 8862
Hoffman, Michael A., II, 14234
Hoffman, Paul D., 9995
Hoffman, Ronald, 1461, 9223, 14380
Hoffman, Saul D., 5618-5619
Hoffman, Steven J., 9728
Hoffman, Tess, 2358
Hoffochwelle, Mary S., 9679
Hofmann, Suellyn M., 14514
Hofrichter, Richard, 5502
Hofstadter, Richard, 10850
Hogan, Dennis P., 5651
Hogan, J.D., 12994
Hogan, Willliam R., 6840
Hoggart, K., 5898
Hogin, Bradley R., 8863
Hohler, Bob, 9527, 13460
Hohri, William, 2203

Holbrook, Thomas M., 8955
Holcomb, Billie D., 10851
Holdeman, Linda L., 141
Holden, Matthew, Jr., 1793, 9014, 9086, 11149
Holder, Calvin, 7568
Holford, David M., 8252
Holian, John, 6268
Holifield, E. Brooks, 12743
Holison, Larry, 3806
Holland, Dorothy C., 4747
Holland, Ronando W., 11665
Holleran, Philip M., 14364
Holley, Dannye, 8864
Holli, Melvin G., 9497, 11595, 11666
Hollinger, Joan H., 1321
Hollingsworth, J. Rogers, 6269
Hollister, Frederick J., 12162
Holloran, Peter C., 1322
Holloway, Joseph E., 392-393
Holloway, S.R., 1794
Holly, Ellen, 9996
Holm, Tom, 10452-10453
Holman, Charles F., III, 6841
Holmes, Doris A., 6772
Holmes, Eleanor H., 2960
Holmes, King H., 6044
Holmes, Malcolm D., 8865, 10454
Holmes, M.D., 6270
Holmes, Peter, 142
Holmes, Samuel J., 6271
Holmes, Steven A., 143-144, 1017, 1194, 1579,
    1948, 2359, 3258, 4748, 5899-5902, 8866,
    9365, 10599-10600, 11667, 12163
Holmes, T. Michael, 9479
Holsinger, M. Paul, 7811
Holstein, J.A., 1882, 11411
Holt, Elvin, 7422
Holt, Jim, 7721
Holt, Sharon Ann, 3259
Holt, Wythe, 11668
Holton, Woody, 9729
Holtzman, Elizabeth, 8867
Holway, John, 13283-13284
Holyan, Regina, 3807
Holzer, Harry J., 2901, 13941
Hondagneu-Sotelo, Pierrette M., 7569, 7570
Honey, Michael K., 1580, 7994-7996
Hong, Kate, 12164
Honigman, J., 11362
Honour, Hugh, 6842
Hood, Marlowe, 7571
Hood, Stafford, 13832-13833
Hoogland, K.A., 145
Hooglund, Eric, 7572
Hook, Eleanor, 10852
Hook, Sidney, 4749, 10853
Hooker, Mark, 2360
Hooker, Richard D., Jr., 10455

Hooks, Bell, pseud. [Watkins, Gloria], 1018, 9998, 12995-12996, 14365-14366 14515-14516
Hoole, S., 4750
Hooler, Clarence O., 7997
Hoose, Phillip M., 13285
Hoover, Herbert T., 8253
Hoover, Karl D., 13676
Hope, John, II, 7998
Hope, Richard O., 10456
Hoppes, Karen E., 12546
Hord, Frederick, 11343
Hordes, Stanley M., 9587
Horn, James, 7484
Horn, Joseph, 2361
Hornblower, Margot, 2031
Horne, Gerald, 146, 443, 733, 1019, 1795, 4751, 6843, 9410, 10854, 14049
Hornick, Michael S., 11150
Hornsby, Alton, Jr., 2651, 11669
Hornstein, Robert, 1
Hornung, Rick, 5903, 8868, 11670
Horovitz, Bruce, 1195-1198, 11229
Horowitz, Bruce, 9999-10002
Horowitz, David A., 7812
Horowitz, Irving Louis, 734
Horowitz, Joy, 10003
Horowitz, Maryanne C., 7712, 12997
Horsman, Reginald, 6844, 12333
Horst, Samuel L., 3808
Hortel, Bradley R., 5653
Horton, Aimee L., 1581
Horton, Carrell P., 14517
Horton, Hayward D., 5591, 13942
Horton, H.D., 5728
Horton, James O., 1796, 5783-5784, 6845, 11230, 14367
Horton, John, 8451
Horton, L., 1796
Horton, Lois E., 11230
Horton, Raymond D., 5402
Horvitz, Eleanor F., 4752
Horwitz, Morton J., 8869-8870
Horwitz, Sari, 10855, 13461
Hoskin, Marilyn, 440
Hoskins, Jim, 821
Hostetler, A.J., 6272
Hougan, Jim, 13677
Houghton, John W., 10856
Houghton, Richard H., III, 2032
Houk, James, 8452
Houlihan, Patrick T., 7030
Houppert, Karen, 3809
House, Ernest R., 147, 5416
House, James S., 6273
Houseman, Alan W., 8871
Houseman, Gerald L., 530
Houston, Charles H., 7999
Houston, Lawrence N., 12286

Houston, Paul, 10004
Houston, Velina H., 12165
Howard, Curtis D., 148
Howard, Elizabeth F., 9229
Howard, J., 2033
Howard, R. Palmer, 6369
Howard, Walter T., 14050-14051
Howard-Pitney, David, 8872
Howe, Irving, 4753, 10857
Howe, K.R., 10858
Howe, Peter J., 5904, 7191-7192, 12076
Howell, D.R., 5417
Howell, Embry M., 6274
Howell, Roy C., 4754
Howell, S.E., 12547
Howington, Arthur F., 8873
Howitt, D., 12255
Howlett, Scott W., 1323
Hoxie, Frederick E., 1705, 2099, 6735, 6791, 6825, 6846-6847, 6866, 6935, 6947, 6957, 9100, 12613
Hoxworth, D.H., 2793
Hoynes, William, 10005
Hraba, Joseph, 1415
Hrdy, S.B., 12998
Hruby, Mary L., 7172
Hruska, Bronwen, 10006
Hsia, Jayjia, 149
Hu, Arthur, 12614
Huang, Hsiao-ping, 2034
Hubbard, Dolan, 14635
Huber, Bettina J., 10859
Hubin, David R., 13834
Hubler, Shaun, 150, 3260, 3810, 9389, 9411, 12999, 14173
Huck, Karen F., 10007
Huckfeldt, Robert, 1797, 11671
Hucles, Harold D., 2139
Huddle, D., 7573
Hudgins, John L., 4755
Hudlin, Reginald, 10118
Hudson, Barbara, 2362-2363
Hudson, Charles M., 6848, 10601
Hudson, Elizabeth, 4756
Hudson, Jill, 11231
Hudson, Larry E., Jr., 5652
Hudson, Richard, 151
Huebner, E. Scott, 13835
Huffman, Terry E., 4757
Hufford, Donald E., 3130
Huggins, Nathan I., 4758, 11129, 13143
Hughes, C. Alvin, 1949
Hughes, Clarence E., 10860
Hughes, Dana, 6275
Hughes, Everett M., 12334
Hughes, Langston, 10008
Hughes, M., 3391, 12275
Hughes, M.A., 7193
Hughes, Marija M., 13000

Hughes, Mark A., 1798, 5808-5809
Hughes, Michael, 5653, 12287
Hughes, Raymond, 13286
Hughes, Robert, 10861-10862
Hugo, Pierre, 152
Huie, H. Mark, 2652
Huizer, G., 12366
Hula, R.C., 7194
Hull, Jon D., 3811, 9507
Hulteen, Bob, 444
Hummels, B., 224
Hummer, Robert A., 6276
Humphreys, Lloyd G., 3199
Humphries, Marilyn L., 7807
Hundley, Kristen, 7195
Hunt, Alfred N., 12225
Hunt, Barbara Ann, 10009
Hunt, Frankie L.C., 2653
Hunt, Jack, 8254
Hunt, J.V., 6278
Hunt, Linda, 7574, 12904
Hunt, R.G., 3441
Hunt, Raymond G., 12249, 14213
Hunter, C., 8946
Hunter, Carol Margaret, 735
Hunter, David W., 13287
Hunter, Herbert M., 13943
Hunter, M., 12905
Hunter, T.P., 11672
Hunter-Gault, Charlayne, 4759
Huntley, Horace, 8000
Hunton, Dorothy, 736
Huntzicker, William E., 6849
Hurlbert, C. Mark, 10863
Hurley, Andrew, 5503
Hurmence, Belinda, 737
Hurns, Walter M., 11673
Hurowitz, J.C., 6279
Hurst, Jack, 7813
Hurst, John, 14235
Hurston, Zora Neale, 8001
Hurt, R. Douglas, 3261, 6850
Hurtado, Aida, 8453, 13001
Hurtado, Albert L., 5905-5906, 8002
Hurtado, Sylvia, 4760-4761
Hurvitz, Nathan, 1020
Hurwitz, Emanuel, 2035
Husemoller, Carl, 1324
Husock, Howard, 531, 2654
Hustoles, Thomas P., 4762
Huston, A.C., 13580
Hustveldt, Lloyd, 10864
Hutcheson, J.D., 11853
Hutchinson, Dennis, 2655
Hutchinson, Earl Ofari, 2364, 6280, 8454,
    10602-10603, 10865, 11674
Hutchison, Ray, 12629
Hutchison, William R., 12744
Hutchison, William T., 12865

Huth, Tom, 11675
Hutton, Frankie P., 10010-10011
Hutton, Mary M.B., 14052
Hux, S., 153
Hwan Kim, Bong, 7483
Hwang, D.H., 10866
Hwang, H-S., 3131
Hyatt, Marshall, 12335
Hyclak, Thomas, 154
Hyde, Arthur, 3812
Hyde, Henry J., 4763
Hyde, Ken, 4764
Hyer, Patricia, 155
Hyllegard, David, 4765-4766
Hylton, Richard D., 1199
Hyman, Harold M., 13678
Hymowitz, Kay S., 10867
Hynes, Charles J., 14053
Hyser, Raymond M., 14023

Ibidunni, A.O., 14236
Ichinokuchi, Tad, 13679
Ichioka, Yuji, 2204, 2225
Idson, T.L., 13244
Ifill, Max B., 13144
Ignatiev, Noel, 1799
Iheanacho, S.O., 12288
Ihlanfeldt, K.R., 5418
Ihle, Elizabeth, 4767
Iiyama, Patty, 2205
Imbeault, Barbara, 6281
Immerwahr, John, 11301-11302
Ingalls, Robert P., 14056
Ingersoll, Gary M., 2656
Ingersoll, Thomas N., 5785
Ingrando, D.P., 7423
Ingulli, Elaine D., 10870
Inniss, Leslie B., 1760, 1800, 11676
Inscoe, John C., 6792, 6794
Inverarity, J., 13944
Ione, Carole, 14369
Ireland, Doug, 11678
Irigaray, Luce, 12906
Irizarry, Annabelle, 1801
Irons, Peter, 1582, 2206-2207
Irvin, Amelia, 5504
Irvine, Jacqueline J., 3816
Irwin, James R., 11232
Isaac, Daniel, 156
Isaac, Katherine, 8874
Isenberg, Sheila, 768
Isham, W.P., 7722
Ison, Paula, 8455
Issacharoff, S., 11679
Itzkoff, Seymour W., 7723
Iudica, Doreen, 12549
Ivers, G., 157
Iverson, Katherine, 3817
Ivins, Molly, 7577

Iwata, Edward, 10013
Iwataki, Miya, 14370

Jabara, A., 10014
Jackman, Mary R., 12432-12433, 12615
Jackson, A.W., 5655
Jackson, Bo, 13288
Jackson, Bryan O., 11456
Jackson, Byden, 9230
Jackson, Carlton, 738
Jackson, Charles C., 2657, 9705
Jackson, David, 11680
Jackson, Derrick , III, 4770-4772
Jackson, Derrick Z., 1325, 2367-2370, 6283-
    6285, 8456, 8875, 10457, 11681, 12336,
    12745, 13289-13290
Jackson, Diana R., 4773
Jackson, Don, 5908, 10015
Jackson, Donald W., 8876
Jackson, Elizabeth K., 10016
Jackson, G., 3818
Jackson, Gerald, 12289
Jackson, Jacquelyn Johnson, 7578-7579
Jackson, James S., 12077, 14518
Jackson, Jesse L., 1021-1023, 11682
Jackson, J.H., 11233
Jackson, Jimmie, 3819
Jackson, John L., 4775
Jackson, John S., 4774
Jackson, Kenneth T., 10872
Jackson, Kenneth W., 4776
Jackson, L. Duane, 1200
Jackson, Leroy F., 8256
Jackson, P., 12434
Jackson, Pamela I., 2371
Jackson, Peter, 7197, 9611
Jackson, Raina, 4777
Jackson, Robert L., 4778
Jackson, Stephanie M., 2658
Jackson, Walter A., 739, 6851
Jacob, Evelyn, 14519
Jacobs, Barbara D., 2659
Jacobs, Donald M., 6852
Jacobs, John, 8003
Jacobs, Paul, 6286, 7606
Jacobs, Sally, 14237
Jacobs, Wilbur R., 6853, 8257
Jacobsen, Darrell D., 72
Jacobsen, J.P., 13002
Jacobson, Cardell, 158, 8004
Jacobson, Derrick Z., 159
Jacobson, Harvey J., 12873
Jacoby, Jeff, 12166
Jacoby, Russell, 8457
Jacoby, Susan, 1802, 12167
Jacoby, Tamar, 740, 11683
Jacques, Jeffrey M., 4779
Jaffe, Harry S., 9452
Jaffe, Mark, 3820

Jaher, Frederic C., 532
Jaimes, M. Annette, 2002, 2036, 8247, 8458,
    9853, 14520, 14575
Jakeman, Robert J., 10458
James, Bernard, 3264
James, Caryn, 1024, 13462
James, Cathy L., 10017
James, C.L.R., 6855
James, David R., 2660, 4191, 4237
James, Franklin, 3189
James, Franklin J., 7198
James, Joy, 4780
James, Parthena L., 10604
James, Portia P., 12746, 12907
James, Stanlie M., 14371
Jameson, Elizabeth, 14372
Jamieson, J.W., 7724-7727
Jamison, Charles N., Jr., 12290
Janken, Kenneth R., 741-742
Janmohamed, Abdul, 8459
Janofsky, Michael, 2961, 13904
Janoski, Thomas, 1416
Janowitz, Morris, 10459
Jarausch, Komad H., 12337
Jaret, Charles, 7424
Jargowsky, Paul A., 3265, 5810-5811
Jarivs, Brian, 13905
Jaroff, Leon, 12435
Jarrell, Robin, 13003
Jarriett, Olga S., 13906
Jarvis, S.R., 10873
Jaschick, Scott, 160-163, 1583-1584, 4781-4786
Jason, Carl E., 2661
Jason, J., 6287
Jayko, Margaret, 13681
Jaynes, Gerald D., 2410, 3266-3268, 3821,
    4787, 5419, 5656-5657, 6288, 8005, 11684,
    12078, 14521
Jean, Clinton M., 394, 1803, 10874
Jeffers, Sidonie C., 2372
Jefferson, Margo, 7425
Jeffries, John, 8047
Jeffries, John C., Jr., 743
Jeffries, Leonard, 4788
Jelen, Ted G., 14238
Jeltz, Wyatt F., 10605
Jen, Gish, 13463
Jencks, Christopher, 1804-1805, 2982, 3269,
    3302, 5812, 5882, 7147, 7199-7202, 11421
Jenifer, Franklyn G., 533, 1025
Jenkins, Adelbert H., 446
Jenkins, Betty L., 9142
Jenkins, David, 395
Jenkins, Kent, Jr., 744
Jenkins, Lynn B., 4003
Jenkins, Mark, 10018
Jenkins, Olga C., 447
Jenkins, Thomas H., 13291
Jenkins, Wilbert L., 9672

Jenkins, William D., 7814
Jenness, Doug, 12436
Jennings, James, 2141, 5817, 10875, 11685-11688, 12168
Jennings, Kenneth M., 13292-13293
Jennings, Thelma, 14373
Jennings, Veronica T., 5910, 6289-6290, 10160, 14057-14058
Jensen, Arthur R., 7728-7729
Jensen, Erik M., 8877
Jensen, Joan M., 8006
Jensen, Leif, 3395, 5658, 7580
Jernudd, Bjorn H., 8460
Jessup, Michael M., 7815
Jett, Stephen C., 10335
Jetter, Alexis, 3822, 4789
Jewell, Karen S., 5659, 14374
Jewell, R.T., 13243
Jewell, Terri L., 14375
Jeyifous, Abiodum, 9231
Jhally, Sut, 9773, 10138
Jimenez, Martha, 8461
Jimenez de Wagenheim, Olga, 6856
Jimenez Montoya, Andres E., 8007-8008
Jiobu, Robert M., 14522
Joe, J., 10336
Johansen, Bruce E., 6857-6859, 8830, 8878
John, Gus, 3823
John, Rupert, 448
Johnny, Ronald E., 5911
Johnson, Alex M., Jr., 8879-8880, 10876, 13836
Johnson, Bill, 2662
Johnson, Charles, 745, 6291
Johnson, Charles, Jr., 10460-10461
Johnson, Charles S., 1405, 14584
Johnson, Clarence B., Sr., 2663
Johnson, Clyde, 8009
Johnson, C.M., 5660
Johnson, D.A., 3377
Johnson, Darrell L., 13464
Johnson, David B., 6292
Johnson, David C., 4790
Johnson, David R., 11689
Johnson, Dianne A., 9232
Johnson, Dirk, 1950, 2142, 2373, 3824, 7203, 7426, 7816, 13837
Johnson, G.D., 4791
Johnson, Glen, 2962
Johnson, Haynes, 9453
Johnson, J., 5815
Johnson, Jacqueline, 746
Johnson, James B., 2477
Johnson, James H., Jr., 10606
Johnson, J.H., Jr., 4792, 10337
Johnson, Joni L., 747
Johnson, Julie, 4793
Johnson, Kirk A., 4794, 10019
Johnson, Larry O., 12326

Johnson, Leola A., 10020
Johnson, Louise A., 2143
Johnson, Melyn, 2208
Johnson, Michael P., 6293
Johnson, N.R., 13294
Johnson, Paul E., 12747
Johnson, Paul N., 7730
Johnson, Rhoda E., 13907
Johnson, Rhonda Shaw, 5912
Johnson, R.J., 10462
Johnson, Robert C., Jr., 164, 2374, 11287, 12908
Johnson, Roberta Ann, 165-166, 11690
Johnson, S.D., 13465
Johnson, Sylvia T., 3825, 10877
Johnson, Terry, 1951
Johnson, Thomas S., 4795
Johnson, Troy R., 11151
Johnson, Violet Mary-Ann, 7581
Johnson, Whittington B., 4796, 5786
Johnston, Allan, 10338
Johnston, David, 5913, 13682-13686
Johnston, Hugh, 13687
Johnston, James H., 10607
Johnston, Lloyd, 6294
Johnston, R.J., 7204
Johus, K., 4508
Jojola, Ted, 10021
Jonassohn, Kurt, 14004
Jone, Carole, 748
Jones, Adrienne Lash, 14376-14377
Jones, Alex S., 10022-10026
Jones, Alice Hanson, 14174
Jones, A.M., 6295
Jones, Augustus J., Jr., 167-168
Jones, Bessie, 749
Jones, Beverly W., 750, 14378
Jones, Bruce A., 10878
Jones, Carter, 6860
Jones, Cathy J., 8462
Jones, Charisse, 751, 2664, 3826-3827, 4798, 5661-5662, 6296, 10027, 12748, 14239
Jones, Charles E., 11691
Jones, Charles H., 4797
Jones, Clifton R., 12437
Jones, Cloyzelle K., 4589
Jones, DeWitt G., 6861
Jones, Dionne J., 6207
Jones, D.J., 4799
Jones, Dorothy, 4048
Jones, Dorothy Knee, 9346
Jones, Dorothy V., 2037
Jones, Edward W., Jr., 11234
Jones, Elaine R., 8882, 11692
Jones, Elias F., 12749
Jones, Evonne P., 4800
Jones, Felecia G., 10028-10029
Jones, G. William, 10030
Jones, Gregg A., 13295

Jones, Hettie, 752
Jones, Howard, 10396
Jones, Jacqueline, 1806, 6862, 14379-14380
Jones, Jacquie, 10031
Jones, James, 449
Jones, James E., Jr., 169, 225, 655, 753, 1476,
    1507, 1585, 1611, 2727, 7020, 7986,
    12029, 13083, 14502, 14511
Jones, James H., 6297
Jones, Jeff, 5505
Jones, John Paul III, 3270
Jones, Judith H., 10879
Jones, Kirkland C., 754
Jones, Lewis W., 755
Jones, Lisa, 396, 5663, 8463, 10032-10033,
    10062, 13004, 13466-13467
Jones, Lowell A., 6298
Jones, Lyle, 3828
Jones, Lynne, 11152
Jones, M., 3829, 13468
Jones, Major J., 12750
Jones, Maldwyn A., 7582
Jones, Maxine D., 4801
Jones, Nathaniel R., 1585
Jones, Norrece T., Jr., 6863, 13145
Jones, Patricia A., 3778, 3830
Jones, Peter d'A., 9497
Jones, Rachel L., 3831, 6299-6300, 10463,
    14240
Jones, Reginald L., 1326, 13838
Jones, Rhett, 11303
Jones, R.S.P., 13469
Jones, Stephen, 170
Jones, Tamara, 12550
Jones, Terry, 5239
Jones, Thomas E., 13358
Jones, Woodrow, Jr., 6507, 14657
Jones-Sneed, Frances M., 9564
Jones-Wilson, Faustine C., 3832-3833
Joondeph, B.W., 2665
Joravsky, Ben, 1740, 2666
Jordan, Cathie, 14519
Jordan, Grant, 11344
Jordan, Mary, 1327, 3834-3836, 4802-4805
Jordan, Robert A., 1328, 2963, 12551
Jordan, Vernon E., Jr., 1026
Jordan, William Chester, 3837
Jordan, Winthrop D., 5664
Jorde, Doris M., 10880
Jorgensen, Joseph G., 9347
Jorgenson, Christabel, 12079
Jorgenson, David E., 12079
Jorgenson, Joseph, 5506
Jorjani, David, 2868
Josefowitz Siegel, Rachael, 13470
Joselit, Jenna W., 2375
Joseph, Antoine, 171, 8010
Joseph, G.G., 10881
Joseph, Jennifer, 9397

Joseph, Joel D., 8883
Joseph, Richard, 10464
Josephy, Alvin M., Jr., 6864-6866
Josey, E.J., 9143
Joughin, Louis, 10882
Joyce, Beverly A., 670
Joyce, Donald F., 9233
Joyce, Joyce A, 9234
Joyce, Robert P., 4806
Joyce, T., 6301
Joyner, Edward T., 3838
Joynson, Robert, 7731
Juarez, R.Z., 6206
Juarez Robles, Jennifer, 11693
Judd, Dennis R., 1563, 1635, 7205
Judd, Elliot L., 8464
Judd, Stephen G., 13688
Judge, Paul C., 1201
Judges, Donald P., 172
Judis, John B., 534, 11694, 12438
Judson, George, 2667-2671, 3839-3840
Judy, Ronald A.T., 9235
Juengst, E.T., 3084
Juhasz, Anne M., 1329
Julian, Elizabeth K., 7206
Julian, George W., 8258
Jungeblut, Ann, 3857
Juska, Sharon, 4807
Justice, Blair, 14059
Justice, William Wayne, 8884
Justus, Joyce B., 173

Kaczorowski, Robert J., 1586-1587
Kadetsky, Elizabeth, 1027, 2964, 7583
Kaestner, Robert, 7207
Kagan, Donald, 10803
Kagay, Michael T., 12080
Kahn, A.J., 5914
Kahn, Alfred J., 3415
Kahn, Eve M., 11235
Kahn, Joseph P., 9528, 9575, 11695
Kahn, Lawrence M., 174, 13296-13297
Kahn, Robert, 13689
Kaine, Timothy M., 7208, 8885
Kairys, David, 8886
Kaiser, Ernest D., 14636
Kaiwar, Vasant, 3440
Kakutani, Michiko, 535, 8465
Kalantzis, Mary, 8466, 10883
Kallal, Edward W., Jr., 7817
Kallan, J.E., 6302
Kalleberg, Arne L., 1807
Kallen, Horace M., 3841
Kallick, D., 5507
Kalmar, Ivan, 7427
Kalt, Joseph P., 2113
Kamabahi, Jeffrey J., 6303
Kamalich, Richard F., 2965
Kamara, A., 7713

Kamara, Mohammed B., 11153
Kamarck, E.C., 5715
Kame'eleihiwa, Lilikala (Lilikala Dorton), 8259
Kamen, Al, 7584
Kamerman, S.B., 5914
Kamerman, Sheila B., 3415
Kamin, Leon, 1027-1028, 7722
Kan, Sergei, 12338
Kanaiaupuni, S.M., 7255
Kanazawa, Tooru J., 9348
Kancewick, Mary, 8887
Kand, K. Connie, 11696
Kane, Thomas J., 4808
Kane, Tim D., 11236
Kanellos, Nicolas, 9236
Kanfer, Stefan, 7428
Kang, Jaime M., 10884
Kang, K. Connie, 11943, 13471
Kanthak, Kris, 4809
Kantor, Paul, 11697
Kantowicz, Edward R., 3873
Kantrowitz, Barbara, 3842, 4810
Kantrowitz, Nathan, 1808
Kapel, David E., 4116
Kaplan, Amy, 3127, 8720, 10465, 12226-
    12227, 12236, 12240, 12248, 14250
Kaplan, David A., 14060
Kaplan, Fred, 10466
Kaplan, George, 6238
Kaplan, H.B., 10462
Kaplan, Janice L., 10034
Kaplan, Louis, 11225
Kaplan, M.S., 12291
Kaplin, William A., 4811
Kapur, Sudarshan, 11698
Karabel, Jerome, 4394, 4812-4813
Karabinus, Robert, 3860
Karcher, Carolyn L., 756, 6867
Kardulias, P. Nick, 6868
Karen, D., 4814-4815
Karenga, Maulana, 11154, 11304, 12439
Karim, Benjamin, 757
Karlan, Pamela S., 2672, 11699-11700
Karlins, Marian, 13472
Karnig, Albert K., 10621, 11701
Karnow, Stanley, 11702
Karp, Robert J., 1330, 6304
Karp, Stan, 3843
Karp, Walter, 1029
Karpoff, J.M., 9349
Karros, Alan L., 12876
Karst, Kenneth L., 1417-1418, 10467
Karwatka, Dennis, 12909
Karweit, Nancy, 3844
Kashefi, M., 11237
Kasinitz, Philip, 7585
Kasiske, Bertram L., 6305
Kass-Simon, Gabriele, 12910, 13068
Kater, John L., Jr., 12751

Kateri Hernandez, Tonya, 14061
Kates, Nick, 13945
Katyal, N.K., 5760
Katz, Dalmas, A., 450
Katz, Irvin, 14241
Katz, J., 536
Katz, Jesse, 7143, 9412, 10608
Katz, Jon, 10035
Katz, Jonathan, 13146
Katz, Martin J., 2966-2967
Katz, Michael B., 1809, 3271-3272, 3845
Katz, P.A., 12191
Katz, Phyllis A., 450, 2214, 2643
Katz, Stephen T., 2038, 6869, 10885
Katz, William Loren, 10036, 10609-10610
Katzenstein, M.F., 13005
Katzman, David M., 758
Kauffman, Albert H., 175
Kauffman, L.A., 10886
Kaufman, Barry, 4816
Kaufman, Joanne, 10037
Kaufman, Jonathan, 1030, 12169
Kaufman, Julie E., 2673
Kaufman, Karen, 13839
Kaufman, Martin, 13232
Kaufman, Michael T., 10038, 13006
Kaufman, Natalie H., 8888
Kaufman, P., 3846
Kaufman, Polly Welts, 2674
Kaus, Mickey, 3273
Kawaguchi, Paul T., 6092
Kaye, Stan, 3847
Kazal-Threshen, D.M., 2675
Kazin, Michael, 12554
Kazyaka, Ann-Marie, 2376, 2968
Kearney, C. Philip, 3848
Kearney, Reginald, 10611
Keating, Pamela, 3631
Keating, W. Dennis, 7209
Keats, Brian E., 10887
Keaulana, Kimo Alama, 9480
Keber, Linda K., 12962
Keckeisen, Robert J., 8260
Keeney, Mark, 7163
Kegay, Michael, 12081
Keil, J.E., 6306-6307
Keil, Thomas J., 2377
Keiser, Richard A., 11703
Keith, Damon J., Jr., 1952
Keith, S.N., 176
Keith, Verna M., 1810
Keith, V.M., 6308
Kelleher, Richard V., 1588, 11704
Keller, Gary D., 10039, 10888
Keller, M.J., 4817
Keller, Robert H., Jr., 8467
Kelley, Kevin J., 4818
Kelley, Lawrence C., 8261
Kelley, Robin D.G., 9339, 11705

Kellogg, Peter J., 12082
Kellough, J. Edward, 177, 5915
Kelly, David H., 10889
Kelly, Gail P., 3817, 7741
Kelly, Kevin, 9237-9238
Kelly, P., 2676
Kelly, Terry, 5526
Kelly, William H., 3274
Kelman, M., 2969
Kelman, W., 13840
Kelmendi, John P., 3849
Kelsey, C., 8011
Kelsey, Frederick T., 8889
Kelsey, Harry, 6870
Kemerer, Frank R., 8890
Kemp, Evan J., Jr., 178, 3746
Kemper, Donald J., 2677
Kempers, Margot, 8262
Kempton, Murray, 10890
Kendler, H.H., 7732
Kendrick, Ann, 11706-11707
Kendrick, Dolores, 9239
Kenneally, Christopher, 13473
Kenneally, James J., 13007
Kennebeck, Edwin, 8891
Kennedy, Donald, 4819
Kennedy, Duncan, 179
Kennedy, J. Michael, 6309, 7818, 12911
Kennedy, John H., 4820
Kennedy, Joseph P., II, 2970
Kennedy, Lisa, 2378
Kennedy, P.W., 12228
Kennedy, Randall L., 180, 2379, 2971-2972,
    4821-4823, 6871, 8892-8897, 9551, 10891,
    12440-12441
Kennedy, R.D., 6310
Kennedy, Robert F., Jr., 5508
Kennedy, Sally J., 5509
Kennedy, Shawn G., 7210
Kennedy, Stetson, 7819, 8898, 13690
Kenny, William R., 2973
Kent, George E., 759
Kent, Ronald C., 8012
Kenworthy, Tom, 5510
Kenzer, Robert C., 1202
Kerber, Linda K., 1419
Kerlow, Eleanor, 4824
Kerman, Cynthia E., 760
Kernfoxworth, M., 11238
Kerr, Peter, 2974
Kerrigan, Colm, 10612
Kerruish, Valerie, 8899
Kersch, Kenneth, 3820
Kershaw, T., 3850
Kerwin, Christine, 1331
Kessel, S.S., 6319
Kessen, Thomas P., 3851
Kessler, Lauren, 2209
Kessler, Sidney H., 537

Kessler-Harris, Alice, 3275, 8013, 8062
Ketabgian, Tamara, 451
Keteyian, Armen, 13373
Ketner, Joseph D., 761
Kettl, P.A., 6311
Key, Oren W., 12752
Keyes, Alan, 11708
Khan, Chandra C., 6312
Khor, Lay Boon, 7677, 13968
Khoury, Muin J., 6375
Kiang, Peter N., 8014, 9529
Kibbe, David C., 11709
Kickingbird, Kirke, 8263
Kidwell, Clar S., 12912
Kiecolt, K.J., 5665, 12067
Kiewiet, D. Roderick, 9375
Kifner, John, 10040, 12083
Kiger, Gary, 431
Kilbaner, Irwin, 1589
Kilborn, Peter T., 181, 2975, 3276, 5916-5917,
    6313, 7586, 8015, 9640
Kilgannon, James, 7211
Killian, Lewis M., 1672, 12339, 14523
Kilpatrick, Anna G., 6872
Kilpatrick, Jack F., 6872
Kilson, Martin L., Jr., 182, 1811, 2976, 4825,
    11710-11712
Kim, Hyung-chan, 12154, 14637
Kim, Illsoo, 13691
Kim, Marlene, 2977-2978
Kimbro, Dennis, 1203
Kimenyi, Mwangi S., 3622, 4826, 13946
Kimmey, Fred M., 8264
Kincaid, John, 11713
Kinder, Donald R., 183, 14242
Kindleberger, Richard, 3852
King, A.G., 1590
King, Colbert I., 13692
King, Dennis, 538, 1031
King, Edith, 13908
King, J., 4827
King, J.E., 3853
King, James D., 11885
King, Joyce E., 10892, 12292
King, Kathleen P., 539
King, M., 7587
King, Mae C., 11714
King, Martin Luther, Jr., 1591
King, Mel, 11687
King, N.J., 184, 2979
King, Patricia, 8900, 11715
King, Richard H., 1420, 1592
King, William M., 10468-10469
Kingrea, Nellie, 2980
Kingsley, David E., 2678
Kingslow, Marcie E., 5337
Kingston, Paul W., 3854
Kinloch, Graham, 14638
Kinney, J.P., 8265

Kinnick, Mary K., 4828
Kinsey, Bernard W., 1204
Kinsley, Michael, 185
Kinsolving, Carey, 7820
Kipen, Howard M., 6314
Kiple, Kenneth F., 6315
Kiple, Virginia H., 6315
Kirby, Jack T., 10041
Kirch, Patrick V., 9481
Kirchheimer, Anne, 2981
Kirkpatrick, Lee A., 12753
Kirp, David L., 3855-3856
Kirsch, Irwin S., 3857
Kirschenman, Joleen, 2982
Kiser, George C., 8016-8017
Kishi, Russell L., 7429
Kissel, Howard, 10042
Kissinger, C. Clark, 9413
Kitchen, Daniel J., 3858
Kitchen, Deborah L., 5666
Kivisto, Peter, 14243
Klamer, Arjo, 9240
Klare, Karl, 8901
Klarman, Michael, 6873, 8902
Klass, Perri, 6316
Klausner, Samuel Z., 540
Kleg, Milton, 3859-3860, 14062
Klehr, Harvey, 11155
Kleiman, H., 186
Kleiman, Michael B., 11716
Klein, B.W., 3277
Klein, Dianne, 7588
Klein, Joe, 1032, 11717
Klein, Kerwin L., 10893
Klein, Michael, 762
Klein, Norman M., 9414
Klein, Stephen P., 2380-2381, 13841
Kleinfeld, Judith, 8018
Kleinkauf, Janice, 4950
Kleinman, J.C., 2320, 6317-6319
Kleinpenning, G., 12170
Kleinwachter, Wolfgang, 8468
Klepfisz, Irena 509
Klepp, Susan E., 763
Kleppner, Paul, 11398
Klerman, Lorraine V., 6320
Kletzer, Lori G., 8019, 13947
Kleven, Thomas, 8864
Kliman, Andrew J., 13948
Kline, Gary, 6321
Klineberg, O., 1334
Kling, Joseph M., 2144
Klingenstein, Susanne, 4829
Kloby, Gerald S., 1812
Klompmaker, John, 3861
Klor de Alva, J. Jorge, 11156
Klos, George E., 6874-6875, 10339, 10613
Klotman, Phyllis R., 10043
Klotter, James C., 3278

Kluegel James R., 30, 12084, 14244
Kluge, P.F., 4830
Kly, Yussuf N., 8903, 11305, 12256, 12754
K'Meyer, Tracy E., 9472
Knapp, M.C., 5420
Knapp, Michael S., 3862
Knee, Stuart, 541
Kneeland, Douglas E., 10044
Knepper, Paul E., 2382-2383, 5761
Knepper, Paula R., 4831
Knights, George P., 10707
Knoepfle, Peg, 2145
Knopke, Harry J., 449, 2586, 2785, 4461,
    12298, 12301, 12611, 12619, 13907, 13913,
    14524
Knouse, Stephen B., 2986, 8020, 8126, 10427,
    10470, 10521
Knowlton, Clark S., 14063
Knox, Kathleen E., 3222
Knox, Margaret L., 10471
Koch, James, 13298
Koch, John, 7430
Kochanek, K.D., 6322
Kochman, T., 11345
Koday, M., 6323
Kodras, Janet E., 3270
Koehler, David H., 12630
Koehler, Lyle, 6876, 14639
Koenenn, Connie, 9358
Koenig, B.A., 3084
Koepke, Jens B., 4832
Koertge, Noretta, 12913
Kohfeld, Carol W., 1797, 11671
Kohl, Herbert, 9241, 10894
Kohlert, Nance, 3279
Kohn, E., 2983
Kohn, Richard H., 10472, 10502
Kolata, Gina, 5667, 6324-6325, 8021
Kolbert, Elizabeth, 6326, 10045-10047
Kolchin, Peter, 6877, 13147
Kolodny, R.L., 542
Kolsky, Thomas A., 1953
Kominski, Robert A., 5261
Kondon, Zak, 764
Kong, Dolores, 6327-6328
Konig, Michael F., 13232
König, Rene, 2039
Koning, Hans, 6878-6879
Konner, Melvin, 6329
Konrad, A.M., 187
Koon, Stacey C., 5918
Koostra, Paul, 13299
Kopecky, Pauline W., 4833
Kopetman, Roxana, 12582
Koppel, Martin, 11718
Koppes, Clayton R., 10048
Kopytoff, Barbara K., 8855-8856
Korbin, Jill E., 3280
Korenman, S., 6211

Koretz, Daniel, 3863, 4834
Korey, William, 8904
Korman, Abraham K., 543
Kornbluh, Felicia, 1593
Kornbluh, Jesse, 1594
Kornblum, William, 1813, 14245
Kornebusch, Karl, 6556
Kornweibel, Theodore, Jr., 765, 13693
Korobkin, Russell, 11719
Kors, Alan C., 4835
Korsmo, Fae L., 8905
Korstad, Robert R., 8022-8023
Koshan, James C., 12552
Kosinski, Jerry, 544
Koski, William S., 3864
Kosmin, Barry A., 3875
Kosmitzki, C., 13474
Kosof, Anna, 1595
Kostelantz, Richard, 9242
Koston, R., 4836
Kotelchuck, M., 6330
Kotkin, Joel, 1814, 9415
Kotlowitz, Alex, 1332
Kourtakis, Bob, 13367
Kousser, J. Morgan, 2984, 3865, 8906, 11720
Kovacic-Fleischer, Candace S., 2985
Kovaleski, Serge F., 14064
Kovel, Joel, 13694
Kovler, Peter B., 12010
Kowalski, Kenneth J., 7212
Kozol, Jonathan, 3866-3868
Kposowa, Augustine J., 7589
Kraft, Scott, 10473
Kraft, Stephanie, 13695
Krahn, H., 8469
Krakoff, Sarah, 1033
Kraly, Ellen P., 1333, 14512
Kramer, Betty Jo, 3869
Kramer, Edward G., 7212
Kramer, Michael, 11721
Kramer, Rita, 10895
Kramer, William M., 600
Krassa, Michael A., 11500
Kraul, Chris, 1205, 7213
Krause, Allen P., 1034
Krause, Dolores R., 4837
Krauss, Celene, 5511
Krauss, Clifford, 5919-5921
Kraut, Alan M., 7590
Krauthammer, Charles, 188, 10896
Krawczynski, Keith, 8024
Kray, S., 10049
Krebs, Bob, 8470
Kremer, Gary R., 766
Kremm, Thomas W., 5946
Krenn, Michael L., 12229
Kreuzer, Terese Loeb, 4839
Kriegel, Leonard, 4840
Krieger, Nancy, 1815, 6331-6335

Krikorian, Greg, 1206
Krmence, A., 7214
Kroch, E., 14175
Kroeber, Alfred L., 8266
Kroll, Michael A., 2384
Krols, Rob, 629
Kropp, Arthur J., 4841
KRS-One, 3870
Krueger, Alan B., 3546-3547, 4432
Krug, Mark, 3871
Krupat, Arnold, 767, 9243, 9314
Krupperman, Karen O., 6880
Kruse, John A., 8018
Kruttschnitt, Candace, 2385
Kryder, D., 10474
Kubey, Robert, 10050
Kubiak, Hieronim, 10634, 13516
Kuchta, E.S., 2488
Kudo, Susumu, 7215
Kuhl, Stefan, 7733, 12553
Kuhn, Clifford M., 9473
Kujovich, Gil, 4842
Kukathas, Chandran, 10897
Kulis, Stephen S., 4843
Kull, Andrew, 8907
Kumamoto, Bob, 13696
Kunjufu, Jawanza, 3872, 4222
Kunstler, Barton, 997
Kunstler, William M., 768, 13697
Kuper, Adam, 10898
Kuper, Leo, 12472
Kurkjian, Stephen, 6009
Kurnick, David, 769
Kurtz, Howard, 8908, 10051-10052, 10614, 11239
Kurtz, Michael L., 11722, 13698
Kurtzman, H.S., 8471
Kurzon, Dennis, 8472
Kushner, James A., 7216-7217
Kushnick, Louis, 3441, 8025
Kusmer, Kenneth L., 2146
Kuttner, Robert, 1816-1817, 11723
Kutzik, David M., 7734
Kwon, S.C., 1207
Kwon, S.Y., 5420
Kwong, Peter, 7591-7592, 14391
Kyle, Charles L., 3873
Kymlicka, Will, 10899

La Brecque, Ron, 4844
La Capra, Dominick, 11578, 12205
La Duke, Winona, 2006, 2147
La Fave, Lawrence, 7431
La France, Joan L., 3874
La Lumia, Joseph, 5190
La Motta, Gregory R., 2040
La Noue, George R., 4845-4846
La Pointe, Clare, 10900
La Van, H.N., 2986

La Veist, Thomas A., 6336-6339
Labaton, Stephen, 2386, 3281, 4847
Labor, Earle, 9244
LaCapra, Dominick, 9245
Lacayo, Richard, 10475
Lacey, L.J., 5668
Lacey, Marc, 6340
Lacey, W., 2679
Lacher, Irene, 10053
Lachman, Seymour P., 3875
LaCost, B.Y., 3719
LaCroix, Sumner J., 8026
Lacy, Michael G., 1596, 12171
Ladd, Everett C., Jr., 4848, 11724
Ladd, Jerrold, 770
Ladner, Joyce A., 771, 1300, 1892, 3213,
    11725, 12319, 14381
Ladson-Billings, G., 3876, 10901
LaDuke, B., 13475
LaFarge, John, 12755
LaFarge, Oliver, 8270
Lafer, G., 13949
Laffoley, Steven, 13699
Lafree, G., 2387
Lagnado, Lucette, 545, 2987-2988
Lahav, P., 8910
Lahr, John, 7432, 9246
Lait, Matt, 3877
Lakoff, Robin, 8473
Lakshmann, India A.R., 2388
Lam, R. Errol, 115, 9137, 14640
Lamar, Howard R., 8027, 8267
Lamar, Jake, 772, 4849
Lamar, Martha, 7218
Lamb, David, 2148, 9752
Lamb, Terrence J., 5923
Lambert, Wallace E., 1334, 11346
Lambropoulos, Vasiclis, 10902
Lammers, John C., 8911
Lamon, Lester C., 3878, 14065
Lamorie, Karen M., 4850
Lamotey, Kofi, 3879
Lamy, Bernhard, 14641
Lancaster, Jane F., 6881-6882
Lancaster, John, 10476
Lande, J.S., 5641
Landerman, Donna, 452
Landers, Jane L., 923, 9461
Landers, Robert K., 10903
Landes, W.M., 189
Landini, Ann L., 10054
Landry, Bart, 1819-1820, 14525
Landry, David M., 11726
Landsman, Gail H., 5924, 10055
Landt, Dan B., 1028
Lane, Daniel M., Jr., 2680
Lane, Linda R., 10477
Lane, Mary Beth, 3880
Lane, Phil, Jr., 14575

Lane, Roger, 9661, 11246
Laness, Thomas, 1035
Laney, Garrine, 190
Lang, Berel, 8474
Lang, Curtis J., 1208
Lang, Kevin, 8475
Lang, Michael H., 7219
Lang, Susan S., 12555
Lang, William L., 9568
Langan, Maria, 4851, 5059
Langbart, David A., 13667
Lange, Ellen E., 4852
Langer, Elinor, 12556
Langham, Don, 4853
Langham, J., 13041
Langhorne, Elizabeth, 5669
Langlois, Judith H., 6341
Langum, David G., 8912, 13476
Lanoue, G.R., 191
Lapchick, Richard E., 13300-13304
Lapp, Michael, 10340-10341
Larber, J., 11240
Larcom, Barbara E.K., 14026
Lardner, David F., 8477
Larew, John, 4854
Larkin, Joseph M., 2681
Larsen, Lauren C., 2041
Larson, Alfred, 14014
Larson, David A., 2989
Larson, John C., 2821
Larson, L.B., 6342
Larson, Louise Leung, 773
Larson, Robert W., 6883
Larson, Tom, 10342
Lasch, Elisabeth D., 2149
Lasch-Quinn, Elisabeth, 7220
Lash, Trude W., 1335
Lash, William H., III, 12230
Laskowsky, Henry J., 10478
Lassman, Barbara, 2682
Lasson, K., 13008
Last, Jonathan M., 6616
Lauber, Diana, 3799
Lauren, Paul G., 12231
Laurentz, Robert, 8028
Lauriault, Robert N., 8029
Laurie, Clayton D., 14066-14067
Laurie, Pantell, 2389
Lauter, Paul, 9247
Lav, Iris, 3283
Lave, James H., 1597
Lavin, David E., 4766
Lavoie, Marc, 13305
Lawrence, Charles R., III, 4855-4857, 12293
Lawrence, Curtis, 7221, 9501, 12756
Lawrence, David, Jr., 10056
Lawrence, D.G., 11727
Lawrence, Ken, 13700
Lawrence, R., 5512

Lawrence-Lightfoot, Sara, 1821
Lawrie, J., 2991
Lawson, Bill E., 2390, 11307, 13156
Lawson, Carol, 1336, 13477
Lawson, Ellen, 4858
Lawson, Raneta J., 2683
Lawson, Steven F., 1598, 11728
Lawton, Millicent, 3881, 10479, 10904
Lay, Shawn, 7825-7826
Laycock, Douglas, 13478
Layzer, David, 7735
Lazare, Daniel, 9579, 10905
Lazarus, Edward, 6344, 8268, 8913
Lazarus, Mark L., III, 8269
Lazear, Edward, 3284
Lazere, Donald, 4859, 10906
Lazere, Edward B., 7222, 7233
Lazo, Robert, 8030
Le Flore, Larry, 2391
Le Melle, Tilden J., 12232
Le Moncheck, Linda, 13009
Le Vine, R.A., 12268
Leach, Carol A., 8914
Leach, Edmund, 10907
Leacock, Eleanor B., 6884
Leahy, E. Molly, 1599
Leake, B.L., 3882
Leake, D.O., 3882
Leana, C.R., 13950
Leap, William L., 8478
Lear, E.N., 192
Leary, Warren E., 6345-6348
Leashore, Bogart R., 5670
Leatherman, Courtney, 4860-4862
Leavitt, J., 7223
LeBlanc, Lawrence, 8916
Lecca, Pedro J., 11241
Lecomte, Monique, 1036
Ledbetter, Billy D., 11729
Ledbetter, James, 10058
Lederer, Katherine, 9565
Lederer, Susan E., 6349
Lederman, Douglas, 4863-4865, 4970
Ledesma, Irene, 8031
Lee, Anne S., 6350
Lee, B.A., 7377
Lee, Barbara A., 2992, 4846
Lee, Barrett A., 7224-7225
Lee, Boon T., 3883
Lee, Chana Kai, 774
Lee, Charles, 5513-5514
Lee, David, 9459
Lee, Dong Ok, 1209
Lee, D.R., 9144
Lee, Everett S., 6350
Lee, Felicia R., 4866-4867, 5671, 6351-6352,
    7226, 8479, 11730, 13479, 13909
Lee, Gary, 1210, 5515, 10615, 11242
Lee, Gretchen, 12557

Lee, Helen Jackson, 9580
Lee, James F., 11731
Lee, Joe A., 4868
Lee, John H., 3884, 10616
Lee, Martha F., 12757
Lee, Martin A., 10059
Lee, Mary Paik, 775, 14383
Lee, Mathelle K., 3885
Lee, Moonlake Lee, 10060
Lee, N'Tanya, 4869
Lee, Pam Tau, 5516
Lee, Patrick, 1211, 7594
Lee, Regina, 7595
Lee, Richard K.C., 9485
Lee, Robert A., 808
Lee, Sally J., 4870
Lee, Samuel T.R., 4871
Lee, Sharon M., 7596, 12172
Lee, Spike, 1037, 10061-10062
Lee, Thea, 13480
Lee, Valerie E., 3886-3887, 14246
Lee, Virginia N., 14068
Lee See, Letha A., 13010
Leeds, Jeff, 4684, 4872
Leeming, David, 776
Lefevre, Patricia, 12758
Leff, Gladys, 777
Leff, Lisa, 2684, 3888, 10908
Leffall, La Salle D., Jr., 6353
Lefkowitz, Mary, 10909-10911
Leggon, C., 12126
Legion, Vicki, 6662
Legters, Lyman H., 2150, 14069
Lehman, C.R., 5420
Lehrer, Evelyn, 14176
Lehrman, Karen, 4873
Lehy, Peter J., 5819
Leibhart, Barbara G., 2151
Leibold, Nora C., 8480
Leibowitz, Arnold H., 2042
Leiby, Richard, 10063
Leicester, U., 3889
Leidholdt, Alexander S., 10064
Leigh, David J., 14526
Leigh, J.P., 14177
Leigh, Wilhelmina A., 5672, 7227-7231
Leighley, J.E., 11732
Leiman, Melvin, 12442
Leininger, Julie, 9504
Lejeune, Catherine, 10912
Leland, John, 10065-10066
Leland, Mickey, 6354
Lemann, Nicholas, 1822-1823, 2152, 2686,
    10343-10345, 11733
Lembcke, Jerry, 12392
Lemons, J. Stanley, 13481
Lemus, Rienzi B., 10480
Lentol, Joseph R., 5517
Lentz, Richard, 10067

Lenz, Gunter H., 9248
Leo, John, 4874-4875, 11243
Leonard, H. Jeffrey, 5518
Leonard, J., 13324
Leonard, Jonathan S., 193-195
Leonard, Paul A., 5925, 7232-7233
Leonard, Rebecca, 13482
Leonard, Wilbert M., II, 13305-13307
Leonardo, Micaela di, 1421, 12443, 14247
Leone, Janice, 4876
Leong, Russell C., 9249
Lerner, Michael, 546, 1038, 11734
Lerner, M.J., 1337
Leroux, Charles, 778
Leschin, Luisa, 13483
Lesher, Dave, 11735, 12085
Lesher, Richard L., 196
Lesher, Stephen, 779
Leslie, C., 4877-4878, 12340
Leslie, Kent A., 14384
Leslie, Paul L., 14385
Leslie, Virginia K.A., 14386
Lesly, Elizabeth, 1212
Lessan, G.T., 2392
Lessenberry, Jack, 4879
Lessinger, Hanna, 5584
Lester, D., 6355
Lester, Julius, 1039, 4881, 14527
Lester, P.M., 10068
Lester, Suzanne S., 3890
Letwin, Daniel L., 8032, 10346
Leuros, Peter, 8418
Leven, C.L., 7234
Levenson, Alvin J., 6356
Levenstein, Harvey A., 7597
Lever, Janet, 4882
Levesque, George A., 2393
Levidow, Les, 5037, 12901
Levin, Doron P., 10069
Levin, Henry M., 3891
Levin, Jack, 2394
Levin, Michael, 197, 4883, 7736
Levin, Murray B., 13701
Levine, Bettijane, 13011
Levine, Burton, 1040
Levine, David A., 9536
Levine, Ellen, 1600
Levine, George, 10913
Levine, Hillel, 7235
Levine, Lawrence W., 780
Levine, Molly M., 10914-10917
Levine, Paul, 10918
Levine, Peter, 13308
Levine, Rhonda F., 11571
Levine, Richard, 5872
Levine, R.M., 10070-10071
Levinson, Arlene, 12444
Levinson, Sanford, 11736
Levi-Strauss, C., 6885

Levitas, Michael, 7236
Levy, Anita, 14387
Levy, Daniel S., 7827
Levy, David W., 13484
Levy, Frank S., 3306, 14178-14179
Levy, J.A., 11240
Levy, Jacques E., 781
Levy, Joe, 10072
Levy, Leonard W., 1601
Levy, Peter B., 1602-1603, 10481
Levy, Renee Gearhart, 4884
Levy, Scott J., 13309
Lew, Bill, 1338
Lew, Julie, 10073
Lew, Walter K., 10617
Lewin, M., 13842
Lewin, Peter, 2916
Lewin, Tamara, 2994, 8917, 12558
Lewin-Epstein, N., 6357
Lewis, Anthony, 11737, 12559
Lewis, Carl, 13310
Lewis, Carrie M., 3388
Lewis, Dan A., 1911, 3892
Lewis, David Levering, 1604
Lewis, Diane E., 1213, 3893, 4885, 7237-7238,
    9530, 11223
Lewis, Diane K., 13012
Lewis, Earl, 924, 6886, 9730
Lewis, Gordon H., 3285
Lewis, Gordon K., 2043, 12233
Lewis, Gregory B., 5926
Lewis, J., 5673
Lewis, James H., 3894-3895
Lewis, L.S., 3854
Lewis, Lisa A., 10074
Lewis, Mark, 4886
Lewis, Neil A., 3896, 8918-8920
Lewis, Oscar, 5674
Lewis, Ronald L., 8033-8034, 10347
Lewis, Rupert, 2044
Lewis, W. Arthur, 3286
Lewis, William Gilbert, 11244
Lewison, Edwin R., 11738
Lewontin, R.C., 13013
Lewter, Merri G., 2153
Lezin, K., 9079
Liberman, Arthur, 547
Licht, Walter, 5423
Lichtblau, Eric, 12086
Lichtenstein, Alexander C., 5762-5763
Lichtenstein, Nelson, 1824, 8023
Lichtenstein, William, 11157
Lichter, Daniel T., 5424, 5620, 13951
Lichter, L.S., 10075
Lichter, S.R., 10075, 11739
Liddell, Felix H., 14590
Liden, Harold, 11158
Lieb, Rebecca, 10076
Lieberman, E., 6358

Lieberman, L., 4887
Lieberman, Myron, 3898
Lieberman, Paul, 2395-2396
Lieberson, Stanley, 2995, 14248, 14528
Liebler, C.M., 10077
Liebman, James S., 2688-2689, 8921
Lief, B.J., 7239
Lieh, T., 10078
Lienesch, Michael, 12759
Liffmann, Karla L., 1605
Liggio, Leonard P., 6887
Light, Audrey, 2816
Lighter, J.E., 8482
Lightfoot, Claude, 11159
Lightfoot, Sara Lawrence, 3899
Lillie-Blanton, Marsha, 6145, 6359
Lim, Shirley Geok-lin, 14388
Limanni, Anthony M., 6888
Limas, Vicki J., 1606
Limerick, Patricia N., 6889-6890, 9482, 11740
Limon, Jose E., 7433
Lincoln, C. Eric, 12760-12762
Lincoln, Kenneth, 7434
Lindenfeld, Frank, 4888
Lindgren, J. Ralph, 4889
Lindner, Charles L., 8922-8923
Lindsay, Drew, 3900
Lindsey, Donal F., 4890
Lindsey, Kenneth P., 6360
Linfield, Michael, 13702
Ling, Peter, 1607
Ling, Susie, 14389
Link, C.R., 3901
Link, Martin A., 6891
Link, William A., 6361
Linn, Robert L., 3902
Linnekin, Jocelyn, 2045
Linton, Ralph M., 8270
Linzer, Peter, 8483
Linzie, Roderick, K., 453
Lippard, Lucy R., 10919
Lippi-Green, Rosina, 2996
Lippy, Charles H., 12763
Lipschultz, Sybil, 8924
Lipset, Seymour M., 198, 1966, 2167, 4848, 11741, 12087
Lipshultz, Robert J., 7598
Lipsky, Michael, 6362
Lipstadt, Deborah E., 548-549, 10079
Lipsyte, Robert, 13311
LiPuma, Edward, 13485
Lisio, Donald J., 11742
Liss, Susan M., 1608
Littell, Marcia S., 550
Little, Cheryl, 7599
Little, D.L., 2318
Little, George, 5927
Little, J.K., 13495
Little, Jonathan D., 9250

Little, Lawrence S, 12764
Little, Monroe H., 4891
Littlefield, Alice, 3903
Littlefield, Daniel C., 397, 13148
Littlefield, Daniel F., Jr., 8317, 10618, 14642
Littlefield, Mary Ann, 10618
Littlejohn, Edward J., 4892
Littman, Mark S., 1825, 3287
Litwack, Leon F., 5787
Liu, Edward, 11743
Liu, J., 2046
Liu, Tessie, 12173
Liu, T.P., 10920
Lively, Adam, 11160
Lively, Donald E., 199, 2997, 8925
Lively, Kit, 4893
Livingston, Ivor L., 6363
Livingstone, D.N., 5519, 12341
Llorens, James L., 11744
Lloyd, David, 8459
Lo, Christina, 7241
Loach, Marva L. De, 9143
Lobaco, Gina, 8695
Lobbia, J.A., 3904
Lochlin, J.C., 7737
Lock, Margaret, 12445
Locke, Alain L., 11306
Locke, Don C., 10921, 13482
Locke, Herbert G., 1041
Locke, Hubert G., 14249
Locke, Mamie E., 14390
Locurto, C., 7738
Locust, Carol, 2998
Loescher, Frank S., 12765
Loevy, Robert D., 1609
Loewen, James W., 10080, 10922-10923, 11745
Loftin, John D., 12766
Loftus, E.F., 13014
Logan, Andy, 1042, 11746-11747
Logan, John R., 7064-7065
Logan, Jonnie Lee, 782
Logan, Paul E., 1043
Logsdon, Joseph, 1422, 9516
Logue, Barbara J., 6364
Logue, Calvin M., 8433, 8484-8485, 8512, 12692
Lohr, Steve, 12914
Loiacono, Stephanie, 13015
Lois, Dale J., 7242
Lokos, Lionel, 200
Lomawaima, K. Tsianina, 3906
Lomax, Melanie E., 5928
Lomeli, Francisco A., 9251, 11127, 11156
Lomotey, Kofi, 4305
London, B., 2120
Long, James E., 2999
Long, Jana, 12767
Long, J.E., 7243, 14180

Long, Jeff, 9706
Long, Richard A., 6892
Long, S., 12104
Long, Stewart, 13016
Longoria, Thomas, Jr., 11748
Longres, John F., Jr., 12294
Loo, Chalsa, 4894
Look, Jeannie, 4895-4896
Lookadoo, Linda K., 3907
Looker, A.C., 6365
Looney, J.G., 5673
Loose, Cindy, 10855, 14064
Lopach, James J., 11749
Lopata, H.Z., 11240
Lopes, A., 13846
Lopes, Grace M., 7852
Lopez, Adalberto, 11866
Lopez, Alfredo, 2047-2048
Lopez, D., 12446
Lopez, Gerald P., 8926-8928
Lopez Gonzalez, Arabia, 9252
Lopez, Jose, 11161
Lopez, Manuel, 1044
Lopez, Manuel Mariano, 7244
Lopez, Patrick F., 4897
Lopez, Steven, 6366
Lopez-Rivera, Oscar, 2049
Lorant, Laurie, 9253
Lorch, Donatella, 5764
Loren, C., 1826
Lorimer, Douglas A., 12342
Loring, Katherine, 10949
Lorini, Alessandra, 9612
Loslier, Luc, 6367
Lothyan, Phillip E., 1423
Lott, Bernice, 10081, 13017-13018
Lott, Eric, 14250
Lotz, David W., 603, 12812
Lotz, Roy, 551
Louie, Vivian, 13486
Louis, C. Benjie, 7339
Loury, Glenn, 2154
Love, Jean C., 8486
Love, R., 8035
Love, Roger, 3288
Love, Sherri, 2397
Love, Spencie, 6368
Love, Wallace B., 6369
Loveland, Christine A., 9180
Low, Ronald, 1339
Low, W.A., 14065
Lowe, David, 12597-12598
Lowe, Denis S., 2690
Lowe, Linda, 6370
Lowe, Lydia, 8487
Lowe, R., 6893
Lowe, Robert E., 3910-3911, 4209
Lowe, Rosemary H., 201
Lowell, Richard, 5520

Lowenthal, David, 10924
Lowery, C.M., 7884
Lowery, Charles D., 1610
Lowie, Robert H., 7739
Lowrie, Samuel H., 13149
Lowry, G.C., 56
Lowry, Ira S., 9426
Lowry, L.D., 202
Lowy, Richard, 12174
Loya, Anamaria C., 3912
Loynd, Ray, 13487
Luban, David, 8929
Lubasch, Arnold, 783
Lubeck, S., 1340
Lubiano, Wahneema, 10082
Lucaites, John L., 8488
Lucal, B., 1827
Lucas, Malcolm M., 8930
Lucas, Maria Elena, 784
Lucas, Tamara, 3913
Lucas, Thomas A., 14071
Luckett, Perry D., 10482
Luder, Elisabeth, 6371
Luebben, Ralph A., 3000
Luebke, Paul, 11750
Lueck, D., 2106
Lueck, Thomas J., 96, 1214
Luedtke, Luther S., 1864, 12962
Luhman, Reid, 8489, 13488
Luker, Kristin, 6372
Luker, Ralph E., 12768
Lum, Darrell H.Y., 9176
Lum, Joann, 14391
Lumsden, Linda, 3777
Lumumba, Chokwe, 13703
Luna, Gaye, 3001
Lundberg, O., 6373
Lundberg, S.J., 203
Lunde, A.S., 6374
Lundy, J., 13704
Lundy-Allen, B., 13942
Lunn, J., 204
Lupo, Alan, 4898
Lurie, E., 12343
Lurie, Nancy, 6884
Lusanne, Clarence, 10083, 11751, 14529
Luskin, R.C., 11752
Lutholtz, M. William, 7828
Luttbeg, Norma R., 12088
Lutz, Chris, 12561
Lutz, Hartmut, 10084
Luvin, Tamar, 8490
Luz, Reyes, Maria de la, 4899
Lyall, Sarah, 11753
Lyden, Fremont J., 2150
Lydon, Mary T., 3289
Lykes, M. Brinton, 3002
Lyles, Barbara D., 14392

Lyman, Stanford M., 1611, 8931, 10085, 12447, 13150
Lyman, Stanley D., 13705
Lynberg, Michele C., 6375
Lynch, Frederick R., 205-206, 12295
Lynch, James, 10925
Lynch, Rene, 2398
Lynch, Robert N., 11754
Lynn, Frank, 11755
Lynn, Lawrence E., Jr., 5812
Lynn, M.L., 12649
Lynn, R., 7740
Lyon, Danny, 1612
Lyon, David, 13706
Lyons, Charles H., 7741
Lyons, Oren, 8932
Lytle, Clifford M., 8762, 11135

Maassen, Gerard H., 13489
Maat, Anasa, 3914
Mabee, Carleton, 785, 3915, 12344, 14393
Mabry, Marcus, 1215, 3916, 4900-4901, 12296, 13490
Mabury, Marcus, 3003
Mac Leod, William C., 3442
Macaulay, Jacqueline, 13491
MacCann, Dormarse C., 9254, 13492
Maccoby, Hyam, 9255
MacCoun, Robert J., 8933
MacDonald, Heather, 4902-4903, 10926
MacDonald, J.M., 1216
MacDonald, John S., 14643
MacDonald, Leatrice, 14643
Macdonald, Mary Lou P., 2691
MacDougall, Jill, 9174
Macenczak, Kimberly P., 3917
MacGregor, Morris J., 10483
Macias, Reynaldo F., 3918, 8491
Maciel, David R., 6894, 8036, 10086
MacKenzie, Melody K., 8934
Mackey, Eric M., 11756
Mackinley, Peter W., 12769
MacKinnon, Catherine A., 13019
Mackintosh, N.J., 7742
Mack-Williams, Voloria (Kibibi) C., 14394
Maclean, N., 552
MacLean, Nancy K., 7829-7830
Macmanus, S.A., 11448
MacMartin, Charley, 4904
MacMillan, Jackie, 13312
Macnicol, John, 1828
Macrae, C.N., 13493
MacRae, D., 4019
MacRobert, Iain, 12770
Madaus, George F., 13843-13844
Madden, J.F., 7193
Maddock, Stella, 14644
Maddox, Lucy, 9256
Madenwald, Abbie M., 3919

Madhubuti, Haki R., 9417, 14395
Madura, William, 147, 5416
Maganini, Stephen, 11757
Magat, Richard, 5234
Magee, Rhonda V., 3290
Maggio, Rosalie, 8492
Maggs, Peter B., 8935
Magnaghi, Russell M., 13151
Magnarella, Paul J., 8936
Magner, Denise K., 1045, 4905-4910
Magubane, Bernard, 398
Mahard, Rita E., 2598
Maher, Timothy W., 5521
Mahfowz, A.M., 12281
Mahnic, Eric, 12089
Mahon, John K., 10484
Mahoney, Brenna B., 3920
Mahoney, Joan, 5675
Mahoney, Kathleen, 8493
Mahoney, Martha, 7245
Maier, Andrea, 1217
Mainfort, Robert C., Jr., 10412
Maingot, Anthony, P., 9462
Mainwaring, W.T., Jr., 1613
Maitzen, Stephen, 3004
Maizlish, Steven, 2782
Majka, Linda C., 5737
Major, Brenda, 12273
Major, Reginald, 11758
Majors, Richard, 1341, 14530
Makofsky, Abraham, 4912
Makue, D.M., 6376
Malamud, Martha A., 10927
Malan, Vernon, 2155
Malcolm, Andrew H., 6377-6378
Malcolm X, 13707
Maldonado, Edwin, 8037
Maldonado, Rita M., 2055, 10350
Maldonado, R.M., 14181
Maldonado-Denis, Manuel, 2050-2054, 10348-10349
Malev, William S., 1046
Malgady, Robert G., 6379
Malina, R.M., 6380
Malitz, Nancy, 11245
Malley, Deborah De Witt, 8038
Maloney, G.D., 5070
Malouf, A.A., 13152
Malouf, C., 13152
Malson, Micheline R., 14396
Maltz, Earl M., 1614, 3005, 13020
Malveaux, Julianne, 3291-3292, 8494, 8937
Mamiija, Lawrence H., 12760
Mancall, Peter C., 6895
Manchester, J.M., 3293
Mancillas, Jorge R., 4913
Mancini, Matthew J., 5765
Mancy, Ardith L., 3294
Mandel, Michael J., 7600

Mandell, Daniel R., 9531
Mandle, Jay R., 3223-3224, 3295, 8039
Mandler, Peter, 3271, 3296
Manegold, Catherine S., 786, 4914
Manes, J., 8575, 8644
Mangan, Katherine S., 4915-4916
Mangold, William D., 6381
Mangrum, Garth, 3345
Mankiller, Wilma, 787
Manly, Howard, 2399-2400, 6603, 9976
Mann, Arthur J., 14142, 14182-14183
Mann, Coramae Rickey, 2401, 8938
Mann, Eric, 788, 5522-5523
Mann, Jim, 7601
Mann, Michael, 1424
Mann, Susan A., 14397
Mannell, Roger, 7431
Mannheim, B., 12366
Manning, Kathleen, 11073
Manning, Stuart, 10928
Manshi, Charles F., 4917
Mansnerus, Laura, 13910
Manta, Ben, 2156
Manton, Kenneth G., 6382-6383
Manuel, Diane, 4918
Manville, Philip B., 1425
Manzagol, Michael, 4919
Maples, Rebeka L., 4920
Mar, Don, 13952-13953
Marable, Manning, 1615-1616, 1830, 4921,
    9537, 10087, 10485, 10929-10932, 11162-
    11163, 11760-11769, 14531
Marable, Virginia M., 14532
Maraniss, David, 4922
Marantz, Steve, 5930, 7099, 7246
Marc, R.D., 6384
Marchetti, Gina, 10088
Marchio, James, 9673
Marcotte, Paul, 7831
Marcum, John, 7247
Marcus, Frances F., 5524, 12562
Marcus, G., 3921
Marcus, Grania B., 3921, 9613
Marcus, Jacob R., 553
Marcuse, Peter, 2157, 7248
Marcy, Sam, 7832
Mardon, Steve, 4923
Mare, R.D., 3712
Marett, C.B., 12126
Marger, Martin, 11347
Margis-Noguera, Taylor, 3922
Margo, Robert A., 3923-3925, 5425-5426,
    6223, 10351, 14533
Margolick, David, 554, 2402-2404, 8939
Margolis, Edwin, 3926
Margolis, Maxine L., 7602
Marian, A.G., 7067
Maril, Robert Lee, 3297, 9707
Marin, Barbara V., 6385

Marin, Gerado, 6385
Marin, Marguerite V., 1954, 1965, 9418
Marina, D., 11246
Marinaccio, James, 10089
Mariner, Wendy K., 6386
Marino, C., 6896
Marisnerus, Laura, 3927
Mark, Gregory Y., 3006
Markowitz, Ruth J., 3928-3929
Marks, Carole, 1831
Marks, G., 12291
Marks, George P., III, 12234
Marks, Paul G., 5676
Markstrom-Adams, Carol, 1371
Marmot, M.G., 6387
Marple, D.P., 13294
Marquart, James W., 2405
Marquez, Benjamin, 1955-1956
Marriott, Michel, 2692-2693, 3930-3932, 4924,
    8495, 10090-10091, 10933-10934
Marsh, Clifton E., 12772
Marsh, Dave, 13708
Marsh, Frances K., 3933
Marshall, D.F., 8496
Marshall, Dale R., 11444, 11770-11771
Marshall, Mary L., 6388
Marshall, Ray, 1590, 3007, 8040
Marshall, Ronald J., 11772
Marshall, S.E., 14398
Marshall, Thurgood, 1617, 8940, 11773
Marston, Linda L., 11774
Marston, Sallie A., 1427, 7603
Marszalek, John F., 1610
Marten, James, 9708
Martens, F.T., 2406
Martin, Anthony C., 4925
Martin, B.L., 14534
Martin, Charles, 8041, 8941
Martin, C.L., 13494-13495
Martin, Douglas, 10619
Martin, Frank, 10935
Martin, Gordon A., Jr., 8942
Martin, J. Malcolm, 12563
Martin, Jeannie, 10936, 10937
Martin, Jean-Pierre, 11334
Martin, Jill E., 1428
Martin, Joel W., 6897
Martin, Judith, 4926, 10938
Martin, Marguerite V., 1957
Martin, Michael, 7743
Martin, Patricia Preciado, 6898
Martin, Philip L., 8042
Martin, Robert F., 8043
Martin, Sandy D., 12773
Martin, Susan E., 207
Martindale, Carolyn, 10092-10093
Martinez, Carlos, 3934
Martinez, Demetria, 5525
Martinez, Deirdre, 3336

Martinez, Elizabeth, 3008, 4927-4929, 6390, 6899, 10620, 11775, 12175
Martinez, Frank, 11776
Martinez, Jose V., Jr., 2056
Martinez, Michael D., 12088
Martinez, Ruben, 5931
Martinez, Ruben O., 4291
Martinez, Thomas M., 10094, 12564, 13496
Martinez, Valerie, 4930
Martinez-Schnell, Beverly, 6389
Martinucci, Suzanne, 9614
Martorella, Peter H., 14062
Marty, Martin E., 12565
Marura, William A., 3935
Marwell, Gerald, 1618
Marx, Andrew, 1958
Marx, Gary T., 13709-13710, 14127
Marx, J., 208
Marx, Jeffrey, 13310
Mascia, Patrick E., 3936
Mascie-Taylor, C.G.N., 7742
Masiel, Richard, 11987
Maslow-Armand, Laura, 2694-2695
Mason, Carol, 1832
Mason, D., 12505
Mason, Phillip L., 3009, 8044
Masotti, Louis H., 13711
Massaro, Toni M., 8497
Massero, Toni Marie, 10939
Massey, C.R., 4931
Massey, Douglas S., 1833-1836, 3214, 3299-3301, 5813, 7078, 7137-7138, 7249-7255
Massey, Grace C., 12257
Massey, James L., 2425, 6900, 14072
Masters, Brooke A., 555, 4932-4935
Mastromarino, Mark A., 14073
Masur, Louis P., 2407
Matabane, Paula W., 10095
Matarese, Linda B., 13021
Mateer, G. Dirk, 3939
Mathabane, Gail, 5677
Mathabane, Mark, 791
Mathews, David, 10940
Mathews, Donald G, 12774
Mathews, Jay, 3010-3011, 9257, 11777
Mathews, Thomas, 209, 12176
Mathis, Chris, 5523
Mathis, William J., 3940
Mathisen, G.S., 13313
Mathisen, J.A., 13313
Matney, Brian K., 2696
Matsuda, Kazue, 2210
Matsuda, Mari J., 210, 8498-8499, 8943-8945, 10941, 14399
Matsumoto, Valerie, 9419
Matsuoka, Jon, 5526
Mattai, P.R., 10942
Mattei, A.R., 2057

Matteson, Kevin, 211
Matthaei, Julie, 6703
Matthews, Anne, 4936, 10943
Matthews, Carolyn R., 8500
Matthews, Dakin, 10096
Matthews, Fred H., 6901, 11348
Matthews, Jim, 1044
Matthews, Victoria Earle, 9258
Mattos Cintron, Wilfredo, 2058-2059
Mattson, Mark T., 6710
Matute-Bianchi, Maria E., 3941, 8535
Mauer, Marc, 2408
Maugh, Thomas H., II, 6391
Maurer, David J., 12566
Maw, Carlyle E., 3635
Max, Daniel, 9259
Maxcy, Spencer J., 10944
Maxted, Julia, 9420
Maxwell, Bill, 4937
Maxwell, Carol J.C., 12775
Maxwell, Madeline, 8501
Maxwell, N.L., 3942
May, Lary, 12043
May, Lee, 9454
May, Mary, 14400
May, Robert E., 10486
Mayberry, Katherine J., 9260
Mayer, Egon, 10097
Mayer, Michael S., 1619
Mayer, Susan E., 3302, 5812, 7200-7202
Mayfield, Bonnie L., 3012
Mayfield, Chris, 2610
Maykovich, Minako K., 13497
Maynard, M., 11285
Mayo, Louise A., 556
Mayo, Nathanette, 8045
Mayo-Smith, R., 7604
Mays, V.M., 14401
Mazama, A., 8502
Mazon, Mauricio, 13498
Mazrui, Ali A., 1047, 13153
Mazunder, Sucheta, 12177, 12345
Mazza, Patrick, 4938
Mazza, Peter, 4939
Mc Cray, Walter A., 12776
Mc Dougall, Harold A., 9521
Mc Loughlin, William G., 12777
McAdam, Douglas, 1620-1621, 11778
McAdams, D. Claire, 5527
McAllister, Bill, 3013, 5932-5933
McAllister, Pam., 452
McAlpine, Robert, 1622
McArdle, Alan, 4692
McArthur, Harvey, 212
McBay, Shirley M., 4940
McBeth, Sally J., 3943
McBride, David, 6392-6395
McBride, Judith Ann, 3944
McBride, William G., 9680

McBroome, Delores N., 9421
McCall, Nathan, 792, 11164
McCallum, Brenda, 8046
McCandless, B.R., 12269
McCann, Carole R., 14402
McCart, Carol L., 10945
McCarthy, C., 10946-10947
McCarthy, Cameron R., 3945-3946, 4941
McCarthy, Claire, 6396
McCarthy, G. Michael, 11779
McCarthy, John R., 4942
McCarthy, John T., 11780
McCarthy, Kathleen D., 14363
McCarthy, Peggy, 3947, 4943
McCarthy, Tim, 12778
McCarus, Ernest, 14535
McCaskill, Barbara Ann, 9261
McCaul, E.J., 3948
McCaul, Robert L., 3949
McCendon, McKee J., 2697
McChesney, Fred S., 8271
McChesney, Robert W., 10098
McClain, Charles J., 6397, 7256
McClain, Paula D., 2465, 10621, 11701,
     14403-14404
McClellan, E. Fletcher, 1959
McClelland, Katherine, 4944, 8946, 14465
McClinton, Gregory L., 8815
McCloskey, Donald N., 14533
McCloud, Aminah B., 12779
McCluggage, Robert W., 8272
McClure, Phyllis, 3950
McCluskey, Audrey T., 3951-3952
McCollum, Heather A., 4945
McCombs, Regina C., 3953
McConahay, John B., 2698, 9435, 13911
McConnell, Malcolm, 12591
McConnell, Michael W., 8947, 10948
McConnell, Scott, 11781
McCord, Colin, 6398
McCorisle, Mac, 11782
McCormack, Arlene, 4946
McCormick, Andy, 4947-4948
McCormick, Angela T., 5678
McCormick E., 13330
McCormick, John, 9508, 9615
McCormick, Joseph P., II, 11933
McCormick, M.C., 6399-6400
McCormick, R.L., 3954
McCormick, Richard P., 4949
McCoy, Clyde, 10352
McCoy, Donald, 1623
McCracken, Robert D., 6401
McCrary, Peyton, 11783-11784
McCrate, Elaine, 5679
McCraw, William, 9262
McCrea, Carrie, 8948
McCullum, Lamela A., 11034
McCunn, Ruthanne Lum, 793

McDade, Laurie, A., 12915
McDermott, John D., 6902
McDevitt, Jack, 1624, 2394
McDonald, Dennis, 3955
McDonald, Janis L., 8949
McDonald, Laughlin, 8950, 11785
McDonald, Roderick A., 13154
McDonnell, Janet A., 8274
McDonnell, Janet E., 8273
McDonnell, Lawrence T., 13155
McDonnell, Patrick J., 5934, 7605-7606
McDougall, Harold A., 1625, 10099
McDowell, Deborah E., 9263
McDowell, Douglas S., 213
McDowell, Edwin, 9264
McDowell, Jeanne, 10100
McDowell, Winston, 9616
McElliot, Mary Ellen, 7883
McElroy, Jerome L., 2012
McElvey, Kay N., 9522
McFadden, Robert D., 2409, 5935, 9617,
     10101
McGahey, Richard, 8047
McFate, Katherine, 3303
McGarry, Richard G., 10102
McGary, Howard J., Jr., 13156
McGeary, Michael G.H., 5812
McGee Banks, Cherry A., 4046
McGee, Celia, 10103
McGee, Henry W., Jr., 7257, 14536
McGee, Jim, 13712
McGee, Leo, 8275-8276
McGehee, Elizabeth, 11786
McGehee, Scott, 9538
McGhee, J.D., 5680
McGhee, Paul E., 7435
McGinnis, Tony, 6903
McGlynn, Frank, 3216, 6877, 12878, 13189,
     14542
McGoun, W.E., 5681
McGovern, Joseph A.H., 4950
McGovney, D.O., 1429
McGowan, David, 7519
McGowan, D.F., 4951
McGowan, Sharon S., 3956
McGrane, Donald J., 1626
McGrary, Howard, Jr., 11307
McGraw, Dan, 7258
McGraw, Marie T., 9731
McGreevy, John T., 10353
McGregor, Alan, 7744
McGregor, Davianna Pomaika'i, 8277
McGrory, Mary, 3957
McGuire, F.A., 12631
McGuire, Phillip, 10487-10488
McGuire, Randall H., 6904
McGunagle, Fred, 7259
McHugh, Blanche, 4952
McHugh, Kevin E., 10354

McIntosh, J.L., 14645
McIntosh, John L., 6402
McIntosh, Peggy, 10949
McIntosh, S., 10956
McIntyre, R., 5682
McJamerson, Evangeline M., 4953
McKanna, Clare V., Jr., 8951-8952, 14074
McKay, Claude, 9265
McKay, Emily G., 12090
McKay, R.H., 3958, 8048
McKee, Jesse O., 14537
McKee, Nancy P., 3304, 3959
McKelvey, Charles, 11165
McKenna, Clare V., Jr., 2410-2411
McKenna, F.R., 10950
McKenna, Kristine, 794
McKenny, Patrick C., 1343
McKenzie-Wharton, Lou B.V., 2699
McKibben, Gordon, 13499
McKillop, Peter, 9615
McKinley, Catherine, 13157
McKinney, Scott, 7260-7262
McKissack, Frederick, 454
McKissack, Patricia, 454
McKiven, Henry Melvin, Jr., 8049
Mclafferty S., 6403
McLanahan, S., 5590
McLanahan, Sara J., 3305
McLanahan, S.S., 5631
McLaren, John, 14132
McLaren, Peter L., 10951, 12448
McLarin, Kimberly J., 2700, 3960-3962
McLaughlin, Andree Nicola, 9167
McLaughlin, F., 13293
McLaughlin, William G., 10622
McLaurin, Melton A., 795
McLean, B., 8503
McLean, J.E., 13845
McLemee, Scott, 11787
McLeod, Jonathan W., 8050
McLeod, Norman C., Jr., 8051
McLoughlin, William G., 6905-6908, 12780-12781
McLoyd, Vonnie C., 5683
McMahon Eileen M., 12782
McManus, Walter S., 8052, 8504
McMath, Robert C., 11230
McMillan, Lewis K., 1048
McMillan, Penelope, 8953
McMillan, Theodore, 2412
McMillen, Liz, 13500
McMillen, Neil R., 9552, 11788
McMillin, D., 4954
McMinn, M.R., 8505
McNabb, Steven, 5936
McNall, Scott G., 6415
McNamara, Martha J., 14594
McNamara, Patricia P., 4955
McNeil, Kurt, 8278

McNeil, Taylor, 2321
McNeil, Teresa B., 3963
McNeill, J.R., 12876
McNertney, Edward M., 10401
McNibb, S., 6404
McNickle, Chris, 11789
McNickle, D'Arcy, 6909-6910
McPartland, James M., 2561
McPheeters, Annie L., 9145
McPherson, James A., 1049, 11790
McPherson, Michael S., 4956
McQuiston, John T., 3014, 11791
McRae, F. Finley, 13314
McRae, M.B., 11247
McShane, Damian, 6405
McShane, S.L., 3015
McTighe, Michael J., 11792
McWhirter, J. Jeffries, 13912
McWhorter, Diane, 7833
McWilliams, Carey, 3016, 6911, 8053-8054, 9422
Meadenka, Kenneth R., 5427
Meaders, Daniel E., 13158
Means, Harrison J., 3964
Means, Howard, 796
Mecklin, J.M., 11308
Medding, Peter Y., 557
Medhurst, Martin, 8954
Medicine, Beatrice, 8506, 14281, 14405
Medina, M., 3965
Medoff, Marshall, 2814, 13315
Medoff, Rafael, 558
Meece, Judith L., 4957
Meeks, Ronald L., 1179
Megdal, S.B., 248
Mehan, H., 3966
Mehler, Barry A., 12346-12348
Mehren, Elizabeth, 797
Meier, August, 798, 1627, 2870-2871, 3967, 5755, 8055, 11725, 12735
Meier, Barry, 1218
Meier, Deborah W., 3968-3969
Meier, Kenneth J., 3017-3018, 3970-3973, 8955
Meier, Matt S., 799, 6911-6913, 14646-14647
Meinig, D.W., 6914
Meisels, M., 11246
Meisenheimer, J.R., II, 7607
Meisenheimer, J.R., 4958
Meisler, Andy, 10105
Melecki, Thomas G., 4959
Melendez, E., 1902, 8102, 10355
Melendez, Edgardo, 2060-2062
Melendez, Edwin, 2061-2062, 8056
Melhem, D.H., 9266
Melmyk, Mary F., 10952
Melosh, Barbara, 6915
Meltzner, Michael, 8956
Melville, Margarita B., 6642
Melzer, Richard, 7436

Memmi, Albert, 12178, 12449
Menacker, Julius, 3974
Menaghan, E.G., 5157
Menand, Louis, 10709, 10953-10955
Menchaca, Martha, 1837, 3975, 14538
Menchik, P.L., 6406
Menciner, Stephanie, 11248
Mendelsohn, Harold, 5835
Mendez, J.L., 2603
Mendez Gonzalez, Rosalinda, 12235
Mendoza, Fernando S., 6407
Mendoza, Manuel, 10106
Mendus, Susan, 8393
Menefee, Selden C., 6916
Menkel-Meadow, Carrie, 8957
Mensh, Elaine, 7745
Mensh, Harry, 7745
Mercer, Jane R., 7746
Mercer, Joyce, 214, 4962-4970
Mercer, Le Ann W., 2413
Merida, Kevin, 5937
Merisotis, J.P., 4971
Merkel, Philip L., 8958
Merl, Jean, 3976-3977, 4972, 10598
Merl, Joan, 3978
Merrell, James H., 6917-6920
Merrill, Christopher, 9483
Merrill Ramrez, Marie A., 13713
Merrimar, W. Richard, 12091
Merritt, Deborah, 5140
Merry, S.E., 8959
Mertz, Elizabeth, 8507
Merwin, W.S., 6921
Messer-Davidow, Ellen, 4973
Messerschmidt, Jim, 5938
Messner, S.F., 2414-2415
Messner, William F., 8057
Mestre, Jose P., 8392
Metz, Holly, 4974
Metzger, Walter P., 10850
Metzler, William H., 14184
Meusner, Jeffrey N., 7608
Meves, Antonio, 9267
Meyer, Bruce, D.D., 1219
Meyer, Eugene L., 7263, 12632
Meyer, Gerald, 11793
Meyer, Josh, 3501, 3980, 10623-10624
Meyer, Madonna H., 6408
Meyer, Marshall W., 5939
Meyer, Melissa L., 6922, 8279
Meyer, P., 10956
Meyer, Sylvan, 10107, 10228
Meyers, Alan F., 6409
Meyers, Christopher, 2416
Meyers, Michael, 1960
Meyerson, Harold, 11794
Meyn, Marianne, 8508
Miah, Malik, 14539
Mial, Joetta M., 4975

Michael, Robert, 559
Michaelides, Sandra, 2701
Michaels, D., 6410
Michaels, Walter B., 12236, 14251
Michaelson, Judith, 10108-10109
Michak, Don, 13714
Michalak, Laurence, 13501
Michel, G.J., 3981
Michel, Richard C., 3306, 14178-14179
Michelman, Frank I., 4976, 8727, 11795
Michelotti, Cecelia, 2702
Mickel, Richard A., 6411
Mickels, Marilyn W., 12783
Mickens, Ronald, 14648
Middleton, Jeanne M., 2703
Middleton, Russell, 560-561, 7437
Middleton, Stephen, 8960-8961
Mieder, Wolfgang, 13502
Mier, Robert, 9498
Migliorino, Ellen G., 6923
Mikell, Edna F., 3982
Miles, Jack, 7609
Miles, Robert, 3443, 10356, 11166, 12450-
    12454
Milic, Mladen, 6417
Milkman, Ruth, 10957
Miller, Alan C., 7610
Miller, Alton, 11796-11797
Miller, Andrew T., 5684
Miller, Arthur G., 13503, 13560, 13581
Miller, Arthur S., 2417
Miller, B., 11798
Miller, Char, 12037
Miller, C.M., 1628
Miller, David, 1050
Miller, E. Ethelbert, 1051
Miller, Edward, 800
Miller, G., 1344, 1882, 11098, 11411
Miller, G.P., 8962
Miller, Gregory R., 7834
Miller, J., 13846
Miller, Jay, 801
Miller, Jerome G., 2418
Miller, John Chester, 13159
Miller, John Daniel, 2704
Miller, Joshua, 6924
Miller, Julie A., 3983, 5940
Miller, K.A., 7611
Miller, Karen K., 4977
Miller, Keith D., 8509
Miller, Kelly, 8058
Miller, Kerby, 10110
Miller, L., 7746
Miller, LaMar P., 13504
Miller, Marc S., 8059
Miller, Margo, 6925
Miller, Mark, 14252
Miller, Marvin D., 562
Miller, Michael V., 3307-3308

Miller, Norman, 2705-2706
Miller, Patrick, 13316
Miller, R. Baxter, 9268
Miller, Randall M., 6926, 10111-10112, 11409, 11800, 13160, 13164, 14301, 14540
Miller, Randi L., 2707-2708
Miller, Robert M., 7835, 14075
Miller, S., 4500
Miller, S.M., 3984
Miller, S.C., 4978
Miller, Sherman N., 10489
Miller, S.M., 5317, 6412
Miller, Stuart Creighton, 12237
Miller, Susan, 3842
Miller, Thomas L., 8280
Miller, Tice, 9193
Miller, Vincent P., 7264
Miller, W., 2676
Miller, Warren E., 11799
Miller, William H., 12179
Miller-Jones, D., 1345, 13847
Millis, Harry A., 7612
Millner, Lois, 6413
Milloy, Courtland, 1961, 3985
Mills, Ami Chen, 13716
Mills, Bette D., 12297
Mills, David, 802, 7438, 9269, 9423, 12567
Mills, Kay, 803-804
Mills, Linda G., 13022
Mills, Nicolaus, 1629
Milner, Neal, 1630
Milofsky, Carl, 13848
Milun, Kathryn, 8314
Min, F.G., 1220
Min, Pyond Gap, 1221
Mincberg, Elliot M., 3986
Mincey, Ronald B., 1838, 1874, 3309
Mindiola, Tatcho, Jr., 3019-3020
Minehan, Cathy E., 7265
Miner, H. Craig, 2158-2159
Minkowitz, Donna, 3987
Minorini, Paul, 3988
Minow, Martha, 3021, 8510, 8964-8966
Mintz, Beth, 6415
Mintz, Lawrence E., 7439
Mintz, Sidney W., 12180, 14542-14543
Miranda, Gloria E., 1839
Miranda, Leticia C., 1346, 3310, 3989
Miranda, Luis A., 2064
Mirande, Alfredo, 6927, 8967
Mirel, Jeffrey, 3990-3991
Miringoff, Marc L., 1347
Mishel, Lawrence R., 3311
Mishkin, Kate, 8511
Miskin, Al, 10113
Misukiewicz, Claude, 12568
Mitchel, Christopher, 7509
Mitchell, Alison, 3022
Mitchell, B.N., 11249

Mitchell, Douglas E., 2731
Mitchell, Emily, 3992
Mitchell, George, 2710
Mitchell, H.L., 455
Mitchell, John L., 2419
Mitchell, Kathy, 5290
Mitchell, M.O., 7230
Mitchell, Robert, 4983
Mitchell-Kernan, Claudia, 5731, 9799
Mitgang, Lee, 3993
Mitson, Betty E., 2200, 12208
Mixon, Gregory L., 14076
Mixon, Harold, 8512
Mixon, J.W., Jr., 216, 330-332
Mjagky, Nina, 12633
Mladenka, Kenneth R., 12634
Mladinic, Antonio, 13422
Moberg, D.O., 12649
Mobley, Joe, 925
Mock, Jere J., 5047
Model, Suzanne, 8060
Modell, John, 3429, 10490
Modgil, C., 7707
Modgil, S., 7707
Modigliani, Andre, 109
Modjeska, Lee, 3023
Modras, Ronald, 563
Moe, Terry M., 3585
Moen, J.R., 3312
Moen, M.C., 12784
Moffat, Susan, 10491-10492
Moffitt, Robert, 3313, 5685
Moghadam, Val, 12455
Mohai, Paul, 5528-5529
Mohammed, Khalid Abdul, 1052
Mohanty, Chandra Talpade, 10958
Mohanty, M.S., 5415
Mohanty, S.P., 10959
Mohawk, John C., 2160
Mohl, Raymond A., 2859, 3314, 7188, 7266, 10625, 11408, 11800
Mokuau, Noreen, 14619
Moldow, Gloria, 6416
Molina, Charles, Jr., 8061
Molina, Liza D., 7267
Mollenkopf, John F., 9618, 11801, 14245
Mollica, Richard F., 6417
Molnar, Alex, 3994, 12456
Momayezi, Nasser, 11802
Momeni, Jamshid A., 7268
Mommsen, Wolfgang J., 12245
Monaco, Anthony, 3315
Monaghan, Peter, 12457
Monday, Jane C., 835
Monet, Don, 2065
Moneyhon, Carl H., 6928
Monfort, Franklin, 2729-2730
Monk, David, 3708
Monk, David H., 5941

Monkawa, David, 13505
Monroe, Suzanne S., 13506
Monroe, Sylvester, 217-218, 1223
Monroy, Douglas G., 1840, 9424, 11803
Montague, Alan, 12569
Montague, Eleanor A., 4985
Monteiro, Tony, 2420, 12252
Montejano, David, 3444-3445, 6929-6930, 9709-9710
Montero, Oscar, 12617
Montgomery, M.R., 4986, 13507
Montgomery, William E., 12785
Monti, Daniel J., 2161
Moody, J. Carroll, 8062
Mooney, Brian C., 7269
Moore, Basil, S., 456
Moore, B.L., 10493
Moore, Charles, 1632
Moore, Dhoruba, 13718
Moore, Donald R., 3812, 3995-3996
Moore, Elsie G.J., 7747
Moore, Emily, 6418
Moore, Gilbert W., 8063
Moore, Helen J., 3024
Moore, Jack B., 12571
Moore, Joan, 1841-1842
Moore, Joan W., 2066, 5814
Moore, John, 3316
Moore, John H., 7270, 9653
Moore, Kelly, 11778
Moore, Leonard J., 7836
Moore, M.R., 8281
Moore, Mavor, 10960
Moore, Michael, 10114
Moore, Richard B., 399
Moore, Robert H., 7032
Moore, S., 2925
Moore, Thelma R., 2711
Moore, T.S., 13954
Moore, William Haas, 6931
Moore, Winfred B., Jr., 2787, 7840, 8248
Mora, Magdalena, 14455
Morain, Dan, 7488
Morales, Alfonso, 8968
Morales, Armando, 5942
Morales Cabrera, Pablo, 6932
Morales, Julio, Jr., 10357-10358
Morales, R., 5428, 14406
Moran, Rachel F., 2712, 8513
Morand D., 11098
More, Winifred B., 13155
Morefield, Richard, 9425
Morefield, Richard H., 7682
Moreland, Lawrence W., 11804
Moreno Fraginals, Manuel, 8064
Moreno, Patricia A., 2713
Morey, Ann I., 4322
Morgan, Dan, 6419
Morgan, Joan, 4987, 13023, 13508

Morgan, Ken, 11167
Morgan, Kenneth, 5766
Morgan, Lynda J., 9732
Morgan, Patricia, 13719
Morgan, Philip D., 6917, 6933, 9674, 13098-13100, 13161
Morgan, S. Philip, 5686
Morgan, Thomas, 12092
Morganthau, Tom, 1348, 3317, 4988
Morgenstern, Dan, 6934
Morgenthau, Tom, 57
Mori, Aisha Kiko, 1349
Morimoto, Toyotomi, 8514
Morin, Raul, 10494
Morin, Richard, 12181
Morley, Jefferson, 3997, 11805
Morrill, Richard L., 2714
Morris, Aldon D., 9340
Morris, Christopher, 13162
Morris, Frank L., 4989, 7748
Morris, J.R., 4990
Morris, Lorenzo, 11806
Morris, Madeline, 13509
Morris, Michael, 8515
Morris, Milton D., 12029
Morris, Nancy E., 2067
Morris, R., 8516, 13849
Morris, Richard B., 8065
Morris, Robert C., 3998-3999
Morris, Robin A., 14488
Morris, Sarah P., 10115, 10961
Morris, William V., 4000
Morrison, James D., 2162
Morrison, Kenneth M., 6935
Morrison, Minion K.C., 11807-11809
Morrison, Peter A., 9426, 11472
Morrison, Richard J., 3285
Morrison, Toni, 8969, 9270
Morrissey, Marietta, 1843
Morrow, Lance, 4991, 9733
Morrow, Victoria P., 10962
Morsch, J., 8970
Morse, Bradford W., 2068
Morse, David, 4992
Morse, J., 7749
Morsy, Soheir A., 13510
Mortenson, Thomas G., 4993-4998
Morton, F.A., 219
Morton, Marian J., 6420
Morton, Patricia, 10963, 14408
Mosco, V., 10116
Moseley, Samuel A., 11811
Moseley-Braun, Carol, 11810
Moses, James C., 2715
Moses, Maryann I.I., 4001
Moses, Stanley, 3926
Moses, Wilson Jeremiah, 14491
Moses, Yolanda T., 4999-5000, 14409
Mosier, Majorie, 5001

Moskos, Charles C., Jr., 10459, 10495-10497, 10538
Mosley, Walter, 9271
Mosley, William, 12787
Moss, Alfred A., Jr., 3998, 6704
Moss, E. Yvonne, 1844, 11812
Moss, Kary L., 13850
Moss, Philip I., 220-221
Moss, R.S., 13163
Motley, Constance Baker, 1633
Mott, Frederick D., 6421
Mott, Patrick, 13720
Mottram, Eric, 7440
Moynihan, Daniel P., 2130
Moynihan, Maria, 13024
Muccigrosso, Robert, 805
Mucha, Janusz, 1845
Muehlberger, Robert J., 14544
Mueller, J.J., 12788
Muenchow, Susan, 4280
Muerty, Komanduri S., 5943
Mufson, Steven, 4002
Muga, David, 12182
Muga, David A., 12182, 12458
Muha, M.J., 12433
Muhammad, Ahvay, 13851
Muhammad, Askia, 1055
Muhly, James D., 10964-10965
Muir, Donal E., 2716, 5002-5004, 12183, 12459
Muir, Leslie W., 2716
Muldoon, James, 13511
Mulkern, John R., 6936
Mullen, Faith E., 12572
Mullen, Phil, 13317
Mullen, Robert W., 8517
Muller, Thomas, 7613
Mulligan, J.G., 3901
Mulligan, Thomas S., 6422
Mullin, Michael, 400
Mullings, Leith, 1616, 1846, 6423
Mullins, Elizabeth, 1847
Mullis, Ina V.S., 4003
Mundt, Robert J., 11640
Munitz, B., 5006
Munk, Erika, 1634
Munkres, Robert L., 5944, 12093
Munoz, Carlos, Jr., 1962, 11813-11814
Munoz, Eric, 6424
Mura, David, 806, 10971
Muravchik, Joshua, 564-565
Murayama, Yuzo, 7614, 11250
Murguia, Edward, 2069, 3086
Muro, Mark, 807, 5007, 8518, 10117
Murphy, Clyde E., 3025
Murphy, Eddie, 10118
Murphy, J., 12349
Murphy, J.P., 7615
Murphy, J.S., 9273

Murphy, James E., 10119
Murphy, John C., 7616
Murphy, Joseph M., 401
Murphy, Marjorie, 8066
Murphy, Penny, 8519
Murphy, R.S., 6425
Murphy, Sharon M., 10119
Murphy, Wanda H., 10498
Murrain, Ethel P.C., 8520
Murray, Carolyn B., 14410
Murray, Charles, 1848, 7718
Murray, C.J.L., 6076
Murray, David, 808-809, 8067
Murray, Hugh, 222, 12789
Murray, Jeffrey, 10972
Murray, Kathleen, 10973
Murray, Pauli, 8971
Murray, Peter C., 12790
Murray, Richard, 11451
Murray, Robert F., 6426
Murray, Vernon G., 13596
Murry, Velma M., 1350
Murty, Komanduri S., 5156
Muse, Clifford L., Jr., 5008-5009
Musicant, Ivan, 10499
Muslin, H.L., 9274
Mutchler, J.E., 6427
Muwakkil, Salim, 1056-1059, 1849, 2422, 5010-5012, 6428, 6937, 8521, 8972, 10121, 10500, 11815-11818, 13025, 13318, 14411, 14545
Mydans, Seth, 810, 5530, 7617, 10122-10123, 10501, 10626, 13955
Myers, Eileen, 5013
Myers, Gerald E., 1116, 8474
Myers, Linda James, 10974
Myers, Martha A., 2423-2425, 6900, 14072
Myers, Patricia, 3318
Myers, Samuel L., Jr., 2303, 2426-2427, 2484, 5610-5611, 5855
Myers, Steven L., 223, 4004, 8522, 10975
Myers, Walter D., 811
Myers-Jones, Holly, 7271
Myerson, Allen R., 1224
Myrick, H., 10124

Nabokov, Peter, 6938, 8282
Nacoste, R.W., 224
Nadeau, Richard, 14546
Naelerio, Ron, 13361
Nagata, D.K., 2211-2212
Nagel, Elizabeth A., 5015
Nagel, Gerald S., 3319
Nagel, J.H., 5945
Naierman, Naomi, 6429
Nain, Gemma Tang, 13026
Naison, Mark, 2428
Naison, Marta, 13319
Nakagawa, Gordon, 2213

Nakanishi, Don T., 2214
Nakano, Erich, 10627
Nakano, Mei, 14412-14413
Nalty, Bernard C., 10483, 10502-10503
Nanda, Serena, 11349
Naples, N.A., 2163
Nappi, Chiara R., 12916
Narasaki, Karen K., 2527
Nardinelli, C., 13320
Nardulli, Peter F., 11862
Nasar, Sylvia, 5016, 14185-14186
Nasaw, David, 12635
Nash, A.E. Keir, 8973
Nash, Gary B., 6939-6940, 9662, 10976,
    11819, 12791, 13164
Nash, Gerald D., 6953, 6986
Nash, Horace D., 6941
Nash, Jeffrey E., 8523
Nash, Philip Tajitsu, 2215
Natanson, Nicholas A., 13512
Nathalang, Matrini, 6430
Nathan, Hans, 7441
Nathan, Joe, 4048
Naughton, Jim, 3027, 11820
Naureckas, Jim, 10184
Navajas, Emma D., 7618
Navarrette, Ruben, Jr., 5019-5021, 7619, 8525
Navarro, Mireya, 6570
Navarro, Vicente, 1850-1852, 6441-6449,
    11821
Navasky, Victor, 8956
Nay, Leslie A., 225
Nazario, Sonia, 6450-6451, 8068
Neal, Diane, 5946
Neal, Fannie Allen, 12298, 13913
Nechyba, T.J., 3322
Neckerman, Kathryn M., 2982
Nedelsky, Jennifer, 8974
Nee, Judy Silva, 2717
Nee, Victor, 1853, 3446
Needleman, Ruth, 8069
Neely, Charlotte, 4009
Negler, J., 11732
Neidert, Lisa J., 3220
Neighbors, Harold W., 6452-6454
Neill, Monty, 13853
Neilson, Melany, 11822
Neisser, Ulric, 1855
Neligh, G., 6455
Nelson, Albert J., 11823
Nelson, Anne, 2070
Nelson, B., 8070
Nelson, Cary, 4360, 11291
Nelson, Dalmas H., 3841
Nelson, Emily, 3323
Nelson, Jack, 566-567, 7837-7838
Nelson, Jill, 5947, 10126
Nelson, Kathryn P., 7272
Nelson, Mack C., 3148

Nelson, M.D., Jr., 6456
Nelson, P.E., 1216
Nelson, Sheila, 4010
Nelson, William E., Jr., 1635, 12792
Nelson, William Javier, 12184
Nelson Salvino, Dana, 9275
Nemeth, Charles P., 226
Nerlove, Marc, 14176
Nesdale, A.R., 13514
Nessen, Joshua, 11824
Nettels, Michael T., 5022-5024, 13854
Neu, Charles E., 10198
Neuberger, M.J., 7620
Neuborne, Burt, 227, 5025
Neufield, Russell, 13722
Neuman, G.L., 8975
Neuwirth, Robert, 5267
Neverdon-Morton, Cynthia, 14414
Nevins, Richard, 9037
Newacheck, P.W., 6457
Newberger, Carolyn, 10127
Newburger, Harriet B., 3028, 7273-7275
Newby, Cassandra L., 9734
Newby, Robert G., 813, 12299
Newcomb, John T., 8527
Newfield, Christopher, 10981
Newhagen, J.E., 10128
Newinger, Sheldon M., 7621
Newman, A.E., 5429
Newman, B.A., 8300
Newman, Harvey K., 12794-12795
Newman, Maria, 5027-5028, 14079
Newman, Mark, 12793
Newman, Richard, 12796
Newman, Robert, 3029
Newman, Roger K., 8976
Newport, Frank, 568
Newsome, Yvonne D., 1061-1062
Newton, Edmund, 5862, 13321
Newton, Huey P., 13723
Newton, Jim, 228, 2430, 5948, 8977-8980,
    12574, 13914
Newton, Judy Ann, 7839, 14080
Newton, Kathy C., 5531
Newton, Michael, 7839, 14080
Newton, N.J., 8981
Ng, Kenneth, 3325
Ng, Man Chak, 8014
Nguyen, Alexander, 5029
Nguyen, B.B.D., 8528
Nichols, Elaine, 926
Nicklin, Julie L., 5030-5033
Nicol V., 3119
Nicola-McLaughlin, Andree, 14415
Niebuhr, Gustav, 1063, 5532
Niedermeyer, Deborah, 8982, 9350
Niehaus, J.A., 6458
Nieli, Russell, 229
Nielsen, Francois, 4011

Nielsen, John T., 7276
Nielsen, Richard A., 8283
Nieman, Donald G., 1395, 2431, 6942, 8529
Niemeyer, Suzanne, 805
Niemi, A.W., Jr., 230, 3030
Nieto, Sonia, 10982
Nightingale, Carl H., 1352, 1963
Nilsen, Alleen P., 7442, 13028
Nilsen, Don L.F., 14649
Nishida, Mo, 5034
Nishizawa, Yoshitaka, 7277
Nistal-Moret, Benjamin, 2071
Niven, Penelope, 753
Nixon, Harold L., 5035
Njeri, Itabari, 5036, 6459, 8530, 9276, 13915, 14254
Nkomo, Stella M., 8071
Noakes, John, 6943, 10129
Nobile, Vince, 10983
Noble, Allen G., 10335, 10364, 10984
Noble, David F., 12917
Noble, D.D., 5037
Nobles, Wade W., 5688, 12300
Noboa, Abdin, 2718
Noboa-Rios, Abdin, 5038
Nodin Valdes, Dennis, 10359
Noel, Peter, 814, 1063-1065, 5039, 8983, 10505, 11826, 12797-12798, 13855-13856
Noell, Jay, 5232
Noer, Thomas J., 12238
Noldin Valdes, Dennis, 8072
Noll, Mark A., 12864
Nomura, Gail M., 9743
Norcini, Marilyn J., 815
Nordheimer, Jon, 1066, 5040-5041, 8531
Nordmann, Christopher A., 5788
Nordquist, Joan, 14650
Nordstrom, Carl, 13165
Nordyke, Eleanor C., 9484-9485
Norgren, Jill, 9035, 11349
Noriega, Chon A., 10130-10131
Norman, David L., 8984
Norman, Jack, 9750
Norman, Mary Ann, 1636
Norman, Michael, 7443
North, Carol S., 7278
North, Oliver L., 816
Northcott, Karen, 13725
Norton, Eleanor Holmes, 3326, 14407
Nossiter, Adam, 1637, 5042, 8985, 14082
Nostrand, Richard L., 6944
Nott, R., 13343
Novick, Michael, 12575-12577
Novick, Peter, 12350
Nsiah-Jefferson, Laurie, 14416
Nuernbery, Susan M., 9277
Nuevo Kerr, Louis Ano, 9497
Numbers, Ronald L., 6460, 6548
Nunberg, Geoffrey, 8532-8533

Nunn, Frederick M., 9586
Nunn, Kenneth B., 8986
Nutter, Jeanne D., 10132
Nutting, Kurt, 2896
Nyankori, J.C.O., 5044
Nybakken, Elizabeth I., 5716
Nybell, L.M., 5637
Nye, M.A., 1638-1639
Nye, William P., 12185

Oakes, J., 3759
Oakes, James, 13166-13167
Oakes, Jeannie, 4012-4013, 12918
Oakes, Penelope J., 13515
Oakland, Thomas, 14666
Obadele, Imari Abuhakari, 11169-11170
Obama, Barack, 2164
O'Barr, Jean, 4342
O'Barr, William M., 1225
Obenzinger, Hilton, 569
Oberly, Jim, 5949
Obermiller, P., 10360
Oberon Garcia, Claire, 9278
Obidinski, Eugene, 13516
Oblinger, Carl D., 9663
Oboler, Suzanne, 8534
O'Brien, Eileen M., 5045-5046
O'Brien, Gail W., 14083
O'Brien, Patrick M., 9664
O'Brien, Raymond C., 3032
O'Brien, Robert M., 2432
O'Brien, Sally, 10133
O'Brien, Sharon, 8987, 11350, 11827
O'Brien, Timothy L., 1208
O'Brien, Tom, 10134
Ocha, Stephen J., 12799
O'Connell, Mary, 4014
O'Connell, Robert M., 8988
O'Connor, Alan, 10985
O'Connor, Alice Mary, 1854
O'Connor, John J., 7444-7445, 10135-10137, 13517-13518
O'Connor, Karen, 1640
O'Connor, M., 157
O'Dell, John H., 9553
Odell, Morgan, 5047
Odlman, B., 6447
O'Donnell, Santiago, 14084
O'Donnell, S.M., 1353
Odum, Howard W., 4015
Odum, Maria, 8989
Odun, Maria, 6461
Officer, James E., 5950, 7409, 9359
Ogbu, John U., 1855, 3698, 3727, 3869, 3941, 4017-4024, 4186, 8535, 10986
O'Gorman, Hubert J., 3604, 13636
Ogot, Bethwell, 13153
Oguntoyinbo, Lekan, 4025
Oh, Angela, 9406

O'Hanlon, Ann, 1641
O'Hare, William P., 1226, 3327, 10361, 11828, 14547
O'Haren, Maureen, 5049
Oishi, Gene, 817
Ojeda Rios, Filiberto, 2072
Okafor, V.O., 402
Okagaki, Lynn, 6505
Okami, P., 1067
Okamura, Raymond Y., 2216, 8990
O'Kane, James M., 2433
Okihiro, Gary Y., 424, 13727
O'Koon, Alan M., 7446
Ola, Akinshiju C., 4026, 5050, 8073
Oldfield, J.R., 11251
Oldroyd, D., 13041
Olds, Madelin J., 13519
O'Leary, Gloria, 7921
Oleksa, Michael, 12800
Olender, Maurice, 12460
Oliensis, Sheldon, 231
Olin, Spencer C., Jr., 9432
Oliphant, Thomas, 11829
Olivas, Michael A., 5051-5053
Oliver, Jennings P., 10987
Oliver, John, 7279
Oliver, M., 5815
Oliver, Melvin L., 1856, 4792, 5054, 10606, 14187-14188
Olivero, J. Michael, 2434
Ollie, Bert W., Jr., 2721
Ollman, B., 4380
Olmos, David R., 6462
Olneck, Michael R., 10988
Olney, James, 818
Olsen, Frances, 8991
Olsen, Frederick H., 10507
Olsen, Laurie, 10989
Olsen, Marvin, 11830
Olson, Bruce A., 14085
Olson, Carol, 5055
Olson, Craig S., 12578
Olson, James S., 8074, 13337
Olson, Lynn, 2722
Olson, Paulette, 3033
Olson, Richard, 12919
Olwell, Robert A., 13168
Olzak, Susan D., 8075, 11252, 14086
O'Malley, Michael, 6945, 9649
O'Malley, Susan G., 14349, 14415
O'Malley, Susan J., 10485
Omatsu, Glenn, 14651
O'Meally, Robert, 6799
Omi, Michael, 8536, 10138, 12461, 14652
Omolade, Barbara, 5689
O'Neal, Patrick H., 7883
O'Neil, Robert M., 8993
O'Neill, June, 232, 3328
O'Nell, Theresa D., 6463

Ong, Paul M., 3329, 8076, 9427, 13953, 13956, 14406
Oommen, T.K., 14548
Oparaocha, Titus E., 6464
Opler, Morris E., 8189
Oppenheimer, Martin, 1642
O'Reagan, K.M., 13957
O'Regan, Katherine, 6465
O'Reilly, Kenneth, 13728-13730
O'Reilly, Richard, 6946, 13883
Oren, Dan A., 5058
Orenstein, Peggy, 10139
Oreskes, Michael, 11831-11832
Orfabea, Gregory, 14653
Orfield, Gary, 2723-2731, 5059-5063, 5430, 5951, 7280, 11833-11834
Orfield, Matthias Nordberg, 8284
Organ, David, 924
Orlans, Harold, 232, 5064-5066
Ornelas, Carlos, 11835
Ornstein, Charles, 5067
Oross, Marianne C., 7281
O'Rourke, Lawrence M., 819
Orozco, Cynthia E., 1643, 1964
Orren, Karen, 4341
Orser, Edward W., 927
Orser, W. Edward, 10362
Ortiz, Alfonso, 6947
Ortiz de Montellano, Bernard, 10990-10992
Ortiz, Flora Ida, 4028
Ortiz, Isidro D., 1965, 11836
Ortiz, Roxanne Dunbar, 2073, 2165, 5816, 11171
Ortiz, Vilma, 8537, 10363
Ortizano, Giacoma L., 10140
Orum, Anthony M., 9711, 11837
Orum, Lori S., 4029-4030, 5068
Osborn, Kevin, 9351
Osborne, A., 1227
Osborne, Newton G., 6466
Osborne, Stephen D., 9279
Osborne, William A., 12801
Osburn, Katherine M.B., 2217, 14417
Oshana, Maryann, 14418
Oshinsky, David M., 5069
Ostenby, Peter M., 13322
Osterhammel, Jurgen, 12245
Osterman, Paul, 3330
Ostling, Richard, N., 12802
Ostow, Mortimer, 571, 12301
Ostrow, Ronald J., 5431, 7282, 7610, 9025, 13731
Ostrower, Francie, 14496
O'Sullivan, Chris, 13029
O'Sullivan, Katherine, 1857
O'Sullivan, Noel, 11517
Oswalt, Wendell H., 6948
Oszuscik, Philippe, 10364
Oteri, L.A., 5070

Otis, Lauren, 9280
O'Tolle, George, 13732
O'Toole, Patrician, 1228
Ottavi, T.M., 5100
Otten, M.W., Jr., 6467
Ottensmann, J.R., 7284
Ouroussoff, Nicolai, 11253
Outlaw, Marpessa Dawn, 12302
Ovando, Carlos J., 8538
Overstreet, Everett L., 9352
Ovington, Mary W., 8077
Ow, Jeffrey A., 13520
Owen, Christopher H., 13169
Owen, David, 13857
Owen, Jean V., 13521
Owens, Charles E., 2435
Owens, Don B., 820
Owens, Leslie H., 13170
Owens, Major R., 1069
Ownby, Ted, 14255
Owsley, Beatrice R., 1229, 6949
Owusu-Bempah, J., 12255
Ozawa, M.N., 5952

Pacheco, Patrick, 10141
Pachon, Harry, 1644
Padilla, A.M., 8379, 8539-8540
Padilla, Felix M., 9499
Padilla, Yolanda C., 12462
Pagden, Anthony, 1998
Page, Catherine M., 5767
Page, Clarence, 1070
Page, Douglas B., 7285
Page, T.W., 7622
Pahl, Jon, 6950
Pain, R., 2436
Paine, Charles, 10993
Painter, Nell Irvin, 5071, 6951, 8078-8080,
    11838, 13030
Pakes, Fraser, 13522
Paley, Vivian Gussin, 13916
Palisi, B.J., 12098
Palladino, Grace, 8081
Pallas, Aaron M., 4031-4032
Palley, Howard A., 2437, 5690
Palm, T., 14200
Palmer, Brian, 9621, 12579, 14087
Palmer, Bryan D., 8541
Palmer, Carolyn, 5072
Palmer, J.L., 1316, 6182
Palmer, Leola, 4033
Palmer, Ransford W. 7623
Palmer, Thomas, 5073, 10994
Palmie, Stephan, 10628
Panella, Frank, 12239
Pao, Angela, 9281
Pappas, Gregory, 6469-6470
Paquette, Jerry, 4034
Paredes, Raymond, 6952

Pareles, Jon, 10143, 12618
Parens, J., 10995
Parenti, Michael, 1858, 10144, 13733-13734
Parham, Thomas A., 5074
Parikh, Sunita, 233
Parins, James W., 14642
Paris, Peter J., 12803
Paris, Phillip L., 4035
Parish, Peter J., 13171
Park, David, 8994
Park, Jeana H., 10145
Park, Jeanne, 13523
Park, Joseph F., 8082-8083
Park, Peter, 1456
Parker, Frank R., 11839-11840
Parker, Johnny C., 234, 5075
Parker, Joseph B., 11726
Parker, Laurence, 13832-13833
Parker, Leann, 173
Parker, Linda C., 234, 5075
Parker, Linda S., 8285
Parker, Maura B., 6320
Parker, Richard A., 7624
Parker, S., 1354
Parker, Tony V., 4036
Parkes, Keith D., 2438
Parkhurst, Jessie W., 14419
Parks, Douglas R., 12835
Parks, Rosa, 821
Parman, Donald L., 6953, 8286
Parr, Susan R., 7382
Parrillo, Vincent N., 13150
Parry, G., 457
Parsons, Dana, 458
Parsons, Talcott, 1430
Partes, A., 14549
Pascal, Anthony M., 13323
Pascoe, P., 5691
Paset, P.S., 5692
Passalacqua, John L.A. de, 1431
Passel, J.S., 7625
Passell, Peter, 1859, 2074, 7286, 7626, 14189
Pasternak, Judy, 2166, 2732, 3034, 14256
Pastor, Manuel, 9428
Patai, Daphne, 3494, 10996
Paterno, Susan, 5954, 6471
Paterson, Kent, 5533
Paterson, T.G., 2089
Patin, Thomas, 14257
Paton, S.E.C., 7447
Patrick, Deval L., 7287
Patrick-Stamp, Leslie Cheryl, 2439
Patterson, E. Britt, 2440
Patterson, Orlando, 1966, 2167, 3331, 8995,
    10997-10998, 12463, 14550
Patterson, Pat, 10146
Patterson, Rosalyn, 12920
Patterson, Thomas C., 10999
Patterson, Tiffany R.L., 822

Patterson, Tim, 14258
Patthey-Chavez, G. Genevieve, 4037
Pattnayak, S.R., 13324
Patton, J.M., 4038
Paul, Ellen F., 1654
Paul, Faith G., 5062-5063, 5076-5077
Paul, Rodman W., 7683
Paulson, Howard W., 5955, 8287
Paust, Jordan J., 6954
Pauwels, Anne, 8542
Pavalko, Ronald W., 7627
Pay, Elaine, 4039
Payette, K.A., 7750
Payne, Charles, 1645, 4040
Payne, Dinah, 13858
Payne, James R., 823-824
Payne, John M., 7288
Payne, Les, 4041, 5956, 10147
Payner, Brook S., 134
Paynter, Robert, 6904
Payton, Brenda, 11841
Payton, Robert L., 11351
Peach, Ceri, 7197
Peak, Ken, 2441
Pear, Robert, 235, 825, 1646, 3332-3333,
    6472, 7289
Pearce, Diana, 7290
Pearce, R.H., 6955
Pearl, Jonathan M., 10148-10149
Pearl, Judith, 10149
Pearlman, Jill, 1071
Pearlstein, Steven, 1230
Pearlsten, Mitchell B., 236
Pearson, Carol S., 4682, 4960, 5079, 5392
Pearson, Edward A., 13172
Pearson, Hugh, 826
Pearson, Jessica S., 5534
Pearson, LaRue C., 12922
Pearson, M., 6473
Pearson, Maggie, 11352
Pearson, Michael, 9282
Pearson, R.W., 1860
Pearson, Ralph L., 5957
Pearson, Robert W., 1776
Pearson, Roger, 7751-7752
Pearson, Ted, 5080
Pearson, Willie, Jr., 12921-12922
Pease, Donald E., 3127, 8720, 9283, 10465,
    12226-12227, 12236, 12240, 12248, 14250
Pease, Edward C., 10150-10151
Pease, Ted, 10152-10153
Peck, Abraham J., 6956
Peck, M.N., 6474
Peckham, H., 5909
Pederson, Paul B., 13919
Peebles, Melvin Van, 10269
Peery, Nelson, 827
Pegues, Robert L., Jr., 8996
Peiss, Judith, 5693

Peller, Gary, 8997-8998, 11842, 12405
Pellicani, Luciano, 11001
Peltzman, S., 4042
Pemberton, Gayle, 1861
Pena, Albert, 14088
Pena, Devon G., 1862
Pena, Laurencio, 8543
Pena, Mario J., 5081
Pencak, William, 9610, 10341
Pendleton, Clarence M., Jr., 237
Penley, L.E., 1231
Penn, Lisha B., 11843
Penna, David, 13962
Pennick, Edward J., 8288
Pennington, Jody, 1232
Pennington, Richard, 13325
Peoples, Gerald C., 5082
Peoples, John A., 5083
Peoples, Morgan D., 11722
Pepion, Kenneth, 5254
Peradotto, John, 11002
Peralez, Jose, 10094
Perdue, Theda, 1863, 6957-6958, 8289, 11172,
    13173
Perea, Juan F., 8544
Pereira, J., 6475
Perelman, S., 14190
Peres, Kenneth R., 5958
Peretti, Burton W., 828
Peretz, Don, 572
Perez Firmat, Gustavo, 14551
Perez, Nelida, 6959
Perez, Sonia M., 3334-3336
Perez-Bustillo, Camilo, 8545
Perez-Stable, E.J., 6476
Perfecto, Ivette, 2094, 11192
Perkins, Carol O., 14420
Perkins, Darlene, 1355
Perkins, Drew A., 2733
Perkins, Jane, 6477
Perkins, Kathy A., 9284, 10154
Perkins, Linda M., 4043, 11254
Perkins, W. Eric, 12367
Perl, Peter, 829
Perlmutter, Philip, 4044, 6960-6961, 8084
Perlo, Victor, 3337
Peroff, Nicholas C., 5959
Perrot, Dominique, 6970, 13528
Perrucci, C.C., 5432, 6478
Perrucci, R., 6478
Perry, Barbara A., 8999
Perry, Bruce, 830, 10155, 11844
Perry, H.L., 11845
Perry, Mary E., 9587
Perry, Michael J., 2734
Perry, P.L., 3035
Perry, Richard, 5084, 6962
Perry, Ronald W., 10450, 10508
Perry, Ruth, 11003

Perry, Theresa, 11004
Perry, Tony, 4045
Persell, C.H., 3618
Persell, Caroline H., 4046, 5085, 7753
Person, Dawn R., 5086
Person-Lynn, Kwaku, 12923
Persons, Stow, 12464
Pertman, Adam, 2400
Pertusati, L., 2735
Perun, Pamela J., 5087
Pescosolido, B.A., 9220
Peshkin, Alan, 4047
Peskin, L., 2731
Peskind, Jennifer, 11005
Pessen, Edward, 1864
Pestello, Fred P., 2697
Pestieau, P., 14190
Pete, Gregory, 7291
Peterkin, Robert, 4048
Peters, Erskine, 5088
Peters, William, 13917
Peterson, Iver, 238, 459, 4049-4050, 11846, 14090
Peterson, Jacqueline, 5694
Peterson, Jonathan, 3338, 9486, 11847
Peterson, Joyce S., 8085
Peterson, Patti M., 2075
Peterson, Paul E., 1805, 1865, 2982, 5882, 7147, 11421
Peterson, Richard H., 3447
Peterson, Susan C., 3036
Peterson, T.R., 8546
Petigny, Alan, 1072
Petitti, D., 6479
Petonito, Gina, 2218
Petras, James, 10509, 11866
Petrin, Ronald A., 11848
Petrini, Christopher J., 2412
Petroni, F.A., 13524
Petrovich, Janice, 4960
Pettigrew, Thomas F., 11849, 12619, 14259
Pettit, Arthur G., 10156
Pettit, Kenneth J., 4051
Petty, Roy, 7152
Pfeffer, J., 187
Pfeffer, Paula F., 831, 1647
Pfeiffenberger, Amy M., 5089
Pfister, Joel, 11006
Pflaum, Susanna W., 4052
Phelan, Pamela E., 239
Phelan, T., 5438, 10367
Phelps, Christopher, 11007, 11850, 12580
Phelps, E., 12465
Philipp, S.F., 12636
Philipps, Jock, 6958
Philips, Chuck, 10157
Philipson, E.H., 6344
Philliber, W., 10352, 10360
Phillipps, John C., 13326

Phillips, Charles D., 2442
Phillips, Christopher W., 9523, 13174
Phillips, Donna C., 4053
Phillips, George H., 3339, 5960, 6963
Phillips, Jan, 7292
Phillips, Kevin, 11851-11852
Phillips, Peter, 3345
Phillips, Romeo E., 12804
Phillips, Tasha, 240
Phillips, William D., Jr., 13175
Phillips, William M., Jr., 1073
Philogene, G., 8547
Philp, Kenneth R., 6964
Philpott, Tom, 10840-10841
Phinney, Jean S., 1356, 12303
Phizacklea, Annie, 3443
Piaget, Jean, 1357
Piatt, Bill, 8548, 8549
Piazza, Thomas, 12111
Picard, Joe, 3591
Pichardo, Nelson A., 8086
Pickering, M., 10158
Pico de Hernandez, Isabel, 12186
Pico, Isabel, 11173, 12620, 13031
Pierammunzi, C.A., 11853
Pierce, Chester M., 10159, 12304
Pierce, Neal R., 2168
Pierre, Robert E., 10160
Pierre-Charles, G., 12466
Pierson, C., 6482
Pierson, William D., 7840
Pilgrim, David, 4054, 5090
Piliavin, J.A., 13918
Piliawsky, Monte, 5091
Pillar, James J, 12805
Piller, Charles, 4055
Pilling, Arnold R., 1866
Pilmer, W., 10161
Pinceti, S., 1432
Pinchbeck, Raymond, 8087
Pincus, F.L., 5092
Pincus, Samuel N., 9000, 9735
Pinder, Margaret E., 10726
Pinderhughes, Dianne M., 1648
Pinderhughes, Howard, 14091
Pinderhughes, Raquel, 1842
Pinkerton, James P., 2443
Pinkney, Alphonso, 1002, 1074, 11174, 14092
Pinzler, Isabelle K., 241, 3037
Piper, Adrian, 14552
Piper-Mandy, Erylene L., 11009
Pitchford, Susan, 13799
Pitsch, Mark, 4056-4057, 5093
Pitt, Leonard M., 6965
Pittman, John, 11309
Pittman, Karen, 1358
Pittman, Ruth, 928
Pittman, Walter E., 14093
Pitts, Bruce, 2444, 9001

Pitts, Robert B., 8088
Pitts, Walter, F., 12806
Pitzl, Mary Jo, 5094
Piven, Francis Fox, 11476
Pizzini, E.L., 4138
Plank, David N., 4058-4059
Plaschke, Bill, 13327
Platt, Anthony M., 5095, 11010
Platt, Tony, 832, 2502, 12467
Platte, Mark, 12581-12582
Player, Mack A., 1433
Ploski, Harry A., 14553
Plotkin, Sidney, 11908
Plotnick, Robert D., 3340
Plummer, Brenda G., 12241
Plunkett, Michael, 9736
Podair, Jerald E., 4060
Podhoretz, Norman, 573
Podilla, Genaro M., 833-834
Poe, S.C., 10510
Pogrebin, Letty Cottin, 1075
Pohlman, Bruce E., 11011
Pohlmann, Marcus D., 11854
Poindexter, Paula, 10162
Poinsett, Alex, 4061, 5096
Pol, Louis G., 6483
Polachek, Solomon, 2965
Pole, J.R., 6940, 6967
Polednak, Anthony P., 6484
Poliakoff, Michael, 11012
Polionard, J.L., 3039, 11855
Polite, Craig K., 2611-2612, 14498
Polite, Vernon C., 4062
Pollack, Andy, 9622, 11014, 11856
Pollack, Phyllis, 13708
Pollard, William R., 11015
Pomeroy, Earl S., 2076
Ponterotto, Joseph G., 12305, 13865, 13919
Pool, Bob, 5098
Pool, K.W., 216
Poole, H. Randall, 5099
Poole, Stafford, 13176
Pope, Christie Farnham, 11016
Pope, Jacqueline, 5817
Pope, Polly, 14191
Pope John Paul II, 12808-12809
Pope-Davis, D.B., 5100
Popkin, S.J., 8089
Popkin, Samuel L., 12096
Popkin, Susan J., 7293
Popov, O., 1867
Porter, C.P., 1359
Porter, Frank W., III, 8290
Porter, Jack N., 1075
Porter, James, 13525
Porter, Judith R., 13378
Porter, Kathryn H., 3341
Porter, Kenneth W., 10629-10633
Porter, Robert B., 5961

Porter, Rosalie Pedalino, 8550-8551
Porterfield, Ernest, 5695
Portes, Alejandro, 9463
Posadas, Barbara M., 8090
Poskocil, Art, 13526
Posner, Prudence S., 2144
Posner, Richard A., 243, 13032
Post, Deborah W., 9003
Post, Robert C., 8552
Postman, Leo, 7781
Poston, D.L., Jr., 3040-3041
Postwan, Sheryl L., 9518
Potter, Jonathan, 8554
Potter, L.B., 6485
Potter, Michael F., 7294
Pottinger, Richard, 5101
Potts, Annette, 10511
Potts, E. Daniel, 10511
Potts, Nancy J., 11857
Poulin, Susan, 3288
Pouncey, Peter R., 5102
Pounder, Robert L., 11018
Poussaint, Alvin, 1360
Poveda, Tony G., 13735
Powell, C., 7447
Powell, John A., 8950
Powell, Kimberly A., 11858
Powell, R.R., 13527
Powell, Thomas R., 6968, 8291
Powell-Griner, Eve, 6381, 6486
Power, C., 6487
Power, Garrett, 11325
Power, M., 5433
Power, Marjory W., 9722
Powers, Ron, 9500
Powers, S., 2459
Powers, William F., 7295-7296
Powledge, Fred, 1649-1650, 11859
Powlishta, K.K., 14421
Poyo, Gerald E., 6969, 9712
Pozzetta, George E., 6926, 7628, 11409, 11800, 14301, 14540
Prager, Jeffrey, 244, 2736, 11860, 12188, 12128, 12468, 12469
Prakasa, Rao V.V., 6488
Prather, Patricia S., 835
Pratkanis, Anthony R., 324, 13408
Pratt, Geronimo j-jaga, 11861
Pratt, Robert A., 2737, 4063
Preiswerk, Roy, 6970, 13528
Press, Andrea L., 10163
Press, Marcia, 13529
Presser, Arlynn L., 2738
Pressley, Sue Anne, 4065, 8555
Prestage, Jewel L., 245, 5103
Preston, Michael B., 11456, 11862
Preston, Samuel H., 5697, 6489
Preston, William, Jr., 10164
Prewitt Diaz, Joseph O., 8556

Price, Alfred D., 7279
Price, Daniel O., 4066, 14554
Price, Edward, 11863
Price, Janet R., 2739, 4067
Price, Monroe E., 8203
Price, Richard, 14543
Prichard, Nancy L., 8091
Priest, Diana H., 4068
Priest, Loring B., 5962
Prieto, Dario O., 6490
Primm, Berry J., 6088
Prince, Hugh B., 11019-11020
Pringle, Peter D., 11021
Pristin, Terry, 10165-10166
Pritchett, Jonathan B., 4069-4071, 13177
Protess, David, 9905
Prothro, E.T., 13530
Prothrow-Stith, Deborah, 14555
Prucha, Francis Paul, 5963-5965
Prude, Jonathan, 8027
Pruitt, Anne S., 5107, 5275
Pryde, Paul, 1184
Prysby, Charles L., 11864
Przybyszewski, Linda C.A., 1434
Ptasiewicz, Seth, 2740
Puddington, Arch, 1077, 11865, 12189
Puente, Teresa, 5108
Puette, William J., 10167
Puffer, Frank, 6492
Puga, Ana, 10168
Pugh, S.L., 10795
Puig, Claudia, 10169
Pukui, Mary Kawena, 9487
Pulido, Alberto L., 12810
Pulido, Laura, 5535
Punter, David 4072
Purdy, D.A., 13328
Purdy, Matthew, 5536
Puta, Manfred, 13033
Putka, Gary, 4073
Putney, Diane T., 6493
Putney, Martha S., 11255

Quadagno, Jill, 5699, 14192
Quam, L., 6494
Quam-Wickham, Nancy, 8092
Quan, D., 9004
Quaye, R., 6495
Quesada, Charo, 7841
Quicke, John C., 13920
Quigley, John M., 7264
Quimby, Ernest, 6496
Quindlen, Anna, 5966, 8557, 11022, 12190, 14094
Quinn, Jane Bryant, 5109
Quinn, Richard, 1035
Quinn, S.C., 6621
Quinn, William W., Jr., 6971, 9005
Quinney, Roger E., 6497

Quint, Howard H., 7564
Quint, Michael, 3042
Quinten, B.T., 5967
Quintero, Marcia Rivera, 12973
Quintero Rivera, Angel G., 1868, 2077-2078, 4075, 6972, 8093, 11176-11177, 11866
Quiroz, Julie Teresa, 3989
Qunitana, S.M., 5110

Raab, Earl, 1078-1079
Rabasa, Jose, 11023
Rabb, Harriet, 4076
Rabino, Linda, 8558
Rabinovitz, Jonathan, 2219, 5111, 13034
Rabinowitz, Howard N., 574, 5968, 6973, 11353
Raboteau, Albert J., 12811-12814
Rachleff, Peter J., 8094, 9737
Racine, Philip N., 7842
Radelet, Joseph, 2741
Radelet, Michael L., 2446
Radhakrishnan, R., 11354
Radosh, Polly F., 2447
Radwin, Eugene, 4078
Radzialowski, Thaddeus C., 10634
Rae, N.C., 11868
Ragsdale, Bruce A., 11869
Ragsdale, John W., Jr., 8292, 9006
Rahming, Melvin B., 7629
Rai, Kul B., 247
Raichle, Donald R., 4079
Rainer, Peter, 10172
Rainerie, Vivian M., 836
Raines, Howell, 837, 11870
Rainey, Kenneth T., 9286
Rainville, R.E., 13330
Rakowsky, Judy, 2448, 7630
Ralph, James R., Jr., 1651-1652
Ralston, Charlie S., 3043
Ramaga, P.V., 11024
Ramazanoglu, Caroline, 11288
Ramey, C.T., 4080, 7756
Ramey, Felicenne H., 5123
Ramey, S.L., 4080
Ramirez, Albert, 11355, 12191
Ramirez, Anthony, 6499
Ramirez, David E., 2449
Ramirez, Deborah A., 9007
Ramirez, Francisco O., 4081, 11131
Ramirez, Rafael L., 1869
Ramirez, Richard, 10513
Ramirez-Barbot, Jaime, 11178
Ramos, George, 7631
Ramos, Moises Rosa, 12815
Ramos Mattei, Andres A., 2079-2080, 13178
Rampersad, Arnold, 616, 838, 9263
Ramsay, E., 929
Ramsey, P.G., 1361
Randel, William P., 7843

Randolph, Laura B., 5124, 5700
Randolph, Robert, 11326
Rankin, Bruce H., 3218, 3343, 8095
Rankin, David C., 9517
Rankin-Hill, L.M., 839
Rans, Geoffrey, 9287
Ransby, Barbara, 840, 5125
Ransford, H.E., 12098
Ransom, Michael R., 248, 5126
Ransom, Roger L., 3101, 6974, 13179-13180
Rapp, Burt, 13736
Rapping, Leonard A., 13323
Rapport, Sara, 5970, 9008
Raskin, A.H., 8096
Raskin, Jamin B., 9009, 11871, 12816
Raskin, Victor, 7448
Rasky, Susan F., 13035
Rasmussen, Cecilia, 841
Raspberry, William, 249, 1080-1081, 1233,
    4082, 8559, 11872, 12471, 13036
Rath, Sura P., 9288
Ratnajeevan, H., 4750
Ratner, Lorman A., 10723
Rauch, Jonathan, 11025
Raudenbush, S.W., 4083
Rauf, M. Naeem, 13737
Rausch, David, 575
Raven, J., 13861
Raver, Anne, 403
Ravitch, Diane, 10683, 11026-11027, 13037
Ravo, Nick, 10173
Rawick, George, 8097
Rawls, Alfred, 2742
Rawls, James J., 5434
Ray, J.J., 12306
Ray, John, 2450, 11028-11029
Ray, Roger B., 8293
Raybon, Patricia, 10174
Rayman, Graham, 10006
Raymond, John, 5127
Rayson, Ann, 842
Razran, I., 13531
Rea, Louis M., 7624
Reardon, Kenneth M., 2169
Reavis, Ralph, 5128
Rebell, Michael A., 250, 8560
Rector, Robert, 1363
Redburn, Tom, 3344
Redding, J. Sanders, 12242
Redenbaugh, Russell G., 5971
Redfern, Bernice, 14422, 14656
Redkey, Edwin S., 10514
Redmond, Patricia, 9161, 9210
Reed, Adolph, Jr., 1870, 11874-11876, 14556
Reed, Christopher R., 11877
Reed, Gerard, 6975
Reed, Harry, 6976
Reed, Ishmael, 1967, 10175
Reed, Julia, 12584

Reed, Little Rock, 2451
Reed, Merl E., 251, 5972, 7942, 13738
Reed, Ralph E., Jr., 5129
Reed, Sally, 1362
Reed, Veronica M., 7297-7298
Reed, Wornie L., 1844, 2452, 3433, 5130,
    6500, 9856, 11812, 13331-13332, 13532,
    14557
Reed-Mundell, C.A., 1653
Rees, A., 2847
Rees, Albert, 3108
Rees, Philip, 12585
Reese, Joan, 10515
Rees-Mogg, William, 7757
Reeve, Frank D., 5973, 8294
Reeves, Garth C., 5131
Register, Charles A., 4673
Regoli, B., 13333
Reich, Alice H., 5134
Reich, Kenneth, 1234, 2453
Reich, Michael, 3044, 3345, 14193
Reich, Robert B., 1871
Reid, Alexander, 5135
Reid, Clifford E., 3045, 7299
Reid, Ellis E., 5136
Reid, Evelyn M., 2743
Reid, Mark A., 10176-10177
Reid, P. Trotman, 13038
Reid, Tim, 10178
Reid-Bookhart, Patricia A., 252
Reidel, M., 2454
Reidinger, Paul, 9010
Reidy, Joseph P., 7169, 8098, 13181
Reidy, Michael J., 7844
Reilly, J., 9289
Reilly, Philip R., 6501
Reiman, Jeffry H., 2455
Reimers, David M., 7632, 12817
Reingold, Nathan, 5137
Reinhart, George R., 9338
Reinhold, Robert, 1235, 5974, 9429-9430,
    9488, 11030
Reinsch, Paul S., 12192
Reisler, Mark, 1435, 8099
Reiss, Matthew, 11878
Reitman, Judith, 2456
Remez, L., 6502
Remnick, David, 11879
Remy, Anselme, 12351
Rendall, Jane, 8393
Renji, Judith, 11031-11032
Reskin, Barbara, 5140
Reskin, Barbara F., 13039
Resnick, David, 11418
Resnick, S., 1872
Resnick, Solomon, 3436
Resnik, Judith A., 5975
Retana, Robert G., 11880
Reuter, Peter, 2457

Revesz, R.L., 843
Rex, John, 11033, 12472, 12505
Rexroat, Cynthia, 3347
Reyes, Maria de la Luz, 11034
Reyhner, J., 4087
Reynolds, Allan G., 11090
Reynolds, C.R., 13845
Reynolds, Craig A., 9290
Reynolds, Donald E., 14096
Reynolds, L.T., 12193
Reynolds, Tracie, 5142
Reynolds, Vernon, 3046, 12473
Reza, H.G., 10516
Rezendes, Michael, 7301, 9533
Rhoades, E.R., 6504
Rhoads, Steven E., 254
Rhoda, Heather, 13739
Rhode, Deborah L., 13040
Rhoden, William C., 5143, 13334
Rhodes, Carroll, 11882
Rhodes, Charles D., 10517
Rhodes, Jane, 11256
Rhodes, J.E., 5612
Rhodes, John, 12818
Riach, P.A., 3047
Riaklin, E., 12194
Ribadeneira, Diego, 2744, 3599, 4088-4094,
    9534, 10179
Ribes Tovar, Federico, 844
Ribowsky, Mark, 845
Ricard, Serge, 1991
Ricciuti, H.N., 6505
Riccucci, Norma M., 255, 8100, 13862
Rice, Bobbylyne, 4095
Rice, D.P., 6506
Rice, E.M., 9349
Rice, F., 1236
Rice, Kym S., 6746
Rice, Mitchell F., 256, 6507, 14657
Rice, Sarah, 846
Rice, T.W., 14260
Rich, Andrea L., 5144
Rich, Frank, 1082, 10180
Rich, J., 3047
Rich, Spencer, 7758
Rich, Wilbur C., 11883
Richard, Alfred C., Jr., 10181
Richard, Ray, 3595
Richards, C., 10182
Richards, David A.J., 9012
Richards, Evelleen, 13041
Richards, Paul, 9569
Richardson, Barbara B., 4097, 5701
Richardson, Bill, 2170
Richardson, C.F., 9713
Richardson, Chad, 7633
Richardson, Henry J., III, 12243
Richardson, Joe M., 4801
Richardson, Lynda, 4098-4099, 5145

Richardson, Marilyn, 10183
Richardson, Richard C., Jr., 5146
Richardson, Tina, 13863
Riches, W.T.M., 1873
Richie, Rob, 10184
Richter, Daniel K., 6977
Richter, William L., 11884
Ricketts, Erol R., 1874-1875
Ricketts, Thomas C., 6212
Rickey, Carrie, 10185
Ricks, Mary F., 4828
Rico, Carlos, 13406
Riddlesperger, James W., Jr., 11885
Ridenhour, Ron, 5147, 11886
Rider, Andrea, 12586
Ridgeway, James, 7845, 10186-11889
Ridgley, Julia, 5148
Riding In, James T., 6978
Ridrigues, Carl A., 5976
Rieder, J., 9624
Riegel, Stephen J., 9013
Riemer, David R., 3348
Ries, Paula, 14423
Ries, Peter W., 6508-6511
Riesenberg, Peter, 1436
Riesman, D., 8561
Riess, Steven A., 13335-13336
Riggs, F.W., 8562, 12195
Rigsby, Enrique Du Bois, 10187
Riker, William H., 1654
Riley, Glenda, 14424
Riley, Michael, 847, 7846, 9641, 11890
Riley, Norman, 1876
Rilloraza, Frances A., 11035
Rimer, Sara, 7634
Rinanelli, Marco, 9518
Rinder, I.D., 7449
Rindo, Ronald J., 9291
Rinehart, Sue T., 6512
Ringle, Ken, 848-849, 1083
Rios-Bustamante, Antonio, 1877
Ripley, C. Peter, 6979, 13182
Ripley, Lee, 7635
Ripley, W.Z., 7636
Rise, Eric W., 2458, 6980
Rishell, Lyle, 10518
Rister, Carl C., 6981
Rithman, S., 2459
Rittenhouse, R.K., 6513
Ritter, Edward H., 4447
Rivera, Angel G., 2081
Rivera, Carla, 12086
Rivera, Dennis, 5508
Rivera, Feliciano, 6912-6913
Rivera, Monte, 11688
Rivera Lugo, Carlos, 2082
Rivers, Eugene F., 5149
Rivlin, Benjamin, 850
Rivlin, Gary, 11891

Roark, Anne C., 6514
Roback, J., 3448, 11356
Robbins, B., 11036
Robbins, Lynn A., 8101
Robbins, Richard, 5151
Robbins, William, 2745
Robbs, Lloyd F., Sr., 257
Robers, C.C., 1388
Roberto, Rita Jean, 1968
Roberts, Alden E., 12244
Roberts, Bruce B., 2919, 3435
Roberts, C., 10188
Roberts, Darrell, 5768
Roberts, Darryl L., 5152
Roberts, D.E., 14425
Roberts, Diane, 13183
Roberts, Frances C., 8295
Roberts, H.W., 6982
Roberts, James B., 2434
Roberts, Julian V., 2460
Roberts, Lawrence E., 11892
Roberts, Randy, 851, 13337
Roberts, Sam, 258, 1084, 2746, 4101, 7303,
    10635-10636, 11893-11895, 12099, 14097
Roberts, Shirley J., 3349
Robertson, M.J., 7315
Robertson, Nan, 10189
Robertson, William E. (Gene), 7304
Robeson, Paul, Jr., 1085, 14558
Robins, K., 5037, 9758
Robins, Natalie, 13740
Robinson, Armstead L, 1627, 1655, 6983
Robinson, B., 14194
Robinson, Carla J., 2171, 7305, 11037
Robinson, Dana A., 2437
Robinson, Donald, 6515, 9014
Robinson, Forrest G., 9216
Robinson, Gary, 4894
Robinson, Gene S., 10190
Robinson, James K., 3048
Robinson, Jeanne B., 5702
Robinson, Robert K., 5153
Robinson, Robert V., 4292
Robinson, Walter S., Jr., 9015
Robles, Al, 9292
Robles, Jennifer, 10637
Robnett, Belinda, 1656-1657
Rocard, Macienne, 9293
Rochin, Refugio Q., 3350
Rochlin, Margy, 5154
Rockoff, Hugh, 14174
Rockwell, Llewellyn H., Jr., 3049
Rockwell, Paul, 259
Rodgers, Daniel T., 8564
Rodgers, Harrell R., Jr., 2747, 3351-3352,
    5703, 11453, 14559
Rodgers, J.L., 3353-3354
Rodgers, J.R., 3353-3354
Rodgers, Jimmie N., 14261

Rodgers, Lawrence R., 10365
Rodgers, Raymond, 14261
Rodgers, W., 3208
Rodin, M.J., 260
Rodriguez, Adriene, 261, 5155
Rodriguez, Antonio H., 10638
Rodriguez, C.E., 8102, 9625
Rodriguez, Carlos, 6516
Rodriguez, Clara E., 1878, 1969, 2083-2084,
    3050, 3355, 5710, 5977, 12196, 13042,
    14430
Rodriguez, Gregory, 12161
Rodriguez, Havidan, 3356
Rodriguez, Luis J., 2461, 9431, 10191
Rodriguez, O., 2462, 6517
Rodriguez, O. Jaime E., 6984
Rodriguez, Rafael, 2102
Rodriguez, Raul, 8453
Rodriguez, Ray, 263
Rodriguez, Richard, 11038
Rodriguez, Roberto, 10581
Rodriguez, Salvador F., 2463
Rodriguez, Santiago, 262
Rodriguez Beruff, Jorge, 10519
Roebuck, Julian B., 5156
Roediger, David, 404, 455, 1879, 8103-8105
Roefs, Wim, 10192
Roehrenbeck, Carol A., 2464
Roemer, John, 2110
Roemer, Multon I., 6421
Roemwe, J.E., 4102
Roff, Sandra, 9146
Rogers, A., 11896
Rogers, Andrei, 10312
Rogers, Edward D., 264
Rogers, Joel A., 7847
Rogers, Kim Lacy, 1659
Rogers, Mary Beth, 2172
Rogers, Patricia, 12296
Rogers, Rebecca A., 11897
Rogers, Richard G., 6518-6520
Rogers, S.J., 5157
Rogers, W. McDowell, 5789
Rogers, William W., 8161
Rogers, Wylie S., 12474
Rogin, Michael P., 10193, 12352
Rogler, Lloyd H., 5704, 6521-6522
Rogosin, H. Rogie, 10345
Rogot, Eugene, 6523-6524
Rohde, Stephen F., 13741
Rohlik, Josef, 3051
Rohrlich, Ted, 3357
Rohrlich-Leavitt, Ruby, 8137
Rohter, Larry, 8565-8566, 10194, 10639,
    11039, 14098
Roiphe, Anne, 1086
Roiphe, Katie, 5158
Roise, Anne, 3052
Roisman, Florence W., 7306-7308

Rokeach, M., 10270
Rolison, Garry, L., 1880, 13958
Rollenhagen, Mark, 9016
Rollings, Willard H., 8296
Rollka, Bodo, 13533
Rolnick, Joshua N., 5159
Romanofsky, Peter, 2123
Romano-V., Octavio L., 852
Romero, Delia W.R., 8567
Romero, Gloria J., 11040
Romero, Mary, 265
Romo, Harriet D., 4103, 10640
Romo, Ricardo, 1660, 6985-6986, 7637
Ronda, Bruce A., 853
Ronda, James P., 9017
Rones, P.L., 3277
Roos, Patricia A., 13039
Root, Marcia P.P., 5705
Roper, Burns W., 12100
Roper, Larry D., 13921
Rosaldo, Renato, 12353
Rosales, Francisco A., 8106
Rosales, Rodolfo, 11898
Roscoe, Wilma J., 5160
Rose, Dan, 9665
Rose, David L., 266
Rose, D.C., 5161
Rose, Douglas, 12587
Rose, Gillian, 13043
Rose, Harold M., 2465, 10641
Rose, Jennifer, 5978, 10195
Rose, Jerome C., 6525-6527
Rose, Lloyd, 9294, 10196
Rose, Margaret, 8107-8108
Rose, Nancy E., 5979
Rose, Patricia S., 267
Rose, Peter, 1087
Rose, S.O., 8109
Rose, Stephen, 1881
Rose, Steven, 12476
Roseberry, William, 11041
Rosen, Benton H., 4752
Rosen, Miriam, 9933
Rosen, Ruth, 5539
Rosenbach, J.H., 7759
Rosenbach, Margo L., 6528
Rosenbaum, Alan S., 576
Rosenbaum, Emily V., 7309-7310
Rosenbaum, James E., 2748, 7311
Rosenbaum, Robert J., 1970
Rosenbaum, S.A., 5435
Rosenbaum, Sara, 6529-6530
Rosenbaum, Stuart E., 12125
Rosenberg, Alan, 1116, 8474
Rosenberg, Charles E., 6531
Rosenberg, David, 8110
Rosenberg, Gerald N., 9018
Rosenberg, Henry, 1088
Rosenberg, Howard, 13535

Rosenberg, Mitchell, 6532
Rosenberg, M.L., 1364
Rosenberg, S., 5433
Rosenberg, Terry J., 3358, 6533
Rosenbery, Howard, 13534
Rosenblatt, Robert A., 7312-7313
Rosenblatt, Roger, 9570
Rosenbloom, David H., 268
Rosenfeld, Megan, 854, 10520
Rosenfeld, Michel, 269-270
Rosenfeld, Paul, 10521
Rosenfield, David, 13560
Rosenstone, Robert A., 7984
Rosenthal, A.M., 1089
Rosenthal, Elisabeth, 6534-6535
Rosenthal, H., 9019
Rosenthal, H.D., 8297
Rosenthal, J.A., 5706
Rosenthal, John N., 7450
Rosenthal, Stuart S., 7154
Rosenwaike, Ira, 6536-6537
Rosenzweig, M.R., 6538
Ross, Andrew, 12197
Ross, Arthur, 7990
Ross, E.A., 12477
Ross, Edward A., 12354
Ross, J.L., 13044
Ross, Joe, 7451
Ross, Michael E., 10197
Ross, Stephen J., 10198
Ross, Steven J., 10199
Ross, Thomas, 271, 272, 8568-8569
Ross, William G., 4104
Rossell, Christine H., 2749-2754
Rosser, Phyllis, 13864
Rossi, Luigi, 13742
Rossi, Peter, 7314
Rosswurm, Steve, 8092, 8111
Rostkowski, Joelle, 14560
Rotberg, Iris C., 4105-4106
Roth, B.M., 12355
Roth, Byron M., 12198
Roth, D., 7315
Rothbell, Gladys W., 13536
Rothblum, E., 8570
Rothbun, Ted A., 6527
Rothenberg, P., 13045
Rothenberg, Paula S., 11042
Rothenberg, Randall, 10200
Rotheram, Mary J., 1356
Rothermund, Dietwar, 4117
Rothman, David J., 2466
Rothman, Robert, 4107
Rothman, S., 7776
Rothman, Sheila M., 6539
Rothstein, Donna S., 4557
Rothstein, Edward, 11257-11258
Rothstein, Mervyn, 9295, 10201
Rothstein, Richard, 5436

Rothstein, Stanley W., 4108
Rothwell, Bruce A., 10522
Roubertoux, Pierre, 7760
Roudevitch, M., 10202
Rountree, E.L., 11043
Rountree, Helen C., 9738
Rouse, Jacqueline A., 855, 14426
Rouse, Joy, 1437
Rouse, Linda P., 13450
Rousseau, M.O., 1882
Rout, Kathleen, 856
Rovaris, Dereck J., 5162
Rowan, Carl T., 857-858
Rowan, G.D., 142
Rowanowski, Michael H., 2220
Rowe, D.C., 1365
Rowe, G.S., 2467
Rowland, D., 6540
Rowse, T., 12621
Royce, Anna Peterson, 12199
Royko, Mike, 14262
Rubenstein, Bruce A., 8298
Rubenstein, Roberta, 9296
Rubin, Bernard, 10203
Rubin, Brad, 5163
Rubin, Diana, 13537
Rubin, Gary E., 1090
Rubin, Jay, 7638
Rubin, Laurie, 3053
Rubin, Lawrence, 11899
Rubin, Margot S., 3054
Rubin, Steven J., 859
Rubinowitz, Leonard S., 4892
Rubio, Phil, 6987
Rucinski, D., 12101
Rucker, Leland, 5164
Rucker, Robert E., 273
Rudnick, Lois, 6699
Rudwick, Elliott M., 6541, 8055, 12735
Ruffing, Lorraine Turner, 11179
Ruggles, Patricia, 3359
Ruggles, Steven, 5707-5708, 7587
Ruiz, Dorothy S., 6542
Ruiz, Raul, 5165
Ruiz, Vicki L., 6784, 6988, 8112, 14332
Rule, Sheila, 10204
Rumbaut, Carmen, 175
Rumbaut, Ruben G., 6104, 6657
Rumberger, R.W., 4109, 8113
Runyan, Timothy J., 9044
Ruoff, A. La Vonne Brown, 9297
Rury, John L., 2173, 4110, 7761
Rusch, R.R., 7759
Rusco, Elmer R., 9020
Rush, David, 6208
Rush, Mark E., 11900
Rushton, J. Philippe, 2468, 7762-7767
Russ, Shlomo M., 577
Russakoff, Dale, 5166

Russell, James W., 10523
Russell, Kathy, 11901
Russell, L.A., 5167
Russell, Margaret M., 10205
Russett, Bruce, 13743
Russo, Andrew, 11902
Russo, Rocco, 4312
Rust, Ben, 3055
Rustin, Bayard, 9432
Ruther, M., 6543
Rutten, Tim, 9433, 11903
Rutti, Ronald, 2755
Ryals, Clyde de L., 4617
Ryan, Alan, 11044
Ryan, Charlotte, 10206
Ryan, Dennis P., 6989
Ryan, Frank, 6544
Ryan, J. Brendan, 9021
Ryan, Jeffrey R., 13744
Ryan, Michael, 12588
Ryan, Roderick, 8114
Ryce, Drew M., 1661
Rynearson, Ann M., 9566

Saad, Henry W., 5168
Sabatier, Renee, 6545
Sabbagh, Suba J., 13538
Sabin, J.I., 9022
Sabinani, H.B., 13865
Sabol, William J., 2426, 2469
Sachar, Howard M., 578
Sachs, Steven J., 1563
Sacks, Karen B., 1091
Sadker, David, 4111
Sadker, Myra, 4111
Saeger, Moe, 8115
Saenger, G., 13539
Saenz, R., 3360, 7316
Saenz, Rogelio, 9714, 10366
Safa, Helen I., 3361, 8116
Safianow, Allen, 7848
Sagatun, Inger J., 2470, 3056
Sage, George H., 13338
Sager, Marilyn, 6530
Sahagun, Louis, 8299, 8571
Sahlins, Marshall, 9489
Said, Edward W., 2085, 11045
Sailes, G.A., 13339, 13540
Sainsbury, John A., 8117
Saks, Eva, 9023
Salamon, Lester, 3057
Salces, Luis M., 11904
Saldivar, Ramon, 8572
Salem, Dorothy C., 6990, 14427-14429
Sales, William W., Jr., 11180
Salleh, Ariel, 5540
Salley, Robert L., 7849
Salloch, Erika, 12356
Salmon, Jacqueline L., 3748

Salmon, Roberto M., 6546
Salmond, John A., 1662, 13745
Salmony, Steven E., 7850
Salstrom, Paul, 6991
Salter, John R., Jr., 1663, 5169
Saltman, Juliet, 7317-7319
Saltzstein, Grace H., 11905
Salvaggio, D.W., 9554
Salvatore, Nick, 1438
Salvino, Dana N., 8573
Salyer, Lucy E., 7639-7640
Salzman, Jack, 1092
Samet, M.J., 5541
Sammons, Vivian, 12924
Samora, Julian, 14099
Sampson, Edward E., 12307
Sampson, Henry T., 9298, 10207
Samson, Jacques, 13340
Samuda, Ronald J., 9462
Samuels, Benjamin, 2756
Samuelson, Franz, 7768
Samuelson, Robert J., 3449
San Juan, E., Jr., 9299-9301, 11046, 11181,
    11357, 12478-12479
San Miguel, Guadalupe, Jr., 2757, 4112-4114
Sanchez, Armand J., 3362
Sanchez, Carmen M.T., 4115
Sanchez, George J., 6992, 9434
Sanchez, Jose R., 7320-7321
Sanchez, Rene, 7322, 10318
Sanchez Korrol, Virginia E., 2174-2175, 14430
Sancho, Anthony R., 2269
Sandalow, T., 5170
Sandefur, Gary D., 3394-3395, 5719
Sander, Richard H., 7323
Sanders, Alain L., 5171
Sanders, Bob Ray, 10208
Sanders, Danielle, 5172
Sanders, Douglas, 9024
Sanders, Heywood, 12037
Sanders, J., 1853
Sanders, Jimmy, 3446
Sanders, Leslie C., 9302
Sanders, Lynn M., 183
Sanders, Rickie, 13046
Sanders, Warren G., Jr., 5173
Sanderson, Steve, 10313
Sandis, E.E., 1884
Sandler, Andrew B., 4116
Sandler, Stanley, 10524
Sandomir, Richard, 13341
Sandoval, Moises, 12819
Sandoval, Raymond E., 2176
Sands, Kathleen M., 14601
Sanford, J.S., 1709
Sanger, David E., 14100
Sanger, Kerran L., 1664
Sanoff, Alvin P., 5174
Santamaria, Ulysses, 1093, 11047

Santana Cooney, Rosemary, 5710
Santiago, A.M., 7324
Santiago, K. Antonio, 14195
Santiago Santiago, Isaura, 4117
Santiago-Valles, Kelvin A., 2086
Santino, Jack, 860
Santiviago, M., 6517
Santos, John F., 6402
Santos, Joseph M., 4118
Santos, R., 5437
Santow, Dan, 4119
Sanua, Marianne, 5175
Saper, Bernard, 7452
Sapiro, Virginia, 1449
Saporta, Sol, 13047
Saravia-Shore, Marietta, 8574
Sardell, Alice, 6547
Sarna, J.D., 7453
Sarna, Jonathan D., 579, 5058
Sarnoski, Dorene R., 5176
Sarrel, Robert, 4120
Sartorius, Rolf, 12622
Sato, Charlene, 8575
Sato, Tadayuki, 580
Satz, Ronald N., 6993
Satzewich, Victor, 10356
Saunders, E., 6142
Sautter, Craig R., 1362
Savage, David G., 2471, 13048
Savage, David S., 9025
Savage, Mark, 9026
Savage, Reginald O., 5177
Savan, Leslie, 10209-10210
Savery, Pancho, 7382
Saville, Julie, 8118-8119
Savitch, Harold V., 5818
Savitt, Todd L., 6460, 6548-6552
Sawer, Mary R., 11906
Sawhill, Isabel V., 1875, 6182, 14196
Sawrey, Robert D., 9651
Sawyer, Marcia R., 9539
Saxton, Alexander, 8120, 9303, 11358, 12480
Sayer, Ian, 13746
Sazama, G.W., 5178
Scadron, S. Michael, 11907
Scales-Trent, Judy, 2758, 9027, 14431
Scanlan, J.P., 3363
Scanlon, Anthony J., 274
Scanlon, J.P., 275
Scannell, James J., 5179
Scaperlanda, Michael A., 3058
Scarano, Francisco A., 8121
Scarborough, C., 8122
Scardino, Albert, 10211
Scarr, Sandra, 7769-7771
Scarry, Elaine, 14251
Schaap, Dick, 13288
Schafer, Ann E., 14432
Schafer, Daniel L., 9464

Schafer, Judith K., 13184
Schaff, Adam, 13541
Schaffer, Daniel, 11317
Schaffer, M.A., 6553
Schaffer, R.C., 6554
Schafran, Lynn H., 9028-9029, 13049
Schappes, Morris U., 1094-1096
Scharf, Lois, 5635
Scharina, Richard G., 9304
Scharnhorst, Gary, 10525
Schatzberg, Rufus, 2472
Schauer, Frederick, 2473
Scheiber, Harry N., 2221, 6994
Scheiber, Jane L., 2221
Scheinin, Richard, 10212
Schemo, Diana J., 5180, 7325, 7851
Scher, Richard K., 1498, 11453
Scherro, Diana J., 5980
Scheuerman, Richard D., 8315
Scheuerman, William E., 11908
Schexnider, Alvin J., 10526
Schick, Frank L., 14561
Schick, Renee, 14561
Schill, Michael, 5455
Schiller, Herbert, 10213
Schilling, R.F., 6555
Schilz, Thomas F., 10527
Schindler, Alexander M., 1097
Schissel, Lillian, 8719
Schlesinger, Arthur M., Jr., 11027, 11048-
    11049
Schlesinger, Mark, 6556
Schliesh, Martin J., 9414
Schlissel, Lillian, 5694
Schlossman, Steven L., 3364
Schmalz, Jeffrey, 1885, 9465
Schmid, Carol, 1439, 8576
Schmidt, Fred H., 11259
Schmidt, James D., 8123
Schmidt, Peter, 2759-2762, 4121-4122, 5181,
    7326, 7641, 8577, 11909
Schmidt, William E., 6557
Schmitt, Eric, 2763, 10528-10529
Schmitz, Betty, 11050
Schmitz, Susanne, 11260
Schnaiberg, Lynn, 4123-4124
Schnapper, Eric, 276
Schnare, Ann B., 7261-7262
Schneider, D., 5805
Schneider, Edgar W., 8578
Schneider, John J., 13342
Schneider, Keith, 4125, 5542-5545, 6558-6561
Schneider, M., 5438, 10367
Schneider, W., 581, 12087
Schockley, E.E., 11910
Schoen, David, 1098, 11051
Schoenberger, R., 4622
Schoenborn, Charlotte A., 6696
Schofield, Janet Ward, 2764-2765, 4126

Scholl, Barry, 8124
Schonbach, Morris, 11911
Schonberger, Howard, 2222
Schor, Joel, 5981
Schram, Sanford F., 3365-3366
Schrecker, Ellen, 6996
Schrender, Yda, 7327
Schroeder, Jeanne L., 13542
Schroeder, Walter A., 405
Schuchter, Arnold, 12820
Schuck, Peter H., 1440-1441
Schuler, J.R., 7328
Schulhofer, Stephen J., 2474
Schulman, Bruce J., 6997
Schulman, M.D., 8300
Schulte, Steven C., 11912
Schultz, Duane, 6998
Schultz, Jon S., 1665
Schultz, T.P., 6538
Schultz, Valerie, 1366
Schumacher, E.J., 2957
Schuman, Howard, 7329, 12102, 12112
Schutz, Charles E., 7454
Schwab, Margo, 5546
Schwabe, Klaus, 12245
Schwalm, Leslie A., 14433
Schwartz, Barry, 11054
Schwartz, Bernard, 277
Schwartz, Deborah R., 5183
Schwartz, Harry, 6999
Schwartz, Harvey, 7000
Schwartz, Herman, 278
Schwartz, John, 8579
Schwartz, Laura J., 5712
Schwartz, Margaret, 14364
Schwartz, Paul H., 9030
Schwartz, Pepper, 4882
Schwarz, John E., 3367
Schwarz, K. Robert, 11261
Schwarz, Philip J., 2475, 9739
Schweik, Susan, 2223
Schwemm, Robert G., 7330
Schweninger, Loren, 1237, 1886, 8301, 13185,
    14197-14198, 14434
Schwenk, Katrin, 11913
Schwer, R. Keith, 7531
Sciolino, Elaine, 13747
Scott, Anne Firor, 7001, 14435
Scott, Barbara Marbien, 14436
Scott, J.A., 4352
Scott, Janny, 4127
Scott, Joan W., 11055-11056, 11262, 13050
Scott, Jonathan, 4598
Scott, Joseph W., 5713
Scott, Marvin B., 279
Scott, Maurice, Jr., 11914
Scott, Ralph, 4128
Scott, Robin F., 2476
Scott, William R., 10530

Scott-Jones, Diane, 4129
Scruggs, Frank, 9031
Scruggs, Marc, 9490
Scully, Gerald W., 13343
Scutt, J.A., 6562
Scuttles, William C., Jr., 406
Seagears, Margaret J., 5184
Seale, Bobby, 5185
Seale, Doris, 9307
Seaman, Louis L., 10531
Searle, John, 11057
Sears, David O., 9435
Sears, Richard, 14437
Seave, Paul L., 5982
Sebok, A.J., 5983
Secada, W.G., 4130
Seccombe, K., 6563
Secor, Robert, 7455
Secret, Philip E., 2477
Sedlacek, W.E., 4567
Sedler, Robert A., 280, 5186-5187
Seeley, David S., 2478
Seem, Susan R., 10408
Seematter, Mary E., 9032
Seff, Monica A., 13353
Sefton, James E., 10642
Segady, Thomas W., 9793
Segal, Daniel, 11058
Segal, D.R., 10533
Segal, Elizabeth A., 3368
Sege, Irene, 2479, 3369, 7331
Segers, Mary C., 319
Segrave, J.O., 13253
Segrest, Mab, 14263
Segura, Denise A., 1887, 8125-8126
Seib, Gerald F., 12103
Seibert, Brant, 8455
Seidel, Gill, 12991, 13065
Seiden, Melvin, 1099
Seidler-Feller, Chaim, 467
Seidman Diamond, Shari, 8957
Seigel, Fred, 11059
Seigle, Larry, 13748
Seijo Bruno, Mini, 11182
Seitz, P., 5437
Selegue, S.M., 5188
Selig, Joel L., 281
Selik, R.M., 6564
Selinker, Michael, 282
Sellers, R.M., 13344
Sells, Cato, 8302
Seltzer, Richard, 12108, 14562
Seltzer, Rick, 7852
Selvin, Paul, 5189
Selznick, Gertrude J., 582
Semons, Maryann, 11060
Semple, Jesse B. [pseud.], 283
Semyenov, Moshe, 8127-8128
Sen, A., 14563

Senecal, Michael D., 12357
Senechal, Roberta, 14101
Senese, Guy B., 11915
Sennett, Richard, 13543
Sera, Kae, 11185
Serafica, Felicisima, 6565
Sereny, Gitta, 9034
Serrano, Richard A., 5984, 13544
Servin, Manuel P., 2476, 8129
Serwatka, Thomas S., 4132
Sessions, William S., 13749-13750
Setser, Gregorio, 1666
Sevenair, John P., 12892
Sexton, Donald E., 3059
Sexton, E.A., 7333
Sexton, Edwin A., 3060
Sexton, Joe, 13345
Sexton, V.S., 12994
Seymour, Cheri, 12589
Shachtman, Marc, 11061
Shadron, Virginia, 9474
Shafer, D. Michael, 10481, 10534
Shaffer, Ralph E., 13186
Shafir, S., 583
Shah, H., 10643
Shaheen, Jack G., 13545-13547
Shakur, Sanjika, a k a Monster Kody Scott, 861
Shalevitz, Judith, 5190
Shalinsky, Audrey C., 9753
Shalom, Stephen R., 584
Shamon, Janet H., 2177
Shanahan, Donald G., Jr., 8303
Shanker, Albert, 284, 2769, 4133-4136, 8130, 13866
Shankman, Arnold, 1100-1101, 7642, 10644
Shanks, Ronald D., 1888
Shanley, Jean M., 3061
Shannon, S.M., 7643
Shapiro, A.L., 11916
Shapiro, Andrew, 7002
Shapiro, Edward S., 585-586
Shapiro, Herbert, 8131
Shapiro, H.R., 1029
Shapiro, Isaac, 3370-3371
Shapiro, John T., 5191
Shapiro, Karin A., 5769
Shapiro, Leonard, 13346
Shapiro, M.J., 8460
Shapiro, Martin M., 13867
Shapiro, Morton O., 4956
Shapiro, R.J., 5715
Shapiro, Robert, 6567
Shapiro, R.S., 6566
Shapiro, R.Y., 12104
Shapiro, Thomas M., 14187-14188
Shapiro, Walter, 1667
Sharbach, Sarah E., 13548
Sharbaugh, C.S., 6330
Sharp, K., 8637

Sharpe, Lora, 13549
Sharps, Ronald L., 12821
Sharpton, A., 11917
Shattuck, Petra T., 9035
Shaw, David, 10214
Shaw, Robert B., 13187
Shaw, Wendy, 9366
Shawki, Ahmed, 13218
Shea, Christine M., 4137
Shea, Christopher, 4865, 5192-5198
Shea, S., 6568
Shebala, Markey, 14438
Sheehan, Bernard W., 7003
Sheehan, Donald, 12246
Sheehan, Henry, 12200
Sheehan, J.B., 2770
Sheehan, Reginald S., 9049
Sheldon, Charles H., 9036
Sheldon, Randall F., 2480
Shell, Marc, 8580
Shelton, Beth Ann, 3062, 7900
Shemlow, Mary, V., 13051
Shen, Fern, 5985
Shenhav, Yehouda, 12902
Shenhaw, Y., 3243
Shenitz, Bruce, 10215
Shenkman, Richard, 7004
Shenon, Philip, 3063, 13751
Shenton, James P., 12246
Shepard, George W., Jr., 13962
Shepard, Gloria, 14439
Shepard, Lorrie A., 13868
Shepard, Paul, 1971
Shepardson, D.P., 4138
Sheperd, J.W., 13493
Sheppard, E., 1889
Sheppard, Tyron J., 9037
Sherburne, Kevin P., 7335
Sheridan, Earl, 1972
Sheridan, Richard B., 10368
Sherk, John, 3619
Sherkat, D.E., 12822
Sherman, J.D., 4139
Sherman, Richard B., 5199
Sherpell, Brenda K., 9147
Sherraden, Michael A., 3371
Sherrill, Rowland A., 9719, 12814
Sherron, Philip, 8132
Sherry, Suzanna, 5200
Sherwin, Richard K., 9038
Sherwood, Tom, 9452
Shields, Patrick M., 3862
Shields, S.W., 3085
Shils, Edward, 11062
Shin, Barbara J.S., 4140
Shin, Eui Hang, 1238
Shindul-Rothschild, Judith, 12986
Shine, Cathy, 2408
Shingles, Richard D., 5986, 12105

Shinn, Vara D., 9715
Shipek, Florence C., 7005
Shipler, David K., 7006
Shipman, Pat, 7772-7773
Shipp, E.R., 6569-6570, 9626
Shirley, Carl R., 9305
Shirley, Don, 10216
Shirley, Paula W., 9305
Shiver, Jube, Jr., 4141
Shklar, Judith N., 1442
Shlay, A.B., 7336-7337
Shoemaker, Nancy, 14440-14441
Shogan, Robert, 11918
Shogren, Elizabeth, 3064, 3372-3373, 3702
Shohat, Ella, 10217, 11063, 13550
Shoop, Julie G., 3065
Shoop, Julie J., 13052
Short, B., 8581
Short, G., 3066
Short, Geoffrey, 587
Short, Thomas, 5201
Shortridge, Barbara G., 14442
Shotland, Jeffrey, 6571
Showmaker, Nancy, 5716
Shrestha, Nanda R., 11263
Shriver, Donald W., Jr., 11919
Shrode, Paul E., 4486
Shropshire, Kenneth L., 13347
Shryer, Tracy, 2310
Shue, Henry, 7957
Shuffelton, Frank, 7455
Shuit, Douglas P., 6572-6575
Shull, Steven A., 1668
Shulman, S., 3374
Shulman, Steven, 350, 3067, 3158, 5896, 8133-8135
Shuptrine, S.C., 6576
Shurkin, Joel N., 7774
Shuster, Beth, 4143
Shweder, Richard A., 13053
Sibert, Anthony, 7456
Sibert, Denise Ji-Ahnte, 7456
Sidanius, J., 11264, 12481
Sidanius, James, 5202
Sidanius, Jim, 2481, 13054
Sidbury, James, 9740
Sidel, Ruth, 5203
Sider, Gerald, 7007, 8582
Sides, W. Hampton, 1973, 2771
Sidey, Hugh, 9555
Siebers, Tobin, 11064
Siegel, Barry, 5204
Siegel, Ed, 10218-10219
Siegel, Evan G.S., 5205
Siegel, Jessica, 5206
Siegelman, P., 2913, 3068
Sifry, Micah L., 588
Sigel, Irving E., 7771
Sigel, Roberta S., 440

Sigelman, Lee, 1669, 12019, 12106, 13079, 13813, 14564
Sikes, Lewright, 6577
Silberman, Neil A., 10535
Silberstein, Fred B., 589
Silcox, Harry C., 11920
Silet, Charles L.P., 13390
Silet, C.L.P., 9787
Silk, Catherine, 460
Silk, John, 460
Silva, Cynthia, 5207
Silver, James W., 8304
Silver, J.H., 5208
Silver, Nina, 1102
Silverberg, David, 590
Silverblatt, Ronnie, 11921
Silverman, Buddy R.S., 13348
Silverman, David, 8017
Silverman, E.R., 6578
Silverman, R.A., 2482
Silverstein, Stuart, 3260, 7644, 8136, 12999
Silvestrini de Pacheco, Blanca, 2483, 8137
Simcox, D., 7573
Simcox, David E., 7579
Simmen, Edward, 2845
Simmons, Cassandra A., 2772
Simmons, Doug, 4144
Simmons, Jerold, 13752
Simmons, Ross, 286
Simmons, S., 6135
Simmons, William S., 13551
Simms, Margaret C., 2427, 2484, 3375, 4145, 14443
Simms-Maddox, Margaret J., 11922
Simon, C., 13320
Simon, Daniel T., 8106
Simon, John, 4117
Simon, Jonathan, 2485
Simon, Richard, 7645
Simon, Rita J., 5717, 13869
Simon, Roger I., 461
Simon, Thomas W., 7338
Simone, Nina, 862
Simons, James, 9039
Simons, Jargaret A., 13055
Simons, Marlene, 863
Simpson, Brooks D., 10536
Simpson, Christopher, 591, 12247, 12590
Simpson, Janice C., 5209, 14565
Simpson, Patricia, 3376
Sims, Calvin, 287, 1239-1240, 1670
Sims, Serbreina J., 5210
Simson, Sharon P., 6579, 6676
Sims-Phillips, Anna, 10246
Sindab, Jean, 14566
Sinden, Peter G., 1103
Singer, Beth J., 11359
Singer, David G., 1104
Singer, Eleanor, 10220

Singer, Joseph W., 8305, 9040
Singer, Merrill, 6580, 12824
Singer, Toba, 11065
Singerman, Robert, 592, 14658
Singh, V.P., 1890
Singlaub, John K., 12591
Singlemann, Joachim, 1923
Singleton, David A., 7339
Singular, Stephen, 12592-12593
Singwaney, Anuradha, 9998
Sinke, Suzanne M., 7667
Sinsheimer, Joseph A., 11923
Sipchen, Bob, 864, 1105, 6581, 9041, 9436, 11066-11067
Sirageldin, I., 14445
Sirefman, Josef P., 7539, 7664, 13336
Sirota, K.L., 11068
Sisk, Glenn N., 2486
Sites, Paul, 1847
Sitton, Tom, 6778, 9388
Sivitz, T.E., 2773
Sizemore, Barbara A., 4146
Sjoquist, David L., 3377, 5418
Skelton, George, 11924
Skemp, Sheila L., 5664
Skerry, Peter N., 11925, 14567
Skidmore, Dave, 7340
Skidmore, Max J., 6582
Skillings, J.H., 12201
Skinner, Elliot P., 407
Skinner, Robert E., 8138
Sklar, Holly, 9883
Sklar, Richard L., 3841
Sklarewitz, Norman, 8583
Skloot, Robert, 9306
Skocpol, Theda, 11926
Skolnick, Jerome H., 5987-5988
Skora, C.L., 3378
Skorapa, Olga L., 865
Skotnes, A., 1241
Skotnes, Andor D., 1671
Skowrovek, Stephen, 4341
Skutnabb-Kangas, Tove, 10760, 12358
Slapin, Beverly, 9307
Slattery, Jim, 1443
Slaughter, Diana T., 4147
Slaughter, John B., 5212, 13303
Slaughter, Thomas P., 13188, 14102
Slavin, Robert E., 2774, 4148
Slawson, Douglas J., 13176
Slee, Amruta, 10221
Sleeper, Jim, 593, 866, 11927-11929
Sleeter, Christine E., 3744, 4149, 11069
Slesnick, D.T., 3379
Sloan, Allan, 288
Sloan, Gene, 12637
Sloan, Kay, 10222
Sloan, Leslie J., 1242
Sloan, William D., 10223

Slonaker, W.M., 3069
Sloss Vento, Adela, 867
Slotkin, Richard, 13552
Small, Christopher, 14568
Smallwood, James M., 7853, 9716
Smedley, Audrey, 12482
Smetak, Jacqueline, 5213
Smien, Eulius, 289
Smiga, George M., 594
Smist, Frank J., Jr., 13753
Smith, A., 13922
Smith, A. Wade, 5214, 12107
Smith, Alan M., 13123
Smith, Albert Joseph, Jr., 11070
Smith, Althea, 13056
Smith, Anna Burtill, 9581
Smith, Barbara Herrnstein, 4632
Smith, Baxter, 13754
Smith, Benjamin T., 3597
Smith, Beverly B., 9308
Smith, Billy G., 763
Smith, Burton M., 8306
Smith, C. Calvin, 10645
Smith, Charlene L., 1367
Smith, Charles U., 1672
Smith, Christopher E., 2487, 9043
Smith, Claire, 13349-13352
Smith, Courtland L., 7775, 12359
Smith, Dale E., 5790
Smith, Darryl F., 13923
Smith, Daryl G., 5215
Smith, D.B., 6583
Smith, Douglas, 2775
Smith, D.P., 6308
Smith, Earl, 290, 5718, 13353
Smith, Edward D., 12825
Smith, Elaine M., 12925
Smith, Elizabeth A., 11072
Smith, Elizabeth M., 7278, 9148
Smith, Eric, 8887
Smith, Eric C., 868
Smith, Eric J., 7646
Smith, Eric L., 7457
Smith, Frank, 4150
Smith, Gaddis, 9044
Smith, G.D., 6584
Smith, Gerald L., 869, 5216
Smith, Gladys E., 2776
Smith, J., 4151
Smith, J. Clay, Jr., 5217, 9045, 11265, 14659
Smith, J. Frazier, 10152
Smith, J. Owens, 11930
Smith, J.P., 291
Smith, James P., 3380-3381, 5719
Smith, Jane M., 2087
Smith, Jessie Carney, 14517
Smith, J.H., 12281
Smith, Joan, 2868
Smith, John David, 6792, 6794, 7008, 12360

Smith, Joyce O., 870
Smith, Kenneth L., 11931
Smith, K.R., 6648
Smith, Lynn, 5720
Smith, Mary J., 9556
Smith, M.D., 2488
Smith, Norman W., 7854
Smith, Patricia, 5721, 6585, 10224-10227, 12826, 13553
Smith, Paul, 1368
Smith, Peggie R., 5439, 8172
Smith, P.J., 2777
Smith, P.K., 14199
Smith, Preston H., 1974
Smith, Raymond T., 13189
Smith, Richard A., 7341-7343
Smith, Robert C., 11932-11933, 12108, 14562
Smith, Robert S., 116
Smith, Rogers M., 1441, 1444-1445
Smith, Ruth S., 1379
Smith, Sam, 13354
Smith, Sherry L., 10537
Smith, S.J., 6586
Smith, Steven D., 9046
Smith, Susan J., 12370
Smith, Susan Lynn, 6587-6588
Smith, Thomas G., 13355
Smith, Tom W., 595-596, 8584, 11934, 12060, 12109-12110, 13554
Smith, Vern E., 4152, 9508, 13755
Smith, Walter E., Jr., 4153
Smith, Warren Thomas, 12827
Smith, Willy D., 4154
Smith, Y.R., 14444
Smith, Z.A., 8197
Smitherman-Donaldson, Geneva, 8389, 8585, 9890
Smith-Irvin, Jeannette, 1975
Smithson, Isaiah, 12981
Smith-Todd, S., 8501
Smits, David D., 5722
Smock, Pamela J., 2778
Smoke, Richard, 7850
Smoler, Fredric, 7458
Smolla, Rodney A., 292, 5218-5219, 7344
Smollar, David, 2779
Smothers, Ronald, 597, 1106, 2780, 3753, 4155-4158, 5220-5222, 8307, 9047-9048, 9341, 9512, 9681, 11935-11938, 13756
Smylie, Mark A., 2643
Smythe, Mabel M., 1932
Snavely, Barbara J., 2781
Snay, Mitchell, 12828
Snead, James, 9309
Snedeker, George, 11939, 12483
Snider, Dixie E., Jr., 6589
Snider, William, 4159-4160
Sniderman, Paul M., 11310, 12111, 12202, 12484-12486

Snifen, Michael J., 2489
Snipp, C. Matthew, 2088, 2133, 2178, 8308, 11266, 14445, 14569-14570
Snow, David, 5819
Snow, Dean R., 7009
Snyder, Robert E., 13757
Snyder-Joy, Zoann Kay, 4161
Snyderman, M., 7776
So Relle, James M., 9717
Sobel, Mechal, 14264
Sobnosky, Matthew J., 8586
Sobol, Thomas, 11071
Soderlund, Jean R., 9662, 10369, 13190, 14446
Sohn, Hongeal, 9310
Soifer, S., 598
Sokoloff, Natalie J., 11267-11268
Solberg, Curtis B., 9394
Solberg, J.E., 9747
Soldatenko, Maria A., 14447
Solinger, R., 14265
Solinger, Regina A., 6590-6591
Solis, Jose, 4162
Sollors, Werner, 5224-5225, 9311, 12204
Solnick, L.M., 5226
Solomon, Alisa, 1107, 14103
Solomon, C.M., 14266
Solomon, Irvin D., 13057
Solomon, Mark I., 2089, 13219
Solomon, Norman, 8587, 10059
Solomos, John, 12258, 12487
Solorzano Bernat, Gloria, 13870
Soltman, Sharon W., 3996
Soltow, Lee, 14200
Somekawa, Ellen, 11072
Sommers, Laurie Kay, 1976
Sommers, Paul M., 13356
Son, In Soo, 294
Sonenshein, Raphael J., 11940-11942
Songer, Donald R., 9049
Sontag, Deborah, 4163, 7647-7652, 12829, 13555
Soo, In Soo, 3070
Sopapavon, Ricardo, 4164
Sorensen, Jonathan R., 2490
Sorenson, R.L., 5161
Sorlie, P., 6592
Sos, R.M., 12958
Soto, L.D., 4165
Soto, Lourdes, 5723
Soucie, J.M., 6593
South, Scott J., 5708, 7345
South, S.J., 2415, 2491
Souza, Steven J., 3071
Sowell, David, 8139
Sowell, Thomas, 295, 1108, 1673, 5228, 7010
Soza, Ramona E., 5989
Spackman, D.G., 6594
Spaid, Elizabeth L., 871
Spaights, Ernest, 12830, 13959

Spalding, Henry D., 7459
Spalding, Phinizy, 12873
Span, Paula, 872
Spann, Girardeau A., 9050
Sparks, L., 8588
Sparks, Randy Jay, 12831-12832
Spayd, Liz, 7089-7090, 7347, 7653
Spearman, Walter, 10107, 10228
Speck, Frank, 3382
Speck, Frank G., 10647
Specktor, Mordicai, 5548
Specter, Michael, 6595
Spector, B., 3072
Spector, Paul, 6596
Speller, Benjamin F., Jr., 9149
Spencer, Buffy, 9642
Spencer, Gary, 5229
Spencer, Hal, 9353
Spencer, Margaret B., 1371
Sperber, Murray, 13357
Spergel, J.A., 2301
Spero, Robert, 1977
Spicer, Edward H., 7011
Spickard, Paul R., 5724
Spiegel, Claire, 6597, 11943
Spigner, Clarence, 6598
Spindel, Donna J., 2492
Spindler, George D., 4167
Spinner, Jeff, 1446
Spiro, Jack D., 529
Spitzberg, Irving J., Jr., 9367
Spivack, John M., 1675
Spivey, Donald, 13358
Spofford, Tim, 5230
Spohn, C., 9051
Spolsky, Bernard, 8519
Sprafka, J. Michael, 6599
Spraggins, Tinsley L., 1243
Spriggs, Matthew, 9491
Sprinker, Michael, 8103
Sproat, John, 2782
Spude, R.L., 8129
Spurlin, Virginia L., 9718
Spurr, Stephen J., 3073
Squire, Madelyn C., 8140
Squires, Gregory D., 1676, 3074, 9750, 11944, 12488
Sreedhar, M.V., 4168
St. Clair, Diane, 14660
St. John, Craig, 7348
St. John, Edward P., 5232
Stacey, Judith, 13058
Stack, Carol, 10321
Stack, Steven, 1723
Staczek, John J., 8589
Stafford, Druicille H., 5233
Stafford, Walter W., 1892, 5440-5441, 7654
Stage, Frances K., 11073
Stahl, Ben, 8141

Stahl, Lori, 10229
Stahly, G.B., 14410
Stahwra, J.M., 7349
Stains, Laurence R., 9666
Stake, R.E., 13832
Stakeman, Randolph, 13191
Stall, Bill, 9437
Stam, Robert, 11063
Stamets, Bill, 10230
Stammer, Larry B., 12833-12834
Stampp, Kenneth M., 11183
Stancik, Edward F., 4169
Standing Bear, Luther, 7012
Stanfield, John H., II, 5234, 10538
Stanfield, John H., III, 12361-12362
Staniland, Martin, 408
Stanley, Alessandra, 5235
Stanley, Harold M., 11945
Stannard, David E., 6600, 12203
Stanton, Bill, 7855
Staples, Brent, 873, 1677, 5236-5239, 11269,
    13556-13557, 14572
Staples, Clifford L., 6601
Staples, Robert, 2090, 2493, 11289, 14104
Stapleton, D.C., 3293
Stapp, Carol B., 9535
Starfield, B., 6457
Stark, Evan, 2494, 13558
Stark, Rodney, 519
Starkey, Hugh, 9067
Starna, William A., 7013, 13192-13193
Starobin, Robert S., 13194
Starr, Kevin, 7655, 9438
Starr, Mark, 4453, 13359
Starr, Paul, 296, 6602
Stauffer, Robert H., 8309
Stauffer, Thomas W., 273
Stavans, Ilan, 618, 1269, 8590
Stavenhagen, Rodolfo, 2091
Stavis, Morton, 11947
Stavitsky, Jerome J., 298
Staw, B.M., 135
Stayton, Richard, 10231
Stea, D., 2179
Steacy, Stephen, 7014
Stead, Robert, 12835
Stearns, Peter N., 11075
Stedman, Raymond W., 13559
Steeh, C., 12112
Steele, Claude M., 299, 4171, 5241
Steele, Ian K., 7015
Steele, James, 11948
Steele, Matthew F., 10539
Steele, R.W., 3075, 11184
Steele, Shelby, 300-301, 11076
Steen, I.F., 3076
Steenland, Sally, 10232
Stefan, S., 1679
Stefancic, Jean, 4525, 8760

Stefon, Frederick J., 4172, 5990
Steger, Michael, 5242
Stegman, L.M., 3077
Stein, A., 1126
Stein, Alan H., 7808
Stein, Charles, 6603
Stein, Eric S., 2783
Stein, Jonathan, 3988
Stein, Judith, 12204
Stein, R.F., 8591
Stein, Robert C., 2784
Stein, Wayne J., 5243
Steinbach, Carol F., 2168
Steinberg, Ronnie, 302
Steinberg, Stephen, 303-304, 582, 1109, 1680,
    1893-1894, 5244, 11949, 14573
Steinerkhamsi, G., 462
Steinfels, Peter, 599
Steinkraus, Warren E., 1681
Steinman, Clay, 9871
Steinmetz, George, 1895
Stekler, Paul J., 11950
Stellings, Brande, 1447
Steltzer, Ulli, 9354
Stempel, Guido H., III, 10153
Stenross, Barbara, 13871
Stent, Gunther, 4926
Stepan, Alfred, 13743
Stepan, Nancy Leys, 12205
Stephan, C.W., 9492
Stephan, Walter G., 2785, 13560
Stephens, Beth, 9052
Stephens, Lester D., 5770
Stephens, Thomas M., 13801
Stephenson, Charles, 7880
Stephenson, Grier, 11951
Stepick, Alex, 9463, 10648
Stern, Carol S., 5245
Stern, D., 4017
Stern, Jane R., 2739, 4067
Stern, Kenneth S., 2495, 5246
Stern, Marc D., 1110
Stern, Mark, 1682-1684
Stern, Norton B., 600, 10649
Sternberg, Robert J., 6505
Sternhell, Carol, 11077
Stetson, Erlene, 874
Stetson, Jeffrey, 305
Stevens, Don, 13758
Stevens, Floraline Q., 4173-4174
Stevens, Jane, 13758
Stevens, Leonard B., 4175
Stevenson, Brenda E., 13195
Stevenson, Marshall Field, Jr., 1098, 1111
Stevenson, Rosemary M., 14661
Stevenson, Thomas H., 13563
Stewart, Abigail J., 13056
Stewart, Donald M., 13872
Stewart, Gail, 3078

Stewart, James B., 601, 5247, 5595, 7231, 13196, 14574
Stewart, Jeffrey C., 11306, 11311
Stewart, Jocelyn Y., 2496, 12638
Stewart, John, 749
Stewart, Joseph, Jr., 306, 3972-3973, 4176-4177
Stewart, Kenneth L., 4178, 7016
Stewart, M.W., 13059
Stewart, R.J., 5248
Stewart, Sharon, 4179
Stewart, William J., 8310
Stickler, K. Bruce, 307
Stiefel, Leanna, 3500
Stielow, Frederick J., 9140
Stiepsu, Judith H., 10540
Stiffarm, Lenore, 14575
Stikes, C. Scully, 5249
Still, Lawrence A., 10233
Stillwaggon, Eileen M., 3384, 3450
Stillwell, Paul, 10541
Stimpson, Catharine R., 308, 5250, 11078
Stinson, James A., 11459, 12113
Stith, Barbara J., 1111-1113
Stock, Carolyn H., 4180
Stocker, Carol, 5251-5252, 14105
Stocking, G.W., 12315
Stoddard, Ellwyn R., 3385, 8142
Stoffle, C.J., 11079, 13564
Stokes, Curtis, 14576
Stokes, Geoffrey, 11952
Stokes, John H., 5253
Stokes, Larry D., 309
Stolarik, Mark M., 7656
Stolberg, Sheryl, 2497-2498, 6604-6607
Stolzenberg, Lisa, 501
Stolzfus, Brenda, 10542
Stone, Alan A., 10234-10235
Stone, Anne J., 14423
Stone, B.J., 13873
Stone, C. Sumner, 10236
Stone, Clarence N., 11953
Stone, Donald P., 4181
Stone, Lorraine, 13060
Stone, Nancy-Stephanie, 13759
Stone, Robert B., 1685
Stone, V.A., 10237
Stoper, Emily, 1686
Storti, Craig, 14106
Story, Rosalyn M., 11270
Stoskopf, Alan L., 1448
Stotland, N.L., 6073
Stotsky, Sandra, 11080
Stott, D.H., 7777
Stott, Richard B., 8143
Stout, Angela K., 7657
Stout, D., 7778
Stout, Hilary, 6608
Stradling, David, 13197

Strane, Susan, 4182
Strasser, Steven, 1114
Stratton, L.S., 13960
Straus, M.A., 13062
Strauss, David A., 3079, 9053
Strauss, Herbert A., 7658
Strauss, Joseph H., 5254
Strauss, Marcy, 8592
Strazheim, M.R., 7350
Strebeigh, Fred, 9054
Strefling, Donna, 4183
Streib, Gordon F., 8144
Streich, Birgit, 10238
Streitfeld, David, 5991-5992
Streit-Matter, R., 875
Strickland, Rennard, 9055-9056, 14107
Stringfellow, Christina H., 2786
Strobel, Fredrick R., 1896
Strober, Myra H., 5738
Strogatz, D.S., 6609
Strom, Margot Stern, 1448
Stroman, Carolyn A., 10162, 10239-10240
Strong, James, 11954
Strong, P.M., 6610
Strossen, Nadine, 5255-5256, 9057
Strough, Kelly, 8145
Strum, Charles, 4184
Strum, Harvey, 2224
Struth, Susan, 13565
Stuart, I.R., 5725
Stuart, Paul H., 5993, 12363
Stuart, Rich, 2397
Stuart, S., 7778
Stuckless, E.R., 8593
Stucky, D., 13304
Stull, Donald D., 2180
Stumbo, Bella, 5994
Sturdvant, Sandra P., 10542
Styron, William, 13198
Su, Frederick, 12972
Suall, Irwin, 12597, 12598
Suardiaz, Debra E., 13061
Suarez-Orozco, Marcelo M., 4185-4186
Sue, D.W., 11081, 12364
Sue, Newton, 310
Sue, S., 12364
Sugarman, David B., 13062
Suggs, Robert E., 311, 1244-1245
Suhl, Isabelle, 9312
Sulek, Robert P., 13360
Sullivan, Andrew, 11082
Sullivan, Deborah A., 6612
Sullivan, Jim, 10241
Sullivan, Joseph W., 7856
Sullivan, Kevin, 2499
Sullivan, Lisa, 5259
Sullivan, Louis W., 6613
Sullivan, Mercer, 2500
Sullivan, Patricia, 1627, 1655

Sullivan, Robert, 11083, 12599, 12836
Sully, Langdon, 5995
Suls, J., 2212
Sulton, A.T., 2531
Sum, Andrew, 3386
Summers, R.J., 312
Sumner, David E., 10242-10243, 12837
Sun, Shirley, 10244
Sundquist, Eric J., 876, 9313
Sung Lee, B., 3387
Sunseri, Alvin R., 13199
Sunstein, Cass R., 1687, 3080, 8594-8595, 9058
Super, David, 3388
Suro, Roberto, 4187, 5549, 8146, 10615, 11955-11958, 12115, 14577
Surpegui, J.A., 9194
Susler, J., 2308
Susser, Mervyn, 6614
Sutch, Richard, 6615, 13180, 13200
Sutherland, Marcia, 5260
Sutter, Valerie O'Connor, 7659
Sutterlin, Rebecca, 5261
Suttles, Gerald D., 8311
Sutton, Imre, 8312
Sutton, R.E., 4188
Suzuki, Bob, 11084
Suzuki, Peter T., 2225, 12365
Svaldi, David, 8596, 14108
Swain, Carol M., 11959-11960
Swain, Johnnie Dee, Jr., 1897
Swallow, S.K., 5550
Swan, Robert J., 877
Swann, Brian, 9314
Swanson, Jane L., 13803
Swarm, Michael, 1761
Swartout, Robert R., Jr., 9568
Swartz, E., 11085
Sweeney, Edwin R., 878
Sweet, L., 9818
Swerdlow, Amy, 5584
Swift, David E., 12838
Swinney, Everette, 7857
Swinth, R.L., 5551
Swinton, David H., 3389, 3451-3452
Swoboda, Frank, 3081, 12839
Sykuta, M.E., 7234
Sylva, Michael F., 9368
Syme, S. Leonard, 6616-6617
Synnott, Marcia G., 2787, 5262
Syrett, H.C., 12246
Szasz, Andrew, 5552
Szasz, Margaret C., 4189-4190
Szathwary, E.J.E., 12998
Szaz, Andrew, 6618
Szckcly, Kalman S., 14640
Szulc, Tad, 11086
Szymanski, Albert, 3083, 8147

Tabariet, Joseph O., 2788
Tabb, W., 2181
Tabor, Mary B.W., 2501, 10245
Taborn, Virginia, 9064
Tachibana, Judy, 5263
Tadman, Michael, 13201
Taeuber, Alma, 2789
Taeuber, Cynthia M., 14448
Taeuber, Karl E., 2790, 4191, 7352
Taguieff, Pierre-Andre, 12207, 12489
Tagupa, William E., 9065
Taibbi, Mike, 10246
Taibi, A.D., 2182
Taitte, W. Lawson, 11351
Tajima, Renee, 10247
Takagi, Dana Y., 313, 5264
Takahashi, Dean, 10248
Takaki, Dana Y., 12490
Takaki, Janie Hitomi, 2226
Takaki, Ronald T., 7017-7020, 11087, 14578
Takara, Kathryn W., 879, 5265
Takayi, Paul, 2502
Takezawa, Yasuko I., 2227, 7461
Talbert, Roy, Jr., 13760
Talbot, Steve, 8148, 11290, 12366
Tam, Shirley S.L., 5996
Tamayo, William R., 7660
Tamez, Elsa, 13063
Tamplin, Arthur R., 5553
Tanaka, Togo, 12208
Tanford, J. Alexander, 9066
Tangri, R.K., 4951
Tani, E., 11185
Taosie, R., 14449
Tapscott, Richard, 5266, 11961
Tarin, P.A., 11079
Tarrow, Norma, 9067
Tarver, Heidi, 8598
Tasang, Daniel C., 13761
Tashman, Billy, 4192, 5267, 11962, 12926
Tasini, Jonathan, 8149
Tassy, Elaine, 1246, 10249
Tate, Claudia, 9315
Tate, Gayle T., 11186
Tate, Greg, 11088
Tate, Katherine T., 11963-11966
Tate, Merze, 9493
Tatel, David S., 5268
Tatum, B.D., 12491, 14267
Tauer, C.A., 3084
Taulbert, Clifton L., 880, 7021, 9557, 10543
Taxman, F.S., 2279
Taylor, Bron R., 314-315
Taylor, Charles, 11089
Taylor, Clarence, 12840-12841
Taylor, D., 2643
Taylor, D. Garth, 3894-3895
Taylor, D.A., 12191
Taylor, Dalmas A., 2214

Taylor, David, 1450
Taylor, D.M., 11090
Taylor, Donald M., 11346
Taylor, Dorceta E., 12639
Taylor, Ella, 10250
Taylor, Hanni U., 8599
Taylor, Hazel, 13064
Taylor, Jerome, 12308
Taylor, John, 11091, 14109
Taylor, Kristin Clark, 14450
Taylor, L.L., 14170
Taylor, Marylee C., 12492, 14269
Taylor, Mary J., 2791
Taylor, Monique M., 7353
Taylor, P.A., 3085
Taylor, Paul S., 8150-8151, 9439
Taylor, Quintard, 9745
Taylor, R., 12842
Taylor, R.D., 4193, 5692
Taylor, R.L., 7779
Taylor, R.J., 5726
Taylor, Robert J., 412
Taylor, Sandra C., 2228
Taylor, Theodore W., 5997
Taylor, Ula Y., 881
Taylor, William Banks, 2503
Taylor, William L., 1566, 1608
Teamoh, George, 882
Teasdale, T.W., 7780
Tedesco, John L., 9316
Tegeler, Philip, 7307-7308
Teicholz, N., 6069
Tein, M.R., 7354
Teitell, Conrad, 8600-8601
Teixeira, Ruy A., 2638, 11967, 13901
Telles, E.E., 3086
Teltsch, Kathleen, 3087, 13924
Telushkin, Joseph, 7462
Tenayuca, Emma, 1978
Tenopyr, Mary L., 13874
Terborg-Penn, Rosalyn, 3088, 11968
Terez, Dennis G., 2792
Tergeist, Peter, 5820
Terkel, Studs, 12116
Terkildsen, N., 11969
Terrell, John U., 12843
Terrell, Robert L., 409
Terris, Daniel, 1372
Terry, Don, 1979, 5442, 7355, 10251, 11970-
    11971, 12844-12845
Terry, Gayle Pollard, 883
Terry, Sara, 12846
Terry, Wallace, 884-885, 10252
Tesner, Michael A., 2504
Tesser, Carmen C., 6848
Tesser, Neil, 10253
Testa, Mark, 7356
Tetlock, P.E., 12485-12486
Tezcatlipoca, Leo Guerra, 8602

Thalmann, Rita, 13065
Thalpa, Megh P., 9355
Thanawala, Kishor, 3390
Thapa, Megh P., 4195
Thatcher, Thomas, II, 2337
Theilmann, John, 11972-11973
Theiss, Evelyn, 4196-4197
Thelen, David, 7022
Thelin, John R., 11092
Thelwell, Michael, 5271-5272, 9317, 11974-
    11976
Theoharis, Athan, 13762-13768, 14662
Thernstrom, Abigail, 11093
Thernstrom, Stephan, 11094-11095
Thibodeau, Marc A., 6362
Thibodeau, Ruth, 10254
Thiederman, Sondra, 11096
Thoele, Mike, 9655
Thoeny, A. Robert, 5024
Thomadsen, Nancy S., 5689, 8780
Thomas, Chleyon D., 930
Thomas, Clarence W., 316-317, 1689, 9068-
    9070, 11977
Thomas, Cornelius C., 8152
Thomas, Duncan, 6137
Thomas, Frances S., 9540
Thomas, Gail E., 5274-5277, 12209-12210,
    12847, 14579
Thomas, Herbert A., Jr., 9513
Thomas, J. Alan, 3089
Thomas, J.K., 3360
Thomas, James D., 6619
Thomas, J.C., 2793
Thomas, Jerry, 5727
Thomas, John K., 9714
Thomas, Joyce, 10544
Thomas, Karen M., 2794
Thomas, Lamont D., 886
Thomas, Laurence M., 1115-1116, 13202
Thomas, Lawrence, 3090
Thomas, Melvin E., 3391, 5728, 14580
Thomas, Pamela D., 2795
Thomas, Patricia J., 10545
Thomas, R. Roosevelt, Jr., 318, 5443
Thomas, Richard K., 6483
Thomas, Richard W., 2184, 9541
Thomas, Stephen B., 6620-6621
Thomas, Suja A., 7357
Thomas, Susan Gregory, 11271
Thomas, Susan L., 3392
Thometz, Carol E., 11978
Thompson, A., 3138
Thompson, Chalmer E., 5278
Thompson, James P., III, 11979
Thompson, James R., 7661
Thompson, John H.L., 1690
Thompson, Julius E., 5279, 10255
Thompson, L., 10310
Thompson, Marilyn W., 1247

Thompson, Mildred, 14451
Thompson, Richard H., 12493
Thompson, Shirley E., 10256
Thompson, T.E., 4365
Thompson, Thomas M., 13203
Thompson, Tracy, 3836, 7358
Thompson, Victoria E., 4198
Thompson, Vincent Bakpetu, 410
Thompson, William, 11155
Thomson, J.J., 5280
Thorin, Elizabeth, 1451
Thornberry, Mary C., 319
Thornbrough, Emma Lou, 9505
Thorne, Christopher, 10546
Thornton, Alvin, 2796
Thornton, Clarence H., 2797
Thornton, John K., 411
Thornton, Leslie J., II, 11097
Thornton, M.C., 10643
Thornton, Michael C., 412, 6661
Thornton, Mona W., 4199
Thornton, Russell, 6622
Thorp, Daniel B., 887
Thurber, Cheryl, 13566, 14452
Thurman, Howard, 888
Thurow, Lester, 1898
Tichenor, D.J., 7662
Tidwell, Billy J., 12494, 13961, 14201
Tidwell, Mike, 5729
Tidwell, John Edgar, 669
Tiefenbacher, J., 5482
Tien, Chang-Lin, 5281, 7663
Tienda, M., 11266, 13936
Tienda, Marta, 1899-1900, 3394-3395, 5658,
    5719, 14473
Tierney, John, 5282, 10257
Tierney, William G., 5283
Tifft, Susan, 5284
Tigar, Michael, 7463
Tijerina, Reies L., 8313
Tilghman, Shirley M., 12928-12929
Till, T.E., 2185
Tillery, Tyrone, 889
Tilly, Chris, 11980, 14202
Tilly, Louise A., 1390, 8798, 11657
Tilove, Jonathan, 14268
Timar, T.B., 4200
Timberlake, Andrea, 14663-14664
Timmer, Doug A., 7359
Timmons, W.H., 7023
Tingley, D.F., 7024
Tinker, George E., 13962
Tin-Mala, 5392
Tinto, V., 5286
Tirado, Amilcar, 6959
Tischler, Barbara L., 10441
Tjosvold, Ida J., 12371
Tobar, Hector, 890, 10650, 11981
Tobias, Henry J., 11982

Tobin, Catherine T., 8153
Tobin, Gary A., 602, 7130, 12848
Tobin, James, 3267
Todd, Gillien, 2798
Todd, J.S., 1669
Todorov, Tzvetan, 7025
Tokarczyk, Michelle M., 5287
Tokayi, D.P., 1691
Tolan, Sandy, 2093
Tolany, Stewart E., 13978
Tolbert, Emory J., 13769
Tolbert, Richard C., 11187
Toll, Robert G., 7026
Toll, William, 1118
Tollett, Kenneth S., Sr., 320, 1119, 5288
Tolnay, Stewart E., 2505, 5708, 10370, 13979,
    14111-14112
Tolson, T.F.J., 5750
Tomaskovic-Devey, Donald, 8154
Tomasky, Michael, 11983
Tomasson, Robert E., 5289
Tomlins, C.L., 8155
Tomlinson, P.S., 4139
Tomlinson, Sally, 32, 375, 4379
Tompkins, Gay M., 2799
Tompkins, Stephen G., 13770
Ton, Paul H., 7356
Toney, Joyce, 7664
Tong, Soo Chung, 10651
Tongchinsub, Helen J., 9318
Tonneson, Thomas V., 1485, 3451, 5288,
    5688, 6423, 7018, 7352, 8148, 11191,
    12009
Toobin, Jeffrey, 9071
Tooker, E., 7027
Toplin, Robert B., 10258
Torgovnick, Marianna De Marco, 9627
Torres, Andrea, 3091, 3396, 5444-5445
Torres, David L., 1901
Torres, Frank, 321
Torres, G., 9072
Torres, Gerald, 8314, 12495
Torres, Luis A., 9319
Torres, R.D., 1902, 2186, 9443
Torres, Richard S., 1980
Torres, Vicki, 9440, 10652
Torres Gonzales, Roame, 4201
Torres-Aponte, Martine, 5290
Torrey, Barbara, 9356
Torrey, J.W., 8603
Torruellas, Rosa M., 4202, 8604
Torry, Saundra, 5291, 9073-9075, 13066
Tostado, Ricardo M., 5430, 7280
Totten, Samuel, 10863
Tougas, F., 322
Tonnesen, Thomas V., 10456
Towers, Karen R.L., 13876
Townsend, Kenneth W., 7028
Townsend, P., 6623

Townsend-Smith, Richard, 323
Towry, M., 2506
Toy, Eckard V., Jr., 7858, 12600-12601
Trafzer, Clifford E., 8315
Traub, James, 1248, 2800, 5292-5295, 10259
Traube, Elizabeth G., 10260
Traugott, Santa A., 11799
Travis, Dempsey T., 891, 11984
Travis, Jack, 11272
Treadwell, David, 1249, 2801, 8316
Trebay, Guy, 11985, 13567
Trebilcock, Bob, 4204
Treese, Joel D., 11869
Trefousse, Hans L., 7029
Trejo, Stephen J., 7496
Tremaine, Richard R., 8605
Trennert, Robert A., 4205
Trent, K., 5730
Trent, S.C., 4206
Trent, William T., 2797, 5297
Trenton, Patricia, 7030
Trescott, Jacqueline, 892, 1120, 5999
Trescott, Martha M., 13068
Tresserras, R., 6625
Trevino, Jesus S., 10261
Trevino, Roberto R., 1903
Trevizo, Dolores, 8156
Tribe, Laurence H., 9076
Trice, H., 11098
Tripp, Joseph F., 2787, 7840, 8248, 13155
Tripp, Steve E., 9741
Trolier, T., 13448
Trombley, William, 4207
Trotsky, Leon, 11188
Trotter, Joe W., Jr., 5821, 9748, 10371
Trouillot, Michel-Rolph, 7711
Trousdale, Ann M., 12849
Troutt, David Dante, 11986
Trow, Martin, 5299
Trowe, Maggie, 7031
Trueba, Henry T., 4208, 7665-7666, 8608
Truelove, C., 14549
Trujillo, Charley, 10547
Truman, G.E., 13069
Trumpbour, John, 5149, 5207, 12317
Trusheim, Dale, 13810
Tsuang, G.W., 5301
Tsukashima, Ronald T., 1121-1122
Tuch, Steven A., 12309, 14269
Tuckel, Peter, 11987
Tucker, Barbara M., 8157
Tucker, F., 14270
Tucker, Gordon, 603
Tucker, M. Belinda, 5731
Tucker, Richard D., 11196
Tucker, Susan, 14453
Tucker, William H., 14581
Tuckman, G., 11361
Tuddenham, Read, 7781

Tullberg, Steven M., 8216
Tuma, Elias H., 14582
Tumulty, Karen, 11988
Turner, Alvin O., 6000
Turner, Bobbie G., 1373
Turner, Castellano B., 12117
Turner, Chris, 12378
Turner, Harry, 7360
Turner, James, 1904, 11189, 12367
Turner, Lorenzo D., 413-415, 5302, 9320
Turner, Margery A., 3092-3094
Turner, Marlene E., 324, 4059
Turner, Patricia A., 10262-10263, 13771
Turner, R.H., 14113
Turner, Richard B., 12850
Turner, Ronald, 325
Turner, Stanton B., 11099
Turoff, Sidney, 14606
Turque, Bill, 326
Tushnet, Mark V., 327, 1692, 7361, 9077-9079, 11989
Tuthill, Nancy M., 1374
Tuttle, William M., Jr., 758
Twale, D.J., 328
Twiggs, Robert D., 8607
Twining, Mary A., 416
Twombly, Robert C., 7032
Twomey, Steve, 8608, 11991
Tyack, David, 4209
Tye, Larry, 2744, 2802-2808, 4210, 10548, 11992, 11993
Tyler, Bruce M., 9441, 10265
Tyler, F.B., 7666
Tyler, Lyon G., 12851
Tyler, S. Lyman, 7033
Tzuriel, D., 3667, 13877

Uchitelle, Louis, 3095
Ubel, Thomas E., 11312
Ugwu-Oju, Dympna, 1376
Uhlander, Carole J., 11994-11995
Ullah, P., 13963
Umemoto, Karen, 5303
Umoja, A.A., 11996
Underhill, Lonnie E., 8317
Underwood, Charles F., 2127
Underwood, James L., 11997
Underwood, Julie K., 2570, 3708, 5941
Underwood, Katherine, 11998
Underwood, Kathleen, 1541
Unselding, Paul J., 10372, 12122
Unsworth, Tim, 12852
Updike, David, 8610
Upp, M.M., 13044
Urban, Wayne J., 893-894, 5307, 7782
Uri, N.D., 330-332
Urofsky, Melvin J., 333, 1101
Useem, Michael, 5317
Usner, Daniel H., Jr., 7034, 10653

Utaumi, K., 13071
Utley, C.A., 13877
Uyeunten, Sandra O., 5733

Vacca, Carolyn, 7365
Vashen, Penny, 10553
Vaillancourt, Meg, 1906
Valdes, Alisa, 13072
Valdez, R. Burciaga, 6641
Valencia, Humberto, 10291
Valencia, Richard R., 3975, 4218, 13878
Valenti, John, 13361
Valenzuela, Abel, 3405
Valk, Barbara G., 14665
Vallangca, Roberto V., 7464
Valle, Victor, 2186, 9443
Vallochi, S., 3453
Valverde, Leonard A., 4219, 12930
Van Brakel, J., 11103
Van Deburg, William L., 14583
Van den Berghe, Pierre L., 11362
Van Dijk, Teun A., 8611-8613, 9890, 10268
Van Geel, Tyll, 4220
Van Haitsma, Martha, 1907
Van Horne, Winston A., 265, 1485, 3451,
    5288, 5688, 6423, 7018, 7352, 8148,
    10456, 11191, 12009
Van Peebles, Mario, 10269
Van Scoy, Holly, 14666
Vandal, Gilles, 14118
Vandel, G., 9519
Vandell M., 9321
Vander Weele, Maribeth, 4221
VanderHill, C.W., 13298
Vanderhoff, J., 7115
Vandermeer, John, 2094, 11192
VanderVelde, Lea S., 8158
Vanderwolf, C.H., 7694
Vandi, A., 11284
Vanfossen, Beth E., 13362
Vann, H., 9831
Vann, K.R., 4222
Vannerman, Reeve, 1908
Varet, Gilbert, 11313
Vargas, Arturo, 8614
Vargas, Zaragosa, 8159
Varma, Premdatta, 1694
Vartabedian, Ralph, 11273, 13775
Vasquez, J.A., 5318
Vasquez, Jesse M., 5319
Vasquez, Olga A., 8615
Vass, Winifred K., 393, 417, 8616
Vasu, Ellen Storey, 3100
Vasu, Michael l., 3100
Vatter, Harold G., 14200
Vaughn, Alden T., 13205
Vecoli, Rudolph J., 7667
Vecsey, Christopher, 5556, 12853
Vedder, R.G., 13964

Vedder, Richard K., 3101, 10372
Veeder, William H., 8321
Vega, W.A., 5735
Velez-i, Carlos G., 6642
Veltman, Calvin J., 8617-8618
Venables, Robert W., 5556
Venet, Wenly H., 13206
Vera, Hernan, 12413
Verbrugge, L., 6643
Verdugo, R.R., 3406
Verdugo, V., 10533
Verhovek, Sam H., 1695, 4223-4225, 7366-
    7367, 7669, 11104, 11274, 12002
Verkerke, J. Hoult, 337, 2952
Verma, Gajendra K., 5320
Vernoff, E., 4380, 6447
Vernon, Amelia W., 9675
Verstegen, Deborah A., 2570
Vertinsky, P.A., 14667
Vervack, Jerry J., 2811
Vetterling-Braggin, Mary, 8619
Viadero, Debra, 895, 1453, 4226, 13879
Vickers, Robert J., 4227
Vidal, Jamie R., 12691, 12854
Vidal de Haynes, Maria R., 2187
Vidman, N., 10270
Vidrine, E., 13220
Vientos Gaston, Nilita, 8620
Vigil, Maurillio E., 1981, 12003
Villamil, Jose J., 2095
Villaraigosa, Antonio, 9406
Villarreal, Roberto E., 12004
Villasenor, Victor, 896
Vinacke, W. Edgar, 13570
Vinas, J., 7316
Vincent, Richard C., 10271
Vincent, Stephen A., 7035
Vincent, Ted, 10272
Vinje, David L., 2188
Vinovskis, M.A., 4228
Viraida, A.R., 11246
Virtanen, Simo V., 338
Virts, Nancy, 3325
Vise, David A., 7368
Vito, G.F., 2377
Vivo, Paquita, 14668
Vizenor, Gerald, 897, 10273
Vobejda, Barbara, 5822, 6644, 10373, 11211
Voelz, Peter M., 10554
Vogel, Jennifer, 6007
Vogel, Virgil J., 7036, 12369
Vogt, Daniel C., 3407
Vold, David J., 4230
Volgy, Thomas J., 3367
Vonnegut, Kurt, 339
Vorenberg, Michael, 7037
Voss, James F., 1345
Vought, H., 7669
Voydanoff, Patricia, 5736-5737

Vroman, Wayne, 3408
Vyas, H.V., 11106
Vyzralek, Frank E., 14119

Wachs, Martin, 11327
Wachter, Kenneth W., 2812
Wacquant, Loic J.D., 1909, 5823, 13363
Waddell, Eileen, 10192
Waddell, Jack O., 5950
Waddoups, Jeffrey, 1910
Wade, Howard P., 9749
Wade, Richard C., 5824
Wade, Wyn C., 7859
Wade-Evans, Florence, 12417
Wade-Gayles, Gloria, 898
Wade-Lewis, Margaret, 899-900
Wagenaar, Hendrick, 1911
Wagener, D.K., 6645
Wagenheim, Karl, 2096
Wagner, Deborah H., 9031
Wagner, J., 340
Wagner, John D., 2557
Wagner, Marsden G., 6646
Wagner, Sally R., 13073, 14454
Wagner, Stephen T., 1124
Wagner-Pacifici, Robin, 6008
Wagoner, Jay J., 7684
Wagstaff, A., 6647
Wahl, Jenny Bourne, 9083
Wainer, Howard, 13880
Wainscott, Stephen H., 3102
Wainstein, N., 5318
Waitzman, N.J., 6648
Wake, Lloyd, 5321
Wakefield, Wanda Ellen, 7365
Wakeman, F., 13776
Walberg, Herbert, 2622
Walcott, Rinaldo, 463
Walcott, Wayne A., 9634
Wald, Alan, 1982, 2097, 5322, 8322
Wald, Kenneth D., 7860
Wald, Priscilla, 12248
Waldinger, Roger, 341, 1252, 2851, 3103,
    7670, 12005
Waldman, Carl, 14669
Waldman, Elizabeth, 14455
Waldman, Peter, 4231
Waldman, Steven, 13364
Waldmann, R.J., 6649
Waldron, Ann, 12602
Walker, Adrian, 3104, 5323, 6009, 11651
Walker, Alice, 14456
Walker, B., 5557
Walker, Clarence E., 7038, 12496
Walker, Deward E., Jr., 6010
Walker, Doris B., 8621
Walker, George E., 9628, 11275
Walker, Harry A., 5738
Walker, Jack L., 1696

Walker, James W. St. G., 13207
Walker, Jimmie, 10274
Walker, Juliet E.K., 1253-1254, 8323
Walker, Laura, 12006
Walker, L.E.A., 14401
Walker, M.A., 28
Walker, Melissa, 1697
Walker, R.W., 3137
Walker, Richard P., 10555
Walker, Roger A., 8622
Walker, Thomas G., 8676
Walker, W. Lawrence, Sr., 5558
Wall, Cheryl A., 9322
Wall, Jim Vander, 2285, 13619-13622, 14612
Wallace, Amy, 12118, 14271
Wallace, D., 6650
Wallace, David T., 12007
Wallace, Michael, 14120
Wallace, Michele, 10275, 13074-13075
Wallace, R., 6651
Wallace, Robert B., 6616
Wallace, S.P., 6652
Wallace, Walter L., 11481
Wallace-Haymore, Denise, 5324
Wallach, Alan, 11107
Wallerstein, Immanuel, 1987, 11108, 12378
Wallimann, I., 2829, 11068, 14006
Wallis, J., 3454
Wallis, Jim, 444
Wallis, John J., 3230
Wallore, Michael, 1718
Walsh, A., 2516
Walsh, Amy, 2813
Walsh, Catherine E., 4018, 4232-4233, 8623-
    8624
Walsh, Edward, 2814, 4234, 7861
Walsh, Lorena S., 8160
Walsh, Mark, 901, 4235
Walter, Robert, 5559
Walters, Donna K.H., 11276, 13076
Walters, Pamela B., 4236-4237
Walters, Ronald W., 418, 1698, 11193, 12008-
    12009, 14272
Waltman, Jerold, 5325
Walton, Hanes, Jr., 1628, 6011, 12010
Walton, Lamont M., 9084
Walton, Scott, 5739
Walzer, Michael, 11109
Wambaugh, Byron L., 9085
Wander, P., 8516
Wang, M.C., 4238-4239
Wannall, W. Raymond, 13777
Ward, David, 5825
Ward, Geoffrey C., 7039, 13262
Ward, Janie Victoria, 14457
Ward, Jerry W., Jr., 9297
Ward, John W., 10556
Ward, Jon A., 5326
Ward, Nicole, 342

Ward, Renee, 10276
Ward, Robert D., 8161
Ward, Wanda E., 5327
Warden, Christina A., 2648
Ware, Leland, 343
Ware, Lowry, 14121
Ware, Vron, 14273
Warlaw, Alvia J., 419
Warmecke, A.M., 11194
Warner, David, 6653
Warner, J.T., 10557
Warner, Robert M., 9151
Warren, Donald, 4043, 11254
Warren, Hanna R., 7040
Warren, Jenifer, 8625
Warren, Kenneth W., 9323
Warren, Nagueyalti, 12011
Warren, Wilson J., 11363
Warshaw, Robin, 5328
Wartberg, Steve, 13365
Wartenberg, Thomas E., 8338
Wasby, Stephen L., 98, 9086
Washburn, J.A., 5329
Washburn, Patrick S., 13778
Washburn, Witcomb E., 12875
Washington, Craig A., 2295
Washington, Harold R., 5330
Washington, J.L., 5331
Washington, Johnny, 11314
Washington, Joseph R., Jr., 358, 12855
Washington, J.R., 5740
Washington, Laura S., 9501
Washington, Mary H., 902
Washington, Robert E., 12497
Washington, Valora, 344, 1378, 5332
Washington-Bolder, Jacqueline, 13221
Wasko, J., 10116
Wasserman, David, 2517
Wasserman, Miriam, 9629
Watanabe, Teresa, 13571
Waters, Enoch P., 10277
Waters, Harry F., 10278
Waters, Mary C., 2995, 14248, 14274, 14528
Waters, Robert C., 2518, 13077
Watkins, Frank, 11475
Watkins, John M., 4240
Watkins, Mel, 7465-7466
Watkins, R., 13192
Watkins, Ralph, 9630, 13193
Watkins, Steve, 3105
Watrous, Peter, 1255, 8626, 10279, 14275
Watson, Alan, 9087
Watson, Bruce W., 13779
Watson, Denton L., 12012
Watson, Frederick D., 2815
Watson, G. Llewellyn, 6731
Watson, Larry D., 9088
Watson, Milton H., 1256
Watson, O. Michael, 5950

Watson, Richard L., Jr., 11281
Watson, Robert W., 8627
Watson, Sidney D., 6654
Watson, Susan, 9538
Watson, Tom, 13366
Watson, Wilbur H., 931
Watterson, K.M., 8628
Watts, Jerry G., 345, 903, 12013-12014
Watts, Jill M., 12856
Watts, R.J., 12310
Watts, Steven, 11110
Watts, T.G., 11392
Watts, Thomas D., 6655, 11241
Watts, Tim J., 14670
Waugh, Earle H., 12761
Waxman, Lisa M., 11590
Waxweiler, Richard J., 6389
Way, P., 8162
Wayne, Leslie, 1257-1258, 7369-7370
Weakley, Vernon S., 5333
Weatherford, Jack, 7041
Weatherford, Willis D., 14584
Weaver, Harold D., 9089
Weaver, Jerry L., 6656
Weaver, John D., 10558
Webb, Walter P., 14123
Weber, David J., 7042-7043
Weber, Devra A., 8163
Weber, Michael J., 4241
Webster, Yehudi O., 14585
Wechsler, Harold S., 5334-5336
Wechsler, Pat, 10280
Weddle, Kevin J., 3106, 10559
Weed, Amy S., 12015
Weed, Elizabeth, 12946
Weeden, L. Darnell, 346-347
Weeks, John R., 6657
Weeks, Louis B., 12857
Weeks, O. Douglas, 12016
Weeks, Philip, 6012
Weeks, Philip C., 7044-7045
Weems, Robert E., Jr., 1259
Weglyn, Michi N., 2230
Wegner, Eldon L., 6658
Wei, William, 12017
Weibel-Orlando, Joan, 9445
Weidemann, Celia J., 5337
Weidner, Catherine S., 4242
Weigel, Russell H., 10281
Weiher, G., 3352
Weiker, Gregory R., 7371
Weil, A.M., 1357
Weil, Richard H., 8324
Weiler, Kathleen, 4243-4244
Weiler, W.C., 5338
Weill, James D., 3409
Weiman, Liza, 4055
Weinberg, Daniel H., 6602
Weinberg, H.A., 5339

Weinberg, Jack, 1699
Weinberg, Jacob, 5340
Weinberg, Marvin L., 13572
Weinberg, Meyer, 3132
Weinberg, Richard A., 7771
Weinberg, Sydney S., 7671
Weiner, Tim, 348, 6013, 13780
Weinraub, Judith, 1260
Weinreb, L.L., 1700
Weinstein, Gerald, 13925
Weinstein, Henry, 604, 2519, 10654, 13078
Weinstein, J., 5341
Weinstein, Steve, 10282
Weintraub, Sidney, 7672-7673
Weir, David, 13600
Weire, Margaret, 11833
Weis, Lois, 4020, 4028, 4040
Weisbord, R.G., 1125-1126
Weisbrot, Robert, 1701
Weisbuch, Robert, 5342
Weisburd, D., 2462
Weisman, Leslie K., 5560
Weisman, Seymour S., 1127
Weiss, Avi, 1128
Weiss, Bernard J., 4669, 5343, 10811
Weiss, J.C., 14124
Weiss, John G., 13881
Weiss, Kenneth R., 10374
Weiss, K.M., 6090
Weiss, Lawrence D., 7046-7047, 8164
Weiss, Marley S., 3107
Weiss, Michael J., 4245
Weiss, Nancy J., 1702
Weiss, Robert G., 349
Weiss, Samuel, 5344-5347
Weissbourd, Richard, 4246
Weisskopf, Richard, 3410, 14204
Weissman, Michaele, 14555
Welch, Finis R., 350, 2816, 3108, 3380-3381, 5348, 5446
Welch, Marvis O., 904
Welch, S., 4677
Welch, Susan, 1912, 12018-12019, 12106, 13079, 14564
Welkos, Robert W., 11277
Wellington, Alison J., 13965
Wellman, David, 8629, 12319
Wells, A., 104
Wells, Amy S., 2817-2818, 4247-4248
Wells Chumm, Eva, 4154
Wells, David I., 12020
Wells, Elmer E., 12311
Wells, Ida B., 14125
Wells, Jovita, 5349
Wells, Julian W., 3109
Wells, Lyn, 7862
Wells-Stevens, Lyndee, 6659
Welsh, Patrick, 4249-4250, 5350
Welte, J.W., 2520

Wendt, A.C., 3069
Wendt, Bruce H., 2098
Wenger, Morton G., 7783
Wenglisky, Harold, 4251
Wennersten, John R., 5351
Wennersten, Ruth E., 5351
Wenze, Gloria T., 11111
Werner, Emmy S., 1379
Werner, John M., 14126
Werum, Regina E., 4252
Wesley, Charles H., 12021
West, Cornel, 1129-1132, 9090, 11112, 11291, 11315, 12022, 12498-12499, 12858, 14516, 14586
West, K.C., 2819
West, Louis Jolyon, 1703
West, Robin, 9091
West, Stephen G., 14046
West, W. Richard, Jr., 1704-1705
Westbury, Susan, 420
Westerhaus, C.F., 351
Westfall, William, 13208
Westling, Louise, 905
Westman, J.C., 3110
Weston, Rafael, 14145
Westphall, Victor, 8325
Westreich, Budd, 605
Wetherell, Margaret, 8554
Wetmore, Ruth Y., 9644
Wetzel, J.R., 5741
Wexler, C., 14127
Weyler, Rex, 6014
Weyr, Thomas, 14587
Weyranch, Walter O., 9092
Wharton, Amy S., 3111, 11278
Wharton, David E., 12932
Whatley, W.C., 8165
Whatley, Warren C., 1261
Wheeler, David L., 5561, 5742
Wheeler, Majorie S., 12023
Wheelock, Anne, 4254
Wherritt, Irene, 8630
Wherry, James D., 6835, 8713
Whetstone, Lauren M., 13926
Whetstone, Muriel L., 2296
Whitaker, Ben, 464
Whitaker, Catherine J., 2521
White, A., 10284
White, Alisa, 10307
White, Bruce, 10560
White, Carmen, 8166
White, Carolyne J., 4047
White, Deborah G., 13209
White, Edward L., III, 9093-9094
White, Forrest R., 2820, 9095
White, Fran, 11195
White, G.C., 7674
White, George, 1262-1263
White, Jack E., 1380

White, James C., 2821
White, John, 12024
White, John V., 9096
White, Lucie E., 8631
White, Michael J., 7372
White, Philip V., 12249
White, Richard, 7048, 8326
White, Ronald C., 12859
White, Sammis B., 4255
White, Shane, 12860
White, Sid, 9747
White, Vilbert L., 1983, 9097
White, Welsh S., 2522
Whitehead, Neil L., 13573
White-Means, Shelley I., 6661
Whitfield, Stephen J., 1133, 7467
Whiting, Albert N., 5355
Whitley, K.J., 11573
Whitman, Mark 4257, 9098
Whitman, Steve, 6662
Whitman, Torrey S., 5791
Whitney, Gleaves, 11114
Whitney, Scott, 9480
Whitney, Stu, 13367
Whittaker, Elvi, 14277
Whittaker, William G., 8167
Whitten, David O., 6663
Whitten, L.A., 5356
Whittier, T.E., 14588
Whittle, Jeff, 6664
Whittler, T.E., 10285
Wibecan, Ken, 8632, 9099, 10286-10288
Wicker, Fred W., 7468
Wicker, Tom, 352, 2523, 10289
Wideman, John Edgar, 906
Wielawski, Irene, 6666
Wiener, Jon, 4617, 5357-5358
Wienk, R., 3112
Wienk, Ronald E., 7374
Wiese, Andrew, 932
Wiese, M.R.R., 4258
Wigderson, Seth M., 8168
Wigdor, Alexander K., 13882
Wigeman, Bobyn, 13080
Wiggins, David K., 13368-13370
Wiggins, Fred, 13890
Wiggins, Sarah Woolfolk, 14225
Wiggins, William H., Jr., 13574
Wilbanks, William, 3113
Wilbekim, Emil, 10561
Wilber, George L., 3412
Wilbert, Deborah G., 14290
Wilcox, C., 6667
Wilcox, Clyde, 12861-12862, 13081, 14458
Wilcox, Steven P., 13871
Wild, C.L., 13842
Wildavsky, Aaron, 11116
Wilde, Larry, 7469-7470
Wildman, S.M., 12990

Wildman, Stephanie M., 2822
Wiley, Ralph, 7471
Wilger, Robert J., 7375-7376
Wilgoren, Debbi, 353
Wilgoren, Jodi, 13883
Wilhite, Al, 11972-11973
Wilken, Paul, 3366
Wilkerson, Frank, 13782
Wilkerson, Isabel, 354, 1913, 2823-2824, 4259-
    4263, 5359-5361, 5743, 6668, 9502, 10290,
    10562, 10655, 12026, 12605, 12863
Wilkerson, Margaret B., 3413
Wilkerson, Martha, 13247, 13998
Wilkes, Robert E., 10291
Wilkie, Curtis, 3414, 4264, 9558
Wilkins, D.E., 6015
Wilkins, Roger W., 355, 1134, 1918, 1984,
    2825, 3136, 3245, 3415, 3455, 5363, 12027
Wilkinson, Alec, 8169
Wilkinson, Charles F., 8328-8329, 9100
Wilkinson, Doris Y., 5362, 5744, 8170, 8633,
    13575, 14459
Wilkinson, R.G., 6669-6670
Will, George F., 2524, 4265, 5364-5365, 7675,
    9324
Will, Jeffry A., 3416
Willhelm, Sidney M., 3417
Williams, Adolphus L., Jr., 356
Williams, B., 3418
Williams, Bruce B., 3114
Williams, Bruce E., 5366
Williams, Christopher C., 10292
Williams, Darrell L., 11405
Williams, David, 7049
Williams, David C., 9101-9102
Williams, David P., III, 13576
Williams, David R., 6671-6673
Williams, Delores S., 13082, 14460
Williams, Donald R., 13966
Williams, Eddie N., 12028-12029
Williams, Elizabeth R., 11117
Williams, Elsie A., 7472
Williams, J.B., 357
Williams, James, 14553
Williams, James D., 10146
Williams, James L., 9559
Williams, J.C., 12500
Williams, John A., 13577
Williams, John E., 13392
Williams, John, 5367
Williams, Juan, 1135, 1706, 4266, 5368, 12030
Williams, Lea E., 5369
Williams, Lena, 1136, 1707, 5447, 5745, 7473-
    7474, 10293, 12211, 12640
Williams, Leon F., 1381
Williams, L.F., 4639, 9953
Williams, Linda F., 11581, 12031
Williams, Loretta J., 358, 12032
Williams, Lou Falkner, 7863

Williams, Norma, 5746
Williams, P.J., 359
Williams, Patricia J., 1708, 2826, 5084, 9103-9107, 13083-13084
Williams, Peter W., 12763
Williams, Portia, 1382
Williams, R., 13371
Williams, R. Hal, 8330
Williams, Randall, 8171
Williams, Rhonda M., 2850, 8172
Williams, Robert A., Jr., 9108-9109, 13085
Williams, Robert L., 7784
Williams, Robin M., Jr., 2140, 3268, 3821, 5657, 6288, 11684, 12078, 14521
Williams, Roger C., 13967
Williams, Stanley (Tookie), 2525
Williams, Terry, 2526-2827, 6674
Williams, Thomas T., 5370
Williams, Vernon J., Jr., 1914, 7050, 12212
Williams, Walter E., 360, 3115
Williams, Walter L., 2099-2101
Williamson, Handy, Jr., 5370
Williamson, Jeffrey G., 7676
Williamson, Lionel, 4455
Williard, Eric, 2828
Willie, Charles V., 1709, 1915, 2830, 4267, 5371-5372, 5747-5749, 14259
Willie, C.V., 2829
Willis, Dana L., 361
Willis, David P., 6675
Willis, Gwendolyn, 13578
Willis, John C., 9726
Willis, John M., 10563
Willis, Susan, 9325
Willis, William S., 10656
Willman, Chris, 7475
Willoughby, John, 9455
Willox-Blau, Pamela, 11279
Wills, David A., 12865
Wills, David W., 12864
Wills, Garry, 8634, 12033-12034, 12866
Wills, T.A., 2212
Willson, Walt, 10657
Wilmore, Gayrand S., 12867-12868
Wilson, Joseph, 1795
Wilson, Ardythe, 2065
Wilson, August, 9326-9327
Wilson, B.M., 9343
Wilson, Basil, 11589, 12869
Wilson, Benjamin F., 5373
Wilson, Carol, 5792, 9110
Wilson, C.E., 12501
Wilson, Charles R., 14037
Wilson, Christopher P., 9328
Wilson, Clint C., II, 10294
Wilson, Clyde N., 397, 8711
Wilson, D., 1916
Wilson, David, 8635
Wilson, David B., 8636

Wilson, David L., 13927
Wilson, Francille R., 8173
Wilson, Franklin D., 2778
Wilson, G., 3419
Wilson, Harry L., 10295
Wilson, James, 1383
Wilson, Joan Hoff, 9111
Wilson, Joseph F., 8174
Wilson, Kenneth L., 4268
Wilson, K.L., 10400
Wilson, Laura B., 6579
Wilson, L.B., 6676
Wilson, Leslie E., 10375
Wilson, Margaret, 9112
Wilson, Margaret A., 4269
Wilson, Merinda D., 5373
Wilson, M.N., 5750
Wilson, Paul, 2831
Wilson, Paula, 1710
Wilson, Phill, 6677
Wilson, Raymond, 907
Wilson, Reginald, 362, 5374-5377
Wilson, S.B., 3116
Wilson, V., 2838
Wilson, Wayne, 13372, 13579
Wilson, William J., 363, 1792, 1909, 1917-1919, 3420-3421, 5826-5827, 12035, 12117, 12502, 12870
Wimmer, K.A., 10296
Winant, Howard, 12036, 12461, 12503, 14652
Winch, C., 8637
Winch, Julie, 1920
Windham, Joseph E., 9113
Windsor, Pat, 606
Winegarden, C.R., 7677, 13968
Winerip, Michael, 4270, 5378
Winfield, Linda F., 4271-4272
Wing, S., 6678
Wingard, D., 6679
Wingfield, Harold L., 364, 5379
Winglee, Marianne, 9334
Winicki, Norine M., 1454
Winkel, F.W., 10298
Winkhurst, David, 11157
Winkler, A.M., 6680
Winkler, Karen J., 1137, 5380, 12213, 14461
Winn, D.W., 6645
Winston, Judith A., 3117, 14462
Winston, Sanford, 12871
Winter, Ella, 6016
Winters, Wendy G., 4273
Wintz, Cary D., 7093, 9684, 9717, 9719, 12037
Wirls, Daniel, 12038
Wirtz, James J., 13783
Wise, Arthur E., 9115-9116
Wise, L.R., 6017
Wise, P., 6681
Wiseman, Michael, 6465

Wishart, David J., 8331
Wishner, A.R., 6682
Wistrich, Robert S., 607
Withall, Keith, 10299
Withey, Ellen, 3118
Witt, Stephanie L., 290, 365-366, 5381
Witte, John, 4274
Wittig, Michele A., 201
Wittke, Carl, 7476
Wogan, P., 8638
Wohlforth, Tim, 13784
Wolcott, James, 7477, 10300
Wolcott, Roger T., 12872
Wolf, C., 14129
Wolf, Eric R., 12504
Wolf, Naomi, 13086
Wolfe, Alan, 5382, 11118, 11361, 14525
Wolfe, Barbara, 1317
Wolfe, Lee M., 5383
Wolfenstein, Eugene V., 12039
Wolff, Alexander, 13373
Wolff, Craig, 6018
Wolff, E.N., 5417, 7940, 14168
Wolff, H.A., 7478
Wolff, R., 1872
Wolfinger, Raymond E., 1711
Wolfley, Jeanette, 12040
Wolfram, Walt, 8639-8640
Wolfson, Adam, 608
Wolfson, Evan, 1712
Wolfson, Nicholas, 5384, 8575, 8644
Wolinsky, Fredric D., 6683
Woliver, Laura R., 1713
Wolkinson, B.W., 3119
Wolkovish-Valkavicius, William, 7864
Woll, Allen L., 10301
Wollons, Roberta, 1384, 3713
Wolohojian, G.R., 2832
Wolpe, Harold, 12505
Wolseley, Roland E., 10302
Wong, Doreena, 2527
Wong, Doris Sue, 9117
Wong, Hertha D., 908
Wong, Ken, 13884
Wong, Sau-Ling Cynthia, 9329
Wong, William, 14130
Wonnell, Christopher T., 367
Wontat, Donald, 9118
Woo, Merle, 1985, 14463
Wood, B. Dan, 368
Wood, Betty, 12873
Wood, Elizabeth P., 5385
Wood, Floris, 12120
Wood, Forrest G., 12874
Wood, Joe, 909-910
Wood, P.B., 7377
Wood, Peter B., 7225
Wood, Peter H., 7051-7052, 12875-12876
Wood, Robert, 2833

Woodard, J. David, 3102
Woodard, Maurice C., 369
Woodard, Michael D., 4272
Wooden-Byrant, Sharon, 911
Woodford, John, 14589
Woodhead, Mary J., 3120
Woodhouse, Charles E., 11982
Woodin, Heather, 4810
Woodman, Harold D., 7053
Woodmansee, John J., 11196
Woodruff, Nan E., 1455, 8176
Woodrum, E., 12877
Woods, Geraldine, 370
Woods, Henry, 2834
Woods, Paula L., 14590
Woods, Randall B., 9511
Woods, Richard D., 912
Woods, Sandra L., 9462
Woods, W. Leon, 9560
Woodson, Carter G., 10658
Woodson, Robert L., Jr., 3422, 12041
Woodward, C. Vann, 4617, 5386, 7054, 11119
Woolbright, Cynthia, 5387
Woolbright, L.A., 2950
Woolf, A.G., 1264
Woolhandler, Steffie, 6684
Woon-Ha, Kim, 13785
Work, John W., 371-372
Workman, Andrew, 12042
Worobey, Jacqueline Lowe, 6040
Worth, D., 6685
Wortham, Anne, 11120
Worthman, Paul B., 8177, 11280
Wriggins, Jennifer, 12949
Wright, Beverly H., 5467-5468
Wright, Bobby E., 5388-5389, 12312
Wright, C.T., 4275
Wright, Donald R., 7055
Wright, Erik O., 1895, 1921-1923
Wright, Gavin, 7056, 8178, 12878-12879
Wright, G.C., 5751
Wright, George C., 14131
Wright, Giles R., 9582, 10376
Wright, James D., 14169
Wright, J.D., 6686
Wright, Jerry, 9395
Wright, John S., 12043
Wright, Kathleen, 7057
Wright, Mary E., 1714
Wright, Michelle D., 14464
Wright, Patricia, 5390
Wright, Paul, 7058
Wright, R. George, 5562, 8641
Wright, Roosevelt, Jr., 6655
Wright, Ted A., 12044
Wrightson, Margaret T., 12630
Wrigley, Julia, 1385
Wroblewski, Roberta, 13580
Wrone, David R., 10659

Wtulich, Josephine, 7678
Wu, Zhijun, 4998
Wunder, John R., 6019, 7059, 8296, 9119-
   9120, 14132-14133
Wunnawa, P.V., 2894
Wurgaft, Nina, 5413
Wurtzel, Elizabeth, 10303
Wuthnow, Robert, 13581
Wyatt, G.E., 2528
Wyckoff, J.H., 4276
Wycliff, Don, 373, 6020, 12934
Wyman, Mark, 7679
Wynes, Charles E., 913
Wyzan, Michael L., 374

X, Cedric, 7785
Xie, Jinjing, 9720

Yacovone, Donald, 12880
Yamamoto, Eric Y., 9121
Yamanaka, K., 14465
Yamashita, Robert C., 1456
Yamauchi, Joanne Sanae, 5392
Yancy, Dorothy C., 914
Yang, B., 6687
Yang, Jeff, 10304
Yang, Jo, 11121
Yankauer, A., 6688
Yanofsky, Saul M., 2835
Yardley, Jonathan, 9330
Yarmolinsky, Adam, 2728
Yarrow, Andrew L., 1266
Yates, James, 915
Yazurlo, Michael V., Sr., 2836
Ybarra, Lea, 10564
Ydstie, John, 3121
Yeakey, Carol C., 4277-4278
Yearwood, Gladstone L., 10305
Yeatman, Anna, 1457
Yeboah, Samuel K., 12214, 12506
Yee, Laura, 2837
Yee, Shirley J., 7060
Yelong, Han, 5393
Yerles, M., 13340
Yetman, Norman R., 13374
Yi, Jeongduk, 10660
Yinger, J. Milton, 12881
Yinger, John, 3122-3123, 7378
Ylisela, James, Jr., 9494
Yoder, Dale, 7786
Yoder, J.D., 3124
Yogev, A., 32, 375, 4379
Yogi, Stan, 14611
Yoon, Yong-Sik, 4279
York, Frederick F., 8332
York, Michael, 3125
Yoshida, Ryo, 12882
Young, A., 6689
Young, A.F., 6721

Young, Alford A., Jr., 14591
Young, Andrew J., 916
Young, Anna B., 5394
Young, Coleman, 917
Young, Crawford, 11364-11365
Young, Gene C., 5395
Young, James H., 6551-6552
Young, Joseph A., 9331
Young, J.T., 12104
Young, Laurette, 2835
Young, Mary E., 7061, 8333-8334, 9122,
   10661, 11197
Young, Peter S., 6690
Young, Philip K.Y., 1267
Young, Robert L., 2529
Young, Rosalie F., 6691
Young, T. Kue, 6692
Young, Thomas J., 6693, 12606, 14134
Young, T.J., 2530
Young, V., 2531
Young-Bruehl, Elizabeth, 3126
Youssef, Z., 13371
Yu, Yuh-Chao, 11316
Yuen, Shirley Mark, 8179
Yuen, Ying Chen, 12045
Yuill, Phyllis J., 9332
Yun, Grace, 13582
Yung, Judith, 14466
Yurco, Frank, 11122
Yusuf, Imtiyaz, 12883
Yuval-Davis, Nira, 11198
Yzaguirre, Raul, 7680

Zack, Naomi, 12215
Zafar, Rafia M., 9333
Zahner, G.E.P., 7379
Zakim, Leonard, 1138
Zalokar, Nadja, 14327, 14467
Zamberana, Ruth E., 14468
Zamora, Del, 10306
Zamora, Emilio, Jr., 8180, 13222
Zane, Nolan, 6694
Zangrando, Robert L., 14135
Zarbin, Earl, 14136
Zarembka, Paul, 1872, 12235
Zarkin, G.A., 6199
Zasloff, Jonathan, 1716
Zatarain, Michael, 7865, 12608
Zatz, Majorie S., 2532
Zavala, Iris M., 2102
Zavaleta, Antonio N., 6380, 6695
Zax, J.S., 12046
Zayas, Luis H., 5396
Zegeye, Abebe, 9420, 12507
Zeiger, Dinah, 5164
Zeigler, Donald J., 2573
Zeigler, Stephen M., 8642
Zeitlin, Maurice, 10565
Zeleny, Carolyn, 9589

Zelman, Donald L., 3423
Zenchelsky, S., 4668
Zentalla, Ana Celia, 8643-8645
Zepeda, Ofelia, 8646
Zepp, Ira G., Jr., 918
Zeskind, Leonard, 12609
Zia, Helen, 12121, 14137
Zieger, Robert H., 7979, 8181
Ziegler, Dhyana, 5397, 10307
Zielinski, Martin A., 12884-12885
Ziesemer, Carol, 7380
Ziglar, William, 14138
Zigler, Edward, 1386-1387, 4280
Zijderveld, Anton C., 7479
Zill, N., 1388
Zill, Nicholas, 6696, 9334
Zillmann, D., 9960
Zimbalist, Andrew, 13375
Zimmerman, Shirley L., 5753
Zingg, Paul J., 13247, 13335, 13358
Zinn, Maxine Baca, 5754

Zion, J.W., 9123
Ziontz, Alvin J., 9124, 11199
Zisman, P., 2838
Zitner, Aaron, 5398
Zoccino, Nanda, 13786
Zodhiates, Philip P., 6021
Zoglin, Kathryn J., 8647
Zoglin, Richard, 7480
Zolbrod, Zoe, 7481
Zollo, Richard P., 10566
Zomalt, Ernest E., 5399
Zophy, Angela H., 7062
Zubrow, E., 6697
Zucker, Bat-Ami, 12047
Zucker, Ben-Ami, 1139
Zuckerman, Donald, 10306
Zuckerman, M., 7787, 13583
Zukin, Sharon, 5828
Zunz, Oliver, 11366
Zweig, Gail R., 9125
Zweigenhaft, Richard L., 5400-5401

SUBJECT INDEX

Numbers refer to entries, not pages.

African Americans:*Affirmative Action;* 26, 48-
50, 58, 79, 103, 112, 134, 148, 182-183,
188, 193-194, 207, 211, 220, 238, 252,
282-283, 290, 294, 306, 326, 338, 342,
344, 373; *Africa;* 376-420; *Anti-racism;*
424, 426, 460; *Autobiography &*
Biography; 609-611, 613-614, 616-617,
619-622, 624, 626-627, 630-650, 652-656,
659-661, 664-669, 671-681, 684-685, 687,
689-695, 697-703, 705-710, 712-731, 733,
735, 738-742, 744-751, 753-755, 757, 759-
762, 764-766, 769-772, 774, 776, 778, 780,
782-783, 785-786, 788-789, 791-792, 795-
797, 800, 802-804, 807, 811-814, 820-822,
826-832, 835, 838-841, 843, 845, 848-851,
854-858, 860-866, 868-870, 872-877, 879-
886, 888-889, 891-894, 898-900, 902-903,
905-906, 909-918; *Black towns;* 919-932;
Blacks & Jews; 933-950, 952-986, 988-
1008, 1010, 1017, 1030, 1037, 1044, 1051,
1053, 1058, 1065, 1067, 1079-1080, 1089,
1091, 1096, 1117, 1121-1122, 1124-1125,
1129, 1133- 1134; *Business;* 1140-1158,
1160-1161, 1163, 1165-1166, 1168, 1171-
1178, 1181-1182, 1184-1191, 1196, 1200,
1202-1204, 1208, 1210-1219, 1224, 1226-
1230, 1232-1233, 1236-1237, 1239-1244,
1246, 1249, 1251, 1253-1256, 1259-1260,
1262-1264, 1266; *Children, effects on;*
1276, 1282-1283, 1299, 1301, 1304, 1306-
1307, 1312-1315, 1323-1324, 1326, 1328-
1329, 1331-1332, 1336, 1341, 1343, 1349-
1350, 1352-1353, 1359-1361, 1368, 1373,
1376, 1378, 1380, 1382; *Civil rights;* 1458-
1459, 1465-1469, 1471, 1473, 1476-1477,
1484-1486, 1488, 1490, 1492, 1497-1509,
1514, 1519, 1521, 1523, 1525-1531, 1534-
1538, 1540-1541, 1543-1544, 1546, 1548-
1552, 1554-1560, 1562, 1564, 1566, 1569-
1571, 1573-1575, 1577-1582, 1585, 1587-
1591, 1594, 1597, 1600, 1607, 1610, 1612-
1613, 1615-1618, 1620, 1625, 1629, 1631-
1634, 1637, 1640-1642, 1644-1645, 1647-
1648, 1650-1652, 1656-1659, 1663, 1669-
1672, 1678, 1680-1681, 1686, 1690, 1692,
1696-1699, 1701-1703, 1707-1708, 1713-
1716; *Class structure;* 1725, 1728, 1734,
1742, 1744, 1746, 1748-1750, 1753, 1757-
1760, 1766-1768, 1772, 1774-1775, 1777-
1779, 1782-1783, 1786-1788, 1790-1792,
1794, 1800, 1803-1805, 1810-1811, 1813,
1815, 1817, 1819-1822, 1825, 1828, 1830-
1831, 1833, 1836, 1844, 1847, 1854, 1857,
1859, 1860, 1874-1876, 1880, 1886 1890-
1894, 1897, 1904-1906, 1909-1910, 1912-
1914, 1916, 1918-1920; *Collective self*
defense; 1926, 1930, 1932, 1935, 1937-
1939, 1941-1943, 1945-1949, 1951-1952,
1958, 1960-1961, 1963, 1966-1967, 1968,
1971-1975, 1979, 1983-1984; *Colonialism;*
2033, 2044, 2075, 2089-2090; *Community*
development; 2107, 2109, 2112-2113, 2119-
2121, 2126-2128, 2130-2132, 2134, 2137-
2141, 2143-2144, 2146, 2149, 2154, 2166-
2167, 2170, 2173, 2177, 2181, 2184-2186;
Crime; 2232-2233, 2238-2239, 2241, 2243-
2247, 2250-2251, 2254-2256, 2259-2262,
2267-2268, 2274-2280, 2282-2283, 2292-
2294, 2297-2301, 2303-2305, 2313-2314,
2319-2320, 2322-2323, 2325-2329, 2333-
2334, 2336, 2339-2340, 2343-2346, 2348-
2357, 2359-2365, 2367-2381, 2384-2385,
2387, 2390-2393, 2396, 2399-2401, 2403-
2409, 2412-2420, 2422-2432, 2434-2435,
2437-2440, 2442, 2445-2446, 2449-2450,
2452-2455, 2457-2458, 2463-2465, 2467,
2469, 2472, 2474-2475, 2477, 2480-2482,
2484-2487, 2489-2494, 2496, 2500-2501,

2503-2507, 2510, 2512-2513, 2516, 2519-
2520, 2522-2526, 2528-2529, 2531-2532;
Desegregation; 2536-2538, 2540, 2542-
2550, 2552-2555, 2557-2559, 2561-2564,
2566-2577, 2579, 2581-2591, 2593-2597,
2599, 2600-2604, 2607-2620, 2623-2626,
2628-2629, 2631, 2633-2635, 2639-2641,
2643, 2645-2653, 2659-2661, 2663-2672,
2674, 2677-2678, 2681-2682, 2684-2688,
2692-2700, 2702-2704, 2715, 2722-2730,
2732, 2736-2737, 2739, 2741, 2746-2751,
2753, 2758, 2760-2761, 2765, 2767, 2770,
2772-2773, 2775-2778, 2782-2784, 2786-
2787, 2790-2791, 2795-2801, 2803-2805,
2807-2813, 2815-2816, 2819-2821, 2824-
2827, 2829-2830, 2834, 2836-2838;
Discrimination; 2848, 2858, 2868, 2887,
2901, 2918, 2923, 2938-2939, 2943, 2947,
2955, 2976, 3014, 3018-3019, 3027, 3034,
3060, 3063-3064, 3088, 3114-3115; *Du
Bois;* 3127-3132; *Economic standards;*
3134, 3139-3140, 3143, 3148, 3158-3160,
3164-3165, 3167, 3170-3172, 3174, 3176,
3181 3184-3186, 3188-3190, 3195-3196,
3200, 3205, 3211-3212, 3214-3216, 3218,
3223-3224, 3232, 3236-3238, 3242-3243,
3247, 3249-3251, 3254, 3259, 3266-3268,
3278, 3281, 3284, 3289-3290, 3292, 3295,
3303, 3309, 3315, 3317, 3320, 3323, 3328,
3337, 3343-3344, 3347, 3374, 3376, 3379-
3380, 3386- 3387, 3389, 3406, 3408, 3414,
3417-3418, 3422; *Economics of racism;*
3427, 3432, 3434, 3453, 3455; *Education,
elementary & secondary;* 3457-3458, 3460-
3461, 3464-3465, 3469-3470, 3476, 3492,
3497, 3502, 3505, 3512, 3521, 3525, 3528-
3530, 3533-3534, 3536, 3547, 3550, 3556-
3557, 3561, 3565-3566, 3577-3578, 3586-
3587, 3597, 3618, 3620-3621, 3624-3625,
3628, 3633, 3638-3640, 3644, 3646-3647,
3652, 3657, 3659, 3663-3665, 3668, 3675,
3679, 3682-3683, 3686, 3693-3698, 3718,
3730-3731, 3736-3739, 3741, 3743, 3753,
3756-3757, 3762, 3767, 3773-3775, 3779-
3780, 3787, 3790-3791, 3793, 3802, 3805,
3808-3809, 3816, 3819, 3821-3822, 3824-
3825, 3828, 3830, 3837, 3841 3844, 3847,
3850-3851, 3863, 3865, 3867, 3872, 3875-
3876, 3878-3879, 3881-3883, 3885, 3888-
3899, 3901, 3915-3916, 3921, 3923-3925,
3930-3931, 3934-3935, 3942, 3949, 3951-
3952, 3956-3957, 3967, 3977, 3990, 3999,
4001-4002, 4010, 4015, 4021, 4026, 4031,
4033, 4038-4039, 4041, 4043, 4047-4063,
4065-4066, 4068-4069, 4073 4076, 4095,
4097, 4101, 4127, 4129, 4132-4133, 4143-
4146, 4154, 4156-4159, 4163, 4171, 4173,
4175-4176, 4181-4182, 4193, 4203, 4206,
4209, 4222, 4230-4231, 4237, 4241-4243,

4252, 4256-4257, 4259, 4261-4264, 4267-
4268, 4271, 4273, 4275; *Education, higher;*
4284, 4288, 4294, 4297-4302, 4306, 4310-
4311, 4314-4319, 4324, 4328, 4332, 4337,
4344, 4348-4349, 4353, 4359, 4367-4372,
4376-4377, 4385, 4390-4391, 4399, 4408,
4413, 4416-4417, 4422, 4432, 4437, 4441,
4444, 4446-4447, 4451-4453, 4455, 4463,
4474-4476, 4478, 4485 4487, 4494-4495,
4501-4504, 4506, 4510, 4520-4521, 4524,
4534-4535, 4538-4539, 4546-4547, 4549,
4551, 4553, 4556-4557, 4560, 4563-4564,
4566, 4571, 4575, 4581-4582, 4590, 4599-
4600, 4602-4603, 4605-4607, 4614, 4618,
4629, 4633, 4636, 4639, 4648, 4652, 4661,
4666, 4672-4674, 4680, 4682- 4685, 4690-
4691, 4694-4698, 4701, 4703-4706, 4710-
4711, 4717 4721, 4726, 4732, 4734, 4736,
4738-4741, 4745, 4748, 4751, 4754-4756,
4758-4759, 4767, 4770-4771, 4773-4774,
4776-4777, 4779-4780, 4785-4788, 4793,
4796, 4798, 4800-4802, 4804, 4808, 4817,
4825, 4836, 4839-4840, 4843, 4858, 4860-
4861, 4863-4864, 4868, 4871, 4881, 4883-
4885, 4888, 4892, 4898, 4900, 4903, 4905,
4907-4910, 4912, 4914-4915, 4918, 4920-
4921, 4923-4924, 4932, 4935, 4938-4939,
4942, 4945, 4947-4949, 4953, 4958, 4964-
4965, 4967-4968, 4970, 4975, 4977, 4983,
4987, 4991, 4994, 4999, 5002-5004, 5008,
5010-5014, 5018, 5022-5024, 5026-5028,
5030-5032, 5035, 5039, 5041-5042, 5044,
5050, 5054-5055, 5061, 5075, 5080, 5082-
5083, 5086, 5093, 5095-5096, 5099, 5102,
5104-5106, 5118, 5136, 5139, 5141-5143,
5145, 5147, 5149, 5151-5152, 5156, 5160,
5162, 5166, 5180-5181, 5184, 5192-5193,
5198-5199, 5209- 5210, 5214, 5216, 5220-
5221, 5223-5226, 5230, 5234-5235, 5238-
5239, 5241, 5247-5249, 5251-5253, 5259-
5260, 5265, 5271, 5273, 5274-5276, 5278-
5279, 5282, 5288, 5294-5295, 5306-5307,
5316, 5324-5325, 5330-5333, 5337, 5340,
5348-5351, 5355-5356, 5359-5362 5366,
5368-5372, 5374, 5379, 5383 5390, 5394-
5395, 5401; *Employment;* 5402, 5405-5408,
5419, 5421, 5425-5426, 5433, 5436, 5438-
5440, 5442, 5445-5446; **Environment;**
5451, 5455, 5467-5468, 5478, 5481, 5524,
5528, 5532, 5544, 5557-5558; *Family;*
5563-5565, 5568-5569, 5575, 5578-5582,
5584, 5586-5587, 5589-5592, 5594-5595,
5602-5603, 5606, 5610-5614, 5617, 5619,
5622-5623, 5625, 5627-5628, 5630, 5632,
5636-5637, 5641-5643, 5645-5650, 5652-
5653, 5655-5657, 5659, 5661, 5665, 5667,
5669-5673, 5675-5677, 5680, 5683-5684,
5687-5690, 5692, 5695-5697, 5700-5703,
5707, 5711, 5713, 5716, 5718, 5720-5721,

5726-5727, 5731, 5742-5745, 5748-5750;
Forced labor; 5756-5759, 5762-5763, 5765,
5768-5770; *Free Blacks;* 5771-5792;
Ghetto; 5793-5805, 5808-5813, 5815, 5817-
5828; *Government & minorities;* 5845,
5847-5848, 5861-5862, 5864, 5872-5873,
5884, 5890-5892, 5895, 5896-5897, 5900,
5912, 5916, 5918-5919, 5928, 5930, 5934,
5943, 5945-5948, 5954, 5956-5957, 5966,
5968-5970, 5972, 5980-5981, 5983, 6008,
6018, 6020; *Health;* 6029, 6037-6039,
6047-6048, 6050, 6055, 6059, 6062, 6066,
6069, 6071-6073, 6077, 6080-6082, 6096,
6099, 6107-6108, 6111-6113, 6123, 6126,
6130, 6139, 6142, 6145, 6148, 6151, 6156,
6158, 6162, 6174, 6177, 6183, 6186, 6190-
6191, 6194, 6197, 6204-6205, 6207, 6209-
6210, 6213-6215, 6218, 6229, 6233-6234,
6242-6245, 6247-6248, 6252, 6259, 6262,
6264-6266, 6271-6272, 6275, 6277, 6283-
6285, 6288-6289, 6291, 6293, 6297, 6299-
6301, 6306-6308, 6315, 6322, 6324, 6328-
6329, 6336-6337, 6339-6341, 6345-6347,
6350-6351, 6353-6354, 6357, 6359-6360,
6363-6364, 6368, 6382-6383, 6393-6395,
6398, 6406, 6410, 6423, 6426, 6431, 6436,
6445, 6453, 6461, 6464, 6467, 6479, 6485-
6486, 6491, 6495-6497, 6500, 6507, 6511,
6513-6514, 6520, 6525-6527, 6541-6542,
6548, 6550-6552, 6554-6555, 6563, 6569-
6570, 6572-6573, 6577, 6585, 6587-6588,
6592, 6599, 6608-6610, 6613, 6615, 6621,
6632-6633, 6641, 6645, 6652, 6661-6663,
6668, 6673, 6675, 6677, 6682; *History;*
6699, 6704, 6708-6710, 6714, 6719-6721,
6726, 6728, 6731, 6739, 6742, 6751, 6757,
6759, 6760-6761, 6765, 6767, 6769, 6771,
6781-6782, 6785, 6788, 6792-6794, 6897-
6804, 6808-6817, 6821, 6827, 6829, 6832,
6836-6838, 6842, 6845, 6851-6852, 6861-
6863, 6867, 6873, 6875, 6877, 6886-6887,
6892-6893, 6900, 6923, 6925-6926, 6928,
6933-6934, 6939, 6941-6943, 6946, 6973-
6974, 6979-6980, 6982-6983, 6987, 6990,
6997, 6999, 7008, 7021-7022, 7026, 7029,
7032, 7034-7035, 7037, 7038-7039, 7050,
7053-7055, 7058; *Housing;* 7072, 7074,
7078, 7087, 7092, 7094, 7105, 7112, 7114,
7131, 7134-7140, 7145-7149, 7151, 7155,
7158-7161, 7164-7165, 7168-7169, 7171-
7172, 7174-7175, 7180, 7182-7183, 7185-
7188, 7190-7194, 7196, 7201-7204, 7206-
7207, 7212, 7214-7216, 7218, 7220, 7225-
7231, 7234, 7237-7239, 7243, 7245-7247,
7249-7251, 7253, 7257-7259, 7262, 7271,
7274-7275, 7279, 7281, 7284-7290, 7293-
7294, 7297, 7299, 7302, 7304-7305, 7309,
7310-7312, 7323, 7325, 7327-7328, 7332,
7338, 7341-7345, 7347-7356, 7361, 7364,

7366-7367, 7372-7377; *Humor;* 7382, 7391,
7393, 7399, 7404, 7416, 7418, 7422, 7425,
7437-7438, 7441, 7443-7444, 7451, 7457,
7459, 7465-7466, 7471-7473, 7476-7477,
7480; *Immigration;* 7492, 7501-7502 7505,
7513, 7531, 7540-7541, 7562, 7578-7579,
7585, 7599, 7616, 7629, 7638, 7642, 7654,
7661, 7664; *IQ & race;* 7689, 7698-7699,
7702, 7707-7714, 7718, 7720-7722, 7726,
7732-7733, 7735-7736, 7739-7742, 7745-
7748, 7753-7754, 7758, 7761, 7765, 7769,
7771-7773, 7778, 7782, 7784, 7785-7787;
Ku Klux Klan; 7799, 7801, 7813; *Labor;*
7867, 7869, 7874, 7876, 7887, 7893, 7895,
7897, 7902, 7907, 7916, 7925, 7928, 7930-
7931, 7933-7938, 7942-7947, 7963, 7968-
7970, 7972-7974, 7976-7979, 7984-7986,
7989-7991, 7994-7996, 7999-8000, 8005,
8009, 8011-8012, 8019, 8022-8024, 8032-
8035, 8039, 8041, 8043-8047, 8049-8051,
8055, 8057-8058, 8060, 8063-8067, 8070-
8071, 8073-8074, 8077-8078, 8081, 8085,
8087-8090, 8094-8095, 8097-8098, 8104-
8105, 8113-8115, 8118-8119, 8121-8122,
8124, 8130-8131, 8133-8135, 8138-8141,
8149, 8152, 8155, 8157, 8160-8161, 8165,
8170, 8172-8174, 8176-8178, 8181; *Land;*
8184-8185, 8193, 8214, 8248, 8250, 8275-
8276, 8288, 8300-8301, 8307, 8323;
Language; 8389, 8394, 8403, 8416, 8433,
8440, 8444, 8452, 8454, 8463, 8477, 8479,
8485, 8502, 8509, 8517, 8520-8521, 8547,
8568, 8573, 8584, 8599, 8616, 8633, 8639;
Law; 8649, 8652\, 8655, 8657-8659, 8663,
8667, 8679-8690, 8692-8693, 8695, 8697,
8702-8711, 8715-8716, 8721, 8723-8729,
8735-8737, 8739-8742, 8744-8748, 8751,
8757, 8760, 8768, 8770-8771, 8774, 8776-
8779, 8782-8784, 8787, 8790, 8792-8793,
8795-8797, 8803-8805, 8809-8810, 8812-
8815, 8817, 8819-8823, 8828, 8831, 8834,
8836-8837, 8841, 8843-8844, 8849-8857,
8862, 8864, 8868, 8872-8873, 8875, 8879-
8883, 8886, 8890-8893, 8895-8897, 8900-
8901, 8903, 8906, 8908-8909, 8918-8923,
8925, 8929-8931, 8940, 8942, 8947, 8950,
8956, 8960, 8972-8973, 8977, 8979-8980,
8985-8986, 8988, 8992, 8994-8995, 8997-
8998, 9000, 9002, 9008, 9012-9014, 9016,
9022-9023, 9027, 9032, 9041-9042, 9044-
9045, 9048, 9050-9051, 9059-9062, 9064,
9066, 9068, 9071, 9079, 9083, 9085-9089,
9091, 9093-9095, 9097-9099, 9103-9107,
9110, 9113, 9118; *Libraries;* 9127, 9133,
9135, 9139, 9142, 9144-9146, 9149;
Literature; 9152-9154, 9159-9162, 9164,
9171, 9173, 9175, 9178-9179, 9181-9183,
9185-9186, 9190, 9192, 9195, 9197, 9199-
9204, 9208-9213, 9215-9216, 9219-9220,

9222-9223, 9225-9226, 9230-9235, 9237,
9239, 9241, 9244, 9246, 9248, 9250, 9253-
9254, 9259, 9261, 9263-9271, 9275-9278,
9280, 9282, 9284, 9286, 9289-9290, 9294-
9295, 9298, 9300, 9302, 9304, 9310-9311,
9313, 9315-9316, 9320, 9322-9323, 9325-
9327, 9331-9333; *Locality - Alabama;* 9335-
9339, 9341-9343; *Locality - Alaska;* 9352;
Locality - Arizona; 9359; *Locality -
Arkansas;* 9360- 9368; *Locality -
California;* 9373, 9376-9377, 9380-9381,
9383, 9385-9387, 9390-9393, 9395-9398,
9406-9410, 9413, 9417, 9420-9421, 9426,
9432, 9435, 9441; *Locality - Colorado;*
9450-9454; *Locality - D.C.;* 9455; *Locality -
Florida;* 9459-9461, 9463-9465; *Locality -
Georgia;* 9466-9474; *Locality - Hawaii;*
9484, 9490, 9493; *Locality - Illinois;* 9494,
9496, 9502; *Locality - Indiana;* 9503, 9505;
Locality - Iowa; 9506-9508; *Locality -
Kansas;* 9509-9511; *Locality - Kentucky;*
9513; *Locality - Louisiana;* 9515-9517,
9519; *Locality - Maryland;* 9521-9523;
Locality - Massachusetts; 9525-9526, 9528,
9530, 9532-9535; *Locality - Michigan;*
9536-9541; *Locality - Mississippi;* 9542-
9560; *Locality - Missouri;* 9561-9565;
Locality - Montana; 9568-9570; *Locality -
Nebraska;* 9571; *Locality - Nevada;* 9573;
Locality - New Hampshire; 9574-9575;
*Locality - New Jersey;*9577, 9579-9582;
Locality - New Mexico; 9583, 9586;
Locality - New York; 9591-9596, 9599-
9610, 9612-9614, 9616-9618, 9620-9624,
9626, 9628, 9630; *Locality - North
Carolina;* 9631-9633, 9635-9643; *Locality -
Ohio;* 9646-9652; *Locality - Oregon;* 9655;
Locality - Pennsylvania; 9656-9665;
Locality - South Carolina; 9667-9675;
Locality - Tennessee; 9677-9681; *Locality -
Texas;* 9682-9684, 9686-9687, 9691-9692,
9697, 9705, 9708, 9713-9720; *Locality -
Virginia;* 9723-9728, 9730-9737, 9739-
9741; *Locality - Washington;* 9742, 9745;
Locality - West Virginia; 9748-9749;
Locality - Wyoming; 9751-9752; *Mass
media;* 9754-9757, 9759, 9763-9764, 9769,
9772, 9774, 9777, 9782, 9784, 9786, 9788-
9799, 9803-9804, 9806-9812, 9814-9815,
9817-9820, 9823-9832, 9834-9843, 9845,
9847, 9849, 9856-9857, 9859, 9863-9864,
9866-9872, 9874-9892, 9895-9900, 9902-
9905, 9914, 9916-9917, 9919, 9922-9923,
9927, 9929-9938, 9940, 9942, 9944-9945,
9948-9956, 9958-9970, 9972-9973, 9975-
9990, 9992, 9994, 9996, 9998, 10001,
10003, 10006-10012, 10015-10020, 10022-
10023, 10026-10038, 10040-10041, 10043-
10048, 10051-10052, 10057-10059, 10061-

10072, 10075, 10077-10078, 10082-10083,
10085, 10087, 10089-10093, 10095-10096,
10099-10101, 10103, 10105, 10107-10110,
10115, 10117-10118, 10120-10121, 10125-
10126, 10128-10129, 10132-10136, 10138-
10147, 10501-10155, 10157-10162, 10166,
10168-10178, 10180, 10182-10185, 10187-
10188, 10190, 10192-10194, 10196-10197,
10200-10202, 10204-10205, 10207-10208,
10211, 10218, 10220-10237, 10239-10246,
10249 10251-10252, 10254-10256, 10258-
10259, 10262-10265, 10268-10269, 10272-
10280, 10283, 10285-10286, 10290-10292,
10294-10295, 10299-10303, 10305;
Migration; 10308, 10313, 10315, 10317-
10319, 10321, 10323-10324, 10326-10332,
10337, 10339, 10342-10347, 10351, 10353,
10361-10372, 10374-10376; *Military;*
10377, 10387-10388, 10391-10400, 10402,
10404, 10408, 10410-10419, 10422-10424,
10429-10434, 10437-10438, 10440-10443,
10445, 10448, 10450-10451, 10454, 10456-
10461, 10463, 10465, 10467-10470, 10473-
10474, 10476-10477, 10480-10483, 10485-
10490, 10493, 10496, 10498, 10500, 10502-
10506, 10508-10509, 10511, 10514-10516,
10518, 10520, 10524-10526, 10530, 10532,
10534, 10536, 10538-10539, 10541, 10544,
10546, 10551, 10553-10554, 10558, 10561-
10562, 10566; *Minorities in conflict;* 10567-
10570, 10572-10583, 10586, 10588, 10590-
10591, 10595-10598, 10601-10605, 10607-
10648, 10650-10661; *Multiculturalism;*
10887, 10915, 10963, 11016, 11120;
Nationalism; 11123-11126, 11129, 11133-
11134, 11138-11141, 11143-11149, 11153-
11155, 11159-11160, 11162-11165, 11167,
11169-11170, 11174, 11180-11189, 11195;
Occupation; 11201-11204, 11206-11207,
11209, 11211-11212, 11214-11216, 11218,
11224-11225, 11227-11228, 11230-11232,
11234-11235, 11244, 11247-11249, 11251-
11258, 11260-11261, 11265, 11267-11268,
11270-11272, 11274-11275, 11277, 11279;
Oppression; 11284-11285, 11287, 11289,
11291; *Philosophy;* 11296, 11299-11300,
11303-11315; *Planning;* 11318-11321,
11324, 11326; *Pluralism;* 11343, 11345;
Politics & racism; 11368-11369, 11372,
11375, 11378, 11380-11382, 11384-11388,
11390, 11392, 11395, 11397-11402, 11404-
11405, 11409-11410, 11413, 11416, 11422-
11423, 11425-11426, 11428-11438, 11440,
11443-11444, 11450, 11452-11455, 11457-
11460, 11463-11464, 11470-11471, 11473-
11477, 11479-11483, 11486, 11488-11489,
11491, 11493-11501, 11506, 11508, 11510-
11511, 11513-11516, 11518-11519, 11521-
11525, 11527, 11531-11532, 11535, 11538-

11539, 11541-11549, 11552, 11554-11556,
11558-11570, 11575-11579, 11581, 11585,
11587-11592, 11594-11595, 11598, 11601-
11604, 11606, 11608-11612, 11614-11617,
11620-11622, 11624-11625, 11629-11631,
11635, 11637-11639, 11641-11646, 11648,
11656-11660, 11665-11674, 11676, 11680,
11682-11684, 11686-11687, 11690-11693,
11695, 11698-11700, 11703-11708, 11710-
11717, 11719-11726, 11728, 11730-11731,
11733, 11738, 11742, 11744-11747, 11750-
11753, 11755-11756, 11758-11786, 11788,
11790-11792, 11795-11798, 11800-11801,
11804-11812, 11815-11820, 11822-11824,
11826, 11828, 11830-11834, 11837-11845,
11847, 11849, 11853-11854, 11856-11865,
11869-11879, 11881-11884, 11891, 11893-
11895, 11900-11901, 11905-11907, 11909-
11910, 11913-11914, 11916-11920, 11922-
11923, 11927-11933, 11935-11942, 11944,
11946-11961, 11963-11966, 11968-11977,
11979, 11983-11986, 11990-11993, 11996-
11997, 12000-12002, 12005-12015, 12018-
12032, 12035-12037, 12039, 12041-12043,
12046-12047; *Public opinion;* 12049-12058,
12060, 12063, 12066, 12068-12069, 12071-
12072, 12074-12078, 12081, 12084, 12089,
12092, 12095, 12101, 12103, 12106-12108,
12111, 12116-12119; *Racism, defining;*
12124, 12128-12131, 12135, 12140-12141,
12143, 12148, 12156-12157, 12164, 12175,
12192, 12212-12213; *Racism, exporting;*
12218, 12223-12224, 12234, 12241;
Racism, institutional; 12250; *Racism,
psychology of;* 12261, 12264-12266, 12275,
12277, 12279-12280, 12282, 12285-12287,
12289, 12292, 12297-12311; *Racism,
scholarly;* 12327, 12329-12330, 12360;
Racism, theory of; 12402, 12405, 12421,
12441, 12461, 12474-12475, 12494, 12496,
12501-12502, 12507; *Religion;* 12643-
12644, 12646-12651, 12653-12654, 12657-
12658, 12661, 12670, 12672, 12676-12684,
12686-12687, 12693-12696, 12698-12707,
12709-12711, 12714-12717, 12720-12724,
12726, 12728-12730, 12732, 12735-12736,
12741-12742, 12746-12748, 12750-12751,
12754-12755, 12757-12758, 12760-12762,
12764-12774, 12776, 12778-12779, 12782-
12783, 12785, 12787-12799, 12801-12804,
12806-12807, 12811-12817, 12820-12822,
12824-12832, 12837-12838, 12840-12842,
12844-12846, 12849-12851, 12855-12860,
12862-12865, 12867-12870, 12873-12874,
12876-12877, 12880-12881, 12884-12885;
Science & technology; 12888, 12891,
12898-12899, 12902, 12905, 12907-12909,
12920-12925, 12932, 12934; *Sexism;*
12946, 12954, 12958, 12967, 12979, 12985,

12990, 12995-12997, 13004, 13006, 13010-
13012, 13015, 13023, 13025-13026, 13029-
13030, 13036, 13038, 13042, 13045, 13054-
13057, 13060, 13064-13065, 13074-13075,
13080-13083; *Slavery;* 13088, 13090-13092,
13094-13100, 13102-13105, 13107-13110,
13112, 13114, 13116-13117, 13119, 13121-
13122, 13124-13127, 13129, 13131-13135,
13137-13140, 13142-13150, 13153-13191,
13194-13198, 13200-13209; *Socialism &
racism;* 13210-13221; *Sports;* 13223-13307,
13309-13347, 13349-13375; *Stereotypes;*
13383-13384, 13386-13387, 13389, 13393-
13395, 13397-13398, 13400, 13403-13404,
13410, 13415, 13419, 13423-13424, 13439-
13441, 13443, 13454, 13456, 13459-13461,
13464, 13466-13467, 13473, 13481-13482,
13484, 13487, 13490, 13492, 13497, 13500,
13508, 13512-13513, 13519, 13524, 13526,
13529, 13532-13533, 13540, 13552-13553,
13556-13558, 13563, 13574-13576;
Surveillance; 13590, 13594, 13600, 13608,
13613-13615, 13620, 13623, 13626, 13634,
13642-13645, 13647-13648, 13651, 13655,
13668-13669, 13671, 13683-13686, 13690,
13692-13693, 13703, 13708, 13711, 13714,
13717-13718, 13723, 13729, 13731, 13738,
13747, 13754-13756, 13769-13774, 13778,
13780; *Tests;* 13798, 13803, 13807-13808,
13814, 13819, 13823, 13835, 13851;
Undoing personal racism; 13901;
Unemployment; 13932, 13938, 13940-
13941, 13943, 13946-13948, 13951-13952,
13957-13959, 13961, 13964, 13966;
Violence vs. Minorities; 13970, 13974
13977-13995, 13997-13999, 14002-14003,
14008-14011, 14013, 14015-14020, 14022-
14023, 14028, 14031-14035, 14037, 14039,
14041-14042, 14044-14056, 14059, 14065,
14068, 14071-14072, 14075-14078, 14083,
14085, 14087, 14089, 14091-14094, 14096-
14098, 14101-14102, 14104-14105, 14109,
14111-14113, 14118, 14121, 14125-14126,
14128, 14131, 14135-14136, 14138; *Wealth
& income;* 14140, 14143-14146, 14148-
14152, 14156, 14158, 14161, 14164, 14171,
14176-14177, 14180, 14192-14193, 14197-
14198, 14200-14201; *Whites;* 14221, 14232,
14240, 14247, 14261; *Women of Color;*
14279-14280, 14282-14283, 14286, 14290,
14298-14301, 14305-14306, 14309-14310,
14315-14319, 14327-14328, 14331, 14333-
14334, 14336, 14338-14339, 14341, 14344-
14346, 14348-14351, 14353-14354, 14356-
14367, 14371, 14373, 14375-14381, 14384-
14386, 14390, 14392-14398, 14401, 14403-
14404, 14407-14411, 14414-14416, 14419-
14420, 14424, 14426-14429, 14431, 14433-
14437, 14439, 14443, 14446, 14450-14453,

14456-14462, 14464, 14467; *General;*
14471-14472, 14474-14476, 14479-14480,
14482, 14486, 14489, 14491-14493, 14495-
14499, 14502, 14504, 14506, 14508-14512,
14514-14518, 14521, 14523-14527, 14529-
14534, 14536, 14539-14541, 14543, 14545,
14547-14548, 14550, 14553-14554, 14556-
14558, 14562, 14564-14566, 14568, 14571-
14572, 14574, 14576, 14579-14581, 14583-
14586, 14588-14591; *Bibliographies;* 14593-
14594, 14596-14597, 14602, 14605-14607,
14613-14618, 14625, 14628-14629, 14632,
14635-14638, 14640, 14643, 14648, 14652,
14657, 14659, 14661, 14663-14664

Arab Americans: *Education, elementary &
secondary;* 4235; *Immigration;* 7572; *Law;*
9009; *Literature;* 9235; *Mass media;* 9771,
9915, 9933, 10014, 10113, 10127, 10212,
10267; *Military;* 10380; *Minorities in
conflict;* 10585, 10637; *Politics & racism;*
11647, 11649; *Racist groups;* 12557;
Sexism; 12953; *Stereotypes;* 13381, 13413,
13417-13418, 13426, 13434, 13445, 13449,
13465, 13501, 13510, 13535, 13538, 13544-
13547, 13555; *Violence vs. Minorities;*
14103; *General;* 14469, 14500, 14535,
14582; *Bibliographies;* 14592, 14653

Asian Americans: *Affirmative action;* 60, 149,
160-161, 177, 240, 313; *Autobiography &
Biography;* 736-737; *Business;* 1156, 1195;
Children, effects on; 1338-1339, 1372;
Class structure; 1853; *Collective self
defense;* 1985; *Desegregation;* 2508;
Discrimination; 2843, 2950; *Economic
standards;* 3147; *Education, higher;* 4880,
4983, 4992, 5029, 5034, 5301, 5303, 5310,
5392; *Employment;* 5406; *Environment;*
5516; *Family;* 5593; *Health;* 6105, 6694;
History; 6901, 7019; *Housing;* 7138, 7253;
Humor; 7411; *Literature;* 9156-9158, 9174,
9228, 9249, 9257, 9292, 9318, 9329;
Locality - Massachusetts; 9529; *Mass
media;* 9779, 9784, 9816, 9848, 9850-9851,
9894, 9971, 9974, 10013, 10017, 10060,
10088, 10125, 10168, 10195, 10232, 10244,
10247, 10297, 10304; *Minorities in conflict;*
10580, 10651; *Multiculturalism;* 11046,
11084; *Occupation;* 11213, 11273; *Politics
& racism;* 11394, 11396, 11605-11606,
11702, 11743, 11924, 11943, 12017; *Public
opinion;* 12086; *Racism, defining;* 12135,
12154, 12200; *Racism, scholarly;* 12345;
Religion; 12775; *Stereotypes;* 13380, 13463,
13471, 13479 13480, 13486, 13497, 13505,
13520, 13523, 13582; *Tests;* 13798 13884;
Violence vs. Minorities; 13971-13972,
13975, 14012, 14015-14016, 14021, 14064,

14068, 14084, 14130, 14137; *Women of
Color;* 14291-14292, 14370, 14388-14389,
14465; *General;* 14505; *Bibliographies;*
14593, 14611, 14619, 14651

Asian Indians: *Civil rights;* 1694;
Discrimination; 2923; *Economics of racism;*
3446; *Education, elementary & secondary;*
3725, 4082, 4121; *Education, higher;*
4327, 4450; *Housing;* 7211; *Immigration;*
7497, 7535, 7584, 7596; *Labor;* 7983,
8014; *Law;* 9004; *Locality - California;*
9404, 9440; *Mass media;* 9998; *Politics &
racism;* 11698; *Racism, defining;* 12177;
Stereotypes; 13421, 13676, 13687; *Violence
vs. Minorities;* 14133

Cambodian Americans: *Literature;* 9177, 9184;
Locality - Hawaii; 9485

Caribbean Americans: *Autobiography &
Biography;* 773; *Colonialism;* 1994, 2010,
2012, 2035, 2040-2041; *Immigration;* 7509,
7513, 7568, 7581, 7585, 7599, 7618, 7623,
7629; *Labor;* 8064, 8157, 8169; *Locality -
Indiana;* 9504; *Migration;* 10310;
Pluralism; 11342; *Women of Color;* 14455;
General; 14477, 14503; *Bibliographies;*
14623-14624

Chinese Americans: *Autobiography &
Biography;* 793; *Colonialism;* 2034; *Crime;*
2284, 2502; *Discrimination;* 2868;
Education, higher; 4647; *Forced labor;*
5764; *Government & minorities;* 5996;
Health; 6397, 6752; *Housing;* 7102, 7241;
Immigration; 7501, 7511-7512, 7558, 7566,
7571, 7591-7592, 7601, 7639, 7640; *Labor;*
7873, 7891, 7945, 8091 8120; *Law;* 8911,
9119-9120; *Literature;* 9281; *Locality -
Nevada;* 9572; *Locality - Washington;*
9744; *Minorities in conflict;* 10592; *Politics
& racism;* 11468, 12045; *Stereotypes;*
13455; *Surveillance;* 13776; *Violence vs.
Minorities;* 14005, 14014, 14060, 14066-
14067, 14106, 14132; *Women of Color;*
14391, 14466

Cuban-Americans: *Community development;*
2187; *Health;* 6407, 6536; *Immigration;*
7520, 7540; *Locality - Florida;* 9460, 9463,
9465; *Minorities in conflict;* 10574, 10628,
10641; *Politics & racism;* 11504, 11677,
11800; *Religion;* 12691; *Sports;* 13275;
General; 14551

Euro-Americans: *Affirmative action;* 348;
Autobiography & Biography; 612-623,

625, 629, 704, 734, 743, 752, 756, 763, 768, 779, 790, 798, 816, 819, 825, 836, 847, 853, 859, 887, 895, 901, 904; *Business;* 1194; *Civil rights;* 1460, 1531, 1653, 1662; *Class structure;* 1719, 1818, 1838, 1859; *Collective self defense;* 1977, 2027; *Concentration camps;* 2196, 2201, 2224; *Crime;* 2375, 2404, 2408, 2446, 2464; *Discrimination;* 2862, 2887, 2900, 2988, 3022; *Economic standards;* 3143, 3190, 3214, 3237, 3243, 3278, 3284, 3289, 3328, 3343, 3387, 3406; *Economics of racism;* 3430, 3434; *Education, elementary & secondary;* 3472, 3480-3481, 3531, 3547, 3598, 3668, 3718, 3739, 3769, 3780, 3823, 3835, 3863, 3865, 3867, 3921, 3928-3929, 3942, 4066, 4076, 4079, 4178, 4199, 4237, 4259; *Education, higher;* 4284, 4314-4315, 4328, 4355, 4399, 4405, 4416, 4432, 4435, 4441, 4456-4457, 4467, 4477, 4482, 4485, 4505, 4522, 4560, 4566, 4591, 4648, 4651, 4661, 4687, 4695, 4697, 4704-4705, 4712, 4721, 4732, 4742, 4749, 4752, 4779, 4782, 4800, 4829, 4850, 4872, 4894, 4898, 4908-4910, 4925, 4944, 4986, 5002-5004, 5022-5023, 5035-5040, 5058, 5069, 5099-5100, 5105, 5118, 5128, 5137, 5159, 5166, 5175, 5193, 5229, 5233, 5235, 5238, 5244, 5282, 5295 5310, 5331-5332, 5334-5335, 5339, 5383, 5385; *Family;* 5569, 5579; *Ghetto;* 5806-5807; *Government & minorities;* 5864, 5900, 5931, 5966; *Health;* 6206, 6224, 6306-6308, 6341, 6357, 6364, 6382-6383, 6393, 6406, 6436, 6464, 6485-6486, 6511, 6520, 6549, 6563, 6573, 6588, 6592, 6599, 6605, 6609, 6660-6661, 6673; *History;* 6705, 6732, 6773, 6914, 6936, 6956, 6989, 7016; *Housing;* 7162, 7184, 7235, 7329, 7346; *Humor;* 7389, 7398, 7407, 7410, 7427-7428, 7432, 7437, 7452-7453, 7462, 7467, 7475; *Immigration;* 7482, 7484, 7492-7494, 7516, 7521, 7556, 7567, 7574, 7608, 7611, 7621, 7627, 7630, 7638, 7648, 7656, 7658, 7667, 7678-7679; *Ku Klux Klan;* 7803, 7852; *Labor;* 8060, 8091, 8103, 8153, 8162; *Language;* 8398, 8489, 8566, 8568, 8589, 8638; *Law;* 8672, 8700, 8867, 8982, 9034; *Literature;* 9169-9170, 9197-9198, 9206, 9218, 9255, 9262, 9274, 9312; *Locality - Louisiana;* 9518; *Locality - Montana;* 9567; *Locality - New Mexico;* 9587; *Locality - New York;* 9595-9596 9601, 9605, 9624, 9626-9627; *Locality - Texas;* 9709; *Locality - Virginia;* 9729; *Mass media;* 9765, 9770, 9776, 9800-9801, 9833, 9861, 9873, 9909, 9912, 9948, 10042, 10076, 10144, 10148-10149, 10210, 10289; *Migration;* 10360; *Military;* 10426; *Minorities in conflict;* 10583, 10585, 10587,

10592, 10594, 10601, 10622, 10634, 10642, 10649, 10656; *Multiculturalism;* 10915, 11023, 11111; *Nationalism;* 11193; *Occupation;* 11222; *Politics & racism;* 11389, 11393, 11417, 11449, 11461, 11478, 11502, 11529, 11570, 11578, 11580, 11606, 11661, 11678, 11681, 11729, 11734, 11737, 11741, 11787, 11789, 11829, 11848, 11867, 11886-11890, 11899, 11911 11955, 11987, 12033, 12034; *Public opinion;* 12048, 12050-12051, 12054-12056, 12058-12060, 12062, 12064-12069, 12071-12072, 12074, 12076, 12078-12080, 12082-12085, 12087-12088, 12091-12095, 12098-12100, 12102-12103, 12109, 12111-12114, 12116, 12118, 12120-12121; *Racism, defining;* 12135, 12143, 12175; *Racism, exporting;* 12244; *Racist groups;* 12508-12511, 12513, 12515-12521, 12523-12553, 12555-12556, 12558-12601, 12603-12609; *Religion;* 12673, 12692, 12712, 12739-12740, 12743, 12759, 12782, 12784, 12795, 12809, 12823, 12830, 12848, 12861; *Science & technology;* 12904; *Sexism;* 13007; *Sports;* 13308, 13348, 13382, 13393, 13395, 13404, 13407, 13423, 13435, 13447, 13467, 13468, 13470, 13482, 13485, 13488, 13497, 13511, 13516-13518, 13526, 13536, 13577, 13581; *Surveillance;* 13742; *Tests;* 13798, 13814, 13863; *Undoing personal racism;* 13890; *Unemployment;* 13938, 13964, 13966; *Violence vs. Minorities;* 14110; *Wealth & income;* 14162, Whites; 14205-14220, 14222-14239, 14241-14277; *Women of Color;* 14311, 14325, 14352; *Bibliographies;* 14658, 14670

Filipino Americans: *Affirmative action;* 329; *Education, higher;* 4333; *Humor;* 7464; *Labor;* 7926, 8090; *Language;* 8339; *Literature;* 9299; *Locality - Louisiana;* 9514; *Locality - Washington;* 9743

Haitians: *Housing;* 7138; *Minorities in conflict;* 10648

Hispanics: *Affirmative action;* 53, 112, 220, 262, 344; *Children, effects on;* 1229, 1279, 1319; *Civil rights;* 1504, 1644; *Class structure;* 1780, 1841, 1901; *Collective self defense;* 1976, 1980; *Community development;* 2115; *Crime;* 2301, 2453, 2501; *Desegregation;* 2539, 2629, 2724-2725, 2727, 2791, 2815; *Discrimination;* 2900, 2907 2929, 2950, 2986, 2989; *Economic standards;* 3144, 3146, 3189-3190, 3214, 3336, 3344, 3405; *Education, elementary & secondary;* 3471, 3475, 3477, 3522, 3527, 3559, 3564, 3635, 3671, 3714,

3720, 3775, 3795, 3803-3804, 3863, 3888, 3934, 3965, 3973, 3984, 3989, 4007-4008, 4011, 4028-4030, 4091, 4094, 4115, 4117, 4123, 4185, 4186, 4202; *Education, higher;* 4289, 4321-4322, 4383, 4436, 4609 4627, 4640, 4704-4705, 4709, 4744, 4885, 4899, 4960, 4983, 4994, 5026, 5038, 5068, 5195, 5274; *Employment;* 5427, 5437, 5440; *Environment;* 5455, 5459; *Family;* 5567, 5735; *Government & minorities;* 5872, 5901, 5910, 5919, 5969; *Health;* 6032, 6040, 6146, 6267, 6299, 6313, 6341, 6365-6366, 6379, 6385, 6425, 6436, 6486, 6517, 6521-6522 6533, 6537, 6555, 6563, 6641; *History;* 6749, 6824, 6944, 6949; *Housing;* 7251, 7253, 7326; *Humor;* 7413, 7619, 7643, 7648; *Ku Klux Klan;* 7841; *Labor;* 7906, 7910, 8020, 8036, 8052, 8056, 8147; *Language;* 8353, 8395, 8424, 8430, 8453, 8470, 8504, 8534, 8537, 8590, 8602, 8617; *Law;* 8862, 8865; *Libraries;* 9140, 9189, 9196, 9236, 9251; *Literature;* 9318; *Locality - Illinois;* 9495; *Locality - Massachusetts;* 9527, 9529; *Mass media;* 9860, 9907, 9926, 10017, 10122-10123, 10125 10168, 10179, 10181, 10232, 10251, 10291; *Migration;* 10354; *Military;* 10427, 10521; *Minorities in conflict;* 10581, 10594-10595, 10614, 10621, 10625, 10635-10636, 10639; *Multiculturalism;* 10707; *Nationalism;* 11130, 11132, 11156; *Occupation;* 11221; *Politics & racism;* 11419, 11444, 11448, 11467, 11472, 11550, 11567-11568, 11584, 11604, 11626, 11651-11652, 11823, 11897, 11904, 11956, 11983, 12003, 12046; *Public opinion;* 12090, 12115, 12118; *Racism, defining;* 12143, 12187, 12191; *Religion;* 12662, 12688-12689, 12708, 12752, 12819; *Science & technology;* 12930; *Sexism;* 13079; *Slavery;* 13150; *Sports;* 13293, 13306, 13352; *Stereotypes;* 13391, 13468, 13548; *Surveillance;* 13751; *Tests;* 13787; *Unemployment;* 13930, 13934, 13936, 13957; *Women of Color;* 14401; *General;* 14473, 14487, 14544, 14549, 14561, 14587; *Bibliographies;* 14598

Japanese Americans: *Black towns;* 806, 817, 842; *Children, effects on;* 1349; *Citizenship;* 1414; *Collective self defense;* 1928, 1931; *Concentration camps;* 2191-2195, 2197-2216, 2218-2223, 2225-2230; *Discrimination;* 2924; *Education, elementary & secondary;* 4045; *Family;* 5733; *History;* 6828, 6888; *Immigration;* 7612, 7614; *Labor;* 8145; *Land;* 8237, 8269; *Language;* 8441, 8514; *Law;* 8763, 9121; *Literature;* 9191; *Locality - Alaska;*

9348; *Locality - California;* 9419; *Mass media;* 9846, 9928, 10209; *Military;*10491-10492, 10528; *Minorities in conflict;* 10611, 10644; *Occupation;* 11250; *Racism, defining;* 12134, 12160, 12208; *Racism, psychology of;* 12882; *Stereotypes;* 13453, 13571; *Surveillance;* 13584, 13679, 13696, 13715, 13727; *Violence vs. Minorities;* 14082, 14100; *Women of Color;* 14412-14413

Korean Americans: *Autobiography & Biography;* 775, 810; *Business;* 1159, 1207, 1209, 1220-1221, 1234-1235, 1238, 1267; *Family;* 5600, 5607; *Locality - California;* 9423; *Mass media;* 9872, 9888, 10145, 10172; *Minorities in conflict;* 10577-10578, 10603, 10616-10617, 10619, 10626-10627, 10655, 10660; *Politics & racism;* 11696; *Racism, defining;* 12164; *Religion;* 12667; *Surveillance;* 13691, 13785; *Violence vs. Minorities;* 14029; *Women of Color;* 14383

Laotian Americans: *Desegregation;* 2578, 2592; *Religion;* 12733

Latinos: *Africa;* 261; *Autobiography & Biography;* 618; *Blacks & Jews;* 951; *Business;* 1162; *Children, effects on;* 1269, 1302, 1346, 1358; *Civil rights;* 1660; *Class structure;* 1834, 1842, 1902; *Collective self defense;* 1965; *Crime;* 2395-2396, 2519; *Discrimination;* 3008; *Economic standards;* 3175, 3253, 3282, 3310, 3334; *Education, elementary & secondary;* 3650, 4037, 4086, 4233; *Education, higher;* 4329, 4612, 4930, 5108, 5110, 5144, 5155, 5276, 5304; *Employment;* 5407, 5412, 5422, 5428, 5430; *Environment;* 5535; *Ghetto;* 5815, 5868, 5931, 5977, 5999; *Health;* 6157, 6285, 6343, 6359, 6476, 6516, 6573, 6580, 6605, 6606; *Housing;* 7125, 7280, 7324, 7360; *Humor;* 7400; *Immigration;* 7522, 7666; *Labor;* 7903, 7907, 8030; *Language;* 8424, 8430, 8443, 8470, 8491, 8576, 8590, 8602, 8630; *Libraries;* 9130-9131; *Locality - California;* 9405, 9412, 9416, 9428, 9443; *Locality - New York;* 9593; *Mass media;* 9805, 9812-9813, 9911, 10106, 10165, 10216, 10253, 10261, 10306; *Minorities in conflict;* 10568, 10579, 10582, 10598, 10602, 10608 10615, 10620, 10623-10624, 10638, 10640, 10643, 10646, 10650, 10652, 10654; *Multiculturalism;* 10839; *Occupation;* 11221; *Politics & racism;* 11374, 11484, 11490, 11532, 11562-11563, 11574, 11606, 11627-11628, 11650, 11653,

11735, 11981, 12004; *Public opinion;*
12061, 12089; *Racism, defining;* 12161,
12187; *Stereotypes;* 13432, 13483; *Tests;*
13798; *Violence vs. Minorities;* 14057-
14058; *Women of Color;* 14382, 14447;
Bibliographies; 14593, 14608, 14622

Mexican Americans: *Affirmative action;* 69,
265; *Autobiography & Biography;* 651,
658, 696, 717, 777, 781, 784, 794, 799,
833-834, 852, 867, 890, 896, 912;
Business; 1170, 1231; *Children, effects
on;* 1273; *Civil rights;* 1584, 1643; *Class
structure;* 1717, 1726, 1739, 1773, 1784,
1837, 1839-1840, 1843, 1862, 1877, 1887,
1903; *Collective self defense;* 1924-1925,
1929, 1933-1934, 1944, 1954-1957, 1962,
1964, 1970, 1978, 1981-1982; *Colonialism;*
1988, 2056, 2066, 2069; *Community
development;* 2104, 2114, 2125, 2156,
2176; *Crime;* 2248, 2331, 2461, 2476;
Desegregation; 2595, 2605, 2616, 2621,
2637, 2659-2660, 2694, 2713, 2723, 2757;
Discrimination; 2839, 2845, 2859, 2862,
2866, 2886, 2948, 2953, 2973, 3019-3020,
3040-3041, 3085-3086; *Economic
standards;* 3163, 3173, 3198, 3202, 3221,
3297, 3304, 3350, 3385, 3406, 3423;
Economics of racism; 3425, 3447;
Education, elementary & secondary; 3459,
3498, 3504, 3519, 3543, 3567, 3627, 3636,
3661, 3701, 3706-3707, 3721, 3735, 3754,
3806, 3912, 3918, 3940-3941, 3959, 3975,
3977, 3979, 4035, 4053, 4057, 4103, 4112-
4114, 4118, 4153, 4178, 4218-4219, 4223,
4225; *Education, higher;* 4291, 4440,
4640-4641, 4693, 4844, 4897, 4913, 4916,
4960, 5021, 5054, 5134, 5165, 5304, 5380;
Family; 5605, 5634-5635, 5640, 5746;
Ghetto; 5814; *Government & minorities;*
5867, 5927, 5942; *Health;* 6024, 6090,
6193, 6206, 6224, 6232, 6309, 6312, 6342,
6357, 6380, 6407, 6536, 6642, 6653, 6695,
6698, 6701-6702, 6718, 6745, 6747, 6750,
6796, 6814, 6818, 6823, 6894; *History;*
6898, 6911-6914, 6916, 6927, 6929-6930,
6952, 6965, 6969, 6984-6986, 6988, 6992,
7016, 7023, 7042-7043, 7047; *Housing;*
7129, 7153, 7176, 7252, 7316; *Humor;*
7394, 7409, 7421, 7433, 7436;
Immigration; 7487, 7490, 7503-7504, 7507-
7508, 7518, 7525-7526, 7534, 7549, 7554-
7555, 7559-7560, 7569-7570, 7597-7598,
7633, 7637, 7655, 7665, 7672-7673, 7681-
7682; *Labor;* 7866, 7870-7872, 7878, 7891,
7896, 7900-7901, 7904, 7911, 7913, 7917,
7919, 7921, 7927, 7929, 7951-7953, 7955-
7959, 7964-7967, 7975, 7982, 7993, 8003,
8007-8008, 8016-8017, 8031, 8038, 8048,

8072, 8082-8083, 8086, 8091, 8099, 8106-
8108, 8112, 8125-8126, 8129, 8142, 8146,
8150-8151, 8159, 8163-8164, 8167, 8180;
Land; 8183, 8186, 8188, 8191, 8194, 8226-
8227, 8238, 8244, 8258, 8267, 8280, 8282,
8313, 8322; *Language;* 8391, 8431, 8448,
8572, 8591, 8602, 8615; *Law;* 8731, 8912,
8926, 8928, 8967-8968, 9081, 9138;
Literature; 9172, 9194, 9217, 9252, 9272,
9293, 9305, 9319; *Locality - Arizona;* 9357;
Locality - California; 9369, 9376, 9400,
9402, 9406, 9410, 9413, 9417-9418, 9420,
9424-9426, 9431, 9434, 9439; *Locality -
Colorado;* 9446; *Locality - Illinois;* 9497;
Locality - Missouri; 9566; *Locality - New
Mexico;* 9585, 9588-9589; *Locality - texas;*
9685, 9689-9690, 9693-9699, 9701-9702,
9703-9704, 9706-9707, 9709-9710, 9712,
9714-9715; *Mass media;* 9862, 9872, 9888,
9920-9921, 10017, 10039, 10086, 10094
10130-10131, 10145, 10156, 10172, 10306,;
Migration; 10359, 10366; *Military;* 10405,
10421, 10486, 10494, 10547, 10564;
Multiculturalism; 10888, 10912;
Nationalism; 11127; *Occupation;* 11236,
11266; *Oppression;* 11281-11283;
Pluralism; 11335; *Politics & racism;* 11503-
11504, 11526, 11564-11566, 11582-11583,
11619 11633, 11677, 11689, 11709, 11748,
11775-11776, 11802-11803, 11813-11814,
11835-11836, 11855, 11880, 11898, 11925,
11941, 11958, 11998, 12016; *Public
opinion;* 12062, 12085; *Racism, defining;*
12135, 12175; *Racism, exporting;* 12223;
Racism, psychology of; 12272, 12291;
Racism, theory of; 12462; *Religion;* 12664,
12680, 12690, 12810; *Socialism & racism;*
13222; *Stereotypes;* 13402, 13406, 13436,
13475-13476, 13496, 13521; *Surveillance;*
13719; *Tests;* 13802, 13870;
Unemployment; 13937; *Violence vs.
Minorities;* 14000-14001, 14015-14016,
14020, 14036, 14063, 14088, 14099, 14123;
Wealth & income; 14165, 14184; *Women
of Color;* 14281, 14285, 14288, 14302,
14314, 14324, 14330, 14335, 14343;
General; 14538, 14567, 14577;
Bibliographies; 14600, 14609, 14646-14647,
14665

Native Americans: *Affirmative action;* 6, 161;
Autobiography & Biography; 615, 628,
644, 657, 662-663, 767, 787, 801, 808-809,
815, 871, 878, 897, 907-908; *Business;*
1142, 1242; *Children, effects on;* 1268,
1271, 1310, 1321, 1374; *Civil rights;* 1606,
1661, 1704-1705; *Class structure;* 1761,
1832, 1863, 1866; *Collective self defense;*
1927, 1940, 1950, 1959; *Colonialism;* 1989,

2002-2007, 2021-2022, 2025, 2029-2030, 2036-2037, 2039, 2065, 2073, 2087-2088, 2093, 2098-2101; *Community development;* 2103, 2105-2106, 2108, 2111, 2116, 2118, 2124, 2129, 2133, 2135, 2142, 2147-2148, 2150-2152, 2155, 2158-2160, 2162, 2165, 2178-2180, 2183, 2188; *Concentration camps;* 2189-2190, 2217; *Desegregation;* 2253, 2258, 2266, 2281, 2341, 2397, 2411, 2441, 2451, 2495, 2530, 2735; *Discrimination;* 2910, 2920, 2998, 3000, 3082; *Economic standards;* 3142, 3191, 3207, 3210, 3244, 3248, 3255, 3261, 3264, 3274, 3276, 3316, 3319, 3339, 3382, 3384, 3397; *Economics of racism;* 3442, 3450; *Education, elementary & secondary;* 3456, 3462, 3490, 3495, 3606-3608, 3632, 3634, 3643, 3662, 3700, 3713, 3807, 3817, 3831, 3861, 3869, 3874, 3890, 3903, 3906, 3917, 3919, 3943, 3954-3955, 3963, 4005, 4009, 4036, 4087, 4161, 4172, 4189-4190, 4205, 4269; *Education, higher;* 4281, 4307, 4320, 4334, 4387, 4417, 4458, 4497-4499, 4548, 4608, 4681, 4757, 4837, 4890, 4912, 4955, 4983, 5045, 5046, 5101, 5172, 5243, 5254, 5283, 5388-5389; *Employment;* 5434; *Environment;* 5450, 5487, 5504-5506, 5510, 5512, 5530, 5541-5542, 5548, 5556; *Family;* 5668, 5681, 5694, 5722; *Government & minorities;* 5830-5831, 5834, 5836, 5839, 5842, 5844, 5846, 5849, 5851, 5853-5854, 5856-5859, 5871, 5874, 5876, 5878-5879, 5883, 5885-5889, 5893-5894, 5903, 5905-5906, 5909, 5911, 5923-5924, 5936, 5938, 5944, 5949-5950, 5955, 5958-5965, 5967, 5973, 5975-5976, 5989-5990, 5993, 5995, 5997, 6000, 6010, 6012, 6014-6015, 6019; *Health;* 6053, 6097, 6147, 6192, 6195, 6310-6311, 6364, 6369, 6402, 6405, 6455, 6463, 6490, 6493, 6502, 6504, 6561, 6581, 6600, 6622, 6634, 6659, 6692-6693, 6697; *History;* 6705-6707, 6711-6713, 6715-6717, 6723-6725, 6727, 6729-6730, 6733, 6735-6737, 6743-6744, 6753-6756, 6762-6763, 6766, 6768, 6770, 6774-6775, 6777, 6780, 6783, 6786, 6789-6791, 6795, 6805-6806, 6815, 6822, 6826, 6830, 6833-6835, 6839, 6844, 6846-6850, 6853-6854, 6857-6860, 6864-6866, 6868-6870, 6872, 6874-6875, 6878, 6880-6882, 6884, 6891, 6896-6897, 6902-6903, 6905-6910, 6914, 6917-6920, 6922, 6931, 6935, 6938, 6947-6948, 6953, 6955, 6957-6959, 6962-6964, 6970-6971, 6975-6978, 6993, 6998, 7003, 7005, 7007, 7009, 7011-7015, 7027-7028, 7030, 7033-7034, 7036, 7040-7042, 7044-7046, 7049, 7051-7052, 7059, 7061; *Housing;* 7082, 7119, 7132, 7270; *Humor;* 7415, 7430, 7434, 7460; *Labor;* 7892,

8002, 8004, 8018, 8101, 8117, 8144, 8148, 8164; *Land;* 8182, 8189-8190, 8192, 8195-8203, 8206-8225, 8228-8236, 8240, 8242-8243, 8245-8247, 8249, 8251-8257, 8260-8266, 8268, 8270-8274, 8279, 8281, 8283, 8285-8287, 8289-8290, 8292-8294, 8296-8298, 8302-8306, 8308, 8310, 8312, 8314-8317, 8321, 8324, 8326, 8329, 8331-8334; *Language;* 8359, 8401, 8404, 8410, 8467, 8470, 8478, 8506, 8516, 8519, 8555, 8571, 8582, 8596, 8635; *Law;* 8689, 8713, 8717-8720, 8722, 8732, 8752, 8761-8762, 8769, 8788, 8818, 8830, 8838, 8877-8878, 8887, 8905, 8913, 8932, 8951-8952, 8981-8982, 8989, 9005-9006, 9015, 9017, 9019-9020, 9026, 9033, 9035, 9040, 9055-9056, 9100-9101, 9108-9109, 9112, 9122-9124; *Literature;* 9163, 9165-9167, 9224, 9243, 9256, 9279, 9287-9288, 9291, 9307, 9314, 9318; *Locality - Alaska;* 9344-9345, 9347, 9349-9351, 9354-9355; *Locality - Arizona;* 9358; *Locality - California;* 9372, 9399, 9445; *Locality - Massachusetts;* 9531; *Locality - New Mexico;* 9584-9585; *Locality - New York;* 9597; *Locality - North Carolina;* 9644; *Locality - North Dakota;* 9645; *Locality - Oklahoma;* 9653; *Locality - Oregon;* 9654; *Locality - South Dakota;* 9676; *Locality - Virginia;* 9729, 9738; *Locality - Washington;* 9743, 9746; *Locality - Wyoming;* 9753; *Mass media;* 9760-9761, 9787, 9852-9854, 9865, 10021, 10049, 10054-10055, 10073, 10084, 10119, 10125, 10168, 10232; *Migration;* 10316, 10320, 10335-10336, 10339; *Military;* 10385, 10389-10390, 10409, 10435-10436, 10439, 10444, 10452-10453, 10471, 10484, 10527, 10535, 10537, 10560; *Minorities in conflict;* 10567, 10569-10570, 10572-10573, 10575-10576, 10583, 10586-10588, 10590-10591, 10596-10597, 10601, 10604-10605, 10607, 10609-10610, 10613, 10618, 10622, 10629-10633, 10642, 10645, 10647, 10649, 10653, 10656-10659, 10661; *Multiculturalism;* 11011, 11071; *Nationalism;* 11135, 11137, 11151, 11171-11172, 11179, 11190, 11197, 11199; *Oppression;* 11286, 11290; *Politics & racism;* 11465-11466, 11485, 11530, 11568, 11636, 11649, 11675, 11749, 11754, 11827, 11846, 11912, 11915, 12040, 12044; *Public opinion;* 12064, 12093; *Racism, defining;* 12158, 12182, 12209; *Racism, exporting;* 12221; *Racism, psychology of;* 12262; *Racism, scholarly;* 12316, 12333, 12338, 12352, 12366; *Racism, theory of;* 12430; *Racist groups;* 12540; *Religion;* 12645, 12663, 12668-12669, 12674-12675, 12722, 12725, 12734, 12737, 12766, 12777-12778, 12780-12781, 12786, 12805 12818,

12835, 12843, 12847, 12853, 12871, 12875; *Science & technology;* 12887, 12894, 12912; *Sexism;* 12944, 13003, 13034, 13073, 13085; *Slavery;* 13101, 13103, 13111, 13120, 13123, 13141, 13150-13152, 13192-13193, 13199; *Socialism & racism;* 13211; *Stereotypes;* 13390, 13405, 13416, 13433, 13446, 13450, 13502, 13506-13507, 13511, 13522, 13551 13559, 13573; *Surveillance;* 13585-13586, 13595, 13618-13619, 13641, 13662, 13697, 13725; *Tests;* 13873; *Unemployment;* 13962; *Violence vs. Minorities;* 14006, 14024, 14040, 14069, 14073-14074, 14107-14108; *Wealth & income;* 14155, 14163, 14166, 14191, *Whites;* 14257; *Women of Color;* 14281, 14284, 14287, 14297, 14304, 14307, 14347, 14405, 14417-14418, 14432, 14438, 14440-14441, 14445, 14449, 14454; *General;* 14484-14485, 14520, 14560, 14569-14570, 14575; *Bibliographies;* 14593, 14601, 14603, 14639, 14642, 14669

Pacific Islanders: *Colonialism;* 2027, 2032, 2034, 2045, 2068; *Education, elementary & secondary;* 3511; *Environment;* 5526; *Family;* 5559; *Government & minorities;* 5978; *Health;* 6033, 6094, 6658; *History;* 6921; *Labor;* 8132, 8209, 8259, 8277, 8285, 8309, 8318, 8320, 8328; *Language;* 8575; *Law;* 8934, 9065; *Locality - Alaska;* 9356; *Locality - Hawaii;* 9480-9481, 9483, 9487-9489, 9491; *Military;* 10507; *Nationalism;* 11136

Puerto Ricans: *Autobiography & Biography;* 711, 844; *Business;* 1167, 1265; *Civil rights;* 1462; *Class structure;* 1743, 1801, 1808, 1823, 1868-1869, 1878, 1884, 1899; *Collective self defense;* 1969; *Colonialism;* 1986, 1990-1993, 1995-1997, 1999, 2008-2011, 2013-2019, 2024, 2028, 2031, 2043, 2047-2055, 2057-2064, 2067, 2070-2072, 2074, 2077-2084, 2086, 2092, 2094-2096, 2102; *Community development;* 2174-2175; *Crime;* 2462, 2483; *Desegregation;* 2718; *Discrimination;* 2981, 3050, 3087, 3118; *Economic standards;* 3156, 3178, 3180, 3183, 3231, 3324, 3335, 3355-3356, 3381, 3396, 3410, 3412; *Education, elementary & secondary;* 3483, 3494, 3588, 3592, 3610, 3687, 4075-4076, 4162, 4165, 4201, 4232, 4380; *Environment;* 4551, 4583, 4827, 4903, 5038, 5081, 5414, 5445; *Family;* 5601, 5674, 5704, 5710, 5723; *Ghetto;* 5816; *Health;* 6027, 6029, 6344, 6357, 6367, 6407, 6536; *History;* 6706, 6738, 6748, 6779, 6787, 6856, 6932, 6972; *Housing;* 7195, 7197, 7320-7321; *Labor;*

7889, 7943, 7954, 8037, 8061, 8093, 8102, 8116, 8121, 8137; *Land;* 8215; *Language;* 8420, 8508, 8556, 8567, 8577, 8604, 8620, 8644; *Literature;* 9267, 9272; *Locality - Illinois;* 9499; *Locality - New York;* 9590, 9611, 9619, 9625; *Locality - Pennsylvania;* 9666; *Mass media;* 9775, 9913; *Migration;* 10309-10310, 10313-10314, 10325, 10333-10334, 10340-10341, 10348-10350, 10355, 10357-10358, 10363; *Military;* 10446, 10519; *Nationalism;* 11128, 11131, 11142, 11150, 11157-11158, 11161, 11175-11178, 11182, 11192; *Occupation;* 1121; *Politics & racism;* 11504, 11533, 11677, 11688, 11866; *Racism, defining;* 12132, 12162, 12176, 12186; *Racism, psychology of;* 12294; *Racism, theory of;* 12421; *Religion;* 12691, 12718, 12815, 12854; *Science & technology;* 12886, 12890; *Sexism;* 12973, 13031; *Slavery;* 13089, 13093, 13113, 13115, 13118, 13128, 13130, 13136, 13178; *Stereotypes;* 13401; *Surveillance;* 13622, 13713, 13722, 13726; *Wealth & income;* 14141-14142, 14154, 14181-14183, 14195, 14204; *Women of Color;* 14278, 14289, 14293-14296, 14321-14322, 14340, 14430; *Bibliographies;* 14595, 14610, 14620, 14668

Romany (Gypsies): *Health;* 6619; *Law;* 9092

Vietnamese Americans: *Crime;* 2286; *Education, elementary & secondary;* 4180; *History;* 6812; *Immigration;* 7550, 7659; *Military;* 10411, 11757, 12244; *Violence vs. Minorities;* 14007

Women: *Affirmative action;* 51, 61, 79, 83, 103, 135, 155-156, 165-166, 177, 186-187, 195, 207, 210, 220-221, 239, 255, 265, 275, 282-283, 322, 330-332, 342, 364-366; *Autobiography & Biography;* 636-637, 640, 645, 651, 654, 656, 658-659, 673-674, 680, 685, 689, 709, 715, 719-720, 724-725, 730-731, 738, 748, 750-751, 756, 759, 771, 774, 782, 784-785, 795, 821-822, 836, 841-842, 862, 865, 872, 874-875, 881, 885, 890, 892, 898, 902, 904-905, 914; *Civil rights;* 1481, 1490, 1549, 1569-1570, 1579, 1584, 1621, 1640-1641, 1643, 1645, 1648, 1656-1657, 1697, 1703; *Class structure;* 1782, 1786, 1815, 1847, 1862, 1887; *Collective self defense;* 1964; *Community development;* 2163; *Crime;* 2250, 2278, 2318, 2340, 2343 2357, 2378, 2401, 2436, 2447, 2470, 2488, 2518, 2528; *Desegregation;* 2631, 2674; *Discrimination;* 2856, 2868, 2887, 2889, 2891, 2897, 2899, 2917, 2919, 2937, 2945, 2951, 2958, 2981, 2992, 2994, 3001-3003, 3005, 3015, 3020,

3022, 3030, 3056, 3069, 3072-3073, 3076, 3088, 3091, 3100, 3116-3117, 3135, 3137, 3141, 3153; *Economic standards;* 3222, 3270-3271, 3275, 3292-3293, 3344, 3351, 3392; *Education, elementary & secondary;* 3494, 3999, 4138, 4156-4158, 4182, 4252; *Education, higher;* 4282, 4331, 4349, 4352, 4373, 4381, 4390, 4395, 4434, 4443-4444, 4459, 4470-4472, 4480, 4516, 4521, 4555, 4561-4562, 4585, 4613, 4635, 4649-4650, 4656, 4662, 4678, 4682, 4726, 4736, 4744, 4747, 4767, 4780, 4791, 4820, 4870, 4873, 4876, 4882, 4889, 4979, 4994, 4999, 5001; *Employment;* 5004, 5079, 5087, 5103, 5126, 5140, 5154, 5157-5158, 5287, 5291, 5338, 5365, 5379, 5381, 5411, 5420, 5433, 5439-5440; *Environment;* 5486, 5511, 5527, 5540, 5560; *Family;* 5563-5564, 5571, 5586, 5591, 5610, 5612, 5615, 5619, 5635, 5643, 5650, 5661, 5689, 5692, 5699, 5701, 5703; *Forced labor;* 5760; *Government & minorities;* 5829, 5861, 5915, 5926, 5970, 5979, 6006, 6013; *Health;* 6031, 6047-6048, 6063, 6073-6075, 6077, 6093, 6101, 6107, 6117, 6119, 6126, 6150, 6153, 6158, 6166, 6186, 6197, 6200, 6206-6210, 6219, 6226, 6266, 6307, 6325, 6330, 6344, 6359, 6376, 6408, 6416, 6418, 6420, 6472, 6479, 6501, 6553, 6556, 6562, 6578, 6587-6588, 6627, 6638, 6642-6643, 6656, 6665, 6667; *History;* 6685, 6703, 6712, 6722, 6741, 6760, 6777, 6784, 6807, 6836, 6876, 6915, 6990, 7001, 7056, 7060, 7062; *Housing;* 7223, 7315, 7331; *Humor;* 7394-7395, 7417, 7423, 7445; *Immigration;* 7553, 7671; *Ku Klux Klan;* 7792, 7807, 7830; *Labor;* 7868, 7890, 7915, 7927, 7938, 7940, 8006, 8013, 8031, 8038, 8069, 8089, 8100, 8107-8109, 8112, 8116, 8122, 8126, 8128, 8137, 8151, 8154, 8170, 8175; *Law;* 8654, 8656, 8671, 8675, 8714, 8719, 8722, 8753, 8780, 8798, 8801, 8839, 8860, 8900, 8914, 8924, 8957, 8963, 8965, 8969,

8991, 9021, 9025, 9027-9029, 9036, 9054,9082, 9084, 9105, 9111, 9125; *Libraries;* 9141-9142; *Literature;* 9158, 9167, 9187, 9223, 9239, 9260-9261, 9325; *Locality - Alaska;* 9346, 9355; *Locality - Georgia;* 9476; *Locality - Hawaii;* 9477; *Locality - New York;* 9625, 9627; *Locality - North Carolina;* 9638; *Locality - Virginia;* 9723; *Mass media;* 9806, 9885, 9887, 9906, 9989-9990, 10006, 10074, 10081, 10115, 10154, 10163, 10189, 10195, 10226, 10232, 10237, 10256, 10260, 10266, 10271, 10304, 10307; *Military;* 10384, 10406-10408, 10441, 10455, 10470, 10477, 10493, 10512, 10540, 10545, 10549, 10550, 10552; *Multiculturalism;* 10949, 10957, 10963, 10996, 11015, 11065; *Occupation;* 11217, 11220, 11227-11228, 11240, 11256, 11262, 11268; *Oppression;* 11285, 11288; *Politics & racism;* 11407, 11433, 11441, 11561, 11591, 11627-11628, 11632, 11634, 11638, 11641, 11657, 11672, 11705, 11714, 11720, 11754, 11823, 11892, 11968, 11988, 12019, 12023, 12038; *Public opinion;* 12086; *Racism, psychology of;* 12281; *Religion;* 12723, 12731, 12741, 12767, 12816; *Science & technology;* 12893, 12895, 12902, 12906, 12910, 12913, 12915-12920, 12925, 12927-12929, 12933; *Sexism;* 12935-13087; *Slavery;* 13157, 13183, 13195, 13206, 13209; *Sports;* 13223, 13236, 13245, 13248, 13255, 13266; *Stereotypes;* 13376, 13378, 13385, 13392, 13404, 13422, 13425, 13429, 13438, 13443, 13466, 13470, 13475, 13494-13495, 13519, 13529, 13542, 13572, 13575, 13579; *Tests;* 13791, 13823; *Undoing personal racism;* 13885; *Unemployment;* 13950; *Wealth & income;* 14174, 14176-14177, *Whites;* 14226-14229; *Women of Color;* 14278-14280, 14282-14307, 14309-14310, 14312-14373, 14375-14386, 14388-14398, 14400-14468; *General;* 14469, 14472; *Bibliographies;* 14598, 14600-14601, 14609, 14616, 14621, 14633, 14639, 14648, 14656, 14663-14664, 14671

About the Compiler

MEYER WEINBERG is Professor Emeritus in the W.E.B. Du Bois Department of Afro-American Studies, University of Massachusetts, Amherst. Professor Weinberg founded and edited *Integrated Education* magazine and the *Research Review of Equal Education.* He is the author of numerous books and articles on the subject of racism.